THE LAW AND POLICY OF

The World Trade Organization

Since the publication ... s first edition, this t... ...NTAL AND AFRICAN STUDIES
and students alike, d.e to its clear introduction to the b... ... f London
and its detailed examination of the law of the World Trade Oganization. The third cuitton
continues to explore the institutional and substantive law of the WTO. Material has been
restructured to closely align with teaching approaches making it even more user-friendly.
It has been updated to incorporate all new developments in the WTO's ever-growing body
of case law. Questions and assignments are integrated to allow students to assess their
understanding, while chapter summaries reinforce learning. Chapters end with an exercise
reflecting real-life trade problems: these challenge students (and practitioners) and enable
them to hone their analytical skills. This title is an essential tool for all WTO law students
and will also serve as the practitioner's introductory guide to the WTO.

Peter Van den Bossche has been a Member of the Appellate Body of the World Trade
Organization since 2009. He is Professor of International Economic Law at Maastricht
University, The Netherlands, and visiting professor at the College of Europe, Bruges; the
World Trade Institute, Berne; the University of Barcelona; and the China–EU School of Law,
Beijing. From 1997 to 2001, he was counsellor at the Appellate Body Secretariat, and in 2001
served as Acting Director of the Secretariat. In the early 1990s, he worked as référendaire
at the European Court of Justice. He studied law at the University of Antwerp (Lic. jur.), the
University of Michigan (LLM) and the European University Institute, Florence (PhD).

Werner Zdouc is Director of the WTO Appellate Body Secretariat since 2006. Mr Zdouc
obtained a law degree from the University of Graz in Austria. He then went on to
earn a PhD from the University of St Gallen in Switzerland, and afterwards an LLM
from Michigan Law School. Mr Zdouc joined the WTO Legal Affairs Division in 1995.
He moved to the Appellate Body Secretariat in 2001. Currently, he is also a lecturer
and visiting professor for international trade law at Vienna Economic University and
the University of Barcelona. From 1987 to 1989 he worked for governmental and
non-governmental development aid organizations.

THE LAW AND POLICY OF

The World Trade Organization

Text, Cases and Materials

THIRD EDITION

Peter Van den Bossche

Werner Zdouc

CAMBRIDGE
UNIVERSITY PRESS

University Printing House, Cambridge CB2 8BS, United Kingdom

Cambridge University Press is part of the University of Cambridge.

It furthers the University's mission by disseminating knowledge in the pursuit of education, learning and research at the highest international levels of excellence.

www.cambridge.org
Information on this title: www.cambridge.org/9781107024496

First published 2013
3rd printing 2014

Printed in the United Kingdom by TJ International Ltd. Padstow Cornwall

A catalogue record for this publication is available from the British Library

ISBN 978-1-107-02449-6 Hardback
ISBN 978-1-107-69429-3 Paperback

CONTENTS

FIGURES

PREFACE

Five years have passed since the publication of the second edition of this book and new developments in the law, and in particular the case law, of the WTO called for an updated and fully revised third edition. This third edition has also been restructured with the intention to make it user-friendlier for both students and practitioners. I was very lucky to find Werner Zdouc willing to share the burden of updating, revising and restructuring this book, and become a co-author of the third edition. Werner focused primarily on Chapters 9 (Economic Emergency Exceptions), 10 (Regional Trade Exceptions), 11 (Dumping) and 12 (Subsidies), while I focused on Chapters 1 (International Trade and the Law of the WTO), 2 (The World Trade Organization), 3 (WTO Dispute Settlement), 4 (Most-Favoured-Nation Treatment), 5 (National Treatment), 6 (Tariff Barriers), 7 (Non-Tariff Barriers), 8 (General and Security Exceptions), 13 (Technical Barriers to Trade), 14 (Sanitary and Phytosanitary Measures), 15 (Intellectual Property Rights) and 16 (Future Challenges). However, we both reviewed and sign for all chapters.

This book reflects the current state of WTO law, in respect of both the covered agreements and the rapidly increasing body of panel and Appellate Body reports. While we mention legal issues still to be adjudicated, we do not express any opinion on how these issues should be decided or, more broadly, how WTO law should develop in the future. Where we quote or refer to various and often divergent statements of negotiators, academics or other eminent experts, we do so in order to give the reader a full picture of open debates. It is evident that the description of the current state of WTO law contained in this book is to be attributed to the authors in their private capacity and does not represent the views of the Appellate Body, its Secretariat or the WTO.

As the first and second edition, this third edition has once again benefitted from the advice, comments and suggestions of many. Werner and I owe thanks to Iveta Alexovicová, Maria Alcover, Ujal Singh Bhatia, Kaarlo Castren, Gian Franco Chianale, Claude Chase, Leila Choukroune, Victoria Donaldson, Lothar Ehring,

Mateo Ferrero, Carlo Gamberale, Susan Hainsworth, Srikanth Hariharan, Valerie Hughes, Johann Human, Arkady Kudryavtsev, Bernard Kuiten, Lauro Locks, Leonardo Macedo, Gabrielle Marceau, Peter Morrison, Jesse Nicol, Fernando Pierola, Maria Pereyra, Denise Prévost, Roy Santana, Andreas Sennekamp, Kelly Kuan Shang, Maarten Smeets, Debra Steger, Paolo Vergano, Hannu Wager, Alan Yanovich and Xiaolu Zhu. We also thank Enrique Arrieta, Samer Budeir, Ahmed Elsisi, Jessica Giovanelli, Gabriel Guardado, Elena Kumashova, and Chengjin Xu for their careful cite checking and cross-referencing. Of course, none of those mentioned above bears any responsibility for any error or omission in this book. Any such error or omission remains the responsibility of the authors. Werner and I are grateful to Sinéad Moloney, Senior Commissioning Editor, Law, at Cambridge University Press and other Cambridge University Press staff, in particular Martin Gleeson, Charles Howell and Helen Francis, for their unfailing and well-organised assistance in matters large and small. We are also grateful to Finola O'Sullivan, Editorial Director, Law, at Cambridge University Press for her continued support for this book.

With the royalties of the first and second editions of this book, the Maastricht University Fund for Education and Research in International Economic Law (MUFERIEL) was established. Over the last eight years this Fund has allowed Maastricht University to give financial assistance to students and scholars from developing countries. The royalties of the third edition will be used for the same purpose.

PETER VAN DEN BOSSCHE
Geneva, March 2013

TABLE OF WTO CASES

The year in brackets following the short name of the case refers to the year in which the panel or Appellate Body report in that case was adopted by the DSB. Where awards or decisions by arbitrators under Articles 21.3(c), 22.6 or 25 of the DSU are concerned, the year in brackets refers to the year in which these awards or decisions were circulated.

Short title	Full case title and citation
China – Electronic Payment Services (2012)	Panel Report, *China – Measures Affecting Electronic Payment Services*, WT/DS413/R, adopted 31 August 2012 343, 406, 409–13, 524, 525–7
China – GOES (2012)	Appellate Body Report, *China – Countervailing and Anti-Dumping Duties on Grain Oriented Flat-Rolled Electrical Steel from the United States*, WT/DS414/AB/R, adopted 16 November 2012 239, 699–700, 702–4, 706, 721, 722, 723, 781–2, 820, 822–3
	Panel Report, *China – Countervailing and Anti-Dumping Duties on Grain Oriented Flat-Rolled Electrical Steel from the United States*, WT/DS414/R, adopted 16 November 2012, upheld by Appellate Body Report WT/DS414/AB/R 757, 816
China – Intellectual Property Rights (2009)	Panel Report, *China – Measures Affecting the Protection and Enforcement of Intellectual Property Rights*, WT/DS362/R, adopted 20 March 2009, DSR 2009:V, 2097 974, 1002–3
China – Publications and Audiovisual Products (2010)	Appellate Body Report, *China – Measures Affecting Trading Rights and Distribution Services for Certain Publications and Audiovisual Entertainment Products*, WT/DS363/AB/R, adopted 19 January 2010, DSR 2010:I, 3 55, 57, 65, 186, 187–188, 407–8, 528–9, 548–50, 570–1
	Panel Report, *China – Measures Affecting Trading Rights and Distribution Services for Certain Publications and Audiovisual Entertainment Products*, WT/DS363/R and Corr.1, adopted 19 January 2010, as modified by Appellate Body Report WT/DS363/AB/R, DSR 2010:II, 261 222, 383–4, 385, 394, 399, 406, 407–8, 409–10, 413, 515, 517–18, 525, 548–0, , 570–1
China – Raw Materials (2012)	Appellate Body Reports, *China – Measures Related to the Exportation of Various Raw Materials*, WT/DS394/AB/R/WT/DS395/AB/R/WT/DS398/AB/R, adopted 22 February 2012 165, 213, 483–4, 485, 486, 503–4, 549–50, 567, 568
	Panel Reports, *China – Measures Related to the Exportation of Various Raw Materials*, WT/DS394/R/WT/DS395/R/WT/DS398/R/and Corr.1, adopted 22 February 2012, as modified by Appellate Body Reports WT/DS394/AB/R/WT/DS395/AB/R/WT/DS398/AB/R 55, 111, 473, 486, 500, 503–4, 505, 549–50, 554, 555, 559–60, 568

Short title	Full case title and citation
EC – Bananas III (1997)	Appellate Body Report, *European Communities – Regime for the Importation, Sale and Distribution of Bananas*, WT/DS27/AB/R, adopted 25 September 1997, DSR 1997:II, 591 46–7, 54, 55–6, 57, 116–17, 118, 158–9, 174, 175–6, 181–2, 199, 201, 209, 210, 230–1, 211–12, 236, 261–2, 300, 318–19, 323–4, 337, 340, 344–5, 382, 384, 395, 413–14, 439, 492, 493, 495, 496, 581
EC – Bananas III (Ecuador) (1997)	Panel Report, *European Communities – Regime for the Importation, Sale and Distribution of Bananas, Complaint by Ecuador*, WT/DS27/R/ECU, adopted 25 September 1997, as modified by Appellate Body Report WT/DS27/AB/R, DSR 1997:III, 1085 175, 273, 280–1, 324–5, 406, 411, 494–5
EC – Bananas III (Guatemala and Honduras) (1997)	Panel Report, *European Communities – Regime for the Importation, Sale and Distribution of Bananas, Complaint by Guatemala and Honduras*, WT/DS27/R/GTM, WT/DS27/R/HND, adopted 25 September 1997, as modified by Appellate Body Report WT/DS27/AB/R, DSR 1997:II, 695 175, 273, 280–1, 323–4, 406, 411, 494–5
EC – Bananas III (Mexico) (1997)	Panel Report, *European Communities – Regime for the Importation, Sale and Distribution of Bananas, Complaint by Mexico*, WT/DS27/R/MEX, adopted 25 September 1997, as modified by Appellate Body Report WT/DS27/AB/R, DSR 1997:II, 803 175, 273, 280–1, 330, 406, 411, 494–5
EC – Bananas III (US) (1997)	Panel Report, *European Communities – Regime for the Importation, Sale and Distribution of Bananas, Complaint by the United States*, WT/DS27/R/USA, adopted 25 September 1997, as modified by Appellate Body Report WT/DS27/AB/R, DSR 1997:II, 943 175, 273, 280–1, 406, 411, 494–5
EC – Bananas III (Article 21.3(c)) (1998)	Award of the Arbitrator, *European Communities – Regime for the Importation, Sale and Distribution of Bananas – Arbitration under Article 21.3(c) of the DSU*, WT/DS27/15, 7 January 1998, DSR 1998:I, 3 199
EC – Bananas III (Article 21.5 – EC)	Panel Report, *European Communities – Regime for the Importation, Sale and Distribution of Bananas – Recourse to Article 21.5 of the DSU by the European Communities*, WT/DS27/RW/EEC, 12 April 1999, and Corr.1, unadopted, DSR 1999:II, 783 162, 207

Short title	Full case title and citation
US – Hot Rolled Steel (Article 21.3(c)) (2002)	Award of the Arbitrator, *United States – Anti-Dumping Measures on Certain Hot Rolled Steel Products from Japan – Arbitration under Article 21.3(c) of the DSU*, WT/DS184/13, 19 February 2002, DSR 2002:IV, 1389 196
US – Lamb (2001)	Appellate Body Report, *United States – Safeguard Measures on Imports of Fresh, Chilled or Frozen Lamb Meat from New Zealand and Australia*, WT/DS177/AB/R, WT/DS178/AB/R, adopted 16 May 2001, DSR 2001:IX, 4051 222, 241, 275–6, 610, 612, 614–15, 616–19, 620–2
US – Large Civil Aircraft (2d complaint) (2012)	Appellate Body Report, *United States – Measures Affecting Trade in Large Civil Aircraft (Second Complaint)*, WT/DS353/AB/R, adopted 23 March 2012 57, 80, 158–9, 186, 206, 234, 288, 745, 752, 754–5, 761, 762, 766–7, 768–9, 790–1, 792, 796, 804, 808–11, 830
	Panel Report, *United States – Measures Affecting Trade in Large Civil Aircraft (Second Complaint)*, WT/DS353/R, adopted 23 March 2012, as modified by Appellate Body Report WT/DS353/AB/R 193, 252
US – Lead and Bismuth II (2000)	Appellate Body Report, *United States – Imposition of Countervailing Duties on Certain Hot Rolled Lead and Bismuth Carbon Steel Products Originating in the United Kingdom*, WT/DS138/AB/R, adopted 7 June 2000, DSR 2000:V, 2595 222, 265, 763
US – Line Pipe (2002)	Appellate Body Report, *United States – Definitive Safeguard Measures on Imports of Circular Welded Carbon Quality Line Pipe from Korea*, WT/DS202/AB/R, adopted 8 March 2002, DSR 2002:IV, 1403 193, 286–7, 607, 610, 618–21, 623, 626, 627, 628–9, 630, 657–8
	Panel Report, *United States – Definitive Safeguard Measures on Imports of Circular Welded Carbon Quality Line Pipe from Korea*, WT/DS202/R, adopted 8 March 2002, as modified by Appellate Body Report WT/DS202/AB/, DSR 2002:IV, 1473 212, 481–2, 493
US – Offset Act (Byrd Amendment) (2003)	Appellate Body Report, *United States – Continued Dumping and Subsidy Offset Act of 2000*, WT/DS217/AB/R, WT/DS234/AB/R, adopted 27 January 2003, DSR 2003:I, 375 174, 175, 199, 230, 233, 237, 239–40, 267–8, 285, 279–85, 678–9, 816, 825

Short title	Full case title and citation
US – Softwood Lumber V (2004)	Appellate Body Report, *United States – Final Dumping Determination on Softwood Lumber from Canada*, WT/DS264/AB/R, adopted 31 August 2004, DSR 2004:V, 1875 221, 236, 239–40, 688–9, 693–5, 713–4
	Panel Report, *United States – Final Dumping Determination on Softwood Lumber from Canada*, WT/DS264/R, adopted 31 August 2004, as modified by Appellate Body Report WT/DS264/AB/R, DSR 2004:V, 1937 689
US – Softwood Lumber V (Article 21.5 – Canada) (2006)	Appellate Body Report, *United States – Final Dumping Determination on Softwood Lumber from Canada – Recourse to Article 21.5 of the DSU by Canada*, WT/DS264/AB/RW, adopted 1 September 2006, DSR 2006:XII, 5087 690, 692
US – Softwood Lumber VI (2004)	Panel Report, *United States – Investigation of the International Trade Commission in Softwood Lumber from Canada*, WT/DS277/R, adopted 26 April 2004, DSR 2004:VI, 2485 707, 708
US – Softwood Lumber VI (Article 21.5 – Canada) (2006)	Appellate Body Report, *United States – Investigation of the International Trade Commission in Softwood Lumber from Canada – Recourse to Article 21.5 of the DSU by Canada*, WT/DS277/AB/RW, adopted 9 May 2006, and Corr.1, DSR 2006:XI, 4865 286, 707, 708, 710–11
US – Stainless Steel (Korea) (2001)	Panel Report, *United States – Anti-Dumping Measures on Stainless Steel Plate in Coils and Stainless Steel Sheet and Strip from Korea*, WT/DS179/R, adopted 1 February 2001, DSR 2001:IV, 1295 503, 688
US – Stainless Steel (Mexico) (2008)	Appellate Body Report, *United States – Final Anti-Dumping Measures on Stainless Steel from Mexico*, WT/DS344/AB/R, adopted 20 May 2008, DSR 2008:II, 513 52, 179, 221–2, 683–4, 691, 693–5
	Panel Report, *United States – Final Anti-Dumping Measures on Stainless Steel from Mexico*, WT/DS344/R, adopted 20 May 2008, as modified by Appellate Body Report WT/DS344/AB/R, DSR 2008:II, 599 221–222, 689
US – Steel Plate (2002)	Panel Report, *United States – Anti-Dumping and Countervailing Measures on Steel Plate from India*, WT/DS206/R and Corr.1, adopted 29 July 2002, DSR 2002:VI, 2073 719, 734

TABLE OF GATT CASES

The year in brackets following the short name of the case refers to the year in which the GATT panel or working party report in that case was adopted. Where unadopted reports are concerned, the year in brackets refers to the year in which these reports were circulated.

Short title	Full case title and citation
Australia – Ammonium Sulphate (1950)	Working Party Report, *The Australian Subsidy on Ammonium Sulphate*, GATT/CP.4/39, adopted 3 April 1950, BISD II, p. 188 361
Belgium – Family Allowances (allocations familiales) (1952)	GATT Panel Report, *Belgian Family Allowances*, G/32, adopted 7 November 1952, BISD 1S, p. 59 323–4, 329
Border Tax Adjustments (1970)	Working Party Report, *Border Tax Adjustments*, L/3464, adopted 2 December 1970, BISD 18S, p. 97 359, 361, 389, 390–1
Canada – FIRA (1984)	GATT Panel Report, *Canada – Administration of the Foreign Investment Review Act*, L/5504, adopted 7 February 1984, BISD 30S, p. 140 354, 383–4, 385
Canada – Herring and Salmon (1988)	GATT Panel Report, *Canada – Measures Affecting Exports of Unprocessed Herring and Salmon*, L/6268, adopted 22 March 1988, BISD 35S, p. 98 566
Canada – Provincial Liquor Boards (US) (1992)	GATT Panel Report, *Canada – Import, Distribution and Sale of Certain Alcoholic Drinks by Provincial Marketing Agencies*, DS17/R, adopted 18 February 1992, BISD 39S, p. 27 383–4, 395, 402
EEC – Animal Feed Proteins (1978)	GATT Panel Report, *EEC – Measures on Animal Feed Proteins*, L/4599, adopted 14 March 1978, BISD 25S, p. 49 7, 326, 358–9, 361, 389, 465

Short title	Full case title and citation
Japan – Leather (US II) (1984)	GATT Panel Report, *Panel on Japanese Measures on Imports of Leather*, L/5623, adopted 15 May 1984, BISD 31S, p. 94 484
Japan – Semi-Conductors (1988)	GATT Panel Report, *Japan – Trade in Semi-Conductors*, L/6309, adopted 4 May 1988, BISD 35S, p. 116 483–4, 485
Japan – SPF Dimension Lumber (1989)	GATT Panel Report, *Canada/Japan – Tariff on Imports of Spruce, Pine, Fir (SPF) Dimension Lumber*, L/6470, adopted 19 July 1989, BISD 36S, p. 167 7, 326, 452–3
Korea – Beef (Australia) (1989)	GATT Panel Report, *Republic of Korea – Restrictions on Imports of Beef – Complaint by Australia*, L/6504, adopted 7 November 1989, BISD 36S, p. 202 465
Spain – Unroasted Coffee (1981)	GATT Panel Report, *Spain – Tariff Treatment of Unroasted Coffee*, L/5135, adopted 11 June 1981, BISD 28S, p. 102 326–7, 361, 452–3
Thailand – Cigarettes (1990)	GATT Panel Report, *Thailand – Restrictions on Importation of and Internal Taxes on Cigarettes*, DS10/R, adopted 7 November 1990, BISD 37S, p. 200 165, 166–7, 383–4, 402
US – Canadian Tuna (1982)	GATT Panel Report, *United States – Prohibition of Imports of Tuna and Tuna Products from Canada*, L/5198, adopted 22 February 1982, BISD 29S, p. 91 566
US – Customs User Fee (1988)	GATT Panel Report, *United States – Customs User Fee*, L/6264, adopted 2 February 1988, BISD 35S, p. 245 323–4, 465, 4689
US – Export Restrictions (Czechoslovakia) (1949)	Contracting Parties Decision, *Article XXI – United States Exports Restrictions*, 8 June 1949, BISD II, p. 28 597
US – Fur Felt Hats (1951)	*Report on the Withdrawal by the United States of a Tariff Concession under Article XIX of the General Agreement on Tariffs and Trade*, GATT/CP/106, adopted 22 October 1951 614
US – Malt Beverages (1992)	GATT Panel Report, *United States – Measures Affecting Alcoholic and Malt Beverages*, DS23/R, adopted 19 June 1992, BISD 39S, p. 206 165, 166–7, 351, 359, 365–6, 383–4, 392, 395, 402
US – MFN Footwear (1992)	GATT Panel Report, *United States – Denial of Most-Favoured-Nation Treatment as to Non-Rubber Footwear from Brazil*, DS18/R, adopted 19 June 1992, BISD 39S, p. 128 322, 323–5

Short title	Full case title and citation
US – Nicaraguan Trade (1986)	GATT Panel Report, *United States – Trade Measures Affecting Nicaragua*, L/6053, 13 October 1986, unadopted 596, 597–8
US – Norwegian Salmon AD (1994)	GATT Panel Report, *Imposition of Anti-Dumping Duties on Imports of Fresh and Chilled Atlantic Salmon from Norway*, ADP/87, adopted 27 April 1994, BISD 41S, p. 229 710–11
US – Section 337 Tariff Act (1989)	GATT Panel Report, *United States Section 337 of the Tariff Act of 1930*, L/6439, adopted 7 November 1989, BISD 36S, p. 345 165, 166–7, 352, 378–9, 3834, 395, 396, 397–8, 399–400, 546, 563–5, 573, 965
US – Spring Assemblies (1983)	GATT Panel Report, *United States – Imports of Certain Automotive Spring Assemblies*, L/5333, adopted 26 May 1983, BISD 30S, p. 107 572–3
US – Sugar (1989)	GATT Panel Report, *United States Restrictions on Imports of Sugar*, L/6514, adopted 22 June 1989, BISD 36S, p. 331 439
US – Sugar Quota (1984)	GATT Panel Report, *United States – Imports of Sugar from Nicaragua*, L/5607, adopted 13 March 1984, BISD 31S, p. 67 595, 597–8
US – Superfund (1987)	GATT Panel Report, *United States – Taxes on Petroleum and Certain Imported Substances*, L/6175, adopted 17 June 1987, BISD 34S, p. 136 165, 166–7, 352, 361, 368
US – Taxes on Automobiles (1994)	GATT Panel Report, *United States – Taxes on Automobiles*, DS31/R, 11 October 1994, unadopted 366
US – Tobacco (1994)	GATT Panel Report, *United States – Measures Affecting the Importation, Internal Sale and Use of Tobacco*, DS44/R, adopted 4 October 1994, BISD 41S, p. 131 358
US – Tuna (Mexico) (1991)	GATT Panel Report, *United States – Restrictions on Imports of Tuna*, DS21/R, 3 September 1991, unadopted, BISD 39S, p. 155 393

1 International Trade and the Law of the WTO

CONTENTS

1 INTRODUCTION

At the Millennium Summit of the United Nations in September 2000, the largest ever meeting of Heads of State and Government, the UN General Assembly solemnly declared:

We will spare no effort to free our fellow men, women, and children from the abject and dehumanizing conditions of extreme poverty, to which more than a billion of them are currently subjected. We are committed to making the right to development a reality for everyone and to freeing the entire human race from want.[1]

1 United Nations General Assembly, *UN Millennium Declaration*, Resolution adopted on 8 September 2000, para. 11.

1

This magnanimous ambition was translated into eight Millennium Development Goals, the most important of which is the eradication of extreme poverty and hunger. The Millennium Development Goals also include achieving universal primary education, promoting gender equality, reducing child and maternal mortality, combating HIV/AIDS, malaria and other diseases, and ensuring environmental sustainability. With regard to the eradication of extreme poverty and hunger, the target set was to *halve* the number of people living in extreme poverty and suffering from hunger by the year 2015.[2] In the *World Development Indicators 2012*, the most recent progress report on the Millennium Development Goals, the World Bank noted:

> We will *not* achieve *all* the targets we set for ourselves, but progress measured against 1990 benchmarks accelerated in the last decade, lifting millions of people out of poverty, enrolling millions of children in school, and sharply reducing loss of life from preventable causes.[3]

While poverty and hunger remain a shameful reality,[4] fewer people – both in absolute numbers and as a percentage of the world population – now live in extreme poverty or suffer from hunger than did two decades ago. The percentage of the world population living on less than US$1.25 a day fell from 43 per cent in 1990 to 22 per cent in 2008.[5] Over the last four years, the global economic crisis has worsened the situation of vulnerable populations and has slowed down poverty reduction in some countries. However, global poverty rates have continued to fall. According to the World Bank, preliminary estimates for 2010 show that the target to halve the number of people living in extreme poverty has been reached five years early. Further progress in poverty reduction is possible and likely by the 2015 target date if developing countries maintain strong economic growth. The reduction in the number of people living in extreme poverty as well as progress on other Millennium Development Goals over the past two decades have been, to a large extent, due to the impressive economic growth rates in developing countries in East Asia and the Pacific region. In China, extreme poverty fell from 60 per cent in 1990 to 13 per cent in 2008. Also, developing countries in South Asia, and in particular India, as well as developing countries in Sub-Saharan Africa have known robust economic growth, which has contributed to the reduction of the percentage of people living in extreme poverty. In South Asia, the poverty rate fell from 54 per cent in 1990 to 36 per cent in 2008. The poverty

---

2 *Ibid.*, para. 19.
3 World Bank, *World Development Indicators 2012*, 1. Emphasis added.
4 According to the latest data available, in 2008, 1.28 billion people lived on less than US$1.25 a day, the standard used by the World Bank to define extreme poverty; 739 million people were without adequate daily food intake; and more than 100 million children under age five remain malnourished. Since 1990, the number of people – in absolute numbers – living in extreme poverty has fallen in all regions except Sub-Saharan Africa, where the rate of population growth exceeded the rate of poverty reduction, increasing the number of extremely poor people from 290 million in 1990 to 356 million in 2008. The largest number of poor people remain in South Asia, where 571 million people live on less than US$1.25 a day. See World Bank, *World Development Indicators 2012*, 2–3.
5 For the data referred to in this paragraph, see *ibid*. 2.

rate in Sub-Saharan Africa fell 4.8 percentage points to less than 50 per cent between 2005 and 2008. This was the largest drop since international poverty rates have been computed. The progress made over the past decades has been impressive, and, importantly, this progress is likely to continue.[6] However, as the World Bank emphasised in its *World Development Indicators 2012*:

hundreds of millions of people will remain mired in poverty, especially in Sub-Saharan Africa and South Asia and wherever poor health and lack of education deprive people of productive employment; environmental resources have been depleted or spoiled; and corruption, conflict, and misgovernance waste public resources and discourage private investment.

Also note that the United Nations Development Programme (UNDP) stated in its *Human Development Report 2011* that:

[f]orecasts suggest that continuing failure to reduce the grave environmental risks and deepening social inequalities threatens to slow decades of sustained progress by the world's poor majority – and even to reverse the global convergence in human development.[7]

The progress made in reducing poverty worldwide should not hide the fact that the income gap between the richest and poorest citizens has continued to grow. In discussing the greatest challenges that the world faces, Jimmy Carter, the former US President, stated in his Nobel Peace Prize Lecture in December 2002:

Among all the possible choices, I decided that the most serious and universal problem is the growing chasm between the richest and poorest people on earth. The results of this disparity are root causes of most of the world's unresolved problems, including starvation, illiteracy, environmental degradation, violent conflict, and unnecessary illnesses that range from guinea worm to HIV/Aids.[8]

In its *Global Risks 2013* report, the World Economic Forum identified severe income disparity as the global risk that is most likely to manifest itself over the next ten years.[9] Such income disparity entrenches corruption and injustice, gives rise to xenophobic nationalism and religious fundamentalism, fosters political instability and leads to violence and economic destruction.

Finally, while their problems are obviously different in nature, scale and/or intensity, many developed countries have, in particular over the last years, experienced little, if any, economic growth, and are struggling with high unemployment. In November 2012, the unemployment rate in the Eurozone was at a record high of 11.8 per cent. In Spain, the unemployment rate was at 26.6 per cent.[10]

One of the defining features of today's world is the process of economic globalisation. The question therefore arises whether this process has contributed

---

6 See *ibid.*, 2.
7 United Nations Development Programme, *Human Development Report 2011*, ii.
8 US President Jimmy Carter, Nobel Lecture, Oslo, 10 December 2002, at http://nobelprize.org/nobel_prizes/peace/laureates/2002/carter-lecture.html.
9 See World Economic Forum, *Global Risks 2013*, 10.
10 See http://epp.eurostat.ec.europa.eu/portal/page/portal/eurostat/home.

to the impressive, albeit still insufficient, progress towards the achievement of the Millennium Development Goals or whether this process has instead aggravated the continuing poverty and hunger in many developing countries, the ever growing gap between the richest and poorest of the world, and the current economic woes of developed countries. This chapter deals in turn with: (1) economic globalisation and international trade; (2) the law of the WTO; (3) the sources of WTO law; and (4) WTO law in context, i.e. its relationship with other international law and national law.

2   ECONOMIC GLOBALISATION AND INTERNATIONAL TRADE

'Economic globalisation' has been a popular buzzword for more than two decades now. Politicians, government officials, businesspeople, trade unionists, environmentalists, church leaders, public health experts, third-world activists, economists and lawyers all speak of 'economic globalisation'. This section deals with economic globalisation and international trade. It discusses: (1) the concept of 'economic globalisation' and the emergence of the global economy; (2) whether economic globalisation, the emergence of the global economy, and, in particular, international trade, are a blessing or curse; (3) what are the arguments for free trade and the arguments for restrictions on trade; and (4) whether international trade can be to the benefit of all.

2.1   Emergence of the Global Economy

Over the past two decades and as a result of the process of economic globalisation, a *global* economy has been emerging, gradually but at an ever-increasing speed replacing the patchwork of national economies. This sub-section discusses in turn: (1) the concept of 'economic globalisation'; (2) the forces driving economic globalisation and creating the global economy; (3) facts and figures on international trade and foreign direct investment in the global economy; and (4) the changing nature of international trade in the global economy.

2.1.1   The Concept of 'Economic Globalisation'

The concepts of 'globalisation', and, in particular, 'economic globalisation', have been used by many to describe one of the defining features of the world in which we live. But what do these terms mean? Joseph Stiglitz, former Chief Economist of the World Bank and winner of the Nobel Prize for Economics in 2001, described the concept of globalisation in his 2002 book, *Globalization and Its Discontents*, as:

the closer integration of the countries and peoples of the world which has been brought about by the enormous reduction of costs of transportation and communication, and the breaking down of artificial barriers to the flow of goods, services, capital, knowledge, and (to a lesser extent) people across borders.[11]

In *The Lexus and the Olive Tree: Understanding Globalisation*, Thomas Friedman, the award-winning journalist of the *New York Times*, defined 'globalisation' as follows:

[I]t is the inexorable integration of markets, nation-states and technologies to a degree never witnessed before – in a way that is enabling individuals, corporations and nation-states to reach around the world farther, faster, deeper and cheaper than ever before, and in a way that is enabling the world to reach into individuals, corporations and nation-states farther, faster, deeper and cheaper than ever before.[12]

Economic globalisation is a multifaceted phenomenon. In essence, however, economic globalisation is the gradual integration of national economies into one borderless global economy. It encompasses both (free) international trade and (unrestricted) foreign direct investment. Economic globalisation affects people everywhere in many aspects of their daily lives. It affects their jobs, their food, their health, their education and their leisure time. Innumerable examples of economic globalisation could be given, ranging from the clothes we wear, the cars we drive, the movies we watch, the bananas we eat, the coffee we drink, the insurance policies we buy, the university education we get, to the mobile phones we so rely on. However, to give but one example, consider the following story which featured in the *Financial Times* in August 2003, but which illustrates today's reality of economic globalisation even better than it did a decade ago:

Clutching her side in pain, the woman with suspected appendicitis who was rushed to a hospital on the outskirts of Philadelphia last week had little time to ponder how dependent her life had become on the relentless forces of globalisation. Within minutes of her arrival at the Crozer-Chester Medical Center, the recommendation on whether to operate was being made by a doctor reading her computer-aided tomography (CAT) scan from a computer screen 5,800 miles away in the Middle East. Jonathan Schlakman, a Harvard-trained radiologist based in Jerusalem, is one of a new breed of skilled professionals proving that geographic distance is no obstacle to outsourcing even the highest paid jobs to overseas locations. The migration of white-collar work has moved up the value chain from call centre operators and back-office clerks to occupations such as equity research, accounting, computer programming and chip design. The trend – still only a trickle at present – may look to some like a temporary fad pursued by companies seeking to cut costs. For trade unions in the US and Europe, it heralds a fundamental restructuring of rich-world economies, akin to the globalisation of manufacturing in the 1980s and the outsourcing of unskilled service jobs in the 1990s. At present, only 35 patients' scans are transmitted each day from US emergency rooms to Dr Schlakman's small team of doctors in Israel. But with senior radiologists costing up to $300,000 a year to hire in the US and many emergency cases arriving at night, the

---

11 J. Stiglitz, *Globalization and Its Discontents* (Penguin, 2002), 9.
12 T. Friedman, *The Lexus and the Olive Tree: Understanding Globalisation*, 2nd edn (First Anchor Books, 2000), 9.

use of medical expertise based in a different time zone and earning less than half US rates is almost certain to rise. 'It's much more expensive to use night staff in the US because they need time off the following day', says Dr Schlakman.[13]

While economic globalisation is often presented as a new phenomenon, it deserves to be mentioned that today's global economic integration is not unprecedented. During the fifty years preceding the First World War, there were also large cross-border flows of goods and capital and, more than now, of people.[14] David Livingstone, the famous nineteenth-century medical missionary and Africa explorer wrote about this period of economic globalisation:

The extension and use of railroads, steamships [and] telegraphs break down nationalities and bring peoples geographically remote into close connection commercially and politically. They make the world one, and capital, like water, tends to a common level.[15]

If one looks at the ratio of trade to GDP, Britain and France are only slightly more open to trade today than they were in 1913, while Japan is less open now than it was then.[16] However, this earlier period of economic globalisation ended abruptly in 1914 and was followed by one of the darkest periods in the history of humankind. Today's process of economic globalisation is strong and gathering ever more strength. However, the extent of global economic integration already achieved can be, and frequently is, exaggerated. International trade should normally force high-cost domestic producers to lower their prices and bring the prices of products and services between different countries closer together. However, large divergences in prices persist. This may be due to, *inter alia*, differences in transport costs, taxes and the efficiency of distribution networks. But this is also due to the continued existence of significant barriers to trade. Furthermore, while goods, services and capital move across borders with greater ease, restrictions on the free movement of workers, i.e. restrictions on economic migration, remain multiple and rigorous.

Questions and Assignments 1.1

How would you define 'economic globalisation'? Does economic globalisation also affect non-economic matters? Give three concrete examples of how *you* are affected by economic globalisation. Is economic globalisation a historically unique and all-pervasive phenomenon?

2.1.2   Forces Driving Economic Globalisation

It is commonly argued that economic globalisation has been driven by two main forces. The first, *technology*, makes globalisation feasible; the second, the

---

13 D. Roberts, E. Luce and K. Merchant, 'Service Industries Go Global', *Financial Times*, 20 August 2003.

14 Also the Roman Empire (27 BC–476 AD) and the Chinese Song dynasty (960–1279) can be seen as (early) examples of economic globalisation.

15 David Livingstone, *The Last Journals of David Livingstone* (originally published in 1880, now published by The Echo Library, 2005), 351.

16 'One World?', *The Economist*, 18 October 1997.

liberalisation of trade and foreign direct investment, makes it happen.[17] Due to technological innovations resulting in a dramatic fall in transport, communication and computing costs, the natural barriers of time and space that separate national economies have been coming down. Between 1920 and 1990, average ocean freight and port charges for US import and export cargo fell by almost 70 per cent. Between 1930 and 1990, average air-transport fares per passenger mile fell by 84 per cent.[18] The cost of a three-minute telephone call between New York and London has fallen from US$300 in 1930 to US$1 in 1997 (in 1996 dollars); the cost of computer processing power has been falling by an average of 30 per cent per year in real terms over recent decades.[19] As noted by Thomas Friedman in his 2005 book, *The World Is Flat – A Brief History of the Globalized World in the Twenty-First Century*:

> Clearly, it is now possible for more people than ever to collaborate and compete in real time with more other people on more different kinds of work from more different corners of the planet and on more equal footing than at any previous time in the history of the world – using computers, e-mail, networks, teleconferencing, and dynamic new software.[20]

The second driving force of economic globalisation has been the liberalisation of international trade and foreign direct investment. Over the last sixty years, most developed countries have gradually but significantly lowered barriers to foreign trade and investment. Over the last twenty years, the liberalisation of trade and investment has become a worldwide trend, including in developing countries, although liberalisation still proceeds at different speeds in different parts of the world. In his book, *Has Globalization Gone Too Far?*, Dani Rodrik, of the John F. Kennedy School of Government at Harvard University, observed with regard to this dimension of globalisation:

> Globalization is not occurring in a vacuum. It is part of a broader trend that we may call marketization. Receding government, deregulation, and the shrinking of social obligations are the domestic counterparts of the intertwining of national economies. Globalization could not have advanced this far without these complementary forces.[21]

While some politicians and opinion-makers claim otherwise, the process of economic globalisation is not irreversible. Lionel Barber, editor of the *Financial Times*, noted in 2004:

> For all its merits, globalization must never be taken for granted. The continued integration of the world economy depends on support not only from rich beneficiaries in the west but increasingly from the still disadvantaged in Africa, India, and Latin America. Cultural barriers also pose increasingly powerful obstacles to globalization. The rise of Islamic

---

17 See also M. Wolf, 'Global Opportunities', *Financial Times*, 6 May 1997.
18 R. Porter, 'The Global Trading System in the 21st Century', in R. Porter, P. Sauvé, A, Subramanian and A. Beviglia Zampetti (eds.), *Efficiency, Equity and Legitimacy: The Multilateral Trading System at the Millennium* (Brookings Institution Press, 2001), 4.
19 'One World?', *The Economist*, 18 October 1997.
20 T. Friedman, *The World is Flat – A Brief History of the Globalised World in the Twenty-first Century* (Farrar, Straus & Giroux, 2005), 8.
21 D. Rodrik, *Has Globalization Gone Too Far?* (Institute for International Economics, 1997), 85.

fundamentalism offers an alternative vision of society, one which will appeal to all those left behind in countries with exploding populations and persistent high unemployment among young people.[22]

However, it would be very difficult, and foolhardy, for governments to reverse the current globalisation process. Three reasons come to mind. First, new technology has created distribution channels especially for services, such as satellite communications and the Internet, that governments with protectionist intentions will find very difficult to control. Secondly, liberal international trade policies now have a firm institutional basis in the multilateral trading system of the WTO, discussed in detail in this book. Thirdly, the price to be paid in terms of economic prosperity for withdrawing from the global economy would be very high. Autarkies do not flourish in today's world. Arguably in recognition of the limited control policy-makers have over the process of globalisation, US President Bill Clinton stated at the 1998 WTO Ministerial Conference in Geneva: 'Globalization is not a policy choice – it is a fact.'[23] However, note that Lord Jordan, former General Secretary of the International Confederation of Free Trades Unions, wrote in December 2000 that globalisation 'is not an unstoppable force of nature, but is shaped by those who set the rules'.[24]

Questions and Assignments 1.2

What explains the process of economic globalisation? Could governments reverse the process of economic globalisation? Should they?

2.1.3 Facts and Figures on International Trade and Foreign Direct Investment

In 1948, world merchandise exports, i.e. exports of goods, amounted to US$59 billion per year. In 2011, world merchandise exports amounted to US$17,816 billion, or almost US$18 trillion, per year.[25] World exports of commercial services, marginal in 1948, amounted in 2011 to US$4,170 billion, or almost US$4.2 trillion.[26] At the height of the global economic crisis, in 2009, world merchandise exports shrunk by 12 per cent in volume terms (the sharpest decline since the Second World War),[27] but in 2010 grew again by 14 per cent and in 2011 by 5 per cent.[28] However, in 2012, world merchandise exports were projected to grow by only 2.5 per cent.[29] The merchandise exports of developed countries

---

22 L. Barber, 'A Symposium of Views: Is Continued Globalisation of the World Economy Inevitable?', *The International Economy*, Summer 2004, 70.

23 See www.wto.org/english/thewto_e/minist_e/min99_e/english/book_e/stak_e_3.htm.

24 B. Jordan, 'Yes to Globalization, But Protect the Poor', *International Herald Tribune*, 21 December 2000.

25 See WTO, *International Trade Statistics 2012*, at www.wto.org/english/res_e/statis_e/its2012_e/its12_world_trade_dev_e.pdf.

26 See *ibid.*

27 The volume of world merchandise exports fell on three other occasions after 1965 (down 0.2 per cent in 2001; down 2 per cent in 1982; and down 7 per cent in 1975). See www.wto.org/english/news_e/pres10_e/pr598_e.htm.

28 See *ibid.*   29 See www.wto.org/english/news_e/pres12_e/pr676_e.htm.

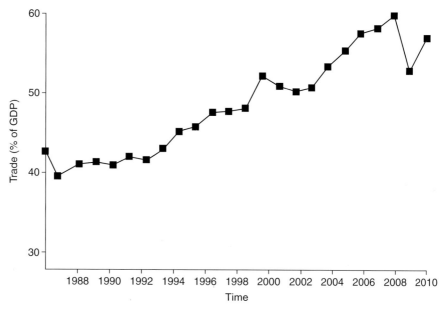

Figure 1.1 Ratio of global trade in merchandise and commercial services to GDP (1988–2010)

were expected to increase by a mere 1.5 per cent, while the merchandise exports of developing countries were expected to increase by 3.5 per cent, confirming a well-established trend of the developing countries outperforming the developed countries. Exports of commercial services shrunk by 12 per cent in 2009, but grew again by 10 per cent in 2010 and 11 per cent in 2011. Like merchandise exports, exports of commercial services were expected to grow considerably less in 2012 than in the two previous years.[30] The global economy, and in particular the economy of developed countries, clearly remains fragile. Recovery from the global economic crisis is a protracted process.

The ratio of global trade in merchandise and commercial services to GDP is a good measurement of economic globalisation.[31] As shown by Figure 1.1, over the past two decades, before the crisis year of 2009, the ratio of global trade to GDP increased significantly, indicating the extent of economic globalisation in these years. As is also shown, in 2010, this trend of ever more economic globalisation picked up again. The ratio of global trade to GDP increased from 37 per cent in 1988 to an all-time high of 59 per cent in 2008, then dropped in 2009 to 51 per cent, but increased again to 56 per cent in 2010.

---

30 See *ibid*.
31 The trade-to-GDP ratio indicates the dependence of domestic producers on foreign demand (exports) and of domestic consumers and producers on foreign supply (imports), relative to the country's economic size (GDP). The trade-to-GDP ratio is a basic indicator of openness to foreign trade and economic integration. See http://data.worldbank.org/news/new-data-visualizers-for-trade-data. For a world map of trade-to-GDP ratios, see www.wto.org/english/res_e/statis_e/statis_maps_e.htm.

Country	1990	2010
Bangladesh	18	43
Brazil	17	23
Canada	53	61
China	31	55
EU (including intra-EU trade)	54	79
India	15	46
Indonesia	45	48
Mexico	38	62
Russia	43	52
South Africa	52	55
South Korea	66	102
United States	20	29

Figure 1.2 Ratio of trade in merchandise and commercial services to GDP for selected countries (1990–2010)

The degree of economic globalisation, when measured as the ratio of trade to GDP, varies from country to country, but has increased in all major trading nations over the past two decades.

As shown by the data in Figure 1.2, the economies of many countries are to a large and ever-increasing degree dependent on trade. This is true for developed as well as developing countries. Note the extent to which, for example China (from 31 to 55 per cent), India (from 15 to 46 per cent), Bangladesh (from 18 to 43 per cent) and Mexico (from 38 to 62 per cent) have 'globalised' over the past two decades. It is interesting, and perhaps surprising to some, that least-developed countries are more 'globalised' than OECD countries. Brazil and the United States have the least 'globalised' economies of all major trading nations. South Korea has the most 'globalised' economy of all major trading nations. Note that the data on the EU include trade between EU Member States, i.e. intra-EU trade. When one considers only EU trade with non-EU countries, the ratio of trade to GDP for the EU was 30 per cent in 2010.[32]

It is not only the value and volume of world trade and the ratio of global trade to GDP that have changed significantly over the years. The share of world trade of various countries and regions of the world also changed significantly.[33] Overall, the

---

32 See http://stat.wto.org/CountryProfile/WSDBCountryPFView.aspx?Language=E&Country=E27.
33 See www.wto.org/english/res_e/statis_e/world_region_export_11_e.pdf, with additional information from WTO, *International Trade Statistics 2007*, at www.wto.org/english/res_e/statis_e/its2007_e/section1_e/i06.xls.

share of world trade of developed countries has in recent years dropped from 67 per cent in 2005 to 58 per cent in 2011, while the share of developing countries has increased from 29 per cent in 2005 to 37 per cent in 2011. Remarkable is the decline of the shares of North America (the United States, Canada and Mexico) from 28.1 per cent in 1948 to 21 per cent in 2005 and 16 per cent in 2011, and the modest increase of the share of Western Europe (primarily the European Union) from 35.1 per cent in 1948 to 39 per cent in 2011 (down from 45.9 per cent in 2003). Equally remarkable are the steep decline of the shares of both Latin America (down from 11.3 per cent to 4 per cent) and Africa (down from 7.3 per cent to 3 per cent) and the significant increase of Asia's share (up from 14 per cent to 29 per cent). The share of the least-developed countries increased in recent years from 0.5 to 1 per cent (although note that it stood at 1.7 per cent in 1970). Also, the composition of the trade of developing countries has changed. While many developing countries remain dependent on their exports of primary commodities, the share of manufactured goods has been growing. Since the early 1990s, there has been a boom in high-technology exports, with countries such as China, India and Mexico emerging as major suppliers of cutting-edge technologies, as well as labour-intensive goods.[34] The data referred to above clearly indicate that there is, with regard to trade in merchandise and commercial services, a 'redistribution of the geopolitical deck of cards on a global scale'.[35]

The leading exporters of merchandise in 2011 were: the European Union (14.9 per cent), China (13.2 per cent), the United States (10.3 per cent), Japan (5.7 per cent) and Korea (3.9 per cent).[36] The leading importers of merchandise were: the European Union (16.2 per cent), the United States (15.6 per cent), China (12.0 per cent), Japan (5.9 per cent) and Korea (3.6 per cent).[37] The leading exporters of commercial services in 2011 were: the European Union (24.7 per cent), the United States (18.3 per cent), China (5.8 per cent), Japan (4.5 per cent) and India (4.3 per cent).[38] The leading importers of commercial services were, in the same order: the European Union (21.1 per cent), the United States (12.9 per cent), China (7.7 per cent), Japan (5.4 per cent) and India (4.1 per cent).[39]

As noted above, next to international trade, the second important aspect of economic globalisation is foreign direct investment (FDI). This book does not

34 *Ibid.*
35 See Pascal Lamy in his welcome address to the participants in the WTO's Public Forum, 24 September 2012. See www.wto.org/english/news_e/sppl_e/sppl244_e.htm.
36 See www.wto.org/english/res_e/statis_e/its2012_e/its12_world_trade_dev_e.pdf. Note that this ranking is on the basis of world merchandise trade excluding intra-EU trade. Also note that the Russian Federation was the 6th biggest exporter of merchandise (3.6 per cent) (before Canada (3.2 per cent) and Hong Kong, China (3.2 per cent)); and that India was the thirteenth (2.1 per cent) and Brazil the sixteenth biggest exporter of merchandise (1.8 per cent).
37 See *ibid.* Note that India was the eighth (3.2 per cent), the Russian Federation the eleventh (2.2 per cent) and Brazil the fifteenth biggest importer of merchandise (1.6 per cent).
38 See *ibid.* Note that the Russian Federation was the eleventh (1.7 per cent) and Brazil the eighteenth biggest exporter of commercial services (1.2 per cent).
39 See *ibid.* Note that the Russian Federation was the ninth (2.9 per cent) and Brazil the tenth biggest importer of commercial services (2.4 per cent).

deal with FDI, but it should be noted that inflows of FDI have – similarly to international trade flows – increased notably over the past decades. In 1990, global FDI flows amounted to US$207 billion. In its *World Investment Report 2012*, the United Nations Conference on Trade and Development (UNCTAD) reported that, in 2011, global FDI flows reached US$1.5 trillion, exceeding the pre-crisis average, albeit still some 23 per cent below the 2007 peak.[40] FDI flows to developed countries increased by 21 per cent, to US$748 billion; FDI flows to developing countries increased by 11 per cent, reaching a record US$684 billion. In 2011, FDI flows to developing countries accounted for 45 per cent of global FDI.[41] Increasingly, companies from developing countries, such as China and India, are in developed and other developing countries.

Questions and Assignments 1.3

Discuss the trends in international trade and foreign direct investment over the past two decades. Do these trends reveal an ever-increasing degree of economic globalisation? Which countries belong to the group of 'top globalisers' and which countries do not? Does the current global economic crisis constitute a turning point in the economic globalisation process? Comment on the developing countries' share in world trade in merchandise and services.

2.1.4   Changing Nature of International Trade in the Global Economy

For many centuries, trade was mostly about products manufactured in country A being exported to country B. However, as has been noted by economists and policy-makers alike, the nature of trade is changing. Trade in the globalised economy of today is increasingly trade in tasks and in value-added. Techno-logical innovations, resulting in much lower transportation and communication costs, as well as the emergence of a 'rules-based', more secure and predictable trading environment (i.e. the prime focus of this book), have allowed producers to fragment production across many countries. Karel De Gucht, the European Commissioner for Trade, noted in April 2012:

Most of you will be familiar with the example of the Nokia smartphone. It is listed as be-ing made in China, but in reality 54% of its value comes from tasks that are carried out in Europe. Key components are produced in other parts of Asia and only the assembly itself actually happens in China.[42]

Today, products and services are often not produced in a single location or by a single producer. Instead, they are 'the end result of a highly coordinated series of steps carried out in many countries around the world by many people with

---

40 See UNCTAD, *World Investment Report 2012*, 24. In 2009, global FDI flows plummeted to US$1.2 trillion. For the next few years, UNCTAD has predicted a moderate but steady rise, with global FDI reaching US$1.9 trillion in 2014. See *ibid.*, 1 and 24.

41 See *ibid.*, 1.

42 Karel De Gucht, 'Trading in Value and Europe's Economic Future', High-Level Conference on 'Competitive-ness, Trade, Environment and Jobs in Europe: Insights from the New World Input Output Database (WIOD)', 16 April 2012, at http://europa.eu/rapid/press-release_SPEECH-12-264_en.htm.

many different skills'. Rather than 'Made in China', 'Made in Australia' or 'Made in Mexico', products and services are now 'Made in the World'.

This reality is not yet reflected in the trade data included in the previous sections of this chapter, as it is currently not yet reflected in the trade statistics generally available. The WTO, the OECD and a large EU-funded coalition of organisations, research institutes and statistical offices have worked together to remedy this problem with trade statistics. In January 2013, the first batch of new trade data reflecting the changing nature of international trade was released. WTO Director-General Pascal Lamy noted on the occasion of this release that these new trade data give us three important insights into today's international trade.[43] First, the new trade data clearly show the importance of trade in services. While trade in services represents about 20 per cent of total trade, its share doubles when one considers its contribution to the value-added that is traded internationally. Secondly, the new trade data highlight the importance of trade in intermediate products and the significance of such trade in improving the competitiveness of the exports. Today, trade in intermediate products accounts for more than half of global merchandise exports; and the average import content of exported goods is 40 per cent. Therefore, in order for exported goods to be competitive on the world market, manufacturers need access to the cheap imported inputs. Thirdly, these new trade data, which reflect imports and exports measured according to their true national content, permit, and indeed require, a redefinition of bilateral trade balances. Such a redefinition results, for example, in a 30 per cent reduction of the politically sensitive current US trade deficit with China.

Acknowledging that the nature of international trade is changing will not only affect the way in which trade data will be gathered in the future. More importantly, it will change – certainly in the longer term – the way in which governments think about trade and trade policy.[44] The acute realisation that cheap imports are the lifeblood of competitive exports is perhaps one of the reasons – next to the strength of the multilateral trading system – why countries did not, as history would expect them to do, react to the global economic crisis with a barrage of restrictions on trade.[45]

2.2   A Blessing or a Curse?

All around the world people feel the effects of economic globalisation and international trade, but these effects are not felt by all in an even or equitable

---

43 See Pascal Lamy, Round Table Discussion on 'New Steps in Measuring Trade in Value Added' at the OECD, Paris on 16 January 2013, at www.wto.org/english/news_e/sppl_e/sppl261_e.htm.

44 See e.g. Global Agenda Council on the Global Trade System, *The Shifting Geography of Global Value Chains: Implications for Developing Countries and Trade Policy* (World Economic Forum, 2012).

45 See also below, pp. 22–6.

way. In the 1990s and early 2000s, the large and often violent street demonstrations that rocked Seattle, Prague, Montreal, Cancún, Washington, Hong Kong, Geneva, Genoa, Zurich and other cities around the world gave expression to many people's dissatisfaction with, and rejection of, economic globalisation and international trade. While such demonstrations seem to be – at least for now – a thing of the past, the debate on the benefits and dangers of economic globalisation and international trade is, in these times of global crises (economic, financial, environmental and food), more relevant than ever.

According to a 2010 survey of public opinion on economic globalisation in the European Union, 56 per cent of Europeans agreed that globalisation is an opportunity for economic growth, while 27 per cent disagreed with this statement.[46] Not surprisingly, many more of the most educated respondents agreed with the statement than did the least educated. Equally unsurprising, Northern Europeans (and in particular the Danes, Swedes and Dutch) significantly more often agreed with the statement than Southern Europeans (and in particular the Italians, French and Greeks).[47] While in the European Union and most other countries, the majority of people is not *opposed* to economic globalisation and international trade, there is widespread concern and considerable anxiety about the harmful effect that economic globalisation and international trade may have: (1) on jobs and wages (affected by delocalisation and outsourcing, or the threat thereof); (2) on the global ecosystem as well as the local environment (by promoting unsustainable patterns of production and consumption); (3) on world poverty and hunger (in the face of growing income disparity between the rich and the poor); (4) on the economic development of developing countries (by obliging these countries to open their markets too far too fast, and not protecting or promoting their export opportunities); (5) on social, labour, health and safety regulation (as a result of regulatory competition resulting in a 'race to the bottom'); (6) on the livelihood of hundreds of millions of small farmers (endangered by the importation of cheap agricultural produce); (7) on cultural identity and diversity (threatened by the rise of a global Anglo Saxon popular monoculture); and (8) on national sovereignty and the democratic process (under threat from international organisations promulgating rules for the global economy beyond the control of individual States).

Radical proponents of economic globalisation and international trade tend to present globalisation and trade as a panacea for many of the world's problems. These cheerleaders of globalisation usually show little sympathy for, or

---

46 European Commission, Standard Eurobarometer 73, *Public Opinion in the European Union*, Report, Volume 2, Spring 2010, 12, at http://ec.europa.eu/public_opinion/archives/eb/eb73/eb73_vol2_en.pdf. Of the 56 per cent agreeing with this statement, 12 per cent totally agreed and 44 per cent tended to agree. Of the 27 per cent disagreeing, 7 per cent totally disagreed and 20 per cent tended to disagree. Note that 17 per cent expressed no opinion.
47 See *ibid.*, 12 and 14.

understanding of, the concerns referred to above.[48] On the contrary, opponents often see economic globalisation and international trade as malignant forces that destroy the livelihood of millions of workers and exacerbate income inequality, social injustice, environmental degradation and cultural homogenisation. They campaign for the replacement of the current 'unfair and oppressive trade system' with a 'new, socially just and sustainable trading framework'. It is unfortunate that the debate on economic globalisation and international trade is often emotionally charged and thus not constructive. Oxfam noted in its 2002 study, *Rigged Rules and Double Standards: Trade, Globalization, and the Fight Against Poverty*, the following:

Current debates about trade are dominated by ritualistic exchanges between two camps: the 'globaphiles' and the 'globaphobes'. 'Globaphiles' argue that trade is already making globalisation work for the poor. Their prescription for the future is 'more of the same'. 'Globaphobes' turn this world-view on its head. They argue that trade is inherently bad for the poor. Participation in trade, so the argument runs, inevitably leads to more poverty and inequality. The corollary of this view is 'the less trade the better'. The anti-globalisation movement deserves credit. It has raised profoundly important questions about social justice – and it has forced the failures of globalisation on to the political agenda. However, the war of words between trade optimists and trade pessimists that accompanies virtually every international meeting is counter-productive. Both world views fly in the face of the evidence – and neither offers any hope for the future.[49]

Oxfam's characterisation of the debate on economic globalisation and international trade in 2002 – unfortunately – still rings true today. While not sharing the extreme positions of anti-globalists and being careful 'not to make the mistake of attributing to globalisation the blemishes of other faces',[50] many observers and scholars recognise both the benefits *and* the dangers of economic globalisation and international trade. In his 2002 book, *Globalization and Its Discontents*, Joseph Stiglitz wrote:

Opening up to international trade has helped many countries grow far more quickly than they would otherwise have done. International trade helps economic development when a country's exports drive its economic growth. Export-led growth was the centrepiece of the industrial policy that enriched much of Asia and left millions of people there far better off. Because of globalization many people in the world now live longer than before and their standard of living is far better. People in the West may regard low-paying jobs at Nike as exploitation, but for many people in the developing world, working in a factory is a far better option than staying down on the farm and growing rice. Globalization has reduced the sense of isolation felt in much of the developing world and has given many people in the developing countries access to knowledge well beyond the reach of even the wealthiest in any country a century ago ... Even when there are negative sides to globalization, there

48 The term 'globalisation's cheerleaders' was used by Dani Rodrik in a 2007 contribution to the *Financial Times*, in which he argued that not the 'protesters on the streets', but these 'cheerleaders' in government or at elite universities in North America and Europe presented the greater menace to globalisation. See D. Rodrik, 'The Cheerleaders' Threat to Global Trade', *Financial Times*, 26 March 2007.
49 Oxfam, *Rigged Rules and Double Standards: Trade, Globalization, and the Fight Against Poverty* (2002), Summary of Chapter 1.
50 J. Bhagwati, 'Globalization in Your Face', *Foreign Affairs*, July/August 2000, 137.

are often benefits. Opening up the Jamaican milk market to US imports in 1992 may have hurt local dairy farmers but it also meant poor children could get milk more cheaply. New foreign firms may hurt protected state-owned enterprises but they can also lead to the introduction of new technologies, access to new markets, and the creation of new industries.[51]

Stiglitz commented that those who vilify globalisation too often overlook its benefits.[52] However, Stiglitz also pointed out:

[T]he proponents of globalization have been, if anything, even more unbalanced. To them, globalization (which typically is associated with accepting triumphant capitalism, American style) *is* progress; developing countries must accept it, if they are to grow and to fight poverty effectively. But to many in the developing world, globalization has not brought the promised economic benefits.[53]

Elsewhere, Stiglitz wrote about the problems and dangers of economic globalisation and international trade:

We should be frank. Trade liberalization, conducted in the wrong way, too fast, in the absence of adequate safety nets, with insufficient reciprocity and assistance on the part of developed countries, can contribute to an increase in poverty ... Complete openness can expose a country to greater risk from external shocks. Poor countries may find it particularly hard to buffer these shocks and to bear the costs they incur, and they typically have weak safety nets, or none at all, to protect the poor. These shocks, resulting essentially from contagion associated with globalization, integration and interdependence can affect workers and employers in the developed world. It must be said, however, that highly industrialized countries are able to deal with these shocks a lot better through re-employment and through other safety nets.[54]

In 2006, Stiglitz further reflected on the dark side of globalisation as follows:

There were once hopes that globalisation would benefit all, both in advanced industrial countries and the developing world. Today, the downside of globalisation is increasingly apparent. Not only do good things go more easily across borders, so do bad; including terrorism ... What is remarkable about globalisation is the disparity between the promise and the reality. Globalisation seems to have unified so much of the world against it, perhaps because there appear to be so many losers and so few winners ... Growing inequality in the advanced industrial countries was a long predicted but seldom advertised consequence: full economic integration implies the equalisation of unskilled wages throughout the world. Although this has not (yet) happened, the downward pressure on those at the bottom is evident. Unfettered globalisation actually has the potential to make many people in advanced industrial countries worse off, even if economic growth increases.[55]

In presenting the *United Nations Millennium Report* to the UN General Assembly in April 2000, the then UN Secretary General Kofi Annan stated:

[T]he benefits of globalization are obvious ... faster growth; higher living standards; and new opportunities, not only for individuals, but also for better understanding between

51 J. Stiglitz, *Globalization and Its Discontents* (Penguin, 2002), 4–5.
52 *Ibid.*, 5.   53 *Ibid.*
54 J. Stiglitz, 'Addressing Developing Country Priorities and Needs in the Millennium Round', in R. Porter and P. Sauvé (eds.), *Seattle, the WTO and the Future of the Multilateral Trading System* (Harvard University Press, 2000), 53–5.
55 J. Stiglitz, 'We Have Become Rich Countries of Poor People', *Financial Times*, 7 September 2006.

nations, and for common action. One problem is that, at present, these opportunities are far from equally distributed. How can we say that the half of the human race, which has yet to make or receive a telephone call, let alone use a computer, is taking part in globalization? We cannot, without insulting their poverty. A second problem is that, even where the global market does reach, it is not yet underpinned, as national markets are, by rules based on shared social objectives. In the absence of such rules, globalization makes many people feel they are at the mercy of unpredictable forces.[56]

On the positive *and* negative aspects of economic globalisation, Pascal Lamy, the WTO Director-General, made the following remarks in August 2007:

Globalization has enabled individuals, corporations and nation-states to influence actions and events around the world – faster, deeper and cheaper than ever before – and equally to derive benefits for them. Trade opening and the vanishing of many walls have the potential for expanding freedom, empowerment, democracy, innovation, social and cultural exchanges, while offering outstanding opportunities for dialogue and understanding. This is the good side of globalization. But the global nature of an increasing number of worrisome phenomena – the scarcity of energy resources, the deterioration of the environment, the migratory movements provoked by insecurity, poverty and political instability or even financial markets volatility, as we have seen in recent weeks – are also by-products of globalization. Indeed, it can be argued that in some instances, globalization has reinforced the strong economies and weakened those that were already weak.[57]

On the positive and negative effects of economic globalisation and international trade on growth, employment and (in)equality in developing countries as well as developed countries, the 2011 study by the International Labour Office (ILO) and the WTO, *Making Globalization Socially Sustainable*, is enlightening and recommended reading.[58]

Questions and Assignments 1.4

What are the main dangers associated with economic globalisation and international trade? Who stands to gain most from economic globalisation and international trade? Who loses?

2.3 Free Trade versus Restricted Trade

For as long as people have traded across borders, the benefits and drawbacks of trade have been debated. This sub-section discusses in turn: (1) the arguments for free trade; and (2) the arguments for restrictions on trade.

2.3.1 Arguments for Free Trade

Most economists agree that countries can benefit from international trade. In 1776, Adam Smith wrote in his classic book, *The Wealth of Nations*:

---

56 See www.un.org/millennium/sg/report/state.htm.

57 P. Lamy, 'Trends and Issues Facing Global Trade', Speech delivered in Kuala Lumpur, Malaysia, 17 August 2007, at www.wto.org/english/news_e/sppl_e/sppl65_e.htm.

58 *Making Globalization Socially Sustainable*, Co-publication by the International Labour Office and the Secretariat of the World Trade Organization, edited by Marc Bacchetta and Marion Jansen (ILO/WTO, 2011).

It is the maxim of every prudent master of a family, never to attempt to make at home what it will cost him more to make than to buy. The tailor does not attempt to make his own shoes, but he buys them from the shoemaker. The shoemaker does not attempt to make his own clothes, but employs a tailor. The farmer attempts to make neither the one nor the other, but employs those different artificers. All of them find it for their interest to employ their whole industry in a way in which they have some advantage over their neighbours, and to purchase with a part of its produce, or what is the same thing, with the price of a part of it, whatever else they have occasion for.

What is prudence in the conduct of every private family, can scarce be folly in that of a great kingdom. If a foreign country can supply us with a commodity cheaper than we ourselves can make it, better buy it of them with some part of the produce of our own industry, employed in a way in which we have some advantage. The general industry of the country ... will not thereby be diminished, no more than the above-mentioned artificers; but only left to find out the way in which it can be employed with the greatest advantage. It is certainly not employed to the greatest advantage, when it is thus directed towards an object which it can buy cheaper than it can make.[59]

Adam Smith's lucid and compelling argument for specialisation and international trade was further built upon by David Ricardo, who, in his 1817 book, *The Principles of Political Economy and Taxation*, developed the theory of 'comparative advantage'. This theory is still the predominant explanation for why countries, even the poorest, can and do benefit from international trade.

What did the classical economist David Ricardo (1772–1823) mean when he coined the term *comparative advantage*? Suppose country A is better than country B at making automobiles, and country B is better than country A at making bread. It is obvious (the academics would say 'trivial') that both would benefit if A specialized in automobiles, B specialized in bread and they traded their products. That is a case of *absolute* advantage. But what if a country is bad at making everything? Will trade drive all producers out of business? The answer, according to Ricardo, is no. The reason is the principle of comparative advantage, arguably the single most powerful insight in economics. According to the principle of comparative advantage, countries A and B still stand to benefit from trading with each other even if A is better than B at making everything, both automobiles and bread. If A is much more superior at making automobiles and only slightly superior at making bread, then A should still invest resources in what it does best – producing automobiles – and export the product to B. B should still invest in what it does best – making bread – and export that product to A, even if it is not as efficient as A. Both would still benefit from the trade. A country does not have to be best at anything to gain from trade. That is *comparative* advantage. The theory is one of the most widely accepted among economists. It is also one of the most misunderstood among non-economists because it is confused with *absolute* advantage. It is often claimed, for example, that some countries have no comparative advantage in anything. That is virtually impossible. Think about it ...[60]

The Ricardo model is of course a vast simplification, in that it is built on two products and two countries only and assumes constant costs and constant prices. Many of the complexities of the modern economy are not taken into account

---

59 A. Smith, *An Inquiry into the Nature and Causes of the Wealth of Nations* (1776), edited by E. Cannan (University of Chicago Press, 1976), Volume 1, 478–9.
60 WTO Secretariat, *Trading into the Future*, 2nd revised edn (WTO, 2001), 9.

in this model. Economists in the twentieth century have endeavoured to refine and build on the classic Ricardo model. While pushing the analysis further, the refined models, such as the Heckscher–Ohlin model,[61] have confirmed the basic conclusions drawn from the Ricardo model concerning the theory of comparative advantage and the gains from trade via specialisation.[62]

While the theory of comparative advantage has won approval from most economists since the early nineteenth century and continues to win approval,[63] Jagdish Bhagwati observed in *Free Trade Today* that it has only infrequently carried credibility with the populace at large. In search of an explanation, he noted that, when asked which proposition in the social science was the most counterintuitive yet compelling, Paul Samuelson, the 1970 winner of the Nobel Prize for Economics, chose the theory of comparative advantage.[64] According to Samuelson, there is essentially only one – but one very powerful – argument for free trade:

Free trade promotes a mutually profitable division of labor, greatly enhances the potential real national product for all nations, and makes possible higher standards of living all over the globe.[65]

Reflecting on the changing nature of international trade in today's global economy, Karel De Gucht, the European Commissioner for Trade, said in 2012:

As we learn more about value chains and trade, we may need to adapt our policies further. But we also need to refine our political discourse on trade to communicate our policies better to the European people. Our findings on global value chains show how interwoven economies are today. It is therefore vital that we convince Europeans that protectionism is not the answer to their concerns. This is not always an easy task. Because, we are saying that in buying something from a distant producer instead of from our neighbour we are actually doing the right thing for the neighbourhood. However true that may be, it can be difficult for people to accept, logically and emotionally. Because when you look at trade only briefly you may jump to the conclusion that imports are bad for jobs and so we should keep them out. You might be willing to accept that we should allow in a few imports, but only in order to compensate our trading partners for letting in our exports. But the insights from global value chains should help people to understand that imports are valuable in

61 The Heckscher–Ohlin model is a general equilibrium mathematical model of international trade. It builds on David Ricardo's theory of comparative advantage by predicting patterns of commerce and production based on the factor endowments of a trading region. The model essentially says that countries will export products that use their abundant and cheap factor(s) of production and import products that use the countries' scarce factor(s). See M. Blaug, *The Methodology of Economics, or, How Economists Explain* (Cambridge University Press, 1992), 286.

62 Note, however, as Jagdish Bhagwati does, that: 'The case of free trade rests on the extension to an open economy of the case for market-determined allocation of resources. If market prices reflect "true" or social costs, then clearly Adam Smith's invisible hand can be trusted to guide us to efficiency; and free trade can correspondingly be shown to be the optimal way to choose trade (and associated domestic production). But if markets do not work well, or are absent or incomplete, then the invisible hand may point in the wrong direction: free trade cannot then be asserted to be the best policy.' See J. Bhagwati, *Free Trade Today* (Princeton University Press, 2002), 12.

63 For a dissenting, neo-Marxist view from legal scholars, see M. H. Davis and D. Neacsu, 'Legitimacy, Globally: The Incoherence of Free Trade Practice, Global Economics and Their Governing Principles of Political Economy', *Kansas City Law Review*, 2001, 733–90.

64 See J. Bhagwati, *Free Trade Today* (Princeton University Press, 2002), 5.

65 P. Samuelson, *Economics*, 10th edn (McGraw-Hill, 1976), 692.

and of themselves. Because today most people in their own daily work have experience of a supply chain, whether within a small company or a large multinational. Few businesses make a product from start to finish and sell it to a consumer themselves. We might make a component, provide legal advice or support the product's sale through marketing. But we know that our work depends on many other people for it to succeed. If we want to earn our living we have to be part of international teams that create wealth. European workers are not solo athletes but relay runners. They need to receive the baton from partners in other parts of the world and then pass it on if they are to cross the finish line. And European decision-makers need to put in place the right conditions to allow these teams to flourish. That is why we need to maintain a policy of open trade if we wish to succeed.[66]

On the question whether free trade indeed leads to greater economic growth, Jagdish Bhagwati observed that:

> those who assert that free trade will also lead necessarily to greater growth *either* are ignorant of the finer nuances of theory and the vast literature to the contrary on the subject at hand *or* are nonetheless basing their argument on a different premise: that is, that the preponderant evidence on the issue (in the postwar period) suggests that freer trade tends to lead to greater growth after all.[67]

A 2001 study by the World Bank showed that the developing countries that increased their integration into the world economy in the 1980s and 1990s achieved higher growth in incomes, longer life expectancy and better schooling. These countries, home to some 3 billion people, enjoyed an average 5 per cent growth rate in income per capita in the 1990s compared to 2 per cent in developed countries overall. Many of these countries, including China and India, have adopted domestic policies and institutions that have enabled people to take advantage of global markets and have thus sharply increased the share of trade in their GDP.[68] These countries have been catching up with the rich ones – their annual growth rates increased from 1 per cent in the 1960s to 5 per cent in the 1990s. In 2010, China and India achieved an economic growth of 10.3 and 10.4 per cent respectively.[69] However, not all developing countries have integrated successfully into the global economy, and not all sections of the population in both developed and developing countries have benefitted from international trade. As a 2000 WTO study, *Trade, Income Disparity and Poverty*, on the relationship between international trade and poverty concluded, the evidence seems to indicate that trade liberalisation is *generally* a positive contributor to poverty alleviation. It allows people to exploit their productive potential, assists economic growth, curtails arbitrary policy interventions and helps to insulate against shocks in the domestic economy. The study warned, however, that most

---

66 Karel De Gucht, 'Trading in Value and Europe's Economic Future', High-Level Conference on 'Competitiveness, Trade, Environment and Jobs in Europe: Insights from the New World Input Output Database (WIOD)', 16 April 2012, at http://europa.eu/rapid/press-release_SPEECH-12-264_en.htm.

67 J. Bhagwati, *Free Trade Today* (Princeton University Press, 2002), 42.

68 See above, pp. 9–10.

69 See *ibid*. Even in 2009, at the height of the global economic crisis, China and India still had an economic growth of 7.2 and 9.2 per cent respectively, while the OECD countries had a negative growth of 3.5 per cent. See *ibid*.

trade reforms will create some losers (some even in the long run). Poverty may be exacerbated temporarily, but the appropriate policy response in those cases is to alleviate the hardship and facilitate adjustments rather than abandon the reform process.[70] A 2003 WTO study, *Adjusting to Trade Liberalization*, concluded that adjustment costs are typically smaller, and sometimes much smaller, than the gains from trade.[71] Also, governments can identify individuals and groups that are likely to suffer from the adjustment process, and they can develop policies to alleviate the burden on those adversely affected.[72]

In its 2002 study, *Rigged Rules and Double Standards: Trade, Globalization, and the Fight Against Poverty*, Oxfam stated:

History makes a mockery of the claim that trade cannot work for the poor. Participation in world trade has figured prominently in many of the most successful cases of poverty reduction – and, compared with aid, it has far more potential to benefit the poor.[73]

Few will question that international trade has the *potential* to make a significant contribution to economic growth and poverty reduction. However, it is definitely not a 'magic bullet for achieving development'.[74] As discussed below, more is needed to achieve sustained economic growth and widespread poverty reduction.[75]

International trade not only has the potential for bringing economic benefits, there may also be considerable non-economic gains. International trade increases both the incentives for not making war and the costs of going to war. International trade intensifies cross-border contacts and exchange of ideas, which may contribute to better mutual understanding. In a free-trading world, other countries and their people are more readily seen as business partners, less as enemies. As Baron de Montesquieu wrote in 1748 in *De l'Esprit des Lois*:

Peace is the natural effect of trade. Two nations who traffic with each other become reciprocally dependent; for if one has an interest in buying, the other has an interest in selling; and thus their union is founded on their mutual necessities.[76]

A country restricting trade directly inflicts economic hardship upon exporting countries. Therefore, trade protectionism is a festering source of conflict. It is often stated that, 'if goods do not cross frontiers, soldiers will'.[77] International

---

70 See D. Ben-David, H. Nordström and A. Winters, *Trade, Income Disparity and Poverty*, Special Studies Series (WTO, 2000), 6.

71 See M. Bacchetta and M. Jansen, *Adjusting to Trade Liberalization: The Role of Policy, Institutions and WTO Disciplines*, Special Studies Series (WTO, 2003), 6.

72 *Ibid.*

73 Oxfam, *Rigged Rules and Double Standards: Trade, Globalization, and the Fight Against Poverty* (2002), Summary of Chapter 2, at www.maketradefair.org.

74 See Justice C. Nwobike, 'The Emerging Trade Regime under the Cotonou Partnership Agreement: Its Human Rights Implications', *Journal of World Trade*, 2006, 292.

75 See below, pp. 26–30.

76 C. de Montesquieu, *De l'Esprit des Lois*, original version available online at http://classiques.uqac.ca/classiques/montesquieu/de_esprit_des_lois/de_esprit_des_lois_tdm.html. An English translation by Thomas Nugent is available at www.constitution.org/cm/sol.htm.

77 P. Lamy, 'Managing Global Security: the Strategic Importance of Global Trade', Speech to the International Institute for Strategic Studies, in Geneva on 8 September 2007, at www.wto.org/english/news_e/sppl_e/sppl66_e.htm.

trade can make an important contribution to peaceful and constructive international relations. Just two weeks after the terrorist attacks of 11 September 2001 on the World Trade Center in New York and on the Pentagon in Washington DC, Robert Zoellick, then the US Trade Representative, made the following simple but profound statement about the importance of continued openness in trade:

> Let me be clear where I stand: Erecting new barriers and closing old borders will not help the impoverished. It will not feed hundreds of millions struggling for subsistence. It will not liberate the persecuted. It will not improve the environment in developing countries or reverse the spread of AIDS. It will not help the railway orphans I visited in India. It will not improve the livelihoods of the union members I met in Latin America. It will not aid the committed Indonesians I visited who are trying to build a functioning, tolerant democracy in the largest Muslim nation in the world.[78]

Two months after the attacks of 11 September 2001, the WTO Members agreed to start the Doha Round, a new round of negotiations on the further liberalisation of international trade.[79] According to WTO Director-General Pascal Lamy, the rationale behind this decision was, and remains, simple: '[T]errorism is about increasing instability; global trade rules are about promoting stability.'[80]

Apart from peaceful relations between nations, open international trade may also promote democracy. In *Free Trade Today*, Jagdish Bhagwati observed:

> One could argue this proposition by a syllogism: openness to the benefits of trade brings prosperity that, in turn, creates or expands the middle class that then seeks the end of authoritarianism. This would fit well with the experience in South Korea, for instance. It was also the argument that changed a lot of minds when the issue of China's entry into the WTO came up in the US Congress recently. I guess there is something to it.[81]

2.3.2 Arguments for Restrictions on Trade

While most economists advise that governments should – in the interest of their country as a whole and that of the world at large – pursue policies aimed at promoting international trade and exchange goods and services on the basis of their comparative advantage, political decision-makers do not necessarily heed this advice. In fact, governments frequently intervene in international trade by adopting trade-restrictive measures. Why do governments restrict international trade? In light of the economic and other benefits of free trade, discussed above, what are the arguments for restrictions on trade?

Governments have multiple, often overlapping, reasons for restricting trade. Governments take trade-restrictive measures for example: (1) to protect a domestic industry and jobs threatened by import competition; (2) to assist the

---

78 As reported by the then WTO Director-General Mike Moore in a speech to the Foreign Affairs Commission of the French Assemblée Nationale in October 2001, available at www.wto.org.

79 On the Doha Round, see below, pp. 87–91.

80 P. Lamy, 'Managing Global Security: The Strategic Importance of Global Trade', Speech to the International Institute for Strategic Studies, in Geneva on 8 September 2007, at www.wto.org/english/news_e/sppl_e/sppl66_e.htm.

81 J. Bhagwati, *Free Trade Today* (Princeton University Press, 2002), 43–4.

establishment of a new industry; (3) to support a domestic industry to establish itself on the world market; (4) to generate government revenue; (5) to protect national security and ensure self-sufficiency; and (6) to protect and promote non-economic societal values and interests, such as public morals, public health, a sustainable environment, human rights, minimum labour standards, consumer safety, and cultural identity and diversity.

An oft-cited reason for governments to restrict trade is the *protection of a domestic industry*, and employment in that industry, from competition arising from imported products, foreign services or service suppliers. As noted in the 2003 WTO study on *Adjusting to Trade Liberalization*:

In the United States, for instance, 45,000 steelworkers have lost their jobs since 1997 and 30 per cent of the country's steel making capacity has filed for bankruptcy since 1998, while steel imports were on the rise. In Mozambique liberalization of trade in cashew nuts resulted in 8,500 of 10,000 cashew processing workers losing their jobs.[82]

When a domestic industry is in crisis and jobs are lost, the political decision-makers may well 'scramble for shelter' by adopting protectionist measures.[83] This may happen even when the decision-makers are well aware that such measures are by no means the best response to the crisis in the industry concerned. While the import competition would probably benefit most of their constituents (through lower prices, better quality and/or more choice), import competition is likely to hurt a small group of their constituents significantly (through lower salaries or job losses). If this small group is vocal and well organised, as it often is, it will put a great deal of pressure on the elected decision-makers to take protectionist measures for the benefit of the few and to the detriment of the many. In such a situation, protectionism can constitute 'good' politics.[84] The *public choice theory* explains that, when the majority of the voters are unconcerned with the (*per capita* small) losses they suffer, the vote-maximising political decision-makers will ignore the interests of the many, and support the interests of the vocal and well-organised few.[85] WTO Director-General Pascal Lamy has called for recognition of the fact that the politics of trade suffer from an 'inbuilt asymmetry'. He noted:

[T]hose who benefit from gains in purchasing power stemming from trade opening are millions, but they are little aware of the source of their gains. Those who suffer from trade opening are thousands who can easily identify the source of their pain. For politicians, such an asymmetry is difficult to cope with and too often the easy way out is to treat foreigners as scapegoats, which we know is one of the safest old tricks of domestic politics.[86]

82 M. Bacchetta and M. Jansen, *Adjusting to Trade Liberalization: The Role of Policy, Institutions and WTO Disciplines*, Special Studies Series (WTO, 2003), 6.
83 'Survey World Trade', *The Economist*, 3 October 1998, 3.
84 B. Hoekman and M. Kostecki, *The Political Economy of the World Trading System: The WTO and Beyond*, 2nd edn (Oxford University Press, 2001), 22.
85 On the role of international trade law in 'helping' national decision-makers to make the 'right' decision, i.e. a decision in the best interest of the country as a whole, see below, p. 32. On measures taken to protect an industry (and jobs) threatened by import competition, see also below, p. 32.
86 P. Lamy, 'Trends and Issues Facing Global Trade', Speech delivered in Kuala Lumpur, Malaysia, on 17 August 2007, at www.wto.org/english/news_e/sppl_e/sppl65_e.htm.

However, as discussed above, trade protectionist measures to protect the interests of some eventually leave everyone worse off. Joseph Stiglitz, reflecting on
his own experience as Chair of the Council of Economic Advisors in the Clinton
Administration, observed in this respect:

> One might have thought that each country would promote liberalization in those sectors
> where it had most to gain from a societal perspective; and similarly, that it would be most
> willing to give up protectionism in those sectors where protection was costing the most. But
> political logic prevails over economic logic: after all, if economic logic dominated, countries
> would engage in trade liberalization on their own. High levels of protection are usually
> indicative of strong political forces, and these higher barriers may be the last to give way ...
> The political force behind the resistance to free trade is a simple one: Although the country
> as a whole may be better off under free trade, some special interests will actually be worse
> off. And although policy could in principle rectify this situation (by using redistribution
> to make everybody better off), in actuality, the required compensations are seldom paid.[87]

A second reason for governments to restrict trade is their wish to assist the
establishment of a new industry, i.e. to offer *infant industry protection*. The
argument for infant industry protection was made by Alexander Hamilton in
1791, Friedrich List in 1841 and John Stuart Mill in 1848, and has been invoked
many times since. In the nineteenth century, the infant manufacturing industries
of the United States and Germany were protected against import competition
on the basis of this argument. Today, this argument may be of particular relevance to developing countries, which may find that, while they have a potential
comparative advantage in certain industries, new producers in these countries
cannot yet compete with established producers in the developed countries. By
means of a customs duty or import restriction, temporary protection is then
given to the national producers to allow them to become strong enough to
compete with well-established producers.[88] The infant industry argument for
protectionist measures has some appeal and validity. However, protecting the
new producers from import competition does not necessarily remedy the problems that caused the new producers to be uncompetitive. Furthermore, the success of an infant industry policy crucially depends on a correct diagnosis of
which industries could over time become competitive. It is often very difficult
for governments to identify, in an objective manner and free from pressure from
special interest groups, the new industries that merit protection. Moreover, in
practice, the protection, which is by nature intended to be temporary, frequently
becomes permanent. When it becomes clear that the protected national industry
will never 'grow up' and will always be unable to face import competition, it is
often politically difficult to remove the protection in place.[89]

---

87 J. Stiglitz, 'Addressing Developing Country Priorities and Needs in the Millennium Round', in R. Porter and
    P. Sauvé (eds.), *Seattle, the WTO and the Future of the Multilateral Trading System* (Harvard University Press,
    2000), 51–3.
88 See below, p. 426 (with regard to customs duties) and pp. 481–2 (with regard to import restrictions).
89 A. Deardorff and R. Stern, 'Current Issues in US Trade Policies: An Overview', in R. Stern (ed.), *US Trade Poli-
    cies in a Changing World Economy* (Massachusetts Institute of Technology Press, 1987), 39–40.

A third reason for governments to take trade-restrictive measures is to support a domestic industry to establish itself on the world market. This *strategic trade policy* argument for restrictions on trade is relatively new. In an industry with economies of scale, a country may, by imposing a tariff or quantitative restriction and thus reserving the domestic market for a domestic firm, allow that firm to cut its costs and undercut foreign competitors in other markets. This may work in an industry where economies of scale are sufficiently large that there is only room for very few profitable companies in the world market. Economists reckon that this might be the case for civil aircraft, semiconductors and cars.[90] The aim of government intervention is to ensure that the domestic rather than a foreign company establishes itself on the world market and thus contributes to the national economic welfare. However, as Paul Krugman noted:

Strategic trade policy aimed at securing excess returns for domestic firms and support for industries that are believed to yield national benefits are both beggar-thy-neighbour policies and raise income at the expense of other countries. A country that attempts to use such policies will probably provoke retaliation. In many (though not all) cases, a trade war between two interventionist governments will leave both countries worse off than if a hands-off approach were adopted by both.[91]

This does not mean that such policies will not be pursued, because, as Krugman also pointed out:

[g]overnments do not necessarily act in the national interest, especially when making detailed microeconomic interventions. Instead, they are influenced by interest group pressures. The kinds of interventions that new trade theory suggests can raise national income will typically raise the welfare of small, fortunate groups by large amounts, while imposing costs on larger, more diffuse groups. The result, as with any microeconomic policy, can easily be that excessive or misguided intervention takes place because the beneficiaries have more knowledge and influence than the losers.[92]

A fourth reason for governments to adopt trade-restrictive measures, and, in particular, customs duties, has always been, and still is, to *generate revenue for government*.[93] Taxing trade is an easy way to collect revenue. While taxation of trade for revenue is no longer significant for developed countries, for many developing-country governments customs duties remain a significant source of revenue.[94]

A fifth reason for governments to restrict trade is to protect *national security* and/or ensure *self-sufficiency*. The steel industry, as well as farmers, can, for example, be heard to argue that their presence and prosperity is essential to the national security of the country. The basic argument is that a country should be able to rely on its domestic industries and farmers to meet its basic needs for vital material and food, because it will be impossible to rely – in times of crisis and conflict – on imports from other countries. Alan Sykes noted in

---

90 'Survey World Trade', *The Economist*, 3 October 1998, 6.
91 P. Krugman, 'Is Free Trade Passé?', *Journal of Economic Perspectives*, 1987, 141.
92 *Ibid.*   93 See below, pp. 470–1.   94 *Ibid.*

this respect that the probability of this type of crisis seems small, and that, if such crisis nevertheless were to arise, it may well be possible to reopen or re-build productive facilities quickly enough to satisfy essential needs.[95] For Sykes, arguments for trade-restrictive measures to protect national security and ensure self-sufficiency rarely hold up to careful scrutiny.[96] Sykes argued that:

> stockpiling during peacetime may well be a superior alternative to the protection of domes-tic capacity. Where the item in question is not perishable, a nation might be better off by buying up a supply of vital material at low prices in an open trading system than to burden itself over time with the high prices attendant on protectionism as a hedge against armed conflict. The funds tied up in a stockpile have some opportunity cost to be sure, but this cost can easily be smaller than the costs of excluding efficient foreign suppliers from the domestic market.[97]

A sixth and ever more prevalent reason for governments to restrict trade is the *protection and promotion of non-economic societal values and interests*, such as public morals, public health, a sustainable environment, human rights, minimum labour standards, consumer safety, and cultural identity and diversity. Measures taken to protect and/or promote these societal values and interests may, intentionally or not, restrict trade in products or services. However, the protection and promotion of these values and interests are core tasks of govern-ment, and, in many instances, trade-restrictive measures may not only be legiti-mate, but also necessary. In other instances, such measures are, however, mere fronts for protectionist measures intended to shield domestic producers from import competition. Domestic producers adversely affected by import competi-tion are generally well aware that trade-restrictive measures are more likely to get adopted if justifications other than protection from import competition are invoked. Protectionism can take on very sophisticated guises.[98]

Questions and Assignments 1.5

Why is it that according to most economists even the poorest countries can, at least in theory, benefit from international trade? Why do governments resort to trade-restrictive measures? Which of the arguments for trade and arguments for restrictions on trade do you find most convincing? Which arguments do you find least convincing?

2.4 International Trade to the Benefit of All?

As discussed in the previous section, governments may in certain situations have good reasons to restrict trade. This will be the case, in particular, when trade-restrictive measures are necessary to protect and/or promote important societal values and interests. However, there is a broad consensus that governments are well advised to adopt free trade policies. As explained above, international trade

---

95 See J. Jackson, W. Davey and A. Sykes, *Legal Problems of International Economic Relations*, 4th edn (Westgroup, 2002), 20–1.
96 *Ibid.*   97 *Ibid.*   98 See below, p. 852.

has the potential of contributing to economic development and lifting people out of poverty.[99] It has realised this potential – albeit to varying degrees – in many countries; over the past two decades, this has been the case, in particular, in Asia. However, at the same time, it is undisputed that not all countries, and within countries not all sections of the population, have benefitted from international trade. In fact, many people have been left behind or are now – because of international trade – worse off than they were before. At the WTO Ministerial Conference in Cancún in September 2003, the then UN Secretary-General Kofi Annan noted, not without a measure of frustration:

> The reality of the international trading system today does not match the rhetoric (of improving the quality of life). Instead of open markets, there are too many barriers that stunt, stifle and starve. Instead of fair competition, there are subsidies by rich countries that tilt the playing field against the poor. And instead of global rules negotiated by all, in the interest of all, and adhered to by all, there is too much closed-door decision-making, too much protection of special interests, and too many broken promises.[100]

In its 2002 study, *Rigged Rules and Double Standards: Trade, Globalization, and the Fight Against Poverty*, Oxfam noted that, just as in any national economy, economic integration in the global economy can be a source of shared prosperity and poverty reduction, or a source of increasing inequality and exclusion. Oxfam stated:

> Managed well, the international trading system can lift millions out of poverty. Managed badly, it will leave whole economies even more marginalised. The same is true at a national level. Good governance can make trade work in the interests of the poor. Bad governance can make it work against them.[101]

In a speech to the G-20 Finance Ministers and Central Bank Governors in November 2001, James Wolfensohn, then President of the World Bank, analysed the challenge to make economic globalisation and international trade to work to the benefit of all. This analysis still holds true today. Wolfensohn first observed:

> In my view, with the improvements in both technology and policies that we have seen over recent decades, some form of globalization is with us to stay. But the kind of globalization is not yet certain: it can be either a *globalization of development and poverty reduction* – such as we have begun to see in recent decades, although this trend still cannot be taken for granted – or a *globalization of conflict, poverty, disease, and inequality*. What can we do to tip the scales decisively toward the right kind of globalization?[102]

To ensure that economic globalisation and international trade contribute to economic development, equity and the well-being of all people, Wolfensohn advocated the following four-point agenda for action: (1) good governance at the

---

99 See above, pp. 2–3.
100 See www.wto.mvs.com/mino3_webcast_e.htm/archives.
101 *Ibid.*
102 'Responding to the Challenges of Globalization', Remarks to the G-20 Finance Ministers and Central Bank Governors by James D. Wolfensohn, President, World Bank Group, Ottawa, 17 November 2001, at www.worldbank.org/html/extdr/extme/jdwsp111701.htm.

national level; (2) a further reduction of trade barriers; (3) more development aid; and (4) better international cooperation and global governance of economic globalisation and international trade. First, with regard to *good governance* at the national level, Wolfensohn stated:

[D]eveloping countries must continue the move toward *better policies, investment climate, and governance*. Despite progress in macroeconomic management and openness, there remain many domestic barriers to integration. Many countries have fallen short in creating an investment climate for productivity, growth, entrepreneurship, and jobs. These domestic barriers include inadequate transport infrastructure, poor governance, bureaucratic harassment of small businesses, a lack of electric power, an unskilled workforce ... And countries also need to make possible the participation of poor people in growth, through support for targeted education, health, social protection, and their involvement in key decisions that shape their lives. Poor people need much greater voice.[103]

Secondly, with regard to the *further reduction of trade barriers*, Wolfensohn noted that:

all countries – developed and developing – must *reduce trade barriers* and give developing countries a better chance in world markets ... Rich countries must increase market access for the exports of developing countries, through both multilateral negotiations and unilateral action, to increase the payoffs to developing-country policy and institutional reforms.[104]

Thirdly, with regard to the *increase in development aid*, Wolfensohn recommended that:

developed countries must *increase development aid*, but allocate it better and cut down the burden its implementation can impose ... The evidence from the Bank's research is that well-directed aid, combined with strong reform efforts, can greatly reduce poverty. If we are serious about ensuring a beneficial globalization and meeting multilateral development goals we have all signed up to, we must double ODA [overseas development aid] from its current level of about $50 billion a year.[105]

Fourthly, with regard to *better international cooperation* and *global governance* of economic globalisation and international trade, Wolfensohn stated that:

we must *act as a global community* where it really matters. Effective globalization requires institutions of global governance, and multilateral action to confront global problems and provide global public goods. This means confronting terrorism, internationalized crime, and money laundering, as we are doing in response to September 11th. But it also means that as a community, we need to address longer-term needs, by: combating communicable diseases like AIDS and malaria; *building an equitable global trading system*; promoting financial stability to prevent deep and sudden crises; and safeguarding the natural resources and environment on which so many poor people depend for their livelihoods. As we do all this, we must bring poor countries into the decision-making of this global community.[106]

According to Wolfensohn, if the international community can act on these four priorities, it will have created the conditions to achieve true global integration and to reach the Millennium Development Goals of halving extreme poverty by 2015.[107]

103 *Ibid.*   104 *Ibid.*   105 *Ibid.*   106 *Ibid.* Emphasis added.   107 See *ibid.*

In the same vein, WTO Director-General Pascal Lamy noted in 2007 when addressing the question of how to ensure that economic globalisation and international trade benefits all, that this question has two sides:

A first one is how to ensure trade benefits are shared more fairly among nations. The second side is how to ensure a better distribution of the benefits stemming from trade within a nation.

On the action that needs to be taken at the *international level* (the 'first side' of the question), Lamy stated:

I believe two elements are fundamental: fairer multilateral trade rules and building of trade capacity in developing countries. One primary objective of the ongoing WTO negotiations under the Doha Development Agenda is precisely to address the remaining imbalances in the WTO rules against developing countries, whether in agriculture or in areas such as textiles or footwear ... But negotiating a fairer playing field, difficult as it is, will not be enough. New trade opportunities do not automatically convert into growth and development. The international community also has a responsibility to make sure poorer countries have the capacity to trade and make full use of the market access opportunities provided to them, through more and better focused Aid for Trade.

On the action that needs to be taken at the *national level* (the 'second side' of the question), Lamy observed that:

[t]rade opening can and does translate into greater growth and poverty alleviation, but this is neither automatic [nor] immediate. Trade opening must be accompanied by a solid domestic agenda to spur on growth and cushion adjustment costs. Appropriate tax policies, competition policy, investment in quality education, social safety nets and innovation fostering healthy environments must all be part of the mix needed for trade to translate into real benefits for the people. In this respect, trade policy cannot be isolated from domestic macroeconomic, social or structural policies. The same trade policy will result in different outcomes depending on the quality of economic policies, and this is true across the board, whether you look at the US, Europe, Japan, or at Vietnam, Cambodia, Kenya or Paraguay.[108]

On the action, both at the national and international level, that needs to be taken to ensure that international trade promotes, rather than hurts, economic growth, employment and equality in developing countries as well as developed countries, refer also to the 2011 study by the International Labour Office and the WTO, *Making Globalization Socially Sustainable.*[109]

Just as Wolfensohn and Lamy have done, Peter Sutherland, former GATT and WTO Director-General and later Chair of BP Amoco and Goldman Sachs International, has also emphasised that more is needed than international trade and economic openness to eradicate poverty and inequality. He already noted in a 1997 contribution to the *International Herald Tribune* that:

108 P. Lamy, 'Trends and Issues Facing Global Trade', Speech delivered in Kuala Lumpur, Malaysia, on 17 August 2007, at www.wto.org/english/news_e/sppl_e/sppl65_e.htm.

109 *Making Globalization Socially Sustainable*, Co-publication by the International Labour Office and the Secretariat of the World Trade Organization, edited by Mac Bacchetta and Marion Jansen (ILO/WTO, 2011).

There are those who oppose redistribution policies in principle, whether in the domestic or the international context. This is wrong. It is morally wrong, it is pragmatically wrong, and we ought not be ashamed to say so. I have been personally and deeply committed to promoting the market system through my entire career. Yet it is quite obvious to me that the market will never provide all of the answers to the problems of poverty and inequality. The fact is that there are those who will not be able to develop their economies simply because market access has been provided. I do not believe that we in the global community will adequately live up to our responsibility if we have done no more than provide the poorest people and the poorest countries with an opportunity to succeed. We must also provide them with a foundation from which they have a reasonable chance of seizing that opportunity – decent health care, primary education, basic infrastructure.[110]

It is clear that international trade and economic openness are necessary but not sufficient conditions for economic development and prosperity. The simple spread of markets will not eliminate poverty. A global economy and more international trade will not automatically lead to rising prosperity for all countries and for all people. In fact, without the international and national action referred to above, international trade will not bring prosperity to all, but, on the contrary, is likely to result in more income inequality, social injustice, environmental degradation and cultural homogenisation.

Questions and Assignments 1.6

Can international trade be of benefit to all countries, and, within countries, to all sections of the population? If so, under what conditions? Are these conditions currently fulfilled? If not, are they likely to be fulfilled in the future?

3   THE LAW OF THE WTO

As discussed above, international trade can make a significant contribution to economic development and prosperity in developed as well as developing countries. However, for this potential to be realised, there must be: good governance at the national level; a further reduction of trade barriers; more development aid; and better international cooperation and global governance of economic globalisation and international trade. This book on the law and the policy of the World Trade Organization (WTO) touches upon the national and international action required in each of these four areas, but deals primarily with the requirement of global governance of international trade. Nobel Peace Prize winner, Muhammad Yunus, founder of the Grameen Bank for the Poor, stated the following in his Nobel Lecture in December 2006:

I support globalization and believe it can bring more benefits to the poor than its alternative. But it must be the right kind of globalization. To me, globalization is like a hundred-lane

110 P. Sutherland, 'Beyond the Market, a Different Kind of Equity', *International Herald Tribune*, 20 February 1997.

highway criss-crossing the world. If it is a free-for-all highway, its lanes will be taken over by the giant trucks from powerful economies. Bangladeshi rickshaw will be thrown off the highway. In order to have a win–win globalization we must have traffic rules, traffic police, and traffic authority for this global highway. Rule of 'strongest takes it all' must be replaced by rules that ensure that the poorest have a place and piece of the action, without being elbowed out by the strong.[111]

This section deals with: (1) the international rules on international trade; and (2) the basic rules of WTO law.

3.1   International Rules on International Trade

This sub-section on the international rules on international trade discusses: (1) the need for international rules; and (2) international economic law and WTO law.

3.1.1   Need for International Rules

Peter Sutherland wrote in 1997:

[T]he greatest economic challenge facing the world is the *need to create an international system* that not only maximizes global growth but also achieves a greater measure of equity, a system that both integrates emerging powers and assists currently marginalized countries in their efforts to participate in worldwide economic expansion … The most important means available to secure peace and prosperity into the future is to *develop effective multilateral approaches and institutions*.[112]

The multilateral approaches and institutions to which Sutherland referred may embrace many structures and take many forms but, as John Jackson noted:

it is very clear that law and legal norms play the most important part of the institutions which are essential to make markets work. The notion that 'rule of law' (ambiguous as that phrase is) or a *rule-based or rule-oriented system* of human institutions is essential to a beneficial operation of markets, is a constantly recurring theme in many writings.[113]

Among the writings to which Jackson referred, note those of Ronald Coase, who in 1960 had already concluded that:

it is evident that, for their operation, markets … require the establishment of legal rules governing the rights and duties of those carrying out transactions … *To realize all the gains of trade* … there has to be a legal system and political order.[114]

But what exactly is the role of legal rules and, in particular, international legal rules in international trade? How do international trade rules allow countries to realise the gains of international trade?

111 Muhammad Yunus, Nobel Lecture, Oslo, 10 December 2006, available at http://nobelprize.org/nobel_prizes/peace/laureates/2006/yunus-lecture-en.html.
112 P. Sutherland, 'Beyond the Market, a Different Kind of Equity', *International Herald Tribune*, 20 February 1997. Emphasis added.
113 J. Jackson, 'Global Economics and International Economic Law', *Journal of International Economic Law*, 1998, 5 (reproduced by permission of Oxford University Press). Emphasis added.
114 R. Coase, *The Firm, the Market and the Law* (reprint of 1960 article), Chapter 5, as quoted by Jackson, *ibid.*, 4. Emphasis added.

There are basically four related reasons why there is a need for international trade rules. First, countries must be restrained from adopting trade-restrictive measures both in their own interest and in the interest of the world economy.[115] International trade rules *restrain countries from taking trade-restrictive measures*. As noted above, national policy-makers may come under considerable pressure from influential interest groups to adopt trade-restrictive measures in order to protect domestic industries from import competition or to enhance their ability to compete abroad. Such measures may benefit the specific, short-term interests of the groups advocating them, but they seldom benefit the larger economic interests of the country adopting them.[116] As Ernst-Ulrich Petersmann observed:

Governments know very well ... that by 'tying their hands to the mast' (like Ulysses when he approached the island of the Sirenes), reciprocal international pre-commitments help them to resist the siren-like temptations from 'rent-seeking' interest groups at home.[117]

In other words, international trade rules are the *shield* behind which a government with the interests of its people in mind can seek protection against the onslaught of politically powerful special interest groups calling for trade-restrictive measures. International trade rules are often referred to by governments when they refuse to give in to demands for trade protectionism. In this way, international trade rules play a very important role in international trade policy. Moreover, countries also realise that, if they take trade-restrictive measures, other countries will do so too. This may lead to an escalation of trade-restrictive measures, a disastrous move for international trade and for global economic welfare. International trade rules help to avoid such escalation.

A second and closely related reason why international trade rules are necessary is the need of traders for a degree of *security and predictability*. Traders operating, or intending to operate, in a country that is bound by international legal rules will be better able to predict how that country will act in the future on matters affecting their operations in that country. The predictability and security resulting from international trade rules will encourage trade and will thus contribute to economic welfare. As John Jackson wrote, international trade rules:

may provide the only predictability or stability to a potential ... trade-development situation. Without such predictability or stability, trade ... flows might be even more risky and therefore more inhibited than otherwise ... To put it another way, the policies which tend to reduce some risks, lower the 'risk premium' required by entrepreneurs to enter into international transactions. This should result in a general increase in the efficiency of various economic activities, contributing to greater welfare for everyone.[118]

---

115 Note, however, that, as discussed throughout this book, there are many instances in which trade-restrictive measures are legitimate, and even called for, to promote or protect important societal values and interests. See e.g. below, pp. 33, 39, 72, and 543–93.
116 See above, p. 25. On the optimal tariff argument and the strategic trade policy argument, see above, p. 25.
117 E. U. Petersmann, *The GATT/WTO Dispute Settlement System: International Law, International Organizations and Dispute Settlement* (Kluwer Law International, 1997), 36–7.
118 J. Jackson, 'Global Economics and International Economic Law', *Journal of International Economic Law*, 1998, 5–6.

A third reason why international trade rules are necessary is that, as a result of the greatly increased levels of trade in goods and services, the *protection and promotion of important societal values and interests* such as public health, a sustainable environment, consumer safety, cultural identity and minimum labour standards is no longer a purely national matter. Attempts to ensure the protection and promotion of these values and interests at the national level alone are doomed to be ineffective and futile. For example, in this age of mass global air travel, an epidemic of an infectious disease, such as SARS or avian flu, cannot be addressed effectively by countries just acting on their own. In the same vein, in a world in which financial products are traded globally and with lightening speed, national regulation of these products was found to be terribly inadequate and at the source of the current global economic crisis. Also, there is general recognition that global warming is unlikely to be addressed in an effective manner by unilateral measures of individual countries. In addition to being ineffective and futile, national measures to address these and other global challenges and risks may well have damaging effects on both the national and global economy. Even when such national measures do not directly or expressly restrict trade, the mere fact that such measures differ from country to country may act as a significant constraint on trade. International trade rules are needed to ensure that countries maintain only those national measures that are necessary for (or at the very least related to) the protection of key societal values and interests.[119] International trade rules may also introduce a degree of harmonisation of domestic regulatory measures and thus promote an effective, international protection of these societal values and interests.[120]

A fourth and final reason why international trade rules are necessary is the need to achieve a *greater measure of equity* in international economic relations. As Father Lacordaire stated in one of his renowned 1835 sermons at the Notre Dame in Paris:

Entre le fort et le faible, entre le riche et le pauvre ... c'est la liberté qui opprime et la loi qui affranchit.[121]

Without international trade rules, binding and enforceable on rich as well as poor countries, and rules recognising the special needs of developing countries, many countries would not be able to integrate fully in the world trading system and derive an equitable share of the gains of international trade.

However, for international legal rules to play these multiple roles, such rules have, of course, to be observed. It is clear that international trade rules are not always followed. Yet, while both the media and academia inevitably pay more

---

119 For a discussion on the protection of key societal values and interests, see below, pp. 543–604, 606–47 and 648–72.

120 See below, pp. 850–92, 894–949 and 951–1016.

121 Translation: 'Between the strong and the weak, between the rich and the poor ... it is freedom which oppresses and the law which sets free.' Abbé Jean-Baptiste Lacordaire (1802–61) was a French Catholic priest, journalist and political activist.

attention to instances of breach, it should be stressed that international trade rules are generally well observed. Countries realise that they cannot expect other countries to observe the rules if they do not do so themselves. The desire to be able to depend on other countries' compliance with the rules leads many countries to observe the rules even though this might be politically inconvenient in a given situation.[122]

All countries and their people benefit from the existence of rules on international trade which make the trading environment more predictable and stable. However, provided the rules take into account their specific interests and needs and leave sufficient 'policy space' to pursue economic development, developing countries, with generally limited economic and political power, should benefit even more from the existence of rules on international trade. The weaker countries are likely to suffer most where the law of the jungle reigns. They are more likely to thrive in a *rules-based*, rather than a power-based, international trading system.

3.1.2   International Economic Law and WTO Law

The legal rules governing trade relations between countries are part of international economic law. International economic law is a very broad field of international law. With regard to 'international economic law', John Jackson noted that:

> [it] is not by any means a new phenomenon although the phrase may be considered relatively new. International law has always had considerable 'economic content', as manifested by international economic institutions and by the international law jurisprudence throughout the centuries devoted to various economic subjects including trade, investment, commerce, and navigation (FCN treaties). In addition, activities of the League of Nations, as well as, more currently, the United Nations, have had a very substantial economic institutional dimension.[123]

Jackson once suggested that 90 per cent of international law work relates in fact to international economic law in one form or another. He also observed that international economic law does not enjoy as much glamour or media attention as work on armed conflicts and human rights seems to do.[124]

International economic law can be defined, broadly, as covering all those international rules pertaining to economic transactions and relations, as well as those pertaining to governmental regulation of economic matters. As such, international economic law includes international rules on trade in goods and services, economic development, intellectual property rights, foreign direct

---

122 See L. Henkin, *How Nations Behave*, 2nd edn (1979), as referred to in J. Jackson, 'Global Economics and International Economic Law', *Journal of International Economic Law*, 1998, 5.

123 J. Jackson, 'International Economic Law: Complexity and Puzzles', *Journal of International Economic Law*, 2007, 3.

124 J. Jackson, 'International Economic Law: Reflections on the "Boilerroom" of International Relations', *American University Journal of International Law and Policy*, 1995, 596.

investment, international finance and monetary matters, commodities, food, health, transport, communications, natural resources, private commercial transactions, nuclear energy, etc. International rules on trade in goods and services, i.e. international trade law, constitute the 'hard core' of international economic law. International trade law consists of, on the one hand, numerous bilateral or regional trade agreements and, on the other hand, multilateral trade agreements. Examples of bilateral and regional trade agreements are manifold. The *North American Free Trade Agreement* (NAFTA) and the *MERCOSUR Agreement* are typical examples of regional trade agreements. The *Trade Agreement between the United States and Israel* and the *Agreement on Trade in Wine between the European Community and Australia* are examples of bilateral trade agreements. The number of multilateral trade agreements is more limited. This group includes, for example, the 1983 *International Convention on the Harmonized Commodity Description and Coding System*, as amended (the '*HS Convention*')[125] and the 1973 *International Convention on the Simplification and Harmonization of Customs Procedures*, as amended (the '*Kyoto Convention*').[126] The most important and broadest of all multilateral trade agreements is the 1994 *Marrakesh Agreement Establishing the World Trade Organization*, commonly referred to as the *WTO Agreement*. It is the law of this Agreement, which is the subject-matter of this book.

3.2   Basic Rules of WTO Law

The law of the WTO is a complex set of rules dealing with trade in goods and services and the protection of intellectual property rights. WTO law addresses a broad spectrum of issues, ranging from tariffs, import quotas and customs formalities to compulsory licensing, food safety regulations and national security measures. However, five groups of basic rules can be distinguished: (1) rules of non-discrimination; (2) rules on market access; (3) rules on unfair trade; (4) rules on the conflict between trade liberalisation and other societal values and interests; and (5) institutional and procedural rules, including those relating to WTO decision-making, trade policy review and dispute settlement. These substantive, institutional and procedural rules of WTO law make up what is commonly referred to as the *multilateral trading system*. Referring to this system, Peter Sutherland and others wrote the following in 2001:

The multilateral trading system, with the World Trade Organization (WTO) at its centre, is the most important tool of global economic management and development we possess.[127]

125 See www.wcoomd.org/~/media/WCO/Public/Global/PDF/Topics/Nomenclature/Instruments%20and%20 Tools/HS%20Nomenclature%202012/NG0163B1.ashx?db=web. See also below, p. 453.
126 See www.wcoomd.org/en/topics/facilitation/instrument-and-tools/conventions/pf_revised_kyoto_conv/ kyoto_new.aspx. See also below, p. 495.
127 P. Sutherland, J. Sewell and D. Weiner, 'Challenges Facing the WTO and Policies to Address Global Governance', in G. Sampson (ed.), *The Role of the World Trade Organization in Global Governance* (United Nations University Press, 2001), 81.

Martin Wolf of the *Financial Times* noted in 2001:

The multilateral trading system at the beginning of the twenty-first century is the most remarkable achievement in institutionalized global economic cooperation that there has ever been.[128]

The following sections of this chapter briefly review the basic rules constituting the multilateral trading system. These rules will be discussed in greater detail in subsequent chapters of this book.

3.2.1   Rules of Non-Discrimination

There are two basic rules of non-discrimination in WTO law: (1) the most-favoured-nation (MFN) treatment obligation; and (2) the national treatment obligation.

The *MFN treatment obligation* requires a WTO Member that grants certain favourable treatment to any given country to grant that same favourable treatment to all other WTO Members. A WTO Member is not allowed to discriminate *between* its trading partners by, for example, giving the products imported from some countries more favourable treatment with respect to market access than the treatment it accords to the 'like' products of other Members.[129] Despite many exceptions and deviations from this obligation, the MFN treatment obligation is arguably the single most important rule in WTO law.[130] Without this rule, the multilateral trading system could and would not exist. Chapter 4 of this book examines in detail this rule as it applies to trade in goods and services.[131]

The *national treatment obligation* requires a WTO Member to treat foreign products, services and service suppliers no less favourably than it treats 'like' domestic products, services and service suppliers. Where the national treatment obligation applies, foreign products, for example, should, once they have crossed the border and entered the domestic market, not be subject to less favourable taxation or regulation than 'like' domestic products. Pursuant to the national treatment obligation, a WTO Member is not allowed to discriminate *against* foreign products, services and service suppliers. The national treatment obligation is an important rule in WTO law which has given rise to many trade disputes. For trade in goods, the national treatment obligation has *general* application to all measures affecting trade in goods.[132] By contrast, for trade in services, the national treatment obligation does not have such general application. It applies only to the extent that a WTO Member has explicitly committed itself to grant 'national treatment' in respect of specific services sectors.[133] Such commitments to give 'national treatment' are made in a Member's Schedule of

---

128 M. Wolf, 'What the World Needs from the Multilateral Trading System', in G. Sampson (ed.), *The Role of the World Trade Organization in Global Governance* (United Nations University Press, 2001), 182.
129 See Article I of the GATT 1994.
130 On the 'exceptions', see e.g. Chapter 8 of this book, at p. 543–604. On the 'deviations', see in particular Chapter 10 of this book, at pp. 648–72.
131 See below, pp. 315–47.   132 See Article III of the GATT 1994.   133 See Article XVII of the GATS.

Specific Commitments on Services. Chapter 5 of this book discusses in detail the national treatment obligation as it applies to trade in goods and services.[134]

3.2.2 Rules on Market Access

WTO law contains four groups of rules regarding market access: (1) rules on *customs duties* (i.e. tariffs); (2) rules on *other duties and financial charges*; (3) rules on *quantitative restrictions*; and (4) rules on *other 'non-tariff barriers'*. These 'other non-tariff barriers' to trade are a very broad, residual category of measures, actions or omissions of Members, including, *inter alia*: the lack of transparency regarding the applicable trade laws, regulations and procedures; the unfair and arbitrary application of trade measures; technical barriers to trade; sanitary and phytosanitary measures; customs formalities and procedures; government procurement laws and practices; and the lack of effective protection of intellectual property rights.

Under WTO law, the imposition of customs duties is not prohibited. In fact, customs duties are a legitimate trade policy instrument, and WTO Members impose customs duties on many products. However, WTO law calls upon WTO Members to negotiate mutually beneficial reductions of customs duties.[135] These negotiations result in tariff concessions or bindings, set out in a Member's Schedule of Concessions. On products for which a tariff concession or binding exists, the customs duties imposed may no longer exceed the maximum level of duty agreed to.[136] Chapter 6 of this book examines the rules applicable to customs duties.[137] It also discusses the rules on other duties and financial charges.[138]

While customs duties are a legitimate trade policy instrument (provided they do not exceed the maximum level agreed to), quantitative restrictions on trade in goods are, as a general rule, forbidden under WTO law.[139] Unless one of many exceptions applies, WTO Members are not allowed to ban the importation or exportation of goods or to subject them to quotas. With respect to trade in services, quantitative restrictions are, in principle, prohibited in services sectors for which specific market-access commitments have been undertaken.[140] In those sectors, quantitative restrictions can only be imposed if they have been inscribed in a Member's Schedule of Specific Commitments. Chapter 7 of this book examines the rules applicable to quantitative restrictions on trade in goods and services.[141]

Among 'other non-tariff barriers', the lack of transparency of national trade regulations definitely stands out as a major barrier to international trade. Uncertainty and confusion regarding the trade rules applicable in

---

134 See below, pp. 403–16.   135 See Article XXVIII*bis* of the GATT 1994.   136 See Article II of the GATT 1994.
137 See below, pp. 420–5.   138 See below, pp. 463–7.   139 See Article XI of the GATT 1994.
140 Article XVI of the GATS. To be precise, the prohibition of Article XVI of the GATS applies to 'market access barriers' as defined in Article XVI:2. All but one category of 'market access barriers' are quantitative restrictions. See below, pp. 515–17.
141 See below, pp. 482–91; 517–18.

other countries has a chilling effect on trade. Likewise, the arbitrary application of these rules also discourages traders and hampers trade. Transparency
and the fair application of trade regulations are therefore part of the basic
rules on market access examined in Chapter 7.[142] Non-tariff barriers to trade,
such as customs formalities and government procurement practices, are, for
many products and in many countries, more important barriers to trade than
customs duties or quantitative restrictions. Chapter 7 also deals with the
rules on many of these non-tariff barriers.[143] As mentioned above, 'other
non-tariff barriers' to trade can also take the form of technical barriers to
trade, sanitary and phytosanitary measures, and the lack of effective protection of intellectual property rights. Due to their importance and detailed
nature, the rules on these 'other non-tariff barriers' are discussed, separately,
in Chapters 13, 14 and 15 of this book respectively.[144] Note that the rules on
technical barriers to trade, the rules on sanitary and phytosanitary measures,
and the rules ensuring a minimum level of protection and enforcement of intellectual property rights have in common that they go far beyond the usual
trade liberalisation rules and venture into 'behind-the-border' regulation to
a greater extent than any other WTO rules. In addition to imposing the usual
WTO disciplines, these rules harmonise, or promote the harmonisation of,
national regulation around international standards.

3.2.3 Rules on Unfair Trade

WTO law, at present, does not provide for general rules on unfair trade practices,
but it does have a number of detailed rules that relate to specific forms of
'unfair' trade. These rules deal with dumping and subsidised trade.

Dumping, i.e. bringing a product onto the market of another country at a
price less than the normal value of that product, is condemned but not prohibited under WTO law. However, when the dumping causes or threatens to cause
material injury to the domestic industry of a Member producing a 'like' product,
WTO law allows that Member to impose anti-dumping duties on the dumped
products in order to offset the dumping.[145] The rules on the imposition of these
anti-dumping duties are examined in Chapter 11.

Subsidies, i.e. financial contributions by governments or public bodies that
confer a benefit, are subject to an intricate set of rules.[146] Some subsidies, such
as export and import substitution subsidies, are, as a rule, prohibited. Other subsidies are not prohibited but, when they cause adverse effects to the interests of

---

142 See below, pp. 498–507; 532–3.
143 See below, pp. 498–541.
144 See below, pp. 850–92, 894–949, and 951–1016.
145 See Article VI of the GATT 1994 and the *Anti-Dumping Agreement.*
146 See Articles VI and XVI of the GATT 1994 and the *Agreement on Subsidies and Countervailing Measures*
(the *'SCM Agreement'*).

other Members, the subsidising Member should withdraw the subsidy or take appropriate steps to remove the adverse effects. If the subsidising Member fails to do so, countermeasures commensurate with the degree and nature of the adverse effect may be authorised.[147] If a prohibited or other subsidy causes or threatens to cause material injury to the domestic industry of a Member producing a 'like' product, that Member is authorised to impose countervailing duties on the subsidised products to offset the subsidisation. Subsidies relating to agricultural products are subject to special (and overall more lenient) rules.[148] The rules applicable to subsidies and countervailing duties are examined in Chapter 12.

3.2.4   Rules on the Conflict Between Trade Liberalisation and Other Societal Values and Interests

Apart from the basic rules referred to above, WTO law also provides for rules that address the conflict between trade liberalisation and other societal values and interests. These rules, which are commonly referred to as 'exceptions', allow WTO Members to deviate – under specific conditions – from basic WTO rules in order to take account of economic and non-economic values and interests that compete or conflict with free trade. The *non-economic* values and interests include the protection of the environment, public health, public morals, national treasures and national security. The relevant rules can be found in, for example, Articles XX and XXI of the GATT 1994 and Articles XIV and XIV *bis* of the GATS. The *economic* interests include: the protection of a domestic industry from serious injury inflicted by an unexpected and sharp surge in imports; the safeguarding of the balance of payments; and the pursuit of regional economic integration. The relevant rules can be found in, for example, Articles XII, XIX and XXIV of the GATT 1994, Articles V, X and XII of the GATS and the *Agreement on Safeguards*. The WTO rules allowing Members to take into account economic or non-economic values and interests that may conflict with free trade are examined in detail in Chapters 8, 9 and 10 of this book.[149]

Recognising the need for positive efforts designed to ensure that developing-country Members, and especially the least-developed countries among them, are integrated into the multilateral trading system, WTO law includes many provisions granting a degree of special and differential treatment to developing-country Members.[150] These provisions attempt to take the special needs of developing countries into account. In many areas, they provide for fewer obligations or differing rules for developing countries as well as for technical assistance. The rules on the special and differential treatment of developing-country Members are discussed throughout this book.[151]

---

147 See Article 7.9 of the *SCM Agreement*.   148 Articles 6–11 of the *Agreement on Agriculture*.
149 See below, pp. 543–604, 606–47 and 648–72.
150 For example, Article XVIII and Part IV of the GATT 1994 as well as the Enabling Clause. See below,
      pp. 426–31 and 663–4.
151 See e.g. below, pp. 299–302, 663–8, 737–9, 834–5, and 1010–11.

3.2.5   Institutional and Procedural Rules

All basic rules referred to above are substantive rules. However, the multilateral trading system also includes, and depends on, institutional and procedural rules relating to WTO decision-making, trade policy review and dispute settlement. The rules regarding the institutions and procedures for the formulation and implementation of trade rules are discussed in detail in Chapter 2. The rules and procedures regarding the settlement of trade disputes are dealt with in Chapter 3.

Questions and Assignments 1.7

Why is there a need for international rules on trade? Who benefits from these rules and why? What is international economic law and what does it cover? How does WTO law relate to international economic law? What are the basic rules that make up the multilateral trading system? What is the most fundamental rule of WTO law? Does WTO law take into account the special situation of developing countries? Does WTO law address the conflict between trade liberalisation and other economic and non-economic societal values and interests?

4   SOURCES OF WTO LAW

WTO law is, by international law standards, a wide-ranging and complex body of law. This section reviews various sources of WTO law. Not all sources of WTO law reviewed below are of the same nature or are on the same legal footing. Some sources provide for specific legal rights and obligations for WTO Members that can be enforced through WTO dispute settlement. Many other sources, reviewed below, do *not* in and of themselves provide for specific, enforceable rights or obligations. They nevertheless assist in 'clarifying' or 'defining' the law that applies between WTO Members on WTO matters.

The principal source of WTO law is the *Marrakesh Agreement Establishing the World Trade Organization*, concluded on 15 April 1994 and in force since 1 January 1995. This section first discusses in some detail this principal source of WTO law. Subsequently, other sources of WTO law are discussed.

4.1   The Marrakesh Agreement Establishing the World Trade Organization

The *Marrakesh Agreement Establishing the World Trade Organization* (the 'WTO Agreement') is the most ambitious and far-reaching international trade agreement ever concluded.[152] It consists of a short basic agreement (of sixteen articles) and numerous other agreements included in the annexes to this basic

---

152   The official version of the *WTO Agreement* and its Annexes is published by the WTO and Cambridge University Press as *The Results of the Uruguay Round of Multilateral Trade Negotiations: The Legal Texts*. The *WTO Agreement* and its Annexes are also available on the WTO website at www.wto.org/english/docs_e/legal_e/legal_e.htm.

agreement. On the relationship between the *WTO Agreement* and the agreements in the annexes as well as on the binding nature of the latter agreements, Article II of the *WTO Agreement* states:

2. The agreements and associated legal instruments included in Annexes 1, 2 and 3 (here-inafter referred to as 'Multilateral Trade Agreements') are integral parts of this Agreement, binding on all Members.

3. The agreements and associated legal instruments included in Annex 4 (hereinafter referred to as 'Plurilateral Trade Agreements') are also part of this Agreement for those Members that have accepted them, and are binding on those Members. The Plurilateral Trade Agreements do not create either obligations or rights for Members that have not accepted them.

While the *WTO Agreement* consists of many agreements, the Appellate Body in one of the first cases before it, *Brazil – Desiccated Coconut (1997)*, stressed that the *WTO Agreement* had been accepted by WTO Members as a 'single undertaking'.[153] All multilateral WTO agreements apply equally and are equally binding on all WTO Members. The provisions of these agreements represent 'an *inseparable package* of rights and disciplines which have to be considered in conjunction'.[154] The *WTO Agreement* is thus a single treaty. However, it should be noted that the agreements making up the *WTO Agreement* were negotiated in multiple separate committees, which operated quite independently and without much co-ordination. Only towards the end of the Uruguay Round were some efforts made at coordinating and harmonising the texts of the various agreements. At that stage, however, the negotiators – for fear of seeing disagreement re-emerge – were often unwilling to change the agreed texts, and some 'inconsistencies' or 'tensions' between the texts remained. Note that Article XVI:3 of the *WTO Agreement* provides:

In the event of a conflict between a provision of this Agreement and a provision of any of the Multilateral Trade Agreements, the provision of this Agreement shall prevail to the extent of the conflict.[155]

Most of the substantive WTO law is found in the agreements contained in Annex 1. This Annex consists of three parts. Annex 1A contains thirteen multilateral agreements on trade in goods; Annex 1B contains the *General Agreement on Trade in Services* (the 'GATS'); and Annex 1C the *Agreement on Trade-Related Aspects of Intellectual Property Rights* (the '*TRIPS Agreement*'). The most important of the thirteen multilateral agreements on trade in goods, contained in Annex 1A, is the *General Agreement on Tariffs and Trade 1994* (the 'GATT 1994'). The plurilateral agreements in Annex 4 also contain provisions of substantive law but they are – as set out in Article II:3 of the *WTO Agreement*, quoted above – only binding upon those WTO Members that are a party

153 See Appellate Body Report, *Brazil – Desiccated Coconut (1997)*, 177.
154 See Appellate Body Report, *Argentina – Footwear (EC) (2000)*, para. 81.
155 On the concept of a 'conflict', see e.g. below, p. 45.

to these agreements. Annexes 2 and 3 cover, respectively, the *Understanding on Rules and Procedures for the Settlement of Disputes* (the 'DSU') and the *Trade Policy Review Mechanism* (the 'TPRM'), and contain procedural provisions. The next sub-sections give a brief description of the agreements annexed to the *WTO Agreement*. For a more in-depth discussion of the substantive, institutional and procedural provisions of these agreements, please refer to Chapters 3 to 15 of this book. Chapter 2 discusses in detail the *WTO Agreement* to which these agreements are annexed.

4.1.1   General Agreement on Tariffs and Trade 1994

The GATT 1994 sets out the basic rules for trade in goods. This agreement is, however, somewhat unusual in its appearance and structure. Paragraph 1 of the introductory text of the GATT 1994 states:

The General Agreement on Tariffs and Trade 1994 ('GATT 1994') shall consist of:

a. the provisions in the General Agreement on Tariffs and Trade, dated 30 October 1947 ...
b. the provisions of the legal instruments set forth below that have entered into force under the GATT 1947 before the date of entry into force of the WTO Agreement ...
c. the Understandings set forth below ... and
d. the Marrakesh Protocol to GATT 1994.

The GATT 1994 would obviously have been a less confusing and more user-friendly legal instrument if the negotiators had drafted a *new* text reflecting the basic rules on trade in goods as agreed during the Uruguay Round. However, as paragraph 1(a) of the introductory text of the GATT 1994, quoted above, shows, the Uruguay Round negotiators chose to *incorporate by reference* the provisions of the GATT 1947 into the GATT 1994.[156] By doing so, they were able to limit the debate on the provisions of the GATT 1994. If the negotiators had opted for a *new* text reflecting the basic rules on trade in goods, it would not have been possible to keep a lid on the many contentious issues relating to the interpretation and application of GATT provisions.[157] The current arrangement obliges one to consult: (1) the provisions of the GATT 1947; (2) the provisions of relevant GATT 1947 legal instruments; and (3) the Understandings agreed upon during the Uruguay Round in order to know what the GATT 1994 rules on trade in goods are. The negotiators were obviously aware that this arrangement might lead to some confusion, especially with regard to the continued relevance of the GATT 1947. They therefore felt the need to state explicitly in Article II:4 of the *WTO Agreement* that:

---

156 Together with the provisions of the GATT 1947, the provisions of the legal instruments that have entered into force under the GATT 1947, referred to in paragraph 1(b) of the introductory text of the GATT 1994, are incorporated into the GATT 1994.

157 It was understood among the negotiators that these issues concerning the interpretation and application of GATT 1947 provisions could and would be addressed through dispute settlement under the *WTO Agreement*. Only a few contentious GATT issues were addressed and resolved during the Uruguay Round negotiations. See the Understandings listed in paragraph 1(c) of the introductory text of the GATT 1994 and included in this instrument.

[t]he General Agreement on Tariffs and Trade 1994 as specified in Annex 1A (hereinafter referred to as 'GATT 1994') is legally distinct from the General Agreement on Tariffs and Trade, dated 30 October 1947 ... (hereinafter referred to as 'GATT 1947').

It should be stressed that the GATT 1947 is, in fact, no longer in force. It was terminated in 1996. However, as explained, its provisions have been incorporated by reference in the GATT 1994.[158]

The GATT 1994 contains rules on: most-favoured-nation treatment (Article I);[159] tariff concessions (Article II);[160] national treatment on internal taxation and regulation (Article III);[161] anti-dumping and countervailing duties (Article VI);[162] valuation for customs purposes (Article VII);[163] customs fees and formalities (Article VIII);[164] marks of origin (Article IX);[165] the publication and administration of trade regulations (Article X);[166] quantitative restrictions (Article XI);[167] restrictions to safeguard the balance of payments (Article XII);[168] administration of quantitative restrictions (Article XIII);[169] exchange arrangements (Article XV);[170] subsidies (Article XVI);[171] State trading enterprises (Article XVII);[172] governmental assistance to economic development (Article XVIII);[173] safeguard measures (Article XIX);[174] general exceptions (Article XX);[175] security exceptions (Article XXI);[176] dispute settlement (Articles XXII and XXIII);[177] regional economic integration (Article XXIV);[178] modification of tariff schedules (Article XXVIII) and tariff negotiations (Article XXVIII*bis*);[179] and trade and development (Articles XXXVI to XXXVIII).[180] A number of these provisions have been amended by one of the Understandings, listed in paragraph 1(c) of the introductory text of the GATT 1994 and contained in the GATT 1994. Note, for example, the *Understanding on the Interpretation of Article II:1(b) of the General Agreement on Tariffs and Trade 1994*;[181] and the *Understanding on the Interpretation of Article XXIV of the General Agreement on Tariffs and Trade 1994*.[182] Finally, note the *Marrakesh Protocol*, which is an important part of the GATT 1994. This Protocol contains the national Schedules of Concessions of all WTO Members. In these national Schedules, the commitments to eliminate or reduce customs duties applicable to trade in goods are recorded.[183] The Protocol is over 25,000 pages long, and is a key instrument for traders and trade officials.

4.1.2 Other Multilateral Agreements on Trade in Goods

In addition to the GATT 1994, Annex 1A to the *WTO Agreement* contains a number of other multilateral agreements on trade in goods. These agreements

---

158 To facilitate the necessary reference to the provisions of the GATT 1947 – and for that reason only – the official WTO *Legal Texts* include the complete text of the GATT 1947. The inclusion of this text should *not* be seen as an indication of the continued application of the GATT 1947.
159 See below, p. 317.   160 See below, pp. 335–6.   161 See below, pp. 350–2.   162 See below, pp. 676–8.
163 See below, pp. 457–60.   164 See below, pp. 468–70.   165 See below, p. 512.   166 See below, pp. 498–507.
167 See below, pp. 482–7.   168 See below, p. 637.   169 See below, pp. 491–5.   170 See below, p. 513.
171 See below, p. 748.   172 See below, p. 513.   173 See below, p. 637.   174 See below, pp. 608–10.
175 See below, pp. 545–81.   176 See below, pp. 595–9.   177 See below, pp. 230–2.   178 See below, pp. 655–64.
179 See below, p. 426.   180 See below, p. 429.   181 See below, pp. 426–9.   182 See below, pp. 465–6.
183 See below, p. 64.

include: (1) the *Agreement on Agriculture*, which requires the use of tariffs instead of quotas or other quantitative restrictions, imposes minimum market access requirements and provides for specific rules on domestic support and export subsidies in the agricultural sector;[184] (2) the *Agreement on the Application of Sanitary and Phytosanitary Measures* (the '*SPS Agreement*'), which regulates the use by WTO Members of measures adopted to ensure food safety and protect the life and health of humans, animals and plants from pests and diseases;[185] (3) the *Agreement on Textiles and Clothing*, which provided for the gradual elimination by 1 January 2005 of quotas on textiles and clothing (and is no longer in force);[186] (4) the *Agreement on Technical Barriers to Trade* (the '*TBT Agreement*'), which regulates the use by WTO Members of technical regulations and standards and procedures to test conformity with these regulations and standards;[187] (5) the *Agreement on Trade-Related Investment Measures* (the '*TRIMS Agreement*'), which provides that WTO Members' regulations dealing with foreign investments must respect the obligations in Article III (national treatment obligation) and Article XI (prohibition on quantitative restrictions) of the GATT 1994;[188] (6) the *Agreement on Implementation of Article VI of the General Agreement on Tariffs and Trade 1994* (the '*Anti-Dumping Agreement*'), which provides for detailed rules on the use of anti-dumping measures;[189] (7) the *Agreement on Implementation of Article VII of the General Agreement on Tariffs and Trade 1994* (the '*Customs Valuation Agreement*'), which sets out in detail the rules to be used by national customs authorities for valuing goods for customs purposes;[190] (8) the *Agreement on Preshipment Inspection*, which regulates activities relating to the verification of the quality, the quantity, the price and/or the customs classification of goods to be exported;[191] (9) the *Agreement on Rules of Origin*, which provides for negotiations aimed at the harmonisation of non-preferential rules of origin, sets out disciplines to govern the application of these rules of origin, both during and after the negotiations on harmonisation, and sets out disciplines applicable to preferential rules of origin;[192] (10) the *Agreement on Import Licensing Procedures*, which sets out rules on the use of import licensing procedures;[193] (11) the *Agreement on Subsidies and Countervailing Measures* (the '*SCM Agreement*'), which provides for detailed rules on subsidies and the use of countervailing measures;[194] and (12) the *Agreement on Safeguards*, which provides for detailed rules on the use of safeguard measures and prohibits the use of voluntary export restraints.[195]

Most of these multilateral agreements on trade in goods provide for rules that are more detailed than, and sometimes possibly in conflict with, the rules contained in the GATT 1994. The Interpretative Note to Annex 1A addresses the

---

184 See below, pp. 488–91, 632–4 and 835–44.   185 See below, p. 895.   186 See below, p. 130.
187 See below, pp. 851–61.   188 See below, pp. 386 and 482–7.   189 See below, pp. 676–8.
190 See below, pp. 457–9.   191 See below, pp. 511–12.   192 See below, pp. 461–3.
193 See below, p. 495.   194 See below, pp. 746–8.   195 See below, pp. 86 and 607–10.

relationship between the GATT 1994 and the other multilateral agreements on trade in goods. It states:

> In the event of conflict between a provision of the General Agreement on Tariffs and Trade 1994 and a provision of another agreement in Annex 1A to the Agreement Establishing the World Trade Organization (referred to in the agreements in Annex 1A as the 'WTO Agreement'), the provision of the other agreement shall prevail to the extent of the conflict.

However, it is only where a provision of the GATT 1994 and a provision of another multilateral agreement on trade in goods are *in conflict* that the provision of the latter will prevail. Provisions are in conflict where adherence to the one provision will necessarily lead to a violation of the other provision and the provisions cannot, therefore, be read as complementing each other.[196] While it is undisputed that a conflict exists when one provision *requires* what another provision *prohibits*, international lawyers tend to disagree on whether such a conflict may exist where one provision expressly *permits* what another provision *prohibits*.

If there is no conflict, both the GATT 1994 and the other relevant multilateral agreement on trade in goods apply. In *Argentina – Footwear (EC) (2000)*, the Appellate Body ruled with regard to the relationship between, and the application of, the safeguard provision of the GATT 1994 (Article XIX) and the *Agreement on Safeguards* that:

> [t]he GATT 1994 and the *Agreement on Safeguards* are *both* Multilateral Agreements on Trade in Goods contained in Annex 1A of the *WTO Agreement*, and, as such, are *both* 'integral parts' of the same treaty, the *WTO Agreement*, that are 'binding on all Members'. Therefore, the provisions of Article XIX of the GATT 1994 *and* the provisions of the *Agreement on Safeguards* are *all* provisions of one treaty, the *WTO Agreement*. They entered into force as part of that treaty at the same time. They apply equally and are equally binding on all WTO Members. And, as these provisions relate to the same thing, namely the application by Members of safeguard measures, the Panel was correct in saying that 'Article XIX of GATT and the Safeguards Agreement must *a fortiori* be read as representing an *inseparable package* of rights and disciplines which have to be considered in conjunction'.[197]

4.1.3 General Agreement on Trade in Services

The *General Agreement on Trade in Services* (the 'GATS') is the first ever multilateral agreement on trade in services. The GATS establishes a regulatory framework within which WTO Members can undertake and implement commitments for the liberalisation of trade in services. The GATS covers measures of Members affecting trade in services.[198] Trade in services is defined in Article I:2 of the GATS as the supply of a service: (1) from the territory of one Member into the

---

196 Note that in international law, there is a strong presumption against conflict as it can be assumed that countries will not undertake conflicting obligations.

197 Appellate Body Report, *Argentina – Footwear (EC) (2000)*, para. 81. On the context in which this finding was made and its practical implications, see below, pp. 608–9.

198 See Article I:1 of the GATS. See also below, p. 337.

territory of any other Member (cross-border supply); (2) in the territory of one Member to a service consumer of any other Member (consumption abroad); (3) by a service supplier of one Member, through a commercial presence in the territory of any other Member (supply through a commercial presence); and (4) by a service supplier of one Member, through the presence of natural persons of a Member in the territory of any other Member (supply through the presence of natural persons).[199] 'Services' includes any service in any sector except services supplied in the exercise of governmental authority.[200] The supply of services includes the production, distribution, marketing, sale and delivery of a service.[201] It is clear from the third mode of supply (i.e. supply through a commercial presence) that the GATS also covers measures relating to foreign investment by suppliers of services.

The GATS contains provisions on: most-favoured-nation treatment (Article II);[202] transparency (Article III);[203] increasing participation of developing countries (Article IV);[204] economic integration (Article V);[205] domestic regulation (Article VI);[206] recognition (Article VII);[207] emergency safeguard measures (Article X);[208] payments and transfers (Article XI);[209] restrictions to safeguard the balance of payments (Article XII);[210] government procurement (Article XIII);[211] general exceptions (Article XIV);[212] security exceptions (Article XIV*bis*);[213] subsidies (Article XV);[214] market access (Article XVI);[215] national treatment (Article XVII);[216] negotiation and schedules of specific commitments (Articles XIX to XXI);[217] dispute settlement (Articles XXII and XXIII);[218] and institutional issues (Articles XXIV to XXVI).[219] Attached to the GATS are a number of annexes, including the Annex on Article II Exemptions,[220] the Annex on Movement of Natural Persons Supplying Services under the Agreement,[221] and the Annexes on Financial Services.[222] The Schedules of Specific Commitments of all WTO Members concerning their market access and national treatment commitments are also attached to the GATS and form an integral part thereof.[223]

On the relationship between the GATS and the GATT 1994, and in particular the question whether they are mutually exclusive agreements, the Appellate Body ruled in *EC – Bananas III (1997)*:

The GATS was not intended to deal with the same subject-matter as the GATT 1994. The GATS was intended to deal with a subject-matter not covered by the GATT 1994, that is,

---

199 See Article I:2(a)–(d) of the GATS. See also below, p. 340.
200 See Article I:3(b) of the GATS. See also below, pp. 338–9.
201 See Article XXVIII(b) of the GATS. See also below, p. 340.
202 See below, pp. 335–8.   203 See below, p. 532.   204 See below, p. 532.   205 See below, pp. 664–7.
206 See below, pp. 533–4.   207 See below, p. 345.   208 See below, p. 635.   209 See below, p. 537.
210 See below, pp. 645–6.   211 See below, p. 535.   212 See below, pp. 583–94.   213 See below, pp. 599–600.
214 See below, pp. 87–94.   215 See below, pp. 516–18.   216 See below, pp. 403–14.   217 See below, pp. 518–27.
218 See below, p. 173.   219 See below, pp. 125–6.   220 See below, pp. 341–2.   221 See below, p. 530.
222 See below, p. 86.
223 See Article XX of the GATS. The Final Act also contains an Understanding on Commitments in Financial Services that is not part of the *WTO Agreement* but which was the basis for post-1995 negotiations on the further liberalisation of trade in financial services. See below, p. 335.

with trade in services ... Given the respective scope of application of the two agreements, they may or may not overlap, depending on the nature of the measures at issue. Certain measures could be found to fall exclusively within the scope of the GATT 1994, when they affect trade in goods as goods. Certain measures could be found to fall exclusively within the scope of the GATS, when they affect the supply of services as services. There is yet a third category of measures that could be found to fall within the scope of both the GATT 1994 and the GATS. These are measures that involve a service relating to a particular good or a service supplied in conjunction with a particular good. In all such cases in this third category, the measure in question could be scrutinized under both the GATT 1994 and the GATS. However, while the same measure could be scrutinized under both agreements, the specific aspects of that measure examined under each agreement could be different. Under the GATT 1994, the focus is on how the measure affects the goods involved. Under the GATS, the focus is on how the measure affects the supply of the service or the service suppliers involved. Whether a certain measure affecting the supply of a service related to a particular good is scrutinized under the GATT 1994 or the GATS, or both, is a matter that can only be determined on a case-by-case basis.[224]

A measure restricting trade in bananas may thus be challenged under both the GATT 1994 (to the extent that it affects trade in bananas) and under the GATS (to the extent that it affects the supply of a service, such as wholesale trading in bananas).

4.1.4 Agreement on Trade-Related Aspects of Intellectual Property Rights

The *Agreement on Trade-Related Aspects of Intellectual Property Rights* (the '*TRIPS Agreement*') is not an agreement concerning trade as such or trade measures in the strict sense of the word. However, the value of many goods and services, particularly those traded by developed countries, is largely determined by the idea, the design or the invention they incorporate. If the value of such goods and services is not protected against the unauthorised use of the incorporated ideas, designs or inventions (for example, if a patented medicine produced by a pharmaceutical company of Member A is produced without authorisation as a generic medicine in Member B),[225] trade in these products or services will be affected. For that reason, developed-country Members sought and obtained the inclusion in the *WTO Agreement* of an agreement specifying minimum standards of protection of intellectual property rights and requiring the effective enforcement of these rights. The *TRIPS Agreement* covers seven types of intellectual property: (1) copyright and related rights (Articles 9–14);[226] (2) trademarks (Articles 15–21); (3) geographical indications (Articles 22–24);[227] (4) industrial designs (Articles 25–26); (5) patents (Articles 27–34);[228] (6) layout-designs (topographies) of integrated circuits (Articles 35–38); and (7) undisclosed information, including trade secrets (Article 39). With regard to these types of intellectual property, the *TRIPS Agreement* provides for minimum standards of protection. With regard to copyright, for example, Article 12 provides:

---

224 Appellate Body Report, *EC – Bananas III (1997)*, para. 221.
225 For a further discussion on the issue of patent protection of medicines, see below, pp. 998–1002.
226 See below, pp. 972–9.   227 See below, pp. 979–88.   228 See below, pp. 993–1002.

Whenever the term of protection of a work, other than a photographic work or a work of applied art, is calculated on a basis other than the life of a natural person, such term shall be no less than 50 years from the end of the calendar year of authorized publication, or, failing such authorized publication within 50 years from the making of the work, 50 years from the end of the calendar year of making.

Furthermore, the *TRIPS Agreement* requires WTO Members to ensure that enforcement procedures and remedies are available to permit effective action against any act of infringement of the intellectual property rights referred to above, including civil and administrative procedures and remedies, provisional measures and criminal procedures (Articles 41–61).[229] Pursuant to Articles 3 and 4 of the *TRIPS Agreement*, each WTO Member must accord other WTO Members national treatment and most-favoured-nation treatment, subject to a number of exceptions.[230] The *TRIPS Agreement* frequently refers to, and incorporates by reference, provisions of other intellectual property agreements, such as the *Paris Convention for the Protection of Industrial Property (1967)*, the *Berne Convention for the Protection of Literary and Artistic Works (1971)*, the *Rome Convention for the Protection of Performers, Producers of Phonograms and Broadcasting Organizations (1961)* and the *Washington Treaty on Intellectual Property in Respect of Integrated Circuits (1989)*, making provisions of these agreements applicable to all WTO Members.[231]

4.1.5 Understanding on Rules and Procedures for the Settlement of Disputes

The *Understanding on Rules and Procedures for the Settlement of Disputes*, commonly referred to as the *Dispute Settlement Understanding* or DSU, is arguably the single most important achievement of the Uruguay Round negotiations.[232] The WTO dispute settlement system applies to all disputes between WTO Members arising under the WTO agreements. In 1997, Renato Ruggiero, then Director-General of the WTO, referred to the dispute settlement system provided for by the DSU as:

in many ways the central pillar of the multilateral trading system and the WTO's most individual contribution to the stability of the global economy.[233]

Building on almost fifty years of experience with settling trade disputes in the context of the GATT 1947, the DSU sets out a dispute settlement system, characterised by compulsory jurisdiction, short timeframes, an appellate review process and an enforcement mechanism.[234] The DSU provides for rules on: the coverage and scope of the dispute settlement system, its administration, its objectives

229 See below, pp. 1002–7.   230 See below, pp. 962–4 and 968–70.
231 E.g. Article 2.1 of the *TRIPS Agreement* (with regard to the *Paris Convention*); and Article 9 of the *TRIPS Agreement* (with regard to the *Berne Convention*). See below, pp. 961–4 and 972–9.
232 See below, pp. 159–60.
233 As reported in WTO, *Trading into the Future*, 2nd revised edn (WTO, 2001), 38.
234 For a full discussion of the WTO dispute settlement system, see below, pp. 156–311.

and its operation (Articles 1–3);[235] on mandatory pre-litigation consultations (Article 4);[236] on good offices, conciliation and mediation (Article 5);[237] on the panel process (Articles 6–16 and 18–20);[238] on the appellate review process (Articles 17–20);[239] on compliance and enforcement (Articles 21–22);[240] on a ban on unilateral action (Article 23);[241] on least-developed-country Members (Article 24);[242] on arbitration as an alternative means of dispute settlement (Article 25);[243] on non-violation and situation complaints (Article 26);[244] and on the role of the WTO Secretariat (Article 27).[245] Attached to the DSU are appendices on: the WTO agreements covered by the DSU (Appendix 1);[246] on special or additional rules and procedures on dispute settlement contained in WTO agreements (Appendix 2);[247] on the working procedures of panels (Appendix 3);[248] and on expert review groups (Appendix 4).[249]

4.1.6 Trade Policy Review Mechanism

It is very important for WTO Members, their companies and citizens involved in trade to be informed as fully as possible about trade regulations and policies of other WTO Members. To that end, many of the WTO agreements referred to above provide for an obligation on WTO Members to inform or notify the WTO of new trade regulations, measures or policies or changes to existing ones.[250] In addition, however, the WTO conducts regular reviews of individual Members' trade policies. The procedural rules for these reviews are set out in Annex 3 on the *Trade Policy Review Mechanism*.[251]

4.1.7 Plurilateral Agreements

All agreements in Annexes 1 to 3 are binding on all WTO Members. Membership of the WTO is conditional upon the acceptance of these 'multilateral agreements'. In contrast, Annex 4 contains two agreements, referred to as 'plurilateral agreements', which are only binding on those WTO Members that are a party to these agreements.[252] The first plurilateral agreement is the *Agreement on Trade in Civil Aircraft*. This is, in fact, an agreement concluded during the 1979 Tokyo Round of trade negotiations. Attempts during the Uruguay Round to negotiate a new agreement failed. The *Agreement on Trade in Civil Aircraft*, which is of particular interest to the United States and the European Communities: (1) provides for duty-free trade in civil aircraft and parts thereof; (2) prohibits quotas and other trade restrictions on civil aircraft; and (3) addresses the issue of government support to aircraft manufacturers. Disputes relating to this agreement *cannot* be brought to the WTO dispute

---

235 See below, pp. 159, 206, 221.   236   See below, pp. 162 and 272.   237 See below, p. 181.
238 See below, pp. 209–31 and 274–83.   239   See below, pp. 231–44 and 283–91.   240 See below, pp. 179–205.
241 See below, p. 306.   242 See below, pp. 299–302.   243 See below, pp. 306–7.   244 See below.
245 See below.   246 See below, p. 163.   247 See below, p. 889.   248 See below, pp. 274–80.
249 See below, p. 227.   250 See e.g. below, pp. 622 and 884.   251 See below, pp. 95–7.
252 When the *WTO Agreement* entered into force on 1 January 1995, Annex 4 included four plurilateral agreements. However, two of those agreements – the *International Dairy Agreement* and the *International Bovine Meat Agreement* – were terminated at the end of 1997.

settlement system for resolution. The second plurilateral agreement is the *Agreement on Government Procurement*. Under GATT 1994 and GATS rules, WTO Members are free to discriminate in favour of domestic products, services and service suppliers in the context of government procurement.[253] This is an important exception to the national treatment obligations of Article III of the GATT 1994 and Article XVII of the GATS.[254] Under the terms of the *Agreement on Government Procurement*, the parties have agreed to accord national treatment in respect of government procurement above certain thresholds by designated government entities.[255] The agreement also obliges parties to make procurement opportunities public, and to provide for a procedure allowing unsuccessful bidders to challenge a procurement award. Disputes under the *Agreement on Government Procurement* can be, and have already been, brought to the WTO dispute settlement system for resolution.[256]

4.1.8   Ministerial Decisions and Declarations

Finally, note the twenty-seven Ministerial Decisions and Declarations, which together with the *WTO Agreement* form the Final Act adopted in Marrakesh in April 1994 at the end of the Uruguay Round negotiations. These Ministerial Decisions and Declarations include, for example, the *Decision on Measures in Favour of Least-Developed Countries*,[257] the *Declaration on the Contribution of the World Trade Organization to Achieving Greater Coherence in Global Economic Policymaking*[258] and the *Decision on the Application and Review of the Understanding on Rules and Procedures Governing the Settlement of Disputes*.[259] These Ministerial Decisions and Declarations do not generate specific rights and obligations for WTO Members, which can be enforced through WTO dispute settlement.

Questions and Assignments 1.8

Look in the WTO's official *Legal Texts* and skim through all the WTO agreements referred to above. Add tabs to your copy of the *Legal Texts* for easy reference to the various agreements. Explain briefly what each of these agreements deals with. What is the difference between multilateral and plurilateral agreements? What is the relationship between the GATT 1994 and other multilateral agreements on trade in goods? Which agreement prevails in case of conflict? When does a conflict exist? What is the relationship between the GATT 1994 and the GATS? Can these two agreements be applied to one and the same measure?

4.2   Other Sources of WTO Law

The *WTO Agreement*, with its multiple annexes, is undisputedly the *principal* source of WTO law. However, this Agreement is not the only source of WTO law. As indicated above, there are also other sources of WTO law. But note, however, that these other sources are *not* of the same nature or on the same legal footing

---

253 See below, pp. 509–11 and 535.
254 See Article III:8(a) of the GATT 1994 and Article XIII of the GATS. See also below, pp. 323 and 535.
255 See below, pp. 509–10.
256 E.g. Panel Report, *Korea – Procurement (2000)*. See below, p. 55.
257 See www.wto.org/english/docs_e/legal_e/legal_e.htm.   258 See *ibid.*, and below, p. 97.   259 See *ibid.*

as the WTO agreements discussed above. The WTO agreements (with the exception of the *Trade Policy Review Mechanism* and the *Agreement on Trade in Civil Aircraft*) provide for specific legal rights and obligations for WTO Members that can be enforced through WTO dispute settlement. *Most* of the other sources reviewed below do *not* in and of themselves provide for specific, *enforceable* rights or obligations. They do, however, assist in 'clarifying' or 'defining' the law that applies between WTO Members on WTO matters. This sub-section discusses in turn: (1) dispute settlement reports; (2) acts of WTO bodies; (3) agreements concluded in the context of the WTO; (4) customary international law; (5) general principles of law; (6) other international agreements; (7) subsequent practice of WTO Members; (8) the negotiating history of WTO agreements; and (9) teachings of the most highly qualified publicists.

4.2.1   Dispute Settlement Reports

Reports of WTO panels and the Appellate Body are the most important source of clarifications and interpretations of WTO law. In addition, reports of GATT 1947 panels are also relevant. In principle, adopted panel and Appellate Body reports are only binding on the parties to a particular dispute.[260] However, in *Japan – Alcoholic Beverages II (1996)* the Appellate Body held with regard to prior GATT panel reports:

Adopted panel reports are an important part of the GATT *acquis*. They are often considered by subsequent panels. They create legitimate expectations among WTO Members, and, therefore, should be taken into account where they are relevant to any dispute.[261]

In adopting this approach, the Appellate Body was clearly inspired by the practice of the International Court of Justice. Article 59 of the *Statute of the International Court of Justice* provides that the decisions of the Court have no binding force except between the parties and in respect of the particular case. However, as the Appellate Body noted:

[t]his has not inhibited the development by that Court (and its predecessor) of a body of case law in which considerable reliance on the value of previous decisions is readily discernible.[262]

Referring to its reasoning in *Japan – Alcoholic Beverages II (1996)*, the Appellate Body stated in *US – Shrimp (Article 21.5 – Malaysia) (2001)*, the Appellate Body added:

This reasoning applies to adopted Appellate Body Reports as well. Thus, in taking into account the reasoning in an adopted Appellate Body Report – a Report, moreover, that was directly relevant to the Panel's disposition of the issues before it – the Panel did not err. The Panel was correct in using our findings as a tool for its own reasoning.[263]

---

260 On the adoption of panel and Appellate Body reports, see below, p. 206–7. With respect to *unadopted* reports, see Panel Report, *Japan – Alcoholic Beverages II (1996)*, para. 6.10. See also Panel Report, *EU – Footwear (China) (2012)*, para. 7.83.
261 Appellate Body Report, *Japan – Alcoholic Beverages II*, 108.
262 *Ibid.*, footnote 30.
263 Appellate Body Report, *US – Shrimp (Article 21.5 – Malaysia) (2001)*, para. 109.

In *US – Oil Country Tubular Goods Sunset Reviews (2005)*, the Appellate Body
stated that:

following the Appellate Body's conclusions in earlier disputes is not only appropriate, but is
what would be expected from panels, especially where the issues are the same.[264]

The issue of the role of precedent in WTO dispute settlement was critical in *US –
Stainless Steel (Mexico) (2008)*. At issue was the Appellate Body's case law – fiercely
contested by the United States – on the WTO consistency of the zeroing methodology to calculate a dumping margin.[265] The panel in *US – Stainless Steel (Mexico)
(2008)* found that it was not, 'strictly speaking, bound by previous Appellate Body
or panel decisions that have addressed the same issue'. The panel noted that the
Appellate Body had stated in earlier cases that panels were 'expected' to take into
account relevant adopted reports. The panel stated that it had done so, but that,
after careful consideration of these reports, it decided that it had 'no option but to
respectfully disagree with the line of reasoning developed by the Appellate Body
regarding the WTO-consistency of simple zeroing in periodic reviews'.[266] Because
it fundamentally disagreed with the Appellate Body's interpretation of the relevant
WTO provision, and agreed with the different interpretation advocated by the United
States in this and prior cases, the panel 'felt compelled to depart' from the Appellate
Body's well-established case law.[267] In its report in this case, the Appellate Body
stated that it was 'deeply concerned' about the panel's decision to depart from the
Appellate Body's well-established case law as the panel's approach had 'serious im-
plications for the proper functioning of the WTO dispute settlement system'.[268] The
Appellate Body stated:

It is well settled that Appellate Body reports are not binding, except with respect to resolving the particular dispute between the parties. This, however, does not mean that subsequent
panels are free to disregard the legal interpretations and the *ratio decidendi* contained in
previous Appellate Body reports that have been adopted by the DSB.[269]

The Appellate Body recalled in this respect its rulings in *Japan – Alcoholic Beverages II (1996)* and *US – Oil Country Tubular Goods Sunset Reviews (2005)*,
both quoted above, and furthermore stated that:

[d]ispute settlement practice demonstrates that WTO Members attach significance to reasoning provided in previous panel and Appellate Body reports. Adopted panel and Appellate
Body reports are often cited by parties in support of legal arguments in dispute settlement
proceedings, and are relied upon by panels and the Appellate Body in subsequent disputes ...
Thus, the legal interpretation embodied in adopted panel and Appellate Body reports becomes part and parcel of the *acquis* of the WTO dispute settlement system.[270]

---

264 Appellate Body Report, *US – Oil Country Tubular Goods Sunset Reviews (2005)*, para. 188.
265 On the zeroing methodology to calculate a dumping margin, see below, p. 689–95.
266 See Panel Report, *US – Stainless Steel (Mexico) (2008)*, para. 7.106.   267 See *ibid*.
268 Appellate Body Report, *US – Stainless Steel (Mexico) (2008)*, para. 162.   269 *Ibid*., para. 158.
270 *Ibid*., para. 160. The Appellate Body also observed that, 'when enacting or modifying laws and national
     regulations pertaining to international trade matters, WTO Members take into account the legal interpreta-
     tion of the covered agreements developed in adopted panel and Appellate Body reports'. See *ibid*.

In other words, whereas the *application* of a provision may be regarded as confined to the context of the case in which it takes place, the relevance of *clarification* contained in adopted Appellate Body reports is not limited to the application of a particular provision in a specific case.[271] Most importantly, the Appellate Body found that:

> [e]nsuring 'security and predictability' in the dispute settlement system, as contemplated in Article 3.2 of the DSU, implies that, *absent cogent reasons*, an adjudicatory body will resolve the same legal question in the same way in a subsequent case.[272]

According to the Appellate Body, the panel's failure to follow previously adopted Appellate Body reports addressing the same issues 'undermines the development of a coherent and predictable body of jurisprudence clarifying Members' rights and obligations under the covered agreements as contemplated under the DSU'.[273] A few months after the adoption of the Appellate Body report in *US – Stainless Steel (Mexico) (2008)*, the panel in *US – Continued Zeroing (2009)*, while expressing doubts regarding the correctness of the Appellate Body's relevant case law but recognising that this case law was well-established, stated:

> [W]e consider that providing prompt resolution to this dispute in this manner will best serve the multiple goals of the DSU, and, on balance, is furthered by following the Appellate Body's adopted findings in this case.[274]

The panel in *US – Continued Zeroing (2009)* thus concluded that the United States acted inconsistently with the *Anti-Dumping Agreement* and the GATT 1994 by applying the zeroing methodology in periodic reviews. The United States appealed this finding of inconsistency, but – not surprisingly – the Appellate Body upheld the panel's finding. In a concurring opinion, one of the members of the division of the Appellate Body hearing the appeal in *US – Continued Zeroing (2009)*, stated as follows:

> In matters of adjudication, there must be an end to every great debate. The Appellate Body exists to clarify the meaning of the covered agreements. On the question of zeroing it has spoken definitively. Its decisions have been adopted by the DSB. The membership of the WTO is entitled to rely upon these outcomes.[275]

4.2.2 Acts of WTO Bodies

Acts of WTO bodies, such as authoritative interpretations under Article IX:2 of the *WTO Agreement* and waivers under Article IX:3 of the *WTO Agreement*, are clearly a source of WTO law which give rise to rights and obligations for WTO Members that can be enforced through the dispute settlement

---

271 See *ibid.*, para. 161.   272 *Ibid.*, para. 160. Emphasis added.   273 *Ibid.*, para. 161.
274 Panel Report, *US – Continued Zeroing (2009)*, para. 7.182.
275 Appellate Body Report, *US – Continued Zeroing (2009)*, para. 312.

system.[276] In this regard, consider, for example, the ruling of the Appellate Body in *EC – Bananas III (1997)* on the European Communities' invocation of the Lomé Waiver as a justification for its breach of the MFN treatment obligations of Articles I:1 and XIII of the GATT 1994.[277] Other acts of WTO bodies are also sources of WTO law and must be taken into account by panels and the Appellate Body. They are a part of WTO law. However, the Appellate Body has not yet ruled explicitly on whether such acts of WTO bodies provide for rights and obligations which can be enforced through the dispute settlement system.[278] In *US – Clove Cigarettes (2012)*, the issue arose whether paragraph 5.2 of the *Doha Ministerial Decision on Implementation-Related Issues and Concerns*, which defined the term 'reasonable interval' in Article 2.12 of the *TBT Agreement* as meaning in most cases a period of at least six months, could be relied on by the complainant in that case.[279] After ruling that paragraph 5.2 of the Decision was not an authoritative interpretation under Article IX:2 of the *WTO Agreement* (because it was not adopted in conformity with the procedure set out in that provision[280]), the Appellate Body ruled with regard to paragraph 5.2 that:

a decision adopted by Members, *other than* a decision adopted pursuant to Article IX:2 of the *WTO Agreement*, may constitute a 'subsequent agreement' on the interpretation of a provision of a covered agreement under Article 31(3)(a) of the *Vienna Convention*.[281]

Therefore, to the extent that an act of a WTO body is a 'subsequent agreement' between Members on the interpretation (or application) of a WTO provision, panels and the Appellate Body *must*, pursuant to Article 31.3(a) of the *Vienna Convention on the Law of Treaties*, take into account such an act when interpreting that provision.[282]

In *US – Tuna II (Mexico) (2012)*, the same issue arose but now with regard to a decision of a technical committee, the TBT Committee.[283] The Appellate Body ruled with regard to the TBT Committee *Decision on Principles for the Development of International Standards, Guides and Recommendations with Relation to Articles 2, 5, and Annex 3 to the Agreement* that:

the TBT Committee Decision can be considered as a 'subsequent agreement' within the meaning of Article 31(3)(a) of the *Vienna Convention*. The extent to which this Decision

---

276 For a discussion of authoritative interpretations and waivers, see below, pp. 139 and 140.

277 See Appellate Body Report, *EC – Bananas III (1997)*, para. 183. On Article I:1 and XIII of the GATT 1994, see below, pp. 317–30 and 538, respectively.

278 For a discussion on the scope of the jurisdiction of the WTO dispute settlement system, see below, pp. 160–72.

279 On Article 2.12 of the *TBT Agreement*, see below, pp. 884–5.

280 See below, p. 139.

281 Appellate Body Report, *US – Clove Cigarettes (2012)*, para. 260.

282 On Article 31.3(a) of the *Vienna Convention*, see below, p. 888.

283 With regard to the legal status of a decision of the SPS Committee, namely, the Decision on Equivalence (see below, pp. 933–4), see Panel Report, *US – Poultry (China) (2010)*, para. 7.136.

will inform the interpretation and application of a term or provision of the *TBT Agreement* in a specific case, however, will depend on the degree to which it 'bears specifically' on the interpretation and application of the respective term or provision.[284]

4.2.3   Agreements Concluded in the Context of the WTO

As discussed in more detail in Chapter 2 of this book, WTO Members have negotiated and concluded, in the framework of the WTO, agreements providing, *inter alia*, for: (1) further market access commitments for specific services and service suppliers; (2) the liberalisation of trade in information technology products; and (3) the accession of some thirty countries to the WTO.[285] These agreements are sources of WTO law and are enforceable in WTO dispute settlement. With regard to the relevance of Protocols of Accession as a source of rights and obligations for Members, consider *China – Auto Parts (2009), China – Publications and Audiovisual Products (2010)* and *China – Raw Material (2012).* Protocols of Accession are integral parts of the *WTO Agreement.*[286] Moreover, the commitments set out in the working party report, which are incorporated in the Protocol by cross-reference, are also binding and enforceable.[287]

4.2.4   Customary International Law

Article 3.2, second sentence, of the DSU provides:

> The Members recognize that [the WTO dispute settlement system] serves to preserve the rights and obligations of Members under the covered agreements, and to clarify the existing provisions of those agreements *in accordance with customary rules of interpretation of public international law.*[288]

The DSU thus explicitly refers to customary international law on treaty interpretation and makes this law applicable in the context of the WTO. It is debated whether other rules of customary international law are also part of WTO law.[289] In *Korea – Procurement (2000),* the panel went so far as to hold that customary international law applies:

> to the extent that the WTO treaty agreements do not 'contract out' from it.[290]

Customary international law is part of general international law and the rules of general international law are, in principle, binding on all States. Each new State, as well as each new treaty, is automatically born into it. This, however, does not

---

284 Appellate Body Report, *US – Tuna II (Mexico) (2012),* para. 372.
285 See below, pp. 86–7.   286 See below, pp. 111, 140 and 153–4.
287 See Panel Reports, *China – Raw Materials (2012),* paras. 7.112 and 7.114.
288 Emphasis added. See also below, pp. 184–94.
289 As discussed in Chapter 3 of this book, this debate is of particular relevance with respect to the available remedies for breach of WTO law. See below, pp. 194–205.
290 Panel Report, *Korea – Procurement (2000),* para. 7.96. This panel report was not appealed.

answer the question whether any such customary international law could be the basis for claims or defences, or, in other words, would be enforceable in WTO dispute settlement. This question is further discussed below.[291]

In addition to the rules of customary international law on treaty interpretation, explicitly referred to in Article 3.2 of the DSU, the Appellate Body and panels have referred to and applied other rules of customary international law. The Appellate Body has made reference to and/or applied customary rules on dispute settlement and, in particular, on standing,[292] representation by private counsel,[293] the burden of proof,[294] and the treatment of municipal law.[295] In addition, panels have referred to and/or applied customary rules on State responsibility and, in particular, rules on countermeasures[296] and attribution.[297] The customary rules on State responsibility and, in particular, rules on compensation of harm caused by unlawful acts, are often referred to as rules that do not apply between WTO Members because WTO law, and in particular the DSU, provides for a *lex specialis*.[298]

4.2.5 General Principles of Law

Like customary international law, general principles of law are part of general international law. As noted in the previous section, rules of general international law are, in principle, binding on all States. Both panels and the Appellate Body have referred to and used general principles of law as a basis for their rulings or in support of their reasoning. In *US – Shrimp (1998)*, the Appellate Body noted with regard to the principle of good faith:

> The chapeau of Article XX is, in fact, but one expression of the principle of good faith. This principle, at once a general principle of law and a general principle of international law, controls the exercise of rights by states. One application of this general principle, the application widely known as the doctrine of *abus de droit*, prohibits the abusive exercise of a state's rights and enjoins that whenever the assertion of a right 'impinges on the field covered by [a] treaty obligation, it must be exercised *bona fide*, that is to say, reasonably'. An abusive exercise by a Member of its own treaty right thus results in a breach of the treaty rights of the other Members and, as well, a violation of the treaty obligation of the Member so acting.[299]

---

291 See below, p. 72.
292 See e.g. Appellate Body Report, *EC – Bananas III (1997)*, para. 133.
293 See e.g. Appellate Body Report, *EC – Bananas III (1997)*, para. 10. See also below, pp. 261–3.
294 See e.g. Appellate Body Report, *US – Wool Shirts and Blouses (1997)*, 14. See also below, pp. 172–8.
295 See e.g. Appellate Body Report, *India – Patents (US) (1998)*, para. 65.
296 See e.g. Decision by the Arbitrators, *Brazil – Aircraft (Article 22.6 – Brazil) (2002)*, para. 3.44 and footnotes 46 and 48.
297 See e.g. Panel Report, *Canada – Dairy (1999)*, para. 7.77 and footnote 427; and Panel Report, *Turkey – Textiles (1999)*, para. 9.33.
298 See below, p. 204–5. Note that Article 55 of the International Law Commission's *Articles on Responsibility of States for Internationally Wrongful Acts*, entitled 'Lex specialis', provides that '[t]hese articles do not apply where and to the extent that the conditions for the existence of an internationally wrongful act or the content or implementation of the international responsibility of a State are governed by special rules of international law'.
299 Appellate Body Report, *US – Shrimp (1998)*, para. 158. See also Appellate Body Report, *US – FSC (2000)*, para. 166.

The principle of due process,[300] the principle of proportionality,[301] the principle of judicial economy,[302] the principle of non-retroactivity[303] and the interpretative principles of effectiveness,[304] of *in dubio mitius*[305] and of *ejusdem generis*[306] have also been applied by panels and the Appellate Body in numerous reports.

4.2.6   Other International Agreements

Other international agreements can also be relevant as sources of WTO law. This is definitely the case when these agreements are incorporated or referred to specifically in a WTO agreement. As mentioned above, the *TRIPS Agreement* incorporates a number of provisions of other intellectual property agreements, such as the *Paris Convention (1967)* and the *Berne Convention (1971)*, thus making provisions of these agreements part of WTO law, applicable to all WTO Members and enforceable through WTO dispute settlement. The *SCM Agreement* refers to the *OECD Arrangement on Guidelines for Officially Supported Export Credits*.[307]

Whether, and, if so, to what extent, other international agreements *not* referred to in a WTO agreement can be a source of WTO law, is a controversial issue. This issue is of particular relevance to multilateral environmental agreements (MEAs) and International Labour Organization (ILO) conventions on minimum labour standards. It is broadly accepted that these other international agreements may play a role in the interpretation of WTO legal provisions. Please refer to the discussion in Chapter 3 of this book on the relevance of other international agreements under Article 31 of the *Vienna Convention* in the interpretation of WTO agreements. It suffices to note here that, in *US – Shrimp (1998)*, the Appellate Body made use of principles laid down in multilateral environmental agreements such as the *United Nations Convention on the Law of the Sea*, the *Convention on Biological Diversity* and the *Convention on the Conservation of Migratory Species of Wild Animals* (CITES) to interpret Article XX of the GATT 1994.[308]

---

300 See e.g. Appellate Body Report, *US – Shrimp (1998)*, para. 182. See also below, pp. 267–8.

301 See e.g. Appellate Body Report, *US – Shrimp (1998)*, para. 141. See also Appellate Body Report, *US – Cotton Yarn (2001)*, para. 120.

302 See e.g. Appellate Body Report, *US – Wool Shirts and Blouses (1998)*, 17–20; and Appellate Body Report, *Australia – Salmon (1998)*, paras. 219–26.

303 See Appellate Body Report, *Brazil – Desiccated Coconut (1997)*, 179; Appellate Body Report, *EC – Bananas III (1997)*, para. 235; and Appellate Body Report, *Canada – Patent Term (2000)*, paras. 71–4.

304 See Appellate Body Report, *US – Gasoline (1996)*, 16; and Appellate Body Report, *Korea – Dairy (2000)*, para. 81.

305 See e.g. Appellate Body Report, *EC – Hormones (1998)*, footnote 154. Note that, in *China – Publications and Audiovisual Products (2010)*, the Appellate Body discussed, but did not apply, the principle of *in dubio mitius*. See Appellate Body Report, *China – Publications and Audiovisual Products (2010)*, para. 411. See also below, pp. 184–94.

306 See Appellate Body Report, *US – Large Civil Aircraft (2nd complaint) (2012)*, para. 615; and Appellate Body Reports, *US – COOL (2012)*, para. 444.

307 See Annex I(k) to the *SCM Agreement*. Grants by governments of export credits that meet the requirements of this Arrangement are not considered an export subsidy prohibited under the *SCM Agreement*.

308 See below, pp. 184–94 and 226–8.

However, it is contested whether these other international agreements (i.e. international agreements to which WTO agreements do not explicitly refer) can be a source of WTO law in the sense that they provide rights and obligations for Members that can be invoked as a basis for claims or defences in WTO dispute settlement. As discussed below, Joost Pauwelyn has argued in this respect that WTO Members cannot base a claim before a WTO panel on the violation of rights and obligations set out in a non-WTO agreement. However, in his opinion, WTO Members that are parties to a particular non-WTO agreement can invoke in a WTO dispute between them the rules of that agreement as a defence against a claim of violation of WTO rules.[309] This position is, however, quite controversial. Other WTO scholars do not agree that rules of non-WTO agreements can be invoked before a panel or the Appellate Body as a defence.[310] In *Mexico – Soft Drinks (2006)*, the Appellate Body held that it saw:

> no basis in the DSU for panels and the Appellate Body to adjudicate non-WTO disputes. Article 3.2 of the DSU states that the WTO dispute settlement system 'serves to preserve the rights and obligations of Members under the *covered agreements*, and to clarify the existing provisions of *those agreements*'. Accepting Mexico's interpretation would imply that the WTO dispute settlement system could be used to determine rights and obligations outside the covered agreements.[311]

The Appellate Body stated that adjudication of disputes under non-WTO agreements 'is not the function of panels and the Appellate Body as intended by the DSU'.[312]

4.2.7 Subsequent Practice of WTO Members

As discussed in Chapter 3 of this book, 'subsequent practice' within the meaning of Article 31.3(b) of the *Vienna Convention* must, pursuant to this provision, be taken into account in the interpretation of the rights and obligations set out in the *WTO Agreement*.[313] Therefore, 'subsequent practice' of the WTO, WTO bodies or WTO Members must be considered to be a source of WTO law. An isolated act, however, is generally not sufficient to establish subsequent practice.[314] In *Japan – Alcoholic Beverages II (1996)*, the Appellate Body stated that 'subsequent practice' within the meaning of Article 31.3(b) must be:

> a 'concordant, common and consistent' sequence of acts or pronouncements which is sufficient to establish a discernible pattern implying the agreement of the parties regarding its interpretation.[315]

309 See J. Pauwelyn, *Conflict of Norms in Public International Law: How WTO Law Relates to Other Norms of International Law* (Cambridge University Press, 2003), 473 and 491.
310 See below, pp. 62–3.
311 Appellate Body Report, *Mexico – Soft Drinks (2006)*, para. 56. Emphasis added. On the underlying legal issue (the applicability of Article XX(d) of the GATT 1994, invoked by Mexico as a defence) and the context in which this statement was made (whether Mexico's measure claimed to have been taken in response to the alleged breach by the United States of its obligations under the NAFTA could be justified under Article XX(d)), see below, p. 560–5.
312 Appellate Body Report, *Mexico – Soft Drinks (2006)*, para. 78.   313 See below, pp. 189–90.   314 See *ibid.*
315 Appellate Body Report, *Japan – Alcoholic Beverages II (1996)*, 106–7. See also Appellate Body Report, *Chile – Price Band System (2002)*, paras. 213–14 and 272; Appellate Body Report, *US – Gambling (2005)*, paras. 192–3; and Appellate Body Report, *EC – Chicken Cuts (2005)*, paras. 259, 265–6 and 271–3.

4.2.8   Negotiating History of WTO Agreements

Pursuant to Article 32 of the *Vienna Convention*, the negotiating history of an agreement may serve as a supplementary means of interpretation. However, as noted in Chapter 3 of this book, there is no formally recorded negotiating history of the WTO agreements, and WTO panels and the Appellate Body have given limited weight to various country-specific and often conflicting negotiating proposals and very little importance to the often contradictory and self-serving *personal* recollections of negotiators.[316] Note that the negotiating history of the GATT 1947 and the 1948 *Havana Charter on an International Trade Organization* have been of some use in the interpretation of the provisions of the GATT 1994.

4.2.9   Teachings of Publicists

Finally, pursuant to Article 38.1 of the *Statute of the International Court of Justice*, the 'teachings of the most highly qualified publicists' are subsidiary means for the determination of rules of international law. WTO panels and the Appellate Body occasionally cite the writings of scholars in support of their reasoning where they found them persuasive.[317]

Questions and Assignments 1.9

Briefly discuss *all* sources of WTO law. Are panel and Appellate Body reports of relevance only to the parties to a dispute? What is the role of precedent in WTO dispute settlement? Why? Have the Appellate Body and panels referred to and applied rules of customary international law and general principles of law? Can multilateral environmental agreements concluded between WTO Members be in any way a source of WTO law? Do decisions of WTO bodies provide for legal rights and obligations for Members? Are such decisions in any way a source of WTO law? Are the negotiating history of the WTO agreements or the personal recollections of negotiators a source of WTO law?

5   WTO LAW IN CONTEXT

Earlier in this chapter, WTO law was described as a significant component of international economic law, which itself is an important part of public international law. However, the relationship between WTO law and *international law* deserves to be explored further. Likewise, the relationship between WTO law and *national law* also raises questions that need to be addressed.

---

316   See below, pp. 192–3.
317   See e.g. Appellate Body Report, *US – Wool Shirts and Blouses (1998)*, footnotes 15 and 16 (on burden of proof). The scholarly writings cited by panels and the Appellate Body often concern general issues of international law or specific legal problems under relevant national law, rather than scholarly writings on WTO law.

5.1 WTO Law and International Law

This section on WTO law and international law deals in turn with: (1) the position of WTO law in international law; and (2) conflicts between WTO agreements and other international agreements.

5.1.1 WTO Law as an Integral Part of International Law

In the past, most handbooks on international law and general courses on this topic gave little or no attention to international trade law. International law commonly excluded the regulation of international trade from its purview. In his 1996 Hague Lecture, Donald McRae noted:

> International trade law and international economic law were not of concern to international lawyers; trade and economic law were not central to the way international lawyers defined their discipline ... Particular social traditions may have played some role in this. In some countries the idea of commerce, of buying and selling, or of economic matters generally, was not viewed with favour. The professions of medicine and law were respectable; those engaged in business did not have the same social status. This, no doubt, helped fashion the attitudes of international lawyers to international trade law and international economic law ... The field of trade law, and that of economic matters generally, are seen as closely intertwined with the field of economics which is perceived as presenting a barrier to those without formal training in that discipline. In his extremely insightful work, *International Law in a Divided World*, Professor Cassese, who does recognize the significance of international economic relations to the study of international law, and devotes a full chapter to it, nevertheless states that 'international economic relations are usually the hunting ground of a few specialists, who often jealously hold for themselves the key to this abstruse admixture of law and economics'.[318]

However, in the current era of globalisation, economic issues and problems have moved to the frontlines of international relations and international law. In a later article, McRae described the work of the WTO as the 'new frontier' of international law.[319] The importance of international economic law and international trade law is now broadly recognised among international lawyers.

It should be noted that, in the past, international trade lawyers were also quite ambivalent with regard to the relationship between international trade law and international law. Many considered international trade law to be a self-contained system of international law.[320] This position has been discredited. International trade law, and in particular WTO law, is now generally considered to be an integral part of international law. WTO Director-General Pascal Lamy, in his address to the European Society of International Law in 2006, noted:

---

318 D. McRae, *The Contribution of International Trade Law to the Development of International Law*, Academy of International Law, *Recueil des Cours*, Volume 260, 1996, 114–15.

319 D. McRae, 'The WTO in International Law: Tradition Continued or New Frontier?', *Journal of International Economic Law*, 2000, 30 and 41.

320 As reported by P. J. Kuijper, 'The Law of GATT as a Special Field of International Law: Ignorance, Further Refinement or Self-Contained System of International Law?', *Netherlands Yearbook of International Law*, 1994, 257.

The effectiveness and legitimacy of the WTO depend on how it relates to norms of other legal systems and on the nature and quality of its relationships with other international organizations ... [T]he WTO, far from being hegemonic, as it is sometimes portrayed to be, recognizes its limited competence and the specialization of other international organizations. In this sense the WTO participates in the construction of international coherence and reinforces the international legal order.[321]

A genuine turning point in the relationship between international law and international trade law was the Appellate Body Report in *US – Gasoline (1996)*. In this report, its very first, the Appellate Body ruled that Article 3.2 of the DSU, which directs panels and the Appellate Body to interpret the WTO agreements according to the 'customary rules of interpretation of public international law', reflects:

a measure of recognition that the *General Agreement* is not to be read in clinical isolation from public international law.[322]

The discussion above of the sources of WTO law shows that WTO law is *not* a closed, self-contained system, isolated from the rest of international law.

5.1.2   Conflicts Between WTO Agreements and Other Agreements

It may happen that the rights and obligations of WTO Members under the WTO agreements are in conflict with their rights and obligations under other international agreements.[323] A classic example of such a conflict is the situation in which a multilateral environmental agreement (an 'MEA') obliges the parties to that agreement to impose quantitative restrictions on trade in certain products whereas the GATT 1994 prohibits such restrictions. WTO Director-General Pascal Lamy has pointed out in this regard:

The WTO, its treaty provisions and their interpretation, confirms the absence of any hierarchy between WTO norms and those norms developed in other forums: WTO norms do not supersede or trump other international norms.[324]

First, it should be noted that WTO rules should, if possible, be interpreted in such a way that they do not conflict with other rules of international law. As Gabrielle Marceau noted:

[p]anels and the Appellate Body have the obligation to interpret the WTO provisions in taking into account all relevant rules of international law applicable to the relations between the WTO Members. One of those rules is the general principle against conflicting interpretation (Article 31.3(c) together with 30 of the Vienna Convention). Therefore, in most cases

---

321 P. Lamy, 'The Place of the WTO and Its Law in the International Legal Order', *European Journal of International Law*, 2007, 977.
322 Appellate Body Report, *US – Gasoline (1996)*, 16.
323 As mentioned above, while it is undisputed that a conflict exists when one provision *requires* what another provision *prohibits*, international lawyers tend to disagree on whether such a conflict may exist where one provision expressly *permits* what another provision *prohibits*. See above, p. 45.
324 P. Lamy, 'The Place of the WTO and Its Law in the International Legal Order', *European Journal of International Law*, 2007, 978.

the proper interpretation of the relevant WTO provisions – themselves often drafted in terms of specific prohibitions leaving open a series of WTO compatible alternative measures – should lead to a reading of the WTO provisions so as to avoid conflict with other treaty provisions.[325]

While there will undoubtedly be many instances in which an adjudicator can interpret WTO rules and non-WTO rules so as to avoid conflict, in some instances this will not be possible. As already briefly mentioned above, Joost Pauwelyn has an innovative and well-thought-out view on the conflict of WTO rules with non-WTO rules.[326] Pauwelyn's view is controversial but has received support from some fellow WTO scholars. Central to Pauwelyn's view is that most WTO obligations are essentially reciprocal in nature.[327] Reciprocal obligations are obligations from which parties to a multilateral treaty may deviate, as long as such deviation does not infringe the rights of third parties. Pauwelyn explains his view on the conflict between WTO rules and non-WTO rules as follows:

In the event of conflict involving WTO provisions, WTO provisions may not always prevail, including before a WTO panel. The trade obligations in the WTO treaty are of the 'reciprocal type'. They are not of an 'integral nature'. Hence, WTO provisions can be deviated from as between a limited number of WTO members only, as long as this deviation does not breach third party rights. Affecting the economic interests of other WTO members does not amount to breaching their WTO rights. Recognizing that WTO obligations are of a reciprocal nature allows for the taking into account of the diversity of needs and interests of different WTO members. It shows that in most cases of conflict between, for example, human rights and environmental conventions (generally setting out obligations of an 'integral type'), on the one hand, and WTO obligations (of the 'reciprocal' type), on the other, the WTO provisions will have to give way.[328]

Pauwelyn is of the view that, in case of conflict, rules of MEAs or other international agreements, such as human rights treaties or ILO conventions, may thus often prevail over rules of WTO law. However, Pauwelyn added:

the fact that non-WTO norms may ... prevail over the WTO treaty, even as before a WTO panel, does not mean that WTO panels must judicially enforce compliance with these non-WTO rules. Non-WTO rules may be part of the applicable law before a WTO panel, and hence offer, in particular, a valid legal defence against claims of WTO breach. However, they cannot form the basis of legal claims, the jurisdiction of WTO panels being limited to claims under WTO covered agreements only.[329]

This particular view of the relationship between WTO rules and conflicting rules of other international agreements is not shared by other WTO scholars. On the

---

325 G. Marceau, 'Conflicts of Norms and Conflicts of Jurisdictions: The Relationship Between the WTO Agreement and MEAs and Other Treaties', *Journal of World Trade*, 2001, 1129.

326 See above, p. 58.

327 Pauwelyn regards *reciprocal* obligations as a 'promise ... made towards each and every state individually' whereas he views *integral* obligations as a 'promise ... towards the collectivity of all state parties taken together'. See J. Pauwelyn, *Conflict of Norms in Public International Law: How WTO Law Relates to Other Norms of International Law* (Cambridge University Press, 2003), 476.

328 *Ibid.*, 491.

329 *Ibid.*

contrary, Gabrielle Marceau has argued that WTO panels confronted with a conflict between a WTO rule and a non-WTO rule may perhaps have alternative courses of action to deal with the conflict, but that:

[a]ny of these courses of action would be possible only to the extent that the conclusions reached by the panels do not constitute an amendment of the WTO, or do not add to or diminish the rights and obligations of WTO Members or do not affect the rights of third WTO Members.[330]

As Marceau noted, and as discussed in Chapter 3 of this book, it is prohibited for panels and the Appellate Body to 'add to or diminish the rights and obligations' of WTO Members, as provided for in the WTO agreements.[331] If panels or the Appellate Body were to allow a respondent to invoke a non-WTO rule in defence against a claim of violation of WTO law, would they then not, in fact, 'add to or diminish the rights and obligations' of WTO Members? As discussed above, in *Mexico – Soft Drinks (2006)*, the Appellate Body saw 'no basis in the DSU for panels and the Appellate Body to adjudicate non-WTO disputes'.[332]

   It is important to note that, to date, a situation of an irreconcilable conflict between an obligation or right under a WTO agreement and an obligation or right under a non-WTO agreement has not yet arisen in WTO dispute settlement.

Questions and Assignments 1.10

Is WTO law a self-contained system of law or is it an integral part of international law? Do you agree with the analysis of Joost Pauwelyn on the relationship between WTO agreements and MEAs? In your opinion, what should a panel do when confronted with a WTO rule that is in conflict with a provision of an MEA concluded *after* the conclusion of the *WTO Agreement*?

5.2   WTO Law and National Law

There are two aspects of the relationship between WTO law and national law that need to be examined: (1) the place of national law in WTO law; and (2) the place of WTO law in the domestic legal order.

5.2.1   National Law in WTO Law

With regard to the place of national law in WTO law, Article XVI:4 of the *WTO Agreement* states:

Each Member shall ensure the conformity of its laws, regulations and administrative procedures with its obligations as provided in the annexed Agreements.

It is a general rule of international law, reflected in Article 27 of the *Vienna Convention on the Law of Treaties*, that:

---

330 G. Marceau, 'Conflicts of Norms and Conflicts of Jurisdictions: The Relationship Between the WTO Agreement and MEAs and Other Treaties', *Journal of World Trade*, 2001, 1130.

331 See below, pp. 184–7.

332 Appellate Body Report, *Mexico – Soft Drinks (2006)*, para. 56.

[a] party may not invoke the provisions of its internal law as justification for its failure to perform a treaty.

In *Brazil – Aircraft (Article 21.5 – Canada) (2000)*, the Appellate Body observed:

We note Brazil's argument before the Article 21.5 Panel that Brazil has a contractual obligation under domestic law to issue PROEX bonds pursuant to commitments that have already been made, and that Brazil could be liable for damages for breach of contract under Brazilian law if it failed to respect its contractual obligations. In response to a question from us at the oral hearing, however, Brazil conceded that *a WTO Member's domestic law does not excuse that Member from fulfilling its international obligations.*[333]

Note, however, that, with regard to measures and actions by regional and local governments and authorities, Article XXIV:12 of the GATT 1994 provides:

Each Member shall take such reasonable measures as may be available to it to ensure observance of the provisions of this Agreement by the regional and local governments and authorities within its territories.[334]

It follows that WTO Members are obliged to enforce compliance with the obligations under the GATT 1994 by regional and local governments and authorities *only* to the extent that they – i.e. the Members – dispose of the necessary constitutional powers to do so.[335] However, note that – as discussed in Chapter 3 of this book – Article 22.9 of the DSU states:

The dispute settlement provisions of the covered agreements may be invoked in respect of measures affecting their observance taken by regional or local governments or authorities within the territory of a Member. When the DSB has ruled that a provision of a covered agreement has not been observed, the responsible Member shall take such reasonable measures as may be available to it to ensure its observance. The provisions of the covered agreements and this Understanding relating to compensation and suspension of concessions or other obligations apply in cases where it has not been possible to secure such observance.[336]

The 1994 *Understanding on the Interpretation of Article XXIV of the GATT 1994* provides for a similar provision.[337] Note that the panel in *Brazil – Retreaded Tyres (2007)* found that the measures of Rio Grande do Sul, a state of the Federative Republic of Brazil, were attributable to Brazil as a WTO Member.[338] The panel also found in that case that the Brazilian government was ultimately responsible for ensuring that its constituent states respected Brazil's obligations under the WTO.[339]

---

333 Appellate Body Report, *Brazil – Aircraft (Article 21.5 – Canada) (2000)*, para. 46. Emphasis added.
334 See also the *Understanding on the Interpretation of Article XXIV of the General Agreement on Tariffs and Trade 1994*, para. 13.
335 T. Cottier and K. Schefer, 'The Relationship Between World Trade Organization Law, National Law and Regional Law', *Journal of International Economic Law*, 1998, 85–6.
336 See below, p. 171.
337 See *Understanding on the Interpretation of Article XXIV of the General Agreement on Tariffs and Trade 1994*, para. 14, last sentence.
338 See Panel Report, *Brazil – Retreaded Tyres (2007)*, para. 7.400.
339 See *ibid.*, para. 7.406.

With respect to the question of how panels and the Appellate Body should handle national law, the Appellate Body held in *India – Patents (US) (1998)* that, in public international law, an international tribunal may treat municipal law in several ways. Municipal law may serve as evidence of facts and may provide evidence of State practice. Municipal law may also constitute evidence of compliance or non-compliance with international obligations. The Appellate Body found support for this position in the ruling of the Permanent Court of International Justice in *Certain German Interests in Polish Upper Silesia*, in which the Court had observed:

It might be asked whether a difficulty does not arise from the fact that the Court would have to deal with the Polish law of July 14th, 1920. This, however, does not appear to be the case. From the standpoint of International Law and of the Court which is its organ, municipal laws are merely facts which express the will and constitute the activities of States, in the same manner as do legal decisions and administrative measures. The Court is certainly not *called upon to interpret* the Polish law as such; but there is nothing to prevent the Court's giving judgment on *the question whether or not*, in applying that law, *Poland is acting in conformity with its obligations* towards Germany under the Geneva Convention.[340]

In *India – Patents (US) (1998)*, the Appellate Body thus concluded:

It is clear that an examination of the relevant aspects of Indian municipal law ... is essential to determining whether India has complied with its obligations under Article 70.8(a). There was simply no way for the Panel to make this determination without engaging in an examination of Indian law. But, as in the *Certain German Interests in Polish Upper Silesia* case ... before the Permanent Court of International Justice, in this case, the Panel was not interpreting Indian law 'as such'; rather, the Panel was examining Indian law solely for the purpose of determining whether India had met its obligations under the *TRIPS Agreement*.[341]

In *China – Auto Parts (2008)*, the Appellate Body summarised its position on the treatment of national law in WTO dispute settlement as follows:

The Appellate Body has explicitly stated that the municipal law of WTO Members may serve not only as evidence of facts, but also as evidence of compliance or non-compliance with international obligations. When a panel examines the municipal law of a WTO Member for purposes of determining whether the Member has complied with its WTO obligations, that determination is a legal characterization by a panel, and is therefore subject to appellate review under Article 17.6 of the DSU. The Appellate Body has reviewed the meaning of a Member's municipal law, on its face, to determine whether the legal characterization by the panel was in error, in particular when the claim before the panel concerned whether a specific instrument of municipal law was, as such, inconsistent with a Member's obligations. We recognize that there may be instances in which a panel's assessment of municipal law will go beyond the text of an instrument on its face, in which case further examination may be required, and may involve factual elements. With respect to such elements, the Appellate Body will not lightly interfere with a panel's finding on appeal.[342]

---

340   [1926] PCIJ Rep., Series A, No. 7, 19. Emphasis added.
341   Appellate Body Reports, *India – Patents (US) (1998)*, para. 66. See also Appellate Body Report, *US – Section 211 Appropriations Act (2002)*, paras. 104–5; Appellate Body Report, *US – Carbon Steel (2002)*, para. 157; Appellate Body Report, *China – Auto Parts (2008)*, paras. 224–5; and Appellate Body Report, *China – Publications and Audiovisual Products (2009)*, paras. 177–8 and 187.
342   Appellate Body Report, *China – Auto Parts (2008)*, para. 225.

5.2.2 WTO Law in National Law

With respect to the role of WTO law in the national legal order, it should first be observed that, where a provision of national law allows different interpretations, this provision should, whenever possible, be interpreted in a manner that avoids any conflict with WTO law. In the United States, the European Union and elsewhere, national courts have adopted this doctrine of *treaty-consistent interpretation*. The European Court of Justice (ECJ) stated in 1996 in *Commission* v. *Germany (International Dairy Arrangement)* with regard to the GATT 1947:

> When the wording of secondary EC legislation is open to more than one interpretation, preference should be given as far as possible to the interpretation which renders the provision consistent with the Treaty ... Similarly, the primacy of international agreements concluded by the Community over the provisions of secondary Community legislation means that such provisions must, so far as is possible, be interpreted in a manner consistent with those agreements.[343]

The ECJ confirmed the doctrine of treaty-consistent interpretation of national/ EC law with regard to the *WTO Agreement* in its judgments in *Hermès* (1998) and *Schieving-Nijstad* (2001).[344] The United States Supreme Court held already in 1804 in *Murray* v. *The Charming Betsy*:

> It has also been observed that an act of Congress ought never to be construed to violate the law of nations if any other possible construction remains.[345]

If a conflict between a provision of national law and a WTO law provision cannot be avoided through treaty-consistent interpretation, the question arises as to whether the provision of WTO law can be invoked before the national court to challenge the legality and validity of the provision of national law. Could a German importer of bananas challenge the EC's import regime for bananas in court on the basis that this regime was inconsistent with, for example, Articles I and XIII of the GATT 1994? Can a US beef exporter challenge the EC import ban on hormone-treated meat on the basis that this ban is inconsistent with the provisions of the *SPS Agreement*? Can a Brazilian steel exporter challenge an anti-dumping duty imposed by India on its hot-rolled steel before an Indian court on the basis that this duty is inconsistent with the provisions of the *Anti-Dumping Agreement*? This is the issue of the 'direct effect' of provisions of WTO law.[346] It is clear that, if provisions of WTO law were to have direct effect and could be invoked to challenge the legality of national measures, this would significantly increase the enforceability and effectiveness of

---

343 Judgment of the Court of 10 September 1996, *Commission of the European Communities* v. *Federal Republic of Germany (International Dairy Arrangement)*, Case C-61/94, [1996] ECR I-3989, para. 52.

344 See Judgment of the Court of 13 September 2001, *Schieving-Nijstad vof and Others* v. *Robert Groeneveld*, Case C-89/99, [2001] ECR I-5851; and Judgment of the Court of 15 June 1998, *Hermès International and FHT Marketing Choice BV*, Case 53/96, [1998] ECR I-3603.

345 *Murray* v. *The Charming Betsy*, 6 US (2 Cranch) 64 (1804).

346 In many jurisdictions, the issue of direct effect, i.e. the issue of direct invocability, is to be distinguished from the issue of direct applicability, i.e. the issue whether a national act of transformation is necessary for an international agreement to become part of national law. On the latter issue, it should be noted that WTO law is directly applicable in the EU legal order. It became part of EU law without any act of transformation.

these provisions, non-compliance with which could and would then be sanctioned by domestic courts.

There is a fierce academic debate on whether provisions of WTO law should be granted direct effect. On that debate, Cottier and Schefer wrote:

Among the scholars writing on the topic of direct effect of international trade agreements, there are three that stand out as the main proponents of the two schools of thought on the issue: Jan Tumlir and Ernst Ulrich Petersmann advocating direct effect and John H. Jackson for the critics of direct effect. A fourth author, Piet Eeckhout, has set out what we call an 'intermediate position' on the issue.[347]

With respect to the arguments of the advocates of the direct effect of WTO rules, Cottier and Schefer noted:

The late Jan Tumlir, whose main thesis supporting direct effect is followed by Ernst Ulrich Petersmann, looks at the direct effect of trade treaties as a weapon against inherently protectionist tendencies in domestic law systems. Tumlir and Petersmann set forth the idea of 'constitutionalizing' international trade principles, elevating the rights of an individual to trade freely with foreigners to the level of a fundamental right. To prevent the erosion of a state's sovereignty, Tumlir suggests granting individuals the right to invoke treaty provisions in front of their domestic courts. Allowing for standing in this way would be available to those citizens harmed by protectionist national policies put into effect by other national interest groups. Thus, direct effect widely defined 'helps to correct the asymmetries in the political process' ... Pleading for keeping the possibility of judicial review open to individuals, Jacques Bourgeois put it quite bluntly: 'Quite simply, what is in the end the use of making law, also international law, designed to protect private parties, if these private parties cannot rely on it?'[348]

For the advocates of direct effect of WTO rules, it is a necessary and effective 'weapon' against national governments that encroach on the right to trade freely with foreigners, a right these advocates consider to be a fundamental right.

John Jackson, and along with him many others, objects to the direct effect of WTO rules. Central to his position against the direct effect of WTO rules is that it might be dangerous for democracy and that it conflicts with the legitimate wish of legislatures to adapt international treaty language to their respective domestic legal systems. Cottier and Schefer noted:

John Jackson ... basically supports US trade policies of denying direct effect due to the imbalances in the institutional balance of government it would cause domestically ... He does ... find the idea of granting standing and allowing for an international treaty to be superior to federal legislation (let alone the constitution) to be dangerous to the idea of democracy and democratic representation of individuals ... While Jackson acknowledges that governments have an obligation to abide by international commitments they undertake, direct effect is not necessary to ensure this. The stronger reasons for denying direct effect are what Jackson calls 'functional arguments'. These arguments include the fact that '[s]ome

---

347 T. Cottier and K. Schefer, 'The Relationship Between World Trade Organization Law, National Law and Regional Law', *Journal of International Economic Law*, 1998, 93.
348 *Ibid.*, 93–5.

constitutions provide for very little democratic participation in the treaty-making process; for example, by giving no formal role to Parliaments or structuring the government so that control over foreign relations is held by certain elites'. There are also legitimate desires of legislatures to adapt international treaty language to their respective domestic legal systems (such as translating the obligations into the native language, using local terms for legal principles, or further explaining certain provisions). And, some governments may want the opportunity to implement the obligations in a national legislative process because 'the act of transformation sometimes becomes part of a purely *internal* power struggle, and may be used by certain governmental institutions to enhance their powers *vis-à-vis* other governmental entities' or 'even, perhaps ... the legislature desires to preserve the *option to breach the treaty* in its method of application'. Even such uses of the separate implementation process are legitimate in Professor Jackson's mind because 'some breaches may be "minor" and therefore *preferable to the alternative of refusing to join the treaty altogether'*. Finally, Jackson argues that if treaties are given direct effect automatically, the characteristic of direct effect itself will not necessarily guarantee that the national courts will apply the treaty rules.[349]

An intermediate position in this debate on the direct effect of WTO law has been taken by Piet Eeckhout. Eeckhout opposes direct effect of WTO law, but concedes that, if a case has been specifically decided by the WTO dispute settlement system, domestic effect should be given to this decision. According to Eeckhout:

[t]he reasons for not granting direct effect – whether it is the agreement's flexibility, or the division of powers between the legislature and the judiciary, or the respect for appropriate dispute settlement forums – cease to be valid where a violation is established.[350]

The *WTO Agreement* could have specified what effect its provisions are to have in the domestic legal order of WTO Members. However, it did not do so. Therefore, although each Member must fully execute the commitments that it has undertaken, it is free to determine the legal means appropriate for attaining that end in its domestic legal system. At present, most WTO Members, including the European Union, the United States, China, India, Japan, South Africa and Canada, refuse to give 'direct effect' to WTO law.[351] Only a few WTO Members give 'direct effect' to WTO law.[352] The ECJ addressed the issue of whether it could review the legality of Community law in the light of WTO law in its judgment of 23 November 1999 in *Portugal* v. *Council*. As the ECJ did not want to deprive: (1) the European Union of the possibility for temporary non-compliance with WTO law provided for in Article 22 of the DSU (the temporary non-compliance argument);[353] and (2) the legislative

---

349 *Ibid.*, 97–8.
350 P. Eeckhout, 'The Domestic Legal Status of the WTO Agreements: Interconnecting Legal Systems', *Common Market Law Review*, 1997, 53.
351 For an overview of whether specific WTO Members give direct effect to WTO law in their domestic legal order, see C. George and S. Orava (eds.), *A WTO Guide for Global Business* (Cameron May, 2002), 398.
352 See above, footnote 351.
353 See Judgment of the Court of 23 November 1999, *Portuguese Republic* v. *Council of the European Union*, Case C-149/96, [1999] ECR I-8395, para. 40. With respect to this possibility for temporary non-compliance with WTO law, see below, pp. 115–18.

or executive organs of the Union of the scope for manoeuvre with respect to compliance enjoyed by their counterparts in the Union's trading partners (the non-reciprocity argument),[354] it concluded:

having regard to their nature and structure, the WTO agreements are not in principle among the rules in the light of which the Court is to review the legality of measures adopted by the Community institutions.[355]

In support of the conclusion reached, the ECJ noted that this interpretation corresponded to what was stated in the Preamble to the Council Decision of 22 December 1994 on the conclusion of the *WTO Agreement*. In the Preamble to this Decision, the Council of Ministers of the European Union stated that:

[b]y its nature, the Agreement Establishing the World Trade Organization, including the Annexes thereto, is not susceptible to being directly invoked in Community or Member State courts.[356]

In its judgment of 14 December 2000 in *Dior* v. *TUK*, the ECJ confirmed its reasoning in *Portugal* v. *Council* and concluded that private persons cannot invoke WTO law before the courts by virtue of Community law.[357] As an exception to the general rule, the ECJ does, however, grant direct effect to provisions of the *WTO Agreement* when the European Union intended to implement a particular obligation assumed in the context of the WTO, *or* where the EU measure refers expressly to the precise provisions of the WTO agreements.[358] Note that, in the 2003 *Biret* v. *Council* cases, the ECJ left open the possibility for an action for damages against the European Union, in a situation in which an EU measure, which was found to be WTO-inconsistent, caused harm after the end of the reasonable period of time for withdrawal or modification of the WTO-inconsistent

354 See Judgment of the Court of 23 November 1999, *Portuguese Republic* v. *Council of the European Union*, Case C-149/96, [1999] ECR I-8395, para. 46.

355 *Ibid.*, para. 47. These arguments were reiterated in Judgment of the Court of 1 March 2005, *Van Parys* v. *Belgisch Interventie- en Restitutiebureau*, Case C-377/02, [2005] ECR I-1465; and Judgment of the Court of First Instance of 3 February 2005, *Chiquita* v. *Commission* Case T-19/01. These arguments have been criticised by e.g. Advocate General Ruiz-Jarabo Colomer in his Opinion of 23 January 2007 in *Merck Genéricos-Produtos Farmacêuticos Lda* v. *Merck & Co. Inc. and Merck Sharp & Dohme Lda*, Case C-431/05, paras. 81–6.

356 Council Decision 94/800/EC of 22 December 1994 concerning the conclusion on behalf of the European Community, as regards matters within its competence, of the agreements reached in the Uruguay Round multilateral negotiations, OJ 1994, L336, 1. Note that the European Commission and the Council of Ministers were in agreement on the issue of 'direct effect' of WTO law. The text adopted by the Council had been proposed by the European Commission.

357 See Judgment of the Court of 14 December 2000, *Parfums Christian Dior SA* v. *TUK Consultancy BV and Assco Gerüste GmbH* and *Rob van Dijk* v. *Wilhelm Layher GmbH & Co. KG and Layher BV*, Joined Cases C-300/98 and C-392/98, [2000] ECR I-11307, paras. 42–4.

358 In its judgment of 22 June 1989 in *Fediol* v. *Commission*, Case 70/87, [1989] ECR 1781, and its judgment of 7 May 1991 in *Nakajima* v. *Council*, Case 69/89, [1991] ECR I-2069, the ECJ gave direct effect to provisions of the GATT 1947 in these circumstances. The ECJ applied its *Fediol/Nakajima* case law to the provisions of the *WTO Agreement* in its judgment of 9 January 2003 in *Petrotub* v. *Council*, Case C-76/00 [2003] ECR I-79, para. 54. That these are the only two exceptions, even in situations where the WTO's Dispute Settlement Body has adopted a report finding the legislation at issue inconsistent with WTO law, was confirmed by the ECJ in its judgment of 1 March 2005 in *Van Parys* v. *Belgisch Interventie- en Restitutiebureau*, Case C-377/02, [2005] ECR I-1465, paras. 39–40 and 52.

measure.[359] However, this possibility was excluded by the Court of First Instance (CFI) in the 2005 *Chiquita Brands* case.[360] It is interesting to note that the domestic courts of several Member States of the European Union have accepted the direct effect of provisions of the *TRIPS Agreement*.[361]

With regard to the domestic law effect of WTO law in the United States, the *Restatement (Third) of Foreign Relations Law of the United States* provides:

> Since generally the United States is obligated to comply with a treaty as soon as it comes into force for the United States, compliance is facilitated and expedited if the treaty is self-executing ... Therefore, if the Executive Branch has not requested implementing legislation and Congress has not enacted such legislation, there is a strong presumption that the treaty has been considered self-executing by the political branches, and *should be considered self-executing by the courts*.[362]

In the United States, trade treaties have historically been granted direct effect in court.[363] As has been the case with a number of other recent trade agreements,[364] the approval of the *WTO Agreement* was made conditional upon the inclusion of a provision in the implementing legislation, explicitly denying direct effect to the Agreement.[365] As David Leebron noted:

> Although Congress specifically approved the agreements, it simultaneously provided 'no provision of any of the Uruguay Round Agreements, nor the application of any such provision to any person or circumstances, that is inconsistent with any law of the United States shall have effect'. Furthermore, Congress mandated that no person other than the United States 'shall have any cause of action or defence under any of the Uruguay Round Agreements' or challenge 'any action or inaction ... of the United States, any state, or any political subdivision of a state on the ground that such action or inaction is inconsistent' with one of those agreements. In short, the Uruguay Agreements themselves are unlikely to be directly applied in any proceedings other than a proceeding brought by the United States for the purpose of enforcing obligations under the agreements.[366]

Likewise, India denies direct effect to WTO law. Indian courts will not consider the consistency of any domestic statute *vis-à-vis* WTO law, as they are constitutionally barred from striking down domestic law on grounds of violation

---

359 See Judgment of the Court of 30 September 2003, *Biret International SA* v. *Council of the European Union*, Case C-93/02, [2003] ECR I-10497; and Judgment of the Court of 30 September 2003, *Etablissements Biret et Cie SA* v. *Council of the European Union*, Case C-94/02, [2003] ECR I-10565.

360 Judgment of the Court of First Instance of 3 February 2005, *Chiquita* v. *Commission*, Case T-19/01, paras. 156–70. See in this regard P. J. Kuijper, 'From Initiating Proceedings to Ensuring Implementation: The Links with the Community Legal Order', in G. Sacerdotti, A. Yanovich and J. Bohanes (eds.), *The WTO at Ten: The Contribution of the Dispute Settlement System* (Cambridge University Press, 2006), 277–8.

361 For Germany, see e.g. Bundesgerichtshof, Urteil vom 25.2.1999 – I ZR 118/96 – *Kopienversanddienst*; OLG München. For Ireland, see e.g. *Allen & Hanbury and Another, Controller of Patents, Designs and Trademarks* (1997); for the Netherlands, see e.g. Rb. 's-Gravenhage 1 April 1998 (kortgeding), BIE 2001, pp. 119–22 Mistral/Tiki – 45(1).

362 *Restatement (Third) of Foreign Relations Law of the United States*, para. 111, Reporters' Notes, reproduced in B. Carter and P. Trimble, *International Law* (Little, Brown and Co., 1991), 151. Emphasis added.

363 See T. Cottier and K. Schefer, 'The Relationship Between World Trade Organization Law, National Law and Regional Law', *Journal of International Economic Law*, 1998, 107.

364 See e.g. the *North American Free Trade Agreement* (NAFTA), 17 December 1992.

365 See Uruguay Round Agreements Act of 1994, 19 USC §3512, Pub. L. No. 104-305 (1996), para. 102(c).

366 D. Leebron, 'Implementation of the Uruguay Round Results in the United States', in J. Jackson and A. Sykes (eds.), *Implementing the Uruguay Round* (Oxford University Press, 1997), 212.

of international law. The issue of direct effect on WTO law in Indian courts arose before the Madras High Court in *Novartis* v. *Union of India*.[367] At issue in *Novartis* v. *Union of India* was the decision of the Indian authorities to deny – on the basis of Section 3(d) of the Indian Patent Act – the pharmaceutical multinational Novartis a patent on Glivec, a cancer medicine, thereby allowing the production of cheap generic copies. Before the Madras High Court, Novartis challenged, *inter alia*, the consistency of Section 3(d) of the Indian Patent Act with the relevant provisions of the *TRIPS Agreement*. The Madras High Court held that, as the WTO provides a comprehensive mechanism for the settlement of disputes in the DSU, any disputes under WTO law are properly litigated through this mechanism.[368]

Questions and Assignments 1.11

Can a WTO Member ever invoke national law as a justification for its failure to comply with WTO obligations? In your opinion, should WTO provisions have direct effect? Does any WTO Member give direct effect to WTO provisions in its internal legal order? Why does the ECJ deny direct effect to provisions of WTO law? Are there any exceptions?

6   SUMMARY

Economic globalisation and, in particular, international trade can make a significant contribution to economic development and prosperity in developed as well as developing countries. International trade has realised this potential – albeit to varying degrees – in many countries. Over the past two decades, this has been the case particularly in Asia. It is, however, undisputed that not all countries, and within countries not all sections of the population, have benefitted from international trade. For the potential of international trade to be realised, there must be: (1) good governance at the national level; (2) a further reduction of trade barriers; (3) more development aid; and (4) better international cooperation and global governance of economic globalisation and international trade. More international trade will not automatically lead to rising prosperity for all countries and for all people. In fact, without national and international action in the four areas referred to above, international trade will not bring prosperity to all; on the contrary, it is likely to result in more income inequality, social injustice, environmental degradation and cultural homogenisation.

International rules on trade are necessary for four related reasons: (1) to restrain countries from taking trade-restrictive measures, both in their own

---

367 See Judgment of the Madras High Court, dated 6 August 2007, published in *Madras Law Journal*, 2007, 1153, also available at http://judis.nic.in/chennai/qrydisp.asp?tfnm=11121.
368 The Madras High Court also refused to exercise its discretion to grant declaratory relief as it would serve no useful purpose to the petitioner.

interest and in the interest of the world economy; (2) to give traders and investors a degree of security and predictability regarding the trade policies of other countries; (3) to allow for the effective protection and promotion of important societal values and interests (such as public health, a sustainable environment, consumer safety, cultural identity and minimum labour standards), while at the same time ensuring that countries maintain only those measures that are necessary for (or at the very least related to) the protection of these values and interests; and (4) to achieve a greater measure of equity in international economic relations. WTO law, which is the core of international economic law, provides for rules on international trade. There are five groups of basic rules of WTO law: (1) the rules of non-discrimination; (2) the rules on market access; (3) the rules on unfair trade; (4) the rules on the conflict between trade liberalisation and other societal values and interests; and (5) institutional and procedural rules.

The principal source of WTO law is the *WTO Agreement*, in force since 1 January 1995. The *WTO Agreement* is a short agreement (of sixteen articles) establishing the World Trade Organization, but it contains, in its annexes, a significant number of agreements with substantive and/or procedural provisions, such as the GATT 1994, the GATS, the *TRIPS Agreement* and the DSU. However, the *WTO Agreement* is not the only source of WTO law. There are also other sources of WTO law, although these other sources are *not* of the same nature nor on the same legal footing as the WTO agreements discussed above. The WTO agreements (with the exception of two) provide for specific legal rights and obligations for WTO Members that can be enforced through WTO dispute settlement. *Most* of the other sources do *not* in and of themselves provide for specific, *enforceable* rights or obligations. They do, however, assist in 'clarifying' or 'defining' the law that applies between WTO Members on WTO matters. These other sources of WTO law include: (1) dispute settlement reports; (2) acts of WTO bodies; (3) agreements concluded in the context of the WTO; (4) customary international law; (5) general principles of law; (6) other international agreements; (7) subsequent practice of WTO Members; (8) the negotiating history of WTO agreements; and (9) teachings of the most highly qualified publicists.

While for many years international trade law was not part of the mainstream of international law, WTO law is now firmly established as an integral part of public international law. However, the relationship between WTO rules and other, conflicting rules of public international law, such as rules of multilateral environmental agreements (MEAs), is controversial. A generally accepted view on this relationship is yet to emerge. With regard to the relationship between WTO law and the national law of WTO Members, it is undisputed that WTO Members must ensure that their respective national laws are consistent with WTO law. Note also that, while some WTO scholars forcefully plead for the granting of direct effect to WTO law in the domestic legal order of WTO Members, in most WTO Members a breach of WTO law cannot be challenged in domestic courts.

Exercise 1: Globaphiles Versus Globaphobes

Last Sunday, more than 50,000 people demonstrated in the streets of Nontes, the capital of Newland, against economic globalisation, free trade and the government's plan to join the WTO. The Republic of Newland is a developing, lower-middle-income country with a population of 30 million people. It has a booming export-oriented toy manufacturing industry and an up-and-coming steel industry. However, many of its other industries are unable to compete with foreign goods and services. The demonstration was organised by the Newland Coalition for a Better World (NCBW), representing Newland's labour unions and its main environmental, consumer and human rights organisations. When small groups of radicals attacked and destroyed a McJohn's restaurant along the route, the police intervened to disperse the demonstrators with tear gas. Three hours of violent clashes between the police and a group of about 500 young demonstrators ensued, leaving several people wounded. At an emergency cabinet meeting called on Sunday evening, the Prime Minister announced that he would invite the Chair of the NCBW to a public debate on economic globalisation, international trade and the government's plan to join the WTO. On Monday, the Chair of the NCBW accepted the challenge. The debate is to be broadcast live on Wednesday evening. You serve on the personal staff of the Prime Minister, and it is your job to prepare him for this important debate by briefing him as fully as possible on all the positive and negative aspects – economic, political and legal – of international trade and WTO membership. With regard to WTO membership, you expect the Chair of the NCBW, a professor of constitutional law, to question, *inter alia*, why it would be in the interest of Newland to 'squander its sovereignty' and accept a host of new international obligations. You expect him to argue that the core WTO rules and disciplines are about opening foreign markets for the benefit of multinationals. From his articles and speeches, you know that the Chair passionately believes that international trade is a malignant force that destroys jobs (as a result of outsourcing and delocalisation) and exacerbates income inequality, social injustice, environmental degradation and cultural homogenisation. Three legal issues are of particular concern to him, namely: (1) whether the *WTO Agreement* encompasses all WTO law (or there is more to WTO law than the rights and obligations set out in the *WTO Agreement*); (2) whether the *WTO Agreement* will prevail over Newland's Constitution and over other international agreements (such as MEAs and ILO conventions to which Newland is a party); and (3) whether WTO law will have, or should have, direct effect in Newland's courts. To prepare the Prime Minister well, you and your colleagues decide to stage a trial debate in which one group, Group A, takes a 'globaphile' position and another group, Group B, a 'globaphobe' position.

2 The World Trade Organization

1 INTRODUCTION

The World Trade Organization was established and became operational on 1 January 1995. It is the youngest of all major international intergovernmental organisations and yet it is possibly – in spite of the challenges it currently faces – one of the most influential in these times of economic globalisation. As Marco Bronckers stated in 2001, it has 'the *potential* to become a key pillar of global governance'.[1] The WTO is also one of the most criticised international organisations.[2] In the late 1990s, it

---

1 M. Bronckers, 'More Power to the WTO?', *Journal of International Economic Law*, 2001, 41 (reproduced by permission of Oxford University Press). Emphasis added.
2 See below, footnote 4 on p. 75.

was referred to as '*un gouvernement mondial dans l'ombre*'.[3] Civil society opponents of the WTO considered it to be 'pathologically secretive, conspiratorial and unaccountable to sovereign States and their electorate'.[4] In these early years of the WTO, developing-country Members considered the WTO to be a 'rich men's club' and objected to their marginalisation in WTO negotiations and decision-making. While parts of civil society remain highly suspicious of the WTO, and the participation of many developing-country Members in WTO negotiations and decision-making can certainly still be improved, the criticism directed at the WTO is now primarily of a different nature. In recent years, developed- and developing-country Members alike have become disenchanted with the WTO for its apparent inability to bring long-running negotiations on further trade liberalisation to a successful close and to agree on new rules addressing the challenges international trade is facing in the twenty-first century.

As discussed in Chapter 1 of this book, in March 2013 WTO Director-General Pascal Lamy compared the multilateral trading system to a computer, and noted that, while the 'hardware' of the system was sufficient, the 'software' was in need of an upgrade.[5] This chapter deals with both the 'hardware' and some of the 'software' of the multilateral trading system. It discusses the distinctive features of the WTO as the principal intergovernmental organisation for international trade and successively addresses: (1) the origins of the WTO; (2) the mandate of the WTO, i.e. its objectives and functions; (3) the membership and institutional structure of the WTO; and (4) decision-making in the WTO.

2 THE ORIGINS OF THE WTO

The origins of the WTO lie in the *General Agreement on Tariffs and Trade* of 1947, now commonly referred to as the 'GATT 1947' but for almost five decades just referred to as the 'GATT'. The study of these origins is relevant because the decisions, procedures and customary practices of the GATT 1947 still guide the WTO in its actions. Article XVI:1 of the *WTO Agreement* states:

Except as otherwise provided under this Agreement or the Multilateral Trade Agreements, the WTO shall be guided by the decisions, procedures and customary practices followed by the Contracting Parties to GATT 1947 and the bodies established in the framework of GATT 1947.

This section will discuss: (1) the genesis of the GATT and its operation as the *de facto* international organisation for international trade until the end of 1994;

---

3 M. Khoh, 'Un gouvernement mondial dans l'ombre', *Le Monde Diplomatique*, May 1997. Translation: 'A lurking world government'.
4 G. de Jonquières, 'Prime Target for Protests: WTO Ministerial Conference', *Financial Times*, 24 September 1999.
5 See Pascal Lamy, 'Changing Landscape of International Trade', www.wto.org/english/news_e/sppl-e/sppl271_e.htm.

and (2) the GATT Uruguay Round of Multilateral Trade Negotiations (1986–94) and the emergence of the WTO, operational as of 1 January 1995.

2.1   The General Agreement on Tariffs and Trade of 1947

For almost five decades, the GATT was the *de facto* international organisation for international trade. This sub-section deals with: (1) the genesis of the GATT and the stillbirth of the International Trade Organization (ITO); and (2) the success and failure of the GATT as *de facto* international trade organisation.

2.1.1   The GATT 1947 and the International Trade Organization

The history of the GATT begins in December 1945 when the United States invited its wartime allies to enter into negotiations to conclude a multilateral agreement for the reciprocal reduction of tariffs on trade in goods. These multilateral tariff negotiations took place in the context of a more ambitious project on international trade. At the proposal of the United States, the newly established United Nations Economic and Social Council adopted a resolution, in February 1946, calling for a conference to draft a charter for an 'International Trade Organization'.[6] At the 1944 Bretton Woods Conference, where the International Monetary Fund (IMF) and the International Bank for Reconstruction and Development (the 'World Bank') were established, the problems of trade had not been taken up as such, but the Conference did recognise the need for a comparable international institution for trade to complement the IMF and the World Bank.[7] A Preparatory Committee was established in February 1946 and met for the first time in London in October 1946 to work on the charter of an international organisation for trade on the basis of a proposal by the United States. The work was continued from April to November 1947 in Geneva. As John Jackson explained:

> The 1947 Geneva meeting was actually an elaborate conference in three major parts. One part was devoted to continuing the preparation of a charter for a major international trade institution, the ITO. A second part was devoted to the negotiation of a multilateral agreement to reduce tariffs reciprocally. A third part concentrated on drafting the 'general clauses' of obligations relating to the tariff obligations. These two latter parts together would constitute the General Agreement on Tariffs and Trade. The 'general clauses' of the draft GATT imposed obligations on nations to refrain from a variety of trade-impeding measures.[8]

The negotiations on the GATT advanced well in Geneva, and by October 1947 the negotiators had reached an agreement. The negotiations on the ITO, however,

---

6 1 UN ECOSOC Res. 13, UN Doc. E/22 (1946). For an overview of the negotiations of the GATT 1947 and the ITO with references to official documents, see *Analytical Index: Guide to GATT Law and Practice* (WTO, 1995), 3–6.
7 See J. Jackson, *The World Trade Organization: Constitution and Jurisprudence* (Royal Institute of International Affairs, 1998), 15–16.
8 *Ibid.*, 16.

were more difficult and it was clear, towards the end of the 1947 Geneva meeting, that the *ITO Charter* would not be finished before 1948. Although the GATT was intended to be attached to the *ITO Charter*, many negotiators felt that it was not possible to wait until the *ITO Charter* was finished to bring the GATT into force. According to Jackson, there were two main reasons for this:

First, although the tariff concessions were still secret, the negotiators knew that the content of the concessions would begin to be known. World trade patterns could thus be seriously disrupted if a prolonged delay occurred before the tariff concessions came into force. Second, the US negotiators were acting under the authority of the US trade legislation which had been renewed in 1945 ... But the 1945 Act expired in mid-1948. Thus, there was a strong motivation on the part of the United States to bring the GATT into force before this Act expired.[9]

It was therefore decided to bring the provisions of the GATT into force immediately. However, this created a new problem. Under the provisions of their constitutional law, some countries could not agree to certain obligations of the GATT (and, in particular, those obligations that might require changes to national legislation) without submitting this agreement to their parliaments. Since they anticipated the need to submit the final draft of the *ITO Charter* to their parliaments in late 1948 or the following year, they feared that 'to spend the political effort required to get the GATT through the legislature might jeopardise the later effort to get the ITO passed'.[10] Therefore, they preferred to take the *ITO Charter* and the GATT to their legislatures as one package.

To resolve this problem, on 30 October 1947, eight of the twenty-three countries that had negotiated the GATT 1947 signed the 'Protocol of Provisional Application of the General Agreement on Tariffs and Trade' (PPA). Pursuant to this Protocol, these Contracting Parties undertook *to apply provisionally as from 1 January 1948* Parts I and III of the GATT 1947 in full, and Part II 'to the fullest extent not inconsistent with existing legislation'.[11] Part II contained most of the substantive provisions, the application of which could require the modification of national legislation and thus the involvement of the legislature. The other fifteen of the original twenty-three Contracting Parties also soon agreed to the provisional application of the GATT 1947 through the PPA. According to the PPA, a GATT Contracting Party was entitled to maintain any provision of its legislation, which was inconsistent with a GATT Part II obligation. The PPA thus provided for an 'existing legislation exception', also referred to as 'grandfather rights'. This was quite 'convenient' and explains why the GATT 1947 itself was never adopted by the Contracting Parties. Until 1996, the provisions of the GATT 1947 were applied through the PPA of 30 October 1947.

9 *Ibid.*, 17–18. 10 *Ibid.*, 18.
11 GATT BISD, Volume IV, 77. Part I of the GATT 1947 contained the MFN obligation and the obligation regarding tariff concessions, and Part III procedural provisions.

In March 1948, the negotiations on the *ITO Charter* were successfully completed in Havana. The Charter provided for the establishment of the ITO, and set out basic rules and disciplines for international trade and other international economic matters. However, the *ITO Charter* never entered into force. While the United States had been the initiator of, and driving force behind, the negotiations on the *ITO Charter*, the United States Congress could not agree to approve it. In 1951, President Truman eventually decided that he would no longer seek Congressional approval of the *ITO Charter*. Since no country was interested in establishing an international organisation for trade of which the United States, the world's leading economy and trading nation, would not be a member, the ITO was 'stillborn'. As the ITO was intended to complete the Bretton Woods structure of international economic institutions, its demise left a significant gap in that structure.

2.1.2   The GATT as a *De Facto* International Organisation for Trade

In the absence of an international organisation for trade, countries gradually turned, from the early 1950s onwards, to the only existing multilateral 'institution' for trade, the GATT 1947, to handle problems concerning their trade relations.[12] Although the GATT was conceived as a multilateral *agreement* for the reduction of tariffs, and *not* an international *organisation*, it would successfully 'transform' itself – in a pragmatic and incremental manner – into a *de facto* international organisation. The 'institutional' provisions in the GATT 1947 were scant.[13] However, over the years, the GATT generated – through experimentation and trial and error – some fairly elaborate procedures for conducting its business.

The GATT was very successful in reducing tariffs on trade in goods, in particular on industrial goods from developed countries. In eight rounds of negotiations between 1947 and 1994,[14] the average level of tariffs imposed by developed countries on industrial products was brought down from over 40 per cent to less than 4 per cent.[15] The first five rounds of negotiations (Geneva (1947), Annecy (1949), Torquay (1951), Geneva (1956) and Dillon (1960–1)) focused on the reduction of tariffs. As from the Kennedy Round (1964–7) onwards, however, the negotiations would increasingly focus on non-tariff barriers (which were becoming a more serious barrier to trade than tariffs). With respect to the reduction of non-tariff barriers, the GATT was notably less successful than it was with the reduction of tariffs. Negotiations on the reduction of non-tariff barriers were much more complex and, therefore, required, *inter alia*, a more

---

12 A second and more modest attempt in 1955 to establish an 'Organization for Trade Cooperation' also failed because the US Congress was again unwilling to give its approval.

13 See Article XXV of the GATT 1947, entitled 'Joint Action by the Contracting Parties'.

14 The first of these rounds of negotiations, in 1947, led to the agreement of the GATT 1947 itself. See above, pp. 76–7.

15 See also below, pp. 78–82.

'sophisticated' institutional framework than that of the GATT. The Kennedy Round produced very few results on non-tariff barriers. The Tokyo Round (1973–9) produced better results; however, a number of the agreements decided upon clearly showed a lack of real consensus among the negotiators and proved to be difficult to implement. Moreover, the Tokyo Round agreements were plurilateral, rather than multilateral, in nature and did not bind many Contracting Parties.[16] In the early 1980s, it was clear that a new round of trade negotiations would be necessary. As Jackson noted:

the world was becoming increasingly complex and interdependent, and it was becoming more and more obvious that the GATT rules were not satisfactorily providing the measure of discipline that was needed to prevent tensions and damaging national activity.[17]

The United States and a few other countries were in favour of a new round of negotiations with a very broad agenda including novel subjects such as trade in services and the protection of intellectual property rights. Other countries objected to such a broad agenda or were opposed to the starting of a round altogether. However, in September 1986, at Punta del Este, Uruguay, the GATT CONTRACTING PARTIES eventually agreed to the start of a new round.

Questions and Assignments 2.1

Briefly outline the historical origins of the GATT. Was the Bretton Woods system of international economic organisations already complete in 1946? If not, what was missing? Explain how the constitutional law of the United States and of other countries played a decisive role in the genesis of the GATT. Why and how did the GATT become the *de facto* international organisation for trade? Did the GATT 1947 ever enter into force? How did the PPA solve the problem faced by those countries that needed parliamentary approval of the GATT 1947? Has the GATT been a success?

2.2   Uruguay Round of Multilateral Trade Negotiations

The 1986 Punta del Este Ministerial Declaration contained a very broad and ambitious mandate for negotiations. According to this Declaration, the Uruguay Round negotiations would cover, *inter alia*, trade in goods (including trade in agricultural products and trade in textiles), as well as – for the first time in history – trade in services. The establishment of a new international organisation for trade was not, however, among the Uruguay Round's initial objectives. The Punta del Este Ministerial Declaration explicitly recognised the need for institutional reforms in the GATT system but the ambitions were limited in this respect. The institutional issues for negotiation identified in the Punta del Este Declaration focused on: regular monitoring of trade policies and practices of

---

16 On the distinction between multilateral and plurilateral agreements, see above, pp. 40–50. Note that the agreements concluded at the end of the Tokyo Round are commonly also referred to as 'codes'.

17 J. Jackson, *The World Trade Organization: Constitution and Jurisprudence* (Royal Institute of International Affairs, 1998), 24.

Contracting Parties; improving the overall effectiveness and decision-making of the GATT; and strengthening the GATT's relationship with the IMF and the World Bank to achieve greater coherence in global economic policy-making.[18]

During the first years of the Uruguay Round negotiations, major progress was made with respect to all of the institutional issues identified in the Punta del Este Ministerial Declaration. In December 1988, at the Montreal Ministerial Mid-Term Review Conference, it was decided in principle to implement, on a provisional basis, a trade policy review mechanism to improve adherence to GATT rules.[19] This Mid-Term Review also resulted in an agreement attempting to create greater cooperation between the GATT, the IMF and the World Bank. In April 1989, it was agreed that, in order to improve the functioning of the GATT, the Contracting Parties would meet at least once every two years at ministerial level.[20] At the time, however, the establishment of a new international trade organisation was not discussed. It was only in February 1990 that the then Italian Trade Minister, Renato Ruggiero (later the second Director-General of the WTO) floated the idea of establishing a new international organisation for trade. A few months later, in April 1990, Canada formally proposed the establishment of what it called a 'World Trade Organization', a fully fledged international organisation which was to administer the different multilateral instruments related to international trade. Along the same lines, in July 1990, the European Community submitted a proposal calling for the establishment of a 'Multilateral Trade Organization'. The European Community argued that the GATT needed a sound institutional framework 'to ensure the effective implementation of the results of the Uruguay Round'.[21]

The reactions of the United States and most developing countries to these proposals were anything but enthusiastic.[22] In 1990, there was still little support for a major institutional overhaul.[23] Fear of supranationalism, the reluctance of major trading nations to give in to voting equality and the traditional worry of national leaders about 'tying their hands' were thought to inhibit the possibility of reconstructing the GATT into an international organisation for trade.[24] The December 1990 Brussels Draft Final Act, discussed

18 *Ministerial Declaration on the Uruguay Round*, GATT MIN.DEC, dated 20 September 1986, Part I, Section E, 'Functioning of the GATT System'.
19 In April 1989, the CONTRACTING PARTIES formally established the Trade Policy Review Mechanism.
20 See T. Stewart, *The GATT Uruguay Round* (Kluwer Law and Taxation, 1993), 1928.
21 See *Communication from the European Community*, GATT Doc. No. MTN.GNG/NG14/W/42, dated 9 July 1990, 2.
22 Many developing countries were hostile to the idea of an international trade organisation, *unless* this organisation was situated within the framework of the United Nations, such as the United Nations Conference on Trade and Development (UNCTAD).
23 J. Jackson, 'Strengthening the International Legal Framework of the GATT–MTN System: Reform Proposals for the New GATT Round 1991', in E. U. Petersmann and M. Hilf (eds.), *The New GATT Round of Multilateral Trade Negotiations: Legal and Economic Problems* (Kluwer, 1991), 17, 21 and 22. See also P. VerLoren van Themaat, in *ibid.*, 29: 'It is highly unlikely that the world's government leaders would be willing, at this point in history, to even start serious discussions about such a new institution.'
24 See J. Jackson, 'Strengthening the International Legal Framework of the GATT–MTN System: Reform Proposals for the New GATT Round 1991', in *ibid.*, 21.

at what was initially planned to be the closing conference of the Uruguay Round, did not contain an agreement with regard to a new international organisation for trade.[25] Albeit for very different reasons, this conference was a total failure, and the Uruguay Round was subsequently suspended.[26] In April 1991, however, the negotiations were taken up again, and, in November 1991, the European Community, Canada and Mexico tabled a joint proposal for an international trade organisation. This joint proposal served as the basis for further negotiations, which resulted, in December 1991, in the draft *Agreement Establishing the Multilateral Trade Organization*. The latter agreement was part of the 1991 Draft Final Act, commonly referred to as the Dunkel Draft, after the then Director-General of the GATT.[27]

For the reasons already referred to above, the United States remained opposed to the establishment of a multilateral trade organization and campaigned against the idea throughout 1992. However, by early 1993 most other participants in the Round were prepared to agree to the establishment of a multilateral trade organisation. This isolation of the United States perhaps explains the turnabout in its position during 1993 when the new Clinton Administration dropped its outspoken opposition of the United States to a new international trade organisation. Nevertheless, uncertainty about US support for such a new international organisation persisted until the last days of the Round.[28] The United States formally agreed to the establishment of the new organisation on 15 December 1993. To the surprise of many, however, the United States demanded a change of name as a condition for giving its consent. The United States suggested that the name of the new organisation should be the 'World Trade Organization' as had originally been proposed by Canada. The proponents of an international trade organisation had opted for 'Multilateral Trade Organization', as was proposed by the European Community, in the hope that this rather technical, and therefore less menacing, name would appease the United States and others opposed to an international organisation perceived as a threat to national sovereignty. Reportedly, the United States did not want to give the European Community the satisfaction of having given the new organisation its name, and further considered that an organisation with such a tongue-twisting and unappealing name as the 'Multilateral Trade Organization' would have a hard time winning the hearts and minds of the American people.[29] The *Agreement Establishing the*

25 *Draft Final Act Embodying the Results of the Uruguay Round of Multilateral Trade Negotiations*, GATT Doc. MTN.TNC/W/35/Rev.1, dated 3 December 1990.

26 The negotiations broke down because of the fundamental disagreement between the European Community and the United States on the issue of agricultural subsidies.

27 *Draft Final Act Embodying the Results of the Uruguay Round of Multilateral Trade Negotiations*, GATT Doc. MTN.TNC/W/FA, dated 20 December 1991.

28 Withholding its consent to a new international trade organisation proved a useful bargaining chip in negotiations with the European Community. See *Financial Times*, 16 December 1993, 5.

29 See *ibid.* Note that the World Trade Organization and the World Tourism Organization concluded an agreement on the use of the abbreviation 'WTO'. To avoid confusion, the World Trade Organization agreed to use a distinct logo and avoid using the abbreviation in the context of tourism. See GATT Doc. MTN.TNC/W/146, 3.

World Trade Organization, commonly referred to as the *WTO Agreement*, was signed in Marrakesh in April 1994, and entered into force on 1 January 1995.[30] A perceptive observer noted:

Those who constructed the WTO are proud of having created what has been described as the greatest ever achievement in institutionalized global economic cooperation.[31]

The Sutherland Report on *The Future of the WTO* noted:

The creation of the World Trade Organization (WTO) in 1995 was the most dramatic advance in multilateralism since the inspired period of institution building of the late 1940s.[32]

Questions and Assignments 2.2

Did the Punta del Este Ministerial Declaration of September 1986 recognise the need for a new international organisation for trade? Briefly outline the events between 1990 and 1995 that led to the establishment of the WTO on 1 January 1995. Which countries were the driving forces behind the establishment of the WTO? Why were other countries opposed to this idea?

3   MANDATE OF THE WTO

The WTO was formally established and became operational on 1 January 1995 when the *WTO Agreement* entered into force. Pursuant to the *WTO Agreement*, the WTO has a broad and ambitious mandate. This section examines two main aspects of this mandate, namely: (1) the objectives of the WTO; and (2) the functions of the WTO.

3.1   Objectives of the WTO

The reasons for establishing the WTO and the policy objectives of this international organisation are set out in the Preamble to the *WTO Agreement*. According to the Preamble, the Parties to the *WTO Agreement* agreed to the terms of this agreement and the establishment of the WTO:

Recognizing that their relations in the field of trade and economic endeavour should be conducted with a view to raising standards of living, ensuring full employment and a large and steadily growing volume of real income and effective demand, and expanding the production of and trade in goods and services, while allowing for the optimal use of the world's resources in accordance with the objective of sustainable development, seeking both to protect and preserve the environment and to enhance the means for doing so in a manner consistent with their respective needs and concerns at different levels of economic development,

---

30 Note that, after the entry into force of the *WTO Agreement* and the establishment of the WTO on 1 January 1995, the WTO and the GATT 1947 existed side by side for one year. The GATT 1947 was terminated only at the end of 1995.

31 G. Sampson, 'Overview', in G. Sampson (ed.), *The Role of the World Trade Organization in Global Governance* (United Nations University Press, 2001), 5.

32 Report by the Consultative Board to the Director-General Supachai Panitchpakdi, *The Future of the WTO: Addressing Institutional Challenges in the New Millennium* (the 'Sutherland Report') (WTO, 2004), para. 1.

Recognizing further that there is need for positive efforts designed to ensure that developing countries, and especially the least developed among them, secure a share in the growth in international trade commensurate with the needs of their economic development ...

The ultimate objectives of the WTO are thus: (1) the increase of standards of living; (2) the attainment of full employment; (3) the growth of real income and effective demand; and (4) the expansion of production of, and trade in, goods and services. However, it is clear from the Preamble that in pursuing these objectives the WTO must take into account the need for preservation of the environment and the needs of developing countries. The Preamble stresses the importance of *sustainable* economic development, i.e. economic development taking account of environmental as well as social concerns. The Preamble also stresses the importance of the *integration* of developing countries, and in particular least-developed countries, in the world trading system. The latter aspects were absent from the Preamble to the GATT 1947.

The statements in the Preamble on the objectives of the WTO are not without legal significance. In *US – Shrimp (1998)*, the Appellate Body stated:

[The language of the Preamble to the *WTO Agreement*] demonstrates a recognition by WTO negotiators that optimal use of the world's resources should be made in accordance with the objective of sustainable development. As this preambular language reflects the intentions of negotiators of the *WTO Agreement*, we believe it must *add colour, texture and shading to our interpretation of the agreements* annexed to the *WTO Agreement*, in this case, the GATT 1994. We have already observed that Article XX(g) of the GATT 1994 is appropriately read with the perspective embodied in the above preamble.[33]

The preambular statements of the objectives of the WTO contradict the contention that the WTO is only about trade liberalisation without regard for the sustainability of economic development, environmental degradation and global poverty.

The Preamble to the *WTO Agreement* also states how the objectives referred to are to be achieved:

Being desirous of contributing to these objectives by entering into reciprocal and mutually advantageous arrangements directed to the substantial reduction of tariffs and other barriers to trade and to the elimination of discriminatory treatment in international trade relations ...

According to the Preamble to the *WTO Agreement*, the two main instruments, or means, to achieve the objectives of the WTO are: (1) the reduction of tariff barriers and other barriers to trade; and (2) the elimination of discriminatory treatment in international trade relations. The reduction of trade barriers and elimination of discrimination were also the two main instruments of the GATT 1947, but the *WTO Agreement* aims at constituting, as the Preamble states in its

---

33 Appellate Body Report, *US – Shrimp (1998)*, para. 153. Emphasis added. For the interpretation of Article XX(g) of the GATT 1994, in light of the Preamble to the *WTO Agreement*, see below, pp. 565–8.

fourth recital, the basis of an integrated, *more* viable and *more* durable multilateral trading system.

In the Doha Ministerial Declaration of 14 November 2001, the WTO Members stated, with regard to the objectives of the WTO and its instruments for achieving these objectives:

International trade can play a major role in the promotion of economic development and the alleviation of poverty. We recognize the need for all our peoples to benefit from the increased opportunities and welfare gains that the multilateral trading system generates. The majority of WTO Members are developing countries. We seek to place their needs and interests at the heart of the Work Programme adopted in this Declaration. Recalling the Preamble to the Marrakesh Agreement, we shall continue to make positive efforts designed to *ensure that developing countries*, and especially the least-developed among them, *secure a share in the growth of world trade* commensurate with the needs of their economic development ...

We strongly reaffirm our commitment to the objective of *sustainable development*, as stated in the Preamble to the Marrakesh Agreement. We are convinced that the aims of upholding and safeguarding an open and non-discriminatory multilateral trading system, and acting for the protection of the environment and the promotion of sustainable development, can and must be mutually supportive.[34]

Questions and Assignments 2.3

What are the objectives of the WTO? Are the economic development of developing countries and environmental protection objectives of the WTO? Explain. What is the legal significance of the Preamble to the *WTO Agreement*? What are the main instruments, or means, of the WTO for achieving its objectives?

3.2   Functions of the WTO

In the broadest of terms, the primary function of the WTO is to:

provide the common institutional framework for the conduct of trade relations among its Members in matters related to the agreements and associated legal instruments included in the Annexes to [the WTO] Agreement.[35]

More specifically, the WTO has been assigned six widely defined functions. Article III of the *WTO Agreement* states:

1. The WTO shall *facilitate the implementation*, administration and operation, and further the objectives, of this Agreement and of the Multilateral Trade Agreements, and shall also provide the framework for the implementation, administration and operation of the Plurilateral Trade Agreements.
2. The WTO shall provide the *forum for negotiations* among its Members concerning their multilateral trade relations in matters dealt with under the agreements in the Annexes to this Agreement. The WTO may also provide a forum for further negotiations among

---

34 Ministerial Conference, *Doha Ministerial Declaration*, WT/MIN(01)/DEC/1, dated 20 November 2001, paras. 2 and 6. Emphasis added.
35 Article II:1 of the *WTO Agreement*.

its Members concerning their multilateral trade relations, and a framework for the implementation of the results of such negotiations, as may be decided by the Ministerial Conference.

3. The WTO shall administer the Understanding on Rules and Procedures Governing the *Settlement of Disputes* (hereinafter referred to as the 'Dispute Settlement Understanding' or 'DSU') in Annex 2 to this Agreement.

4. The WTO shall administer the *Trade Policy Review Mechanism* (hereinafter referred to as the 'TPRM') provided for in Annex 3 to this Agreement.

5. With a view to achieving greater coherence in global economic policy-making, the WTO shall *cooperate*, as appropriate, with the International Monetary Fund and with the International Bank for Reconstruction and Development and its affiliated agencies.[36]

In addition to the five functions of the WTO explicitly referred to in Article III of the *WTO Agreement*, technical assistance to developing-country Members, to allow the latter to integrate into the world trading system, is, undisputedly, also an important sixth function of the WTO.[37]

This section will examine the following functions of the WTO: (1) the facilitation of the implementation of the WTO agreements; (2) negotiations on trade matters; (3) the settlement of disputes; (4) trade policy review; (5) cooperation with other organisations; and (6) technical assistance to developing countries.

3.2.1   Facilitation of the Implementation of the WTO Agreements

According to Article III of the *WTO Agreement*, the first function of the WTO is to facilitate the implementation, administration and operation of the *WTO Agreement* and the multilateral and plurilateral agreements annexed to it.[38] The WTO is also entrusted with the task of furthering the objectives of these agreements. For two concrete examples of what this function of 'facilitating' and 'furthering' entails, refer to the work of the WTO Committee on Sanitary and Phytosanitary Measures (the 'SPS Committee') and the work of the WTO Committee on Safeguards.[39] Article 12, paragraph 2, of the *SPS Agreement* states that the SPS Committee shall, *inter alia*:

encourage and facilitate *ad hoc* consultations or negotiations among Members on specific sanitary or phytosanitary issues. The Committee shall encourage the use of international standards, guidelines or recommendations by all Members and, in this regard, shall sponsor technical consultation and study with the objective of increasing coordination and integration between international and national systems and approaches for approving the use of food additives or for establishing tolerances for contaminants in foods, beverages or feedstuffs.

---

36 Emphasis added.
37 See Ministerial Conference, *Doha Ministerial Declaration*, WT/MIN(01)/DEC/1, dated 20 November 2001, para. 38. See also below, p. 85.
38 For an overview of these agreements, see above, pp. 40–50.
39 For a further discussion of these and other examples, see below, pp. 622 (Committee on Safeguards), 733 (Dumping Committee), 833 (Subsidies Committee), 887 (TBT Committee), 941 (SPS Committee).

Pursuant to Article 13 of the *Agreement on Safeguards*, the tasks of the Committee on Safeguards include:

a.   to monitor, and report annually to the Council for Trade in Goods on, the general implementation of this Agreement and make recommendations towards its improvement;

b.   to find, upon request of an affected Member, whether or not the procedural requirements of this Agreement have been complied with in connection with a safeguard measure, and report its findings to the Council for Trade in Goods;

c.   to assist Members, if they so request, in their consultations under the provisions of this Agreement.

This function of facilitating the implementation, administration and operation of the WTO agreements and furthering the objectives of these agreements is an essential function of the WTO. It involves most of its bodies and takes up much of their time.[40]

Questions and Assignments 2.4

Give two concrete examples of how the WTO facilitates the implementation, administration and operation of the *WTO Agreement* other than the examples given in this sub-section.

3.2.2   Negotiations on New Trade Rules

A second function of the WTO is to provide a forum for negotiations amongst WTO Members on new trade rules. The WTO provides 'the' forum for negotiations on matters already covered by the WTO, and the WTO is 'a' forum among others with regard to negotiations on matters not yet addressed. To date, WTO Members have negotiated and concluded, in the framework of the WTO, trade agreements providing, *inter alia*, for: (1) further market access commitments for specific services and service suppliers (on financial services,[41] on basic telecommunications services,[42] and on the movement of natural persons[43]); (2) the liberalisation of trade in information technology products;[44] (3) the amendment of the *TRIPS Agreement* regarding the rules on compulsory licensing to ensure

---

40 For a discussion on these WTO bodies, see below, pp. 53–5.

41 See *Second Protocol to the General Agreement on Trade in Services*, S/L/11, dated 24 July 1995; and *Fifth Protocol to the General Agreement on Trade in Services*, S/L/45, dated 3 December 1997.

42 See *Fourth Protocol to the General Agreement on Trade in Services*, S/L/20, dated 30 April 1996.

43 See *Third Protocol to the General Agreement on Trade in Services*, S/L/12, dated 24 July 1995.

44 See *Agreement on Trade in Information Technology Products (ITA)*, in *Ministerial Declaration on Trade in Information Technology Products*, adopted on 13 December 1996 and entered into force on 1 July 1997. The ITA was agreed at the close of the Singapore Ministerial Conference in December 1996. The ITA provides for the elimination of customs duties and other duties and charges on information technology products by the year 2000 on an MFN basis. The implementation of the ITA was contingent on approximately 90 per cent of world trade in information technology products being covered by the ITA. On 26 March 1997, that criterion was met. In 2012, seventy Members, representing 97 per cent of world trade in information technology products, were party to the ITA. In May 2012, it was announced that informal bilateral and plurilateral talks were about to start on the expansion of the ITA. See www.wto.org.

access for developing countries to pharmaceutical products;[45] (4) the amendment of the *Agreement on Government Procurement* to set the basis for expanded coverage of and disciplines under this Agreement;[46] and (5) the accession of thirty countries to the WTO.[47] Furthermore, negotiations within the WTO have resulted in a number of decisions by WTO bodies, such as the 2001 Ministerial Decision on implementation-related issues and concerns,[48] and the 2011 Decision of the SPS Committee on SPS-related private standards.[49]

Before the establishment of the WTO, multilateral trade negotiations under the GATT were primarily conducted in specially convened, 'time-limited' rounds of negotiations covering a wide range of issues.[50] The WTO provides for a *permanent* forum for negotiations in which each trade matter can be negotiated separately and on its own merits. It was initially thought that consequently there would be no need anymore for specially convened rounds of negotiations. However, soon after the establishment of the WTO, its Members considered that, to negotiate successfully on further trade liberalisation at the multilateral level, they needed the political momentum, and the opportunity for package deals, brought by the old GATT-type round of negotiations. Therefore, WTO Members decided at the Doha Ministerial Conference in November 2001 to start such a round of multilateral trade negotiations.[51] This round is commonly referred to as the 'Doha Round'.[52] Pursuant to the Doha Ministerial Declaration, the Doha Round negotiations should have been concluded no later than 1 January 2005. However, this and subsequent deadlines were not met and the negotiations are currently still ongoing.

The Doha Ministerial Declaration provided for an ambitious agenda for negotiations. These negotiations include matters on which WTO Members had already agreed in the *WTO Agreement* to continue negotiations, such as: (1) trade in agricultural products;[53] and (2) trade in services.[54] In fact, negotiations on

45 See *Protocol Amending the TRIPS Agreement*, WT/L/641, dated 8 December 2005. See below, pp. 141 and 1000.
46 See *Protocol Amending the Agreement on Government Procurement*, GPA/113, dated 2 April 2012. See below, pp. 509–11 and 535–7.
47 On accession protocols, such as the *Protocol on the Accession of the People's Republic of China*, see below, pp. 109–13.
48 See Ministerial Conference, *Decision of 14 November on Implementation-Related Issues and Concerns*, WT/MIN(01)/17, dated 20 November 2001. See also below, p. 139.
49 See Committee on Sanitary and Phytosanitary Measures, *Decision of the Committee on Actions regarding SPS-Related Private Standards*, G/SPS/55, dated 6 April 2011. See also below, footnote 21 of page 901.
50 See above, pp. 78–82, and below, pp. 87–94.
51 Note that the WTO Members already tried, but dismally failed, to start such round of multilateral trade negotiations at the ill-fated Seattle Ministerial Conference in November–December 1999. See above, p. 14, and below, p. 99. Also note that the willingness of WTO Members to agree to the launch of the Doha Round in November 2001 was related to the need for the international community to express its faith in international cooperation and negotiations after the terrorist attacks on the United States of 11 September 2001.
52 In the Doha Ministerial Declaration, the WTO Members stressed their 'commitment to the WTO as the unique forum for global trade rule-making and liberalization'. See Ministerial Conference, *Doha Ministerial Declaration*, WT/MIN(01)/DEC/1, dated 20 November 2001, para. 4.
53 See Article 20 of the *Agreement on Agriculture*.
54 See Article XIX of the GATS.

these matters had already started in early 2000. Furthermore, the Doha Round negotiations include negotiations on: (1) problems of developing-country Members with the implementation of the existing WTO agreements (the so-called 'implementation issues'); (2) market access for non-agricultural products (NAMA); (3) TRIPS issues such as access for developing countries to essential medicines and the protection of geographical indications; (4) rules on relating to dumping, subsidies and regional trade agreements; (5) dispute settlement; and (6) special and differential treatment for developing-country Members and least-developed-country Members.[55] The stated ambition of the Doha Round negotiations was, and still is, to place economic development and poverty alleviation at the heart of the multilateral trading system.[56]

In view of many distinct matters on the agenda of the Doha Round negotiations, it is important to note that the Doha Ministerial Declaration stated that 'the conduct, conclusion and entry into force of the outcome of the negotiations shall be treated as parts of a single undertaking'.[57] Under this 'single undertaking' approach to the negotiations, there is no agreement on anything until there is an agreement on everything.[58]

Some WTO Members, and in particular the then European Communities, wanted an even broader agenda for the Doha Round. They also wanted the WTO to start negotiations on, for example, the relationship between trade and investment, the relationship between trade and competition law and the relationship between trade and core labour standards. There was, however, strong opposition, especially among developing-country Members, to the inclusion of some or all of these matters on the agenda of the Round. At the Doha Ministerial Conference, WTO Members decided that there would be no negotiations, within the context of the WTO, on the relationship between trade and core labour standards.[59] However, with respect to what is commonly referred to as the 'Singapore issues'[60] – namely: (1) the relationship between trade and investment; (2) the relationship between trade and competition law; (3) transparency in government procurement, and (4) trade facilitation[61] – the WTO Members decided in Doha that negotiations would start after they had agreed, by 'explicit consensus', on the modalities of these negotiations.[62] This agreement on the modalities of the

---

55 For a complete list of the matters on the agenda of the Doha Round, see Ministerial Conference, *Doha Ministerial Declaration*, WT/MIN(01)/DEC/1, dated 20 November 2001.

56 See *ibid.*, para. 2.

57 *Ibid.*, para. 47. The only subject-matter exempted from the 'single undertaking' approach are the negotiations on the improvements to and clarifications of the *Dispute Settlement Understanding*. See *ibid.* See also below, pp. 91–2.

58 Note, however, that para. 47 of the Doha Ministerial Declaration provides room for deviation from the 'single undertaking' approach when it states: 'However, agreements reached at an early stage may be implemented on a provisional or a definitive basis.' See *ibid.*

59 WTO Members took 'note of work under way in the International Labour Organization (ILO) on the social dimension of globalization'. See Ministerial Conference, *Doha Ministerial Declaration*, WT/MIN(01)/DEC/1, dated 20 November 2001, para. 8.

60 At the Singapore Ministerial Conference in December 1996, these issues were first identified as possible issues for further negotiations within the WTO.

61 On 'trade facilitation', see below, pp. 508–9.

62 Note that the concept of 'explicit consensus' was a *novum* in WTO law. See below, p. 137, footnote 326.

negotiations on the Singapore issues was to be reached at the next session of the Ministerial Conference in Cancún in September 2003. However, at this session, no such agreement was reached. Developing-country Members were unwilling to consent to the request of the European Communities and others to start negotiations on the Singapore issues. Moreover, at the Cancún Ministerial Conference, it became clear that little progress had been achieved on most of the issues on which Members had been negotiating since the start of the negotiations in February 2002. As was the case during the Uruguay Round negotiations, agricultural subsidies and market access for agricultural products were again the most contentious issues on the negotiating table.[63] The Cancún Ministerial Conference turned out to be a dismal failure, with nothing agreed upon.[64] In diplomatic language masking the deep sense of failure and disappointment, the Ministerial Statement adopted at the close of the Conference on 14 September 2003 read:

> All participants have worked hard and constructively to make progress as required under the Doha mandates. We have, indeed, made considerable progress. However, more work needs to be done in some key areas to enable us to proceed towards the conclusion of the negotiations in fulfilment of the commitments we took at Doha.[65]

The deadlock in the negotiations after the Cancún Ministerial Conference was only overcome during the summer of 2004 when, following weeks of intense discussions, a new Doha Work Programme was adopted by the General Council on 1 August 2004.[66] In its Decision of 1 August, the General Council called on all Members 'to redouble their efforts towards the conclusion of a balanced overall outcome of the Doha Development Agenda'.[67] A key element of the Decision of the General Council was not to start negotiations on the Singapore issues with the exception of the issue of trade facilitation.[68] The 'redoubling of efforts' did not, however, have the results hoped for. At the Hong Kong Ministerial Conference in December 2005, agreement was reached on the elimination of agricultural export subsidies by 2013.[69] This was in itself a significant achievement but of little value if no agreement was also reached on all other major issues on the negotiating table, such as market access for agricultural products, domestic support for agricultural production, market access for non-agricultural

---

63 See below, p. 81, footnote 26 and 90.
64 Note that, in the run-up to the Cancún Ministerial Conference, the General Council of the WTO did reach an agreement on the waiver to the *TRIPS Agreement* enabling the import by developing countries of generic medicines produced under compulsory licences. See General Council, *Decision on the Implementation of Paragraph 6 of the Doha Declaration on TRIPS and Public Health*, WT/L/540, dated 1 September 2003. See further below, p. 122, footnote 243.
65 Ministerial Conference, *Ministerial Statement*, WT/MIN(03)/20, dated 23 September 2003, para. 3.
66 See General Council, *Doha Work Programme Decision adopted by the General Council on 1 August 2004*, WT/L/579, dated 2 August 2004.
67 *Ibid.*, para. 3.
68 See below, pp. 88–9.
69 See Ministerial Conference, *Hong Kong Ministerial Declaration*, WT/MIN(05)/DEC, dated 22 December 2005, para. 6 The elimination of export subsidies by 2013 was an important concession on the part of the European Communities.

products (NAMA), and the liberalisation of trade in services. With regard to these other issues, Members were unfortunately only able to agree to disagree and to put forward the summer of 2006 as a new deadline for agreement on the broad lines of an overall deal on NAMA. When that deadline was missed, WTO Director-General Lamy decided at the end of July 2006 to suspend the negotiations. In February 2007, the negotiations were resumed. In the summer of 2008, a breakthrough in the negotiations seemed within reach but failed to materialise. The mini-ministerial meeting in July 2008 in Geneva failed over the inability to reach agreement on a special safeguard mechanism (SSM) for the protection of poor farmers in developing-country Members. However, Ambassador Servansing from Mauritius, the Coordinator and Chief Negotiator of the ACP Group in Geneva, noted:

> The SSM was only the immediate trigger that precipitated the failure. The real causes were more fundamental ... The underlying reason was the growing development deficit that slowly crept into the negotiations and emptied the development ambition of the DDA [Doha Development Agenda] mandate. There was a clear feeling among the developing countries that the imbalances that the DDA was meant to correct were not being addressed and the outcome was being skewed more in their disfavour. While in agriculture, higher ambition, which served a developmental objective, was being consistently diluted through multiple flexibilities for developed countries, in NAMA the developmental concerns of protecting industrial development and employment in developing countries were being denied by a predatory mercantilist approach of seeking higher market access in developing countries.[70]

For a detailed and technical account of the negotiations, refer to the regular reports of the Chair of the Trade Negotiations Committee to the General Council, which are an excellent, and sobering, public source of information.[71] Many reasons have been advanced to explain why the Doha Round negotiations have been, and are, so difficult, including: (1) the increase in the WTO membership and its diversity, and the emergence of developing-country Members as full participants in the negotiations;[72] (2) the difficulties arising from the fact that the decision on the ultimate result of the negotiations, but also the decisions on all intermediate steps in the negotiations, must be adopted by consensus;[73] (3) the fact that the decision to launch the Doha Round was ill-prepared and not based on a consensus regarding necessary economic reforms;[74] (4) the fact that the 'easy' steps in the process of trade liberalisation have all been taken in previous negotiations and that what is now 'left' includes primarily trade barriers or distortions fiercely defended by strong domestic interests; (5) the ambitious

70 Shree B. C. Servansing, 'Non-Agricultural Market Access (NAMA) – Balancing Development and Ambition', in P. Mehta, A. Kaushik and R. Kaukab (eds.), *Reflections from the Frontline: Developing Country Negotiators in the WTO* (CUTS International, 2012), 88–9.
71 See, for example, General Council, *Minutes of Meeting of 31 July 2008*, WT/GC/M/115, dated 10 October 2008.
72 See below, pp. 136–8.   73 See below, p. 100.
74 As discussed above, the launch of the Doha Round has been seen as a 'political response' by the international community to the terrorist attacks on the United States of 11 September 2001. See above, pp. 21–2.

agenda of the negotiations and the 'single undertaking' approach;[75] (6) the fact that Members are unwilling to agree to new rights and obligations formulated in ambiguous wording (a technique much used in other international negotiations to overcome deadlock) because such ambiguously worded rights and obligations may later be 'clarified' in the context of the WTO's binding dispute settlement system in a manner inconsistent with their interests;[76] and finally (7) a general questioning of economic globalisation and a reduced enthusiasm for further trade liberalisation, in particular since the outbreak of the global economic and financial crisis in the summer of 2007.

In April 2011, Director-General Lamy, in his capacity as Chair of the Trade Negotiations Committee,[77] presented to the Members the so-called 'Easter Package', a document reflecting the work done so far.[78] For the first time since the start of the negotiations almost ten years earlier, Members had 'the opportunity to consider the entire Doha package in all market access and regulatory areas'.[79] This document showed that in many areas progress had been made, but it also made clear that Members had still to come to an agreement on many core issues, in particular on NAMA. The issue of market access for industrial products, a 'classic mercantilist issue' which had been 'the bread and butter' of the negotiations since the start, divided Members as no other issue.[80] Chapter 6 of this book discusses this issue in greater detail.[81] Director-General Lamy reported to the Members that it appeared that the 'political gap' which separated Members was 'not bridgeable' at that time.[82] The Members, concurring with Lamy's assessment, subsequently made an effort to agree by the next Ministerial Conference in December 2011, on a smaller 'package' of issues. These issues related primarily to issues of particular interest to the least-developed-country Members (such as duty-free and quota-free market access and associated rules of origin; cotton subsidies; and a waiver of the GATS MFN treatment obligation). However, such narrow focus was not acceptable to all Members. Director-General Lamy thus presented a non-exhaustive list of other issues, such as trade facilitation, export competition and fisheries subsidies ('LDC plus' issues), which could be part of the smaller package to be agreed on by December 2011. In July 2011 it was clear, however, that Members would not be able to agree on a 'LDC plus' package.

The Doha Round negotiations were in a deep crisis. Even an intermediate agreement on a smaller package of issues, a so-called 'Doha Lite', was not possible. At the Geneva Ministerial Conference in December 2011, the Chair of the Ministerial Conference said in his Concluding Statement:

---

75 See above, p. 88.   76 See below, p. 676.   77 See below, p. 94, footnote 95.
78 The 'Easter Package' consisted of documents of the chairs of the negotiating committees on the work done by their committee, as well as an accompanying report by Pascal Lamy. See www.wto.org/english/tratop_e/dda_e/chair_texts11_e/chair_texts11_e.htm.
79 See *WTO Annual Report 2012*, 22.
80 See Opening Remarks of Director-General Pascal Lamy at the informal TNC meeting of 29 April 2011, www.wto.org/english/news_e/news11_e/tnc_dg_infstat_29apr11_e.htm.
81 See below, pp. 436–8.   82 See *WTO Annual Report 2012*, 22.

Ministers deeply regret that, despite full engagement and intensified efforts to conclude the Doha Development Agenda single undertaking since the last Ministerial Conference, the negotiations are at an impasse.

Ministers acknowledge that there are significantly different perspectives on the possible results that Members can achieve in certain areas of the single undertaking. In this context, it is unlikely that all elements of the Doha Development Round could be concluded simultaneously in the near future.[83]

Members did, however, express their willingness to continue with the Doha Round negotiations. As reflected in the Chair's Concluding Statement, Members recognised:

[the] need to more fully explore different negotiating approaches while respecting the principles of transparency and inclusiveness.[84]

Members declared themselves willing to abandon the 'single undertaking' approach.[85] They agreed to advance negotiations on issues where progress can be achieved with the aim of reaping an 'early harvest', i.e. concluding provisional or definitive agreements *before* the full conclusion of the single undertaking.[86] Finally, Members stressed that:

they will intensify their efforts to look into ways that may allow Members to overcome the most critical and fundamental stalemates in the areas where multilateral convergence has proven to be especially challenging.[87]

Half a year later, in July 2012, Director-General Lamy reported to the General Council as follows:

[P]rogress and activity have been mixed, to use diplomatic language ... [W]e have to recognize that prolonged and dogmatic discussions about whether or not to deliver on everything or a few things or nothing at all have not and will not take us very far. The only thing we know is that an 'all' or 'nothing' does not work. A 'my way or the highway' is the best way to ensure paralysis ... [T]he guidance from Ministers is clear ... [U]ltimately the ball lies in your court. You, the negotiators, have to achieve the needed substantive and balanced progress across all areas of our negotiations that you all say you desire.[88]

However, this call on Geneva-based negotiators to show flexibility and creativity should not be misunderstood as implying that the impasse in the negotiations is mainly due to disagreement on technical trade issues. The impasse is primarily political and must be addressed at the (highest) political level.[89]

---

83 Chairman's Concluding Statement, WT/MIN(11)/11, dated 11 December 2011, p. 3.
84 *Ibid.*
85 While the emphasis since the start of the Doha Round had always been on the 'single undertaking' approach, note that the 2001 Doha Ministerial Declaration itself provided room for deviation from this approach. As discussed above, para. 47 of the Declaration states: 'However, agreements reached at an early stage may be implemented on a provisional or a definitive basis.' See above, p. 88, footnote 57.
86 See *ibid.*   87 *Ibid.*
88 Report by the Chairman of the Trade Negotiations Committee to the General Council on 25 July 2012, www.wto.org/english/news_e/news12_e/gc_rpt_25jul12_e.htm.
89 See also Pascal Lamy, *Strengthening the Multilateral Trading System*, speech delivered at the Singapore Schuman Lecture Series of the European Chamber of Commerce in Singapore on 21 September 2012.

However, regional trade agreements, which are negotiated and concluded in ever-increasing number,[90] have diverted, and continue to divert, political attention (and negotiating resources) away from the Doha Round negotiations. Also, the agenda of the Doha Round, agreed upon more than a decade ago, may have become in view of the rapidly changing reality of international trade, outdated, i.e. insufficiently focused on more pressing problems faced by the multilateral trading system today (such as export restrictions and trade-related energy and investment issues).[91] Finally, the rapidly increasing importance of emerging economies in the global economy, their growing assertiveness within the WTO, and the divergence of their interests (with those of developed countries but also *inter se*) make the successful conclusion of multilateral trade negotiations, such as the Doha Round negotiations, an ever more formidable challenge. In December 2012, it was reported that in 2012 the Doha Round negotiations on topics such as trade facilitation, agriculture, special and differential treatment, least-developed-country issues, and dispute settlement had advanced to at least some extent, while the negotiations on topics such as services had barely moved at all, and were unlikely to move forward in the near future.[92]

A possible indication of things to come are the current talks – outside the Doha Round negotiations – among a group of about twenty developed- and developing-country Members on a Trade in Services Agreement (TISA), a plurilateral agreement on an ambitious liberalisation of trade in services, building upon but going far beyond the existing GATS. Tellingly, this group of Members, referred to as the 'Real Good Friends of Services' (RGF), includes the European Union and the United States but not Brazil, China or India. The latter Members have warned of the consequences for the multilateral trading system of adopting a plurilateral approach to negotiations on trade liberalisation in reaction to the impasse in the Doha Round negotiations.[93]

Contrary to some alarmist commentary in the media, the impasse in the Doha Round negotiations does not herald the imminent demise of the WTO. As discussed above and below, the WTO fulfils, besides the function of negotiating new trade rules, also other important functions, and does so quite successfully.[94] However, failure to update and add to the current WTO rules in order to keep these rules adapted to the ever-changing reality of international trade and the

---

90 It has been argued that this proliferation of regional trade agreements was, and is, to a large degree triggered by the failure to bring the Doha Round negotiations to a successful conclusion. On the proliferation of regional trade agreements, see below, pp. 650–5.

91 On the rapidly changing reality of international trade, see Chapter 1 of this book, at pp. 12–13.

92 See *Bridges Weekly Trade News Digest*, 12 December 2012.

93 See *Bridges Weekly Trade News Digest*, 4 April 2012, 11 July 2012, 26 September 2012 and 12 December 2012. Other Members involved include Australia, Canada, Colombia, Costa Rica, Hong Kong China, Iceland, Israel, Japan, Mexico, New Zealand, Norway, Pakistan, Panama, Peru, South Korea, Switzerland, Chinese Taipei, and Turkey.

94 See above, p. 75, and below, pp. 157–9. Moreover, while unsuccessful in the context of the Doha Round negotiations, it must be noted that the WTO has been successful in its function as a forum for negotiations and agreeing on new rules in several areas. See above, p. 91.

needs of WTO Members will, over time, weaken the rules-based multilateral trading system and result in a 'creeping return of the law of the jungle'.[95]

Questions and Assignments 2.5

Has the WTO thus far been successful as a forum for the negotiation of new multilateral trade agreements? What is on the agenda of the Doha Round? What is not on the agenda? Find out exactly what the Doha Ministerial Declaration of November 2001 says about the relationship between trade and core labour standards. What, in your opinion, are the main reasons for the failure of Members to conclude the Doha Round negotiations? Should Members proceed with the Doha Round negotiations and, if so, how? Are plurilateral negotiations on trade liberalisation a 'useful' alternative to the Doha Round negotiations? Does the impasse in the Doha Round negotiations herald the imminent demise of the WTO?

3.2.3 Dispute Settlement

A third and very important function of the WTO is the administration of the WTO dispute settlement system. As stated in Article 3.2 of the *Dispute Settlement Understanding*:

The dispute settlement system of the WTO is a central element in providing security and predictability to the multilateral trading system.

The prompt settlement of disputes under the WTO agreements is essential for the effective functioning of the WTO and for maintaining a proper balance between the rights and obligations of Members.[96] The WTO dispute settlement system serves: (1) to preserve the rights and obligations of Members under the WTO agreements; and (2) to clarify the existing provisions of those agreements.[97] However, the dispute settlement system is explicitly proscribed from adding to or diminishing the rights and obligations provided in the WTO agreements.[98]

The WTO dispute settlement system, referred to as the 'jewel in the crown' of the WTO, has been operational for eighteen years now, and has arguably been the most prolific of all State-to-State dispute settlement systems in that period. Since 1 January 1995, 454 disputes have been brought to the WTO for resolution.[99] Some of these disputes, involving, for example, national legislation on public health or environmental protection, were politically sensitive and have attracted considerable attention from the media.[100] With its compulsory jurisdiction, its strict timeframes, the possibility of appellate review and the detailed mechanism to ensure compliance with recommendations and rulings, the WTO dispute settlement system is unique among international dispute settlement

---

95 See Opening Remarks of Director-General Pascal Lamy at the informal TNC meeting of 29 April 2011, www. wto.org/english/news_e/news11_e/tnc_dg_infstat_29apr11_e.htm.
96 See Article 3.3 of the DSU.   97 See Article 3.2, second sentence, of the DSU.
98 See Article 3.2, last sentence, of the DSU.
99 I.e. the number of requests for consultations notified to the DSB until 31 December 2012. See www. worldtradelaw.net/dsc/database/searchcomplaints.asp.
100 Other disputes, such as those concerning the methodologies used by domestic trade remedy authorities (see e.g. below, pp. 692–6 and 159) are also, at least in some Members, politically very sensitive, albeit they do not attract much attention in the non-specialized media.

systems. Chapter 3 examines in detail the basic principles, institutions and procedures of the WTO dispute settlement system.[101]

3.2.4 Trade Policy Review

A fourth function of the WTO is the administration of the Trade Policy Review Mechanism (TPRM).[102] The TPRM provides for the regular *collective* appreciation and evaluation of the full range of *individual* Members' trade policies and practices and their impact on the functioning of the multilateral trading system.[103] The purpose of the TPRM is: (1) to achieve greater transparency in, and understanding of, the trade policies and practices of Members; and (2) to contribute to improved compliance by all Members with their WTO obligations.[104]

Under the TPRM, the trade policies and practices of all Members are subject to *periodic review*. The frequency of review is determined by reference to each Member's share of world trade in a recent representative period.[105] The four largest trading entities, i.e. the European Union, the United States, Japan and China, are subject to review every two years. The next sixteen are reviewed every four years. Other Members are reviewed every six years, except that for least-developed-country Members a longer period may be fixed.[106]

Trade policy reviews are carried out by the Trade Policy Review Body (TPRB)[107] on the basis of two reports: a report supplied by the Member under review, in which the Member describes the trade policy and practices it pursues; and a report, drawn up by the WTO Secretariat, based on the information available to it and that provided by the Member under review.[108] These reports, together with the concluding remarks by the TPRB Chair and the minutes of the meeting of the TPRB, are published shortly after the review and are a valuable source of information on a WTO Member's trade policy. The reports and the minutes of the TPRB are searchable by country and available on the WTO website as WT/TPR documents.

In 2012, the TPRB carried out twenty reviews.[109]

It is important to note that the TPRM is not intended to serve as a basis for the enforcement of specific obligations under the WTO agreements or for dispute

---

101 See below, pp. 156–310.
102 See Annex 3 to the *WTO Agreement*, entitled 'Trade Policy Review Mechanism'.
103 See Trade Policy Review Mechanism, para. A(i).   104 See above pp. 8–12.   105 See *ibid.*, para. C(ii).
106 Exceptionally, in the event of changes in a Member's trade policies or practices that may have a significant impact on its trading partners, the Member concerned may be requested by the TPRB, after consultation, to bring forward its next review. See *ibid.*
107 See below, pp. 122–4.
108 The two reports cover all aspects of the Member's trade policy broadly speaking, including its domestic laws and regulations; the institutional framework; bilateral, regional and other preferential agreements; the wider economic needs; and the external environment.
109 In 2012, Members reviewed the trade policy and practices of Bangladesh, China, Colombia, Cote d'Ivoire, the East African Community (Burundi, Kenya, Rwanda, Tanzania and Uganda), Guinea-Bissau, Iceland, Israel, Korea, Kuwait, Nepal, Nicaragua, Norway, Philippines, Saudi Arabia, Singapore, Togo, Trinidad and Tobago, Turkey, the United Arab Emirates, the United States and Uruguay. See www.wto.org/english/tratop_e/tpr_e/tpr_e.htm.

settlement procedures.[110] However, by *publicly* deploring inconsistencies with WTO law of a Member's trade policy or practices, the TPRM intends to 'shame' Members into compliance and to support domestic opposition to trade policy and practices inconsistent with WTO law. Likewise, by *publicly* praising WTO-consistent trade policies, the TPRM bolsters, both internationally and domestically, support for such policies. By way of example, note the remarks made by the TPRB Chair at the conclusion of the trade policy review of Bangladesh in 2006. In these concluding remarks, the TPRB Chair stated:

Members commended Bangladesh's efforts to ensure steady growth of GDP through prudent macroeconomic policies and reforms in certain areas, despite endogenous and exogenous challenges. While noting efforts to improve governance, certain Members encouraged Bangladesh to increase its capacity for revenue collection and move away from dependence on tariffs and other border charges as a main source of revenue. Some Members considered that there was room for progress in implementing privatization plans. Members congratulated Bangladesh on its increased Foreign Direct Investment inflows during the period under review and encouraged further improvements in the foreign investment framework. Members noted that Bangladesh's comprehensive poverty reduction strategy had led to an improvement of certain social indicators, including the share of people living below the poverty line. Trade and trade policy measures were an integral part of these efforts.[111]

Trade policy reviews of developing-country Members also give an opportunity to identify the needs of these countries in terms of technical and other assistance. The remarks of the TPRB Chair at the conclusion of the trade policy review of Pakistan in 2002 are also noteworthy:

Purely as an aside, and as much a comment on the review process as on this Review, I was struck by [Pakistan's] Secretary Beg's remarks that questions had given his delegation food for considerable thought and that sources of information had been found of which he was unaware. This goes to the heart of our work: not only do we learn a lot about the Member, but often the Member learns a lot about itself.[112]

Apart from carrying out individual trade policy reviews, the TPRB also undertakes an *annual overview* of developments in the international trading environment, which have an impact on the multilateral trading system. To assist the TPRB with this review, the Director-General presents an *annual report* setting out the major activities of the WTO and highlighting significant policy issues affecting the trading system.

In the context of the global financial and economic crisis, WTO Director-General Pascal Lamy took in February 2009 the initiative to report regularly to the TPRB on developments in trade as a result of the crisis. At the request of the G-20 leaders, the WTO Secretariat, together with the OECD and UNCTAD Secretariats, also prepares regular reports on trade and investment measures taken by

---

110 See Trade Policy Review Mechanism, para. A(i).
111 Trade Policy Review Body – Review of Bangladesh – TPRB's Evaluation, PRESS/TPRB/269, dated 13 and 15 September 2006.
112 Trade Policy Review Body – Review of Pakistan – TPRB's Evaluation, PRESS/TPRB/187, dated 25 January 2002.

the G-20 countries in the face of the crisis.[113] Chapter 1 of this book refers to the findings of these reports.[114]

Questions and Assignments 2.6

What is the objective of the Trade Policy Review Mechanism? Is trade policy review under the WTO comparable with WTO dispute settlement? Find the latest trade policy review reports concerning China, the European Union, Argentina and Burkina Faso on the WTO website. Find also the latest WTO Annual Report and *World Trade Report*.

3.2.5   Cooperation with Other Organisations

Article III:5 of the *WTO Agreement* refers specifically to cooperation with the IMF and the World Bank. Such cooperation is mandated by the need for greater coherence in global economic policy-making. The 'linkages' between the different aspects of global economic policy (financial, monetary and trade) require that the international institutions with responsibilities in these areas follow coherent and mutually supportive policies.[115] The WTO has concluded agreements with both the IMF and the World Bank to give form to the cooperation required by Article III:5 of the *WTO Agreement*.[116] These agreements provide for consultations and the exchange of information between the WTO Secretariat and the staff of the IMF and the World Bank. The WTO, the IMF and the World Bank now cooperate quite closely on a day-to-day basis, in particular in the area of technical assistance to developing countries. Along with three other international organisations,[117] the IMF, the World Bank and the WTO participate actively in the Enhanced Integrated Framework for Trade-Related Technical Assistance (EIF) to help the least-developed countries expand their exports.[118] Furthermore, the IMF and the World Bank have observer status in the WTO, and the WTO attends the meetings of the IMF and the World Bank. Officials of the three organisations meet regularly to discuss issues of global economic policy coherence.

Pursuant to Article V:1 of the *WTO Agreement*, the WTO is also to cooperate with other international organisations. Article V, which is entitled 'Relations with Other Organizations', states in its first paragraph:

> The General Council shall make appropriate arrangements for effective cooperation with other intergovernmental organizations that have responsibilities related to those of the WTO.

The WTO has made cooperation arrangements with, *inter alia*, the World Intellectual Property Organization (WIPO) and the United Nations Conference on

---

113 The first such report is dated 14 September 2009 and is, as are later reports, available on the WTO website.

114 See above, pp. 12–14.

115 See also *Declaration on the Contribution of the World Trade Organization to Achieving Greater Coherence in Global Economic Policymaking*, Final Act Embodying the Results of the Uruguay Round of Multilateral Trade Negotiations, para. 5.

116 See *Agreement between the International Monetary Fund and the World Trade Organization*, contained in Annex I to WT/GC/W/43, dated 4 November 1996; and the *Agreement between the International Bank for Reconstruction and Development and the International Development Association and the World Trade Organization*, contained in Annex II to WT/GC/W/43, dated 4 November 1996.

117 UNCTAD, the ITC and the UNDP.   118 See below, p. 104.

Trade and Development (UNCTAD). In these and other international organisations the WTO has observer status. The WTO and UNCTAD also cooperate in a joint venture, the International Trade Centre (ITC). The ITC works with developing countries and economies in transition to set up effective trade promotion programmes to expand their exports and improve their import operations.

The WTO Director-General participates in the meetings of the United Nations Chief Executives Board (CEB), a body consisting of the heads of UN organisations. The objective of the CEB is to enhance international cooperation on global issues, such as, currently, the international response to the global economic crisis.

In addition, the WTO Secretariat has concluded a large number of so-called Memoranda of Understanding (MOUs) with other international secretariats. These MOUs provide mainly for technical assistance from the WTO to these other secretariats or the geographical regions in which they work. In September 2003, for example, the then WTO Director-General, Supachai Panitchpakdi, and the Secretary-General of the ACP Group, Jean-Robert Goulongana, signed an MOU committing both organisations to cooperate more closely to provide training, technical assistance and support to negotiators of the ACP Member States in the Doha Round.[119] Almost 140 international intergovernmental organisations have been granted formal or *ad hoc* observer status with WTO councils and committees.[120] Likewise, the WTO participates in the work of many international organisations. In all, the WTO Secretariat maintains working relations with almost 200 international organisations active in areas of interest to the WTO.[121]

Apart from cooperating with international intergovernmental organisations, the WTO also cooperates with non-governmental organisations (NGOs). Article V:2 of the *WTO Agreement* states:

> The General Council may make appropriate arrangements for consultation and cooperation with non-governmental organizations concerned with matters related to those of the WTO.

On 18 July 1996, the General Council thus adopted a set of guidelines clarifying the framework for relations with civil society in general and NGOs in particular.[122] In these guidelines, the General Council explicitly recognised 'the role NGOs can play to increase the awareness of the public in respect of WTO activities'.[123] However, the General Council was equally clear that NGOs could not, and should not, be *directly* involved in the work of the WTO. A very modest 'breakthrough' of sorts in the relationship between the WTO and civil society

---

119 The ACP (African, Caribbean and Pacific) Group comprises seventy-nine members, forty of which are least-developed countries, most of them from Africa. The objective of the ACP Group is to contribute to the economic development and social progress of its Member States. See also below, pp. 102–4.

120 See www.wto.org/english/thewto_e/coher_e/coher_e.htm and www.wto.org/english/thewto_e/igo_obs_e.htm.

121 See www.wto.org/english/thewto_e/coher_e/coher_e.htm.

122 *Guidelines for Arrangements on Relations with Non-Governmental Organizations*, Decision adopted by the General Council on 18 July 1996, WT/L/162, dated 23 July 1996.

123 *Ibid.*

was realised in the context of the Singapore Ministerial Conference in December 1996, when NGOs were invited to attend the plenary meetings of the Ministerial Conference.[124] However, the 108 NGOs that attended did not have observer status; they were only passive auditors, and were not allowed to make any statements. Not surprisingly, this degree of involvement did not satisfy civil society, and their dissatisfaction expressed itself in publications and in public debates as well as in large and rowdy demonstrations. The expression of this dissatisfaction reached its apex on the streets of Seattle during the 1999 Ministerial Conference in that American city. Overnight, the global public became familiar with the WTO through images of violent protest against it. In the year following the Seattle debacle, the General Council held informal but intensive consultations on the issue of the involvement of civil society in the work of the WTO.[125] From these consultations, it was clear that no Member wished to undermine the intergovernmental character of the WTO. Moreover, most, if not all, Members were of the opinion that the dialogue with civil society is first and foremost a responsibility for Member governments and should take place at the national level. However, the positions of Members differed significantly on whether civil society, and in particular NGOs, can and should play a greater role in the work of the WTO. On the one hand, the position championed by many of the industrialised Members was (and is) that the involvement of NGOs in the work of the WTO should be a 'two-way street'. The involvement of NGOs should be a 'give and take' relationship; it involves not only informing NGOs about the work and activities of the WTO but also being informed by NGOs on issues of relevance to the WTO. On the other hand, the position of many developing-country Members was (and is) that the relationship between the WTO and NGOs can only be a 'one-way street'. Treading on (very) thin ice, the then WTO Director-General, Mike Moore, noted in March 2002 with regard to the role of NGOs in the WTO:

> The WTO will always remain an inter-governmental organization, because ultimately it is always our member Governments and Parliaments that must ratify any agreements we conclude. We need to encourage better-focused and more constructive inputs from civil society. *They should be given a voice, but not a vote.*[126]

Many Members would not agree to give NGOs 'a voice' in the WTO. The debate on the desirability of the involvement of NGOs in the work of the WTO is a complex one, with both arguments in favour and arguments against such greater involvement. There are four main *arguments in favour* of greater NGO involvement. First, NGO participation will enhance the WTO decision-making process because NGOs have a wealth of specialised knowledge, resources and analytical capacity that governments do not necessarily have. Secondly, public confidence

---

124 Moreover, an NGO centre with facilities for organising gatherings and workshops was set up alongside the official conference centre.

125 This issue is also referred to as the 'external transparency' issue. See also below, footnote 372, p. 145.

126 M. Moore, *How Trade Liberalization Impacts on Employment*, Speech to the International Labour Organization, 18 March 2002. Emphasis added.

in the WTO will increase when NGOs have the opportunity to be heard and to observe the decision-making process. Thirdly, transnational interests and concerns may not be adequately represented by any national government. By allowing NGO involvement in WTO discussions, the WTO would hear about these interests and concerns. Fourthly, hearing NGOs at the WTO can compensate for the fact that NGOs are not always and everywhere heard at the national level. There are equally four main *arguments against* greater involvement of NGOs in the work of the WTO. First, NGO involvement may lead the decision-making process to be captured by special interests. Secondly, many NGOs are neither accountable to an electorate nor representative in a general way, and may thus lack legitimacy. NGOs typically advocate relatively narrow interests. Thirdly, WTO decision-making, with its consensus requirement, is already very difficult. NGO involvement will make negotiations and decision-making even more difficult. Fourthly, since developed-country NGOs are usually better organised and funded than developing-country NGOs, greater NGO involvement would introduce another element of asymmetry in WTO negotiations. Note that most developing-country Members object to greater involvement of NGOs in the WTO because they view many NGOs, and in particular NGOs focusing on environmental or labour issues, as inimical to their interests.[127]

Since Seattle, the WTO's relationship with civil society has much improved, and this not as a result of a major institutional reform but as a result of a number of concrete, pragmatic initiatives by the WTO Secretariat.[128] Today, 'cooperation' with civil society essentially focuses on: (1) symposia or public fora;[129] (2) regular briefings for NGOs on the work of WTO bodies and trade topics of specific interest;[130] (3) the dissemination to WTO Members and the general public of NGO position papers and studies;[131] and (4) the setting up of an NGO centre during ministerial conferences to facilitate the lobbying work of NGOs in the margin of these meetings. The WTO also collaborates with certain NGOs to deliver technical assistance.[132]

One of the most successful outreach activities of the WTO is the annual WTO Public Forum. First organised in 2001, the Public Forum 'has become one of the

---

127 With regard to developing-country NGOs focusing on environmental and labour issues, it has been alleged that the source of funding of these NGOs is not always transparent and may come from developed-country Members.

128 Note also that the mobilisation of civil society against economic globalisation has weakened in force (see above, p. 75); and that the WTO's weakness as a global rule-maker, apparent from its failure to reach agreement in the context of the Doha Development Round negotiations, has made it a much less appealing target for protest. Some would say that civil society has lost interest in the WTO.

129 On the 2011 WTO Public Forum, see below, p. 101.

130 In 2011, the WTO Secretariat undertook 21 NGO briefings. From 2007 to 2011, the WTO Secretariat organised 118 NGO briefings. See *WTO Annual Report 2012*, 127.

131 Note, however, that in 2011 NGOs submitted only three contributions for posting on the WTO website.

132 Note, in this regard, for example, the collaboration with the International Centre for Trade and Sustainable Development (ICTSD) on technical assistance relating to WTO dispute settlement, and in particular the Specialized Training Course on WTO Litigation, organised in April–May 2012. This course also involved the Advisory Centre on WTO Law (ACWL) (see below, p. 301).

most important meeting grounds for dialogue'.[133] In September 2012, the 2012 Public Forum attracted 1,200 participants, among which many NGO representatives, but also government officials, business representatives, academics, students, officials of other international organisations, parliamentarians, lawyers and journalists. Under the title 'Is Multilateralism in Crisis?', the 2012 Public Forum addressed – over three days and in forty-four sessions – issues ranging from, on one end of the spectrum, the benefits and dangers of preferential, plurilateral and bilateral approaches to trade liberalisation, to, on the other end, agricultural innovation, water, food security for least-developed countries and fair trade in the twenty-first century.[134]

The improved and timely access to WTO documents has also contributed to the improvement of the relationship between the WTO and civil society. In the Doha Ministerial Declaration of November 2001, Members stated:

[W]e are committed to making the WTO's operations more transparent, including through more effective and prompt dissemination of information, and to improve dialogue with the public.[135]

In May 2002, WTO Members agreed, after years of discussion, to accelerate the de-restriction of official WTO documents. Pursuant to the Decision of the General Council of 14 May 2002 on *Procedures for the Circulation and De-restriction of WTO Documents*, most WTO documents are now immediately available to the public and those documents that are initially restricted are de-restricted sooner.[136]

Questions and Assignments 2.7

Why and how does the WTO cooperate with international intergovernmental organisations? Why and how does the WTO cooperate with NGOs? Find out on the WTO website about the next WTO/NGO event and about the programme of this year's WTO Public Forum. Would the WTO benefit from a greater role for NGOs in WTO negotiations and decision-making processes?

3.2.6   Technical Assistance to Developing Countries

The functions of the WTO listed in Article III of the *WTO Agreement* do not explicitly include technical assistance to developing-country Members. Yet this is, in practice, an important function of the WTO. Of course, it could be argued that this function is implied in the other functions discussed above, in particular the function of facilitating the implementation, administration and operation, and of furthering the objectives, of the *WTO Agreement*. However, in view of its importance, it deserves to be mentioned separately.

---

133   See *WTO Annual Report 2012*, 126.
134   For a complete overview of the programme of the 2012 WTO Public Forum, see www.wto.org/english/forums_e/public_forum12_e/public_forum12_e.htm.
135   Ministerial Conference, *Doha Ministerial Declaration*, WT/MIN(01)/DEC/1, dated 20 November 2001, para. 10.
136   See General Council, *Procedures for the Circulation and De-restriction of WTO Documents*, WT/L/452, dated 16 May 2002.

In order to exercise their rights and obligations under the *WTO Agreement*, to reap the benefits of their membership of the WTO and to participate fully and effectively in trade negotiations, most developing-country Members need to have more expertise and resources in the area of trade law and policy. This is recognised in many WTO agreements, including the *SPS Agreement*, the *TBT Agreement*, the *TRIPS Agreement*, the *Customs Valuation Agreement* and the *Dispute Settlement Understanding*, which all specifically provide for technical assistance to developing-country Members. This technical assistance may take the form of bilateral assistance, given by other Members, or multilateral assistance, given by, *inter alia*, the WTO.

In the Doha Ministerial Declaration of November 2001, the Ministerial Conference declared that:

technical cooperation and capacity building are core elements of the development dimension of the multilateral trading system.[137]

As an essential element of the Doha Development Agenda, the WTO embarked in 2002 on a programme of greatly enhanced support for developing countries in the form of trade-related technical assistance and training.[138] Under the current Biennial Technical Assistance and Training Plan 2012–2013, the WTO budget for trade-related technical assistance and training amounts to CHF24.2 million for 2012 and CHF24.3 million for 2013.[139] Of this, only about one-fifth comes out of the regular WTO budget. Most comes out of the Doha Development Agenda Global Trust Fund, commonly referred to as the Global Trust Fund or 'GTF'.[140] The GTF is a fund to which Members make *voluntary* contributions. Ensuring timely and adequate levels of funding is obviously a significant challenge, especially in these times of global economic crisis and budget austerity measures by Member governments. However, note that funding levels for 2011 were reportedly sufficient to meet needs.[141]

The WTO's technical assistance and training activities come in many different forms and sizes. In 2011, the WTO organised 267 different activities, either in Geneva or around the world. The technical assistance and training activities undertaken by the WTO include: (1) e-learning courses;[142] (2) regional trade policy

---

137 Ministerial Conference, *Doha Ministerial Declaration*, WT/MIN(01)/DEC/1, dated 20 November 2001, para. 38.
138 For an overview, see M. Smeets, 'Trade Capacity Building in the WTO: Main Achievements Since Doha and Key Challenges', *Journal of World Trade*, forthcoming 2013.
139 See Committee on Trade and Development, *Biennial Technical Assistance and Training Plan 2012–2013 (Revision)*, WT/COMTD/W/180/Rev.1, dated 3 February 2012, 81. CHF24.2 million and CHF24.3 million is equivalent to €20.1 million/US$24.7 million and €20.2 million/US$24.8 million respectively (August 2012 exchange rates).
140 *Ibid.*
141 See *WTO Annual Report 2012*, 122. Also note that, for the *Biennial Technical Assistance and Training Plan 2012–2013*, the budget for WTO technical assistance and training was revised downwards in light of the budget constraints experienced by Members. See WT/COMTD/W/180/Rev.1, dated 3 February 2012, para. 6.
142 There were twenty-six online courses open on a dedicated e-platform accessible from the WTO website. Note that successful participation in these e-learning courses is a prerequisite for eligibility to apply for the trade policy courses mentioned under points (2) and (3) of this list. In 2011, over 5,000 people enrolled in these e-learning courses. See *WTO Annual Report 2012*, 121.

courses and seminars;[143] (3) advanced trade policy courses and seminars held in Geneva;[144] (4) *technical support missions* to specific developing-country Members;[145] (5) the 'WTO reference centres' in developing countries;[146] (6) support for teaching and research on the WTO and international trade;[147] and (7) the 'Geneva Week'.[148] These technical assistance and training activities are coordinated by the Institute for Training and Technical Cooperation (ITTC), which was established within the WTO Secretariat in 2003. The ITTC implements a biennial technical assistance and training plan (TA Plan), adopted by the WTO Committee on Trade and Development, in which all WTO Members are represented.[149]

In recent years, trade-related official development assistance (ODA) has amounted to about US$40 billion a year.[150] The technical assistance and training activities of the WTO – in this larger context very modest – are part of the broader spectrum of bilateral, regional and multilateral efforts to enhance the delivery of 'Aid for Trade'. The Aid for Trade Initiative was launched at the Hong Kong Ministerial Conference in December 2005, and concerns all ODA specifically targeted at assisting developing countries, and in particular least-developed countries, in developing trade-related skills and infrastructure.[151] In addition to the activities listed above, the WTO's role in the context of Aid for Trade is to: (1) ensure that the many national, regional and international donors and organisations understand the *trade-related* needs of developing countries and least-developed countries; (2) encourage them to meet those needs; (3) facilitate and coordinate the efforts made in this respect by different donors and organisations; (4) support improved ways of monitoring and evaluating Aid for Trade; and (5) encouraging mainstreaming of trade into national development strategies.

---

143 In 2011, four three-month courses were held in Colombia, India, Swaziland and Benin. Two shorter courses were held in Turkey and the United Arab Emirates. Moreover, the WTO organised at least one subject-specific regional seminar or workshop per month, in particular on NAMA and other market-access-related subjects. See *ibid.*

144 In 2011, two three-month advanced courses on trade policy (one in English and one in Spanish) and a number of shorter advanced courses focusing on specific topics, such as technical barriers to trade, SPS measures, intellectual property and WTO dispute settlement, were held at the WTO headquarters in Geneva. See *ibid.*

145 Such technical missions are undertaken at the request of the developing-country Member concerned to: (i) assist developing-country Members on specific tasks related to the implementation of obligations under the WTO agreements (such as the adoption of trade legislation or notifications), and/or (ii) provide support to mainstream trade into national plans for economic development.

146 In 2011, nine WTO reference centres were established in developing-country Members. See *ibid.*, p. 120.

147 This support is provided through the WTO Chairs Programme, which now encompasses fifteen universities in developing-country Members and least-developed-country Members, and the Academic Support Programme, which supports academic institutions from developing-country and least-developed-country Members outside the scope of the WTO Chairs Programme. See *WTO Annual Report 2012*, 131.

148 The 'Geneva Week' is a special week-long event which brings to Geneva representatives of developing-country Members without a permanent representation (see below, p. 120) to brief them on recent developments at the WTO. In 2011, the WTO organised the 'Geneva Week' twice, once back-to-back with the Geneva Ministerial Conference in December 2011. See *WTO Annual Report 2012*, 121.

149 See below, p. 126. For the current biennial technical assistance and training plan, see WT/COMTD/W/180/Rev.1, dated 3 February 2012.

150 See *WTO Annual Report 2012*, pp. 113–14.

151 See Ministerial Declaration adopted on 18 December 2005 at the Hong Kong Ministerial Conference (6th MC), see WT/MIN(05)/DEC, dated 22 December 2005, para. 57.

The main mechanism through which least-developed countries access Aid for Trade resources is the Enhanced Integrated Framework for Least-Developed Countries (EIF). The WTO is one of the six partner agencies of the EIF, along with the IMF, the World Bank, UNCTAD, UNDP and the ITC. The EIF Executive Secretariat is housed at the WTO.[152]

In 2007, the WTO took the initiative to organise the First Global Review of Aid for Trade, a two-day meeting attended by donor governments, other international organisations, civil society and the private sector, to assess critically the success of the Aid for Trade initiative. The Third Global Review, which took place in July 2011, showed that trade-related assistance has helped to alleviate poverty by increasing export performance and employment.[153] Trade is increasingly an integral part of national development policies. The Review noted a substantial increase in Aid for Trade over the years but also highlighted the need to: (1) ensure additional and predictable Aid for Trade flows; (2) measure the effectiveness of Aid for Trade; and (3) ensure that Aid for Trade is always compatible with the goals of sustainable development.[154] The Fourth Global Review will take place in 2013.

Questions and Assignments 2.8

Give a brief overview of the technical assistance and training activities of the WTO. How does the WTO coordinate its technical assistance efforts with the efforts of other organisations and donors? Look up how much of the WTO budget of the current year is earmarked for technical cooperation, trade policy courses and the WTO contribution to the International Trade Centre. Are there other funds available for WTO technical assistance and training activities?

4   MEMBERSHIP AND INSTITUTIONAL STRUCTURE

The *institutional structure* of the WTO differs little from that of many other intergovernmental international organisations. By contrast, its *membership* has features that are uncommon among these organisations. Below, both the WTO's membership and its institutional structure will be discussed in turn.

4.1   Membership of the WTO

With 159 Members,[155] representing 99.5 per cent of the world population and 97 per cent of world trade, the WTO is a universal organisation.[156] This section

---

152 Note in this context also the *Standards and Trade Development Facility*: see below, p. 947.
153 See the OECD/WTO study on Aid for Trade at a Glance 2011: Showing Results (OECD Publishing, 2011).
154 See *WTO Annual Review 2012*, pp. 113–15. In view of the need to ensure that Aid for Trade is always compatible with the goals of sustainable development, the 2012–13 Aid for Trade work programme is based around the theme 'Deepening Coherence'.
155 Tajikistan joined the WTO as its 159th Member on 2 March 2013.
156 Calculated on the basis of data available on the website of the World Bank and the WTO.

will consecutively deal with: (1) the current membership of the WTO; (2) accession to the WTO; (3) waivers and opt-outs; and (4) withdrawal, suspension and expulsion.

4.1.1   Current Membership

The composition of the current membership of the WTO is very diverse as well as confusing. It includes States but also separate customs territories; it includes all developed countries but also most developing countries; it includes the European Union but also all EU Member States; and it features multiple, often overlapping, groups, coalitions and alliances pursuing different goals.

First, the WTO membership does not include only States. Separate customs territories possessing full autonomy in the conduct of their external commercial relations and in the other matters covered by the *WTO Agreement* can also be WTO Members.[157] There are currently three WTO Members which are not States but separate customs territories: Hong Kong, China (commonly referred to as Hong Kong), Macau, China (commonly referred to as Macau) and Chinese Taipei (which joined the WTO as the Separate Customs Territory of Taiwan, Penghu, Kinmen and Matsu).[158]

Secondly, three-quarters of the 159 Members of the WTO are developing countries. There is no WTO definition of a 'developing country'. The status of 'developing-country Member' is based, to a large extent, on self-selection. Members announce whether they consider themselves 'developing' countries.[159] As discussed throughout this book, developing-country Members benefit from special and differential treatment under many of the WTO agreements and may receive WTO technical assistance.[160] Other Members can, and occasionally do, challenge the decision of a Member to claim developing-country member status and to make use of special and differential treatment provisions available to developing countries. For some Members, such as China, the status of 'developing-country Member' was part of the accession negotiations.[161]

The group of WTO developing-country Members is very diverse in its composition. This group includes: continent-sized countries and minuscule island States; fast-growing, export-oriented emerging economies and quasi-autarkic countries; agricultural-products-exporting countries and net-food-importing countries; mineral-rich countries and countries less endowed by nature; and democratic, well-governed countries and totalitarian, corruption-riddled countries.

---

157 See Article XII:1 of the *WTO Agreement*. The Explanatory Notes attached to the *WTO Agreement* stipulate that the 'terms "country" or "countries" as used in this Agreement and the Multilateral Trade Agreements are to be understood to include any separate customs territory Member of the WTO'.

158 On the European Union, see below, pp. 106–7.

159 Note that, in the context of the national Generalized Systems of Preferences (GSP), adopted under the Enabling Clause of the GATT 1994 (see below, pp. 331–4), it is, on the contrary, the preference-giving Member that decides which countries qualify for the preferential tariff treatment.

160 See e.g. below, pp. 663, 668, 834, 1010 and 301.

161 See Report of the Working Party on the Accession of China, WT/ACC/CHN/49, dated 1 October 2001, paras. 8 and 9.

The group of WTO developing-country Members includes: upper-middle income countries, such as Brazil, China, Russia, South Africa, Ecuador and Saint Lucia; lower-middle income countries, such as India, Pakistan, Nigeria, Egypt, Ghana and Tonga; and low income countries, such as Bangladesh, Cambodia, Haiti, Kenya, Mali and Nepal.[162] As discussed in Chapter 1 as well as later in this chapter, over the last decade, developing-country Members, and in particular the emerging economies among them, have played an ever more important role in the WTO, not so much because of their numbers but because of their increasing importance in the global economy.[163]

Among the low income country Members, there are currently thirty-four least-developed countries. Least-developed-country Members constitute one-fifth of the WTO membership. The WTO recognises as least-developed countries those countries which have been designated as such by the United Nations.[164] As discussed throughout this book, least-developed-country Members benefit from *additional* special and differential treatment.[165] By far the most populous of the least-developed-country Members is Bangladesh. The group of least-developed-country Members further includes many African countries, such as Angola, Mozambique and Tanzania, and a few Asian countries, such as Cambodia, Laos and Myanmar.

A third aspect of the diverse and confusing nature of the current WTO membership is the status of the European Union and its twenty-seven Member States.[166] Article XI:1 of the *WTO Agreement* explicitly provides for the WTO membership of the 'European Communities', now referred to as the 'European Union'.[167] At the same time, all EU Member States are also WTO Members. This 'dual' membership reflects the division of competence between the European Union and its Member States in the various policy areas covered by the *WTO*

---

162 For this classification of countries as upper middle income (GNI per capita of US$4,036 to US$12,475), lower-middle income (GNI per capita of US$1,026 to US$4,035) and low income (GNI per capita of US$1,025 or lower), see the World Bank website.

163 See above, pp. 8–12, and below, pp. 144–8. On the question whether 'emerging economies' should still benefit from special and differential treatment linked to the status of developing-country Member, see below, pp. 663–4.

164 The United Nations designates forty-eight countries as least-developed. See UNCTAD, *The Least Developed Countries Report 2012*, UNCTAD/LDC/2012. Note that the share of world trade of the least-developed countries is 1.1 per cent of the total. See also above, pp. 11–12.

165 See above, p. 114.

166 Note that Croatia is set to become the twenty-eighth Member State of the European Union on 1 July 2013.

167 On 29 November 2009, the World Trade Organization received a Verbal Note (WT/L/779) from the Council of the European Union and the Commission of the European Communities stating that, by virtue of the *Treaty of Lisbon amending the Treaty on European Union and the Treaty establishing the European Community* (done at Lisbon, 13 December 2007), as of 1 December 2009, the 'European Union' replaces and succeeds the 'European Community'. On 13 July 2010, the World Trade Organization received a second Verbal Note (WT/Let/679) from the Council of the European Union confirming that, with effect from 1 December 2009, the European Union replaced the European Community and assumed all the rights and obligations of the European Community in respect of all WTO agreements. Note that the Verbal Notes refer to the 'European Community' rather than the 'European Communities', the term used in Article XI:1 of the *WTO Agreement*. In *EC and certain member States – Large Civil Aircraft (2011)*, the Appellate Body stated that it 'understand[s] the reference in the Verbal Notes to the "European Community" to be a reference to the "European Communities"'. See Appellate Body Report, *EC and certain member States – Large Civil Aircraft (2011)*, footnote 1.

Agreement. However, it is important to note the following. First, both the European Union and all EU Member States are *full* Members of the WTO and that all rights and obligations of the *WTO Agreement* apply equally to all of them. Secondly, in practice, it is the European Commission that will act and speak for the European Union *and* all EU Member States in WTO meetings and negotiations.[168]

A fourth aspect of the diverse and confusing nature of the current WTO membership is that the membership features multiple, often overlapping, groups, coalitions and alliances pursuing different goals.[169] The developing-country Members, the least-developed-country Members, and the European Union and its Member States are not the only distinguishable groups within the WTO membership. Other formal or informal groups and alliances exist in the WTO. Some of these groups have been formed to defend common interests and advance common positions; they coordinate (or try to coordinate) positions and, when appropriate, speak in unison. This category of groups includes the Association of South East Asian Nations (ASEAN), the Group of Latin America and Caribbean Countries (GRULAC) and the African, Caribbean and Pacific Group (ACP). However, the North American Free Trade Agreement (NAFTA) and the Southern Common Market (MERCOSUR), while constituting significant efforts at regional economic integration, have not, or have hardly ever, spoken with one voice within the WTO. A well-known and quite effective alliance of a different kind was the Cairns group of nineteen agricultural-products-exporting developed and developing countries, including Canada, Australia, Brazil and Indonesia. This group was set up in the mid-1980s to campaign for agricultural trade liberalisation and was an important force in negotiations on trade in agricultural products. However, at the Cancún Ministerial Conference in September 2003, the Cairns group seemed to have all but disappeared. In the run-up to, and at, the Cancún Ministerial Conference, a new influential group of developing countries, including China, India, Indonesia, Brazil, Egypt, Argentina and South Africa, emerged. This group, commonly referred to as the 'G-20',[170] forcefully demanded the dismantling of the trade-distorting and protectionist agricultural policies of the European Union, the United States and other industrialised countries.[171]

---

168 This is not the case for matters relating to the WTO budget. In particular, in the Budget Committee, the EU Member States, and not the European Commission, are active. On the contributions by the European Union and its Member States to the WTO budget, see below, pp. 149–51.

169 For a list of, and a map showing geographically, the groupings, coalitions and alliances of WTO Members, see www.wto.org/english/tratop_e/dda_e/negotiating_groups_maps_e.htm.

170 Note that, *outside* the WTO, the 'G-20' commonly refers to a different group of countries, consisting of the major (developed as well as developing) economies, which as a group account for more than 80 per cent of the gross world product, 80 per cent of world trade and two-thirds of the world's population. This group has met regularly since 2008 to discuss international (economic) issues.

171 The G-20 includes countries from Africa (Egypt, Nigeria, South Africa, Tanzania and Zimbabwe), from Asia (China, India, Indonesia, Pakistan, Philippines and Thailand) and from Latin America (Argentina, Bolivia, Brazil, Chile, Cuba, Mexico, Paraguay and Venezuela). Contrary to what the term 'G-20' seems to imply, the *number* of countries that are members of the G-20 has in fact varied over time.

Also in Cancún, a new group known as the ACP/LDC/AU alliance, but also referred to as the 'G-90', emerged as the 'representative' of the interests of the poorest countries.[172] Among the many other 'common interest' groups, coalitions and alliances, note the 'Cotton Four' or 'C-4', a group of four West African cotton-producing Members, campaigning against the 'unfair' practices of the United States and the European Union affecting trade in cotton.[173] As discussed below, 'common interest' groups, coalitions and alliances play an important role in helping developing-country Members to overcome, or at least mitigate, their lack of resources and expertise, and to participate more effectively in WTO negotiations and decision-making.[174]

Other groups have been formed to allow for discussion in small(er) groups of Members, to agree new initiatives, to break deadlocks and to achieve compromises. The best-known example of such a group was the 'Quad', which during the Uruguay Round and in the early years of the WTO was the group of the then four largest trading entities, i.e. the European Communities, the United States, Japan and Canada. The Quad was at the core of all negotiations. However, the Quad has now been replaced by a new group of key WTO Members, the G-5, consisting of the European Union, the United States, India, Brazil and China.[175] As already noted above, without agreement among these key Members, progress within the WTO on the further liberalisation and/or regulation of trade is not feasible. This shift in political power within the WTO reflects the growing importance of China, India and Brazil in the world economy.[176]

Finally, note that, in addition to Members, the WTO also has twenty-six Observer Governments. With the exception of the Holy See, these Observer Governments must start accession negotiations within five years of becoming an Observer. Intergovernmental international organisations, such as the UN, the IMF, the World Bank, UNCTAD, the FAO, WIPO and the OECD, have also permanent Observer status. Other international organisations have Observer status in the WTO bodies that deal in particular with the matters within their mandate. As such, the Joint FAO/WHO Codex Alimentarius Commission has Observer status

---

172 This group is made up of the ACP countries, the least-developed countries and the countries of the African Union.

173 Note further the following 'common interest' groups: G-10 (regarding non-trade concerns in agriculture); G-33 ('Friends of Special Products' in agriculture); NAMA-11 (regarding limits on market opening for industrial products); Small, Vulnerable Economies (SVEs); Friends of Fish (FoFs); Friends of Anti-Dumping Negotiations (FANs); Recently Acceded Members (RAMs); and the Informal Group of Developing Countries (formerly the G-110) (G-90, plus countries belonging to the G-20, G-33, NAMA-11 and the SVE Group).

174 See below, pp. 105–9.

175 Next to the G-5, also the G-7, consisting of the G-5 plus Japan and Australia, has played a role since the demise of the Quad in efforts to agree on new initiatives, to break deadlocks and to achieve compromises. This was the case, for example, during the intense Doha Round negotiations in July 2008. Note that, *outside* the WTO, the 'G-7' refers to a different group of countries, namely, the group of the major developed economies, which have met regularly since 1975 to discuss international (economic) issues. Since 1997, Russia also participates in these meetings (transforming the G-7 into the G-8). Finally, note that the term 'G-5' is occasionally (and confusingly) also used to refer to the group of the five major emerging economies (Brazil, China, India, Mexico and South Africa).

176 See above, p. 1018.

in the WTO SPS Committee; and the Convention on International Trade in Endangered Species (CITES) has Observer status in the WTO Committee on Trade and Environment.[177]

Questions and Assignments 2.9

Can non-State entities become Members of the WTO? If so, give three examples of such Members. When will a country 'qualify' as a developing-country Member or as a least-developed-country Member? Is it easy or common for developing-country Members of the WTO to speak with one voice? Do the Member States of the EU speak with one voice in the context of the WTO? Do all EU Member States have *full* WTO membership? Since when has the European Union, rather than the European Communities, been a Member of the WTO? What is the *raison d'être* of the 'G-20' and the 'G-5'? What does the FANs group lobby for? Comment on the demise of the 'Quad' and the emergence of the 'G-5'.

4.1.2   Accession

Becoming a Member of the WTO is not an easy matter. This sub-section discusses the accession process and looks at some past accessions and ongoing accession negotiations.

The *WTO Agreement* initially provided for two ways of becoming a WTO Member. The first, 'original membership', was provided for in Article XI:1 of the *WTO Agreement*, and allowed Contracting Parties to the GATT 1947 (and the European Communities) to join the WTO by: (1) accepting the terms of the *WTO Agreement* and the Multilateral Trade Agreements; and (2) making concessions and commitments for both trade in goods and services (embodied in national goods and services schedules respectively). This way of becoming a WTO Member was only available at the time of establishment of the WTO.[178] Of the 159 WTO Members, 123 are 'original Members' in that they became Members pursuant to Article XI:1 of the *WTO Agreement*.[179]

The second way of becoming a WTO Member is through accession, and this way is open indefinitely. The procedure for accession is set out in Article XII of the *WTO Agreement*. To become a WTO Member through accession, a State or customs territory has to negotiate the terms of accession with the current Members. The applicant for membership must in principle always accept the terms of the *WTO Agreement* and all Multilateral Trade Agreements. This is not up for negotiation.[180] The accession negotiations focus on: (1) whether the legislation

---

177   For an exhaustive list of all international organisations having Observer status in the WTO or in one or more WTO bodies, see www.wto.org/english/thewto_e/igo_obs_e.htm, visited on 15 February 2013.

178   The term 'original membership' is a misnomer. It suggests that there are two sorts of membership with different rights and obligations. This is not the case. In principle, all Members have the same membership rights and obligations. The term 'original membership' is used merely to distinguish between the different ways of acquiring membership. It must be noted, however, that, in the context of WTO accession negotiations, applicants for membership have in certain cases been forced to accept 'WTO-plus' obligations and/or 'WTO-minus' rights. See below, p. 113.

179   Yugoslavia is the only GATT Contracting Party which did not become a WTO Member in this way.

180   However, there may be negotiations on whether the applicant for membership should be allowed a transitional period for compliance with specific obligations.

and practices of the applicant for membership are WTO-consistent, and, if not, what needs to be done to make them so; and (2) the market access concessions (for trade in goods) and commitments (for trade in services) the applicant for membership has to make. With regard to the latter, it could be said that the price of the 'ticket of admission' is negotiated. When a State or customs territory accedes to the WTO, it instantly benefits from all the efforts that WTO Members have undertaken in the past to reduce barriers to trade and increase market access. In return for the access to the markets of current Members that a new Member will obtain, that new Member will itself have to open up its market to the current Members. The extent of the market access concessions and commitments that an applicant for membership will be expected to make, or in other words the price of the 'ticket of admission' that it will be expected to pay, will depend to a large extent on its level of economic development.

Generally speaking, there are four phases in the accession process. In the first phase – the 'tell-us-about-yourself' phase[181] – the State or customs territory applying for membership has to report on all aspects of its trade and economic policies that are relevant to the obligations under the WTO agreements, and has to submit a memorandum on these policies to the WTO. A WTO working party, established especially to deal with the request for accession and composed of all (interested) WTO Members, will, on the basis of this 'memorandum on the foreign trade regime' and additional information supplied later, examine with care the WTO-consistency of the relevant legislation and practices of the applicant for membership.

When the working party has made satisfactory progress with its examination of the trade and economic policies of the applicant for membership, the second phase is initiated. In this phase – the 'work-out-with-us-individually-what-you-have-to-offer' phase – individual Members and the applicant for membership start bilateral negotiations on market access. Since different Members obviously have different export interests, these negotiations cannot but be bilateral. However, the new Member's market access concessions and commitments, made in any of the bilateral negotiations, will eventually apply equally to all WTO Members as a result of the MFN treatment obligation.[182] These bilateral market access negotiations can be very difficult.

When the working party has fully completed its examination of the WTO-consistency of relevant legislation and practices of the applicant *and* individual Members and the applicant for membership have successfully concluded the their bilateral market access negotiations, the third phase of the accession process can start. In this phase – the 'let-us-draft-membership-terms' phase – the working party finalises the terms of accession which are set out in: (1) a working party report; (2) a draft 'protocol of accession'; and (3) the draft 'goods schedule'

---

181 For the name given to this and the other phases, see the WTO website, www.wto.org.
182 On the MFN treatment obligation, see above, p. 36, and below, pp. 315–47.

and 'services schedule', which list all of the market access concessions and commitments of the applicant for membership. This package is submitted to the Ministerial Conference or the General Council.

In the fourth and final phase of the accession process – the 'decision' phase – the Ministerial Conference or the General Council decides, in practice by consensus, on the application for membership.[183] In case of a positive decision, the candidate for membership accedes to the WTO thirty days after it has deposited its instrument of ratification of the protocol of accession. Note that protocols of accession become integral parts of the *WTO Agreement* and are enforceable in dispute settlement.[184]

Even when no major problems are encountered, accession negotiations typically take much time. The shortest accession negotiation to date was that of Kyrgyzstan, lasting two years and ten months. The accession negotiations with Algeria have been going on since 1987.[185] The delays in completing accession negotiations have been severely criticised. However, this situation is not only the result of hard bargaining on the part of WTO Members or political factors. It is also a result of the tardy supply of information by the applicant and the slow pace at which it makes the necessary amendments to its legislation and practices.[186] It can take years to draft, approve and apply the new legislation required for accession to the WTO. As noted by the Minister of Industry and Commerce of Laos at the conclusion of Laos' accession negotiations in September 2012:

> We ... underestimated the difficult negotiations we would have to undergo at the internal front. Quite frankly, trying to convince our trading partners of the position of Lao PDR only to go home, and to convince our internal partners of the justification of the reforms requested, was one of our most difficult and hard tasks.[187]

Over the last five years, Cape Verde (2008), Ukraine (2008), Montenegro (2012), Samoa (2012), Russia (2012), Vanuatu (2012), Laos (2013) and Tajikistan (2013) joined the WTO. Russia was the last major country to join the WTO. On 16 December 2011, the Ministerial Conference adopted the Protocol on the Accession of the Russian Federation, and Russia subsequently became a Member of the WTO on 22 August 2012.[188] While quite different from the accession negotiations with China,

---

183 On decision-making within the WTO, see below, pp. 136–47.

184 See above, p. 55. The terms of accession are set out in the Protocol of Accession *and* the accompanying working party report. The commitments set out in the working party report, and incorporated in the Protocol by cross-reference, are binding and enforceable. See Panel Reports, *China – Raw Materials (2012)*, paras. 7.112 and 7.114.

185 Algeria originally applied to become a Contracting Party to the GATT 1947 (as it then was).

186 Least-developed countries, in particular, often lack the administrative capacity to conduct the complex negotiations and to draft and apply the necessary changes in national legislation and practices. On General Council guidelines to facilitate the accession of least-developed countries to the WTO (adopted in 2002 and 2012), see below, p. 112.

187 See *Bridges Weekly*, 3 October 2012.

188 Note that, at the time of the adoption of the Russian Accession Protocol, the United States invoked the 'non-application' clause of Article XIII of the *WTO Agreement* with regard to Russia, and Russia invoked this clause against the United States. See below, p. 117.

discussed below,[189] the accession negotiations with Russia were also fraught with disagreements and obstacles.[190] They took eighteen years to complete. In order to join the WTO, Russia had to bring 300 legal acts into conformity with WTO law and had to make substantial market access concessions and commitments.[191] However, according to Russia's Minister of Economic Development, the benefits of accession are expected to be numerous, and include: (1) 'improved quality of goods'; (2) 'a signal to investors of a better business climate'; and (3) 'having access to the WTO's dispute settlement system'.[192]

In December 2012, there were twenty-four States negotiating their accession to the WTO, including Algeria, Iran, Iraq, Serbia and nine least-developed countries.[193] On 25 July 2012, the General Council approved, at the recommendation of the Sub-Committee on Least-Developed Countries, new guidelines to facilitate and speed up accession negotiations with least-developed countries.[194] Of particular interest is that the General Council's Decision sets out concrete guidelines for Members on how to apply 'restraint' when seeking concessions and commitments from least-developed countries applying for membership.

The most difficult and most important accession negotiations ever conducted were those with the People's Republic of China. In 1947, China was one of the original signatories of the GATT, but, after the revolution in 1949, the Chinese nationalist government in Chinese Taipei announced that China would leave the GATT system. The Government of the People's Republic of China in Beijing never recognised this withdrawal decision and, in 1986, it notified the GATT of its wish to resume its status as a GATT Contracting Party. The GATT CONTRACTING PARTIES considered, however, that China would have to negotiate its re-accession. In 1987, a GATT Working Party on the Accession of China was established, and in 1995 this Working Party was converted into a WTO Working Party. The accession negotiations with China eventually took almost fifteen years and resulted in a legal text of some 900 pages. On 10 November 2001, in Doha, the Ministerial Conference approved by consensus the Protocol on the

---

189 See below, pp. 472–4. Unlike Russia's main exports (oil, gas and minerals), China's main exports (manufactured products) competed with, and constituted a threat to, products of the then WTO Members.

190 The last obstacle to overcome was the opposition of neighbouring WTO Member Georgia to Russia's accession. In 2008, Russia and Georgia fought a brief war over South Ossetia, a disputed border area. A last-minute deal brokered by Switzerland ensured that Georgia did not block the consensus on Russia's accession. On decision-making on accession, see below, pp. 137–8.

191 See WT/L/839, dated 17 December 2011, containing the Decision of the Ministerial Conference of 16 December 2011, with, in an annex, Russia's Protocol of Accession. See also the Report of the Working Party on the Accession of Russia, WT/ACC/RUS/70, dated 17 November 2011.

192 'After Eighteen Year "Marathon", Russia Crosses WTO Finish Line', *Bridges Daily Update*, 17 December 2011.

193 *WTO Accessions, 2012 Annual Report by the Director-General*, WT/ACC/19, 3 December 2012.

194 This Decision, which is set out in document WT/COMTD/LDC/21, dated 6 July 2012, strengthens the General Council Decision of 10 December 2002 on the facilitation and acceleration of the negotiations for the accession of LDCs to the WTO, contained in document WT/L/508, dated 20 January 2003. Note that, since 1995, only six least-developed countries (Cambodia (2004), Nepal (2004), Cape Verde (2008), Samoa (2012), Vanuatu (2012) and Laos (2013)) acceded to the WTO pursuant to Article XII of the *WTO Agreement*. As of 6 December 2012, nine least-developed countries were in the process of negotiating their accession to the WTO, of which Yemen was reportedly close to concluding its accession negotiations.

Accession of the People's Republic of China.[195] On 11 December 2001, China formally became a Member of the WTO.

In order to join the WTO, China agreed to: (1) important market access concessions and commitments; (2) some, as they have been called, 'WTO-plus' obligations and 'WTO-minus' rights; and (3) more generally, offer a more predictable environment for trade and foreign investment in accordance with WTO rules. While China reserves the right of exclusive State trading for products such as cereals, tobacco, fuels and minerals, and maintains some restrictions on transportation and distribution of goods inside the country, many of the restrictions on foreign companies were to be eliminated or considerably eased after a three-year phase-out period. During a twelve-year period starting from the date of accession, a special transitional safeguard mechanism applied. This mechanism allowed other WTO Members to restrict – more easily than under the normal rules on safeguard measures – imports of products of Chinese origin that cause or threaten to cause market disruption to their domestic producers.[196] China is also bound under its Protocol of Accession not to impose export duties on most of its exports, while most WTO Members are not subject to such obligation.[197] On the other hand, measures adversely affecting imports from China in a manner inconsistent with WTO obligations, are phased out, or otherwise dealt with, by the Members maintaining such measures in accordance with mutually agreed terms and timetables specified in an annex to the Protocol of Accession.[198]

Questions and Assignments 2.10

Is the country of which you are a national an 'original Member' of the WTO? Does it matter whether it is or not? Why are WTO accession negotiations often so difficult and take so long? Discuss the various steps in the process of accession to the WTO. Did some applicants for WTO membership have to accept 'WTO-plus' obligations and/or 'WTO-minus' rights to be able to join the WTO?

4.1.3   Special and Differential Treatment

As discussed above, many WTO Members are developing countries and thirty-four of them are least-developed countries.[199] Their level of economic development and, with a few exceptions, their participation in international trade are obviously not on a par with those of developed-country Members. As explicitly stated in the Preamble to the *WTO Agreement*, there is:

---

195 See WT/L/432, dated 23 November 2001, containing the Decision of the Ministerial Conference of 10 November 2001, with, in Annex, the Protocol on the Accession of the People's Republic of China. See also the Report of the Working Party on the Accession of China, WT/ACC/CHN/49, dated 1 October 2001.
196 See below, pp. 634–5. Note in this regard the *China – Tyres (2011)* dispute. For a discussion on the additional safeguard system for Chinese textiles, see also below, p. 634, footnote 146.
197 See below, pp. 473–4. Note in this regard the *China – Raw Materials (2012)* dispute.
198 See 'WTO Successfully Concludes Negotiations on China's Entry', WTO Press/243, dated 17 September 2001.
199 See above, p. 106.

need for positive efforts designed to ensure that developing countries, and especially the least developed among them, secure a share in the growth in international trade commensurate with the needs of their economic development.

The 'positive efforts' in favour of developing countries undertaken by the WTO take many forms. Almost all WTO agreements have provisions providing for 'special and differential treatment' for developing-country Members to facilitate their integration into the world trading system and to promote their economic development. These 'special and differential treatment' provisions can be subdivided into six categories: (1) provisions aimed at increasing the trade opportunities of developing-country Members; (2) provisions under which WTO developed-country Members should safeguard the interests of developing-country Members; (3) provisions allowing for flexibility of commitments, of action, and use of policy instruments; (4) provisions on transitional time periods; and (5) provisions on technical assistance. In many cases, *additional* special and differential treatment is provided for least-developed-country Members. Therefore, with regard to membership rights and obligations, not all Members are equal. For good reason, there are at least three different categories of Members: developed-country Members, developing-country Members, and least-developed-country Members.[200]

A detailed overview of all WTO 'special and differential treatment' provisions, agreement by agreement, can be found in the 2001 Note by the WTO Secretariat on *Implementation of Special and Differential Treatment Provisions in WTO Agreements and Decisions*.[201] In this book, the 'special and differential treatment' provisions are discussed in the context of the rules to which they relate. For example, Chapter 6 on 'Tariff barriers' discusses Article XXXVI:8 of the GATT 1994, which provides that, in tariff negotiations with developed-country Members, developing-country Members are expected to 'reciprocate' only to the extent that is consistent with their development, financial and trade needs.[202]

Note that many 'special and differential treatment' provisions are couched in hortatory language, or at most entail 'best endeavour' obligation.[203] Not surprisingly, developing-country Members have therefore expressed serious concerns regarding the effectiveness of these provisions to address the problems they face. It was therefore agreed that, as part of the Doha Round negotiations, all 'special and differential treatment' provisions shall be reviewed 'with a view of strengthening them and making them more precise, effective and operational'.[204]

---

200 In addition, there may be Members, which, as a result of the terms of their Protocol of Accession, are subject to 'WTO plus' obligations and 'WTO-minus' rights. See below, p. 473.

201 See Committee on Trade and Development, *Implementation of Special and Differential Treatment Provisions in WTO Agreements and Decisions*, Note by the WTO Secretariat, WT/COMTD/W/77/Rev.1, dated 21 September 2001, para. 3. See also the addenda to this Note and, in particular, Addendum 4, WT/COMTD/W/77/Rev.1/Add.4, dated 7 February 2002.

202 See below, pp. 429–31 .

203 See, for example, Article 15 of the *Anti-Dumping Agreement*, discussed below, pp. 737–9; or Article 10.1 of the *SPS Agreement*, discussed below, pp. 939–40.

204 See Doha Ministerial Declaration, para. 44.

Developed-country Members have, however, insisted on the need to differentiate among developing-country Members between, on the one hand, 'emerging economies', of which the GDP in some cases equals or even surpasses the GDP of some EU Member States, and, on the other hand, other developing-country Members still in need of special and differential treatment. Not surprisingly, emerging economies have shown little enthusiasm for such differentiation. Disagreement on who still 'deserves' special and differential treatment is one of the causes for the impasse in the Doha Round negotiations, discussed above.[205]

4.1.4   Waivers and Opt-Outs

Article XVI:4 of the *WTO Agreement* provides that:

> Each Member shall ensure the conformity of its laws, regulations and administrative procedures with its obligations as provided in the annexed Agreements.[206]

However, when a Member finds it difficult, if not impossible, to meet an obligation under one of the WTO agreements, that Member can request the WTO to waive the 'problematic' obligation. Pursuant to Article IX:3 of the *WTO Agreement*, 'exceptional circumstances' may justify such a waiver.[207] The decision of the Ministerial Conference (or the General Council) granting the waiver shall state the exceptional circumstances, the terms and conditions governing the application of the waiver and the date on which the waiver shall be terminated.[208] In 2012, the General Council granted four new waivers and extended two previously granted waivers; there were in total twenty-two waivers in force in 2012.[209]

As is provided in Article IX:4 of the *WTO Agreement*, any waiver granted for a period of more than one year is reviewed annually. The General Council examines whether the exceptional circumstances justifying the waiver still exist and whether the terms and conditions attached to the waiver have been met. On the basis of this annual review, the waiver may be extended, modified or terminated.

One of the most important waivers, which was in force from 2001 to 2007, was a waiver of the MFN treatment obligation of Article I:1 of the GATT 1994, granted to the then European Communities, with respect to preferential tariff treatment given to products of African, Caribbean and Pacific countries under the terms of the Cotonou *ACP–EC Partnership Agreement*. Similar waivers, currently in force, are: (1) the waiver granted to the European Union allowing

---

205 See above, pp. 87–94.
206 With regard to reservations to the provisions of the WTO agreements, note that Article XVI:5 of the *WTO Agreement* provides that no reservations may be made in respect of provisions of the *WTO Agreement*, and reservations in respect of any of the provisions of the Multilateral Trade Agreements may only be made to the extent provided for in those Agreements. See e.g. Article 15.1 of the *TBT Agreement*, which states that no reservations may be entered without the consent of the other Members.
207 Note that, for waivers of GATT 1994 obligations, provisions of the *Understanding in Respect of Waivers of Obligations under the General Agreement on Tariffs and Trade 1994* also apply.
208 Article IX:4 of the *WTO Agreement*. As discussed below, decisions on waivers are, in practice, always taken by consensus. See below, pp. 115–17.
209 See WT/GC/W/665, dated 10 January 2013.

it to grant preferential tariff treatment to countries of the Western Balkans to 'promote economic expansion and recovery';[210] and (2) the waiver granted to the United States allowing it to provide duty-free treatment to products from Sub-Saharan African countries under the African Growth and Opportunity Act (AGOA) to 'alleviate poverty and promote stability and sustainable economic development in sub-Saharan Africa'.[211]

A well-known waiver is the waiver granted to Members producing, under a compulsory licence, essential medicines for HIV, malaria and other life-threatening diseases for export to eligible least-developed countries.[212] Under this waiver, the obligations under Article 31(f) and (h) of the *TRIPS Agreement* are waived to give least-developed-countries access to these essential medicines.[213] Another waiver worth noting is the waiver granted to a large group of Members to allow these Members to take domestic measures under the Kimberley Process aimed at banning trade in conflict diamonds, also referred to as 'blood diamonds'.[214] Under this waiver, the obligations under Articles I, XI and XIII of the GATT 1994 are waived.[215] Among the waivers approved in 2012, note the waiver granted to the European Union allowing the latter to lift for two years customs duties on certain products from Pakistan to help that country recover from the devastating 2010 floods.[216] Under this waiver, the obligations under Articles I and XIII of the GATT 1994 are waived.[217]

In *EC – Bananas III (1997)*, the then European Communities argued that the Lomé Waiver, which waived the provisions of Article I:1 of the GATT 1994, should be interpreted to waive also the provisions of Article XIII of the GATT 1994. In that case, the panel accepted this argument to the extent that 'the scope of Article XIII:1 is identical with that of Article I'.[218] The Appellate Body reversed this finding, and noted, with regard to the nature and the interpretation of waivers, the following:

Although the WTO Agreement does not provide any specific rules on the interpretation of waivers, Article IX of the WTO Agreement and the Understanding in Respect of Waivers

---

210　See General Council Decision of 30 November 2011, WT/L/836, dated 5 December 2011. This waiver will expire on 31 December 2016.

211　See General Council Decision of 27 May 2009, WT/L/754, dated 29 May 2009. This waiver will expire on 30 September 2015.

212　See General Council Decision of 30 August 2003, WT/L/540, dated 2 September 2003. This waiver will terminate for each Member on the date on which an amendment to the *TRIPS Agreement* replacing its provisions takes effect for that Member. See below, p. 1000.

213　See below, pp. 999–1000.

214　See General Council Decision of 15 December 2006, WT/L/676, dated 19 December 2006. This waiver was granted to Australia, Botswana, Brazil, Canada, Croatia, India, Israel, Japan, Korea, Mauritius, Mexico, Norway, the Philippines, Sierra Leone, Chinese Taipei, Thailand, the United Arab Emirates, the United States and Venezuela, and any other Member that has notified the CTG since December 2006 that it wishes to be covered by this waiver. This waiver was extended by the General Council at its meeting of 11 December 2012.

215　On these GATT 1994 obligations, see below, pp. 317–34, 482–90 and 492–500.

216　See www.wto.org/english/news_e/news12_e/good_02feb12_e.htm.

217　On these GATT 1994 obligations, see below, pp. 317–34 and 492–500.

218　Panel Report, *EC – Bananas III*, para. 7.107.

of Obligations under the General Agreement on Tariffs and Trade 1994, which provide requirements for granting and renewing waivers, stress the exceptional nature of waivers and subject waivers to strict disciplines. Thus, waivers should be interpreted with great care.[219]

In addition to the possibility to waive obligations under the WTO agreements, the *WTO Agreement* also provides for an 'opt-out' possibility. For political or other reasons (including economic reasons), a Member may not want the WTO rules to apply to its trade relations with another Member. Article XIII of the *WTO Agreement*, entitled 'Non-Application of Multilateral Trade Agreements between Particular Members', states in its first paragraph:

This Agreement and the Multilateral Trade Agreements in Annexes 1 and 2 shall not apply as between any Member and any other Member if either of the Members, at the time either becomes a Member, does not consent to such application.

It is thus possible for a Member to prevent WTO rules from applying to its trade relations with another Member. However, the 'non-application' or 'opt-out' clause has to be invoked at the time that this Member, or the other, joins the WTO. The 'opt-out' clause cannot be invoked at any later time. The decision to opt out must be notified to the Ministerial Conference (or the General Council) before the latter decides on the accession. In practice, the importance of the 'non-application' clause under the *WTO Agreement* has been limited. Since 1995, this clause has been invoked eleven times (including eight times by the United States)[220] but only two of these invocations are currently still in force.[221] Most recently, in December 2011, the United States invoked the 'non-application' clause when the Protocol on the Accession of the Russian Federation was adopted and the US Congress had not yet adopted legislation allowing for Russia to be granted MFN status.[222] Russia reciprocated by also invoking Article XIII against the United States. In December 2012, the US Congress adopted the necessary legislation and Russia was granted MFN status.[223] The United States subsequently revoked its invocation of the 'non-application' clause against Russia and so did Russia *vis-à-vis* the United States.[224]

---

219 Appellate Body Report, *EC – Bananas III (1997)*, para. 185.
220 See *WTO Analytical Index 2012*, Volume 1, 57. The United States invoked the 'non-application' clause of Article XIII:1 of the *WTO Agreement* with respect to Armenia, Georgia, Kyrgyzstan, Moldova, Mongolia, Romania and Vietnam. Since the publication of the *WTO Analytical Index 2012*, the United States has further invoked the 'non-application' clause with respect to Russia.
221 Still in force are the invocations of the opt-out clause of Turkey against Armenia (WT/L/501, dated 29 November 2002) and of El Salvador against China (WT/L/429, dated 5 November 2001) and of Russia against the United States (WT/L/838, dated 16 December 2011). While both documents (WT/L/837 and WT/L/838) are dated 16 December, they concern communications, dated 15 December, addressed to, and received by, the Chair of the Ministerial Conference before the decision on Russia's accession.
222 Some Members of Congress objected to granting Russia MFN status, or, as it is now referred to in US law, 'permanent normal trade relations' status because of concerns regarding specific trade issues (such as Russia's use of SPS measures to restrict imports of US-produced meat and weak enforcement of intellectual property rights) and/or concerns regarding human rights and foreign policy issues. See W. H. Cooper, *Permanent Normal Trade Relations (PNTR) Status for Russia and US–Russian Economic Ties*, Congressional Research Service Report for Congress, 15 June 2012.
223 See W. H. Cooper, *Permanent Normal Trade Relations (PNTR) Status for Russia and US – Russian Economic Ties*, Congressional Research Service Report for Congress, 17 December 2012.
224 In December 2012, the United States also revoked its invocation of the 'non-application' clause against Moldova. See *ibid.*

Questions and Assignments 2.11

What is a 'waiver' of WTO obligations and under what conditions can it be granted? Find out how many and which waivers currently apply in favour of India and the European Union. Can the European Union invoke the 'non-application' clause against a WTO Member that is guilty of gross violations of human rights or acts of aggression against other countries?

4.1.5   Withdrawal, Suspension and Expulsion

Article XV:1 of the *WTO Agreement* states:

> Any Member may withdraw from this Agreement. Such withdrawal shall apply both to this Agreement and the Multilateral Trade Agreements and shall take effect upon the expiration of six months from the date on which written notice of withdrawal is received by the Director-General of the WTO.

WTO Members may thus, at any time, unilaterally withdraw from the WTO. A withdrawal only takes effect, however, upon the expiration of six months from the notification of the decision to withdraw.[225] Note that, when a Member withdraws from the WTO, it cannot remain a party to any of the Multilateral Trade Agreements. Withdrawal is thus an 'all or nothing' option. There is no such thing as a WTO *à la carte*.[226] To date, no Member has ever withdrawn from the WTO. A group of Caribbean banana-producing countries, very disappointed with the outcome of the *EC – Bananas III (1997)* dispute, reportedly 'threatened' at one point to withdraw from the WTO but did not do so.

The *WTO Agreement* does – except in one specific situation – not provide for the suspension or expulsion of a Member.[227] There is no procedure to suspend or exclude from the WTO Members that systematically breach their obligations under the WTO agreements.[228] There are also no rules or procedures for the suspension or expulsion of Members that are guilty of gross violations of human rights or acts of aggression.

Questions and Assignments 2.12

Can a Member withdraw from the WTO? If so, how? Can a WTO Member, guilty of gross violations of human rights or acts of aggression against other countries, be expelled from the WTO?

4.2   Institutional Structure of the WTO

To carry out the functions and tasks entrusted to the WTO, the *WTO Agreement* provides for manifold bodies. The basic institutional structure of the WTO is set out in Article IV of the *WTO Agreement*, and is shown in Figure 2.1. Subordinate

---

225 The notification to withdraw is made to the WTO Director-General.

226 Except, of course, with regard to the (currently two) plurilateral agreements. See above, pp. 49–50.

227 Note that the expulsion of a Member is provided for in case of the non-acceptance of certain amendments to the WTO agreements. See below, p. 141.

228 Note, however, the possibility for the DSB to authorise under Article 22.6 of the DSU the suspension of concessions or other obligations with respect to a Member that fails to comply with dispute settlement decisions. See below, p. 296.

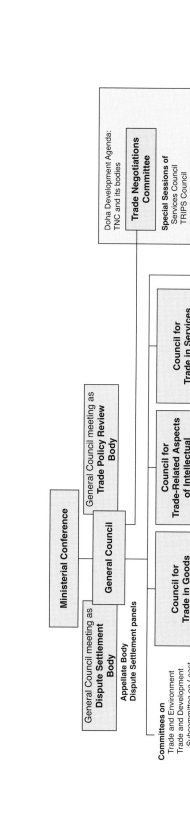

Figure 2.1 WTO organisation chart

Ministerial Conference

General Council meeting as
**Dispute Settlement
Body**

General Council

General Council meeting as
**Trade Policy Review
Body**

Appellate Body
Dispute Settlement panels

**Council for
Trade in Goods**

**Council for
Trade-Related Aspects
of Intellectual
Property Rights**

**Council for
Trade in Services**

Doha Development Agenda:
TNC and its bodies

**Trade Negotiations
Committee**

Committees on
Trade and Environment
Trade and Development
  *Subcommittee on Least-
  Developed Countries*
Regional Trade Agreements
Balance of Payments
Restrictions
Budget, Finance and
  Administration

Working parties on
Accession

Working groups on
Trade, Debt and Finance
Trade and Technology
Transfer

Committees on
Market Access
Agriculture
Sanitary and Phytosanitary Measures
Technical Barriers to Trade
Subsidies and Countervailing Measures
Anti-Dumping Practices
Customs Valuation
Rules of Origin
Import Licensing
Trade-Related Investment Measures
Safeguards

Working party on
State-Trading Enterprises

Committees on
Trade in Financial Services
Specific Commitments

Working parties on
Domestic Regulation
GATS Rules

Plurilateral Committees on
Trade in Civil Aircraft
Government Procurement
Information Technology Agreement

Special Sessions of
Services Council
TRIPS Council
Dispute Settlement Body
Agriculture Committee
  Cotton Sub-Committee
Trade and Development Committee
Trade and Environment Committee

Negotiating groups on
Market Access
Rules
Trade facilitation

Date	Time	Meeting
3–4	10:00	General Council
8	10:00	Negotiating Group on Trade Facilitation (followed by Inf.)
9 + 11	10:00	Trade Policy Review Body – Norway
9	15:00	Working Party on the Accession of Tajikistan
10	10:00	Sub-Committee on Least-Developed Countries
15 + 17	10:00	Trade Policy Review Body – Bangladesh
15–16	10:00	Workshop – Sanitary and Phytosanitary Measures
16	10:00	Committee on Market Access
18–19	10:00	Committee on Sanitary and Phytosanitary Measures
22	10:00	Committee on Safeguards
22	15:00	Working Group on Trade and Transfer of Technology
23	10:00	Committee on Budget, Finance and Administration
23	–	Committee on Subsidies and Countervailing Measures – Special Meeting followed by Regular Committee
23	–	Dispute Settlement Body
24	10:00	Committee on Anti-Dumping Practices – Informal Group on Anti-Circumvention followed by the Working Group on Implementation
25	–	Negotiating Group on Rules (Technical Group)
29	15:00	Committee on Import Licensing Fax
30 + 1 November	10:00	Trade Policy Review Body – Israel
31	10:00	Committee on Government Procurement

Figure 2.2 Programme of WTO meetings in October 2012

committees and working groups have been added to this structure by later decisions.

At present, the WTO has a total of thirty-five standing bodies and about thirty *ad hoc* bodies.[229] Many of these WTO bodies meet on a regular basis, making for a heavy workload for WTO diplomats. In 2012, WTO bodies held nearly 500 formal and informal meetings. For many developing-country Members, with only a small, and sometimes no, permanent representation in Geneva, this workload is a daunting challenge.[230] The schedule of meetings at the WTO is posted on the WTO website. Consider the schedule of meetings in October 2012, as shown in Figure 2.2.

229 Most of these *ad hoc* bodies are working groups on accession. This group of *ad hoc* bodies also includes the bodies especially established for the Doha Round negotiations. See below, pp. 125–27.

230 Most WTO Members have a 'permanent representation', also referred to as a 'permanent mission', in Geneva. This is, however, often a 'permanent representation' to *all* Geneva-based international organisations, which means that the limited human and other resources are spread (thinly) over a great number of meetings and activities. A number of developed-country as well as developing-country Members have a separate 'permanent representation' to the WTO. This is the case, for example, for Brazil, China, India, the European Union, Honduras, Japan, Malaysia, the Philippines and the United States. The meetings of WTO bodies are usually attended by diplomats from the permanent representation, but often government officials specialising in a specific subject-matter are flown in from the capital to attend important meetings in Geneva and present their governments' views. This is obviously, however, not an option for many developing-country Members. Furthermore, there are about twenty developing-country Members that do not even have a permanent representation in Geneva. See above, p. 103, footnote 148.

The institutional structure of the WTO includes, at the highest level, the Ministerial Conference, at a second level, the General Council, the Dispute Settlement Body (DSB) and the Trade Policy Review Body (TPRB) and, at lower levels, specialised councils, committees, working groups and working parties. Furthermore, and not reflected in the organisational chart shown in Figure 2.1, the institutional structure of the WTO includes judicial and other non-political bodies, as well as the WTO Secretariat. This sub-section examines in turn these various elements of the institutional structure of the WTO. In addition, this sub-section also briefly discusses political bodies lacking the formal institutional structure of the WTO.

Questions and Assignments 2.13

Look up the programme of meetings at the WTO for this month. Which of these meetings would you definitely want/need to attend if you were a small, sugar-exporting, least-developed-country Member (with a diplomatic staff of two for all international organisations in Geneva)?

4.2.1   Ministerial Conference

Article IV:1 of the *WTO Agreement* states:

> There shall be a Ministerial Conference composed of representatives of all the Members, which shall meet at least once every two years. The Ministerial Conference shall carry out the functions of the WTO and take actions necessary to this effect. The Ministerial Conference shall have the authority to take decisions on all matters under any of the Multilateral Trade Agreements, if so requested by a Member, in accordance with the specific requirements for decision-making in this Agreement and in the relevant Multilateral Trade Agreement.

The Ministerial Conference is the 'supreme' body of the WTO. It is composed of minister-level representatives from *all* Members and has decision-making powers on *all* matters under *any* of the multilateral WTO agreements.[231] Decisions by the Ministerial Conference are binding on Members.[232] In addition to this very broad decision-making power, the Ministerial Conference has been explicitly granted a number of specific powers, such as: (1) adopting authoritative interpretations of the WTO agreements;[233] (2) granting waivers;[234] (3) adopting amendments;[235] (4) making decisions on accession;[236] (5) appointing the Director-General;[237] and (6) adopting staff regulations.[238]

---

231 For the Rules of Procedure for the Ministerial Conference, see WT/L/161, dated 25 July 1996.
232 However, whether these decisions can be enforced through WTO dispute settlement is another matter dealt with both above, p. 52 and below, p. 189.
233 Article IX:2 of the *WTO Agreement*. See below, p. 139.
234 Article IX:3 of the *WTO Agreement*. See below, p. 140.
235 Article X of the *WTO Agreement*. See below, p. 140.
236 Article XII of the *WTO Agreement*. See below, pp. 109–13.
237 Article VI:2 of the *WTO Agreement*.
238 Article VI:3 of the *WTO Agreement*. See below, p. 134. Note also that, pursuant to Article XII:5(b) and XII:6 of the GATS, the Ministerial Conference also has the power to establish certain procedures in connection with balance-of-payments restrictions (see below, pp. 645–6). Pursuant to Article 64.3 of the *TRIPS Agreement*, the Ministerial Conference has the power to extend the non-application of non-violation complaints to the *TRIPS Agreement* (see below, p. 1010).

The Ministerial Conference is not often in session. Since 1995, there have only been eight sessions of the Ministerial Conference, each lasting a few days only: Singapore (1996),[239] Geneva (1998),[240] Seattle (1999),[241] Doha (2001),[242] Cancún (2003),[243] Hong Kong (2005),[244] Geneva (2009)[245] and Geneva (2011).[246] Sessions of the Ministerial Conference are major media events and focus the minds of the political leaders of WTO Members on the current challenges to, and the future of, the multilateral trading system. They offer a much-needed opportunity to give political leadership and guidance to the WTO and its actions.[247] The 9th Session of the Ministerial Conference will be held in Bali, Indonesia, in December 2013.

4.2.2   General Council, DSB and TPRB

Article IV:2 of the *WTO Agreement* states:

There shall be a General Council composed of representatives of all the Members, which shall meet as appropriate. In the intervals between meetings of the Ministerial Conference, its functions shall be conducted by the General Council. The General Council shall also carry out the functions assigned to it by this Agreement. The General Council shall establish its rules of procedure and approve the rules of procedure for the Committees provided for in paragraph 7.

The General Council is composed of ambassador-level diplomats and meets at least every two months.[248] All WTO Members are represented in the General Council. As with all other WTO bodies, except the Ministerial Conference, the General Council meets on the premises of the WTO in Geneva. Each year, the General Council elects its Chair from among its members.[249] The Chair of the General Council holds the highest elected office within the WTO. In February

---

239 For the Ministerial Declarations adopted on 13 December 1996 at the Singapore Ministerial Conference (1st MC), see WT/MIN(96)/DEC, dated 18 December 1996, and WT/MIN(96)/16, dated 13 December 1996.

240 For the Ministerial Declarations adopted on 20 May 1998 at the Geneva Ministerial Conference (2nd MC), see WT/MIN(98)/DEC/1, dated 25 May 1998, and WT/MIN(98)/DEC/2, dated 25 May 1998.

241 No Ministerial Declaration was adopted at the Seattle Ministerial Conference in November/December 1999 (3rd MC).

242 For the Ministerial Declarations and Decisions adopted on 14 November 2001 at the Doha Ministerial Conference (4th MC), see WT/MIN(01)/DEC/1, dated 20 November 2001, WT/MIN(01)/DEC/2, dated 20 November 2001, WT/MIN(01)/15, dated 14 November 2001, WT/MIN(01)/16, dated 14 November 2001, and WT/MIN(01)/17, dated 20 November 2001.

243 No Ministerial Declaration was adopted at the Cancún Ministerial Conference in September 2003 (5th MC). However, the Ministerial Conference did issue on 14 September 2003 a Ministerial Statement. See WT/MIN(03)/20, dated 23 September 2003.

244 For the Ministerial Declaration adopted on 18 December 2005 at the Hong Kong Ministerial Conference (6th MC), see WT/MIN(05)/DEC, dated 22 December 2005.

245 No Ministerial Declaration was adopted at the Geneva Ministerial Conference in November 2009 (7th MC).

246 No Ministerial Declaration was adopted at the Geneva Ministerial Conference in December 2011 (8th MC). For the Ministerial Decisions adopted at this session on 17 December 2011, see WT/L/842–848, dated 19 December 2011. For the Chair's Concluding Statement on 17 December 2011, see WT/MIN(11)/11, dated 11 December 2011.

247 Note, however, that there was no Ministerial Conference in 2007, as it was not considered useful to have a session at that time due to the lack of progress in the Doha Round negotiations.

248 For the Rules of Procedure of the General Council, see WT/L/161, dated 25 July 1996.

249 The Chair of the General Council alternates between ambassadors from developed-country and developing-country Members.

General Council

3–4 October 2012

Proposed agenda

I.   Report by the Chairman of the Trade Negotiations Committee
II. Work Programme on Small Economies – Report by the Chairman of the dedicated session of the Committee on Trade and Development
III. Situation regarding the rights to the Havana Club rum trademark in the United States – Communication from Cuba
IV. Improving the guidelines for granting intergovernmental organizations permanent observer status in the WTO – Statement by the Chair
V.   Committee on Budget, Finance and Administration – Reports on meetings of July and September 2012
VI. WTO pension plan ...
VII. Appointment of officers to WTO bodies – Negotiating Group on Market Access and Working Group on Trade, Debt and Finance – Statement by the Chair
     Other business

Figure 2.3 Proposed agenda for the meeting of the General Council of 3–4 October 2012

2013, the General Council elected Shahid Bashir, Pakistan's Ambassador and Permanent Representative to the WTO, as its Chair for 2013.[250]

The General Council is responsible for the continuing, 'day-to-day' management of the WTO and its many activities. In between sessions of the Ministerial Conference, the General Council exercises the full powers of the Ministerial Conference. In addition, the General Council also carries out some functions specifically assigned to it. The General Council is responsible for adopting the annual budget and the financial regulations[251] and for making appropriate arrangements for effective cooperation with international organisations and NGOs.[252] By way of example of the matters dealt with by the General Council, consider the proposed agenda for the meeting of the General Council of 3–4 October 2012, set out in Figure 2.3.

Rule 37 of the *Rules of Procedure for the Meetings of the General Council* states:

The meeting of the General Council shall ordinarily be held in private. It may be decided that a particular meeting or meetings should be held in public.

In practice, the General Council always meets behind closed doors. After the meeting, the Chair may issue a *communiqué* to the press.[253] The Chair and/or the

---

250 The list of the 2013 chairs of all WTO bodies can be found on the WTO website.
251 Article VII:3 of the *WTO Agreement*. See also below, p. 142.
252 Article V:1 of the *WTO Agreement*. See also above, pp. 97–101.
253 See Rule 38 of the Rules of Procedure for the Meetings of the General Council, WT/L/161, dated 25 July 1996.

Director-General, assisted by the WTO spokesperson, usually hold a press conference after the meeting. The minutes of a meeting of the General Council (as are the minutes of meetings of all WTO bodies except the TPRB) are 'restricted' documents, i.e. not available to the public, until they are 'de-restricted' under the rules on the de-restriction of official documents.[254] The lack of transparency and openness of the General Council and other WTO bodies compares unfavourably with many UN bodies.[255]

The functions specifically assigned to the General Council also cover dispute settlement and trade policy review. Article IV:3 and 4 of the *WTO Agreement* state respectively:

3. The General Council shall convene as appropriate to discharge the responsibilities of the Dispute Settlement Body provided for in the Dispute Settlement Understanding. The Dispute Settlement Body may have its own chairman and shall establish such rules of procedure as it deems necessary for the fulfilment of those responsibilities.
4. The General Council shall convene as appropriate to discharge the responsibilities of the Trade Policy Review Body provided for in the TPRM. The Trade Policy Review Body may have its own chairman and shall establish such rules of procedure as it deems necessary for the fulfilment of those responsibilities.

The General Council, the DSB and the TPRB are, in fact, the same body. The DSB and the TPRB are the *alter ego* of the General Council; they are two emanations of the General Council. When the General Council administers the WTO dispute settlement system, it convenes and acts as the DSB. When the General Council administers the WTO trade policy review mechanism, it convenes and acts as the TPRB. To date, the DSB and the TPRB have always had a different Chair from the General Council,[256] and both the DSB and the TPRB have developed their own Rules of Procedure, which take account of the special features of their work.[257]

The DSB has a regular meeting once a month, but, in between, additional meetings (called 'special meetings') may be requested by WTO Members in order to enable them to exercise their rights within specified timeframes as provided for in the DSU.[258] In 2012, for example, the DSB met in total eighteen times.

---

254 General Council, Decision on *Procedures for the Circulation and Derestriction of WTO Documents*, WT/L/452, dated 16 May 2002.
255 Note, however, that the transparency and openness of these UN bodies may be deceptive.
256 Note, however, that it is an established practice that the Chair of the DSB in year *n* becomes the Chair of the General Council in year *n* + 1. In line with this practice, Ambassador Elin Johansen from Norway, who was DSB Chair in 2011, was General Council Chair in 2012; and Ambassador Shahid Bashir from Pakistan, who was DSB Chair in 2012, is General Council Chair in 2013.
257 For the Rules of Procedure for the TPRB, see Trade Policy Review Body, *Rules of Procedure for Meetings of the Trade Policy Review Body*, WT/TPR/6/Rev.1, dated 10 October 2005. For the Rules of Procedure for the DSB, see below, p. 207, footnote 268. Note that the TPRB and the DSB follow, *mutatis mutandis* and with certain deviations, the Rules of Procedure for the General Council (WT/L/160).
258 See below, p. 207.

Questions and Assignments 2.14

Discuss the composition and the scope of the decision-making competence of the Ministerial Conference. What is the relationship between the Ministerial Conference and the General Council? What is the relationship between the General Council and the DSB? Look up who serves this year as the Chair of the DSB and the TPRB. Find the minutes of the last meeting of the General Council. What issues were on the agenda of this meeting? What does this tell you about the General Council?

4.2.3   Specialised Councils, Committees, Working Groups and Working Parties

At the level below the General Council, the DSB and the TPRB, there are three so-called specialised councils provided for in Article IV:5 of the *WTO Agreement*: the Council for Trade in Goods (CTG),[259] the Council for Trade in Services (CTS)[260] and the Council for TRIPS.[261] These specialised councils assist the General Council and operate under its general guidance. The CTG, CTS and TRIPS Council oversee, respectively, the functioning of the WTO agreements on trade in goods, the GATS and the *TRIPS Agreement*. These specialised councils carry out the functions assigned to them by the *WTO Agreement*,[262] by their respective agreements[263] and by the General Council. Overall, however, few specific powers have been entrusted to the specialised councils, and their general power to *oversee* the functioning of relevant agreements does not explicitly include the power to take any decision. An often-cited example of an instance in which a WTO body went beyond its powers relates to the CTS and, in particular the CTS's decision to extend the deadline for the entry into force of the result of negotiations on emergency safeguard measures in the field of services. Article X:1 of the GATS sets this deadline explicitly at 'not later than three years from the date of entry into force of the *WTO Agreement*', i.e. on 1 January 1998. This treaty-mandated deadline was extended five times by the CTS even though the CTS did not have any apparent legal mandate to do so.[264] The political need to extend the deadline prevailed over any jurisdictional concern.

---

259 For the Rules of Procedure for the CTG, see WT/L/79, dated 7 August 1995.
260 For the Rules of Procedure for the CTS, see S/L/15, dated 19 October 1995.
261 For the Rules of Procedure for the Council for TRIPS, see IP/C/1, dated 28 September 1995.
262 See Article IX:2 of the *WTO Agreement* which provides that the Ministerial Conference and the General Council may only exercise their authority to adopt authoritative interpretations of the multilateral trade agreements of Annex 1 on the basis of a recommendation from the specialised council overseeing the functioning of the agreement at issue. See below, pp. 139–42. The specialised councils also play a role in the procedure for the adoption of waivers and the amendment procedure. See Article IX:3(b) and Article X:1 of the *WTO Agreement*. See below, pp. 140–2 and 140–1.
263 The GATS explicitly empowers the CTS to develop disciplines on domestic regulation, and to establish rules and procedures for the rectification and modification of services schedules. See Articles VI:4 and XXI:5 of the GATS. The *TRIPS Agreement* empowers the TRIPS Council to extend, upon a duly motivated request, the ten-year transition period for the implementation of the *TRIPS Agreement* granted to the least-developed-country Members. See Article 66.1 of the *TRIPS Agreement*.
264 The most recent extension was decided on in March 2004, and on that occasion the CTS decided to extend the deadline for an indefinite period. See Decision of the Council for Trade in Services, adopted on 15 March 2004, S/L/159, dated 17 March 2004.

The specialised councils meet as necessary. In 2012, for example, the CTG met four times in formal session and the CTS met four times.[265] Furthermore, these specialised councils also met informally. All WTO Members are represented in these specialised councils, although some Members, in particular developing-country Members, may find it difficult to attend all meetings.

In addition to the three specialised councils, there are numerous committees and working parties that assist the Ministerial Conference and the General Council in carrying out their functions. The committees include the Committee on Trade and Environment (CTE), which was established by the 1994 Ministerial Decision on Trade and Environment, adopted in Marrakesh on 14 April 1994. Another important committee is the Committee on Trade and Development (CTD), which is explicitly provided for in Article IV:7 of the *WTO Agreement* and was established by the General Council in 1995.[266] In 1996, the General Council also established the Committee on Regional Trade Agreements (CRTA).[267] Furthermore, all but one of the multilateral agreements on trade in goods provide for a committee to carry out certain functions relating to the implementation of the particular agreement.[268] All of these committees are under the authority of, and report to, the CTG. In practice, however, they tend to be relatively independent, arguably due to the technical nature of their work. Note, by way of example, the SCM Committee. Article 24.1 of the *SCM Agreement* states:

There is hereby established a Committee on Subsidies and Countervailing Measures composed of representatives from each of the Members. The Committee shall elect its own Chairman and shall meet not less than twice a year and otherwise as envisaged by relevant provisions of this Agreement at the request of any Member. The Committee shall carry out responsibilities as assigned to it under this Agreement or by the Members and it shall afford Members the opportunity of consulting on any matter relating to the operation of the Agreement or the furtherance of its objectives. The WTO Secretariat shall act as the secretariat to the Committee.[269]

Note that, under Article 27.4 of the *SCM Agreement*, the SCM Committee has the power to determine whether a request by a developing-country Member to extend the special transitional period for the maintenance of export subsidies is justified.[270] Such specific decision-making powers to add to, or diminish, the obligations of certain Members are, however, quite exceptional.[271]

265 In addition, the CTG and the CTS met three and two times respectively in informal session.
266 At the same meeting of the General Council on 31 January 1995, at which the Committee on Trade and Development, the Committee on Balance-of-Payment Restrictions and the Committee on the Budget, Finance and Administration were established (see WT/GC/M/1, dated 28 February 1995).
267 See WT/GC/M/10, dated 6 March 1996, para. 11.
268 The exception is the *Agreement on Preshipment Inspection*. However, the CTG established a Committee on Preshipment Inspection.
269 The powers of the Committee on Anti-Dumping (AD) Practices, the Committee on Customs Valuation (CV) and the Committee on Technical Barriers to Trade (TBT) are worded in similar terms.
270 Furthermore, Article 29.4 of the *SCM Agreement* gives the SCM Committee the power to allow Members in the process of transformation into a market economy to derogate from their notified programmes and measures and their timeframes. See also above, p. 834, footnote 472.
271 Another example is the power given to the TBT Committee under Article 12.8 of the *TBT Agreement* relating to granting exceptions from TBT obligations to developing-country Members. See also below, pp. 886–7.

Furthermore, Article IV:6 of the *WTO Agreement* provides that the specialised councils may also establish subsidiary bodies as required. For example, the CTS created the Working Party on Professional Services. A number of committees also have this power to establish subordinate bodies where necessary.[272]

Subsidiary bodies set up to study and report on a particular issue are usually referred to as 'working parties' or 'working groups'.[273] In December 2012, there were twenty-four working parties on the accession of would-be Members.

When a working party, a committee or a specialised council is called upon to take a decision but is unable to do so, the applicable Rules of Procedure commonly require the matter to be referred to a higher body if a Member so requests.

The Plurilateral Agreements, i.e. the *Agreement on Trade in Civil Aircraft* and the *Agreement on Government Procurement*, provide for a Committee on Trade in Civil Aircraft and a Committee on Government Procurement respectively. These bodies carry out the functions assigned to them under those agreements. They operate within the institutional framework of the WTO, keeping the General Council informed of their activities on a regular basis.[274]

4.2.4   Trade Negotiations Committee

The Doha Round negotiations are conducted in the Trade Negotiations Committee (TNC) and its subordinate negotiating bodies.[275] The TNC was established at the Doha Ministerial Conference in November 2001.[276] This body supervises the overall conduct of the negotiations under the authority of the General Council. The TNC reports on the progress of the negotiations to each regular meeting of the General Council. The 'detailed' negotiations take place either in special sessions of standing WTO bodies or in specially created negotiating groups. At its first meeting on 28 January and 1 February 2002, the TNC established two such new negotiating groups, one on market access and one on rules. Most of the negotiations, however, take place in special sessions of standing WTO bodies (such as the Dispute Settlement Body, the Council for Trade in Services and the Committee on Agriculture). The TNC and its negotiating bodies consist of all the WTO Members and all countries negotiating accession to the WTO.[277] On 1 February 2002, the TNC decided that the WTO Director-General would *ex officio* chair the TNC. The TNC is the only political WTO body chaired by a WTO official, rather than an ambassador or senior diplomat of a Member.[278] In 2012, the TNC met once.[279]

---

272 See e.g. Article 13.2 of the *TBT Agreement*.
273 See, for example, the Working Group on Trade, Debt and Finance, and the Working Party on State Trading Enterprises.
274 See Article IV:8 of the *WTO Agreement*.   275 See above, p. 127.
276 See Ministerial Conference, *Doha Ministerial Declaration*, WT/MIN(01)/DEC/1, dated 20 November 2001, para. 46.
277 Note, however, that decisions on agreements, that would result from the negotiations, are taken by WTO Members only.
278 Note that the choice of the WTO Director-General as Chair of the TNC is controversial among WTO Members.
279 Some of the negotiating bodies met much more. For example, the Special Session of the Dispute Settlement Body met seven times in informal session and the Negotiating Group on Market Access met once in formal session and six times in informal session.

4.2.5   Political Bodies Lacking in the Formal Institutional Structure

While the WTO's institutional structure is in many respects similar to that of other intergovernmental organisations, it does not have, unlike, for example, the United Nations, the IMF and the World Bank, an 'executive body' consisting of the most important Members and a selection of other Members. In the aforementioned organisations an executive body facilitates decision-making by concentrating discussions in a smaller but representative group of members, or by taking certain decisions for the whole membership. Also, unlike intergovernmental organisations such as the OECD and the ILO, the WTO does not have any permanent body in which stakeholders other than governments are represented.

As noted above, all political WTO bodies comprise all 159 WTO Members. However, it is clear that it is impossible to negotiate effectively with such a large number, or even with the lower number that is likely to turn up for meetings. Over the years, informal 'solutions', such as 'green room meetings', have been developed to address, or at least mitigate, this problem. These informal 'solutions', and in particular green room meetings, are discussed later in this chapter.[280] However, as noted above, the WTO institutional structure does not currently provide for a formal solution to this problem in the form of an 'executive body'. There have been a few proposals to create such an executive body to facilitate decision-making within the WTO. The 2004 Sutherland Report on *The Future of the WTO*, for example, recommended that the informal 'mini-ministerials' should be replaced by a permanent 'senior level consultative body'.[281] In order for this body to be effective, its membership should not exceed thirty Members. While most seats might be filled on a 'rotating basis', taking into account different criteria, such as 'geographical areas, regional trading arrangements or mixed constituencies', the permanent presence of certain Members would be a 'must', given the significance of their trade flows.[282] However, this and similar proposals have not received much support from WTO Members.[283] Disagreement on its composition is likely to be the major stumbling block for the establishment of a formal, permanent 'executive body'.

In addition to an 'executive body', the WTO also does not have any permanent consultative body in which representatives of national parliaments or NGOs are represented. As is the case in other international organisations, such a body could serve as a forum for 'dialogue' between the WTO and civil society. In 2001, Pascal Lamy, the then European Trade Commissioner, proposed the establishment of a WTO Parliamentary Consultative Assembly.[284] While there

---

280 See below, pp. 144–8.

281 See Report by the Consultative Board to the Director-General Supachai Panitchpakdi, *The Future of the WTO: Addressing Institutional Challenges in the New Millennium* (the 'Sutherland Report') (WTO, 2004), para. 323. This 'senior level consultative body' would be similar to the Consultative Group of 18 (CG-18), a body which operated in the GATT for many years.

282 *Ibid.*, para. 325.

283 See, for example, General Council, *Minutes of Meeting*, WT/GC/M/91, dated 26 January 2005, 20.

284 See speech given in Berlin on 26 November 2001.

seems to be little support among Members for the establishment of such an assembly, it should be noted that, in recent years, contacts with national parliamentarians have been greatly enhanced through regular visits to capitals by the WTO Director-General and through various seminars and briefings with the Inter-Parliamentary Union and, *inter alia*, the European Parliament and the US Congress.[285] Since 2003, the Inter-Parliamentary Union (IPU) and the European Parliament have organised a number of sessions of the Parliamentary Conference on the WTO. The 2011 session was, for the first time, hosted by the WTO, and was attended by some 300 parliamentarians from around the world.[286]

As discussed above, it has been argued that 'outside voices', such as expert NGOs, can provide valuable advice to Members.[287] The WTO could obtain such advice through permanent consultative bodies of individuals and/or NGOs reflecting a broad range of views and interests. However, suggestions to establish such consultative bodies have received little support from Members to date. In 2003, Supachai Panitchpakdi, the then WTO Director-General, established on his own initiative two advisory bodies: the Informal NGO Advisory Body, made up of eleven high-level representatives from NGOs, and the Informal Business Advisory Body, which comprised fourteen captains of industry from developed as well as developing-country Members. Both bodies were to advise the WTO Director-General, channel the positions of civil society and global business on trade issues to the WTO, and ultimately aim at facilitating mutual understanding. However, this initiative died a silent death. Note that, in April 2012, Director-General Pascal Lamy established the Panel on Defining the Future of Trade. This twelve-strong panel is composed of representatives of the business community, such as the President and CEO of a Brazilian aircraft manufacturer, representatives of civil society, such as the Secretary-General of the International Trade Union Confederation, and former politicians, such as the former President of Botswana. This panel is to examine and analyse the challenges to global trade in the twenty-first century, and submit a report with its findings in April 2013.

4.2.6 Judicial, Quasi-Judicial and Other Non-Political Bodies

All the WTO bodies discussed above are political in nature. The WTO also has a number of judicial, quasi-judicial and other non-political bodies. The most prominent among the judicial and quasi-judicial bodies are the standing Appellate Body and the *ad hoc* dispute settlement panels respectively. These bodies are discussed in detail in Chapter 3 of this book.[288]

The WTO also has other non-political bodies. An example of such a body is the Permanent Group of Experts (PGE) provided for under the *SCM Agreement*.

---

285 In 2011, the WTO also organised two regional workshops for parliamentarians: one in Singapore (for the ASEAN-plus region) and one in Vanuatu (for the Pacific region). See *WTO Annual Report 2012*, 128.
286 See *WTO Annual Report 2012*, 128.
287 See above, pp. 98–101.   288 See below, pp. 205–44.

The PGE consists of five independent persons with a high level of expertise in the fields of subsidies and trade relations. The members of the PGE are appointed by the SCM Committee. The PGE may be requested to assist a dispute settlement panel in determining whether a subsidy is a prohibited subsidy.[289] The PGE may also be requested by the SCM Committee for an advisory opinion on the existence and nature of any subsidy.[290] Furthermore, a WTO Member may request the PGE for a confidential advisory opinion on the nature of any subsidy proposed to be introduced or currently maintained by that Member.[291] Reportedly, to date no use has yet been made of the PGE.

Until 1 January 2005, a prime example of a non-political body was the Textile Monitoring Body (TMB), provided for in the *Agreement on Textiles and Clothing*. The TMB was to examine all relevant measures taken by Members and assess their consistency with the *Agreement on Textiles and Clothing*. The eleven members of the TMB were appointed by Members designated by the CTG but were to discharge their functions in an independent and impartial manner (not as the representative of a WTO Member). As discussed in Chapter 1, the *Agreement on Textiles and Clothing* ceased to be in force on 1 January 2005 and, as of that date, the TMB also ceased to exist.[292]

4.2.7   WTO Secretariat

The WTO Secretariat is based in Geneva at the Centre William Rappard (CWR), beautifully situated by the Lac Léman.[293] The Secretariat has regular staff of 629 persons.[294] This makes it undoubtedly one of the smallest secretariats of any of the major international organisations. However, as Hoekman and Kostecki observed:

> The small size of the secretariat is somewhat misleading ... [T]he WTO is a network-based organization. The WTO secretariat and the national delegates in Geneva work in close cooperation with numerous civil servants in their respective capitals. The total size of the network is impossible to determine, but certainly spans at least 5,000 people.[295]

As discussed below, the Secretariat's prime function is to keep the 'WTO network' operating smoothly.[296]

The WTO Secretariat is headed by a Director-General, who is appointed by the Ministerial Conference.[297] The Ministerial Conference adopts regulations

---

289 See Articles 4.5 and 24.3 of the *SCM Agreement*.   290 See *ibid.*, Article 24.3.
291 See *ibid.*, Article 24.4.   292 See above, p. 44. See also below, pp.
293 Note that the WTO does not have any offices outside Geneva.
294 See www.wto.org/english/thewto_e/secre_e/intro_e.htm. In September 2012, of these 629 regular staff, 342 are women and 287 are men. However, only one out of four directors is a woman. The WTO website notes elsewhere that the WTO Secretariat has 677 staff on the regular budget. This number includes temporary staff paid from the regular budget (see the WTO website version of the *WTO Annual Report 2012*, 142, available at www.wto.org/english/res_e/booksp_e/anrep_e/anrep12_e.pdf).
295 B. Hoekman and M. Kostecki, *The Political Economy of the World Trading System: The WTO and Beyond*, 2nd edn (Oxford University Press, 2001), 55.
296 See below, pp. 130–36.
297 See Article VI:1 and 2 of the *WTO Agreement*.

setting out the powers, duties, conditions of service and the term of office of the Director-General.[298] In the brief history of the WTO, the appointment of the Director-General has often been a contentious matter.[299] In particular, the process of appointing a successor for Renato Ruggiero,[300] the WTO's second Director-General, was particularly divisive. After a year of discussions, WTO Members finally agreed in July 1999 to an unprecedented term-sharing arrangement under which Mike Moore, of New Zealand,[301] was appointed as Director-General for a term of three years beginning on 1 September 1999, and Supachai Panitchpakdi, of Thailand,[302] was appointed for a three-year term beginning on 1 September 2002. The current Director-General, Pascal Lamy, of France,[303] took office on 1 September 2005. He was reappointed for a second, four-year term, starting on 1 September 2009. This second term expires on 31 August 2013.

Chastised by the bruising experience of the 1998–9 appointment process, discussed above, the General Council adopted in December 2002 new procedures for the appointment of a Director-General.[304] Under these new procedures, the appointment process shall start nine months prior to the expiry of the term of an incumbent Director-General. The various steps of the process are carefully set out. The process shall be conducted by the Chair of the General Council, assisted by the Chairs of the Dispute Settlement Body and the Trade Policy Review Body acting as facilitators. Only WTO Members may nominate candidates.[305] While the Sutherland Report on *The Future of the WTO* found these procedures to be steps in the right direction, it stated that it:

would favour the abandonment of the agreement that permits WTO Members to make nominations only of their own nationals or that candidates must have the backing of their own

---

298 See Article VI:2 of the *WTO Agreement*.

299 To date, the following persons have served as WTO Director-General: Peter Sutherland from Ireland (January 1995–April 1995); Renato Ruggiero from Italy (May 1995–April 1999); Mike Moore from New Zealand (September 1999–August 2002); Supachai Panitchpakdi from Thailand (September 2002–August 2005); and Pascal Lamy from France (September 2005 to present).

300 Renato Ruggiero of Italy was Italy's Trade Minister during the Uruguay Round. He has been credited for being the first senior government official to propose the establishment of an international organisation for trade to replace the GATT. See above, p. 80. He also held posts in private companies such as the car manufacturer Fiat and the energy firm ENI. After leaving the WTO, Ruggiero briefly served as Italy's Foreign Minister.

301 Mike Moore, a former printer, social worker and trade union researcher, was the youngest Member of Parliament ever elected in New Zealand. In the 1980s, he served six years as New Zealand's Minister of Overseas Trade and Marketing, and was New Zealand's Prime Minister for a brief period in 1990.

302 Supachai Panitchpakdi held a range of senior government positions in Thailand and was in charge of Thailand's participation in the final stages of the Uruguay Round negotiations. At the time of his appointment to the post of WTO Director-General, Supachai served as Thailand's Deputy Prime Minister and Minister of Commerce. After leaving the WTO, Supachai was appointed Secretary-General of UNCTAD.

303 Pascal Lamy served as the EU Trade Commissioner for five years until shortly before his appointment as WTO Director-General. Lamy began his career in the French civil service, served as Chief of Staff to Jacques Delors, President of the European Commission, and later was CEO of the bank Crédit Lyonnais.

304 See General Council, *Decision on the Procedures for the Appointment of Directors-General*, adopted 10 December 2002, WT/L/509, dated 20 January 2003.

305 According to the General Council Decision of 10 December 2002, a candidate for the post of WTO Director-General should have extensive experience in international relations, encompassing economic, trade and/or political experience; a firm commitment to the work and objectives of the WTO; proven leadership and managerial ability; and demonstrable communication skills.

governments. Indeed, there would be more logic in disallowing such national nominations completely. Any tendency towards alternating between developing and developed countries and any regional sequencing should be avoided. By the same token we would favour reducing the intensity of candidate 'campaigns'. A further option requiring that an initial independent search for appropriate candidates be carried out may be worth further examination.[306]

The overriding objective of Members is to reach a decision on the appointment of a Director-General by consensus. However, note that the new procedures explicitly state:

If, after having carried out all the procedures set out above, it has not been possible for the General Council to take a decision by consensus by the deadline provided for the appointment, Members should consider the possibility of recourse to a vote as a last resort by a procedure to be determined at that time. Recourse to a vote for the appointment of a Director-General shall be understood to be an exceptional departure from the customary practice of decision-making by consensus, and shall not establish any precedent for such recourse in respect of any future decisions in the WTO.[307]

By 31 December 2012, nine candidates to succeed Pascal Lamy as Director-General were nominated by their respective governments.[308] In January 2013, each of these candidates made a presentation to the General Council on their vision for the WTO, followed by a question-and-answer session, and started an intensive campaign in support of their candidacy.[309] On 8 May 2013, the General Council recommended Mr Roberto Carvalho de Azevêdo as the next Director-General, to take office on 1 September 2013.

With regard to the role of the Director-General and the WTO Secretariat, it is important to note that the Members of the WTO set the policy agenda and take all policy decisions. Neither the Director-General nor the WTO Secretariat has any autonomous policy decision-making powers. The Director-General and the WTO Secretariat act primarily as an 'honest broker' in, or a 'facilitator' of, the decision-making processes within the WTO. They are not expected to act as initiators of proposals for action or reform. In such a seemingly modest role, the Director-General and the WTO Secretariat can, however, make an important contribution to the building of consensus among Members on a specific agreement or decision. As noted above, the Director-General serves *ex officio* as Chair of the Trade Negotiations Committee, which oversees the Doha Round negotiations.[310] Speaking about his role as Director-General and the role of the WTO Secretariat, Supachai Panitchpakdi noted in January 2003:

306 Report by the Consultative Board to the Director-General Supachai Panitchpakdi, *The Future of the WTO: Addressing Institutional Challenges in the New Millennium* (the 'Sutherland Report') (WTO, 2004), para. 352.
307 See General Council, *Decision on the Procedures for the Appointment of Directors-General*, adopted 10 December 2002, WT/L/509, dated 20 January 2003, para. 21. On decision-making in the WTO, see below, pp. 131–4.
308 Mr Taeho Bark (Republic of Korea), Mr Herminio Blanco (Mexico), Mr Roberto Carvalho de Azevêdo (Brazil), Ms Anabel González (Costa Rica), Mr Tim Groser (New Zealand), Mr Ahmad Thougan Hindawi (Jordan), Ms Amina C. Mohamed (Kenya), Mr Alan John Kwadwo Kyerematen (Ghana), and Ms Mari Elka Pangestu (Indonesia).
309 After their presentation to the General Council, each of the candidates held a press conference, which was webcasted and can be viewed at http://gaia.world-television.com/wto/2013/dgsel_webcast_e.htm.
310 See above, p. 127.

As you know the WTO is, if I may use the cliché, a 'member-driven' organization. In the negotiations, Member governments negotiate directly with each other. As Chairman of the TNC, I shall be doing my utmost to keep all Members on board, facilitate their discussions, mediate in their problems and consult with all. And the WTO Secretariat, through its technical assistance work programme, is working hard to help developing and least-developed-country Members prepare effectively for the negotiations. But we cannot make any decisions on behalf of Members, we cannot unplug blockages when Members' positions are intractable and we cannot force consensus. It is Members who have the very difficult responsibility of developing policy positions, negotiating concessions and deciding how far they are able to go in any given area.[311]

The main duties of the WTO Secretariat are: (1) to provide technical, secretarial and professional support for the many WTO bodies (including the writing of the minutes of the meetings of these bodies; and the organization of the biennial sessions of the Ministerial Conference); (2) to provide technical assistance to developing-country Members; (3) to monitor and analyse developments in world trade; (4) to advise governments of countries wishing to become Members of the WTO; and (5) to provide information to the public and the media. As discussed in Chapter 3, the WTO Secretariat also provides administrative support and legal assistance for WTO dispute settlement panels.[312]

Developing-country Members have been apprehensive regarding the role of the WTO Secretariat and the Director-General of the WTO in negotiations and debates on policy matters. In 2002, in a joint communication, addressing, *inter alia*, the issue of the role of the Secretariat and the Director-General at sessions of the Ministerial Conference, fifteen developing-country Members, led by India, stated:

The Secretariat and the Director-General of the WTO ... should assume a neutral/impartial and objective role. They shall not express views explicitly or otherwise on the specific issues being discussed in the Ministerial Conference.[313]

The Sutherland Report on *The Future of the WTO* recommended, however, that the Director-General and the WTO Secretariat take on a greater, more proactive role. The Report stated:

The WTO needs a convincing and persistent institutional voice of its own. If Members are not prepared to defend and promote the principles they subscribe to, then the Secretariat must be free to do so ... Further, a clearer – though always careful – lead on policy issues should be emerging from the Secretariat. Members should not be afraid of asking the Secretariat to provide policy analysis.[314]

---

311 See Supachai Panitchpakdi, *Build Up: The Road to Mexico*, speech on 8 January 2003 at Plenary Session XI of the Partnership Summit 2003 in Hyderabad.

312 See below, pp. 216–17. Note that the Appellate Body has its own Secretariat, which is separate from and independent of the WTO Secretariat, but which shares the same facilities and makes use of the general support services of the WTO Secretariat (translation, library, etc.). See below, p. 235.

313 Communication from Cuba, Dominican Republic, Egypt, Honduras, India, Indonesia, Jamaica, Kenya, Malaysia, Mauritius, Pakistan, Sri Lanka, Tanzania, Uganda and Zimbabwe, *Preparatory Process in Geneva and Negotiating Procedure at the Ministerial Conferences*, WT/GC/W/471, dated 24 April 2002, para. (i).

314 Report by the Consultative Board to the Director-General Supachai Panitchpakdi, *The Future of the WTO: Addressing Institutional Challenges in the New Millennium* (the 'Sutherland Report') (WTO, 2004), paras. 361 and 366.

With regard to the status of the Director-General and WTO staff as *independent* and *impartial* international officials, Article VI:4 of the *WTO Agreement* states:

> The responsibilities of the Director-General and of the staff of the Secretariat shall be exclusively international in character. In the discharge of their duties, the Director-General and the staff of the Secretariat shall not seek or accept instructions from any government or any other authority external to the WTO. They shall refrain from any action which might adversely reflect on their position as international officials. The Members of the WTO shall respect the international character of the responsibilities of the Director-General and of the staff of the Secretariat and shall not seek to influence them in the discharge of their duties.

As noted above, the WTO Secretariat is headed by the WTO Director-General. The Director-General is assisted by four Deputy Directors-General (DDGs), also political appointees serving for a limited period of time. They are appointed by the Director-General – in consultation with WTO Members – and form, together with the Director-General, the senior management of the WTO Secretariat. Currently, Alejandro Jara (of Chile), Valentine Sendanyoye Rugwabiza (of Rwanda), Harsh V. Singh (of India) and Rufus H. Yerxa (of the United States) serve as DDGs under Pascal Lamy. The number of DDGs has been the subject of discussions in the General Council.[315] While it is argued that there could be fewer than four, having four DDGs makes it possible for the main regions of the world to be represented in senior management.

The WTO Secretariat is organised into divisions with a functional role (e.g. the Rules Division, the Services Division and the Market Access Division), divisions with an information and liaison role (e.g. the Information and Media Relations Division) and divisions with a supporting role (e.g. the Administration and General Services Division and the Language Services and Documentation Division). Divisions are normally headed by a Director, who reports to one of the WTO's four DDGs or directly to the Director-General.[316] In addition to the Divisions, the WTO Secretariat also includes the Institute for Training and Technical Cooperation (ITTC), which was established in 2003 to ensure a coherent and coordinated approach to capacity-building and technical assistance. Figure 2.4 shows the organisation of the WTO Secretariat.

The Director-General appoints the staff and determines their duties and conditions of service in accordance with the Staff Regulations adopted by the Ministerial Conference.[317]

---

315 See statement by Ambassador Ali Mchumo, Chair of the General Council, at the meeting on 6 October 1999, WT/GC/27, dated 12 October 1999.

316 Five (or one-quarter) of the twenty directors at the WTO are women.

317 See Article VI:3 of the *WTO Agreement*. According to the *Staff Regulations*, the paramount objective in the determination of conditions of service is to secure staff members of the highest standards of competence, efficiency and integrity and to meet the requirements of the WTO taking into account the needs and aspirations of the staff members. The Director-General has established and administers *Staff Rules*. The *Staff Rules* implement the provisions of the *Staff Regulations*. The Director-General furthermore issues staff administrative memoranda in elaboration of the *Staff Rules*.

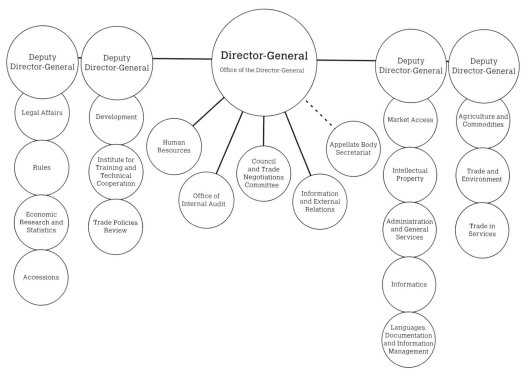

Figure 2.4 WTO Secretariat organization chart as of 31 December 2011

Seventy-six different nationalities are represented in the staff of the WTO Secretariat.[318] Nationals of France, the United Kingdom, Spain, Switzerland, the United States and Canada are best represented among the staff.[319] The representation of developing-country nationals in the staff is growing but remains a matter of concern.[320] There are no formal or informal national or regional quotas for WTO Secretariat officials.[321] Still, ensuring the broadest possible diversification of the WTO Secretariat is an important objective of the WTO's recruitment policy. Most of the professional staff are lawyers or economists. The working languages within the WTO Secretariat are English, French and Spanish, with English being the language most frequently used.

The WTO Secretariat has an internship programme for graduate students who wish to gain practical experience and deeper knowledge of the activities of the WTO. Only a limited number of internships are available. The eligibility

318 See *WTO Annual Report 2012*, 142, available at www.wto.org/english/res_e/booksp_e/anrep_e/anrep12_ e.pdf.
319 See *ibid*. 14. One hundred and seventy-seven are from France, 66 from the United Kingdom, 43 from Spain, 36 from Switzerland, 28 from the United States and 24 from Canada.
320 There are sixty-three officials are from South and Central America, 65 from Asia and 38 from Africa. Respectively nine, nine and thirteen staff are from Brazil, China and India. See *ibid*.
321 Vacancies are the subject of open competition. The final selection of professional staff is done on the basis of a written exam and an interview. The recruitment process is highly competitive. All vacancy notices are posted on the WTO website.

requirements, as well as the terms and conditions of the internship and the application procedure, are set out on the WTO website.

Questions and Assignments 2.15

What is the main task of the WTO's specialised councils, committees, working parties and working groups? How do these WTO bodies differ from each other? Where do the Doha Round negotiations take place? In your opinion, should the WTO have an executive body and/or a consultative assembly? Is the WTO controlled by 'faceless international bureaucrats'? Discuss the role and the powers of the WTO Director-General and the WTO Secretariat.

5   DECISION-MAKING IN THE WTO

The WTO decision-making process has been criticised for being undemocratic, non-transparent and accountable to no one. A decade ago, in 2003, War on Want, a British NGO fighting poverty in developing countries, noted:

From formulating the agenda to reaching a decision, the process is dominated by the most powerful and richest countries. As such, negotiations at the WTO are fertile ground for horse-trading that inevitably favour those with greatest financial and political might. To keep on top of the massive agenda at the WTO, rich countries, such as US, EU, Japan and Canada, have large teams of well-resourced specialists in Geneva. Half of the poorest countries in the WTO cannot even afford one.[322]

This section examines WTO decision-making in theory and in practice, and will, by discussing participation in WTO decision-making, allow the careful reader to assess what extent the criticism by War on Want and others was valid in 2003 and/or is still valid in 2013.

5.1   WTO Decision-Making in Theory

The standard decision-making procedure for WTO bodies is set out in Article IX:1 of the *WTO Agreement*, which states:

The WTO shall continue the practice of decision-making by consensus followed under GATT 1947. Except as otherwise provided, where a decision cannot be arrived at by consensus, the matter at issue shall be decided by voting. At meetings of the Ministerial Conference and the General Council, each Member of the WTO shall have one vote ... Decisions of the Ministerial Conference and the General Council shall be taken by a majority of the votes cast, unless otherwise provided in this Agreement or in the relevant Multilateral Trade Agreement.[323]

---

322   Excerpt from *5th Ministerial: Free Trade on Trial*, available at www.waronwant.org.

323   The Rules of Procedure of the various WTO bodies set out the quorum requirement. For example, Rule 16 of the *Rules of Procedure for the Meetings of the General Council* states: 'A simple majority of the Members shall constitute a quorum.' Most WTO bodies have the same quorum requirement. Currently, seventy-six of the WTO Members must be present at the meeting in order to take valid decisions. In practice, the quorum is not checked.

However, Article 2.4 of the DSU and Articles VII:3, IX:2, IX:3, X and XII:2 of the *WTO Agreement* provide for special decision-making procedures. This sub-section first deals with the standard decision-making procedure and subsequently with the special procedures. Keep in mind that what is explained in this section is WTO decision-making *in theory*. WTO decision-making *in practice* is discussed in the next section.[324]

5.1.1   Standard Procedure

Pursuant to Article IX:1 of the *WTO Agreement*, Members first try to take decisions *by consensus*. Footnote 1 to Article IX defines consensus decision-making by WTO bodies as follows:

> The body concerned shall be deemed to have decided by consensus on a matter submitted for its consideration, if no Member, present at the meeting when the decision is taken, *formally* objects to the proposed decision.[325]

In other words, unless a Member *explicitly* objects to the proposed decision, that decision is taken.[326] No voting takes place.[327] Decision-making by consensus gives all Members *veto power*.[328] John Jackson noted, however, in this respect:

> the practice ... is that some countries that have difficulty with a particular decision will nevertheless remain silent out of deference to countries with a substantially higher stake in the pragmatic economic consequences of a decision.[329]

Decision-making by consensus involves a degree of deference to economic power. It is 'only' when important national, economic or other interests are at stake that a WTO Member would consider blocking the consensus.[330]

As Hoekman and Kostecki noted, decision-making by consensus is a useful device to ensure that only decisions which have a good chance of being implemented are adopted because the decisions adopted are all decisions to which there was no major opposition. However, Hoekman and Kostecki also observed that, as further discussed below,[331] decision-making by consensus:

---

324 See below, pp. 142–8.   325 Emphasis added.

326 Note that the Doha Ministerial Declaration of November 2001 introduced the concept of 'explicit consensus' (for decisions on the inclusion of 'Singapore issues' in the agenda of the Doha Development Round). See above, pp. 88–9. It is not clear what is meant by 'explicit consensus'. The inclusion of this concept in the Doha Ministerial Declaration was, however, a condition of India and other developing-country Members agreeing to the Declaration. At the close of the Doha Ministerial Conference, the Conference Chair, the Qatari Finance, Economy and Trade Minister Youssef Hussain Kamal, stated that 'his understanding of the requirement of "explicit consensus" was that it would give each member the right to take a position on modalities that would prevent negotiations from proceeding after the next Ministerial Conference until that member is prepared to join in an explicit consensus'. If this is indeed the meaning of the concept of 'explicit consensus', the question arises whether an 'explicit' consensus differs from a 'normal' consensus.

327 In decision-making by consensus, unlike in decision-making by unanimity, no voting takes place.

328 As noted in the Sutherland Report, however, the definition of consensus favours Members that can afford to be present at all meetings, since absence does not defeat a consensus. See Report by the Consultative Board to the Director-General Supachai Panitchpakdi, *The Future of the WTO: Addressing Institutional Challenges in the New Millennium* (the 'Sutherland Report') (WTO, 2004), para. 282.

329 J. Jackson, *The World Trade Organization: Constitution and Jurisprudence* (Royal Institute of International Affairs, 1998), 46.

330 See *ibid*.   331 See below, p. 138, footnote 332.

reinforces conservative tendencies in the system. Proposals for change can be adopted only if unopposed, creating the potential for paralysis.[332]

If consensus cannot be achieved, Article IX:1, second sentence, of the *WTO Agreement* provides for voting. For a decision to be adopted, it must have a simple majority of the votes cast. Pursuant to Article IX:1, third sentence, each Member has one vote.[333] However, there is one exception to this rule. Article IX:1, fourth sentence, states:

> Where the European Communities exercise their right to vote, they shall have a number of votes equal to the number of their member States which are Members of the WTO.

In a footnote to this sentence, it is further explained that the total number of votes of the European Communities, now referred to as the European Union, *and* the EU Member States shall in no case exceed the number of the EU Member States. It is thus clear that either the European Union *or* the EU Member States (each individually) will participate in a vote. Who participates in a vote is not a matter of WTO law but of EU constitutional law. For reasons relating to the practice of WTO decision-making, discussed below, the fact that the European Union currently has twenty-seven votes and the United States, China and India only one, does not have much, if any, impact on the political decision-making processes at the WTO.[334]

As already discussed above, it should be pointed out that, as a rule, the European Commission speaks for the European Union *and* the EU Member States at meetings of WTO bodies, even if those bodies deal with matters that are not within the exclusive competence of the European Union.[335] Delegates from the EU Member States attend the meetings but do not speak. The EU Member States speak (and vote, if a vote is called) only with regard to budgetary, finance and administrative matters.[336] Furthermore, the Ministers of the EU Member States make short formal statements at the biennial sessions of the Ministerial Conference.

Questions and Assignments 2.16

What is decision-making by consensus? Does decision-making by consensus amount to a veto power for each WTO Member? Can WTO bodies take decisions by voting? Do all WTO Members have the same number of votes? How many votes do the United States, the European Union, China, Belgium and Saint Lucia have? In your opinion, should the number of votes of Members be related to the size of their population or their share of world trade?

332 B. Hoekman and M. Kostecki, *The Political Economy of the World Trading System: The WTO and Beyond,* 2nd edn (Oxford University Press, 2001), 57.
333 Compare this with decision-making and voting in the IMF or the World Bank. In the IMF, for example, each member country is assigned a quota, based on its relative position in the world economy. This quota largely determines a member's voting power in IMF decision-making.
334 See below, pp. 136–48.
335 See Article 207 of the *Treaty on the Functioning of the European Union,* Official Journal, C 83, 30 March 2010.
336 Note that the EU Member States, and not the European Union, contribute to the WTO budget. See below, pp. 150–1.

5.1.2   Special Procedures

In addition to the standard decision-making procedure, provided for in Article IX:1 of the *WTO Agreement* and discussed in the previous sub-section, the *WTO Agreement* sets out a number of decision-making procedures which deviate from the standard procedure. This sub-section briefly discusses these special procedures.[337]

With regard to decision-making by the DSB, Article 2.4 of the DSU states that the DSB shall take decisions by consensus. As discussed in detail in Chapter 3, the DSB takes certain decisions, such as the decisions on the establishment of a panel, on the adoption of dispute settlement reports, or on the authorisation of retaliation measures, by *negative consensus*.[338] Other decisions, such as the appointment of Members of the Appellate Body, are taken by a *positive consensus*.[339]

With regard to authoritative interpretations of provisions of the *WTO Agreement* and the multilateral agreements of Annex 1, 2 and 3, Article IX:2 of the *WTO Agreement* states that the Ministerial Conference and the General Council shall have the *exclusive authority* to adopt such interpretations,[340] and that the decision to adopt an authoritative interpretation shall be taken by a *three-quarter majority* of the Members.[341] To date, the WTO has not made any *explicit* use of the possibility to adopt 'authoritative interpretations'. The Doha Ministerial Decision on *Implementation-Related Issues and Concerns* contains a number of provisions which are obviously interpretations of provisions of the WTO agreements. However, in its Preamble, the Decision does not explicitly refer to Article IX:2 of the *WTO Agreement* and at least some of these interpretations were adopted without a recommendation of the relevant specialised council.[342] Note that the Appellate Body ruled in *US – Clove Cigarettes (2012)* that paragraph 5.2 of this Decision – which defines the term 'reasonable interval' in Article 2.12 of the *TBT Agreement* was at least six months[343] – was not an authoritative interpretation because it was not based on a recommendation of the Council on Trade in Goods.[344] The Appellate Body emphasised that:

> the recommendation from the relevant Council is an *essential element* of Article IX:2, which constitutes the legal basis upon which the Ministerial Conference or the General Council exercise their authority to adopt interpretations of the *WTO Agreement*.[345]

---

337 Note that not all special decision-making procedures are discussed below. Not discussed is, for example, Article 12.1 of the *SPS Agreement*, pursuant to which the SPS Committee always takes its decisions by consensus.

338 See below, pp. 204–7.

339 See below, p. 206.

340 On the difference between 'authoritative interpretations' of provisions of WTO agreements by the Ministerial Conference and the General Council, on the one hand, and 'clarification' of those provisions by panels and the Appellate Body, see above, p. 125, footnote 262 and below, pp. 184–7.

341 Recall that, in the case of an interpretation of a multilateral trade agreement in Annex 1, the Ministerial Conference and the General Council shall adopt an authoritative interpretation on the basis of a recommendation by the Council overseeing the functioning of that Agreement. See above, footnote 262, p. 125.

342 See above, footnote 262, p. 125.

343 On Article 2.12 of the *TBT Agreement*, see below, pp. 884–7.

344 See Appellate Body Report, *US – Clove Cigarettes (2012)*, para. 255.

345 *Ibid.*, para. 254. Emphasis added.

With regard to decisions on the accession of new Members, Article XII:2 of the *WTO Agreement* provides that such decisions are taken by the Ministerial Conference (or the General Council) by a *two-thirds majority* of the Members. However, on 15 November 1995, the General Council agreed that, for decisions on accession, it will first seek to reach *consensus*.[346] Only when a decision cannot be arrived at by consensus shall the matter be decided by a two-thirds majority vote.[347] To date, only the 1995 decision on the accession of Ecuador was taken by majority vote.

With regard to decisions to waive an obligation imposed on a Member, Article IX:3 of the *WTO Agreement* distinguishes between waivers of obligations under the *WTO Agreement* and waivers of obligations under the multilateral trade agreements of Annex 1. Decisions on waivers of the first type require consensus and, if consensus cannot be reached within a time period not exceeding ninety days, a *three fourths majority* of the Members.[348] Decisions on waivers of the more common, second type require a *three fourths majority* of the Members.[349] However, on 15 November 1995, the General Council decided that – in spite of Article IX:3 – it would also with regard to this second type of waivers first seek to reach *consensus*.[350] Only when a decision cannot be arrived at by consensus shall the matter be decided by a three-quarters majority.

With regard to decisions on amendments of the *WTO Agreement* and the multilateral agreements of Annexes 1, 2, and 3, Article X of the *WTO Agreement* sets out a complex regime. In general terms, the amendment procedure is as follows. Individual Members or one of the three specialised councils (the CTG, CTS and the TRIPS Council)[351] initiate the amendment procedure by submitting an amendment proposal to the Ministerial Conference or the General Council. In a first period of at least ninety days, the Ministerial Conference or the General Council tries to reach *consensus* on the proposal for amendment. If consensus cannot be reached, the Ministerial Conference or the General Council will resort to voting. To be adopted, the proposal for amendment requires a *two-thirds majority* of the Members. Once adopted by consensus or by a two-thirds majority, the amendment is forthwith submitted to the Members for acceptance in accordance with their national constitutional requirements and procedures. An amendment shall take effect for the Members that have accepted the amendment upon

346 See Statement by the Chairman, as agreed by the General Council on 15 November 1995, *on Decision-Making Procedures under Articles IX and XII of the WTO Agreement*, WT/L/93, dated 24 November 1995, first paragraph.
347 *Ibid.*
348 See Article IX:3(a) and the chapeau of Article IX:3 of the *WTO Agreement*.
349 See the chapeau of Article IX:3 of the *WTO Agreement*. Note that a request for a waiver concerning the multilateral agreements of Annex 1 shall be submitted initially to the relevant specialised council for consideration during a time-period which shall not exceed ninety days. See Article IX:3(b) of the *WTO Agreement*.
350 See General Council Decision of 15 November 1995 on *Decision-Making Procedures under Articles IX and XII of the WTO Agreement*, WT/L/93, dated 24 November 1995, first paragraph.
351 See above, pp. 125–7.

acceptance by two-thirds of the Members.[352] As a rule, the amendment is effective only in respect of those Members that have accepted it.[353] However, Article X:2 lists a number of fundamental provisions (concerning the MFN treatment obligation under the GATT 1994, the GATS and the *TRIPS Agreement*, the GATT 1994 tariff schedules and WTO decision-making and amendment) which have to be accepted by all Members before they can take effect. Moreover, a decision to amend the DSU must be made by consensus, and amendments to the DSU take effect for all Members upon approval by the Ministerial Conference. Amendments to the DSU are not submitted to the Members for acceptance.[354] Article X:4 also provides that amendments that do not alter the rights and obligations of the Members take effect for *all* Members upon acceptance by *two-thirds* of the Members. Finally, Article X:3 states in pertinent part:

> The Ministerial Conference may decide by a three-fourths majority of the Members that any amendment made effective under this paragraph is of such a nature that any Member which has not accepted it within a period specified by the Ministerial Conference in each case shall be free to withdraw from the WTO or to remain a Member with the consent of the Ministerial Conference.

While conveyed in diplomatic language, this means, in effect, that a Member that refuses to accept certain amendments may be expelled from the WTO.[355] The actual importance of this provision, however, seems limited. Note that this power also existed under the GATT 1947 but was never used.[356] It is likely that this will also be the case in the WTO.

The first, and thus far only, amendment to the WTO agreements was adopted by the General Council in December 2005 and concerned an amendment to the *TRIPS Agreement*.[357] Pursuant to the amendment decision, an Article 31*bis* is inserted after Article 31 of the *TRIPS Agreement* and an Annex to the *TRIPS Agreement* is inserted after Article 73 thereof. As discussed in Chapter 15, the amendment concerns a relaxation of the obligations of Members when they export to certain eligible developing countries pharmaceutical products produced under a compulsory licence.[358] Pursuant to Article X:3 of the *WTO Agreement*, this amendment will take effect when two-thirds of the Members have accepted the amendment in accordance with their national constitutional requirements and procedures. As of 1 March 2013, only seventy-two Members had notified their acceptance of the amendment.[359] Therefore, this amendment, agreed on in December 2005, has yet to take effect.

---

352 See Article X:3 of the *WTO Agreement*. See, however, Article X:4 of the *WTO Agreement*, discussed below, with regard to amendments that do not alter the rights and obligations of Members.
353 See *ibid.*   354 See *ibid.*, Article X:8.   355 See above, p. 118, footnote 227.
356 See *Analytical Index: Guide to GATT Law and Practice*, 6th edn (GATT, 1994), 934.
357 General Council, *Decision of 6 December 2005 on the Amendment of the TRIPS Agreement*, WT/L/641, dated 8 December 2005.
358 See below, pp. 998–1001.
359 See www.wto.org/english/tratop_e/trips_e/amendment_e.htm. Note that the European Union notified its acceptance and did so also on behalf of the twenty-seven EU Member States.

Finally, with regard to decisions on the annual budget and financial regulations, Article VII:3 of the *WTO Agreement* provides that the General Council
adopts the annual budget and the financial regulations by a *two-thirds majority*
of the votes cast but comprising more than half of the Members of the WTO.

Questions and Assignments 2.17

How does the WTO decide on waivers of WTO obligations? What is the difference between
'authoritative interpretations' under Article IX:2 of the *WTO Agreement* and 'amendments'
under Article X thereof? Should Members wish to amend Article III of the GATT 1994 or
Article 5 of the DSU, what are the procedural requirements for such amendments? Has the
WTO Agreement already been amended?

5.2   WTO Decision-Making in Practice

Although the *WTO Agreement* provides for the possibility to take decisions by
voting, it is very exceptional for bodies to vote. In practice, WTO decisions are
taken by consensus. In 1999, when discussion on the selection of a new Director-General became deadlocked, some developing countries suggested that the
decision on the new Director-General should be taken by vote (as provided for
in Article IX:1 of the *WTO Agreement*). However, this suggestion was not well
received, in particular by the developed countries, which argued that this was
'contrary to the way things were done in the WTO'.[360] Jackson wrote in 1998:

[T]he spirit and practice of the GATT has always been to try to accommodate through
consensus negotiation procedures the views of as many countries as possible, but certainly
to give weight to the views of countries that have power in the trading system. This is not
likely to change.[361]

In a speech in February 2000 at UNCTAD X in Bangkok, a few weeks after
the failure of the Seattle Ministerial Conference, Mike Moore, the then WTO
Director-General, stated:

[T]he consensus principle which is at the heart of the WTO system – and which is a fundamental democratic guarantee – is not negotiable.[362]

It cannot be disputed that decisions taken by consensus have more 'democratic
legitimacy' than decisions taken by majority vote. At the same time, it should
be noted that the consensus requirement does, of course, make decision-making
in the WTO difficult and susceptible to paralysis. After the failure of the Cancún

---

360 Note, however, that the *Decision on the Procedures for the Appointment of Directors-General*, adopted in
     2002, states that: 'Members should consider the possibility of recourse to a vote as a last resort by a proce-
     dure to be determined at that time.' See General Council, *Decision on the Procedures for the Appointment of
     Directors-General*, adopted 10 December 2002, WT/L/509, dated 20 January 2003, para. 21. See also above,
     pp. 136–41.
361 J. Jackson, *The World Trade Organization: Constitution and Jurisprudence* (Royal Institute of International
     Affairs, 1998), 45.
362 M. Moore, *Back on Track for Trade and Development*, keynote address at UNCTAD X, Bangkok, on 16 Feb-
     ruary 2000.

Ministerial Conference in September 2003, the *Financial Times* reported on the frustration of the European Union with the consensus requirement as follows:

Mr Lamy [the EU's trade commissioner] also expanded on his calls for a sweeping overhaul of the way in which the 146-strong WTO operates, and promised that the EU would come up with a set of reform proposals. His comments made clear that he is primarily concerned with the body's consensus-driven approach. 'I think it's above dispute that the principle of the permanent sit-in of 146 trade ministers in order to take a number of very detailed decisions. is a theory that visibly does not work', he said. A Commission official said Mr Lamy was not yet in a position to come up with a set of rounded proposals but that they were likely to address the WTO's most obvious shortfalls. 'Everything needs to be done by consensus. Even the agenda needs to be decided by consensus. And the powers of the WTO director-general are very limited', the official said. 'All that is incredibly complicated with 146 members.'[363]

According to the 2004 Sutherland Report on *The Future of the WTO*, there is definitely 'a larger sense of legitimacy' for decisions adopted by consensus.[364] The Sutherland Report noted, however, that:

[a]s the number of Members grows larger and larger (now 148, perhaps going to 170 and more), it becomes harder and harder to implement needed measures that require decisions, even when there is a vast majority of the Members that desire a measure. The consensus requirement can result in the majority's will being blocked by even one country. If the measure involved a fundamental change, such difficulty would probably be worthwhile, as adding a measure of 'constitutional stability' to the organization. But often there are non-fundamental measures at stake, some of which are just fine-tuning to keep the rules abreast of changing economic and other circumstances.[365]

The Sutherland Report recommended that:

WTO Members give serious further study to the problems associated with achieving consensus in light of possible distinctions that could be made for certain types of decisions, such as purely procedural issues.[366]

The Sutherland Report also recommended that:

WTO Members cause the General Council to adopt a Declaration that a Member considering blocking a measure which otherwise has very broad consensus support shall only block such consensus if it declares in writing, with reasons included, that the matter is one of vital national interest to it.[367]

Questions and Assignments 2.18

Why are WTO Members so hesitant to resort to decision-making by voting? Would decision-making by voting be to the advantage of the developing-country Members?

363 T. Buck, 'EU May Rethink Multilateral Trade Role', *Financial Times*, 16 September 2003.
364 Report by the Consultative Board to the Director-General Supachai Panitchpakdi, *The Future of the WTO: Addressing Institutional Challenges in the New Millennium* (the 'Sutherland Report') (WTO, 2004), para. 282.
365 *Ibid.*, para. 283. As noted by the Sutherland Report, observers of WTO decision-making sometimes contend that consensus decision-making is not a problem as they do not observe many instances in which consensus is blocked. However, it should be noted that 'almost all potential decisions are prepared informally in advance and usually do not move to a formal proposition in a decision-making body if they are not ripe for consensus'. See *ibid.*, para. 285.
366 *Ibid.*, para. 288.   367 *Ibid.*, para. 289.

5.3 Participation in WTO Decision-Making

As discussed above, in practice the WTO takes decisions by consensus. As such, the WTO seems to ensure the participation of all Members, including developing-country Members. However, it is obviously neither possible nor practical to involve directly all 159 Members in negotiations aimed at reaching agreement on controversial issues. It is likely that such broad participation would make these negotiations ineffective. Over the years, mechanisms have, therefore, been developed to facilitate negotiations and decision-making in the WTO. The best-known and most frequently used of these mechanisms is the 'green room meeting'.[368] Green room meetings bring together the major powers in the WTO (which obviously include the European Union, the United States, China, Brazil and India) *and* a select number of other Members, which either are the coordinator/representative of a larger group of Members (such as, for example, the least-developed-country Members) or have a particular interest in the subject-matter under discussion.[369] In green room meetings, ministers, ambassadors or senior officials of the twenty or so Members invited meet under the chairship of the WTO Director-General or the chair of a WTO council or committee to explore possible approaches to the key issues under discussion and to reach, if possible, a preliminary agreement. Such preliminary agreement is then subsequently presented to the rest of the WTO membership for adoption. As noted above, this mechanism was much criticised at the ill-fated Seattle Ministerial Conference.[370] Peter Sutherland wrote in this respect:

Ironically, in Seattle, WTO Director-General Mike Moore and US Trade Representative Charlene Barshefsky, the co-chairs of the Ministerial Meeting, made a concerted, good-faith effort to broaden the participation of delegations in the negotiations. They divided the Ministerial agenda into several sections, created working groups for each, and invited all delegations to participate in all the working groups. Their goal was to keep Green Rooms to a minimum. But developing country delegations, in particular, had difficulty covering all of the working groups, and as the Ministerial week proceeded and agreements remained elusive, the temptation to pull together smaller groups of countries for harder bargaining – Green Rooms, in other words – understandably grew. In communiqués released towards the end of the week, large groupings of African and Latin American countries denounced what they described as the Ministerial's exclusive and non-democratic negotiating structure.[371]

368 See above, pp. 144–8. Other mechanisms are 'mini-ministerials', ambassadorial group meetings (AGMs) and 'heads of delegation meetings' (HODs). These mechanisms are not discussed in this book.

369 While green room meetings are frequently held in the conference room of the WTO Director-General, the term 'green room' does not refer to a specific location. In fact, green room meetings can be, and are, held anywhere. The term 'green room' has its origins in British theatre and refers to the space where actors would wait when they were not required on stage. However, an alternative and more colourful explanation for the use of the term 'green room' is that the conference room of the GATT Director-General, where the first green room meetings were held, had green wallpaper. While this conference room has fortunately been redecorated since, the term 'green room' stuck.

370 See above, p. 87, footnote 51.

371 P. Sutherland, J. Sewell and D. Weiner, 'Challenges Facing the WTO and Policies to Address Global Governance', in G. Sampson (ed.), *The Role of the World Trade Organization in Global Governance* (United Nations University Press, 2001), 87–8.

In the first half of 2000, after the debacle of the Seattle Ministerial Conference in November and December 1999, Members conducted intensive consultations on the issue of the effective participation of developing countries in WTO decision-making.[372] These consultations, however, did not result in any reform of the WTO's institutional structure or its decision-making process. In fact, the consultations indicated that Members thought that there was no need for such reform. At the General Council meeting of 17–19 July 2000, the Chair of the General Council summarised the outcome of the consultations as follows:

First, within the framework of the WTO Agreement it seemed that Members generally did not see the need for any major institutional reform which could alter the basic character of the WTO as a Member-driven organization and its decision-making process. There was also a strong commitment of the Members to reaffirm the existing practice of taking decisions by consensus. Second, Members seemed to recognize that interactive open-ended informal consultation meetings played an important role in facilitating consensus decision-making. As a complement to, but in no way a replacement of this open-ended consultation process, consultations might also take place with individual Members or groups of Members.[373]

While the consultations of 2000 did not result in any reform of the WTO's decision-making process, they did, however, serve to 'clear the air' and rebuild a degree of confidence in the process after the Seattle debacle. In order to ensure that negotiations conducted by only a select group of Members, such as green room meetings, contribute to the achievement of genuine consensus among all Members, it was recognised that there was a need: (1) to inform all Members that such negotiations conducted by a select group of Members were taking place; (2) to allow all interested Members to make their views known in such negotiations; (3) not to make any assumptions on the representation of Members by other Members in such negotiations; and (4) to report back promptly on the results of the negotiations to all Members.[374] The consultations of 2000 also made clear that the WTO needed: (1) to schedule its meetings carefully so as to avoid overlapping meetings as much as possible; and (2) to ensure prompt and efficient dissemination of information and documents to Members, and, in particular, to non-resident Members and Members with small missions. Since 2000, improvements along these lines have been made to the WTO decision-making process. The success of the Doha Ministerial Conference and the launch of the Doha Round at the end of 2001 may be considered as an early result of improvements made. Note, however, that these improvements fell short of the expectations of some Members and that the discussion on how to improve the WTO's decision-making process continued in 2002 and thereafter.[375]

---

372 As a sort of shorthand, this issue was also referred to as the 'internal transparency' issue. The 'internal transparency' issue was distinguished from the 'external transparency' issue, which related to the involvement of civil society in WTO decision-making. See above, p. 99, footnote 125.
373 General Council, *Minutes of Meeting*, WT/GC/M/57, dated 14 September 2000, para. 134.
374 See *ibid*.
375 See General Council, *Minutes of Meetings*, WT/GC/M/73, dated 11 March 2002; WT/GC/M/74, dated 1 July 2002; WT/GC/M/75, dated 27 September 2002; and WT/GC/M/77, dated 13 February 2002. See also Communication from Cuba, Dominican Republic, Egypt, Honduras, India, Indonesia, Jamaica, Kenya, Malaysia, Mauritius, Pakistan, Sri Lanka, Tanzania, Uganda and Zimbabwe, *Preparatory Process in Geneva and Negotiating Procedure at the Ministerial Conferences*, WT/GC/W/471, dated 24 April 2002.

The challenges facing WTO Members, and in particular many developing-country Members, in WTO negotiations and decision-making are well illustrated by the account that Mark Pearson gave of the LDC Group's participation in the (ultimately unsuccessful) Hong Kong Ministerial Conference in December 2005. The task of co-ordinating the LDC Group, i.e. the group of least-developed-country Members, rotates every six months between those least-developed country Members that have a permanent mission in Geneva. In the run-up to, and at, the Hong Kong Ministerial Conference, Zambia acted as the LDC Coordinator. The Zambian diplomats were assisted in this task by Mark Pearson, Director of the Regional Trade Facilitation Programme, a UK-funded programme to promote and improve trade in southern Africa. The following personal account by Pearson gives a rare view behind the 'closed doors' of WTO negotiations and decision-making. Pearson wrote:

Zambia, as LDC Coordinator, was invited to the Green Room consultation process. The Green Room process ... is meant to assist the WTO to broker deals in seemingly difficult situations. There do not seem to be any rules as to who is invited to the Green Room but all Group Coordinators are invited plus other influential countries. Some Groups or countries (including US, EU and South Africa) had two Ministers present, one Trade Minister and one Agricultural Minister. The rules are strict and each Minister is allowed to be accompanied by only one official (1+1). Only Ministers can sit at the table and only Ministers can speak. The meeting is done in English and, if necessary (such as for Japan and Senegal), personal interpretation is done.

Prior to Hong Kong the information was that the conference centre was covered by WiFi so the team opted to use WiFi enabled PDAs to communicate between the [Green Room] and the support team outside. As it turned out, there was WiFi throughout the Conference Centre except in the Green Room. Communication was done by SMS and Blackberry (USTR are issued with Blackberrys as standard) and by going out of the [Green Room], into an anteroom where other officials were allowed, to consult.

The negotiating process in Hong Kong was tortuous in that there was a [Green Room] meeting held for 5 consecutive nights (Tuesday to Saturday) and two other [Green Room] meetings during the day. For two nights the [Green Room meetings] went throughout the night and for the other 3 nights the meetings went on to around 3.00 am to 4.00 am. On Saturday night the [Green Room] started at 10.30 pm and finished at 9.00 am the next morning.

The [Green Room] process in HK started with Agriculture, then moved to NAMA then Services then Development. Special and Different Treatment (SDT) for LDCs, which was really the only development aspect discussed (apart from Cotton, which was discussed as part of Agriculture), was, therefore, always discussed in the early hours of the morning when Ministers were at their most tired, with lowest concentration levels and lowest tolerance levels. There was a need to take these external factors into account in the negotiations. The positions and the arguments had to be expressed in a simplified, quickfire manner as, by the time the LDC slot came up, Ministers were in no mood for long and detailed presentations and discussions.

Although there is only one official inside the [Green Room] there is a need for other officials to be available during the [Green Room] consultations. These other officials waited in anterooms. So it was not only the Minister and his official who lacked sleep. In the case of the LDCs it was the whole of the core negotiating team who had to stay up most of the night and then function effectively the next day.

After the final [Green Room] process, which ended at 9.00 am on Saturday, we went back to the full LDC Group to explain what the outcome of the [Green Room] process had been.

There were attempts by one or two LDCs to convince the LDC Group to walk away from the agreement reached in the [Green Room]. On the one hand there was the opinion that what had been agreed was of no value to the LDCs as it did not offer any more than what was already offered by EBA and AGOA. The other view was that the [Green Room] agreement was a platform from which further progress could be made, and that if the Group walked away from this deal it would be a long time before the Group could be as organised as it was then to launch a similar offensive. The Coordinator suggested that the text agreed in the [Green Room] could be accepted by the LDCs if it was adopted as a 'framework' agreement, with the modalities to be worked out after HK. This compromise was acceptable to the LDC Group and this is how the text was accepted by the LDC Group.[376]

With regard to negotiations and decision-making, the main challenge for the WTO and its 159 Members is to strike an appropriate *balance* between inclusiveness, transparency and efficiency. To date, green room meetings (as they have evolved over time) are the WTO's best effort to strike such balance. Disparities in economic and political power will of course always affect, if not determine, the weight of Members in the WTO negotiations and decision-making. No institutional mechanism can ever totally 'undo' these differences. However, in recent years, the WTO is definitely no longer the 'rich men's club' that the GATT, its predecessor, was, or that the WTO in its early years arguably also was. As discussed in Chapter 1 and noted earlier in this chapter, over the last decade, developing-country Members, and in particular the emerging economies among them, have played an ever more important role in the WTO because of their increasing importance in the global economy.[377] The Coordinator and Chief Negotiator of the ACP Group in Geneva, Ambassador Servansing from Mauritius,[378] wrote in 2012, referring to the crucial NAMA negotiations in the context of the Doha Round, that:

the dominant role of developed countries in determining the contours of a deal for the rest is no longer on the cards.[379]

Also in 2012, Ambassador Bhatia from India,[380] wrote:

At the heart of the present impasse in the [Doha Round] negotiations are the changes in the political economy of the organisation since the conclusion of the Uruguay Round. In previous Rounds under the aegis of the GATT, developed countries played a pre-eminent role in agenda setting as well as in shaping the final outcomes. Developing countries while active in varying degrees were not always sufficiently well organized to translate their

---

376 Mark Pearson, *Assisting the LDCs in WTO Trade Negotiations: A Personal Assessment*, dated December 2005, available at the website of the Regional Trade Facilitation Programme, www.rtfp.africonnect.com. Note that Pearson often referred to the green room process as the Chairman's Consultative Group (CCG), as it was then renamed. However, for clarity, references to the 'CCG' have been replaced with 'Green Room'. In the last paragraph, 'EBA' refers to the European Union's Everything But Arms Regulation and 'AGOA' to the United States' African Growth and Opportunity Act.
377 See above, pp. 20–22 and 106–9.
378 Ambassador Shree B. C. Servansing is the Permanent Representative of Mauritius to the United Nations and other international organisations in Geneva.
379 Shree B. C. Servansing, 'Non-Agricultural Market Access (NAMA) – Balancing Development and Ambition', in P. Mehta, A. Kaushik and R. Kaukab (eds.), *Reflections from the Frontline: Developing Country Negotiators in the WTO* (CUTS International, 2012), 94.
380 Ambassador Ujal Singh Bhatia was the Permanent Representative of India to the WTO from 2004 to 2010. Since December 2011, Ambassador Bhatia is a Member of the WTO Appellate Body. See below, 232.

interests and concerns in key areas into negotiated outcomes. However, the Doha Round has witnessed unprecedented engagement of developing countries, both in their individual capacity, as well as through their various coalitions.[381]

As noted above, three developing-country Members, Brazil, China and India, are now part of the very select group of Members, whose consent is necessary to get anything done within the WTO.[382] A larger group of emerging economies among the developing-country Members, including Argentina, Chile, Indonesia, Malaysia, Mexico, Pakistan, Peru, Philippines, Thailand, Turkey and Venezuela, have in recent years – acting on their own, but more commonly as part of a group, coalition or alliance – significantly gained in influence in WTO negotiations and decision-making. Many other developing-country Members, including of course the least-developed-country Members, still lack in resources and expertise to participate effectively in WTO negotiations and decision-making.[383] Nevertheless, these Members have increasingly been able to make their voice heard and their concerns considered in WTO negotiations and decision-making. This has been the result of: (1) trade-related technical assistance and training, discussed above;[384] and (2) the systematic coordination of positions and the pooling of resources and expertise in groups, coalitions and alliances of developing-country Members with common interests, also discussed above.[385] Overall, developing-country Members are now participating in WTO negotiations and decision-making in a much more active and effective manner than ever before. However, as already suggested above, there is a drawback to this welcome development.[386] The active and effective participation of a greater number of Members with very different economic and trade interests has inevitably made WTO negotiations and decision-making also more difficult than ever before.

Questions and Assignments 2.19

Can developing-country Members effectively participate in WTO negotiations and decision-making? If not, why? What are green room meetings? Could the WTO function without green room or similar meetings? How can the effective participation of developing-country Members best be ensured?

6   OTHER ISSUES

The final section on 'other issues' addresses briefly issues relating to the legal status of the WTO under international law and issues relating to the WTO budget.

381 Ujal S. Bhatia, 'G20 – Combining Substance with Solidarity and Leadership', in P. Mehta, A. Kaushik and R. Kaukab (eds.), *Reflections from the Frontline: Developing Country Negotiators in the WTO* (CUTS International, 2012), 239.
382 See above, 148.
383 In addition to the relative lack of experienced trade negotiators, two particular problems faced by many of these developing-country Members are: (1) the lack of effective coordination between ministries and government agencies; and (2) the lack of a structured, i.e. institutionalised, dialogue with domestic stakeholders. These problems often result in a situation in which a Member does not have a clear picture of its offensive and defensive interests in specific negotiations.
384 See above, pp. 101–4.   385 See above, pp. 106–8.   386 See above, p. 93.

6.1 Legal Status of the WTO

Pursuant to Article VIII of the *WTO Agreement*, the WTO has legal personality, and shall be accorded by each of its Members such legal capacity as well as such privileges and immunities as may be necessary for the exercise of its functions.[387] The privileges and immunities to be accorded by a Member to the WTO, its officials, and the representatives of its Members shall be similar to the privileges and immunities stipulated in the 1947 United Nations *Convention on the Privileges and Immunities of the Specialised Agencies.*[388] Article III, Section 4, of this Convention stipulates that:

> The specialized agencies ... shall enjoy immunity from every form of legal process except in so far as in any particular case they have expressly waived their immunity.

The privileges and immunities which Switzerland accords to the WTO, its officials and the representatives of WTO Members are set out in detail in the 1995 *WTO Headquarters Agreement* concluded between the WTO and Switzerland.[389]

It deserves to be mentioned that the WTO is *not* part of the UN 'family'. It is a fully independent international organisation with its own particular 'corporate' culture. John Jackson noted, with regard to the question of the 'specialised-agency-of-the-UN' status for the WTO, that this question:

> was explicitly considered and explicitly rejected by the WTO members, possibly because of the skepticism of some members about the UN budgetary and personnel policies and their alleged inefficiencies.[390]

However, this 'separateness' does not preclude that the WTO maintains a close working relationship with many UN organisations and agencies.[391]

6.2 WTO Budget

The total WTO budget for 2012 amounted to CHF196 million (Swiss francs).[392] In comparison with the annual budget of other international organisations or

---

387 See Article VIII:1 and 2 of the *WTO Agreement.* With regard to the privileges and immunities of WTO staff and the representatives of the WTO Members, see Article VIII:3 of the *WTO Agreement*: 'The officials of the WTO and the representatives of the Members shall similarly be accorded by each of its Members such privileges and immunities as are necessary for the independent exercise of their functions in connection with the WTO.'

388 Article VIII:4 of the *WTO Agreement.*

389 For the *WTO Headquarters Agreement*, see WT/GC/1 and Add.1.

390 J. Jackson, *The World Trade Organization: Constitution and Jurisprudence* (Royal Institute of International Affairs, 1998), 52.

391 See above, pp. 97–101.

392 See *WTO Annual Report 2012*, 148. Of these CHF196 million, CHF190 million is for the WTO Secretariat, and CHF6 million is for the Appellate Body and its Secretariat. Of the total budget of CHF196 million, CHF127 million, or 65 per cent, was for staff costs. The WTO budget adopted for 2013 amounted to CHF197 million. Compared to 2011, there was a zero nominal growth in 2012 and a 0.61 per cent growth in 2013. CHF196 million and CHF197 million is equivalent to €163.2 million/US$200.6 million and €164.1 million/US$201.6 million respectively (August 2012 exchange rates). Over the last decade, the WTO budget has gradually been increased. In 2008, the WTO budget amounted to CHF184.8 million; and in 2003 to CHF154.9 million.

some NGOs, the WTO's annual budget is quite modest. In 2001, the then WTO Director-General, Mike Moore, noted that the World Wildlife Fund had three times the resources of the WTO.[393] The modest budget of the WTO reflects the small size of the Secretariat and the relatively limited scope of the WTO's activities outside Geneva. Peter Sutherland has, however, criticised the limited size of the WTO budget:

> Lacking either the courage of their own convictions or confidence in their ability to prevail over domestic opposition, the chief financial backers of the WTO have failed to provide adequate funding for a WTO Secretariat (by far the smallest of all the major multilateral institutions) that is already overburdened by technical assistance demands as well as dispute settlement cases and new accessions.[394]

Pursuant to Article VII:1 of the *WTO Agreement*, the WTO Director-General presents a budget proposal to the Committee on Budget, Finance and Administration, which will review the proposal and make recommendations thereon to the General Council. As discussed above, Article VII:3 of the *WTO Agreement* provides that the General Council adopt the budget by a *two-thirds majority* of the votes cast but comprising more than half of the Members of the WTO. However, in practice, the budget is adopted by consensus.

With respect to the financial contributions to be made by Members to the budget of the WTO, the WTO *Financial Regulations*, as last amended by the General Council in May 2007, set out: (1) the scale of contributions apportioning the expenses of the WTO among its Members; and (2) the measures to be taken in respect of Members in arrears.[395] Pursuant to Article VII:4 of the *WTO Agreement*, each Member shall promptly contribute to the WTO its share in the expenses of the WTO in accordance with the *Financial Regulations*.[396]

As provided for in the *Financial Regulations*, the contribution of a Member to the WTO budget is established on the basis of that Member's international trade (imports plus exports) in relation to the total international trade of all WTO Members.[397] In other words, a Member's contribution is based on that Member's share in international trade. Members of which the share in the total international trade of all WTO Members is less than 0.015 per cent make a minimum contribution to the budget of 0.015 per cent.[398] The European Union does not contribute to the WTO budget. The twenty-seven EU Member States contribute

---

393   Reported by F. Lewis, 'The Anti-Globalization Spoilers Are Going Global', *International Herald Tribune*, 6 July 2001.
394   P. Sutherland, J. Sewell and D. Weiner, 'Challenges Facing the WTO and Policies to Address Global Governance', in G. Sampson (ed.), *The Role of the World Trade Organization in Global Governance* (United Nations University Press, 2001), 82.
395   For the currently applicable *Financial Regulations of the World Trade Organization*, see WT/L/156/Rev.2, dated 21 May 2007. For the currently applicable detailed *Financial Rules of the World Trade Organization*, see WT/L/157/Rev.1, dated 21 May 2007.
396   Note that, in addition to the contributions made by Members, the WTO has miscellaneous income from contributions made by Observer countries (see above, pp. 149–52) and the sale of publications.
397   See Regulation 12.2 of the *Financial Regulations of the World Trade Organization*.
398   See *ibid.*, Regulation 12.7.

to the WTO budget, and their contribution is by far the largest. This is because, in calculating the contribution of the EU Member States, not only trade between the EU with other WTO Members but also trade between the EU Member States, is taken into account. Together, the EU Member States contributed, in 2012, 40.4 per cent of the WTO budget; the United States 12.2 per cent; China 7.3 per cent; Japan 4.8 per cent; Canada 2.9 per cent; Korea 2.7 per cent; Hong Kong 2.6 per cent; Singapore 2.2 per cent; Mexico 1.8 per cent; India 1.7 per cent; Chinese Taipei 1.6 per cent; Saudi Arabia 1.2 per cent; Australia 1.2 per cent; Malaysia 1.1 per cent; Brazil 1.1 per cent; Norway 0.9 per cent; Indonesia 0.8 per cent; and South Africa 0.6 per cent.[399] At the end of 2011, there were nine Members with arrears in contributions.[400]

In addition to the annual budget, the WTO also manages a number of trust funds, which have been contributed to by Members. Trust funds such as the Doha Development Agenda Global Trust Fund are used in support of special activities for technical assistance and training meant to enable least-developed and developing countries to make better use of the WTO and draw greater benefit from the multilateral trading system.

In March 2008, the Office of Internal Audit (OIA) was established to undertake the independent examination and evaluation of the WTO's financial and budgetary control systems and processes, with the aim of ensuring that the contributions by Members to the WTO budget are used 'efficiently and effectively to obtain the best value for money'.[401] In 2011, the OIA issued two reports: one on the cleaning and maintenance services and the other on security and safety activities.[402] The WTO accounts are also subject to external audits.[403] The main findings of the 2011 Audit Report include the following:

The headquarters renovation-extension project should be completed in 2012, with a slight delay but within the planned budgets. The cost of the common facilities, not originally planned, exceeds the budget foreseen at the end of 2011, but additional work has been done.[404]

The six external auditors conducting the 2011 audit certified that the accounts for the financial year 2011 'present fairly the financial position of the WTO as at 31 December 2011'.[405]

399   See *WTO Annual Report 2012*, 150–1.
400   See *ibid.*, 148. Only four Members had arrears of more than three years. Of those, three Members (Burundi, the Democratic Republic of the Congo and Mauritania) accepted in 2011 a payment plan. See *ibid.*
401   *Ibid.*, 152. Regulation 41(d) of the *Financial Regulations of the World Trade Organization*, WT/L/156/Rev.2, dated 21 May 2007, provides the relevant legal basis.
402   In its report on cleaning and maintenance services, the OIA noted that the provider of these services had been contracted (by the GATT and the WTO) for thirty-two years in succession. The report identified opportunities for improving the terms and conditions of contract, and to enhance compliance with the terms and conditions of contract by the provider. See *WTO Annual Report 2012*, 152.
403   See Regulations 46 and 47 of the *Financial Regulations of the World Trade Organization*, WT/L/156/Rev.2, dated 21 May 2007.
404   *Report on the Financial Statements for the Financial Year Ended 31 December 2012 and Performance Audit*, WT/BFA/W/279, dated 14 August 2012, 3.
405   *Ibid.*, 49.

Questions and Assignments 2.20

Can legal proceedings be brought against the WTO before a court of a WTO Member? Please comment on the 'separateness' of the WTO from the UN 'family'. How is the WTO financed? How is the decision on the annual budget and on the contributions of Members to that budget taken? Who is the biggest contributor to the WTO budget? Why? How does the WTO ensure that Members get 'the best value for money'?

7 SUMMARY

The WTO is a young international organisation with a long history. The origins of the WTO lie in the GATT 1947, which for almost fifty years was – after the 'stillbirth' of the ITO – the *de facto* international organisation for trade. While the GATT was successful with respect to the reduction of tariffs, effectively addressing the problems of international trade in goods and services in the era of economic globalisation would require a more 'sophisticated' institutional framework. The Uruguay Round negotiations resulted, in December 1993, in an agreement on the establishment of the World Trade Organization, which was subsequently signed in Marrakesh, Morocco, in April 1994. The WTO has been operational since 1 January 1995.

Pursuant to the Preamble to the *WTO Agreement*, the ultimate objectives of the WTO are: (1) the increase of standards of living; (2) the attainment of full employment; (3) the growth of real income and effective demand; and (4) the expansion of production of, and trade in, goods and services. However, it is clear from the Preamble that, in pursuing these objectives, the WTO must take into account the need for sustainable development and the needs of developing countries. The two main instruments, or means, to achieve the objectives of the WTO are: (1) the reduction of trade barriers; and (2) the elimination of discrimination.

The primary function of the WTO is to provide the common institutional framework for the conduct of trade relations among its Members. More specifically, the WTO has been assigned six widely defined functions: (1) to facilitate the implementation, administration and operation of the WTO agreements; (2) to be a forum for negotiations on new trade rules; (3) to settle trade disputes between its Members; (4) to review the trade policies of its Members; (5) to cooperate with other international organisations and non-governmental organisations; and (6) to give technical assistance to developing-country Members to allow them to integrate into the world trading system and reap the benefits of international trade.

Since the accession of China in December 2001 and even more so with the accession of Russia in 2012, the WTO is a universal organisation. Its 159 Members account for almost all international trade. Three out of every four

WTO Members are developing countries. It is noteworthy that not only States but also autonomous customs territories can be, and are, Members of the WTO. Equally noteworthy is that both the European Union *and* all EU Member States are Members of the WTO. Accession to the WTO is a difficult process, since applicants for membership have to: (1) negotiate an 'entrance ticket' of market access concessions and commitments; and (2) bring their national legislation and practices into conformity with the WTO agreements. With regard to membership rights and obligations, not all Members are equal. For good reason, there are at least three different categories of Members: developed-country Members, developing-country Members; and least-developed-country Members. The latter two categories benefit from some degree of 'special and differential treatment' under most of the WTO agreements. All WTO Members can, and do, in exceptional circumstances obtain temporary waivers of WTO obligations. They can also, but have not done so to date, withdraw from the WTO. With one insignificant exception, the *WTO Agreement* does not provide for the possibility to expel Members from the WTO.

The WTO has a complex institutional structure which includes: (1) at the *highest* level, the Ministerial Conference, which is in session only for a few days every two years; (2) at a *second* level, the General Council, which exercises the powers of the Ministerial Conference in between its sessions; and the Dispute Settlement Body (DSB) and the Trade Policy Review Body (TPRB), which are both emanations of the General Council; and (3) at *lower* levels, specialised councils and manifold committees, working parties and working groups. The current Doha Round negotiations are conducted in special sessions of existing WTO bodies and in two specially created, negotiating groups. The conduct of these negotiations is supervised by the Trade Negotiations Committee (TNC), which regularly reports to the General Council. Furthermore, the institutional structure of the WTO includes judicial, quasi-judicial and other non-political bodies as well as the WTO Secretariat, headed by the WTO Director-General. The WTO is a 'Member-driven' organisation. The Members – and not the Director-General or the WTO Secretariat – set the agenda, make proposals and take decisions. The Director-General and the WTO Secretariat act primarily as an 'honest broker' in, or a 'facilitator' of, the political decision-making processes in the WTO. In such a seemingly modest role, the Director-General and the WTO Secretariat can, however, make an important contribution to the building of consensus among Members on a specific agreement or decision. Unlike other international organisations, the WTO does not have a permanent body through which the 'dialogue' between the WTO and civil society can take place. Furthermore, all WTO bodies (except for the non-political bodies) comprise all 159 Members of the WTO. The WTO does not have an executive body, comprising only core WTO Members, to facilitate negotiations and decision-making. However, it is obviously neither possible nor practical to involve directly all 159 Members in negotiations aimed at reaching agreement on controversial issues. Over the years, mechanisms have, therefore, been developed to facilitate negotiations and decision-making in the WTO. The best-known and most frequently used of these mechanisms is the 'green room meeting'. Since the ill-fated Seattle Ministerial Conference in 1999, a number of practical improvements have been made to the 'green room meetings' to ensure that negotiations taking place between the select number of Members invited to attend the 'green room meeting', contribute to the achievement of genuine consensus among all Members.

With respect to decision-making by WTO bodies, one must distinguish between WTO decision-making in theory and decision-making in practice. The *WTO Agreement* provides for a standard decision-making procedure, which applies as the default procedure, and a number of special procedures for specific decisions. *In theory*, WTO Members, under the standard and most of the special procedures, take decisions by consensus, and, if that is not possible, by majority voting. In the latter case, every Member has one vote, except the European Union, which has as many votes as there are EU Member States (currently twenty-seven). *In practice*, however, the WTO very seldom resorts to voting. WTO decisions are made almost exclusively by consensus. Decision-making by consensus is at the heart of the WTO system and is regarded as a fundamental democratic guarantee. However, the consensus requirement renders decision-making by the WTO difficult and susceptible to paralysis.

In recent years, the WTO is definitely no longer the 'rich men's club' that the GATT, its predecessor, was, or that the WTO in its early years arguably also was. Three developing-country Members, Brazil, China and India, are now part of the very select group of Members, whose consent is necessary to get anything done within the WTO. A larger group of emerging economies among the developing-country Members, have in recent years – acting on their own, but more commonly as part of a group, coalition or alliance – significantly gained in influence in WTO negotiations and decision-making. Many other developing-country Members, including of course the least-developed-country Members, still lack in resources and expertise to participate effectively in WTO negotiations and decision-making. Nevertheless, these Members have increasingly been able to make their voice heard and their concerns considered in WTO negotiations and decision-making. This has been the result of: (1) trade-related technical assistance and training; and (2) the systematic coordination of positions and the pooling of resources and expertise in groups, coalitions and alliances of developing-country Members with common interests. However, the active and effective participation of a greater number of Members with very different economic and trade interests has inevitably made WTO negotiations and decision-making more difficult than ever before.

Exercise 2: To Join or not to Join?

The Parliament of the Republic of Newland has approved – by a narrow margin – the government's plans to start negotiations on accession to the WTO. However, the opposition continues its campaign against Newland's accession to the WTO in the hope of turning public opinion in Newland against WTO membership. In a series of interviews and speeches, the charismatic leader of the opposition claims that: (1) for many years Newland's best diplomats and negotiators will be caught up in never-ending, very complex negotiations on accession; (2) Newland will be forced to make many amendments to its domestic legislation; (3) Newland will be forced to accept obligations to which current WTO Members are not subject; (4) if Newland were unable to meet some of its obligations under the *WTO Agreement*, it would have no other option than to withdraw from the WTO; (5) as a Member, Newland will have to grant market access to goods and services from Evilland, an original WTO Member, but a country with a notoriously bad human rights record; (6) the WTO is controlled by the European Union (which holds no less than twenty-seven votes) and the United States; (7) Newland, as a developing country, will not be able to participate effectively in WTO negotiations and decision-making; (8) the WTO is directed by a group of faceless international officials of French nationality, headed by a Director-General, who is also of French nationality and is handpicked by the 'Quad'; (9) the confidentiality of government-to-government negotiations on trade matters is not guaranteed as special interest groups have access to meetings of WTO bodies and have immediate access to all official documents; and (10) NGOs, none of which is friendly to the economic and trade interests of Newland, have a voice in WTO decision-making. A recent poll showed that the opposition's campaign against WTO accession is succeeding and that public opinion in Newland is turning against accession. To reverse the tide, Newland's government decides to engage in a debate with the opposition in Parliament. The Minister of Foreign Affairs has taken it upon herself to reply to each of the 10 claims of the opposition leader. She wishes to do so, whenever possible, with legal, rather than political, arguments. You have been instructed to prepare speaking notes for the Minister.

3 WTO Dispute Settlement

CONTENTS

1 INTRODUCTION

As discussed in Chapter 1, the WTO agreements provide for many wide-ranging and broadly formulated rules concerning international trade in goods, trade in services and trade-related aspects of intellectual property rights.[1] In view of the importance of their impact, economic and otherwise, it is not surprising that WTO Members do not always agree on the correct interpretation and application of these rules. In fact, Members frequently argue about whether or not a particular law or practice constitutes a violation of a right or obligation provided for in a WTO agreement. The WTO has a remarkable system to settle disputes between WTO Members concerning their rights and obligations under the WTO agreements. As mentioned in Chapter 2, dispute settlement is one of the core functions of the WTO.[2]

The WTO dispute settlement system has been operational for eighteen years now. In that period it has arguably been the most prolific of all international State-to-State dispute settlement systems. Between 1 January 1995 and 31 December 2012, a total of 454 disputes have been brought to the WTO for resolution.[3] In more than a fifth of the disputes brought to the WTO, the parties were able to reach an amicable solution through consultations, or the dispute was otherwise resolved without recourse to adjudication. In other disputes, parties have resorted to adjudication. Between 1 January 1995 and 31 December 2012, such adjudication resulted in 183 reports of dispute settlement panels and 109 reports of the Appellate Body.[4] During the same period, the International Court of Justice (ICJ) in The Hague rendered fifty-four judgments and six advisory opinions, and the International Tribunal for the Law of the Sea (ITLOS) in Hamburg rendered sixteen judgments and one advisory opinion.[5] Also in comparison to its 'predecessor', the GATT dispute settlement system, the WTO dispute settlement system has obviously been very active. During the forty-seven years that the GATT dispute settlement system was operational (from 1948 to 1994), only 132 GATT dispute settlement reports were issued.[6] Most importantly, however, in more than eight out of ten disputes in which the respondent had to withdraw (or amend) a WTO-inconsistent measure, it did so in a timely manner.[7]

---

1 See above, pp. 34–50.   2 See above, p. 21.
3 I.e. the number of requests for consultations notified to the DSB until 31 December 2012. See www.worldtradelaw.net/dsc/database/searchcomplaints.asp.
4 See www.worldtradelaw.net/reports/wtopanels/wtopanels.asp and www.worldtradelaw.net/reports/wtoab/abreports.asp. Note that when two or more reports are contained *in one document* (see e.g. *Philippines – Distilled Spirits (2012)*), these reports are counted as one for the purpose of this count. Also note that these numbers include Article 21.5 'compliance' reports (see below, p. 293) as well as reports in the very few cases in which the complaint or appeal was withdrawn while the case was pending before a panel or the Appellate Body (see below, pp. 177 (re panels) and 286–7 (re appeals)).
5 See www.icj-cij.org and www.itlos.org.
6 See www.worldtradelaw.net/reports/gattpanels/gattpanels.asp. This number includes some chair's rulings and decisions by the Contracting Parties in the late 1940s.
7 See below, p. 293.

The WTO dispute settlement system has been used by developed-country Members and developing-country Members alike.[8] In 2000, 2001, 2003, 2005, 2008, 2010 and 2012, developing-country Members brought more disputes to the WTO for resolution than developed-country Members.[9] While many disputes are between developed-country Members, developing-country Members have frequently used the WTO dispute settlement system to resolve trade disputes between them.[10] Particularly note-worthy is the successful use of the dispute settlement system by small, sometimes very small, developing-country Members against the largest among the developed-country Members.[11] In the WTO, might is not necessarily right.

A number of disputes brought to the WTO dispute settlement system have triggered considerable controversy and public debate and have attracted much media attention. This has been the case, for example, for disputes on national legislation for the protection of public health or the environment, such as the *EC – Hormones (1998)* dispute on the European Union's import ban on meat from cattle treated with growth hormones (complaints by the United States and Canada);[12] the *US – Shrimp (1998)* dispute on the US import ban on shrimp harvested with nets that kill sea turtles (complaints by India, Malaysia, Pakistan and Thailand);[13] the *Brazil – Retreaded Tyres (2007)* dispute on a Brazilian ban on the import of retreaded tyres for environmental reasons (complaint by the European Union);[14] the *EC – Approval and Marketing of Biotech Products (2006)* dispute on measures affecting the approval and marketing of genetically modified products in the European Union (complaint by the United States, Canada and Argentina); the *US – Clove Cigarettes (2012)* dispute concerning a tobacco-control measure taken by the United States that prohibits cigarettes with 'characterizing flavours' other than tobacco or menthol (complaint by Indonesia); the *US – Tuna II (Mexico) (2012)* dispute concerning US regulation on the use of the dolphin-safe label on tuna cans; and the currently pending *Canada – Feed-In Tariff/Renewable Energy* dispute concerning measures relating to renewable energy generation (complaints by the European Union and Japan). Also, the *EC – Bananas III (1997)* dispute on the European Communities' preferential import regime for bananas was, for many years, headline news (complaints by Ecuador,

8 The most active user of the system has been the United States, closely followed by the European Union. The system has, however, also been used 'against' the United States more often than against any other Member, the European Union being a distant second in this respect. For statistics on complainants and respondents in WTO dispute settlement, see www.worldtradelaw.net.
9 In 1995, 2006, 2009 and 2011, developing-country and developed-country Members initiated the same number of cases. From 1996 to 1999, in 2002, 2004 and 2007 developed-country Members initiated more cases than developing-country Members. The most active users of the system among developing-country Members have been Brazil, India, Argentina, Thailand, Chile and China. The most frequent respondents among developing-country Members have been China, India, Argentina, Brazil, Mexico, Chile and Turkey. See www.wto.org/english/tratop_e/dispu_e/dispu_e.htm.
10 See *ibid.*
11 E.g. the dispute between Antigua and Barbuda (a Caribbean island State with less than 90,000 inhabitants) and the United States, *US – Gambling (2005)*. See below, pp. 587 and 594.
12 See below, pp. 911–22. 13 See below, pp. 554–9. 14 See below, pp. 261, 897–900, 919.

Guatemala, Honduras, Mexico and the United States).[15] Other highly 'sensitive' disputes include the *EC and certain member States – Large Civil Aircraft (2011)* and *US – Large Civil Aircraft (2nd complaint) (2012)* disputes concerning subsidies to Airbus and Boeing respectively (complaints by the United States and the European Union respectively).[16] The latter two disputes were undoubtedly the biggest and most complex disputes handled by the WTO dispute settlement system to date. Many trade remedy cases, and in particular those concerning zeroing,[17] also caused much commotion, although perhaps more among the industries or companies directly affected (and their interest groups and lawyers) than among the general public.

   The WTO dispute settlement system, which has been in operation since 1 January 1995, was not established out of the blue. It is not an entirely novel system. On the contrary, this system is based on, and has taken on board, almost fifty years of experience in the resolution of trade disputes in the context of the GATT 1947. Article 3.1 of the DSU states:

> Members affirm their adherence to the principles for the management of disputes heretofore applied under Articles XXII and XXIII of GATT 1947 and the rules and procedures as further elaborated and modified herein.

The GATT 1947 contained only two brief provisions on dispute settlement (Articles XXII and XXIII), which neither explicitly referred to 'dispute settlement' nor provided for detailed procedures to handle disputes. However, the GATT Contracting Parties 'transformed', in a highly pragmatic manner over a period of five decades, what was initially a rudimentary, power-based system for settling disputes through diplomatic negotiations into an elaborate, rules-based system for settling disputes through adjudication. While for decades quite successful in resolving disputes to the satisfaction of the parties,[18] the GATT dispute settlement had some serious shortcomings which became ever more acute in the course of the 1980s. The most important shortcoming related to the fact that the findings and conclusions of the panels of experts adjudicating disputes only became legally binding when adopted *by consensus* by the GATT Council. The responding party could thus prevent any unfavourable conclusions from becoming legally binding upon it. As discussed in this chapter, the WTO dispute settlement system, negotiated during the Uruguay Round and provided for in the *Understanding on Rules and Procedures for the Settlement of Disputes*, commonly referred to as the *Dispute Settlement Understanding* or DSU, remedied this and a number of other shortcomings

---

15 See below, p. 203.   16 See below, p. 791.

17 On the 'zeroing' methodology, i.e. a methodology to calculate anti-dumping margins, see below, pp. 692–6.

18 On the GATT dispute settlement system, see R. E. Hudec, D. L. M. Kennedy and M. Sgarbossa, 'A Statistical Profile of GATT Dispute Settlement Cases: 1948–1989', *Minnesota Journal of Global Trade*, 1993, 285–7. Hudec has also been quoted as saying with regard to the success of the GATT dispute settlement system that 'accomplishments to this point, if not unique, are at least rare in the history of international legal institutions'.

of the GATT dispute settlement system.[19] The DSU is generally considered to be one of the most important achievements of the Uruguay Round negotiations.[20] Claus-Dieter Ehlermann, a former Appellate Body Member and top EU official, noted in 2003 that the successful negotiation of the DSU is 'an extraordinary achievement that comes close to a miracle'.[21]

It is not the ambition of this chapter to give a detailed account of the evolution and current operation of the WTO dispute settlement system, the manifold relevant provisions in the WTO agreements and the impressive body of case law on those provisions. The relevant section in the 2012 WTO Analytical Index runs over 400 pages. This chapter will also not address in any detail the many proposals for the improvement of the WTO dispute settlement which have been tabled by Members over the last twelve years in the context of the Doha Round negotiations.[22] Instead, this chapter focuses on the basics of WTO dispute settlement and addresses in turn: (1) the jurisdiction of the WTO dispute settlement system; (2) access to WTO dispute settlement; (3) the key features of WTO dispute settlement; (4) the institutions of WTO dispute settlement; (5) the process of WTO dispute settlement; and (6) developing-country Members and WTO dispute settlement.

2 JURISDICTION OF THE WTO DISPUTE SETTLEMENT SYSTEM

The WTO dispute settlement system stands out by virtue of the nature as well as the scope of its jurisdiction. This section examines these two aspects – nature and scope – of the jurisdiction of the WTO dispute settlement system in turn.

2.1 Nature of the Jurisdiction

Unlike the jurisdiction of other important State-to-State dispute settlement mechanisms, such as the International Court of Justice or the International Tribunal for the Law of the Sea, the jurisdiction of the WTO dispute settlement system is: (1) compulsory; (2) exclusive; and (3) only contentious (i.e. not advisory).

2.1.1 Compulsory Jurisdiction

The jurisdiction of the WTO dispute settlement system is compulsory in nature. A responding Member has, as a matter of law, no choice but to accept the jurisdiction of the WTO dispute settlement system. Note that Article 6.1 of the DSU states:

---

19 As discussed in Chapter 1, the DSU is attached to the *WTO Agreement* as Annex 2 thereto. See above, p. 48.
20 On the Uruguay Round negotiations, see above, p. 79.
21 C.-D. Ehlermann, 'Six Years on the Bench of the "World Trade Court": Some Personal Experiences as Member of the Appellate Body of the World Trade Organization', *Journal of World Trade*, 2002, 639.
22 For a general overview of the DSU reform negotiations, see below, p. 303.

If the complaining party *so requests*, a *panel* shall *be established* at the latest at the DSB meeting following that at which the request first appears as an item on the DSB's agenda, unless at that meeting the DSB decides by consensus not to establish a panel.[23]

Unlike in other international dispute settlement systems, there is no need for the parties to a dispute, arising under the covered agreements, to accept, in a separate declaration or separate agreement, the jurisdiction of the WTO dispute settlement system to adjudicate the dispute. Membership of the WTO constitutes consent to, and acceptance of, the jurisdiction of the WTO dispute settlement system.

2.1.2   Exclusive Jurisdiction

The jurisdiction of the WTO dispute settlement system is also exclusive. Article 23.1 of the DSU states:

When Members seek the redress of a violation of obligations or other nullification or impairment of benefits under the covered agreements or an impediment to the attainment of any objective of the covered agreements, they shall have recourse to, and abide by, the rules and procedures of this Understanding.

Pursuant to this provision, a complaining Member is obliged to bring any dispute arising under the covered agreements to the WTO dispute settlement system.[24] The panel in *US – Section 301 Trade Act (2000)* ruled that Article 23.1 of the DSU:

imposes on all Members [a requirement] to 'have recourse to' the multilateral process set out in the DSU when they seek the redress of a WTO inconsistency. In these circumstances, Members have to have recourse to the DSU dispute settlement system to the *exclusion* of any other system, in particular a system of unilateral enforcement of WTO rights and obligations.[25]

Article 23.1 of the DSU both ensures the exclusivity of the WTO *vis-à-vis* other international fora *and* protects the multilateral system from unilateral conduct.[26] As Article 23.2(a) of the DSU provides, Members are prohibited from making a determination to the effect that a violation has occurred, that benefits have been nullified or impaired, or that the attainment of any objective of the covered agreements has been impeded, *except* through recourse to dispute settlement in accordance with the rules and procedures of the DSU. While Members can only have recourse to the WTO dispute settlement system to resolve their disputes, this does not mean that these disputes can only be resolved through consultations between the parties or adjudication by a WTO panel and the Appellate Body. It should be noted that the WTO dispute settlement system provides for

---

23 Emphasis added.   24 On the concept of 'covered agreement', see below, p. 163.

25 Panel Report, *US – Section 301 Trade Act (2000)*, para. 7.43. Emphasis added. The panel noted that this 'exclusive dispute resolution clause' is an important new element of Members' rights and obligations under the DSU. *Ibid.*

26 See Panel Report, *EC – Commercial Vessels (2005)*, para. 7.193. On the multilateral nature of WTO dispute settlement, see below, p. 182.

several methods to resolve disputes. *Consultations* between the parties, provided for in Article 4 of the DSU, and *adjudication* by a panel and the Appellate Body, provided for in Articles 6 to 20 of the DSU, are by far the methods most frequently used, and therefore the focus of this chapter. However, the WTO dispute settlement system also provides for other dispute settlement methods, and in particular: *arbitration*; and *good offices, conciliation* and *mediation*, which are briefly discussed below.[27]

2.1.3   Contentious Jurisdiction

Unlike the International Court of Justice or the International Tribunal for the Law of the Sea, the WTO dispute settlement system has only contentious, and not advisory, jurisdiction. In *US – Wool Shirts and Blouses (1997)*, the Appellate Body held:

> Given the explicit aim of dispute settlement that permeates the DSU, we do not consider that Article 3.2 of the DSU is meant to encourage either panels or the Appellate Body to 'make law' by clarifying existing provisions of the WTO Agreement *outside the context of resolving a particular dispute.*[28]

The WTO dispute settlement system is called upon to clarify WTO law only in the context of an actual dispute.[29] In *EC – Commercial Vessels (2005)*, the panel declined to address a matter before it because it did not consider that 'an abstract ruling on hypothetical future measures' was either necessary or helpful to the resolution of that dispute.[30]

Questions and Assignments 3.1

Can a WTO Member refuse to submit to the jurisdiction of the WTO dispute settlement system? Can a WTO Member submit a dispute arising under one of the covered agreements to the International Court of Justice? Does the exclusive jurisdiction of the WTO dispute settlement system mean that all disputes arising under the covered agreements are to be resolved through consultations and adjudication by a WTO panel and/or the Appellate Body? In your opinion, would it be useful for the WTO dispute settlement system to have advisory jurisdiction?

2.2   Scope of the Jurisdiction

This section on the scope of the jurisdiction of the WTO dispute settlement system deals with two separate but obviously closely related questions, namely: (1) which disputes are subject to WTO dispute settlement?; and (2) which measures can be subject to WTO dispute settlement?

---

27   On the various methods of WTO dispute settlement, see below, p. 180.
28   Appellate Body Report, *US – Wool Shirts and Blouses (1997)*, 340. Emphasis added.
29   See also below, p. 184.
30   See Panel Report, *EC – Commercial Vessels (2005)*, para. 7.30. Note, however, that the panel in *EC – Bananas III (Article 21.5 – EC) (1999)* considered it did have jurisdiction in spite of the fact that there were no respondents in this case. The panel ruled against the European Communities and the report was never put on the agenda of the DSB for adoption and remained unadopted.

2.2.1 Disputes Subject to WTO Dispute Settlement

Article 1.1 of the DSU states, in relevant part:

> The rules and procedures of this Understanding shall apply to disputes brought pursuant to the consultation and dispute settlement provisions of the agreements listed in Appendix 1 to this Understanding (referred to in this Understanding as the 'covered agreements').

The WTO dispute settlement system thus has jurisdiction *ratione materiae* over disputes between WTO Members arising under the 'covered agreements'. The covered agreements, referred to in Appendix 1 to the DSU, include the *WTO Agreement*, the GATT 1994 and all other multilateral agreements on trade in goods, the GATS, the *TRIPS Agreement*, the DSU and the plurilateral *Agreement on Government Procurement*.[31] It is clear that the scope of jurisdiction of the WTO dispute settlement system is very broad as it ranges from disputes over measures regarding customs duties, disputes regarding sanitary measures, disputes regarding subsidies, disputes regarding measures affecting market access for services, to disputes regarding intellectual property rights enforcement measures.

2.2.2 Measures Subject to WTO Dispute Settlement

While the DSU refers in many of its provisions to the 'measure' or 'measures' that can be subject to WTO dispute settlement, it does, however, not define this term.[32] In *US – Corrosion-Resistant Steel Sunset Review (2004)*, the Appellate Body ruled that:

> [i]n principle, any act or omission attributable to a WTO Member can be a measure of that Member for purposes of dispute settlement proceedings.[33]

However, this general statement leaves a number of questions regarding the precise scope of the measures that can be challenged in WTO dispute settlement proceedings unanswered. The following paragraphs focus on seven 'atypical' measures that can be the 'measure at issue' in WTO disputes: (1) action or conduct by private parties attributable to a Member; (2) measures that are no longer in force; (3) legislation 'as such' (as opposed to the actual application of this legislation in specific cases); (4) discretionary legislation (as opposed to mandatory legislation); (5) unwritten 'norms or rules' of Members; (6) ongoing conduct by Members; and (7) measures by regional and local authorities.

The question whether *action or conduct by private parties*, the first category of 'atypical' measures mentioned above, can be subject to WTO dispute settlement arises because the WTO agreements, as is traditionally the case with international agreements, bind the States that are party to them, not private parties. As clearly stated by the panel in *Japan – Film (1998)*:

---

31 Only two WTO agreements are not 'covered agreements': the *Trade Policy Review Mechanism* and the plurilateral *Agreement on Trade in Civil Aircraft*.

32 The term 'measure(s)' appears over twenty-five times in the DSU.

33 Appellate Body Report, *US – Corrosion-Resistant Steel Sunset Review (2004)*, para. 81.

As the WTO Agreement is an international agreement, in respect of which only national governments and separate customs territories are directly subject to obligations, it follows by implication that the term *measure* in Article XXIII:1(b) and Article 26.1 of the DSU, as elsewhere in the WTO Agreement, refers only to policies or actions of governments, not those of private parties.[34]

Nevertheless, the panel in *Japan – Film (1998)* recalled that various GATT panels have had to deal with the question whether:

what appear on their face to be private actions may nonetheless be attributable to a government because of some governmental connection to or endorsement of those actions.[35]

For private actions to be attributed to a government – and therefore potentially be subject to WTO dispute settlement – there has to be a certain level of government involvement in the private action. The panel in *Japan – Film (1998)* ruled in this respect:

[P]ast GATT cases demonstrate that the fact that an action is taken by private parties does not rule out the possibility that it may be deemed to be governmental if there is sufficient government involvement with it. It is difficult to establish bright-line rules in this regard, however. Thus, that possibility will need to be examined on a case-by-case basis.[36]

Each case will have to be examined on its facts to determine whether the level of *government involvement* in the actions of private parties is such that these actions can be properly attributed to a Member. Note in this regard Article 8 of the International Law Commission's *Articles on Responsibility of States for Internationally Wrongful Acts*, which states:

The conduct of a person or group of persons shall be considered an act of a State under international law if the person or group of persons is in fact acting on the instructions of, or under the direction or control of, that State in carrying out the conduct.[37]

Any measure, including action or conduct by private parties, which can be properly attributed to a WTO Member, can be challenged in WTO dispute settlement proceedings.[38]

The second category of 'atypical' measures, which can be subject to WTO dispute settlement, are *measures that are no longer in force*. As the Appellate Body noted

34 Panel Report, *Japan – Film (1998)*, para. 10.52.   35 *Ibid.*   36 *Ibid.*, para. 10.56.
37 Article 8, *Articles on Responsibility of States for Internationally Wrongful Acts 2001*, in *Yearbook of the International Law Commission*, 2001, Volume II (Part Two). Text reproduced as it appears in the annex to General Assembly resolution 56/83 of 12 December 2001, and corrected by document A/56/49(Vol.I)/Corr.4.
38 Note Article I:3(a)(ii) of the GATS which defines 'measures by Members' as including measures 'taken by non-governmental bodies', i.e., private parties, 'in the exercise of powers delegated by central, regional or local governments or authorities'. See below, p. 171. Query whether measures that cannot be attributed to a Member cannot be subject to WTO dispute settlement. Note in this regard Article 11.3 of the *Agreement on Safeguards*, which stipulates that 'Members shall not encourage or support the adoption or maintenance by public and private enterprises of non-governmental measures equivalent to those referred to in [Article 11.1]'. Article 11.1 of the *Agreement on Safeguards* mentions, *inter alia*, voluntary export restraints, orderly marketing agreements, and any other similar measures on the export or the import side. Footnote 4 to that paragraph lists export moderation, export-price or import-price monitoring systems, export or import surveillance, compulsory import cartels, and discretionary export or import licensing schemes, any of which afford protection.

in *China – Raw Materials (2012)*, the DSU does not specifically address whether a WTO panel may or may not make findings and recommendations with respect to a measure that expires or is repealed during the course of the panel proceedings. Panels have made findings on expired measures in some cases and declined to do so in others, depending on the particularities of the disputes before them.[39] In *US – Upland Cotton (2005)*, the Appellate Body stated in this regard:

> Whether or not a measure is still in force is not dispositive of whether that measure is currently affecting the operation of any covered agreement. Therefore, we disagree with the United States' argument that measures whose legislative basis has expired are incapable of affecting the operation of a covered agreement in the present and that, accordingly, expired measures cannot be the subject of consultations under the DSU.[40]

A measure that is no longer in force can be challenged in WTO dispute settlement proceedings if that measure still affects the operation of a covered agreement. As discussed below, a Member may have recourse to WTO dispute settlement whenever it considers that benefits accruing to it are being impaired by a measure taken by another Member.[41] A Member may have reason to consider that a measure, which has expired, nevertheless still impairs benefits accruing to it.[42] While a measure that has expired can be subject to WTO dispute settlement, the fact that a measure has expired may affect the recommendations a panel may make under Article 19.1 of the DSU. It is clear that a panel cannot recommend the withdrawal of a measure that has already expired.[43] However, in *China – Raw Materials (2012)*, the Appellate Body noted that a recommendation made with respect to a measure that has expired is 'prospective in nature in the sense that it has an effect on, or consequences for, a WTO Member's implementation obligations that arise after the adoption of a panel and/or Appellate Body report by the DSB'.[44]

The third category of 'atypical' measures, which can be subject to WTO dispute settlement, concerns *legislation 'as such'*.[45] It is clear that the WTO consistency of the actual application of specific national legislation can be challenged in WTO dispute settlement proceedings. However, can national legislation as such, i.e. independently from its application in specific cases, be challenged in WTO dispute settlement proceedings? In *US – 1916 Act (2000)*, the Appellate Body recalled the GATT practice in this respect as follows:

> Prior to the entry into force of the *WTO Agreement*, it was firmly established that Article XXIII:1(a) of the GATT 1947 allowed a Contracting Party to challenge legislation as such, independently from the application of that legislation in specific instances.[46]

---

39 See Appellate Body Reports, *China – Raw Materials (2012)*, para. 263.
40 Appellate Body Report, *US – Upland Cotton (2005)*, para. 262.   41 See below, pp. 172–3.
42 See Appellate Body Report, *US – Upland Cotton (2005)*, para. 264.   43 See *ibid.*, para. 272.
44 Appellate Body Reports, *China – Raw Materials (2012)*, para. 260.
45 While 'legislation as such' is referred to as a category of 'atypical' measures, it should be emphasised that 'legislation as such' is frequently subject to WTO dispute settlement.
46 Appellate Body Report, *US – 1916 Act (2000)*, para. 60. In a footnote, the Appellate Body referred, for example, to the GATT panel reports in *US – Superfund (1987)*; *US – Section 337 (1989)*; *Thailand – Cigarettes (1990)*; and *US – Malt Beverages (1992)*. The reference to these GATT panel reports should not be read as an endorsement of these reports.

The Appellate Body noted that a number of WTO panels have – following this GATT practice – dealt with dispute settlement claims brought against a Member on the basis of its legislation *as such*, independently from the application of that legislation in specific instances.[47] As already noted above, in *US – Corrosion-Resistant Steel Sunset Review (2004)*, the Appellate Body stated in this regard that:

[i]n principle, any act or omission attributable to a WTO Member can be a measure of that Member for purposes of dispute settlement proceedings.[48]

The Appellate Body noted in particular that, in addition to acts applying legislation in a specific situation, also 'acts setting forth rules or norms that are intended to have general and prospective application' can be the subject of WTO dispute settlement.[49] According to the Appellate Body, this is so because the disciplines of the WTO and its dispute settlement system:

are intended to protect not only existing trade but also the security and predictability needed to conduct future trade. This objective would be frustrated if instruments setting out rules or norms inconsistent with a Member's obligations could not be brought before a panel once they have been adopted and irrespective of any particular instance of application of such rules or norms.[50]

The Appellate Body also pointed out that, if legislation could not be challenged as such but only in the instances of its application, this would lead to a multiplicity of litigation.[51] Allowing claims against legislation as such thus 'serves the purpose of preventing future disputes by allowing the root of WTO-inconsistent behaviour to be eliminated'.[52] The Appellate Body did, however, emphasise, in *US – Oil Country Tubular Goods Sunset Reviews (2004)*, the *seriousness* of 'as such' claims, stating:

By definition, an 'as such' claim challenges laws, regulations, or other instruments of a Member that have general and prospective application, asserting that a Member's conduct – not only in a particular instance that has occurred, but in future situations as well – will necessarily be inconsistent with that Member's WTO obligations. In essence, complaining parties bringing 'as such' challenges seek to prevent Members *ex ante* from engaging in certain conduct. The implications of such challenges are obviously more far-reaching than 'as applied' claims.[53]

The fourth category of 'atypical' measures, which can be subject to WTO dispute settlement, concerns *discretionary legislation*, i.e. legislation that leaves authorities leeway as to what action (WTO-consistent or WTO-inconsistent) to take (whereas mandatory legislation does not leave such leeway). The Appellate Body in *US – 1916 Act (2000)* noted that, in *examining* claims relating to legislation 'as such':

---

47 See, e.g. panel reports in *Japan – Alcoholic Beverages II (1996)*; *Canada – Periodicals (1997)*; *EC – Hormones (1998)*; *Korea – Alcoholic Beverages (1999)*; *Chile – Alcoholic Beverages (2000)*; *United States – FSC (2000)*; and *United States – Section 110(5) Copyright Act (2000)*.
48 Appellate Body Report, *US – Corrosion-Resistant Steel Sunset Review (2004)*, para. 81.
49 *Ibid.*, para. 82.   50 *Ibid.*, para. 82.   51 See *ibid.*   52 *Ibid.*
53 Appellate Body Report, *US – Oil Country Tubular Goods Sunset Reviews (2004)*, para. 172.

panels developed the concept that mandatory and discretionary legislation should be distinguished from each other, reasoning that only legislation that mandates a violation of GATT obligations can be found as such to be inconsistent with those obligations.[54]

The discussion on the relevance of the distinction between mandatory and discretionary legislation has been marred by confusion. It is important to observe that this distinction does not relate to the question, addressed above, whether legislation 'as such' can be challenged in WTO dispute settlement proceedings. Legislation 'as such' can be challenged regardless of whether it is mandatory or discretionary.[55] As clearly stated by the Appellate Body in *US – Corrosion-Resistant Steel Sunset Review (2004)*, the mandatory or discretionary nature of legislation is 'relevant, *if at all*, only as part of the panel's assessment of whether the measure is, as such, inconsistent with particular obligations'.[56] The Appellate Body has not, as yet, been required to pronounce generally upon the continuing relevance or significance of the distinction between mandatory and discretionary legislation.[57] In *US – Corrosion-Resistant Steel Sunset Review (2004)*, the Appellate Body did observe, however, that 'the import of the "mandatory/discretionary distinction" may vary from case to case', and cautioned 'against the application of this distinction in a mechanistic fashion'.[58] An early illustration of the fact that the import of the 'mandatory/discretionary distinction' may vary from case to case, are the findings of the panel in *US – Section 301 Trade Act (2000)*. The panel in that case rejected the presumption, implicit in the argument of the United States, that no WTO provision ever prohibits discretionary legislation. At issue in *US – Section 301 Trade Act (2000)* was Article 23 of the DSU, which requires Members to abstain from unilateral determinations of inconsistency with WTO law.[59] According to the panel, the duty of Members under Article 23 is meant to guarantee other Members, as well as the marketplace and those who operate in it, that no such unilateral determinations of inconsistency with WTO law will be made.[60] The panel noted:

When a Member imposes unilateral measures in violation of Article 23 in a specific dispute, serious damage is created both to other Members and the market-place. However, in our view, the creation of damage is not confined to actual conduct in specific cases. A law reserving the right for unilateral measures to be taken contrary to DSU rules and procedures,

---

54 Appellate Body Report, *US – 1916 Act (2000)*, para. 60. In a footnote, the Appellate Body referred, for example, to the panel reports in *US – Superfund (1987)*; *US – Section 337 (1989)*; *Thailand – Cigarettes (1990)*; and *US – Malt Beverages (1992)*.
55 See Appellate Body Report, *US – Corrosion-Resistant Steel Sunset Review (2004)*, para. 88.
56 *Ibid.*, para. 89. Emphasis added.
57 See Appellate Body Report, *US – 1916 Act (2000)*, para. 99; Appellate Body Report, *US – Countervailing Measures on Certain EC Products (2003)*, para. 159, n. 334; and Appellate Body Report, *US – Corrosion-Resistant Steel Sunset Review (2004)*, para. 93. In these reports, the Appellate Body declined to answer the question of the continuing relevance of the distinction between mandatory and discretionary legislation.
58 Appellate Body Report, *US – Corrosion-Resistant Steel Sunset Review (2004)*, para. 93. Moreover, note that the 'discretionary' nature of legislation does not merely depend on the characterization under municipal law but requires a more rigorous examination of the nature and character of the legislation concerned.
59 See also below, p. 183.   60 See Panel Report, *US – Section 301 Trade Act (2000)*, para. 7.95.

may – as is the case here – constitute an ongoing threat and produce a 'chilling effect' causing serious damage in a variety of ways.[61]

The panel subsequently ruled with regard to the measure at issue in *US – Section 301 Trade Act (2000)*:

The *discretion* given to the [US Trade Representative] to make a determination of inconsistency creates a real risk or threat for both Members and individual economic operators that determinations prohibited under Article 23.2(a) will be imposed. The USTR's *discretion* effectively to make such determinations removes the guarantee which Article 23 is intended to give not only to Members but indirectly also to individuals and the marketplace.[62]

The panel concluded, therefore, that the statutory language of Section 304 of the Trade Act of 1974, although it was not mandatory but discretionary in nature, was *prima facie* inconsistent with Article 23 of the DSU (in view of the particular nature of the obligation in Article 23).[63]

   The fifth category of 'atypical' measures, which can be subject to WTO dispute settlement, are *unwritten 'norms or rules'* or *practices* of Members. The Appellate Body first addressed the question whether practices of Members can be challenged in WTO dispute settlement proceedings in *US – Zeroing (EC) (2006)*. In that case, the United States argued on appeal that the panel had erred in finding that the zeroing methodology, which was not expressed in writing, was a measure that can be challenged, as such, in dispute settlement proceedings. In response, the Appellate Body first observed that – as discussed above – it had ruled in *US – Corrosion-Resistant Steel Sunset Review (2004)* that, '[i]n principle, any act or omission attributable to a WTO Member can be a measure of that Member for purposes of dispute settlement proceedings'[64] and that '"acts setting forth rules or norms that are intended to have general and prospective application" are measures subject to WTO dispute settlement'.[65] Subsequently, the Appellate Body ruled that the determination whether a measure can be challenge in WTO dispute settlement proceedings 'must be based on the "content and substance" of the alleged measure, and "not merely on its form".'[66] Accordingly, the Appellate Body found that:

the mere fact that a 'rule or norm' is not expressed in the form of a written instrument, is not determinative of the issue of whether it can be challenged, as such, in dispute settlement proceedings.[67]

Based on its review of the DSU and the *Anti-Dumping Agreement*, the agreement at issue in this case, the Appellate Body saw:

---

61 *Ibid.*, para. 7.88.   62 *Ibid.*, para. 7.96. Emphasis added.
63 See *ibid.*, para. 7.97. The panel report in *US – Section 301 Trade Act (2000)* was not appealed.
64 Appellate Body Report, *US – Zeroing (EC) (2006)*, para. 188, referring to Appellate Body Report, *US – Corrosion-Resistant Steel Sunset Review (2004)*, para. 81. See above, pp. 163–4.
65 Appellate Body Report, *US – Zeroing (EC) (2006)*, para. 189, referring to Appellate Body Report, *US – Corrosion-Resistant Steel Sunset Review (2004)*, para. 82. See above, p. 166.
66 Appellate Body Report, *US – Zeroing (EC) (2006)*, para. 192, referring to Appellate Body Report, *US – Corrosion-Resistant Steel Sunset Review (2004)*, para. 87.
67 Appellate Body Report, *US – Zeroing (EC) (2006)*, para. 192.

no basis to conclude that 'rules or norms' can be challenged, as such, only if they are expressed in the form of a written instrument.[68]

In fact, both participants in this case, the United States and the European Union, agreed that an 'as such' challenge can, in principle, be brought against a measure that is not expressed in the form of a written document.[69] However, the Appellate Body agreed with the United States that:

> a panel must not lightly assume the existence of a 'rule or norm' constituting a measure of general and prospective application, especially when it is not expressed in the form of a written document.[70]

The Appellate Body thus ruled that, when bringing a challenge against such an unwritten 'rule or norm', a complaining party must clearly establish: (1) that the 'rule or norm' is attributable to the responding Member; (2) the precise content of the 'rule or norm'; and (3) that the 'rule or norm' does have general and prospective application.[71] The Appellate Body emphasised that 'it is only if the complaining party meets this high threshold, and puts forward sufficient evidence with respect to each of these elements', that a panel can find that an unwritten 'rule or norm' may be challenged, as such.[72] The evidence referred to may include proof of the systematic application of the unwritten 'rule or norm'.[73] Applying its test to the facts in *US – Zeroing (EC) (2006)*, the Appellate Body considered that:

> the evidence before the Panel was sufficient to identify the precise content of the zeroing methodology; that the zeroing methodology is attributable to the United States, and that it does have general and prospective application.[74]

The Appellate Body thus concluded that the zeroing methodology was an unwritten 'rule or norm' that could be challenged in WTO dispute settlement proceedings.[75]

The sixth category of 'atypical' measures, which can be subject to WTO dispute settlement, concerns '*ongoing conduct*' of Members. In *US – Continued Zeroing (2009)*, the question arose whether 'the continued use of the zeroing methodology in successive proceedings in which duties resulting from the 18 anti-dumping duty orders are maintained, constitute "measures" that can be challenged in WTO dispute settlement'.[76] The Appellate Body agreed with the complainant, the European Union, that this continued use did indeed constitute 'measures' that can be challenged in WTO dispute settlement.[77] In reaching this

---

68 See *ibid.*, para. 193.   69 See *ibid.*, para. 194.   70 *Ibid.*, para. 196.

71 See *ibid.*, para. 198.   72 *Ibid.*, para. 198.   73 See *ibid.*, para. 198.

74 *Ibid.*, para. 204. Note that the Appellate Body emphasised that this evidence consisted of considerably more than a string of cases, or repeat action, based on which the panel would have simply divined the existence of a measure in the abstract. See *ibid.*

75 See *ibid.*, para. 205. On zeroing, see below, pp. 192–6.

76 Appellate Body Report, *US – Continued Zeroing (2009)*, para. 185. On the 'zeroing methodology', see below, p. 193.

77 See *ibid.*, para. 185.

conclusion, the Appellate Body observed that measures 'as such' and measures 'as applied', discussed above, are not the only types of measures that may be subject to challenge in WTO dispute settlement.[78] The Appellate Body stated:

> [I]n order to be susceptible to challenge, a measure need not fit squarely within one of these two categories, that is, either as a rule or norm of general and prospective application, or as an individual instance of the application of a rule or norm.[79]

The Appellate Body saw no reason to exclude 'ongoing conduct' that consists of the use of the zeroing methodology from challenge in WTO dispute settlement.[80] The Appellate Body explained that 'successive determinations by which duties are maintained are connected stages in each of the 18 cases involving imposition, assessment, and collection of duties under the same anti-dumping duty order'.[81] For the Appellate Body, the 'use of the zeroing methodology in a string of these stages [was] the allegedly unchanged component of each of the 18 measures at issue' and it was 'with respect to this "ongoing conduct" that the European Communities brought its challenge, seeking its cessation'.[82]

In light of the Appellate Body's analysis in *US – Continued Zeroing (2009)*, the United States argued in *EC and certain member States – Large Civil Aircraft (2011)* that what it referred to as the 'launch aid programme', i.e. the 'systematic and coordinated' provision of launch aid by France, Germany, Spain and the United Kingdom for the development of various models of Airbus large civil aircraft was 'ongoing conduct', and, as such, a measure subject to challenge in WTO dispute settlement proceedings.[83] The Appellate Body in that case did not exclude, as a general proposition:

> the possibility that concerted action or practice could be susceptible to challenge in WTO dispute settlement.[84]

The Appellate Body added that it did not consider that a complainant would necessarily be required to demonstrate the existence of a rule or norm of general and prospective application in order to show that such concerted action or practice exists.[85]

The seventh and final category of 'atypical' measures, which can be subject to WTO dispute settlement, are *measures by regional or local authorities*. It is clear that measures by the central government of Members can be challenged in WTO dispute settlement proceedings and it is undisputed that the central government includes all branches of government (legislative, executive and judicial). In *US – Shrimp (1998)*, the Appellate Body ruled that a WTO Member

78 See *ibid.*, para. 179.   79 *Ibid.*, para. 179.   80 See *ibid.*, para. 181.
81 *Ibid.*   82 *Ibid.*
83 See Appellate Body Report, *EC and certain member States – Large Civil Aircraft (2011)*, para. 475.
84 *Ibid.*, para. 794.
85 See *ibid.*, para. 794. Note, however, the Appellate Body found in *EC and certain member States – Large Civil Aircraft (2011)* that the alleged 'launch aid programme' was not within the panel's terms of reference. The Appellate Body therefore did not consider the arguments regarding the alleged 'launch aid programme'. See *ibid.*, paras. 795–6, and below, p. 808.

'bears responsibility for acts of all its departments of government, including its judiciary'.[86] However, do the 'acts of all its departments of government' to which the Appellate Body refers include acts of regional or local authorities? This question may be of particular relevance to Members with a federal system of government under which the federal government may have little control over measures taken by sub-federal levels of government. As discussed in Chapter 1, Article 22.9 of the DSU states:

> The dispute settlement provisions of the covered agreements may be invoked in respect of measures affecting their observance taken by regional or local governments or authorities within the territory of a Member. When the DSB has ruled that a provision of a covered agreement has not been observed, the responsible Member shall take such reasonable measures as may be available to it to ensure its observance. The provisions of the covered agreements and this Understanding relating to compensation and suspension of concessions or other obligations apply in cases where it has not been possible to secure such observance.[87]

This appears to give a clear answer to the question whether measures by regional or local authorities can be challenged in WTO dispute settlement proceedings. Even in situations in which the central government lacks the authority under its constitution to 'control' regional or local authorities, measures by these regional or local authorities can be subject to WTO dispute settlement. Dispute settlement proceedings against such measures can be brought against the Member concerned.[88]

A final remark may be made on measures adopted or maintained by Member States of the European Union. As discussed in Chapter 2, both the European Union and all its twenty-seven Member States are WTO Members. Measures by EU Member States can, and have been, challenged in dispute settlement proceedings brought: (1) against the EU Member State concerned;[89] (2) against the European Union and the EU Member State(s) concerned;[90] or (3) against the European Union alone.[91] In all disputes involving measures of EU Member States, it was always the European Union which made the submissions and defended the EU Member State measure(s) concerned.[92]

---

86 Appellate Body Report, *US – Shrimp (1998)*, para. 173, referring in footnote to Appellate Body Report, *United States – Gasoline (1996)*, p. 28.

87 See also *Understanding on the Interpretation of Article XXIV of the General Agreement on Tariffs and Trade 1994*, para. 14, last sentence, and above, p. 64.

88 Note that, unlike under the GATT 1994, under the GATS, measures by regional or local authorities are explicitly found to be attributable to the Member concerned. Article I:3(a)(i) of the GATS explicitly defines 'measures by Members' as 'measures by central, regional or local authorities'. Compare with Article XXIV:12 of the GATT 1994. See above, p. 163–4.

89 See e.g. *Belgium – Administration of Measures Establishing Customs Duties for Rice* (DS 210), concerning measures imposed by Belgium. In this dispute, a mutually agreed solution was notified to the DSB by the United States and the European Commission.

90 See e.g. *EC and certain member States – Large Civil Aircraft (2011)*, concerning measures by Germany, France, Spain and the United Kingdom, and the EU. See also above, pp. 106, 170.

91 See e.g. *EC – Asbestos (2001)*, concerning measures imposed by France. See also above, p. 138.

92 See Panel Report, *EC and certain member States – Large Civil Aircraft (2011)*, footnote 2047.

Questions and Assignments 3.2

Which of the WTO agreements are not 'covered agreements'? Can a Member challenge the WTO consistency of a measure by a private party? Can a Member challenge the WTO consistency of a measure that is no longer in force? Can a measure that is not yet in force be challenged in WTO dispute settlement? Can a Member challenge national legislation as such, i.e. independently from any application of this legislation in specific cases? What is the relevance of the distinction between mandatory and discretionary legislation? Can an unwritten 'norm or rule' or practice of a Member be challenged in WTO dispute settlement proceedings? In addition to rules or norms of general and prospective application (measures 'as such'), or individual instances of the application of a rule or norm (measures 'as applied'), can 'ongoing conduct' also be subject to WTO dispute settlement? Can national court decisions be challenged in WTO dispute settlement proceedings as WTO-inconsistent? Can measures of regional or local authorities of a Member be subject to WTO dispute settlement?

3 ACCESS TO THE WTO DISPUTE SETTLEMENT SYSTEM

It is clear and undisputed that access to the WTO dispute settlement system is limited to Members of the WTO. The Appellate Body ruled in *US – Shrimp (1998)*:

It may be well to stress at the outset that access to the dispute settlement process of the WTO is limited to Members of the WTO. This access is not available, under the *WTO Agreement* and the covered agreements as they currently exist, to individuals or international organizations, whether governmental or non-governmental.[93]

The WTO dispute settlement system is a *government-to-government* dispute settlement system for disputes concerning rights and obligations of WTO Members. Only WTO Members can have recourse to WTO dispute settlement; only they are entitled to initiate proceedings against breaches of WTO law. The WTO Secretariat cannot prosecute breaches of WTO law on its own motion nor are other international organisations, non-governmental organisations, industry associations, companies or individuals entitled to do so. While it is clear that only Members have access to the WTO dispute settlement system, the question arises whether WTO membership alone suffices to allow recourse to WTO dispute settlement or whether Members must have a specific trade or legal interest in having recourse.

3.1 Right of Recourse to WTO Dispute Settlement

Each covered agreement contains one or more consultation and dispute settlement provisions. These provisions set out when a Member can have recourse to

---

93 Appellate Body Report, *US – Shrimp (1998)*, para. 101.

WTO dispute settlement. For the GATT 1994, the relevant provisions are Articles XXII and XXIII. Of particular importance is Article XXIII:1 of the GATT 1994, which states:

If any Member should consider that any benefit accruing to it directly or indirectly under this Agreement is being nullified or impaired or that the attainment of any objective of the Agreement is being impeded as the result of

(a) the failure of another Member to carry out its obligations under this Agreement, or
(b) the application by another Member of any measure, whether or not it conflicts with the provisions of this Agreement, or
(c) the existence of any other situation,

the Member may, with a view to the satisfactory adjustment of the matter, make written representations or proposals to the other Member or Members which it considers to be concerned.[94]

The consultation and dispute settlement provisions of most other covered agreements incorporate, by reference, Articles XXII and XXIII of the GATT 1994. For example, Article 11.1 of the *SPS Agreement*, entitled 'Consultations and Dispute Settlement', states:

The provisions of Articles XXII and XXIII of GATT 1994 as elaborated and applied by the Dispute Settlement Understanding shall apply to consultations and the settlement of disputes under this Agreement, except as otherwise specifically provided herein.

With regard to a Member's right to have recourse to WTO dispute settlement, the Appellate Body held in *India – Quantitative Restrictions (1999)*:

This dispute was brought pursuant to, *inter alia*, Article XXIII of the GATT 1994. According to Article XXIII, any Member which considers that a benefit accruing to it directly or indirectly under the GATT 1994 is being nullified or impaired as a result of the failure of another Member to carry out its obligations, may resort to the dispute settlement procedures of Article XXIII. The United States considers that a benefit accruing to it under the GATT 1994 was nullified or impaired as a result of India's alleged failure to carry out its obligations regarding balance-of-payments restrictions under Article XVIII:B of the GATT 1994. Therefore, the United States was entitled to have recourse to the dispute settlement procedures of Article XXIII with regard to this dispute.[95]

As was the case in *India – Quantitative Restrictions (1999)*, the nullification or impairment of a benefit (or the impeding of the realisation of an objective) may, and most often will, be the result of a violation of an obligation prescribed by a covered agreement (see Article XXIII:1(a)). Nullification or impairment may, however, also be the result of 'the application by another Member of any measure, whether or not it conflicts with the provisions' of a covered agreement (see Article XXIII:1(b) and Article 26.1 of the DSU). Nullification or impairment

---

94 Note that there is no need to exhaust local remedies before having recourse to WTO dispute settlement.
95 Appellate Body Report, *India – Quantitative Restrictions (1999)*, para. 84.

may equally be the result of 'the existence of any other situation' (see Article XXIII:1(c) and Article 26.2 of the DSU). Unlike other international dispute settlement systems, the WTO system thus provides for three types of complaint: (1) 'violation' complaints; (2) 'non-violation' complaints; and (3) 'situation' complaints.[96] In the case of a 'non-violation' complaint or a 'situation' complaint, the complainant must demonstrate that there is nullification or impairment of a benefit or that the achievement of an objective is impeded. The panel in *Japan – Film (1998)* stated with regard to non-violation claims that it must be demonstrated: (1) that the imported products at issue are subject to and *benefiting from* a relevant market access concession; (2) that the *competitive position* of the imported products is being upset (i.e. 'nullified or impaired'); and (3) that the competitive position is being upset by (i.e. 'as the result of') the application of a *measure not reasonably anticipated*.[97] According to the panel in *EC – Asbestos (2001)*, nullification or impairment would exist, in the case before it, if the measure:

ha[s] the effect of *upsetting* the *competitive relationship* between Canadian asbestos and products containing it, on the one hand, and substitute fibres and products containing them, on the other.[98]

In the case of a 'violation' complaint, however, there is no need for the complainant to show nullification or impairment of a benefit. There is a *presumption* of nullification or impairment when the complainant demonstrates the existence of the violation. Article 3.8 of the DSU states:

In cases where there is an infringement of the obligations assumed under a covered agreement, the action is considered *prima facie* to constitute a case of nullification or impairment. This means that there is normally a presumption that a breach of the rules has an adverse impact on other Members parties to that covered agreement, and in such cases, it shall be up to the Member against whom the complaint has been brought to rebut the charge.[99]

In only a few cases to date has the respondent argued that the alleged violation of WTO law did not nullify or impair benefits accruing to the complainant. In no case has the respondent been successful in rebutting the presumption of

---

96 Note, however, that, pursuant to Article XXIII:3 of the GATS, situation complaints are not possible in disputes arising under the GATS; and that, pursuant to Article 64.2 and 3 of the *TRIPS Agreement* and successive ministerial decisions, non-violation complaints and situation complaints are *currently* not possible in disputes arising under the *TRIPS Agreement*. See below, p. 1010.

97 See Panel Report, *Japan – Film (1998)*, para. 10.82. With regard to what a complainant must show in a non-violation complaint, see also *ibid.*, para. 9.5.

98 Panel Report, *EC – Asbestos (2001)*, para. 8.288. Emphasis added. With respect to non-violation complaints, see also Appellate Body Report, *EC – Asbestos (2001)*, paras. 38 and 185–6.

99 In *US – Offset Act (Byrd Amendment) (2003)*, the Appellate Body concluded, pursuant to Article 3.8 of the DSU, that, to the extent that it had found the measure to be inconsistent with Article 18.1 of the *Anti-Dumping Agreement* and Article 32.1 of the *SCM Agreement*, 'the [Offset Act] nullifies or impairs benefits accruing to the appellees in this dispute under those Agreements'. See Appellate Body Report, *US – Offset Act (Byrd Amendment) (2003)*, paras. 300–4. See also Appellate Body Report, *EC – Bananas III (1997)*, paras. 249–54; and Appellate Body Report, *EC – Export Subsidies on Sugar (2005)*, paras. 293–300.

nullification or impairment. For instance, in *EC – Export Subsidies on Sugar (2005)*, the panel found, and the Appellate Body upheld on appeal, that the European Communities did not rebut the presumption of nullification or impairment.[100] It has been suggested that this presumption of nullification or impairment is in fact not rebuttable.[101]

Violation complaints are by far the most common type of complaint. To date, there have been only seven disputes in which a non-violation complaint was filed.[102] Note that the Appellate Body stated in *EC – Asbestos (2001)* that:

the ['non-violation' nullification or impairment] remedy ... 'should be approached with caution and should remain an exceptional remedy'.[103]

None of the non-violation complaints brought to the WTO to date has been successful.[104] Moreover, there has never been any adjudication of situation complaints.[105] The difference between the WTO system and other international dispute settlement systems with regard to causes of action is, therefore, of little practical significance.

In *EC – Bananas III (1997)*, the Appellate Body held:

[W]e believe that a Member has broad discretion in deciding whether to bring a case against another Member under the DSU. The language of Article XXIII:1 of the GATT 1994 and of Article 3.7 of the DSU suggests, furthermore, that a Member is expected to be largely self-regulating in deciding whether any such action would be 'fruitful'.[106]

The first sentence of Article 3.7 of the DSU, to which the Appellate Body refers, states:

Before bringing a case, a Member shall exercise its judgement as to whether action under these procedures would be fruitful.

---

100 See Appellate Body Report, *EC – Export Subsidies on Sugar (2005)*, para. 298. *In EC – Bananas III (1997)*, the European Communities also attempted – unsuccessfully – to rebut the presumption of nullification and impairment with respect to the Panel's findings of violation of the GATT on the basis that the United States has never exported bananas to the European Communities. See Panel Report, *EC – Bananas III (1997)*, para. 7.398.

101 Note that the panel in *EC – Bananas III (1997)* expressed doubts whether this presumption could be rebutted. See Panel Report, *EC – Bananas III (1997)*, para. 7.398.

102 Note that Article 26.1 of the DSU provides for some special procedural rules applicable to non-violation complaints. For a list of disputes in which a non-violation claim was made (up to 30 September 2011), see *WTO Analytical Index (2012)*, Volume II, 1883. For a recent example of non-violation claims, see Panel Reports, *US – COOL (2012)*, paras. 7.900–7.907.

103 Appellate Body Report, *EC – Asbestos (2001)*, para. 186. This was reiterated by the panel in *US – Offset Act (Byrd Amendment) (2003)* with regard to non-violation complaints under the *SCM Agreement*. See Panel Report, *US – Offset Act (Byrd Amendment) (2003)*, para. 7.125.

104 Note, however, that, in all disputes in which there was a non-violation complaint, there were also violation complaints. These violation complaints were often successful. See e.g. *US – Gasoline (1996)*; *EC – Hormones (1998)*; *Korea – Procurement (2000)*; *US – Offset Act (Byrd Amendment) (2003)*; and *China – Auto Parts (2009)*.

105 See GATT Analytical Index (WTO, 1995), 668–91. Pursuant to Article 26.2 of the DSU, the procedural rules of the Decision of 12 April 1989, and not the rules of the DSU, apply to situation complaints. As a result, reports addressing a situation complaint would have to be adopted by consensus, rather than by reverse consensus.

106 Appellate Body Report, *EC – Bananas III (1997)*, para. 135. The Appellate Body also noted in *EC – Bananas III (1997)* that the DSU neither explicitly stated nor implied that a Member must have a 'legal interest' to have recourse to WTO dispute settlement. See *ibid.*, para. 132.

The Appellate Body explicitly agreed with the statement of the panel in *EC – Bananas III (1997)* that:

> with the increased interdependence of the global economy ... Members have a greater stake in enforcing WTO rules than in the past since any deviation from the negotiated balance of rights and obligations is more likely than ever to affect them, directly or indirectly.[107]

Note that, in *EC – Bananas III (1997)*, the Appellate Body decided that the United States could bring a claim under the GATT 1994 despite the fact that the United States does not export bananas. In coming to this decision, the Appellate Body considered the fact that the United States is a producer and a potential exporter of bananas, the effects of the EC banana regime on the US internal market for bananas and the fact that the US claims under the GATS and the GATT 1994 were inextricably interwoven. The Appellate Body subsequently concluded:

> Taken together, these reasons are sufficient justification for the United States to have brought its claims against the EC banana import regime under the GATT 1994.[108]

The Appellate Body added, however, that:

> [t]his does not mean, though, that one or more of the factors we have noted in this case would necessarily be dispositive in another case.[109]

In *Mexico – Corn Syrup (Article 21.5 – US) (2001)*, the Appellate Body ruled with respect to the role of panels in assessing a Member's decision to have recourse to WTO dispute settlement:

> Given the 'largely self-regulating' nature of the requirement in the first sentence of Article 3.7, panels and the Appellate Body must presume, whenever a Member submits a request for establishment of a panel, that such Member does so in good faith, having duly exercised its judgement as to whether recourse to that panel would be 'fruitful'. Article 3.7 neither requires nor authorizes a panel to look behind that Member's decision and to question its exercise of judgement.[110]

A Member's decision to start WTO dispute settlement proceedings is thus largely beyond judicial review. The 'hands-off' approach of panels was clearly reflected in *Colombia – Ports of Entry (2009)*. In this case, the panel found that:

> [i]t is satisfied that a sufficient basis exists for Panama to bring its claim under Article I:1 of the GATT 1994, with respect to subject textiles ... and footwear ... As noted, Panama ... has stated its interest in exporting domestically produced footwear ... in the future, and stated its potential to manufacture textiles in the future. In the Panel's view, Panama has sufficiently demonstrated its interest in a determination of rights and obligations under the WTO Agreement.[111]

Accordingly, the panel concluded that Panama was entitled to bring, and had sufficient interest to initiate and proceed with, an Article I:1 claim against

---

107 *Ibid.*, para. 136. Here the Appellate Body referred to Panel Reports, *EC – Bananas III (1997)*, para. 7.50.
108 Appellate Body Report, *EC – Bananas III (1997)*, para. 138.   109 *Ibid.*
110 Appellate Body Report, *Mexico – Corn Syrup (Article 21.5 – US) (2001)*, para. 74. The Appellate Body referred to its earlier finding, quoted above, in *EC – Bananas III (1997)*, para. 135.
111 Panel Report, *Colombia – Ports of Entry (2009)*, para. 7.329.

Colombia.[112] Note, however, that, although a Member's decision to have recourse to WTO dispute settlement is largely beyond judicial review, it is apparent from the 'success rate' of complainants in WTO dispute settlement that Members do duly exercise their judgment as to whether recourse to WTO dispute settlement will be '*fruitful*'.[113] To date, panels have agreed with the complainant in 89 per cent of disputes brought before them that the respondent acted inconsistently with WTO law.[114]

3.2   Access of Members other than the Parties

In addition to the complainant and, albeit not by its own choice, the respondent, other Members may also have access to WTO dispute settlement proceedings. As discussed in more detail below, if consultations are conducted pursuant to Article XXII of the GATT 1994 (rather than Article XXIII) thereof, any Member, which has a 'substantial trade interest' in the consultations, can be allowed to join, i.e. to participate, in these consultations.[115] More importantly, any Member, having a 'substantial interest' in a matter before a panel and having notified its interest in a timely manner to the DSB, may be a third party in the panel proceedings;[116] and any Member, who was a third party in the panel proceedings, may be a third participant in the Appellate Body proceedings.[117] Third parties and third participants have a *right* to be heard by the panel and the Appellate Body respectively. While only Members having a 'substantial interest' in the matter before the panel may become third parties, it is very rare for parties to challenge the third party status of a Member claiming to have such an interest.

3.3   Indirect Access to the WTO Dispute Settlement System

As discussed above, only WTO Members have access to the WTO dispute settlement system. Companies, industry associations or NGOs cannot have recourse to WTO dispute settlement, nor can they join consultations or be a third party or third participant in panel or Appellate Body proceedings. Yet, it would be incorrect to state that companies, industry associations and NGOs are not 'involved' in WTO dispute settlement. It is undisputed that most of the disputes brought to the WTO dispute settlement system are brought by Members *at the*

---

112 See *ibid.*, para. 7.330.
113 Note also that the limitation of retaliation to nullification and impairment suffered operates as a disincentive to bringing cases where there is no actual or reasonably potential trade interest. See also below, p. 201.
114 See www.worldtradelaw.net/dsc/database/violationcount.asp. Eighty-nine per cent is the percentage of disputes in which panels found *at least one* WTO inconsistency.
115 See Article 4.11 of the DSU. For a further discussion of the right to join consultations, see below, p. 272.
116 See Article 10 of the DSU. On the rights of third parties in panel proceedings, see below, p. 309.
117 See Article 17.4 of the DSU. On the rights of third participants in Appellate Body proceedings, see below, p. 289.

instigation of a company or industry association. Companies and industry associations are the 'driving force' behind the initiation of dispute settlement proceedings in most cases. In fact, it is hard to identify cases in which this was not so. Moreover, companies or industry associations will not only lobby governments to bring dispute settlement cases to the WTO, they (and their law firms) will often also play an important, 'behind-the-scenes' role in planning the legal strategy and drafting the submissions. It could be argued that companies and industry associations have an 'indirect' access to the WTO dispute settlement system and make abundant use of this 'indirect' access. The legal system of some WTO Members explicitly provides for the possibility for companies and industry associations to bring a violation of WTO obligations, by another WTO Member, to the attention of their government and to 'induce' their government to start WTO dispute settlement proceedings against that Member. In EU law, this possibility is provided for under the Trade Barriers Regulation;[118] in US law, under Section 301 of the 1974 Trade Act;[119] and, in Chinese law, under the Investigation Rules of Foreign Trade Barriers.[120] In many other Members, the process of lobbying the government to bring WTO cases has not been regulated and institutionalised in the same manner, but the process is no less present. In addition to this 'indirect' access, it should also be noted that, according to the Appellate Body, companies and industry associations as well as NGOs can be 'involved' in panel and Appellate Body proceedings as an *amicus curiae*. This controversial case law is discussed later in this chapter.[121]

Questions and Assignments 3.3

Who has access to the WTO dispute settlement system? When can WTO Members have recourse to WTO dispute settlement? List the different causes of action provided for in Article XXIII:1 of the GATT 1994. How can a complainant show nullification or impairment of a benefit accruing to it under a covered agreement? Can the presumption of nullification or impairment, provided for in Article 3.8 of the DSU, be rebutted? In your opinion, why have there been so few 'non-violation' complaints? Do the dispute settlement provisions of the GATS and the *TRIPS Agreement* provide for non-violation and situation complaints? Can a Member bring a case against another Member regardless of its 'interest' in the outcome of the case? Is a Member's decision to have recourse to WTO dispute settlement subject to judicial review? Do you agree that companies and industry associations can be considered to have 'indirect' access to the WTO dispute settlement system? Discuss the importance of the EU's Trade Barriers Regulation in this context.

---

118 Council Regulation (EC) No. 3286/94 on Community procedures for the exercise of rights under international trade rules, in particular those established under the WTO, OJ 1994, L349, 71, as amended by Council Regulation (EC) No. 356/95, OJ 1995, L41, 3.

119 Section 301(a)(1) of the Trade Act 1974, 19 USC 2411(a)(1).

120 Investigation Rules of Foreign Trade Barriers, entered into force on 1 March 2005. The English translation of these rules is available on the official website of the Ministry of Commerce of China. See http://english.mofcom.gov.cn/aarticle/policyrelease/domesticpolicy/200503/20050300029640.html, visited on 15 February 2013.

121 On *amicus curiae* briefs, see below, pp. 265–7.

4 KEY FEATURES OF WTO DISPUTE SETTLEMENT

The prime object and purpose of the WTO dispute settlement system is the *prompt settlement of disputes* between WTO Members concerning their respective rights and obligations under WTO law, and to provide *security and predictability* to the multilateral trading system. As stated in Article 3.3 of the DSU, the prompt settlement of disputes is:

essential to the effective functioning of the WTO and the maintenance of a proper balance between the rights and obligations of Members.[122]

Article 3.2 of the DSU states:

The dispute settlement system of the WTO is a central element in providing security and predictability to the multilateral trading system. The Members recognize that it serves to preserve the rights and obligations of Members under the covered agreements, and to clarify the existing provisions of those agreements ...

According to the panel in *US – Section 301 Trade Act (2000)*, the WTO dispute settlement system is one of the *most important instruments* of the WTO in protecting the security and predictability of the multilateral trading system.[123] As discussed in Chapter 1 of this book in the context of the sources of WTO law and the role of 'precedent' in WTO dispute settlement, the Appellate Body ruled in *US – Stainless Steel (Mexico) (2008)* that ensuring security and predictability, as contemplated in Article 3.2 of the DSU, implies that, absent cogent reasons, an adjudicatory body will resolve the same legal question in the same way in a subsequent case.[124]

The importance of WTO dispute settlement to the multilateral trading system is uncontested, and the frequent and successful recourse to WTO dispute settlement to date confirms and reinforces this importance.[125] This section describes key features of WTO dispute settlement, which, in addition to the compulsory and exclusive jurisdiction of the WTO dispute settlement system, discussed above, and the process of WTO dispute settlement, discussed below, contribute to, if not explain, the importance and success of WTO dispute settlement to date. Some of these features set apart the WTO dispute settlement system from other international dispute settlement mechanisms.[126] This section discusses in turn: (1) the single, comprehensive and integrated nature of the WTO dispute

---

122 The Appellate Body referred to this principle of 'prompt settlement of disputes' in, e.g. Appellate Body Report, *US – Upland Cotton (Article 21.5 – Brazil) (2008)*, para. 246; and in Appellate Body Report, *US – Zeroing (Japan) (Article 21.5 – Japan) (2009)*, para. 122.

123 See Panel Report, *US – Section 301 Trade Act*, para. 7.75.

124 See Appellate Body Report, *US – Stainless Steel (Mexico) (2008)*, para. 160. See also above, p. 53.

125 See above, p. 157, and also below, p. 302.

126 With regard to the compulsory jurisdiction, see above, p. 126. With regard to e.g. remedies, appellate review and timeframes, see below, pp. 124 (remedies), 231 (appellate review), 246 (timeframes), respectively.

settlement system; (2) the methods of WTO dispute settlement; (3) the multilateral nature of WTO dispute settlement; (4) the preference for mutually acceptable solutions; (5) the mandate to clarify WTO provisions; and (6) remedies for breach of WTO law. Other key features, such as the short timeframes, confidentiality and transparency, and appellate review, are discussed separately in subsequent sections of this chapter.

4.1   Single, Comprehensive and Integrated System

The DSU provides for a single dispute settlement system applicable to disputes arising under any of the covered agreements.[127] This is different from the pre-WTO situation when each of the GATT agreements had its own dispute settlement system and the jurisdiction of each of these systems was limited to disputes arising under a specific agreement. Needless to say that this created a degree of confusion and uncertainty, especially when a measure was allegedly inconsistent with more than one GATT agreement. While the DSU now provides for a single WTO dispute settlement system, some of the covered agreements provide for some special and additional rules and procedures 'designed to deal with the particularities of dispute settlement relating to obligations arising under a specific covered agreement'.[128] Pursuant to Article 1.2 of the DSU, these special or additional rules and procedures *prevail* over the DSU rules and procedures to the extent that there is a 'difference' between them. The Appellate Body in *Guatemala – Cement I (1998)* ruled in this regard:

> [I]f there is no 'difference', then the rules and procedures of the DSU apply *together with* the special or additional provisions of the covered agreement. In our view, it is only where the provisions of the DSU and the special or additional rules and procedures of a covered agreement *cannot* be read as *complementing* each other that the special or additional provisions are to *prevail*.[129]

The special and additional rules and procedures of a particular covered agreement combine with the generally applicable rules and procedures of the DSU 'to form a comprehensive, integrated dispute settlement system for the *WTO Agreement*'.[130]

4.2   Different Methods of Dispute Settlement

As noted above, the WTO dispute settlement system provides for several dispute settlement methods. In addition to *consultations*, i.e. negotiations, between the

---

127 See Appellate Body Report, *Guatemala – Cement I (1998)*, para. 64.   128 *Ibid.*, para. 66.

129 *Ibid.*, para. 65. The Appellate Body further noted that: 'A special or additional provision should only be found to *prevail* over a provision of the DSU in a situation where adherence to the one provision will lead to a violation of the other provision, that is, in the case of a *conflict* between them.' See *ibid*. See also Appellate Body Report, *US – Hot-Rolled Steel (2001)*, paras. 55 and 62, and below, p. 734, with regard to Article 17.6 of the *Anti-Dumping Agreement*.

130 Appellate Body Report, *Guatemala – Cement I (1998)*, para. 66.

parties, provided for in Article 4 of the DSU, and *adjudication* by a panel and the Appellate Body, provided for in Articles 6 to 20 of the DSU, which are by far the methods most frequently used and the methods focused on in this chapter, the WTO dispute settlement system also provides for other dispute settlement methods, and in particular: arbitration; and good offices, conciliation and mediation. Pursuant to Article 25 of the DSU, parties to a dispute arising under a covered agreement may decide to resort to *arbitration* as an alternative means of binding dispute settlement, rather than have the dispute adjudicated by a panel and the Appellate Body.[131] When parties opt for arbitration, they must agree on the procedural rules that will apply to the arbitration process; and they must explicitly agree to abide by the arbitration award.[132] Arbitration awards need to be consistent with WTO law,[133] and must be notified to the DSB where any Member may raise any point relating thereto.[134] To date, Members have resorted only once to arbitration under Article 25 of the DSU.[135] The DSU also provides for arbitration in Articles 21.3(c) and 22.6. As discussed below, these arbitration procedures concern specific issues that may arise in the *context* of a dispute, such as the determination of the reasonable period of time for implementation (Article 21.3(c) of the DSU) and the appropriate level of retaliation (Article 22.6 of the DSU).[136] Members frequently resort to arbitration under Article 21.3(c) or 22.6. As mentioned above, the DSU also provides for *good offices, conciliation* and *mediation* as methods of dispute settlement. These dispute settlement methods are provided for in Article 5 of the DSU. Their use may be requested at any time by any party to a dispute. They may begin at any time and be terminated at any time.[137] Their use requires the agreement of all parties to the dispute.[138] Proceedings involving good offices, conciliation and mediation are confidential, and without prejudice to the rights of either party in any further proceedings under the DSU.[139] Pursuant to Article 5.6 of the DSU, the WTO Director-General may, acting in an *ex officio* capacity, offer good offices, conciliation or mediation with a view to assisting Members to settle a dispute.[140] However, similar to

---

131 Article 25.1 of the DSU refers to 'expeditious' arbitration, suggesting that this dispute settlement method will be quicker and more efficient than adjudication pursuant to Articles 6 to 20 of the DSU.

132 See Articles 25.2 and 25.3 of the DSU.

133 See Article 3.5 of the DSU.

134 See Article 25.3 of the DSU.

135 In 2001, the United States and the European Communities resorted to arbitration under Article 25 to resolve a dispute on the appropriate level of compensation due by the United States after it failed to comply with the panel report in *US – Section 110(5) Copyright Act (2000)*. See Award of the Arbitrators, *US – Section 110(5) Copyright Act (Article 25) (2001)*, Recourse to Arbitration under Article 25 of the DSU, WT/DS160/ARB25/1, dated 9 November 2001. See below, p. 199.

136 See below, pp. 196 and 200–202.

137 See Article 5.3 of the DSU.

138 See Article 5.1 of the DSU.

139 See Article 5.2 of the DSU.

140 In July 2001, the Director-General reminded Members of his availability to help settle disputes through good offices, mediation or conciliation. See Communication from the Director-General, *Article 5 of the Dispute Settlement Understanding*, WT/DSB/25, dated 17 July 2001.

arbitration under Article 25 of the DSU, Members have made little use of these dispute settlement methods.[141]

4.3 Multilateral Dispute Settlement

The object and purpose of the WTO dispute settlement system is for Members to settle disputes with other Members through the *multilateral* procedures of the DSU, rather than through *unilateral* action. Article 23.1 of the DSU states:

> When Members seek the redress of a violation of obligations or other nullification or impairment of benefits under the covered agreements or an impediment to the attainment of any objective of the covered agreements, they shall have recourse to, and abide by, the rules and procedures of this Understanding.

According to the Appellate Body in *US – Certain EC Products (2001)*, Article 23.1 of the DSU imposes a general obligation to redress a violation of WTO law through the multilateral DSU procedures, and not through unilateral action.[142] Pursuant to Article 23.2 of the DSU, WTO Members may not make a *unilateral* determination that a violation of WTO law has occurred and may not take retaliation measures *unilaterally* in the case of a violation of WTO law.[143]

It has been argued that concerns regarding unilateral action taken by the United States against what it considered to be violations of GATT law were the driving force behind the Uruguay Round negotiations on dispute settlement, which eventually resulted in the DSU. During the 1980s, the United States

---

141 To date there has been no reported instance of the use of the dispute settlement methods referred to in Article 5 of the DSU. See *WTO Analytical Index (2012)*, Volume II, 1555–6. However, note the successful mediation of Deputy Director-General Rufus Yerxa in 2002 in a dispute between the European Communities and the Philippines and Thailand on the tariff treatment of canned tuna (see Communication from the Director-General, *Request for Mediation by the Philippines, Thailand and the European Communities*, WT/GC/66, dated 16 October 2002; WT/GC/66/Add.1, dated 23 December 2002; and Joint Communication from the European Communities, Thailand and the Philippines, *Request for Mediation by the Philippines, Thailand and the European Communities*, WT/GC/71, dated 1 August 2003; and the unsuccessful good offices of Norway's foreign minister, Jonas Gahr Store, in 2006 in the *EC – Bananas III* dispute between the European Communities and Ecuador on the WTO-consistency of the EC's new 'tariff-only' banana import regime (see *Bridges Weekly Trade News Digest*, 22 November 2006). Ecuador subsequently resorted to an Article 21.5 compliance procedure to assess the WTO-consistency of the EC's new banana import regime. Also note that the Decision of 5 April 1966 on Procedures under Article XXIII of the GATT (BISD 14S/18) for disputes between a complaining developing country and a responding developed country, referred to in Article 3.12 of the DSU and discussed below at p. 300, contemplate compulsory good offices by the WTO Director-General. This mechanism was instrumental in the final settlement of the *EC – Bananas III* dispute.

142 Appellate Body Report, *US – Certain EC Products (2001)*, para. 111. The panel in this case noted that unilateral action is contrary to the essence of the multilateral trading system because such action threatens the system's stability and predictability. See Panel Report, *US – Certain EC Products (2001)*, para. 6.14.

143 The panel in *EC – Commercial Vessels (2005)* held that the obligation to have recourse to the DSU when Members seek the redress of a violation covers *any act of a Member* in response to what it considers to be a violation of a WTO obligation. See Panel Report, *EC – Commercial Vessels (2005)*, para. 7.207. Note, however, that the Appellate Body found in *US/Canada – Continued Suspension (2008)* that statements made in the DSB regarding the WTO consistency of measures of other Members are 'generally diplomatic or political in nature' and 'do not have the legal status of a definitive determination in themselves'. See Appellate Body Report, *US/Canada – Continued Suspension (2008)*, para. 398. The Appellate Body also found that, by maintaining the suspension of concessions authorised by the DSB after the European Communities had notified an implementation measure, the United States and Canada were not seeking redress of a violation. See *ibid.*, para. 393.

increasingly took unilateral action against purported GATT violations by other countries. The United States did so under Section 301 of the Trade Act of 1974, and, with the adoption of the Trade and Competitiveness Act of 1988, the United States considerably expanded its ability to take such unilateral action. Many other countries considered this unilateral action to be a form of 'vigilante justice' and demanded that the United States cease to act unilaterally against purported violations of GATT law. The United States, however, argued that the existing GATT dispute settlement system was too weak to protect US trade interests effectively.[144] Robert Hudec noted:

> This United States counter-attack against the procedural weaknesses of the existing dispute settlement system led other governments to propose a deal. In exchange for a US commitment not to employ its Section 301-type trade restrictions, the other GATT governments would agree to create a new and procedurally tighter dispute settlement system that would meet US complaints.[145]

In this way, agreement was eventually reached on the current WTO dispute settlement system. It is unlikely that, without, on the one hand, the frustration of the United States with the GATT dispute settlement system and, on the other hand, the concerns of other GATT Contracting Parties about US unilateralism in international trade disputes, the Uruguay Round negotiators would ever have been able to agree on a dispute settlement system as far-reaching, innovative and effective as the current WTO system.

4.4 Preference for Mutually Acceptable Solutions

Article 3.7 of the DSU states, in relevant part:

> The aim of the dispute settlement mechanism is to secure a positive solution to a dispute. A solution mutually acceptable to the parties to a dispute and consistent with the covered agreements is clearly to be preferred.

The DSU thus expresses a clear preference for solutions mutually acceptable to the parties reached through negotiations, rather than solutions resulting from adjudication. In other words, the DSU prefers parties *not* to go to court, but to settle their dispute amicably out of court. Accordingly, each dispute settlement process must start with consultations (or an attempt to have consultations) between the parties to the dispute.[146] To resolve disputes through consultations is obviously cheaper and more satisfactory for the long-term trade relations with the other party to the dispute than adjudication by a panel. Note, however, that any mutually agreed solution reached through consultations needs to be consistent with WTO law,[147] and must be notified to the DSB, where any Member

---

144 This weakness was primarily the result of the requirement that panel reports had to be adopted by consensus to become legally binding.

145 R. E. Hudec, 'The New WTO Dispute Settlement Procedure', *Minnesota Journal of Global Trade*, 1999, 13.

146 On consultations, see also below, p. 269.   147 See Articles 3.5 and 3.7 of the DSU.

may raise any point relating thereto.[148] For a further discussion on consultations and mutually agreed solutions, refer to sub-section 6.2 of this chapter on the process of WTO dispute settlement.[149]

Questions and Assignments 3.4

What is the prime object and purpose of the WTO dispute settlement system? Why is the WTO dispute settlement important to the multilateral trading system? The WTO dispute settlement system has been defined as 'a comprehensive, integrated dispute settlement system'. What does this mean and why is this important? Identify the special or additional rules and procedures contained in the *Anti-Dumping Agreement* and discuss whether these rules and procedures prevail over the rules and procedures of the DSU. Briefly discuss the different methods of dispute settlement provided for in the DSU and the use made by Members of each of these methods. What is the WTO dispute settlement system's preferred method of dispute settlement? Why? Does Article 23 of the DSU prohibit *any* form of unilateral conduct by Members when seeking redress of a violation of WTO obligations or does it prohibit only the unilateral suspension of concessions or other obligations? Explain how concerns regarding unilateral action taken by the United States in international trade disputes were the driving force behind the Uruguay Round negotiations which resulted in the DSU.

4.5   Mandate to Clarify WTO Provisions

Article 3.2, second sentence, of the DSU states that the WTO dispute settlement system serves not only 'to preserve the rights and obligations of Members under the covered agreements', but also 'to clarify the existing provisions of those agreements'. This sub-section discusses in turn: (1) the scope and nature of this mandate to clarify, i.e. to interpret, the provisions of the covered agreements; (2) the general rule of interpretation set out in Article 31 of the *Vienna Convention on the Law of Treaties*; and (3) supplementary means of interpretation set out in Article 32 of the *Vienna Convention*.

4.5.1   Scope and Nature of the Mandate to Clarify

As stated above, Article 3.2, second sentence, of the DSU mandates the WTO dispute settlement system with the task of clarification of the existing provisions of the covered agreements. As the past eighteen years of WTO dispute settlement have shown, many provisions of the covered agreements are a masterpiece of 'constructive ambiguity'.[150] There is, therefore, much need for clarification in particular dispute settlement proceedings. However, the scope and nature of this clarification mandate is circumscribed. Article 3.2, third sentence, provides:

Recommendations and rulings of the DSB cannot add to or diminish the rights and obligations provided in the covered agreements.

---

148 See Article 3.6 of the DSU.   149 See below, p. 269.
150 It is often such 'constructive ambiguity' that allowed negotiators to conclude the negotiations and agree on the provisions of an agreement.

In the same vein, Article 19.2 of the DSU states:

> In accordance with paragraph 2 of Article 3, in their findings and recommendations, the panel and Appellate Body cannot add to or diminish the rights and obligations provided in the covered agreements.

While allowing the WTO dispute settlement system to clarify WTO law, Articles 3.2 and 19.2 explicitly preclude the system from adding to or diminishing the rights and obligations of Members. The DSU thus explicitly cautions against 'judicial activism'. WTO panels and the Appellate Body are not to take on the role of 'legislator'.[151] Furthermore, as noted in Chapter 2 of this book, pursuant to Article IX:2 of the *WTO Agreement*, it is the exclusive competence of the Ministerial Conference and the General Council to adopt 'authoritative' interpretations of the provisions of the *WTO Agreement* and the Multilateral Trade Agreements.[152] Article 3.9 of the DSU stipulates that the provisions of the DSU are without prejudice to the rights of Members to seek such 'authoritative' interpretation. In *US – Certain EC Products (2001)*, the Appellate Body held:

> Determining what the rules and procedures of the DSU *ought to be* is not our responsibility nor the responsibility of panels; it is clearly the responsibility solely of the Members of the WTO.[153]

Note that, in *Chile – Alcoholic Beverages (2000)*, Chile argued before the Appellate Body that the panel had acted inconsistently with Articles 3.2 and 19.2 of the DSU as it had added to the rights and obligations of Members. The Appellate Body found, however that:

> [w]e have difficulty in envisaging circumstances in which a panel could add to the rights and obligations of a Member of the WTO if its conclusions reflected a correct interpretation and application of provisions of the covered agreements.[154]

For panels and the Appellate Body to stay within their mandate to clarify existing provisions, it is therefore important that they interpret and apply the provisions concerned correctly. Article 3.2 of the DSU explicitly states in this respect that the dispute settlement system serves:

> to clarify the existing provisions of [the covered] agreements *in accordance with customary rules of interpretation of public international law*.[155]

---

151   WTO Members losing a dispute sometimes raise accusations of judicial activism. By way of example, note the reaction of Sander Levin, a senior US Congressman from Michigan, to the Appellate Body report in *US – Zeroing (Japan) (2007)* that 'the Appellate Body was overstepping its mandate, "changing the rules in the middle of the game"' and that 'the Appellate Body is required to apply obligations that the United States and other WTO Members have negotiated – not create obligations out of thin air'. See *Bridges Weekly Trade News Digest*, 17 January 2007. Likewise, United States Trade Representative Ron Kirk reacted to some adverse findings in the Appellate Body report in *US – Anti-Dumping and Countervailing Duties (China) (2011)* as follows: 'I am deeply troubled by this report. It appears to be a clear case of overreaching by the Appellate Body. We are reviewing the findings closely in order to understand fully their implications.' See www.ustr.gov/about-us/press-office/press-releases/2011/march/ustr-statement-regarding-wto-appellate-body-report-c.

152   For a discussion on Article IX:2 of the *WTO Agreement*, see above, p. 139.

153   Appellate Body Report, *US – Certain EC Products (2001)*, para. 92. Emphasis added.

154   Appellate Body Report, *Chile – Alcoholic Beverages (2000)*, para. 79.

155   Emphasis added.

A correct interpretation of a WTO provision is thus an interpretation in accordance with customary rules of interpretation of public international law. In its very first report, the report in *US – Gasoline (1996)*, the Appellate Body noted with regard to the general rule of interpretation in Article 31 of the *Vienna Convention*:

Th[is] 'general rule of interpretation' [set out in Article 31(1) of the *Vienna Convention on the Law of Treaties*] has attained the status of a rule of customary or general international law. As such, it forms part of the 'customary rules of interpretation of public international law' which the Appellate Body has been directed, by Article 3(2) of the *DSU*, to apply in seeking to clarify the provisions of the [WTO agreements].[156]

In its second report, the report in *Japan – Alcoholic Beverages II (1996)*, the Appellate Body added:

There can be no doubt that Article 32 of the *Vienna Convention*, dealing with the role of supplementary means of interpretation, has also attained the same status [of a rule of customary international law].[157]

In accordance with Articles 31 and 32 of the *Vienna Convention on the Law of Treaties*, panels and the Appellate Body interpret provisions of the covered agreements in accordance with the ordinary meaning of the words of the provision in their context and in light of the object and purpose of the agreement involved; and, if necessary and appropriate, they have recourse to supplementary means of interpretation. While the mandate of panels and the Appellate Body to clarify the provisions of the covered agreements is – as discussed above – limited by Articles 3.2 and 19.2 of the DSU and 'judicial activism' is not condoned, note that the Appellate Body held in *Japan – Alcoholic Beverages II (1996)* with regard to the degree of 'flexibility' and 'interpretability' of the covered agreements that:

WTO rules are reliable, comprehensible and enforceable. WTO rules are not so rigid or so inflexible as not to leave room for reasoned judgements in confronting the endless and ever-changing ebb and flow of real facts in real cases in the real world. They will serve the multilateral trading system best if they are interpreted with that in mind. In that way, we will achieve the 'security and predictability' sought for the multilateral trading system by the Members of the WTO through the establishment of the dispute settlement system.[158]

As the Appellate Body's interpretation of the term 'exhaustible natural resources' of Article XX(g) of the GATT 1994 in *US – Shrimp (1998)* demonstrated, the

---

156 Appellate Body Report, *US – Gasoline (1996)*, 15–16.
157 Appellate Body Report, *Japan – Alcoholic Beverages II (1996)*, 104. Also the rule reflected in Article 33 of the *Vienna Convention* regarding plurilingual treaties has been used by panels and the Appellate Body in the interpretation of provisions of WTO agreements. See e.g. Appellate Body Report, *US – Anti-Dumping and Countervailing Duties (China) (2011)*, paras. 330–2. Other customary rules or principles of interpretation which panels and/or the Appellate Body have already had recourse to (or at least discussed) are the *in dubio mitius* rule (see *EC – Hormones (1998)* and *China – Publications and Audiovisual Products (2010)*) and the *ejusdem generis* rule (see *US – COOL (2012)* and *US – Large Civil Aircraft (2nd complaint) (2012)*). See above, p. 57.
158 Appellate Body Report, *Japan – Alcoholic Beverages II (1996)*, 122–3.

meaning of a term may evolve over time.[159] An 'evolutionary' interpretation of terms and provisions of WTO law is not excluded.

With regard to one of the most controversial interpretations of the Appellate Body, namely, the interpretation of the relevant provisions of the *Anti-Dumping Agreement* which led the Appellate Body to rule that the United States' zeroing methodology is WTO-inconsistent,[160] one of the Members of the Appellate Body in *US – Continued Zeroing (2009)* stated in a concurring opinion:

The interpretation of the covered agreements requires scrupulous adherence to the disciplines of the customary rules of interpretation of public international law ... Just as the interpreter of a treaty strives for coherence, there is an inevitable recognition that a treaty bears the imprint of many hands. And what is left behind is a text, sometimes negotiated to a point where an agreement to regulate a matter could only be reached on the basis of constructive ambiguity, carrying both the hopes and fears of the parties. Interpretation is an endeavour to discern order, notwithstanding these infirmities, without adding to or diminishing the rights and obligations of the parties.[161]

4.5.2 Article 31 of the Vienna Convention

Article 31 of the *Vienna Convention on the Law of Treaties*, entitled 'General Rule of Interpretation', states in its first paragraph:

A treaty shall be interpreted in good faith in accordance with the ordinary meaning to be given to the terms of the treaty in their context and in the light of its object and purpose.

As the panel in *US – Section 301 Trade Act (2000)* observed:

Text, context and object-and-purpose correspond to well established textual, systemic and teleological methodologies of treaty interpretation, all of which typically come into play when interpreting complex provisions in multilateral treaties. For pragmatic reasons the normal usage, and we will follow this usage, is to start the interpretation from the ordinary meaning of the 'raw' text of the relevant treaty provisions and then seek to construe it in its context and in the light of the treaty's object and purpose. However, the elements referred to in Article 31 – text, context and object-and-purpose as well as good faith – are to be viewed as one holistic rule of interpretation rather than a sequence of separate tests to be applied in a hierarchical order. Context and object-and-purpose may often appear simply to confirm an interpretation seemingly derived from the 'raw' text. In reality it is always some context, even if unstated, that determines which meaning is to be taken as 'ordinary' and frequently it is impossible to give meaning, even 'ordinary meaning', without looking also at object-and-purpose.[162]

The panel in *US – Section 301 Trade Act (2000)* thus stressed that the elements of Article 31 of the *Vienna Convention* – text, context and object-and-purpose – constitute 'one holistic rule of interpretation', and not 'a sequence of separate tests to be applied in a hierarchical order'.[163] To determine the ordinary meaning

---

159 For a discussion of this interpretation of the term 'exhaustible natural resources', see below, pp. 565–6.
160 On the zeroing methodology to calculate a dumping margin, see below, p. 692.
161 Appellate Body Report, *US – Continued Zeroing (2009)*, para. 306.
162 Panel Report, *US – Section 301 Trade Act (2000)*, para. 7.22.
163 *Ibid.* See also Appellate Body Report, *China – Publications and Audiovisual Products (2010)*, para. 176, where the Appellate Body stated that interpretation under Article 31 of the *Vienna Convention* is 'ultimately a holistic exercise that should not be mechanically subdivided into rigid components'.

of a term, it makes sense to start with the dictionary meaning of that term but, as the Appellate Body noted more than once, a term often has several dictionary meanings and dictionary meanings thus leave many interpretative questions open.[164] The ordinary meaning of a term cannot be determined outside the context in which the term is used and without consideration of the object and purpose of the agreement at issue.[165]

In *Japan – Alcoholic Beverages II (1996)*, the Appellate Body stated:

Article 31 of the *Vienna Convention* provides that the words of the treaty form the foundation for the interpretive process: 'interpretation must be based above all upon the text of the treaty'. The provisions of the treaty are to be given their ordinary meaning in their context. The object and purpose of the treaty are also to be taken into account in determining the meaning of its provisions.[166]

The duty of an interpreter is to examine the words of the treaty to determine the *common* intentions of the parties to the treaty.[167] The panel in *US – Corrosion-Resistant Steel Sunset Review (2004)* declined to consider Japan's arguments regarding the object and purpose of the *Anti-Dumping Agreement* on the basis that:

Article 31 of the *Vienna Convention* requires that the text of the treaty be read in light of the object and purpose of the treaty, not that object and purpose alone override the text.[168]

One of the corollaries of the 'general rule of interpretation' of Article 31 of the *Vienna Convention* is that interpretation must give meaning and effect to *all* the terms of a treaty (i.e. the interpretative principle of effectiveness). An interpreter is not free to adopt a reading that would result in reducing whole clauses or paragraphs of a treaty to redundancy or inutility.[169] Furthermore, the Appellate Body in *EC – Hormones (1998)* cautioned interpreters as follows:

The fundamental rule of treaty interpretation requires a treaty interpreter to read and interpret the words actually used by the agreement under examination, and not words the interpreter may feel should have been used.[170]

In *India – Patents (US) (1998)*, the Appellate Body ruled that the principles of treaty interpretation 'neither require nor condone' the importation into a treaty of 'words that are not there' or 'concepts that were not intended'.[171]

---

164 See Appellate Body Report, *Canada – Aircraft (1999)*, para. 153; and Appellate Body Report, *EC – Asbestos (2001)*, para. 92.
165 On the concept of 'ordinary meaning', see also Appellate Body Report, *EC – Chicken Cuts (2005)*, paras. 170–87.
166 Appellate Body Report, *Japan – Alcoholic Beverages II (1996)*, 104.
167 See e.g. Appellate Body Report, *India – Patents (US) (1998)*, para. 45; and Appellate Body Report, *EC – Computer Equipment (1998)*, para. 84. Note that, in both these cases, the Appellate Body rejected the relevance of the 'legitimate expectations' of *one of the parties* in the interpretation of the meaning of the provision at issue.
168 Panel Report, *US – Corrosion-Resistant Steel Sunset Review (2004)*, para. 7.44.
169 See Appellate Body Report, *US – Gasoline (1996)*, 21. See also e.g. *Canada – Dairy (1999)*, para. 135.
170 Appellate Body Report, *EC – Hormones (1998)*, para. 181.
171 Appellate Body Report, *India – Patents (US) (1998)*, para. 45.

As stated above, the words used must be interpreted in their context. In fact, the ordinary meaning of the words used can often only be determined when considered in their context. As Article 31.2 of the *Vienna Convention* states, the relevant context includes, in addition to the rest of the text of the agreement, the Preamble and annexes, also: (1) any agreement relating to the treaty which was made between all the parties in connection with the conclusion of the treaty (see Article 31.2(a)); and (2) any instrument which was made by one or more parties in connection with the conclusion of the treaty and accepted by the other parties as an instrument related to the treaty. In *EC – Chicken Cuts (2005)*, the Appellate Body found that the Harmonized Commodity Description *and Coding System*, commonly referred to as the 'Harmonized System' and discussed in Chapter 6 of this book,[172] serves as 'context' within the meaning of Article 31.2(a) of the *Vienna Convention* for the purpose of interpreting the WTO agreements.[173] The Appellate Body referred to the 'close link' between the Harmonized System and the WTO and the 'broad consensus' among Members to use the Harmonized System.[174]

Pursuant to Article 31.3 of the *Vienna Convention*, a treaty interpreter must take into account together with the context: (1) any subsequent agreement between the parties regarding the interpretation of the treaty or the application of its provisions (see Article 31.3(a)); (2) any subsequent practice in the application of the treaty which establishes the agreement of the parties regarding its interpretation (see Article 31.3(b)); and (3) any relevant rules of international law applicable in the relations between the parties (see Article 31.3(c)). It is important to note the mandatory nature of Article 31.3. As the wording of its chapeau ('[t]here shall be taken into account') indicates, Article 31.3 mandates a treaty interpreter to take into account subsequent agreements, subsequent practice and relevant rules of international law; it does not merely give a treaty interpreter the option of doing so.[175] With regard to *subsequent agreements* within the meaning of Article 31.3(a), note that the Appellate Body considered in *US – Clove Cigarettes (2012)* that a decision by the Ministerial Conference, namely, the *Doha Ministerial Decision on Implementation-Related Issues and Concerns*, and in particular paragraph 5.2 thereof, constituted a subsequent agreement between the parties, within the meaning of Article 31.3(a).[176]

---

172 See below, p. 453.

173 See Appellate Body Report, *EC – Chicken Cuts (2005)*, paras. 197–9. Note, however, that, in *US – Gambling (2005)*, the Appellate Body ruled that the panel in that case erred in categorising document W/120 and the 1993 Scheduling Guidelines as 'agreements' within the meaning of Article 31.2(a) of the *Vienna Convention*. See Appellate Body Report, *US – Gambling (2005)*, paras. 175–6.

174 See Appellate Body Report, *EC – Chicken Cuts (2005)*, paras. 197–9.

175 See Panel Reports, *EC – Approval and Marketing of Biotech Products (2006)*, para. 7.69. While the panel made this observation on the mandatory nature in particular with regard to Article 31.3(c), the same reasoning applies to the other paragraphs of Article 31.3.

176 See Appellate Body Report, *US – Clove Cigarettes (2012)*, para. 268. With regard to the question whether a TBT Committee decision could be considered to be a 'subsequent agreement', see Appellate Body Report, *US – Tuna II (Mexico) (2012)*, para. 372. See also above, p. 54, and below, p. 888.

With regard to *subsequent practice* within the meaning of Article 31.3(b), the Appellate Body stated in *Japan – Alcoholic Beverages II (1996)*:

[I]n international law, the essence of subsequent practice in interpreting a treaty has been recognized as a 'concordant, common and consistent' sequence of acts or pronouncements which is sufficient to establish a discernible pattern implying the agreement of the parties regarding its interpretation. An isolated act is generally not sufficient to establish subsequent practice; it is a sequence of acts establishing the agreement of the parties that is relevant.[177]

With regard to *relevant rules of international law* within the meaning of Article 31.3(c), the panel in *EC – Approval and Marketing of Biotech Products (2006)* noted:

Textually, this reference [to relevant rules of international law] seems sufficiently broad to encompass all generally accepted sources of public international law, that is to say, (i) international conventions (treaties), (ii) international custom (customary international law), and (iii) the recognized general principles of law. In our view, there can be no doubt that treaties and customary rules of international law are 'rules of international law' within the meaning of Article 31(3)(c).[178]

Earlier, the Appellate Body had already held in *US – Shrimp (1998)* that general principles of international law are 'rules of international law' within the meaning of Article 31.3(c).[179] However, the panel in *EC – Approval and Marketing of Biotech Products (2006)* pointed out that Article 31.3(c) of the *Vienna Convention* contains an important limitation, namely, that only those rules of international law 'applicable in the relations between the parties' are to be taken into account. It held 'the parties' to mean those States that have consented to be bound by the treaty being interpreted (i.e. *all* WTO Members).[180] According to the panel, a treaty interpreter is not *required* to have regard to treaties signed by only some WTO Members as context under Article 31.3(c) of the *Vienna Convention*, but would have the *discretion* to use such treaties as informative tools in establishing the ordinary meaning of the words used.[181] The panel's finding that 'rules of international law' within the meaning of Article 31.3(c) do not include treaties signed by only some WTO Members has been criticised by some international law scholars, who have noted that:

[b]earing in mind the unlikeliness of a precise congruence in the membership of most important multilateral conventions, it would become unlikely that *any* use of conventional international law could be made in the interpretation of such conventions. This would have the ironic effect that the more the membership of a multilateral treaty such as the WTO covered agreements expanded, the more those treaties would be cut off from the rest of

---

177 Appellate Body Report, *Japan – Alcoholic Beverages II (1996)*, 105–6. See also above, p. 58; and Panel Report, *US – FSC (2000)*, para. 7.75; Panel Report, *Canada – Patent Term (2000)*, para. 5.5 and para. 6.89, footnote 48; and Appellate Body Report, *Chile – Price Band System (2002)*, para. 272.
178 Panel Reports, *EC – Approval and Marketing of Biotech Products (2006)*, para. 7.67.
179 See Appellate Body Report, *US – Shrimp (1998)*, para. 158.
180 Panel Reports, *EC – Approval and Marketing of Biotech Products (2006)*, para. 7.68.
181 See *ibid.*, paras. 7.92–7.93.

international law. In practice, the result would be the isolation of multilateral agreements as 'islands' permitting no references *inter se* in their application.[182]

Note, however, that the panel in *EC – Approval and Marketing of Biotech Products (2006)* did not rule that a treaty interpreter may not take into account treaties to which not all WTO Members are a party, but that a treaty interpreter is not required to do so.[183] In *EC and certain member States – Large Civil Aircraft (2011)*, the Appellate Body ruled that an interpretation of 'the parties' in Article 31.3(c) should be guided by the Appellate Body's statement in *EC – Computer Equipment (1998)* that 'the purpose of treaty interpretation is to establish the common intention of the parties to the treaty'. This suggests that one must exercise caution in drawing from an international agreement to which not all WTO Members are party.[184] However, the Appellate Body also recognised in *EC and certain member States – Large Civil Aircraft (2011)* that:

a proper interpretation of the term 'the parties' must also take account of the fact that Article 31(3)(c) of the Vienna Convention is considered an expression of the 'principle of systemic integration' which, in the words of the International Law Commission, seeks to ensure that 'international obligations are interpreted by reference to their normative environment' in a manner that gives 'coherence and meaningfulness' to the process of legal interpretation.[185]

The Appellate Body therefore concluded in *EC and certain member States – Large Civil Aircraft (2011)* that:

[i]n a multilateral context such as the WTO, when recourse is had to a non-WTO rule for the purposes of interpreting provisions of the WTO agreements, a delicate balance must be struck between, on the one hand, taking due account of an individual WTO Member's international obligations and, on the other hand, ensuring a consistent and harmonious approach to the interpretation of WTO law among all WTO Members.[186]

In *EC and certain member States – Large Civil Aircraft (2011)*, the Appellate Body did not decide on whether the non-WTO agreement invoked by the European Union, namely, the 1992 Agreement between the European Community and the United States on trade in civil aircraft, was a 'rule of international law' within the meaning of Article 31.3(c). The Appellate Body did not need to decide on this question since it determined that the 1992 Agreement was not a 'relevant' rule of international law. It was not a 'relevant' rule because it did not – contrary to what the European Union argued – concern the subject-matter of the WTO provision at issue.[187]

Finally, as discussed above, interpretation pursuant to Article 31 requires a treaty interpreter to consider the terms used 'in the light of the object and

---

182 International Law Commission, 58th Session, *Fragmentation of International Law: Difficulties Arising from the Diversification and Expansion of International Law*, Report of the Study Group of the International Law Commission, finalised by Martti Koskenniemi, A/CN.4/L.682, 13 April 2006, para. 471.

183 Moreover, note that, in *EC – Approval and Marketing of Biotech Products (2006)*, not even all parties to the dispute, let alone all WTO Members, were parties to the non-WTO agreements at issue.

184 See Appellate Body Report, *EC and certain member States – Large Civil Aircraft (2011)*, para. 845.

185 *Ibid.*   186 *Ibid.*   187 *Ibid.*, para. 855.

purpose' of the treaty. With regard to the 'object and purpose', the Appellate Body agreed with the panel in *EC – Chicken Cuts (2005)*, that:

> the security and predictability of 'the reciprocal and mutually advantageous arrangements directed to the substantial reduction of tariffs and other barriers to trade' is an object and purpose of the WTO Agreement, generally, as well as of the GATT 1994.[188]

Of particular interest in this case is that the Appellate Body emphasised that the starting point for ascertaining 'object and purpose' is the treaty itself, *in its entirety*, but that Article 31.1 did not exclude taking into account the object and purpose of particular treaty provisions, if doing so assists the interpreter in determining the treaty's object and purpose on the whole.[189] The Appellate Body did not consider it necessary 'to divorce a treaty's object and purpose from the object and purpose of specific treaty provisions, or *vice versa*'.[190] The Appellate Body stated:

> To the extent that one can speak of the 'object and purpose of a treaty provision', it will be informed by, and will be in consonance with, the object and purpose of the entire treaty of which it is but a component.[191]

4.5.3 Article 32 of the Vienna Convention

Article 32 of the *Vienna Convention*, entitled 'Supplementary Means of Interpretation', states:

> Recourse may be had to supplementary means of interpretation, including the preparatory work of the treaty and the circumstances of its conclusion, in order to confirm the meaning resulting from the application of article 31, or to determine the meaning when the interpretation according to article 31:
>
> a. leaves the meaning ambiguous or obscure; or
> b. leads to a result which is manifestly absurd or unreasonable.

As the Appellate Body observed in *EC – Computer Equipment (1998)*, the application of the general rule of interpretation set out in Article 31 of the *Vienna Convention*, and discussed above, will usually allow a treaty interpreter to establish the meaning of a term. However, if that is not the case, Article 32 of the *Vienna Convention* allows a treaty interpreter to have recourse to supplementary means of interpretation, including the preparatory work of the treaty and the circumstances of its conclusion.[192] A treaty interpreter may also have recourse to Article 32 in order to confirm, i.e. further support, the interpretation resulting from the application of the general rule of interpretation of Article 31.

With regard to the 'preparatory work of the treaty', commonly also referred to as the 'negotiating history' of a treaty, it must be noted that there exists

---

188 Appellate Body Report, *EC – Chicken Cuts (2005)*, para. 243.
189 See *ibid.*, para. 238.   190 *Ibid.*   191 *Ibid.*
192 Appellate Body Report, *EC – Computer Equipment (1998)*, para. 86. See also Appellate Body Report, *Canada – Dairy (1999)*, para. 138.

no officially recorded negotiating history of the WTO agreements (unlike for the GATT 1947 and the 1948 *Havana Charter for an International Trade Organization*).[193] It is, therefore, not surprising that panels and the Appellate Body have made little use of the 'preparatory work of the treaty' in their interpretative efforts.[194] Panels and the Appellate Body have given limited weight to various country-specific and often conflicting negotiating proposals and very little importance to the often contradictory and self-serving *personal* recollections of negotiators. In *US – Line Pipe (2002)*, the Appellate Body noted that the 'negotiating history' of Article XIX of the GATT 1947 and of the WTO *Agreement on Safeguards* did not provide much guidance on the interpretative question at issue in that case.[195] Note, however, that the panel in *US – Large Civil Aircraft (2nd complaint) (2012)* observed that a reference to governmental 'purchases of services' was initially included in the draft, but was removed from the final version, of Articles 1.1 and 14(d) of the *SCM Agreement*. The panel attached significance to this fact in its interpretation of these provisions.[196]

With regard to 'the circumstances of [the] conclusion' of a treaty, the Appellate Body considered in *EC – Computer Equipment (1998)*, that Article 32 permits, in appropriate cases, the examination of the historical background against which the treaty was negotiated. In this case, the Appellate Body considered that the tariff classification practice in the European Communities during the Uruguay Round was part of 'the circumstances of [the] conclusion' of the *WTO Agreement* and could therefore be used as a supplementary means of interpretation within the meaning of Article 32 of the *Vienna Convention*.[197] In *EC – Poultry (1998)*, the Appellate Body considered a pre-WTO bilateral agreement between the parties to the dispute (i.e. the *Oilseeds Agreement*) to be part of the historical background to be taken into account when interpreting the provision at issue.[198] In *US – Gambling (2005)*, the Appellate Body used two documents ('Scheduling Guidelines') drawn up by the Secretariat during the Uruguay Round services negotiations to assist Members in drafting their GATS Schedules of Specific Commitments, as supplementary means of interpretation with regard to the United States' Services Schedule.[199]

---

193 In *India – Quantitative Restrictions (1999)*, for example, the Appellate Body explicitly noted 'the absence of a record of the negotiations' on the 1994 WTO Understanding at issue in that case. See Appellate Body Report, *India – Quantitative Restrictions (1999)*, para. 94.

194 The Appellate Body referred to the negotiating history of the provision at issue in *Canada – Periodicals (1997)*. However, the negotiating history referred to was the negotiating history of the *Havana Charter*. See Appellate Body Report, *Canada – Periodicals (1997)*, 34.

195 See Appellate Body Report, *US – Line Pipe (2002)*, para. 175.

196 See Panel Report, *US – Large Civil Aircraft (2nd complaint) (2012)*, paras. 7.963–7.964.

197 See Appellate Body Report, *EC – Computer Equipment (1998)*, para. 92.

198 See Appellate Body Report, *EC – Poultry (1998)*, para. 83. See also Appellate Body Report, *Canada – Dairy (1999)*, para. 139.

199 See Appellate Body Report, *US – Gambling (2005)*, para. 196. In this regard, the Appellate Body disagreed with the panel that these documents were part of the 'context' for interpretation of the United States' Schedule, under Article 31.2(a) of the *Vienna Convention*. See also below, p. 528.

Questions and Assignments 3.5

Why is the panels' and Appellate Body's task to clarify existing provisions of the covered agreements an important task? Does the DSU allow for 'judicial activism'? How does Article 3.2 of the DSU try to ensure that panels and the Appellate Body remain within their 'clarification' mandate'? Why are Articles 31 and 32 of the *Vienna Convention on the Law of Treaties* relevant to the interpretation and clarification of the provisions of the covered agreements? How do panels and the Appellate Body have to interpret provisions of the covered agreements? Can panels or the Appellate Body base their interpretation of a provision of the covered agreements on the 'legitimate expectations' of one of the parties to the dispute? What does the 'principle of effectiveness' require panels and the Appellate Body to do when they interpret provisions of the covered agreements? Give an example of a 'subsequent agreement' within the meaning of Article 31.3(a) of the *Vienna Convention* which has been considered by the Appellate Body in interpreting a provision of the *TBT Agreement*. What is the relevance of non-WTO agreements and customary international law in the interpretation of provisions of the covered agreements? Can agreements to which not all WTO Members are a party be relevant in the interpretation of a provision of a covered agreement? What can panels and the Appellate Body use as supplementary means of interpretation and when can they do so?

4.6   Remedies for Breach

The DSU provides for three types of remedy for breach of WTO law: one final remedy, namely, the withdrawal (or modification) of the WTO-inconsistent measure; and two temporary remedies which can be applied pending the withdrawal (or modification) of the WTO-inconsistent measure, namely, compensation *and* suspension of concessions or other obligations (commonly referred to as 'retaliation'). The DSU makes clear that compensation and/or the suspension of concessions or other obligations are *not* alternative remedies, which Members may want to apply *instead of* withdrawing (or modifying) the WTO-inconsistent measure.[200] Article 22.1 of the DSU explicitly states:

Compensation and the suspension of concessions or other obligations are *temporary measures* available in the event that the recommendations and rulings are not implemented within a reasonable period of time. However, neither compensation nor the suspension of concessions or other obligations is preferred to full implementation of a recommendation to bring a measure into conformity with the covered agreements.[201]

This sub-section discusses in turn the final remedy and the two temporary remedies for breach of WTO law. It also briefly examines whether other types of remedy may be available.

---

200 Note that the 2004 Sutherland Report observed in this respect: 'It has even been argued by some that a WTO Member finding itself in a losing position in the WTO dispute settlement system has a free choice on whether or not to actually implement the obligations spelled out in the adopted Appellate Body or panel reports: the alternatives being simply to provide compensation or endure retaliation. This is an erroneous belief.' See Report by the Consultative Board to the Director-General Supachai Panitchpakdi, *The Future of the WTO: Addressing Institutional Challenges in the New Millennium* (the 'Sutherland Report') (WTO, 2004), para. 241.
201 Emphasis added.

4.6.1 Withdrawal of the WTO-Inconsistent Measure

Article 3.7, fourth sentence, of the DSU states:

In the absence of a mutually agreed solution, the first objective of the dispute settlement mechanism is usually to secure the withdrawal of the measures concerned if these are found to be inconsistent with the provisions of any of the covered agreements.

Furthermore, Article 3.7, fifth sentence, suggests that the withdrawal of the WTO-inconsistent measure should normally be 'immediate'.[202] Article 19.1 of the DSU provides:

Where a panel or the Appellate Body concludes that a measure is inconsistent with a covered agreement, it shall recommend that the Member concerned bring the measure into conformity with that agreement ...

Such a recommendation, once adopted by the DSB, is legally binding on the Member concerned.[203] With regard to recommendations and rulings adopted by the DSB, Article 21.1 of the DSU provides that:

Prompt compliance with recommendations or rulings of the DSB is essential in order to ensure effective resolution of disputes to the benefit of all Members.[204]

While Article 3.7 of the DSU refers to the withdrawal of the measure found to be WTO-inconsistent, the withdrawal or the modification of the WTO-inconsistent aspects or elements of such a measure usually suffices to bring the measure into conformity with WTO law pursuant to the recommendations or rulings of the DSB.[205] Prompt or immediate compliance with the DSB recommendations and rulings, i.e. prompt or immediate withdrawal or modification of the WTO-inconsistent measure, is essential to the effective functioning of the WTO and is the primary obligation. However, if it is impracticable to comply immediately with the recommendations and rulings, and this may often be the case, the Member concerned has, pursuant to Article 21.3 of the DSU, a reasonable period of time in which to do so. The 'reasonable period of time for implementation' may be: (1) agreed on by the parties to the dispute; or (2) determined through binding arbitration at the request of either party.[206] In most cases – in particular in recent years – the parties to the dispute succeed in agreeing on what constitutes a 'reasonable period of time for implementation'. In seventy-four cases to date,

---

202 As discussed below, Article 3.7 provides: 'The provision of compensation should be resorted to only if the *immediate* withdrawal of the measure is impracticable ... '. Emphasis added.

203 On the adoption of recommendations and rulings of panel reports, see below, p. 282.

204 Emphasis added.

205 While it is appropriate for panels and the Appellate Body to rule on the WTO-consistency of measures that are no longer in force (see above, pp. 164–5), it is not 'appropriate' for them to recommend that a measure that is no longer in force be brought into conformity. In *Dominican Republic – Import and Sale of Cigarettes (2005)*, the Appellate Body upheld the panel's ruling to this effect. See Appellate Body Report, *Dominican Republic – Import and Sale of Cigarettes (2005)*, para. 129.

206 See Article 21.3(b) and (c) of the DSU. See also below, pp. 291–3. Note that Article 21.3(a) also provides for the possibility that the DSB decides on the reasonable period of time for implementation. The DSB has never done so. Since the DSB must take such decision by consensus, it would always require the agreement of the parties to the dispute.

the parties were able to agree on the reasonable period of time for implementation.[207] The period agreed on ranges from four months and fourteen days (*US – Wheat Gluten (2001)*) to twenty-four months (*Dominican Republic – Import and Sales of Cigarettes (2005)*).[208] In twenty-six cases to date, the 'reasonable period of time for implementation' was decided through binding arbitration under Article 21.3(c) of the DSU.[209] The latter provision states:

In such arbitration, a guideline for the arbitrator should be that the reasonable period of time to implement panel or Appellate Body recommendations should not exceed 15 months from the date of adoption of a panel or Appellate Body report. However, that time may be shorter or longer, depending upon the particular circumstances.

Since the Article 21.3(c) arbitration in *EC – Hormones (1998)*, it is generally accepted and clearly reflected in practice, that the fifteen-month period mentioned in Article 21.3(c) of the DSU is a mere guideline for the arbitrator and that it is neither an '*outer* limit' nor, of course, *a floor* or '*inner* limit' for a 'reasonable period of time for implementation'.[210] In *EC – Hormones (1998)*, the arbitrator ruled that the 'reasonable period of time for implementation', as determined under Article 21.3(c), should be:

the shortest period possible within the legal system of the Member to implement the recommendations and rulings of the DSB.[211]

While this has become the core rule in establishing the reasonable period of time for implementation, the arbitrator in *US – Gambling (2005)* stated:

Yet, it is useful to recall that the DSU does not refer to the 'shortest period possible for implementation within the legal system' of the implementing Member. Rather, this is a convenient phrase that has been used by previous arbitrators to describe their task. I do not, however, view this standard as one that stands in isolation from the text of the DSU. In my view, the determination of the 'shortest period possible for implementation' can, and must, also take due account of the two principles that are expressly mentioned in Article 21 of the DSU, namely reasonableness and the need for prompt compliance. Moreover, as differences in previous awards involving legislative implementation by the United States have shown, and as the text of Article 21.3(c) prescribes, each arbitrator must take account of 'particular circumstances' relevant to the case at hand.[212]

Moreover, as the arbitrator in *Korea – Alcoholic Beverages (1999)* ruled, a Member is not required to utilise extraordinary legislative procedures, rather than the normal procedure, in order to shorten the period of implementation.[213] In

---

207 See www.worldtradelaw.net/dsc/database/implementationprovision.asp.
208 See www.worldtradelaw.net/dsc/database/implementationperiod.asp.
209 See www.worldtradelaw.net/dsc/database/rptawards.asp. On the appointment of an Article 21.3(c) arbitrator and the Article 21.3(c) arbitration proceeding, see below, pp. 291–3.
210 See e.g. Award of the Arbitrator, *US – Hot-Rolled Steel (Article 21.3 (c)) (2002)*, para. 25.
211 Award of the Arbitrator, *EC – Hormones (Article 21.3 (c)) (1998)*, para. 26.
212 Award of the Arbitrator, *US – Gambling (Article 21.3(c)) (2005)*, para. 44.
213 See Award of the Arbitrator, *Korea – Alcoholic Beverages (Article 21.3(c)) (1999)*, para. 42. In *Canada – Autos (2000)*, the arbitrator held that the question whether a Member could take 'extraordinary action' to bring about compliance was not even relevant to the determination of the reasonable period of time. See Award of the Arbitrator, *Canada – Autos (Article 21.3(c)) (2000)*, para. 53.

EC – Hormones (1998), the arbitrator also noted that, when implementation does not require changes in legislation but can be effected by administrative means, the reasonable period of time 'should be considerably less than 15 months'.[214] In *Canada – Pharmaceutical Patents (2000)*, the arbitrator listed a number of other 'particular circumstances' that can influence what the shortest period possible for implementation may be within the legal system of the implementing Member. Apart from the means of implementation (legislative or administrative), this arbitrator referred to the complexity of the proposed implementation[215] and the legally binding, as opposed to the discretionary, nature of the component steps in the process leading to implementation.[216] The legislative calendar of Members will have a bearing on the reasonable period of time on a case-by-case basis.[217] Also, the time taken for previous legislation on the same subject-matter to pass through parliament would be relevant for an Article 21.3(c) arbitration.[218] The domestic political or economic situation in the Member concerned is not relevant in determining the 'reasonable period of time for implementation'.[219] The absence of a political majority to adopt implementing measures or economic hardship resulting from implementation, for example, are not taken into consideration by the arbitrator in determining the 'reasonable period of time for implementation'.[220] The need for consultations with government departments and stakeholders is in itself not a reason for more time for implementation.[221] Note that the arbitrator in *EC – Tariff Preferences (2004)* considered that the EU enlargement was a relevant factor in the determination of the reasonable period of time for implementation in that case. The implementing Member bears the burden of proof that the period of time it seeks is a *reasonable* period of time within the meaning of Article 21.3 of the DSU.[222]

---

214 See Award of the Arbitrator, *EC – Hormones (Article 21.3(c)) (1998)*, para. 25. See also e.g. Award of the Arbitrator, *EC – Chicken Cuts (Article 21.3(c)) (2006)*, para. 67.

215 Note that the complexity of the proposed implementation must be a 'particular circumstance'. On this ground, a number of arbitrators have refused to accept the 'complexity' argument made by the respondent. See e.g. Award of the Arbitrator, *US – Offset Act (Byrd Amendment) (Article 21.3(c)) (2003)*, paras. 60–1; and Award of the Arbitrator, *EC – Export Subsidies on Sugar (Article 21.3(c)) (2005)*, para. 88.

216 See Award of the Arbitrator, *Canada – Pharmaceutical Patents (Article 21.3(c)) (2000)*, paras. 48–52.

217 See e.g. Award of the Arbitrator, *US – Gambling (Article 21.3(c)) (2005)*, para. 52.

218 See *ibid.*, para. 55.

219 With regard to developing-country Members, see, however, Article 21.2 of the DSU, discussed below, p. 198.

220 Note, however, that the arbitrator in *Chile – Price Band System (2002)* considered that the unique role and *impact* of the Price Band System on Chilean society was a relevant factor in his determination of the reasonable period of time for implementation. See Award of the Arbitrator, *Chile – Price Band System (Article 21.3(c)) (2003)*, para. 48.

221 See e.g. Award of the Arbitrator, *Canada – Autos (Article 21.3(c)) (2000)*, para. 49. For a more liberal view on the relevance of the need for consultations, see Award of the Arbitrator, *Chile – Price Band System (Article 21.3(c)) (2003)*, paras. 41–2. The need for 'serious debate' and the 'political contentiousness' of the proposed measure are, however, not grounds for a longer period of implementation. See Award of the Arbitrator, *EC – Export Subsidies on Sugar (Article 21.3(c)) (2005)*, paras. 89–90.

222 See Award of the Arbitrator, *EC – Export Subsidies on Sugar (Article 21.3(c)) (2005)*, para. 59. The original complainant may be expected to point at the economic harm suffered by its exporters. However, the arbitrator in *US – Offset Act (Byrd Amendment) (Article 21.3(c)) (2003)* explicitly stated that such harm did not, and could not, impact on what the reasonable period of time for implementation was. See Award of the Arbitrator, *US – Offset Act (Byrd Amendment) (Article 21.3(c)) (2003)*, para. 79.

Article 21.2 of the DSU requires that, in determining the 'reasonable period of time for implementation', particular attention should be paid to matters affecting the interests of developing-country Members.[223] On that legal basis, the arbitrator in *Indonesia – Autos (1998)* ruled:

Indonesia is not only a developing country; it is a developing country that is currently in a dire economic and financial situation. Indonesia itself states that its economy is 'near collapse'. In these very particular circumstances, I consider it appropriate to give full weight to matters affecting the interests of Indonesia as a developing country pursuant to the provisions of Article 21.2 of the DSU. I, therefore, conclude that an additional period of six months over and above the six-month period required for the completion of Indonesia's domestic rule-making process constitutes a reasonable period of time for implementation of the recommendations and rulings of the DSB in this case.[224]

It is clear that the mere fact that either of the parties to a dispute is a developing-country Member does not *ipso facto* affect the determination of the period of time for implementation unless such party is able to substantiate why the otherwise normal period for implementation should cause it hardship.[225]

Finally, it should be emphasised that the mandate of an Article 21.3(c) arbitrator relates to determining the 'reasonable period of time for implementation'.[226] As the arbitrator in *US – COOL (2012)* stated:

Like previous arbitrators, I consider that my mandate relates to the *time* by when the implementing Member must achieve compliance, not to the *manner* in which that Member achieves compliance ... Yet, *when* a Member must comply cannot be determined in isolation from the means used for implementation. In order 'to determine *when* a Member must comply, it may be necessary to consider *how* a Member proposes to do so'. Thus, the means of implementation that are available to the Member concerned, and that this Member intends to use, are relevant for a determination under Article 21.3(c).

The implementing Member has 'a measure of discretion in choosing the *means* of implementation, as long as the means chosen are consistent with the recommendations and rulings of the DSB and with the covered agreements'. As stated by previous arbitrators, 'the implementing Member does not have an unfettered right to choose any method of implementation.' I must consider, in particular, 'whether the implementing action falls within the range of permissible actions that can be taken in order to implement the DSB's recommendations and rulings'. In other words, the chosen method must be capable of placing the implementing Member into compliance within a reasonable period of time in accordance with the guidelines contained in Article 21.3(c).[227]

---

223 Note that Article 21.2 directs an arbitrator to pay attention to matters affecting the interests of *both* complaining and implementing developing-country Members. See Award of the Arbitrator, *EC – Export Subsidies on Sugar (Article 21.3(c)) (2005)*, para. 99.

224 Award of the Arbitrator, *Indonesia – Autos (Article 21.3(c)) (1998)*, para. 24. However, note that 'criteria' for the determination of 'the reasonable period of time' are not 'qualitatively' different for developed and for developing-country Members. See Award of the Arbitrator, *Chile – Alcoholic Beverages (Article 21.3(c)) (2000)*, para. 45.

225 See e.g. Award of the Arbitrator, *US – Offset Act (Byrd Amendment) (Article 21.3(c)) (2003)*, para. 81; and Award of the Arbitrator, *EC – Tariff Preferences (Article 21.3(c)) (2004)*, para. 59.

226 See Award of the Arbitrator, *Korea – Alcoholic Beverages (Article 21.3(c)) (1999)*, para. 45. See also below, p. 196.

227 Award of the Arbitrator, *US – COOL (2012)*, paras. 68–9.

To date, the 'reasonable period of time for implementation' determined through arbitration ranges between six months (in *Canada – Pharmaceutical Patents (2000)*) and fifteen months and one week (in *EC – Bananas III (1997)*).[228] The average time granted for implementation as a 'reasonable period' under Article 21.3 arbitrations to date is just under twelve months.[229] Members should make good use of the time following an adverse ruling to bring about compliance as the obligation to implement starts at the moment of the adoption of the report by the DSB, and *not* at the moment of the arbitrator's award setting the reasonable period of time.

Note that, in more than four out of five disputes in which the responding party had to bring its challenged measure or legislation into conformity with WTO law, this was done within the 'reasonable period of time for implementation'. In most cases, therefore, the responding party implements the recommendations and rulings adopted by the DSB in a timely manner. However, in some of these cases, Article 21.5 'compliance' proceedings are initiated to assess whether measures taken to comply with DSB rulings are fully, only partially or not at all WTO-consistent.[230] The media and academia tend to focus on disputes in which there is no, or only partial, implementation within the reasonable period of time, as was, or is, the case in, for example, *EC – Bananas III (1997)*, *EC – Hormones (1998)*, *US – FSC (2000)*, *US – Section 110(5) Copyright Act (2000)*, *US – Hot-Rolled Steel (2001)*, *US – Section 211 Appropriations Act (2002)*, *US – Offset Act (Byrd Amendment) (2003)*, *EC – Approval and Marketing of Biotech Products (2006)*, *US – Zeroing (EC) (2006)*, *US – Zeroing (EC) (2007)* and *US – Upland Cotton (2008)*.[231] However, the overall record of compliance with the recommendations and rulings adopted by the DSB is quite positive and encouraging. One can conclude on the basis of this record of compliance that the WTO dispute settlement system 'works'. Nevertheless, it is useful to consider the following sobering story regarding the *US – Cotton Yarn (2001)* dispute between Pakistan and the United States in which the United States implemented the recommendations and rulings of the DSB *within* the reasonable period of time:

Finally, complying with the recommendations of the DSB and the Appellate Body of the WTO, the US government in November 2001 lifted the quota restriction on Pakistani imports, much to the relief of the Pakistani manufacturers and exporters. The whole process, from the day the quota restraints were imposed to the day they were lifted, lasted for almost two years and nine months, covering almost the entire period of the three-year transitional

228 See Award of the Arbitrator, *Canada – Pharmaceutical Patents (Article 21.3(c)) (2000)*, paras. 62–4; and Award of the Arbitrator, *EC – Bananas III (Article 21.3(c)) (1998)*, paras. 18–20.

229 See www.worldtradelaw.net/dsc/database/implementaverage.asp.

230 On the Article 21.5 'compliance' proceedings, see below, p. 293.

231 In some of these cases, the DSB's recommendations and rulings have been implemented, but *US – Section 110(5) Copyright Act (2000)*, *US – Hot-Rolled Steel (2001)*, *US – Section 211 Appropriations Act (2002)* and *EC – Approval and Marketing of Biotech Products (2006)* are examples of non-compliance many years after the end of the reasonable period of time for implementation. These cases remain under DSB surveillance. See below, p. 292.

safeguard measure-quota restraint employed by the United States. The following comment by Akbar Sheikh after being congratulated by Ambassador Don Johnson for winning the case aptly summarizes the feeling at that time:

> At the end of the day both parties won, Pakistan because it got a decision in its favour and the United States because it was able to keep the quota restraints for almost the entire three-year period, thanks to the duration of the case.[232]

As discussed in detail below, any disagreement as to (1) the existence of measures taken to comply with the recommendations and rulings or (2) the WTO consistency of these measures, shall be settled through proceedings which are provided for in Article 21.5 of the DSU (therefore commonly referred to as Article 21.5 'compliance' proceedings).[233]

4.6.2   Compensation

As noted above, only the withdrawal (or modification) of the WTO-inconsistent measure constitutes a final remedy for breach of WTO law.[234] However, if a Member has not withdrawn or modified the WTO-inconsistent measure by the end of the 'reasonable period of time for implementation', the DSU provides for the possibility of recourse to *temporary* remedies, namely: (1) compensation; or (2) suspension of concessions or other obligations, commonly referred to as 'retaliation'. This sub-section briefly deals with the less important – and hardly used – of the two temporary remedies, namely, compensation. Compensation within the meaning of Article 22 of the DSU is: (1) voluntary, i.e. the complainant is free to accept or reject compensation; and (2) forward looking, i.e. the compensation concerns only the nullification or impairment (i.e. the harm) that will be suffered in the future. Compensation must be consistent with the covered agreements. To date, parties have been able to agree on compensation in very few cases. In *Japan – Alcoholic Beverages II (1996)*, for example, the parties agreed on compensation which took the form of temporary, additional market access concessions for certain products of export interest to the original complainants.

4.6.3   Retaliation

As is explicitly stated in Article 3.7 of the DSU, the suspension of concessions or other obligations, commonly referred to as 'retaliation', is a measure of 'last resort'. When the 'reasonable period of time for implementation' has expired and the parties have not been able to agree on compensation, the original complaining party may request authorisation from the DSB to retaliate against the offending party by suspending concessions or other obligations with respect to that offending party. Since the DSB decides on such a request by reverse

---

232 T. Hussain, 'Victory in Principle: Pakistan's Dispute Settlement Case on Combed Cotton Yarn Exports to the United States', in P. Gallagher, P. Low and A. Stoler (eds.), *Managing the Challenges of WTO Participation: 45 Case Studies* (Cambridge University Press, 2005), 469.
233 See below, p. 293.   234 See above, p. 195.

consensus, the granting of authorisation is quasi-automatic.[235] To date, requests for authorisation to retaliate were filed in twenty-two cases.[236] Note, however, that these requests were often not further pursued.[237]

With regard to the concessions or other obligations that may be suspended, Article 22.3 of the DSU provides that: (1) the complaining party should first seek to suspend concessions or other obligations with respect to the same sector(s) as that in which a violation was found; (2) if that is not practicable or effective, the complaining party may seek to suspend concessions or other obligations in other sectors under the same agreement; and (3) if also that is not practicable or effective, the complaining party may seek to suspend concessions or other obligations under another covered agreement.[238] In other words, if the violation of WTO law concerns an obligation regarding trade in goods, or regarding trade in financial services, or regarding the protection of patents, suspension of concessions or other obligations should first be sought in the *same* sector. If this is not 'practicable' or 'effective', then suspension may be sought in another sector or under another agreement. This is known as 'cross-retaliation'. To date, cross-retaliation has been requested, and authorised, only a few times. In *EC – Bananas III (1997)*, Ecuador requested, and the DSB authorised, retaliation under an agreement (the *TRIPS Agreement*) other than the agreements at issue in that dispute (the GATT 1994 and the GATS).[239] Similarly, in *US – Upland Cotton (2005)*, the complaining party (Brazil) requested, and the DSB authorised, retaliation under the *TRIPS Agreement*, even though no violations of the obligations under that Agreement were found.[240]

With regard to the level of retaliation, Article 22.4 of the DSU provides:

> The level of the suspension of concessions or other obligations authorized by the DSB shall be equivalent to the level of the nullification or impairment.

While the purpose of retaliation measures is to induce compliance, the arbitrators in *EC – Bananas III (US) (Article 22.6 – EC) (1999)* found that nothing in Article 22 of the DSU could be read as a justification for retaliation measures 'of a *punitive* nature'.[241] The DSB can only authorise retaliation measures *equivalent* to the level of nullification or impairment. Determining the level of the nullification or impairment resulting from the WTO-inconsistent measure(s) may, however, be a difficult and contentious exercise. Pursuant to Article 22.6 of the

---

235 See below, pp. 206–7, 290.
236 See www.worldtradelaw.net/dsc/database/retaliationrequests.asp. The total number of requests for authorisation to retaliation stands at thirty-five. In disputes with multiple complainants, there may be multiple requests. See e.g. *US – Offset Act (Byrd Amendment) (2003)* in which there were eight separate requests for authorisation.
237 See below, p. 202.
238 For definitions of, for example, the concept of 'sectors', and further rules, see Article 22.3(d)–(g) of the DSU.
239 See Dispute Settlement Body, *Minutes of Meeting held on 18 May 2000*, WT/DSB/M/80, dated 26 June 2000, paras. 48–58.
240 See Dispute Settlement Body, *Minutes of Meeting held on 19 November 2009*, WT/DSB/M/276, dated 29 January 2010, paras. 84–7.
241 Decision by the Arbitrators, *EC – Bananas III (US) (Article 22.6 – EC) (1999)*, para. 6.3.

DSU, disputes between the parties on the level of nullification or impairment, and thus on the appropriate level of retaliation, are to be resolved through arbitration by the original panel.[242] As is clear from Article 22.6 itself, the Article 22.6 arbitrators can also review whether a retaliating Member has:

> considered the necessary facts objectively and whether, on the basis of these facts, it could plausibly arrive at the conclusion that it was not practicable or effective to seek suspension within the same sector under the same agreements, or only under another agreement.[243]

To date, Article 22.6 arbitrators have determined the appropriate level of retaliation in nine cases.[244] Typically, the Article 22.6 arbitrators determine the appropriate level of retaliation, to be (considerably) lower than the level of retaliation requested. An extreme example of this was *US – Gambling (2005)* in which Antigua and Barbuda requested retaliation in the amount of US$3,443 million per year, and the Article 22.6 arbitrators set the appropriate level of retaliation at US$21 million per year.[245] The level of retaliation requested has ranged from less than €1.3 million per year in *US – Section 110(5) Copyright Act (2000)* to US$12 billion per year in *US – Large Civil Aircraft (2nd complaint) (2012).*[246]

To date, the DSB has authorised the taking of retaliation measures in nine cases.[247] However, in only four of these cases did the complaining parties actually suspend concessions or other obligations. This was the case in *EC – Bananas III (1997)* (retaliation by the United States for an amount of US$191.4 million per year), in *EC – Hormones (1998)* (retaliation by the United States and Canada for an amount of US$116.8 million and C$11.3 million per year respectively), in *US – FSC (2000)* (retaliation by the European Communities for an amount of US$4,043 million per year) and in *US – Offset Act (Byrd Amendment) (2003)* (retaliation by the European Communities, Canada and Japan for an amount of US$27.8 million, US$11.2 million and US$52.1 million, respectively per year). Retaliation often takes the form of a drastic *increase* in the customs duties (e.g. an increase up to 100 per cent *ad valorem*) on selected products of export interest to the offending party. In *US – FSC (2000)*, however, the European Communities opted for retaliation measures on selected products consisting of an

---

242 On the procedural aspects of these Article 22.6 arbitration proceedings, see below, p. 296.

243 Decision by the Arbitrators, *EC – Bananas III (Ecuador) (Article 22.6 – EC) (2000)*, para. 52.

244 See www.worldtradelaw.net/dsc/database/suspensionawards.asp.

245 See www.worldtradelaw.net/dsc/database/retaliationrequests.asp and www.worldtradelaw.net/dsc/database/suspensionawards.asp.

246 Note that the request in *US – Section 110(5) Copyright Act (2000)* was not further pursued; and that the request in *US – Large Civil Aircraft (2nd complaint) (2012)* is pending.

247 The DSB authorised retaliatory measures in *EC – Bananas III (1997)* (US); *EC – Bananas (Ecuador)*; *EC – Hormones (1998)* (US and Canada); *Brazil – Aircraft (1999)* (Canada); *US – FSC (2000)* (EC); *Canada – Aircraft Credits and Guarantees (2002)* (Brazil); *US – Offset Act (Byrd Amendment) (2003)* (Brazil, Canada, Chile, EC, India, Japan, Korea and Mexico); *US – Upland Cotton (2005)* (Brazil); and *US – Gambling (2005)*. See www.worldtradelaw.net/dsc/database/suspensionawards.asp. Note that, in *US – Section 110(5) Copyright Act (2000)*, the original complainant, the European Union, has not (to date) pursued its request for authorisation to retaliate. Also in *US – Gambling (2005)*, the original complainant, Antigua and Barbuda, did for many years not pursue its request for authorisation. However, at the DSB meeting of 28 January 2013, Antigua and Barbuda requested the DSB to authorise retaliation measures against the United States, and the DSB did so.

additional customs duty of 5 per cent, increased each month by 1 per cent up to a maximum of 17 per cent. Retaliation can also take the form of the suspension of 'obligations' rather than the suspension of tariff 'concessions'. For example, retaliation can consist of the non-protection of the intellectual property rights of products originating in the offending party.[248] It is clear that retaliation puts economic and political pressure on the offending party to comply with the recommendations and rulings. The producers of the products or services hit by the retaliation – typically not the beneficiaries of the WTO-inconsistent measure – will lobby energetically for the withdrawal or modification of the WTO-inconsistent measure. By strategically selecting the products and services of the offending party hit by the retaliation, the complaining party can maximise the economic pain inflicted and the political commotion generated.

Retaliation measures are by nature *trade destructive* and the complaining party imposing these measures is also negatively affected by them. In particular, for developing-country Members, applying retaliation measures is often not a genuine option. In *EC – Bananas III (1997)*, Ecuador was authorised to (cross-) retaliate for an amount of US$201.6 million per year but found it impossible to make use of this possibility without causing severe harm to its own economy. This and later cases, especially cases involving developing-country complainants, have given rise to doubts as to the effectiveness of retaliation as a (temporary) remedy for breach of WTO law. However, in *EC – Bananas III (1997)* and in *US – FSC (2000)*, the retaliation measures imposed by the United States on the European Communities and imposed by the European Communities on the United States respectively, have arguably led to some degree of compliance with the recommendations and rulings in those disputes.[249]

It is debated whether a Member authorised to retaliate may periodically (e.g. every six months) rotate, i.e. change, the products or services on which the retaliation measures are applied. This issue, commonly referred to as the 'carousel retaliation', arose because US legislation foresees a periodic shift in the focus of retaliation measures to maximise their impact. It is clear that rotation of the products or services on which the retaliation measures are applied would 'inflict' harm on a wider section of producers and exporters of the Member concerned and thus add to the pressure on that Member to comply with WTO law. It has been argued, however, that a periodic rotation in the products and services 'hit' by the retaliation measure cannot be allowed since it would result in retaliation measures going beyond the level of nullification or impairment caused.

248 Such retaliation was authorised in *EC – Bananas III (1997)* (retaliation by Ecuador against the European Communities); and in *US – Upland Cotton (2005)* (retaliation by Brazil against the United States). In neither case, however, was this retaliation actually carried out.

249 Note that, in both cases, the implementing measures taken 'under pressure' from retaliation were later challenged and found to be WTO-inconsistent. See *US – FSC (Article 21.5 – EC II) (2006)*; and *EC – Bananas III (Article 21.5 – Ecuador II)/EC – Bananas III (Article 21.5 – US) (2008)*. However, in both disputes, eventually, the WTO-inconsistent measures were withdrawn or modified to the satisfaction of the complainants.

4.6.4 Other Remedies

Under customary international law, a breach of an international obligation leads to responsibility entailing certain legal consequences. The first legal consequence of international responsibility is the obligation to cease the illegal conduct.[250] According to the International Law Commission's *Articles on Responsibility of States for Internationally Wrongful Acts*, the injured State is furthermore entitled to claim 'full reparation' in the form of: (1) restitution in kind; (2) compensation; (3) satisfaction; and (4) assurances and guarantees of non-repetition.[251] Restitution in kind means that the wrong-doing State has to re-establish the situation that existed before the illegal act was committed.[252] If damage is not made good by restitution, the State responsible for the internationally wrongful act is under an obligation to compensate for the damage caused by this act.[253] Compensation covers any economically assessable damage suffered by the injured State and may include interest, and also, under certain circumstances, lost profits.[254] The DSU does not contain a rule providing for the compensation of damage suffered.[255] However, the question is whether the rules of customary international law on State responsibility, as reflected in the International Law Commission's *Articles on Responsibility of States for Internationally Wrongful Acts*, apply to breaches of WTO law. Are the only possible remedies for breach of WTO law the remedies explicitly provided for in the provisions of the DSU quoted and discussed above? Or, in the absence of a specific rule in the DSU excluding compensation of damage suffered, is the customary international law rule on compensation applicable? Note that Article 55 of the *Articles on Responsibility of States for Internationally Wrongful Acts*, entitled 'Lex Specialis', states:

> These articles do not apply where and to the extent that the conditions for the existence of an internationally wrongful act or the content or implementation of the international responsibility of a State are governed by special rules of international law.

By providing a detailed set of rules regarding the legal consequences of a breach of WTO law, the DSU has contracted out of customary international law on State responsibility and that the rule on compensation for damage suffered therefore does not apply.[256] This issue is part of the larger issue of the relationship between WTO law and other international law, discussed in Chapter 1 of this book.[257]

While controversial, in very specific circumstances, repayment of sums illegally received could constitute a remedy for breach of WTO law. Article 4.7

---

250 See Article 30 of the *Articles on Responsibility of States for Internationally Wrongful Acts 2001*, in *Yearbook of the International Law Commission*, 2001, Volume II (Part Two). Text reproduced as it appears in the annex to General Assembly resolution 56/83 of 12 December 2001, and corrected by document A/56/49(Vol.I)/Corr.4.

251 See *ibid.*, Article 34.   252 See *ibid.*, Article 35.

253 See *ibid.*, Article 36(a).   254 See *ibid.*, Article 36(b).

255 Compensation under Article 22 of the DSU concerns only damages suffered after the reasonable period of time for implementation. See above, p. 200.

256 See also above, p. 56.   257 See above, p. 60.

of the *SCM Agreement* states that, if a measure is found to be a prohibited subsidy, the panel shall recommend that the subsidising Member withdraw the subsidy without delay. As discussed in Chapter 12 of this book, the panel in *Australia – Automotive Leather II (Article 21.5 – US) (2000)* concluded that, in the circumstances of that case, repayment is necessary in order to 'withdraw' the prohibited subsidies found to exist.[258] However, the panel's ruling in *Australia – Automotive Leather (Article 21.5 – US) (2000)* that, at least with regard to prohibited subsidies, the DSU not only provides for a 'prospective' but also for a 'retrospective' remedy was criticised by many WTO Members, including *both* parties to this dispute.[259]

Questions and Assignments 3.6

What are the remedies for breach of WTO law? Must Members comply with the recommendations and rulings adopted by the DSB 'immediately' or within a 'reasonable period of time'? Who determines the 'reasonable period of time for implementation'? How is the 'reasonable period of time for implementation' determined? What are the rules applicable to compensation within the meaning of Article 22 of the DSU? When may a complaining party retaliate against a responding party for breach of WTO law? What is 'cross retaliation', and when will it be allowed? Who decides on the level of retaliation and on what basis? Have complaining parties frequently retaliated against a responding party for breach of WTO law? Has retaliation been an effective temporary remedy for breach of WTO law? Do WTO rules on remedies deviate from customary international law on remedies? If so, does customary international law nevertheless apply? In your opinion, should a Member that causes significant damage to the economy of another Member as a result of breach of WTO law compensate this damage? Should customs duties, which were imposed in violation of WTO law, be repaid to the importer?

5   INSTITUTIONS OF WTO DISPUTE SETTLEMENT

Among the institutions involved in WTO dispute settlement, one can distinguish between *political institutions*, such as the Dispute Settlement Body, and *judicial-type institutions*, such as the *ad hoc* dispute settlement panels and the standing Appellate Body. While the WTO has entrusted the adjudication of disputes to panels and the Appellate Body, the Dispute Settlement Body continues to play an active role in the WTO dispute settlement system. Also other institutions as well as persons contribute to the functioning of this system. This section deals in turn with: (1) the Dispute Settlement Body; (2) panels; and (3) the Appellate Body. In conclusion, this section also briefly discusses the other institutions, bodies and persons involved in WTO dispute settlement.

---

258 See Panel Report, *Australia – Automotive Leather II (Article 21.5 – US) (2000)*, para. 6.48. For a full discussion of this ruling, see below, p. 777.

259 The panel report was not appealed because the parties to this dispute, the United States and Australia, had agreed at the outset of the Article 21.5 'compliance' proceeding not to appeal the panel report.

5.1 Dispute Settlement Body

As already noted in Chapter 2 of this book, the Dispute Settlement Body, commonly referred to as the 'DSB', is an emanation, or an *alter ego*, of the WTO's General Council.[260] Article IV:3 of the *WTO Agreement* states, in relevant part:

> The General Council shall convene as appropriate to discharge the responsibilities of the Dispute Settlement Body provided for in the Dispute Settlement Understanding. The Dispute Settlement Body may have its own chairman and shall establish such rules of procedure as it deems necessary for the fulfilment of those responsibilities.

When the General Council administers the WTO dispute settlement system, it convenes and acts as the DSB. Like the General Council, the DSB is composed of diplomats representing all WTO Members.[261] With respect to the functions of the DSB, Article 2.1 of the DSU broadly defines these functions as the *administration* of the dispute settlement system and then specifies them by stating:

> Accordingly, the DSB shall have the authority to establish panels, adopt panel and Appellate Body reports, maintain surveillance of implementation of rulings and recommendations, and authorize suspension of concessions and other obligations under the covered agreements.

However, the administration of the dispute settlement system is not limited to these functions. It also includes, for example, the appointment of the Members of the Appellate Body,[262] and the adoption of the rules of conduct for WTO dispute settlement.[263] Article 2.4 of the DSU stipulates that, where the DSU provides for the DSB to take a decision, such a decision is always taken by consensus.[264] It is important to note, however, that, for some key decisions, such as: (1) the decision on the establishment of panels; (2) the adoption of panel and Appellate Body reports; and (3) the authorisation of suspension of concession and other obligations, the consensus requirement is in fact a 'reverse' or 'negative' consensus requirement.[265] With respect to the DSB's decision to adopt an Appellate Body report, for example, Article 17.14 of the DSU states, in relevant part:

> An Appellate Body report shall be adopted by the DSB ... unless the DSB decides by consensus not to adopt the Appellate Body report within 30 days following its circulation to the Members.

---

260 See above, p. 124.
261 See Article IV:2 of the *WTO Agreement*. Where the DSB administers the dispute settlement provisions of a WTO plurilateral trade agreement, only those WTO Members that are parties to that agreement may participate in the decisions or actions taken by the DSB with respect to that dispute. See Article 2.1 of the DSU.
262 See below, p. 232.   263 See above, p. 122.
264 Footnote 1 to the DSU states: 'The DSB shall be deemed to have decided by consensus on a matter submitted for its consideration, if no Member, present at the meeting of the DSB when the decision is taken, formally objects to the proposed decision.' On decision-making by consensus, see also above, p. 139.
265 See Articles 6.1, 16.4, 17.14 and 22.6 of the DSU. Other decisions of the DSB, such as the appointment of the Members of the Appellate Body, are taken by 'normal' consensus. Note, however, that, with regard to the 'decision' to initiate the information-gathering procedure under Annex V to the *SCM Agreement*, the Appellate Body ruled that paragraph 2 of Annex V imposes 'an obligation on the DSB to initiate an Annex V procedure upon request', and that such DSB action 'occurs automatically when there is a request for initiation of an Annex V procedure and the DSB establishes a panel'. See Appellate Body Report, *US – Large Civil Aircraft (2nd complaint) (2012)*, para. 531. See also below, p. 810.

The 'reverse' consensus requirement means that the DSB is deemed to take a decision unless there is a consensus among WTO Members *not* to take that decision. Since there will usually be at least one Member with a strong interest in the establishment of a panel, the adoption of the panel and/or Appellate Body reports or the authorisation to suspend concessions, it is unlikely that there will be a consensus in the DSB *not* to adopt these decisions.[266] As a result, decision-making by the DSB on these matters is, for all practical purposes, automatic and a matter of course. Furthermore, it should be noted that the DSU provides for strict timeframes within which decisions on these matters must be taken.[267] The DSB meets as often as necessary to carry out its functions within the timeframes provided in the DSU. In practice, the DSB holds one regular meeting per month and, in addition, special meetings when the need for a meeting arises. In 2012, the DSB met eighteen times. By way of example, consider the agenda of the DSB meeting of 28 January 2013, as shown in Figure 3.1.

Meetings of the DSB are always held in Geneva, usually last a few hours and are well attended. With minor deviations regarding Observers (Chapter IV) and the Chair (Chapter V), the Rules of Procedure for the General Council apply to the meetings of the DSB.[268] In 2012, Ambassador Shahid Bashir of Pakistan served as Chair of the DSB. In February 2013, Ambassador Jonathan T. Fried of Canada was elected to serve as DSB Chair in 2013.

As a result of the fact that the DSB takes the core dispute settlement decisions referred to above by reverse consensus, the DSB's impact on, and influence over, consultations and adjudication by panels and the Appellate Body in specific disputes is very limited. The involvement of the DSB is, to a large extent, a legacy of the past in which trade dispute settlement was more diplomatic and political than judicial in nature.[269] Nevertheless, the involvement of the DSB in each major step of a dispute fulfils three useful purposes: (1) it keeps all WTO Members directly informed of WTO dispute settlement; (2) it ensures multilateral surveillance of DSB recommendations and rulings, thereby exerting pressure on the offending party to comply; and (3) it gives WTO Members a designated political forum in which issues arising from the use of the dispute settlement system can be debated.

Questions and Assignments 3.7

What are the functions of the DSB in the WTO dispute settlement system? Is it common for political institutions to play an active role in dispute settlement systems? Does the DSB play a significant role in WTO dispute settlement or is its role more a 'symbolic' one? Explain.

266 Note, however, that, in very exceptional circumstances, it is possible that no Member puts the adoption of the report on the agenda of the DSB and that the report therefore remains unadopted. This happened with the Panel Report, *EC – Bananas III (Article 21.5 – EC)*, circulated on 12 April 1999.
267 For example, the decision to adopt an Appellate Body report shall be taken within thirty days following its circulation to the Members (see Article 17.14 of the DSU). If there is no meeting of the DSB scheduled during this period, such a meeting shall be held for this purpose (see footnote 8 to the DSU).
268 See WT/Air/4068, dated 18 January 2013.
269 See above, p. 159.

1. Surveillance of implementation of recommendations adopted by the DSB
    A. United States – Section 211 Omnibus Appropriations Act of 1998: status report by the United States (WT/DS176/11/add.122)
    B. United States – Anti-Dumping Measures on Certain Hot-Rolled Steel Products from Japan: status report by the United States (WT/DS184/15/add.122)
    C. United States – Section 110(5) of the US Copyright Act: status report by the United States (WT/DS160/24/add.97)
    D. European Communities – Measures Affecting the Approval and Marketing of Biotech Products: status report by the European Union (WT/DS291/37/add.60)
    E. United States – Anti-Dumping Administrative Reviews and other Measures related to Imports of Certain Orange Juice from Brazil: status report by the United States (WT/DS382/10/Add.13)
    F. Thailand – Customs and Fiscal Measures on Cigarettes from the Philippines: status report by Thailand (WT/DS371/15/add.9)
    G. United States – Anti-Dumping Measures on Certain Shrimp from Viet Nam: status report by the United States (WT/DS404/11/Add.8)
    H. Philippines – Taxes on Distilled Spirits: status report by Philippines (WT/DS396/15/add.3 – WT/DS403/15/add.3)
    I. China – Measures related to the Exportation of Various Raw Materials: status report by China (WT/DS394/19/add.1 – WT/DS395/18/add.1 – WT/DS398/17/add.1)
    J. United States – Measures affecting the Production and Sale of Clove Cigarettes: status report by the United States (WT/DS406/11/add.1)

2. United States – Continued Dumping and Subsidy Offset Act of 2000: implementation of the recommendations adopted by the DSB
    A. Statements by the European Union and Japan

3. Argentina – Measures affecting the Importation of Goods
    A. Request for the establishment of a panel by the European union (WT/DS438/11)
    B. Request for the establishment of a panel by the United States (WT/DS444/10)
    C. Request for the establishment of a panel by Japan (WT/DS445/10)

4. United States – Measures affecting the Importation of Animals, Meat and other Animal Products from Argentina
    A. Request for the establishment of a panel by Argentina (WT/DS447/2)

5. United States – Anti-Dumping Measures on Certain Shrimp from Viet Nam
    A. Request for the establishment of a panel by Viet Nam (WT/DS429/2/Rev.1)

6. United States – Measures affecting the Cross Border Supply of Gambling and Betting Services
    A. Recourse to Article 22.7 of the DSB by Antigua and Barbuda (WT/DS285/25)

7. Statement by Brazil regarding requests for preliminary rulings

8. Proposed nominations for the indicative list of governmental and non-governmental panelists (WT/DSB/W/497)

Figure 3.1 Agenda of the DSB meeting of 28 January 2013

5.2 Panels

The actual adjudication of disputes brought to the WTO is carried out, at the first-instance level, by *ad hoc* dispute settlement panels. This section discusses: (1) the establishment of panels; (2) the composition of panels; (3) the mandate of panels; and (4) panel reports.

5.2.1 Establishment of Panels

WTO dispute settlement panels are not standing bodies. They are *ad hoc* bodies established for the purpose of adjudicating a particular dispute and are dissolved once they have accomplished this task. The complainant must request the DSB to establish a panel. Such a 'request for the establishment of a panel', also referred to as a 'panel request', serves two essential purposes: (1) it defines the scope of the dispute and delimits the jurisdiction of the panel;[270] and (2) it serves the due process objective of notifying the respondent and third parties of the nature of the complainant's case.[271] The panel request is thus a document of critical importance in WTO dispute settlement.

Pursuant to Article 6.2 of the DSU, the panel request must be made in writing and must: (1) indicate *whether* consultations were held;[272] (2) identify the *specific* measures at issue; and (3) provide a brief summary of the legal basis of the complaint *sufficient* to present the problem clearly.[273] In light of the critical importance of the panel request, in particular for defining the scope of the dispute and delimiting the jurisdiction of the panel, it is not surprising that in many WTO disputes the question arises whether the panel request meets the second and third requirement of Article 6.2. In *EC and certain member States – Large Civil Aircraft (2011)*, the Appellate Body ruled that:

---

270 Note that, in the exceptional situation in which the parties agree to special terms of reference for the panel, the panel request does not define the scope of the dispute. On the jurisdiction of panels, i.e. their terms of reference, see below, p. 218.

271 See Appellate Body Report, *EC and certain member States – Large Civil Aircraft (2011)*, paras. 639 and 786. See also e.g. Appellate Body Report, *EC – Bananas III (1997)*, para. 142; Appellate Body Report, *US – Carbon Steel (2002)*, para. 126; and Appellate Body Report, *EC – Chicken Cuts (2005)*, para. 155. As the Appellate Body explained in *EC and certain member States – Large Civil Aircraft (2011)*, it is in defining the scope of the dispute and delimiting the jurisdiction of the panel, that the panel request fulfils its due process objective. Note that 'this due process objective is not constitutive of, but rather follows from, the proper establishment of a panel's jurisdiction'. See Appellate Body Report, *EC and certain member States – Large Civil Aircraft (2011)*, para. 640.

272 On the relationship between the request for consultations and the panel request, see below, p. 269. In *Mexico – Corn Syrup (Article 21.5 – US) (2001)*, the Appellate Body held that the purpose of the requirement to indicate whether consultations were held 'seems to be primarily informational'. Failure to indicate in the panel request whether consultations were held, does not invalidate the authority of the panel. What matters is whether consultations were actually held. See Appellate Body Report, *Mexico – Corn Syrup (Article 21.5 – US) (2001)*, para. 70.

273 Article 6.2 of the DSU. Note that Article 6.2 of the DSU also applies to requests for the establishment of a panel under Article 21.5 of the DSU, but it needs to be interpreted in the light thereof, and, as a result, its requirements need to be adapted to compliance proceedings. See Appellate Body Report, *US – FSC (Article 21.5 – EC II) (2006)*, paras. 52–69. See also below, p. 211.

determining whether a panel request is 'sufficiently precise' so as to conform to Article 6.2 requires a panel to scrutinize carefully the panel request, read as a whole, and on the basis of the language used.[274]

It is important to note insufficient precision of the panel request regarding the specific measure at issue and/or the legal basis for the complaint cannot be 'subsequently "cured" by a complaining party's argumentation in its first written submission to the panel or in any other submission or statement made later in the panel proceeding'.[275]

Whether or not the 'specific measure at issue' is sufficiently identified in the panel request, as required by Article 6.2 of the DSU, depends in essence on the ability of the respondent to defend itself given the actual reference to the measure at issue.[276] In *Canada – Wheat Exports and Grain Imports (2004)*, the panel noted that:

the fact that a panel request does not specify by name, date of adoption, etc. the relevant law, regulation or other legal instrument to which a claim relates does not necessarily render the panel request inconsistent with Article 6.2, provided that the panel request contains sufficient information that effectively identifies the precise measures at issue.[277]

In *EC and certain member States – Large Civil Aircraft (2011)*, the Appellate Body ruled with regard to the question whether the complainant, the United States, had sufficiently identified a French research and technology development (R&TD) funding measure in the panel request, that:

[this] may ... depend on the extent to which that measure is specified in the public domain. We do not understand Article 6.2 to impose a standard that renders it more difficult to challenge a measure simply because information in the public domain concerning that measure is of a general character.[278]

Taking into account the public information that existed regarding the French R&TD funding measure at the time of the United States' panel request, the Appellate Body considered that the description of this measure in the panel request was sufficiently precise for this measure to be within the panel's jurisdiction.[279] With regard to a Spanish R&TD funding measure, the Appellate Body came to the opposite conclusion because precise information on this measure was readily available in the public domain at the time of the United States' panel request.[280]

274 Appellate Body Report, *EC and certain member States – Large Civil Aircraft (2011)*, para. 641. See also *ibid.*, para. 787.
275 Appellate Body Report, *EC – Bananas III (1997)*, para. 143. See also Appellate Body Report, *EC and certain member States – Large Civil Aircraft (2011)*, paras. 642 and 787. The Appellate Body considered the principle that defects in the panel request cannot be 'cured' to be paramount in the assessment of the jurisdiction of the panel. See *ibid.*, para. 642.
276 See e.g. Appellate Body Report, *EC – Computer Equipment (1998)*, para. 70. See also e.g. Panel Report, *Argentina – Footwear (EC) (2000)*, para. 8.35 (on subsidiary or implementing measures or later modifications to measures which were not explicitly identified); Appellate Body Report, *EC – Chicken Cuts (2005)*, paras. 163–9 (on the identification of the products to which the measure at issue applied); and Panel Report, *Canada – Aircraft Credits and Guarantees (2002)*, paras. 7.21–7.55 (on an umbrella term used in a request sufficing to indicate more precise matters and general commercial terms used to identify specific measures).
277 Panel Reports, *Canada – Wheat Exports and Grain Imports (2004)*, para. 6.10.
278 Appellate Body Report, *EC and certain member States – Large Civil Aircraft (2011)*, para. 641.
279 See *ibid.*   280 See *ibid.*, para. 646.

Also, in *EC and certain member States – Large Civil Aircraft (2011)*, the Appellate Body considered that while it was uncontested that numerous references in the United States' panel request could be read to refer to individual provisions of Launch Aid/Member State Financing (LA/MSF), the same references could not 'be read simultaneously to refer to a *distinct* measure, consisting of an unwritten LA/MSF Programme'.[281] The Appellate Body thus found that the alleged LA/MSF Programme was not within the panel's jurisdiction 'because it was not identified in the request for the establishment of a panel, as required by Article 6.2 of the DSU'.[282] Note that the European Union did *not* raise before the Appellate Body the issue of whether the alleged LA/MSF Programme was within the jurisdiction of the panel. However, as the Appellate Body ruled in *US – Carbon Steel (2002)*, 'certain issues going to the jurisdiction of a panel are so fundamental that they may be considered at any stage in a proceedings'.[283] In *EC and certain member States – Large Civil Aircraft (2011)*, the Appellate Body deemed it necessary to consider this issue on its own motion.[284]

The question has arisen whether the requirement of Article 6.2 to 'identify the specific measures at issue' also means that the specific *products* at issue must be identified in the panel request. In *EC – Chicken Cuts (2005)*, the Appellate Body held:

Article 6.2 of the DSU does not refer to the identification of the products at issue; rather, it refers to the identification of the specific measures at issue. Article 6.2 contemplates that the identification of the products at issue must flow from the specific measures identified in the panel request. Therefore, the identification of the product at issue is generally not a separate and distinct element of a panel's terms of reference; rather, it is a consequence of the scope of application of the specific measures at issue. In other words, it is the *measure* at issue that generally will define the *product* at issue.[285]

With regard to the requirement that the panel request must 'provide a brief summary of the legal basis of the complaint sufficient to present the problem clearly', the Appellate Body noted that the DSU demands only a *brief* summary of the legal basis of the complaint.[286] The summary must, however, be one 'sufficient to present the problem clearly'.[287] In order for a panel request to 'present the problem clearly', it must 'plainly connect the challenged measure(s) with the provision(s) of the covered agreements claimed to have been infringed'.[288] All the claims, but *not* the arguments,[289] must be specified sufficiently in the panel

---

281 *Ibid.*, para. 790.   282 *Ibid.*, para. 795.
283 Appellate Body Report, *US – Carbon Steel (2002)*, para. 123.
284 Appellate Body Report, *EC and certain member States – Large Civil Aircraft (2011)*, para. 791.
285 Appellate Body Report, *EC – Chicken Cuts (2005)*, para. 165. Note, however, that in some instances the products covered in a panel request can have the effect of potentially qualifying the scope of substantive measures before the panel. See e.g. Panel Report, *Dominican Republic – Import and Sale of Cigarettes (2005)*, paras. 7.94–7.103.
286 See Appellate Body Report, *Korea – Dairy (2000)*, para. 120.   287 *Ibid.*
288 Appellate Body Report, *US – Oil Country Tubular Goods Sunset Review (2005)*, para. 162.
289 The *arguments* are set out and progressively clarified in the written submissions to the panel and at the panel meetings.

request.[290] In *EC – Bananas III (1997)*, the Appellate Body found that, in view of the particular circumstances of that case, the listing of the articles of the agreements alleged to have been breached satisfied the minimum requirement of Article 6.2 of the DSU.[291] In *Korea – Dairy (2000)*, however, the Appellate Body noted that, where the articles listed establish not one single, distinct obligation but, rather, multiple obligations, the listing of articles of an agreement, in and of itself, may fall short of the standard of Article 6.2 of the DSU.[292] The Appellate Body held that the question of whether the mere listing of the articles suffices must be examined on a case-by-case basis.

In *US – Carbon Steel (2002)*, the Appellate Body noted that, in considering the sufficiency of a panel request, a panel must consider the panel request *as a whole*, and may take into account the 'attendant circumstances'.[293] The Appellate Body also stated in this case that 'submissions and statements made during the course of the panel proceedings may be consulted in order to confirm the meaning of the words used in the panel request'.[294] While, as noted above, a panel request cannot be 'cured' by a complaining party's argumentation in subsequent submissions,[295] a panel may look at these submissions when it considers the sufficiency of the panel request.[296] In *EC and certain member States – Large Civil Aircraft (2011)*, the Appellate Body stated:

> Although subsequent events in panel proceedings, including submissions by a party, may be of some assistance in confirming the meaning of the words used in the panel request, those events cannot have the effect of curing the failings of a deficient panel request. In every dispute, the panel's terms of reference must be objectively determined on the basis of the panel request as it existed at the time of filing.[297]

---

290 See Appellate Body Report, *EC – Bananas III (1997)*, para. 143. Note that the Appellate Body ruled in *EC – Tariff Preferences (2004)* that in the particular circumstances of that case 'a complaining party challenging a measure taken pursuant to the Enabling Clause must allege more than mere inconsistency with Article I:1 of the GATT 1994, for to do only that would not convey the "legal basis of the complaint sufficient to present the problem clearly"'. See Appellate Body Report, *EC – Tariff Preferences (2004)*, para. 110. See also below, pp. 209–10. 'See also below, p. 260.'

291 See Appellate Body Report, *EC – Bananas III (1997)*, para. 141.

292 See Appellate Body Report, *Korea – Dairy (2000)*, para. 124. The panel in *Korea – Various Measures on Beef (2001)* held that a mere listing of articles may suffice to cover other provisions or annexures not expressly mentioned in the request, if the nature of the legal determination of the issues covered by the enumerated provisions would be 'inextricably linked' to a consideration of consistencies under such other provisions or annexures. See Panel Report, *Various Measures on Beef (2001)*, paras. 813–15, upheld in Appellate Body Report, *Korea – Various Measures on Beef (2001)*, paras. 76–89. For decisions that found a claim in the panel request not to be 'integrally linked' or 'not related in any self-evident way' with another provision that was argued only in the written submissions, see Panel Report, *US – Line Pipe (2002)*, paras. 7.116–7.126; and Panel Report, *Egypt – Steel Rebar (2002)*, para. 7.31.

293 See Appellate Body Report, *US – Carbon Steel (2002)*, paras. 128–33.

294 Appellate Body Report, *US – Carbon Steel (2002)*, para. 127. See also e.g. Panel Report, *Mexico – Anti-Dumping Measures on Rice (2005)*, para. 7.30, where the panel held that the listing of provisions allegedly violated, taken '*together with the narrative*' that accompanied the list, was sufficient to present the problem clearly to the responding Member.

295 See above, p. 210, referring to Appellate Body Report, *EC – Bananas III (1997)*, para. 143.

296 See Panel Report, *US – FSC (Article 21.5 – EC II) (2006)*, para. 7.83, where the panel found that 'a complainant's first written submission may confirm the meaning of the words used in the panel request'.

297 Appellate Body Report, *EC and certain member States – Large Civil Aircraft (2011)*, para. 642.

In *China – Raw Materials (2012)*, the Appellate Body, reaffirming and usefully summarising its prior case law,[298] concluded that a substantial section of the complainants' panel requests did not satisfy the requirement in Article 6.2 of the DSU to provide 'a brief summary of the legal basis of the complaint sufficient to present the problem clearly'.[299] The claims allegedly identified in that section of the complainants' panel requests were therefore not within the terms of reference of the panel, and the panel erred in making findings regarding those claims. The Appellate Body declared these findings 'moot and of no legal effect'.[300]

A panel request is addressed to the Chair of the DSB. It is subsequently circulated to all WTO Members, and posted on the WTO website, as a WT/DS document. If the complaining party so requests, a meeting of the DSB for the purpose of establishing a panel shall be convened within fifteen days of the request.[301] The panel is established *at the latest* at the second DSB meeting at which the panel request is discussed. At this meeting, the panel is established *unless* the DSB decides by consensus *not* to establish a panel ('reverse consensus'). Since this is unlikely, the establishment of a panel by the DSB is 'quasi-automatic'. A panel can be, and occasionally is, established at the first DSB meeting at which the panel request is considered. At this meeting, the establishment of the panel requires a 'normal consensus' decision of the DSB. The panel can thus only be established at the first DSB meeting if the respondent does not object to its establishment. Often, however, the respondent objects to the panel's establishment at the first DSB meeting, arguing that it 'hopes' and 'believes' that a mutually agreed solution to the dispute can still be found.

The decision of the DSB on the establishment of a panel is usually preceded by short statements by the parties to the dispute setting forth their respective positions. Decisions to establish a panel very seldom give rise to much debate within the DSB. A practice has evolved whereby, immediately after the DSB's decision to establish the panel, other Members may, at the DSB meeting itself, notify their interest in the dispute and reserve their third party rights; or, alternatively, they may do so in writing within ten days as of the DSB meeting.[302]

---

298 See Appellate Body Reports, *China – Raw Materials (2012)*, para. 219–20.
299 See *ibid.*, para. 234.
300 See *ibid.*, para. 235.
301 Note, however, that, as for all WTO meetings, Members must be given at least ten days' advance notice of the meeting. See footnote 5 to Article 6.1 of the DSU.
302 See above p. 177, and below, p. 280. In *EC – Export Subsidies on Sugar (2005)*, Kenya (twenty-eight days) and Côte d'Ivoire (sixty-eight days) made a request to participate as third parties long after the establishment of the panel (but before the panel was composed). While the parties objected to the participation of these two Members, the panel allowed them to take part in the panel proceedings as third parties. See Panel Report, *EC – Export Subsidies on Sugar (2005)*, para. 2.4. Also in cases where the third party request was made *after* the composition of the panel, panels have accepted this request. See e.g. Panel Report, *Turkey – Rice (2007)*, para. 6.9. In the latter case, the third party request was made 151 days after the establishment of the panel.

Where more than one Member requests the establishment of a panel related to the same matter, Article 9.1 of the DSU states that:

a single panel may be established to examine these complaints taking into account the rights of all Members concerned. A single panel *should* be established to examine such complaints *whenever feasible.*

In *US – Steel Safeguards (2003)*, the DSB at first established multiple panels to hear and decide similar complaints by the European Communities, Japan, Korea, China, Switzerland, Norway, New Zealand and Brazil. Subsequently, the United States and the complainants reached an agreement on the establishment of a single panel, under Article 9.1, to hear the matter at issue.

In cases in which it is not possible to establish a single panel to examine complaints relating to the same matter, Article 9.3 of the DSU requires that – to the extent possible – the same persons shall serve as panellists on each of the separate panels and that the timetable for the panel process in such disputes shall be harmonised. This was done, for example, in *EC – Hormones (1998)* and *US – 1916 Act (2000)*.[303]

The DSU does not deal with the situation in which a Member files a second panel request on the same matter. A Member may do this in order to clarify and/or extend the scope of its first panel request. This happened, for example, in *Canada – Wheat Exports and Grain Imports (2004)* and in *US – Large Civil Aircraft (2nd complaint) (2012)*. In both cases, the complainant, the United States and the European Communities, respectively, filed a second panel request. In *Canada – Wheat Exports and Grain Imports (2004)*, it was decided that the panellists that composed the panel established pursuant to the first panel request would also compose the panel established pursuant to the second panel request, and that the proceedings of both panels would be harmonised pursuant to Article 9.3 of the DSU.[304] In *US – Large Civil Aircraft (2nd complaint) (2012)*, a second panel was established pursuant to the second panel request. Subsequently, the first panel, which had a different composition, from the second panel, became inactive.[305]

5.2.2   Composition of Panels

As set forth in Article 8.5 of the DSU, panels are normally composed of three persons. The parties to the dispute can agree, within ten days from the establishment of the panel, to a panel composed of five panellists. However, to date, this has never occurred in WTO dispute settlement. Pursuant to Article 8.1 of the DSU, panels must be composed of well-qualified governmental and/or

---

303   See Panel Report, *EC – Hormones (US) (1998)* and Panel Report, *EC – Hormones (Canada) (1998)*; and Panel Report, *US – 1916 Act (EC) (2000)* and Panel Report, *US – 1916 Act (Japan) (2000)*.

304   See Panel Reports, *Canada – Wheat Exports and Grain Imports (2004)*, paras. 1.11–1.12.

305   At the request of the parties, the panel established pursuant to the first panel request agreed 'to set aside the original timetable for the dispute until an unspecified date in the future'. See Communication from the Chairman of the Panel, *US – Large Civil Aircraft*, WT/DS317/6, dated 18 April 2006.

non-governmental individuals. By way of guidance, the DSU indicates that these individuals can be:

persons who have served on or presented a case to a panel, served as a representative of a Member or of a contracting party to GATT 1947 or as a representative to the Council or Committee of any covered agreement or its predecessor agreement, or in the Secretariat, taught or published on international trade law or policy, or served as a senior trade policy official of a Member.[306]

Article 8.2 of the DSU stipulates that panellists should be selected with a view to ensuring their independence, providing a sufficiently diverse background and a wide spectrum of experience. Nationals of Members that are parties or third parties to the dispute shall not serve on a panel concerned with that dispute unless the parties to the dispute agree otherwise.[307] While this is not common, parties have in some cases agreed on a panellist who is a national of one of the parties.[308] When a dispute occurs between a developing-country Member and a developed-country Member, the panel shall, if the developing-country Member so requests, include at least one panellist from a developing-country Member.[309] In many panels dealing with disputes involving a developing-country Member, at least one of the panellists is indeed a national of a developing-country Member.[310]

To date, panellists have been predominantly current or retired government trade officials with a background in law. Many among them are Geneva-based diplomats of WTO Members. A considerable number of academics and private trade law practitioners have also served as panellists. The DSU explicitly provides, however, that panellists shall serve in their individual capacities and not as government representatives. Members shall therefore not give panellists any instructions nor seek to influence them with regard to matters before a panel.[311] It is also significant that at least half of the panellists have already served on a GATT or WTO panel before. In other words, many panellists serve more than once as panellist.[312]

Once a panel is established by the DSB, the parties to the dispute will try to reach an agreement on the composition of the panel. The WTO Secretariat shall propose nominations for the panel to the parties to the dispute. The DSU requires the parties to the dispute not to oppose the Secretariat's nominations except for compelling reasons.[313] However, in practice, parties often reject these nominations

---

306 Article 8.1 of the DSU.   307 See Article 8.3 of the DSU.
308 For an example of a dispute in which the parties agreed on the appointment of nationals, see *US – Zeroing (EC) (2006)*, a dispute between the European Communities and the United States. The panel in this dispute included William Davey from the United States and Hans-Friedrich Beseler from Germany.
309 See Article 8.10 of the DSU.
310 Note, for example, that the panel in *China – Rare Earths* is composed of three nationals of developing-country Members.
311 See Article 8.9 of the DSU.
312 For a list of all persons who served as panellists to date and the panels on which they served, see www.worldtradelaw.net/dsc/database/panelistcases.asp.
313 See Article 8.6 of the DSU.

initially proposed by the WTO Secretariat without much justification, except that they consider that a proposed panellist may hold views that are not in line with the argument(s) they wish to advance. In practice, the composition of the panel is often a difficult and contentious process, which may take many weeks. If the parties are unable to agree on the composition of the panel within twenty days of its establishment by the DSB, either party *may* request the Director-General of the WTO to determine the composition of the panel.[314] Within ten days of such a request, the Director-General shall – after consulting the parties to the dispute and the Chair of the DSB and of the relevant WTO council or committee – appoint the panellists whom he considers most appropriate. In recent years, the Director-General has determined the composition of most panels.[315]

To assist in the selection of panellists, the WTO Secretariat maintains a list of governmental and non-governmental individuals possessing the required qualifications to serve as panellists.[316] Members periodically suggest names of individuals for inclusion on this list, and those names are added to the list upon approval by the DSB. However, this list is merely *indicative* and individuals not included in this list may be selected as panellists. In fact, most first-time panellists were not on the list at the time of their selection.[317]

When hearing and deciding a WTO dispute, panellists are subject to the *Rules of Conduct for the Understanding on Rules and Procedures Governing the Settlement of Disputes* (the '*Rules of Conduct*').[318] To preserve the integrity and impartiality of the WTO dispute settlement system, the *Rules of Conduct* require that panellists:

shall be independent and impartial, shall avoid direct or indirect conflicts of interest and shall respect the confidentiality of proceedings.[319]

To ensure compliance with the *Rules of Conduct*, panellists must disclose:

the existence or development of any interest, relationship or matter that the person could reasonably be expected to know and that is likely to affect, or give rise to justifiable doubts as to, that person's independence or impartiality.[320]

---

314 See Article 8.7 of the DSU. Often, however, parties will allow more time to reach an agreement on the composition of a panel instead of requesting the Director-General to decide on the composition. If neither party pushes for the composition of the panel, the panel may remain 'in limbo' indefinitely.

315 In 2010, 2011 and 2012, respectively 78, 60 and 83 per cent of the panels were composed by the Director-General. Overall, i.e. since 1995, the Director-General composed 61 per cent of the panels. In three cases, a party or third party challenged before the panel the decision of the Director-General on the composition of the panel. See *Guatemala – Cement II (2000)*; *US – Upland Cotton (Article 21.5 – Brazil) (2008)*; and *US – Zeroing (EC) (Article 21.5 – EC) (2009)*. Panels always found that they had no authority to rule on the propriety of its own composition. See e.g. Panel Report, *US – Zeroing (EC) (Article 21.5 – EC) (2009)*, para. 8.17, as upheld by Appellate Body Report, *US – Zeroing (EC) (Article 21.5 – EC) (2009)*, para. 172.

316 See Article 8.4 of the DSU. For the most recent consolidated list, see WT/DSB/44/Rev.21, dated 7 January 2013.

317 This is also due to the fact that the vast majority of individuals on the indicative list are nationals of Members that are frequently involved in dispute settlement proceedings as parties or third parties.

318 WT/DSB/RC/1, dated 11 December 1996. As discussed below, these *Rules of Conduct* also apply to Appellate Body Members (see below, p. 233), arbitrators (see below, p. 244) and the support staff (see below, pp. 217 and 244).

319 Para. II(1) of the *Rules of Conduct*.

320 Para. III(1) of the *Rules of Conduct*. This information shall be disclosed to the Chair of the DSB for consideration by the parties to the dispute. See para. VI(4)(a) of the *Rules of Conduct*. Panellists are subject to this disclosure obligation prior to as well as after the confirmation of their appointment as panellist. See paras. VI(4)(a) and (5).

This disclosure obligation includes information on financial, professional and other active interests as well as considered statements of personal opinion on issues relevant to the dispute and employment or family interests.[321] Parties can request the disqualification of a panellist on the ground of *material* violation of the obligations of independence, impartiality, confidentiality or the avoidance of direct or indirect conflicts of interest.[322] The evidence of such material violation is provided to the Chair of the DSB, who will, in consultation with the Director-General of the WTO and the chairs of the relevant WTO bodies, decide whether a material violation has occurred. If it has, the panellist is replaced. To date, no panellist has ever been found to have committed a material violation of the *Rules of Conduct*. However, very exceptionally, a panellist has resigned from the panel, at his or her own initiative, after a party raised concerns about a possible conflict of interest.[323]

Panels are assisted by the WTO Secretariat. Pursuant to Article 27.1 of the DSU, the WTO Secretariat has the responsibility of assisting panels, especially on the legal, historical and procedural aspects of the matters dealt with, and of providing secretarial and technical support. The Legal Affairs Division and the Rules Division are the main divisions of the WTO Secretariat that assist dispute settlement panels. Generally speaking, panels considering cases related to anti-dumping, countervailing and safeguard measures and State trading are assisted by staff from the Rules Division. Panels considering other cases are assisted by an interdisciplinary team (i.e. economists and lawyers) drawn from the Legal Affairs Division and other divisions of the WTO Secretariat. For example, for a dispute concerning an SPS measure, a team composed of staff from the Agriculture and Commodities Division and staff from the Legal Affairs Division will assist the panel. Officials of the WTO Secretariat assigned to assist panels are also subject to the *Rules of Conduct* and bound by the obligations of independence, impartiality, confidentiality and the avoidance of direct or indirect conflicts of interest.[324]

Questions and Assignments 3.8

What are the requirements that a panel request must meet? Why is it important that a panel request is sufficiently precise? How does one determine whether a panel request is sufficiently precise? Who establishes a panel? How are panels established? What happens in case more than one Member requests the establishment of a panel related to the same matter? Who decides on the composition of panels? Describe the relevant procedure. What are the required qualifications for a panellist? Is it, in your opinion, inappropriate for a national

---

321 See Annex 2 to the *Rules of Conduct*.   322 See para. VIII of the *Rules of Conduct*.

323 For example, in *Turkey – Textiles (1999)*, Robert Hudec resigned from the panel within three weeks of its composition. See Panel Report, *Turkey – Textiles (1999)*, para. 1.6, and WT/DS34/4, dated 23 July 1998. The panel report itself does not give any indication as to the reason for Hudec's resignation, but reportedly one of the parties raised a concern regarding an unpublished conference paper by Hudec, which was of relevance to the dispute but the existence of which had not been disclosed to the parties.

324 See above, pp. 216–7.

of a party or third party to the dispute to sit on the panel? What are the key obligations for panellists under the *Rules of Conduct*? By whom and on what grounds can panellists be disqualified? What is the role of the WTO Secretariat in panel proceedings? In your opinion, can this role be problematic? If so, how?

5.2.3   Mandate of Panels

As stated above, at the first-instance level, the adjudication of disputes is carried out by panels. This sub-section deals with the various aspects of the mandate of panels, i.e. the scope and nature of the task(s) entrusted to panels. This sub-section will discuss in turn: (1) the terms of reference of a panel; (2) the standard of review to be applied by panels; (3) the exercise of judicial economy; (4) acts *ultra petita*; and (5) the use of experts by panels.

First, with regard to the *terms of reference of a panel*, Article 7.1 of the DSU states that, unless the parties agree otherwise within twenty days from the establishment of the panel, a panel is given the following *standard* terms of reference:

> To examine in the light of the relevant provisions in (name of the covered agreement(s) cited by the parties to the dispute), the *matter referred to the DSB* by (name of party) *in document* ... and make such findings as will assist the DSB in making the recommendations or in giving the rulings provided for in that/those agreement(s).[325]

The 'matter referred to the DSB' consists of two elements: (1) the specific measure(s) at issue; and (2) the legal basis of the complaint, i.e. the claims of WTO-inconsistency.[326] The 'document' referred to in these standard terms of reference is the panel request. Hence, a claim falls within the panel's terms of reference, i.e. within the jurisdiction of the panel, only if that claim is identified in the panel request.[327] In *EC – Tube or Pipe Fittings (2003)*, the panel found that Brazil's claims under Articles 6.9, 6.13, 9.3 and 12.1 of the *Anti-Dumping Agreement* were not within its terms of reference as these provisions 'do not appear in the list of provisions' in the panel request, 'nor are they referred to in the ensuing description of allegations in that document'. Likewise, as discussed above in relation to *EC and certain member States – Large Civil Aircraft (2011)* and *China – Raw Materials (2012)*, specific measures or claims are only within the terms of reference, i.e. within the jurisdiction, of the panel, when these measures or claims are sufficiently identified in the panel request.[328] A panel may consider only the specific measures and the claims relating to these measures that it has authority to consider under its terms of reference.[329] A panel is *bound* by its terms of reference.[330]

---

325 Emphasis added.
326 See Appellate Body Report, *Guatemala – Cement I (1998)*, paras. 72 and 76.
327 Note that, in case of a broadly phrased panel request, it may be necessary to examine the complainant's submissions closely to determine precisely which claims have been made and fall under the panel's terms of reference. See Appellate Body Report, *Chile – Price Band System (2002)*, para. 165. However, as discussed above, later submissions and statements cannot cure any defects in the panel request. See above, pp. 209–10, 212.
328 See above, p. 211.
329 See Appellate Body Report, *India – Patents (US) (1998)*, para. 92. A panel cannot assume jurisdiction that it does not have. See *ibid*.
330 See *ibid.*, para. 93.

Within twenty days of the establishment of the panel, the parties to the dispute *can* agree on *special* terms of reference for the panel, i.e. terms of reference that are not determined by the complainant's panel request.[331] However, it very rarely occurs that parties agree on *special* terms of reference.[332] If no agreement on *special* terms of reference is reached within twenty days of the establishment of the panel, the panel shall have *standard* terms of reference, determined – as explained above – by the complainant's panel request.

Two further questions deserve to be mentioned with respect to a panel's terms of reference, i.e. its jurisdiction, namely: (1) which measures *can* be within panel's terms of reference; and (2) whether a panel *can* decline to exercise jurisdiction which it has according to its terms of reference. With regard to the first question, please refer to the comprehensive discussion above regarding the measures, which can be subject to WTO dispute settlement.[333] It suffices to note here that, as the Appellate Body ruled in *EC – Chicken Cuts (2005)*, measures included in a panel's terms of reference must be measures that are *in existence* at the time of the establishment of the panel.[334] With regard to the second question, note that the Appellate Body held in *Mexico – Taxes on Soft Drinks (2006)*:

A decision by a panel to decline to exercise validly established jurisdiction would seem to 'diminish' the right of a complaining Member to 'seek the redress of a violation of obligations' within the meaning of Article 23 of the DSU, and to bring a dispute pursuant to Article 3.3 of the DSU. This would not be consistent with a panel's obligations under Articles 3.2 and 19.2 of the DSU. We see no reason, therefore, to disagree with the Panel's statement that a WTO panel 'would seem … not to be in a position to choose freely whether or not to exercise its jurisdiction'.[335]

Secondly, with regard to the *standard of review* to be applied by panels in assessing the WTO consistency of the measure at issue in a dispute, Article 11 of the DSU stipulates:

The function of panels is to assist the DSB in discharging its responsibilities under this Understanding and the covered agreements. Accordingly, a panel should make an objective assessment of the matter before it, including an objective assessment of the facts of the case and the applicability of and conformity with the relevant covered agreements, and make

---

331 See Article 7.1 of the DSU.
332 See e.g. Panel Report, *Brazil – Desiccated Coconut (1997)*, para. 9. Note that this is the only example mentioned in the *WTO Analytical Index (2012)*, Volume II, 1622–3.
333 See above, p. 163.
334 See Appellate Body Report, *EC – Chicken Cuts (2005)*, para. 156. For a particular 'exception' to this rule, see Appellate Body Report, *Chile – Price Band System (2002)*, para. 144.
335 Appellate Body Report, *Mexico – Taxes on Soft Drinks (2006)*, para. 53. Note, however, that the Appellate Body in para. 54 of its Report was careful to stress that it was not expressing any views on whether there may be other circumstances in which legal impediments could exist that would preclude a panel from ruling on the merits of the claims before it. In view of the scope of Mexico's appeal, it was not necessary for the Appellate Body to express a view on this issue. For a further discussion, see Chapter 10 of this book, on regional trade agreements, at p. 648.

such other findings as will assist the DSB in making the recommendations or in giving the rulings provided for in the covered agreements.[336]

In *EC – Hormones (1998)*, the Appellate Body noted that Article 11 of the DSU:

articulates with great succinctness but with sufficient clarity the appropriate standard of review for panels in respect of both the ascertainment of facts and the legal characterization of such facts under the relevant agreements.[337]

With regard to the ascertainment of facts, i.e. *fact-finding*, panels have 'to make an objective assessment of the facts'. With regard to the legal characterization of such facts under the relevant agreement, i.e. the *assessment of WTO consistency*, Article 11 imposes the same standard on panels, namely, 'to make an objective assessment' of the applicability of and conformity with the relevant covered agreement.[338]

In many appeals, the Appellate Body has been called upon to assess whether the panel had correctly discharged its duty under Article 11 of the DSU 'to make an objective assessment of the matter before it'. In *Brazil – Retreaded Tyres (2007)*, the Appellate Body ruled that a panel must consider all the evidence presented to it, assess its credibility and determine its weight.[339] However, the requirements of Article 11 of the DSU go beyond this. The abundant case law on these requirements was conveniently summarised by the Appellate Body in *EC – Fasteners (China) (2011)*. In that case, the Appellate Body held that, pursuant to Article 11 of the DSU, a panel, as a trier of facts: (1) must base its findings on a sufficient evidentiary basis on the record;[340] (2) may not apply a double standard of proof;[341] (3) must treat evidence in an 'even-handed' manner;[342] (4) must consider evidence before it in its totality (which includes consideration of submitted evidence in relation to other evidence);[343] and (5) should not disregard evidence that is relevant to the case of one of the parties.[344] The Appellate Body also recalled in *EC – Fasteners (China) (2011)* that a panel is 'entitled, in the exercise of its discretion, to determine that certain elements of evidence should be accorded more weight than other elements'.[345] A panel is not required

---

336   Note that Article 11 of the DSU states that 'a panel *should* make an objective assessment of the matter'. Emphasis added. In *Canada – Aircraft (1999)*, the Appellate Body noted in this respect, be it in a different context, that, 'although the word "should" is often used colloquially to imply an exhortation, or to state a preference, it is not always used in those ways. It can also be used "to express a duty [or] obligation".' It is in this way that the word 'should' is used in Article 11 of the DSU. See Appellate Body Report, *Canada – Aircraft (1999)*, para. 187.

337   Appellate Body Report, *EC – Hormones (1998)*, para. 116. See also Panel Report, *US – Underwear (1997)*, paras. 7.10, 7.12 and 7.13; and Panel Report, *US – Wool Shirts and Blouses (1997)*, paras. 7.16 and 7.17.

338   See Appellate Body Report, *Chile – Price Band System (2002)*, para. 172; and Appellate Body Report, *Dominican Republic – Import and Sale of Cigarettes (2005)*, para. 105.

339   See Appellate Body Report, EC – Fasteners (China) (2011), para 441, referring to *Brazil – Retreaded Tyres (2007)*, para. 185.

340   See *ibid.*, referring to *US – Continued Zeroing (2009)*, para. 338.

341   See *ibid.*, referring to *Korea – Dairy (2000)*, para. 137.

342   See *ibid.*, referring to *US – Upland Cotton (Article 21.5 – Brazil) (2008)*, para. 292.

343   See *ibid.*, referring to *US – Continued Zeroing (2009)*, para. 331.

344   See *ibid.*, referring to *US/Canada – Continued Suspension (2008)*, paras. 553 and 615.

345   See *ibid.*, referring to *EC – Asbestos (2001)*, para. 161.

to accord to the evidence the weight that one of the parties believes should be accorded to it.[346] Also, a panel 'is not required to discuss, in its report, each and every piece of evidence'.[347] Finally, note that the Appellate Body ruled in *US – Continued Zeroing (2009)* that:

> Article 11 requires a panel to test evidence with the parties, and to seek further information if necessary, in order to determine whether the evidence satisfies a party's burden of proof.[348]

The panel in *US – Stainless Steel (Mexico) (2008)* expressed, in the context of the divisive debate on the role of precedent in WTO dispute settlement, the view that the concern over the preservation of a consistent line of case law should not override a panel's task of carrying out an objective examination of the matter before it, as required under Article 11 of the DSU. The panel noted that, in two previous cases, the Appellate Body had reversed decisions of panels that found a particular practice of zeroing to be WTO-consistent and that its own reasoning was very similar to that of those two panels. Nonetheless, referring to the obligation under Article 11 of the DSU to carry out an objective examination of the matter, that panel 'felt compelled to depart' from the Appellate Body's approach.[349] The Appellate Body reversed the panel's finding. It noted that it is 'well settled that Appellate Body reports are not binding, except with respect to resolving the particular dispute between the parties'.[350] However, this 'does not mean that subsequent panels are free to disregard the legal interpretations and the *ratio decidendi* contained in previous Appellate Body reports that have been adopted by the DSB'.[351] It found that the general provisions of Article 3 of the DSU, and in particular paragraph 2 thereof, inform the obligation under Article 11 of the DSU for panels to carry out an objective examination of the matter.[352] Paragraph 2 of Article 3 provides that '[t]he dispute settlement system of the WTO is a central element in providing security and predictability to the multilateral trading system'.[353] The Appellate Body clarified that, in the hierarchical structure of the dispute settlement system, panels and the Appellate Body have distinct roles to play, and stated that ensuring 'security and predictability' in the dispute settlement system, as contemplated in Article 3.2 of the DSU, implies that, absent cogent reasons, an adjudicatory body will resolve the same legal

---

346 See Appellate Body Report, *Korea – Alcoholic Beverages (1999)*, para. 164.
347 Appellate Body Report, *Brazil – Retreaded Tyres (2007)*, para. 202.
348 Appellate Body Report, *US – Continued Zeroing (2009)*, para. 347.
349 See Panel Report, *US – Stainless Steel (Mexico) (2008)*, paras. 7.105–7.106. On the debate on the role of precedent in WTO dispute settlement, see above, pp. 51–2.
350 See Appellate Body Report, *Japan – Alcoholic Beverages II (1996)*, 106–8. See also Appellate Body Report, *US – Softwood Lumber V (2004)*, paras. 109–12; and Appellate Body Report, *US – Shrimp (Article 21.5 – Malaysia) (2001)*, para. 109. While Appellate Body reports adopted by the DSB shall be accepted unconditionally by the parties to the dispute, it is the exclusive authority of the Ministerial Conference and the General Council to adopt, pursuant to Article IX:2 of the *WTO Agreement*, interpretations that are binding upon the WTO membership.
351 Appellate Body Report, *US – Stainless Steel (Mexico) (2008)*, para. 158.
352 See *ibid.*, para. 157.   353 See above, p. 53.

question in the same way in a subsequent case. The Appellate Body concluded that the panel's failure to follow previously adopted Appellate Body reports addressing the same issues undermines the development of a coherent and predictable body of jurisprudence clarifying Members' rights and obligations under the covered agreements.[354] It added that dispute settlement practice demonstrates that 'WTO Members attach significance to reasoning provided in previous panel and Appellate Body reports. Adopted panel and Appellate Body reports are often cited by parties in support of legal arguments in dispute settlement proceedings, and are relied upon by panels and the Appellate Body in subsequent disputes.'[355] As the Appellate Body stated in *US – Stainless Steel (Mexico)*:

[T]he legal interpretation embodied in adopted panel and Appellate Body reports becomes part and parcel of the *acquis* of the WTO dispute settlement system.[356]

In other words, whereas the *application* of a provision may be regarded as confined to the context of the case in which it takes place, the relevance of *clarification* contained in adopted Appellate Body reports is not limited to the application of a particular provision in a specific case.[357]

With regard to the standard of review for panels, two more observations should be made, both relating to cases in which panels are not, but national authorities are, the first trier of facts. First, as the Appellate Body found in *US – Lamb (2001)*, the appropriate standard is neither a '*de novo* review' of the facts nor 'total deference' to the parties. However, some degree of deference is due to the factual determinations by national authorities.[358] Secondly, Article 11 of the DSU sets forth the appropriate standard of review for panels for disputes under all but one of the covered agreements. Only for disputes under the *Anti-Dumping Agreement* is there a 'special' standard of review, which is set out in Article 17.6 of the *Anti-Dumping Agreement* and discussed in Chapter 11 of this book.[359]

While uncommon, it has happened in a few disputes that the respondent did not make any argument to contest the complainant's claims of inconsistency. It is important to note that in such cases the panel must also make an objective assessment of the matter as required by Article 11 of the DSU, and it must assess whether the complainant made a *prima facie* case.[360]

Thirdly, with regard to the exercise of *judicial economy*, note that complainants often assert with regard to one and the same measure numerous violations under various agreements. It is well-established case law that panels are not required to examine each and every one of the legal claims that a complainant makes. In *US – Wool Shirts and Blouses (1997)*, the Appellate Body had already ruled that panels:

354 See Appellate Body Report, *US – Stainless Steel (Mexico) (2008)*, para. 161.
355 *Ibid.*, para. 160.   356 *Ibid.*   357 See *ibid.*, para. 161.
358 See Appellate Body Report, *US – Lamb (2001)*, paras. 106–7.
359 See below, p. 734.
360 See e.g. Panel Report, *US – Shrimp (Ecuador) (2007)*, paras. 7.1–7.11; and Panel Report, *China – Publications and Audiovisual Products (2010)*, para. 7.942.

need only address those claims which must be addressed in order to resolve the matter in issue in the dispute.[361]

A panel has discretion to determine the claims it must address in order to resolve the dispute between the parties effectively.[362] The Appellate Body has, however, cautioned panels to be careful when exercising judicial economy. To provide only a partial resolution of a dispute may be false judicial economy since the issues that are not resolved may well give rise to a new dispute.[363] As the Appellate Body stated in *Australia – Salmon (1998)*, a panel has to address:

> those claims on which a finding is necessary in order to enable the DSB to make sufficiently precise recommendations and rulings so as to allow for prompt compliance by a Member with those recommendations and rulings 'in order to ensure effective resolution of disputes to the benefit of all Members'.[364]

For an example of manifestly false judicial economy, refer to *US – Export Subsidies on Sugar (2005)*, in which the panel, after finding that the export subsidies at issue were inconsistent with the *Agreement on Agriculture* exercised judicial economy with regard to the claim of inconsistency with the *SCM Agreement*. The Appellate Body held that this was false judicial economy constituting a breach of Article 11 of the DSU because the remedies under the *SCM Agreement* would be different and more specific than those under the *Agreement on Agriculture*.[365]

In *Argentina – Preserved Peaches (2003)*, Chile insisted that the panel rule on all the claims presented 'in order to ensure that Argentina does not continue to violate these agreements as it has done'. The panel observed, however, that Chile did not offer any explanation as to why ruling on *all* claims would achieve this objective. Having concluded that the measure at issue was inconsistent with various WTO provisions and that further findings on the other Chilean claims would not alter that conclusion and would not further assist the DSB in making sufficiently precise recommendations (to allow for prompt compliance by Argentina), the panel chose to exercise judicial economy on these other claims.[366] Panels frequently exercise judicial economy with regard to claims before them. However, in some instances, panels may decide to continue their legal analysis and

---

361 Appellate Body Report, *US – Wool Shirts and Blouses (1997)*, 340.
362 See Appellate Body Report, *India – Patents (US) (1998)*, para. 87. A panel is never required to exercise judicial economy (see Appellate Body Report, *US – Lead and Bismuth II (2000)*, para. 71; and Appellate Body Report, *US – Gambling (2005)*, paras. 343–4), but, when it does exercise judicial economy, it should state so explicitly for the purposes of transparency and fairness to the parties (see Appellate Body Report, *Canada – Autos (2000)*, para. 117).
363 The Appellate Body found that the panels had erred in exercising judicial economy in e.g. Appellate Body Report, *Australia – Salmon (1998)*; and Appellate Body Report, *Japan – Agricultural Products II (1999)*.
364 Appellate Body Report, *Australia – Salmon (1998)*, para. 223. See also Appellate Body Report, *Japan – Agricultural Products II (1999)*, para. 111; Appellate Body Report, *US – Wheat Gluten (2001)*, para. 183; and Appellate Body Report, *US – Lamb (2001)*, para. 194.
365 See Appellate Body Report, *US – Export Subsidies on Sugar (2005)*, paras. 334–5.
366 See Panel Report, *Argentina – Preserved Peaches (2003)*, paras. 7.141–7.142. For similar conclusions, see e.g. Panel Report, *EC – Sardines (2002)*, paras. 7.147–7.152; Appellate Body Report, *US – Anti-Dumping Measures on Oil Country Tubular Goods (2005)*, para. 178; Appellate Body Report, *US – Zeroing (EC) (2006)*, para. 250; and Panel Report, *Mexico – Steel Pipes and Tubes (2007)*, para. 7.400.

to make factual findings beyond those that are strictly necessary to resolve the dispute because this 'may assist the Appellate Body should it later be called upon to complete the analysis'.[367]

Since panels may exercise judicial economy with regard to *claims*, it is not surprising that they may also exercise judicial economy with regard to *arguments* made by a party with regard to a claim. As long as it is clear in a panel report that a panel has reasonably considered a claim, the fact that a particular *argument* relating to that claim is not addressed is not inconsistent with Article 11 of the DSU.[368] In *Dominican Republic – Import and Sale of Cigarettes (2005)*, the Appellate Body ruled that:

> there is no obligation upon a panel to consider each and every argument put forward by the parties in support of their respective cases, so long as it completes an objective assessment of the matter before it, in accordance with Article 11 of the DSU.[369]

In *EC – Fasteners (China) (2011)*, the Appellate Body rejected China's contention that the panel erred by not addressing one of its main arguments concerning a claim. The Appellate Body found that:

> a panel has the discretion 'to address only those arguments it deems necessary to resolve a particular claim' and 'the fact that a particular argument relating to that claim is not specifically addressed in the "Findings" section of a panel report will not, in and of itself, lead to the conclusion that that panel has failed to make the "objective assessment of the matter before it" required by Article 11 of the DSU'.[370]

Fourthly, with regard to acting *ultra petita*, i.e. making a finding on a claim that does not fall within its terms of reference, the Appellate Body found in *Chile – Price Band System (2002)* that a panel acting *ultra petita* does not make an objective assessment of *the matter before it*, and thus acts inconsistently with Article 11 of the DSU.[371] However, if the panel's finding relates to a *claim* which does fall within its terms of reference, it is not restricted to considering only those *legal arguments* made by the parties to the dispute. The Appellate Body ruled in *EC – Hormones (1998)* that:

> nothing in the DSU limits the faculty of a panel freely to use arguments submitted by any of the parties – or to develop its own legal reasoning – to support its own findings and conclusions on the matter under its consideration.[372]

---

367 Appellate Body Report, *US – Gambling (2005)*, para. 344. On the 'completing of the legal analysis' by the Appellate Body, see below, pp. 242–3.

368 See Appellate Body Report, *EC – Poultry (1998)*, para. 135.

369 Appellate Body Report, *Dominican Republic – Import and Sale of Cigarettes (2005)*, para. 125. The Appellate Body referred in a footnote to Appellate Body Report, *EC – Poultry (1998)*, para. 135. On this matter, see also Appellate Body Report, *US – Anti-Dumping Measures on Oil Country Tubular Goods (2005)*, paras. 131–6.

370 Appellate Body Report, *EC – Fasteners (China) (2011)*, para. 511.

371 See Appellate Body Report, *Chile – Price Band System (2002)*, para. 173. In *Chile – Price Band System (2002)*, the panel made findings regarding Article II:1(b), second sentence of the GATT 1994, while Argentina, the complainant, had not made any claim of inconsistency with that provision.

372 Appellate Body Report, *EC – Hormones (1998)*, para. 156. See also Panel Report, *Australia – Automotive Leather II (Article 21.5 – US) (2000)*, para. 6.19.

A panel, which uses legal arguments or reasoning that have not been submitted or developed by any of the parties to the dispute, does not act *ultra petita*. Panels are restricted to the claims falling within their terms of reference but they are not restricted to the legal arguments and reasoning submitted or developed by the parties.[373]

Fifthly, with regard to the use by panels of experts, note that disputes brought to panels for adjudication often involve complex factual, technical and scientific issues. These issues frequently play a central role in WTO dispute settlement proceedings. Article 13 of the DSU gives a panel the authority to seek information and technical advice from any individual or body, which it deems appropriate.[374] Panels may consult experts to obtain their opinion on certain aspects of the matter under consideration. As the Appellate Body ruled in *Argentina – Textiles and Apparel (1998)*, '[t]his is a grant of discretionary authority'.[375] In *US – Shrimp (1998)*, the Appellate Body further stated:

[A] panel ... has the authority to *accept or reject* any information or advice which it may have sought and received, or to *make some other appropriate disposition* thereof. It is particularly within the province and the authority of a panel to determine the *need for information and advice* in a specific case, to ascertain the *acceptability* and *relevancy* of information or advice received, and to decide *what weight to ascribe to that information or advice* or to conclude that no weight at all should be given to what has been received.[376]

This authority is 'indispensably necessary' to enable a panel to discharge its duty under Article 11 of the DSU to 'make an objective assessment of the matter before it'.[377] Note that, while the authority under Article 13 to seek information is 'discretionary', failure by the panel to seek information necessary to make an objective assessment of the facts may, as discussed above, amount to a violation of Article 11 of the DSU.[378]

To date, panels have consulted experts in, for example, *EC – Hormones (1998)*, *Australia – Salmon (1998)*, *Japan – Agricultural Products II (1999)*, *EC – Asbestos (2001)*, *Japan – Apples (2003)*, *EC – Approval and Marketing of Biotech Products (2006)*, *US/Canada – Continued Suspension (2008)* and *Australia – Apples (2010)*, which were all disputes involving complex scientific

373 See *ibid.*

374 In addition to Article 13 of the DSU, panels have either the possibility or the obligation to consult experts under a number of other covered agreements: see Article XV:2 of the GATT 1994; Article 11.2 of the *SPS Agreement* (see below, p. 943); Articles 14.2 and 14.3 of the *TBT Agreement* (see below, p. 889); Articles 19.3 and 19.4 of, and Annex II to, the *Agreement on Customs Valuation*; and Articles 4.5 and 24.3 of the *SCM Agreement* (see above, pp. 129–30, and below, pp. 777 and 833).

375 Appellate Body Report, *Argentina – Textiles and Apparel (1998)*, para. 84. This case concerned the question whether the panel was obliged to consult the IMF with regard to Argentina's imposition of import surcharges. The Appellate Body noted that the only provision that *requires* consultation of the IMF is Article XV:2 of the GATT (dealing with problems of monetary reserves, balances of payments or foreign exchange arrangements).

376 Appellate Body Report, *US – Shrimp (1998)*, para. 104.

377 *Ibid.*, para. 106. See also Appellate Body Report, *US – Continued Zeroing (2009)*, para. 347.

378 See Appellate Body Report, *US – Large Civil Aircraft (2nd complaint) (2012)*, para. 1145.

issues.[379] In these cases, the panels typically selected the experts in consultation with the parties; presented the experts with a list of questions to which each expert individually responded in writing; and finally called a special meeting with the experts at which the panel's questions as well as other questions were discussed with the panellists and the parties. The panel report usually contained both the written responses of the experts to the panel's questions as well as a transcript of the discussions at the meeting with the panel.[380] Note that experts consulted by the panel are subject to the Rules of Conduct and must therefore be independent and impartial, avoid conflicts of interest, and respect the confidentiality of the proceedings.[381] In *US/Canada – Continued Suspension (2008)*, the Appellate Body – while recognising the difficulty in selecting experts who have the required level of expertise and are acceptable to the parties – found that the institutional affiliation of two of the panel experts 'was likely to affect or give justifiable doubts as to their independence or impartiality', given that studies made by their institution were at the heart of the controversy between the parties.[382] The Appellate Body thus concluded that the panel had infringed the due process rights of the European Communities in this case.

Under Article 13 of the DSU, a panel may not only consult individual experts and scientists; it may also consult specialised international organisations.[383] For example, in *EC – Approval and Marketing of Biotech Products (2006)*, the panel sought information from the Secretariat of the Convention on Biological Diversity, the Codex Alimentarius Commission, the Food and Agriculture Organization, the International Plant Protection Convention, the International Organization for Epizootics, the UN Environment Programme and the World Health Organization.[384] In *EC – Chicken Cuts (2005)* and *China – Auto Parts (2008)*, the panel sought information from the World Customs Organization.[385] In *Dominican Republic – Import and Sale of Cigarettes (2005)*, the panel consulted with the International Monetary Fund;[386] and, in *EC – Trademarks and Geographical Indications (2005)*, the panel requested from the World Intellectual Property Organization 'assistance in the form of any factual information available to it relevant to the interpretation of certain provisions of the *Paris Convention for the Protection of Industrial Property*'.[387]

---

379 See *WTO Analytical Index (2012)*, Volume II, 1718.

380 However, confidential information must not be revealed without formal authorisation from the individual, body or authorities of the Member providing the information.

381 See above, p. 216.

382 See Appellate Body Report, *US/Canada – Continued Suspension (2008)*, paras. 480–1.

383 Such consultations of specialised international organisations are also possible under the other legal bases for consultations listed in footnote 374 above. For a list of proceedings in which information was sought from other international organisations, see *WTO Analytical Index (2012)*, Volume II, 1715.

384 See Panel Reports, *EC – Approval and Marketing of Biotech Products (2006)*, paras. 7.19 and 7.31–7.32.

385 See Panel Report, *EC – Chicken Cuts (2005)*, paras. 7.52–7.53 (complaint by Brazil) and paras. 7.52–7.53 (complaint by Thailand).

386 See Panel Report, *Dominican Republic – Import and Sale of Cigarettes (2005)*, paras. 1.8 and 7.138–7.154.

387 Panel Reports, *EC – Trademarks and Geographical Indications (2005)*, paras. 2.16–2.18 (complaint by Australia) and paras. 2.16–2.18 (complaint by the US).

Apart from consulting individual experts and international organisations, a panel can, with respect to a factual issue concerning a scientific or other technical matter, request a report in writing from an expert review group.[388] Rules for the establishment of such a group and its procedures are set forth in Appendix 4 to the DSU. Expert review groups are under the authority of the panel and report to the panel. The panel decides their terms of reference. The report of an expert review group is advisory only; it does not bind the panel. To date, panels have made no use of this possibility to request an advisory report from an expert review group. Panels have preferred to seek information from experts directly and on an individual basis.[389]

It should be noted that, while a panel has broad authority to consult experts to help it to understand and evaluate the evidence submitted and the arguments made by the parties, a panel may not – with the help of its experts – make the case for one or the other party. In *Japan – Agricultural Products II (1999)*, the Appellate Body held:

> Article 13 of the DSU and Article 11.2 of the *SPS Agreement* suggest that panels have a significant investigative authority. However, this authority cannot be used by a panel to rule in favour of a complaining party which has not established a *prima facie* case of inconsistency based on specific legal claims asserted by it. A panel is entitled to seek information and advice from experts and from any other relevant source it chooses, pursuant to Article 13 of the DSU and, in an SPS case, Article 11.2 of the *SPS Agreement*, to *help it to understand and evaluate the evidence* submitted and the arguments made by the parties, but not to make the case for a complaining party.[390]

In *Japan – Apples (2003)*, Japan referred to this finding by the Appellate Body to challenge on appeal the panel's use of experts. Japan argued that the United States had not made claims or submitted evidence in respect of the risk of transmission of fire blight by apples other than mature symptomless apples, yet the panel had made findings of fact with regard to these 'other' apples. Japan claimed that the panel had thus exceeded the bounds of its investigative authority. The Appellate Body rejected Japan's argument, finding that the panel had acted within the limits of its investigative authority, as:

> it did nothing more than assess the relevant allegations of fact asserted by Japan, in the light of the evidence submitted by the parties and the opinions of the experts.[391]

The Appellate Body thus clarified that a panel may use the evidence of its experts to assist it in assessing not only the claims of the complaining Member, but also the allegations of the responding Member. In doing so, it cannot be said to be exceeding its authority.

---

388 See Article 13.2 of the DSU.
389 The DSU leaves it to the discretion of a panel to determine whether the establishment of an expert review group is necessary or appropriate. See Appellate Body Report, *EC – Hormones (1998)*, para. 147.
390 Appellate Body Report, *Japan – Agricultural Products II (1999)*, para. 129. Emphasis added. See further Appellate Body Report, *Japan – Apples (2003)*, para. 158.
391 Appellate Body Report, *Japan – Apples (2003)*, para. 158.

Questions and Assignments 3.9

What are, and where do we find, the terms of reference of a panel? Why are the terms of reference of a panel important? How should the precise scope of a panel's terms of reference be determined? What is the standard of review to be applied by a panel in assessing the WTO consistency of the measure at issue in a dispute? When does a panel not meet the requirement of Article 11 of the DSU to make an objective assessment of the matter before it? Does a panel have to address and decide on every claim of the complainant? Can the panel ignore an explicit request of the complainant to rule on a particular claim? Can a panel develop an 'original' legal reasoning in its report that is not in any way based on legal arguments made by any of the parties to the dispute? When can panels make use of experts? Which experts may panels consult? Who selects the experts? Do panels have broad investigative authority? What are the limits of this authority? Find in a panel report a section dealing with the testimony and questioning of experts.

5.2.4   Requirements for Panel Reports

Article 12.7 of the DSU requires that a panel submits its findings to the DSB in the form of a written report, and that this report sets out: (1) the findings of fact; (2) the applicability of relevant provisions; and (3) the basic rationale behind any findings and recommendations that it makes.[392] In *Mexico – Corn Syrup (Article 21.5 – US) (2001)*, the Appellate Body stated that Article 12.7 sets a 'minimum standard' for the basic rationale with which panels must support their findings and recommendations.[393] The Appellate Body explained further:

> In our view, the duty of panels under Article 12.7 of the DSU to provide a 'basic rationale' reflects and conforms with the principles of fundamental fairness and due process that underlie and inform the provisions of the DSU. In particular, in cases where a Member has been found to have acted inconsistently with its obligations under the covered agreements, that Member is entitled to know the reasons for such finding as a matter of due process. In addition, the requirement to set out a 'basic rationale' in the panel report assists such Member to understand the nature of its obligations and to make informed decisions about: (i) what must be done in order to implement the eventual rulings and recommendations made by the DSB; and (ii) whether and what to appeal. Article 12.7 also furthers the objectives, expressed in Article 3.2 of the DSU, of promoting security and predictability in the multilateral trading system and of clarifying the existing provisions of the covered agreements, because the requirement to provide 'basic' reasons contributes to other WTO Members' understanding of the nature and scope of the rights and obligations in the covered agreements.[394]

In a few cases to date, parties have challenged a panel report before the Appellate Body for lack of a basic rationale behind the panel's findings and recommendations. In *Argentina – Footwear (EC) (2000)*, the Appellate Body found as follows:

> In this case, the Panel conducted *extensive* factual and legal analyses of the competing claims made by the parties, set out numerous factual findings based on detailed consideration of

---

392 Note the special requirements for panel reports in cases where parties have reached a mutually acceptable solution during the panel proceedings (see Article 12.7 of the DSU). See e.g. Panel Report, *Japan – Quotas on Laver*.
393 See Appellate Body Report, *Mexico – Corn Syrup (Article 21.5 – US) (2001)*, para. 106.
394 *Ibid.*, para. 107.

the evidence before the Argentine authorities as well as other evidence presented to the Panel, and provided extensive explanations of how and why it reached its factual and legal conclusions. Although Argentina may not agree with the rationale provided by the Panel, and we do not ourselves agree with all of its reasoning, we have no doubt that the Panel set out, in its Report, a 'basic rationale' consistent with the requirements of Article 12.7 of the DSU.[395]

In *Chile – Price Band System (Article 21.5 – Argentina) (2007)*, the Appellate Body curtly observed that:

[t]he mere fact that Chile disagrees with the substance of [the Panel's] reasoning cannot suffice to establish a violation of Article 12.7.[396]

In a dispute involving a developing-country Member, the panel report must explicitly indicate how the panel has taken account of any special or differential treatment provision that the developing-country Member has invoked before the panel. In *India – Quantitative Restrictions (1999)*, for example, the panel specifically referred to this requirement and noted:

In this instance, we have noted that Article XVIII:B as a whole, on which our analysis throughout this section is based, embodies the principle of special and differential treatment in relation to measures taken for balance-of-payments purposes. This entire part G therefore reflects our consideration of relevant provisions on special and differential treatment, as does Section VII of our report (suggestions for implementation).[397]

Where a panel concludes that a Member's measure is inconsistent with a covered agreement, it shall recommend that the Member concerned bring that measure into conformity with that agreement.[398] The recommendations and rulings of a panel are *not* legally binding by themselves. They become legally binding only when they are adopted by the DSB and thus have become the recommendations and rulings of the DSB.[399] In addition to making recommendations and rulings, the panel may suggest ways in which the Member concerned could implement those recommendations.[400] These suggestions are not legally binding on the Member concerned (even after the report is adopted).[401] However, because the panel making the suggestions might later be called upon to assess the sufficiency of the implementation of the recommendations, such suggestions are likely to have a certain impact.[402] To date, few panels have made use of this authority to make suggestions regarding implementation of their recommendations.[403]

---

395 Appellate Body Report, *Argentina – Footwear (EC) (2000)*, para. 149.
396 Appellate Body Report, *Chile – Price Band System (Article 21.5 – Argentina) (2007)*, para. 247. See also Appellate Body Report, *US – Steel Safeguards (2003)*, para. 507.
397 Panel Report, *India – Quantitative Restrictions (1999)*, para. 5.157.
398 See Article 19.1 of the DSU.
399 On the adoption of panel reports, see above, pp. 51, 206, and below, p. 282.
400 See Article 19.1 of the DSU.
401 On the legal effect of suggestions, see Appellate Body Report, *EC – Bananas III (Ecuador) (Article 21.5 – Ecuador II)/EC – Bananas III (US) (Article 21.5 – US) (2008)*, paras. 321–6.
402 See below, p. 293.
403 See e.g. Panel Report, *Mexico – Steel Pipes and Tubes (2007)*, paras. 8.12–8.13.

In fact, panels often refuse to make such suggestions. The panel in *EC – Tariff Preferences (2004)* explained its refusal as follows:

[I]n light of the fact that there is more than one way that the European Communities could bring its measures into conformity with its obligations under GATT 1994 and the fact that the European Communities has requested a waiver which is still pending, the Panel does not consider it appropriate to make any particular suggestions to the European Communities as to how the European Communities should bring its inconsistent measures into conformity with its obligations under GATT 1994.[404]

However, in *EC – Export Subsidies on Sugar (2005)*, in light of the concerns expressed by developing-country third parties with regard to their preferential access to the EC market for their sugar exports, the panel in that case suggested that:

[i]n bringing its exports of sugar into conformity with its obligations under Article 3.3 and 8 of the *Agreement on Agriculture*, the European Communities consider measures to bring its production of sugar more in line with domestic consumption whilst respecting its international commitments with respect to imports, including its commitments to developing countries.[405]

Pursuant to Article 14.3 of the DSU, panellists can express a separate opinion in the panel report, be it dissenting or concurring. However, if they do, they must do so anonymously. To date, there have only been nine panel reports setting out a separate opinion of one of the panellists.[406]

In cases in which the DSB decides to establish one panel to hear complaints of several Members,[407] any party may, pursuant to Article 9.2 of the DSU, request a separate report from the panel. As such, the panel in *United States – Steel Safeguards (2003)* decided 'to issue its Reports in the form of one document constituting eight Panel Reports' with a common cover page and a common descriptive part.[408] Note that, in *US – Offset Act (Byrd Amendment) (2003)* concerning complaints by Australia, Brazil, Canada, Chile, the European Communities, India, Indonesia, Japan, Korea, Mexico and Thailand, the Appellate Body upheld the panel's refusal to issue, at the request of the United States, a separate report for the complaint brought by Mexico because the United States filed that request too late.[409]

Panel reports are always circulated to WTO Members, and made available to the public, in English, French and Spanish. Reports are not circulated until all

---

404 Panel Report, *EC – Tariff Preferences (2004)*, para. 8.3.
405 Panel Report, *EC – Export Subsidies on Sugar (2005)*, para. 8.7.
406 See *WTO Analytical Index (2012)*, Volume II, 1720. Four of those separate opinions were referred to as 'dissenting opinions'. See e.g. Panel Report, *EC – Tariff Preferences (2004)*, paras. 9.1–9.21; Panel Report, *US – Zeroing (EC) (2006)*, paras. 7.285 and 9.1–9.62; and Panel Report, *Canada – Feed-in Tariff Programme (2012)*, paras. 9.1–9.3.
407 See above, p. 214.
408 Separate panel reports were also issued as a single document in, for example, *EC – Approval and Marketing of Biotech Products (2006)*; *Canada – Wheat Exports and Grain Imports (2004)*; and *Philippines – Distilled Spirits (2012)*. Separate panel reports were issued in different documents in, for example, *EC – Chicken Cuts (2005)*, *EC – Trademarks and Geographical Indications (2005)*, *EC – Export Subsidies on Sugar (2005)* and *EC – Bananas III (1997)*.
409 See Appellate Body Report, *US – Offset Act (Byrd Amendment) (2003)*, paras. 305–17.

three language versions are available. Most reports are written in English and then translated into French and Spanish. However, there have been a few panel reports written in Spanish,[410] and at least one written in French.[411] Panel reports often are several hundred pages long. The longest reports to date were *EC – Approval and Marketing of Biotech Products (2006)* (1,087 pages) and *EC and certain member States – Large Civil Aircraft (2011)* (1,044 pages).

Questions and Assignments 3.10

What are the (formal) requirements that a panel report must meet under the DSU? Can a panellist have his or her dissenting opinion noted in the panel report? What is the difference between a recommendation of a panel and a suggestion of a panel?

5.3   The Appellate Body

Article 17.1 of the DSU provides for the establishment of a standing Appellate Body to hear appeals from reports of panels. The DSB established the Appellate Body in February 1995.[412] The WTO dispute settlement system is one of very few international dispute settlement mechanisms that provide for appellate review and has an appellate court. In 2003, Claus-Dieter Ehlermann referred to the Appellate Body as the 'World Trade Court'.[413] This section discusses: (1) the membership and structure of the Appellate Body; (2) the scope of appellate review; (3) the mandate of the Appellate Body; and (4) the requirements for Appellate Body reports.

5.3.1   Membership and Structure of the Appellate Body

Unlike panels, the Appellate Body is a permanent international tribunal.[414] The Appellate Body is composed of seven judges referred to as 'Members' of the Appellate Body.[415] With respect to the required qualifications of Members of the Appellate Body, Article 17.3 of the DSU states in relevant part:

The Appellate Body shall comprise persons of recognized authority, with demonstrated expertise in law, international trade and the subject-matter of the covered agreements generally. They shall be unaffiliated with any government.

It is understood that the expertise of Appellate Body Members should be of a type that allows them to resolve 'issues of law covered in the panel report and

---

410 See e.g. Panel Report, *Mexico – Tubes and Pipes (2007)*; and Panel Report, *Dominican Republic – Safeguard Measures on Polypropylene Bags (2012)*.
411 See e.g. Panel Report, *EC – Asbestos (2001)*.
412 See Recommendations by the Preparatory Committee for the WTO approved by the Dispute Settlement Body on 10 February 1995, *Establishment of the Appellate Body*, WT/DSB/1, dated 19 June 1995.
413 See C.-D. Ehlermann, 'Six Years on the Bench of the World Trade Court: Personal Experiences as a Member of the Appellate Body of the World Trade Organization', *Journal of World Trade*, 2003, 605.
414 See Article 17.1 of the DSU.
415 Note that, in the context of the DSU reform negotiations, the European Union has proposed providing the DSB with the power to modify the number of Appellate Body Members, when necessary, to deal with the workload.

legal interpretations developed by the panel'.[416] While the overriding concern is to provide highly qualified Members for the Appellate Body,[417] Article 17.3 also requires that:

[t]he Appellate Body membership shall be broadly representative of membership in the WTO.

Therefore, factors such as different geographical areas, levels of development and legal systems are taken into account.[418] In its *Decision Establishing the Appellate Body*, the DSB stated:

The success of the WTO will depend greatly on the proper composition of the Appellate Body, and persons of the highest calibre should serve on it.[419]

In early 2013, the composition of the Appellate Body was as follows: Mr Ujal Singh Bhatia (India), Mr Seung Wha Chang (Korea), Mr Thomas R. Graham (United States), Mr Ricardo Ramírez-Hernández (Mexico), Mr Peter Van den Bossche (European Union), Mr David Unterhalter (South Africa) and Ms Zhang Yuejiao (China).[420] Appellate Body Members are not required to reside permanently in Geneva and most do not. However, Article 17.3 of the DSU requires that they 'be available at all times and on short notice'.[421] Article 17.2 of the DSU states with respect to the appointment of Appellate Body Members and their term of office:

The DSB shall appoint persons to serve on the Appellate Body for a four-year term, and each person may be reappointed once.

The Members of the Appellate Body thus serve a term of four years, which can be renewed once. Pursuant to Article 2.4 of the DSU, the DSB takes the decision on the appointment of Appellate Body Members by consensus. It takes this decision on the recommendation of a Selection Committee, composed of the Chairs of the General Council, the DSB, the Council for Trade in Goods, the Council for Trade in Services, and the TRIPS Council and the WTO Director-General. The Selection Committee selects among candidates nominated by WTO Members.

As already noted, Appellate Body Members shall not be affiliated with any government.[422] They must exercise their office without accepting or seeking instructions from any international, governmental or non-governmental organisation or

---

416 Recommendations by the Preparatory Committee for the WTO approved by the Dispute Settlement Body on 10 February 1995, *Establishment of the Appellate Body*, 10 February 1995, WT/DSB/1, dated 19 June 1995, para. 5.

417 See *ibid.*, para. 6.   418 See *ibid.*   419 *Ibid.*, para. 4.

420 For biographical information on the current and former Members of the Appellate Body and their respective terms of office, see www.wto.org/english/tratop_e/dispu_e/ab_members_descrp_e.htm.

421 Note that Appellate Body Members have 'part-time' appointments. This arrangement reflects the expectation on the part of WTO Members, in 1995, that the Appellate Body would not be so 'busy' as to justify a full-time employment arrangement. While the caseload has gone up and down since 1996, in many years Appellate Body membership has been *more* than a full-time job. The demands of the job have been such that it is difficult, and at times impossible, for Appellate Body Members to pursue other professional activities.

422 See Article 17.3 of the DSU.

any private source.[423] During their term of office, Members must not accept any employment nor pursue any professional activity that is inconsistent with their duties and responsibilities.[424] The Members of the Appellate Body are *mutatis mutandis* subject to the same *Rules of Conduct* as those applicable to panellists, discussed above.[425] Under these Rules, Appellate Body Members:

> shall be independent and impartial, shall avoid direct or indirect conflicts of interest and shall respect the confidentiality of proceedings.[426]

They are required 'to disclose the existence or development of any interest, relationship or matter' that is 'likely to affect, or give rise to justifiable doubts' as to their 'independence or impartiality'.[427] They may not participate in the consideration of any appeal that would create a direct or indirect conflict of interests. Parties can request the disqualification of an Appellate Body Member on the ground of a material violation of the obligations of the *Rules of Conduct*. It is, however, for the Appellate Body itself, and not for the Chair of the DSB (as is the case for panellists), to decide whether a material violation has occurred and, if so, to take appropriate action.[428]

As to the institutional structure of the Appellate Body, note first of all that the Appellate Body does not hear or decide appeals *en banc*. It hears and decides appeals in divisions of three Members.[429] Pursuant to Rule 6(2) of the *Working Procedures for Appellate Review*, commonly referred to as the *Working Procedures*, the Members constituting the division hearing and deciding a particular appeal are selected on the basis of *rotation*, taking into account the principles of random selection and unpredictability and opportunity for all Members to serve, regardless of their nationality.[430] Unlike in the process for panellist selection, the nationality of Appellate Body Members is irrelevant. Appellate Body Members can, and will, sit in cases to which their countries of origin are party. The Members of a division select their presiding Member.[431] Pursuant to Rule 7(2) of the *Working Procedures*, the responsibilities of the presiding Member shall include: (1) coordinating the overall conduct of the appeal proceeding; (2) chairing all oral hearings and meetings related to that appeal; and (3) coordinating the drafting of the appellate report.

---

423 See Rule 2(3) of the *Working Procedures*.   424 See Rule 2(2) of the *Working Procedures*.

425 See above, p. 216.   426 Para. II(1) of the *Rules of Conduct*.

427 Para. III(1) of the *Rules of Conduct*. This information shall be disclosed to the Appellate Body for its consideration whether the Member concerned should hear a particular appeal. Appellate Body Members remain subject to this disclosure obligation throughout the Appellate Body proceeding. See para. VI(4)(b) and (5) of the *Rules of Conduct*.

428 See *ibid*.

429 See Article 17.1 of the DSU and Rule 6(1) of the *Working Procedures*.

430 Another Member selected pursuant to Rule 6(2) shall replace a Member unable to serve on a division for a reason set out in Rule 6(3). In *US – Softwood Lumber IV (2004)* and *US – Offset Act (Byrd Amendment) (2003)*, for example, Mr Giorgio Sacerdoti was selected to replace Mr Arumugamangalam V. Ganesan, who had to step down for 'serious personal reasons'. See Appellate Body Report, *US – Softwood Lumber IV (2004)*, para. 10; and Appellate Body Report, *US – Offset Act (Byrd Amendment) (2003)*, para. 8.

431 See Rule 7(1) of the *Working Procedures*.

All decisions relating to an appeal are taken by the division assigned to that appeal. However, to ensure consistency and coherence in its case law and to draw on the individual and collective expertise of all seven Members, the division responsible for deciding an appeal exchanges views with the other Members on the issues raised by the appeal.[432] This exchange of views, which may take two to three days (or longer), is held before the division has come to any definitive views on the issues arising in the appeal.[433] While it is for the Appellate Body Members on the division to decide on the issues arising in the appeal and they are free not to take into account any 'advice' by other Members, the exchange of views, and the importance given to it, has undoubtedly contributed to the quality and consistency of the Appellate Body's case law and the limited number of separate opinions.[434]

A division makes every effort to take its decision on the appeal by consensus. However, if a decision cannot be reached by consensus, the *Working Procedures* provide that the matter at issue be decided by majority vote.[435] Pursuant to Article 17.11 of the DSU, individual Members may express separate opinions in the report, but these opinions (whether concurring or dissenting) must be anonymous. Separate opinions are rare in Appellate Body reports. To date, in only six Appellate Body reports has an Appellate Body Member expressed an individual opinion.[436]

In addition to their meetings to exchange views on each appeal, all seven Appellate Body Members also convene on a regular basis to discuss matters of policy, practice and procedure.[437] If the Appellate Body is called upon to take a decision, it will try to do so by consensus. However, if it fails to reach a consensus, the decision will be taken by majority vote.

Each year the Appellate Body Members elect a chair from among themselves.[438] In 2013, Mr Ricardo Ramírez-Hernández serves as the Chairperson of the Appellate Body. Rule 5(3) of the *Working Procedures* states that the Chair shall be responsible for the overall direction of the Appellate Body business. His or her responsibilities shall include: (1) the supervision of the internal functioning of the Appellate Body; and (2) any such other duties as the Members may agree to entrust to him/her.

---

432 See Rule 4(3) of the *Working Procedures*. Each Member therefore receives all documents filed in an appeal. A Member who has a conflict of interest under the *Code of Conduct* shall not take part in the work of a division or the exchange of views.
433 See also below, p. 289.
434 On separate opinions, see e.g. above, p. 187, and below, p. 391, footnote 224, p. 763, footnote 95, and p. 841, footnote 504.
435 See Rule 3(2) of the *Working Procedures*.
436 On the separate opinion(s) in *EC – Asbestos (2001)*, see below, p. 391; in *US – Upland Cotton (2005)*, see above, p. 841; in *US – Continued Zeroing (2009)*, see above, p. 53 and 187; in *US – Zeroing (Article 21.5 – EC) (2009)*, see above, p. 53; and in *EC and certain member States – Large Civil Aircraft (2011)*, see below, p. 763, footnote 95. For the separate opinion in *US – Large Civil Aircraft (2nd complaint) (2012)*, see Appellate Body Report, *US – Large Civil Aircraft (2nd complaint) (2012)*, footnotes 1118, 1130 and 1153.
437 See Rule 4 of the *Working Procedures*.
438 See Rule 5(1) of the *Working Procedures*. While the term of office of the chair is one year, the Appellate Body may exceptionally decide to extend the term of office for an additional period of up to one year.

The Appellate Body has its own secretariat, which is separate from and independent of the WTO Secretariat.[439] The Appellate Body Secretariat provides the Appellate Body with legal and administrative support.[440] The *Rules of Conduct* and their requirements of independence, impartiality and confidentiality apply to the staff of the Appellate Body Secretariat.[441] The Appellate Body Secretariat has its offices in the Centre William Rappard, the lakeside premises of the WTO Secretariat in Geneva. All meetings of the Appellate Body or of divisions of the Appellate Body, as well as the oral hearings in appeals, are also held on these premises.

Questions and Assignments 3.11

How and by whom are Members of the Appellate Body appointed? Is the current composition of the Appellate Body consistent with the relevant DSU provisions? What requirements apply to Appellate Body Members during their term in office? How are the Appellate Body divisions that hear and decide particular appeals composed? In your opinion, is it appropriate that a Member of the Appellate Body with the nationality of one of the participants may sit on the division hearing and deciding the appeal? How has the Appellate Body been able to maintain consistency in its case law in spite of the fact that appeals are never heard or decided *en banc*? What are the key obligations under the *Rules of Conduct* relevant for Appellate Body Members? Can Appellate Body Members be disqualified? If so, by whom and on what grounds?

5.3.2   Scope of Appellate Review

As stated above, appellate review of panel reports is entrusted to the Appellate Body. This sub-section deals with the scope of this review, and focuses on the following two questions: (1) who can appeal; and (2) what can be appealed.

First, with regard to the question who can appeal, Article 17.4 states in clear terms:

Only parties to the dispute, not third parties, may appeal a panel report.

However, while third parties or other WTO Members cannot appeal a panel report, third parties, i.e. WTO Members, which have notified the DSB of a substantial interest in the dispute at the time of the establishment of the panel,[442] can participate in the Appellate Body proceedings.[443] Members which were not third parties in the panel proceedings, cannot participate in Appellate Body proceedings.[444]

In Appellate Body proceedings, the parties are referred to as 'participants'. The participant that appeals a panel report is called the 'appellant', while the

---

439 See Recommendations by the Preparatory Committee for the WTO approved by the Dispute Settlement Body on 10 February 1995, *Establishment of the Appellate Body*, 10 February 1995, WT/DSB/1, dated 19 June 1995, para. 17.

440 Article 17.7 of the DSU. At present, the Appellate Body Secretariat consists of a director, fourteen staff lawyers (including temporary staff) and four support staff.

441 See above, p. 216.

442 Or within ten days of the establishment of the panel. See above, p. 213.

443 On the participants' rights in Appellate Body proceedings, see below, p. 289.

444 Note, however, that these Members may submit an *amicus curiae* brief. See below, pp. 266–7.

participant responding to an appeal is called the 'appellee'. Once one of the participants has appealed certain aspects of a panel report, it is not uncommon for other participants to 'cross-appeal' other aspects of the report.[445] A participant cross-appealing is known as an 'other appellant'. Third parties choosing to participate in the Appellate Body proceedings are referred to as 'third participants'.

Secondly, with regard to the question what can be appealed, Article 17.6 of the DSU states:

An appeal shall be limited to issues of law covered in the panel report and legal interpretations developed by the panel.

In *EC – Hormones (1998)*, the Appellate Body found that factual findings of panels are, in principle, excluded from the scope of appellate review. The Appellate Body stated:

Under Article 17.6 of the DSU, appellate review is limited to appeals on questions of law covered in a panel report and legal interpretations developed by the panel. Findings of fact, as distinguished from legal interpretations or legal conclusions, by a panel are, in principle, not subject to review by the Appellate Body.[446]

In many cases, the characterisation of findings as findings on issues of fact, rather than on issues of law or legal interpretations, is fairly straightforward. In *EC – Hormones (1998)*, the Appellate Body noted that:

[t]he determination of whether or not a certain event did occur in time and space is typically a question of fact.[447]

In that dispute, the Appellate Body found that the panel's findings regarding whether or not international standards had been adopted by the Codex Alimentarius Commission were findings on issues of fact and were, therefore, not subject to appellate review. In other cases, the task of distinguishing between findings on issues of fact and findings on issues of law can be a complex exercise. The Appellate Body has made it clear, however, that findings involving the application of a legal rule to a specific fact or a set of facts are findings on issues of law and thus fall within the scope of appellate review. As stated in *EC – Hormones (1998)*:

[t]he consistency or inconsistency of a given fact or set of facts with the requirements of a given treaty provision is ... a legal characterization issue. It is a legal question.[448]

---

445 See below, p. 286.
446 Appellate Body Report, *EC – Hormones (1998)*, para. 132. See also Appellate Body Report, *EC – Bananas III (1997)*, para. 239.
447 Appellate Body Report, *EC – Hormones (1998)*, para. 132.
448 *Ibid.* Considerable reliance has been placed by later decisions on this proposition. For example, in *US – Softwood Lumber V (2004)*, the Appellate Body found that the question as to whether the particular approach adopted by a domestic authority was fair and even-handed was a 'legal characterization' of facts, and thus subject to appellate review. See Appellate Body Report, *US – Softwood Lumber V (2004)*, para. 163. Similarly, in *US – Anti-Dumping Measures on Oil Country Tubular Goods (2005)*, the Appellate Body held that the qualitative assessment of facts against a legal requirement is a 'legal characterization of [those] facts', and thus subject to appellate review. See Appellate Body Report, *US – Anti-Dumping Measures on Oil Country Tubular Goods (2005)*, para. 195.

The Appellate Body had used similar reasoning in *Canada – Periodicals (1997)* to explain why the panel's determination of 'like products', for the purposes of Article III:2 of the GATT 1994, was subject to appellate review:

> The determination of whether imported and domestic products are 'like products' is a process by which legal rules have to be applied to facts.[449]

Furthermore, as the Appellate Body ruled in *US – Section 211 Appropriations Act (2002)*, also the scope and content of the municipal law of a Member, as determined by a panel, for the purpose of ascertaining the Member's compliance with WTO obligations, is a question of law, which the Appellate Body can review.[450]

In brief, pursuant to Article 17.6 of the DSU, the Appellate Body can review a panel's interpretation of WTO provisions as well as the panel's application of these provisions to the facts in the case at hand. However, there is more. As explained below, the Appellate Body can also review whether a panel has made an objective assessment of the facts as a panel is required to do under Article 11 of the DSU.[451] As a panel's factual determinations are, in principle, not subject to appellate review, a panel's weighing and assessment of evidence before it is also, in principle, not subject to appellate review.[452] In *EC – Hormones (1998)*, the Appellate Body found:

> Determination of the credibility and weight properly to be ascribed to (that is, the appreciation of) a given piece of evidence is part and parcel of the fact finding process and is, in principle, left to the discretion of a panel as the trier of facts.[453]

In *Korea – Alcoholic Beverages (1999)*, in which Korea sought to cast doubt on certain studies relied on by the panel in that case, the Appellate Body stated:

> The Panel's examination and weighing of the evidence submitted fall, in principle, within the scope of the Panel's discretion as the trier of facts and, accordingly, outside the scope of appellate review. This is true, for instance, with respect to the Panel's treatment of the Dodwell Study, the Sofres Report and the Nielsen Study. We *cannot second-guess* the Panel in appreciating either the evidentiary value of such studies or the consequences, if any, of alleged defects in those studies. Similarly, it is not for us to review the relative weight ascribed to evidence on such matters as marketing studies.[454]

---

449 Appellate Body Report, *Canada – Periodicals (1997)*, 468.
450 See Appellate Body Report, *US – Section 211 Appropriations Act (2002)*, paras. 105–6, relying on Appellate Body Report, *India – Patents (US) (1998)*, paras. 65–6 and 68.
451 On a panel's obligations under Article 11 of the DSU, see above, pp. 219–25.
452 Note that, in *US – Offset Act (Byrd Amendment) (2003)*, Canada argued on appeal that Article 17.6 of the DSU prohibited the United States from challenging 'the credibility and weight the Panel attached' to two letters that had been in evidence before it. The Appellate Body, however, rejected Canada's claim. It found that the comments by the United States formed part of the latter's challenge to the panel's legal findings. Whether these findings were supported by those letters was, according to the Appellate Body, an issue of law on which it had the authority to rule. See Appellate Body Report, *US – Offset Act (Byrd Amendment) (2003)*, para. 220.
453 Appellate Body Report, *EC – Hormones (1998)*, para. 132.
454 Appellate Body Report, *Korea – Alcoholic Beverages (1999)*, para. 161. Emphasis added.

Panels thus have wide-ranging discretion in the consideration and weight they give to the evidence before them.[455] However, a panel's discretion in the consideration and weight it gives to evidence is *not* unlimited.[456] A panel's factual determinations must be consistent with Article 11 of the DSU, i.e. consistent with the standard of review the panel must apply.[457] As noted by the Appellate Body in *EC – Hormones (1998)*:

> Whether or not a panel has made an objective assessment of the facts before it, as required by Article 11 of the DSU, is also a legal question which, if properly raised on appeal, would fall within the scope of appellate review.[458]

Therefore, a factual finding may be subject to appellate review when the appellant alleges that this finding was not reached in a manner consistent with the requirements of Article 11 of the DSU. In *Philippines – Distilled Spirits (2012)*, the Appellate Body ruled:

> We recall that Article 11 of the DSU requires a panel to 'consider all the evidence presented to it, assess its credibility, determine its weight, and ensure that its factual findings have a proper basis in that evidence'. Within these parameters, 'it is generally within the discretion of the panel to decide which evidence it chooses to utilize in making findings', and panels 'are not required to accord to factual evidence of the parties the same meaning and weight as do the parties'. For a claim under Article 11 to succeed, the Appellate Body must be satisfied that the panel has exceeded its authority as initial trier of facts, which requires it to provide 'reasoned and adequate explanations and coherent reasoning', base its finding on a sufficient evidentiary basis, and treat evidence with 'even-handedness'.[459]

It is clear that not every error by a panel amounts to a violation of Article 11 of the DSU. As the Appellate Body ruled in *EC – Fasteners (China) (2011)*:

> It is incumbent on a participant raising a claim under Article 11 on appeal to explain *why* the alleged error *meets* the standard of review under that provision ... In particular, when alleging that a panel ignored a piece of evidence, the mere fact that a panel did not explicitly refer to that evidence in its reasoning is insufficient to support a claim of violation under Article 11. Rather, a participant must explain why such evidence is so material to its case that the panel's failure explicitly to address and rely upon the evidence has a bearing on the objectivity of the panel's factual assessment.[460]

In *US – Steel Safeguards (2003)*, the Appellate Body noted that a challenge under Article 11 of the DSU 'must not be vague or ambiguous', but, rather, must be clearly articulated and substantiated with specific arguments.[461] A claim that a panel failed to conduct an objective assessment of the matter is, according to the Appellate Body:

---

455 See also e.g. Appellate Body Report, *Australia – Salmon (1998)*, para. 261; Appellate Body Report, *India – Quantitative Restrictions (1999)*, para. 143; and Appellate Body Report, *Korea – Dairy (2000)*, para. 137.

456 See Appellate Body Report, *Korea – Alcoholic Beverages (1999)*, para. 162.

457 See above, pp. 219–22.

458 Appellate Body Report, *EC – Hormones (1998)*, para. 132. See also e.g. Appellate Body Report, *Korea – Alcoholic Beverages (1999)*, para. 162.

459 Appellate Body Reports, *Philippines – Distilled Spirits (2012)*, para. 235.

460 Appellate Body Report, *EC – Fasteners (China) (2011)*, para. 442.

461 See Appellate Body Report, *US – Steel Safeguards (2003)*, para. 498.

not to be made lightly, or merely as a subsidiary argument or claim in support of a claim of a panel's failure to construe or apply correctly a particular provision of a covered agreement.[462]

In view of the distinction between the respective roles of the Appellate Body and panels, the Appellate Body will not 'interfere lightly' with the panel's fact-finding authority,[463] and 'cannot base a finding of inconsistency under Article 11 simply on the conclusion that [it] might have reached a different factual finding from the one the panel reached'.[464]

In a number of appeals to date, the appellant claimed with regard to specific findings that the panel erred in its application of the law to the facts *as well as* in its duty to make an objective assessment of the facts under Article 11 of the DSU.[465] While both claims of error are within the appellate jurisdiction of the Appellate Body under Article 17.6 of the DSU, it is important to determine which claim of error is properly made with regard to specific findings. This is so because the threshold for a finding that a panel erred in its duty to make an objective assessment of the facts is much higher than the threshold for a finding that the panel erred in its application of the law to the facts. In *China – GOES (2012)*, the Appellate Body observed the following in this respect:

In most cases ... the issue raised by a particular claim 'will either be one of application of the law to the facts or an issue of the objective assessment of facts, and not both'. The Appellate Body has found that allegations implicating a panel's appreciation of facts and evidence fall under Article 11 of the DSU. By contrast, '[t]he consistency or inconsistency of a given fact or set of facts with the requirements of a given treaty provision is ... a legal characterization issue' and is therefore a legal question.[466]

With regard to the question whether the Appellate Body may consider 'new facts' on appeal, the Appellate Body held in *US – Offset Act (Byrd Amendment) (2003)* that it had no authority to do so, even if these new facts are contained in documents that are 'available on the public record'.[467] In *US – Softwood Lumber V (2004)*, Canada asked that the United States be requested to submit certain

---

462 *Ibid.* An Article 11 claim of error must stand on its own.
463 See e.g. Appellate Body Report, *US – Carbon Steel (2002)*, para. 142.
464 Appellate Body Report, *US – Wheat Gluten (2001)*, para. 151.
465 As the Appellate Body explained in *EC and certain member States – Large Civil Aircraft (2011)*, a failure to make a claim under Article 11 of the DSU on an issue that the Appellate Body determines to concern a factual assessment (rather than the application of the law to the facts) may have serious consequences for the appellant. Therefore, an appellant may 'feel safer putting forward both a claim that the Panel erred in the application of the law to the facts *and* a claim that the panel failed to make an objective assessment of the facts under Article 11 of the DSU'. See Appellate Body Report, *EC and certain member States – Large Civil Aircraft (2011)*, para. 872.
466 Appellate Body Report, *China – GOES (2012)*, para. 183. See also Appellate Body Report, *EC and certain member States – Large Civil Aircraft (2011)*, para. 872.
467 See Appellate Body Report, *US – Offset Act (Byrd Amendment) (2003)*, paras. 221–2. Note, however, that a new fact in a document that is publicly available may *in principle* be considered on appeal if the document is expressly referred to in the measure in question and its contents were discussed before the panel. The other party may have to establish prejudice in entertaining such a document so as to render it inadmissible before the Appellate Body. See Appellate Body Report, *Chile – Price Band System (2002)*, para. 13.

documents to the Appellate Body. The Appellate Body declined to do so, stating that:

> the materials at issue constituted new factual evidence and, therefore, pursuant to Article 17.6 of the DSU, fell outside the scope of the appeal.[468]

However, data need not be presented to the Appellate Body in *precisely* the same manner as before the panel. If the data presented on appeal can be clearly traced to the data in the panel record and the way in which such data has been converted can be readily understood, the evidence presented on appeal will not amount to 'new evidence', excluded by Article 17.6.[469]

With regard to 'new arguments' (as opposed to 'new facts'), the Appellate Body held in *Canada – Aircraft (1999)* that 'new arguments' on appeal cannot be rejected 'simply because they are new'. However, the Appellate Body recognised that Article 17.6 of the DSU forecloses the possibility for the Appellate Body to decide on a new argument that would involve reviewing new facts.[470] In *US – FSC (2000)*, the United States asked the Appellate Body to address a matter that it had not argued before the panel. The Appellate Body ruled:

> In our view, [the] examination of the substantive issues raised ... would be outside the scope of our mandate under Article 17.6 of the DSU, as this argument does not involve either an 'issue of law covered in the panel report' or 'legal interpretations developed by the panel'. The Panel was simply not asked to address the issues raised by the United States' new argument. Further, the new argument now made before us would require us to address legal issues quite different from those which confronted the Panel and which may well require proof of new facts.[471]

The Appellate Body had occasion in *EC – Poultry (1998)* to note that Article 17.6, read together with Article 17.13, discussed below, precludes from appellate review comments[472] or statements[473] by the panel (as opposed to legal findings and conclusions).

Note that during the first years of the WTO dispute settlement system, all panel reports were appealed. The first panel report that was *not* appealed was the report in *Japan – Film (1998)*. To date, 67 per cent of the circulated panel reports have been appealed.[474] This high rate of appeal is not necessarily a reflection of the quality of the panel reports but rather of the fact that appealing an unfavourable panel report is a rational decision for a losing party to take. As discussed above, in most disputes the panel finds against the respondent, at least in respect of part of the complainant's claims.[475] Often the respondent

---

468 Appellate Body Report, *US – Softwood Lumber V (2004)*, para. 9.
469 See Appellate Body Report, *Chile – Price Band System (2002)*, para. 13. See also e.g. Appellate Body Report, *EC – Export Subsidies on Sugar (2005)*, para. 242.
470 See Appellate Body Report, *Canada – Aircraft (1999)*, para. 211.
471 Appellate Body Report, *US – FSC (2000)*, para. 103.
472 See Appellate Body Report, *EC – Poultry (1998)*, para. 107.
473 See Appellate Body Report, *US – Wool Shirts and Blouses (1997)*, 338.
474 See www.worldtradelaw.net/dsc/database/appealcount.asp.
475 See above, p. 177.

will consider that it has little to lose by appealing.[476] On the contrary, an appeal – even if eventually unsuccessful – will allow a party, found to have acted inconsistently with WTO law, to delay the moment at which it has to bring its legislation or policy into consistency by usually three months. An appeal will also demonstrate to domestic constituencies that a Member has exhausted *all* legal means available to avert what may be economically painful and/or politically sensitive changes to national legislation or policies.

5.3.3 Mandate of the Appellate Body

The mandate of the Appellate Body is set out in Articles 17.12 and 17.13 of the DSU. Article 17.12 states:

> The Appellate Body shall address each of the issues raised in accordance with paragraph 6 during the appellate proceeding.

Article 17.13 states:

> The Appellate Body may uphold, modify or reverse the legal findings and conclusions of the panel.

With regard to Article 17.12 of the DSU, it should be noted that the Appellate Body has repeatedly ruled that this provision does not preclude it from exercising judicial economy.[477] Underlying this position may be the reasoning that expressly exercising judicial economy with regard to an issue (as opposed to remaining silent on that issue) is considered to amount to 'addressing' the issue.

When the Appellate Body agrees with both the panel's reasoning and the conclusion regarding the WTO-consistency of a measure, it *upholds* the relevant findings. When the Appellate Body agrees with the conclusion but not with the reasoning leading to that conclusion, it *modifies* the relevant findings. If the Appellate Body disagrees with the conclusion regarding the WTO-consistency of a measure, it *reverses* the relevant findings. In practice, however, the distinction between 'upholding' and 'modifying' is not always as clear-cut as suggested above, and the Appellate Body may 'uphold' a panel finding even though it amends or supplements the panel's reasoning leading to this finding.[478]

When the Appellate Body upholds all findings appealed, it upholds the panel report *as a whole*. In very few panel reports appealed the Appellate Body found such fundamental error that it could not but reverse the whole report.[479] In most

---

476 However, when a respondent fears that after the Appellate Body has considered the issues that may be raised on appeal, it might find itself 'worse off', it is likely to decide not to appeal an adverse panel report. Examples of such panel reports may be *US – Section 301 Trade Act (2000)*.

477 See e.g. Appellate Body Report, *US – Upland Cotton (2005)*, paras. 761–2.

478 See e.g. Appellate Body Report, *US – Hot-Rolled Steel (2001)*, paras. 90 and 158; and Appellate Body Report, *US – Lamb (2001)*, para. 188.

479 For examples of panel reports reversed, see e.g. the reports in *Guatemala – Cement I (1998)* and *Canada – Dairy (Article 21.5 – New Zealand and US) (2001)*.

appeals, the results of the appellate review were mixed. Some of the findings appealed were upheld, some modified and/or reversed. The panel report as a whole therefore was modified.

Although Article 17.13 of the DSU allows the Appellate Body only to uphold, modify or reverse the panel's findings appealed, the Appellate Body has, in a number of cases, gone beyond that mandate and has, explicitly or implicitly, 'completed the legal analysis'. As noted above, a complainant often makes claims of inconsistency with multiple provisions of WTO law with regard to the measure at issue. Once the panel has found inconsistency with one or some of these provisions, the panel may decide, for reasons of judicial economy, not to make findings with respect to the claims of inconsistency with other provisions. The need for 'completing the legal analysis' may arise when a dispute could potentially remain unresolved due to the Appellate Body's disposition of a claim on appeal. For example, if the panel report is appealed and the Appellate Body reverses the panel's findings of inconsistency with WTO provisions A and B, the question arises as to what the Appellate Body can do with regard to the claims of inconsistency with WTO provision C, which the panel, in its exercise of judicial economy, did not address. The question of whether the Appellate Body can complete the legal analysis also arises in cases in which a panel concludes that a provision or provisions of WTO law (e.g. the *TBT Agreement*, as was the case in *EC – Asbestos (2001)*) is not applicable in the case at hand but in which, on appeal of this finding of inapplicability, the Appellate Body comes to the opposite conclusion.

In many domestic judicial systems, the appeals court would in similar situations 'remand' the case to the court of first instance. However, the DSU does not provide the Appellate Body with the authority to remand a dispute to the panel. In the absence of a remand authority, the Appellate Body is left with two options: (1) either to leave the dispute unresolved; or (2) to go on to 'complete the legal analysis'. In *Canada – Periodicals (1997)*, the Appellate Body stated:

> We believe the Appellate Body *can, and should,* complete the analysis of Article III:2 of the GATT 1994 in this case by examining the measure with reference to its consistency with the second sentence of Article III:2, *provided that there is a sufficient basis in the Panel Report to allow us to do so.*[480]

In the circumstances of that case, the Appellate Body considered that it would be 'remiss in not completing the analysis of Article III:2'.[481] However, the Appellate Body has 'completed the legal analysis' only in cases in which there were sufficient factual findings in the panel report or undisputed facts in the panel record to enable it to carry out the legal analysis.[482] In practice, the

---

480 Appellate Body Report, *Canada – Periodicals (1997)*, 469. Emphasis added.
481 *Ibid.*
482 See Appellate Body Report, *Australia – Salmon (1998)*, para. 118. See also Appellate Body Report, *EC – Export Subsidies on Sugar (2005)*, para. 340.

Appellate Body has often found it impossible to 'complete the legal analysis' due to insufficient factual findings in the panel report or a lack of undisputed facts in the panel record.[483] Highly contested and complicated facts have also discouraged the Appellate Body from completing the analysis.[484] In addition, the Appellate Body has declined to complete the legal analysis because of the novel character of the claims, which the panel did not address. Claims are 'novel' when they concern issues, which have not yet been dealt with in the WTO case law, as was the case in *EC – Asbestos (2001)* with regard to Articles 2.1, 2.2, 2.4 and 2.8 of the *TBT Agreement*.[485] The Appellate Body will also decline to complete the legal analysis when a panel is thought to have improperly excluded evidence, or erred in its assessment of evidence, and the Appellate Body would have to examine the evidence in order to complete the legal analysis.[486] Finally, the Appellate Body will not complete the legal analysis if the completion is not necessary to resolve the dispute. For example, in *US – Steel Safeguards (2003)*, the Appellate Body refused to address a substantive issue that arose as a result of reversing a panel reasoning because addressing that issue would in no event have disturbed the panel's ultimate finding.[487] While the Appellate Body has completed the legal analysis in a number of cases, it has often declined to do so for the reasons set out above. In *EC and certain member States – Large Civil Aircraft (2011)*, the Appellate Body observed that 'in deciding whether to complete the legal analysis it has exercised "restraint" in past disputes'.[488]

Questions and Assignments 3.12

Can third parties or other WTO Members, which are directly and adversely affected by a panel report, appeal that report? What is an 'other appellant'? What explains the high rate of appeals of panel reports? What can be appealed? How does one distinguish between issues of law and issues of fact? Can factual findings ever be the subject of appeal? Can the Appellate Body review the weighing of evidence by a panel? Can the Appellate Body consider 'new facts' and/or 'new arguments' in the course of appellate review proceedings? When does the Appellate Body uphold, when does it modify and when does it reverse the legal findings and conclusions of the panel under appellate review? Why and when does the Appellate Body 'complete the legal analysis'? Are there arguments for the proposition that the Appellate Body should under no circumstances 'complete the legal analysis'? In your opinion, should the Appellate Body have the power to remand cases to the panel?

---

483 See e.g. Appellate Body Report, *US – Zeroing (EC) (2006)*, paras. 228 and 243; and Appellate Body Report, *EC and certain member States – Large Civil Aircraft (2011)*, paras. 1143–7.
484 See Appellate Body Report, *US – Softwood Lumber VI (Article 21.5 – Canada) (2006)*, paras. 157–61.
485 See Appellate Body Report, *EC – Asbestos (2001)*, para. 82.
486 See Appellate Body Report, *US – Countervailing Duty Investigation on DRAMs (2005)*, paras. 196–7.
487 See Appellate Body Report, *US – Steel Safeguards (2003)*, paras. 430–1.
488 Appellate Body Report, *EC and certain member States – Large Civil Aircraft (2011)*, para. 1140.

5.4   Other Entities Involved in WTO Dispute Settlement

Apart from the DSB, panels and the Appellate Body, there are a number of other institutions, bodies and persons involved in the WTO's efforts to resolve disputes between its Members, including: (1) the Chair of the DSB;[489] (2) the WTO Director-General;[490] (3) arbitrators under Articles 21.3, 22.6 and 25 of the DSU;[491] (4) experts under Articles 13.1 and 13.2 of the DSU, Article 11.2 of the *SPS Agreement* and Article 14 of the *TBT Agreement*;[492] (5) Expert Review Groups under Article 13.2 of and Appendix 4 to the DSU;[493] (6) Technical Expert Groups under Article 14.3 of and Annex 2 to the *TBT Agreement*;[494] (7) the Permanent Group of Experts under Article 4.5 of the *SCM Agreement*;[495] and (8) the Facilitator under Annex V.4 to the *SCM Agreement*.[496] The institutions, bodies or persons listed above, such as arbitrators, experts and expert groups, which directly participate in panel or Appellate Body proceedings, are subject to the *Rules of Conduct*, discussed earlier.[497]

6   PROCESS OF WTO DISPUTE SETTLEMENT

Having discussed in previous sections the jurisdiction, the object and purpose, and the structure, role and operation of the institutions of WTO dispute settlement, this section finally focuses on the process of WTO dispute settlement. The WTO dispute settlement process may – and often does – entail four major steps: (1) consultations; (2) panel proceedings; (3) Appellate Body proceedings; and (4) implementation and enforcement. As already indicated above, the process always starts with *consultations*, or at least an attempt by the complainant to involve the respondent in consultations, to resolve the dispute amicably. If that is not possible, the complainant can refer the dispute to a panel for adjudication. The *panel proceedings* will result in a panel report. This report can be appealed to the Appellate Body. The *Appellate Body proceedings* will result in an Appellate Body report upholding, modifying or reversing the panel report. The panel report, or, in the case of an appeal, the Appellate Body report *and* the panel report, will be adopted by the Dispute Settlement Body. After the adoption of the reports, the respondent, if found to be in breach of WTO law, will have to implement the recommendations and rulings adopted by the DSB. This *implementation and enforcement* of the adopted recommendations and rulings constitute the last major step in the WTO dispute settlement process.

489 See e.g. above, pp. 216 and 217, and below, pp. 274 and 283.
490 See e.g. above, pp. 181–2 and 216 and below, p. 292.
491 See e.g. above, p. 196 and below, pp. 291–2 and 296.
492 See e.g. above, p. 225, and below, pp. 889, 924 and 943–4.   493 See below, p. 227.
494 See below, p. 889.
495 See below, p. 777.   496 See e.g. above, p. 206, footnote 265, and below, pp. 810–11.
497 See para. IV(1) of the *Rules of Conduct*.

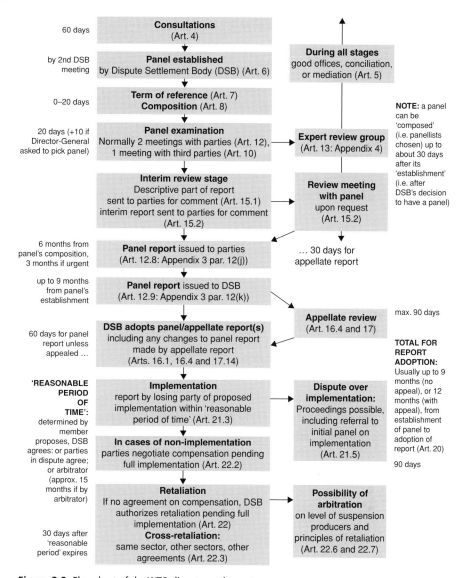

Figure 3.2 Flowchart of the WTO dispute settlement process

Figure 3.2, a flowchart prepared by the WTO Secretariat, reflects the four major steps, adding some additional detail, which is discussed below. It is, however, not the ambition of this section to inform the reader in detail of the multiple procedural provisions of WTO dispute settlement. Rather, this section will first include six general observations on the WTO dispute settlement process, and, then, in a broad manner, deal in turn with each of the major steps in the WTO dispute settlement process, as listed above.

6.1   General Observations on the WTO Dispute Settlement Process

The WTO dispute settlement process has many noteworthy features, but there are six features that are particularly so, partly because they distinguish WTO dispute settlement from other international dispute settlement mechanisms. This sub-section discusses these features, namely: (1) the short timeframe for each of the steps in the process; (2) the confidentiality and resulting lack of transparency of the process; (3) the burden of proof in WTO dispute settlement proceedings; (4) the important role of private legal counsel in representing parties in WTO dispute settlement; (5) the controversial issue of *amicus curiae* briefs; and (6) the obligation on Members to act in good faith in WTO dispute settlement proceedings, and the obligation on panels and the Appellate Body to ensure due process in these proceedings. With regard to these features, and in particular with regard to confidentiality and the role of private legal counsel, there has been a remarkable evolution since the initiation of the WTO dispute settlement system in 1995. Also, with regard to timeframes and confidentiality, there has been – and continues to be – a marked tension between theory and practice, i.e. between the world of legal requirements and noble ambitions on the one hand, and the world of limited resources and short-term political convenience on the other hand.

6.1.1   Timeframe

One of the most striking features of the WTO dispute settlement process when compared with other international (or national) dispute settlement mechanisms or judicial systems are the short timeframes within which, in particular, the panel and Appellate Body proceedings must be completed. Also, the consultation and implementation stages of the WTO dispute settlement process are subject to (strict) timeframes.[498]

Pursuant to Article 12.8 of the DSU, the period in which a panel must conduct its examination, from the date that the composition and terms of reference of the panel have been agreed upon until the date the final report is issued to the parties, shall, as a general rule, not exceed six months. When a panel considers that it cannot issue its report within six months, it shall inform the DSB in writing of the reasons for the delay, together with an estimate of the period within which it will issue its report. However, as stated in Article 12.9 of the DSU, in no case should the period from the establishment of the panel to the circulation of the report to the Members exceed nine months.[499] Even shorter timeframes (generally half of the standard timeframe) apply for panel proceedings in cases

---

498   On the timeframes for consultation and implementation stages, see below, pp. 271, and 291–8. and above, pp. 195–200, respectively.

499   See Article 12.9 of the DSU. When compared to the timeframe of Article 12.8, the timeframe of Article 12.9 starts earlier (the establishment of the panel precedes its composition) and finishes later (the panel report is first issued to the parties and later circulated). See also below, pp. 247–8, 277 and 303.

of urgency (including disputes relating to perishable goods) and with respect to disputes regarding subsidies under the *SCM Agreement*.[500] Also, the Article 21.5 compliance panel proceedings are subject to a shorter timeframe than the standard panel proceedings.[501]

In practice, however, the panel proceedings often exceed the standard timeframes of six and nine months. On average, a panel process – from the establishment of the panel until the circulation of the panel report – lasts 456 days, or approximately fifteen months.[502] The reasons for exceeding the DSU timeframes include: the complexity of the case; the need to consult experts; the availability of experts; problems with scheduling meetings; and the time taken to translate the report. The longest panel proceedings to date have been those in *US – Large Civil Aircraft (2nd complaint) (2012)*, which lasted for 61 months; and in *EC and certain member States – Large Civil Aircraft (2011)*, which lasted for 59.2 months.[503] In *EC – Approval and Marketing of Biotech Products (2006)* and *US/Canada – Continued Suspension (2008)*, it took the panel, respectively, 36.9 months and 37.3 months to complete the panel proceedings.[504] In *EC – Approval and Marketing of Biotech Products (2006)*, the chair of the panel raised the long delay in this case as an issue of systemic concern. In a letter to the Chair of the DSB, the chair of the panel stated:

With the circulation of its Reports, the Panel is completing more than two and a half years of legal proceedings. This is an unusually long period of time for WTO panel proceedings, considering also that Article 3.3 of the DSU stresses the importance of the prompt settlement of disputes. But the number of claims and products involved in this case was unprecedented and the record before the Panel immense. An estimated 7–8 work years of professional Secretariat staff time (not including translation and support staff time) have gone into the preparation of these Reports, not counting the time invested by the Panellists. This quite simply means that panels are unable to complete proceedings concerning such disputes within the 6–9 month timeframe laid down in Article 12.9 of the DSU, without additional resources being made available to the Secretariat for this purpose. [505]

With regard to the timeframe for Appellate Body proceedings, Article 17.5 of the DSU provides that, as a general rule, the proceedings shall not exceed sixty days from the date a party to the dispute formally notifies its decision to appeal to the date the Appellate Body circulates its report. When the Appellate Body believes that it cannot render its report within sixty days, it shall inform the DSB in writing of the reasons for the delay together with an estimate of the

---

500 See Article 12.8 of the DSU and Article 4 of the *SCM Agreement*. See below, p. 776, 811.
501 On the Article 21.5 compliance panel proceedings, see below, p. 293. According to Article 21.5 of the DSU, such proceedings should not take more than ninety days.
502 See www.worldtradelaw.net/dsc/database/paneltiming.asp. This is the average length of original, as opposed to Article 21.5 compliance panel proceedings. See below, p. 293.
503 See www.worldtradelaw.net/dsc/database/paneltiming.asp.
504 See *ibid*.
505 See Communication from the Chair of the Panel, *EC – Approval and Marketing of Biotech Products (2006)*, WT/DS291/32, WT/DS292/26 and WT/DS293/26, dated 29 September 2006, para. 1.

period within which it will submit its report. As Article 17.5 explicitly states, 'in no case shall the proceedings exceed ninety days'.[506] As for panel proceedings, even shorter timeframes (generally half of the standard timeframes) apply for Appellate Body proceedings in cases of urgency (including disputes relating to perishable goods) and with respect to disputes regarding subsidies under the *SCM Agreement*.[507]

In practice, the Appellate Body has, in almost all cases, taken more than sixty days to complete the appellate review.[508] However, except in 2011 and 2012, the Appellate Body has been able to complete the appellate review proceedings in ninety days in most cases.[509] The longest Appellate Body proceedings to date have been those in *US – Large Civil Aircraft (2nd complaint) (2012)*, which lasted for 346 days; and in *EC and certain member States – Large Civil Aircraft (2011)*, which lasted for 301 days.[510] Recall that the panel proceedings in these cases lasted 1,868 days and 1,806 days, respectively.[511] The time taken to complete these very complex and voluminous aircraft subsidy cases had a knock-on effect on the time taken for the other Appellate Body proceedings in 2011 and 2012. In this period, seven of the ten other proceedings took longer than ninety days. To date, Appellate Body proceedings have taken on average ninety-six days, rather than the ninety days allowed for under Article 17.5 of the DSU.[512] By way of example, note that in *US – Tuna II (Mexico) (2012)*, which took 117 days rather than ninety days, the Chair of the Appellate Body informed the Chair of the DSB on 20 March 2012 as follows:

The Appellate Body will not be able to circulate its Report within 90 days. This is due in part to the size of this appeal, including the number and complexity of the issues raised by the participants. It is also due to the large caseload that the Appellate Body was, and is, facing, and scheduling constraints resulting therefrom.[513]

---

506 Note that Article 12.9 of the DSU, with regard to the timeframe for panel proceedings, uses the word 'should', rather than 'shall'. This implies more 'flexibility' for panels than for the Appellate Body with regard to the timeframes set out in Articles 12.9 and 17.5 respectively.

507 See Article 17.5 of the DSU and Article 4 of the *SCM Agreement*.

508 During the first years of its operation, the Appellate Body succeeded only a few times in completing appellate review proceedings within the sixty-day timeframe. See e.g. *Japan – Alcoholic Beverages (1996)*, *US – Wool Shirts and Blouses (1997)*, *Canada – Periodicals (1997)*, *Brazil – Aircraft (Article 21.5 – Canada) (2000)* and *Canada – Aircraft (Article 21.5 – Brazil) (2000)*. It has not done the same since May 2000. For *India – Autos (2002)*, see above, p. 286.

509 Before 2011, the Appellate Body took longer than ninety days to complete its proceedings in e.g. *EC – Hormones (1998)* (114 days), *EC – Asbestos (2001)* (140 days), *US – Upland Cotton (2005)* (136 days) and *EC – Export Subsidies on Sugar (2005)* (105 days). The reasons for the delay in the proceedings included the complexity of the appeal, an overload of work, a delay in translation of the submissions or the report, and the death of an Appellate Body Member hearing the appeal. The latter happened in *US – Lead and Bismuth II (2000)* where Mr Christopher Beeby, a Member of the Appellate Body division hearing the appeal, passed away six days after the oral hearing.

510 See www.worldtradelaw.net/dsc/database/abtiming.asp.

511 See above, p. 247.

512 See www.worldtradelaw.net/dsc/database/abtiming.asp. However, if the 2011–12 aircraft subsidies cases are not included in the calculation of the average time taken, the average time for Appellate Body proceedings is very close to ninety days.

513 Communication from the Appellate Body, *US – Tuna II (Mexico)*, WT/DS381/12, dated 22 March 2012.

Some Members, and in particular the United States and Japan, have repeatedly criticised the Appellate Body for exceeding the ninety-day timeframe without the express consent of the parties. At the DSB meeting of 23 July 2012, a number of WTO Members made comments on the Appellate Body's circulation of reports beyond the ninety-day time-limit set forth in Article 17.5 of the DSU.[514] Almost all Members recognised that, while in the great majority of cases the Appellate Body has respected the ninety-day time-limit, the workload faced by the Appellate Body, compounded by the increasing complexity of the issues raised, makes it impossible for the Appellate Body to meet the ninety-day deadline in some cases. Many Members also recognised the high quality of Appellate Body reports and the importance of high-quality Appellate Body reports. However, Members disagreed on two issues, namely: (1) whether the ninety-day time-limit set out in Article 17.5 was a rigid one that must be enforced in all circumstances; and (2) what actions the Appellate Body should take when circulation of reports within the ninety-day time-limit was not possible.

The United States and Costa Rica asserted that Article 17.5 of the DSU does not allow for exceptions and must be strictly enforced. In case of inevitable delay, the Appellate Body should, according to the United States and some other Members: (1) consult with the parties to the dispute; (2) communicate the reasons for the delay to the DSB; and (3) obtain the agreement of the parties to circulate its report beyond the ninety-day time-limit.[515] Japan stressed that any departure from the ninety-day deadline set out in the DSU must be of a temporal or emergency nature and be limited to address exceptional circumstances. Japan also believed that, in the interest of legal certainty regarding the process of adoption of Appellate Body reports by the DSB, it is essential that the Appellate Body seeks the agreement of the parties that they will deem Appellate Body reports circulated beyond the ninety-day time-limit to be reports circulated within the ninety-day time-limit. Given the general principle of 'prompt settlement' set out in Article 3.3 of the DSU and the categorical nature of the ninety-day time-limit set out in Article 17.5 of the DSU, Japan stated that the ninety-day time-limit should be observed strictly. However, Japan also stated that: (1) it appreciated that the heavy workload and the complexity of appeals posed a difficult challenge to the Appellate Body; and (2) it valued the high quality of Appellate Body reports. Australia stated that the Appellate Body should consult with the parties about the likely timing of the circulation of its report whenever it will go beyond the ninety-day time-limit, and that the outcome of these consultations should be notified to the DSB. However, in contrast to the United States and some other Members, Australia did not think

---

514 Dispute Settlement Body, *Minutes of Meeting held on 23 July 2012*, WT/DSB/M/320, dated 28 September 2012, paras. 97–109.
515 The United States and Guatemala argued in this respect that the Appellate Body should return to its pre-2011 practice, under which the Appellate Body consulted with the parties and obtained their agreement whenever it had to circulate its report after the deadline provided for in the DSU.

that the Appellate Body should obtain the agreement of the parties to the dispute for going beyond the ninety-day time-limit. Brazil took the position that it is necessary to allow for some flexibility with regard to the ninety-day time-limit. Both Brazil and China emphasised that there should be no obligation on the Appellate Body either to consult with or to obtain agreement from the parties when circulation beyond the ninety-day time-limit is inevitable. According to Brazil and China, notification to the parties and to the DSB that the Appellate Body report will be circulated beyond the ninety-day time-limit is sufficient. While recognising the importance of the ninety-day time-limit, both Brazil and China recognised that, given the challenges and difficulties faced by the Appellate Body, it may be impossible for the latter to complete its work within ninety days. The European Union did not address the question of what actions the Appellate Body should take when it has to delay the circulation of a report. Rather, it trusted that the Appellate Body will deal with the issue with fairness and transparency. The European Union took note of Article 17.12 of the DSU, which mandates the Appellate Body to address 'each of the issues raised ... during the appellate proceeding', as well as Article 3.2 of the DSU, which provides that the WTO dispute settlement system is to 'preserve the rights and obligations of Members under the covered agreements'. Concretely, the European Union pointed to the situations where parties filed simultaneously more appeals than the Appellate Body is objectively able to handle and where individual appeals are voluminous or contain complex issues so that even the entire devotion of the Appellate Body's resources would be insufficient to fulfil its tasks within the ninety-day time-limit. In the view of the European Union, a high-quality Appellate Body report produced beyond the ninety-day time-limit is to be preferred over, and contributes to a rule-based system more than, a low-quality report produced within ninety days. With regard to the consequences of circulating an Appellate Body report beyond the ninety-day time-limit, a number of Members noted that the rule of reverse-consensus adoption of Appellate Body reports applied to *all* reports, regardless of whether they were circulated within or beyond the ninety-day time-limit.

Note that no other international court or tribunal operates with similarly short timeframes. These time-limits, and in particular the time-limits for appellate review, have been criticised as excessively short and demanding for both the parties to the dispute and the Appellate Body. As a result of these time-limits, however, there is no backlog of cases at either the panel or appellate level. Moreover, it is of great importance that the dispute settlement process is short and comes to a determination regarding the WTO consistency of the measure at issue quickly because, as discussed above, the WTO dispute settlement system does not provide for compensation of harm caused by the measure at issue during the time that the dispute settlement process is running.[516]

---

516 See above, p. 204.

6.1.2 Confidentiality and Transparency

The second principal feature of the WTO dispute settlement process is its confidentiality and resulting lack of transparency. The DSU provides that consultations, panel proceedings and Appellate Body proceedings shall be 'confidential'.[517] This confidentiality requirement relates to: (1) the written submissions of parties and third parties; (2) the meetings of panels with the parties and hearings of the Appellate Body; and (3) to some extent, the reports of panels. The confidentiality of the WTO dispute settlement process is considered indispensable by some Members and companies, while the lack of transparency necessarily resulting from this confidentiality has been criticised by other Members and civil society.

First, with regard to the written submissions of parties and third parties, Article 18.2 of the DSU states that 'written submissions to the panel or the Appellate Body shall be treated as confidential'.[518] Parties may only make their *own* submissions available to the public.[519] While a few Members do so in a consistent manner (see e.g. the United States and the European Union), most Members choose to keep their submissions confidential.[520] The DSU provides that a party to a dispute must, upon request of any WTO Member, provide a non-confidential summary of the information contained in its submissions that could be disclosed to the public.[521] However, this provision does not provide for a deadline by which such a non-confidential summary must be made available. In the few instances in which WTO Members requested such a summary, it was usually made available too late to be of any practical relevance.

In WTO dispute settlement, access to and/or knowledge of sensitive and confidential business information may be indispensable for parties to make their case, and for panels and the Appellate Body to decide, on the WTO consistency of the measure at issue. Recognising that parties, and more specifically the companies concerned, have a legitimate interest in protecting such information submitted to a panel, the panels in *Canada – Aircraft (1999)* and *Brazil – Aircraft (1999)* adopted special procedures governing business confidential information (BCI) that go beyond the protection afforded by Article 18.2 of the DSU.[522] Whether

---

517 See Article 4.6 of the DSU (with regard to consultations), Appendix 3 to the DSU (with regard to panel proceedings) and Article 17.10 of the DSU (with regard to Appellate Body proceedings).

518 See Articles 18.2 and 17.10, and Appendix 3, para. 3, of the DSU.

519 See in this respect also Panel Report, *Argentina – Poultry Anti-Dumping Duties (2003)*, paras. 7.13–7.16.

520 As Article 18.2, first sentence, of the DSU explicitly states, a party can of course not keep its submissions confidential from the other party or parties to the dispute. Any submission filed with, and more broadly any evidence or information given to, the panel must be shared with the other party. This also follows from Article 18.1 of the DSU, which prohibits *ex parte* communications between the panel and one of the parties. See also below, pp. 252, 278.

521 See Article 18.2 of the DSU.

522 See Panel Report, *Canada – Aircraft (1999)*, Annex 1; and Panel Report, *Brazil – Aircraft (1999)*, Annex 1. Under the Procedures Governing Business Confidential Information adopted by the panel in *Canada – Aircraft (1999)*, the BCI was to be stored in a safe in a locked room at the premises of the relevant Geneva missions, with restrictions imposed on access; and was to be returned or destroyed after completion of the panel proceedings. Note that, in spite of these procedures, Canada refused to submit certain confidential business information because the procedures did not, according to Canada, provide the requisite level of protection. On the consequences of such a refusal to submit information requested by the panel, see below, p. 278.

panels consider the adoption of special procedures for the protection of business confidential information appropriate, however, varies from case to case.[523] In *EC – Export Subsidies on Sugar (2005)*, for example, the panel rejected a request for special procedures, noting that normal DSU confidentiality rules were sufficient,[524] while in, for example, *EC and certain member States – Large Civil Aircraft (2011)*, *Philippines – Distilled Spirits (2012)* and *US – Large Civil Aircraft (2nd complaint) (2012)* the panels did adopt special procedures.[525] While panels are willing to provide additional protection of BCI, the panel in *Canada – Dairy (Article 21.5 – New Zealand and United States) (2001)* made it clear that the party requesting BCI protection must explain to the panel the nature of the information it seeks to protect and justify the insufficiency of the standard confidentiality requirements.[526] Also, the party that has concerns about the protection of business confidential information must *request* the panel to adopt special procedures to handle such information. In other words, parties cannot just invoke the business confidential nature of certain information as a 'justification' for not submitting the information without having at least requested the panel to adopt special procedures. In *Korea – Certain Paper (2005)*, a dispute concerning anti-dumping duties on paper from Indonesia, Korea had requested that representatives of the Indonesian paper industry who were part of the Indonesian delegation leave the room as business confidential information would be discussed. Moreover, Korea wanted to withdraw its written submissions and provide non-confidential versions to Indonesia. In response, the panel ruled with regard to the presence of the representatives of the Indonesian paper industry that Indonesia was entitled to determine the composition of its delegation in the proceedings, and that it was responsible for all members of its delegation.[527] With regard to Korea's proposal to withdraw its existing submissions and submit non-confidential versions of those submissions to Indonesia, the panel in *Korea – Certain Paper (2005)* ruled as follows:

[C]onsidering the fact that Article 18.1 of the DSU precludes *ex parte* communications between the Panel and a party, we stated that while we would entertain any request by Korea to withdraw its submissions or to redact from them certain information, in such a case the submissions withdrawn or information redacted would no longer be before the Panel.[528]

In *Turkey – Rice (2007)*, Turkish officials informed the panel that they '[did] not feel comfortable in risking information leaks and possible criminal accusations

---

523 For a list of panel proceedings in which parties requested BCI protection and the action taken by the panel (up to 30 September 2011), see *WTO Analytical Index (2012)*, Volume II, 1763–4.
524 See Panel Report, *EC – Export Subsidies on Sugar (2005)*, para. 2.17.
525 See Panel Report, *EC and certain member States – Large Civil Aircraft (2011)*, Annex E; Panel Reports, *Philippines – Distilled Spirits (2012)*, Annex G-4; and Panel Report, *US – Large Civil Aircraft (2nd complaint) (2012)*, Annex D.
526 See Panel Report, *Canada – Dairy (Article 21.5 – New Zealand and United States) (2001)*, paras. 2.20–2.21.
527 See Panel Report, *Korea – Certain Paper (2005)*, para. 7.11.
528 Panel Report, *Korea – Certain Paper (2005)*, para. 7.17.

of violation of Turkish law on confidentiality'.[529] The panel noted, however, that Turkey did not request the adoption of special procedures for handling confidential information during the panel proceedings, even though the complainant, the United States, suggested this possibility.[530]

With regard to the confidentiality of Appellate Body proceedings, the Appellate Body ruled in *Canada – Aircraft (1999)*, after carefully considering all the requirements already provided for in the DSU to protect the confidentiality of Appellate Body proceedings, that:

we do not consider that it is necessary, under all the circumstances of this case, to adopt *additional* procedures for the protection of business confidential information in these appellate proceedings. [531]

The Appellate Body considered the protection offered by the confidentiality requirements of Articles 17.10 and 18.2 of the DSU more than sufficient. However, a decade later, in *EC and certain member States – Large Civil Aircraft (2011)*, the Appellate Body took a different approach and provided for detailed additional procedures for the protection of business confidential information (BCI) and highly sensitive business information (HSBI). For a full exposition of these detailed additional procedures, refer to the Appellate Body's Procedural Ruling and Additional Procedures to Protect Sensitive Information of 10 August 2010.[532] By way of example, note that, to protect HSBI, the additional procedures required that:

[a]ll HSBI shall be stored in a combination safe in a designated secure location on the premises of the Appellate Body Secretariat. Any computer in that room shall be a stand-alone computer, that is, not connected to a network. Appellate Body Members and assigned Appellate Body Secretariat staff may view HSBI only in the designated secure location referred to above. HSBI shall not be removed from this location, except as provided in paragraph (x) or in the form of handwritten notes that may be used only on the Appellate Body Secretariat's premises and shall be destroyed once no longer in use.[533]

Secondly, with regard to the confidentiality of panel meetings and Appellate Body hearings, paragraph 2 of Appendix 3 of the DSU provides that the meetings of the panel with the parties 'take place behind closed doors'; and Article 17.10 of the DSU states that the proceedings of the Appellate Body, and thus also the Appellate Body hearings, are 'confidential'. As a rule, nobody, except the parties themselves and the officials of the WTO Secretariat assisting the panel, is allowed to attend all meetings of the panel with the parties. Third parties are usually invited to attend only one session of the

529 Panel Report, *Turkey – Rice (2007)*, para. 7.92.
530 See *ibid.*, para. 7.103.
531 Appellate Body Report, *Canada – Aircraft (1999)*, para. 147. See also Appellate Body Report, *Brazil – Aircraft (1999)*, para. 125.
532 See Appellate Body Report, *EC and certain member States – Large Civil Aircraft (2011)*, Annex III.
533 See *ibid.*, para. 28(ix).

first substantive panel meeting.[534] The 2004 Sutherland Report noted in this respect that:

the degree of confidentiality of the current dispute settlement proceedings can be seen as damaging to the WTO as an institution.[535]

The Report therefore recommended that, as a matter of course, the panel meetings and Appellate Body hearings should generally be open to the public.[536] Certain WTO Members share this view, as evidenced by the opening of panel meetings and Appellate Body hearings to public observation in disputes in which those Members were parties. At the request of the parties, the panel in *US/Canada – Continued Suspension (2008)*, complaint by the European Communities, authorised in September and October 2006 the real time closed-circuit television broadcast of its meetings with experts and the parties to a separate viewing room at WTO Headquarters in Geneva.[537] In July 2007, the panel in *EC and certain member States – Large Civil Aircraft (2011)* was more cautious (because of concerns regarding the protection of BCI) and merely allowed its second meeting with the parties to be video-taped and broadcast in an edited version two days later in Geneva.[538] In November 2007, the panel in *EC – Bananas III (Article 21.5 – US) (2008)* decided to allow the delegates of WTO Members and members of the general public to observe the panel's meeting with the parties from the public gallery above the meeting room. As only a limited number of places was available, prior registration with either party in this dispute, the United States or the European Communities, was required to secure a seat.[539] Note that, in *Brazil – Retreaded Tyres (2007)*, the Centre for International Environmental Law (CIEL) requested the panel to allow the webcasting of the first meeting of the panel with the parties. After consultations with the parties, Brazil and the European Communities, and in light of the views expressed by them, the panel informed CIEL that its meetings with the parties would be held in closed sessions in accordance with the working procedures adopted by the panel at the beginning of the proceedings.[540] The legal basis for the panel to allow public observation of its meetings is to be found in Article 12.1 of the DSU. As discussed below, Article 12.1 provides that panels shall follow the *Working Procedures*

534 See below, pp. 280, 289.
535 Report by the Consultative Board to the Director-General Supachai Panitchpakdi, *The Future of the WTO: Addressing Institutional Challenges in the New Millennium* (the 'Sutherland Report') (WTO, 2004), para. 261 (emphasis omitted).
536 See *ibid.*, para. 262.
537 The 200 places reserved for the public were allocated on a first-come-first-served basis upon receipt of the completed application form. However, despite the frequent calls by civil society for increased transparency of dispute settlement proceedings, few attended the meetings of the panel. See Communication from the Chair of the Panels, *US/Canada – Continued Suspension*, WT/DS320/8, WT/DS321/8, dated 2 August 2005.
538 The delayed broadcasting allowed the parties and the panel to verify that no business confidential information would be inadvertently disclosed in showing the videotape. See also e.g. in *US – Large Civil Aircraft (2nd complaint) (2012)*.
539 See Panel Report, *EC – Bananas III (Article 21.5 – US) (2008)*, para. 1.11.
540 See Panel Report, *Brazil – Retreaded Tyres (2007)*, para. 1.9.

in Appendix 3 unless the panel decides otherwise after consulting the parties to the dispute. Paragraph 2 of the *Working Procedures* in Appendix 3 provides that: 'The panel shall meet in closed session.' Pursuant to Article 12.1, however, panels can – after consulting the parties – deviate from this rule and open up the panel meetings to the public.

The legal basis for allowing public observation of Appellate Body hearings was less obvious. The question whether the Appellate Body could allow public observation of its hearings first arose in *US/Canada – Continued Suspension (2008)*, when all participants (the European Communities, the United States and Canada) requested the Appellate Body to allow public observation of the hearing in this case.[541] However, some of the third participants in this case, namely, Brazil, China, India and Mexico, strongly objected to the request to allow public observation.[542] They pointed out that Article 17.10 of the DSU explicitly states that:

[t]he proceedings of the Appellate Body shall be confidential.

According to these third participants, the confidentiality requirement in Article 17.10 is absolute and permits no derogation. The Appellate Body disagreed. According to the Appellate Body, Article 17.10 must be read in context, particularly in relation to Article 18.2 of the DSU. The second sentence of Article 18.2 expressly provides that '[n]othing in this Understanding shall preclude a party to a dispute from disclosing statements of its own positions to the public'. Thus, under Article 18.2, second sentence, the parties may decide to forego confidentiality protection in respect of their statements of position.[543] The Appellate Body observed that notices of appeal as well as Appellate Body reports are disclosed to the public, and that the latter contain summaries of the participants' and third participants' written and oral submissions and frequently quote directly from them. Clearly, in practice, the confidentiality requirement in Article 17.10 has its limits; confidentiality under the DSU is 'relative and time-bound'.[544] The Appellate Body noted that there are different sets of relationships that are implicated in Appellate Body proceedings, namely: (1) a relationship between the participants and the Appellate Body; and (2) a relationship between the third participants and the Appellate Body.[545] According to the Appellate Body:

The requirement that the proceedings of the Appellate Body are confidential affords protection to these separate relationships and is intended to safeguard the interests of the participants and third participants and the adjudicative function of the Appellate Body, so as to foster the system of dispute settlement under conditions of fairness, impartiality,

---

541 See Appellate Body Report, *US/Canada – Continued Suspension (2008)*, Annex IV, para. 1. Annex IV contains the Procedural Ruling of 10 July 2008 to allow public observation of the oral hearing.

542 *Ibid.*, para. 1. Note that other third participants, namely, Australia, Chinese Taipei, New Zealand and Norway, supported the request to allow public observation of the Appellate Body oral hearing. See *ibid.*

543 See *ibid.*, para. 4. The Appellate Body further referred to Article 18.2, third and fourth sentences, for contextual support for the view that the confidentiality rule in Article 17.10 is not absolute. See *ibid.*

544 See *ibid.*, para. 5.   545 See *ibid.*, para. 6.

independence and integrity. In this case, the participants have jointly requested authorization to forego confidentiality protection for their communications with the Appellate Body at the oral hearing. The request of the participants does not extend to any communications, nor touches upon the relationship, between the third participants and the Appellate Body. The right to confidentiality of third participants *vis-à-vis* the Appellate Body is not implicated by the joint request. The question is thus whether the request of the participants to forego confidentiality protection satisfies the requirements of fairness and integrity that are the essential attributes of the appellate process and define the relationship between the Appellate Body and the participants. If the request meets these standards, then the Appellate Body would incline towards authorizing such a joint request.[546]

The Appellate Body subsequently noted that the DSU does not specifically provide for an oral hearing at the appellate stage. The oral hearing was instituted by the Appellate Body in its *Working Procedures*, which were drawn up pursuant to Article 17.9 of the DSU, and the conduct and organisation of the oral hearing 'falls within the authority of the Appellate Body (*compétence de la compétence*) pursuant to Rule 27 of the *Working Procedures*'.[547] The Appellate Body thus concluded that it holds:

the power to exercise control over the conduct of the oral hearing, including authorizing the lifting of confidentiality at the joint request of the participants as long as this does not adversely affect the rights and interests of the third participants or the integrity of the appellate process.[548]

The Appellate Body authorised public observation of its oral hearing in *US/ Canada – Continued Suspension (2008)* by means of real time closed-circuit television broadcast to a separate viewing room at WTO Headquarters in Geneva.[549] To safeguard the rights of confidentiality of the third participants, which did not agree to public observation, the transmission was turned off during statements made by those third participants. To date, the Appellate Body has allowed public observation of its hearings either through real time or delayed closed-circuit television broadcast to a separate viewing room in all cases in which the participants requested public observation to be allowed.[550] Note that, in *US – COOL (2012)*, the Appellate Body allowed public observation of its hearing at the request of two of the three participants in this case, namely, the European Union and the United States, and the fact that the other participant, Mexico, did not object to public

---

546 *Ibid.*, para. 6.   547 *Ibid.*, para. 7.

548 *Ibid.* The Appellate Body emphasised that authorising the participants' request to forego confidentiality did not affect the rights of third participants to preserve the confidentiality of their communications with the Appellate Body. See *ibid.*

549 See *ibid.*, para. 11.

550 This was the case in *US/Canada – Continued Suspension (2008)*; *EC – Bananas III (Article 21.5 – Ecuador II and US)*; *US – Continued Zeroing (2009)*; *US – Zeroing (Article 21.5 – EC) (2009)*; *US – Zeroing (Article 21.5 – Japan) (2009)*; *Australia – Apples (2010)*; *EC and certain member States – Large Civil Aircraft (2011)*; *US – Large Civil Aircraft (2nd complaint) (2012)*; *US – COOL (2012)*; and *Canada – Renewable Energy (2013)*. In cases involving BCI, the broadcast was delayed. See e.g. *EC and certain member States – Large Civil Aircraft (2011)*.

observation in the case at hand. Mexico did, however, maintain its objection in principle to opening up the hearings of the Appellate Body to the public.

Thirdly, with regard to the confidentiality of panel reports, note that the interim report of the panel and the final panel report, as long as it has merely been issued to the parties to the dispute, are confidential.[551] The final panel report only becomes a public document when it is circulated to all WTO Members. In reality, however, the interim report, and even more so the final report issued to the parties, are frequently 'leaked' to the media.[552] In *US – Gambling (2005)*, the panel regretted the breach of the duty of confidentiality by the parties, and stated that 'disregard for the confidentiality requirement contained in the DSU affects the credibility and integrity of the WTO dispute settlement process, of the WTO and of WTO Members and is, therefore, unacceptable'.[553] Note that there is no interim review of Appellate Body reports, and that Appellate Body reports are issued to the parties and circulated to all WTO Members at the same time and are as of that moment a public document.[554] Unlike for panel reports, the problem of 'leaking' Appellate Body reports does therefore not present itself.

6.1.3 Burden of Proof

The DSU does not contain any specific rules concerning the burden of proof in WTO dispute settlement proceedings. However, in *US – Wool Shirts and Blouses (1997)*, the Appellate Body noted:

[W]e find it difficult, indeed, to see how any system of judicial settlement could work if it incorporated the proposition that the mere assertion of a claim might amount to proof. It is, thus, hardly surprising that various international tribunals, including the International Court of Justice, have generally and consistently accepted and applied the rule that the party who asserts a fact, whether the claimant or the respondent, is responsible for providing proof thereof. Also, it is a generally accepted canon of evidence in civil law, common law and, in fact, most jurisdictions, that the burden of proof rests upon the party, whether

---

551 On interim review and the interim report, and the issuance of panel reports to the parties, see below, pp. 281–2.

552 An infamous example of leaked interim panel reports were the reports in *EC – Approval and Marketing of Biotech Products (2006)*. The panel in that case expressed its grave concern about the effect of such breaches on the integrity of the WTO dispute settlement system. It referred specifically to the adverse effect this may have on the willingness of private parties to make available business confidential information that may be crucial to the resolution of a dispute, and to the possibility that, as a result of the public discussion of the interim findings, the panel or Secretariat may be exposed to political pressure. See Panel Reports, *EC – Approval and Marketing of Biotech Products (2006)*, paras. 6.183–6.196. Interestingly, the panel took the unprecedented step of explaining some of its findings in a letter to the parties, as it was concerned that certain aspects of the leaked findings had 'inadvertently or on purpose' been misconstrued in the civil society discussion of the interim reports. This letter is appended to the panel reports as Annex K. The panel reports state, however, that the letter 'is not part of the Panel's findings and is not intended to modify them in any way'. See Panel Reports, *EC – Approval and Marketing of Biotech Products (2006)*, para. 6.3, footnote 170.

553 Panel Report, *US – Gambling (2005)*, paras. 5.3–5.13. Note that further concerns were put forward by the panel in *US – Gambling (Article 21.5 – Antigua and Barbuda) (2007)*, where, according to the panel, the United States seemed to imply that the leak would have taken place in Geneva, as a breach of confidentiality by the panel or the WTO Secretariat, assertions that the panel rejected 'forcefully'. See Panel Report, *US – Gambling (Article 21.5 – Antigua and Barbuda) (2007)*, paras. 5.2–5.10.

554 See below, pp. 282–3.

complaining or defending, who asserts the affirmative of a particular claim or defence. If that party adduces evidence sufficient to raise a presumption that what is claimed is true, the burden then shifts to the other party, who will fail unless it adduces sufficient evidence to rebut the presumption.[555]

The burden of proof in WTO dispute settlement proceedings is thus on the party, the complainant *or* the respondent, that asserts the affirmative of a particular claim or defence.[556] The burden of proof shifts to the other party when sufficient evidence is adduced to raise a presumption that what is claimed is true. Precisely how much and precisely what kind of evidence is required to establish such a presumption 'will necessarily vary from measure to measure, provision to provision, and case to case'.[557]

In *EC – Hormones (1998)*, the Appellate Body further clarified the burden of proof in WTO dispute settlement proceedings, and stated with respect to disputes under the *SPS Agreement*:

The initial burden lies on the complaining party, which must establish a *prima facie* case of inconsistency with a particular provision of the *SPS Agreement* on the part of the defending party, or more precisely, of its SPS measure or measures complained about. When that *prima facie* case is made, the burden of proof moves to the defending party, which must in turn counter or refute the claimed inconsistency.

... It is also well to remember that a *prima facie* case is one which, in the absence of effective refutation by the defending party, requires a panel, as a matter of law, to rule in favour of the complaining party presenting the *prima facie* case.[558]

With regard to the concept of a '*prima facie* case', the Appellate Body further stated in *US – Gambling (2005)*:

A *prima facie* case must be based on 'evidence *and* legal argument' put forward by the complaining party in relation to each of the elements of the claim. A complaining party may not simply submit evidence and expect the panel to divine from it a claim of WTO-inconsistency. Nor may a complaining party simply allege facts without relating them to its legal arguments.

... The evidence and arguments underlying a *prima facie* case, therefore, must be sufficient to identify the challenged measure and its basic import, identify the relevant WTO provision and obligation contained therein, and explain the basis for the claimed inconsistency of the measure with that provision.[559]

The above should not be understood as imposing a requirement on panels to make an explicit ruling on whether the complainant has established a *prima*

555 Appellate Body Report, *US – Wool Shirts and Blouses (1997)*, 335. Note that, in *Japan – Apples (2003)*, the Appellate Body stated: 'It is important to distinguish, on the one hand, the principle that the complainant must establish a *prima facie* case of inconsistency with a provision of a covered agreement from, on the other hand, the principle that the party that asserts a fact is responsible for providing proof thereof. In fact, the two principles are distinct.' See Appellate Body Report, *Japan – Apples (2003)*, para. 157.
556 This basic rule on burden of proof identified by the Appellate Body in *US – Wool Shirts and Blouses (1997)* has since been consistently applied by panels, the Appellate Body and arbitrators.
557 Appellate Body Report, *US – Wool Shirts and Blouses (1997)*, 335.
558 Appellate Body Report, *EC – Hormones (1998)*, paras. 98 and 104.
559 Appellate Body Report, *US – Gambling (2005)*, paras. 140–1. See also e.g. Appellate Body Report, *Canada – Wheat Exports and Grain Imports (2004)*, para. 191.

facie case of violation *before* they may proceed to examine the respondent's defence and evidence.[560] The jurisprudence of the Appellate Body regarding the rules on burden of proof is well summarised by the panel in *US – Section 301 Trade Act (2000)*, where it is stated:

> In accordance with this jurisprudence, both parties agreed that it is for the EC, as the complaining party, to present arguments and evidence sufficient to establish a *prima facie* case in respect of the various elements of its claims regarding the inconsistency of Sections 301–310 with US obligations under the WTO. Once the EC has done so, it is for the US to rebut that *prima facie* case. Since, in this case, both parties have submitted extensive facts and arguments in respect of the EC claims, our task will essentially be to balance all evidence on record and decide whether the EC, as party bearing the original burden of proof, has convinced us of the validity of its claims. In case of uncertainty, i.e. in case all the evidence and arguments remain in equipoise, we have to give the benefit of the doubt to the US as defending party.[561]

As stated by the panel in *US – Section 301 Trade Act (2000)*, the task of a panel is essentially to *balance all evidence* on record and decide whether the party bearing the original, i.e. the ultimate, burden of proof has convinced it of the validity of its claims. Moreover, the panel in the same case made an important observation on the relevance of the rules on burden of proof with respect to issues of fact as opposed to issues of legal interpretation. The panel noted that:

> the party that alleges a specific fact – be it the EC or the US – has the burden to prove it. In other words, it has to establish a *prima facie* case that the fact exists. Following the principles set out in the previous paragraph, this *prima facie* case will stand unless sufficiently rebutted by the other party.
>
> The factual findings in this Report were reached [by] applying these principles. Of course, when it comes to deciding on the correct interpretation of the covered agreements a panel will be aided by the arguments of the parties but not bound by them; its decisions on such matters must be in accord with the rules of treaty interpretation applicable to the WTO.[562]

With regard to the burden of establishing the correct legal interpretation of provisions of the covered agreements, the Appellate Body further clarified in *EC – Tariff Preferences (2004)*:

> Consistent with the principle of *jura novit curia*, it is not the responsibility of the European Communities to provide us with the legal interpretation to be given to a particular provision in the Enabling Clause; instead, the burden of the European Communities is to adduce sufficient evidence to substantiate its assertion that the Drug Arrangements comply with the requirements of the Enabling Clause.[563]

560 See Appellate Body Report, *Korea – Dairy (2000)*, para. 145. See also e.g. Appellate Body Report, *Thailand – H-Beams (2001)*, para. 134.
561 Panel Report, *US – Section 301 Trade Act (2000)*, para. 7.14.
562 *Ibid.*, paras. 7.15 and 7.16.
563 Appellate Body Report, *EC – Tariff Preferences (2004)*, para. 105. In a footnote, the Appellate Body added that the principle of *jura novit curia* was articulated by the International Court of Justice as follows: 'it being the duty of the Court itself to ascertain and apply the relevant law in the given circumstances of the case, the burden of establishing or proving rules of international law cannot be imposed upon any of the parties, for the law lies within the judicial knowledge of the Court.' See International Court of Justice, Merits, *Case Concerning Military and Paramilitary Activities in and against Nicaragua (Nicaragua* v. *United States of America)*, 1986 ICJ Reports, 14, para. 29.

Thus, the burden of establishing what the applicable rule of WTO law is, and how that rule must be interpreted, is not on the parties but on the panel and the Appellate Body. In *India – Quantitative Restrictions (1999)*, the Appellate Body considered that:

> the invocation of the proviso to Article XVIII:11 does not give rise to a burden of proof issue insofar as it relates to the interpretation of what policies may constitute a 'development policy' within the meaning of the proviso.[564]

As discussed above, the basic rule is that the burden of proof rests on the party, the complainant *or* the respondent, that asserts the affirmative of a particular claim or defence.[565] It follows that, when a respondent invokes an exception provision as an affirmative defence, the burden of proof is on the respondent. Note, however, that, in *EC – Tariff Preferences (2004)*, the Appellate Body imposed on the complainant a legal responsibility 'to raise a defence' as an issue in a dispute. With regard to the Enabling Clause,[566] and in view of the specific characteristics and the special nature of the Enabling Clause, the Appellate Body ruled that:

> although a responding party must defend the consistency of its preference scheme with the conditions of the Enabling Clause and must prove such consistency, a *complaining* party has to define the parameters within which the *responding* party must make that defence.[567]

The Appellate Body thus concluded that it is the responsibility of the complaining party to identify those provisions of the Enabling Clause with which the scheme is allegedly inconsistent. The Appellate Body emphasised, however, that the responsibility of the complaining party in such an instance should not be overstated. The Appellate Body noted that the responsibility of the complaining party:

> is merely to *identify* those provisions of the Enabling Clause with which the scheme is allegedly inconsistent, without bearing the burden *of establishing* the facts necessary to support such inconsistency.[568]

The latter burden remains on the responding party invoking the Enabling Clause as a defence.

With regard to the kind of evidence a complainant must produce, the Appellate Body found in *US – Carbon Steel (2002)* as follows:

---

564 Appellate Body Report, *India – Quantitative Restrictions (1999)*, para. 136.
565 See above, pp. 257–68.
566 On the Enabling Clause of the GATT 1994, see below, pp. 330–4, 663–4, 670.
567 Appellate Body Report, *EC – Tariff Preferences (2004)*, para. 114. The Appellate Body considered that: '[A] complaining party challenging a measure taken pursuant to the Enabling Clause must allege more than mere inconsistency with Article I:1 of the GATT 1994, for to do only that would not convey the "legal basis of the complaint sufficient to present the problem clearly".' This is because every measure undertaken pursuant to the Enabling Clause would necessarily be inconsistent with Article I, if assessed on that basis alone, but it would be exempted from compliance with Article I because it meets the requirements of the Enabling Clause. See Appellate Body Report, *EC – Tariff Preferences (2004)*, para. 110.
568 *Ibid.*, para. 115.

[A] responding Member's law will be treated as WTO-consistent until proven otherwise. The party asserting that another party's municipal law, as such, is inconsistent with relevant treaty obligations bears the burden of introducing evidence as to the scope and meaning of such law to substantiate that assertion. Such evidence will typically be produced in the form of the text of the relevant legislation or legal instruments, which may be supported, as appropriate, by evidence of the consistent application of such laws, the pronouncements of domestic courts on the meaning of such laws, the opinions of legal experts and the writings of recognized scholars. The nature and extent of the evidence required to satisfy the burden of proof will vary from case to case.[569]

Finally, note that the panel in *EC – Approval and Marketing of Biotech Products (2006)* addressed the question of when a provision should be characterised as an *exception* to another provision, and when it should instead be characterised as a *right creating an exemption* from the scope of application of another provision.[570] Referring to the findings of the Appellate Body in *EC – Tariff Preferences (2004)*,[571] the panel in *EC – Approval and Marketing of Biotech Products (2006)* found that a provision can be characterised as a right (rather than as an exception) in relation to another provision if the relationship between them is one:

where one provision permits, in certain circumstances, behaviour that would otherwise be inconsistent with an obligation in another provision, [where] one of the two provisions refers to the other provision, [and] where one of the provisions suggests that the obligation is not applicable to the said measure.[572]

Otherwise, the permissive provision is characterised as an exception or defence. The panel in *EC – Approval and Marketing of Biotech Products (2006)* subsequently addressed the implications for the burden of proof regarding a provision embodying a right rather than an exception. According to the panel, in cases where the complainant claims a violation of a provision embodying a *right creating an exemption* from the scope of application of another provision, it is incumbent on the complainant, and not the respondent, to prove that the challenged measure is also inconsistent with at least one of the requirements of the provision creating the exemption. As the panel stated:

If such non-compliance is demonstrated, then, and only then, does the relevant obligation … apply to the challenged … measure.[573]

The relationship between the rules on burden of proof and the authority of panels to seek expert advice is examined above.[574]

6.1.4 Role of Private Legal Counsel

The DSU does not explicitly address the issue of representation of the parties before panels or the Appellate Body. In *EC – Bananas III (1997)*, the issue arose

569 Appellate Body Report, *US – Carbon Steel (2002)*, para. 157.
570 See Panel Reports, *EC – Approval and Marketing of Biotech Products (2006)*, para. 7.2985.
571 See Appellate Body Report, *EC – Tariff Preferences (2004)*, para. 88.
572 Panel Reports, *EC – Approval and Marketing of Biotech Products (2006)*, para. 7.2985.
573 *Ibid.*, para. 7.2976.   574 See above, p. 227.

whether private legal counsel, i.e. legal counsel not in government employ, may represent a party or third party in WTO dispute settlement proceedings. The United States objected to the presence at the panel meeting of a private legal counsel acting on behalf of a third party to the case, Saint Lucia, a tiny Caribbean banana-producing island State with a very significant interest in the outcome of the case. The panel ruled, in line with the established practice in GATT dispute settlement, that only government officials could represent parties and third parties. However, when this issue arose again in the Appellate Body proceedings in this case, the Appellate Body took a very different approach from the panel. The Appellate Body noted that nothing in the *WTO Agreement* or the DSU, or in customary international law or the prevailing practice of international tribunals, prevents a WTO Member from determining the composition of its own delegation in WTO dispute settlement proceedings.[575] The Appellate Body thus ruled that a party can decide that private legal counsel forms part of its delegation and will represent it in Appellate Body proceedings. As a result, the Appellate Body allowed Saint Lucia to be represented by private legal counsel. The Appellate Body noted in its ruling:

that representation by counsel of a government's own choice may well be a matter of particular significance – especially for developing-country Members – to enable them to participate fully in dispute settlement proceedings.[576]

While the ruling of the Appellate Body concerned the proceedings before this body, the reasoning of this ruling is equally relevant for panel proceedings. This was confirmed in the panel report in *Indonesia – Autos (1998)*, adopted one year after the Appellate Body report in *EC – Bananas III (1997)*. The panel in *Indonesia – Autos (1998)* rejected the request of the United States to exclude Indonesia's private legal counsel from the panel meetings, stating:

[I]t is for the Government of Indonesia to nominate the members of its delegation to meetings of this Panel, and we find no provision in the WTO Agreement or the DSU, including the standard rules of procedure included therein, which prevents a WTO Member from determining the composition of its delegation to WTO panel meetings.[577]

At present, private legal counsel is involved in almost all panel and Appellate Body proceedings, and acts on behalf of WTO Members in these proceedings.[578] A question which arises as a result of this involvement is which, if any, rules of conduct apply to private legal counsel active in WTO dispute settlement. In *EC – Tariff Preferences (2004)*, the European Communities objected to the 'joint representation' by the Advisory Centre on WTO Law (ACWL) of both India, the complainant, and Paraguay, a third party.[579] The panel was thus confronted with

---

575 See Appellate Body Report, *EC – Bananas III (1997)*, para. 10.
576 Appellate Body Report, *EC – Bananas III (1997)*, para. 12.
577 Panel Report, *Indonesia – Autos*, para. 14.1.
578 Note that private legal counsel is usually also already involved in the consultations.
579 On the ACWL, see below, pp. 301–2.

the question of whether the same legal counsel could represent simultaneously a complaining party and a third party.[580] In response to this question, the panel first noted that:

the WTO has not itself elaborated any rules governing the ethical conduct of legal counsel representing WTO Members in particular disputes.[581]

The panel subsequently noted, however, that:

[a]s a general matter ... it is the responsibility of legal counsel to ensure that it is not placing itself in a position of actual or potential conflict of interest when agreeing to represent, and thereafter representing, one or more WTO Members in a dispute under the DSU.[582]

As the panel observed, bar associations in many jurisdictions have elaborated rules of conduct dealing explicitly with conflicts of interest through joint representation.[583] As India and Paraguay had been fully informed about their joint representation by the ACWL and had given their written consent to such representation, the panel did not see any problem with the joint representation in this case. However, it is useful to make two observations of a more general nature with regard to the rules of conduct applicable to private legal counsel. First, the Member, for which private legal counsel acts, is responsible for the compliance by counsel with the relevant rules of the DSU (such as the confidentiality requirement), as counsel is part of the delegation of that Member.[584] Secondly, while private legal counsel will usually be subject to the rules of conduct of his or her bar association or professional organisation, it may be argued that there is need for specific rules of conduct for private legal counsel acting in WTO dispute settlement proceedings.

6.1.5   Amicus Curiae Briefs

As discussed above, the WTO dispute settlement system is a government-to-government dispute settlement system for disputes concerning the rights and obligations of WTO Members. Individuals, companies, industry associations, labour unions, international organisations and NGOs have no direct access to the WTO dispute settlement system.[585] They cannot bring claims of violation of WTO rights or obligations. Moreover, under the current rules, they do not have the *right* to be heard in the proceedings. However, under Appellate Body case law, panels and the Appellate Body have the authority to accept and consider written briefs submitted by individuals, companies or organisations.[586] The acceptance

---

580 See Panel Report, *EC – Tariff Preferences (2004)*, para. 7.3.
581 *Ibid.*, para. 7.5.   582 *Ibid.*, para. 7.9.   583 See *ibid.*, para. 7.10.
584 See, in this respect, Appellate Body Report, *Thailand – H-Beams (2001)*, paras. 62–78. In this case, Hogan & Hartson LLP withdrew as Poland's legal counsel after Thailand's appellant submission had been 'leaked' and the Appellate Body had instituted an investigation into this breach of the confidentiality of the Appellate Body proceedings.
585 On 'indirect' access to the WTO dispute settlement system, see above, pp. 128–9, 177–8.
586 Note that panels and the Appellate Body also have the authority to accept and consider briefs submitted by Members which are not parties or third parties. See above, pp. 163–7.

by panels and the Appellate Body of these briefs, which are commonly referred to as *amicus curiae* briefs ('friend of the court' briefs), has been controversial and criticised by most WTO Members.

With respect to the authority of *panels* to accept and consider *amicus curiae* briefs, the Appellate Body noted in *US – Shrimp (1998)*, first, the *comprehensive* nature of the authority of a panel – under Article 13 of the DSU – to 'seek' information and technical advice from 'any individual or body' it may consider appropriate, or from 'any relevant source'.[587] Secondly, the Appellate Body considered it also pertinent to note that Article 12 of the DSU authorises panels to develop their own working procedures, which should provide *sufficient flexibility* so as to *ensure high-quality panel reports* while *not unduly delaying the panel process*.[588] The Appellate Body found that:

[t]he thrust of Articles 12 and 13, taken together, is that the DSU accords to a panel ... ample and extensive authority to undertake and to control the process by which it informs itself both of the relevant facts of the dispute and of the legal norms and principles applicable to such facts.[589]

According to the Appellate Body, that 'authority, and the breadth thereof, is indispensably necessary' to enable a panel to make an objective assessment of the matter before it, as it is required to do pursuant to Article 11 of the DSU.[590] On the basis of Articles 11, 12 and 13 of the DSU, the Appellate Body thus came to the conclusion in *US – Shrimp (1998)* that panels have the authority to accept and consider *amicus curiae* briefs. To date, a few panels did, on the basis of this ruling of the Appellate Body, accept and consider *amicus curiae* briefs.[591] This was the case, for example, in *US – Tuna II (Mexico) (2012)*. The panel in this case considered the information contained in the *amicus curiae* brief submitted by Humane Society International and American University's Washington College of Law.[592] The panel noted that where it considered the information in the *amicus curiae* submission relevant, it 'sought the views of the parties in accordance with the requirements of due process'.[593] The panel added that it deemed it appropriate to refer to this information in its findings to the extent that one of the parties had cited or referred to the brief during the panel proceedings.[594] In many other disputes, however, panels refused to accept or consider *amicus curiae* briefs submitted to them.[595]

---

587 See Appellate Body Report, *US – Shrimp (1998)*, para. 104. On Article 13 of the DSU, see (above) 225–7, (below) 278.
588 See *ibid.*, para. 105. On Article 12 of the DSU, see below, p. 275.
589 *Ibid.*, para. 106.
590 See *ibid.* On Article 11 of the DSU, see above, pp. 219–22.
591 For a list of *amicus curiae* briefs *received* by panels up to 30 September 2011, see *WTO Analytical Index (2012)*, Volume II, 1712–3.
592 See Panel Report, *US – Tuna II (Mexico) (2012)*, para. 7.9.
593 *Ibid.*   594 See *ibid.*
595 See, e.g. Panel Report, *EC – Bed Linen (2001)*, para. 6.1, footnote 10; Panel Reports, *EC – Export Subsidies on Sugar (2005)*, paras. 2.20 and 7.76–7.85; Panel Reports, *EC – Approval and Marketing of Biotech Products (2006)*, paras. 7.10–7.11; and Panel Report, *US – Zeroing (EC) (2006)*, para. 1.7.

With respect to the authority of the Appellate Body to accept and consider *amicus curiae* briefs submitted in Appellate Body proceedings, the Appellate Body noted in *US – Lead and Bismuth II (2000)* that, pursuant to Article 17.9 of the DSU and Rule 16(1) of the *Working Procedures for Appellate Review*, it has broad authority to adopt procedural rules which do not conflict with any rules and procedures in the DSU or the covered agreements.[596] On that basis, the Appellate Body concluded that

> as long as we act consistently with the provisions of the DSU and the covered agreements, we have the legal authority to decide whether or not to accept and consider any information that we believe is pertinent and useful in an appeal.[597]

In *US – Lead and Bismuth II (2000)*, the Appellate Body did not find it necessary to take the two *amicus curiae* briefs filed into account in rendering its decision.[598]

In October 2000, the Appellate Body division hearing the appeal in *EC – Asbestos (2001)* adopted an Additional Procedure to deal with *amicus curiae* briefs which the division expected to receive in great numbers in that dispute.[599] This Additional Procedure set out substantive and procedural requirements to be met by any person or entity, other than a party or a third party to this dispute, wishing to file a written brief with the Appellate Body. The Additional Procedure provided, for example, for a requirement to apply for leave to file, and for a maximum page limit (twenty) on the *amicus curiae* briefs that would be allowed to be filed. In the *EC – Asbestos (2001)* appeal, the Appellate Body received eleven applications for leave to file an *amicus curiae* brief, but decided to deny all applications for failure to comply sufficiently with the substantive requirements for filing an *amicus curiae* brief. While, in the end, the Appellate Body did not allow any *amicus curiae* brief to be filed, many WTO Members were infuriated by the Appellate Body's adoption of the Additional Procedure and its apparent willingness to accept and consider *amicus curiae* briefs where certain requirements are fulfilled. On 20 November 2000, a special meeting of the General Council was convened to discuss this issue. The discussion at this meeting reflected the deep division between the vast majority of WTO Members opposing the Appellate Body's case law on this issue and the United States, which fully supported this case law. At the end of this tumultuous meeting, the Chair of the General Council concluded that he believed that there had been a large sentiment, expressed by almost all delegations, that there was a need to put

---

596 Appellate Body Report, *US – Lead and Bismuth II (2000)*, para. 39.

597 *Ibid.* Note that the Appellate Body indicated in *EC – Sardines (2002)* that it would refuse to accept and consider *amicus curiae* briefs if this would interfere with the 'fair, prompt and effective resolution of trade disputes'. This could arise, for example, if an *amicus curiae* brief were to be submitted at a very late stage in the appellate proceedings, with the result that accepting the brief would impose an undue burden on other participants. See Appellate Body Report, *EC – Sardines (2002)*, para. 167.

598 See Appellate Body Report, *US – Lead and Bismuth II (2000)*, para. 42.

599 See Appellate Body Report, *EC – Asbestos (2001)*, paras. 51–2. The Additional Procedure was adopted pursuant to Rule 16(1) of the *Working Procedures for Appellate Review*. See below, p. 284.

clear rules in place for *amicus curiae* briefs, and he called for further consultations on the content of such rules. The Chair finally also stated:

> [I]n light of the views expressed and in the absence of clear rules, he believed that the Appellate Body should exercise extreme caution in future cases until Members had considered what rules were needed.[600]

There are two main reasons for the antagonism of many Members at that time, especially developing-country Members, against *amicus curiae* briefs. First, Members feared that the need to consider and react to *amicus curiae* briefs would take up scarce legal resources and will further bend the WTO dispute settlement proceedings in favour of Members with more legal resources at their disposal. Secondly, developing-country Members in particular believed that the most vocal and best-funded NGOs (such as Greenpeace, WWF and labour unions) often took positions that are considered 'unfriendly' to the interests and policies of developing-country Members. However, in recent years it has become clear that this is not (or no longer) necessarily the case.[601]

To date, WTO Members have been unable to adopt any clear rules on *amicus curiae* briefs.[602] The Appellate Body has repeatedly confirmed its case law on its authority (and that of panels) to accept and consider *amicus curiae* briefs. To date, a total of fifty-eight *amicus curiae* briefs have been submitted in sixteen Appellate Body proceedings.[603] However, in no proceeding thus far did the Appellate Body consider it useful to consider *amicus curiae* briefs submitted to it.[604]

The *amicus curiae* brief filed by Morocco in the appellate proceedings in *EC – Sardines (2002)* is of particular interest. Morocco, which had not reserved third party rights in this dispute, was the first WTO Member to file an *amicus curiae* brief. Peru, the complainant in *EC – Sardines (2002)*, argued that the Appellate Body should not accept or consider this brief. In considering the issue, the Appellate Body first recalled its case law on *amicus curiae* briefs and then noted:

> We have been urged by the parties to this dispute not to treat Members less favourably than non-Members with regard to participation as *amicus curiae*. We agree. We have not. And we will not. As we have already determined that we have the authority to receive an *amicus curiae* brief from a private individual or an organization, *a fortiori* we are entitled to accept

---

600 General Council, *Minutes of Meeting held on 22 November 2000*, WT/GC/M/60, dated 23 January 2001, para. 120.

601 Consider e.g. the position taken by NGOs on the *TRIPS Agreement* and access to essential medicines (see below, pp. 998–9) or on subsidies on agricultural exports (see below, pp. 835–42).

602 Members have made proposals both for the prohibition (e.g. India; and the Africa Group) and for admittance of *amicus curiae* briefs (e.g. the European Union) in the context of DSU review negotiations.

603 Most recently, *amicus curiae* briefs were submitted in *US – Clove Cigarettes (2012)* and *US – Tuna II (2012)*.

604 Even in *US – Countervailing Measures on Certain EC Products (2003)*, a dispute in which both the complainant (the European Union) and the respondent (the United States) explicitly agreed that the Appellate Body had the authority to accept and consider an *amicus curiae* brief from an industry association received in the course of the appeal, the Appellate Body decided not to take the brief into account 'as we do not find it to be of assistance in this appeal'. See Appellate Body Report, *US – Countervailing Measures on Certain EC Products (2003)*, paras. 10 and 76.

such a brief from a WTO Member, provided there is no prohibition on doing so in the DSU. We find no such prohibition.[605]

The Appellate Body therefore concluded that it was entitled to accept the *amicus curiae* brief submitted by Morocco, and consider it.[606] Having concluded that it had the authority to accept the *amicus curiae* brief filed by Morocco, the Appellate Body then considered whether this brief could assist it in this appeal. Morocco's *amicus curiae* brief provided mainly factual information, which is, in view of the mandate of the Appellate Body under Article 17.6 of the DSU, no longer pertinent in Appellate Body proceedings.[607] Morocco also put forward arguments relating to legal issues.[608] However, the Appellate Body decided not to make findings on these specific issues and, therefore, Morocco's arguments on these issues did not assist the Appellate Body in this appeal.[609]

6.1.6 Good Faith and Due Process

Finally, it is important to make a few observations regarding: (1) the obligation on Members to use WTO dispute settlement proceedings in good faith; and (2) the obligation on panels and the Appellate Body to ensure due process in WTO dispute settlement proceedings.

Article 3.10 of the DSU provides that the use of the dispute settlement procedures 'should not be intended or considered as contentious acts' and that all Members must 'engage in these procedures in good faith in an effort to resolve the dispute'.[610] Engaging in dispute settlement *in good faith*, i.e. with the genuine intention to see the dispute resolved, is part of the object and purpose of the WTO dispute settlement system.[611] In *US – FSC (2000)*, the Appellate Body found that the United States had failed to act in good faith, by failing to bring procedural deficiencies 'seasonably and promptly' to the attention of the complainant and the panel, so that corrections, if needed, could have been made.[612] In *Argentina – Poultry Anti-Dumping Duties (2003)*, Argentina argued that Brazil failed to act in good faith by first challenging Argentina's anti-dumping measure before a MERCOSUR Ad Hoc Tribunal and then, having lost that case, challenging the same measure in WTO dispute settlement proceedings.[613] The

---

605 Appellate Body Report, *EC – Sardines (2002)*, para. 164.

606 See *ibid.*, para. 167. The quote cited by the Appellate Body comes from Appellate Body Report, *US – FSC (2000)*, para. 166.

607 See Appellate Body Report, *EC – Sardines (2002)*, para. 169. On the mandate of the Appellate Body under Article 17.6 of the DSU, see above, pp. 239–42.

608 Morocco's brief contained arguments relating to Article 2.1 of the *TBT Agreement* and the GATT 1994.

609 See Appellate Body Report, *EC – Sardines (2002)*, para. 314.

610 Note that Article 4.3 of the DSU also refers to 'good faith', where it requires that the respondent enter into consultations in 'good faith'.

611 On the relationship between 'good faith' and 'estoppel', see Panel Report, *EC and certain member States – Large Civil Aircraft (2011)*, para. 7.101, where it is stated that the good faith obligation of Article 3.10 of the DSU can reasonably be analysed 'in the light of the general international law principle of estoppel'.

612 See Appellate Body Report, *US – FSC (2000)*, para. 165–6. See also below, p. 275.

613 See also above, pp. 172–7.

panel, referring to the findings of the Appellate Body in *US – Offset Act (Byrd Amendment) (2003)*, held:

[W]e consider that two conditions must be satisfied before a Member may be found to have failed to act in good faith. First, the Member must have violated a substantive provision of the WTO agreements. Second, there must be something 'more than mere violation'.[614]

As Argentina had not argued that Brazil had violated any substantive provision of the WTO agreements in bringing its case, the first requirement was not met, and the panel did not find a violation of the principle of good faith.[615]

With regard to the obligation for panels and the Appellate Body to ensure due process in WTO dispute settlement proceedings, the Appellate Body ruled in *Chile – Price Band System (2002)*, that due process is an obligation inherent to the WTO dispute settlement system.[616] According to the Appellate Body in *US/Canada – Continued Suspension (2008)* the protection of due process is an essential feature of a rules-based system of adjudication, such as that established under the DSU.[617] In *Thailand – Cigarettes (Philippines) (2011)*, the Appellate Body ruled that:

[d]ue process is a fundamental principle of WTO dispute settlement. It informs and finds reflection in the provisions of the DSU.[618]

The principle of due process guarantees that proceedings are conducted 'with fairness and impartiality, and that one party is not unfairly disadvantaged with respect to other parties in a dispute'.[619] The due process obligation requires panels and the Appellate Body to afford parties an adequate opportunity to pursue their claims, make out their defences, and establish the facts in the context of proceedings conducted in a balanced and orderly manner, according to established rules.[620] In the interest of 'due process', parties should also bring alleged procedural deficiencies to the attention of a panel or the Appellate Body at the earliest possible opportunity.[621]

Questions and Assignments 3.13

How long are panel and Appellate Body proceedings allowed to take under the DSU, and how long do they take in practice? Why do panels and the Appellate Body exceed the timeframes provided for in the DSU? Please comment on the following statement: 'While WTO dispute settlement proceedings are short, and often much shorter than comparable international or national proceedings, the time taken by WTO dispute settlement proceedings

---

614 Panel Report, *Argentina – Poultry Anti-Dumping Duties (2003)*, para. 7.36. See also Appellate Body Report, *US – Offset Act (Byrd Amendment) (2003)*, para. 298.
615 See Panel Report, *Argentina – Poultry Anti-Dumping Duties (2003)*, para. 7.36.
616 See Appellate Body Report, *Chile – Price Band System (2002)*, para. 176.
617 See Appellate Body Report, *US/Canada – Continued Suspension (2008)*, para. 433.
618 Appellate Body Report, *Thailand – Cigarettes (Philippines) (2011)*, para. 147.
619 Appellate Body Report, *US/Canada – Continued Suspension (2008)*, para. 433.
620 See Appellate Body Report, *Thailand – Cigarettes (Philippines) (2011)*, para. 147.
621 See Appellate Body Report, *US – Carbon Steel (2002)*, para. 123. See also e.g. Appellate Body Report, *Canada – Wheat Exports and Grain Imports (2004)*, para. 205.

is always too long'. Under WTO law, do citizens have a right of access to the submissions made by their and other governments to panels and the Appellate Body? Do WTO Members have a right of access to the submissions made by other Members in panel or Appellate Body proceedings? Are panel and Appellate Body reports confidential documents? Are meetings of panels or the hearings of the Appellate Body open to the public? What is the legal basis in the DSU for allowing public observation of panel meetings and Appellate Body hearings? In your opinion, should all panel meetings and Appellate Body hearings be open to the public? In your opinion, should confidential business information, submitted by the parties to a panel or the Appellate Body, be given *additional* protection? Describe the additional procedures adopted by the Appellate Body in *EC and certain member States – Large Civil Aircraft (2011)* to protect confidential business information (BCI) and highly sensitive business information (HSBI). Who has the burden of proof in WTO dispute settlement proceedings? Does the burden of proof ever shift between the parties? When has a *prima facie* case of inconsistency been made? Will a panel consider the arguments and evidence advanced by the respondent before the complainant has made a *prima facie* case with respect to its claims? How does one distinguish between an exception to another WTO provision *and* a right creating an exemption from the scope of application of another WTO provision? What are the implications for the burden of proof of this distinction? When and why does the complainant have the responsibility 'to raise a defence' in WTO dispute settlement proceedings? What is the legal basis for allowing the involvement of private legal counsel in the WTO dispute settlement process? In your opinion, what are the positive and/or negative aspects of this involvement? Do panels and the Appellate Body have the authority to accept and consider *amicus curiae* briefs? Do NGOs have a right to submit *amicus curiae* briefs? Did panels and the Appellate Body ever consider *amicus curiae* briefs in their deliberations? Why are most WTO Members highly critical of the Appellate Body's approach to the *amicus curiae* brief issue? Do you consider this criticism justified? What does the obligation on panels and the Appellate Body to ensure due process in WTO dispute settlement proceedings entail?

6.2   Consultations

As noted above, the DSU expresses a clear preference for resolving disputes amicably rather than through adjudication.[622] To that end, WTO dispute settlement proceedings always start with consultations (or, at least, an attempt to have consultations) between the parties to the dispute.[623] In *Mexico – Corn Syrup (Article 21.5 – US) (2001)*, the Appellate Body stressed the importance of consultations in WTO dispute settlement as follows:

Through consultations, parties exchange information, assess the strengths and weaknesses of their respective cases, narrow the scope of the differences between them and, in many cases, reach a mutually agreed solution in accordance with the explicit preference expressed in Article 3.7 of the DSU. Moreover, even where no such agreed solution is reached, consultations provide the parties an opportunity to define and delimit the scope of the dispute between them. Clearly, consultations afford many benefits to complaining and responding parties, as well as to third parties and to the dispute settlement system as a whole.[624]

---

622 See above, p. 183.
623 See Article 4 of the DSU. Note in particular Article 4.5 but also Articles 4.3 and 4.7 of the DSU.
624 Appellate Body Report, *Mexico – Corn Syrup (Article 21.5 – US) (2001)*, para. 54.

As already noted, the resolution of disputes through consultations is obviously more cost-effective and more satisfactory for the long-term trade relations with the other party to the dispute than adjudication by a panel.[625] Consultations enable the disputing parties to understand better the factual situation and the legal claims in respect of the dispute. Such understanding may allow them to resolve the matter without further proceedings and, if not, will at least allow a party to learn more about the facts and the legal arguments that the other party is likely to use when the dispute goes to adjudication. In this way, the consultations *can* serve as an informal pre-trial discovery mechanism. Their primary object and purpose, however, is to settle the dispute amicably.

This sub-section discusses the following issues that arise with respect to consultations, namely: (1) their initiation; (2) their conduct; and (3) their outcome.

6.2.1   Initiation of Consultations

Any WTO Member considering that a benefit accruing to it under the *WTO Agreement* is being impaired or nullified by measures taken by another WTO Member may request consultations with that other Member.[626] WTO Members are required to accord sympathetic consideration to, and afford adequate opportunity for, consultations.[627] Consultations can be requested pursuant to *either* Article XXII of the GATT 1994 (or the corresponding provision in other covered agreements), *or* Article XXIII of the GATT 1994 (or the corresponding provision in other covered agreements). The Member requesting consultations is free to choose either type of consultations. For the initiation of consultations, the choice made does not make any difference. However, as discussed below, this choice does affect the conduct of the consultations.[628]

A request for consultations, giving the reasons for the request, must be submitted in writing and must identify: (1) the measure at issue; and (2) the legal basis for the complaint.[629] The request for consultations circumscribes the scope of the dispute.[630] All requests for consultations are to be notified to the DSB by the Member requesting consultations.[631] Requests for consultations are available on the WTO website as a WT/DS document.

With respect to the relationship between the request for consultations and the later panel request,[632] the Appellate Body noted, in *Brazil – Aircraft (1999)*, that Articles 4 and 6 of the DSU do *not* require a *precise and exact identity* between the specific measures and claims of WTO-inconsistency that were the subject of consultations and the specific measures and claims of WTO-inconsistency that were identified in the panel request. What is important is that the essence of the

625 See above, p. 183.   626   On access to WTO dispute settlement, see above, p. 172.
627 See Article 4.2 of the DSU.   628 See below, p. 272.   629 See Article 4.4 of the DSU.
630 See Appellate Body Report, *Mexico – Corn Syrup (Article 21.5 – US) (2001)*, para. 54.
631 See Article 4.4 of the DSU.
632 On the request for the establishment of a panel, see above, pp. 161, 218.

challenged measures and claims has not changed.[633] Note that, in *US – Certain EC Products (2001)*, the Appellate Body found that, while a specific measure was explicitly referred to in the panel request, it was not referred to in the request for consultations, and for that reason was not properly before the panel.[634] The Appellate Body ruled in *US – Upland Cotton (2005)* that measures or claims not listed in the consultation request cannot be added to the panel request, and can therefore not be within the panel's jurisdiction.[635] In the same case, the Appellate Body also ruled that the scope of the consultations is determined by the request for consultations, rather than by what actually happened, i.e. what actually was discussed, during the consultations.[636]

6.2.2   Conduct of Consultations

Parties have broad discretion with regard to the manner in which consultations are to be conducted. The DSU provides few rules on the conduct of consultations. The consultation process essentially is meant to resolve a dispute by diplomatic means. In *India – Patents (US) (1998)*, the Appellate Body noted:

All parties engaged in dispute settlement under the DSU must be fully forthcoming *from the very beginning* both as to the claims involved in a dispute and as to the facts relating to those claims. Claims must be stated clearly. Facts must be disclosed freely. This must be so in consultations as well as in the more formal setting of panel proceedings. In fact, the demands of *due process* that are implicit in the DSU make this especially necessary during consultations. For the claims that are made and the facts that are established during consultations do much to shape the substance and the scope of subsequent panel proceedings.[637]

Unless otherwise agreed, the Member to which a request for consultations is made must *reply* to the request within ten days of the date of its receipt, and enter into consultations within a period of no more than thirty days after the date of receipt of the request.[638] It must enter into consultations in good faith and with a view to reaching a mutually satisfactory solution. If the Member does not respond within ten days after the date of receipt of the request, or does not enter into consultations within a period of no more than thirty days (or a period otherwise mutually agreed), then the Member that requested the consultations may proceed directly to request the establishment of a panel. As the Appellate Body noted in *Mexico – Corn Syrup (Article 21.5 – US) (2001)*, in such a case the

---

633   See Appellate Body Report, *Brazil – Aircraft (1999)*, para. 132. See e.g. also Appellate Body Report, *US – Zeroing (Japan) (2007)*, paras. 89–96 (with regard to the challenged measures); and Appellate Body Report, *Mexico – Anti-Dumping Measures on Rice (2005)*, para. 138 (with regard to the claims of WTO-inconsistency made).

634   See Appellate Body Report, *US – Certain EC Products (2001)*, paras. 69–82.

635   See Appellate Body Report, *US – Upland Cotton (2005)*, paras. 284–5. As discussed above, however, the Appellate Body has said that it does not believe that 'Articles 4 and 6 of the DSU ... require a *precise and exact identity* between the specific measures that were the subject of consultations and the specific measures identified in the request for the establishment of a panel'. See Appellate Body Report, *Brazil – Aircraft (1999)*, para. 132. See also above, pp. 210–13.

636   See *ibid.*, paras. 286–7.

637   Appellate Body Report, *India – Patents (US) (1998)*, para. 94. Emphasis added.

638   See Article 4.3 of the DSU. For the deadlines applicable in cases of urgency, see Article 4.8 of the DSU.

respondent, by its own conduct, relinquishes the potential benefits that could be derived from consultations.[639]

While the request for consultations is notified to the DSB and posted on the WTO website, Article 4.6 of the DSU stipulates that the consultations themselves shall be confidential.[640] However, the requirement of confidentiality does not mean that information acquired during consultations may not be used during panel proceedings between the same parties on the same matter. It means that the information acquired may not be disclosed to anyone not involved in the consultations.[641] In addition to stipulating that the consultations shall be confidential, Article 4.6 of the DSU also states that the consultations shall be 'without prejudice to the rights of any Member in any further proceedings.' Therefore, evidence pertaining to settlement offers made during the consultations is 'of no legal consequence to the later stages' of WTO dispute settlement proceedings. On this basis, the panel in *US – Underwear (1997)* refused to consider as evidence the settlement proposals made by the United States during consultations, which had been submitted to it by Costa Rica. The panel emphasised that:

Article 4.6 of the DSU makes it clear that offers made in the context of consultations are, in case a mutually agreed solution is not reached, of no legal consequence to the later stages of dispute settlement, as far as the rights of the parties to the dispute are concerned.[642]

As noted above, a Member can request consultations pursuant to *either* Article XXII (or corresponding provisions) *or* Article XXIII of the GATT 1994 (or corresponding provisions).[643] Members are free to choose between either type of consultations. With regard to the conduct of the consultations, there is, however, a significant difference between these types of consultations. Only in the context of consultations pursuant to Article XXII (or corresponding provisions) can a Member other than the consulting Members be allowed to participate in the consultations.[644] A Member that considers that it has a 'substantial trade interest' may notify the consulting Members and the DSB of such interest within ten days after the date of the circulation of the request for consultations.[645] Provided that the respondent to the dispute agrees that the claim of substantial interest is well founded, this Member shall join in the consultations. If consultations are instead conducted pursuant to Article XXIII (or corresponding provisions), it is not possible for other Members to join in the consultations.

Generally, consultations are held in Geneva and involve Geneva-based diplomats as well as capital-based trade officials and private lawyers of the parties to

639 See Appellate Body Report, *Mexico – Corn Syrup (Article 21.5 – US) (2001)*, para. 59.
640 In *Canada – Wheat Exports and Grain Imports (2004)*, the panel granted Canada's request in the interim review stage that specific references to discussions and events that occurred during consultations between the parties be deleted from the final panel report. See Panel Report, *Canada – Wheat Exports and Grain Imports (2004)*, paras. 5.4–5.10.
641 See e.g. Panel Report, *Korea – Alcoholic Beverages (1999)*, para. 10.23.
642 Panel Report, *US – Underwear (1997)*, para. 7.27.
643 See above, pp. 214 and 270.   644 See above, p. 280.   645 See Article 4.11 of the DSU.

the dispute (and Members allowed to join the consultations).[646] The WTO Secretariat is neither present at, nor in any other way associated with, the consultations. As the Appellate Body noted in *US – Upland Cotton (2005)*:

> There is no public record of what actually transpires during consultations and parties will often disagree about what, precisely, was discussed.[647]

Occasionally, respondents have argued that the consultations held had not been adequate or meaningful or that the complainant had not engaged in consultations in good faith.[648] The panel in *Korea – Alcoholic Beverages (1999)* ruled in this respect that it was not for panels to assess the 'adequacy' of consultations.[649] Consultations are a matter reserved for the parties. What takes place in these consultations is not the concern of panels. Panels may only ascertain whether consultations were held or at least were requested.[650] Note, however, that, if a respondent raises in a timely manner the lack of a request for consultations or the lack of consultations, a panel would have to conclude that it has no authority to hear and decide the dispute.[651]

6.2.3   Outcome of Consultations

If consultations are successful and lead to a mutually agreed solution to the dispute, this solution must be notified to the DSB.[652] Any Member may raise any point relating to this notified solution at meetings of the DSB.[653] Note that mutually agreed solutions must be consistent with WTO law.[654] As discussed above, consultations have frequently been successful in resolving disputes.[655]

If consultations between the parties fail to settle the dispute within sixty days of the receipt of the request for consultations, the complainant may request the DSB to establish a panel to adjudicate the dispute.[656] In many cases, however,

---

646 Note, however, that the consultations between the European Union and the Philippines in *Philippines – Distilled Spirits (2012)* were held in Manila. See Panel Reports, *Philippines – Distilled Spirits (2012)*, para. 1.2.

647 Appellate Body Report, *US – Upland Cotton (2005)*, para. 287.

648 See the requirements in Articles 3.10 and 4.2 of the DSU. Also note Article 4.10 of the DSU, which provides that during consultations Members 'should' give special attention to the particular problems and interests of developing-country Members.

649 See Panel Report, *Korea – Alcoholic Beverages (1999)*, para. 10.19. See also e.g. *US – Poultry (China) (2010)*, para. 7.35.

650 See Panel Reports, *EC – Bananas III (1997)*, para. 7.19.

651 The lack of prior consultations is, however, not a defect that a panel must examine on its own motion. See Appellate Body Report, *Mexico – Corn Syrup (Article 21.5 – US) (2001)*, para. 64. See also below, footnote 656.

652 See Article 3.6 of the DSU. The mutually agreed solutions must also be notified to other relevant bodies, such as the TRIPS Council in a dispute concerning rights and obligations of Members under the *TRIPS Agreement*. For a list of all mutually agreed solutions notified to the DSB up to 30 September 2011, see *WTO Analytical Index (2012)*, Volume II, 1530–1.

653 See *ibid*. Any Member may also raise any point relating to notified solutions at meetings of other relevant WTO bodies.

654 See Article 3.5 of the DSU.   655 See above, p. 183.

656 The complainant may also request a panel *during* the sixty-day period if the consulting parties jointly consider that consultations have failed to settle the dispute. See Article 4.7 of the DSU. Another possible situation is that the respondent does not object, explicitly and in a timely manner, to the failure of the complainant to request or engage in consultations. In such situation, the respondent may be deemed to have consented to the lack of consultations. See Appellate Body Report, *Mexico – Corn Syrup (Article 21.5 – US) (2001)*, para. 63.

the complainant will not, immediately upon the expiration of the sixty-day period, request the establishment of a panel but will allow for more time to settle the dispute through consultations.

For consultations involving a measure taken by a developing-country Member, Article 12.10 of the DSU explicitly provides that the parties may agree to extend the sixty-day period. If, after the sixty-day period has elapsed, the consulting parties cannot agree that the consultations have concluded, the Chair of the DSB shall decide, after consultation with the parties, whether to extend this period and, if so, for how long.

Consultations between the parties with the aim of settling the dispute can, and do, continue *during* the panel proceedings. Article 11 of the DSU provides that panels should consult the parties to the dispute regularly and give them an adequate opportunity to develop a mutually satisfactory solution.[657] There have been a number of disputes in which a mutually agreed solution was reached while the dispute was already before a panel.[658] In such a case, Article 12.7 of the DSU provides that the panel report 'shall be confined to a brief description of the case and to reporting that a solution has been reached'.

Questions and Assignments 3.14

Apart from settling the dispute amicably, what is the purpose of consultations? What must be contained in the request for consultations? How do requests for consultations relate to panel requests, and what is the importance of this relationship for the terms of reference of a panel? What is the 'sanction' for not holding (or requesting) consultations before requesting the establishment of a panel? Will consultations always last at least sixty days? Can consultations last longer than sixty days? Can a panel find that the complainant did not engage in consultations in good faith as required by Article 3.10 of the DSU? Can other Members join consultations between the parties to a dispute? May WTO Members resolve a dispute amicably by *agreeing* to a solution, which deviates from the *WTO Agreement*? Does the DSU provide any special rules for developing-country Members engaged in consultations?

6.3   Panel Proceedings

As noted above, when consultations are unsuccessful,[659] the complainant may decide to advance to the next stage of the process of WTO dispute settlement, namely, the panel proceedings. The basic rules governing panel proceedings are set out in Article 12 of the DSU. Article 12.1 of the DSU directs a panel to follow the *Working Procedures* contained in Appendix 3 to the DSU, while at the same time authorising a panel to do otherwise after consulting the parties to the dispute. While Article 12.1 of the DSU merely requires that the panel 'consult'

---

657 See Article 11 of the DSU.

658 See e.g. *EC – Scallops* (complaints by Canada, Peru and Chile (1996)); *EC – Butter* (complaint by New Zealand ((1996)) *US – DRAMs (Article 21.5 – Korea)* (complaint by Korea (2006)); and *Japan – Quotas on Laver* (complaint by Korea (2006)).

659 For the exceptional situation in which the complainant can request the establishment of a panel without having had consultations with the respondent, see above, p. 209.

the parties, panels are often hesitant to deviate from the *Working Procedures* contained in Appendix 3 without the 'consent' of the parties. Moreover, panels usually agree to requests on procedural issues tabled by the parties jointly.[660] In *EC – Hormones (1998)*, the Appellate Body noted that panels enjoy:

a margin of discretion to deal, always in accordance with due process, with specific situations that may arise in a particular case.[661]

In *India – Patents (US) (1998)*, however, the Appellate Body cautioned panels as follows:

Although panels enjoy some discretion in establishing their own working procedures, this discretion does not extend to modifying the substantive provisions of the DSU. To be sure, Article 12.1 of the DSU says: 'Panels shall follow the Working Procedures in Appendix 3 unless the panel decides otherwise after consulting the parties to the dispute.' Yet that is *all* that it says. Nothing in the DSU gives a panel the authority either to disregard or to modify other explicit provisions of the DSU.[662]

Article 12.2 of the DSU requires that panel procedures provide sufficient flexibility so as to ensure high-quality panel reports while not unduly delaying the panel process. Since the *Working Procedures* contained in Appendix 3 to the DSU are rudimentary, most panels now find it useful, if not necessary, to adopt more detailed *ad hoc* working procedures.[663] As the Appellate Body stated in *Thailand – Cigarettes (Philippines) (2011)*:

Panel working procedures should both embody and reinforce due process ... As the Appellate Body has previously observed, the use by panels of detailed standardized working procedures promotes fairness and the protection of due process.[664]

Generally speaking, the parties to a dispute enjoy a high degree of discretion to argue before panels in the manner they deem appropriate. This discretion, however, does not detract from their obligation under the DSU to engage in dispute settlement proceedings 'in good faith in an effort to resolve the dispute'.[665] Both the complaining and the responding Members must comply with the requirements of the DSU in good faith. In *US – FSC (2000)*, the Appellate Body held:

By good faith compliance, complaining Members accord to the responding Members the full measure of protection and opportunity to defend, contemplated by the letter and spirit of the procedural rules. The same principle of good faith requires that responding Members seasonably and promptly bring claimed procedural deficiencies to the attention of the

---

660 Note, however, that the discretion of panels is limited in that panels cannot modify the rules set out in the DSU itself.
661 Appellate Body Report, *EC – Hormones (1998)*, para. 152, footnote 138.
662 Appellate Body Report, *India – Patents (US) (1998)*, para. 92. In this case, the Appellate Body reversed a decision by the panel that it would consider all claims made prior to the end of the first substantive meeting. All parties had agreed with this panel decision.
663 For an example of such *ad hoc* panel working procedures, see Panel Reports, *US – Steel Safeguards (2003)*, para. 6.1. While these working procedures are *ad hoc*, they often include *standardised* provisions.
664 Appellate Body Report, *Thailand – Cigarettes (Philippines) (2011)*, para. 148. On 'due process' in WTO dispute settlement, see above, pp. 267–9.
665 Article 3.10 of the DSU.

complaining Member, and to the DSB or the Panel, so that corrections, if needed, can be made to resolve disputes. The procedural rules of WTO dispute settlement are designed to promote, not the development of litigation techniques, but simply the fair, prompt and effective resolution of trade disputes.[666]

Note that, in *EC – Tube or Pipe Fittings (2003)*, Brazil's first written submission did not contain paragraph or line numbering. The panel noted in this respect that it 'would appreciate efforts on the part of the parties to facilitate the task of the Panel in examining the matter referred to [it]', and 'invite[d] Brazil to submit a paragraph-numbered version of its first submission to facilitate referencing by the Panel and the parties'.[667] Brazil accordingly submitted a revised, paragraph-numbered version of its first written submission to the panel.[668]

This sub-section discusses the following issues which arise with respect to panel proceedings: (1) the initiation of panel proceedings; (2) the written submissions and panel meetings; (3) panel deliberations and interim review; and (4) the adoption or appeal of panel reports.

Questions and Assignments 3.15

Who decides on the working procedures for the panels and on the timetable for the panel's work? Which requirements do the working procedures and the timetable have to meet? Is a panel free to deviate from Appendix 3 to the DSU as well as other provisions of the DSU if all parties to the dispute agree? How much discretion do parties enjoy regarding the manner in which they argue before panels?

6.3.1   Initiation of Panel Proceedings

As discussed above, when consultations are unsuccessful, the complainant may request the establishment of a panel.[669] The DSB usually establishes the panel by reverse consensus at the second meeting at which it discusses the panel request.[670] Subsequently, the parties agree on the composition of the panel or, if they fail to do so, the WTO Director-General decides on the composition of the panel.[671] Once composed, the panel will – whenever possible within a week of its composition – fix the timetable for its work on the basis of the 'proposed timetable for panel work' set out in Appendix 3 to the DSU.[672] At that time the panel may also decide on detailed *ad hoc* working procedures.[673] Before deciding on the timetable and *ad hoc* working procedures, the panel will consult with the parties at what is commonly referred to as the 'organisational meeting'.[674]

666 Appellate Body Report, *US – FSC (2000)*, para. 166. See also Appellate Body Report, *US – Lamb (2001)*, para. 115.
667 Panel Report, *EC – Tube or Pipe Fittings (2003)*, para. 7.40.
668 See *ibid.*, para. 7.41.   669 See above, pp. 273–4.   670 See above, p. 206.   671 See above, p. 216.
672 See Article 12.3 of the DSU. The timetable includes precise deadlines for written submissions by the parties, which the parties must respect (see Article 12.5 of the DSU). In determining the timetable, the panel must provide sufficient time for the parties to prepare their submissions (see Article 12.4 of the DSU).
673 See above, p. 275.
674 See Articles 12.3 and 12.5 of the DSU.

Note with regard to the decision on the timetable for the panel proceedings that Article 12.10 of the DSU provides that:

in examining a complaint against a developing country Member, the panel shall accord sufficient time for the developing country Member to prepare and present its argumentation.

In *India – Quantitative Restrictions (1999)*, for example, India requested additional time from the panel in order to prepare its first written submission. Noting the DSU's strict timeframe for the panel process, the United States objected to this request. Referring to Article 12.10 and taking into account 'the administrative reorganization taking place in India as a result of the recent change in government', the panel decided to grant India an additional period of ten days to prepare its submission.[675]

Note that, pursuant to Article 12.12 of the DSU, the panel may, at the request of the complaining party, at any time during the panel proceedings, suspend its work for a maximum period of twelve months. While not common, this does happen occasionally.[676] The authority of the panel lapses if the work of the panel is suspended for more than twelve months.[677]

6.3.2   Written Submissions and Panel Meetings

Each of the parties to a dispute submits two written submissions to the panel: (1) a 'first written submission'; and (2) a 'rebuttal submission'. In their first written submissions, the parties present the facts of the case as they see them and their arguments relating to the alleged inconsistencies with WTO law.[678] In their rebuttal submissions, they reply to the argument and evidence submitted by the other party.[679] As the Appellate Body ruled in *US – Shrimp (1998)*, the parties have a *legal right* to make the above-mentioned submissions to the panel, and the panel in turn is *obliged in law* to accept and give due consideration to these submissions.[680]

After the first written submissions of the parties have been filed, the panel holds its first substantive meeting with the parties.[681] At this meeting, the panel first asks the complainant to present its case, and then gives the respondent the

---

675   See Panel Report, *India – Quantitative Restrictions (1999)*, para. 5.10. A similar request for additional time to prepare written submissions was made by China to the panel in *China – Raw Materials (2012)* because it had to respond to the submissions by three complainants (the European Union, Mexico and the United States).

676   See e.g. Panel Report, *EC – Butter (1999)*, para. 12.

677   See e.g. in *US – The Cuban Liberty and Democratic Solidarity Act (Helms–Burton Act)* (complaint by the EC); and *India – Wines and Spirits* (complaint by the EC). Note that it is for the complainant to request the panel to resume its work.

678   Note that, even if the complainant fails to include any arguments on certain claims in its first written submission, these claims, if properly identified in the panel request, remain within the terms of reference of the panel. See Appellate Body Report, *EC – Bananas III (1997)*, paras. 145–7.

679   The first written submission of the complainant is usually filed two to three weeks in advance of the first written submission of the respondent. The rebuttal submissions are filed simultaneously. See Article 12.6 of, and para. 12 of Appendix 3 to, the DSU. On the 'late' submission of evidence, see below, p. 279.

680   See Appellate Body Report, *US – Shrimp (1998)*, para. 101. This is also the case for submissions by third parties but not for submissions by any other Member or person (*amicus curiae* briefs). See above, pp. 263–7.

681   See para. 4 of Appendix 3 to the DSU.

opportunity to react to the case brought against it.[682] The panel holds a second substantive meeting with the parties after the rebuttal submissions have been filed.[683] While not mandatory, panel meetings are always held on the premises of the WTO Secretariat in Geneva. A panel meeting may take one or more days. While initially far less formal and less 'court-like' than the oral hearings of the Appellate Body, WTO panel meetings have become increasingly formal in recent years.[684] All *ex parte* communications with the panel, on matters under consideration, are explicitly proscribed.[685] As already discussed, until 2006 panels always met in closed session with only the delegations of the parties present. In recent years, however, panel meetings with the parties are open to public observation if the parties so agree and the panel so rules.[686]

The panel may, at any time, put questions to the parties and ask them for explanations either in the course of a meeting or in writing.[687] The DSU provides panels with discretionary authority to request and obtain information from *any* Member, including *a fortiori* a Member, which is a party to the dispute before the panel.[688] The parties are under an *obligation* to provide the panel with the information or the documents that the panel requests. Article 13.1 of the DSU states, in relevant part:

A Member *should* respond promptly and fully to any request by a panel for such information as the panel considers necessary and appropriate.[689]

In *Canada – Aircraft (1999)*, the Appellate Body ruled that the word 'should' in Article 13.1 is used in a normative sense.[690] As held by the Appellate Body in this case, it is within the discretion of panels to draw adverse inferences from the fact that a party has refused to provide information requested by the panel. However, the Appellate Body stressed that panels must draw inferences on the basis of all the facts of record (and not only the refusal to provide information).[691]

---

682 See para. 5 of Appendix 3 to the DSU.
683 Additional meetings with the parties may be scheduled if required: para. 12 of Appendix 3 to the DSU. In practice, however, very few panels have had additional meetings with the parties.
684 See below, pp. 283–92.
685 See Article 18.1 of the DSU. As already mentioned, in *Turkey – Rice (2007)*, the respondent, Turkey, proposed that it would provide certain information to the panel on condition that these documents would not be made available to the complainant, the United States. The panel refused this condition, as it would violate Article 18.1 of the DSU. See Panel Report, *Turkey – Rice (2007)*, para. 7.100. See also Panel Report, *Korea – Certain Paper (2005)*, paras. 7.13–7.18.
686 See above, p. 255.
687 See para. 8 of Appendix 3 to the DSU. During panel meetings, parties may also question each other. This does not happen during hearings of the Appellate Body.
688 See Article 13.1 of the DSU. On the discretionary nature of this authority to request information, see e.g. Appellate Body Report, *EC – Bed Linen (Article 21.5 – India) (2003)*, paras. 165–7; and Panel Report, *EC – Selected Customs Matters (2006)*, paras. 7.77–7.83.
689 Emphasis added.
690 See Appellate Body Report, *Canada – Aircraft (1999)*, para. 187.
691 See *ibid.*, paras. 204–5; and Appellate Body Report, *US – Wheat Gluten (2001)*, paras. 173–6. In *US – Upland Cotton (2005)*, the United States responded in part to the request of the panel to provide certain information and also argued that other information could not be provided. The panel ultimately, based on all of the information before it, determined that it was not necessary to draw adverse inferences in respect of information allegedly not submitted by the United States. See Panel Report, *US – Upland Cotton (2005)*, paras. 7.20–7.42 and 7.609–7.633. See also Panel Report, *Canada – Aircraft Credits and Guarantees (2002)*, paras. 7.379–7.386.

The DSU does not establish precise rules or deadlines for the submission of evidence by a party to the dispute. In *Argentina – Textiles and Apparel (1998)*, the panel allowed the United States to submit certain evidence two days before the second substantive meeting. Argentina appealed the panel's decision to admit this evidence. The Appellate Body rejected the appeal by noting that neither Article 11 of the DSU nor the *Working Procedures* set out in Appendix 3 thereof establish time-limits for the submission of evidence to a panel.[692] The Appellate Body acknowledged that the DSU clearly contemplates two distinct stages in panel proceedings: a first stage during which the parties should set out their case in chief, including a full presentation of the facts on the basis of submission of supporting evidence; and a second stage which is generally designed to permit 'rebuttals' by each party of the arguments and evidence submitted by the other party.[693] Nevertheless, unless specific deadlines for the submission of evidence are set out in the *ad hoc* working procedures of the panel, parties can submit new evidence as late as the second substantive meeting with the panel.[694] The panel must, of course, always be careful to observe due process, which, *inter alia*, entails providing the parties with adequate opportunity to respond to the evidence submitted.[695] Most panels now have *ad hoc* working procedures that set out precise deadlines for the submission of evidence.[696]

With regard to temporal limitations on the evidence submitted, the Appellate Body ruled in *EC – Selected Customs Matters (2006)* that, while there are temporal limitations on the measures that may be within a panel's terms of reference, 'such limitations do not apply in the same way to evidence'. The Appellate Body found that '[e]vidence in support of a claim challenging measures that are within a panel's terms of reference, may pre-date or post-date the establishment of the panel'.[697] Note, however, that, with regard to trade remedy cases, a different rule applies. As the Appellate Body ruled in *US – Cotton Yarn (2001)* and later cases, the WTO consistency of anti-dumping, countervailing and safeguard

---

692 See Appellate Body Report, *Argentina – Textiles and Apparel (1998)*, para. 79. See also Panel Report, *Canada – Aircraft (1999)*, paras. 9.75–9.78.

693 See Appellate Body Report, *Argentina – Textiles and Apparel (1998)*, para. 79. See also Panel Report, *Korea – Commercial Vessels (2005)*, paras. 7.277–7.279.

694 In *EC – Selected Customs Matters (2006)*, the Appellate Body upheld the panel's decision to exclude evidence contained in exhibits provided by the European Communities at the interim review stage. The Appellate Body noted that 'the interim review stage is not an appropriate time to introduce new evidence'. See Appellate Body Report, *EC – Selected Customs Matters (2006)*, paras. 248, 250 and 259. See also Panel Reports, *EC – Approval and Marketing of Biotech Products (2006)*, paras. 6.134 and 6.162–6.164. However, note that the panel in *US – Anti-Dumping Measures on Oil Country Tubular Goods (2005)* saw 'no harm' in accepting a letter from the United States drawing the panel's attention to the Appellate Body Report in *US – Gambling (2005)*, circulated after the interim report was issued. See Panel Reports, *US – Anti-Dumping Measures on Oil Country Tubular Goods (2005)*, paras. 6.24–6.25.

695 Appellate Body Report, *Argentina – Textiles and Apparel (1998)*, paras. 80–1; and Appellate Body Report, *Australia – Salmon (1998)*, para. 272.

696 Under these rules, the submission of evidence after the deadline will nevertheless be allowed when there is 'good cause' to do so. The panel in *US – Offset Act (Byrd Amendment) (2003)* accepted evidence submitted after the deadline, stating that 'good cause' for acceptance existed. See Panel Report, *US – Offset Act (Byrd Amendment) (2003)*, para. 7.2.

697 Appellate Body Report, *EC – Selected Customs Matters (2006)*, paras. 177–89 and 249–54. See also Panel Report, *Japan – Apples (2003)*, paras. 8.55–8.56.

measures needs to be determined in the light of the evidence and facts on record before the national authority at the time when the latter made the relevant determinations.[698]

Finally, as discussed above, any WTO Member having a substantial interest in a matter before a panel and having notified its interest in a timely manner to the DSB shall have an opportunity to be heard by the panel and to make written submissions to the panel.[699] These third parties to the dispute are invited by the panel to present their views during a special session of the first substantive meeting.[700] Their written submissions to the panel are shared with the parties to the dispute.[701] Third parties, however, only receive the first written submissions of the parties.[702] It is clear from the above that the rights of third parties to participate in the panel proceedings are, as a rule, somewhat limited. In a number of cases, however, third parties have sought and obtained enhanced third party rights. In *EC – Bananas III (1997)*, for example, third party developing-country Members that had a major interest in the outcome of this case, were allowed to attend the entire first and second substantive meetings of the panel with the parties, as well as to make statements at both meetings. Third parties were also granted enhanced third party rights in, for example, *EC – Hormones (1998), EC – Tariff Preferences (2004)* and *EC – Export Subsidies on Sugar (2005)*.[703] Note that the grant of enhanced third party rights is within 'the sound discretion' of the panel, although '[s]uch discretionary authority is, of course, not unlimited and is circumscribed, for example, by the requirements of due process'.[704] Third parties were refused enhanced third party rights in, for example, *EC and certain member States – Large Civil Aircraft (2011)*. The panel in this case justified its refusal to grant Brazil enhanced third party rights as follows:

While we accept that Brazil … ha[s] an interest in the aircraft sector, we consider this interest to be insufficient to justify granting enhanced third party rights … Brazil has not explained

---

698 See below, p. 673 (for anti-dumping measures), p. 748 (for countervailing measures) and p. 610 (for safeguard measures).

699 See Article 10.2 of the DSU. See also above, p. 177.

700 See Article 10.2 of, and para. 6 of Appendix 3 to, the DSU.

701 Article 10.2 of the DSU. These submissions are reflected in, or attached to, the panel report.

702 See Article 10.3 of the DSU.

703 The panel in *EC – Bananas III (1997)*, however, refused the third parties participation in the interim review process. See Panel Reports, *EC – Bananas III (1997)*, para. 7.9. In *EC – Hormones (1998)*, enhanced third party rights were granted due to the fact that the third parties in the two disputes were complainants in a parallel panel procedure concerning the same EC measure, to be dealt with by the same panellists. See Panel Report, *EC – Hormones (US) (1998)*, para. 8.15; and Panel Report, *EC – Hormones (Canada) (1998)*, paras. 8.12–8.20 (upheld by the Appellate Body: see Appellate Body Report, *EC – Hormones (1998)*, paras. 150–4). The panel in *EC – Tariff Preferences (2004)* allowed third parties some participation in the interim review process by allowing them to review the summary of their respective arguments in the draft descriptive part of the panel report. See Panel Report, *EC – Tariff Preferences (2004)*, para. 1.10. In this case, eleven of the eighteen third parties had requested enhanced third party rights. The panel decided to grant additional rights to *all* third parties. See Panel Report, *EC – Tariff Preferences (2004)*, Annex A, para. 7. See also Panel Reports, *EC – Export Subsidies on Sugar (2005)*, paras. 2.5–2.9, where, following a request for enhanced third party rights by the fourteen ACP sugar-producing third parties, the panel decided to grant additional rights to *all* third parties.

704 Appellate Body Report, *US – 1916 Act (2000)*, paras. 149 and 150. In this case, the Appellate Body upheld the panel's decision not to grant enhanced third party rights.

how, in the light of the foregoing, the measures at issue have a significant economic or trade policy effect on Brazil. While we accept that Brazil has a general systemic interest in the interpretation of the SCM Agreement, this does not differentiate Brazil from any other WTO Member, whether appearing as a third party in this dispute or not.[705]

6.3.3   Panel Deliberations and Interim Review

As provided for in Article 14 of the DSU, panel deliberations are confidential.[706] The reports of panels are drafted without the presence of the parties to the dispute; they are drafted in light of the information provided and the statements made during the proceedings.[707]

Having completed a draft of the descriptive (i.e. facts and argument) sections of its report, the panel issues, pursuant to Article 15 of the DSU, this draft to the parties for their comments.[708] Following the expiration of the time period for comments, the panel subsequently issues an interim report to the parties, including both the descriptive sections and the panel's findings and conclusions.[709] A party may submit written comments on the interim report and request the panel to review particular aspects of the report. The parties are given an opportunity to comment on each other's comments on the interim report in writing. At the request of a party, the panel may hold a further meeting with the parties on the issues identified in the written comments.[710] In recent years, however, parties have rarely requested such an interim review meeting with the panel.[711] Instead, parties have responded in writing on each others' interim review comments. The final panel report must include a summary and discussion of the arguments made at the interim review stage.[712]

In *US/Canada – Continued Suspension (2008)*, the European Communities stated in its interim review request that the errors in the panel reports were so numerous and serious that it was not possible in the time available to 'provide a detailed and complete list of all omissions and errors', and that it may 'make all its comments' at the appeal stage.[713] The panel expressed 'surprise' by the choice of the European Communities to 'make all its comments' before the Appellate Body rather than before the panel, 'at the procedural stage expressly designed for the purpose of considering any and all comments on the interim report'.[714]

The comments made by the parties at the interim review stage frequently give rise to corrections of technical errors or unclear drafting. However, panels seldom changed the conclusions reached in their reports in any substantive way

---

705 Panel Report, *EC and certain member States – Large Civil Aircraft (2011)*, para. 7.167.
706 See Article 14.1 of the DSU.   707 See Article 14.2 of the DSU.
708 See Article 15.1 of the DSU.   709 See Article 15.2 of the DSU.   710 See *ibid.*
711 Note that there was an interim review meeting in *Thailand – Cigarettes (Philippines) (2011)*. See Panel Report, *Thailand – Cigarettes (Philippines) (2011)*, para. 6.1.
712 See Article 15.3 of the DSU. If no comments are received from any party within the comment period, the interim report shall be considered the final panel report. See Article 15.3 of the DSU.
713 See e.g. Panel Report, *US/Canada – Continued Suspension (2008)*, para. 6.14.
714 *Ibid.*, para. 6.15.

as a result of the comments made by parties, although it should be noted that there have been some panels that have done so.[715] To safeguard the 'ability' of the panel to alter the conclusions reached in its interim report in light of comments made by parties, it is important that this report remains confidential. A panel will be 'disinclined' to make substantive changes to its report if the latter is already in the public domain. Disregard for the confidentiality of the interim report is therefore a matter of systemic concern. In *EC – Approval and Marketing of Biotech Products (2006)*, the panel sharply criticised two NGOs, Friends of the Earth Europe and the Institute of Agriculture and Trade Policy, for having posted the interim report on their websites.[716] It is clear that the interim report in this case was leaked in order to bring political pressure to bear on the panel during the interim review process. Interim review is an unusual feature in judicial or quasi-judicial dispute settlement proceedings.[717]

6.3.4   Adoption or Appeal of Panel Reports

The final panel report is first *issued* to the parties to the dispute, and some weeks later, once the report is available in the three working languages of the WTO, it is *circulated* to the general WTO membership. Once circulated to WTO Members, the panel report is an unrestricted document available to the public. On the day of its circulation, a panel report is posted on the WTO's website as a WT/DS document. Panel reports are also included in the official *Dispute Settlement Reports of the World Trade Organization*, published by Cambridge University Press.[718]

According to Article 16.4 of the DSU, within sixty days after the date of circulation of the panel report to the Members, the report is adopted at a DSB meeting unless: (1) a party to the dispute formally notifies the DSB of its decision to appeal; or (2) the DSB decides by consensus not to adopt the report. Note that, in some cases, the parties reached a procedural agreement to request the DSB to extend the sixty-day deadline for the adoption or appeal of the panel report.[719] Typically, these requests have been made, and the DSB has granted such requests, to manage workload and scheduling difficulties at the stage of the Appellate Body proceedings.

If a panel report is appealed, it is not discussed by the DSB until the appellate review proceedings are completed and the Appellate Body report – together

---

715 See e.g. Panel Reports, *EC – Approval and Marketing of Biotech Products (2006)*, para. 8.18 (with regard to the US complaint) and para. 8.36 (with regard to the Canadian complaint); Panel Report, *Korea – Certain Paper (2005)*, paras. 6.3–6.5 and 7.106–7.112; and Panel Report, *US – Carbon Steel (2002)*, paras. 7.24 and 8.120–8.145.

716 See Panel Reports, *EC – Approval and Marketing of Biotech Products (2006)*, para. 7.696.

717 See also Communication from the Chair of the Panel, *EC – Approval and Marketing of Biotech Products (2006)*, WT/DS291/32, WT/DS292/26 and WT/DS293/26, dated 29 September 2006, para. 2.

718 See www.cambridge.org/gb/knowledge/series/series_display/item3937379/?site_locale=en_GB.

719 See e.g. in *EC – Export Subsidies on Sugar (2005)*; *Brazil – Retreaded Tyres (2007)*; *US – Anti-Dumping and Countervailing Duties (China) (2011)*; *EC – Fasteners (2011)*; *US – Tyres (2011)*; *US – Clove Cigarettes (2011)*; *US – Tuna II (2011)*; and *US – COOL (2012)*.

with the panel report – comes before the DSB for adoption. When the DSB does consider and debate a panel report, the parties to the dispute, as well as all other Members, have the right to comment on the report. All views expressed shall be fully recorded in the minutes of the DSB meeting.[720] In order to provide sufficient time for the Members to review panel reports, the reports shall not be considered for adoption by the DSB until twenty days after they have been circulated.

As the Appellate Body noted in *EC – Bed Linen (Article 21.5 – India) (2003)*, a panel report that is adopted by the DSB must be treated by the parties to a particular dispute 'as a final resolution to that dispute'.[721]

Questions and Assignments 3.16

Describe the various steps in panel proceedings. What is the purpose of the 'organisational meeting', which the panel will have with parties soon after its composition? Can developing-country Members request additional time to prepare their written submissions? Briefly describe the purpose and content of the various written submissions of the parties to the panel. When will a panel have its first and second 'substantive meeting' with the parties? Are *ex parte* communications with the panel allowed? Are parties to a dispute obliged to provide the panel with the information or the documents that the panel requests? What are the consequences of a failure or refusal to provide information or documents requested by a panel? Can parties submit new evidence to the panel at any stage of the panel proceedings? What are the rights of third parties in panel proceedings? Why have these third party rights been extended in a few disputes? In your opinion, is interim review of panel reports useful and/or appropriate in the current WTO dispute settlement system? Discuss the importance of the confidentiality of the interim report. Is a panel report that is appealed, considered by the DSB for adoption? Do parties have an opportunity to comment on a panel report prior to its adoption by the DSB? Within what period can and must a panel report be adopted or rejected by the DSB? Can the adoption of a panel report be blocked? Look up what Members had to say on the panel report in *China – Electronic Payment Services (2012)*. Can panel proceedings be suspended indefinitely?

6.4   Appellate Body Proceedings

Almost seven out of ten panel reports circulated to date were appealed to the Appellate Body.[722] In contrast to panels, the Appellate Body has detailed standard working procedures set out in the *Working Procedures for Appellate Review* (the '*Working Procedures*').[723] Pursuant to Article 17.9 of the DSU, the Appellate Body has the authority to draw up these *Working Procedures* itself, in consultation with the Chair of the DSB and the WTO Director-General. In addition, where a procedural question arises that is not covered by the *Working Procedures*, the division hearing the appeal may, 'in the interest of fairness and orderly procedure in the

---

720 See Articles 16.1 and 16.3 of the DSU.
721 See Appellate Body Report, *EC – Bed Linen (Article 21.5 – India) (2003)*, para. 95.
722 See above, p. 240.
723 *Working Procedures for Appellate Review*, WT/AB/WP/6, dated 16 August 2010. This is a consolidated, revised version of the original *Working Procedures for Appellate Review*, WT/AB/WP/1, dated 15 February 1996.

conduct of the appeal', adopt an appropriate procedure for the purpose of that appeal.[724] The Additional Procedure adopted in the context of *EC – Asbestos (2001)* in respect of the filing of *amicus curiae* briefs, discussed above, is arguably the best-known example of the use of this authority.[725] More recently, the Appellate Body divisions in *EC and certain member States – Large Civil Aircraft (2011)* and *US – Large Civil Aircraft (2nd complaint) (2012)* adopted, *inter alia*, Additional Procedures for the protection of business confidential information (BCI) and highly sensitive business information (HSBI) submitted by the parties in these disputes.[726]

This sub-section discusses the following key aspects of the Appellate Body proceedings and issues that arise with respect to these proceedings: (1) the initiation of Appellate Body proceedings; (2) written submissions and the oral hearing; (3) the exchange of views and deliberations; and (4) the adoption of the Appellate Body report.

6.4.1   Initiation of Appellate Body Proceedings

Pursuant to Rule 20(1) of the *Working Procedures*, appellate review proceedings commence with a party's notification in writing to the DSB of its decision to appeal *and* the simultaneous filing of a notice of appeal with the Appellate Body. The notice of appeal must adequately identify the findings or legal interpretations of the panel that are being appealed as erroneous. To this end, Rule 20(2)(d) of the *Working Procedures* requires that a notice of appeal include: (1) identification of the alleged errors made by the panel; (2) a list of the legal provision(s) of the covered agreements that the panel is alleged to have erred in interpreting or applying; and (3) an indicative list of the paragraphs of the panel report containing the alleged errors.[727] Before the 2010 amendment to the *Working Procedures*, the underlying rationale of Rule 20(2)(d) was to require the appellant to provide notice of the alleged error(s) in the panel report that the appellant intended to argue on appeal. The notice of appeal was not expected to contain the reasons why the appellant regards the appealed findings or interpretations as erroneous.[728] Citing the relevant parts of the challenged panel report and basing claims on specifically identified legal provisions was considered sufficient to indicate the 'nature of the appeal' to which the other party must respond.[729] In *EC – Export Subsidies on Sugar (2005)*, Australia contended that the notice of appeal of the European Communities did not satisfy the 'due process requirements' of Rule 20(2)(d). The Appellate Body noted, however, that:

[i]n its Notice of Appeal, the European Communities 'seeks review' of six 'conclusion[s]' and 'related legal findings and interpretations' set out in certain specified paragraphs of the Panel Reports. The European Communities summarizes the substance of each contested conclusion and the related legal findings and interpretations. The Notice of Appeal also contains a list of the legal provisions of the covered agreements that the Panel is alleged to have erred in interpreting or applying.[730]

As this notice of appeal would allow the appellees to make a proper defence, the Appellate Body subsequently concluded that the notice satisfied the requirements of Rule 20(2)(d) of the *Working Procedures*.[731] If the notice of appeal failed to give the appellee sufficient notice of a claim of error, that claim could not, and would not, be considered by the Appellate Body. As further discussed below, since the 2010 amendment of the *Working Procedures*, the notice of appeal and the appellant submission are filed on the same day, and the notice of appeal has thus lost its function of giving 'advance' notice of the appellant's claims of error.[732] However, the notice of appeal still fulfils the important task of setting out, in brief and clearly, what the appeal is about. The notice of appeal still delineates the Appellate Body's terms of reference in a specific appeal. It is important that all claims made on appeal are *expressly* and *sufficiently* identified in the notice of appeal. In *US – Upland Cotton (2005)*, the Appellate Body held in that respect:

We acknowledge that the wording ... of the United States' Notice of Appeal (and, in particular, the use of the words 'for example') suggests that the findings listed ... are simply *examples* of findings challenged ... [being] an illustrative rather than exhaustive list of the findings that the United States intends to challenge. [A]n illustrative list is not conclusive as to whether the Notice of Appeal contains a sufficient reference to the Panel's findings ... for us to conclude that these findings are included in the United States' appeal.[733]

With regard to the issue of a panel's jurisdiction, however, the Appellate Body held in *US – Offset Act (Byrd Amendment) (2003)* that this issue is so fundamental that it is appropriate to consider claims that a panel has exceeded its jurisdiction even if such claims were not raised in the notice of appeal.[734] In the interest of due process, it would of course be preferable for the appellant to raise such an important issue, as the panel's jurisdiction, in the notice of appeal.

A party can appeal a panel report as soon as the report is circulated to WTO Members, and it can do so as long as the report has not yet been adopted by the DSB. In practice, parties usually appeal shortly before the meeting of the DSB that would consider the adoption of the panel report.

---

730 Appellate Body Report, *EC – Export Subsidies on Sugar (2005)*, para. 344.
731 See *ibid.*, paras. 344–5. See also e.g. Appellate Body Report, *US – Upland Cotton (2005)*, paras. 494–5 and *US – Offset Act (Byrd Amendment) (2003)*, para. 206.
732 See below, p. 287.
733 Appellate Body Report, *US – Upland Cotton (2005)*, para. 495.
734 See Appellate Body Report, *US – Offset Act (Byrd Amendment) (2003)*, para. 208.

Upon the commencement of an appeal, the Appellate Body division responsible for deciding the appeal draws up an appropriate working schedule in accordance with the time periods stipulated in the *Working Procedures*.[735] The working schedule sets forth precise dates for the filing of documents and includes a timetable of the division's work.[736] This working schedule, together with information on the composition of the Appellate Body division hearing the appeal, will be communicated to the parties within one or two days after the filing of the appeal. In exceptional circumstances, where strict adherence to a time period would result in manifest unfairness, a party or third party to the dispute may request modification of the working schedule for the appeal. This possibility is provided for in Rule 16(2) of the *Working Procedures* and has been used occasionally.[737]

If the other party to the dispute decides to 'cross appeal' pursuant to Rule 23 of the *Working Procedures*, it must file a 'notice of other appeal' within five days of the first notice.[738] The notice of other appeal must meet the same requirements as the first notice.[739]

A party to a dispute may not only initiate an appeal, it may – pursuant to Rule 30(1) of the *Working Procedures* – also withdraw that appeal at any stage of the appellate review process. Such a withdrawal leads normally to the termination of the appellate review. This was the case in *India – Autos (2002)*, where the Appellate Body issued, subsequent to the withdrawal, a brief report on the procedural history and the reason for not having completed its work namely, India's withdrawal of its appeal.[740] However, in some cases, parties withdrew their appeal in order to submit a new one. This happened, for example, in *EC – Sardines (2002)*. In this case, Peru contended that the appeal of the European Communities was insufficiently clear. In response, the European Communities withdrew its appeal and filed a more detailed one. The Appellate Body rejected Peru's claim that the withdrawal of the European Communities' appeal was invalid and clarified that there was no indication in Rule 30 that the right of withdrawal only encompasses unconditional withdrawal.[741] Conditions are allowed as long

---

735 See Rule 26(1) of the *Working Procedures*.   736 See Rule 26(2) of the *Working Procedures*.

737 Instances of extension have been where a Member has a deadline for written submission or a hearing in another WTO dispute, very close to the initial date set for filing of submissions (see Appellate Body Report, *Chile – Price Band System (Article 21.5 – Argentina) (2007)*, para. 11); where lead counsel for a party had prior commitments (see Appellate Body Report, *US – Softwood Lumber VI (Article 21.5 – Canada) (2006)*, para. 13); and where suspected bioterrorist attacks prevent internal consultations in legislative circles of a Member (see Appellate Body Report, *US – FSC (Article 21.5 – EC) (2002)*, para. 8). A hearing can also be brought forward if parties do not object (see Appellate Body Report, *US – Softwood Lumber V (Article 21.5 – Canada) (2006)*, footnote 29 to para. 9). While translation of documents is a valid ground for extension (see Appellate Body Report, *Guatemala – Cement I (1998)*, para. 4), it will not be unfair to decline a request for extension where documents requiring translation would be made available earlier than expected (see Appellate Body Report, *Mexico – Anti-Dumping Measures on Rice (2005)*, paras. 9–10).

738 On 'cross appeals', see above, p. 236.   739 See Rule 23(2) of the *Working Procedures*.

740 See Appellate Body Report, *India – Autos (2002)*, paras. 14–18.

741 See Appellate Body Report, *EC – Sardines (2002)*, para. 141. The Appellate Body ruled: 'While it is true that nothing in the text of Rule 30(1) explicitly permits an appellant to exercise its [Rule 30(1)] right subject to conditions, it is also true that nothing in the same text prohibits an appellant from doing so.' See *ibid*.

as they do not undermine the fair, prompt and effective resolution of the dispute and as long as the disputing party involved acts in good faith.[742] In *US – Softwood Lumber IV (2004)*, the United States filed a notice of appeal on 2 October 2003 and withdrew this notice the following day 'for scheduling reasons'. The withdrawal was conditional upon the right to re-file the notice of appeal at a later date, and, on 21 October 2003, the United States re-filed a 'substantively identical' notice of appeal.[743] This technique of withdrawal and re-filing of the notice of appeal has also been used in order to resolve workload and scheduling problems the Appellate Body is faced with. The Appellate Body allows an appellant to attach conditions to the withdrawal of its notice of appeal, saving its right to file a replacement notice.[744]

Note that Rule 23*bis* of the *Working Procedures* set out detailed rules for the amendment of a notice of appeal or notice of other appeal. Upon a request of the appellant or other appellant the division may authorise the amendment of a notice, taking into account the ninety-day timeframe for appellate review and the interests of fairness and orderly procedure.

6.4.2   Written Submissions and the Oral Hearing

On the same day as the filing of the notice of appeal, the appellant must file a written submission.[745] This written submission sets out a precise statement of the grounds of appeal, including the specific allegations of legal errors in the panel report, and the legal arguments in support of these allegations.[746] The parties to the dispute that have filed a notice of other appeal must file an other appellant's submission on the same day as the filing of the notice of other appeal.[747] Within eighteen days of the filing of the notice of appeal, any party that wishes to respond to allegations of legal errors, whether raised in the submission of the original appellant or in the submission(s) of other appellants, may file an appellee's submission.[748] The appellee's submission(s) set(s) out a precise statement of the grounds for opposing the specific allegations of legal errors raised in the (other) appellant's submission(s) and includes legal arguments in support thereof.[749] Third participants' submissions have to be filed within twenty-one days from the

---

742 See *ibid.*   743 See Appellate Body Report, *US – Softwood Lumber IV (2004)*, para. 6.
744 In *US – Line Pipe (2002)* and *US – FSC (2000)*, for example, the Appellate Body division and the appellees had prior knowledge of, and agreed to, the United States' reservation that it would file a fresh notice of appeal on withdrawing its initial notice under Rule 30(1). See Appellate Body Report, *US – Line Pipe (2002)*, para. 13; and Appellate Body Report, *US – FSC (2000)*, para. 4. However, as the Appellate Body ruled in *EC – Sardines (2002)*, such prior notice or agreement is not a precondition and a requirement for validity of the withdrawal and replacement of a notice of appeal. See Appellate Body Report, *EC – Sardines (2002)*, para. 138, footnote 31.
745 See Rule 21(1) of the *Working Procedures*.
746 See Rule 21(2) of the *Working Procedures*. The submission also sets out the nature of the decision or ruling sought.
747 See Rule 23(3) of the *Working Procedures*.
748 See Rules 22(1) and 23(4) of the *Working Procedures*.
749 See Rules 22(2) and 23(4) of the *Working Procedures*.

filing of the notice of appeal.[750] Should a participant or a third participant fail to file a submission within the required time periods, the division, after hearing the views of the participants, issues such order, including dismissal of the appeal, as it deems appropriate.[751]

The division responsible for deciding the appeal holds an oral hearing. According to the *Working Procedures*, the oral hearing is, as a general rule, held between thirty and forty-five days after the notice of appeal is filed.[752] The purpose of the oral hearing is to provide participants with an opportunity to present and argue their case before the division, in order to clarify the legal issues in the appeal. At the hearing, the appellant(s), appellee(s) and third participants first make brief opening statements on the core legal issues raised in the appeal.[753] After the oral presentations, the participants answer detailed questions posed by Appellate Body Members serving on the division regarding the issues raised in the appeal. At the end of the oral hearing, the participants are given the opportunity to make a brief concluding statement. In recent years, the oral hearing has usually been completed in two days. In complex cases, however, the oral hearing may take (much) longer. In *EC and certain member States – Large Civil Aircraft (2011)* and *US – Large Civil Aircraft (2nd complaint) (2012)*, the oral hearing took nine days and eight days, respectively. In both these disputes, the oral hearing took place in two sessions, each covering different issues.[754]

At any time during the appellate proceedings, the division may address questions to, or request additional memoranda from, any participant or third participant and specify the time periods by which written responses or memoranda shall be received.[755] Any such questions, responses or memoranda are made available simultaneously to the other participants and third participants in the appeal who are then given an opportunity to respond.[756]

Throughout the proceedings, the participants and third participants are precluded from having *ex parte* communications with the Appellate Body in respect of matters concerning the appeal. Neither a division nor any of its Members may

---

750 A third participant that does not wish to file a written submission may notify the Secretariat that it intends to appear at the oral hearing and whether it intends to make an oral statement. See Rules 24(1), 24(2) and 24(4) of the *Working Procedures*.

751 See Rule 29 of the *Working Procedures*. To date, there has been no need for such an order. Note also that Rule 18(5) provides for a procedure for parties and third parties to request authorisation to correct clerical errors (such as 'typographical mistakes, errors of grammar, or words or numbers placed in the wrong order') in the documents submitted.

752 See Rule 27(1) of the *Working Procedures*.

753 See Rule 27(3) of the *Working Procedures*. Any third participant may also make an oral presentation and may be questioned at the oral hearing. See below, pp. 288–90.

754 See Appellate Body Report, *EC and certain member States – Large Civil Aircraft (2011)*, paras. 19 and 26; and Appellate Body Report, *US – Large Civil Aircraft (2nd complaint) (2012)*, para. 32. The oral hearing took place on 11–17 November and 9–14 December 2010. In *US – Large Civil Aircraft (2nd complaint) (2012)*, the oral hearing took place on 16–19 August and 11–14 October 2011. In *EC and certain member States – Large Civil Aircraft (2011)*, a special oral hearing was held on 3 August 2010 to explore the issues relating to the additional procedures to protect BCI and HSBI.

755 See Rule 28(1) of the *Working Procedures*.

756 See Rule 28(2) of the *Working Procedures*. See also e.g. Appellate Body Report, *US – Section 211 Appropriations Act (2002)*, para. 13.

meet with or contact a participant or third participant in the absence of the other participants and third participants.[757]

As discussed above, the rights of third parties in panel proceedings are limited.[758] Normally, third parties only attend, and are heard at, a special session of the first substantive meeting of the panel, and receive the first written submissions of the parties only. Third participants, i.e. third parties participating in Appellate Body proceedings, have more comprehensive rights. In appellate review proceedings, third participants receive all submissions of the participants and have a right to file a written submission themselves, within twenty-one days of the filing of the notice of appeal, containing the grounds and legal arguments in support of their position.[759] A third participant has the right to participate in the oral hearing when: (1) it has filed a written submission; or (2) it has notified the Appellate Body Secretariat of its intention to participate in the oral hearing within twenty-one days of the notice of appeal.[760] A third party that has neither filed a written submission nor notified its intention to participate in the oral hearing within twenty-one days may still participate in the oral hearing. It may, at the discretion of the division and taking into account the requirements of due process, be allowed to make an oral statement at the hearing and respond to questions asked by the division.[761]

6.4.3 Exchange of Views and Deliberations

As noted above, the division responsible for deciding an appeal will exchange views on issues raised by the appeal with the other Members of the Appellate Body, before finalising its report.[762] The exchange of views puts into practice the principle of collegiality set out in the *Working Procedures*.[763] Depending on the number and complexity of the issues under discussion, this process usually takes place over two or more days, after the division has had its first deliberations on the issues raised by the appeal. For the importance of the exchange of views, please refer to section 5.3.1 above on the 'Membership and Structure of the Appellate Body'.[764]

Following the exchange of views, the division continues its deliberations and drafts the report. While initially Appellate Body reports were short (and lacked paragraph numbering), over the years the reports became much longer, due to: (1) the increased number of panel findings and legal interpretations developed by panels that are appealed; and (2) the increased complexity of the appeals. The longest report to date, the report in *EC and certain member States – Large Civil Aircraft (2011)*, is 645 pages long.

---

757 See Article 18.1 of the DSU and Rule 19(1) of the *Working Procedures*. Also, a Member of the Appellate Body who is not assigned to the division hearing the appeal shall not discuss any aspect of the subject-matter of the appeal with any participant or third participant. See Rule 19(3) of the *Working Procedures*.
758 See above, pp. 177, 280.   759 See Rule 24(1) of the *Working Procedures*.
760 See Rule 27(3) of the *Working Procedures*. Third participants are encouraged to file written submissions to facilitate their positions being taken into account. See Rule 24(3) of the *Working Procedures*.
761 See Rule 27(3)(b) and (c) of the *Working Procedures*.   762 See above, p. 234.
763 See Rule 4 of the *Working Procedures*.   764 See above, p. 234.

6.4.4   Adoption of Appellate Body Reports

When the report is finalised, the three Members of the division sign it. The report is then translated so that it is available in all three languages of the WTO.[765] After translation, the report is circulated to the WTO Members as an unrestricted document available to the public. The Appellate Body report is posted on the WTO website as a WT/DS document. Appellate Body reports are also included in the official *Dispute Settlement Reports of the World Trade Organization*, published by Cambridge University Press.[766]

Within thirty days following circulation of the Appellate Body report, the Appellate Body report *and* the panel report as upheld, modified or reversed by the Appellate Body are adopted by the DSB *unless* the DSB decides by consensus not to adopt the reports.[767] As stated in Article 17.14 of the DSU:

> The adopted Appellate Body report must be accepted unconditionally by the parties to the dispute.

The adoption procedure is, however, without prejudice to the right of Members to express their views on an Appellate Body report.[768] WTO Members often take full advantage of this opportunity to comment on the reports at the meeting of the DSB at which they are adopted. Generally, the winning party briefly praises the Appellate Body (and the panel) while the losing party is more critical. In recent years, participants and third participants tend to make more substantive comments on the findings and reasoning contained in the reports and on systemic implications of the rulings for future cases. The views of WTO Members on Appellate Body reports (and panel reports) are fully recorded in the minutes of the DSB meeting.

As the Appellate Body noted in *US – Shrimp (Article 21.5 – Malaysia) (2001)*, an Appellate Body report that is adopted by the DSB must be treated by the parties to a particular dispute 'as a final resolution to that dispute'.[769]

Questions and Assignments 3.17

How are the *Working Procedures for Appellate Review* established? What can a division hearing an appeal do when a procedural question arises that is not covered by the *Working Procedures*? Describe the various steps in appellate review proceedings. How and when can an appellate review proceeding be initiated? At what point in time are appellate review proceedings most frequently initiated? What is the function of a notice of appeal? Briefly describe the written submissions of the participants in appellate review proceedings. When does the Appellate Body meet with the participants in the appeal? Briefly describe the

---

765 In all appellate review proceedings to date, English has been the working language of the Appellate Body, and the Appellate Body reports were all drafted in English and then translated into French and Spanish. In a few appellate review proceedings, participants or third participants filed submissions or made oral statements in French or Spanish. When requested, interpretation is provided at the oral hearing.

766 See www.cambridge.org/gb/knowledge/series/series_display/item3937379/?site_locale=en_GB.

767 See Article 17.14 of the DSU. On the reverse consensus requirement, see above, p. 207.

768 See Article 17.14, last sentence, of the DSU.

769 See Appellate Body Report, *US – Shrimp (Article 21.5 – Malaysia) (2001)*, para. 97.

organisation of an oral hearing of the Appellate Body. Are *ex parte* communications with the Appellate Body allowed? Can the Appellate Body – like panels – consult experts? Can participants, and in particular developing-country participants, request additional time to prepare their written submissions in Appellate Body proceedings? Can an appeal be withdrawn in order to file a new appeal? Compare the rights of third parties in panel proceedings with the rights of third participants in Appellate Body proceedings. When is an Appellate Body report considered by the DSB for adoption? Is a panel report that has been reversed by the Appellate Body adopted by the DSB? If so, why? Look up what Members had to say on the Appellate Body report in *US – Tuna II (Mexico) (2012)*.

6.5   Implementation and Enforcement

If a panel and/or the Appellate Body concludes that the responding Member acted inconsistently with its obligations under one or more of the covered agreements, the process of WTO dispute settlement reaches its final stage, namely, the stage of the implementation and enforcement of the recommendations and rulings of the panel and/or the Appellate Body, as adopted by the DSB. Within thirty days of the adoption of the panel and/or Appellate Body report, the Member concerned must inform the DSB of its intentions in respect of the implementation of the recommendations and rulings.[770] This sub-section discusses the following procedural issues, which arise with respect to the implementation and enforcement of recommendations and rulings: (1) arbitration on the 'reasonable period of time for implementation'; (2) the surveillance of implementation by the DSB; (3) disagreement on implementation; and (4) arbitration on, and authorisation of, suspension of concessions or other obligations.

6.5.1   Arbitration on the 'Reasonable Period of Time for Implementation'

As discussed above, prompt or immediate compliance with the recommendations and rulings of the panel and/or the Appellate Body, as adopted by the DSB, is essential for the effective functioning of the WTO and the primary obligation of the Member concerned.[771] Prompt or immediate compliance with the recommendations and rulings means prompt or immediate withdrawal or modification of the WTO-inconsistent measure. However, if it is 'impracticable' to comply with the recommendations and rulings immediately – and this may often be the case – the Member concerned has, pursuant to Article 21.3 of the DSU, a reasonable period of time in which to do so.[772]

As discussed above, in most cases to date, the parties reach agreement on the 'reasonable period of time for implementation'.[773] However, if no agreement can be reached within forty-five days of the adoption of the recommendations and rulings, the original complainant can refer the matter to arbitration under Article 21.3(c) of the DSU. The parties must agree on an arbitrator, and, if they

---

770 See Article 21.3 of the DSU.   771 See above, p. 195.
772 See Article 21.3(a), (b) and (c) of the DSU.   773 See above p. 195.

cannot do so within ten days, either party may request the Director-General of the WTO to appoint an arbitrator.[774] The Director-General will consult the parties and appoint an arbitrator within ten days. The DSU does not provide for any rule or guideline as to the professional or other requirements persons should meet to serve as an Article 21.3(c) arbitrator. However, a practice has developed that present or former Members of the Appellate Body serve as Article 21.3(c) arbitrators. They do so not as Members of the Appellate Body but in a personal capacity.

While not set out in the DSU, the arbitration proceedings involve the sequential filing of written submissions and an oral hearing. The DSU does require that the arbitration proceedings do not exceed ninety days commencing on the date of the adoption of the panel and Appellate Body reports by the DSB. As this requirement is often not realistic, it is – with the agreement of the parties – commonly set aside. The arbitration award indicating the 'reasonable period of time for implementation' is issued to the parties and circulated to all WTO Members. Note that, unlike panel or Appellate Body reports, an Article 21.3(c) arbitration award is *not* adopted by the DSB. An arbitration award is posted as a WT/DS document on the WTO website.

6.5.2   Surveillance of Implementation by the DSB

During the 'reasonable period of time for implementation', the DSB keeps the implementation of adopted recommendations and rulings under surveillance.[775] At any time following adoption of the recommendations and rulings, any WTO Member may raise the issue of implementation at the DSB. Starting six months after establishment of the reasonable period of time, the issue of implementation is placed on the agenda of each DSB meeting and remains on the DSB's agenda until the issue is resolved. At least ten days prior to such a DSB meeting, the Member concerned must provide the DSB with a status report on its progress in the implementation of the recommendations or rulings.[776] Note that, pursuant to Article 22.8 of the DSU, the DSB shall 'continue to keep under surveillance the implementation of adopted recommendations or rulings' also after the reasonable period of time has expired and this for as long as there is no implementation. For example, at the DSB meeting of 31 August 2012, the United States presented its 118th status report on its implementation of the recommendations and rulings in *US – Section 211 Appropriations Act (2002)*.[777] At this meeting, the European Union (the complainant), Angola, Argentina, Bolivia,

---

774 To date, the parties have been able to agree on the Article 21.3(c) arbitrator in most cases.

775 See Article 21.6 of the DSU.

776 See Article 21.6 of the DSU. The status reports under Article 21.6 of the DSU are posted on the WTO website as WT/DS documents. For the debate on these reports, see the minutes of the relevant DSB meeting (WT/DSB/M/...).

777 Status Report by the United States, *US – Section 211 Appropriations Act (2002)*, WT/DS176/11/Add.117, dated 21 August 2012.

Brazil, Chile, China, Cuba, Dominican Republic, Ecuador, Mexico, Nicaragua, Venezuela and Vietnam expressed (grave) concerns about the United States' failure to implement the recommendations and rulings in this case adopted by the DSB in 2002.[778] The United States responded that 'there were bills pending in the current Congress that would address the WTO findings in this matter in different ways'.[779]

6.5.3   Disagreement on Implementation

Before the expiry of the reasonable period of time, the respondent must withdraw or modify the measure that was found to be WTO-inconsistent. In other words, the respondent must take the appropriate implementing measures. It is, however, not uncommon for the original complainant and respondent to disagree on whether any implementing measure is taken or whether the implementing measure taken is WTO-consistent. Article 21.5 of the DSU provides that such disagreement as to the existence, or consistency with WTO law, of implementing measures shall be decided:

through recourse to these dispute settlement procedures, including wherever possible resort to the original panel.

It is now generally accepted that recourse to 'these dispute settlement procedures' means recourse to the procedures set out in Articles 4 to 20 of the DSU.[780] The normal procedures discussed in previous sections apply with a few deviations. The most notable of these deviations is that Article 21.5 requires that the panel circulate its report within ninety days after the date of the referral of the matter to it.[781] However, this timeframe is not realistic, as is demonstrated by the fact that the average duration of Article 21.5 compliance proceedings is now 246 days, i.e. more than double the time allowed.[782]

The issue of which measures fall within the scope of jurisdiction of a 'compliance' panel, or, in other words, when a measure is a 'measure taken to comply with the recommendations and rulings', was addressed by the Appellate Body in *US – Softwood Lumber IV (Article 21.5 – Canada) (2005)*. The Appellate Body

---

778 Dispute Settlement Body, *Minutes of Meeting held on 31 August 2012*, WT/DSB/M/321, dated 7 November 2012, paras. 4–17.

779 *Ibid.*, para. 18.

780 While Article 21.5 refers to 'these procedures', there was initially considerable disagreement among Members as to which procedures were included. It is now generally accepted that 'these procedures' include appellate review pursuant to Article 17 of the DSU. Note that, in *US – FSC (Article 21.5 – EC II) (2006)*, the Appellate Body ruled that the rules of Article 6.2 with regard to the request for the establishment of a panel (and the sufficiency thereof) applied in the context of an Article 21.5 procedure, albeit that Article 6.2 needs to be interpreted in light of Article 21.5. See Appellate Body Report, *US – FSC (Article 21.5 – EC II) (2006)*, para. 59; and see also above p. 209. It is still disputed by some WTO Members that 'these procedures' also include consultations pursuant to Article 4 of the DSU.

781 For the timeframe of the standard panel proceedings, see above, p. 246. Another notable deviation is that the complainant and respondent will each file only one submission to the panel and the panel will have only one meeting with the parties. See above, p. 293.

782 See www.worldtradelaw.net/dsc/database/paneltiming1.asp.

noted that the limits on the claims that can be raised in Article 21.5 proceedings 'should not allow circumvention by Members by allowing them to comply through one measure, while, at the same time, negating compliance through another'.[783] According to the Appellate Body, for a new measure to be a 'measure taken to comply with the recommendations and rulings' within the meaning of Article 21.5 of the DSU, there have to be 'sufficiently close links' between the original measure and the new measure so that the latter can be characterised as 'taken to comply' with the recommendations and rulings concerning the original measure.[784] Also note that, as the Appellate Body ruled in *Canada – Aircraft (Article 21.5 – Brazil) (2000)*:

> in carrying out its review under Article 21.5 of the DSU, a panel is not confined to examining the 'measures taken to comply' from the perspective of the claims, arguments and factual circumstances that related to the measure that was the subject of the original proceedings. Although these may have some relevance in proceedings under Article 21.5 of the DSU, Article 21.5 proceedings involve, in principle, not the original measure, but rather a new and different measure which was not before the original panel.[785]

If an Article 21.5 panel were restricted to examining the new measure from the perspective of the claims, arguments and factual circumstances that related to the original measure, the effectiveness of an Article 21.5 review would be seriously undermined because an Article 21.5 panel would then be unable to examine fully the 'consistency with a covered agreement of the measures taken to comply', as required by Article 21.5 of the DSU.[786] The Appellate Body accordingly ruled in *Canada – Aircraft (Article 21.5 – Brazil) (2000)* that the panel was not merely mandated to see if the revised subsidy programme of Canada had dropped the WTO-inconsistent aspects that the original dispute pertained to, but was also mandated to consider Brazil's new claim that the revised programme was inconsistent with Article 3.1(a) of the *SCM Agreement*. Inconsistency with Article 3.1(a) of the *SCM Agreement* had not been an issue before the original panel but this did not prevent the Article 21.5 panel from examining this claim. In *EC – Bed Linen (Article 21.5 – India) (2003)*, the Appellate Body found that:

> *new* claims, arguments, and factual circumstances different from those raised in the original proceedings [may be raised], because a 'measure taken to comply' may be *inconsistent* with WTO obligations *in ways different* from the original measure ... [A]n Article 21.5 panel could not properly carry out its mandate to assess whether a 'measure taken to comply' is *fully consistent* with WTO obligations if it were precluded from examining claims additional to, and different from, the claims raised in the original proceedings.[787]

The panel in *US – Gambling (Article 21.5 – Antigua and Barbuda) (2007)* addressed the question whether Article 21.5 could be used by the respondent

---

783 Appellate Body Report, *US – Softwood Lumber IV (Article 21.5 – Canada) (2005)*, para. 72.
784 See Appellate Body Report, *Canada – Aircraft (Article 21.5 – Brazil) (2000)*, para. 36.
785 *Ibid.*, para. 41.   786 See *ibid.*
787 Appellate Body Report, *EC – Bed Linen (Article 21.5 – India) (2003)*, para. 79.

to re-litigate the WTO-consistency of a measure already found to be WTO-inconsistent. In this case, the United States requested that the 'compliance' panel re-examine the WTO-consistency of its original measure 'based on new evidence and arguments not previously available to the Panel or the Appellate Body'.[788] The panel rejected this request of the United States. The panel found that compliance entails a *change* relevant to the measure. This may take various forms, including the repeal or modification of the measure at issue, a change in the way the measure is applied, or changes in the factual or legal background that modify the effects of the measure.[789] In this case, no such changes had occurred.[790] The panel made clear that the respondent's original defence cannot be re-litigated in an Article 21.5 proceeding on the basis of new arguments or evidence.[791] To reassess the consistency of the original measure would, according to the panel, mean that the original conclusion in the Appellate Body report was not final.[792]

To date, Members have initiated forty-three Article 21.5 'compliance' proceedings;[793] and twenty-nine Article 21.5 panel reports and eighteen Article 21.5 Appellate Body reports have been circulated.[794] In four disputes, there were two successive Article 21.5 'compliance' proceedings.[795] In most Article 21.5 procedures thus far, the original panel served as the compliance panel.[796]

Like 'original' panel and Appellate Body reports, Article 21.5 'compliance' panel and Appellate Body reports become legally binding on the parties only after adoption by the DSB. The DSB adopts these reports by reverse consensus within thirty days after circulation.

An important difference between the recommendations and rulings of 'original' reports and Article 21.5 'compliance' reports is that the respondent does not benefit from a reasonable period of time to implement the recommendations and rulings of Article 21.5 reports. Immediately after the adoption of these report(s), the complainant can request authorisation from the DSB to suspend the application of concessions or other obligations to the respondent.

---

788 See Panel Report, *US – Gambling (Article 21.5 – Antigua and Barbuda) (2007)*, para. 6.40. The original complainant, Antigua and Barbuda, argued before the panel that the United States had taken no measures to comply with the DSB rulings as the measures challenged in the original proceeding had not been amended, supplanted or otherwise changed. The US countered that the 'measures taken to comply' can be the same measures at issue in the original proceeding. By bringing new evidence that these measures satisfy the requirements of the chapeau of Article XIV, the US submitted that it had complied with the DSB rulings. See *ibid.*, para. 6.4.

789 *Ibid.*, paras. 6.20–6.22.   790 See *ibid.*, para. 6.27.   791 *Ibid.*, paras. 6.15–6.16.

792 See *ibid.*, para. 6.55. As the panel pointed out, this would be 'contrary to the obligation on parties to a dispute, under Article 17.14 of the DSU, "unconditionally" to accept an Appellate Body report that has been adopted by the DSB'. See *ibid.*, para. 6.57.

793 See www.worldtradelaw.net/dsc/database/searchcomplaintscompliance.asp.

794 See www.worldtradelaw.net/dsc/database/art215reports1.asp.

795 See *Brazil – Aircraft (Article 21.5 – Canada II) (2001)*; *Canada – Dairy (Article 21.5 – New Zealand and US II) (2003)*; *US – FSC (Article 21.5 – EC II) (2006)*; and *EC – Bananas III (Article 21.5 – Ecuador II) (2008)*.

796 Note, however, that in, for example, *US – Softwood Lumber IV (Article 21.5 – Canada) (2005)* and *Chile – Price Band System (Article 21.5 – Argentina) (2007)* certain panellists of the original panel were replaced because they had the nationality of third parties in the Article 21.5 proceedings.

6.5.4 Compensation or Retaliation

If the respondent fails to implement the recommendations and rulings correctly within the reasonable period of time agreed by the parties or determined by an arbitrator, the respondent will, at the request of the complainant, enter into negotiations with the latter party in order to come to an agreement on mutually acceptable compensation.[797] If satisfactory compensation is not agreed upon within twenty days of the expiry of the reasonable period of time, the complainant may request authorisation from the DSB to suspend the application to the respondent of concessions or other obligations under the covered agreements.[798] In other words, it may seek authorisation to retaliate. The DSB must decide on the authorisation to retaliate within thirty days of the expiry of the reasonable period of time.[799] As discussed above, the DSB decides on the authorisation to retaliate by reverse consensus; the authorisation is thus quasi-automatic.[800]

However, if the non-complying Member objects to the level of suspension proposed, or claims that the principles and procedures for suspension set out in Article 22.3 of the DSU have not been followed,[801] the matter may be referred to arbitration before the DSB takes a decision.[802] This arbitration under Article 22.6 of the DSU is carried out by the original panel, if the same members are available, or by an arbitrator appointed by the Director-General.[803] The arbitration must be completed within sixty days of expiry of the reasonable period of time,[804] and a second arbitration or appeal is not possible.[805] The DSB is informed promptly of the decision of the arbitrator and grants, by reverse consensus, the requested authorisation to suspend concessions or other obligations to the extent that the request is consistent with the decision of the arbitrators.[806] Decisions by the arbitrators under Article 22.6 of the DSU are circulated to WTO Members, and posted on the WTO website as WT/DS documents.

Finally, there are two issues with regard to the decision-making on retaliation that are currently not, or not adequately, dealt with in the DSU and have, therefore, given rise to considerable controversy, namely: (1) the 'sequencing issue'; and (2) the 'post-retaliation issue'.[807]

With regard to the 'sequencing issue', recall that if the respondent fails to implement the recommendations and rulings within the 'reasonable period of time' and agreement on compensation cannot be reached, the complainant

---

797 See Article 22.2 of the DSU. On compensation under Article 22, see above, p. 295.
798 See Article 22.2 of the DSU.   799 See *ibid.*
800 See above, p. 296.   801 See above, p. 201.
802 See Article 22.6 of the DSU. On the appropriate level of suspension and on the principles and procedures of suspension, see above, p. 193.
803 See Article 22.6 of the DSU.   804 See *ibid.* In practice, this timeframe has proven to be unrealistic.
805 See Article 22.7 of the DSU.
806 See *ibid.* Note that the Decision of the Arbitrators under Article 22.6 is notified to the DSB but is not adopted by it.
807 Both issues are on the agenda of the Doha Round negotiations on DSU reform. See above, p. 88.

may request the DSB authorisation to retaliate.[808] However, it is clear that such
retaliation is *only* called for when the respondent has failed to take a WTO-
consistent implementing measure. As also discussed above, the complainant and
the respondent may disagree on whether such implementing measure exists or
whether it is WTO-consistent. To resolve such disagreements, the DSU provides
for the Article 21.5 procedure. However, due to 'sloppy' drafting of the DSU,
there is a conflict between the timeframe for this Article 21.5 procedure and the
timeframe within which authorisation for the suspension of concessions and
other obligations must be requested and obtained from the DSB. Pursuant to
Article 22.6, the authorisation for retaliation must be granted by the DSB within
thirty days of the expiry of the reasonable period of time. It is clear that it is not
possible to obtain authorisation for retaliation within thirty days, in cases where
the complainant must first submit the disagreement on implementation to an
Article 21.5 'compliance' panel. In *EC – Bananas III (1997)*, this inconsistency
led in 1999 to a serious institutional crisis in which the United States insisted on
its right to obtain authorisation for retaliation and the European Communities
asserted that an Article 21.5 'compliance' panel first had to establish that the
implementing measures taken by the European Communities were not WTO-
consistent. Eventually, a pragmatic compromise was found to defuse the crisis.
However, the problem of the relationship between these two procedures (referred
to as the 'sequencing issue') remains, and a change to the DSU is required to
resolve the problem. In the meantime, parties commonly agree, on an *ad hoc*
basis, that the procedure of examining the WTO-consistency of the implementing measures will need to be terminated before the authorisation for retaliation
measures may be granted.[809] As the European Communities noted in a communication of March 2002:

> In light of the practice followed consistently since [1999], it would appear that Members
> now broadly agree that completing the procedure established under Article 21.5 DSU is a
> prerequisite for invoking the provisions of Article 22 DSU, in case of disagreement among
> the parties about implementation.[810]

However, this does not mean that the DSU does not need to be amended on this
point in order to ensure legal certainty and predictability of the system for all
its Members.

---

808 See above, p. 200.
809 See e.g. Understanding between the European Union and the United States Regarding Procedures under
  Articles 21 and 22 of the DSU, *European Communities and certain member States – Large Civil Aircraft
  (2011)*, WT/DS316/21, dated 17 January 2012.
810 Communication from the European Communities, *Contribution of the European Communities and its Member
  States to the Improvement of the WTO Dispute Settlement Understanding*, TN/DS/W/1, dated 13 March 2002,
  4. While there is broad agreement that retaliation cannot be authorised before an Article 21.5 'compliance'
  ruling is made, this agreement is 'operationalised' in two different ways: (1) in some cases both Article 21.5
  and 22.6 proceedings are initiated at the end of the reasonable period of time for implementation, and the
  Article 22.6 proceeding is suspended until completion of the Article 21.5 proceeding; and (2) in other cases
  only the Article 21.5 proceeding is initiated and the parties agree that the respondent will not object to a
  request for authorisation of retaliation in the DSB once the Article 21.5 'compliance' proceeding is completed.

With regard to the 'post-retaliation issue', note that the DSU currently does not provide for a procedure for the withdrawal or termination of the authorisation to retaliate. The lack of such procedure is of course not a problem when the complainant is satisfied that the respondent has withdrawn or the WTO-inconsistent measure. A problem arises, however, when the complainant is not satisfied that the respondent has withdrawn or adequately modified the WTO-inconsistent measure and thus maintains the retaliation measure. This situation arose in *EC – Hormones (1998)*, and led the European Communities to initiate new dispute settlement proceedings against the United States and Canada in an effort to secure the lifting of their retaliation measures. In *US/Canada – Continued Suspension (2008)*, the Appellate Body held:

Members must act in a cooperative manner so that the normal state of affairs, that is, compliance with the covered agreements and absence of the suspension of concessions, may be restored as quickly as possible. Thus, both the suspending Member and the implementing Member share the responsibility to ensure that the application of the suspension of concessions is 'temporary' ... Where, as in this dispute, an implementing measure is taken and Members disagree as to whether this measure achieves substantive compliance, both Members have a duty to engage in WTO dispute settlement in order to establish whether the conditions in Article 22.8 have been met and whether, as a consequence, the suspension of concessions must be terminated. Once substantive compliance has been confirmed through WTO dispute settlement procedures, the authorization to suspend concessions lapses by operation of law (*ipso jure*).[811]

The Appellate Body recommended that the DSB request Canada, the United States and the European Communities:

to initiate Article 21.5 proceedings without delay in order to resolve their disagreement as to whether the European Communities has removed the measure found to be inconsistent in *EC – Hormones* and whether the application of the suspension of concessions by the United States remains legally valid.[812]

Questions and Assignments 3.18

What is the object and purpose of an Article 21.3(c) proceeding? Who can serve as an Article 21.3(c) arbitrator? What is the mandate of Article 21.3(c) arbitrators? Find the Article 21.3(c) award in *US – COOL (2012)*. What was the ruling of the arbitrator in that case? Find the latest Article 21.6 status report in *US – Section 211 Appropriations Act (2002)*. How did the WTO Members react to this report? When will an Article 21.5 procedure be initiated? What are the differences between the 'original' proceedings and the Article 21.5 'compliance' proceedings? Which measures can be the subject of an Article 21.5 procedure? To what extent can 'new' claims of WTO-inconsistency be made in an Article 21.5 procedure? Can an Article 21.5 proceeding be used to re-litigate the WTO-consistency of the measure that was found to be WTO-inconsistent? When *must* the respondent enter into negotiations on compensation? When may the complainant request the DSB to authorise retaliation measures? Who decides on the level of retaliation? Explain briefly what the so-called 'sequencing issue' is and how it is 'handled' now. What is the procedure for terminating retaliation?

811 Appellate Body Report, *US/Canada – Continued Suspension (2008)*, para. 310.
812 See *ibid.*, para. 737.

7   DEVELOPING-COUNTRY MEMBERS AND WTO DISPUTE SETTLEMENT

As noted above, developing-country Members have made much use of the WTO dispute settlement system. In many years since 2000, developing-country Members, as a group, have brought more disputes to the WTO than developed-country Members.[813] To date, Brazil (twenty-six complaints), Mexico (twenty-three complaints), India (twenty-one complaints), Argentina (eighteen complaints), Thailand (thirteen complaints), China (eleven complaints) and Chile (ten complaints) are among the biggest users of the system. The 2004 Sutherland Report observed, with regard to the record of complaints under the WTO dispute settlement system, that:

[o]ne of the interesting facets of this record of complaints is a much greater participation of developing countries than was the case in the GATT dispute settlement system. Of course, the major trading powers continue to act either as complainant or respondent in a very large number of cases. Given their large amount of trade with an even greater number of markets, it could hardly be otherwise. Yet, developing countries – even some of the poorest (when given the legal assistance now available to them) – are increasingly taking on the most powerful. That is how it should be.[814]

Developing-country Members have used the WTO dispute settlement system to bring cases against the economic superpowers and have done so successfully. *US – Underwear*, a complaint by Costa Rica, and even more so *US – Gambling (2005)*, a complaint by Antigua and Barbuda, are well-known examples of successful 'David versus Goliath' use of the system. Developing-country Members have also used the system against other developing-country Members. Examples of such use of the system are *Turkey – Textiles (1999)*, a complaint by India; *Chile – Price Band System (2002)*, a complaint by Argentina; *Thailand – Cigarettes (Philippines) (2011)*, a complaint by the Philippines; and *Dominican Republic – Safeguard Measures (2012)*, complaints by Costa Rica, El Salvador, Guatemala and Honduras. To date, least-developed-country Members have used the WTO dispute settlement system only once. In February 2004, Bangladesh requested consultations with India on the imposition of anti-dumping duties by India on batteries from Bangladesh.[815] To date, the WTO dispute settlement system has never been used *against*

---

813 Developing-country Members brought more disputes to the WTO than developed-country Members in 2000, 2001, 2003, 2005, 2008, 2010 and 2012. See above, p. 158.

814 Report by the Consultative Board to the Director-General Supachai Panitchpakdi, The Future of the WTO: Addressing Institutional Challenges in the New Millennium (the 'Sutherland Report') (WTO, 2004), para. 222.

815 Request for Consultations by Bangladesh, *India – Anti-Dumping Measure on Batteries from Bangladesh*, WT/DS306/1, dated 2 February 2004. On 20 February 2006, the parties informed the DSB that a mutually satisfactory solution to the matter had been achieved. The anti-dumping measure addressed in the request for consultations had been terminated by India. See Notification of Mutually Satisfactory Solution, *India – Anti-Dumping Measure on Batteries from Bangladesh*, WT/DS306/3, dated 23 February 2006.

least-developed-country Members. Note in this respect that Article 24.1 of the DSU requires Members to 'exercise due restraint' in using the WTO dispute settlement system in disputes involving a least-developed-country Member. The DSU contains in addition a number of other provisions providing for special treatment or consideration for developing-country Members involved in WTO dispute settlement. This section examines these provisions. It also discusses the legal assistance available to developing-country Members involved in WTO dispute settlement.

7.1   Special Rules for Developing-Country Members

The DSU recognises the difficulties developing-country Members may encounter when they are involved in WTO dispute settlement. Therefore, the DSU contains some special rules for developing-country Members. Such special DSU rules are found in Article 3.12 (regarding the application of the 1966 Decision),[816] Article 4.10 (regarding consultations), Article 8.10 (regarding the composition of panels), Article 12.10 (regarding consultations and the time to prepare and present arguments), Article 12.11 (regarding the content of panel reports), Article 21.2 (regarding implementation of adopted recommendations and rulings), Article 21.7 (regarding the DSB surveillance of the implementation of adopted recommendations or rulings), Article 24 (regarding least-developed countries) and Article 27 (on the assistance of the WTO Secretariat). Most of these special rules for developing countries are discussed above.[817] The special rules, for the most part, have these special rules have been of limited significance to date.

7.2   Legal Assistance for Developing-Country Members

Many developing-country Members do not have the specialised 'in-house' legal expertise to participate in the most effective manner in WTO dispute settlement. However, as discussed above, WTO Members can be assisted and represented by private legal counsel in WTO dispute settlement proceedings.[818] The Appellate Body noted in *EC – Bananas III (1997)*:

that representation by counsel of a government's own choice may well be a matter of particular significance – especially for developing-country Members – to enable them to participate fully in dispute settlement proceedings.[819]

816 Decision of 5 April 1966 on Procedures under Article XXIII of the GATT, BISD 14S/18. Article 3.12 of the DSU allows a developing-country Member that brings a complaint against a developed-country Member to invoke the provisions of the Decision of 5 April 1966 of the GATT Contracting Parties. These provisions may be invoked as an 'alternative' to the provisions contained in Articles 4, 5, 6 and 12 of the DSU. To date, the provisions of the 1966 Decision have been 'invoked' only once, on 21 March 2007, in a complaint brought by Colombia against the European Communities' new 'tariff-only' regime for bananas applied from 1 January 2006. See Request for Consultations by Colombia, *European Communities – Regime for the Importation of Bananas*, WT/DS361/1. The reason for the lack of enthusiasm for the provisions of the 1966 Decision is undoubtedly that the DSU provisions afford developing-country complaining parties treatment at least as favourable as, if not more favourable than, the treatment afforded by the 1966 Decision.
817 See e.g. above, pp. 198, 215, 229, 274 and 277–80.
818 See above, p. 262.   819 Appellate Body Report, *EC – Bananas III (1997)*, para. 12.

However, assistance and representation by private legal counsel has its costs, and these costs may be quite burdensome for developing-country Members. Other forms of assistance are needed to: (1) lower further the threshold for developing-country Members, and, in particular, low-income-country and least-developed-country Members, to bring complaints against other Members; or (2) support developing-country Members against whom complaints are brought by other Members. The WTO Secretariat assists all Members in respect of dispute settlement when they so request. However, the DSU recognises that there may be a need to provide additional legal advice and assistance to developing-country Members.[820] To meet this additional need, Article 27.2 of the DSU requires that the WTO Secretariat make qualified legal experts available to help any developing-country Member that so requests.[821] The extent to which the Secretariat can assist developing-country Members is, however, limited by the requirement that the Secretariat's experts give assistance in a manner 'ensuring the continued impartiality of the Secretariat'.[822]

Effective legal assistance for developing-country Members in dispute settlement proceedings is given by the Geneva-based Advisory Centre on WTO Law (ACWL). The ACWL is an intergovernmental organisation, fully independent of the WTO, which functions essentially as a law firm specialising in WTO law, providing legal services and training exclusively to developing-country and economy-in-transition members of the ACWL and *all* least-developed countries. The ACWL provides support at all stages of WTO dispute settlement proceedings at discounted rates. The ACWL currently has forty-one members: eleven developed countries and thirty developing countries and economies-in-transition.[823] The services of the ACWL are at present available to a total of seventy-three countries. On the occasion of the official opening of the ACWL on 5 October 2001, Mike Moore, then WTO Director-General, said:

> The International Court of Justice has a small fund out of which costs of legal assistance can be paid for countries who need such help. But today marks the first time a true legal aid centre has been established within the international legal system, with a view to combating the unequal possibilities of access to international justice as between States.[824]

Since its establishment, the ACWL has become a major player in WTO dispute settlement. During the period from 2001 to 2012, the ACWL provided support in almost forty WTO dispute settlement proceedings.[825] In addition, the ACWL provides free of charge legal advice on substantive and procedural aspects of WTO law.[826] Finally, the ACWL also offers training courses and seminars on

---

820 See Article 27.2 of the DSU.

821 For this purpose, the Institute for Training and Technical Cooperation, a division of the WTO Secretariat, presently employs two independent consultants on a permanent part-time basis. See *WTO Analytical Index (2012)*, Volume II, 1884.

822 Article 27.2, final sentence, of the DSU.   823 See www.acwl.ch/e/members/Introduction.html.

824 Inauguration of the ACWL: Speech delivered by Director-General of the WTO, 5 October 2001, at www.acwl.ch/e/news/milestone_0004.html.

825 See www.acwl.ch/e/disputes/WTO_disputes.html.   826 See www.acwl.ch/e/legal_advice/legal_advice.html.

WTO law and policy and provides for the Secondment Programme for Trade Lawyers, under which government lawyers from least-developed countries and developing-country ACWL members join the staff of the ACWL for a period of nine months.[827]

Questions and Assignments 3.19

Does the DSU take the particular situation of developing-country Members into account? Do developing-country Members involved in WTO dispute settlement benefit from legal assistance? By whom and under what conditions is this assistance granted?

8   FUTURE CHALLENGES TO WTO DISPUTE SETTLEMENT

In 1996, the then WTO Director-General Renato Ruggiero referred to the WTO dispute settlement system as 'the jewel in the crown of the WTO'. While obviously not perfect, the WTO dispute settlement system has by and large lived up to, if not surpassed, Ruggiero's high expectations. The frequent use by a significant number of developed- as well as developing-country Members to resolve often politically sensitive issues, and the high degree of compliance with the recommendations and rulings, testify to the success of the WTO dispute settlement system. The 2004 Sutherland Report on *The Future of the WTO* stated:

> The current WTO dispute settlement procedures – constructed with painstaking, innovative, hard work during the Uruguay Round – are to be admired, and are a very significant and positive step forward in the general system of rules-based international trade diplomacy. In many ways, the system has already achieved a great deal, and is providing some of the necessary attributes of 'security and predictability', which traders and other market participants need, and which is called for in the Dispute Settlement Understanding (DSU), Article 3.[828]

The WTO dispute settlement system makes an important contribution to the objective that within the WTO 'right prevails over might'. As the legendary Julio Lacarte Muró, the first Chair of the Appellate Body, remarked, the system works to the advantage of all Members, but it especially gives security to developing-country Members that have often, in the past, lacked the political or economic clout to enforce their rights and to protect their interests.[829]

While there exists much satisfaction with the performance of the WTO dispute settlement system, there have been negotiations on its further improvement ever

---

827 See www.acwl.ch/e/training/training.html.
828 Report by the Consultative Board to the Director-General Supachai Panitchpakdi, *The Future of the WTO: Addressing Institutional Challenges in the New Millennium* (the 'Sutherland Report') (WTO, 2004), para. 213.
829 See J. Lacarte and P. Gappah, 'Developing Countries and the WTO Legal and Dispute Settlement System', *Journal of International Economic Law*, 2000, 400. Ambassador Lacarte Muró served as the Deputy Executive Secretary of the GATT in 1947–8, and as Permanent Representative of Uruguay to the GATT in the 1960s, 1980s and early 1990s. He was the Chair of the Uruguay Round committee that negotiated the DSU.

since 1998.[830] Currently, DSU reform negotiations take place in the context of the Doha Round negotiations.[831] The proposals for improvement tabled and discussed since the start of these negotiations are many and wide-ranging.[832] A few of these proposals suggest quite radical reforms to the system, such as the EU proposals for the replacement of the *ad hoc* panels with a permanent panel body or a roster of permanent panellists (these proposals are currently no longer actively considered); and the US proposals for more Member-control over WTO dispute settlement, and in particular over panel and Appellate Body reports (these proposals to curtail the WTO dispute settlement system are still being considered). Most proposals for improvement are, however, more technical in nature, although they may touch on politically sensitive issues. Examples of such proposals are the proposals on: (1) timeframes and time-saving by, for example, halving the time for mandatory consultations, and establishing panels by reverse consensus at the *first* DSB meeting; (2) improved conditions for Members seeking to join consultations; (3) the notification of mutually agreed solutions; (4) the facilitation of panel composition; (5) the extension of third party rights; (6) the protection of business confidential information; (7) the issue of *amicus curiae* briefs; (8) enhanced transparency through opening panel meetings and Appellate Body hearings to the public; (9) the suspension of panel proceedings; (10) the introduction of remand in Appellate Body proceedings; (11) the 'sequencing' issue; (12) the 'post-retaliation' issue; (13) the promotion of prompt and effective compliance by strengthening the remedies available for breach of WTO law, including collective retaliation and monetary compensation; and (14) the strengthening of special and differential treatment for developing-country Members.

In July 2008, the Chair of the DSB Special Session issued under his own responsibility a consolidated draft legal text, which has been the basis for the DSU reform negotiations since.[833] In April 2011, the Chair last reported on the state of play of the negotiations as follows:

Participants have engaged in our recent work in a constructive spirit, and we have made measurable progress in a number of areas ... Specifically, we are close to an understanding on draft legal text on sequencing, we have identified key points of convergence on post-retaliation, and we have conducted constructive work on third-party rights, timesavings and various aspects of effective compliance. We have also discussed certain aspects of flexibility and Member-control, and in that context, made substantial progress towards draft legal text on the suspension of panel proceedings ... Nonetheless, much work remains

---

830 As agreed at the time of the adoption of the *WTO Agreement*, the WTO Members first reviewed the DSU in 1998 and 1999.

831 See Ministerial Conference, *Doha Ministerial Declaration*, WT/MIN(01)/DEC/1, dated 20 November 2001, para. 30.

832 All publicly available documents relating to the DSU reform negotiations can be found on the WTO website as TN/DS documents.

833 This text was initially circulated as an informal document (JOB(08)/81) on 18 July 2008 but it is reproduced as Appendix A to the 2011 Report of the Chair of the DSB Special Session to the Trade Negotiations Committee, TN/DS/25, dated 21 April 2011.

to be done in order to reach agreement ... In addition to completing the work on the issues referred to above, we will need to discuss also panel composition, remand, mutually agreed solutions, strictly confidential information, transparency and *amicus curiae* briefs and developing country interests, including special and differential treatment.[834]

As the Chair noted, a successful conclusion to the negotiations will 'require additional flexibility in Members' positions'.[835] To date, Members have not been able to reach agreement on the reform of the DSU.

However, the problem of the WTO dispute settlement system in the years to come may not be its shortcomings and Members' inability to address these shortcomings. Its problem will rather be its success, discussed throughout this chapter. This success has created an unwelcome institutional imbalance in the WTO between its 'judicial' branch and its political, 'rule-making' branch. As discussed in Chapter 2, the WTO has not been very successful in negotiating new and/or improved rules for the multilateral trading system.[836] Confronted with the ineffectiveness of the political branch of the WTO, WTO Members may be ever more tempted to use the dispute settlement system to bring about new or improved rules to address the manifold problems confronting the multilateral trading system. Already in 2001, Claude Barfield of the Washington-based American Enterprise Institute suggested that the WTO dispute settlement system is 'substantively and politically unsustainable'. Barfield suggested that governments may only continue to obey its rulings if its powers are curbed.[837] While strongly disagreeing with Barfield's prescription, others have also warned against excessive reliance by WTO Members on adjudication, instead of seeking political agreement on new rules, to resolve problems arising in trade relations.[838]

9   SUMMARY

The WTO has a remarkable system to settle disputes between its Members concerning their rights and obligations under the WTO agreements. This system is based on the dispute settlement system of the GATT. The latter system evolved between the late 1940s and the early 1990s from a system that was primarily a power-based system of dispute settlement through diplomatic negotiations, into a rules-based system of dispute settlement through adjudication. The WTO dispute settlement system, one of the most significant achievements of the Uruguay

---

834 Special Session of the Dispute Settlement Body, *Report by the Chairman, Ambassador Ronald Saborio Soto, to the Trade Negotiations Committee*, TN/DS/25, 21 April 2011, paras. 3 and 4.
835 *Ibid.*, para. 4.
836 See above, p. 92, and below, p. 436.
837 See C. Barfield, *Free Trade, Sovereignty, Democracy: The Future of the World Trade Organization* (American Enterprise Institute Press, 2001), 1–68.
838 See C.-D. Ehlermann, *Some Personal Experiences as Member of the Appellate Body of the WTO*, Policy Papers, RSC No. 02/9 (European University Institute, 2002), 14.

Round, is a further step in that process of progressive 'judicialisation' of the settlement of international trade disputes. Since January 1995, the WTO dispute settlement system has been widely used and its 'output', in terms of the number of dispute settlement reports, has been remarkable. Both developed- and developing-country Members have frequently used the system to resolve their trade disputes, and these disputes have concerned a very broad range of matters under WTO law.

The jurisdiction of the WTO dispute settlement system is compulsory, exclusive and contentious in nature. Furthermore, it is very broad in scope. It covers disputes arising under the *WTO Agreement*, the DSU, all multilateral agreements and one plurilateral agreement on trade in goods, the GATS and the *TRIPS Agreement* (commonly referred to as the covered agreements). In principle, any act or omission attributable to a WTO Member can be a measure that is subject to WTO dispute settlement. Measures that can be subject to WTO dispute settlement include a number of 'atypical' measures, such as: (1) action or conduct by private parties attributable to a Member; (2) measures that are no longer in force; (3) legislation 'as such' (as opposed to the actual application of this legislation in specific cases); (4) discretionary legislation (as opposed to mandatory legislation); (5) unwritten 'norms or rules' of Members; (6) ongoing conduct by Members; and (7) measures by regional and local authorities.

Access to the WTO dispute settlement system is limited to WTO Members. A WTO Member can have recourse to the system when it claims that a benefit accruing to it under one of the covered agreements is being nullified or impaired. A complainant will almost always argue that the respondent violated a provision of WTO law and file a violation complaint. If the violation is shown, there is a presumption of nullification or impairment of a benefit. Alternatively, a complainant can file a non-violation complaint (seldom done) or situation complaint (never done). NGOs, industry associations, companies or individuals have no direct access to the WTO dispute settlement system. However, it should be noted that most disputes are brought to the WTO for resolution at the instigation of companies and industry associations (i.e. indirect access).

The prime object and purpose of the WTO dispute settlement system is the prompt settlement of disputes between WTO Members and to provide security and predictability to the multilateral trading system. WTO dispute settlement has six key features, which in addition to the compulsory and exclusive jurisdiction of the WTO dispute settlement system and the process of WTO dispute settlement contribute to, if not explain, the importance and success of WTO dispute settlement to date. Some of these features set apart the WTO dispute settlement system from other international dispute settlement mechanisms. *First*, the WTO dispute settlement system is a single, comprehensive and integrated dispute settlement system. The rules of the DSU apply to all disputes arising under the covered agreements while some of these covered agreements provide for some special and additional rules and procedures 'designed to deal with the particularities of dispute settlement relating to obligations arising under a specific covered agreement'. *Secondly*, the DSU provides for several methods to settle disputes between WTO Members: consultations or negotiations (Article 4 of the DSU); adjudication by panels and the Appellate Body (Articles 6 to 20 of the DSU); arbitration (Articles 21.3(c), 22.6 and 25 of the DSU); and good offices, conciliation and mediation (Article 5 of the DSU). Of these methods, arbitration under Article 25 and good offices, conciliation and mediation under Article 5 have only played a marginal role; in almost all WTO disputes, Members had recourse to consultations, and, if those were unsuccessful, adjudication. *Thirdly*, pursuant to Article 23 of the DSU, Members must settle disputes with other Members over compliance with WTO obligations through the *multilateral* procedures of the DSU, rather than through *unilateral* action. Concerns regarding unilateral action taken by the United States against what it considered to be violations of GATT law were the driving force behind the Uruguay Round negotiations on dispute settlement, which eventually resulted in the DSU. *Fourthly*, the WTO dispute settlement system prefers Members to resolve a dispute through consultations, resulting in a mutually acceptable solution, rather than through adjudication. In other words, the DSU prefers parties *not* to go to court, but to settle their dispute amicably out of court. *Fifthly*, pursuant to Article 3.2, second sentence, of the DSU, the WTO dispute settlement system serves not only 'to preserve the rights and obligations of Members under the covered agreements', but also 'to clarify the existing provisions of those agreements'. The scope and nature of this clarification mandate is, however, circumscribed by Article 3.2, third sentence, and Article 19.2 of the DSU, which explicitly preclude the system from adding to or diminishing the rights and obligations of Members. The DSU does not condone judicial activism. For panels and the Appellate Body to stay within their mandate to clarify existing provisions and not stray into judicial activism, it is therefore important that they interpret and apply the provisions concerned correctly, i.e. in accordance with customary rules of interpretation of international law, as codified in Articles 31 and 32 of the *Vienna Convention on the Law of Treaties*. Pursuant to Articles 31 and 32, panels and the Appellate Body interpret provisions of the covered agreements in accordance with the ordinary meaning of the words of the provision in their context and in light of the object and purpose of the agreement involved; and, if necessary and appropriate, they have recourse to supplementary means of interpretation. *Sixthly*, the DSU provides for three types of remedy for breach of WTO law: one final remedy, namely, the withdrawal (or modification) of the WTO-inconsistent measure; and two temporary remedies which can be applied awaiting the withdrawal (or modification) of the WTO-inconsistent measure, namely, compensation *and* suspension of concessions or other obligations (commonly referred to as 'retaliation'). A

measure which was found to be WTO-inconsistent must be withdrawn immediately or, if that is impracticable, within a 'reasonable period of time'. In more
than four out of five disputes, the offending party withdraws (or modifies) the
WTO-inconsistent measure by the end of the 'reasonable period of time'. However, when the offending party fails to do so, and the parties were subsequently
unable to agree on compensation for the harm that will result from the lack of
compliance, the original complaining party may request authorisation from the
DSB to retaliate against the offending party by suspending concessions or other
obligations with respect to that offending party. Retaliation, often in the form of
a drastic increase in the customs duties on strategically selected products, puts
economic and political pressure on the offending party to withdraw (or modify)
its WTO-inconsistent measure(s). Subject to certain conditions, the retaliation
may take the form of the suspension of obligations under agreements other
than those with regard to which a violation was found in the underlying dispute
(i.e. cross-retaliation). To date, Members applied retaliation measures in four
disputes, while the number of disputes in which the DSB authorised Members
to do so was significantly higher. The effectiveness and/or appropriateness of
retaliation – which is by definition trade destructive – as a temporary remedy
for breach of WTO law is the subject of debate.

Among the institutions involved in WTO dispute settlement one must distinguish between a political institution, the Dispute Settlement Body or DSB, and
two independent, judicial-type institutions, the dispute settlement panels and
the Appellate Body. The DSB, which is composed of all WTO Members, administers the dispute settlement system. It has the authority to establish panels, adopt
panel and Appellate Body reports, and authorise retaliation in case of non-
compliance. It takes decisions on these important matters by *reverse consensus*.
As a result, the DSB decisions on these matters are quasi-automatic.

The actual adjudication of disputes brought to the WTO is done, at the first-
instance level, by dispute settlement panels and, at the appellate level, by the
Appellate Body. Panels are *ad hoc* bodies established for the purpose of adjudicating a particular dispute and are dissolved once they have accomplished this
task. A panel is established by the DSB at the request of the complainant. At the
latest at the second DSB meeting at which the panel request is discussed, the
panel is established by reverse consensus. The parties decide on the composition
of the panel by mutual accord. However, if they fail to do so within twenty days
after the establishment of the panel, either party can ask the Director-General
of the WTO to appoint the panellists. As a rule, panels are composed of three
well-qualified governmental and/or non-governmental individuals, who are not
nationals of the parties or third parties to the dispute. Pursuant to the *Rules of
Conduct* for WTO dispute settlement, panellists must be independent and impartial, avoid direct and indirect conflicts of interest and respect the confidentiality

of proceedings. Almost all panels have standard terms of reference, which refer back to the complainant's request to establish a panel. Hence, a claim and/or measure falls within the panel's terms of reference, i.e. within its jurisdiction, only if that claim or measure is identified in the panel request. The standard of review of panels, as set forth in Article 11 of the DSU, is 'to make an objective assessment of the matter'. Pursuant to Article 11 of the DSU, a panel, as a trier of facts: (1) must base its findings on a sufficient evidentiary basis on the record; (2) may not apply a double standard of proof; (3) must treat evidence in an 'even-handed' manner; (4) must consider evidence before it in its totality (which includes consideration of submitted evidence in relation to other evidence); and (5) should not disregard evidence that is relevant to the case of one of the parties. Panels may exercise judicial economy; they need only address (but at the same time are required to address at least) those claims which must be addressed in order to resolve the matter at issue in the dispute. A panel report must, at a minimum, set out the findings of fact, the applicability of relevant provisions and the basic rationale behind any findings and recommendations it makes. Where a panel concludes that a Member's measure is inconsistent with WTO law, it shall recommend that the Member concerned bring that measure into conformity with WTO law. The recommendations and rulings of the panel become legally binding when they are adopted – by reverse consensus – by the DSB.

The Appellate Body is a standing, i.e. permanent, international tribunal of seven individuals of recognised authority, appointed by the DSB for a term of four years (renewable once). Pursuant to the *Rules of Conduct* for WTO dispute settlement, Members of the Appellate Body must be independent and impartial, avoid direct and indirect conflicts of interest and respect the confidentiality of proceedings. The composition of the Appellate Body shall be broadly representative of WTO membership. The Appellate Body hears and decides appeals in divisions of three of its Members. Only parties to the dispute can appeal a panel report. An appeal is limited to issues of law covered in the panel report and legal interpretations developed by the panel. Issues of fact cannot be appealed. However, the treatment of the facts or evidence by a panel may raise the question of whether the panel has made an objective assessment of the facts as required under Article 11 of the DSU. This is a legal issue and can therefore be examined by the Appellate Body. The Appellate Body may uphold, modify or reverse the legal findings and conclusions of the panel that were appealed. On occasion, the Appellate Body has also – in the absence of the authority to remand a case to the panel – felt compelled to 'complete the legal analysis' on issues not addressed by the panel. It has done so in order to provide a prompt resolution of the dispute.

The WTO dispute settlement process may – and often does – entail four major steps: (1) consultations; (2) panel proceedings; (3) Appellate Body proceedings; and (4) implementation and enforcement. The four-step WTO dispute settlement process has six features that are particularly noteworthy, partly because they distinguish WTO dispute settlement – in both positive and negative ways – from other international dispute settlement mechanisms. These six features are: (1) the short timeframe for each of the steps in the process; (2) the confidentiality and resulting lack of transparency of the process; (3) the burden of proof in WTO dispute settlement proceedings, which is on the party that asserts the affirmative of a particular claim or defence; (4) the important role of private legal counsel in representing parties in WTO dispute settlement; (5) the acceptance and consideration by panels and the Appellate Body of *amicus curiae* briefs; and (6) the obligation on Members to act in good faith in WTO dispute settlement proceedings, and the obligation on panels and the Appellate Body to ensure due process in these proceedings.

The WTO dispute settlement process always begins with consultations (or, at least, an attempt to have consultations) between the parties to the dispute. The consultations enable the disputing parties to understand better the factual situation and the legal claims in respect of the dispute. Parties have broad discretion regarding the manner in which consultations are to be conducted. The consultation process essentially tries to resolve a dispute by diplomatic means and has frequently been successful in resolving disputes. However, if consultations do not resolve the dispute within sixty days after the request for consultations, the complainant may request the DSB to establish a panel.

The basic rules governing panel proceedings are set out in Article 12 of the DSU. Article 12.1 of the DSU directs a panel to follow the *Working Procedures* contained in Appendix 3 to the DSU, but at the same time authorises a panel to do otherwise. A panel will – whenever possible within one week of its composition – fix the timetable for its work and decide on detailed *ad hoc* working procedures. Each party to a dispute normally submits two written submissions to the panel: a 'first written submission' and a 'rebuttal submission'. During the proceedings, the panel will meet with the parties twice, first after the filing of the 'first written submissions' and then after the filing of the 'rebuttal submissions'. Unless specific deadlines for the submission of evidence are set out in the *ad hoc* working procedures of the panel (which is often the case now), parties can submit new evidence as late as the second meeting with the panel. The panel must of course always be careful to ensure due process. Panels have the discretionary authority to seek information and technical advice from any source including experts, in order to help them to understand and evaluate the evidence submitted and the arguments made by the parties. The parties are under an obligation to provide the panel with the information or the documents that the panel requests at any time during the proceedings. The rights of third parties to participate in the panel proceedings are limited but have been, in some cases, extended. Panels submit their draft reports to the parties for comment in a so-called 'interim review'. After this interim review, the panel finalises the report, issues it to the parties and eventually – when the report is available in the three official languages of the WTO – circulates the report to all Members, at which time it is also made public. Panel proceedings in theory should not exceed nine months, but in practice panel proceedings take, on average, fifteen months. Within sixty days of its circulation, a panel report is either adopted by the DSB by negative consensus or appealed to the Appellate Body.

In contrast to panels, the Appellate Body has detailed standard working procedures set out in the *Working Procedures for Appellate Review*. Appellate Body proceedings are initiated by a notice of appeal. A party to the dispute other than the original appellant may also appeal alleged legal errors in the panel report by filing a notice of other appeal. The appellant's and other appellant's submissions are filed at the same time as the notice of appeal or the notice of other appeal. The appellee's submission(s) and the third participants' submissions are due within, respectively, eighteen and twenty-one days after the date of the notice of appeal. An oral hearing generally takes place between day 30 and day 45 after the date of the notice of appeal. Compared to panel proceedings, third parties have broader rights to participate in Appellate Body proceedings. After the oral hearing and before finalising its report, the division responsible for deciding an appeal will always exchange views on the issues raised by the appeal with the Members of the Appellate Body not serving on the division. When the report is available in the three official languages of the WTO, it is circulated to all WTO Members and made public. Article 17.5 of the DSU requires that Appellate Body proceedings not exceed ninety days, and, in most cases, the Appellate Body has been able to complete its review within that very short timeframe. Within thirty days of its circulation, the Appellate Body report, together with the panel report, as upheld, modified or reversed by the Appellate Body, is adopted by the DSB by reverse consensus.

Recommendations and rulings of panels and/or the Appellate Body, as adopted by the DSB, must be implemented immediately or within a 'reasonable period of time'. Usually the parties are able to agree on the duration of that period, but, if they cannot, the 'reasonable period of time' can – at the request of either party – be determined through binding arbitration (under Article 21.3(c) of the DSU). During the 'reasonable period of time for implementation', the DSB keeps the implementation of adopted recommendations and rulings under surveillance. If by the end of the reasonable period there is disagreement as to the existence or the WTO-consistency of the implementing measures, this dispute is resolved in Article 21.5 compliance proceedings. If the offending party is found to have failed to implement the recommendations and rulings within the 'reasonable period of time' and agreement on compensation cannot be reached, the complainant may request authorisation from the DSB to retaliate against the offending party. A practice has developed under which the parties agree to resort first to an Article 21.5 'compliance' proceeding before obtaining authorisation from the DSB to retaliate (i.e. the sequencing issue). Under the Article 21.5 'compliance' proceeding, disagreement as to the existence or consistency with WTO law of implementing measures shall be decided through recourse to the DSU dispute settlement procedures, including, wherever possible, resort to the original panel. If the respondent did indeed fail to implement, the DSB can at the request of the complainant, authorise retaliation measures by reverse consensus. If the non-complying Member objects to the level of suspension proposed or claims that the principles and procedures for suspension have not been followed, the matter may be referred to arbitration (under Article 22.6 of the DSU) before the DSB takes a decision.

In recognition of the difficulties developing-country Members may encounter when they are involved in WTO dispute settlement, the DSU contains some special rules for developing-country Members. Most of these rules are, however, of limited significance. Effective legal assistance to developing-country Members in dispute settlement proceedings is given by the Geneva-based Advisory Centre on WTO Law (ACWL), which is established as an independent, international organisation that offers legal advice and representation to its developing-country Members and to least-developed countries.

The WTO system for resolving trade disputes between WTO Members has been a remarkable success in many respects. However, the current system can undoubtedly be further improved. In the context of the Doha Round, WTO Members are currently negotiating on proposals for the clarification and amendment of the DSU. The main challenge to the WTO dispute settlement system is, however, not its further improvement but the dangerous imbalance between the WTO's highly efficient judicial arm and its far less effective political negotiating arm.

Exercise 3: Right Over Might

ClearScreen Inc. of Compucity, Richland, is the world's largest producer and exporter of LED displays. In recent years, however, ClearScreen has encountered ever more competition from LED display producers from Newland. To protect ClearScreen and other Richland LED display producers from import competition, the Government of Richland decided last month to limit the importation of LED displays to 1 million units per year. The Association of Newland Consumer Electronics Manufacturers (ANCEM) is very concerned about Richland's import quota on LED displays and has been able to convince the Government of Newland to challenge the WTO-consistency of this measure. As a lawyer in the Brussels-based law firm Dupont, Bridge & Brucke, you have been asked by the Government of Newland to advise on the procedural and systemic issues arising in the course of the dispute settlement proceedings in Geneva. In the course of the proceedings, the following situations arise on which your advice is requested:

(1)   To mitigate the damage to Newland's LED display producers and employment in this industry, it is important to act quickly against Richland's import quota. Newland's Minister of Foreign Affairs therefore instructs Newland's Permanent Representative to the WTO, Ambassador Rita Montesdeoca de Murillo, to request the establishment of a panel at the next meeting of the DSB. Does Newland act in accordance with the DSU by requesting the establishment of a panel in this way? If not, could the DSB refuse to establish the panel?

(2)   Richland's Permanent Representative to the WTO, Ambassador Dr Heinrich Schiller, reportedly receives instructions from his government to block or, if that is impossible, to delay the establishment *and* composition of a panel as much as possible. What can the Permanent Representative of Richland do? Can he refuse to accept the jurisdiction of the WTO to settle this dispute and suggest that Richland and Newland take the dispute to the International Court of Justice?

(3)   The Government of Richland announces that it will insist that the panel includes five members, of which at least one is a national of Richland and none are nationals of developing-country Members. Among the five panellists, it wants two economists and one engineer. None of the panellists should be a former or current Geneva diplomat. The instructions of the Government of Richland are not to agree to a panel the composition of which does not meet these 'requirements'. The Government of Newland cannot agree to Richland's 'requirements' and instructs its Permanent Representative to expedite the process of composing the panel. What can the Permanent Representative of Newland do?

(4)   Poorland, a neighbour of Newland and a WTO Member, would like to be a third party in this dispute. Is this possible? Can Richland prevent Poorland from becoming a third party in this dispute?

(5)   In the interest of transparency, the Government of Richland would like the meetings of the panel with the parties to be open to other WTO Members as well as to the general public. Newland would prefer to hold the meetings with the panel behind closed doors. What will and/or can the panel do?

(6)   In its first written submission, Newland requests the panel to examine not only the import quota on LED displays (the measure at issue identified in the panel request) but also an import quota on digital TV decoders, imposed at the same time as the quota on LED displays. Moreover, Newland wants the panel to find that the import quota on LED displays is not only in breach of Article XIX of the GATT 1994 and the *Agreement on Safeguards* (as it stated in its panel request)

but also in violation of Article XIII of the GATT 1994. How will the panel react to these demands by Newland?

(7) Newland also argues in its first written submission that the burden is on Richland to demonstrate that it has acted consistently with its obligations under Article XIX of the GATT 1994 since Article XIX constitutes an exception to the basic prohibition of quantitative restrictions set out in Article XI of the GATT 1994. On whom does the burden of proof rest in this dispute?

(8) The Newland Brotherhood of Workers, the National Association of Electronics Producers of Richland, and 'Fair Deal', a non-governmental organisation that focuses on the problems of developing countries, all send *amicus curiae* briefs to the chair of the panel. The brief of the National Association of Electronics Producers of Richland was published in the *Financial Times* and the *Wall Street Journal* a week earlier and received a lot of attention. The chair of the panel also receives a brief from Southland, a developing-country Member which is a major exporter of consumer electronics, including LED displays. What should the panel do with these unsolicited briefs? The Newland Brotherhood of Workers and the National Association of Electronics Producers of Richland have expressed a wish to receive all the briefs submitted by the parties to the panel and to attend the panel meetings. Is this possible? Will you, as a private lawyer, be allowed to attend the panel meetings and speak for Newland?

(9) ClearScreen has demanded from the panel that information that ClearScreen considers to be BCI will not be made available to the lawyers representing the Government of Newland and the lawyers representing the Newland LED display producers. How will the panel react to this demand?

(10) Newland argues in its rebuttal submission that the panel should interpret the provisions of the *Agreement on Safeguards* in light of the object and purpose of the *WTO Agreement* and in light of the alleged intention of the negotiators to limit the use of safeguard measures. Can the panel follow the interpretative approach suggested by Newland?

(11) One week before the second substantive meeting with the panel, Newland submits to the panel a 100-page document on the Uruguay Round negotiations, which it claims supports its position. The panel would like to get the advice of a number of eminent international trade law scholars and of former Uruguay Round negotiators on this issue. What can the panel do?

(12) In its interim report, the panel finds in favour of Newland and recommends that the DSB requests that Richland bring the measure at issue in this dispute into conformity with its obligations under the GATT 1994 and the *Agreement on Safeguards*. The panel suggests that this can best be achieved by prompt removal of the quota. Richland's Minister of Trade denounces the panel's ruling as a legal travesty and announces that Richland will appeal as soon as possible. Is Richland's Minister of Trade allowed to make such a statement? When and how can Richland appeal the panel report?

(13) Richland appeals the panel's interpretation of Article XIX of the GATT 1994 and several provisions of the *Agreement on Safeguards*. It also appeals the panel's finding that the imports of LED displays from Newland did not cause or threaten to cause serious injury to the domestic industry of Richland. In its notice of appeal, Richland also calls upon the Appellate Body 'to complete the legal analysis when required'. Does the Appellate Body have the mandate to review the findings appealed by Richland? Can the Appellate Body complete the legal analysis?

(14) Newland objects to the composition of the division of the Appellate Body that hears the appeal. One of the Appellate Body Members is a national of Richland and has acted in the past as counsel to a Richland consumer electronics company. What can Newland do?

(15) While the panel ruled in its favour, Newland is not 'happy' with some of the panel's legal findings and would like to appeal these findings. Can it still do so once Richland has initiated appellate review proceedings?

(16) Newland insists that it needs more time to prepare its appellee's submission and argues that the date set for the oral hearing is not convenient. What can Newland do? Under what circumstances will Richland also need to submit an appellee's submission? When can the parties expect the report of the Appellate Body?

(17) The Appellate Body upholds the panel report. After the DSB adopts the Appellate Body report and the panel report as upheld, Richland announces that it will comply with the DSB's recommendations and rulings but that it is unable to do so immediately. Newland contends that it is possible to withdraw the quota promptly. What can Newland do next?

(18) After the expiry of the reasonable period of time for implementation (determined at five months), Richland claims that it has implemented the recommendations and rulings of the panel. Newland is baffled by this claim since the import quota is still in force. Can Newland take retaliatory measures?

4 Most-Favoured-Nation Treatment

CONTENTS

1 INTRODUCTION

As discussed in Chapter 1, discrimination in matters relating to trade breeds resentment and poisons the economic and political relations between countries.[1] Moreover, discrimination makes scant economic sense as, generally speaking, it distorts the market in favour of goods and services that are more expensive and/or of lower quality. Non-discrimination is, therefore, a key concept in WTO law and policy. The importance of eliminating discrimination is highlighted in the Preamble to the *WTO Agreement*, where the 'elimination of discriminatory treatment in international trade relations' is identified as one of the two main means by which the objectives of the WTO may be attained.[2]

1 See above, pp. 21–2.   2 See above, p. 83.

As stated in Chapter 1, there are two main non-discrimination obligations under WTO law: the most-favoured-nation (MFN) treatment obligation and the national treatment obligation.[3] In simple terms, an MFN treatment obligation relates to whether a country favours some countries over others. An MFN treatment obligation prohibits a country to discriminate *between* other countries. A national treatment obligation relates to whether a country favours itself over other countries. A national treatment obligation prohibits a country to discriminate *against* other countries. The national treatment obligation under WTO law will be discussed in the next chapter; the MFN treatment obligation under WTO law is the topic of this chapter. This MFN treatment obligation applies to trade in goods as well as trade in services. The key provision dealing with the MFN treatment obligation for measures affecting trade in goods is Article I:1 of the GATT 1994. The key provision dealing with the MFN treatment obligation for measures affecting trade in services is Article II:1 of the GATS. This chapter discusses these MFN treatment obligations in turn.[4]

With regard to the MFN treatment obligation under Article I:1 of the GATT 1994, the questions that may arise include the following:

(1) Can Richland, a WTO Member, impose a 10 per cent *ad valorem* customs duty on beer from Newland, also a WTO Member, while imposing a 5 per cent *ad valorem* customs duty on beer from Oldland, another WTO Member?

(2) Can Richland impose a 10 per cent domestic sales tax on soft drinks from Newland while imposing a 5 per cent domestic sales tax on mineral water from Oldland?

(3) Can Richland impose on soft drinks a labelling requirement to indicate the sugar content while not imposing such a requirement on fruit juice?

With regard to the MFN treatment obligation under Article II:1 of the GATS, the following questions may arise:

(1) Can Richland allow doctors from Newland to practise medicine in its territory but bar doctors from Oldland from doing so?

(2) Can Richland impose strict qualification requirements on nannies from Oldland while leaving the qualifications of domestic workers from Newland largely unregulated?

(3) Can Richland impose a 20 per cent domestic tax on English-language courses, while exempting French-language courses from domestic taxation?

---

3 See above, p. 36.
4 As discussed in Chapter 15 of this book, Article 4 of the *TRIPS Agreement* provides for an MFN treatment obligation with regard to intellectual property rights. See below, pp. 968–70.

2 MOST-FAVOURED-NATION TREATMENT UNDER THE GATT 1994

Article I of the GATT 1994, entitled 'General Most-Favoured-Nation Treatment', states in paragraph 1:

With respect to customs duties and charges of any kind imposed on or in connection with importation or exportation or imposed on the international transfer of payments for imports or exports, and with respect to the method of levying such duties and charges, and with respect to all rules and formalities in connection with importation and exportation, and with respect to all matters referred to in paragraphs 2 and 4 of Article III, any advantage, favour, privilege or immunity granted by any [Member] to any product originating in or destined for any other country shall be accorded immediately and unconditionally to the like product originating in or destined for the territories of all other [Members].[5]

The GATT 1994 contains a number of other provisions requiring MFN or MFN-like treatment, such as: Article III:7 (regarding local content requirements); Article V (regarding freedom of transit); Article IX:1 (regarding marks of origin); Article XIII:1 (regarding the non-discriminatory administration of quantitative restrictions); and Article XVII (regarding State trading enterprises). Article XX of the GATT 1994, and in particular the chapeau of this 'general exceptions' provision, also contains an MFN-like obligation.[6] The very existence of these MFN-type clauses demonstrates the pervasive character of the MFN principle of non-discrimination.[7] Other multilateral agreements on trade in goods such as the *TBT Agreement*, the *SPS Agreement*, the *Agreement on Rules of Origin* and the *Agreement on Import Licensing Procedures* likewise require MFN treatment.[8] However, this section is only concerned with the MFN treatment obligation set out in Article I:1 of the GATT 1994.

2.1 Nature of the MFN Treatment Obligation of Article I:1 of the GATT 1994

As the Appellate Body observed in *EC – Tariff Preferences (2004)*, it is well settled that the MFN treatment obligation set out in Article I:1 of the GATT 1994 is a 'cornerstone of the GATT' and 'one of the pillars of the WTO trading system'.[9]

---

5 Paragraphs 2, 3 and 4 of Article I of the GATT 1994 deal with so-called colonial preferences and allow the continuation of such preferences, albeit within certain limits. While important and controversial when the GATT 1947 was negotiated, these colonial preferences are now of very little significance and will therefore not be discussed.
6 See below, pp. 574–81.
7 See Appellate Body Report, *Canada – Autos (2000)*, para. 82.
8 See below, pp. 863 (TBT), 921–3 (SPS), 461–2 (ROOs), and 496 (Import licensing).
9 Appellate Body Report, *EC – Tariff Preferences (2004)*, para. 101 (quoting Appellate Body Report, *Canada – Autos (2000)*, para. 69).

The importance of the MFN treatment obligation to the multilateral trading system is undisputed.[10] However, as discussed in Chapter 10 of this book, in the last fifteen years there has been a proliferation of customs unions, free trade agreements and other arrangements, which provide for preferential, i.e. discriminatory, treatment in trade relations between WTO Members.[11] Considering this proliferation, the 2004 Sutherland Report on *The Future of the WTO* arrived, not without some pathos, at the following conclusion:

> [N]early five decades after the founding of the GATT, MFN is no longer the rule; it is almost the exception. Certainly, much trade between the major economies is still conducted on an MFN basis. However, what has been termed the 'spaghetti bowl' of customs unions, common markets, regional and bilateral free trade areas, preferences and an endless assortment of miscellaneous trade deals has almost reached the point where MFN treatment is exceptional treatment.[12]

As discussed in Chapter 10, the situation may not be as dramatic as suggested in the Sutherland Report.[13] While MFN treatment is in practice perhaps less prevalent than one might expect of 'one of the pillars of the WTO trading system', it undoubtedly is, and remains, a principal obligation for WTO Members.

As the Appellate Body stated in *Canada – Autos (2000)*, Article I:1 of the GATT 1994 prohibits discrimination *between* like products *originating in*, or destined for, different countries.[14] In other words, Article I:1 prohibits WTO Member Richland from giving products from WTO Member Newland treatment less favourable than the treatment it gives to like products from any other WTO Member or other country. Also, Article I:1 prohibits Richland from giving products destined for Newland treatment less favourable than the treatment it gives to like products *destined for* any other WTO Member or other country. The principal purpose of the MFN treatment obligation of Article I:1 is to ensure all WTO Members *equality of opportunity* to import from, or to export to, other WTO Members (or any other country). In *EC – Bananas III (1997)*, the Appellate Body stated, with respect to WTO non-discrimination obligations (such as the obligation set out in Article I:1):

> [...]ns is that like products should be treated
> [...]icipant disputes that all bananas are like
> [...]y to *all* imports of bananas, irrespective of
> [...]ivides these imports for administrative or

[...], the Appellate Body stated that 'most-favoured-
[...]oth central and essential to assuring the success of

[...]upachai Panitchpakdi, *The Future of the WTO*:
[...](the 'Sutherland Report') (WTO, 2004), para. 60.

[...]4.
[...] Original emphasis.

In *EC – Bananas III (1997)*, the measure at issue was the import regime for bananas of the European Communities under which bananas from Latin American countries ('dollar bananas') were treated less favourably than bananas from, broadly speaking, former European colonies ('ACP bananas').

Article I:1 of the GATT 1994 covers not only 'in law', or *de jure*, discrimination but also 'in fact', or *de facto*, discrimination. In other words, Article I:1 applies not only to 'origin-based' measures (which are discriminatory by definition), but also to measures which, on their face, appear 'origin-neutral' but are *in fact* discriminatory. A measure may be said to discriminate in law (or *de jure*) in a case in which it is clear from reading the text of the law, regulation or policy that it treats the product from one WTO Member less favourably than the like product from another WTO Member or country. For example, if Richland imposed a customs duty of 10 per cent *ad valorem* on chocolate from Newland while imposing a customs duty of 20 per cent *ad valorem* on chocolate from other WTO Members, the imposition of the 20 per cent customs duty on other WTO Members constitutes 'in law' or *de jure* discrimination. However, if the measure at issue does not appear on its face to discriminate against particular WTO Members, it may still constitute 'in fact' or *de facto* discrimination if, on reviewing all the facts relating to the application of the measure, it becomes clear that it treats, in practice or in fact, the product from one WTO Member less favourably than the like product from another WTO Member or country. For example, if Richland imposes a customs duty of 10 per cent *ad valorem* on chocolate made with milk from cows that spent at least six months per year at an altitude of more than 1,500 metres, while imposing a customs duty of 20 per cent *ad valorem* on chocolate made with other milk, the imposition of the 20 per cent customs duty may well constitute 'in fact' or *de facto* discrimination. This would be so if, in fact, in Newland, cows spent at least six months per year at an altitude of more than 1,500 metres, while the highest point in Oldland, a major chocolate producer and exporter, is 300 metres above sea level.[16] The panel in *Canada – Pharmaceutical Patents (2000)* noted that:

de facto discrimination is a general term describing the legal conclusion that an ostensibly neutral measure transgresses a non-discrimination norm because its actual effect is to impose differentially disadvantageous consequences on certain parties, and because those differential effects are found to be wrong or unjustifiable.[17]

While instances of *de jure* discrimination still occur, ever more sophisticated legislators and/or regulators of WTO Members are more likely to adopt measures that constitute *de facto* discrimination.

16 It is assumed here that chocolate made with milk from highland cows is 'like' chocolate made with milk from lowland cows. For the discussion on the concept of 'likeness', see below, pp. 325–8.
17 Panel Report, *Canada – Pharmaceutical Patents (2000)*, para. 7.101. Note that *Canada – Pharmaceutical Patents* concerned the national treatment obligation under Article III:4 of the GATT and not the MFN treatment obligation under Article I:1 thereof. However, this does not affect the relevance of the panel statement quoted.

In *Canada – Autos (2000)*, the Appellate Body rejected, as the panel had done, Canada's argument that Article I:1 does not apply to measures which appear, on their face, to be 'origin-neutral' *vis-à-vis* like products.[18] According to the Appellate Body, measures which appear, on their face, to be 'origin-neutral' can still give certain countries more opportunity to trade than others and can, therefore, be in violation of the non-discrimination obligation of Article I:1. The measure at issue in *Canada – Autos (2000)* was a customs duty exemption accorded by Canada to imports of motor vehicles by certain manufacturers.[19] Formally speaking, there were no restrictions on the origin of the motor vehicles that were eligible for this exemption. In practice, however, the manufacturers imported only their own make of motor vehicle and those of related companies. As a result, only motor vehicles originating in a small number of countries benefited *de facto* from the exemption.

Previously, the panel in *EEC – Imports of Beef (1981)* found that EC regulations, making the suspension of an import levy on beef conditional on the production of a certificate of authenticity, were inconsistent with the MFN treatment obligation of Article I:1 of the GATT 1947 after it was established that the only certifying agency authorised to produce a certificate of authenticity was an agency in the United States.[20] While on its face the EC regulations at issue applied in the same way to all imported beef, irrespective of its origin, it is clear that these regulations *de facto* discriminated against beef from Canada, the complainant in this case.

Questions and Assignments 4.1

Discuss the importance of the MFN treatment obligation of Article I:1 of the GATT 1994 in the multilateral trading system. What is the principal purpose of the MFN treatment obligation of Article I:1? Does the MFN treatment obligation of Article I:1 cover both *de jure* and *de facto* discrimination? Explain the difference between *de jure* and *de facto* discrimination. Which of these types of discrimination is currently more common and constitutes the greater challenge to the multilateral trading system? Give two examples of *de facto* discrimination from the WTO/GATT case law.

2.2 MFN Treatment Test of Article I:1 of the GATT 1994

Article I:1 of the GATT 1994 sets out a four-tier test of consistency with the MFN treatment obligation. There are four questions which must be answered to determine whether or not a measure affecting trade in goods is consistent with the MFN treatment obligation of Article I:1, namely:

- whether the measure at issue is a measure covered by Article I:1;
- whether that measure grants an '*advantage*';

---

18 See Appellate Body Report, *Canada – Autos (2000)*, para. 78.
19 This exemption was granted to car manufacturers when their production of motor vehicles in Canada reached a minimum amount of Canadian value added (CVA) and a certain production-to-sales ratio in Canada.
20 See Panel Report, *EEC – Imports of Beef (1981)*, paras. 4.2 and 4.3.

- whether the products concerned are '*like products*'; and
- whether the advantage at issue is *accorded 'immediately and unconditionally'* to all like products concerned, irrespective of their origin or destination.[21]

Below, each element of this four-tier test of consistency will be discussed in turn.

To date, WTO Members have been found to have acted inconsistently with the MFN treatment obligation of Article I:1 of the GATT 1994 in eleven disputes.[22]

2.2.1   Measure Covered by Article I:1

The MFN treatment obligation of Article I:1 of the GATT 1994 concerns 'any advantage, favour, privilege or immunity' granted by any Member to any product originating in, or destined for, any other country with respect to: (1) customs duties; (2) charges of any kind imposed *on* or *in connection with* importation or exportation (e.g. import surcharges, export duties, customs fees, or quality inspection fees); (3) charges imposed on the international transfer of payments for imports or exports; (4) the method of levying such duties and charges, such as the method of assessing the base value on which the duty or charge is levied; (5) all rules and formalities in connection with importation and exportation; (6) internal taxes or other internal charges (i.e. the matters referred to in Article III:2 of the GATT 1994); and (7) laws, regulations and requirements affecting internal sale, offering for sale, purchase, transportation, distribution or use of any product (i.e. the matters referred to in Article III:4 of the GATT 1994).

In brief, the MFN treatment obligation of Article I:1 covers both border measures and internal measures. The *border measures* include, in particular, customs duties, other charges on imports and exports, import and export prohibitions and quotas, tariff quotas, import licences, and customs formalities. The *internal measures* include, in particular, internal taxes on products and internal regulations affecting the sale, distribution or use of products. Generally, there has been little debate about the kind of measures covered by Article I:1. Both panels and the Appellate Body have recognised that Article I:1 covers a broad range of measures.

In the past, there has been some debate on the applicability of Article I:1 to safeguard measures, anti-dumping duties and countervailing duties. With regard to safeguard measures, the *Agreement on Safeguards* makes it clear that the MFN

---

21 Note that the panel in *Indonesia – Autos (1998)* set out a three-tier, rather than a four-tier, test of consistency with the MFN treatment obligation. Under the panel's test, the first and second questions were merged. See Panel Report, *Indonesia – Autos (1998)*, para. 14.138.

22 See *EC – Bananas III (1997)*; *Indonesia – Autos (1998)*; *EC – Bananas III (Article 21.5 – Ecuador) (1999)*; *Canada – Autos (2000)*; *US – Certain EC Products (2001)*; *EC – Tariff Preferences (2004)*; *EC – Bananas III (Article 21.5 – Ecuador II) (2008)*; *EC – Bananas III (Article 21.5 – US) (2008)*; *Colombia – Ports of Entry (2009)*; *US – Poultry (China) (2010)*; and *EU – Footwear (China) (2012)*.

treatment obligation normally applies to safeguard measures. Article 2.2 of the *Agreement on Safeguards* states:

Safeguard measures shall be applied to a product being imported irrespective of its source.

However, as further discussed in Chapter 9 of this book, the *Agreement on Safeguards* does allow, under certain conditions, the discriminatory use of safeguard measures.[23] With regard to countervailing duties, the panel in *US – MFN Footwear (1992)* found:

the *rules and formalities* applicable to countervailing duties, including those applicable to the revocation of countervailing duty orders, are rules and formalities imposed in connection with importation, within the meaning of Article I:1.[24]

In principle, countervailing duties as well as anti-dumping duties fall within the scope of the MFN treatment obligation of Article I:1. Article 9.2 of the *Anti-Dumping Agreement* provides:

When an anti-dumping duty is imposed in respect of any product, such anti-dumping duty shall be collected in the appropriate amounts in each case, on a *non-discriminatory basis* on imports of such product from all sources found to be dumped and causing injury ...[25]

Article 19.3 of the *SCM Agreement* contains a very similar provision. As further discussed in Chapters 11 and 12 of this book, where the relevant facts concerning dumping or subsidisation of products of different origins are the same, anti-dumping duties or countervailing duties should be applied without discrimination.[26] However, it should be noted that the relevant facts concerning dumping or subsidisation of products from different origins will more often than not differ from one country of origin to another country of origin.

While Article I:1 of the GATT 1994 covers a broad range of measures, the panel in *EC – Commercial Vessels (2005)* made it clear that the scope of application of Article I:1 is not unlimited. This dispute concerned EC subsidies to support the building of commercial vessels in the European Union. Korea claimed that these subsidies were inconsistent with Article I:1. As noted above, Article I:1 applies to 'all matters referred to in paragraphs 2 and 4 of Article III'. According to Korea, the subsidies at issue were measures within the meaning of Article III:4 and therefore covered by Article I:1. Having found that the EC subsidies at issue were covered by Article III:8(b) and that Article III:4 therefore did *not* apply,[27] the panel turned to the question whether the subsidies were consequently outside the scope of the MFN obligation in Article I:1. In replying to this question, the panel stated:

[T]he phrase 'matters referred to in ...' in Article I:1 refers to the subject-matter of those provisions in terms of their substantive legal content. Understood in this sense, it is clear

---

23 See below, pp. 625–7.   24 Panel Report, *US – MFN Footwear (1992)*, para. 6.8. Original emphasis.
25 Emphasis added.   26 See below, p. 725.
27 Panel Report, *EC – Commercial Vessels (2005)*, para. 7.75. On Article III:8(b) of the GATT 1994, see below, p. 351.

to us that the 'matters referred to in paragraphs 2 and 4 of Article III' cannot be interpreted without regard to limitations that may exist regarding the scope of the substantive obligations provided for in these paragraphs. If ... a particular measure is not subject to the obligations of Article III, that measure in our view does not form part of the 'matters referred to' in Articles III:2 and 4. Thus, since Article III:8(b) provides that Article III 'shall not prevent the payment of subsidies exclusively to domestic producers', such subsidies are not part of the subject-matter of Article III:4 and cannot be covered by the expression 'matters referred to in paragraphs 2 and 4 of Article III' in Article I:1.[28]

To the extent that measures covered by Article III:8(b) (i.e. subsidies to domestic producers) fall outside the scope of application of Article III:2 and 4, these measures also fall outside the scope of application of Article I:1. The same logic would seem to apply to laws, regulations and requirements governing government procurement, which – as discussed below – are excluded from the scope of application of Article III:4 pursuant to Article III:8(a).[29]

Finally, note that, pursuant to Article XXIV:3(a) of the GATT 1994, a measure that grants an advantage to adjacent countries in order to facilitate frontier traffic, is not subject to the MFN treatment obligation of Article I:1.

2.2.2   Measure Granting an 'Advantage'

The second element of the test of consistency with the MFN treatment obligation of Article I:1 of the GATT 1994 relates to the question of whether the measure at issue grants an '*advantage*'. The text of Article I:1 of the GATT 1994 refers to 'any advantage, favour, privilege or immunity granted by any [Member]'. In light of the use of the word 'any', it is not surprising that the term 'advantage' has been given a broad meaning in the case law.[30] The panel in *EC – Bananas III (1997)* considered that a measure granting an 'advantage' within the meaning of Article I:1 is a measure that creates 'more favourable competitive opportunities' or affects the commercial relationship between products of different origins.[31] The Appellate Body held in this case:

---

28 *Ibid.*, para. 7.83.
29 See below, p. 351. Note, however, that Article III:1(b) of the plurilateral *Agreement on Government Procurement* imposes on those WTO Members which are a party to this Agreement an MFN treatment obligation with regard to laws, regulations and requirements governing government procurement. On measures regarding government procurement and the plurilateral *Agreement on Government Procurement*, see below, pp. 386, 509–11 and 535–7.
30 See Panel Report, *Belgium – Family Allowances (allocations familiales) (1952)*, para. 3; Panel Report, *US – Customs User Fee (1988)*, para. 122; Panel Report, *US – MFN Footwear (1992)*, para. 6.9; and Panel Report, *Colombia – Ports of Entry (2009)*, paras. 7.340 and 7.345. Note, however, that the panel in *US – Anti-Dumping and Countervailing Duties (China) (2011)* found that China had failed to establish the existence of an 'advantage' within the meaning of Article I:1, and therefore rejected China's claim of inconsistency with the MFN treatment obligation of Article I:1. See Panel Report, *US – Anti-Dumping and Countervailing Duties (2011)*, paras. 14.150–14.182.
31 See Panel Report, *EC – Bananas III (Guatemala and Honduras) (1997)*, para. 7.239. See also Panel Report, *Colombia – Ports of Entry (2009)*, para. 7.341; and Panel Report, *US – Poultry (China) (2010)*, para. 7.415. The panel in *US – Poultry (China) (2010)* found that, when a measure creates market access opportunities and affects the commercial relationship between products of different origins, that measure grants an 'advantage' within the meaning of Article I:1 of the GATT 1994. See Panel Report, *US – Poultry (China) (2010)*, para. 7.417. At issue in this case was the opportunity to export poultry products to the United States. This opportunity was considered to be a 'very favourable market opportunity and not having such an opportunity would mean a serious competitive disadvantage'. See *ibid.*, para. 7.416.

[T]he Panel found that the procedural and administrative requirements of the activity function rules for importing third-country and non-traditional ACP bananas differ from, and go significantly beyond, those required for importing traditional ACP bananas. This is a factual finding. Also, a broad definition has been given to the term 'advantage' in Article I:1 of the GATT 1994 by the panel in [*US – MFN Footwear (1992)*] ... For these reasons, we agree with the Panel that the activity function rules are an 'advantage' granted to bananas imported from traditional ACP States, and not to bananas imported from other Members, within the meaning of Article I:1.[32]

In *Canada – Autos (2000)*, the Appellate Body further clarified the meaning of the term 'advantage' and thus the scope of the MFN treatment obligation by ruling:

Article I:1 requires that '*any advantage*, favour, privilege or immunity granted by any Member to *any product* originating in or destined for any other country shall be accorded immediately and unconditionally to the like product originating in or destined for the territories of *all other Members*.' (emphasis added) The words of Article I:1 refer not to *some* advantages granted 'with respect to' the subjects that fall within the defined scope of the Article, but to '*any advantage*'; not to *some* products, but to '*any product*'; and not to like products from *some* other Members, but to like products originating in or destined for '*all other*' Members.[33]

In other words, the term 'advantage' in Article I:1 refers to *any* advantage granted by a Member to *any* like product from or for another country.[34]

By way of example, note that the panel in *Colombia – Ports of Entry (2009)* found that Colombian customs regulations on the importation of textiles, apparel and footwear required importers of goods arriving from Panama to submit import declarations in advance, and, accordingly, to pay customs duties and taxes in advance, while importers of goods from other countries were not required to file import declarations in advance. On this basis, the panel concluded that the Colombian customs regulations granted an advantage within the meaning of Article I:1 of the GATT 1994 to the goods from countries other than Panama.[35]

The question has arisen whether a Member could offset less advantageous treatment of a product under certain circumstances with more advantageous treatment of that product under other circumstances and thus avoid inconsistency with Article I:1. In line with earlier case law concerning Article III:4, the panel in *US – MFN Footwear (1992)* categorically rejected such possibility and ruled that Article I:1 does not permit 'balancing' less advantageous treatment with more advantageous treatment.[36] The panel noted that:

---

32 Appellate Body Report, *EC – Bananas III (1997)*, para. 206.
33 Appellate Body Report, *Canada – Autos (2000)*, para. 79. Original emphasis.
34 Note that the MFN treatment obligation of Article I:1 of the GATT 1994 clearly concerns not only advantages granted to other WTO Members, but also advantages granted to non-WTO Members. However, now that the membership of the WTO is universal and trade between WTO Members comprises 97 per cent of all international trade, this particular aspect of the MFN treatment obligation is of little significance anymore.
35 See Panel Report, *Colombia – Ports of Entry (2009)*, para. 7.352.
36 See Panel Report, *US – MFN Footwear (1992)*, para. 6.10. The panel in *US – Section 337 Tariff Act (1989)* rejected a similar 'balancing' argument in the context of the national treatment obligation in Article III:4. See Panel Report, *US – Section 337 Tariff Act (1989)*, para. 5.14. See also below, p. 965.

[i]f such a balancing were accepted, it would entitle a contracting party to derogate from the most-favoured-nation obligation in one case, in respect of one contracting party, on the ground that it accords more favourable treatment in some other case in respect of another contracting party. In the view of the Panel, such an interpretation of the most-favoured-nation obligation of Article I:1 would defeat the very purpose underlying the unconditionality of that obligation.[37]

Questions and Assignments 4.2

What are the constituent elements of the MFN treatment test of Article I:1 of the GATT 1994? To which kind of measures, generally speaking, does Article I:1 apply? Does the MFN treatment obligation apply to safeguard measures, anti-dumping duties, and/or countervailing duties? Does the MFN treatment obligation apply to subsidies to domestic producers? What constitutes an 'advantage' within the meaning of Article I:1? Why did the panel in *Colombia – Ports of Entry (2009)* find that the measure at issue granted an advantage within the meaning of Article I:1? Does Article I:1 permit 'balancing' less advantageous treatment with more advantageous treatment?

2.2.3 'Like Products'

The third element of the test of consistency with the MFN treatment obligation of Article I:1 of the GATT 1994 relates to the question of whether the products at issue are '*like products*'. Article I:1 concerns any product originating in or destined for any other country and requires that an advantage granted to such products shall be accorded to 'like products' originating in or destined for the territories of all other Members. It is only between 'like products' that the MFN treatment obligation applies and discrimination within the meaning of Article I:1 of the GATT 1994 may occur. Products that are not 'like' may be treated differently; different treatment of products that are not 'like' will not constitute discrimination within the meaning of Article I:1. For the application of the MFN treatment obligation of Article I:1, it is therefore important to be able to determine whether, for example, a sports utility vehicle (SUV) is 'like' a family car; orange juice is 'like' tomato juice; a laptop is 'like' a tablet computer; pork is 'like' beef; or whisky is 'like' brandy within the meaning of Article I:1.

The concept of 'like products' is used not only in Article I:1 but also in Articles II:2(a), III:2, III:4, VI:1(a), IX:1, XI:2(c), XIII:1, XVI:4 and XIX:1 of the GATT 1994. Nevertheless, the concept of 'like products' is not defined in the GATT 1994.[38] In its examination of the concept of 'like products' under Article III:4, the Appellate Body in *EC – Asbestos (2001)* considered that the dictionary meaning of 'like' suggests that 'like products' are products that share a number

---

37 Panel Report, *US – MFN Footwear (1992)*, para. 6.10. See also Panel Report, *EC – Bananas III (Ecuador) (1997)*, para. 7.239.

38 Note that the concept of 'like product' is also used in the *Anti-Dumping Agreement*, the *SCM Agreement* and the *Agreement on Safeguards* and that this concept is defined in these agreements. See below, pp. 685 (A-DA), 779–80 (SCM) and 616 (Safeguards).

of identical or similar characteristics.[39] However, as the Appellate Body already noted in *Canada – Aircraft (1999)*, 'dictionary meanings leave many interpretive questions open'.[40] With regard to the concept of 'like products', there are three questions of interpretation that need to be resolved: (1) which characteristics or qualities are important in assessing 'likeness'; (2) to what degree or extent must products share qualities or characteristics in order to be 'like products'; and (3) from whose perspective 'likeness' should be judged.[41]

It is generally accepted that the concept of 'like products' has a different scope or 'width' in the different contexts in which it is used. In *Japan – Alcoholic Beverages II (1996)*, the Appellate Body illustrated the possible differences in the scope of the concept of 'like products' in different provisions of the *WTO Agreement* by evoking the image of an accordion:

> The accordion of 'likeness' stretches and squeezes in different places as different provisions of the *WTO Agreement* are applied. The width of the accordion in any one of those places must be determined by the particular provision in which the term 'like' is encountered as well as by the context and the circumstances that prevail in any given case to which that provision may apply.[42]

In other words, products such as orange juice and tomato juice may be 'like' under one provision of the GATT 1994 and not 'like' under another provision.

The meaning of the phrase 'like products' in Article I:1 was addressed in a few GATT working party and panel reports.[43] In *Spain – Unroasted Coffee (1981)*, the panel had to decide whether various types of unroasted coffee ('Colombian mild', 'other mild', 'unwashed Arabica', 'Robusta' and 'other') were 'like products' within the meaning of Article I:1. Spain did not apply customs duties to 'Colombian mild' and 'other mild', while it imposed a 7 per cent customs duty on the other three types of unroasted coffee. Brazil, which exported mainly 'unwashed Arabica', claimed that the Spanish tariff regime was inconsistent with Article I:1. In examining whether the various types of unroasted coffee were 'like products' to which the MFN treatment obligation applied, the panel considered: (1) the physical characteristics of the products;[44] (2) their end-use; and (3) tariff regimes of other Members. The panel found that:

---

39 See Appellate Body Report, *EC – Asbestos (2001)*, para. 91. The reference to 'similar' as a synonym of 'like' also echoes the language of the French version of Article III:4, '*produits similaires*', and the Spanish version, '*productos similares*'. See *ibid*. On the Appellate Body's analysis of the concept of 'like products' in *EC – Asbestos (2001)*, see above, p. 188.

40 Appellate Body Report, *Canada – Aircraft (1999)*, para. 153. See also Appellate Body Report, *EC – Asbestos (2001)*, para. 92.

41 See Appellate Body Report, *EC – Asbestos (2001)*, para. 92.

42 Appellate Body Report, *Japan – Alcoholic Beverages II (1996)*, 114.

43 See e.g. Working Party Report, *Australian Subsidy on Ammonium Sulphate (1950)*, para. 8; and Panel Report, *EEC – Animal Feed Proteins (1978)*, para. 4.2. See also Panel Report, *Japan – SPF Dimension Lumber (1989)*, paras. 5.13 and 5.14.

44 These physical characteristics included the organoleptic properties (i.e. the taste, smell, aroma, etc.) of the different types of coffee. The panel found that the differences between the different kinds of coffee in organoleptic properties (differences mainly resulting from geographical factors, cultivation methods, the processing of the beans and the genetic factor) were not sufficient to consider the different types of coffee not to be 'like products'. See Panel Report, *Spain – Unroasted Coffee (1981)*, para. 4.6.

unroasted coffee was mainly, if not exclusively, sold in the form of blends, combining various types of coffee, and that coffee in its end-use, was universally regarded as a well-defined and single product intended for drinking.[45]

The panel also found that:

no other contracting party applied its tariff régime in respect of unroasted, non-decaffeinated coffee in such a way that different types of coffee were subject to different tariff rates.[46]

On the basis of these findings, the panel in *Spain – Unroasted Coffee (1981)* concluded that the different types of unroasted coffee should be considered to be 'like products' within the meaning of Article I:1.[47]

In addition to the physical characteristics of the products, their end-use and the tariff regimes of other Members (the criteria used by the panel in *Spain – Unroasted Coffee (1981)*), a WTO panel examining whether products are 'like' within the meaning of Article I:1 would now definitely also consider consumers' tastes and habits as well as any other relevant criterion. Since the case law on 'likeness' within the meaning of Article I:1 of the GATT 1994 is limited, the more extensive case law on 'likeness' within the meaning of Article III of the GATT 1994, discussed in Chapter 5, should be considered carefully, even though one should be cautious regarding a wholesale transfer of this case law.[48] In the context of Article III:2, first sentence, and Article III:4 of the GATT 1994, the Appellate Body found that the determination of whether products are 'like products' is, fundamentally, 'a determination about the nature and extent of a competitive relationship between and among products'.[49] To make such a determination, a panel examines on a case-by-case basis *all* relevant criteria or factors, including: (1) the products' properties, nature and quality, i.e. their physical characteristics; (2) the products' end-uses; (3) consumers' tastes and habits, also referred to as consumers' perceptions and behaviour, in respect of the products; and (4) the products' tariff classification. It is reasonable to expect that this case law regarding Article III will inform the interpretation of the concept of 'like products' in Article I:1. Future case law will clarify whether the concept of 'like products' in Article I:1 has as narrow a scope as the concept of 'like products' in Article III:2, first sentence; as broad a scope as the concept of 'like products' in Article III:4; or a scope that lies somewhere in between. In other words, future

---

45 *Ibid.*, para. 4.7.   46 *Ibid.*, para. 4.8.

47 See *ibid.*, paras. 4.6–4.9. In *EEC – Animal Feed Proteins (1978)*, the panel decided, on the basis of such factors as 'the number of products and tariff items carrying different duty rates and tariff bindings, the varying protein contents and the different vegetable, animal and synthetic origins of the protein products', that the various protein products at issue could not be considered as 'like products' within the meaning of Articles I and III of the GATT 1947. See Panel Report, *EEC – Animal Feed Proteins (1978)*, para. 4.2. It has been suggested that some GATT panels, and in particular the panel in *Japan – SPF Dimension Lumber (1989)*, considered tariff classification as the dominant criterion to establish 'likeness' within the meaning of Article I:1. See Panel Report, *Japan – SPF Dimension Lumber (1989)*, para. 5.13.

48 On the meaning of 'like products' in Article III of the GATT 1994, see below, pp. 355–6 and 360–8.

49 Appellate Body Report, *EC – Asbestos (2001)*, para. 99. See also Appellate Body Reports, *Philippines – Distilled Spirits (2012)*, para. 170. See below, pp. 362–3 and 378.

case law will tell whether the accordion of 'likeness' stretches or squeezes in Article I:1 of the GATT 1994.[50]

It is much debated whether, under current WTO law, a product's process and production method (PPM) is relevant in determining whether products are 'like' if the PPM by which a product is made does *not* affect the physical characteristics of the product. The traditional view is that such non-product-related processes and production methods (NPR-PPMs) are not relevant. Consequently, products produced in an environmentally unfriendly manner cannot be treated less favourably than products produced in an environmentally friendly manner on the sole basis of the difference in NPR-PPMs. Note, however, in this respect, the discussion on the concept of 'likeness' in Article III:4 in the context of the *EC – Asbestos (2001)* dispute.[51]

While the determination of whether products are 'like' is often a significant challenge, note that the panels in *Colombia – Ports of Entry (2009)* and *US – Poultry (China) (2010)* – inspired by panel reports in disputes concerning Article III of the GATT 1994[52] – have side-stepped the issue of 'likeness' and have proceeded on the *assumption* that there are 'like' products concerned.[53] The panel in *US – Poultry (China) (2010)* ruled:

> The funding restriction imposed by Section 727 [i.e. the measure at issue] is origin-based in respect of the products it affects, i.e. poultry products from China, and not from any other WTO Member. By targeting only China, Section 727 imposes origin-based discrimination.
>
>   Given this origin-based distinction the Panel believes it is appropriate to follow prior panels that have used a hypothetical like products analysis. In this sense, for the purposes of determining whether an advantage has been accorded immediately and unconditionally to other WTO Members and not to China, the Panel will assume that poultry products originating from China are like products to those originating from other WTO Members.[54]

This ruling, and the ruling of the panel in *Colombia – Ports of Entry (2009)*, stand for the proposition that it may be assumed that there are 'like' products when the measure at issue distinguishes between products solely on the basis of their origin. These rulings were not appealed.

Questions and Assignments 4.3

Is there *one* concept of 'like products' in WTO law? How is a panel to determine whether products are 'like products' within the meaning of Article I:1 of the GATT 1994? Is beef from cattle kept, fed, transported and slaughtered in accordance with animal welfare requirements 'like' beef from cattle treated in a less 'humane' manner?

---

50 The question arises whether the case law since *Japan – SPF Dimension Lumber (1989)* suggests that the accordion of 'likeness' stretches *and* squeezes in Article I:1, depending on the measure at issue (e.g. customs duties *versus* internal taxation or regulation).
51 See below, pp. 387–92.
52 Both panels referred to Panel Report, *Indonesia – Autos (1998)*, para. 14.113; and Appellate Body Report, *Canada – Periodicals (1997)*, 466. See below, p. 780 and see above, p. 237.
53 See *Colombia – Ports of Entry (2009)*, para. 7.357; and *US – Poultry (China) (2010)*, paras. 7.431–7.432.
54 *US – Poultry (China) (2010)*, paras. 7.431–7.432.

2.2.4   Advantage Accorded 'Immediately and Unconditionally'

The fourth and final element of the test of consistency with the MFN treatment obligation of Article I:1 relates to the question of whether the advantage granted by the measure at issue is accorded 'immediately and unconditionally' to all like products irrespective of their origin or destination. Article I:1 of the GATT 1994 requires that any advantage granted by a WTO Member to imports from, or exports to, any country must be granted 'immediately and unconditionally' to imports from, or exports to, all other WTO Members.

There is little debate on the meaning of the requirement to accord an advantage 'immediately' to all like products. 'Immediately' means 'without delay, at once, instantly'. No time should lapse between granting an advantage to a product and according that advantage to all like products.

More problematic is the meaning of the requirement to accord an advantage 'unconditionally'. According to the panel in *Indonesia – Autos (1998)*, the requirement to accord an advantage 'unconditionally' means that such advantage:

> cannot be made conditional on any criteria that [are] not related to the imported product itself.[55]

Two years later, the panel in *Canada – Autos (2000)* rejected the interpretation of Article I:1 advocated in this case by Japan, the complainant, according to which the term 'unconditionally' in Article I:1 must be interpreted to mean that subjecting an advantage to conditions not related to the imported product itself is *per se* inconsistent with Article I:1.[56] The panel in *Canada – Autos (2000)* ruled that:

> whether conditions attached to an advantage granted in connection with the importation of a product offend Article I:1 depends upon whether or not such conditions discriminate with respect to the origin of products.[57]

However, four years later, the panel in *EC – Tariff Preferences (2004)* stated without any reference to the interpretation of the term 'unconditionally' in the panel report in *Canada – Autos (2000)* that:

> the Panel sees no reason not to give that term its ordinary meaning under Article I:1, that is, 'not limited by or subject to any conditions'.[58]

---

55 Panel Report, *Indonesia – Autos (1998)*, para. 14.143. In support of this statement, the panel referred to Panel Report, *Belgium – Family Allowances (allocations familiales) (1952)*. See *ibid.*, para. 14.144. Note that the panel in *EEC – Imports of Beef (1981)* and the GATT Working Party Report in *Accession of Hungary (1973)* took a similar (strict) approach to the requirement that advantages shall be granted 'unconditionally'.

56 See Panel Report, *Canada – Autos (2000)*, para. 10.29.

57 Panel Report, *Canada – Autos (2000)*, para. 10.29.

58 Panel Report, *EC – Tariff Preferences (2004)*, para. 7.59. The panel acknowledged the European Union's argument that conditionality in the context of traditional MFN clauses in bilateral treaties may relate to conditions of trade compensation for receiving MFN treatment, but it did not consider this to be the full meaning of 'unconditionally' under Article I:1. See *ibid.*

In two more recent panel reports, namely, the reports in *Colombia – Ports of Entry (2009)* and in *US – Poultry (China) (2010)*, the panels explicitly referred to the interpretation of the term 'unconditionally' in the panel report in *Canada – Autos (2000)*.[59] The panel in *Colombia – Ports of Entry (2009)* stated:

[T]he Panel reiterates the view expressed in *Canada – Autos* that conditions attached to an advantage granted in connection with the importation of a product will violate Article I:1 when such conditions discriminate with respect to the origin of products.[60]

By way of conclusion, a comment may be made on two uncontroversial but important aspects of the MFN treatment obligation of Article I:1 of the GATT 1994. A complainant has to show neither any *actual trade effects* nor the *discriminatory intent* of the measure at issue to be successful in claiming inconsistency with the MFN treatment obligation of Article I:1. Note in this respect that the panel in *EC – Bananas III (1997)* found that it is the mere fact of creating *more favourable competitive opportunities* for some WTO Members only that triggers the inconsistency with the MFN treatment obligation of Article I:1 of the GATT 1994.[61]

Questions and Assignments 4.4

When is an advantage accorded 'immediately' and 'unconditionally' within the meaning of Article I:1 of the GATT 1994? Why is it not necessary to show either any *actual trade effects* or the *discriminatory intent* of the measure at issue to be successful in claiming inconsistency with the MFN treatment obligation of Article I:1?

2.3   Most-Favoured-Nation Treatment Obligation and the Enabling Clause of the GATT 1994

An important exception to the MFN treatment obligation of Article I:1 of the GATT 1994, and arguably the most significant special and differential treatment provision in WTO law, is the 1979 GATT Decision on Differential and More Favourable Treatment, Reciprocity and Fuller Participation of Developing Countries, commonly referred to as the 'Enabling Clause'.[62] The Enabling Clause, which is now an integral part of the GATT 1994,[63] states, in paragraph 1:

---

59 See Panel Report, *Colombia – Ports of Entry (2009)*, paras. 7.362–7.366; and Panel Report, *US – Poultry (China) (2010)*, paras. 7.437–7.440.

60 Panel Report, *Colombia – Ports of Entry (2009)*, para. 7.366.

61 See Panel Report, *EC – Bananas III (Mexico) (1997)*, para. 7.239.

62 GATT Document L/4903, dated 28 November 1979, BISD 26S/203. The Enabling Clause was adopted by the GATT CONTRACTING PARTIES in the context of the Tokyo Round of Multilateral Trade Negotiations. Note that the Enabling Clause replaced, and expanded, a 1971 *Waiver Decision on the Generalized System of Preferences*, GATT Document L/3545, dated 25 June 1971, BISD 18S/24. This Waiver Decision was in turn adopted to give effect to the *Agreed Conclusions* of the UNCTAD Special Committee on Preferences, adopted in 1970. These *Agreed Conclusions* recognised in para. I:2 that preferential tariff treatment accorded under a generalised scheme of preferences was key for developing countries '(a) to increase their export earnings; (b) to promote their industrialization; and (c) to accelerate their rates of economic growth'.

63 The Enabling Clause is one of the 'other decisions of the CONTRACTING PARTIES' within the meaning of para. 1(b)(iv) of Annex 1A incorporating the GATT 1994 into the *WTO Agreement*. See Appellate Body Report, *EC – Tariff Preferences (2004)*, para. 90 and footnote 192.

Notwithstanding the provisions of Article I of the General Agreement, [Members] may accord differential and more favourable treatment to developing countries, without according such treatment to other [Members].

2.3.1 Preferential Tariff Treatment for Developing Countries Under the Enabling Clause

Paragraph 2(a) of the Enabling Clause provides that the differential and more favourable treatment referred to in paragraph 1 includes:

Preferential tariff treatment accorded by [developed-country Members] to products originating in developing countries in accordance with the Generalized System of Preferences ...[64]

As the Appellate Body ruled in *EC – Tariff Preferences (2004)*, the Enabling Clause operates as an 'exception' to Article I:1 of the GATT 1994.[65] Paragraph 1 of the Enabling Clause explicitly exempts Members from complying with the obligation contained in Article I:1 for the purposes of providing differential and more favourable treatment to developing countries.[66] The Enabling Clause authorises developed-country Members to grant enhanced market access to products from developing countries extending beyond the access granted to like products from developed countries.[67] The Enabling Clause thus permits Members to provide 'differential and more favourable treatment' to developing countries in spite of the MFN treatment obligation of Article I:1, which normally requires that such treatment be extended to all Members 'immediately and unconditionally'. What is more, WTO Members are *not merely allowed* to deviate from Article I:1 in the pursuit of 'differential and more favourable treatment' for developing countries; they are *encouraged* to do so.[68] Note that most developed-country Members grant preferential tariff treatment to imports from developing countries under their respective Generalized System of Preferences (GSP) schemes. The Enabling Clause plays a vital role in promoting trade as a means of stimulating economic growth and development.[69]

---

64 The footnote in the original reads: 'As described in the Decision of the Contracting Parties of 25 June 1971, relating to the establishment of "generalized, non-reciprocal and non-discriminatory preferences beneficial to the developing countries" (BISD 18S/24).'

65 See Appellate Body Report, *EC – Tariff Preferences (2004)*, para. 99. On this point, the Appellate Body upheld the finding of the panel; see Panel Report, *EC – Tariff Preferences (2004)*, para. 7.53. The European Communities argued in *EC – Tariff Preferences (2004)* that the Enabling Clause, reflecting the fundamental objective of assisting developing-country Members, is not an exception to Article I:1 of the GATT 1994 but exists 'side-by-side and on an equal level' with Article I:1. The Appellate Body disagreed and ruled that: 'characterising the Enabling Clause as an exception, in our view, does not undermine the importance of the Enabling Clause within the overall framework of the covered agreements and as a "positive effort" to enhance economic development of developing-country Members. Nor does it "discourag[e]" developed countries from adopting measures in favour of developing countries under the Enabling Clause.' Appellate Body Report, *EC – Tariff Preferences*, para. 95.

66 See *ibid.*, para. 90.   67 See *ibid.*, para. 106.   68 See *ibid.*, para. 111.

69 See *ibid.*, para. 106. Note, however, that the Sutherland Report is very critical of the functioning of the GSP in practice. See Report by the Consultative Board to the Director-General Supachai Panitchpakdi, The Future of the WTO: Addressing Institutional Challenges in the New Millennium (the 'Sutherland Report') (WTO, 2004), paras. 88–102.

Before the Enabling Clause can successfully be invoked, certain conditions must be fulfilled. The deviation from the MFN obligation of Article I:1 is allowed only when, and to the extent that, the conditions set out in paragraphs 3 and 4 of the Enabling Clause are met. Paragraph 3 sets out the following substantive conditions:

Any differential and more favourable treatment provided under this clause:

a. shall be designed to facilitate and promote the trade of developing countries and not to raise barriers to or create undue difficulties for the trade of any other [Members];
b. shall not constitute an impediment to the reduction or elimination of tariffs and other restrictions to trade on a most-favoured-nation basis;
c. shall in the case of such treatment accorded by [developed-country Members] to developing countries be designed and, if necessary, modified, to respond positively to the development, financial and trade needs of developing countries.

Paragraph 4 sets out the procedural conditions for the introduction, modification and withdrawal of a preferential measure for developing countries. Pursuant to paragraph 4, Members granting preferential tariff treatment to developing countries must notify the WTO and afford adequate opportunity for prompt consultations at the request of any interested Member with respect to any difficulty or matter that may arise.

2.3.2   Additional Preferential Tariff Treatment Under the Enabling Clause

In *EC – Tariff Preferences (2004)*, the question arose as to whether the European Communities could grant *additional* preferential tariff treatment to certain developing countries to the exclusion of others. Council Regulation (EC) No. 2501/2001 of 10 December 2001, the EC's former Generalized System of Preferences Regulation,[70] provided for five preferential tariff 'arrangements', namely: (1) the 'General Arrangements'; (2) special incentive arrangements for the protection of labour rights; (3) special incentive arrangements for the protection of the environment; (4) special arrangements for least-developed countries; and (5) special arrangements to combat drug production and trafficking. The General Arrangements, which provide for tariff preferences for all developing countries, and the special arrangements for least-developed countries, were, and still are, not problematic. Both arrangements were, and are, justified under the Enabling Clause: the General Arrangements under paragraph 2(a), discussed above; and the special arrangements for least-developed countries under paragraph 2(d). The latter provision states that the Enabling Clause also covers:

[s]pecial treatment of the least developed among the developing countries in the context of any general or specific measures in favour of developing countries.

However, questions as to GATT-consistency arose with regard to the other preferential arrangements, i.e. the special incentive arrangements for the protection

---

70 OJ 2001, L346, 1.

of labour rights, the special incentive arrangements for the protection of the environment and the special arrangements to combat drug production and trafficking. Only some developing countries were beneficiaries of these special arrangements. For example, preferences under the special incentive arrangements for the protection of labour rights and the special incentive arrangements for the protection of the environment were restricted to those countries that were 'determined by the European Communities to comply with certain labour [or] environmental policy standards', respectively. Preferences under the special arrangements to combat drug production and trafficking (the 'Drug Arrangements') were provided only to eleven Latin American countries and Pakistan.[71]

While India, the complainant in *EC – Tariff Preferences (2004)*, challenged, in its panel request, the WTO-consistency of the Drug Arrangements as well as the special incentive arrangements for the protection of labour rights and the environment, it later decided to limit its complaint to the Drug Arrangements. Accordingly, the *EC – Tariff Preferences (2004)* dispute, and the rulings in this case, only concerned the WTO-consistency of the Drug Arrangements. However, it is clear that the rulings in this case may also be of relevance to other special arrangements.

The main substantive issue disputed between India and the European Communities in *EC – Tariff Preferences (2004)* was whether the Drug Arrangements were consistent with paragraph 2(a) of the Enabling Clause, and, in particular, the requirement of non-discrimination in footnote 3 thereto, quoted above.[72] With regard to paragraph 2(a) and its footnote, the panel in *EC – Tariff Preferences (2004)* found that:

the clear intention of the negotiators was to provide GSP equally to all developing countries and to eliminate all differentiation in preferential treatment to developing countries.[73]

As the Drug Arrangements do not provide identical tariff preferences to *all* developing countries, the panel concluded that the Drug Arrangements were inconsistent with paragraph 2(a) of the Enabling Clause and, in particular, the requirement of non-discrimination in footnote 3 thereto.[74] According to the panel, the term 'non-discriminatory' in footnote 3 requires that identical tariff preferences under GSP schemes be provided to all developing countries without differentiation.[75]

On appeal, the Appellate Body reversed this finding.[76] After a careful examination of the text and context of footnote 3 to paragraph 2(a) of the Enabling

---

71 See Appellate Body Report, *EC – Tariff Preferences (2004)*, para. 3. Preferences under the Drug Arrangements were provided to Bolivia, Colombia, Costa Rica, Ecuador, El Salvador, Guatemala, Honduras, Nicaragua, Pakistan, Panama, Peru and Venezuela.
72 The requirement of non-discrimination is derived from the words 'non-discriminatory preferences' in footnote 3. See above, p. 331, footnote 64.
73 Panel Report, *EC – Tariff Preferences (2004)*, para. 7.144.   74 See *ibid.*, para. 7.177.
75 See *ibid.*, paras. 7.161 and 7.176.
76 See Appellate Body Report, *EC – Tariff Preferences (2004)*, para. 174.

Clause, and the object and purpose of the *WTO Agreement* and the Enabling Clause, the Appellate Body came to the conclusion that:

the term 'non-discriminatory' in footnote 3 does not prohibit developed-country Members from granting different tariffs to products originating in different GSP beneficiaries, provided that such differential tariff treatment meets the remaining conditions in the Enabling Clause. In granting such differential tariff treatment, however, preference-granting countries are required, by virtue of the term 'non-discriminatory', to ensure that identical treatment is available to all similarly situated GSP beneficiaries, that is, to all GSP beneficiaries that have the 'development, financial and trade needs' to which the treatment in question is intended to respond.[77]

In other words, a developed-country Member may grant additional preferential tariff treatment to some, and not to other, developing-country Members, as long as additional preferential tariff treatment is available to all *similarly situated* developing-country Members. *Similarly situated* developing-country Members are all those that have the development, financial and trade needs to which additional preferential tariff treatment is intended to respond. The determination of whether developing-country Members are similarly situated must be based on objective criteria. With respect to the Drug Arrangements of the European Communities, however, the Appellate Body found in *EC – Tariff Preferences (2004)* that these arrangements provided for a *closed* list of twelve identified beneficiaries and contained no criteria or standards to provide a basis for distinguishing developing-country Members which are beneficiaries under the Drug Arrangements from other developing-country Members.[78] The Appellate Body therefore upheld – albeit for very different reasons – the panel's conclusion that the European Communities 'failed to demonstrate that the Drug Arrangements are justified under paragraph 2(a) of the Enabling Clause'.[79]

Questions and Assignments 4.5

What does the Enabling Clause of the GATT 1994 allow Members to do that they would otherwise not be allowed to do? Where in the GATT 1994 can the Enabling Clause be found? Is it appropriate and correct to identify the Enabling Clause as an 'exception' to the basic MFN

---

77 *Ibid.*, para. 173.   78 See *ibid.*, paras. 187 and 188.
79 *Ibid.*, para. 189. On 27 June 2005, the EC adopted Council Regulation (EC) No. 980/2005, replacing Council Regulation (EC) No. 221/2003 and establishing a new scheme of preferential tariff arrangements. The preferential tariff arrangements were reduced from five to three: (1) the 'General Arrangements'; (2) the 'special incentive arrangement for sustainable development and good governance' (GSP+); (3) the 'Everything But Arms' (EBA) arrangement. While the 'General Arrangements' provided tariff preferences for all developing countries, the GSP+ was available only to developing countries that have ratified and implemented a number of international conventions set out in Annex 3 to the Regulation. The GSP+ system replaced the Drug Arrangements (and the special incentive arrangements referred to above) so as to comply with the Appellate Body's ruling in *EC – Tariff Preferences (2004)*. It applied to 'vulnerable' countries meeting a set of objective criteria set out in Articles 9 and 10 of the Regulation. Note that the following countries are eligible for GSP+: Bolivia, Colombia, Costa Rica, Ecuador, El Salvador, Georgia, Guatemala, Honduras, Moldova, Mongolia, Nicaragua, Panama, Peru, Sri Lanka and Venezuela. Finally, the EBA arrangement extends duty-free and quota-free market access to least-developed countries, save for arms and ammunition. The Regulation applied from 1 January 2006 until 31 December 2008, but the GSP+ provisions were already applied from 1 July 2005. See WTO Secretariat, *Trade Policy Review Report – European Communities*, WT/TPR/S/177, dated 22 January 2007, 35–6.

treatment obligation of the GATT 1994? Does the Enabling Clause allow developed-country Members to treat certain developing-country Members more favourably than others?

3   MOST-FAVOURED-NATION TREATMENT UNDER THE GATS

As mentioned above, the MFN treatment obligation is also one of the basic provisions of the GATS. This section examines: (1) the nature of the MFN treatment obligation provided for in Article II:1 of the GATS; and (2) the test of consistency with Article II:1.

3.1   Nature of the MFN Treatment Obligation of Article II:1 of the GATS

Article II:1 of the GATS states as follows:

> With respect to any measure covered by this Agreement, each Member shall accord immediately and unconditionally to services and service suppliers of any other Member treatment no less favourable than that it accords to like services and service suppliers of any other country.

Article II:1 prohibits discrimination *between* like services and service suppliers from different countries. In other words, Article II:1 prohibits WTO Member Richland to give services and service suppliers from WTO Member Newland treatment less favourable than the treatment it gives to like services and service suppliers from any other WTO Members or other country. The principal purpose of the MFN treatment obligation of Article II:1 of the GATS is to ensure all WTO Members *equality of opportunity* to supply like services.

Article II:1 is supplemented by a number of other MFN or MFN-like provisions found elsewhere in the GATS. These provisions include: Article VII (regarding recognition of education or experience obtained); Article VIII (regarding monopolies and exclusive service suppliers); Article X (regarding future rules on emergency safeguard measures); Article XII (regarding balance of payments measures); and Article XXI (regarding the modification of schedules).[80] Article XIV of the GATS, and in particular the chapeau of this 'general exceptions' provision, also contains an MFN-like obligation.[81]

The Appellate Body in *EC – Bananas III (1997)* found that the MFN treatment obligation of Article II:1 of the GATS applies both to *de jure* and to *de facto* discrimination.[82] The Appellate Body came to this conclusion in spite of the fact that Article II of the GATS, unlike Article XVII thereof, does not explicitly

---

80 See also Article 5(a) of the GATS *Annex on Telecommunications* and the Preamble to the GATS *Understanding on Commitments in Financial Services.*
81 See below, pp. 574–81.
82 With respect to the concepts of *de jure* and *de facto* discrimination, see above, pp. 319–20.

state that it applies to *de facto* discrimination.[83] The European Communities had argued in this case that, if the negotiators of the GATS had wanted Article II:1 to cover also *de facto* discrimination, they would have explicitly said so. The Appellate Body disagreed and ruled:

[t]he obligation imposed by Article II is unqualified. The ordinary meaning of this provision does not exclude *de facto* discrimination. Moreover, if Article II was not applicable to *de facto* discrimination, it would not be difficult – and, indeed, it would be a good deal easier in the case of trade in services, than in the case of trade in goods – to devise discriminatory measures aimed at circumventing the basic purpose of that Article.[84]

An example of *de jure* discrimination inconsistent with Article II:1 would be a regulation of WTO Member Richland on content quota for TV broadcasting that gives TV series produced in Spain (such as *Amar en tiempos revueltos*[85]) preference over TV series produced in other WTO Members (such as *Friends*). Such a measure discriminates explicitly on the basis of the origin of the service and therefore constitutes *de jure* discrimination. An example of *de facto* discrimination inconsistent with Article II:1 may be a regulation of Richland on content quota for TV broadcasting that gives TV series with a storyline based on historical events (such as *Amar en tiempos revueltos*) preference over TV series with a storyline based on silly everyday events of life (such as *Friends*). Although this measure does not distinguish between the services on the basis of national origin, it may *de facto* offer less favourable treatment to some WTO Members than to others because they do not, or are less likely to, make TV series with a storyline based on historical events.[86]

Questions and Assignments 4.6

Are the MFN clauses of the GATS and of the GATT 1994 similar in wording? Are they similar in nature? Does Article II:1 of the GATS also prohibit *de facto* discrimination? Explain. Give an example of a *de facto* discriminatory measure inconsistent with Article II:1 of the GATS. Would a regulation of Richland on content quota for TV broadcasting that gives TV series in Spanish (such as *Amar en tiempos revueltos*) preference over TV series in other languages (such as *Friends*) constitute *de jure* or *de facto* discrimination inconsistent with Article II:1 of the GATS?

3.2   MFN Treatment Test of Article II:1 of the GATS

As the Appellate Body found in *Canada – Autos (2000)*, the wording of Article II:1 of the GATS suggests that the test of consistency with the MFN treatment obligation of this provision proceeds in *three* steps.[87] There are three questions

---

83 See below, p. 344.
84 Appellate Body Report, *EC – Bananas III (1997)*, para. 233.
85 Translation: 'To love in troubled times'.
86 It is assumed here that TV series with a story line based on historical events *and* TV series with a story line based on silly everyday events of life are 'like' services. For the discussion on the concept of 'likeness' of services and services suppliers under Article II:2 of the GATS, see below, pp. 342–4.
87 See Appellate Body Report, *Canada – Autos (2000)*, paras. 170–1.

which need to be answered to determine whether or not a measure is consistent with the MFN treatment obligation of Article II:1 of the GATS, namely:

- whether the measure at issue falls *within the scope of application* of *Article II:1* of the GATS;
- whether the services or service suppliers concerned are '*like services*' or '*like service suppliers*'; and
- whether like services or service suppliers are accorded *treatment no less favourable*.

Below, each element of this three-tier test of consistency will be discussed in turn.[88]

To date, WTO Members have been found to have acted inconsistently with the MFN treatment obligation of Article II:1 of the GATS in three disputes.[89]

3.2.1 Measure Covered by Article II:1

The first element of the test of consistency with the MFN treatment obligation of Article II:1 of the GATS is whether the measure at issue is covered by, i.e. falls within the scope of application of, Article II:1 of the GATS. To answer this question, one must assess whether the measure at issue is a measure to which the GATS applies. However, some measures to which the GATS applies are exempted from the MFN treatment obligation of Article II:1. One must, therefore, also always assess whether the measure at issue is not one of the measures exempted from the MFN treatment obligation.

Article I:1 of the GATS states with regard to the measures to which the obligations of the GATS apply that:

[t]his Agreement applies to measures by Members affecting trade in services.

Therefore, for the GATS to apply to a measure, that measure must be: (1) a measure by a Member; and (2) a measure affecting trade in services.

A 'measure by a Member' is a very broad concept. Article XXVIII(a) of the GATS defines a 'measure' for the purposes of the GATS to be:

any measure by a Member, whether in the form of a law, regulation, rule, procedure, decision, administrative action, or any other form.

Article I:3(a) of the GATS further clarifies that 'measures by Members' means measures taken by central, regional or local governments and authorities.[90] Measures taken by non-governmental bodies are also 'measures by Members' when they are taken in the exercise of powers delegated by central, regional

---

88 See below, pp. 337–42, 342–4 and 344–5.
89 See *EC – Bananas III (1997)*; *EC – Bananas III (Article 21.5 – Ecuador) (1999)*; and *EC – Bananas III (US) (Article 22.6 – EC) (1999)*. There was no finding of inconsistency in *Canada – Autos (2000)*; the Appellate Body reversed the panel's finding of inconsistency.
90 See also above, pp. 170–1.

or local governments or authorities.[91] For example, in many WTO Members, the government has delegated the regulation of the legal or medical profession to the relevant professional association and, consequently, a measure taken by such association in the exercise of this delegated authority is considered to fall within the scope of 'measures by Members' within the meaning of Article II:1 of the GATS. In brief, a 'measure by a Member' within the meaning of Article II:1 can therefore be a national parliamentary law as well as municipal decrees or rules adopted by professional associations.

With regard to the concept of 'measures affecting trade in services', note that Article XXVIII(c) of the GATS gives a number of examples of such measures, including measures in respect of the purchase, payment or use of a service and measures in respect of the access to services which are required to be offered to the public generally. The concept of a 'measure affecting trade in services' was clarified by the Appellate Body in *Canada – Autos (2000)*. The measure at issue in that case was an import duty exemption accorded by Canada to imports of motor vehicles by certain manufacturers. The complainants, the European Communities and Japan, argued that this measure was inconsistent with Article II:1 of the GATS as it accorded 'less favourable treatment' to certain Members' services and service suppliers than to those of other Members. The panel found that the import duty exemption was indeed inconsistent with Article II:1 of the GATS. In addition to appealing this finding, Canada challenged, as a threshold matter, the panel's finding that the measure at issue fell within the scope of application of Article II:1 of the GATS. According to Canada, the measure at issue was not a measure 'affecting trade in services'. The Appellate Body stated that two key issues must be examined in order to determine whether a measure is one 'affecting trade in services', namely: (1) whether there is 'trade in services' in the sense of Article I:2; and (2) whether the measure at issue 'affects' such trade in services within the meaning of Article I:1.[92]

With respect to the question of whether there is 'trade in services', note that the GATS does not define what a 'service' is. Article I:3(b) of the GATS, however, states that the term 'services' includes:

any service in any sector except services supplied in the exercise of governmental authority.

'Services supplied in the exercise of governmental authority' are defined in Article I:3(c) of the GATS as any services which are supplied neither on a commercial basis nor in competition with one or more service suppliers. It is clear that what are 'services supplied in the exercise of governmental authority' differ

---

91 See *ibid.*
92 Appellate Body Report, *Canada – Autos (2000)*, para. 155. Note that the Appellate Body eventually reversed the panel's conclusion that the import duty exemption was inconsistent with the requirements of Article II:1 of the GATS. However, it did so, not because it came to the conclusion that Canada acted consistently with its MFN treatment obligation, but because the panel failed to substantiate its conclusion that the import duty exemption was inconsistent with Article II:1 of the GATS. See *ibid.*, paras. 182–3.

from WTO Member to WTO Member. For most WTO Members, police protection and penitentiary services are 'services supplied in the exercise of governmental authority'. However, for a growing number of WTO Members, services that were traditionally considered to be 'services supplied in the exercise of governmental authority', such as primary health care, basic education, mail delivery, rail transport and garbage disposal, have in recent years been subject to privatisation, and, consequently, measures affecting such services now fall within the scope of application of the GATS.[93] Services which the government offers on a commercial basis and/or in competition with one or more (private) service suppliers are not 'services supplied in the exercise of governmental authority' and, therefore, 'services' within the meaning of Article I:3(b).

While the GATS does not define 'services', Article I:2 thereof defines 'trade in services' as 'the supply of a service' in any one of four listed 'modes of supply'. Article I:2 states:

For the purpose of this Agreement, trade in services is defined as the supply of a service:

(a) from the territory of one Member into the territory of any other Member;
(b) in the territory of one Member to the service consumer of any other Member;
(c) by a service supplier of one Member, through commercial presence in the territory of any other Member;
(d) by a service supplier of one Member, through presence of natural persons of a Member in the territory of any other Member.

These four modes of supply of services are commonly referred to as:

- 'cross border supply' (mode 1), such as legal advice given by a lawyer in Richland to a client in Newland;
- 'consumption abroad' (mode 2), such as medical treatment given by a doctor in Richland to a patient from Newland who comes to Richland for treatment;
- 'commercial presence' (mode 3), such as financial services supplied in Newland by a bank from Richland through a branch office established in Newland;[94] and
- 'presence of natural persons' (mode 4), such as the programming services supplied in Newland by a computer programmer from Richland, who travels to Newland to supply such services.[95]

---

93 Note also that many measures affecting services in the air transport sector do not fall within the scope of application of the GATS. See GATS *Annex on Air Transport Services*, para. 2.
94 Note that, pursuant to Article XXVIII(d) of the GATS, 'commercial presence' means any type of business or professional establishment, including through the constitution, acquisition or maintenance of a juridical person, or the creation or maintenance of a branch or a representative office, within the territory of a Member for the purpose of supplying a service.
95 It is estimated that cross-border supply of services and supply of services through commercial presence each represent around 40 per cent of total world trade in services; consumption abroad represents around 20 per cent. Supply through the presence of natural persons is, to date, insignificant. See WTO Secretariat, Market Access: Unfinished Business, Special Studies Series 6 (WTO, 2001), 105.

Furthermore, Article XXVIII(b) makes clear that the 'supply of a service' includes the production, distribution, marketing, sale and delivery of a service.

Clearly, the concept of 'trade in services' within the meaning of Article I:1 is very broad. The panel in *Mexico – Telecoms (2004)* clarified the meaning of two of the modes of supply, namely, 'cross-border supply' and 'commercial presence'. The question in *Mexico – Telecoms (2004)* was whether telecommunication services, provided by a United States service provider to consumers in Mexico without operating or being present in Mexico, could be considered services supplied 'cross-border' within the meaning of Article I:2(a) of the GATS. The panel found that Article I:2(a) does not require the presence of the supplier in the territory of the country where the service is provided.[96] With regard to 'commercial presence' within the meaning of Article I:2(c), the panel stated:

> The definition of services supplied through a commercial presence makes explicit the location of the service supplier. It provides that a service supplier has a commercial presence – any type of business or professional establishment – *in the territory* of any other Member. The definition is silent with respect to any other territorial requirement (as in cross-border supply under mode 1) or nationality of the service consumer (as in consumption abroad under mode 2). Supply of a service through commercial presence would therefore not exclude a service that originates in the territory in which a commercial presence is established (such as Mexico), but is delivered into the territory of any other Member (such as the United States).[97]

With regard to the question of whether the measure at issue *affects* trade in services within the meaning of Article I:1, the Appellate Body clarified in *EC – Bananas III (1997)* the term 'affecting' as follows:

> In our view, the use of the term 'affecting' reflects the intent of the drafters to give a broad reach to the GATS. The ordinary meaning of the word 'affecting' implies a measure that has 'an effect on', which indicates a broad scope of application. This interpretation is further reinforced by the conclusions of previous panels that the term 'affecting' in the context of Article III of the GATT is wider in scope than such terms as 'regulating' or 'governing'.[98]

For a measure to affect trade in services, the measure is not required to regulate or govern the trade in, i.e. the supply of, services. A measure is covered by the GATS if it *affects* trade in services, even though the measure may regulate other matters, such as trade in goods.[99] A measure affects trade in services when the measure bears upon 'the conditions of competition in supply of a service'.[100]

---

96 The panel noted that the words of Article I:2(a) do not address the service supplier or specify where the services supplier must operate, or be present in some way, much less imply any degree of presence of the supplier in the territory into which the service is supplied. See Panel Report, *Mexico – Telecoms (2004)*, para. 7.30.

97 *Ibid.*, para. 7.375. Original emphasis.

98 Appellate Body Report, *EC – Bananas III (1997)*, para. 220.

99 See Panel Reports, *EC – Bananas III (1997)*, para. 7.285.

100 See *ibid.*, para. 7.281. Regarding the question whether measures adopted by regional and local governments and authorities can 'affect the supply of a service', see Panel Report, *US – Gambling (2005)*, para. 6.252. With regard to the function of the term 'affecting' in the context of Article I:1 of the GATS, see Appellate Body Report, *US – FSC (Article 21.5 – EC) (2002)*, para. 209.

In brief, the concept of 'measures by Members affecting trade in services' is, in all respects, a concept with a broad meaning. Consequently, the scope of measures to which the MFN treatment obligation applies is likewise broad.

As noted above, to answer the question whether the measure at issue is covered by Article II:1, it does not suffice to determine whether that measure is a measure to which the GATS applies. It must also be established whether or not the measure at issue is exempted from the MFN treatment obligation of Article II:1 of the GATS. Unlike under the GATT 1994, the GATS allows Members *to exempt* measures from the MFN treatment obligation. Article II:2 of the GATS provides:

A Member may maintain a measure inconsistent with paragraph 1 provided that such a measure is listed in, and meets the conditions of, the Annex on Article II Exemptions.

Members could list measures in the Annex on Article II Exemptions *until* the date of entry into force of the *WTO Agreement*. For original Members, this meant until 1 January 1995.[101] About two-thirds of WTO Members have listed MFN exemptions. In total, Members have listed over 400 exempted measures. The exempted measures often concern maritime transport, audiovisual, financial and business services, bilateral investment treaties and measures regarding the presence of natural persons. The list of exempted measures that a particular Member has included in the Annex on Article II Exemptions can be found – and easily consulted – on the WTO website.[102] Note, by way of example, that the European Union included in its list of exempted measures:

Measures granting the benefit of any support programmes (such as Action Plan for Advanced Television Services, MEDIA or EURIMAGES) to audiovisual works, and suppliers of such works, meeting certain European origin criteria.[103]

This allows the European Union to give support to, for example, Canadian filmmakers, while denying such support to US filmmakers.

Paragraph 6 of the Annex on Article II Exemptions states that, in principle, the exemptions should not exceed ten years. Therefore, one might have expected that most, if not all, exemptions under Article II:2 would have come to an end by 1 January 2005.[104] However, this did not happen. Relying on the language

---

101 For WTO Members that have acceded to the WTO pursuant to Article XII of the *WTO Agreement* after 1 January 1995, exemptions from the MFN treatment obligation of Article II:1 of the GATS were part of their accession negotiations and needed to be agreed on before accession. After the *WTO Agreement* has entered into force for a particular Member, that Member can only exempt a measure from the application of the MFN obligation under Article II:1 by obtaining a waiver from the MFN obligation pursuant to Article IX:3 of the *WTO Agreement* (see paragraph 2 of the Annex on Article II Exemptions). On waivers, see above, pp. 115–6.

102 See www.wto.org.

103 See European Communities and Their Member States, *Final List of Article II (MFN) Exemptions*, GATS/ EL/31, 15 April 1994.

104 This is so at least for original Members. For Members that acceded to the WTO pursuant to Article XII of the *WTO Agreement*, the date on which the ten-year period expires will be later than 1 January 2005.

of paragraph 6 (which states that 'in principle' exemptions 'should not' exceed ten years), many Members continue to apply the exemptions they listed in the Annex on Article II Exemptions.

Pursuant to paragraph 3 of the Annex on Article II Exemptions, all exemptions granted for a period of more than five years are reviewed by the Council for Trade in Services. As stated in paragraph 4 of the Annex, the Council examines whether the conditions that created the need for the exemption still prevail. If the Council concludes that these conditions are no longer present, the Member concerned would arguably be obliged to accord MFN treatment in respect of the measure previously exempted from this obligation. Perhaps not surprisingly,[105] the reviews that took place in 2000, 2004–5 and 2010–11 did not result in any finding that a listed exemption was no longer justified.[106] As observed by Hong Kong, China, during the 2010–11 review, 'most, if not all, MFN exemptions that had been listed, persisted'.[107]

Finally, note that, pursuant to Article II:3 of the GATS, a measure that grants advantages to adjacent countries in order to facilitate trade in services between contiguous frontier zones is not subject to the MFN treatment obligation of Article II:1. For Article II:3 to apply, it is required, however, that the services concerned are both locally produced and consumed. An example of such services would be taxi services between Geneva and 'la France voisine' (i.e. neighbouring France).

Questions and Assignments 4.7

What are the constituent elements of the MFN treatment test of Article II:1 of the GATS? What measures are covered by the GATS? What measures are not covered? In your opinion, are measures affecting basic education and primary health care in your country subject to the MFN treatment obligation of Article II:1 of the GATS? Give an example (other than those given above) of each mode of supply of services. Can an import prohibition on products containing asbestos be a measure covered by the GATS? Can Members exempt measures for an indefinite period of time from the application of the MFN treatment obligation under Article II:1 of the GATS? Name two measures that the United States and India exempted from the MFN treatment obligation pursuant to Article II:2 of the GATS.

3.2.2 'Like Services' or 'Like Service Suppliers'

Once it has been established that the measure at issue is covered by Article II:1 of the GATS, the second element of the three-tier test of consistency with the MFN treatment obligation of Article II:1 of the GATS comes into play. Namely, it must be determined whether the services or services suppliers concerned are

---

105 Note that, in practice, the Council on Trade in Services makes its decisions by consensus, and a finding that an exemption is no longer justified would thus require the consent of the Member that listed the exemption. On WTO decision-making, see above, pp. 136–48.

106 See S/C/M/44, dated 21 June 2000; S/C/M/76, dated 4 February 2005; S/C/M/78, dated 17 May 2005; S/C/M/79, dated 16 August 2005; and S/C/M/105, dated 6 June 2011. The next review will take place no later than 2016. See S/C/M/105, dated 6 June 2011, paras. 35–6.

107 See S/C/M/105, dated 6 June 2011, para. 31.

'like services' or 'like service suppliers'. It is only between 'like services' and between 'like service suppliers' that the MFN treatment obligation applies and that discrimination within the meaning of Article II:1 of the GATS may occur. Services or service suppliers that are not 'like' may be treated differently; different treatment of services or service suppliers that are not 'like' will not constitute discrimination within the meaning of Article II:1. For the application of the MFN treatment obligation of Article II:1, it is therefore important to be able to determine whether, for example, movie actors are 'like' stage actors, whether the distribution of books is 'like' the distribution of e-books; whether doctors with a German medical degree are 'like' doctors with a Chinese medical degree; whether Internet gambling is 'like' casino gambling; and whether a 500-partner law firm is 'like' a sole legal practitioner.

As noted above, the term 'services' is not defined in the GATS, but Article I:3(c) states that 'services' includes 'any service in any sector except services supplied in the exercise of governmental authority'. The term 'service supplier' is defined in the GATS. Article XXVIII(g) provides that a 'service supplier' is 'any person who supplies a service', including natural and legal persons as well as service suppliers providing their services through forms of commercial presence, such as a branch or a representative office. The terms '*like* services' and '*like* service suppliers*' are not defined in the GATS and, to date, there is very little relevant case law on the meaning of these terms in Article II:1. The panels in *EC – Bananas III (1997)* and *Canada – Autos (2000)* found that, to the extent that service suppliers provide 'like services', they are 'like service suppliers'.[108] However, the question arises whether this is always the case, or whether, for example, the size of the service suppliers, their assets and the nature and extent of their expertise must also be taken into account when deciding whether service suppliers providing 'like services' are 'like service suppliers'.[109]

Note that there is more case law on the meaning of the terms 'like services' and 'like service suppliers' in Article XVII:1 of the GATS. As discussed in Chapter 5, this case law indicates that the determination of whether services or service suppliers are 'like' under Article XVII:1 'should be made on a case-by-case basis'; 'should be based on arguments and evidence that pertain to the competitive relationship of the services being compared'; and 'must be made on the basis of the evidence as a whole'.[110] Services are 'like' for the purposes of Article XVII:1 if 'it is determined that the services in question in a particular case are essentially or generally the same in competitive terms'.[111] It is reasonable to expect that this case law regarding Article XVII:1 will inform the

---

108 See Panel Report, *EC – Bananas III (1997)*, para. 7.322; and Panel Report, *Canada – Autos (2000)*, para. 10.248.

109 See in this regard the statement regarding 'likeness' under Article XVII:1 of the GATS made by the panel in *China – Electronic Payment Services (2012)*, para. 7.705. See below, p. 412.

110 Panel Report, *China – Electronic Payment Services*, paras. 7.701–7.702. See below, pp. 410–11.

111 *Ibid.*, para. 7.702. See below, p. 411.

interpretation of the terms 'like services' and 'like service suppliers' in Article II:1 of the GATS.

Questions and Assignments 4.8

How would you determine whether services or service suppliers are 'like' within the meaning of Article II:1 of the GATS? Is retail banking 'like' private banking? Is home insurance 'like' car insurance? Are nannies 'like' domestic workers?

3.2.3 Treatment no Less Favourable

The third and final element of the test of consistency with the MFN treatment obligation of Article II:1 of the GATS relates to the treatment accorded to 'like services' and 'like service suppliers'. A WTO Member must accord, immediately and unconditionally, to services and service suppliers of any given WTO Member 'treatment no less favourable' than the treatment it accords to 'like services' and 'like service suppliers' of any other country. Article II of the GATS does not provide any guidance as to the meaning of the concept of 'treatment no less favourable'. However, as discussed below, Article XVII of the GATS on the national treatment obligation contains guidance on the meaning of the concept of 'treatment no less favourable'.[112] Article XVII:3 states:

Formally identical or formally different treatment shall be considered to be less favourable if it modifies the conditions of competition in favour of services or service suppliers of the Member compared to the like services or service suppliers of any other Member.

In the context of Article XVII, a measure thus accords 'less favourable treatment' if it *modifies* the *conditions of competition* in favour of the domestic service or service supplier. As the Appellate Body cautioned in *EC – Bananas III (1997)*, it should not be assumed that, in interpreting Article II:1, and in particular the concept of 'treatment no less favourable', the guidance of Article XVII equally applies to Article II:1. However, as noted above, the Appellate Body has already concluded that the concept of 'treatment no less favourable' in Article II:1 and Article XVII of the GATS should be interpreted to include both *de facto* as well as *de jure* discrimination although only Article XVII states so explicitly.[113] Moreover, note that the panel in *EC – Bananas III (Article 21.5 – Ecuador) (1999)* found that the import licensing measures were inconsistent with the MFN treatment obligation of Article II:1, because Ecuador, the complainant, had shown that:

its service suppliers do not have opportunities to obtain access to import licences on terms equal to those enjoyed by service suppliers of EC/ACP origin under the revised regime and carried on from the previous regime.[114]

Also note that the Appellate Body stated in *EC – Bananas III (1997)* that it saw no specific authority in Article II:1 of the GATS for the proposition, advanced

---

112 See below, pp. 412–14.
113 See Appellate Body Report, *EC – Bananas III (1997)*, para. 234. See also above, p. 336.
114 Panel Report, *EC – Bananas III (Article 21.5 – Ecuador) (1999)*, para. 6.133.

by the European Union, that the 'aims and effects' of a measure are relevant in determining whether that measure is inconsistent with the MFN treatment obligation of Article II:1.[115]

Finally, pursuant to Article VII of the GATS, entitled 'Recognition', a Member may recognise the education or experience obtained, requirements met or licences or certificates granted in a particular country. Such recognition may be based upon an agreement or arrangements with the country concerned or may be accorded autonomously. In either case, such recognition, when it benefits the services or service suppliers of one or some WTO Members but not the like services or service suppliers of other WTO Members, will be consistent with the MFN treatment obligation if it meets the requirements of Article VII. Article VII:2, first sentence, requires a WTO Member, which has negotiated a recognition agreement or arrangement with another Member, to afford 'adequate opportunity' for other interested Members to negotiate their accession to such an agreement or arrangement or to negotiate a comparable one with it. Article VII:2, second sentence, provides that a WTO Member, which accords recognition autonomously, must afford 'adequate opportunity' for any other Member to demonstrate that education, experience, licences or certifications obtained or requirements met in that other Member's territory should be recognised. Moreover, Article VII:3 states:

A Member shall not accord recognition in a manner which would constitute a means of discrimination between countries in the application of its standards or criteria for the authorization, licensing or certification of services suppliers, or a disguised restriction on trade in services.

Recognition under Article VII is further discussed in Chapter 7 of this book.[116]

Questions and Assignments 4.9

When is treatment accorded to services or service suppliers of a Member *less favourable* than that accorded to like services or like service suppliers of any other country? Can formally identical treatment be considered to be *less favourable* treatment within the meaning of Article II:1 of the GATS? Is the regulatory intent of a measure affecting trade in services relevant in determining whether this measure is consistent with Article II:1 of the GATS?

4 SUMMARY

There are two main rules of non-discrimination in WTO law: the most-favoured-nation (MFN) treatment obligation, discussed in this chapter, and

115 See Appellate Body Report, *EC – Bananas III (1997)*, para. 241. The Appellate Body came to the same finding regarding the national treatment obligation of Article XVII:1 of the GATS. See below, p. 414.
116 See below, p. 536.

the national treatment obligation, discussed in the next chapter. In simple terms, an MFN treatment obligation relates to whether a country favours some countries over others. An MFN treatment obligation prohibits a country to discriminate *between* other countries. The MFN treatment obligation under WTO law applies to trade in goods as well as trade in services. The key provision that deals with the MFN treatment obligation for measures affecting trade in goods is Article I:1 of the GATT 1994. The key provision that deals with the MFN treatment obligation for measures affecting trade in services is Article II:1 of the GATS.

Article I:1 of the GATT 1994 prohibits discrimination *between* like products originating in, or destined for, different countries. The principal purpose of the MFN treatment obligation of Article I:1 is to ensure all WTO Members *equality of opportunity* to import from, or to export to, other WTO Members. The MFN treatment obligation of Article I:1 applies to *de jure* as well as *de facto* discrimination. There are four questions which must be answered to determine whether or not a measure affecting trade in goods is consistent with the MFN treatment obligation of Article I:1, namely: (1) whether the measure at issue is a measure covered by Article I:1; (2) whether that measure grants an '*advantage*'; (3) whether the products concerned are '*like products*'; and (4) whether the advantage at issue is *accorded* '*immediately and unconditionally*' to all like products concerned irrespective of their origin or destination. An important exception to the MFN treatment obligation of Article I:1 of the GATT 1994 and arguably the most significant special and differential treatment provision in WTO law is the Enabling Clause of the GATT 1994. The Enabling Clause allows, under certain conditions, developed-country Members to grant preferential tariff treatment to imports from developing countries. This exception therefore allows Members to deviate from the basic MFN treatment obligation of Article I:1 of the GATT 1994 to promote the economic development of developing-country Members. Under specific conditions, the Enabling Clause also allows developed-country Members to grant additional preferential tariff treatment to some developing countries to the exclusion of others.

Article II:1 of the GATS prohibits discrimination *between* like services and service suppliers from different countries. The principal purpose of the MFN treatment obligation of Article II:1 is to ensure all WTO Members *equality of opportunity* to supply like services. The MFN treatment obligation of Article II:1 applies to *de jure* as well as *de facto* discrimination. There are three questions which must be answered to determine whether or not a measure is consistent with the MFN treatment obligation of Article II:1 of the GATS, namely: (1) whether the measure at issue is covered by Article II:1; (2) whether the services or service suppliers concerned are '*like services*' or '*like service suppliers*'; and (3) whether like services or service suppliers are accorded *treatment no less favourable*.

Exercise 4: Tyres

Since colonial times, Newland has been a major producer and exporter of natural rubber. In recent years, RichYear Inc., the biggest tyre producer of Richland, has made significant investments in new production facilities in Newland. While at present still modest in size, the tyre industry in Newland is expected to grow further in the near future and employ more people. Currently, Newland still imports most of its tyres from Richland and Oldland.[117] Ever more of the tyres imported from Richland – especially tyres in the lower price brackets – are made from synthetic rubber rather than natural rubber. Tyres from Oldland remain primarily tyres made from natural rubber.

To support its infant tyre industry, Newland imposes a special import charge on tyres imported from Richland of N$5 pre tyre.[118] No such charge is levied on tyres from other countries. Also, tyres made from synthetic rubber are subject to a value added tax (VAT) of 25 per cent *ad valorem*, while tyres made from natural rubber are subject to a 15 per cent VAT.

Since last year, when a case of serious customs fraud was discovered, Newland has required that all tyres be imported through two designated ports of entry only. This requirement does not apply, however, to tyres imported from neighbouring Nearland, a country currently negotiating accession to the WTO.

Shortly after joining the WTO, Newland imposed an export duty on the natural rubber destined for Richland. No such duty applies to natural rubber exported to any other country.

In Newland, tyres made from natural rubber originating in Oldland may be sold by the importer directly to the final consumer (rather than to car repair shops or specialised tyre replacement and fitting workshops). Tyres made from natural rubber originating in Richland may also be sold directly to the final consumer, but only on the condition that the imported tyres are accompanied by a certificate that the tyres are indeed made from natural rubber. All other tyres (and in particular tyres made from synthetic rubber) may only be sold by the importer to car repair shops or specialised tyre replacement and fitting workshops.

OldTyres Inc., a big tyre manufacturer from Oldland, has established in Newland a chain of specialised tyre replacement and fitting workshops, which has allowed it to boost its sales of tyres. Inspired by this example, RichYear Inc. wants to establish a chain of car repair shops. RichYear is told that it would be allowed to establish – as did OldTyres from Oldland – specialised tyre replacement and fitting workshops, but that it would not be authorised to establish car repair shops. In Newland, all car repair shops are owned and run by the Ministry of Transport.

RichYear also wants engineers from Richland to advise it on tyre production at its new production facilities in Newland. Newland only allows engineers from Oldland,

117 Newland and Richland are already known to you. Oldland is a developed country and an original Member of the WTO. Until 1960, Newland was part of the colonial empire of Oldland.
118 N$ stands for Newland dollars and N$1 is €1.

where the same language is spoken as in Newland, to work as engineers in Newland. In justification of its ban on engineers who are not native speakers, Newland points out that engineering advice misunderstood because of language difficulties has in the past led to serious accidents.

You are an associate with the Washington-based law firm Laker & McCartney. Your firm has been requested by RichYear Inc. to give legal advice on all the issues raised above. You have been instructed to limit your legal brief to the question of whether there are violations of the MFN treatment obligations under WTO law.[119]

119 For the purpose of this exercise, assume that the list of measures included by Newland in the Annex on Article II Exemptions is identical to the list included by China. As instructed, you will not address questions relating to the consistency of the measures at issue with other WTO agreements (such as the *TBT Agreement* or the *SCM Agreement*) or questions relating to the possible justification of inconsistencies with the MFN treatment obligations under the 'general' or other exceptions provided for in the GATT 1994 or the GATS. For a discussion on these questions, see below.

5 National Treatment

CONTENTS

1 INTRODUCTION

As stated in Chapter 1, there are two main non-discrimination obligations under WTO law: the most-favoured-nation (MFN) treatment obligation, discussed in the previous chapter, and the national treatment obligation, which is discussed in this chapter. In simple terms, a national treatment obligation relates to whether a country favours itself over other countries. A national treatment obligation prohibits a country to discriminate *against* other countries. The national treatment obligation under WTO law applies – albeit not in the same manner – to trade in goods as well as trade in services. The key provisions dealing with the national treatment obligation for measures affecting trade in goods are Articles III:2 and

III:4 of the GATT 1994. The key provision dealing with the national treatment obligation for measures affecting trade in services is Article XVII:1 of the GATS. In this chapter, we will discuss these national treatment obligations in turn.[1]

Discrimination *against* foreign products, services or service suppliers, as compared to like domestic products, services or service suppliers, occurs frequently. There is often widespread popular support for such discrimination. To many, it is only normal that their government accords treatment more favourable to domestic products, services or service suppliers than it accords to products, services or service suppliers of foreign origin. However, for the reasons already set out in Chapters 1 and 4 of this book, discrimination is clearly ill-advised from an international relations perspective and makes scant sense from an economic perspective.[2] Therefore, WTO law seeks to eliminate discrimination *against* foreign products, services and service suppliers. It succeeds in doing so to varying degrees.

With regard to the national treatment obligation under Article III of the GATT 1994, the questions that may arise include the following: (1) Can Richland, a WTO Member, impose a 10 per cent sales tax on beer imported from Newland, also a WTO Member, while imposing a 5 per cent sales tax on domestic beer? (2) Can Richland impose a 10 per cent sales tax on soft drinks imported from Newland while imposing a 5 per cent sales tax on domestic mineral water? (3) Can Richland impose on soft drinks a labelling requirement to indicate the sugar content while not imposing such a requirement on fruit juice?

With regard to the national treatment obligation under Article XVII of the GATS, the following questions may arise: (1) Can Richland bar all foreign doctors from practising medicine in its territory? (2) Can Richland impose strict qualification requirements on nannies from Oldland while leaving the qualifications of domestic workers from Richland itself largely unregulated? (3) Can Richland, a country with a large French-speaking minority, impose a 20 per cent tax on language courses, while exempting French-language courses from taxation?

2 NATIONAL TREATMENT UNDER THE GATT 1994

Article III of the GATT 1994, entitled 'National Treatment on Internal Taxation and Regulation', states, in relevant part:

1. The [Members] recognize that internal taxes and other internal charges, and laws, regulations and requirements affecting the internal sale, offering for sale, purchase,

---

1 As discussed in Chapter 15, the *TRIPS Agreement* also provides for a national treatment obligation. See below, pp. 962–8.
2 See above, p. 36 and pp. 315–16.

transportation, distribution or use of products, and internal quantitative regulations requiring the mixture, processing or use of products in specified amounts or proportions, should not be applied to imported or domestic products so as to afford protection to domestic production.

2. The products of the territory of any [Member] imported into the territory of any other [Member] shall not be subject, directly or indirectly, to internal taxes or other internal charges of any kind in excess of those applied, directly or indirectly, to like domestic products. Moreover, no [Member] shall otherwise apply internal taxes or other internal charges to imported or domestic products in a manner contrary to the principles set forth in paragraph 1.

3. ...

4. The products of the territory of any [Member] imported into the territory of any other [Member] shall be accorded treatment no less favourable than that accorded to like products of national origin in respect of all laws, regulations and requirements affecting their internal sale, offering for sale, purchase, transportation, distribution or use ...

Other paragraphs of Article III deal with the application (or non-application) of the national treatment obligation to particular kinds of measures, such as: local content requirements (paragraph 5);[3] government procurement (paragraph 8(a)); subsidies to domestic producers (paragraph 8(b)); internal maximum price control measures (paragraph 9); and screen quotas for cinematograph films (i.e. movies) (paragraph 10). This chapter does not discuss the rules relating to these specific kinds of measures in any detail. It is sufficient to mention here that, pursuant to paragraph 5, local content requirements are prohibited. Pursuant to paragraph 8(a), the national treatment obligation does not apply to laws, regulations or requirements governing government procurement.[4] Pursuant to paragraph 8(b), the national treatment obligation does not prevent the payment of subsidies exclusively to domestic producers. However, the panel in *Italy – Agricultural Machinery (1958)* already gave a narrow interpretation to this exemption from the national treatment obligation of Article III. If paragraph 8(b) were to be interpreted broadly, any discrimination against imports could be qualified as a subsidy to domestic producers and thus render the discipline of Article III meaningless. The panel in *US – Malt Beverages (1992)* therefore found that the term 'payment of subsidies' in paragraph 8(b) refers only to direct subsidies involving a payment, not to other subsidies, such as tax credits or tax reductions.[5] With regard

---

3 Local content requirements are internal quantitative regulations, which require that a specific amount or proportion of a product must be supplied from domestic sources.

4 However, Article III:1(a) of the plurilateral *Agreement on Government Procurement* imposes on those WTO Members, which are a party to this Agreement, a national treatment obligation. On measures regarding government procurement and the plurilateral *Agreement on Government Procurement*, see above, p. 163, and below, pp. 509–10.

5 See Panel Report, *US – Malt Beverages (1992)*, para. 5.8. On Article III:8(b), see also Appellate Body Report, *Canada – Periodicals (1997)*, pp. 32–5; and Panel Report, *EC – Commercial Vessels (2005)*, paras. 7.55–7.75. Also note that, while the payment of a subsidy to domestic producers escapes the disciplines of Article III of the GATT 1994, the disciplines of the *SCM Agreement* may well apply. See below, p. 775.

to paragraph 10 of Article III, note that pursuant to this provision the national treatment obligation does not apply to screen quotas for movies.[6]

The paragraphs of Article III, quoted or referred to above, should always be read together with the Note *Ad* Article III contained in Annex I, entitled 'Notes and Supplementary Provisions', of the GATT 1994. As discussed below, this is important in particular with regard to the obligation under Article III:2, second sentence.[7]

Note that Article XX of the GATT 1994 as well as other multilateral agreements on trade in goods, such as the *TBT Agreement*, the *SPS Agreement* and the *Agreement on Trade-Related Investment Measures*, also provide for a national treatment obligation.[8] However, this section is only concerned with the national treatment obligation set out in Article III of the GATT 1994.

2.1 Nature of the National Treatment Obligation of Article III of the GATT 1994

This sub-section on the nature of the national treatment obligation of Article III of the GATT 1994 deals with: (1) the object and purpose of this obligation; (2) two issues relating to the scope of this obligation (namely, the issue of *de jure* and *de facto* discrimination, and the issue of internal *versus* border measures); and (3) the structure of Article III.

2.1.1 The Object and Purpose of the National Treatment Obligation

As noted above, Article III of the GATT 1994 prohibits discrimination *against* imported products. Generally speaking, it prohibits Members from treating imported products less favourably than like domestic products once the imported product has entered the domestic market, i.e. once it has been cleared through customs.

In *Japan – Alcoholic Beverages II (1996)*, the Appellate Body stated with respect to the purpose of the national treatment obligation of Article III:

> The broad and fundamental purpose of Article III is to avoid protectionism in the application of internal tax and regulatory measures. More specifically, the purpose of Article III 'is to ensure that internal measures "not be applied to imported or domestic products so as to afford protection to domestic production"'. Toward this end, Article III obliges Members of the WTO to provide equality of competitive conditions for imported products in relation to domestic products.[9]

---

6 On screen quotas for movies, see further Article IV(a) of the GATT 1994.

7 See below, p. 370. The Note *Ad* Article III also clarifies the scope of the measures (internal measures *versus* border measures) to which Article III applies. See below, p. 354.

8 See below, p. 567, pp. 863–72, pp. 908–10 and p. 386.

9 Appellate Body Report, *Japan – Alcoholic Beverages II (1996)*, 109. In the footnotes to this paragraph, the Appellate Body refers to the following panel reports: Panel Report, *US – Section 337 Tariff Act (1989)*, para. 5.10; Panel Report, *US – Superfund (1987)*, para. 5.1.9; and Panel Report, *Italy – Agricultural Machinery (1958)*, para. 11.

In *Korea – Alcoholic Beverages (1999)*, the Appellate Body identified the objectives of Article III as 'avoiding protectionism, requiring equality of competitive conditions and protecting expectations of equal competitive relationships'.[10] In *EC – Asbestos (2001)*, the Appellate Body stated that the purpose of Article III is:

> to prevent Members from applying internal taxes and regulations in a manner which affects the competitive relationship, in the marketplace, between the domestic and imported products involved, 'so as to afford protection to domestic production'.[11]

As Article III not merely requires equality of competitive conditions between imported and domestic products, but also protects 'the *expectations* of equal competitive relationships', the actual trade effects of the measure at issue are not dispositive of the consistency with Article III. A measure can be found to be inconsistent with Article III even when the effect of the measure on the volume of imports is insignificant or even non-existent.[12]

Panels and scholars have affirmed that one of the main purposes of Article III is to guarantee that internal measures of WTO Members do not undermine their commitments on tariffs under Article II.[13] Note, however, that the Appellate Body stressed in *Japan – Alcoholic Beverages II (1996)* that the purpose of Article III is broader. The Appellate Body stated:

> The sheltering scope of Article III is not limited to products that are the subject of tariff concessions under Article II. The Article III national treatment obligation is a *general prohibition* on the use of internal taxes and other internal regulatory measures so as to afford protection to domestic production. This obligation clearly extends also to products not bound under Article II.[14]

In brief, the national treatment obligation of Article III of the GATT 1994 is an obligation of *general application* that applies both to measures affecting products with regard to which Members have made tariff concessions and to measures affecting products with regard to which Members have not done so.[15]

2.1.2 *De Jure* and *De Facto* Discrimination

Article III of the GATT 1994 covers not only 'in law' or *de jure* discrimination; it also covers 'in fact' or *de facto* discrimination. The concepts of *de jure* and *de facto* discrimination were discussed at length in the previous chapter.[16] An

---

10 Appellate Body Report, *Korea – Alcoholic Beverages (1999)*, para. 120. See also Appellate Body Report, *Canada – Periodicals (1997)*, 464.
11 Appellate Body Report, *EC – Asbestos (2001)*, para. 98. Original emphasis.
12 See Appellate Body Report, *Japan – Alcoholic Beverages II (1996)*, 109, referring in footnote to Panel Report, *US – Superfund (1987)*, para. 5.1.9. In the same paragraph, the Appellate Body even stated that the actual trade effects were 'irrelevant'.
13 See e.g. Panel Report, *Japan – Alcoholic Beverages II (1996)*, para. 6.13. With regard to the commitments on tariffs under Article II of the GATT, see below, p. 438
14 Appellate Body Report, *Japan – Alcoholic Beverages II (1996)*, 16. Emphasis added.
15 Note the difference with the national treatment obligation of Article XVII:1 of the GATS. See below, p. 403.
16 See above, p. 319.

example of a *de jure* discriminatory measure to which the national treatment obligation of Article III has been applied is the measure at issue in *Korea – Various Measures on Beef (2001)*.[17] In that case, the disputed measure was an 'origin-based' dual retail distribution system for the sale of beef. Under this system, *imported* beef was to be sold in specialist stores selling only imported beef or in separate sections of supermarkets. An example of a *de facto* discriminatory measure to which the national treatment obligation of Article III has been applied is the measure at issue in *Japan – Alcoholic Beverages II (1996)*.[18] In that case, the disputed measure was tax legislation that provided for higher taxes on, for example, whisky, brandy and vodka (whether domestic or imported) than on shochu (whether domestic or imported). On its face, this Japanese tax legislation was 'origin-neutral'. However, in fact, it discriminated against imported alcoholic beverages.[19]

2.1.3 Internal Measures Versus Border Measures

Article III applies only to internal measures, not to border measures. Other GATT provisions, such as Article II on tariff concessions and Article XI on quantitative restrictions, apply to border measures. Since Article III and Articles II and XI provide for very different rules, it is important to determine whether a measure is an internal or a border measure. It is not always easy to distinguish an internal measure from a border measure when the measure is applied to imported products at the time or point of importation. The Note *Ad* Article III clarifies:

> Any internal tax or other internal charge, or any law, regulation or requirement of the kind referred to in paragraph 1 which applies to an imported product and to the like domestic product and is collected or enforced in the case of the imported product at the time or point of importation, is nevertheless to be regarded as an internal tax or other internal charge, or a law, regulation or requirement of the kind referred to in paragraph 1, and is accordingly subject to the provisions of Article III.

It follows that, if the importation of a product is barred at the border because that product fails, for example, to meet a public health or consumer safety requirement that applies also to domestic products, the consistency of this import ban with the GATT is to be examined under Article III.[20] However, the Note *Ad* Article III, quoted above, leaves it unclear whether Article XI could also apply to such a measure. In *India – Autos (2002)*, the panel noted on the relationship between Article III and Article XI of the GATT 1994 that:

> it ... cannot be excluded *a priori* that different aspects of a measure may affect the competitive opportunities of imports in different ways, making them fall within the scope either of Article III (where competitive opportunities on the domestic market are affected) or of Article XI (where the opportunities for importation itself, i.e. entering the market, are affected),

---

17 See below, p. 395.   18 See below, p. 360.   19 See further below, p. 362, p. 363 and p. 372.
20 See Panel Report, *Canada – FIRA (1984)*, para. 5.14.

or even that there may be, in perhaps exceptional circumstances, a potential for overlap between the two provisions, as was suggested in the case of state trading.[21]

The panel in *India – Autos (2002)* further considered that:

[t]he fact that the measure applies only to imported products need not [be], in itself, an obstacle to its falling within the purview of Article III. For example, an internal tax, or a product standard conditioning the sale of the imported but not of the like domestic product, could nonetheless 'affect' the conditions of the imported product on the market and could be a source of less favorable treatment. Similarly, the fact that a requirement is imposed as a condition on importation is not necessarily in itself an obstacle to its falling within the scope of Article III:4.[22]

As discussed below, in *China – Auto Parts (2009)*, the question whether the measures concerned were subject to Article III (applicable to internal measures) or Article II (applicable to border measures) was a threshold issue in that case.[23]

2.1.4   Articles III:1, III:2 and III:4

As stated above, and as explicitly noted by the Appellate Body in *Japan – Alcoholic Beverages II (1996)*, Article III:1 articulates a general principle that internal measures should not be applied so as to afford protection to domestic production. According to the Appellate Body in *Japan – Alcoholic Beverages II (1996)*:

This general principle informs the rest of Article III. The purpose of Article III:1 is to establish this general principle as a guide to understanding and interpreting the specific obligations contained in Article III:2 and in the other paragraphs of Article III, while respecting, and not diminishing in any way, the meaning of the words actually used in the texts of those other paragraphs.[24]

The general principle that internal measures should not be applied so as to afford protection to domestic production is elaborated on in Article III:2 with regard to internal taxation and in Article III:4 with regard to internal regulation. In Article III:2, two non-discrimination obligations can be distinguished: one obligation is set out in the first sentence of Article III:2, relating to internal taxation of 'like products'; and the other obligation is set out in the second sentence of Article III:2, relating to internal taxation of 'directly competitive or substitutable products'. The sub-sections below discuss in turn the national treatment tests for internal taxation (on like products and on directly competitive or substitutable products) under Article III:2, first and second sentence, and for internal regulation under Article III:4.

---

21 Panel Report, *India – Autos (2002)*, para. 7.224.
22 *Ibid.* para. 7.306. The panel applied this finding subsequently to the 'indigenisation' condition, at issue in this case. See *ibid.*, paras. 7.307–7.317.
23 See below, p. 356.
24 Appellate Body Report, *Japan – Alcoholic Beverages II (1996)*, 111. See also Appellate Body Report, *EC – Asbestos (2001)*, para. 93.

Questions and Assignments 5.1

What is the purpose of the national treatment obligation set out in Article III of the GATT 1994? Can measures that do not have an adverse effect on the volume of imported products sold on the domestic market be found to be inconsistent with Article III of the GATT 1994? Does Article III apply to border measures? How and why does one distinguish between border measures and internal measures? What is the function of Article III:1?

2.2 National Treatment Test for Internal Taxation on Like Products

Article III:2, first sentence, of the GATT 1994 states:

The products of the territory of any [Member] imported into the territory of any other [Member] shall not be subject, directly or indirectly, to internal taxes or other internal charges of any kind in excess of those applied, directly or indirectly, to like domestic products.

In *Canada – Periodicals (1997)*, the Appellate Body found:

there are two questions which need to be answered to determine whether there is a violation of Article III:2 of the GATT 1994: (a) whether imported and domestic products are like products; and (b) whether the imported products are taxed in excess of the domestic products. If the answers to both questions are affirmative, there is a violation of Article III:2, first sentence.[25]

However, before addressing the questions set out by the Appellate Body in *Canada – Periodicals (1997)*, it has to be determined whether the measure at issue is an 'internal tax or other internal charge of any kind' within the meaning of Article III:2, first sentence. In *China – Auto Parts (2009)*, the Appellate Body referred to this question as a 'threshold issue'.[26] This question constitutes in fact a third tier or element of the test under Article III:2, first sentence, which must be addressed first.

The three-tier test of consistency of internal taxation with Article III:2, first sentence, requires the examination of:

- whether the measure at issue is an *internal tax or other internal charge* on products;
- whether the imported and domestic products are *like products*; and
- whether the imported products are *taxed in excess* of the domestic products.

Recall that Article III:1 provides that internal taxation must not be applied so as to afford protection to domestic production. However, according to the Appellate Body in *Japan – Alcoholic Beverages II (1996)*, the presence of a protective application need not be established separately from the *specific* requirements of Article III:2, first sentence.[27] Whenever imported products from one

---

25 Appellate Body Report, *Canada – Periodicals (1997)*, 468.
26 See Appellate Body Reports, *China – Auto Parts (2009)*, para. 181.
27 See Appellate Body Report, *Japan – Alcoholic Beverages II (1996)*, 111–12.

Member are subject to taxes in excess of those applied to like domestic products in another Member, this is deemed to 'afford protection to domestic production' within the meaning of Article III:1.[28]

Below, each element of the three-tier test of consistency will be discussed in turn.

To date, WTO Members have been found to have acted inconsistently with Article III:2, first sentence in ten disputes.[29]

Questions and Assignments 5.2

What are the constituent elements of the national treatment test of Article III:2, first sentence, of the GATT 1994? Is it necessary to examine whether the internal taxation on like products is or is not applied 'so as to afford protection to domestic production'?

2.2.1 'Internal Taxes ...'

Article III:2, first sentence, of the GATT 1994 concerns 'internal taxes and other charges of any kind' which are applied 'directly or indirectly' on products. Examples of such internal taxes or other internal charges on products are value added taxes (VAT), sales taxes and excise duties.[30] Income taxes are not covered by Article III:2, first sentence, since they are not internal taxes or other internal charges on *products*.[31] Likewise, customs duties or other border charges are not covered since they are not *internal* taxes or other *internal* charges on products. In *China – Auto Parts (2009)*, the panel had to determine whether the charges at issue in that case were an 'internal charge' (as argued by the complainants) or a 'customs duty' (as argued by China). With the exception of one particular charge, the panel found that the charges were an 'internal charge', and thus concluded that the national treatment obligation of Article III:2, first sentence, applied.[32] In addressing this issue, the Appellate Body noted that 'the time at which a charge is collected or paid is not decisive' when determining whether a charge is an internal charge or a border charge (such as a customs duty).[33] In other words, it is not because a charge is paid at the time of importation that it is a customs duty or other border charge within the meaning of Article II:1,

---

28 See also Panel Report, *Argentina – Hides and Leather (2001)*, para. 11.137.

29 See *Japan – Alcoholic Beverages II (1996)*, *Canada – Periodicals (1997)*, *Indonesia – Autos (1998)*, *Argentina – Hides and Leather (2001)*, *Dominican Republic – Import and Sale of Cigarettes (2005)*, *Mexico – Taxes on Soft Drinks (2006)*, *China – Auto Parts (2009)*, *Colombia – Ports of Entry (2009)*, *Thailand – Cigarettes (Philippines) (2011)* and *Philippines – Distilled Spirits (2012)*.

30 With regard to 'other [internal] charges', the panel in *Argentina – Hides and Leather (2001)* noted that the term 'charge' denotes, *inter alia*, a 'pecuniary burden' and a 'liability to pay money laid on a person', and concluded that two of the measures at issue, while not taxes in their own right, were tax measures within the meaning of Article III:2 because they imposed a 'pecuniary burden' and created 'a liability to pay money'. See Panel Report, *Argentina – Hides and Leather (2001)*, para. 11.143.

31 With regard to taxes on *income*, note that an income tax regulation can be considered to be an internal regulation and thus to fall within the scope of Article III:4 of the GATT 1994, discussed below, p 382–6. See also Panel Report, *US – FSC (Article 21.5 – EC) (2002)*, para. 8.145. With regard to taxes on *services* and the applicability of Article III:2, first sentence, see Panel Report, *Mexico – Taxes on Soft Drinks (2006)*, para. 8.152.

32 See Panel Reports, *China – Auto Parts (2009)*, para. 7.212.

33 See Appellate Body Reports, *China – Auto Parts (2009)*, para. 162.

and not an internal charge within the meaning of Article III:2. According to the Appellate Body, what is important for the applicability of Article III:2 is that:

the *obligation* to pay a charge must accrue due to an internal event, such as the distribution, sale, use or transportation of the imported product.[34]

A determination of whether a particular measure falls within the scope of Article III:2 must be made in the light of the characteristics of the measure and the circumstances of the case. The Appellate Body observed that in many cases this is 'a straightforward exercise', but that in other cases a panel may face a 'more complex' challenge.[35] Note, in particular, that neither the way in which a measure is characterised in a Member's domestic law nor the intent of a Member's legislator is dispositive of the characterisation of such measure under WTO law as an internal tax or a border charge.[36]

Subject to Article III:2, first sentence, are 'internal taxes and other charges of any kind' which are applied 'directly or indirectly' on products. The words 'applied *directly or indirectly* on products' should be understood to mean 'applied *on or in connection with* products'. According to the panel in *Japan – Alcoholic Beverages I (1987)*, the term 'indirect taxation' refers to taxes imposed on the raw materials used in the product during the various stages of its production.[37] The panel in *Mexico – Taxes on Soft Drinks (2006)* found that non-cane sugar sweeteners were 'indirectly' subject to the soft drink tax when they were used in the production of soft drinks.[38]

In *US – Tobacco (1994)*, the panel examined the question of whether financial penalty provisions for the enforcement of a domestic content requirement for tobacco could be qualified as 'internal taxes or other charges of any kind' within the meaning of Article III:2, first sentence. The panel found that a financial penalty provision for the enforcement of a domestic law is not an 'internal tax or charge of any kind'.[39] Such a penalty provision is an internal regulation within the meaning of Article III:4 of the GATT 1994, as discussed below.[40]

Also, the panel in *EEC – Animal Feed Proteins (1978)* did not consider a security deposit to be a fiscal measure within the meaning of Article III:2, although this deposit accrued to the EEC when the buyers of vegetable proteins failed to fulfil the obligation to purchase milk powder. The panel considered the security

---

34 *Ibid.* Original emphasis.
35 See *ibid.*, para. 171. See in this context also *India – Additional Import Duties (2008)*, in which the panel agreed with the parties that the measures at issue were border charges within the meaning of Article II:1, and not internal charges within the meaning of Article III:2. See Appellate Body Report, *India – Additional Import Duties (2008)*, footnote 304 to para. 153.
36 See Appellate Body Reports, *China – Auto Parts (2009)*, para. 178.
37 See Panel Report, *Japan – Alcoholic Beverages I (1987)*, para. 5.8.
38 See Panel Report, *Mexico – Taxes on Soft Drinks (2006)*, para. 8.45. The panel in *Mexico – Taxes on Soft Drinks (2006)* also found that, while on its face the distribution tax is a tax on the provision of certain services, in the circumstances of this case it is also a tax applied *indirectly* on soft drinks and syrups. See Panel Report, *Mexico – Taxes on Soft Drinks (2006)*, para. 8.152.
39 See Panel Report, *US – Tobacco (1994)*, para. 80.   40 See below, pp. 382–6.

deposit, including any associated cost, to be only an enforcement mechanism for the purchase requirement and, as such, its GATT consistency should be examined, together with the purchase requirement, under Article III:4.[41]

The issue of border tax adjustment must also be mentioned in this context. Border tax adjustments are:

any fiscal measures which put into effect, in whole or in part, the destination principle (i.e. which enable exported products to be relieved of some or all of the tax charged in the exporting country in respect of similar domestic products sold to consumers on the home market and which enable imported products sold to consumers to be charged with some or all of the tax charged in the importing country in respect of similar domestic products).[42]

Such a fiscal measure involving the imposition of taxes by the importing country is obviously a fiscal measure which falls within the scope of application of Article III:2.[43]

Finally, with regard to 'tax administration' and 'tax collection' measures, the panel in *Argentina – Hides and Leather (2001)* rejected the contention of Argentina that such measures do not fall under Article III:2. The panel stated:

We agree that Members are free, within the outer bounds defined by such provisions as Article III:2, to administer and collect internal taxes as they see fit. However, if, as here, such 'tax administration' measures take the form of an internal charge and are applied to products, those measures must, in our view, be in conformity with Article III:2.[44]

In *US – Malt Beverages (1992)*, the panel considered a measure preventing imported products from being sold in a manner that would enable them to avoid taxation, to be a measure within the scope of Article III:2, first sentence, because it assigned a higher tax rate to the imported products.[45] Most recently, the Appellate Body ruled in *Thailand – Cigarettes (Philippines) (2011)* that:

even if a measure at issue consisted solely of administrative requirements, we do not exclude the possibility that such requirements may have a bearing on the respective tax burdens on imported and like domestic products, and may therefore be subject to Article III:2.[46]

Questions and Assignments 5.3

Does income tax fall within the scope of application of Article III:2 of the GATT 1994? How can one distinguish between an 'internal tax' and a border tax? Give an example of an internal tax 'applied indirectly' to products. Are a security deposit or a financial penalty provision internal tax measures within the meaning of Article III:2? What is border tax adjustment and does it fall within the scope of application of Article III:2? Does Article III:2 affect the freedom of Members to administer and collect internal taxes on products as they see fit?

41 See Panel Report, *EEC – Animal Feed Proteins (1978)*, para. 4.4.
42 Working Party Report, *Border Tax Adjustments (1970)*, BISD 18S/97, para. 4.
43 See *ibid.*, para. 14.
44 Panel Report, *Argentina – Hides and Leather (2001)*, para. 11.144. The panel argued that excluding 'tax administration' measures from the scope of Article III:2 would 'create a potential for abuse and circumvention of the obligations contained in Article III:2'. See *ibid.*
45 See Panel Report, *US – Malt Beverages (1992)*, paras. 5.21–5.22.
46 Appellate Body Report, *Thailand – Cigarettes (Philippines) (2011)*, footnote 144 to para. 114.

2.2.2 'Like Products'

The second element of the test of consistency with the national treatment obligation of Article III:2, first sentence, of the GATT 1994 relates to the question of whether the products at issue are '*like products*'. It is only between 'like' imported and domestic products that the national treatment obligation applies and discrimination within the meaning of Article III:2, first sentence, may occur. Imported and domestic products that are not 'like' may be treated differently; different treatment of such 'unlike' products will not constitute discrimination within the meaning of Article III:2, first sentence. For the application of the national treatment obligation of Article III:2, first sentence, it is therefore important to be able to determine whether, for example, a sports utility vehicle (SUV) is 'like' a family car; orange juice is 'like' tomato juice; a laptop is 'like' a tablet computer; pork is 'like' beef; or whisky is 'like' brandy within the meaning of Article III:2, first sentence.

Just as the concept of 'like products' in Article I:1 of the GATT 1994, the concept of 'like products' in Article III:2, first sentence, is not defined in the GATT 1994. There are, however, a number of GATT and WTO dispute settlement reports that shed light on the meaning of the concept of 'like products' in Article III:2, first sentence.

Under the Japanese tax system at issue in *Japan – Alcoholic Beverages II (1996)*, the internal tax imposed on domestic shochu was the same as that imposed on imported shochu; the higher tax imposed on imported vodka was also imposed on domestic vodka. Identical products (not considering brand differences) were thus taxed identically. However, the question in that case was whether shochu and vodka should be considered to be 'like products'. If shochu and vodka were 'like products', vodka could not be taxed in excess of shochu. As already discussed above in the context of 'likeness' under Article I:1 of the GATT 1994, the Appellate Body in *Japan – Alcoholic Beverages II (1996)* stated:

> The concept of 'likeness' is a relative one that evokes the image of an accordion. The accordion of 'likeness' stretches and squeezes in different places as different provisions of the *WTO Agreement* are applied. The width of the accordion in any one of those places must be determined by the particular provision in which the term 'like' is encountered as well as by the context and the circumstances that prevail in any given case to which that provision may apply.[47]

With respect to 'like products' in Article III:2, first sentence, the Appellate Body in *Japan – Alcoholic Beverages II (1996)* ruled that the 'accordion of "likeness" is meant to be narrowly squeezed'.[48] According to the Appellate Body, the concept of 'like products' in Article III:2, first sentence, should be construed narrowly because of the existence of the concept of 'directly competitive or substitutable products' used in the second sentence of Article III:2.[49] If 'like

---

47 Appellate Body Report, *Japan – Alcoholic Beverages II (1996)*, 114.   48 *Ibid.*
49 *Ibid.*, 112–13. See also Appellate Body Report, *EC – Asbestos (2001)*, paras. 94–5.

products' in Article III:2, first sentence, were to be given a broad meaning, the scope of this concept would be identical, or at least largely overlap, with the concept of 'directly competitive or substitutable products' in Article III:2, second sentence, and thus render Article III:2, second sentence, redundant. Such interpretation would be inconsistent with the interpretative principle of effectiveness, as discussed in Chapter 3 of this book.[50] To give meaning to the concept of 'directly competitive or substitutable products' in Article III:2, second sentence, the concept of 'like products' in Article III:2, first sentence, must be construed narrowly.

In *Japan – Alcoholic Beverages II (1996)*, the Appellate Body expressly agreed with the basic approach for determining 'likeness' set out in the working party report in *Border Tax Adjustments (1970)*.[51] In this report, a working party established by the GATT Council in 1968 found with regard to the term 'like' that:

the interpretation of the term should be examined on a case-by-case basis ... Some criteria were suggested for determining, on a case-by-case basis, whether a product is 'similar': the product's end-uses in a given market; consumers' tastes and habits, which change from country to country; the product's properties, nature and quality.[52]

This basic approach was followed in almost all post-1970 GATT panel reports involving a GATT provision in which the concept of 'like products' was used.[53] According to the Appellate Body in *Japan – Alcoholic Beverages II (1996)*, this approach should be helpful in identifying on a case-by-case basis the range of 'like products' that falls within the limits of Article III:2, first sentence, of the GATT 1994. However, the Appellate Body added:

In applying the criteria cited in [the working party report in] *Border Tax Adjustments* to the facts of any particular case, and in considering other criteria that may also be relevant in certain cases, panels can only apply their best judgement in determining whether in fact products are 'like'. This will always involve an unavoidable element of individual, discretionary judgement.[54]

In *Japan – Alcoholic Beverages II (1996)*, the Appellate Body called upon panels to consider, in addition to the *Border Tax Adjustments* criteria, also 'other criteria that may be relevant'.[55] One of such criteria considered by panels and

---

50 See above, p. 188.
51 The working party considered the concept of 'like' or 'similar' products as used throughout the GATT.
52 Working Party Report, *Border Tax Adjustments (1970)*, BISD 18S/97, para. 18.
53 See e.g. GATT working party or panel reports in *Australia – Ammonium Sulphate (1950)*, *EEC – Animal Feed Proteins (1978)*, *Spain – Unroasted Coffee (1981)*, *Japan – Alcoholic Beverages I (1987)* and *US – Superfund (1987)*.
54 Appellate Body Report, *Japan – Alcoholic Beverages II (1996)*, 113–14. The Appellate Body disagreed with the panel's observation in para. 6.22 of the panel report that distinguishing between 'like products' and 'directly competitive or substitutable products' under Article III:2 is 'an arbitrary decision'. According to the Appellate Body, it is 'a discretionary decision that must be made in considering the various characteristics of products in individual cases'. Appellate Body Report, *Japan – Alcoholic Beverages II (1996)*, 114.
55 See above in the quote from Appellate Body Report, *Japan – Alcoholic Beverages II (1996)*, 113–14.

the Appellate Body has been the tariff classification of the products at issue.[56] The Appellate Body acknowledged in *Japan – Alcoholic Beverages II (1996)* that classification under the same Harmonized System tariff heading or sub-heading can provide a 'useful basis for confirming 'likeness' in products'.[57] However, this is only so if the tariff heading is sufficiently detailed.[58] 'Other criteria that may be relevant' have also included internal regulations, or the internal regulatory framework or regime, applicable to the products at issue.[59] Regulations, or the regulatory framework or regime, applicable to the products at issue may indicate that consumers perceive the products as having similar or distinct characteristics.[60] Also, the price level of the products at issue and the expendable income of the population has been considered a criterion that may be relevant in deciding on whether products are 'like' within the meaning of Article III:2, first sentence.[61]

Note that the Appellate Body ruled in *Canada – Periodicals (1997)*:

As Article III:2, first sentence, normally requires a comparison between imported products and like domestic products, and as there were no imports of split-run editions of periodicals because of the import prohibition in Tariff Code 9958 ... *hypothetical imports* of split-run periodicals have to be considered.[62]

The Appellate Body thus provides for a 'hypothetical like products' analysis in cases where there are no imports because of, for example, an import prohibition.[63]

The current state of the law regarding the determination of 'likeness' under Article III:2, first sentence, is best reflected in the Appellate Body reports in *Philippines – Distilled Spirits (2012)*. Taking as a given that the concept of 'like products' in Article III:2, first sentence, should be construed narrowly for the reasons set out above, the Appellate Body ruled in this case, as it had already done in *EC – Asbestos (2001)* with regard to the concept of 'like products' in Article III:4,[64] that:

---

56 Note that the tariff classification of the products concerned by other countries was a criterion considered by the panel in *Spain – Unroasted Coffee (1981)*. See above, p. 193. See most recently in Panel Report, *Thailand – Cigarettes (Philippines) (2011)*, para. 7.433; Panel Reports, *Philippines – Distilled Spirits (2012)*, para. 7.63; and Appellate Body Reports, *Philippines – Distilled Spirits (2012)*, para. 161.

57 Appellate Body Report, *Japan – Alcoholic Beverages II (1996)*, 116. See also Appellate Body Reports, *Philippines – Distilled Spirits (2012)*, para. 161.

58 See Appellate Body Reports, *Philippines – Distilled Spirits (2012)*, para. 161.

59 See Panel Report, *Thailand – Cigarettes (Philippines) (2011)*, para. 7.441; and Panel Reports, *Philippines – Distilled Spirits (2012)*, paras. 7.72–7.73. See also Appellate Body Reports, *Philippines – Distilled Spirits (2012)*, paras. 118 and 169.

60 By way of example, note that, in the European Union and in the United States, whisky made from sugar cane molasses cannot be marketed and sold as 'whisky'. This internal regulation may be an indication that consumers in those countries perceive these products as having quite distinct physical properties. See Appellate Body Reports, *Philippines – Distilled Spirits (2012)*, para. 167.

61 See Panel Report, *Thailand – Cigarettes (Philippines) (2011)*, para. 7.428; and Panel Reports, *Philippines – Distilled Spirits (2012)*, para. 7.59. See below, pp. 364 and 356.

62 Appellate Body Report, *Canada – Periodicals (1997)*, 466. Emphasis added.

63 See also Panel Report, *Indonesia – Autos (1998)*, para. 14.113; and Panel Report, *Colombia – Ports of Entry (2009)*, para. 7.356. Note that the 'hypothetical like products approach' has also been applied in another context. See above, p. 328, and below, p. 368 and p. 394.

64 See below, p. 387.

the determination of 'likeness' under Article III:2, first sentence, of the GATT 1994 is, fundamentally, a determination about the nature and extent of a competitive relationship between and among products.[65]

To make such a determination, a panel examines on a case-by-case basis all relevant criteria, including: (1) the products' properties, nature and quality, i.e. their physical characteristics; (2) the products' end-uses; (3) consumers' tastes and habits, also referred to as consumers' perceptions and behaviour, in respect of the products; and (4) the products' tariff classification.[66] With regard to these criteria, the Appellate Body observed that they are not exhaustive and also not treaty text, but rather:

tools available to panels for organizing and assessing the evidence relating to the competitive relationship between and among the products ...[67]

The Appellate Body added to this that, while the criteria are 'distinct', they are not mutually exclusive.[68] Certain evidence may well fall, and can be examined, under more than one criterion.[69] As to the relative importance of each of these criteria, the Appellate Body noted that:

while in the determination of 'likeness' a panel may logically start from the physical characteristics of the products, none of the criteria a panel considers necessarily has an overarching role in the determination of 'likeness' under Article III:2 of the GATT 1994.[70]

As the Appellate Body explained, products that have very similar physical characteristics may not be 'like', within the meaning of Article III:2, if their competitiveness or substitutability is low, while products that present physical differences may still be considered 'like' if such physical differences have a limited impact on the competitive relationship among the products.[71]

In *Japan – Alcoholic Beverages II (1996)*, shochu and vodka were found to be 'like products' within the meaning of Article III:2, first sentence.[72] In

---

65 See Appellate Body Reports, *Philippines – Distilled Spirits (2012)*, para. 170.

66 See *ibid.*, para. 118. On other possible criteria, see below, p. 375.

67 Appellate Body Reports, *Philippines – Distilled Spirits (2012)*, para. 131. In its report in *EC – Asbestos (2001)*, the Appellate Body had already made this observation in the context of the 'likeness' analysis under Article III:4 of the GATT 1994. See below, p. 389.

68 See Appellate Body Reports, *Philippines – Distilled Spirits (2012)*, para. 131. On the distinctiveness of the criteria, see Appellate Body Report, *EC – Asbestos (2001)*, para. 111. See below, p. 387.

69 See Appellate Body Reports, *Philippines – Distilled Spirits (2012)*, para. 131. The evidence at issue in *Philippines – Distilled Spirits (2012)* concerned the perceptibility of differences in physical characteristics. Such evidence can be examined both under the 'physical characteristics' criterion and under the criterion of 'consumers' tastes and habits'. Note that, in *EC – Asbestos (2001)*, the Appellate Body considered health risks under the 'physical characteristics' criterion as well as under the criterion of 'consumers' tastes and habits'. See Appellate Body Report, *EC – Asbestos (2001)*, paras. 114 and 120.

70 Appellate Body Reports, *Philippines – Distilled Spirits (2012)*, para. 119.

71 See *ibid.*, para. 120.

72 See Panel Report, *Japan – Alcoholic Beverages II (1996)*, para. 6.23, referring to the panel report in *Japan – Alcoholic Beverages I (1987)*. The panel found that shochu and vodka were 'like products' because 'they were both white/clean spirits, made of similar raw materials, and the end-uses were virtually identical'. The panel also found that the traditional Japanese consumer habits with regard to shochu provided no reason for not considering vodka to be a 'like' product. The panel found that shochu and a number of other alcoholic beverages were not 'like products' because of the 'substantial noticeable differences' in physical characteristics such as the use of additives (for liqueurs and gin), the use of ingredients (for rum) and appearance (for whisky and brandy). As discussed below, the panel would, however, find shochu and these other alcoholic beverages 'directly competitive or substitutable' within the meaning of Article III:2, second sentence. See below, p. 372.

Korea – Alcoholic Beverages (1999), however, soju and vodka were not found to be 'like products'.[73] In *Mexico – Taxes on Soft Drinks (2006)*, soft drinks sweetened with beet sugar or high fructose corn syrup (HFCS) and soft drinks sweetened with cane sugar were considered to be 'like products' within the meaning of Article III:2, first sentence.[74] In the same case, beet sugar and cane sugar were also considered to be 'like products' but cane sugar and HFCS were not.[75] In *Philippines – Distilled Spirits (2012)*, distilled spirits of a specific type (such as whisky and brandy) made from designated raw materials (and in particular sugar cane) and distilled spirits of the same type made from other raw materials (cereals for whisky and grapes for brandy) were found to be 'like products' within the meaning of Article III:2, first sentence.[76] In the latter case, the Appellate Body found that:

as long as the differences among the products, including a difference in the raw material base, leave fundamentally unchanged the competitive relationship among the final products, the existence of these differences does not prevent a finding of 'likeness' if, by considering all factors, the panel is able to come to the conclusion that the competitive relationship among the products is such as to justify a finding of 'likeness' under Article III:2.[77]

While examining the concept of 'directly competitive or substitutable products' within the meaning of Article III:2, second sentence, the Appellate Body in *Canada – Periodicals (1997)* as well as in *Korea – Alcoholic Beverages (1999)* observed that products that are perfectly substitutable would be 'like products' within the meaning of Article III:2, first sentence.[78] However, the Appellate Body in *Philippines – Distilled Spirits (2012)* noted in this regard:

We do not understand the statements by the Appellate Body in *Canada – Periodicals* and in *Korea – Alcoholic Beverages* to mean that *only* products that are perfectly substitutable can fall within the scope of Article III:2, first sentence. This would be too narrow an interpretation and would reduce the scope of the first sentence essentially to identical products. Rather, we consider that, under the first sentence, products that are close to being perfectly substitutable can be 'like products', whereas products that compete to a lesser degree would fall within the scope of the second sentence.[79]

According to the panel in *Dominican Republic – Import and Sale of Cigarettes (2005)*, the actual price at which products are sold on the market of the importing country is a criterion – in addition to the criteria already discussed

---

73 See Panel Report, *Korea – Alcoholic Beverages (1999)*, para. 10.104. These products were, however, considered to be directly competitive or substitutable within the meaning of the second sentence of Article III:2. See below, p. 372.

74 See Panel Report, *Mexico – Taxes on Soft Drinks (2006)*, para. 8.136.

75 See *ibid.*, paras. 8.36 and 8.78. Cane sugar and HFCS were, however, considered to be directly competitive or substitutable within the meaning of the second sentence of Article III:2. See below, p. 400.

76 See Appellate Body Reports, *Philippines – Distilled Spirits (2012)*, para. 172.

77 *Ibid.*, para. 125.

78 In *Canada – Periodicals (1997)*, the Appellate Body stated: 'A case of perfect substitutability would fall within Article III:2, first sentence, while we are examining the broader prohibition of the second sentence.' Appellate Body Reports, *Canada – Periodicals (1997)*, 473. See also Appellate Body, *Korea – Alcoholic Beverages (1999)*, para. 118.

79 Appellate Body Reports, *Philippines – Distilled Spirits (2012)*, para. 149. Original emphasis.

above – to be considered when determining whether products are 'like' within the meaning of Article III:2, first sentence.[80] Also, the panel in *Philippines – Distilled Spirits (2012)* recognised the relevance of the price of products in the determination of whether products are 'like'.[81] In this case, the Philippines contended that imported 'non-sugar-based' spirits were priced regularly above PHP150 per bottle, that only 1.8 per cent of its population could afford these imported distilled spirits, and that the imported 'non-sugar-based' spirits and the much cheaper domestic 'sugar-based' spirits were, therefore, not in competition, i.e. were not 'like products'. The panel considered price and expendable income to be a relevant criterion for determining 'likeness', but came to the conclusion that, while a large proportion of the Philippine population had indeed a limited ability to purchase distilled spirits beyond certain price levels, the Philippine market was *not* divided into two segments (namely, high-priced imported spirits *and* low-priced domestic spirits).[82] In *Thailand – Cigarettes (Philippines) (2011)*, the panel found that it was not required that 'all' imported cigarettes and 'all' domestic cigarettes were like, and it limited its examination to whether the imported and domestic cigarettes 'within particular price segments' were 'like'.[83]

In *US – Malt Beverages (1992)*, the panel held that legislation giving special tax exemptions to products of small firms (whether domestic or foreign) would constitute discrimination against imports from a larger foreign firm and therefore infringe Article III because its products would be treated less favourably than the like products of a small domestic firm.[84] According to the panel in *US – Malt Beverages (1992)*, the fact that products were produced by small, artisanal *or* large, industrial firms (i.e. a process and production method (PPM) of the products concerned) was irrelevant in the determination of their 'likeness'. While there has been no further attempt in dispute settlement cases to refer to PPMs in the determination of 'likeness' in Article III:2, first sentence, it is not clear whether this 1992 panel statement on the irrelevance of PPMs reflects the current state of the law.[85]

The panel in *US – Malt Beverages (1992)* also considered, however, with regard to the determination of 'likeness' that:

the like product determination under Article III:2 also should have regard to the purpose of the Article ... The purpose ... is ... not to prevent contracting parties from using their fiscal and regulatory powers for purposes other than to afford protection to domestic production. Specifically, the purpose of Article III is not to prevent contracting parties from

---

80 See Panel Report, *Dominican Republic – Import and Sale of Cigarettes (2005)*, paras. 7.333–7.336. Note, however, that a price difference between the imported and the domestic product may be a consequence of discriminatory discrimination.

81 See Panel Reports, *Philippines – Distilled Spirits (2012)*, para. 7.59.

82 See Panel Reports, *Philippines – Distilled Spirits (2012)*, para. 7.59. On the basis of the evidence before it, the panel found that there were in fact lower-priced imported 'non-sugar-based' spirits that competed with domestic 'sugar-based' spirits, as well as high-priced domestic 'sugar-based' spirits that competed with imported 'non-sugar-based' spirits. See *ibid.*

83 Panel Report, *Thailand – Cigarettes (Philippines) (2011)*, para. 7.428. This finding was not appealed.

84 See Panel Report, *US – Malt Beverages (1992)*, para. 5.19.

85 For a discussion on the relevance of PPMs in the determination of 'likeness' in Article III:4, see below, p. 393.

differentiating between different product categories for policy purposes unrelated to the protection of domestic production ... Consequently, in determining whether two products subject to different treatment are like products, it is necessary to consider whether such product differentiation is being made 'so as to afford protection to domestic production'.[86]

The panel found domestic wine containing a particular local variety of grape to be 'like' imported wine not containing this variety of grape after considering that the purpose of differentiating between the wines was to afford protection to the local production of wine. The panel noted that the United States did not advance any alternative policy objective for the differentiation. According to the panel, the reason for the product differentiation was to be considered when deciding on the 'likeness' of products. The panel in *US – Malt Beverages (1992)* thus for the first time referred to a 'regulatory intent' approach, more commonly referred to as an 'aim-and-effect' approach, to the determination of 'likeness' of products.

In a dispute concerning, *inter alia*, special tax levels for luxury vehicles, *US – Taxes on Automobiles (1994)*, the panel elaborated on the 'aim-and-effect' approach to determining 'likeness'.[87] The United States imposed a retail excise tax on cars with prices above US$30,000 and the panel had to determine whether cars with prices above and below US$30,000 were 'like products'. The complainant in this dispute, the European Community, argued before the panel that 'likeness' should be determined on the basis of criteria such as the end-use of the products, their physical characteristics and tariff classification. The United States contended that the key factor in determining 'likeness' should be whether the measure was applied 'so as to afford protection to domestic industry'. The panel reasoned that the determination of 'likeness' would, in all but the most straightforward cases, have to include an examination of the *aims and effects* of the particular tax measure. According to the panel in *US – Taxes on Automobiles (1994)*, 'likeness' should be examined in terms of whether the less favourable treatment was based on a regulatory distinction made so as to afford protection to domestic production. *In casu*, the panel decided that the luxury tax was not implemented to afford protection to the domestic production of cars and that, therefore, cars above and below US$30,000 could not, for the purpose of the luxury tax, be considered as 'like products' under Article III:2, first sentence.[88]

The 'aim-and-effect' test for determining 'likeness' was, however, explicitly rejected in 1996 by the panel in *Japan – Alcoholic Beverages II (1996)*. The panel found as follows:

the proposed aim-and-effect test is not consistent with the wording of Article III:2, first sentence. The Panel recalled that the basis of the aim-and-effect test is found in the words 'so as to afford protection' contained in Article III:1. The Panel further recalled that Article

---

86 Panel Report, *US – Malt Beverages (1992)*, paras. 5.24–5.25.
87 Panel Report, *US – Taxes on Automobiles (1994)*, para. 5.10.
88 Note that the panel report in *US – Taxes on Automobiles (1994)* was never adopted by the GATT Contracting Parties.

III:2, first sentence, contains no reference to those words. Moreover, the adoption of the aim-and-effect test would have important repercussions on the burden of proof imposed on the complainant. The Panel noted in this respect that the complainants, according to the aim-and-effect test, have the burden of showing not only the effect of a particular measure, which is in principle discernible, but also its aim, which sometimes can be indiscernible. The Panel also noted that very often there is a multiplicity of aims that are sought through enactment of legislation and it would be a difficult exercise to determine which aim or aims should be determinative for applying the aim-and-effect test.[89]

In further support of its rejection of the aim-and-effect test in determining 'likeness' in the context of Article III:2, the panel in *Japan – Alcoholic Beverages II (1996)* also noted:

the list of exceptions contained in Article XX of GATT 1994 could become redundant or useless because the aim-and-effect test does not contain a definitive list of grounds justifying departure from the obligations that are otherwise incorporated in Article III ... [I]n principle, a WTO Member could, for example, invoke protection of health in the context of invoking the aim-and-effect test. The Panel noted that if this were the case, then the standard of proof established in Article XX would effectively be circumvented. WTO Members would not have to prove that a health measure is 'necessary' to achieve its health objective. Moreover, proponents of the aim-and-effect test even shift the burden of proof, arguing that it would be up to the complainant to produce a *prima facie* case that a measure has both the aim and effect of affording protection to domestic production and, once the complainant has demonstrated that this is the case, only then would the defending party have to present evidence to rebut the claim.[90]

The Appellate Body in *Japan – Alcoholic Beverages II (1996)* implicitly affirmed the panel's rejection of the 'aim-and-effect' (or 'regulatory intent') approach to determining whether products are 'like'.[91]

Finally, while the determination of whether products are 'like' within the meaning of Article III:2, first sentence, may often be quite problematic, there have been disputes concerning Article III:2, first sentence, in which panels have side-stepped the 'likeness' issue and have proceeded on the *assumption* that there are 'like' products.[92] The panels in these disputes have assumed that there are 'like' products when the measure at issue distinguishes between products solely on the basis of their origin. The panel in *Indonesia – Autos (1998)* stated:

Under the Indonesian car programmes the distinction between the products for tax purposes is based on such factors as the nationality of the producer or the origin of the parts and components contained in the product ... In our view, such an origin-based distinction in respect of internal taxes suffices in itself to violate Article III:2, without the need to demonstrate the existence of actually traded *like* products.[93]

---

89 Panel Report, *Japan – Alcoholic Beverages II (1996)*, para. 6.16.
90 *Ibid.*, para. 6.17. For a detailed discussion of Article XX of the GATT 1994 and the conditions it imposes for the justification of an otherwise GATT-inconsistent measure, see below, pp. 545–83.
91 The Appellate Body stated: 'With these modifications to the legal reasoning in the Panel Report, we affirm the legal conclusions and the findings of the Panel with respect to "like products" in all other respects.' Appellate Body Report, *Japan – Alcoholic Beverages II (1996)*, 115.
92 See also above, pp. 325–9 (regarding 'likeness' under Article I:1 of the GATT 1994) and below, pp. 382–6 (regarding 'likeness' under Article III:4).
93 Panel Report, *Indonesia – Autos (1998)*, para. 14.113. Emphasis added.

The panel in *Colombia – Ports of Entry (2009)* stated:

> where a WTO Member imposes an origin-based distinction with respect to internal taxes, imported and domestic products may be considered as like products, and a case-by-case determination of 'likeness' between the foreign and domestic would be unnecessary.[94]

Questions and Assignments 5.4

Why must the concept of 'like products' in Article III:2, first sentence, of the GATT 1994 be construed narrowly? What is the basic approach followed by most panels and the Appellate Body in determining 'likeness' within the meaning of Article III:2, first sentence? Can it be that products considered to be 'like' under Article I:1 are not 'like' under Article III:2, first sentence? Why did the panel in *Japan – Alcoholic Beverages II (1996)* reject the 'aim-and-effect' approach, or 'regulatory intent' approach, to the determination of whether products are 'like'?

2.2.3   Taxes 'in Excess of'

The third and last element of the test of consistency with the national treatment obligation of Article III:2, first sentence, relates to the question of whether the imported products are *taxed in excess* of the domestic products. Pursuant to Article III:2, first sentence, internal taxes on imported products should not be 'in excess of' the internal taxes applied to 'like' domestic products. In *Japan – Alcoholic Beverages II (1996)*, the Appellate Body established a strict benchmark for the 'in excess of' requirement. The Appellate Body ruled that the prohibition of discriminatory taxes in Article III:2, first sentence, is not qualified by a *de minimis* standard. According to the Appellate Body, 'even the smallest amount of "excess" is too much'.[95]

Furthermore, the prohibition of discriminatory taxes in Article III:2, first sentence, is not conditional on a 'trade effects test'. As already discussed above, the Appellate Body stated in *Japan – Alcoholic Beverages II (1996)*:

> it is irrelevant that the 'trade effects' of the tax differential between imported and domestic products, as reflected in the volumes of imports, are insignificant or even non-existent; Article III *protects expectations* not of any particular trade volume but rather *of the equal competitive relationship* between imported and domestic products.[96]

---

94   Panel Report, *Colombia – Ports of Entry (2009)*, para. 7.182. See also Appellate Body Report, *Canada – Periodicals (1997)*, 466; and Panel Report, *Indonesia – Autos (1998)*, para. 14.113. The panel in *Colombia – Ports of Entry (2009)* noted that both the Appellate Body and panels have previously recognised the possibility of the existence of hypothetical like products.

95   Appellate Body Report, *Japan – Alcoholic Beverages II (1996)*, 23. With respect to the absence of a *de minimis* standard, note that the panel in *US – Superfund (1987)* already ruled that, although the rate of tax applied to the imported petroleum was merely 3.5 cents per barrel higher than the rate applied to the like domestic petroleum, the US tax on petroleum was inconsistent with Article III:2, first sentence. See Panel Report, *US – Superfund (1987)*, para. 5.1.1. In *Argentina – Hides and Leather (2001)*, the panel rejected Argentina's argument that the tax burden differential between imported and domestic products was *de minimis* because it would only exist for a thirty-day period. See Panel Report, *Argentina – Hides and Leather (2001)*, para. 11.245. See also Panel Report, *Colombia – Ports of Entry (2009)*, para. 7.195; and Panel Report, *China – Auto Parts (2009)*, para. 7.221.

96   Appellate Body Report, *Japan – Alcoholic Beverages II (1996)*, 110. Emphasis added.

In *Argentina – Hides and Leather (2001)*, the panel emphasised that Article III:2, first sentence, requires a comparison of *actual tax burdens* rather than merely of nominal tax rates. The panel ruled:

> Article III:2, first sentence, is not concerned with taxes or charges as such or the policy purposes Members pursue with them, but with their economic impact on the competitive opportunities of imported and like domestic products. It follows, in our view, that what must be compared are the tax burdens imposed on the taxed products.[97]

The panel noted that, if Article III:2, first sentence, would not require a comparison of actual tax burdens, Members could easily evade the prohibition on tax discrimination by, for example, using different methods of computing tax bases for imported and domestic products resulting in a greater actual tax burden for imported products.[98]

In *Thailand – Cigarettes (Philippines) (2011)*, the tax measure at issue imposed the same nominal value added tax (VAT) rate, 7 per cent *ad valorem*, on domestic as well as imported cigarettes. However, resellers of domestic cigarettes incurred no VAT liability while resellers of imported cigarettes did incur VAT liability, and this liability was not offset automatically.[99] Resellers of imported cigarettes had to satisfy certain administrative requirements in order for the VAT paid to be offset against the VAT due. The Appellate Body 'agree[d] with the Panel that Thailand subjects imported cigarettes to internal taxes in excess of those applied to like domestic cigarettes, within the meaning of Article III:2, first sentence, of the GATT 1994'.[100]

A Member which applies higher taxes on imported products in some situations but 'balances' this by applying lower taxes on the imported products in other situations also acts inconsistently with the national treatment obligation of Article III:2, first sentence. The panel in *Argentina – Hides and Leather (2001)* ruled:

> Article III:2, first sentence, is applicable to each individual import transaction. It does not permit Members to balance more favourable tax treatment of imported products in some instances against less favourable tax treatment of imported products in other instances.[101]

Questions and Assignments 5.5

Is the size of the tax differential important under Article III:2, first sentence, of the GATT 1994? Is Article III:2, first sentence, concerned with the nominal tax rate or the actual tax burden on like products? Does Article III:2, first sentence, allow balancing less favourable tax treatment of imported products in some instances against more favourable tax treatment of imported products in other instances?

---

97 Panel Report, *Argentina – Hides and Leather (2001)*, para. 11.182.
98 See *ibid.*, para. 11.183. See already Panel Report, *Japan – Alcoholic Beverages I (1987)*, para. 5.8. See also Panel Report, *Colombia – Ports of Entry (2009)*, paras. 7.188–7.196.
99 In respect of sales of domestic cigarettes, only Thailand Tobacco Monopoly (TTM), the only manufacturer of cigarettes in Thailand, was subject to VAT.
100 Appellate Body Report, *Thailand – Cigarettes (Philippines) (2011)*, para. 116.
101 Panel Report, *Argentina – Hides and Leather (2001)*, para. 11.260.

2.3 National Treatment Test for Internal Taxation on Directly Competitive or Substitutable Products

The second sentence of Article III:2 of the GATT 1994 states:

Moreover, no [Member] shall otherwise apply internal taxes or other internal charges to imported or domestic products in a manner contrary to the principles set forth in paragraph 1.

As discussed above, the relevant leading principle set forth in paragraph 1 of Article III is that internal taxes and other internal charges:

should not be applied to imported or domestic products so as to afford protection to domestic production.

Furthermore, the Note *Ad* Article III provides with respect to Article III:2:

A tax conforming to the requirements of the first sentence of paragraph 2 would be considered to be inconsistent with the provisions of the second sentence only in cases where competition was involved between, on the one hand, the taxed product and, on the other hand, a directly competitive or substitutable product which was not similarly taxed.

The relationship between the first and the second sentence of Article III:2 was addressed by the Appellate Body in *Canada – Periodicals (1997)*, a dispute concerning, *inter alia*, a Canadian excise tax on magazines. The Appellate Body considered that, if an internal tax on products is found to be consistent with Article III:2, first sentence, there is a need to examine further whether the measure is consistent with Article III:2, second sentence.[102] As the Appellate Body stated in *Japan – Alcoholic Beverages II (1996)* and again in *Canada – Periodicals (1997)*, Article III:2, second sentence, contemplates a 'broader category of products' than Article III:2, first sentence.[103] With regard to this broader category of products, it sets out a different test of consistency.[104] In *Japan – Alcoholic Beverages II (1996)*, the Appellate Body stated:

three separate issues must be addressed to determine whether an internal tax measure is inconsistent with Article III:2, second sentence. These three issues are whether:

1. the imported products and the domestic products are 'directly competitive or substitutable products' which are in competition with each other;
2. the directly competitive or substitutable imported and domestic products are 'not similarly taxed'; and
3. the dissimilar taxation of the directly competitive or substitutable imported [and] domestic products is 'applied ... so as to afford protection to domestic production'.[105]

---

102 See Appellate Body Report, *Canada – Periodicals (1997)*, 468.
103 See *ibid.*, 470. See also Appellate Body Report, *Japan – Alcoholic Beverages II (1996)*, 112.
104 See also Appellate Body Reports, *Philippines – Distilled Spirits (2012)*, para. 190.
105 Appellate Body Report, *Japan – Alcoholic Beverages II (1996)*, 116. See also Appellate Body Report, *Canada – Periodicals (1997)*, 470; Appellate Body Report, *Chile – Alcoholic Beverages (2000)*, para. 47; and Appellate Body Reports, *Philippines – Distilled Spirits (2012)*, para. 190.

However, before this test of consistency of internal taxation with Article III:2, second sentence, of the GATT 1994 can be applied, it must be established that the measure at issue is an 'internal tax or other internal charge' within the meaning of Article III:2, second sentence.

Therefore, the four-tier test of consistency of internal taxation with Article III:2, second sentence, requires the examination of:

- whether the measure at issue is an *internal tax or other internal charge* on products;
- whether the imported and domestic products are *directly competitive or substitutable*;
- whether the imported and domestic products are *dissimilarly taxed*; and
- whether the dissimilar taxation is applied so as to afford protection to domestic production.

Below, each element of this four-tier test of consistency will be discussed in turn.[106]

To date, WTO Members have been found to have acted inconsistently with Article III:2, second sentence, in seven disputes.[107]

Questions and Assignments 5.6

What are the constituent elements of the national treatment test under Article III:2, second sentence, of the GATT 1994? What is the relationship between the first and the second sentences of Article III:2?

2.3.1 'Internal Taxes ...'

As is the case with Article III:2, first sentence, Article III:2, second sentence, of the GATT 1994 is also concerned with 'internal taxes or other internal charges' which are applied 'directly or indirectly' on products. For a discussion on the meaning and scope of these concepts, recall the discussion above in the subsection dealing with Article III:2, first sentence.[108] With regard to this constituent element of the national treatment test, there is no difference between the first and the second sentences of Article III:2.

2.3.2 'Directly Competitive or Substitutable Products'

The second element of the test of consistency with the national treatment obligation of Article III:2, second sentence, relates to the question of whether the imported and domestic products concerned are 'directly competitive or substitutable products'. The national treatment obligation of Article III:2, second

---

106 See below, pp. 372, 378 and 379.
107 See *Japan – Alcoholic Beverages II (1996), Canada – Periodicals (1997), Indonesia – Autos (1998), Korea – Alcoholic Beverages (1999), Chile – Alcoholic Beverages (2000), Mexico – Taxes on Soft Drinks (2006)* and *Philippines – Distilled Spirits (2012)*.
108 See above, pp. 365–70.

sentence, of the GATT 1994 applies to 'directly competitive or substitutable products'. As with the concept of 'like products' discussed above, the concept of 'directly competitive or substitutable products' is not defined in the GATT 1994. However, the relevant case law to date provides us with a number of examples of products that panels and/or the Appellate Body have found to be 'directly competitive or substitutable' on the market of a particular Member. In *Canada – Periodicals (1997)*, the 'directly competitive or substitutable products' were the imported split-run periodicals and domestic non-split-run periodicals at issue in that case.[109] In *Japan – Alcoholic Beverages II (1996)* and *Korea – Alcoholic Beverages (1999)*, the traditional local alcoholic beverages, shochu and soju respectively, were found to be 'directly competitive or substitutable' with imported 'Western-style' liquors, such as whisky, vodka, brandy, cognac, rum, gin and liqueurs.[110] In *Chile – Alcoholic Beverages (2000)*, the domestically produced pisco was considered 'directly competitive or substitutable' with imported distilled spirits, such as whisky, brandy and cognac.[111] In *Mexico – Taxes on Soft Drinks (2006)*, the 'directly competitive or substitutable products' were the domestic cane sugar and imported high fructose corn syrup.[112] Most recently, in *Philippines – Distilled Spirits (2012)*, domestic distilled spirits from designated raw materials (and in particular sugar cane) were found to be 'directly competitive or substitutable' with imported distilled spirits from other raw materials (such as cereals, grapes etc.).[113]

In *Canada – Periodicals (1997)*, the Appellate Body ruled that, to be 'directly competitive or substitutable' within the meaning of Article III:2, second sentence, products do not – contrary to what Canada had argued – have to be perfectly substitutable. The Appellate Body noted:

A case of perfect substitutability would fall within Article III:2, first sentence, while we are examining the broader prohibition of the second sentence.[114]

109 See Appellate Body Report, *Canada – Periodicals (1997)*, 474. A split-run periodical is a periodical with different editions distributed in different countries, in which part of the editorial material is the same or substantially the same as editorial material that appears in other editions but in which advertisements differ (as they are focused on the local market of a specific edition). The Appellate Body found split-run and non-split-run periodicals to be directly competitive or substitutable products insofar as they are part of the same segment of the Canadian market for periodicals.
110 See Panel Report, *Japan – Alcoholic Beverages II (1996)*, para. 6.32 ('whisky, brandy, gin, genever, rum, and liqueurs', para. 6.28); and Panel Report, *Korea – Alcoholic Beverages (1999)*, para. 10.98 ('vodka, whiskies, rum, gin, brandies, cognac, liqueurs, tequila and ad-mixtures', para. 10.57). Recall that, in *Japan – Alcoholic Beverages (1996)*, shochu and vodka were found to be 'like products' under Article III:2, first sentence. See above, p. 360.
111 See Panel Report, *Chile – Alcoholic Beverages (2000)*, para. 7.83.
112 See Panel Report, *Mexico – Taxes on Soft Drinks (2006)*, para. 8.78. Recall that, in this case, the domestic cane sugar and the imported beet sugar were found to be 'like products' under Article III:2, first sentence. Also, the domestic soft drinks sweetened with cane sugar and imported soft drinks sweetened with beet sugar or HFCS were found to be 'like products'. See above, p. 364.
113 See Appellate Body Reports, *Philippines – Distilled Spirits (2012)*, para. 242. Recall that, in this case, distilled spirits of a specific type (such as whisky and brandy) made from designated raw materials (and, in particular, sugar cane) and distilled spirits of the same type made from other raw materials (cereals for whisky and grapes for brandy) were found to be 'like products'. See above, p. 364.
114 Appellate Body Report, *Canada – Periodicals (1997)*, 473. As to the implications of this statement for the scope of the concept of 'like products', see above, p. 364.

With regard to the relationship between the concept of 'like products' of Article III:2, first sentence, and the concept of 'directly competitive or substitutable products' of Article III:2, second sentence, the Appellate Body stated in *Korea – Alcoholic Beverages (1999)*:

'Like' products are a subset of directly competitive or substitutable products: all like products are, by definition, directly competitive or substitutable products, whereas not all 'directly competitive or substitutable' products are 'like'. The notion of like products must be construed narrowly but the category of directly competitive or substitutable products is broader.[115]

As to the meaning of the concept of 'directly competitive or substitutable products', the Appellate Body further stated in *Korea – Alcoholic Beverages (1999)* that products are 'competitive' or 'substitutable' when:

they are interchangeable or if they offer, as the Panel noted, 'alternative ways of satisfying a particular need or taste'.[116]

The words 'competitive' or 'substitutable' are qualified by the word 'directly'. In the context of Article III:2, second sentence, the word 'directly' suggests a 'degree of proximity' in the competitive relationship between the domestic and the imported products.[117] According to the Appellate Body in *Philippines – Distilled Spirits (2012)*, the requisite degree of competition is met where the imported and domestic products are characterised by a high, but imperfect, degree of substitutability.[118]

In *Korea – Alcoholic Beverages (1999)*, the Appellate Body further clarified the concept of 'directly competitive or substitutable products' by noting that:

Competition in the market place is a dynamic, evolving process. Accordingly, the wording of the term 'directly competitive or substitutable' implies that the competitive relationship between products is *not* to be analyzed *exclusively* by reference to *current* consumer preferences.[119]

According to the Appellate Body, the word 'substitut*able*' indicates that:

the requisite relationship *may* exist between products that are not, at a given moment, considered by consumers to be substitutes but which are, nonetheless, *capable* of being substituted for one another.[120]

In assessing whether products are 'directly competitive or substitutable', a panel must thus consider not only extant demand (or current competition) but also

---

115 Appellate Body Report, *Korea – Alcoholic Beverages (1999)*, para. 118. In a footnote, the Appellate Body referred to the Appellate Body Report, *Japan – Alcoholic Beverages II (1996)*, and Appellate Body Report, *Canada – Periodicals (1997)*.

116 *Ibid.*, para. 115.

117 *Ibid.*, para. 116.

118 See Appellate Body Reports, *Philippines – Distilled Spirits (2012)*, para. 205. In a footnote, the Appellate Body refers to Appellate Body Report, *Korea – Alcoholic Beverages (1999)*, para. 118; Appellate Body Report, *Canada – Periodicals (1997)*, 473; and also Appellate Body Report, *US – Cotton Yarn (2001)*, footnote 68 to para. 97.

119 Appellate Body Report, *Korea – Alcoholic Beverages (1999)*, para. 114. Original emphasis.

120 *Ibid.* Original emphasis.

latent demand (or potential competition). As the Appellate Body noted in *Korea – Alcoholic Beverages (1999)*, particularly in a market where there are barriers to trade or to competition, there may well be latent demand.[121] In *Philippines – Distilled Spirits (2012)*, the Appellate Body held that:

> instances of *current* substitution are likely to *underestimate* latent demand for imported spirits as a result of distortive effects introduced by the excise tax at issue.[122]

The tax measure at issue as well as (current and prior) other protectionist taxation, import restrictions and regulatory measures can have the effect of creating, and even freezing, consumer preferences for domestic products.[123] It is thus highly relevant to examine latent demand. The competitive relationship between products is clearly not to be analysed by reference to *current* consumer preferences only.[124]

In justification of its position that when determining whether products are 'directly competitive or substitutable' a panel should also consider *latent* demand, and thus *potential* competition, the Appellate Body stated in *Korea – Alcoholic Beverages (1999)*:

> In view of the objectives of avoiding protectionism, requiring equality of competitive conditions and protecting expectations of equal competitive relationships, we decline to take a static view of the term 'directly competitive or substitutable'. The object and purpose of Article III confirms that the scope of the term 'directly competitive or substitutable' cannot be limited to situations where consumers *already* regard products as alternatives. If reliance could be placed only on current instances of substitution, the object and purpose of Article III:2 could be defeated by the protective taxation that the provision aims to prohibit.[125]

In brief, products are considered to be 'directly competitive or substitutable' when they are interchangeable or when they offer alternative ways of satisfying a particular need or taste. In examining whether products are 'directly competitive or substitutable', an analysis of *latent* as well as *extant* demand is required

---

121 See *ibid.*, para. 115.
122 Appellate Body Reports, *Philippines – Distilled Spirits (2012)*, para. 226.
123 See Appellate Body Report, *Korea – Alcoholic Beverages (1999)*, para. 120 (quoting Panel Report, *Japan – Alcoholic Beverages II (1996)*, para. 6.28); and Appellate Body Reports, *Philippines – Distilled Spirits (2012)*, para. 226. The Appellate Body noted in *Korea – Alcoholic Beverages (1999)* and again in *Philippines – Distilled Spirits (2012)* that current demand for products is a function of actual retail prices, which could be distorted by the tax measure at issue *and* other related effects, such as higher distribution costs, lower volumes, and economies of scale (see paras. 122–3 and para. 221 respectively). For these reasons, the Appellate Body did not agree with the Philippines that an analysis of potential competition is limited to an assessment of whether competition would otherwise occur if the challenged taxation were not in place. According to the Appellate Body, such a 'but for' test reflects an overly restrictive interpretation of the term 'directly competitive or substitutable' products, one which assumes that internal taxation is the *only* factor restricting potential substitutability. See Appellate Body Reports, *Philippines – Distilled Spirits (2012)*, para. 227.
124 As the Appellate Body noted in *Philippines – Distilled Spirits (2012)*, it follows from this that for products to be 'directly competitive or substitutable', Article III:2, second sentence, does not require – contrary to what was argued by the Philippines in this case – 'identity in the "nature and frequency" of the consumer's purchasing behaviour'. If that were the case, the competitive relationship between the imported and domestic products in a given market would only be assessed with reference to *current* consumer preferences. See Appellate Body Reports, *Philippines – Distilled Spirits (2012)*, para. 217.
125 Appellate Body Report, *Korea – Alcoholic Beverages (1999)*, para. 120.

since 'competition in the marketplace is a dynamic, evolving process' and the object and purpose of Article III is, fundamentally, 'protecting expectations of equal competitive relationships'.[126]

With respect to the criteria to be taken into account in establishing whether products are 'directly competitive or substitutable' within the meaning of Article III:2, second sentence, the Appellate Body agreed with the panel in *Japan – Alcoholic Beverages II (1996)* that, in addition to the products' physical characteristics, end-use and tariff classification, a panel needs to look at the 'market place'.[127] The Appellate Body held:

> The GATT 1994 is a commercial agreement, and the WTO is concerned, after all, with markets. It does not seem inappropriate to look at competition in the relevant markets as one among a number of means of identifying the broader category of products that might be described as 'directly competitive or substitutable'.[128]
>
> Nor does it seem inappropriate to examine elasticity of substitution as one means of examining those relevant markets.[129]

The Appellate Body thus considered an examination of the cross-price elasticity of demand in the relevant market, as a means of establishing whether products are 'directly competitive or substitutable' in that market. However, in *Korea – Alcoholic Beverages (1999)*, the Appellate Body was careful to stress that cross-price elasticity of demand for products is not the decisive criterion in determining whether these products are 'directly competitive or substitutable'. The Appellate Body agreed with the panel's emphasis on the 'quality' or 'nature' of competition rather than the 'quantitative overlap of competition'. The Appellate Body shared the panel's reluctance to rely unduly on quantitative analyses of the competitive relationship. In the Appellate Body's view, an approach that focused solely on the quantitative overlap of competition would, in essence, make cross-price elasticity the decisive criterion in determining whether products are 'directly competitive or substitutable'.[130] Making cross-price elasticity the decisive criterion would likely result in underestimating latent demand and potential competition between the products at issue and, therefore, result in an incomplete, i.e. wrong, assessment of whether these products are 'directly competitive or substitutable' within the meaning of Article III:2, second sentence.

In *Philippines – Distilled Spirits (2012)*, the panel came to the conclusion that the products at issue – distilled spirits made from designated raw materials (and in particular sugar cane) and distilled spirits made from other raw materials (such as cereals, grapes etc.) – were 'directly competitive or substitutable' by considering the following criteria: (1) the competitive relationship between the products at issue in the Philippines' market; (2) the products' channels of

---

126 *Ibid.*, paras. 114–20.
127 See Appellate Body Report *Japan – Alcoholic Beverages II (1996)*, 117.
128 *Ibid.*   129 *Ibid.*
130 See Appellate Body Report, *Korea – Alcoholic Beverages (1999)*, para. 134.

distribution; (3) their physical characteristics; (4) their end-uses and marketing; (5) their tariff classification; and (6) internal regulations regarding these products.[131] With regard to the first of these criteria, namely, the competitive relationship between the products at issue, the Appellate Body found on appeal that:

the Panel did not err in its assessment of the competitive relationship between the imported and domestic distilled spirits at issue in the Philippine market. In our view, studies showing a significant degree of substitutability in the Philippine market between imported and domestic distilled spirits, as well as instances of price competition and evidence of actual and potential competition between imported and domestic distilled spirits in the Philippine market, sufficiently support the Panel's conclusion that there is 'a direct competitive relationship [in the Philippines] between domestic and imported distilled spirits, made from different raw materials'.[132]

Subsequently, the Appellate Body concluded:

This factor, combined with the other elements upon which the Panel relied, such as overlap in the channels of distribution, and similarities in the products' physical characteristics, end-uses, and marketing, sufficiently supports the Panel's finding that all imported and domestic distilled spirits at issue are 'directly competitive or substitutable' within the meaning of Article III:2, second sentence, of the GATT 1994.[133]

Note that, with regard to the relevance of 'price' in the determination of whether products are 'directly competitive or substitutable', the Appellate Body noted in *Philippines – Distilled Spirits (2012)* that:

price is very relevant in assessing whether imported and domestic products stand in a sufficiently direct competitive relationship in a given market. This is because evidence of price competition indicates that the imported product exercises competitive constraints on the domestic product, and *vice versa*. In this respect, we agree with the Philippines that evidence of major price differentials could demonstrate that the imported and domestic products are in completely separate markets.[134]

However, the panel in *Philippines – Distilled Spirits (2012)* made a factual finding that there was overlap in the prices of imported and domestic distilled spirits in the Philippines, and that such overlap was not 'exceptional' but rather occurred for both high- and low-priced products.[135] This factual finding was not challenged on appeal.[136]

In establishing whether products are 'directly competitive or substitutable' in the market of the responding Member, the market situation in *other* Members may be relevant and can be taken into consideration. In *Korea – Alcoholic Beverages (1999)*, the Appellate Body stated:

It is, of course, true that the 'directly competitive or substitutable' relationship must be present in the market at issue, in this case, the Korean market. It is also true that consumer

---

131 See Appellate Body Reports, *Philippines – Distilled Spirits (2012)*, para. 198. On appeal, the Philippines challenged only the panel's assessment of the competitive relationship between the products concerned in the Philippine market. See *ibid.*, para. 199.

132 *Ibid.*, para. 242.   133 *Ibid.*   134 *Ibid.*, para. 215.

135 See Panel Reports, *Philippines – Distilled Spirits (2012)*, para. 7.118.

136 Appellate Body Reports, *Philippines – Distilled Spirits (2012)*, para. 214. The Philippines argued instead that existing price overlaps do not show a sufficiently direct degree of competition.

responsiveness to products may vary from country to country. This does not, however, preclude consideration of consumer behaviour in a country other than the one at issue. It seems to us that evidence from other markets may be pertinent to the examination of the market at issue, particularly when demand on that market has been influenced by regulatory barriers to trade or to competition.[137]

The Appellate Body emphasised that obviously not every other market will be relevant to the market at issue. However, if another market has characteristics similar to the market at issue, then evidence of consumer demand in that other market may be of some relevance to the market at issue.[138]

The question has arisen as to whether, in examining whether products are 'directly competitive or substitutable', it is necessary to scrutinise products on an item-by-item basis or whether it is permitted to group products together for the purpose of this examination. In *Korea – Alcoholic Beverages (1999)*, the panel compared soju (the domestic Korean liquor at issue in this case) with imported liquor products (vodka, whisky, rum, gin, brandy, cognac, liqueurs, tequila and ad-mixtures) on a group basis, rather than on an item-by-item basis. Korea appealed the panel's 'grouping' of products, but the Appellate Body rejected this appeal.[139] The Appellate Body first noted that the question whether, and to what extent, products can be grouped is a matter to be decided on a case-by-case basis, and that, in this case, the panel decided to group the imported products at issue on the basis that, 'on balance, all of the imported products specifically identified by the complainants have sufficient common characteristics, end-uses and channels of distribution and prices'.[140] The Appellate Body then observed that the panel's subsequent analysis of the physical characteristics, end-uses, channels of distribution and prices of the imported products confirmed the correctness of its decision to group the products for analytical purposes. The Appellate Body also observed that, where appropriate, the panel did take account of individual product characteristics.[141]

In *Philippines – Distilled Spirits (2012)*, the Philippines argued on appeal that the panel incorrectly found direct competition between the imported and domestic distilled spirits at issue on the basis of a 'narrow segment' of the population having 'access' to imported distilled spirits. The Philippines contended that Article III:2, second sentence, requires that competition be assessed in relation to the market that is most representative of the 'market as a whole'. The Appellate Body considered that:

the Panel was correct in concluding that Article III of the GATT 1994 'does not protect just *some* instances or *most* instances, but rather, it protects *all* instances of direct competition'.[142]

137 Appellate Body Report, *Korea – Alcoholic Beverages (1999)*, para. 137.
138 See *ibid.*, para. 137.
139 See *ibid.*, para. 144. According to the Appellate Body, 'grouping' is an *analytical tool* to minimise repetition when examining the competitive relationship between a large number of differing products. Some grouping is almost always necessary in cases arising under Article III:2, second sentence. See Appellate Body Report, *Korea – Alcoholic Beverages (1999)*, para. 142.
140 See *ibid.*, para. 143, quoting from para. 10.60 of the panel report.   141 See *ibid.*, para. 144.
142 Appellate Body Reports, *Philippines – Distilled Spirits (2012)*, para. 221, referring to Panel Report, *Chile – Alcoholic Beverages (2000)*, para. 7.43.

And that:

> it was reasonable for the Panel to conclude that actual competition in a segment of the market *further supports* its conclusion that imported and domestic distilled spirits are capable of being substituted in the Philippines.[143]

Questions and Assignments 5.7

When are products 'directly competitive or substitutable' within the meaning of Article III:2, second sentence, of the GATT 1994? What criteria can be taken into account in determining whether products are 'directly competitive or substitutable'? How important is the 'cross-price elasticity of demand' of products in determining whether such products are 'directly competitive or substitutable'? In determining whether products are 'directly competitive or substitutable', does one consider only extant demand and actual competition or also latent demand and potential competition? Why? How relevant is the fact that products are directly competitive and substitutable on the market of *other* Members? How relevant is the price differential between products? Can products that are in competition in one segment of the market be found 'directly competitive or substitutable' within the meaning of Article III:2, second sentence?

2.3.3   Dissimilar Taxation

The third element of the test of consistency with the national treatment obligation of Article III:2, second sentence, of the GATT 1994 relates to the question of whether the products at issue are 'not similarly taxed', i.e. whether they are dissimilarly taxed. If imported products and directly competitive or substitutable domestic products are 'similarly taxed', there is no inconsistency with Article III:2, second sentence. While under Article III:2, first sentence, even the slightest tax differential leads to the conclusion that the internal tax imposed on imported products is GATT-inconsistent, under Article III:2, second sentence, the tax differential has to be more than *de minimis* to support a conclusion that the internal tax imposed on imported products is GATT-inconsistent. In *Japan – Alcoholic Beverages II (1996)*, the Appellate Body explained:

> To interpret 'in excess of' and 'not similarly taxed' identically would deny any distinction between the first and second sentences of Article III:2. Thus, in any given case, there may be some amount of taxation on imported products that may well be 'in excess of' the tax on domestic 'like products' but may not be so much as to compel a conclusion that 'directly competitive or substitutable' imported and domestic products are 'not similarly taxed' for the purposes of the *Ad* Article to Article III:2, second sentence.[144]

Whether any particular differential amount of taxation is *de minimis* or not, or, in other words, whether products are 'similarly taxed' or not, must be determined on a case-by-case basis.[145] Note that the Appellate Body found in

---

143   Appellate Body Reports, *Philippines – Distilled Spirits (2012)*, para. 222. Emphasis added.
144   Appellate Body Report, *Japan – Alcoholic Beverages II (1996)*, 118. On the *de minimis* standard, see also Appellate Body Report, *Canada – Periodicals (1997)*, 474; Panel Report, *Indonesia – Autos (1998)*, para. 14.116; and Appellate Body Report, *Chile – Alcoholic Beverages (2000)*, para. 49.
145   See Appellate Body Report, *Japan – Alcoholic Beverages II (1996)*, 118.

Canada – Periodicals (1997) that the amount of the tax differential was 'far above the *de minimis* threshold', considering that the amount was 'sufficient to prevent the production and sale of split-run periodicals in Canada'.[146] In *Philippines – Distilled Spirits (2012)*, the imported distilled spirits were taxed ten to forty times more than the domestic distilled spirits. Not surprisingly, the panel in that case found that the products at issue were 'not taxed similarly'.[147]

Note that there is also 'dissimilar taxation' when only *some* of the imported products are not taxed similarly. The Appellate Body stated in *Canada – Periodicals (1997)* that:

> dissimilar taxation of even *some* imported products as compared to directly competitive or substitutable domestic products is inconsistent with the provisions of the second sentence of Article III:2.[148]

Questions and Assignments 5.8

Is the size of the tax differential important under Article III:2, second sentence, of the GATT 1994?

2.3.4 'So as to Afford Protection to Domestic Production'

The fourth and last element of the test of consistency with the national treatment obligation of Article III:2, second sentence, of the GATT 1994 relates to the question of whether dissimilar taxation is applied 'so as to afford protection to domestic production'.

This fourth element of the consistency test must be distinguished from the third element of the test, discussed above, namely, whether there is dissimilar taxation. In *Japan – Alcoholic Beverages II (1996)*, the Appellate Body noted:

> [T]he Panel erred in blurring the distinction between [the issue of whether the products at issue were 'not similarly taxed'] and the entirely separate issue of whether the tax measure in question was applied 'so as to afford protection'. Again, these are separate issues that must be addressed individually.[149]

It must be stressed that WTO Members are allowed to apply dissimilar taxes on directly competitive or substitutable products as long as these taxes are not applied so as to afford protection to domestic production. As to how to establish whether a tax measure was applied so as to afford protection to domestic production, the Appellate Body noted in *Japan – Alcoholic Beverages II (1996)*:

> As in [the GATT panel report on *Japan – Alcoholic Beverages I (1987)*], we believe that an examination in any case of whether dissimilar taxation has been applied so as to afford

---

146 Appellate Body Report, *Canada – Periodicals (1997)*, 474.
147 See Panel Reports, *Philippines – Distilled Spirits (2012)*, para. 7.154.
148 Appellate Body Report, *Canada – Periodicals (1997)*, 474. Emphasis added. To support this conclusion, the Appellate Body referred to the panel in *US – Section 337 Tariff Act (1989)* concerning treatment less favourable under Article III:4 of the GATT. See Panel Report, *US – Section 337 Tariff Act (1989)*, para. 5.14. See below, p. 395.
149 Appellate Body Report, *Japan – Alcoholic Beverages II (1996)*, 119.

protection requires a comprehensive and objective analysis of the structure and application of the measure in question on domestic as compared to imported products. We believe it is possible to examine objectively the underlying criteria used in a particular tax measure, its structure, and its overall application to ascertain whether it is applied in a way that affords protection to domestic products.

Although it is true that the aim of a measure may not be easily ascertained, nevertheless its protective application can most often be discerned from the design, the architecture, and the revealing structure of a measure.[150]

Thus, to determine whether the application of a tax measure affords protection to domestic production, a panel must examine the design, the architecture, the structure and the overall application of the measure.[151] For example, if the tax measure operates in such a way that the lower tax bracket covers primarily domestic production, whereas the higher tax bracket embraces primarily imported products, the implication is that the tax measure is applied so as to afford protection to domestic production. More difficult is the situation that arose in *Chile – Alcoholic Beverages (2000)*, where 75 per cent of the domestically produced products fell in the lower tax bracket and 95 per cent of the imported products fell in the higher tax bracket, *but* at the same time the majority of the products falling in that higher tax bracket were domestically produced products.[152] The Appellate Body noted that this did not exclude that the tax measure was inconsistent with Article III:2, second sentence. The Appellate Body pointed out that Article III:2, second sentence:

provides for equality of competitive conditions of *all* directly competitive or substitutable imported products, in relation to domestic products, and not simply, as Chile argues, those imported products within a particular [tax bracket].[153]

As the Appellate Body acknowledged in *Japan – Alcoholic Beverages II (1996)*, the very magnitude of the tax differential may be evidence of the protective application of a tax measure. Most often, however, other factors will also be considered.[154] As the Appellate Body found in *Korea – Alcoholic Beverages (1999)*, the protective application of dissimilar taxation can only be determined 'on a case-by-case basis, taking account of all relevant facts'.[155]

In *Korea – Alcoholic Beverages (1999)*, Korea argued that a finding that an internal tax measure affords protection 'must be supported by proof that the tax

---

150 *Ibid.*, 120.
151 The *subjective intent* of the legislator or regulator is irrelevant (see below, p. 381). What needs to be examined and identified are the tax measure's 'objectives or purposes as revealed or objectified in the measure itself'. See Appellate Body Report, *Chile – Alcoholic Beverages (2000)*, para. 71.
152 See Panel Report, *Chile – Alcoholic Beverages (2000)*, para. 7.158.
153 Appellate Body Report, *Chile – Alcoholic Beverages (2000)*, para. 67. See also Appellate Body Reports, *Philippines – Distilled Spirits (2012)*, para. 221; and see above, p. 377.
154 Note that, in *Korea – Alcoholic Beverages (1999)*, *Chile – Alcoholic Beverages (2000)* and *Philippines – Distilled Spirits (2012)*, both the tax differential (in all three cases quite substantial) *and* the design, architecture and structure of the tax measure at issue were examined. See Appellate Body Report, *Korea – Alcoholic Beverages (1999)*, para. 150; Appellate Body Report, *Chile – Alcoholic Beverages (2000)*, para. 71; and Appellate Body Reports, *Philippines – Distilled Spirits (2012)*, para. 255.
155 Appellate Body Report, *Korea – Alcoholic Beverages (1999)*, para. 137.

difference has some identifiable trade effect'.[156] However, the Appellate Body curtly rejected this argument, pointing out that 'Article III is not concerned with trade volumes' and that thus a complaining party did not have 'to prove that tax measures are capable of producing any particular trade effect'.[157]

With regard to the relevance of the intent of the legislator or regulator, the Appellate Body in *Japan – Alcoholic Beverages II (1996)* noted:

[Whether a tax measure is applied so as to afford protection to domestic production] is not an issue of intent. It is not necessary for a panel to sort through the many reasons legislators and regulators often have for what they do and weigh the relative significance of those reasons to establish legislative or regulatory intent. If the measure is applied to imported or domestic products so as to afford protection to domestic production, then it does not matter that there may not have been any desire to engage in protectionism in the minds of the legislators or the regulators who imposed the measure. It is irrelevant that protectionism was not an intended objective if the particular tax measure in question is nevertheless, to echo Article III:1, '*applied* to imported or domestic products so as to afford protection to domestic production'. This is an issue of how the measure in question is *applied*.[158]

The *subjective intent* of the legislator or regulator is irrelevant. As the Appellate Body stated in *Chile – Alcoholic Beverages (2000)*:

We called for examination of the design, architecture and structure of a tax measure precisely to permit identification of a measure's objectives or purposes as revealed or objectified in the measure itself.[159]

In *Chile – Alcoholic Beverages (2000)*, Chile argued that the internal taxation on alcoholic beverages at issue in that case was aimed at, among other things, reducing the consumption of alcoholic beverages with higher alcohol content. The Appellate Body held that the mere statement of such or other objectives pursued by Chile did not constitute effective rebuttal on the part of Chile of the alleged protective application of the internal taxation on alcoholic beverages.[160]

Note, however, that, in *Canada – Periodicals (1997)*, the Appellate Body did seem to attach at least some importance to statements of representatives of the Canadian Government about the policy objectives of the tax measure at issue.[161]

Questions and Assignments 5.9

How does one establish whether internal taxes on directly competitive or substitutable products have been applied so as to afford protection to domestic production? Is the intent of the legislator relevant in deciding whether an internal tax is inconsistent with the national treatment obligation of Article III:2, second sentence, of the GATT 1994?

---

156 *Ibid.*, para. 153.   157 *Ibid.*
158 Appellate Body Report, *Japan – Alcoholic Beverages II (1996)*, 119.
159 Appellate Body Report, *Chile – Alcoholic Beverages (2000)*, para. 71.
160 See *ibid.* The Chilean tax system had two levels of taxation on alcoholic beverages (27 per cent *ad valorem* and 47 per cent *ad valorem*) separated by only 4 degrees of alcohol content.
161 See Appellate Body Report, *Canada – Periodicals (1997)*, 475–6. *In casu*, these statements of Canadian officials confirmed that the tax measure was indeed applied so as to afford protection to domestic production.

2.4   National Treatment Test for Internal Regulation

The national treatment obligation under Article III of the GATT 1994 does not only concern internal taxation dealt with in Article III:2. Article III also concerns internal regulation, dealt with primarily in Article III:4. Article III:4 states, in relevant part:

The products of the territory of any [Member] imported into the territory of any other [Member] shall be accorded treatment no less favourable than that accorded to like products of national origin in respect of all laws, regulations and requirements affecting their internal sale, offering for sale, purchase, transportation, distribution or use.

In *Korea – Various Measures on Beef (2001)*, the Appellate Body stated:

For a violation of Article III:4 to be established, three elements must be satisfied: that the imported and domestic products at issue are 'like products'; that the measure at issue is a 'law, regulation, or requirement affecting their internal sale, offering for sale, purchase, transportation, distribution, or use'; and that the imported products are accorded 'less favourable' treatment than that accorded to like domestic products.[162]

In other words, the three-tier test of consistency of internal regulation with Article III:4 requires the examination of:

* whether the measure at issue is a *law, regulation or requirement* covered by Article III:4;
* whether the imported and domestic products are *like products*; and
* whether the imported products are accorded *less favourable treatment*.

Unlike Article III:2, second sentence, Article III:4 does *not* specifically refer to Article III:1. Therefore, while Article III:1 has 'particular contextual significance in interpreting Article III:4, as it sets forth the "general principle" pursued by that provision',[163] a determination of whether there has been a violation of Article III:4 does *not* require a separate consideration of whether a measure 'afford[s] protection to domestic production'.[164] The test of consistency with Article III:4 thus has three, rather than four, elements.

Below, each element of this three-tier test of consistency will be discussed in turn.

To date, WTO Members have been found to have acted inconsistently with Article III:4 in sixteen disputes.[165]

---

162   Appellate Body Report, *Korea – Various Measures on Beef (2001)*, para. 133.
163   Appellate Body Report, *EC – Asbestos (2001)*, para. 93.
164   Appellate Body Report, *EC – Bananas III (1997)*, para. 216.
165   See *US – Gasoline (1996)*; *Canada – Periodicals (1997)*; *EC – Bananas III (1997)*; *Korea – Various Measures on Beef (2001)*; *US – FSC (Article 21.5 – EC) (2002)*; *India – Autos (2002)*; *Canada – Wheat Exports and Grain Imports (2004)*; *EC – Trade Marks and Geographical Indications (2005)*; *Dominican Republic – Import and Sale of Cigarettes (2005)*; *Mexico – Taxes on Soft Drinks (2006)*; *EC – Approval and Marketing of Biotech Products (2006)*; *Turkey – Rice (2007)*; *Brazil – Retreaded Tyres (2007)*; *China – Auto Parts (2009)*; *China – Publications and Audiovisual Products (2010)*; and *Thailand – Cigarettes (Philippines) (2011)*. No inconsistency with Article III:4 was found in *Japan – Film (1998)*; *EC – Poultry (1998)*; *Canada – Autos (2000)*; and *EC – Asbestos (2001)*.

What are the constituent elements of the national treatment test of Article III:4 of the GATT 1994? In this context, what is the importance of Article III:1?

2.4.1 'Laws, Regulations and Requirements Affecting ...'

Article III:4 concerns 'all laws, regulations and requirements affecting [the] internal sale, offering for sale, purchase, transportation, distribution or use [of products]'. Broadly speaking, the national treatment obligation of Article III:4 applies to domestic regulations affecting the sale and use of products. The panel in *Italy – Agricultural Machinery (1958)* ruled that:

> the text of paragraph 4 referred both in English and French to laws and regulations and requirements *affecting* internal sale, purchase, etc., and not to laws, regulations and requirements governing the conditions of sale or purchase. The selection of the word 'affecting' would imply, in the opinion of the Panel, that the drafters of the Article intended to cover in paragraph 4 not only laws and regulations which directly governed the conditions of sale or purchase but also any laws or regulations which might adversely modify the conditions of competition between the domestic and imported products on the internal market.[166]

The panel thus interpreted the scope of application of Article III:4 broadly as including all measures that may modify the conditions of competition in the market. In *US – FSC (Article 21.5 – EC) (2002)*, the Appellate Body affirmed this broad interpretation of the word 'affecting'.[167]

The panel in *US – Section 337 Tariff Act (1989)* addressed the issue of whether only substantive laws, regulations and requirements *or* also procedural laws, regulations and requirements can be regarded as 'affecting' the internal sale of imported goods. Referring back to the paragraph from *Italy – Agricultural Machinery (1958)* quoted above, the panel found that such *procedural* measures are also covered by Article III:4, as otherwise circumvention of the national treatment obligation would be easy.[168]

According to GATT and WTO case law, Article III:4 applies, *inter alia*, to: (1) minimum price requirements applicable to domestic and imported beer;[169] (2) the requirement that imported beer and wine be sold only through in-State wholesalers or other middlemen;[170] (3) a ban on cigarette advertising;[171] (4) trade-related investment measures;[172] (5) requirements that imported cigarettes cannot leave the bonded warehouse unless the tax stamps are affixed to each

---

166 Panel Report, *Italy – Agricultural Machinery (1958)*, para. 12.
167 See Appellate Body Report, *US – FSC (Article 21.5 – EC) (2002)*, para. 210. Moreover, as the panel in *India – Autos (2002)* stated, and the Appellate Body affirmed in *China – Auto Parts (2009)*, the fact that a measure is not primarily aimed at *regulating* the sale, offering for sale, purchase, transportation, distribution and use of the products at issue 'is not an obstacle to its "affecting" them'. See Appellate Body Reports, *China – Auto Parts (2009)*, para. 194.
168 See Panel Report, *US – Section 337 Tariff Act (1989)*, para. 5.10.
169 See Panel Report, *Canada – Provincial Liquor Boards (US) (1992)*, para. 5.30.
170 See Panel Report, *US – Malt Beverages (1992)*, para. 5.32.
171 See Panel Report, *Thailand – Cigarettes (1990)*, para. 78.
172 See Panel Report, *Canada – FIRA (1984)*, paras. 5.12 and 6.1.

cigarette packet in the presence of a tax inspector;[173] (6) regulation resulting in higher railway transportation costs for imported grain;[174] (7) regulation prohibiting storage of grain of foreign origin in grain elevators containing domestic grain;[175] (8) a requirement to purchase paddy rice from domestic producers to obtain the right to import rice at reduced tariff levels;[176] (9) an obligation to dispose of ten used tyres as a prerequisite for the importation of one retreaded tyre;[177] (10) regulation requiring that all imported newspapers and periodicals be distributed through only one particular distribution channel;[178] (11) regulation subjecting imported sound recordings intended for electronic distribution to content review regimes;[179] and (12) VAT-related administrative requirements imposed on resellers of imported cigarettes.[180] It is clear from this *illustrative* list of 'laws, regulations and requirements ...' within the meaning of Article III:4 that the scope of this concept is very broad. Panels and the Appellate Body have drawn the outer limits of this concept generously.

In *EC – Bananas III (1997)*, the Appellate Body agreed with the panel that Article III:4 was applicable to the EC requirements at issue. This was contested by the European Communities on the ground that import licensing was a border measure and not an internal measure within the scope of Article III:4. However, the Appellate Body ruled with regard to the EC requirements at issue, which concerned the *distribution* of banana import licences among eligible operators *within* the European Union, that:

[t]hese rules go far beyond the mere import licence requirements needed to administer the tariff quota ... These rules are intended, among other things, to cross-subsidize distributors of EC (and ACP) bananas and to ensure that EC banana ripeners obtain a share of the quota rents. As such, these rules affect 'the internal sale, offering for sale, purchase ...' within the meaning of Article III:4, and therefore fall within the scope of this provision.[181]

In *Canada – Autos (2000)*, the panel held that a measure can be considered to be a measure affecting, i.e. having an effect on, the internal sale or use of imported products even if it is not shown that *under the current circumstances* the measure has an impact on the decisions of private parties to buy imported products. The panel noted:

The word 'affecting' in Article III:4 of the GATT has been interpreted to cover not only laws and regulations which directly govern the conditions of sale or purchase but also any laws or regulations which *might* adversely modify the conditions of competition between domestic and imported products.[182]

173 See Panel Report, *Dominican Republic – Import and Sale of Cigarettes (2005)*, paras. 7.170–7.171.
174 See Panel Reports, *Canada – Wheat Exports and Grain Imports (2004)*, paras. 6.331–6.332.
175 See *ibid.*, para. 6.262.   176 See Panel Report, *Turkey – Rice (2007)*, para. 7.219.
177 See Panel Report, *Brazil – Retreaded Tyres (2007)*, para. 7.433.
178 See Panel Report, *China – Publications and Audiovisual Products (2010)*, para. 7.1513.
179 See *ibid.*, para. 7.1595.
180 See Panel Report. *Thailand– Cigarettes (Philippines) (2011)*, para. 7.665.
181 Appellate Body Report, *EC – Bananas III (1997)*, para. 211.
182 Panel Report, *Canada – Autos (2000)*, para. 10.80. Emphasis added. This follows from the fact that, to show inconsistency with Article III:4, it is not necessary to establish that the measure at issue has *actual* adverse trade effects. See below, p. 381.

While, to date, most cases involving Article III:4 concerned *generally applicable* 'laws' and 'regulations', i.e. measures that apply across the board, Article III:4 also covers 'requirements' which may apply to *isolated cases only*.[183] The panel in *Canada – FIRA (1984)* noted:

> The Panel could not subscribe to the Canadian view that the word 'requirements' in Article III:4 should be interpreted as 'mandatory rules applying across-the-board' because this latter concept was already more aptly covered by the term 'regulations' and the authors of this provision must have had something different in mind when adding the word 'requirements'. The Panel also considered that, in judging whether a measure is contrary to obligations under Article III:4, it is not relevant whether it applies across-the-board or only in isolated cases. Any interpretation which would exclude case-by-case action would, in the view of the Panel, defeat the purposes of Article III:4.[184]

The question has arisen whether a 'requirement' within the meaning of Article III:4 necessarily needs to be a government-imposed requirement, or whether a (voluntary) action by a private party can constitute a 'requirement' to which Article III:4 applies.[185] In *Canada – Autos (2000)*, the panel examined commitments by Canadian car manufacturers to increase the value added to cars in their Canadian plants. These commitments were communicated in letters addressed to the Canadian Government. The panel characterised these commitments as 'requirements' subject to Article III:4. According to the panel, (voluntary) private action can be a 'requirement' within the meaning of Article III:4 if, and only if, there is such a *nexus*, i.e. a close link, between that action and the action of a government, that the government must be held responsible for that private action.[186] Such nexus may exist, for example, when a Member makes the grant of an advantage (such as an exemption from customs duties) conditional upon the private action concerned.[187] Note that the panel in *China – Publications and Audiovisual Products (2010)* found with regard to one of the measures at issue in that case, namely, the distribution duopoly for films, that the United States, the complainant, had not established that the distribution duopoly was attributable to China and that, therefore, the consistency of this measure with Article III:4 could not be challenged in WTO dispute settlement.[188]

---

183 See Panel Report, *Canada – FIRA (1984)*, para. 5.5. See also Panel Report, *India – Autos (2002)*, paras. 7.189–7.191; and Panel Reports, *China – Auto Parts (2009)*, paras. 7.241 and 7.243.

184 Panel Report, *Canada – FIRA (1984)*, para. 5.5. The measures at issue in *Canada – FIRA (1984)* were written undertakings by investors to purchase goods of Canadian origin in preference to imported goods or in specified amounts or proportions, or to purchase goods from Canadian sources.

185 On the general question whether actions by private parties can be challenged in WTO dispute settlement, see Panel Reports, *China – Auto Parts (2009)*, paras. 7.242–7.243.

186 See Panel Report, *Canada – Autos (2000)*, para. 10.107. See also Panel Report, *Canada – Periodicals (1997)*, paras. 5.33–5.36; Panel Report, *India – Autos (2002)*, paras. 7.177–7.194; and Panel Report, *Turkey – Rice (2007)*, paras. 7.217–7.226. For older case law, see *Canada – FIRA (1984)*, para. 5.4; and Panel Report, *EEC – Parts and Components (1990)*, para. 5.21.

187 See Panel Report, *Canada – Autos (2000)*, para. 10.106.

188 See Panel Report, *China – Publications and Audiovisual Products (2010)*, paras. 7.1693–7.1694. Also note the Appellate Body's statement in *Korea – Various Measures on Beef (2001)* that dual distribution systems are not measures within the scope of Article III:4 when they are 'solely the result of private entrepreneurs acting on their own calculation of comparative costs and benefits of differentiated distribution systems' (para. 149). See also above, p. 354.

While Article III:2 concerns internal taxation and Article III:4 internal regulation, the panel in *Mexico – Taxes on Soft Drinks (2006)* found that:

the soft drink tax, the distribution tax and the bookkeeping requirements may be considered as measures that affect the internal use in Mexico of non-cane sugar sweeteners, such as beet sugar and [high fructose corn syrup], within the meaning of Article III:4 of the GATT 1994.[189]

Taxes can thus be measures subject to Article III:4. Note that, in *China – Auto Parts (2009)*, the same legal provisions of Chinese law were found to be inconsistent with both Article III:2 and Article III:4.[190]

The *Agreement on Trade-Related Investment Measures* (the *TRIMS Agreement*) contains an illustrative list of trade-related investment measures that are inconsistent with Article III:4.[191] This illustrative list includes measures that require the purchase or use by an enterprise of products of domestic origin; or require that an enterprise's purchases or use of imported products be limited to an amount related to the volume or value of local products that it exports.

As discussed above, Article III:8 of the GATT 1994 explicitly excludes two kinds of measure from the scope of application of Article III:4, namely: laws, regulations or requirements governing government procurement (see Article III:8(a)); and the payment of subsidies exclusively to domestic producers (see Article III:8(b)).[192]

Questions and Assignments 5.11

What laws, regulations and requirements fall within the scope of application of Article III:4 of the GATT 1994? Can a measure be considered to be a measure affecting the internal sale of imported products within the meaning of Article III:4 if: (a) it does not regulate the sale, offering for sale, purchase, transportation, distribution or use of the products at issue; or (b) it is not shown that *under current circumstances* the measure has an impact on the decisions of private parties to buy imported products? Is the national treatment obligation of Article III:4 applicable to border measures such as import licensing? Is the national treatment obligation of Article III:4 applicable to measures that do not apply generally across the board, but only to isolated cases? Can an action by a private person, company or organisation constitute a measure within the meaning of Article III:4? Does the national treatment obligation of Article III apply to regulations concerning government procurement or to subsidies to domestic producers? Can internal taxes within the meaning of Article III:2 be subject to the national treatment requirement of Article III:4?

2.4.2 'Like Products'

The second element of the test of consistency with the national treatment obligation of Article III:4 relates to the question of whether the imported and domestic products concerned are 'like'. As with Articles I:1 and III:2, first sentence, both discussed above, the non-discrimination obligation of Article III:4 only

---

189 Panel Report, *Mexico – Taxes on Soft Drinks (2006)*, para. 8.113.
190 Appellate Body Reports, *China – Auto Parts (2009)*, paras. 183 and 197.
191 See Article 2.2 of, and the Annex to, the *TRIMS Agreement*.
192 See above, p. 351.

applies to 'like products'. Therefore, it is also important for the application of the national treatment obligation of Article III:4 to be able to determine whether, for example, a sports utility vehicle (SUV) is 'like' a family car; orange juice is 'like' tomato juice; a laptop is 'like' a tablet computer; pork is 'like' beef; or whisky is 'like' brandy. As discussed above, the answer to these questions may be different in the context of Article III:4 of the GATT 1994 than in the context of other non-discrimination provisions of the GATT 1994.[193] The answer may also be different from the market of one WTO Member to the market of another WTO Member. Products that are 'like' in Richland are not necessarily 'like' in Newland.

The Appellate Body considered the meaning of the concept of 'like products' in Article III:4 in *EC – Asbestos (2001)*. In its report in that case, the Appellate Body first noted that the concept of 'like products' was also used in Article III:2, first sentence, and that, in *Japan – Alcoholic Beverages II (1996)*, it had held that the scope of 'like products' was to be construed 'narrowly' in that provision.[194] The Appellate Body then examined whether this interpretation of 'like products' in Article III:2 could be taken to suggest a similarly narrow reading of 'like products' in Article III:4, since both provisions form part of the same Article. The Appellate Body recalled its considerations in *Japan – Alcoholic Beverages II (1996)* that led it to conclude in that case that the concept of 'like products' in Article III:2, first sentence, must be construed narrowly,[195] and observed:

In construing Article III:4, the same interpretive considerations do not arise, because the 'general principle' articulated in Article III:1 is expressed in Article III:4, not through two distinct obligations, as in the two sentences in Article III:2, but instead through a single obligation that applies solely to 'like products'. Therefore, the harmony that we have attributed to the two sentences of Article III:2 need not and, indeed, cannot be replicated in interpreting Article III:4. Thus, we conclude that, given the textual difference between Articles III:2 and III:4, the 'accordion' of 'likeness' stretches in a different way in Article III:4.[196]

Having distinguished the concept of 'like products' in Article III:4 from the concept in Article III:2, first sentence, the Appellate Body then proceeded to examine the meaning of this concept in Article III:4. It first recalled that, in *Japan – Alcoholic Beverages II (1996)*, it had ruled that the broad and fundamental purpose of Article III is to avoid protectionism in the application of internal tax and regulatory measures.[197] As is explicitly stated in Article III:1, the purpose of Article III is to ensure that internal measures 'not be applied to imported and domestic products so as to afford protection to domestic production'. To this end, Article III obliges WTO Members to provide equality of competitive conditions

---

193 On the 'accordion of likeness', see above, p. 360.
194 Appellate Body Report, *EC – Asbestos (2001)*, para. 93. The Appellate Body referred to Appellate Body Report, *Japan – Alcoholic Beverages II (1996)*, 112 and 113, and also to Appellate Body Report, *Canada – Periodicals (1997)*, 473. See above, p. 364.
195 Appellate Body Report, *EC – Asbestos (2001)*, para. 95. For the Appellate Body's considerations in *Japan – Alcoholic Beverages II (1996)*, see above, p. 360.
196 Appellate Body Report, *EC – Asbestos (2001)*, para. 96.
197 See above, p. 352.

for imported products in relation to domestic products.[198] This 'general principle' is not explicitly invoked in Article III:4. Nevertheless, it does 'inform' that provision.[199] The Appellate Body in *EC – Asbestos (2001)* thus reasoned that the term 'like product' in Article III:4 must be interpreted to give proper scope and meaning to the anti-protectionism principle of Article III:1.[200] It is clear that an internal regulation can *only* afford protection to domestic production if the internal regulation addresses domestic and imported products that are in a competitive relationship. In the absence of a competitive relationship between the domestic and imported products, internal regulation cannot be applied to these products so as to afford protection to domestic production. The Appellate Body thus came to the following conclusion with respect to the meaning of 'like products' in Article III:4:

[A] determination of 'likeness' under Article III:4 is, fundamentally, a determination about the nature and extent of a competitive relationship between and among products.[201]

Note that the Appellate Body referred to both the nature *and* the extent of a competitive relationship between and among products. A mere economic analysis of the cross-price elasticity of demand for the products at issue will not suffice to determine whether these products are 'like'. 'Likeness' is a matter of judgment – qualitatively as well as quantitatively.

Having concluded that the determination of 'likeness' is a determination of the nature and extent of a competitive relationship between and among the products at issue, the Appellate Body subsequently noted in *EC – Asbestos (2001)* that it is mindful that there is a spectrum of degrees of 'competitiveness' of products in the marketplace, and that it is difficult, if not impossible, in the abstract, to indicate precisely where on this spectrum the word 'like' in Article III:4 of the GATT 1994 falls.[202] The Appellate Body found, however, that:

[i]n view of [the] different language [of Articles III:2 and III:4], and although we need not rule, and do not rule, on the precise product scope of Article III:4, we do conclude that the product scope of Article III:4, although broader than the *first* sentence of Article III:2, is certainly *not* broader than the *combined* product scope of the *two* sentences of Article III:2 of the GATT 1994.[203]

Moreover, the Appellate Body found that the product scope of Article III:4 and that of Article III:2, first *and* second sentence, cannot be significantly different.[204]

---

198 See Appellate Body Report, *Japan – Alcoholic Beverages II (1996)*, 109–10.   199 *Ibid.*, 111.
200 See Appellate Body Report, *EC – Asbestos (2001)*, para. 98.
201 *Ibid.*, para. 99. As discussed above, in *Philippines – Distilled Spirits (2011)*, the Appellate Body ruled that the same basic test applies to determine whether products are 'like' within the meaning of Article III:2, first sentence, of the GATT 1994. See above, p. 363. As discussed below, in *US – Clove Cigarettes (2012)*, the Appellate Body ruled that this test also applies to determine whether products are 'like' within the meaning of Article 2.1 of the *TBT Agreement*. See below, p. 866.
202 Appellate Body Report, *EC – Asbestos (2001)*, para. 96.
203 *Ibid.* The panel in *Mexico – Taxes on Soft Drinks (2006)* therefore concluded that, as it had found cane sugar and beet sugar to be 'like' under Article III:2, first sentence, these products could also be considered 'like' under Article III:4. See Panel Report, *Mexico – Taxes on Soft Drinks (2006)*, para. 8.105.
204 See Appellate Body Report, *EC – Asbestos (2001)*, para. 99.

As pointed out by the Appellate Body, there is no sharp distinction between fiscal measures covered by Article III:2, and regulatory measures, covered by Article III:4. Both forms of measure can often be used to achieve the same ends. Therefore, 'it would be incongruous' if, due to significant difference in the product scope of these two provisions, Members were prevented from using one form of measure (fiscal measures) to protect domestic production of certain products, but were able to use another form of measure (regulatory measures) to achieve the same ends. According to the Appellate Body, '[t]his would frustrate a consistent application of the "general principle" in Article III:1'.[205]

Having reached a conclusion on the meaning and the scope of the concept of 'like products' under Article III:4, the Appellate Body turned in *EC – Asbestos (2001)* to the question of *how* one should determine whether products are 'like' within the meaning of Article III:4. The Appellate Body first noted:

As in Article III:2, in this determination, '[n]o one approach ... will be appropriate for all cases'. Rather, an assessment utilizing 'an unavoidable element of individual, discretionary judgement' has to be made on a case-by-case basis.[206]

The Appellate Body then recalled that, in analysing 'likeness', panels and the Appellate Body itself had followed, and further developed, the approach outlined in the working party report in *Border Tax Adjustments (1970)*.[207] According to the Appellate Body, this approach has, essentially, consisted of employing four general criteria in analysing 'likeness': (i) the properties, nature and quality of the products; (ii) the end-uses of the products; (iii) consumers' tastes and habits – also referred to as consumers' perceptions and behaviour – in respect of the products; and (iv) the tariff classification of the products.[208] These four criteria comprise four categories of 'characteristics' that the products involved might share: (i) the physical properties of the products; (ii) the extent to which the products are capable of serving the same or similar end-uses; (iii) the extent to which consumers perceive and treat the products as alternative means of performing particular functions in order to satisfy a particular want or demand; and (iv) the international classification of the products for tariff purposes.[209] The Appellate Body hastened to add, however, that, while these general criteria, or

---

205 *Ibid.* The panel in *Mexico – Taxes on Soft Drinks (2006)* therefore concluded that cane sugar and high fructose corn syrup (HFCS), which were considered 'directly competitive or substitutable' within the meaning of Article III:2, second sentence, were in a close competitive relationship and could thus be considered 'like' products within the meaning of Article III:4. See Panel Report, *Mexico – Taxes on Soft Drinks (2006)*, para. 8.106.

206 Appellate Body Report, *EC – Asbestos (2001)*, para. 101.

207 See *ibid.* In a footnote to para. 101, the Appellate Body referred to Appellate Body Report, *Japan – Alcoholic Beverages II (1996)*, 113. It also referred to Panel Report, *US – Gasoline (1996)*, para. 6.8, where the approach set out in the working party report in *Border Tax Adjustments (1970)* was adopted in a dispute concerning Article III:4 of the GATT 1994.

208 See Appellate Body Report, *EC – Asbestos (2001)*, para. 101. The Appellate Body noted in a footnote to para. 101 that the fourth criterion, tariff classification, was not mentioned in the working party report in *Border Tax Adjustments (1970)*, but was included by subsequent panels (see e.g. Panel Report, *EEC – Animal Feed Proteins (1978)*, para. 4.2; and Panel Report, *Japan – Alcoholic Beverages I (1987)*, para. 5.6).

209 See Appellate Body Report, *EC – Asbestos (2001)*, para. 101.

groupings of potentially shared characteristics, provide a framework for analysing the 'likeness' of particular products, they are 'simply tools to assist in the
task of sorting and examining the relevant evidence'.[210] The Appellate Body
stressed that these criteria are 'neither a treaty-mandated nor a closed list of
criteria that will determine the legal characterisation of products'.[211] In each
case, *all* pertinent evidence, whether related to one of these criteria or not, must
be examined and considered by panels to determine whether products are – or
could be – in a competitive relationship in the marketplace, i.e. are 'like'.[212] The
Appellate Body also found:

> When all the relevant evidence has been examined, panels must determine whether that
> evidence, *as a whole*, indicates that the products in question are 'like' in terms of the legal
> provision at issue.[213]

It follows that, in and of itself, evidence under one of the criteria cannot be
determinative on the 'likeness' of products. A panel always has to examine the
totality of the relevant evidence.

In *EC – Asbestos (2001)*, the Appellate Body was highly critical of the manner in which the panel examined the 'likeness' of the products at issue in that
case, namely, chrysotile asbestos fibres and cement-based products containing
chrysotile asbestos fibres on the one hand *and* PCG fibres and cement-based
products containing PCG fibres on the other hand.[214] The Appellate Body criticised the panel for not examining each of the criteria set forth in the working
party report in *Border Tax Adjustments (1970)*[215] and for not examining these
criteria separately.[216] The Appellate Body also disagreed with the panel's refusal
to consider the health risks posed by asbestos in the determination of 'likeness',
stating that panels must evaluate *all* of the relevant evidence.[217] According to
the Appellate Body, the carcinogenic or toxic nature of chrysotile asbestos fibres
constitutes a defining aspect of the physical properties of those fibres and must
therefore be considered when determining 'likeness' under Article III:4.[218] According to the Appellate Body, 'evidence relating to health risks may be relevant
in assessing the *competitive relationship in the marketplace* between allegedly
"like" products'.[219] The Appellate Body also noted that consumers' tastes and

---

210 See *ibid.*, para. 102.   211 See *ibid.*   212 See *ibid.*, para. 103.   213 *Ibid.* Emphasis added.
214 *Ibid.*, para. 109. PCG fibres are PVA, cellulose and glass fibres.
215 The panel declined to examine the third criterion (consumers' tastes and habits) and dismissed the fourth
    criterion (tariff classification) as non-decisive. With respect to consumers' tastes and habits, for example, the
    Appellate Body was very critical of the panel for declining to examine this criterion because, as the panel stated,
    'this criterion would not provide clear results'. See Appellate Body Report, *EC – Asbestos (2001)*, para. 122.
216 In the course of the examination of the first criterion (the properties, nature and quality of the products), the
    panel relied on the second criterion (end-use) to come to the 'conclusion' that the products were like.
217 Appellate Body Report, *EC – Asbestos (2001)*, para. 113.   218 See *ibid.*, para. 114.
219 *Ibid.*, para. 115. According to the Appellate Body, considering evidence relating to the health risks
    associated with a product, under Article III:4, does not nullify the effect of Article XX(b) of the GATT 1994.
    For a discussion on Article XX of the GATT 1994, see below, pp. 554–60. The fact that an interpretation
    of Article III:4 taking into account health risks, implies a less frequent recourse to Article XX(b) does
    not deprive the exception in Article XX(b) of effetciveness. On the rules of treaty interpretation and
    effectiveness, see above, p. 188.

habits regarding asbestos fibres or PCG fibres are very likely to be shaped by the health risks associated with a product which is known to be highly carcinogenic (as asbestos fibres are).[220]

With regard to the second and third criteria set out in the working party report in *Border Tax Adjustments (1970)*, i.e. end-uses and consumers' tastes and habits, the Appellate Body found in *EC – Asbestos (2001)*:

> Evidence of this type is of particular importance under Article III of the GATT 1994, precisely because that provision is concerned with competitive relationships in the marketplace. If there is – or could be –*no* competitive relationship between products, a Member cannot intervene, through internal taxation or regulation, to protect domestic production. Thus, evidence about the extent to which products can serve the same end-uses, and the extent to which consumers are – or would be – willing to choose one product instead of another to perform those end-uses, is highly relevant evidence in assessing the 'likeness' of those products under Article III:4 of the GATT 1994.[221]

According to the Appellate Body in *EC – Asbestos (2001)*, evidence relating to end-uses and consumers' tastes and habits is *especially* important in cases where the evidence relating to properties establishes that the products at issue are physically quite different. In such cases, in order to overcome this indication that products are *not* 'like', a higher burden is placed on complaining Members to establish that, despite the pronounced physical differences, there is a competitive relationship between the products such that *all* of the evidence, taken together, demonstrates that the products are 'like' under Article III:4.[222]

With respect to end-uses, the Appellate Body further found that, while it is certainly relevant that products have similar end-uses for a 'small number of ... applications', a panel must also consider the other, *different* end-uses of products. It is only by forming a complete picture of the various (similar as well as different) end-uses of a product that a panel can assess the significance of the fact that products share a limited number of end-uses.[223]

In general, the Appellate Body confirmed in *EC – Asbestos* the prior case law by upholding the market-based, economic interpretation of the concept of 'likeness' (and thus confirmed the marketplace approach to determining 'likeness').[224] At the same time, however, the Appellate Body 'remedied' the narrow scope given to the concept of 'likeness' in prior case law by allowing non-economic interests and values, such as health, to be considered in the determination of 'likeness'.

After reversing the panel's findings, in *EC – Asbestos (2001)*, on the 'likeness' of chrysotile asbestos fibres and PCG fibres, the Appellate Body itself examined

---

220 See *ibid.*, para. 122.   221 *Ibid.*, para. 117.   222 See *ibid.*, paras. 117 and 118.
223 See *ibid.*, para. 119.
224 Note, however, that, in a separate 'concurring' opinion, one of the Appellate Body Members on the division in *EC – Asbestos (2001)* considered that 'the necessity or appropriateness of adopting a "fundamentally" economic interpretation of the "likeness" of products under Article III:4 of the GATT 1994 does not appear to me to be free from substantial doubts'. See *ibid.*, para. 154. According to that Appellate Body member, it is difficult to imagine what evidence relating to economic competitive relationships as reflected in end-uses and consumers' tastes and habits could outweigh the undisputed deadly nature of chrysotile asbestos fibres, compared with PCG fibres. See *ibid.*, para. 152.

the 'likeness' of these products and came to the conclusion that the evidence was certainly far from sufficient to satisfy the complainant's burden of proving that chrysotile asbestos fibres are 'like' PCG fibres under Article III:4. The Appellate Body considered that the evidence tended rather to suggest that these products are not 'like products'.[225]

Two additional observations on the determination of 'likeness' under Article III:4 of the GATT 1994 are called for: one observation regarding the 'regulatory intent' or 'aim-and-effect' approach discussed above in the context of Article III:2, first sentence, of the GATT 1994;[226] and one observation regarding the relevance of processes and production methods (PPMs) discussed above in the context of Article I of the GATT 1994.[227] With regard to the former, note that in *US – Malt Beverages (1992)*, the panel considered the regulatory intent (or aim) of the measure in determining whether low alcohol beer and high alcohol beer were 'like products' within the meaning of Article III:4. In this regard, the panel recalled its earlier statement on like product determinations under Article III:2, first sentence,[228] and held that:

> in the context of Article III, it is essential that such determinations be made not only in the light of such criteria as the products' physical characteristics, but also in the light of the purpose of Article III, which is to ensure that internal taxes and regulations 'not be applied to imported or domestic products so as to afford protection to domestic production'.[229]

The panel noted that, on the basis of their 'physical characteristics', low and high alcohol beers were 'similar'. However, in order to determine whether low and high alcohol beers were 'like products' under Article III:4, the panel considered that it had to examine whether the purpose of the distinction between low and high alcohol beers was 'to afford protection to domestic production'. The panel noted that the United States argued that the distinction was made to encourage the consumption of low rather than high alcohol beer. The panel eventually concluded that the purpose of the regulatory distinction was not to afford protection to domestic production and that low and high alcoholic beers were, therefore, not 'like products'.[230]

For reasons discussed above, this 'regulatory intent' or 'aim-and-effect' approach to the determination of 'likeness' has been discredited and abandoned by WTO panels and the Appellate Body.[231] A first indication that WTO panels would not follow this approach was given in *US – Gasoline (1996)*, in which the panel found that chemically identical imported and domestic gasoline were 'like products' because 'chemically identical imported and domestic gasoline by definition have exactly the same physical characteristics, end-uses, tariff

---

225 See *ibid.*, para. 141. Also, with regard to the products containing asbestos and PCG fibres, the Appellate Body concluded that Canada had not satisfied the burden of proof that these products were 'like'. See *ibid.*, para. 147.
226 See above, p. 366.   227 See above, p. 328.   228 See above, p. 365.
229 Panel Report, *US – Malt Beverages (1992)*, para. 5.71.
230 See *ibid.*, paras. 5.25–5.26 and 5.71–5.76.   231 See above, pp. 366–8.

classification, and are perfectly substitutable'.[232] The intent or the aim of the regulatory distinction made was not given any consideration in determining 'likeness'. Shortly after *US – Gasoline (1996)*, the 'regulatory intent' or 'aim-and-effect' approach to the determination of 'likeness' was explicitly rejected in *Japan – Alcoholic Beverages II (1996)*.[233]

With regard to the processes and production methods, which do not affect the characteristics or properties of the products concerned (NPR-PPMs), note that the panel in *US – Tuna (Mexico) (1991)* found that differences in NPR-PPMs are not relevant in determining 'likeness'. The panel stated:

> Article III:4 calls for a comparison of the treatment of imported tuna *as a product* with that of domestic tuna *as a product*. Regulations governing the taking of dolphins incidental to the taking of tuna could not possibly affect tuna as a product.[234]

Thus, whether tuna was fished in a dolphin-friendly manner or not (i.e. an NPR-PPM) was, according to the panel in *US – Tuna (Mexico) (1991)*, of no relevance in determining whether the imported tuna was 'like' the domestic tuna. However, as reflected above, the concept of 'likeness' has evolved since *US – Tuna (Mexico) (1991)*.[235] The question of whether NPR-PPMs may be of relevance in the determination of 'likeness' now requires a more nuanced answer than that given by the panel in *US – Tuna (Mexico) (1991)*.[236] It should be noted that NPR-PPMs may have an impact on consumers' perceptions and behaviour, and thus on the nature and the extent of the competitive relationship between products. If the consumers in a particular market shun carpets made by children, a situation may arise in which there is in fact no (or only a weak) competitive relationship between these carpets and carpets made by adults. In light of the nature and the extent of the competitive relationship between them, carpets made by children and carpets made by adults could in such a situation be found to be not 'like'. While this differs from market to market, an increasing number of consumers is interested in, and sensitive to, the labour, environmental and other conditions under which products are produced. However, more often, consumers are, in their choice between products, primarily guided by the price and quality of the products, rather than the conditions under which these products were produced.

Finally, it should be noted that, while the 'likeness' of products is often a controversial issue in disputes concerning Article III:4, there have been a number of disputes in which panels have side-stepped the 'likeness' issue and have proceeded on the *assumption* that there are 'like' products.[237] The panels in these

---

232 Panel Report, *US – Gasoline (1996)*, para. 6.9.   233 See above, pp. 366 and 367.
234 Panel Report, *US – Tuna (Mexico) (1991)*, para. 5.15. Note that this report was never adopted.
235 See above, p. 386.
236 As discussed in Chapter 13 of this book, the issue of 'likeness' of tuna fished in a dolphin-friendly manner and tuna fished otherwise re-emerged in *US – Tuna II (Mexico) (2012)*, albeit not under Article III:4, but under Article 2.1 of the *TBT Agreement*. See below, pp. 865–7.
237 See also above, pp. 325–8 (regarding 'likeness' under Article I:1 of the GATT 1994), and pp. 360–8 (regarding 'likeness' under Article III:2, first sentence).

disputes have assumed that there are 'like' products when the measure at issue distinguishes between products solely on the basis of their origin. In *Canada – Wheat Exports and Grain Imports (2004)*, for example, the measures at issue provided either for requirements applicable *only* to imported grain[238] or benefits granted *only* to domestic grain.[239] 'Likeness' was therefore considered not to be an issue in *Canada – Wheat Exports and Grain Imports (2004)*.[240] The panel found that:

[g]iven the existence of an origin-based distinction in [the measure at issue], the United States need only demonstrate that there *can or will be* domestic and imported products that are like.[241]

The panel in *China – Publications and Audiovisual Products (2010)* stated the view that:

when origin is the sole criterion distinguishing the products, it is sufficient for purposes of satisfying the 'like product' requirement for a complaining party to demonstrate that there *can or will be* domestic and imported products that are 'like'.[242]

However, in disputes concerning measures that are, on their face, 'origin-neutral', such as *EC – Asbestos (2001)*, the 'likeness' of the products concerned is usually at the core of the dispute.[243] Note that, in *EC – Asbestos (2001)*, the Appellate Body stated not without a touch of despair regarding the 'likeness' analysis in the context of disputes concerning measures that are, on their face, 'origin-neutral':

There will be few situations where the evidence on the 'likeness' of products will lend itself to 'clear results'. In many cases, the evidence will give conflicting indications, possibly within each of the four criteria.[244]

Questions and Assignments 5.12

Should the concept of 'like products' in Article III:4 of the GATT 1994 be interpreted in the same manner as in Article III:2, first sentence? What is the relevance of the general principle of Article III:1 to the interpretation of the concept of 'like products' in Article III:4? How do the product scopes of the Article III:2 and Article III:4 compare? Which factors should be taken into account in determining whether products are 'like' within the meaning of Article III:4? What is the ultimate basis for determining the 'likeness' of products? Can two products that have substantially different physical characteristics be 'like products' within the meaning of Article III:4? Would the Appellate Body Member who wrote the separate opinion in *EC – Asbestos (2001)* agree? What is the relevance of the 'regulatory intent' of a measure and the NPR-PPMs of products in the determination of likeness under Article III:4? In which disputes is the issue of 'likeness' typically *not* problematic?

238 See Panel Reports, *Canada – Wheat Exports and Grain Imports (2004)*, para. 6.165.
239 See *ibid.*, paras. 6.262 and 6.331–6.332.   240 See *ibid.*, paras. 6.164, 6.264 and 6.333.
241 *Ibid.*, para. 6.262. Emphasis added.
242 Panel Report, *China – Publications and Audiovisual Products (2010)*, para. 7.1446. Emphasis added. This approach to likeness has also been referred to as the 'hypothetical like products approach'. See above, p. 328 and p. 362.
243 See above, p. 354.   244 Appellate Body Report, *EC – Asbestos (2001)*, para. 120.

2.4.3 'Treatment no Less Favourable'

The third and last element of the test of consistency with the national treatment obligation of Article III:4 relates to the question of whether the measure at issue accords 'treatment no less favourable'. The fact that a measure distinguishes between 'like products' does not suffice to conclude that this measure is inconsistent with Article III:4.[245] As the Appellate Body noted in *EC – Asbestos (2001)*:

> A complaining Member must still establish that the measure accords to the group of 'like' *imported* products 'less favourable treatment' than it accords to the group of 'like' *domestic* products. [246]

The panel in *US – Section 337 Tariff Act (1989)* interpreted 'treatment no less favourable' as requiring 'effective equality of opportunities'.[247] In later GATT and WTO reports, panels and the Appellate Body have consistently interpreted 'treatment no less favourable' in the same way.[248] In *US – Gasoline (1996)*, a dispute concerning legislation designed to prevent and control air pollution, the panel recalled the ruling in *US – Section 337 Tariff Act (1989)* that the words 'treatment no less favourable' in Article III:4 call for effective equality of competitive opportunities for imported products, and then found:

> since ... imported gasoline was effectively prevented from benefiting from as favourable sales conditions as were afforded domestic gasoline ... imported gasoline was treated less favourably than domestic gasoline.[249]

In *Korea – Various Measures on Beef (2001)*, a dispute concerning a dual retail distribution system for the sale of beef under which *imported* beef was, *inter alia*, to be sold in specialised stores selling only imported beef or in separate sections of supermarkets, the panel ruled that 'any regulatory distinction that is based exclusively on criteria relating to the nationality or the origin of the products is incompatible with [Article III:4 of the GATT 1994]'.[250] The Appellate Body disagreed with the panel and reversed this ruling. According to the Appellate Body, the formal difference in treatment between domestic and imported products is neither necessary nor sufficient for a violation of Article III:4. Formally different treatment of imported products does not necessarily constitute less favourable treatment while the absence of formal difference in treatment does not necessarily mean that there is no less favourable treatment.[251] The Appellate Body stated in *Korea – Various Measures on Beef (2001)*:

---

245 See below, p. 396.
246 Appellate Body Report, *EC – Asbestos (2001)*, para. 100.
247 Panel Report, *US – Section 337 Tariff Act (1989)*, para. 5.11.
248 See e.g. Panel Report, *Canada – Provincial Liquor Boards (US) (1992)*, paras. 5.12–5.14 and 5.30–5.31; Panel Report, *US – Malt Beverages (1992)*, para. 5.30; Panel Report, *US – Gasoline (1996)*, para. 6.10; Panel Reports, *EC – Bananas III (1997)*, paras. 7.179–7.180; and Panel Report, *Japan – Film (1997)*, para. 10.379.
249 Panel Report, *US – Gasoline (1996)*, para. 6.10.
250 Panel Report, *Korea – Various Measures on Beef (2001)*, para. 627.
251 See also Panel Report, *US – Section 337 Tariff Act (1989)*, para. 5.11; and Panel Report, *US – Gasoline (1996)*, para. 6.25.

We observe ... that Article III:4 requires only that a measure accord treatment to imported products that is 'no less favourable' than that accorded to like domestic products. A measure that provides treatment to imported products that is *different* from that accorded to like domestic products is not necessarily inconsistent with Article III:4, as long as the treatment provided by the measure is no 'less favourable'. According 'treatment no less favourable' means, as we have previously said, according *conditions of competition* no less favourable to the imported product than to the like domestic product.[252]

As the Appellate Body noted in *EC – Asbestos (2001)*, a Member may draw distinctions between products which have been found to be 'like', without, for this reason alone, according to the group of imported products 'less favourable treatment' than that accorded to the group of 'like' domestic products.[253] The Appellate Body's interpretation of 'treatment no less favourable' focuses on the *conditions of competition* between imported and domestic like products and, as a result, a measure according formally *different* treatment to imported products does not *per se*, that is, necessarily, violate Article III:4.[254] Why this is so was persuasively explained by the panel in *US – Section 337 Tariff Act (1989)*. The panel in that case had to determine whether US procedures for patent infringement claims, which were formally different for imported and for domestic products, violated Article III:4. The panel ruled:

On the one hand, [Members] may apply to imported products *different* formal legal requirements if doing so would accord imported products more favourable treatment. On the other hand, it also has to be recognised that there may be cases where the application of formally *identical* legal provisions would in practice accord less favourable treatment to imported products and a [Member] might thus have to apply different legal provisions to imported products to ensure that the treatment accorded them is in fact no less favourable.[255]

From this, the Appellate Body concluded in *Korea – Various Measures on Beef (2001)*:

A formal difference in treatment between imported and like domestic products is thus neither necessary, nor sufficient, to show a violation of Article III:4. Whether or not imported products are treated 'less favourably' than like domestic products should be assessed instead by examining whether a measure modifies the *conditions of competition* in the relevant market to the detriment of imported products.[256]

Under current case law, a measure gives rise to 'treatment less favourable' inconsistent with Article III:4 when it modifies the conditions of competition in the relevant market to the detriment of the imported products. In *Dominican Republic – Import and Sale of Cigarettes (2005)*, for example, the panel found with respect to the tax stamp to be affixed to all cigarette packets marketed in the Dominican Republic that:

---

252 Appellate Body Report, *Korea – Various Measures on Beef (2001)*, para. 135.
253 See Appellate Body Report, *EC – Asbestos (2001)*, para. 100.
254 See Appellate Body Report, *Korea – Various Measures on Beef (2001)*, para. 136. See also, for example, Panel Report, *India – Autos (2002)*, para. 7.199.
255 Panel Report, *US – Section 337 Tariff Act (1989)*, para. 5.11. Emphasis added.
256 Appellate Body Report, *Korea – Various Measures on Beef (2001)*, para. 137.

although the tax stamp requirement is applied in a formally equal manner to domestic and imported cigarettes, it does modify the conditions of competition in the marketplace to the detriment of imports. The tax stamp requirement imposes additional processes and costs on imported products. It also leads to imported cigarettes being presented to final consumers in a less appealing manner.[257]

As already noted above, the Appellate Body ruled in *EC – Asbestos (2001)* that for a measure to be inconsistent with Article III:4 that measure must accord:

to the group of 'like' *imported* products 'less favourable treatment' than it accords to the group of 'like' *domestic* products.[258]

When establishing whether there is 'treatment less favourable', what is to be compared is the treatment given to the *group* of imported products as a whole and the treatment given to the *group* of like domestic products as a whole.[259] However, this does not mean that for there to be 'treatment less favourable', every single product in the group of imported products must be given treatment less favourable compared to every single product in the group of like domestic products. A measure, which does not accord treatment less favourable to *some* products in the group of imported products, may still be found to accord 'treatment less favourable' to the whole *group* of imported products.

The panel in *US – Gasoline (1996)* ruled that under Article III:4, as under Articles I:1 and III:2,[260] balancing *less* favourable treatment to some imported products with *more* favourable treatment to other imported products does not save a measure from a finding of inconsistency. In *US – Gasoline (1996)*, the panel rejected the US contention that the regulation at issue was not inconsistent with Article III:4 because it treated imported products and domestic products 'equally overall'.[261] The panel noted that:

the argument that on average the treatment provided was equivalent amounted to arguing that *less* favourable treatment in one instance could be *offset* provided that there was correspondingly *more* favourable treatment in another. This amounted to claiming that less favourable treatment of particular imported products in some instances would be balanced by more favourable treatment of particular products in others.[262]

The panel rejected this argument, recalling that the panel in *US – Section 337 Tariff Act (1989)* had already held that:

the 'no less favourable' treatment requirement of Article III:4 has to be understood as applicable to each individual case of imported products. The Panel rejected any notion of balancing more favourable treatment of some imported products against less favourable treatment

---

257 Panel Report, *Dominican Republic – Import and Sale of Cigarettes (2005)*, para. 7.196. The panel noted that the Dominican Republic could have chosen to apply the tax stamp requirement in a different manner to imported products than on domestic products, to ensure that the treatment accorded to them is *de facto* not less favourable. See *ibid.*, para. 7.197.
258 Appellate Body Report, *EC – Asbestos (2001)*, para. 100.
259 See *ibid.*   260 See above, pp. 323–5 and pp. 368–9.
261 See Panel Report, *US – Gasoline (1996)*, para. 6.14.
262 *Ibid.* The panel referred to Panel Report, *US – Section 337 Tariff Act (1989)*, para. 5.14.

of other imported products. If this notion were accepted, it would entitle a [Member] to derogate from the no less favourable treatment obligation in one case, or indeed in respect of one [Member], on the ground that it accords more favourable treatment in some other case, or to another [Member]. Such an interpretation would lead to great uncertainty about the conditions of competition between imported and domestic products and thus defeat the purposes of Article III.[263]

In brief, under Article III:4, as under Articles I:1 and III:2,[264] balancing *less* favourable treatment to some imported products with *more* favourable treatment to other imported products does not save a measure from a finding of inconsistency.

In *Canada – Wheat Exports and Grain Imports (2004)*, the panel stated that the measures at issue (i.e. a prohibition on depositing foreign grain in Canadian grain elevators unless specifically authorised; the granting of a standing mixing authorisation for Eastern Canadian grain only; and the application of a revenue cap for rail transportation of Western Canadian grain only) would appear to be inconsistent with Article III:4 of the GATT 1994 because imported grain is treated less favourably than like domestic grain.[265] However, as the panel noted, Canada argued with regard to, for example, the first of the measures at issue (the authorisation requirement for foreign grain to be deposited in grain elevators) that the measure at issue:

does not adversely affect the conditions of competition for imported grain as compared with like domestic grain. More particularly, Canada argues that the authorization process is not onerous; that elevator operators are very familiar with the process; that authorizations are consistently granted; that the CGC [Canadian Grain Commission] has discretion to always authorize receipt of foreign grain; and that advance authorization may be obtained.[266]

The panel recognised that there may be legitimate reasons for Canada to treat domestic grain and 'like' imported grain differently, for example because the latter has not been subjected to the Canadian quality assurance system, which imposes certain restrictions and conditions on Canadian grain, including with respect to production.[267] However, it was not clear to the panel how the arguments put forward by Canada to justify the difference in treatment between domestic grain and 'like' imported grain could support the conclusion that the measure at issue treated imported grain 'no less favourably' than 'like' domestic grain. The panel, therefore, confirmed its provisional conclusion that the authorisation requirement for foreign grain to enter grain elevators is, as such, inconsistent with Article III:4 of the GATT 1994.[268] Moreover, the panel also made clear that a *de*

---

263 Panel Report, *US – Section 337 Tariff Act (1989)*, para. 5.14. See in this context also Appellate Body Report, *Thailand – Cigarettes (Philippines) (2011)*, para. 139.
264 See above, pp. 323–5 and pp. 368–9.
265 See Panel Reports, *Canada – Wheat Exports and Grain Imports (2004)*, paras. 6.187, 6.290 and 6.352.
266 *Ibid.*, para. 6.188.   267 See *ibid.*, para. 6.209.
268 See *ibid.*, para. 6.214. Similar findings were made with regard to Canada's defences relating to the advantage of standing mixing authorisation it granted to Eastern Canadian grain only and relating to the revenue cap on rail transportation of Western Canadian grain. See *ibid.*, paras. 6.297 and 6.359.

minimis impact of the measure does not prevent it from finding that the measure treated imported products less favourably. The panel stated:

That the requirement in question may not be very onerous in commercial and/or practical terms does not, in our view, detract from the fact that it is an additional requirement not imposed on like domestic grain.[269]

In a footnote, the panel noted that neither the text of Article III:4 nor GATT/WTO case law indicates that there is a *de minimis* exception to the 'no less favourable treatment' requirement in Article III:4.[270]

As the Appellate Body found in *US – FSC (Article 21.5 – EC) (2002)*, and reaffirmed in *Thailand – Cigarettes (Philippines) (2011)*, an examination of whether a measure involves less favourable treatment 'need not be based on the actual effects of the contested measure in the marketplace'.[271] The fact that no 'actual effects' of the measure in the market are required means that 'potential effects' of the measure may suffice as a basis for a finding that a measure involves 'less favourable treatment'. Above, it has been explained why this is so.[272] The panels in *India – Autos (2002)* and *China – Publications and Audiovisual Products (2010)* considered that, for a measure to afford 'less favourable treatment' to imported products, it is required that this measure 'is more than likely'[273] or 'may reasonably be expected'[274] to modify adversely the conditions of competition. The Appellate Body in *Thailand – Cigarettes (Philippines) (2011)*, however, found that an analysis of 'less favourable treatment' should not be anchored in an assessment of the degree of likelihood that an adverse impact on competitive conditions will materialise. The Appellate Body ruled:

Rather, an analysis under Article III:4 must begin with careful scrutiny of the measure, including consideration of the design, structure, and expected operation of the measure at issue. Such scrutiny may well involve – but does not require – an assessment of the contested measure in the light of evidence regarding the actual effects of that measure in the market.[275]

It is clear that measures imposing an additional administrative burden or hurdle on imported products may modify the competitive conditions of such products in the marketplace, and may thus be found to accord 'treatment less favourable'. The panel in *US – Section 337 Tariff Act (1989)* found that the fact that patent infringement claims regarding *imported* products could be brought in the US International Trade Commission (USITC), in a federal district court, or in both fora, while patent infringement claims regarding *domestic* products could only be

---

269 Panel Report, *Canada – Wheat Exports and Grain Imports (2004)*, para. 6.190.
270 See *ibid.*, footnote 281 to para. 6.190.
271 Appellate Body Report, *US – FSC (Article 21.5 – EC) (2002)*, para. 215; and Appellate Body Report, *Thailand – Cigarettes (Philippines) (2011)*, para. 135. Of course, nothing *prevents* a panel from considering evidence relating to actual effects of the contested measure in the market place. See *ibid.*, para. 129.
272 See above, p. 353.   273 Panel Report, *India – Autos (2002)*, para. 7.201.
274 Panel Report, *China – Publications and Audiovisual Products (2010)*, para. 7.1471.
275 Appellate Body Report, *Thailand – Cigarettes (Philippines) (2011)*, para. 134.

brought in a federal district court, constituted less favourable treatment for the imported products.[276] In *Thailand – Cigarettes (Philippines) (2011)*, however, the Appellate Body added a cautionary note in this respect:

[W]here a Member's legal system applies a single regulatory regime to both imported and like domestic products, with the sole difference being that an additional requirement is imposed only on imported products, the existence of this additional requirement may provide a significant indication that imported products are treated less favourably. Because, however, the examination of whether imported products are treated less favourably 'cannot rest on simple assertion', close scrutiny of the measure at issue will normally require further identification or elaboration of its implications for the conditions of competition in order properly to support a finding of less favourable treatment under Article III:4 of the GATT 1994.[277]

In other words, the mere existence of an additional requirement on imported products does *not automatically* lead to the conclusion that imported products are accorded 'treatment less favourable'.

Finally, note that, in *Korea – Various Measures on Beef (2001)*, the Appellate Body found that a measure, which does *not legally require* certain treatment of imports, may still be considered to accord 'treatment less favourable'. This may be so when such measure creates incentives for market participants to behave in certain ways, and thereby has the 'practical effect' of treating imported products less favourably.[278] Following this line of reasoning, the panel in *Mexico – Taxes on Soft Drinks (2006)* found with respect to the tax exemptions at issue in that case:

The challenged measures create an economic incentive for producers to use cane sugar as a sweetener in the production of soft drinks and syrups, instead of other non-cane sugar sweeteners such as beet sugar or HFCS ... These measures do not legally impede producers from using non-cane sugar sweeteners ... However, they significantly modify the conditions of competition between cane sugar, on the one hand, and non-cane sugar sweeteners, such as beet sugar or HFCS, on the other.[279]

As discussed above, the Appellate Body ruled in *Korea – Various Measures on Beef (2001)* that imported products are treated less favourably than like products if a measure modifies the conditions of competition in the relevant market *to the detriment of imported products*.[280] However, it has been argued by some that the Appellate Body ruled in *Dominican Republic – Import and Sale of Cigarettes*

276 See Panel Report, *US – Section 337 Tariff Act (1989)*, para. 5.18.
277 Appellate Body Report, *Thailand – Cigarettes (Philippines) (2011)*, para. 130. Note that the Appellate Body in this case indicated that 'the Panel might have made further inquiry into the issue', but found that 'the Panel's analysis was sufficient to support its finding that the additional administrative requirements modify the conditions of competition to the detriment of imported cigarettes'. See *ibid.*, para. 138.
278 See Appellate Body Report, *Korea – Various Measures on Beef (2001)*, para. 144–5. See also Appellate Body Reports, *China – Auto Parts (2009)*, paras. 195 and 196; and Appellate Body Reports, *US – COOL (2012)*, para. 288. For a detailed discussion of *US – COOL (2012)*, see below, p. 858.
279 Panel Report, *Mexico – Taxes on Soft Drinks (2006)*, para. 8.117. 'HFCS' stands for 'high fructose corn syrup'.
280 See above, p. 396.

(2005) that panels, in examining whether a measure accords treatment less favourable, should inquire further whether 'the detrimental effect is unrelated to the foreign origin of the product'.[281] The relevant measure in *Dominican Republic – Import and Sale of Cigarettes (2005)* was a requirement that importers and domestic producers post a bond of 5 million Dominican pesos (RD$). Honduras argued that the requirement to post a bond of RD$5 million accorded 'less favourable treatment' to imported cigarettes because, as the sales of domestic cigarettes are greater than those of imported cigarettes on the Dominican Republic market, the per unit cost of the bond requirement for imported cigarettes is higher than for domestic products.[282] The panel in *Dominican Republic – Import and Sale of Cigarettes (2005)* found that Honduras had failed to establish that the measure at issue accorded less favourable treatment to imported cigarettes.[283] On appeal, the Appellate Body upheld the panel's finding.[284] In its report, the Appellate Body stated, *inter alia*, that:

the existence of a detrimental effect on a given imported product resulting from a measure does not necessarily imply that this measure accords less favourable treatment to imports if the detrimental effect is explained by factors or circumstances unrelated to the foreign origin of the product, such as the market share of the importer in this case.[285]

In *US – Clove Cigarettes (2012)*, the Appellate Body recognised that this statement, 'when read in isolation, could be viewed as suggesting that further inquiry into the rationale for the detrimental impact is necessary'.[286] The Appellate Body noted, however, that it rejected Honduras' claim under Article III:4 because 'the difference between the per-unit costs of the bond requirement alleged by Honduras is explained by the fact that the importer of Honduran cigarettes has a smaller market share than two domestic producers'.[287] Thus, in *Dominican Republic – Import and Sale of Cigarettes (2005)*, the Appellate Body merely held that the higher *per unit* costs of the bond requirement for imported cigarettes did not conclusively demonstrate less favourable treatment, because such costs were not attributable to the specific measure at issue but, rather, were a function of sales volumes. The Appellate Body noted that it had already ruled in *Thailand – Cigarettes (Philippines) (2011)* that to support a finding of 'treatment less favourable' under Article III:4:

there must be in every case a genuine relationship between the measure at issue and its adverse impact on competitive opportunities for imported versus like domestic products.[288]

281 See e.g.: United States' appellant's submission in *US – Clove Cigarettes (2012)*, para. 101, referred to in Appellate Body Report, *US – Clove Cigarettes (2012)*. footnote 372 to para. 17. See also Panel Report, *EC – Approval and Marketing of Biotech Products (2006)*, para. 7.2514.
282 See Appellate Body Report, para. 96.
283 See Panel Report, *Dominican Republic – Import and Sale of Cigarettes (2005)*, paras. 7.311 and 7.316.
284 See Appellate Body Report, *Dominican Republic – Import and Sale of Cigarettes (2005)*, para. 96.
285 *Ibid.*
286 Appellate Body Report, *US – Clove Cigarettes (2012)*, footnote 372 to para. 179. For a discussion on *US – Clove Cigarettes (2012)*, see below, pp. 863–72.
287 *Ibid.*
288 Appellate Body Report, *Thailand – Cigarettes (Philippines) (2011)*, para. 134.

Thus, a finding of 'treatment less favourable' does not require that the detrimental impact of the measure on the conditions of competition is related to the foreign origin of the products, but does require that there is a *genuine relationship* between the measure and the detrimental impact. In other words, if a genuine relationship between the measure and the detrimental impact exists, the measure may be found to accord 'treatment less favourable' even if the detrimental impact can be explained by factors or circumstances that are unrelated to the foreign origin of the product.

GATT and WTO panels and the Appellate Body have found a wide variety of measures inconsistent with the national treatment obligation of Article III:4. In addition to the reasoning discussed above, the following reasoning by panels or the Appellate Body is also noteworthy and further illustrates the broad scope of the national treatment obligation of Article III:4. With respect to minimum price requirements, the panel in *Canada – Provincial Liquor Boards (US) (1992)* ruled that:

> minimum prices applied equally to imported and domestic beer did not necessarily accord equal conditions of competition to imported and domestic beer. Whenever they prevented imported beer from being supplied at a price below that of domestic beer, they accorded in fact treatment to imported beer less favourable than that accorded to domestic beer: when they were set at the level at which domestic brewers supplied beer – as was presently the case in New Brunswick and Newfoundland – they did not change the competitive opportunities accorded to domestic beer but did affect the competitive opportunities of imported beer which could otherwise be supplied below the minimum price.[289]

With respect to a general ban on cigarette advertising, the panel in *Thailand – Cigarettes (1990)* noted:

> It might be argued that such a general ban on all cigarette advertising would create unequal competitive opportunities between the existing Thai supplier of cigarettes and new, foreign suppliers and was therefore contrary to Article III:4.[290]

The panel in *US – Malt Beverages (1992)* found with regard to regulations concerning internal transportation that:

> the requirement for imported beer and wine to be transported by common carrier, whereas domestic in-state beer and wine is not so required, may result in additional charges to transport these imported products and therefore prevent imported products from competing on an equal footing with domestic like products.[291]

Questions and Assignments 5.13

Can a Member treat 'like' products differently without acting inconsistently with Article III:4 of the GATT 1994? What treatment of imported products constitutes 'treatment less

---

289 Panel Report, *Canada – Provincial Liquor Boards (US) (1992)*, para. 5.30.
290 Panel Report, *Thailand – Cigarettes (1990)*, para. 78. Note that such a general ban on cigarette advertising was not the measure at issue in this case but a suggested alternative measure of which the panel considered the GATT-consistency.
291 Panel Report, *US – Malt Beverages (1992)*, para. 5.50.

favourable' within the meaning of Article III:4? Can a measure that potentially (but not actually) modifies the conditions of competition on the market to the detriment of the imported products be considered to involve 'less favourable treatment' within the meaning of Article III:4? Is there a '*de minimis* test' or a 'balancing justification' under Article III:4? Is there tension between, on the one hand, the fact that balancing *less* favourable treatment with *more* favourable treatment does not save a measure from a finding of 'treatment less favourable', and, on the other hand, the fact that to find 'treatment less favourable' a measure must accord to the *group* of imported products 'less favourable treatment' than it accords to the *group* of 'like' domestic products? Give three examples of internal regulations which panels found to be inconsistent with Article III:4 of the GATT 1994. Can a measure be found to accord 'treatment less favourable' when the detrimental impact of that measure on the conditions of competition is not related to the foreign origin of the products concerned?

3 NATIONAL TREATMENT UNDER THE GATS

Article XVII of the GATS, which is entitled 'National Treatment', states, in paragraph 1:

In the sectors inscribed in its Schedule, and subject to any conditions and qualifications set out therein, each Member shall accord to services and service suppliers of any other Member, in respect of all measures affecting the supply of services, treatment no less favourable than that it accords to its own like services and service suppliers.

This section first explores the nature of the national treatment obligation of Article XVII:1 of the GATS and then discusses the test of consistency with this obligation.[292]

3.1 Nature of the National Treatment Obligation of Article XVII:1 of the GATS

The national treatment obligation of Article XVII:1 of the GATS is different from the national treatment obligation of Article III of the GATT 1994. As discussed above, the national treatment obligation of Article III of the GATT 1994 has *general* application to all measures affecting trade in goods.[293] On the contrary, the national treatment obligation for trade in services of Article XVII:1 of the GATS does not have such general application; it does not apply to all measures affecting trade in services. The national treatment obligation *only* applies to a measure affecting trade in services *to the extent* that a WTO Member has explicitly committed itself to grant 'national treatment' in respect of the specific services sector concerned. Such commitments are set out in a Member's 'Schedule of Specific Commitments', also referred to as its 'Services Schedule'. These commitments to

---

292 On the relationship between the national treatment obligation of Article XVII:1 of the GATS and the market access obligation of Article XVI:1 of the GATS, see below, pp. 525–7.
293 See above, p. 353.

grant national treatment are often made subject to certain conditions, qualifications and limitations, which are also set out in the Schedule. A Member can, for example, grant national treatment in a specific services sector only with respect to certain modes of supply (such as cross-border supply) and not others (such as commercial presence).[294] Typical national treatment limitations included in Services Schedules relate to: (1) nationality or residence requirements for service suppliers; (2) requirements to invest a certain amount of assets in local currency; (3) restrictions on the purchase of land by foreign service suppliers; (4) special subsidy or tax privileges granted only to domestic service suppliers; and (5) differential capital requirements and special operational limits applying only to operations of foreign service suppliers.[295]

Note, by way of example, the national treatment column of the Services Schedule of the European Union and its Member States with respect to higher education services, as included in Figure 5.1. It appears from this Schedule that the European Union and its Member States agreed to accord national treatment to higher education services supplied in mode 1 ('cross-border supply') (with a qualification by Italy), mode 2 ('consumption abroad') and mode 3 ('commercial presence'). However, no commitment to accord national treatment is made with regard to mode 4 ('presence of natural persons'), except commitments made for all services sectors (see 'horizontal commitments').[296]

To determine the scope of the national treatment obligation of a Member, or to determine whether, in respect of a specific services sector, a Member must grant national treatment to services and service suppliers of other Members, it is necessary to examine the commitments, conditions, qualifications and limitations set out in the Member's Schedule very carefully. The Services Schedules of Members can be found on the WTO website.[297]

Generally speaking, many Members, especially developing-country Members, have made national treatment commitments with regard to a limited number of services sectors only, and when commitments are made, they are often accompanied by extensive limitations. Negotiations on more ambitious national treatment commitments are an important element of the ongoing negotiations on trade in services in the context of the Doha Round.

As all other non-discrimination obligations in both the GATT 1994 and the GATS, also the national treatment obligation of Article XVII:1 of the GATS covers both *de jure* and *de facto* discrimination.[298] In fact, unlike for other non-discrimination obligations, for the national treatment obligation under the

---

294 On the modes of supply of services, see above, p. 339.
295 See WTO Secretariat, *Market Access: Unfinished Business*, Special Series Studies 6 (WTO, 2001), 103.
296 On 'horizontal commitments', see above, p. 523.
297 See www.wto.org/english/tratop_e/serv_e/serv_commitments_e.htm, visited on 15 February 2013. For an explanation on how to 'read' Services Schedules, see below, pp. 522–9.
298 See e.g. Panel Report, *EC – Bananas III (Article 21.5 – Ecuador) (1999)*, para. 6.126; and Decision by the Arbitrators, *EC – Bananas III (US) (Article 22.6 – EC) (1999)*, paras. 5.89–5.95.

Sector or Sub-Sector	Limitations on Market Access	Limitations on National Treatment
C. Higher Education Services (CPC 923)	5. PRIVATELY FUNDED EDUCATION SERVICES	
	1) F: Condition of nationality. However, third country nationals can have authorization from competent authorities to establish and direct an education institution and to teach.	1) I: Condition of nationality for service providers to be authorised to issue state recognised diplomas.
	2) None	2) None
	3) E, I: Needs test for opening of private universities authorised to issue recognised diplomas or degrees; producers involves an advice of the Parliament. GR: Unbound for education institutions granting recognised State diplomas.	3) None
	4) Unbound except as indicated in the horizontal section and subject to the following specific limitations: DK: Condition of nationality for professors. F: Condition of nationality. However, third country nationals may obtain authorization from competent authorities to establish and direct an education institution and to teach. I: Condition of nationality for service providers to be authorised to issue state recognised diplomas.	4) Unbound except as indicated in the horizontal section

Figure 5.1 Excerpt from the Services Schedule of the European Union and its Member States

GATS, the treaty text clearly indicates that *de facto* discrimination is covered by this obligation. As discussed further below, Article XVII:3 states:

Formally identical or formally different *treatment* shall be considered to be less favourable if it modifies the conditions of competition in favour of services or service suppliers of the Member compared to like services or service suppliers of any other Member.[299]

The 2001 *Scheduling Guidelines* give the following example of a *de facto* discriminatory measure:

A measure [which] stipulates that prior residency is required for the issuing of a licence to supply a service.[300]

With regard to this measure, the *Scheduling Guidelines* note:

Although the measure does not formally distinguish service suppliers on the basis of national origin, it *de facto* offers less favourable treatment to foreign service suppliers because

---

299 Emphasis added.
300 *Guidelines for the Scheduling of Specific Commitments under the General Agreement on Trade in Services*, adopted by the Council for Trade in Services on 23 March 2001, S/L/92, dated 28 March 2001, 6.

they are less likely to be able to meet a prior residency requirement than like service suppliers of national origin.[301]

The panel in *China – Electronic Payment Services (2012)* deduced from Article XVII:3 that the objective of the national treatment obligation of Article XVII:1 is 'to ensure equal competitive opportunities for like services [and like service suppliers] of other Members'.[302]

Questions and Assignments 5.14

In your country, are health care and legal services subject to the national treatment obligation of Article XVII:1 of the GATS? Are these services subject to the national treatment obligation in the European Union, the United States, China, India and Brazil? Give an example of a *de facto* discriminatory measure affecting trade in services (other than the example given above).

3.2 National Treatment Test of Article XVII:1 of the GATS

In its analysis of the consistency of the EC licensing regime for the importation of bananas with the national treatment obligation under Article XVII:1 of the GATS, the panel in *EC – Bananas III (1997)* noted:

In order to establish a breach of the national treatment obligation of Article XVII, three elements need to be demonstrated: (i) the EC has undertaken a commitment in a relevant sector and mode of supply; (ii) the EC has adopted or applied a measure affecting the supply of services in that sector and/or mode of supply; and (iii) the measure accords to service suppliers of any other Member treatment less favourable than that it accords to the EC's own like service suppliers.[303]

The panels in *China – Publications and Audiovisual Products (2010)* and *China – Electronic Payment Services (2012)* structured their analysis of the consistency with Article XVII:1 of the measures at issue in these cases along the same broad lines.[304]

Article XVII:1 of the GATS thus sets out a four-tier test of consistency with the national treatment obligation thereof. This test of consistency requires the examination of:

- whether, and to what extent, a *national treatment commitment* was made in respect of the relevant services sector;
- whether the measure at issue is a *measure by a Member affecting trade in services*, i.e. a measure to which the GATS applies;
- whether the foreign and domestic services or service suppliers are '*like services*' or '*like service suppliers*'; and
- whether the foreign services or service suppliers are accorded '*treatment no less favourable*'.

---

301 *Ibid.*   302 Panel Report, *China – Electronic Payment Services (2012)*, para. 7.700.
303 Panel Reports, *EC – Bananas III (1997)*, para. 7.314. See also Panel Report, *EC – Bananas III (Article 21.5 – Ecuador) (1999)*, para. 6.100.
304 See, for example, Panel Report, *China – Publications and Audiovisual Products (2010)*, paras. 7.942 *et seq.*

Below, each element of this four-tier test of consistency will be discussed in turn.[305]

To date, WTO Members have been found to have acted inconsistently with the national treatment obligation of Article XVII:1 of the GATS in six disputes.[306]

3.2.1   National Treatment Commitment

As explained above, the national treatment obligation of Article XVII:1 of the GATS does not apply generally to all trade in services. The national treatment obligation applies only to the extent that a WTO Member has explicitly committed itself to grant 'national treatment' in respect of a specific services sector.[307] In applying Article XVII:1, panels must therefore first examine the responding Member's Services Schedule to establish whether, and to what extent, that Member has made a national treatment commitment with respect to the services sector at issue in the dispute.

In *China – Publications and Audiovisual Products (2010)*, the issue arose whether China had made a national treatment commitment with respect to the distribution of sound recordings through electronic means. China argued that the entry 'Sound recording distribution services' under the heading 'Audiovisual Services' (sector 2.D) in China's Services Schedule, with regard to which it had made a national treatment commitment, does *not* extend to the distribution of sound recordings through electronic means. According to China, the entry at issue covers only the distribution of sound recordings in physical form, for example, music embedded on compact discs (CDs). This dispute thus called for an interpretation of China's Services Schedule and in particular the meaning and scope of the entry 'Sound recording distribution services'. After interpreting this entry in accordance with Articles 31 and 32 of the *Vienna Convention on the Law of Treaties*, the panel concluded that China's commitment in the entry 'Sound recording distribution services' covers both physical distribution as well as the electronic distribution of sound recordings.[308] The Appellate Body upheld the panel's finding. After reviewing the panel's reasoning, the Appellate Body concluded that the panel did not err in its consideration of dictionary definitions of the terms 'sound recording' and 'distribution'.[309] Furthermore, the Appellate Body was persuaded that, on balance, the analysis of a number of contextual elements (such as China's Services Schedule, provisions of the GATS,

---

305 See below, pp. 407–8, pp. 408–9, pp. 409–12 and pp. 412–14.

306 See *EC – Bananas III (1997)*; *EC – Bananas III (Article 21.5 – Ecuador) (1999)*; *EC – Bananas III (US) (Article 22.6 – EC) (1999)*; *Canada – Autos (2000)*; *China – Publications and Audiovisual Products (2010)*; and *China – Electronic Payment Services (2012)*.

307 On the concept of 'services sectors', see below. A list of the services sectors is contained in GATT Secretariat, *Note by the Secretariat, Services Sectoral Classification List*, MTN.GNS/W/120, dated 10 July 1991. A Member's national treatment commitments are set out in its Services Schedule. See below, pp. 522–7.

308 See Panel Report, *China – Publications and Audiovisual Products (2010)*, para. 7.1265.

309 See Appellate Body Report, *China – Publications and Audiovisual Products (2010)*, para. 357.

and the Services Schedules of other Members) supported the interpretation of China's commitment on 'Sound recording distribution services' as including the electronic distribution of sound recordings.[310] With regard to the object and purpose of the GATS, the Appellate Body noted that it did not consider that the principle of progressive liberalisation – a core purpose of the GATS – lends support to an interpretation that would constrain the scope and coverage of specific commitments that have already been undertaken by Members.[311] More generally, the Appellate Body considered in *China – Publications and Audiovisual Products (2010)* that the terms used in China's Services Schedule ('sound recording' and 'distribution') are 'sufficiently generic that what they apply to may change over time'.[312] Even more generally, the Appellate Body noted in this respect that the Services Schedules, like the GATS itself and all WTO agreements, constitute 'multilateral treaties with continuing obligations that WTO Members entered into for an indefinite period of time'.[313] The Appellate Body further stated that:

interpreting the terms of GATS specific commitments based on the notion that the ordinary meaning to be attributed to those terms can only be the meaning that they had at the time the Schedule was concluded would mean that very similar or identically worded commitments could be given different meanings, content, and coverage depending on the date of their adoption or the date of a Member's accession to the treaty. Such interpretation would undermine the predictability, security, and clarity of GATS specific commitments ...[314]

3.2.2 'Measures by Members Affecting Trade in Services'

The second element of the test of consistency with the national treatment obligation of Article XVII:1 of the GATS relates to the question of whether the measure at issue is a measure by a Member affecting trade in services, i.e. a measure to which the GATS applies. As discussed above in the context of the MFN treatment obligation of Article II:1 of the GATS, the concept of a 'measure by a Member' is broad, including not only measures of central government or authorities but also measures of regional and local governments and authorities as well as – in specific circumstances – measures of non-governmental bodies.[315]

The concept of a 'measure affecting trade in services' has been clarified by the Appellate Body in *Canada – Autos (2000)*, where it stated that two key issues must be examined to determine whether a measure is one 'affecting trade in services', namely, first, whether there is 'trade in services' in the sense of Article I:2, and, secondly, whether the measure at issue 'affects' such trade in services within the meaning of Article I:1.[316] Recall, with respect to the first question, the broad scope of the concept of 'trade in services', including all services except services supplied in the exercise of governmental authority. Trade in services

---

310 See *ibid.*, para. 387.   311 See *ibid.*, para. 394.   312 *Ibid.*, para. 396.
313 *Ibid.*   314 *Ibid.*, para. 397.   315 See above, p. 322.
316 See Appellate Body Report, *Canada – Autos (2000)*, para. 155. See above, p. 338.

includes services supplied in any of the four distinct modes of supply (cross-border supply, consumption abroad, commercial presence and the presence of natural persons).[317] With respect to the second question, recall that, for a measure to 'affect' trade in services, this measure need not regulate or govern the trade in, i.e. the supply of, services. A measure affects trade in services when the measure bears 'upon the conditions of competition in supply of a service'.[318] The panel in *China – Publications and Audiovisual Products (2010)* noted in the context of its assessment of the prohibition on wholesale trading of reading materials that the term 'affecting' is wider in scope than 'regulating' or 'governing', and thus concluded that the measures at issue 'affect' the supply of reading materials distribution services for the purpose of Article XVII:1.[319]

3.2.3 'Like Services' or 'Like Service Suppliers'

The third element of the test of consistency with the national treatment obligation of Article XVII:1 of the GATS relates to the question of whether the foreign and domestic services or service suppliers are 'like services' or 'like service suppliers'. It is only between 'like services' or 'like service suppliers' that the national treatment obligation applies and that discrimination within the meaning of Article XVII:1 of the GATS may occur. Services or service suppliers that are not 'like' may be treated differently; different treatment of services or service suppliers that are not 'like' will not constitute discrimination within the meaning of Article XVII:1. For the application of the national treatment obligation of Article XVII:1, it is therefore important to be able to determine whether, for example, movie actors are 'like' stage actors, whether the distribution of books is 'like' the distribution of e-books; whether doctors with a foreign medical degree are 'like' doctors with a domestic medical degree; whether Internet gambling is 'like' casino gambling; and whether a 500-partner law firm is 'like' a sole practitioner.

As already noted above in Chapter 4, the GATS does not define the terms 'like services' and 'like service suppliers'. However, unlike in the context of the MFN treatment obligation under the GATS, there is useful case law regarding the meaning of the terms 'like services' and 'like service suppliers' in the context of the national treatment obligation. The panel in *China – Publications and Audiovisual Products (2010)* noted in the context of its assessment of the consistency of the prohibition on wholesale trading of reading materials with Article XVII:1 that:

[t]he measures at issue distinguish between suppliers that may be permitted to engage in the wholesale of imported reading materials and suppliers that are prohibited from engaging in this service, based exclusively on the suppliers' origin. When origin is the only factor on which a measure bases a difference of treatment between domestic service suppliers and foreign suppliers, the 'like service suppliers' requirement is met, provided there will, or

---

317 See above, p. 404.   318 See above, p. 405.
319 See Panel Report, *China – Publications and Audiovisual Products (2010)*, para. 7.971.

can, be domestic and foreign suppliers that under the measure are the same in all material respects except for origin.[320]

However, the panel observed that, in cases where a difference of treatment is not exclusively linked to the origin of service suppliers, but to other factors, a more detailed (and undoubtedly more demanding) analysis would probably be required to determine whether service suppliers on either side of the dividing line are, or are not, 'like'.[321] *China – Electronic Payment Services (2012)* was such a case.[322] Referring to the considerable body of case law on 'likeness' in the context of Article III of the GATT 1994,[323] the panel first observed that it did not assume that 'without further analysis, [it] may simply transpose' to trade in services the criteria or analytical framework used to determine 'likeness' in the context of Article III of the GATT 1994.[324] The panel noted that there are 'important dissimilarities' between the two areas of trade, such as the intangible nature of services, their supply through four different modes, and possible differences in how trade in services is conducted and regulated.[325] The determination of 'likeness' in the context of Article XVII:1 of the GATS undoubtedly raises even more difficult conceptual problems than the determination of 'likeness' in the context of Article III of the GATT 1994.

The panel in *China – Electronic Payment Services (2012)* observed that the dictionary defines 'like' as:

[h]aving the same characteristics or qualities as some other person or thing; of approximately identical shape, size, etc., with something else; similar.[326]

According to the panel, this range of meanings suggests that:

for services to be considered 'like', they need not necessarily be exactly the same, and that in view of the references to 'approximately' and 'similar', services could qualify as 'like' if they are essentially or generally the same.[327]

The panel further noted that the dictionary definition of 'like' made clear that something or someone is 'like' *in some respect*, such as – in the terms of the definition – the 'shape, size, etc.' of a thing or person. To determine in what respect services need to be essentially the same for them to be 'like', the panel subsequently turned to consider the context of the term 'like services', and, in

---

320 *Ibid.*, para. 7.975. In support of this ruling, the panel referred to Panel Report, *Canada – Wheat Exports and Grain Imports (2004)*, paras. 6.164–6.167, and Panel Report *Argentina – Hides and Leather (2001)*, paras. 11.168–11.169. Although these cases concern trade in goods, the panel considered that the same reasoning applies in the context of Article XVII:1 of the GATS. See also Panel Report, *China – Electronic Payment Services (2012)*, para. 7.695.

321 See Panel Report, *China – Publications and Audiovisual Products (2010)*, para. 7.975. See also Panel Report, *China – Electronic Payment Services (2012)*, para. 7.697.

322 See Panel Report, *China – Electronic Payment Services (2012)*, para. 7.697.

323 See above, pp. 360–8.

324 See Panel Report, *China – Electronic Payment Services (2012)*, para. 7.698.

325 See *ibid.*

326 Panel Report, *China – Electronic Payment Services (2012)*, para. 7.699.

327 *Ibid.*

particular, Article XVII:3 of the GATS. As discussed below, Article XVII:3 clarifies the 'treatment no less favourable' requirement of Article XVII:1 and states that a Member is deemed to provide less favourable treatment if it 'modifies the conditions of competition in favour of services ... of [that] Member compared to like services ... of any other Member'.[328] According to the panel, this suggests that:

> like services are services that are in a competitive relationship with each other (or would be if they were allowed to be supplied in a particular market).[329]

The panel argued that this is so because:

> only if the foreign and domestic services in question are in such a competitive relationship can a measure of a Member modify the conditions of competition in favour of one or other of these services.[330]

Consistent with the approach to 'likeness' under Article III of the GATT 1994, the panel in *China – Electronic Payment Services (2012)* ruled that any determination of 'likeness' under Article XVII:1 of the GATS should 'take into account the particular circumstances of each case', or, in other words, 'should be made on a case-by-case basis'.[331] Also consistent with the approach to 'likeness' under Article III of the GATT 1994, the panel held that a determination of 'likeness' under Article XVII:1 of the GATS:

> should be based on arguments and evidence that pertain to the competitive relationship of the services being compared.[332]

Moreover, such determination of 'likeness':

> must be made on the basis of the evidence as a whole. [333]

According to the panel in *China – Electronic Payment Services (2012),* services are 'like' for the purposes of Article XVII:1 if:

> it is determined that the services in question in a particular case are essentially or generally the same in competitive terms.[334]

With regard to the 'likeness' of service suppliers, the panel in *China – Electronic Payment Services (2012)* recalled that the panel in *EC – Bananas III (1997)* had found that, to the extent that service suppliers provide 'like services', they are 'like service suppliers'.[335] The panel in *China – Electronic Payment Services (2012)* agreed that the fact that service suppliers provide like services might in some cases 'raise a presumption' that they are 'like' service suppliers. However,

---

328 See below, p. 412.   329 Panel Report, *China – Electronic Payment Services (2012)*, para. 7.700.
330 *Ibid.*
331 *Ibid.*, para. 7.701. For the relevant case law under Article III of the GATT 1994, see above, p. 406 and p. 410.
332 *Ibid.*, para. 7.702. For the relevant case law under Article III of the GATT 1994, see above, p. 406 and p. 410.
333 *Ibid.* For the relevant case law under Article III of the GATT 1994, see above, p. 406 and p. 410.
334 *Ibid.*
335 See Panel Report, *EC – Bananas III (1997)*, para. 7.322. The panel in *EC – Bananas III (1997)* made this statement with regard to both Article II:1 and Article XVII:1 of the GATS. See above, p. 343.

the panel cautioned that, in the specific circumstances of other cases, a separate inquiry into the 'likeness' of the suppliers may be called for.[336] 'Like service suppliers' determinations should be made on a case-by-case basis.[337]

3.2.4 'Treatment no Less Favourable'

The fourth and final element of the test of consistency with the national treatment obligation of Article XVII:1 of the GATS relates to the question of whether the foreign services or service suppliers are accorded treatment no less favourable than 'like' domestic services or service suppliers. Paragraphs 2 and 3 of Article XVII:1 clarify the requirement of 'treatment no less favourable' set out in paragraph 1 by stating:

2. A Member may meet the requirement of paragraph 1 by according to services and service suppliers of any other Member, either formally identical treatment or formally different treatment to that it accords to its own like services and service suppliers.
3. Formally identical or formally different treatment shall be considered to be less favourable if it modifies the conditions of competition in favour of services or service suppliers of the Member compared to like services or service suppliers of any other Member.

It follows that a Member that gives formally identical treatment to foreign and domestic services or service suppliers may nevertheless be in breach of the national treatment obligation. This happens if that Member, by giving formally identical treatment, modifies the conditions of competition in favour of the domestic services or service suppliers. Also, a Member that gives formally *different* treatment to foreign and domestic services or service suppliers does not act in breach of the national treatment obligation if that Member, by giving formally *different* treatment, does not modify the conditions of competition in favour of the domestic services and service suppliers. The latter would obviously be the case if the different treatment would be in favour of the foreign services or service suppliers but it may also be that a formally different treatment has no impact on the conditions of competition. As the panel in *China – Electronic Payment Services (2012)* noted:

subject to all other Article XVII conditions being fulfilled, formally identical or different treatment of service suppliers of another Member constitutes a breach of Article XVII:1 if and only if such treatment modifies the conditions of competition to their detriment.[338]

Note that the panel in this case proceeded with its examination of this fourth and last element of the national treatment test of Article XVII:1 in two steps. First, it analysed whether, and, if so, how, the measures at issue provided for different treatment between domestic services and service suppliers and 'like'

---

336 See Panel Report, *China – Electronic Payment Services (2012)*, para. 7.705. *In casu*, the panel considered no such 'separate inquiry' necessary. See *ibid.*, para. 7.706.
337 See *ibid.*, para. 7.705.   338 *Ibid.*, para. 7.687.

services and service suppliers of other Members. Secondly, it examined whether any different treatment amounts to less favourable treatment.[339] *In casu*, the panel found that there was such different treatment;[340] and that this different treatment amounted to less favourable treatment.[341]

As already discussed above, for the national treatment obligation of Article XVII:1 of the GATS (unlike for other non-discrimination obligations), the treaty text itself, and in particular Article XVII:3, clearly indicates that *de facto* discrimination is covered by this national treatment obligation.[342] Recall that the panel in *EC – Bananas III (Article 21.5 – Ecuador) (1999)* and the arbitrators in *EC – Bananas III (Article 22.6 – US) (1999)* found that certain measures under the revised EC banana import regime accorded to foreign service suppliers, and in particular service suppliers of Ecuador and the United States, *de facto* less favourable conditions of competition than to 'like' EC service suppliers.[343]

In *China – Publications and Audiovisual Products (2010)*, the panel found in the context of its assessment of the prohibition on wholesale trading of reading materials that:

[s]ince the measures at issue have the effect of prohibiting foreign service suppliers from wholesaling imported reading materials, while like Chinese suppliers are permitted to do so, these measures clearly modif[y] the conditions of competition to the detriment of the foreign service supplier and thus constitutes 'less favourable treatment' in terms of Article XVII.[344]

With respect to *inherent* competitive disadvantages resulting from the fact that the service or service supplier is foreign and not domestic, footnote 10 to Article XVII:1 states:

Specific commitments assumed under this Article shall not be construed to require any Member to compensate for any inherent competitive disadvantages which result from the foreign character of the relevant services or service suppliers.

The panel in *Canada – Autos (2000)*, however, stressed the limited scope of this provision as follows:

Footnote 10 to Article XVII only exempts Members from having to compensate for disadvantages due to the foreign character in the application of the national treatment provision; it does not provide cover for actions which might modify the conditions of competition against services or service suppliers which are already disadvantaged due to their foreign character.[345]

Finally, note that the Appellate Body stated in *EC – Bananas III (1997)* that it saw no specific authority in Article XVII:1 of the GATS for the proposition,

---

339 See *ibid.*, para. 7.689.   340 See *ibid.*, paras. 7.709, 7.722 and 7.733.
341 See *ibid.*, paras. 7.712, 7.714, 7.725 and 7.736.   342 See above, p. 405.
343 See Panel Report, *EC – Bananas III (Article 21.5 – Ecuador) (1999)*, para. 6.126; and Decision by the Arbitrators, *EC – Bananas III (US) (Article 22.6 – EC) (1999)*, paras. 5.89–5.95. The measures at issue concerned the criteria for acquiring 'newcomer' status under the revised EC licensing procedures.
344 Panel Report, *China – Publications and Audiovisual Products (2010)*, para. 7.996.
345 Panel Report, *Canada – Autos (2000)*, para. 10.300.

advanced by the European Union, that the 'aims and effects' of a measure are in any way relevant in determining whether that measure is inconsistent with the national treatment obligation of Article XVII:1.[346] Recall that the Appellate Body came to the same finding with regard to the MFN treatment obligation under Article II:1 of the GATS.[347]

Questions and Assignments 5.15

What are the elements of the test of consistency with the national treatment obligation of Article XVII:1 of the GATS? How shall panels interpret Members' national treatment commitments set out in their Services Schedules? Can a national treatment commitment cover a type of service that did not yet exist (for example, because it was not yet technologically feasible or economically viable) at the time the commitment was made? Which measures are 'measures affecting trade in services'? How does one determine whether services or service suppliers are 'like' within the meaning of Article XVII:1? Are all banking services 'like services' within the meaning of Article XVII:1? Are all law firms 'like service suppliers' within the meaning of Article XVII:1? When is there 'treatment less favourable' within the meaning of Article XVII:1? Would subsidies granted only to *domestic* film producers, hospitals or schools be inconsistent with the national treatment obligation of Article XVII:1? In answering this question, focus on the legality of such subsidies when granted by your country. Can a measure, which grants a subsidy to both domestic and foreign service suppliers be inconsistent with the national treatment obligation of Article XVII:1 of the GATS? Does the two-step approach to establishing 'treatment less favourable' followed by the panel in *China – Electronic Payment Services (2012)* suggest that a measure which provides for formally identical treatment, cannot be found to accord 'treatment less favourable'?

4   SUMMARY

There are two main non-discrimination obligations under WTO law: the most-favoured-nation (MFN) treatment obligation, discussed in the previous chapter, and the national treatment obligation, which is discussed in this chapter. In simple terms, a national treatment obligation relates to whether a country favours itself over other countries. A national treatment obligation prohibits a country to discriminate *against* other countries. The national treatment obligation under WTO law applies – albeit not in the same manner – to trade in goods as well as trade in services. The key provision that deals with the national treatment obligation for measures affecting trade in goods is Article III of the GATT 1994. The key provision that deals with the national treatment obligation for measures affecting trade in services is Article XVII:1 of the GATS.

The principal purpose of the national treatment obligation of Article III of the GATT 1994 is to *avoid protectionism* in the application of internal tax and regulatory measures. As is explicitly stated in Article III:1, the purpose of Article III is to ensure that internal measures 'not be applied to imported and domestic

---

346 See Appellate Body Report, *EC – Bananas III (1997)*, para. 241.
347 See above, p. 330.

products so as to afford protection to domestic production'. To this end, Article III obliges WTO Members to provide *equality of competitive conditions* for imported products in relation to domestic products. More, Article III protects the *expectations* of an equal competitive relationship between imported and domestic products.

The test of consistency of internal taxation with the national treatment obligation of Article III:2, first sentence, of the GATT 1994 requires the examination of: (1) whether the measure at issue is an *internal tax or other internal charge* on products; (2) whether the imported and domestic products are *like products*; and (3) whether the imported products are *taxed in excess* of the domestic products.

Article III:2, second sentence, also concerns national treatment with respect to internal taxation, but it contemplates a 'broader category of products' than Article III:2, first sentence. It applies to 'directly competitive or substitutable products'. Article III:2, second sentence, of the GATT 1994 sets out a different test of consistency, which requires the examination of: (1) whether the measure at issue is an *internal tax or other internal charge* on products; (2) whether the imported and domestic products are *directly competitive or substitutable*; (3) whether these products are *dissimilarly taxed*; and (4) whether the dissimilar taxation is applied *so as to afford protection to domestic production*.

The national treatment obligation of Article III of the GATT 1994 concerns not only internal taxation, but also internal regulation. The national treatment obligation for internal regulation is set out in Article III:4. To determine whether a measure is consistent with the national treatment obligation of Article III:4 of the GATT 1994, there is a three-tier test which requires the examination of: (1) whether the measure at issue is a law, regulation or requirement covered by Article III:4; (2) whether the imported and domestic products are 'like products'; and (3) whether the imported products are accorded 'treatment no less favourable'.

The national treatment obligation with respect to measures affecting trade in services is set out in Article XVII:1 of the GATS. The national treatment obligation of Article XVII:1 is different from the national treatment obligation of Article III of the GATT 1994. While the national treatment obligation of Article III of the GATT 1994 has general application to all measures affecting trade in goods, the national treatment obligation of Article XVII:1 of the GATS *only* applies to a measure affecting trade in services *to the extent* that a WTO Member has explicitly committed itself to grant 'national treatment' in respect of the specific services sector concerned. Such commitments are set out in a Member's Services Schedule. Often these commitments are subject to conditions and qualifications limiting the scope of the commitment. To determine whether a measure is consistent with the national treatment obligation of Article XVII:1 of the GATS, there is a four-tier test, which requires the examination of: (1) whether, and to what extent, a *national treatment commitment* was made in respect of the relevant services sector; (2) whether the measure at issue is a *measure by a Member affecting trade in services*; (3) whether the foreign and domestic services or service suppliers are '*like services*' or '*like service suppliers*'; and (4) whether the foreign services or service suppliers are granted '*treatment no less favourable*'.

Generally speaking, internal measures (whether taxation or regulation) are inconsistent with the national treatment obligations under the GATT 1994 and the GATS when they modify the conditions of competition in the relevant market to the detriment of the imported products, foreign services or foreign service suppliers.

Exercise 5: Beer

Traditionally, Newland is a wine-drinking country. However, recent market research has shown that demand for beer in Newland is steadily growing. RichBrew Inc. of Richland, one of the world's largest beer producers, therefore wants to increase its exports of specialty beers,[348] ordinary beer and non-alcoholic beer to Newland. Before its accession to the WTO, Newland limited the importation of beer of any kind to a meagre 50,000 hectolitres per year. This quantitative restriction was put into place in the late 1950s to protect the many winegrowers in Newland from competition from imported beer. The National Association of Wineries (NAW) was, and still is, a powerful lobby in Newland politics. Beer production in Newland has always been and remains small.

On accession to the WTO, Newland abolished the quantitative restriction on the importation of beer. However, around the same time, it revised its tax regime for alcoholic and non-alcoholic beverages. In addition to a value added tax (VAT) of 21 per cent *ad valorem* applied to all alcoholic beverages, the following excise tax rates currently apply: N$5 ppl on wine; N$6 ppl on ordinary beer; and N$15 ppl on specialty beers.[349]

Non-alcoholic beer is not subject to excise tax. However, non-alcoholic beer is subject to a VAT of 21 per cent *ad valorem* whereas soft drinks are subject to a VAT of 15 per cent *ad valorem*. As stated above, all alcoholic beverages are subject to a 21 per cent VAT but resellers of imported alcoholic beverages are subject to more onerous VAT-related administrative requirements.

At the time of importation, the Newland Customs Service imposes a charge of N$0.5 per litre on alcoholic beverages that are, after importation, bottled in aluminium cans rather than glass bottles.

---

348 The specialty beers concerned are primarily blond ales with an alcohol content of 8–9 per cent, almost as high as wine.

349 N$ stands for Newland dollars, and 'ppl' for 'per proof litre'. Since alcoholic beverages have different alcohol contents (proof), the specific excise tax applicable to a particular alcoholic beverage will vary depending on its alcohol contents per litre. N$1 equals €1.

In Newland, beer, whether domestic or imported, may only be sold by licensed beer merchants; it may not be sold in supermarkets. No such restrictions exist on the sales of domestic or imported wine.

RichBrew Inc. not only wants to sell its beer in Newland's supermarkets, it also wants to establish a wholesale trade company in Newland as well as a network of retail shops to handle the distribution and sales of its beer. RichBrew has been told it can do neither because it is not a company incorporated in Newland.

Pursuant to the *Fair Competition Act* of 1991, imported as well as domestic beer and wine are subject to a minimum price requirement, annually set by the Ministry of Commerce of Newland. Furthermore, Newland prohibits the use of additives in lager while leaving the use of additives in specialty beers and wine unregulated.

In support of the national wine industry, Newland's National Federation of Restaurateurs, a government-sponsored organisation, has instructed its 10,000 members not to serve beer with traditional Newland dishes. Municipal authorities in Newland's main wine-producing region prohibit serving beer on weekends. Note also that, since the *Armed Forces Reform Act* of 1996, the armed forces of Newland are required by law to buy domestic alcoholic beverages to serve in army mess halls.

As stated above, beer production in Newland has always been and remains small. The Newland beer industry consists primarily of microbreweries, which produce beer in a more environment-friendly manner than RichBrew Inc. As part of its environmental policy, the Government of Newland intends to lower the excise tax on beer produced by microbreweries to N$5 ppl (instead of the N$6 ppl (for ordinary beer) and N$15 ppl (for specialty beer) currently applied). Also, the Government of Newland intends to give financial incentives (i.e. subsidies) to Newland-based beer merchants engaged in the retail selling of beer from microbreweries.

Finally, RichBrew Inc. has recently acquired a moribund brewery in Newland, and, in order to revive this brewery, it wants to employ in Newland brew masters from Richland. However, RichBrew Inc. has been informed that, under Newland's *Regulated Professions Act* of 1997, only brew masters with a degree obtained in Newland are allowed to work in Newland.[350] Newland argues that brewmasters trained in Richland are not 'like' brewmasters trained in Newland.

You are an associate with the Brazilian law firm Nogueira Neto Avogados. Your firm has been hired by RichBrew Inc. to give legal advice on all the issues raised above. You have been instructed to limit your legal brief to the question of whether there are violations of the national treatment obligations under WTO law.[351]

---

350 *Ibid.* Brew masters are chemical *engineers* specialised in beer production.
351 For the purpose of this exercise, assume that the Services Schedule of Newland is identical to the Services Schedule of Brazil. As instructed, you will not address questions relating to the consistency of the measures at issue with other WTO agreements (such as the *TBT Agreement* or the *SCM Agreement*) or questions relating to the possible justification of inconsistencies with the national treatment obligations under the 'general' or other exceptions provided for in the GATT 1994 or the GATS. For a discussion on these questions, see below.

6 Tariff Barriers

CONTENTS

1 INTRODUCTION

There can be no international trade without access to the domestic markets of other countries, and it is essential for traders in goods and services that this access is secure and predictable. Therefore, rules on market access are at the core of WTO law. Market access for goods and services from other countries may be impeded or restricted in many different ways, but two main categories of barriers to market access can be distinguished: (1) tariff barriers; and (2) non-tariff barriers. The category of tariff barriers primarily includes customs duties, but also other duties and charges on imports (and exports). Tariff barriers are particularly relevant for trade in goods; they are of marginal importance for trade in services. The category of non-tariff barriers is a residual category that includes quantitative restrictions (such as quotas) and 'other non-tariff barriers' (such as lack of transparency of trade regulation, unfair and arbitrary application of trade regulation, customs formalities, technical barriers to trade, sanitary and phytosanitary measures, and government procurement practices). These 'other non-tariff barriers' undoubtedly constitute the largest and most diverse sub-category of non-tariff barriers. Unlike tariff barriers, non-tariff barriers significantly affect both trade in goods and trade in services.

As set out in the Preamble to the *WTO Agreement*, WTO Members pursue the objectives of higher standards of living, full employment, growth and economic development by:

entering into reciprocal and mutually advantageous arrangements directed to the substantial reduction of tariffs and other barriers to trade.

The substantial reduction of tariff and non-tariff barriers to trade is, together with the elimination of discrimination, the key instrument of the WTO to achieve its overall objectives.[1] As discussed in Chapter 1 of this book, few economists and trade policy-makers dispute that further trade liberalisation *can* make a significant contribution to the economic development of countries.[2] The possible annual increase in global GDP resulting from the ongoing Doha Round negotiations on the reduction of customs duties is conservatively estimated to be US$63 billion.[3] Significantly, developing-country Members are expected to benefit more than developed-country Members from a successful conclusion of these tariff negotiations.[4]

As already noted in Chapter 1, some barriers to market access, such as quantitative restrictions on trade in goods, are prohibited, while other barriers, such as customs duties, are allowed in principle and are only limited to the extent of a Member's specific agreement. Thus, different rules apply to different forms of barriers. This difference in rules reflects a difference in the negative effects they have on trade and on the economy.[5] The rules on non-tariff barriers will be examined in the next chapter. The rules on tariff barriers are discussed in this chapter, which, first, deals with rules on customs duties on imports, secondly,

1 See above, p. 83.   2 See above, p. 21.
3 See Gary Clyde Hufbauer, Jeffrey J. Schott and Woan Foong Wong, 'Figuring out the Doha Round', *Policy Analysis in International Economics*, No. 91 (Peterson Institute for International Economics, 2010), 35. On the Doha Round negotiations on the reduction of customs duties on non-agricultural products (the NAMA negotiations), see below, pp. 433–8.
4 See *ibid.* According to this study, the overall Doha Round package would result for the developing-country Members in a 1.3 per cent gain in GDP, while for developed-country Members the package would result in a 0.3 per cent gain.
5 See below, p. 422.

with rules on other duties and charges on imports, and, thirdly, with customs duties and other duties and charges on exports. Since tariff barriers are not imposed on trade in services, this chapter only addresses tariff barriers on trade in goods.[6]

2   CUSTOMS DUTIES ON IMPORTS

A very common and widely used barrier to market access for goods are customs duties, also referred to as tariffs, on imports. This section discusses: (1) the definition and types of customs duties on imports; (2) the purpose of customs duties on imports; (3) customs duties as a lawful instrument of protection; (4) negotiations on the reduction of customs duties; (5) tariff concessions and Schedules of Concessions; (6) protection of tariff concessions; (7) modification or withdrawal of tariff concessions; and (8) the imposition of customs duties on imports.

2.1   Definition and Types

The term 'customs duty' is not defined in the GATT 1994 or in any of the other multilateral agreements on trade in goods. Moreover, these agreements use not only the term 'customs duty' but also the term 'tariff' (equally undefined), and they use these terms as synonyms. The GATT 1994 and the other multilateral agreements on trade in goods also do not set out the different types of customs duties. However, for the reasons explained below, it is important to define what a customs duty is, as well as to distinguish between the various types of customs duties. This sub-section addresses the definition and types of customs duties on imports in turn.

2.1.1   Definition of a Customs Duty on Imports

Generally speaking, a customs duty or tariff on imports is a financial charge or tax on imported goods, due because of their importation. Market access for the goods concerned is conditional upon the payment of the customs duty. In *EC – Poultry (1998)*, the Appellate Body held that:

---

6   Note, however, that tariff barriers imposed on trade in goods may relate to goods which contain services outputs, embedded in digital form, for example a DVD containing audio-visual material or software, professional advice, *or* embedded in a non-digital form, for example in a book containing professional advice. The notion of a 'tariff barrier' on trade in services has also arisen in cases where there is *no embedding* of a service output in a good. The prime example is the so-called 'bit tax', which could theoretically be imposed 'at the border' on electronic communications containing services outputs, or 'digital products'. In 1998, Members agreed to maintain the practice not to impose customs duties on electronic transmissions. This and later 'moratorium' decisions reflect the concern of Members regarding such tariff barriers. For the currently applicable 'moratorium' decision, see Ministerial Conference, Decision of 17 December 2011, *Work Programme on Electronic Commerce*, WT/L/843, dated 19 December 2011.

it is upon entry of a product into the customs territory, but before the product enters the domestic market, that the *obligation* to pay customs duties ... accrues.[7]

As discussed in Chapter 5 of this book, the panel in *China – Auto Parts (2009)* had to determine whether the charges at issue in that case were 'internal charges' (as argued by the complainants) or 'customs duties' (as argued by China).[8] With the exception of one particular charge, the panel found that the charges were not 'customs duties' but 'internal charges'.[9] In addressing this issue, the Appellate Body noted that 'the time at which a charge is collected or paid is not decisive' in determining whether a charge is a customs duty or an internal charge.[10] Customs duties may be collected after the moment of importation, and internal charges may be collected at the moment of importation.[11] What is important in determining whether a charge is a border charge (such as a customs duty) or an internal charge is whether the *obligation* to pay that charge accrues due to the importation or to an internal event (such as the distribution, sale, use or transportation of the imported product).[12] For a charge to constitute a customs duty, the *obligation* to pay it must accrue at the moment and by virtue of or on importation.[13] A determination of whether a particular charge is a customs duty or an internal charge must be made in light of the characteristics of the measure and the circumstances of the case. As noted in Chapter 5, the Appellate Body observed that in many cases this is 'a straightforward exercise', but that in other cases a panel may face a 'more complex' challenge.[14] However, neither the way in which a measure is characterised in a Member's domestic law nor the intent of a Member's legislator is dispositive of the characterisation of such measure under WTO law as a customs duty or internal charge.[15]

2.1.2 Types of Customs Duties

Customs duties are either *ad valorem* or non-*ad valorem*. An *ad valorem* customs duty on a good is an amount based on the value of that good. It is a percentage

---

7 Appellate Body Report, *EC – Poultry (1998)*, para. 145. Emphasis added.   8 See above, p. 357.

9 See Panel Reports, *China – Auto Parts (2009)*, para. 7.212. Since they were internal charges, they were subject to the national treatment obligation of Article III:2, first sentence. See above, p. 357.

10 See Appellate Body Reports, *China – Auto Parts (2009)*, para. 162.

11 See Note *Ad* Article III of the GATT 1994, as discussed in Chapter 5 of this book. See above, p. 354.

12 See Appellate Body Reports, *China – Auto Parts (2009)*, para. 162. See also Panel Reports, *China – Auto Parts (2009)*, paras. 7.128–7.129.

13 See Appellate Body Reports, *China – Auto Parts (2009)*, para. 158. With regard to the difference between a 'customs duty' and 'other duties and charges on imports', see below, p. 364.

14 See Appellate Body Reports, *China – Auto Parts (2009)*, para. 171. See in the context also *India – Additional Import Duties (2008)*, in which the panel agreed with the parties that the measures at issue were border charges within the meaning of Article II:1, and not internal charges within the meaning of Article III:2. See Appellate Body Report, *India – Additional Import Duties (2008)*, footnote 304 to para. 153.

15 See Appellate Body Reports, *China – Auto Parts (2009)*, para. 178. Note that the 1973 *Kyoto International Convention on the Simplification and Harmonization of Customs Procedures*, to which many WTO Members are a party, defines 'customs duties' as 'the duties laid down in the Customs tariff to which goods are liable on entering ... the Customs territory'. Therefore, according to the *Kyoto Convention*, but contrary to the ruling of the Appellate Body in *China – Auto Parts (2009)*, a duty is a customs duty because a country characterises it as such by including it in its national customs tariff. See *International Convention on the Simplification and Harmonization of Customs Procedures* (as amended), done at Kyoto, 18 May 1973, General Annex, Chapter 2, E8./F11.

of the value of the imported good, for example a 15 per cent *ad valorem* duty on computers. In that case, the duty on a computer worth €1,000 will be €150. Non-*ad valorem* customs duties (or NAV duties) can be specific, compound, mixed or 'other' customs duties.[16] A specific customs duty on a good is an amount based on a unit of quantity such as weight (kg), length (m), area (m^2), volume (m^3 or l) or numbers (pieces, pairs, dozens, or packs) of that good, for example a duty of €100 per hectolitre of vegetable oil or a duty of €3,000 on each car. A compound customs duty is a duty comprising an *ad valorem* duty to which a specific duty is added or, less frequently, subtracted, for example a customs duty on wool of 10 per cent *ad valorem* and €50 per tonne. In that case, the duty on three tonnes of wool worth €1,000 per tonne will be €450. A mixed customs duty is a duty that can be either an *ad valorem* duty or a specific duty, subject to an upper and/ or a lower limit, for example a customs duty on shirts of 10 per cent *ad valorem* or €4 per shirt, whichever duty is the higher. Finally, 'other' non-*ad valorem* customs duties, also referred to as technical customs duties, are duties determined by technical factors often related to the content, composition or nature of the goods concerned.[17]

Ad valorem customs duties are by far the most common type of customs duties.[18] They are preferable to non-*ad valorem* duties for several reasons. First, *ad valorem* duties are more transparent than non-*ad valorem* duties. The protectionist impact and the negative effect on prices for consumers are easier to assess for *ad valorem* duties than for non-*ad valorem* duties. The lack of transparency of non-*ad valorem* duties makes it easier for special interest groups to obtain government support for high levels of protection.[19] Secondly, by definition, *ad valorem* customs duties are index-linked. In times of inflation, the government's tariff revenue will keep up with price increases and the level of protection will remain the same. By contrast, non-*ad valorem* duties will constantly have to be changed to maintain the same real tariff revenue or maintain the same level of protection. Thirdly, non-*ad valorem* duties 'punish' efficiency, because the cheaper like products are subject to a higher duty in *ad valorem* terms. Overall, with respect to industrial products, non-*ad valorem* duties are unusual.[20] With respect to agricultural products, however, non-*ad valorem* duties, and in particular compound duties, are still common.[21]

---

16 See Negotiating Group on Market Access, Note by the Secretariat, *Incidence of Non-Ad Valorem Tariffs in Members' Tariff Schedules and Possible Approaches to the Estimation of Ad Valorem Equivalents*, TN/MA/S/10/Rev.1, dated 18 July 2005, para. 3.

17 See *ibid.*   18 See *ibid.*, paras. 5–7.

19 See WTO Secretariat, Market Access: Unfinished Business, Special Studies Series 6 (WTO, 2001), 9.

20 For only five Members, more than 5 per cent of their tariff lines for industrial products are bound in non-*ad valorem* terms. Only Switzerland uses non-*ad valorem* terms for all its non-zero duties. See TN/MA/S/10/Rev.1, dated 18 July 2005, para. 5. Note that the General Council, in its Decision of 1 August 2004 on the Doha Work Programme, decided that 'all non-*ad valorem* duties [on non-agricultural products] shall be converted to *ad valorem* equivalents on the basis of a methodology to be determined' (WT/L/579, dated 2 August 2004, Annex B, para. 5).

21 WTO Secretariat, *Market Access: Unfinished Business*, Special Studies Series 6 (WTO, 2001), 46 and 47. That is the case, for example, for the European Union and the United States.

Ad valorem or non-*ad valorem* duties can be MFN duties, preferential duties or neither of the two. *MFN duties* are the 'standard' customs duties applicable to all other WTO Members in compliance with the non-discrimination MFN treatment obligation of Article I:1 of the GATT 1994.[22] *Preferential duties* are customs duties applied to specific countries pursuant to conventional or autonomous arrangements under which products from these countries are subject to duties lower than MFN duties.[23] For example, the customs duties applied by the European Union and sixteen Caribbean countries on each other's products under the terms of the *CARIFORUM–EC Economic Partnership Agreement* are conventional preferential duties.[24] The customs duties applied by the European Union on products from developing countries under the EU's Generalized System of Preferences (GSP) are autonomous preferential duties.[25] Finally, there are customs duties that are neither MFN duties nor preferential duties. These are the duties applicable to goods from countries which are not WTO Members and do not benefit from MFN treatment.[26] However, since the number of countries that are not Members of the WTO is now very small and their share in world trade is negligible, the latter category of customs duties is therefore of limited importance.

2.1.3 National Customs Tariff

As stated above, the terms 'customs duty' and 'tariff' are used as synonyms in the multilateral agreements on trade in goods. However, the term 'tariff' has a second meaning, different from 'customs duty'. A 'tariff', or 'customs tariff', is also a structured list of product descriptions and their corresponding customs duty. The customs duties or tariffs, which are due on importation, are set out in a country's customs tariff.[27] Most national customs tariffs now follow or reflect the structure set out in the Harmonized Commodity Description and Coding System, usually referred to as the 'Harmonized System' or 'HS' discussed in detail later in this chapter.[28]

Figure 6.1, an excerpt from the customs tariff of India, shows that the MFN customs duties on cocoa are 30 per cent *ad valorem*. India's customs duties on

---

22 See above, p. 331.
23 The existence of preferential duties makes it important to determine the country of origin of products. On rules of origin, see below, pp. 460–1.
24 See *CARIFORUM–EC Economic Partnership Agreement*, signed on 15 October 2008. Under this Agreement, goods from the CARIFORUM countries (with the exception of rice and sugar) may be imported into the European Union free of customs duties.
25 See below.
26 Note that non-WTO Members may benefit from MFN treatment under the terms of bilateral or regional trade agreements.
27 The 'national' customs tariff of the European Union is referred to as the Common Customs Tariff. See Council Regulation (EEC) No. 2658/87 of 23 July 1987 on the tariff and statistical nomenclature and on the Common Customs Tariff, OJ 1987, L256, 7 September 1987. Every year, the European Commission adopts a Regulation reproducing a complete version of the Common Customs Tariff, taking into account Council and Commission amendments of that year. The Regulation is published in the *Official Journal of the European Communities* no later than 31 October. It applies from 1 January of the following year.
28 See below, pp. 453–6.

Tariff item	Description of goods	Unit	Rate of duty	
			Standard	Preferential areas
1801 00 00	COCOA BEANS, WHOLE OR BROKEN, RAW OR ROASTED	kg	30%	
1802 00 00	COCOA SHELLS, HUSKS, SKINS AND OTHER COCOA WASTE	kg	30%	
1803	COCOA PASTE, WHETHER OR NOT DEFATTED			
1803 10 00	- Not defatted	kg	30%	
1803 20 00	- Wholly or partly defatted	kg	30%	
1804 00 00	COCOA BUTTER, FAT AND OIL	kg	30%	
1805 00 00	COCOA POWDER, NOT CONTAINING ADDED SUGAR OR OTHER SWEETENING MATTER	kg	30%	
1806	CHOCOLATE AND OTHER FOOD PREPARATIONS CONTAINING COCOA			
1806 10 00	Cocoa powder, containing added sugar or other sweetening matter	kg	30%	
1806 20 00	Other preparations in blocks, slabs or bars weighing more than 2 kg or in liquid, paste, powder, granular or other bulk form in containers or immediate packings, of a content exceeding 2 kg	kg	30%	
	- Other, in blocks, slabs or bars:			
1806 31 00	-- Filled	kg	30%	
1806 32 00	-- Not filled	kg	30%	
1806 90	- Other:			
1806 90 10	--- Chocolate and chocolate products	kg	30%	
1806 90 20	--- Sugar confectionary containing cocoa	kg	30%	
1806 90 30	--- Spreads containing cocoa	kg	30%	
1806 90 40	--- Preparations containing cocoa for making beverages	kg	30%	
1806 90 90	--- Other	kg	30%	

Figure 6.1 Excerpt from the customs tariff of India, 2013

some goods are even higher than 30 per cent, while on other goods they are lower. The customs duty on, for example, tariff item 1704 10 00 ('Chewing gum ...') is 45 per cent *ad valorem* and the customs duty on tariff item 8703 21 10 ('Vehicles principally designed for the transport of more than seven persons, including the driver') is 100 per cent *ad valorem*. The customs duty on tariff item

2501 00 10 ('Common salt ...') is 10 per cent *ad valorem*. As discussed below, average customs duties imposed by developing-country Members are, generally speaking, considerably higher than those of developed-country Members.[29]

Many WTO Members have an online database of the customs duties they apply. The website of the World Customs Organization gives easy access to many of these databases, including the TARIC database of the European Union.[30] However, information on customs duties is perhaps most conveniently obtained via the WTO's Tariff Analysis Online (for registered users only) or, for less sophisticated searches, via the Tariff Download Facility (for all users).[31] Also quite useful and presenting data in an easily accessible and graphic way is the International Trade and Market Access interactive tool, launched by the WTO Secretariat in November 2012.[32]

Questions and Assignments 6.1

What is a customs duty and how can it be distinguished from an internal tax? What is a tariff? What are specific customs duties, and how do they differ from *ad valorem* customs duties? What are MFN customs duties? Find out and compare the MFN customs duties imposed by the European Union, the United States, China, South Africa, Bangladesh and Poland on cocoa powder (HS 1805 00) and road tractors (HS 8701 20). If you are a national of a WTO Member other than those Members referred to above, find out as well the MFN customs duties your government imposes on cocoa powder and tractors.

2.2 Purpose of Customs Duties on Imports

Customs duties or tariffs on imports serve two main purposes. First, customs duties are a source of revenue for governments. In fact, it is one of the oldest ways for a government to collect revenue.[33] This purpose is now less important for industrialised countries with a well-developed system of direct and indirect taxation. For many developing countries, however, customs duties are an important source of government revenue. In comparison with income taxes and sales taxes, customs duties are easy to collect. Imports are relatively easy to monitor and the collection of customs duties can be concentrated in a few points of entry. Secondly, customs duties are used to protect and/or promote domestic

---

29 See below, pp. 427–8. However, note also that India reduced its overall applied rate between 2001/2 and 2006/7 from 32.3 per cent to 15.8 per cent, and between 2006/7 and 2010/11 from 15.1 per cent to 12 per cent. See WTO Secretariat, *Trade Policy Review Report – India, Revision*, WT/TPR/S/182/Rev.1, dated 24 July 2007, vii, para. 2; and WTO Secretariat, *Trade Policy Review Report – India, Revision*, WT/TPR/S/249/Rev.1 dated 10 October 2011, para. 28.

30 See www.wcoomd.org. For the TARIC database, see http://ec.europa.eu/taxation_customs/dds2/taric/taric_consultation.jsp.

31 See www.wto.org/english/tratop_e/tariffs_e/tariff_data_e.htm. The information on customs duties in Tariff Analysis Online (http://tariffanalysis.wto.org) and the Tariff Download Facility (http://tariffdata.wto.org) is drawn from the WTO's Integrated Database (IDB), which is fed with the information that Members annually supply on the customs duties they apply. Anybody can register as a user of Tariff Analysis Online, but only WTO Members have access to import statistics beyond six digits.

32 See www.wto.org/english/res_e/statis_e/statis_e.htm.

33 There is historical evidence of the imposition of customs duties in the ancient Egyptian, Indian and Chinese civilisations. See H. Asakura, *World History of the Customs and Tariffs* (World Customs Organization, 2003), 19–105.

industries. The customs duties imposed on imported products make the 'like' domestic products relatively cheaper, giving them a price advantage and thus some degree of protection from import competition. Developing countries are likely to use customs duties to protect infant industries (and thus as an instrument of economic development policy), while developed countries use them more often to protect industries in decline.[34]

2.3 Customs Duties as a Lawful Instrument of Protection

In principle, WTO Members are free to impose customs duties on imported products. WTO law, and in particular the GATT 1994, does not prohibit the imposition of customs duties on imports.[35] This is in sharp contrast to the general prohibition on quantitative restrictions, discussed in Chapter 7 of this book.[36] In *India – Additional Import Duties (2008)*, the Appellate Body stated:

Tariffs are legitimate instruments to accomplish certain trade policy or other objectives such as to generate fiscal revenue. Indeed, under the GATT 1994, they are the preferred trade policy instrument, whereas quantitative restrictions are in principle prohibited. Irrespective of the underlying objective, tariffs are permissible.[37]

Customs duties, unlike quantitative restrictions, represent an instrument of protection against imports generally allowed by the GATT 1994.[38]

2.4 Negotiations on the Reduction of Customs Duties

While WTO law does not prohibit customs duties, it does recognise that customs duties constitute an obstacle to trade. Article XXVIII*bis* of the GATT 1994, therefore, calls upon WTO Members to negotiate the reduction of customs duties. This article provides, in relevant part:

[T]hus negotiations on a reciprocal and mutually advantageous basis, directed to the substantial reduction of the general level of tariffs and other charges on imports and exports and in particular to the reduction of such high tariffs as discourage the importation even of minimum quantities, and conducted with due regard to the objectives of this Agreement and the varying needs of individual [Members], are of great importance to the expansion of international trade. The [Members] may therefore sponsor such negotiations from time to time.

Note that Article XXVII:1 of the GATT 1994 calls upon developed-country Members to accord, in the interest of the economic development of developing-country Members:

---

34 Note in addition that customs duties can also be used to promote a *rational* allocation of scarce foreign exchange (by imposing low duties on capital goods (e.g. industrial machinery) and high duties on luxury goods (e.g. SUVs or perfumes)).

35 Note, however, that Article V:3 of the GATT 1994 does prohibit customs duties on goods *in transit*.

36 See below, pp. 479–542.

37 Appellate Body Report, *India – Additional Import Duties (2008)*, para. 159.

38 The reasons behind the GATT's preference for customs duties are discussed below, p. 487.

Implementation period	Round covered	Weighted tariff reduction
1948	Geneva (1947)	−26
1959	Annecy (1949)	−3
1952	Torquay (1959–51)	−4
1956–8	Geneva (1955–6)	−3
1962–4	Dillon Round (1961–2)	−4
1968–72	Kennedy Round (1964–7)	−38
1980–7	Tokyo Round (1973–9)	−33
1995–9	Uruguay Round (1986–94)	−38

Figure 6.2 Sixty years of GATT/WTO tariff reductions

high priority to the reduction and elimination of barriers to products currently or potentially of particular export interest to [developing-country Members].[39]

2.4.1 Success of Past Tariff Negotiations

Under the GATT 1947, negotiations on the reduction of customs duties, commonly and in short referred to as tariff negotiations, took place primarily in the context of eight successive 'Rounds' of trade negotiations. In fact, the first five of these Rounds (Geneva, Annecy, Torquay, Geneva and Dillon) were exclusively dedicated to the negotiation on the reduction of tariffs. The sixth, seventh and eighth Rounds (Kennedy, Tokyo and Uruguay) had an increasingly broader agenda, although the negotiation of tariff reductions remained an important element on the agenda of these Rounds. The eight GATT Rounds of trade negotiations were very successful in reducing customs duties. In the late 1940s, the average duty on industrial products imposed by developed countries was about 40 per cent *ad valorem*. As a result of the eight GATT Rounds, the average duty of developed-country Members on industrial products is now below 3.8 per cent *ad valorem*.[40] Figure 6.2 sets out the tariff reductions achieved by the GATT/WTO over the past sixty years.

2.4.2 Importance of Customs Duties as Trade Barriers

Economists often consider a customs duty below 5 per cent *ad valorem* to be a nuisance rather than a barrier to trade. Nevertheless, customs duties remain a significant barrier in international trade for several reasons. First, most developing-country Members still impose relatively high customs duties. Many of them

---

39 Note, however, that Article XXXVII qualifies its call to give high priority to the reduction and elimination of barriers with the words 'except when compelling reasons ... make it impossible'.
40 See 'Tariffs: more bindings and closer to zero' in *Understanding the WTO: The Agreements*, at www.wto.org/english/thewto_e/whatis_e/tif_e/agrm2_e.htm.

have a simple average duty ranging between 10 and 15 per cent *ad valorem.*[41] The simple average duty of Argentina is 13.6 per cent, of Bangladesh 14.4 per cent, of Brazil 13.7 per cent, China 9.6 per cent, India 12.6 per cent, Mexico 8.3 per cent, Nigeria 11.7 per cent and Pakistan 13.9 per cent.[42] In comparison, the simple average applied MFN duty of Japan is 5.3 per cent, the European Union 5.3 per cent, Canada 4.5 per cent, United States 3.5 per cent, and Hong Kong, China 0 per cent.[43] Secondly, developed-country Members as well as developing-country Members still have high, to very high, duties on specific groups of 'sensitive' industrial and agricultural products.[44] With respect to industrial products, these so-called 'tariff peaks' are quite common for textiles and clothing, leather and, to a lesser extent, transport equipment.[45] With respect to agricultural products, under the *WTO Agreement on Agriculture*, all non-tariff barriers to trade have been eliminated and substituted by customs duties at often very high levels.[46] Thirdly, in very competitive markets and in trade between neighbouring countries, a very low duty may still constitute a barrier.

In addition, customs duties may also impede the economic development of developing-country Members to the extent that duties increase with the level of processing that products have undergone. The duties on processed and semi-processed products are often higher than the duties on non-processed products and raw materials. This phenomenon is referred to as 'tariff escalation'. Tariff escalation discourages manufacturing or processing in countries where those non-processed products or raw materials are produced, often developing countries.[47] The customs duties of Canada and Australia increase at each production stage. US customs duties increase significantly only between raw materials and semi-processed products. The same holds true for the customs duties of Japan. On average, the customs duties of the European Union appear to de-escalate, i.e. they are higher on raw materials than on semi-processed or processed

---

41 The simple average duties referred to in this paragraph are simple average applied MFN duties on all products (agricultural and non-agricultural). See WTO/ITC/UNCTAD, *World Tariff Profiles 2012*, available at www.wto.org/english/res_e/booksp_e/tariff_profiles12_e.pdf.

42 See *ibid.*   43 See *ibid.*

44 See *ibid.* For example, the average duty imposed by the European Union on products in the product group 'dairy products' is 55.2 per cent; on products in the product group 'sugars and confectionary' 29.1 per cent; and on products in the product group 'clothing' 11.5 per cent. The average duty imposed by India on products in the product group 'tea and coffee' is 56.1 per cent; on products in the product group 'beverages and tobacco' 70.8 per cent; on products in the product group 'sugars and confectionary' 34.4 per cent; and on products in the product group 'fish and fish products' 29.1 per cent. The average duty imposed by Brazil on products in the product group 'clothing' is 35 per cent; on products in the product group 'textiles' 23.3 per cent; and on products in the product group 'transport equipment' 18.3 per cent.

45 Tariff peaks are tariffs that exceed a selected reference level. The OECD distinguishes between 'national peaks' and 'international peaks'. 'National peaks' are tariffs which are three times or more than the national mean tariff. 'International peaks' are tariffs of 15 per cent or more. See WTO Secretariat, *Market Access: Unfinished Business*, Special Studies Series 6 (WTO, 2001), 12.

46 See below, p. 488.

47 Note that Article XXVIII:1 of the GATT 1994 calls upon developed-country Members to accord 'high priority to the reduction and elimination of barriers to products currently or potentially of particular export interest to [developing-country Members], including customs duties and other restrictions *which differentiate unreasonably between such products in their primary and in their processed forms*' (emphasis added). See, in this respect, however, also pp. 426–7, footnote 39.

products.[48] However, this is not always the case. As a clear example of tariff escalation, consider that the MFN duty applied by the European Union on cotton is zero per cent; on cotton yarn between 4 and 4.4 per cent; on woven fabric of cotton 8 per cent; and on men's or boy's shirts of cotton 12 per cent.

Questions and Assignments 6.2

Why do countries impose customs duties on imports? Is the imposition of customs duties prohibited under WTO law? What does Article XXVIII*bis* of the GATT 1994 provide for? Have past efforts to reduce customs duties through negotiations been successful? Are customs duties still a major barrier to trade? What is 'tariff escalation' and why is it a problem?

2.4.3 Basic Rules Governing Tariff Negotiations

As noted above, Article XXVIII*bis* of the GATT 1994 calls for negotiations on the reduction of customs duties, in short tariff negotiations, on a 'reciprocal and mutually advantageous basis'. Furthermore, as discussed in Chapter 4 of this book, Article I:1 of the GATT 1994 requires that with respect to customs duties any advantage granted by any Member to any product originating in any other country shall be accorded immediately and unconditionally to the like product originating in all other Members.[49] The basic principles and rules governing tariff negotiations are thus: (1) the principle of reciprocity and mutual advantage; and (2) the most-favoured-nation (MFN) treatment obligation.

The principle of reciprocity and mutual advantage, as applied in tariff negotiations, entails that, when a Member requests another Member to reduce its customs duties on certain products, it must be ready to reduce its own customs duties on products which the other Member exports, or wishes to export. For tariff negotiations to succeed, the tariff reductions requested must be considered to be of equivalent value to the tariff reductions offered. There is no agreed method to establish or measure reciprocity. Each Member determines for itself whether the economic value of the tariff reductions received is equal to the value of the tariff reductions granted. Although some Members apply rather sophisticated economic methods to measure reciprocity, in general the methods applied are basic. The final assessment of the 'acceptability' of the outcome of tariff negotiations is primarily political in nature.[50]

The principle of reciprocity does not apply, at least not to its full extent, to tariff negotiations between developed- and developing-country Members. Article XXXVI:8 of Part IV ('Trade and Development') of the GATT 1994 provides:

[Developed-country Members] do not expect reciprocity for commitments made by them in trade negotiations to reduce or remove tariffs and other barriers to the trade of [developing-country Members].

48 See WTO Secretariat, *Market Access: Unfinished Business*, Special Studies Series 6 (WTO, 2001), 12 and 13, and Table II.3.

49 See above, p. 329.

50 Note that the principle of reciprocity applies not only to tariff negotiations adopting a product-by-product approach but also to tariff negotiations adopting a formula approach (be it a linear reduction approach or a non-linear reduction approach) or a sectoral approach. See below, p. 433.

This provision is further elaborated in the 1979 Tokyo Round Decision on Differential and More Favourable Treatment, Reciprocity and Fuller Participation of Developing Countries, commonly referred to as the Enabling Clause, which provides, in paragraph 5:

[Developed-country Members] shall ... not seek, neither shall [developing-country Members] be required to make, concessions that are inconsistent with the latter's development, financial and trade needs.

In tariff negotiations between developed- and developing-country Members, the principle of *relative* reciprocity applies. In tariff negotiations with developed-country Members, developing-country Members are expected to 'reciprocate' only to the extent consistent with their development, financial and trade needs. With respect to least-developed-country Members, paragraph 6 of the Enabling Clause furthermore instructs developed-country Members to exercise the 'utmost restraint' in seeking any concessions for commitments made by them to reduce or remove tariffs.

Note, however, that paragraph 7 of the Enabling Clause states, in pertinent part:

[Developing-country Members] expect that their capacity to make contributions or negotiated concessions ... would improve with the progressive development of their economies and improvement in their trade situation and they would accordingly expect to participate more fully in the framework of rights and obligations under the General Agreement.

Because of the principle of relative reciprocity, few developing-country Members agreed to any reductions of their customs duties up to and including the Tokyo Round. Before the Uruguay Round, tariff negotiations were, in practice, primarily conducted between developed-country Members. This changed in the Uruguay Round when almost all developing-country Members got involved in the tariff reduction negotiations, albeit that the reductions agreed to were – in accordance with the principle of relative reciprocity – smaller than the reductions agreed to by developed-country Members. The increased willingness of developing-country Members to participate actively in tariff reduction negotiations during the Uruguay Round can be attributed to two factors. First, a number of developing-country Members had made significant progress in their economic development. Secondly, a fundamental change had occurred in the trade policy of many developing-country Members. In the 1980s, many developing-country Members moved away from protectionist trade policies to more open and liberal trade policies.[51]

As noted above, tariff negotiations are governed not only by the principle of reciprocity (full or relative) but also by the MFN treatment obligation set out in Article I:1 of the GATT 1994. Any tariff reduction a Member grants to any country

---

51 See *Business Guide to the World Trading System*, 2nd edn (International Trade Centre/Commonwealth Secretariat, 1999), 59.

as the result of tariff negotiations with that country must be granted to all other Members, immediately and unconditionally. This considerably complicates tariff negotiations. Member A, interested in exporting product *a* to Member B, will request Member B to reduce its customs duties on product *a*. In return for such a reduction, Member A will offer Member B, interested in exporting product *b* to Member A, a reduction of its customs duties on product *b*. As a result of the MFN treatment obligation, the tariff reductions to which Members A and B agree would also benefit all other Members. However, Members A and B will be hesitant to give other Members the benefit of the tariff reductions 'without getting something in return'. Member A is therefore likely to put a hold on the agreement to reduce the customs duty on product *b* until it has been able 'to get something in return' from, for example, Member C which also exports product *b* to Member A and would thus also benefit from the reduction of the customs duty on product *b*. Likewise, Member B will be hesitant to reduce the customs duty on product *a* as long as Member D, which also has an interest in exporting product *a* to Member B, has not given Member B 'something in return' for this reduction. In tariff negotiations, Members may try to benefit from tariff reductions agreed between other Members without giving anything in return. If their export interests are small, they are likely to succeed and will therefore be 'free-riders'. The free-rider problem can be mitigated by opting for an approach to tariff negotiations other than the product-by-product approach described above. Other approaches to tariff negotiations include the formula approach (be it the linear reduction approach or the non-linear reduction approach) and the sectoral approach, all discussed below.[52]

Questions and Assignments 6.3

What are the basic principles and rules governing tariff negotiations? Does the principle of reciprocity also apply to tariff negotiations between developed- and developing-country Members? Why does the MFN treatment obligation complicate tariff negotiations? What does the term 'free-rider' refer to in tariff negotiations?

2.4.4 Organisation of Tariff Negotiations

Tariff negotiations can be organised in different ways. As Article XXVIII*bis* of the GATT 1994 provides, tariff negotiations may be carried out: (1) on a selective product-by-product basis; or (2) by the application of such multilateral procedures as may be accepted by the Members concerned. Negotiators may thus opt for different tariff reduction approaches or methodologies, also referred to in WTO-speak as 'modalities'.[53]

52 In fact, as discussed in the next section of this chapter, the increasing complexity of multilateral (as opposed to bilateral) tariff negotiations has led to the abandonment of the product-by-product approach to multilateral tariff negotiations. Note, however, that the principle of reciprocity (full or relative) and the MFN treatment obligation continue to be the underlying principles governing the negotiations.

53 For a detailed discussion of the different approaches to tariff negotiations, see Patrick Low and Roy Santana, 'Trade Liberalization in Manufactures: What Is Left After the Doha Round?', *Journal of International Trade and Diplomacy*, November 2008.

During the first GATT Rounds (up to and including the 1961–2 Dillon Round), negotiators opted for a *product-by-product approach* to tariff negotiations. Under this approach, each of the participants in the tariff negotiations submits first its request list and then its offer list, identifying respectively the products with regard to which it is seeking and is willing to make tariff reductions. The negotiations take place between the principal suppliers and importers of each product. However, the product-by-product approach has one major disadvantage. For practical reasons, the number of products that can be subject to this kind of tariff negotiation is necessarily limited, and the product coverage of the tariff reductions that can be achieved is thus 'restricted'.

The product-by-product approach to tariff negotiations is still used, in bilateral or plurilateral negotiations outside a Round, both for Article XXVIII renegotiations and for tariff negotiations in the context of the accession of new Members to the WTO. However, since the 1963–7 Kennedy Round, the product-by-product approach has no longer been used as the main approach in multilateral tariff negotiations. Multilateral tariff negotiations have been primarily conducted on the basis of a *formula approach*. Under the formula approach, tariff reductions that are derived from the application of a mathematical formula, result in either a linear reduction (linear reduction approach) or a non-linear reduction (non-linear reduction approach). These 'formula approach' negotiations always involve: (1) the selection of an appropriate formula; and (2) the identification of products to which the formula will not apply. With respect to the latter products, the tariff negotiations may be conducted on a product-by-product basis. For the Kennedy Round tariff negotiations, a *linear reduction approach* to tariff negotiations was adopted. While successful, this linear reduction approach also presented problems. Contracting Parties with low average customs duties argued that it was not reasonable to expect them to cut these duties by the same percentage as Contracting Parties with high customs duties. It is clear that a 50 per cent reduction of a customs duty of 40 per cent still leaves a 20 per cent customs duty in place, i.e. a significant degree of protection from import competition. However, a 50 per cent reduction of a customs duty of 10 per cent leaves only a 5 per cent customs duty. To mitigate this problem, the negotiators in the Tokyo Round (1973–9) applied a *non-linear reduction approach*, often referred to as the 'Swiss formula', which requires larger cuts of higher customs duties than of lower customs duties.

In the Uruguay Round tariff negotiations (1986–94), the negotiators applied different approaches, or modalities, to reduce agricultural and non-agricultural customs duties. Customs duties on agricultural products were reduced using the 'Uruguay Round formula', whereby developed-country Members eventually had to reduce customs duties on a simple average basis by 36 per cent, with a minimum reduction of 15 per cent for each tariff line.[54] Developing-country Members

---

54 These modalities for the tariff negotiations on non-agricultural products, which were set out in the so-called 'Dunkel text' of 1991, were never accepted by the Uruguay Round participants (see GATT document MTN. GNG/MA/W/24). However, in 1992, the participants proceeded to table comprehensive draft schedules which were in line with these modalities.

were required to do two-thirds of that effort.[55] With regard to the reduction of customs duties on non-agricultural products, the negotiators were never able to agree on the specific approach to apply to the tariff negotiations. In 1990, they did agree, however, on the result to be achieved, namely, an overall tariff reduction of at least 33 per cent. Each participant in the negotiations was free to determine the manner in which it would reach that reduction target.[56] Different participants applied different approaches. While some participants, and in particular Canada, the European Union and Japan, applied a formula to produce their initial offers, others, and in particular the United States, engaged in product-by-product negotiations. Subsequently, in 1993, Canada, the European Union, Japan and the United States announced they had reached an agreement on a number of elements they considered necessary for a final agreement on a global and balanced package, which included the large-scale use of the *sectoral approach* to tariff negotiations. The sectoral approach is an approach in which negotiators aim at reducing or eliminating tariffs in a specific sector (such as the chemical products, pharmaceuticals, construction equipment, medical equipment and beer sectors).[57]

Between the end of the Uruguay Round and the start of the current Doha Round, a group of WTO Members agreed to eliminate all customs duties on information technology products (i.e. computers, telecommunications equipment, semiconductors, etc.). At the Singapore Ministerial Conference in 1996, twenty-nine Members adopted the *Ministerial Declaration on Trade in Information Technology Products* and thus agreed to the *Agreement on Trade in Information Technology Products* (ITA) attached to the Ministerial Declaration.[58] The ITA provided for participants to eliminate duties completely on information technology products by 1 January 2000. The ITA entered into force in 1997 when forty Members, accounting for more than 90 per cent of world trade in information technology products, had adopted the Agreement. At present, seventy-four Members, accounting for 97 per cent of world trade in information technology products, have adopted the Agreement.[59] As a result of the ITA, virtually all trade in information technology products is now free from customs duties. Over the last fifteen years, world exports of information technology products have increased by almost 200 per cent, and amounted in 2010 to US$1.4 trillion or 9.5 per cent of world trade in goods.[60]

The Doha Ministerial Declaration of November 2001, in which the WTO Members agreed to start the Doha Round, provided little guidance with respect to the approach to be taken to the Doha Round tariff negotiations on non-agricultural

---

55 I.e. reduce customs duties on a simple average by 24 per cent, with a minimum reduction of 10 per cent for each tariff line.
56 See Negotiating Group on Market Access, Note by the Secretariat, *Sector Specific Discussions and Negotiations on Goods in the GATT and WTO*, TN/MA/S/13, dated 24 January 2005.
57 See *ibid.*
58 Ministerial Conference, *Singapore Ministerial Declaration on Trade in Information Technology Products*, WT/MIN(96)/16, dated 13 December 1996.
59 See WTO Secretariat, *15 Years of the Information Technology Agreement: Trade, Innovation and Global Production Networks* (WTO, 2012), 3.
60 *Ibid.*

products. However, the level of ambition of these tariff negotiations was clearly high. The Doha Ministerial Declaration states, in relevant part:

We agree to negotiations which shall aim, *by modalities to be agreed*, to reduce or as appropriate eliminate tariffs, including the reduction or elimination of tariff peaks, high tariffs, and tariff escalation, as well as non-tariff barriers, in particular on products of export interest to developing countries. Product coverage shall be comprehensive and without *a priori* exclusions. The negotiations shall take fully into account the special needs and interests of developing and least-developed country participants, including through less than full reciprocity in reduction commitments.[61]

The approach to be taken to these tariff negotiations – negotiations commonly referred to as negotiations on non-agricultural market access or NAMA negotiations – was further 'clarified' by the General Council in its Decision of 1 August 2004. In this Decision, the General Council stated:

We recognize that a *formula approach* is key to reducing tariffs, and reducing or eliminating tariff peaks, high tariffs, and tariff escalation. We agree that the Negotiating Group should continue its work on a non-linear formula applied on a line-by-line basis which shall take fully into account the special needs and interests of developing and least-developed country participants, including through less than full reciprocity in reduction commitments.

We recognize that a *sectoral tariff component*, aiming at elimination or harmonization is another key element to achieving the objectives of paragraph 16 of the Doha Ministerial Declaration with regard to the reduction or elimination of tariffs, in particular on products of export interest to developing countries.[62]

At the subsequent Ministerial Conference in Hong Kong in December 2005, Members were unable to agree on the specific approach to (or, in WTO-speak, the modalities of) the NAMA negotiations.[63] After the Hong Kong Ministerial Conference, the positions of developed-country and developing-country Members in the NAMA negotiations became increasingly polarised. Developed-country Members wanted developing-country Members, and in particular emerging economies, to agree to a much greater reduction of tariff bindings than the latter were willing to accept.[64] Against this background, Ambassador Don Stephenson, the Chair of the Negotiating Group on Non-Agricultural Market Access (NAMA), proposed in July 2007 the first 'NAMA Draft Modalities' with regard to the tariff negotiations on non-agricultural products.[65] The Chair proposed to conduct the

---

61 Ministerial Conference, *Doha Ministerial Declaration*, WT/MIN(1)/DEC/1, dated 20 November 2001, para. 16. Emphasis added.

62 See General Council, *Doha Work Programme, Framework for Establishing Modalities in Market Access for Non-Agricultural Products*, WT/L/579, dated 2 August 2004, Annex B, paras. 4 and 7. Emphasis added. See paras. 5, 6 and 8–13 for further details on the 'initial elements' for future work on the modalities for the Doha Round tariff negotiations.

63 Ministerial Conference, *Hong Kong Ministerial Declaration*, WT/MIN(05)/DEC, dated 22 December 2005, 4–5. However, Members were able – four years after the start of the Doha Round – to frame better the agenda of the NAMA negotiations.

64 The European Union and the United States needed more market access for non-agricultural goods to balance the liberalisation of trade in agricultural goods requested by developing-country Members.

65 Negotiating Group on Market Access, *Draft NAMA Modalities*, JOB(07)/126, dated 17 July 2007. This draft was revised by the Chair in February 2008. See Negotiating Group on Market Access, *Draft Modalities for Non-Agricultural Market Access*, TN/MA/W/103, dated 8 February 2008.

tariff reduction negotiations primarily on the basis of a *non-linear reduction approach*, commonly referred to as the 'Swiss formula'. As explained above, the 'Swiss formula' requires larger cuts of higher customs duties than of lower customs duties. According to the 'Swiss formula', which applies on a line-by-line basis, the tariff reductions will be calculated as follows:

$$t_1 = \frac{(a \text{ or } b) \times t_0}{(a \text{ or } b) + t_0}$$

where:

t_1 is the final bound rate of duty

t_0 is the base rate of duty

a is the coefficient for developed Members, and is in the range 8–9

b is the coefficient for developing Members, and is in the range 19–23.[66] Note that the 'Swiss formula' provides for different coefficients for developed- and developing-country Members.[67] Least-developed-country Members would not be required to undertake tariff reduction commitments.

The Chair's July 2007 proposals for tariff negotiations on non-agricultural products were not received with much enthusiasm. Many developing-country Members had grave concerns regarding the 'Swiss formula' as well as other issues, which they considered were not satisfactorily addressed, such as the issue of preference erosion and the issue of sectoral tariff elimination. They considered that the specific interests of developing countries were not sufficiently taken into account. The *Financial Times* reported on the reaction of developing-country Members to the Chair's proposals, as follows:

Serious opposition emerged ... to new proposals to cut manufacturing tariffs in the troubled Doha round of trade talks, with a group of developing countries saying the draft agreement was unacceptable. The group, led by South Africa and including Argentina and Venezuela, wants to continue protecting its industry against imports ... Mr Stephenson's [Canadian Ambassador] paper, released this week ... suggested a ceiling of 19–23 per cent for developing country industrial tariffs. The group wanted a ceiling of more than 30 per cent.[68]

Developed-country Members were also dissatisfied with the Chair's proposals, as the proposals were not, in their opinion, sufficiently ambitious in reducing customs duties.[69] The Chair's proposals triggered intense negotiations, which made

---

66 Negotiating Group on Market Access, *Draft NAMA Modalities*, JOB(07)/126, dated 17 July 2007, para. 5.

67 As an exception, the Chair proposed that developing-country Members with a binding coverage of non-agricultural tariff lines of less than 35 per cent would be exempted from making tariff reductions through the formula. Instead, they would be expected to bind 90 per cent of non-agricultural tariff lines at an average level that does not exceed the overall average of bound tariffs for all developing countries after full implementation of current concessions (28.5 per cent). The developing countries concerned are Cameroon, Congo, Côte d'Ivoire, Cuba, Ghana, Kenya, Macao, Mauritius, Nigeria, Sri Lanka, Suriname and Zimbabwe. See *ibid.*, para. 8.

68 See A. Beattie, 'Attack on Doha Talks Plan to Cut Tariffs', *Financial Times*, 25 July 2007.

69 This was so, in particular, because developing-country Members would in fact only be required to cut 'water' (i.e. the difference between the bound and the applied duties) and would, therefore, fail to create new market access opportunities. On 'water', see below, p. 448. Moreover, developed-country Members considered that emerging economies should join a number of sectoral tariff elimination initiatives.

meaningful progress by providing, for example, for more flexible modalities for certain categories of developing-country Members.[70] However, these negotiations eventually ended in failure at the mini-ministerial meeting in Geneva in July 2008.[71]

As discussed in Chapter 2 of this book, in April 2011, WTO Director-General Pascal Lamy presented to the Members the so-called 'Easter Package', a document reflecting the work done in the Doha Round negotiations so far.[72] This document showed that in many areas progress had been made, but it also made clear that Members had still to come to an agreement on many core issues, in particular on NAMA. The issue of market access for industrial products, a 'classic mercantilist issue' which had been 'the bread and butter' of the negotiations since the start, divided Members as no other issue.[73] Developed-country Members demanded, in particular from emerging economies, a substantial and meaningful 'Swiss-formula' cut in tariff bindings, combined with tariff elimination in important sectors. Emerging economies considered that these demands would: (1) lower their tariff bindings to a point where their policy space would be greatly reduced; and (2) have huge adverse impacts – especially as a result of sectoral tariff elimination – on their industrial development prospects. In his report to Members when presenting the 'Easter Package' in April 2011, Director-General Lamy concluded:

There are fundamentally different views on the ambition provided by the Swiss formula as it currently stands, on whether the contributions between different members are proportionate and balanced as well as on what is the contribution of sectorals. I believe we are confronted with a clear political gap which, as things stand, under the NAMA framework currently on the table, and from what I have heard in my consultations, is not bridgeable today.[74]

As discussed in Chapter 2 of this book, the Members subsequently made an effort to agree by the next Ministerial Conference in December 2011, on a smaller 'package' of issues relating primarily to issues of particular interest to the least-developed-country Members (an LDC package), including duty-free and quota-free market access and associated rules of origin. However, such narrow focus was not acceptable to all Members and agreement was subsequently sought on

---

70 A 'sliding scale' with five options was established for developing-country Members applying the formula. Moreover, separate and more flexible modalities were established for 'small, vulnerable economies' (SVEs), 'Members with low binding coverage', and 'recently acceded Members' (RAMs).

71 See above, p. 90.   72 See above, p. 91.

73 See Opening Remarks of Director-General Pascal Lamy at the informal TNC meeting of 29 April 2011, www.wto.org/english/news_e/news11_e/tnc_dg_infstat_29apr11_e.htm. As Lamy noted, trade negotiators have haggled over market access for industrial products for more than sixty years and they were eventually always able to find a compromise, 'using a mix of imagination, determination and spirit of compromise'. It was, therefore 'deeply disappointing that no ground for compromise has been found on the issue of industrial tariffs yet'. See *ibid.*

74 Report by the Director-General on his consultations on NAMA sectoral negotiations, WT/TN/C/14, dated 21 April 2011, para. 14.

a somewhat extended package of issues, including for example trade facilitation and export competition (an 'LDC plus' package).[75]

Ambassador Servansing from Mauritius, the Coordinator and Chief Negotiator of the ACP Group in Geneva, noted in 2012:

> It could be said that the NAMA negotiations ultimately floundered on the conflict between market access mercantilism on the one hand and development concerns on the other. But, this failure in large measure also shows the complexity of finding a new balance in global economic governance in today's globalised world.[76]

In the context of the Doha Round, Members are, in addition to tariff negotiations on non-agricultural products, also engaged in tariff negotiations on agricultural products. Reflecting the dissatisfaction of some countries with the result reached in the Uruguay Round regarding agricultural trade, Article 20 of the *Agreement on Agriculture* provided, as part of the so-called 'built-in agenda', for the restart of negotiations on agricultural trade, including tariff negotiations on agricultural products, by the end of 1999. The need for further negotiations on agricultural tariff reductions was particularly 'acute' since the Uruguay Round 'tariffication exercise' (discussed in Chapter 7 of this book) resulted in many (prohibitively) high tariff bindings.[77] Pursuant to paragraph 13 of the Doha Ministerial Declaration of November 2001, these negotiations were made a core part of the agenda of the Doha Round negotiations. As in the NAMA negotiations, discussed above, in the agricultural tariff negotiations the major challenge is to agree on the approach to be taken to the tariff reduction. Since the early years of the Doha Round negotiations, Members are discussing a tiered formula approach to the agricultural tariff negotiations. Under this approach, developed countries would reduce their customs duties on agricultural products in equal annual instalments over a number of years in accordance with a formula that provides for larger reductions in the higher tiers of customs duties. For example, duties in the tier from 21 to 50 per cent would be reduced by x per cent, while duties in the tier from 51 to 75 per cent would be reduced by $x + y$ per cent. In addition, developed-country Members would have to achieve a minimum average cut of their customs duties on agricultural products. Developing-country Members would also have to reduce their customs duties on agricultural products but would have to do so over a longer period in accordance with a tiered formula similar to the formula for developed-country Members but which provides for relatively smaller reductions in each tier. Also developing-country Members would have to achieve a minimum average cut of their customs duties on agricultural products but this minimum average cut would be smaller than for developed-country

---

75 See above, p. 91.

76 See Shree B. C. Servansing, 'Non-Agricultural Market Access (NAMA) – Balancing Development and Ambition', in P. Mehta, A. Kaushik and R. Kaukab (eds.), Reflections from the Frontline: Developing Country Negotiators in the WTO (CUTS International, 2012), 94.

77 On the tariffication exercise, see below, pp. 488–9.

Members. Small, vulnerable economies (SVEs) and recently acceded Members (RAMs) would be allowed to reduce their customs duties on agricultural products by a smaller amount than other developing-country Members. While various proposals have been worked out in excruciating technical detail,[78] final agreement on the tiered formula to be applied in the agricultural tariff negotiations has not been reached to date. Before agreeing on any tariff reduction formula, Members want to address numerous related concerns, such as the designation and treatment of 'sensitive products', the designation and treatment of 'special products', tariff escalation, tariff simplification, tariff quotas, cotton market access and the special safeguard mechanism (SSM), as well as broader issues such as agricultural export subsidies and domestic support.[79] Note, however, that – as discussed above – the current impasse in the Doha Round negotiations is caused not by disagreement on agricultural tariff reduction (or other agricultural trade issues), but by the fundamentally different views on non-agricultural market access (NAMA).

2.5   Tariff Concessions and Schedules of Concessions

The results of tariff negotiations are referred to as 'tariff concessions' or 'tariff bindings'. This sub-section discusses the concept of 'tariff concessions' or 'tariff bindings', and explains where they can be found and how they are to be interpreted.

2.5.1   Tariff Concessions or Tariff Bindings

A tariff concession, or a tariff binding, is a commitment not to raise the customs duty on a certain product above an agreed level. As a result of the Uruguay Round tariff negotiations, almost all customs duties imposed by developed-country Members are now 'bound', i.e. are subject to a maximum level.[80] Most Latin American developing-country Members have bound all customs duties.[81] However, for Asian and African developing-country Members the situation is more varied. While Members such as Indonesia and South Africa have bound more than 95 per cent of their customs duties, India and Thailand have bound about 75 per cent; Hong Kong, China, 45.6 per cent; Zimbabwe, 21.9 per cent; Bangladesh, 15.5 per cent; and Cameroon, 13.3 per cent.[82]

---

78 See, for example, Negotiating Group on Agriculture, *Report by the Chairman, H. E. Mr David Walker, to the Trade Negotiations Committee*, TN/AG/26, dated 21 April 2011, which contains in an annex the Revised Draft Modalities for Agriculture, TN/AG/W/4/Rev.4, dated 6 December 2008.

79 On agricultural export subsidies and domestic support, see below, p. 837.

80 For both the European Union and the United States, the binding coverage is 100 per cent. See WTO/ITC/UNCTAD, *World Tariff Profiles 2012*, available at www.wto.org/english/res_e/booksp_e/tariff_profiles12_e.pdf.

81 Note that many Latin American Members apply a 'uniform ceiling binding', i.e. they have bound their customs duties to a single maximum level. For Chile, for example, this uniform maximum level is 25 per cent.

82 See WTO/ITC/UNCTAD, *World Tariff Profiles 2012*, available at www.wto.org/english/res_e/booksp_e/tariff_profiles12_e.pdf. Note that these percentages are not weighted according to trade volume or value. With regard to Hong Kong, China, note also that, while a high percentage of customs duties is unbound, the applied duties are zero.

2.5.2   Schedules of Concessions

The tariff concessions or bindings of a Member are set out in that Member's Schedule of Concessions (also referred to as a Goods Schedule). Each Member of the WTO has a schedule, except when the Member is part of a customs union, in which case the Member has a common schedule with the other members of the customs union.[83] The Schedules of Concessions resulting from the Uruguay Round negotiations are all annexed to the *Marrakesh Protocol* to the GATT 1994. Pursuant to Article II:7 of the GATT 1994, the Schedules of Members are an integral part of the GATT 1994. The Schedules are available on the WTO website.[84] Information on tariff bindings can also be obtained via Tariff Analysis Online or, for less sophisticated searches, via the Tariff Download Facility.[85] Also the International Trade and Market Access interactive tool is quite useful.[86]

Each Schedule of Concessions contains four parts. The most important part, Part I, sets out the MFN concessions with respect to agricultural products and non-agricultural products. Furthermore, a Schedule sets out preferential concessions (Part II), concessions on non-tariff measures (Part III) and specific commitments on domestic support and export subsidies on agricultural products (Part IV). Figure 6.3 sets out an excerpt from Chapter 18 of the Schedule of Concessions of the European Union.

It is not possible for Members to agree in their Schedules to treatment that is inconsistent with the basic GATT obligations. In *EC – Bananas III (1997)*, the Appellate Body addressed the question of whether the allocation of tariff quotas agreed to and inscribed in the EC's Schedule was inconsistent with Article XIII of the GATT 1994. The Appellate Body referred first to the report of the panel in *US – Sugar (1989)*, which stated, *inter alia*:

Article II permits contracting parties to incorporate into their Schedules acts yielding rights under the General Agreement but not acts diminishing obligations under that Agreement.[87]

Subsequently, the Appellate Body ruled in *EC – Bananas III (1997)*:

This principle is equally valid for the market access concessions and commitments for agricultural products contained in the Schedules annexed to the GATT 1994. The ordinary meaning of the term 'concessions' suggests that a Member may yield rights and grant benefits, but it cannot diminish its obligations.[88]

---

83 E.g. the twenty-seven Member States of the European Union do not have their 'own' individual schedule. Their common schedule is the Schedule of the European Communities, now the European Union.

84 See www.wto.org/english/tratop_e/schedules_e/goods_schedules_table_e.htm.

85 See www.wto.org/english/tratop_e/tariffs_e/tariff_data_e.htm. The information on tariff bindings in Tariff Analysis Online and the Tariff Download Facility is based on the WTO's Consolidated Tariff Schedules (CTS) database. As discussed above, Tariff Analysis Online and the Tariff Download Facility also contain information on the applied duties. That information is drawn from the WTO's Integrated Database (IDB), which is fed with the information that Members annually supply on the duties they apply.

86 See www.wto.org/english/res_e/statis_e/statis_e.htm.

87 GATT Panel Report, *US – Sugar (1989)*, para. 5.2.

88 Appellate Body Report, *EC – Bananas III (1997)*, para. 154. The Appellate Body confirmed this ruling in Appellate Body Report, *EC – Poultry (1998)*, para. 98.

SCHEDULE LXXX – EUROPEAN COMMUNITIES
PART I – MOST-FAVOURED-NATION TARIFF
SECTION I – Agricultural Products
SECTION I – A Tariffs

Tariff item number	Description of products	Base rate of duty			Bound rate of duty		Implementation period from/to	Special safeguard	Initial negotiating right	Other duties and charges	Comments
		Ad valorem (%)	Other	U/B/C	Ad valorem (%)	Other					
1801.00.00	Cocoa beans, whole or broken, raw or roasted	3.0			0.0						
1802.00.00	Cocoa shells, husks, skins and other cocoa waste	3.0			0.0						
1803	Cocoa pastes, whether or not defatted :										
1803.10.00	- Not defatted	15.0			9.6						
1803.20.00	- Wholly or partly defatted	15.0			9.6						
1804.00.00	Cocoa butter, fat and oil	12.0			7.7						
1805.00.00	Cocoa powder, not containing added sugar or other sweet-ening matter	16.0			8.0						
1806	Chocolate and other food preparations containing cocoa:										
1806.10	- Cocoa powder, containing added sugar or other sweet-ening matter:										

Code	Description				
1806.10.10	-- Containing no more or less than 5% by weight of sucrose (including invert sugar expressed as sucrose) or iso-glucose expressed as sucrose	10.0		8.0	
1806.10.30	-- Containing 5% or more but less than 65% by weight of sucrose (including invert sugar expressed as sucrose) or iso-glucose expressed as sucrose	10.0	+ 315 ECU/T	8.0	+ 252 ECU/T
1806.10.30	-- Containing 65 % or more but less than 80 % by weight of sucrose (including invert sugar expressed as sucrose) or isoglucose expressed as sucrose	10.0	+ 393 ECU/T	8.0	+ 314 ECU/T
1806.10.90	-- Containing 80 % or more by weight of sucrose (including invert sugar expressed as sucrose) or isoglucose expressed as sucrose	10.0	+ 524 ECU/T	8.0	+ 419 ECU/T
1806.20	- Other preparations in block slabs or bars weighing more than 2 kg or in liquid, paste, powder, granular or other bulk form in containers or immediate packings, of a content exceeding 2 kg:				

Figure 6.3 Excerpt from the EU Goods Schedule

Tariff item number	Description of products	Base rate of duty			Bound rate of duty		Implementation period from/to	Special safeguard	Initial negotiating right	Other duties and charges	Comments
		Ad valorem (%)	Other	U/B/C	Ad valorem (%)	Other					
1806.20.70	-- Chocolate milk crumb, containing a combined weight of less than 25% of cocoa butter and milkfat and containing less than 18% by weight of cocoa butter	22.3	*		15.4	*					* see annex 1
1806.20.80	-- Other	12.0	* MAX 27% + AD S/Z		8.3	* MAX 18.7% + AD S/Z					* see annex 1
	- Other, in blocks, slabs or bars:										
1806.31.00	-- Filled	12.0	* MAX 27% + AD S/Z		8.3	* MAX 18.7% + AD S/Z					* see annex 1
1806.32.50	-- Not filled	12.0	* MAX 27% + AD S/Z		8.3	* MAX 18.7% + AD S/Z					* see annex 1
1806.90.49	- Other	12.0	* MAX 27% + AD S/Z		8.3	* MAX 18.7% + AD S/Z					* see annex 1

Figure 6.3 (*Cont.*)

Most Schedules are structured according to the Harmonized Commodity Description and Coding System ('Harmonized System' or 'HS'), discussed below. Although the format is not identical in all cases, they generally contain the following information for each product subject to tariff concessions: (1) HS tariff item number; (2) description of the product; (3) base rate of duty; (4) bound rate of duty; (5) initial negotiating rights (INR);[89] (6) other duties and charges;[90] and (7) for agricultural products only, special safeguards.[91]

Note that the Schedules of the major trading entities such as the European Union and the United States, which have made tariff concessions on virtually all products, are lengthy and detailed. The file containing the Schedule of the European Union on the WTO's website is 759KB in size. By contrast, the Schedules of many developing-country Members are general and short. The files containing the Schedules of Botswana and the Dominican Republic are only 12 and 13KB respectively.[92]

2.5.3   Interpretation of Tariff Schedules and Concessions

Since the tariff schedules are an integral part of the GATT 1994 pursuant to Article II:7 thereof, they are part of a 'covered agreement' under the DSU.[93] Article 3.2 of the DSU therefore applies to the interpretation of tariff schedules and the concessions set out therein. As discussed in Chapter 3 of this book, Article 3.2 of the DSU provides that the provisions of the covered agreements are to be clarified in accordance with customary rules of interpretation of public international law, which have been codified in Articles 31 and 32 of the *Vienna Convention on the Law of Treaties*.[94] In *EC – Computer Equipment (1998)*, at issue was a dispute between the United States and the European Communities on whether the EC's tariff concessions regarding automatic data-processing equipment applied to local area network (LAN) computer equipment.[95] The panel based its interpretation of the EC's tariff concessions on the 'legitimate expectations' of the exporting Member, *in casu*, the United States. On appeal, the Appellate Body rejected this approach to the interpretation of tariff concessions, ruling as follows:

The purpose of treaty interpretation under Article 31 of the *Vienna Convention* is to ascertain the *common* intentions of the parties. These *common* intentions cannot be ascertained

---

89 See below, p. 450.   90 See below, p. 464.

91 See below, p. 632. Since the Schedules are structured according to the Harmonized System, the periodic amendments to the Harmonized System to take account of changes in technology and patterns in international trade will give rise to changes in the Schedules.

92 See www.wto.org/english/tratop_e/schedules_e/goods_schedules_e.htm.

93 On the concept of 'covered agreement', see above, p. 163.   94 See above, pp. 187–94.

95 In the context of the Uruguay Round tariff negotiations, the European Communities agreed to a tariff binding for automatic data processing equipment of 4.9 per cent (to be reduced to 2.5 per cent for some products or duty-free for others). According to the United States, during and shortly after the Uruguay Round, the European Communities classified LAN computer equipment as automatic data processing equipment. Later, however, it started classifying LAN computer equipment as telecommunications equipment, a product category subject to generally higher duties, in the range of 4.6–7.5 per cent (to be reduced to 3–3.6 per cent).

on the basis of the subjective and unilaterally determined 'expectations' of *one* of the parties to a treaty. Tariff concessions provided for in a Member's Schedule – the interpretation of which is at issue here – are reciprocal and result from a mutually advantageous negotiation between importing and exporting Members. A Schedule is made an integral part of the GATT 1994 by Article II:7 of the GATT 1994. Therefore, the concessions provided for in that Schedule are part of the terms of the treaty. As such, the only rules which may be applied in interpreting the meaning of a concession are the general rules of treaty interpretation set out in the Vienna Convention.[96]

The Appellate Body furthermore noted with respect to the lack of clarity of tariff concessions and tariff schedules:

Tariff negotiations are a process of reciprocal demands and concessions, of 'give and take'. It is only normal that importing Members define their offers (and their ensuing obligations) in terms which suit their needs. On the other hand, exporting Members have to ensure that their corresponding rights are described in such a manner in the Schedules of importing Members that their export interests, as agreed in the negotiations, are guaranteed ... [T]he fact that Members' Schedules are an integral part of the GATT 1994 indicates that, while each Schedule represents the tariff commitments made by *one* Member, they represent a common agreement among *all* Members.

For the reasons stated above, we conclude that the Panel erred in finding that 'the United States was not required to clarify the scope of the European Communities' tariff concessions on LAN equipment'. We consider that any clarification of the scope of tariff concessions that may be required during the negotiations is a task for *all* interested parties.[97]

Note that, at the very end of the Uruguay Round, a special arrangement was made to allow the negotiators to check and control, through consultations with their negotiating partners, the scope of tariff concessions agreed to. This 'process of verification' took place from 15 February to 25 March 1994.[98]

As discussed above, most schedules are structured according to the Harmonized System. The Uruguay Round tariff negotiations were held on the basis of the Harmonized System's nomenclature; requests for, and offers of, concessions were normally made in terms of this nomenclature. In *EC – Chicken Cuts (2005)*, the Appellate Body stated that:

[these] circumstances confirm that, prior to, during, as well as after the Uruguay Round negotiations, there was broad consensus among the GATT Contracting Parties *to use* the Harmonized System as the basis for their WTO Schedules, notably with respect to agricultural products. In our view, this consensus constitutes an 'agreement' between WTO Members 'relating to' the WTO Agreement that was 'made in connection with the conclusion of' that Agreement, within the meaning of Article 31(2)(a) of the Vienna Convention. As such, this agreement is 'context' under Article 31(2)(a) for the purpose of interpreting the WTO agreements, of which the EC Schedule is an integral part.[99]

---

96 Appellate Body Report, *EC – Computer Equipment (1998)*, para. 84.
97 *Ibid.*, paras. 109 and 110.   98 See MTN.TNC/W/131, dated 21 January 1994.
99 Appellate Body Report, *EC – Chicken Cuts (2005)*, para. 199. See also Appellate Body Reports, *China – Auto Parts (2009)*, para. 149. Already in *EC – Computer Equipment (1998)*, the Appellate Body expressed surprise that in that case neither the European Communities nor the United States argued before the panel that the Harmonized System and its Explanatory Notes were relevant in the interpretation of the EC's Goods Schedule. See Appellate Body Report, *EC – Computer Equipment (1998)*, para. 89.

The Appellate Body thus considered that the Harmonized System is relevant for purposes of interpreting tariff commitments in the Members' Schedules.[100] The Appellate Body also considered that Chapter Notes and Explanatory Notes to the Harmonized System could also be relevant for interpretation purposes.[101]

Finally, note that the consistent classification practice at the time of the tariff negotiations is also relevant to the interpretation of tariff concessions.[102] As the Appellate Body noted in *EC – Computer Equipment (1998)*, the classification practice during the Uruguay Round is part of 'the circumstances of [the] conclusion' of the *WTO Agreement*. Therefore, this practice may be used as a supplementary means of interpretation within the meaning of Article 32 of the *Vienna Convention*.[103]

Questions and Assignments 6.4

What are tariff concessions or tariff bindings? Where can you find the tariff concessions or tariff bindings agreed to by a Member? Do Argentina, Mali, Thailand and the Netherlands each have a tariff schedule? Find out what, if any, is the tariff binding of your country on cocoa powder and on road tractors. How are tariff schedules and tariff concessions to be interpreted? Whose obligation is it to ensure that the scope of tariff concessions is unambiguous?

2.6 Protection of Tariff Concessions

As noted above, under WTO law customs duties are not prohibited. It was envisaged, however, that customs duties would be 'bound' and then progressively reduced through rounds of negotiations. WTO rules on customs duties relate primarily to the protection of tariff concessions agreed to in the context of tariff negotiations. The basic rules are set out in Article II:1 of the GATT 1994.

2.6.1 Articles II:1(a) and II:1(b), First Sentence, of the GATT 1994

Article II:1 of the GATT 1994 states:

a.   Each [Member] shall accord to the commerce of the other [Members] treatment no less favourable than that provided for in the appropriate Part of the appropriate Schedule annexed to this Agreement.

b.   The products described in Part I of the Schedule relating to any [Member], which are the products of territories of other [Members], shall, on their importation into the territory to which the Schedule relates, and subject

---

100 See Appellate Body Report, *EC – Chicken Cuts (2005)*, para. 199. Note that the panel in *EC – IT Products (2010)* stated that it does not follow from the Appellate Body's case law that the Harmonized System will necessarily be relevant in interpreting *all* tariff concessions, including tariff concessions that are not based on the Harmonized System. See Panel Report, *EC – IT Products (2010)*, para. 7.443.
101 See Appellate Body Report, *EC – Chicken Cuts (2005)*, paras. 219–29.
102 On tariff classification, see below, pp. 452–6.
103 See above, pp. 192–4. See also Appellate Body Report, *EC – Computer Equipment (1998)*, paras. 92 and 95. Note that, while the prior classification practice of only *one* of the parties may be relevant, it is clearly of more limited value than the practice of all parties. See *ibid.*, para. 93.

to the terms, conditions or qualifications set forth in that Schedule, be exempt from ordinary customs duties in excess of those set forth and provided therein.

Article II:1(a) provides that Members shall accord to the commerce of other Members, that is, in any case the products imported from other Members, *treatment no less favourable* than that provided for in their Schedule.[104] Article II:1(b), first sentence, provides that products described in Part I of the Schedule of any Member shall, on importation, be *exempt from ordinary customs duties in excess of* those set out in the Schedule. This means that products may not be subjected to customs duties above the tariff concessions or bindings. With respect to the relationship between Article II:1(a) and Article II:1(b), first sentence, the Appellate Body noted in *Argentina – Textiles and Apparel (1998)*:

> Paragraph (a) of Article II:1 contains a general prohibition against according treatment less favourable to imports than that provided for in a Member's Schedule. Paragraph (b) prohibits a specific kind of practice that will always be inconsistent with paragraph (a): that is, the application of ordinary customs duties in excess of those provided for in the Schedule.[105]

The requirement of Article II:1(b), first sentence, that a Member may not impose customs duties *in excess of* the duties set out in its Schedule was at issue in *Argentina – Textiles and Apparel (1998)*. In its Schedule, Argentina has bound its customs duties on textiles and apparel to 35 per cent *ad valorem*. In practice, however, these products were subject to the higher of *either* a 35 per cent *ad valorem* duty *or* a minimum specific import duty (the so-called 'DIEM'). The panel found the DIEM to be inconsistent with Argentina's obligations under Article II:1(b) of the GATT 1994 for two reasons: (1) because Argentina applied a different *type* of import duty (a specific duty) than that set out in its Schedule (an *ad valorem* duty); and (2) because the DIEM would, in certain cases, be in excess of the binding of 35 per cent *ad valorem*. On appeal, the Appellate Body agreed with the panel that the DIEM was inconsistent with Argentina's obligations under Article II:1(b), but it modified the panel's reasoning. The Appellate Body first noted:

> The principal obligation in the first sentence of Article II:1(b) ... requires a Member to refrain from imposing ordinary customs duties *in excess of* those provided for in that Member's Schedule. However, the text of Article II:1(b), first sentence, does not address whether applying a *type* of duty different from the *type* provided for in a Member's Schedule is inconsistent, in itself, with that provision.[106]

According to the Appellate Body, the application of a type of duty different from the type provided for in a Member's Schedule is only inconsistent with

---

104 The question whether the concept of the 'commerce of other [Members]' refers not only to the imports from other Members but also to the exports to other Members, has not yet been addressed in WTO dispute settlement. See below, p. 472.

105 Appellate Body Report, *Argentina – Textiles and Apparel (1998)*, para. 45.

106 *Ibid.*, para. 46.

Article II:1(b) *to the extent that* it results in customs duties being imposed in excess of those set forth in that Member's Schedule.[107]

As Article II:1(b), first sentence, explicitly states, the obligation to exempt products from customs duties in excess of those set forth in the Schedule is 'subject to the terms, conditions or qualifications set forth in that Schedule'. In *Canada – Dairy (1999)*, the Appellate Body ruled in this respect:

In our view, the ordinary meaning of the phrase 'subject to' is that such concessions are without prejudice to and are *subordinated to*, and are, therefore, *qualified by*, any 'terms, conditions or qualifications' inscribed in a Member's Schedule … A strong presumption arises that the language which is inscribed in a Member's Schedule under the heading, 'Other Terms and Conditions', has some *qualifying* or *limiting* effect on the substantive content or scope of the concession or commitment.[108]

Some of the disputes under Article II:1(a) and (b), first sentence, of the GATT 1994 do not directly stem from duties or charges imposed in excess of those contained in the Schedules of Concessions. In *EC – Chicken Cuts (2005)*, the European Communities did not deviate from the customs duties as contained in its Schedule of Concessions. It did, however, reclassify a certain type of chicken meat, namely, frozen boneless chicken cuts impregnated with salt, under a different tariff heading (heading 02.07 'Meat and edible offal, of the poultry of heading No. 0105, fresh, chilled or frozen').[109] Under that particular tariff heading, the customs duty imposed was higher than under the heading that applied according to the complainants in the case (heading 02.10 'Meat and edible meat offal, salted, in brine, dried, smoked; edible flours and meals of meat or meat offal'). As in *EC – Computer Equipment (1998)*, discussed above, the outcome of the *EC – Chicken Cuts (2005)* dispute depended on the interpretation of the tariff headings, and, in this case more specifically, on the interpretation of the term 'salted'. According to the European Communities, the key element under heading 02.10 was preservation and therefore the term 'salted' implied that the meat should be impregnated with salt sufficient to ensure long-term preservation. The complainants, Thailand and Brazil, contended that 'salted' did not imply long-term preservation and that the salted chicken cuts at issue thus fell within

107 See *ibid.*, para. 55. On this basis, the Appellate Body found the DIEM regime inconsistent with Article II:1(b), first sentence, of the GATT 1994.
108 Appellate Body Report, *Canada – Dairy (1999)*, para. 134. At issue in *Canada – Dairy (1999)* was a tariff quota for fluid milk of 64,500 tonnes included in Canada's Schedule. In the column 'Other Terms and Conditions' of Canada's Schedule, it states that 'this quantity [64,500 tonnes] represents the estimated annual cross-border purchases imported by Canadian consumers'. In practice, Canada restricted imports under the 64,500 tonnes tariff quota to dairy products for the personal use of the importer and his household not exceeding C$20 in value for each importation. The United States contested that the restriction of access to imports for personal use not exceeding C$20 in value constituted a violation of Article II:1(b) of the GATT 1994. The panel agreed with the United States. The panel found that the 'condition' in Canada's Schedule is *descriptive* and does not establish restrictions on access to the tariff quota for fluid milk. The Appellate Body disagreed with the panel that the 'condition' was merely descriptive, and concluded that the limitation of cross-border purchases to 'Canadian consumers' referred to in Canada's Schedule justifies Canada's effective limitation of access to the tariff quota to imports for 'personal use'. However, the Appellate Body found that the C$20 value limitation was not contained in Canada's Schedule. See *ibid.*, para. 143.
109 See Panel Report, *EC – Chicken Cuts (2005)*, paras. 7.46–7.47.

heading 02.10. Both the panel and the Appellate Body came to the conclusion that 'salted' did not imply long-term preservation in any way and that therefore the chicken cuts did fall under the more favourable tariff heading 02.10.[110] The European Communities had thus acted inconsistently with Article II:1(a) and (b) by wrongly classifying the chicken cuts, which resulted in treatment less favourable than that provided for in its Schedule.[111] To date, WTO Members have been found to have acted inconsistently with the obligations under Articles II:1(a) and II:1(b), first sentence, of the GATT 1994 in eight disputes[112]

2.6.2   Tariff Concessions and Customs Duties Actually Applied

Note the difference between tariff concessions or bindings and the customs duties actually applied. As the Appellate Body observed in *Argentina – Textiles and Apparel (1998)*:

> A tariff binding in a Member's Schedule provides an upper limit on the amount of duty that may be imposed, and a Member is permitted to impose a duty that is less than that provided for in its Schedule.[113]

For many Members, tariff bindings for industrial products are considerably higher than the customs duties actually applied to these products. This means that the customs duties applied are significantly lower than the maximum levels agreed upon. This is in particular the case for developing-country Members. Figure 6.4 shows simple average tariff bindings and applied duties of selected Members. For example, the simple average tariff binding of India is 48.7 per cent, while its simple average applied duty is 12.6 per cent. Likewise, the simple average tariff binding of Brazil is 31.4 per cent, while its simple average applied duty is 13.7 per cent. In WTO-speak, the difference between the tariff binding and the applied duty is referred to as 'water' or 'binding overhang'. The presence of 'water' reflects a unilateral lowering of tariff barriers and thus allows for better market access. In this respect, 'water' is very welcome. However, 'water' also gives the importing Members concerned ample opportunity to increase the applied duties. Importing Members have the discretion to increase the applied duty to the level of the tariff binding. Therefore, when there is a lot of 'water',

---

110 This conclusion was reached by applying the customary rules of interpretation of public international law, as codified in Articles 31 and 32 of the *Vienna Convention on the Law on Treaties*. Note, however, that the Appellate Body reversed the panel's conclusion that: 'the European Communities' practice of classifying, between 1996 and 2002, the products at issue under heading 02.10 of the EC Schedule "amounts to subsequent practice" within the meaning of Article 31.3(b) of the Vienna Convention'. See Appellate Body Report, *EC – Chicken Cuts (2005)*, para. 276.

111 See *ibid.*, paras. 346, 347(b)(i), (ii) and (iii) and 347 (c)(i), (ii) and (iii).

112 See *Argentina – Textiles and Apparel (1998)*; *Canada – Dairy (1999)*; *Korea – Various Measures on Beef (2001)*; *EC – Chicken Cuts (2005)*; *EC – Bananas III (Article 21.5 – Ecuador II)/EC – Bananas III (Article 21.5 – US) (2008)*; *China – Auto Parts (2009)*; *US – Zeroing (Japan – Article 21.5 – Japan) (2009)*; and *EC – IT Products (2010)*. Note that, in *EC – Computer Equipment (1998)*, the Appellate Body reversed the panel's finding of inconsistency for the reasons discussed above, and did not complete the legal analysis. See above, p. 443.

113 Appellate Body Report, *Argentina – Textiles and Apparel (1998)*, para. 46.

	Bound rate	MFN applied rate
Argentina	31.8	13.6
Brazil	31.4	13.7
Burundi	67.6	12.5
China	10	9.6
European Union	5.2	5.2
India	48.7	12.6
Japan	5.3	5.3
Kuwait	97.2	4.7
Malaysia	23	6.5
Nigeria	119.1	11.7
United States	3.5	3.5

Figure 6.4 Tariff rates: bound and applied

i.e. when the difference between the tariff bindings and the applied duties is large, exporting Members and traders have much less security and predictability with respect to the level of duties that will actually be applied on their products. However, as is clear in the Doha Round tariff negotiations,[114] Members, and in particular developing-country Members, are often hesitant to agree to lower bindings and to give up their 'water', even when their applied duties have for years been much lower than their bindings. Agreeing to lower bindings means giving up economic and fiscal policy space.

Questions and Assignments 6.5

Which provisions of the GATT 1994 prohibit the imposition of customs duties higher than the tariff concession or binding? What is the relationship between Article II:1(a) and Article II:1(b), first sentence? Is the application of a type of duty different from the type provided for in a Member's Schedule inconsistent with Article II:1(b), first sentence? Can tariff concessions or bindings be subject to terms and conditions? If so, give a concrete example of such a term or condition. Can a Member impose customs duties lower than the tariff concession or binding? Is 'water' a problem?

2.7 Modification or Withdrawal of Tariff Concessions

As discussed above, Members may not apply customs duties above the tariff concessions or bindings agreed to in tariff negotiations and reflected in their Schedules. However, the GATT 1994 provides a procedure for the modification

114 See above, pp. 427–8.

or withdrawal of agreed tariff concessions. Article XXVIII:1 of the GATT 1994 states, in pertinent part:

[A Member] ... may, by negotiation and agreement ... modify or withdraw a concession included in the appropriate schedule annexed to this Agreement.

The negotiations on the modification or withdrawal of tariff concessions are to be conducted with: (1) the Members that hold so-called 'Initial Negotiating Rights' (INRs); and (2) any other Member that has a 'principal supplying interest'. In addition, consultations should be held with Members having a 'substantial interest'. The Members holding INRs are those Members with which the concession was bilaterally negotiated, initially. As mentioned above, INRs are commonly, though not always, specified in the Schedule of the Member granting the concession, but can also be determined on the basis of the negotiation records. Due to the approach to tariff negotiations adopted during the Uruguay Round,[115] many tariff concessions did not result from bilateral negotiations and thus INRs are much less common in respect of concessions agreed during the Uruguay Round. It was therefore agreed in the *Understanding on Article XXVIII* that:

Any Member having a principal supplying interest ... in a concession which is modified or withdrawn shall be accorded an initial negotiating right.[116]

A Member has a 'principal supplying interest' if, as provided in Note *Ad* Article XXVIII, paragraph 1.4:

that [Member] has had, over a reasonable period of time prior to the negotiations, a larger share in the market of the applicant [Member] than a Member with which the concession was initially negotiated or would ... have had such a share in the absence of discriminatory quantitative restrictions maintained by the applicant [Member].

The *Understanding on Article XXVIII*, paragraph 1, further elaborates on the concept of 'principal supplying interest' as follows:

[T]he Member which has the highest ratio of exports affected by the concession (i.e. exports of the product to the market of the Member modifying or withdrawing the concession) to its total exports shall be deemed to have a principal supplying interest if it does not already have an initial negotiating right or a principal supplying interest as provided for in paragraph 1 of Article XXVIII.

Pursuant to Article XXVIII, the *negotiations* on the modification or withdrawal of a tariff concession are to be conducted only with the Members holding INRs or those having a principal supplying interest. However, the Member wishing to modify or withdraw a tariff concession must *consult* any other Member that has a substantial interest in such concession.[117] The Note *Ad* Article XXVIII, paragraph 1.7, states:

---

115 See above, pp. 432–3.
116 *Understanding on the Implementation of Article XXVIII of the GATT 1994*, para. 7.
117 See Article XXVIII:1 of the GATT 1994. The Ministerial Conference determines which Members have a 'substantial interest'. See *ibid.*

The expression 'substantial interest' is not capable of a precise definition and accordingly may present difficulties ... It is, however, intended to be construed to cover only those [Members] which have, or in the absence of discriminatory quantitative restrictions affecting their exports could reasonably be expected to have, a significant share in the market of the [Member] seeking to modify or withdraw the concession.

A 'significant share', required to claim a 'substantial interest', has generally been considered to be 10 per cent of the market of the Member seeking to modify or withdraw a tariff concession.

With respect to the objective of the negotiations and agreement on the modification or withdrawal of tariff concessions, Article XXVIII:2 provides:

In such negotiations and agreement ... the [Members] concerned shall endeavour to maintain a general level of reciprocal and mutually advantageous concessions not less favourable to trade than that provided for in this Agreement prior to such negotiations.

When a tariff concession is modified or withdrawn, compensation in the form of new concessions needs to be granted to maintain a general level of concessions not less favourable to trade.[118]

It follows from the above that the modification or withdrawal of a tariff binding is based on the principle of renegotiation and compensation. However, if the negotiations fail to lead to an agreement, Article XXVIII:3(a) provides, in relevant part, that:

[T]he [Member] which proposes to modify or withdraw the concession shall, nevertheless, be free to do so.

In that case, any Member holding an INR, any Member having a principal supplying interest *and* any Member having a substantial interest shall be free to withdraw substantially equivalent concessions.[119]

In 2012, Ukraine requested – less than four years after its accession to the WTO – the renegotiation of its tariff bindings on 371 tariff lines. Both the size and the timing of this request for renegotiation alarmed many Members. At the General Council meeting of 26 September 2012, EU Ambassador Angelos Pangratis stated:

The EU is of the firm opinion that the procedure set out in Article XXVIII GATT is not meant for renegotiating a significant part of the accession commitments of WTO members ... The EU considers that Ukraine's request raises very obvious and very serious systemic concerns as it risks undermining the credibility of members' commitments to their WTO obligations.[120]

---

118 See Award of the Arbitrator, *EC–ACP Partnership Agreement – Recourse to Arbitration Pursuant to the Decision of 14 November 2001*.
119 See Article XXVIII:3 of the GATT 1994.
120 *Bridges Weekly Trade News Digest*, 3 October 2012. Argentina, Australia, Brazil, Canada, Chile, China, Colombia, Ecuador, El Salvador, Guatemala, Hong Kong, China, Korea, Malaysia (on its own behalf and on behalf of the ASEAN countries), Mexico, New Zealand, Norway, Switzerland, Turkey, Uruguay and the United States raised similar concerns. No Member spoke up in Ukraine's defence. See *Bridges Weekly Trade News Digest*, 3 October 2012 and 17 October 2012.

In support of its request for renegotiation of so many of its tariff bindings, Ukraine argued that, on joining the WTO in 2008, it agreed on very low tariff bindings 'with the expectation that the ongoing Doha Round talks would lead to additional liberalisation among other WTO members with more protected economies'.[121] As such additional liberalisation has clearly not been realised, Ukraine argued that 'today's reality [now] makes the adjustment necessary'.[122]

Finally, note that Article XVIII:7 of the GATT 1994 allows developing-country Members to *modify or withdraw a tariff concession* in order to promote the establishment of a particular industry.[123] However, the developing-country Member concerned must enter into negotiations with the Members primarily affected by the modification or withdrawal of the tariff concession in order to come to an agreement on compensatory adjustment.[124] If no agreement is reached, it is for the General Council to decide whether the compensatory adjustment offered is adequate. Where the General Council considers the compensation to be adequate, the developing-country Member is then free to modify or withdraw the tariff concession provided that, at the same time, it gives effect to the compensatory adjustment. Should the General Council find the compensation offered to be inadequate, but also that every reasonable effort was made to offer adequate compensation, the developing-country Member may proceed with the modification or withdrawal of the tariff concession.[125] Any other Member affected by the modification or withdrawal is then free to modify or withdraw substantially equivalent concessions with regard to the developing-country Member concerned.[126] Under the GATT 1947, the GATT Council was generous in allowing developing-country Members to modify or withdraw tariff concessions without requiring any compensatory adjustment. As discussed in Chapter 1 of this book, the contribution of the exception under Article XVIII:7 to the economic development of developing countries has been limited.[127] In fact, the infant-industry-protection exception under Article XVIII:7 has not been invoked by any developing-country Member since the entry into force of the *WTO Agreement* in 1995.[128]

Questions and Assignments 6.6

Can tariff concessions or bindings, set forth in a Member's Schedule, be modified or withdrawn? Which Members hold INRs? Which Members have a 'principal supplying interest' and which Members have a 'substantial interest' in the concession to be modified or withdrawn? Why is this important? Can a tariff concession or binding be modified or withdrawn without agreement on compensation? In the absence of such an agreement, can the unsatisfied

121 See *Bridges Weekly Trade News Digest*, 17 October 2012.
122 See *ibid*.
123 For a discussion of the 'infant industry' argument for trade-restrictive measures, see above, p. 24.
124 See Article XVIII:7(a) of the GATT 1994.
125 See Article XVIII:7(b) of the GATT 1994.
126 See *ibid*.   127 See above, p. 456.
128 Committee on Trade and Development, *Implementation of Special and Differential Treatment Provisions in WTO Agreements and Decisions*, Note by the WTO Secretariat, Addendum 4, WT/COMTD/W/77/Rev.1/Add.4, dated 7 February 2002, 2.

Member retaliate by withdrawing equivalent concessions? Does such withdrawal apply on an MFN basis or can it be done only *vis-à-vis* the Member that withdraws or modifies its bindings?

2.8 Imposition of Customs Duties on Imports

In addition to rules for the protection of tariff concessions, WTO law also provides for rules on the manner in which customs duties must be imposed. The imposition of customs duties may require three determinations to be made: (1) the determination of the proper classification of the imported good, which allows customs authorities to determine which duty to levy; (2) the determination of the customs value of the imported good; and (3) the determination of the origin of the imported good.

The need for these determinations follows from the fact that customs duties differ from good to good (customs classification); are usually *ad valorem* duties and thus calculated on the basis of the value of the products concerned (customs valuation); and may differ depending on the exporting country (determination of origin).

2.8.1 Customs Classification

As illustrated above when discussing *EC – Computer Equipment (1998)* and *EC – Chicken Cuts (2005)*, the imposition of customs duties requires the determination of the proper customs classification of the imported good.[129] WTO law does not *specifically* address the issue of customs classification. In *Spain – Unroasted Coffee (1981)*, the panel ruled that:

> there was no obligation under the GATT to follow any particular system for classifying goods, and that a contracting party had the right to introduce in its customs tariff new positions or sub-positions as appropriate.[130]

However, in classifying products for customs purposes, Members have of course to consider their general obligations under the WTO agreements, such as the MFN treatment obligation. As discussed in Chapter 4 of this book, the panel in *Spain – Unroasted Coffee (1981)* ruled that:

> whatever the classification adopted, Article I:1 required that the same tariff treatment be applied to 'like products'.[131]

Specific rules on classification can be found in the *International Convention on the Harmonized Commodity Description and Coding System* (the '*HS Convention*'), which entered into force on 1 January 1988 and to which most WTO Members are a party.[132] The Harmonized Commodity Description and Coding System,

---

129 See above, pp. 445 and 447.
130 Panel Report, *Spain – Unroasted Coffee (1981)*, para. 4.4.
131 *Ibid.* See also above, pp. 429–31; and Panel Report, *Japan – SPF Dimension Lumber (1989)*, para. 5.9.
132 *International Convention on the Harmonized Commodity Description and Coding System*, Brussels, 14 June 1983, as amended by the Protocol of Amendment of 24 June 1986, available at www.wcoomd.org/home_wco_topics_hsoverviewboxes_hsconvention.htm.

commonly referred to as the 'Harmonized System' or 'HS', is an *international commodity classification system*, developed under the auspices of the Brussels-based Customs Cooperation Council (CCC), known today as the World Customs Organization (WCO).[133] As of 1 January 2013, 207 countries, territories or customs or economic unions are applying the Harmonized System.[134]

The Harmonized System consists of 21 sections covering 97 chapters, 1,241 headings and over 5,000 commodity groups. The sections and chapters are:

- Section I (Chapters 1–5, live animals and animal products);
- Section II (Chapters 6–14, vegetable products);
- Section III (Chapter 15, animal or vegetable fats and oils);
- Section IV (Chapters 16–24, prepared foodstuffs, beverages and spirits, tobacco);
- Section V (Chapters 25–7, mineral products);
- Section VI (Chapters 28–38, chemical products);
- Section VII (Chapters 39–40, plastics and rubber);
- Section VIII (Chapters 41–3, leather and travel goods);
- Section IX (Chapters 44–6, wood, charcoal, cork);
- Section X (Chapters 47–9, wood pulp, paper and paperboard articles);
- Section XI (Chapters 50–63, textiles and textile products);
- Section XII (Chapters 64–7, footwear, umbrellas, artificial flowers);
- Section XIII (Chapters 68–70, stone, cement, ceramic, glass);
- Section XIV (Chapter 71, pearls, precious metals);
- Section XV (Chapters 72–83, base metals);
- Section XVI (Chapters 84–5, electrical machinery);
- Section XVII (Chapters 86–9, vehicles, aircraft, vessels);
- Section XVIII (Chapters 90–2, optical instruments, clocks and watches, musical instruments);
- Section XIX (Chapter 93, arms and ammunition);
- Section XX (Chapters 94–6, furniture, toys, miscellaneous manufactured articles); and
- Section XXI (Chapter 97, works of art, antiques).[135]

In the Harmonized System, each commodity group has a six-digit HS code.[136] For example, the HS Code for 'Electric trains, including tracks, signals and other

---

133 The Harmonized System was developed not only for customs classification purposes, but also for the collection of trade statistics and for use in the context of various types of transactions in international trade (such as insurance and transport).

134 See www.wco.org. The *HS Convention* has 145 Contracting Parties (including the European Union and all EU Member States).

135 Chapters 98 and 99 are reserved for special use by Contracting Parties. Most Members do not use these chapters.

136 Note, however, that, pursuant to Article 3.3 of the *HS Convention*, parties to the Convention can, and do, use more than six-digit codes. Article 3.3 of the *HS Convention*. See, for example, Figures 6.1 and 6.3, at p. 424 and pp. 440–42, respectively.

accessories therefor; reduced-size (scale) model assembly kits' is 9503 30. Of this code, the first two digits refer to the Chapter, in this case Chapter 95 ('Toys, games and sport requisites; parts and accessories thereof'), while the first four digits refer to the heading, in this case Heading 95.03 ('Tricycles, scooters, pedal cars and similar wheeled toys; dolls' carriages; dolls; other toys; reduced-size (scale) models and similar recreational models working or not; puzzles of all kinds').

To keep the Harmonized System up to date, to include new products (resulting from new technologies) and to take account of new developments in international trade, the Harmonized System is revised every four to six years.[137]

To allow for a systematic and uniform classification of goods, the Harmonized System not only provides for a structured list of commodity descriptions and related numerical codes, but also compromises: (1) Chapter, Heading and Subheading Notes; and (2) General Rules for the Interpretation of the Harmonized System. The Chapter, Heading and Subheading Notes, which precede the chapters of the Harmonized System are the most important source for determining classification in case of doubt. The General Rules for the Interpretation of the Harmonized System, set out in an annex to the *HS Convention*, provide that the classification of goods shall be governed, *inter alia*, by the following principles: (1) incomplete or unfinished goods are classified as finished goods (in the event that they do not have their own line) when the goods already have the essential character of the complete or finished goods;[138] (2) when goods are, *prima facie*, classifiable under two or more headings, classification shall be effected as follows: (a) the heading which provides the most specific description shall be preferred to headings providing a more general description;[139] (b) when goods cannot be classified as provided under (a), mixtures, composite goods consisting of different materials or made up of different components, and goods put up in sets for retail sale, shall be classified as if they consisted of the material or component which gives them their essential character;[140] and (c) when goods cannot be classified as provided under (a) or (b), they shall be classified under the heading which occurs last in numerical order among those which equally merit consideration;[141] and (3) goods which cannot be classified in accordance with the above rules shall be classified under the heading appropriate to the goods to which they are most akin, i.e. with which they bear most likeness.[142]

In addition to the Chapter, Heading and Subheading Notes and the General Rules for the Interpretation of the Harmonized System, the Explanatory Notes and Classification Opinions are also of importance. As stated in Article 8.2 of the *HS Convention*, the Explanatory Notes and Classification Opinions serve to

---

137 See Article 16 of the *HS Convention*. To date, there have been revisions in 1992, 1996, 2002, 2007 and 2012. The next revision is to take place in 2017.
138 See General Rules for the Interpretation of the Harmonized System, para. 2(a).
139 *Ibid.*, para. 3(a).
140 *Ibid.*, para. 3(b).   141 *Ibid.*, para. 3(c).   142 *Ibid.*, para. 4.

secure uniformity in the interpretation and application of the Harmonized System. The Explanatory Notes are commentaries on the Harmonized System finalised by the WCO Harmonized System Committee (HSC) and adopted by the WCO Council, while the Classification Opinions are decisions taken by the WCO's HSC on the classification of specific products.[143]

WTO Members are not obliged under the GATT 1994 to adopt the Harmonized System.[144] However, as already noted, most WTO Members are a party to the *HS Convention*. Article 3.1(a) of this Convention provides, in relevant part, that a party to the *HS Convention*:

undertakes that, in respect of its customs tariff and statistical nomenclatures:

i.   it shall use all the headings and subheadings of the Harmonized System without addition or modification, together with their related numerical codes;
ii. it shall apply the General Rules for the Interpretation of the Harmonized System and all the Section, Chapter and Subheading Notes, and shall not modify the scope of the Sections, Chapters, headings or subheadings of the Harmonized System; and
iii. it shall follow the numerical sequence of the Harmonized System.

Consequently, most WTO Members use the Harmonized System, its Section, Chapter and Subheading Notes and its General Rules for the Interpretation in their national customs tariffs and for the customs classification of goods. Although the Harmonized System is not a WTO agreement, as discussed above, the Appellate Body ruled in *EC – Chicken Cuts (2005)* and confirmed in *China – Auto Parts (2009)* that the Harmonized System is relevant for the interpretation of WTO Schedules and the tariff bindings contained therein.[145]

Disputes between the importer and the relevant customs authorities on proper classification are resolved by national courts or tribunals.[146] Parties to the *HS Convention* may bring a dispute to the WCO for settlement under Article 10 thereof.[147]

Questions and Assignments 6.7

Are there any WTO rules on tariff classification? What is the Harmonized System? Discuss the key principles that govern the classification of goods set forth in the General Rules for the Interpretation of the Harmonized System. Are these rules of any relevance in disputes on WTO rights and obligations?

143 They are published in four volumes in English and French but are also available on CD-ROM and online, as part of a database giving the HS classification of more than 200,000 goods. Information about all HS publications can be found at www.publications.wcoomd.org.
144 Note, however, that the WTO *Agreement on Agriculture*, when defining its product scope, does refer to the Harmonized System, and in particular to HS Chapters 1 to 24. See Article 2 of and Annex 1 to the *Agreement on Agriculture*.
145 See above, p. 445.
146 Article X of the GATT 1994 concerns the access to national courts and tribunals. See below, p. 498.
147 Pursuant to Article 10 of the *HS Convention*, any dispute between CONTRACTING PARTIES concerning the interpretation or application of the Convention shall, so far as possible, be settled by negotiation. Any dispute, which is not so settled shall be referred to the HS Committee. If the HS Committee is unable to settle the dispute, it shall refer the matter to the WCO Council. The parties to the dispute may agree in advance to accept the recommendations of the HS Committee or the WCO Council as binding.

2.8.2   Valuation for Customs Purposes

As previously explained, most customs duties are *ad valorem*. The customs administrations must therefore determine the value of the imported goods in order to be able to calculate the customs duty due. Unlike for customs classification, the WTO agreements provide for rules on customs valuation. These rules, which are crucial to ensure that the value of the tariff concessions is not nullified or undermined, are set out in: (1) Article VII of the GATT 1994, entitled 'Valuation for Customs Purposes'; (2) the Note *Ad* Article VII; and (3) the WTO *Agreement on the Implementation of Article VII of the GATT 1994*.[148] The latter agreement, commonly referred to as the *Customs Valuation Agreement*, elaborates the provisions of Article VII in order to provide greater uniformity and certainty in their implementation.

The core provision of Article VII on customs valuation is found in paragraph 2(a), which states:

> The value for customs purposes of imported merchandise should be based on the *actual value* of the imported merchandise on which duty is assessed, or of like merchandise, and should *not* be based on the value of merchandise of national origin or on arbitrary or fictitious values.[149]

Paragraph 2(b) of Article VII defines the concept of the 'actual value' of goods as the price at which such or like goods are sold or offered for sale in the ordinary course of trade under fully competitive conditions. Elaborating on and elucidating Article VII:2 of the GATT 1994, Article 1.1 of the *Customs Valuation Agreement* provides:

> The customs value of imported goods shall be the *transaction value*, that is the price actually paid or payable for the goods when sold for export to the country of importation adjusted in accordance with the provisions of Article 8.[150]

The primary basis for the customs value is thus the 'transaction value' of the imported goods, i.e. the price actually paid or payable for the goods. This price is normally shown in the invoice, contract or purchase order.[151] Article 1.1 is to

---

148 The WTO *Agreement on the Implementation of Article VII of the GATT 1994* replaced the 1979 Tokyo Round *Agreement on the Implementation of Article VII of the GATT*, but is not significantly different from this 1979 Agreement.

149 Emphasis added.

150 Emphasis added. Note that, in the proviso to Article 1.1, a number of situations are identified in which the transaction value cannot be used to determine the customs value. This is, for example, the case when there are certain restrictions on the use or disposition of the goods. Furthermore, as a rule, the buyer and seller should not be related (within the meaning of Article 15) but, if they are, the use of the transaction value is still acceptable if this relationship did not influence the price (see Article 1.2(a)) or the transaction value closely approximates a test value (see Article 1.2(b)). See also Panel Report, *Thailand – Cigarettes (Philippines) (2011)*, paras. 7.143–7.173.

151 Pursuant to Article 17 of the *Customs Valuation Agreement*, customs authorities have the right to 'satisfy themselves as to the truth or accuracy of any statement, document or declaration'. In cases of doubt as to the truth or accuracy, customs authorities will first request the importer to provide further information and clarification. If reasonable doubt persists, the customs authorities will not determine the customs value on the basis of the transaction value but will apply a different method of valuation (see below, pp. 475–6).

be read together with Article 8, which provides for *adjustments* to be made to the price actually paid or payable, as discussed below.

Articles 2–7 of the *Customs Valuation Agreement* provide methods for determining the customs value whenever it cannot be determined under the provisions of Article 1. These methods to determine the customs value, other than the 'transaction value' method of Article 1, are, first, the 'transaction value of identical or similar goods' method set out in Articles 2 and 3; secondly, the deductive value method set out in Article 5; thirdly, the computed value method set out in Article 6; and, fourthly, the fall-back method set out in Article 7. These methods to determine the customs value of imported goods are to be applied in the above order.[152]

Under the *deductive value method*, the customs authorities try to determine the customs value based on information provided by the importer concerning the price at which the imported goods are subsequently sold. This is done by determining the unit price at which the imported goods, or identical or similar imported goods, are sold at the greatest aggregate quantity to an unrelated buyer in the country of importation.[153] The greatest aggregate quantity is the greatest number of units sold at one price.[154] A number of elements are then 'deducted' (i.e. subtracted) from this price, including commissions paid to distributors in the importing country, the costs of transport and insurance in the country of importation, and customs duties and other internal taxes paid.

Under the *computed value method*, customs authorities try to 'compute' (i.e. reconstruct) the value of the good at the time of exportation based on information provided by the manufacturer, who is often located in the exporting country. The computed value is the sum of the production cost (i.e. the cost of materials and fabrication), profit and general expenses and other expenses (e.g. transport costs to the place or port of importation).[155]

The *fall-back method*, set out in Article 7.1, applies when the customs value cannot be determined under any of the other four methods. Under this method, the customs value shall be:

determined using reasonable means consistent with the principles and general provisions of this Agreement and of Article VII of the GATT 1994 and on the basis of the data available in the country of importation.[156]

---

152 See Article 4 and the General Note in Annex I to the *Customs Valuation Agreement*. Note, however, that, at the request of the importer, the order of application of the deductive method (Article 5) and the computed method (Article 6) may be reversed (*ibid.*).

153 Goods are 'identical' if they are the same in all respects, including physical characteristics, quality and reputation. 'Similar goods' means goods which, although not alike in all respects, have like characteristics and like component materials which enable them to perform the same functions and to be commercially interchangeable. In addition, goods shall not be regarded as 'similar' or 'identical' unless they are produced in the same country as the goods being valued. See Article 15.2 of the *Customs Valuation Agreement*.

154 See Article 5 and the Note to Article 5 in Annex I to the *Customs Valuation Agreement*. Since the deductive value method uses the sale price in the country of importation as a basis for the calculation of the customs value, a number of deductions (for profits, general expenses, transport, etc.) are necessary to reduce the sale price to the relevant customs value. See also Panel Report, *Thailand – Cigarettes (Philippines) (2011)*, paras. 7.345–7.362.

155 See Article 6 and the Note to Article 6 in Annex I to the *Customs Valuation Agreement*.

156 Paragraph 2 of the Note to Article 7 in Annex 1 to the *Customs Valuation Agreement* states: 'The methods of valuation to be employed under Article 7 should be those laid down in Articles 1 through 6 but a reasonable flexibility in the application of such methods would be in conformity with the aims and provisions of Article 7.'

However, as explicitly stated in Article 7.2(a)–(g), the customs value of imported goods may never be determined on the basis of, for example: the selling price in the country of importation of goods produced in that country; the price of goods on the domestic market of the country of exportation; minimum customs values; or arbitrary or fictitious values.

In *Colombia – Ports of Entry (2009)*, one of the measures at issue was a Colombian regulation requiring customs authorities to use indicative prices for the customs valuation of imported products, unless the transaction value was higher than the indicative price. The panel found this regulation to be inconsistent with the obligation to conduct customs valuations of imported goods based on the sequential application of the methods established by Articles 1, 2, 3, 5 and 6 of the *Customs Valuation Agreement*.[157] Moreover, the panel found that Colombia's use of indicative prices did not constitute a 'reasonable means' of customs valuation within the meaning of Article 7.1 of the *Customs Valuation Agreement*, as it was inconsistent with Article 7.2(b) and (f) thereof.[158]

As mentioned above, the customs value of imported goods is – if possible (and, usually, this *is* possible) – determined on the basis of the transaction value of these goods. This transaction value must, however, be adjusted as provided for in Article 8 of the *Customs Valuation Agreement*. Pursuant to Article 8.1, the following costs and values, for example, must be added to the price actually paid or payable for the imported products: (1) commissions and brokerage;[159] (2) the cost of packing;[160] (3) royalties and licence fees related to the goods being valued that the buyer must pay;[161] and (4) the value of any part of the proceeds of any subsequent resale that accrues to the seller.[162]

Pursuant to Article 8.2, each Member is free either to include or to exclude from the customs value of imported goods: (1) the cost of transport to the port or place of importation; (2) loading, unloading and handling charges associated with the transport to the port or place of importation; and (3) the cost of insurance. Note in this respect that most Members take the CIF price as the basis for determining the customs value, while Members such as the United States, Japan and Canada take the (lower) FOB price.[163]

To date, WTO Members have been found to have acted inconsistently with the obligations under Article VII of the GATT 1994 and the *Customs Valuation Agreement* in two disputes.[164]

Questions and Assignments 6.8

Why must customs administrations determine the value of imported goods? Which provisions set out the WTO rules on customs valuation? What is the principal, and most common,

---

157 See Panel Report, *Colombia – Ports of Entry (2009)*, para. 7.152.   158 See *ibid.*, para. 7.153.
159 See Article 8.1(a)(i) of the *Customs Valuation Agreement*.   160 See *ibid.*, Article 8.1(a)(iii).
161 See *ibid.*, Article 8.1(c).   162 See *ibid.*, Article 8.1(d).
163 CIF (cost, insurance and freight) and FOB (free on board) are International Commercial terms (INCO terms). CIF means that the seller must pay the costs, insurance and freight involved in bringing the goods to the named port of destination. FOB means that the buyer has to bear all costs and risks of loss of, or damage to, the goods from the point that the goods pass the ship's rail at the named port of shipment.
164 See *Colombia – Ports of Entry (2009)*; and *Thailand – Cigarettes (Philippines) (2011)*.

method for determining the customs value of imported goods? Briefly discuss other methods for determining the customs value of imported products. Must the cost of the packaging and/or the cost of transport to the port or place of importation be included in the customs value of imported goods?

2.8.3   Determination of Origin

In spite of the MFN treatment obligation, discussed in Chapter 4 of this book, the customs duties applied to imported goods may differ depending on the country from which the goods originate. For example, goods *from* developing-country Members commonly benefit from lower import duties in developed-country Members than do goods from other developed-country Members;[165] and no customs duties apply to goods *from* Members that are a party to the same free trade agreement.[166] Moreover, only the goods *from* WTO Members benefit under WTO law from MFN treatment with respect to customs duties. It is, therefore, important to determine the origin of imported goods, and this is not always an easy determination to make. As noted in Chapter 1 of this book, when discussing the global value chain, many industrial products, available on the market today, are produced with inputs and raw materials from more than one country.[167] For example, in the case of cotton shirts, it is possible that the cotton used in their production is manufactured in country A, the textile woven, dyed and printed in country B, the cloth cut and stitched in country C and the shirts packed for retail in country D before being exported to country E.[168]

The rules to determine the origin of imported goods differ from Member to Member, and many Members use different rules of origin depending on the purpose for which the origin is determined.[169] Generally speaking, the national rules of origin currently applied by Members use one or more of three methods to determine origin: (1) the method of 'value added'; (2) the method of 'change in tariff classification'; and (3) the method of 'qualifying processes'. Under national rules of origin using the method of 'value added', a good will be considered to have originated in country X if in that country a specified percentage (for example, 50 per cent) of the value of the good was added. Under national rules of origin using the method of 'change in tariff classification', a good will be considered to have originated in country X if, as a result of processing in that country, the tariff classification of the product changes. Finally, under national rules of origin using the method of 'qualifying processes', a good will be

---

165 On preferential customs duties for developing-country Members under the Enabling Clause of the GATT 1994, see above, p. 331.

166 On customs duties in the context of customs unions and free trade agreements pursuant to Article XXIV of the GATT 1994, see below, pp. 658–60.

167 See below, pp. 656–62.

168 See *Business Guide to the World Trading System*, 2nd edn (International Trade Centre/Commonwealth Secretariat, 1999), 155.

169 E.g. whether the origin of imported products is determined for the imposition of ordinary customs duties, anti-dumping or countervailing duties or the administration of country-specific tariff quota shares.

considered to have originated in country X if a particular technical manufacturing or processing operation relating to the good took place in that country.[170]

The GATT 1947 had no specific rules on the determination of the origin of imported goods, and the GATT 1994 still provides no specific rules on this matter. However, the negotiators during the Uruguay Round recognised the need for multilateral disciplines on rules of origin in order to prevent these rules from being a source of uncertainty and unpredictability in international trade. The consensus on the need for such disciplines resulted in the *Agreement on Rules of Origin*, which is part of Annex 1A to the WTO Agreement.

The *Agreement on Rules of Origin* makes a distinction between: (1) non-preferential rules of origin; and (2) preferential rules of origin. Non-preferential rules of origin are rules of origin used in non-preferential trade policy instruments (relating to, *inter alia*, MFN treatment, anti-dumping and countervailing duties, safeguard measures, origin marking or tariff quotas).[171] Most of the disciplines set out in the *Agreement on Rules of Origin* concern *non-preferential* rules of origin.[172] However, Annex II to the *Agreement on Rules of Origin* sets out some disciplines for *preferential* rules of origin. Preferential rules of origin are rules of origin applied by Members to determine whether goods qualify for preferential treatment under contractual or autonomous trade regimes (leading to the granting of tariff preferences going beyond the application of the MFN treatment obligation).[173] Note that 19 per cent of world trade is conducted on a preferential basis.[174]

With respect to *non-preferential* rules of origin, the *Agreement on Rules of Origin* provides for a work programme on the harmonisation of these rules.[175] Pursuant to Article 9.2 of the *Agreement on Rules of Origin*, this Harmonization Work Programme should have been completed by July 1998. However, the WTO Members failed to meet this deadline. In fact, work on the harmonisation of non-preferential rules of origin is still ongoing.[176]

The failure of WTO Members to agree, to date, on harmonised rules of origin does not, however, mean that no WTO disciplines apply to non-preferential rules of origin. Article 2 of the *Agreement on Rules of Origin* contains a rather extensive list of multilateral disciplines for rules of origin already applicable during the 'transition period', i.e. the period until the Harmonization Work

---

170 Members may also have a list of processes and operations, such as packaging, simple painting or dilution with water, that are considered insufficient to confer origin.
171 See Article 1.2 of the *Agreement on Rules of Origin*.   172 See *ibid.*, Article 1.1.
173 See *ibid.*, Article 1.1 and Annex II.2.   174 See below, p. 650.
175 See Article 9.1 of the *Agreement on Rules of Origin*. This work programme is to be undertaken in conjunction with the World Customs Organization.
176 See WTO Secretariat, *Report (2011) of the Committee on Rules of Origin to the Council for Trade in Goods*, G/L/975, dated 2 November 2011. At its meeting on 27 July 2007, the General Council recognised that delegations in the Committee on Rules of Origin felt that the difficulties they had encountered on certain core issues relating to the harmonisation of rules of origin required guidance from the General Council on how to take these issues forward. It was therefore agreed that the Committee would suspend work on these issues until such guidance was forthcoming, but would continue work on technical issues. See *ibid.*, para. 5.

Programme is completed. These multilateral disciplines applicable during the transitional period include: (1) a transparency requirement, namely, the rules of origin must clearly and precisely define the criteria they apply; (2) a prohibition on using rules of origin as instruments to pursue trade objectives; (3) a requirement that rules of origin shall not themselves create restrictive, distorting or disruptive effects on international trade; (4) a national treatment requirement, namely, that the rules of origin applied to imported products shall not be more stringent than the rules of origin applied to determine whether or not a good is domestic; (5) an MFN requirement, namely, that rules of origin shall not discriminate between other Members, irrespective of the affiliation of the manufacturers of the good concerned; (6) a requirement that rules of origin shall be administered in a consistent, uniform, impartial and reasonable manner; (7) a requirement that rules of origin state what confers origin (a positive standard) rather than state what does *not* confer origin (a negative standard); (8) a requirement to publish laws, regulations, judicial decisions, etc., relating to rules of origin; (9) requirements regarding the issuance of assessments of origin (no later than 150 days after the request) and the validity of the assessments (in principle, three years); (10) a prohibition on the retroactive application of new or amended rules of origin; (11) a requirement that any administrative action relating to the determination of origin is reviewable promptly by independent tribunals; and (12) a requirement to respect the confidentiality of information provided on a confidential basis.[177] Note that many of these disciplines are in fact the specific application of general GATT obligations (such as Articles I, III and X of the GATT 1994) to national non-preferential rules on the determination of origin.

To date, there has only been one dispute before a panel dealing with rules of origin. In *US – Textiles Rules of Origin (2003)*, India claimed that the United States applied rules of origin on textiles and certain other products that were inconsistent with several obligations under Article 2 of the *Agreement on Rules of Origin*. The panel in *US – Textiles Rules of Origin (2003)* noted that Article 2 does not provide what WTO Members must do, but rather what they should not do,[178] and that:

[b]y setting out what Members cannot do, these provisions leave for Members themselves discretion to decide what, within those bounds, they can do. In this regard, it is common ground between the parties that Article 2 does not prevent Members from determining the criteria which confer origin, changing those criteria over time, or applying different criteria to different goods.[179]

---

177 See Articles 2(a)–(k) of the *Agreement on Rules of Origin*.
178 See Panel Report, *US – Textiles Rules of Origin (2003)*, para. 6.23.
179 *Ibid.*, para. 6.24. India argued that rules of origin applied by the United States on its textile imports were inconsistent with Articles 2(b), (c) and (d) of the *Agreement on Rules of Origin*. The panel found with regard to all claims that India did not adduce sufficient evidence to make a *prima facie* case of inconsistency. See Panel Report, *US – Textiles Rules of Origin (2003)*, paras. 6.118; 6.190–6.191, 6.221 and 6.231; and 6.271–6.272.

Once the Harmonization Work Programme is completed, all Members will apply only one set of non-preferential rules of origin for all purposes.[180] As provided for in Article 3 of the *Agreement on Rules of Origin*, the disciplines set out in Article 2, already applicable, will continue to apply.[181] Moreover, Article 3 makes clear that, under the harmonised rules (still to be agreed on), Members will be required to determine as the country of origin of imported goods: (1) the country where the goods have been wholly obtained; or (2) the country where the last substantial transformation to the goods has been carried out.[182] However, to date, Members have been unsuccessful in reaching consensus either on detailed rules regarding the requirements for a good to be 'wholly obtained' in one country,[183] or on the criteria for a 'substantial transformation' (a change in tariff classification and/or a specific percentage of value added).

The disciplines on rules of origin discussed above concern only non-preferential rules of origin. However, as already noted, Annex II to the *Agreement on Rules of Origin* provides – in the form of a 'Common Declaration' – for some disciplines applicable to preferential rules of conduct. Pursuant to Annex II, the general principles and requirements set out in the *Agreement on Rules of Origin* in respect of transparency, positive standards, administrative assessments, judicial review, non-retroactivity of changes and confidentiality apply also to *preferential* rules of origin. The results of the Harmonization Work Programme, however, will not apply to preferential rules of origin.

To date, no WTO Member has been found in dispute settlement proceedings to have acted inconsistently with the obligations under *the Agreement on Rules of Origin*.[184]

Questions and Assignments 6.9

Why is it important to determine the origin of imported goods? How do Members commonly determine the origin of goods? Why is there a need for multilateral disciplines on rules of origin? Are there any WTO rules on the determination of the origin of goods? Briefly describe the disciplines currently applicable to non-preferential rules of origin. Discuss the rules that will be applicable once the Harmonization Work Programme is completed. Are there any multilateral disciplines applicable on preferential rules of origin?

3   OTHER DUTIES AND CHARGES ON IMPORTS

In addition to customs duties on imports, tariff barriers on imports can also take the form of 'other duties and charges'. This section deals in turn with: the definition and types of 'other duties and charges on imports'; the rule applicable

---

180 See Article 3(a) of the *Agreement on Rules of Origin*.
181 See *ibid.*, Article 3(c)–(i) and Article 9(c)–(g).   182 See *ibid.*, Article 3(b).
183 The question of, for example, which minimal operations or processes can and cannot, by themselves, confer origin on a good is a matter of current debate.
184 With regard to *US – Textiles Rules of Origin (2003)*, see above, p. 462, footnote 179.

to such measures; and the measures exempted from the scope of application of this rule.

3.1 Definition and Types

'Other duties and charges on imports' are financial charges or taxes, *other than* ordinary customs duties,[185] which are levied on imported products and are due because of their importation. In *India – Additional Import Duties (2008)*, the Appellate Body held that 'other duties and charges on imports', also referred to as 'ODC' on imports:

> are defined in relation to duties covered by the first sentence of Article II:1(b), such that ODCs encompass only duties and charges that are not [ordinary customs duties].[186]

'Other duties and charges on imports' form a *residual* category encompassing financial charges on imports that are not ordinary customs duties or customs duties *sensu stricto*.[187] The difference between ordinary customs duties and other duties and charges was at issue in *Chile – Price Band System (2002)*.[188] The panel in this case distinguished ordinary customs duties from other duties and charges by considering that customs duties:

> always relate to either the value of the imported goods, in the case of *ad valorem* duties, or the volume of the imported goods, in the case of specific duties. Such ordinary customs duties, however, do not appear to involve the consideration of any other, exogenous, factors, such as, for instance, fluctuating world market prices. We therefore consider that ... an 'ordinary' customs duty, that is, a customs duty *sensu stricto*, is to be understood as referring to a customs duty which is not applied on the basis of factors of an exogenous nature.[189]

On appeal, the Appellate Body disagreed with the panel that what distinguishes ordinary customs duties from other duties and charges is that the former are applied on the basis of the value or volume of the imported products, and not on the basis of factors of an exogenous nature.[190] The Appellate Body thus reversed the panel's finding but did not offer much further guidance on the distinction

---

185 The term '*ordinary* customs duties' (emphasis added) is used in Article II:1(b), first sentence, of the GATT 1994. The panel in *Chile – Price Band System (2002)* used the term 'customs duties *sensu stricto*'. See below, footnote 187.

186 Appellate Body Report, *India – Additional Import Duties (2008)*, para. 151.

187 See also Panel Report, *Dominican Republic – Safeguard Measures (2012)*, paras. 7.79 and 7.85; and Panel Report, *Dominican Republic – Import and Sale of Cigarettes (2005)*, para. 7.113. The panel in this case also referred to the *travaux préparatoires* concerning the *Understanding on the Interpretation of Article II:1 (b) of the GATT 1994*, where it is stated that it would be impossible to draw up an exhaustive list of ODCs since it is always possible for governments to invent new charges. See *ibid.*, para. 7.114.

188 As discussed above, the Appellate Body in *China – Auto Parts (2009)* addressed the question whether the charges at issue in that dispute were a customs duty or an internal charge. The Appellate Body ruled in this respect that what is important in determining whether a charge is a border charge (such as a customs duty) or an internal charge is whether the obligation to pay that charge accrues due to the importation or to an internal event (such as the distribution, sale, use or transportation of the imported product). This usefully distinguishes border charges from internal charges, but is of little help in distinguishing, within the category of border charges, between customs duties *and* other duties and charges.

189 Panel Report, *Chile – Price Band System (2002)*, para. 7.52. See also *ibid.*, para. 7.104.

190 See Appellate Body Report, *Chile – Price Band System (2002)*, para. 278.

between ordinary customs duties and other duties and charges, except that an essential feature of ordinary customs duties is that 'any change in them is discontinuous and unrelated to an underlying scheme or formula'.[191]

Examples of 'other duties and charges on imports' identified in GATT/WTO case law are: (1) an import surcharge, i.e. a duty imposed on an imported product in addition to the ordinary customs duty;[192] (2) a security deposit to be made on the importation of goods;[193] (3) a statistical tax imposed to finance the collection of statistical information, with no maximum limit;[194] (4) a customs fee with no maximum limit;[195] (5) a transitional surcharge for economic stabilisation imposed on imported goods;[196] and (6) a foreign exchange fee imposed on imported goods.[197]

3.2   Rule Regarding Other Duties or Charges on Imports

To protect the tariff bindings set forth in the Schedules and to prevent 'circumvention' of the prohibition of Article II:1(b), first sentence, of the GATT 1994, to impose ordinary customs duties in excess of the bindings, WTO law provides for a rule on other duties and charges on imports. With regard to products subject to a tariff binding, Article II:1(b), second sentence, of the GATT 1994 requires that *no* other duties or charges be imposed *in excess of* those: (1) already imposed at the 'date of this Agreement'; or (2) provided for in mandatory legislation in force on that date. However, under the GATT 1947, there was considerable uncertainty and confusion regarding the 'date of this Agreement' and thus regarding the maximum level of other duties or charges on imports that could be imposed.[198] Therefore, the Uruguay Round negotiators agreed on the *Understanding on the Interpretation of Article II:1(b) of the GATT 1994*, commonly referred to as the *Understanding on Article II:1(b)*. This Understanding states, in relevant part:

In order to ensure transparency of the legal rights and obligations deriving from paragraph 1(b) of Article II, the nature and level of any 'other duties or charges' levied on bound tariff items, as referred to in that provision, shall be recorded in the Schedules of Concessions annexed to GATT 1994 against the tariff item to which they apply.[199]

The Understanding thus requires Members to record in their Schedules all other duties or charges on imports imposed on products subject to a tariff binding. As noted above, the Uruguay Round Schedules have a special column for 'other

---

191 *Ibid.*, para. 233.   192 See e.g. *Korea – Beef (Australia) (1989)*.
193 See e.g. *EEC – Minimum Import Prices (1978)*; and *EEC – Animal Feed Proteins (1978)*.
194 See e.g. *Argentina – Textiles and Apparel (1998)*.
195 See e.g. *United States – Customs User Fee (1988)*. A customs fee is a financial charge imposed for the processing of imported goods by the customs authorities.
196 See e.g. *Dominican Republic – Import and Sale of Cigarettes (2005)*.
197 *Ibid.*
198 See *Analytical Index: Guide to GATT Law and Practice* (WTO, 1995), 84–5.
199 *Understanding on the Interpretation of Article II:1(b) of the GATT 1994* (hereinafter '*Understanding on Article II:1(b)*'), para. 1.

duties or charges'.[200] The other duties or charges on imports must be recorded in the Schedules at the levels applying on 15 April 1994.[201] The other duties or charges on imports are 'bound' at these levels.[202]

It follows from Article II:1(b), second sentence, and from the Understanding, that Members may: (1) impose only other duties and charges on imports that have been properly recorded in their Schedules; and (2) impose other duties and charges on imports only at a level that does not exceed the level recorded in their Schedules.

In *Chile – Price Band System (2002)*, the panel, having found that the Chilean Price Band System (PBS) duties were not 'ordinary customs duties' but were 'other duties or charges', examined whether these duties were inconsistent with Article II:1(b), second sentence. The panel ruled:

> Pursuant to the Uruguay Round Understanding on the Interpretation of Article II:1(b), such other duties or charges had to be recorded in a newly created column 'other duties and charges' in the Members' Schedules ... Other duties or charges must not exceed the binding in this 'other duties and charges' column of the Schedule. If other duties or charges were not recorded but are nevertheless levied, they are inconsistent with the second sentence of Article II:1(b), in light of the Understanding on the Interpretation of Article II:1(b). We note that Chile did not record its PBS in the 'other duties and charges' column of its Schedule. We therefore find that the Chilean PBS duties are inconsistent with Article II:1(b) of GATT 1994.[203]

In *Dominican Republic – Import and Sale of Cigarettes (2005)*, the panel found that the two 'other duties or charges' at issue in this case, namely, the transitional surcharge for economic stabilisation and the foreign exchange fee imposed on imported products, had not been recorded in a legally valid manner in the Schedule of Concessions of the Dominican Republic.[204] With regard to the transitional surcharge for economic stabilisation, the panel came to the following conclusion:

> For all legal and practical purposes, what was notified by the Dominican Republic in document G/SP/3 is equivalent to 'zero' in the Schedule. The Panel finds that the surcharge as an 'other duty or charge' measure is applied in excess of the level 'zero' pursuant to the

200 See above, pp. 440–3.
201 See *Understanding on Article II:1(b)*, para. 2. Note, however, that paragraph 4 of the *Understanding on Article II:1(b)* states: 'Where a tariff item has previously been the subject of a concession, the level of "other duties or charges" recorded in the appropriate Schedule shall not be higher than the level obtaining at the time of the first incorporation of the concession in that Schedule.'
202 Note that paragraph 1 of the *Understanding on Article II:1(b)* states that the recording in the Schedules does not change the legal character of the 'other duties or charges' and that paragraphs 4 and 5 provide that – with certain restrictions in time – the Members can challenge the GATT-consistency of recorded 'other duties or charges'. See Panel Report, *Argentina – Textiles and Apparel (1998)*, para. 6.81.
203 Panel Report, *Chile – Price Band System (2002)*, paras. 7.105 and 7.107–7.108. On appeal, the Appellate Body found that the panel's finding on Article II:1(b), second sentence, related to a claim that had not been made, and this finding was therefore in violation of Article 11 of the DSU. As a result, the Appellate Body reversed the finding. See above, p. 464.
204 The panel ruled that the recording of the Selective Consumption Tax, i.e. an internal tax, could not be used as legal basis to justify the current transitional surcharge or the foreign exchange fee. See Panel Report, *Dominican Republic – Import and Sale of Cigarettes (2005)*, para. 7.86.

Schedule. Therefore, the surcharge measure is inconsistent with Article II:1(b) of the GATT 1994.[205]

With regard to the foreign exchange fee, the Panel came to the same conclusion.[206]

On the legal effects of the scheduling of other duties or charges on imports, note that, in *Argentina – Textiles and Apparel (1998)*, Argentina argued that, since its 3 per cent statistical tax was included in its Schedule of Concessions (Schedule LXIV), there was no violation of Article II:1(b) of the GATT 1994. The panel disagreed with Argentina, and noted that:

[t]he provisions of the WTO Understanding on the Interpretation of Article II:1(b) of GATT 1994, dealing with 'other duties and charges', make clear that including a charge in a schedule of concessions in no way immunizes that charge from challenge as a violation of an applicable GATT rule.[207]

To date, WTO Members have been found to have acted inconsistently with the obligations under Article II:1(b), second sentence of the GATT 1994 in two disputes.[208]

3.3   Measures Exempted from the Rule

There are a number of 'other duties and charges on imports' that are exempted from the rule that Members may not impose such duties or charges unless recorded and not in excess of the recorded level. Pursuant to Article II:2 of the GATT 1994, Members may – despite their obligation under Article II:1(b), second sentence – impose on an imported product: (1) a financial charge equivalent to an internal tax on the like domestic product imposed consistently with Article III:2 of the GATT 1994 (border tax adjustment) (see Article II:2(a));[209] (2) WTO-consistent anti-dumping or countervailing duties (see Article II:2(b)); or (3) fees or other charges 'commensurate' with, i.e. matching, the cost of the services rendered (see Article II:2(c)). In *India – Additional Import Duties (2008)*, the Appellate Body ruled with regard to Article II:2(a) that:

Article II:2(a), subject to the conditions stated therein, *exempts* a charge from the coverage of Article II:1(b).[210]

---

205 *Ibid.*, para. 7.89.   206 See *ibid.*, para. 7.121.

207 Panel Report, *Argentina – Textiles and Apparel (1998)*, para. 6.81. See also above, p. 448.

208 See *Argentina – Textiles and Apparel (1998)*; and *Dominican Republic – Import and Sale of Cigarettes (2005)*. With regard to *Chile – Price Band System (2002)*, see above, p. 464, footnote 187. With regard to *India – Additional Import Duties (2008)*, the Appellate Body found that the panel erred in its interpretation of Article II:1 (b), second sentence, and was unable to complete the legal analysis.

209 See Appellate Body Report, *India – Additional Import Duties (2008)*, paras. 170, 172 and 180. On the concept of 'border tax adjustment', see above, p. 359. On the requirements of Article III:2 of the GATT 1994, see above, p. 356.

210 Appellate Body Report, *India – Additional Import Duties (2008)*, para. 153. Emphasis added. Note that the Appellate Body found that, where there is a reasonable basis to understand that the challenged measure may not result in a violation of Article II:1(b) because it satisfies the requirements of Article II:2(a), then the complaining party bears some burden of establishing that the conditions of Article II:2(a) are not met. See *ibid.*, para. 192.

In the same vein, but with regard to Article II:2(b), in *US – Zeroing (Japan) – (Article 21.5 – Japan) (2009)*, the Appellate Body upheld the panel's approach to Article II:2(b) as providing a *safe harbour* to Article II:1 to the extent that the anti-dumping duties concerned were applied in a WTO-consistent manner.[211]

Most case law on Article II:2 relates to Article II:2(c). The requirement set out in this provision, namely, that the fees or other charges concerned must be commensurate with the cost of the services, is also reflected in Article VIII:1(a) of the GATT 1994. The latter provision requires that:

All fees and charges of whatever character (other than import or export duties and other than taxes within the purview of Article III) imposed by [Members] on or in connection with importation or exportation shall be limited in amount to the approximate cost of services rendered and shall not represent an indirect protection to domestic products or a taxation of imports or exports for fiscal purposes.[212]

The fees and charges for services rendered within the meaning of Article II:2(c) and Article VIII:1(a) include, pursuant to Article VIII:4, fees and charges relating to: (1) consular transactions, such as consular invoices and certificates; (2) quantitative restrictions; (3) licensing; (4) exchange control; (5) statistical services; (6) documents, documentation and certification; (7) analysis and inspection; and (8) quarantine, sanitation and fumigation. With respect to the concept of 'services' used in this context, the panel in *US – Customs User Fee (1988)* stated, not without wit:

Granted that some government regulatory activities can be considered as 'services' in an economic sense when they endow goods with safety or quality characteristics deemed necessary for commerce, most of the activities that governments perform in connection with the importation process do not meet that definition. They are not desired by the importers who are subject to them. Nor do they add value to the goods in any commercial sense. Whatever governments may choose to call them, fees for such government regulatory activities are, in the Panel's view, simply taxes on imports. It must be presumed, therefore, that the drafters meant the term 'services' to be used in a more artful political sense, i.e. government activities closely enough connected to the processes of customs entry that they might, with no more than the customary artistic licence accorded to taxing authorities, be called a 'service' to the importer in question.[213]

In *US – Customs User Fee (1988)*, the financial charge at issue was a merchandise-processing fee, in the form of an *ad valorem* charge without upper limits. The complainants, the European Communities and Canada, challenged the GATT-consistency of an *ad valorem* charge without upper limit. The panel in this case noted that the requirement of Article VIII:1(a) that a fee or charge

---

211 See Appellate Body Report, *US – Zeroing (Japan) – (Article 21.5 – Japan) (2009)*, para. 209.
212 Note that there is a slight difference in wording between the two 'cost of services' limitations stated in Articles II:2(c) and VIII:1(a), i.e. 'commensurate with the cost of services rendered' and 'limited in amount to the approximate cost of services rendered'. However, the panel in *US – Customs User Fee (1988)*, after reviewing both the drafting history and the subsequent application of these provisions, concluded that no difference of meaning had been intended.
213 Panel Report, *US – Customs User Fee (1988)*, para. 77.

be 'limited in amount to the approximate cost of services rendered' is in fact a dual requirement: (1) the fee or charge in question must first involve a 'service' rendered; and (2) the level of the charge must not exceed the approximate cost of that service.[214] With respect to the first element of this dual requirement, the panel in *Argentina – Textiles and Apparel (1998)* further clarified that the fee or charge in question must involve a 'service' rendered to the *individual* importer in question.[215] Services rendered to foreign trade operators in general and for-eign trade as an activity *per se* would fail to meet this first element of the dual requirement.[216] With respect to the second element of the dual requirement, the panel in *US – Customs User Fee (1988)* stated that:

> the term 'cost of services rendered' in Articles II:2(c) and VIII:1(a) must be interpreted to refer to the cost of the customs processing for the individual entry in question and accord-ingly that the *ad valorem* structure of the United States merchandise processing fee was inconsistent with the obligations of Articles II:2(c) and VIII:1(a) to the extent that it caused fees to be levied in excess of such costs.[217]

In *Argentina – Textiles and Apparel (1998)*, the panel found that Argentina's 3 per cent *ad valorem* statistical tax on imports was inconsistent with Article VIII:1(a) of the GATT 1994 'to the extent it results in charges being levied in excess of the approximate costs of the services rendered'.[218] As the panel ex-plained, an *ad valorem* charge with no maximum limit, as was the case with Argentina's statistical tax,

> by its very nature, is not 'limited in amount to the approximate cost of services rendered'. For example, high-price items necessarily will bear a much higher tax burden than low-price goods, yet the service accorded to both is essentially the same. An unlimited *ad val-orem* charge on imported goods violates the provisions of Article VIII because such a charge cannot be related to the cost of the service rendered.[219]

Note that the panel in *Argentina – Textiles and Apparel (1998)* also found that the statistical tax was inconsistent with Article VIII:1(a) because this tax – according to Argentina's own admission – was imposed for 'fiscal purposes', which is explicitly prohibited under Article VIII:1(a).

Questions and Assignments 6.10

What are 'other duties or charges on imports' within the meaning of Article II:1(b), second sentence, of the GATT 1994? Give three examples of such duties or charges. Are 'other

---

214 See *ibid.*, para. 69. See also Panel Report, *Argentina – Textiles and Apparel (1998)*, para. 6.74; and Panel Report, *US – Certain EC Products (2001)*, para. 6.69.

215 See Panel Report, *US – Customs User Fee (1988)*, para. 80.

216 See Panel Report, *Argentina – Textiles and Apparel (1998)*, para. 6.74.

217 Panel Report, *US – Customs User Fee (1988)*, para. 86. Underlining in the original deleted.

218 Panel Report, *Argentina – Textiles and Apparel (1998)*, para. 6.80.

219 *Ibid.*, para. 6.75. Note that, in the context of the Doha Round negotiations on trade facilitation (see above, p. 437), it has been proposed that 'the cost of services rendered shall be understood to refer broadly to all costs related to the provision of services including reasonable infrastructure-related, capital cost recovery, and continuing personnel training, equipment and software upgrades and maintenance related costs and expenses'. See Negotiating Group on Trade Facilitation, *Draft Consolidated Negotiating Text*, TN/TF/W/165/Rev.13, dated 24 October 2012, Article 6.1(2).

duties or charges on imports' permitted in the same way as customs duties are? Which 'other duties or charges on imports' are permitted under the GATT 1994? Find an example of a product on which the country of which you are a national imposes an 'other duty or charge on importation'. Which 'other duties or charges' are allowed on imported products irrespective of a Member's obligations under Article II:1(b), second sentence, of the GATT 1994? When are customs fees or charges covered by Article II:2(c) of the GATT 1994?

4   CUSTOMS DUTIES AND OTHER DUTIES AND CHARGES ON EXPORTS

As noted above, tariff barriers to trade in goods apply not only to imports. While much less common than customs duties and other duties and charges on imports, Members also impose customs duties and other duties and charges on exports, often in brief referred to as 'export duties'.[220] This section discusses in turn: (1) the definition and purpose of export duties; and (2) WTO rules applicable to export duties.

4.1   Definition and Purpose

Generally speaking, an export duty, be it a customs duty or another duty or charge on exports, is a financial charge or tax on exported products, due because of their exportation. Market exit of the products concerned is conditional upon the payment of the export duty. Like import duties, export duties have a long history, but, unlike the former, the latter largely fell into disuse in the mid-nineteenth century.[221] While there have always been some countries that applied export duties on some products, these 'sporadic' export duties were considered to be much less problematic to international trade than the 'omnipresent' import duties. As noted below, this was, and still is, clearly reflected in the GATT/WTO rules on export duties, or rather the paucity of these rules. Possibly because of this paucity of rules, there has, however, been a proliferation of the use of export duties in recent years. At present, export duties are most commonly imposed on raw materials and agricultural products, which are in short supply on the world market.

---

220 Unlike for customs duties and other duties and charges on imports, there is no need to distinguish between customs duties and other duties and charges on exports, since there is no difference in the rules that apply to customs duties on exports on the one hand and other duties and charges on exports on the other hand. See below, p. 471.

221 In the seventeenth century, England imposed export duty on more than 200 goods, but in 1842 all export duties were abolished. France abolished export duties in 1857 and Prussia in 1865. See www.britannica.com/EBchecked/topic/583535/tariff#ref592273.

Like customs duties and other duties and charges on imports, export duties serve two main purposes. First, export duties are a source of revenue for governments. Some mineral-rich developing-country Members depend on export duties for much of their revenue. Secondly, export duties are used to protect and/or promote domestic industries. Some Members consider export duties to act as 'indirect subsidies' to domestic down-stream industries.[222] By imposing export duties, exportation is commercially less attractive and goods are less likely to be exported, thus reserving them for use by domestic down-stream industries. For example, by imposing an export duty on forest products, a Member will protect and/or promote the domestic milling, furniture and paper industries. An export duty will stem the exportation of forest products and ensure the availability of forest products for domestic down-stream industries, often at prices lower than they would be if exportation were not impeded. In other words, export duties may give the domestic down-stream industries a cost advantage in comparison with foreign down-stream industries.[223] In some cases, export duties on agricultural products, in particular, may also be used to safeguard, in times of international scarcity, domestic supply of food products at affordable prices. In the context of its WTO accession negotiations, with regard to the purpose pursued by its export duties, Russia explained as follows:

> [I]n 1998 export duties had been imposed on raw materials and semi-finished goods, mainly for fiscal purposes, and now ranged from 3 to 50 per cent, with a few exceptions where higher export duties were applied. In very few cases (oil seeds, raw hides and skins), export duties had been imposed to ensure greater availability of raw materials for the domestic industry. Export duties on non-ferrous and ferrous metals waste and scrap (and those in the guise of other products, e.g. used axle-boxes) had been imposed to address problems of environmental protection.[224]

4.2   Rules Applicable on Export Duties

Neither the GATT 1994 nor any of the other multilateral agreements on trade in goods prohibits or specifically regulates export duties, be it customs duties or other duties and charges on exports. While the WTO agreements do not *specifically* regulate export duties, there are some general GATT obligations which also apply to export duties. This is the case, for example, for Article I:1 of the GATT

---

222 *Report of the Working Party on the Accession of Russia*, WT/ACC/RUS/70, dated 17 November 2011, para. 629.

223 In situations in which a country produces a substantial share of the world output of a good (for example, a rare mineral), that country can, by imposing an export duty, push up the world price of that good. This would disadvantage foreign down-stream industries in comparison to the domestic down-stream industries, which would have access to this good at a lower price.

224 *Report of the Working Party on the Accession of Russia*, WT/ACC/RUS/70, dated 17 November 2011, para. 626. See also *ibid.*, paras. 631–3. Russia also indicated that, over the last few years, the overall number of products subject to export duties had been reduced from 1,200 to 310 tariff lines. See *ibid.*, para. 627.

1994, which sets out the MFN treatment obligation.[225] In short, if a Member imposes an export duty on a product exported to another Member, it must impose the same export duty on all like products exported to all other Members.

As discussed above, the GATT 1994 does not prohibit customs duties on imports but encourages negotiations on the lowering of these duties and protects the results of these negotiations. Pursuant to Articles II:1(a) and II:1(b), first sentence, of the GATT 1994, a Member is not allowed to impose customs duties on imports of a product above the relevant binding, i.e. the maximum level it has agreed on.[226] Some Members have agreed to bindings with regard to their export duties and have included these bindings in their Goods Schedule.[227] It is the subject of debate whether Article II:1(a) also applies to, and thus provides protection for, bindings regarding customs duties on exports. It has been observed that Article II:1(a) states:

Each [Member] shall accord *to the commerce* of the other [Members] treatment no less favourable than that provided for in the appropriate Part of the appropriate Schedule annexed to this Agreement.[228]

It has been argued that the term 'commerce' in Article II:1(a) refers to both imports and exports. What is clear is that the obligation set out in Article II:1(b), first sentence, does not apply to customs duties on exports as it explicitly refers to the 'importation' of products. For the same reason, Article II:1(b), second sentence, which concerns other duties and charges, also does not apply to export duties.

While the GATT 1994 or the other multilateral agreements on trade in goods do not prohibit or specifically regulate export duties, some WTO accession protocols do. The best-known example of such accession protocol is the 2001 *Protocol on the Accession of the People's Republic of China*.[229] Paragraph 11.3 of China's Accession Protocol contains specific obligations with respect to export duties, and provides that:

China shall *eliminate* all taxes and charges applied to exports unless specifically provided for in Annex 6 of this Protocol or applied in conformity with the provisions of Article VIII of the GATT 1994.[230]

Annex 6 to China's Accession Protocol, entitled 'Products Subject to Export Duty', lists eighty-four different products, such as live eels fry, bones and horn-cores, yellow phosphorus, alloy pig iron, copper alloys and unwrought aluminium. The Note to Annex 6 states that:

---

225 See above, p. 321. See also Articles VII, VIII and XVII of the GATT 1994.
226 See above, p. 446.
227 Part I, Section 2, of the Goods Schedule of Australia, for example, provides in the 'Notes' column with regard to eleven tariff lines that 'there shall be no export duty on this product'. See Schedule I, annexed to the *Marrakesh Protocol* of the GATT 1994, www.wto.org/english/tratop_e/schedules_e/goods_schedules_table_e.htm.
228 Emphasis added. Also note that Article XXVIII*bis* of the GATT 1994, which calls for negotiations on the reduction of customs duties, expressly refers to customs duties on imports *and* exports.
229 See WT/L/432, dated 23 November 2001. See also above, pp. 112–13.
230 Emphasis added.

China confirmed that the tariff levels included in this Annex are *maximum levels* which will not be exceeded.[231]

In *China – Raw Materials (2012)*, the question arose whether China's export duties on bauxite, coke, fluorspar, magnesium, manganese, silicon metal, zinc and yellow phosphorus were inconsistent with paragraph 11.3 of China's Accession Protocol. The panel found that, with the exception of yellow phosphorus, none of these raw materials is listed in Annex 6 to China's Accession Protocol and that China therefore acted inconsistently with paragraph 11.3 of the Accession Protocol when it imposed export duties on these raw materials.[232] With regard to yellow phosphorus, which is included in the list of Annex 6, the complainants contended that China imposed a 'special' export duty of 50 per cent *ad valorem* on yellow phosphorus pursuant to the 2009 Tariff Implementation Program, while it had committed, pursuant to paragraph 11.3 of and Annex 6 to its Accession Protocol, not to exceed a maximum export duty of 20 per cent on yellow phosphorous. The panel, however, agreed with China that China had removed the 'special' export duty rate as of 1 July 2009, before the date of the panel's establishment and therefore did not make any finding on the WTO-consistency of this measure.[233]

China's Accession Protocol is not the only accession protocol, which provides for 'WTO-plus' obligations with regard to export duties. As already noted above, Russia imposed export duties on a significant number of goods, including minerals, petrochemicals, natural gas, raw hides and skins, wood, ferrous and non-ferrous metals and scrap.[234] The 2011 *Protocol on the Accession of the Russian Federation* and, in particular, the Schedule of Concessions and Commitments on Goods of the Russian Federation annexed to the Protocol, provides that the goods described in 'Part V' of that Schedule are, subject to the relevant terms, conditions or qualifications, *exempt from export duties in excess* of those set-forth therein.[235] During its accession negotiations, Russia emphasised that export duties were permitted under WTO rules, and that many Members applied export duties as an instrument of trade policy.[236] However, as part of the deal on

---

231 Emphasis added. The Note to Annex 6 also states: 'China confirmed furthermore that it would not increase the presently applied rates, except under exceptional circumstances. If such circumstances occurred, China would consult with affected members prior to increasing applied tariffs with a view to finding a mutually acceptable solution.'

232 See Panel Reports, *China – Raw Materials (2012)*, para. 7.77 (for bauxite), para. 7.81 (for coke), para. 7.85 (for fluorspar), para. 7.89 (for magnesium), para. 7.93 (for manganese), para. 7.98 (for silicon metal) and para. 7.101 (for zinc). Note that China did not invoke Article VIII of the GATT 1994 in justification of the export duties at issue. However, with regard to most of the export duties, China did invoke Articles XX(b) or XX(g) of the GATT 1994 in justification of the inconsistency with paragraph 11.3 of its Accession Protocol. As discussed in Chapter 8 of this book, the panel found – as upheld by the Appellate Body – that Article XX did not apply in the case at hand. See above, p. 555.

233 See Panel Reports, *China – Raw Materials (2012)*, para. 7.71.

234 See above, p. 471. For a complete list of the export duties applied by Russia, see *Report of the Working Party on the Accession of Russia*, WT/ACC/RUS/70, dated 17 November 2011, Table 32.

235 See Annex 1 to WT/L/839, dated 17 December 2011, which contains Russia's Goods Schedule, circulated as WT/ACC/RUS/70/Add.1.

236 *Report of the Working Party on the Accession of Russia*, WT/ACC/RUS/70, dated 17 November 2011, para. 635.

its accession to the WTO, Russia was required to agree on maximum levels for its export duties. It deserves to be noted that the obligation with regard to export duties undertaken by Russia is less far reaching than the obligation undertaken by China.

In the context of the Doha Round negotiations, the European Union has advocated for specific WTO rules on export duties confirming and operationalising the basic GATT disciplines (and exceptions), while allowing flexibility to small developing-country Members and least-developed-country Members.[237] However, to date, it has been unsuccessful in garnering sufficient support for such rules on export duties.

5 SUMMARY

Market access for goods and services from other countries can be, and frequently is, impeded or restricted in various ways. There are two main categories of barriers to market access: (1) tariff barriers; and (2) non-tariff barriers. This chapter deals with tariff barriers. The category of tariff barriers includes: (1) customs duties on imports; (2) other duties and charges on imports; and (3) export duties (i.e. customs duties and other duties and charges on exports). Different rules apply to these different types of tariff barrier.

A customs duty or tariff on imports is a financial charge or tax on imported goods, due because of their importation. Market access for the goods concerned is conditional upon the payment of the customs duty. Customs duties are *ad valorem* specific, compound, mixed or otherwise. *Ad valorem* customs duties are by far the most common type of customs duties. The customs duties or tariffs, which are due on importation, are set out in a country's national customs tariff. Most national customs tariffs follow or reflect the structure set out in the Harmonized Commodity Description and Coding System, usually referred to as the 'Harmonized System' or 'HS'.

WTO law, and in particular the GATT 1994, does not prohibit the imposition of customs duties on imports. Customs duties, unlike quantitative restrictions discussed in Chapter 7, represent an instrument of protection against imports generally allowed by the GATT 1994. Article XXVIII*bis* of the GATT 1994 does, however, call upon WTO Members to negotiate the reduction of customs duties. The eight GATT Rounds of trade negotiations have been very successful in reducing customs duties. Nevertheless, customs duties remain a significant barrier in international trade, and further negotiations on the reduction of tariffs are

---

237 See Negotiating Group on Market Access, Communication from the European Communities, *Market Access for Non-Agricultural Products, Revised Submission on Export Taxes*, TN/MA/W/101, dated 17 January 2008.

therefore necessary. The basic principles and rules governing tariff negotiations are: (1) the principle of reciprocity and mutual advantage; and (2) the most-favoured-nation (MFN) treatment obligation. The principle of reciprocity does not apply in full to tariff negotiations between developed- and developing-country Members. Members can adopt different approaches, or modalities, to tariff negotiations, including the product-by-product approach, the formula approach (be it the linear reduction approach or the non-linear reduction approach), the sectoral approach, or a combination of these approaches.

The results of tariff negotiations are referred to as 'tariff concessions' or 'tariff bindings'. A tariff concession, or tariff binding, is a commitment not to raise the customs duty on a certain product above an agreed level. The tariff concessions or bindings made by a Member are set out in that Member's Schedule of Concessions (also referred to as a Goods Schedule). The Schedules of Concessions resulting from the Uruguay Round negotiations are all annexed to the *Marrakesh Protocol* to the GATT 1994 and are an integral part thereof. Therefore, the tariff schedules and tariff concessions must be interpreted in accordance with the rules of interpretation set out in Article 31 and 32 of the *Vienna Convention on the Law of Treaties*.

Article II:1(a) of the GATT 1994 provides that Members shall accord to products imported from other Members *treatment no less favourable* than that provided for in their Schedules. Article II:1(b), first sentence, of the GATT 1994 provides that products described in Part I of the Schedule of any Member shall, on importation, be *exempt from ordinary customs duties in excess of* those set out in the Schedule. This means that products may not be subjected to customs duties above the tariff concessions or bindings. Note, however, that Article XXVIII of the GATT 1994 provides a procedure for the modification or withdrawal of the agreed tariff concessions.

In addition to the rules to protect tariff concessions, WTO law also provides for some rules on the manner in which customs duties must be imposed. The imposition of customs duties may require three determinations to be made: (1) the determination of the proper classification of the imported good; (2) the determination of the customs value of the imported good; and (3) the determination of the origin of the imported good. The WTO agreements do not specifically address the issue of customs classification. However, in classifying products for customs purposes, Members have of course to consider their general obligations under the WTO agreements, such as the MFN treatment obligation. *Specific* rules on classification can be found in the *HS Convention*, to which most WTO Members are a party.

Unlike for customs classification, the *WTO Agreement* provides for rules on customs valuation. These rules are set out in: Article VII of the GATT 1994; the Note *Ad* Article VII; and the WTO *Customs Valuation Agreement*. The primary basis for the customs value is the 'transaction value' of the imported goods, i.e. the price actually paid or payable for the goods. This price is normally shown in the invoice, contract or purchase order, albeit that a number of adjustments usually have to be made. If the customs value cannot be established in this manner, it must be established pursuant to the alternative methods set out in the *Customs Valuation Agreement*.

The GATT 1994 provides no specific disciplines on rules of origin. However, the negotiators during the Uruguay Round recognised the need for multilateral disciplines on rules of origin in order to prevent these rules from being a source of uncertainty and unpredictability in international trade. The consensus on the need for such disciplines resulted in the WTO *Agreement on Rules of Origin*. With respect to *non-preferential* rules of origin, the *Agreement on Rules of Origin* provides for a work programme on the harmonisation of these rules. While the completion of the work programme is long overdue, Members have not yet been able to reach agreement on harmonised rules of origin. Until the successful completion of this work programme, Article 2 of the *Agreement on Rules of Origin* contains a list of multilateral disciplines on the application and administration of rules of origin applicable during the current 'transition period'. After harmonised rules of origin have been agreed on, these disciplines will continue to apply. With respect to *preferential* rules of origin, Annex 2 to the *Agreement on Rules of Origin* provides for a more modest list of multilateral disciplines on the application and administration of rules of origin.

In addition to 'ordinary' customs duties on imports, tariff barriers on imports can also take the form of other duties and charges on imports. 'Other duties and charges on imports' are financial charges or taxes, *other than* ordinary customs duties, which are levied on imported products and are due because of their importation. Pursuant to Article II:1(b), second sentence, of the GATT 1994 and the *Understanding on Article II:1(b)*, Members may: (1) impose only other duties and charges on imports that have been properly recorded in their Schedules; and (2) impose other duties and charges on imports only at a level that does not exceed the level recorded in their Schedules. There are, however, a number of 'other duties and charges on imports' that are *exempted* from the rule that Members may not impose such duties or charges unless recorded and not in excess of the recorded level. Pursuant to Article II:2 of the GATT 1994, Members may – in spite of their obligation under Article II:1(b), second sentence – impose on imported products: (1) a financial charge equivalent to an internal tax on the like domestic product imposed consistently with Article III:2 of the GATT 1994 (border tax adjustment); (2) WTO-consistent anti-dumping or countervailing duties; or (3) fees or other charges 'commensurate' with, i.e. matching, the cost of the services rendered.

Tariff barriers to trade in goods apply not only to imports. While much less common than customs duties and other duties and charges on imports, Members also impose export duties. An export duty, be it a customs duty or another duty or charge on exports, is a financial charge or tax on exported products, due because of their exportation. Market exit of the products concerned is conditional upon the payment of the export duty. Neither the GATT 1994 nor any of the other multilateral agreements on trade in goods prohibits or specifically regulates export duties. Note that some WTO accession protocols, including China's Accession Protocol (2001) and Russia's Accession Protocol (2011) do prohibit or specifically regulate export duties.

Exercise 6: Carlie goes to Europe

Dolls Я Us is a toy manufacturer from Goldtown, Richland, with production facilities in Richland, Newland and Farawayland.[238] Dolls Я Us produces a wide range of toys but is best known for a doll named Carlie. In view of Carlie's success in the United States, Dolls Я Us wants to explore the possibility of marketing Carlie in the United Kingdom. Carlie is a Barbie-like doll with a plastic body, artificial hair and three sets of clothes. The plastic body parts are produced in Newland. The hair and the clothes are produced in Farawayland. Carlie is only assembled and packaged in Richland. It is expected to sell at £10 per doll in the United Kingdom.

The UK's Customs Service has informed Dolls Я Us that the customs duty on Carlie will amount to 15 per cent *ad valorem* and that the value will be determined on the basis of the sales price on the domestic market in Richland. Dolls Я Us challenges both the level of the duty and the manner in which the Customs Service intends to determine the value of the dolls for customs purposes. It also disagrees with the Customs Service that the country of origin of Carlie is Richland and not Newland. Furthermore, Dolls Я Us considers that Carlie is not really a toy but rather a collector's item. Finally, it wonders whether, for the customs classification of Carlie, it makes a difference whether Carlie is imported as a finished product or in parts still to be assembled.

The UK Customs Service also informs Dolls Я Us that all imported dolls are subject to an import surcharge of £0.30 per doll as well as a special customs-handling fee of 0.2 per cent *ad valorem*. This fee goes to the Customs Service's Fund for Disfavoured Children.

To boost its sales of Carlie in the United Kingdom, Dolls Я Us plans to send buyers of this doll, upon their request, short movies on the wondrous adventures of Carlie. These movies are sent from Richland by e-mail. Dolls Я Us is concerned about the rumour that the European Commission is considering the introduction of a customs duty on movies imported into the European Union via the Internet.

238 Farawayland is a least-developed currently negotiating its accession to the WTO.

The Government of Newland, eager to promote the development of its toy industry, has announced that they will introduce an export duty of 10 per cent *ad valorem* on plastic body parts of dolls.

Dolls Я Us is 'disappointed' by the information received from the UK's Customs Service, and concerned about the rumours on the 'movies duty' as well as about Newland's planned introduction of an export duty. It has asked its law firm, Gandhi, Bhatia & Ganesan, an Indian law firm with offices in London, for legal advice on the WTO-consistency of the various measures referred to above. You are a junior lawyer working at Gandhi, Bhatia & Ganesan and you have been tasked with preparing a note on the legal advice sought by Dolls Я Us. The senior partner of the law firm has warned you not to forget to check the EU's Goods Schedule as well as the EU's Common Customs Tariff.

7 Non-Tariff Barriers

CONTENTS

1   INTRODUCTION

As mentioned in Chapter 6, not only tariff barriers but also a wide range of non-tariff barriers restrict trade.[1] While tariff barriers were systematically reduced since the late 1940s as a result of successive rounds of tariff negotiations, non-tariff barriers have in recent decades gradually become an ever more prominent instrument of protection. The term 'non-tariff barrier' is not defined in WTO law, but this important residual category of barriers to trade can be understood to include all government imposed and sponsored actions or omissions that act as prohibitions or restrictions on trade, other than ordinary customs duties and other duties and charges on imports and exports.[2]

Unlike tariff barriers, non-tariff barriers not only affect trade in goods but also trade in services.[3]

This chapter deals in turn with: (1) quantitative restrictions on trade in goods; (2) 'other non-tariff barriers' on trade in goods; (3) market access barriers to trade in services; and (4) other barriers to trade in services. Note, however, that this chapter does not deal with two specific types of 'other non-tariff barriers' to trade in goods, namely, technical barriers to trade and sanitary and phytosanitary measures. Due to their importance and detailed nature, the rules on these 'other non-tariff barriers' are discussed, separately, in Chapters 13 and 14 of this book respectively.[4] While non-tariff barriers have become a prominent instrument of protection, they often also serve important public policy objectives, such as public health, consumer safety and environmental protection. To the extent that they do so, their elimination or liberalisation may not be desirable at all. That is the case in particular, but not only, for the 'other non-tariff barriers' discussed in Chapters 13 and 14, WTO law regulates these other non-tariff barriers with a view to allowing their use but minimising discrimination and their adverse impact on trade.

Finally, this chapter does not deal either with non-tariff barriers to trade resulting from the lack of effective protection of intellectual property rights. The WTO rules addressing these barriers, i.e. the WTO rules ensuring a minimum

---

1   In this book, the term 'non-tariff barrier' (NTB) encompasses the term 'non-tariff measure' (NTM), a term in vogue and referred to in the title of the WTO's World Trade Report 2012, *Trade and Public Policies: A Closer Look at Non-Tariff Measures in the 21st Century* (WTO, 2012). However, the term 'non-tariff barrier' is broader than the term 'non-tariff measure' as it also includes barriers to trade other than measures, such as the lack of transparency. See below, pp. 498–502.

2   See also Roy Santana and Lee Ann Jackson, 'Identifying Non-Tariff Barriers: Evolution of Multilateral Instruments and Evidence From the Disputes (1948–2011)', *World Trade Review*, 2012, 465.

3   On tariff barriers to trade in services, see above, p. 419. As discussed, tariff barriers to trade in services do not currently exist, but the debate, and the current WTO moratorium, on the 'bit tax', i.e. a tax imposed 'at the border' on electronic communications containing services outputs, shows that tariff barriers *can* exist for trade in services.

4   See below, pp. 851, 852 and 896.

level of protection and enforcement of intellectual property rights, are dealt with in Chapter 15 of this book.[5]

2   QUANTITATIVE RESTRICTIONS ON TRADE IN GOODS

The archetypical non-tariff barrier to trade is a quantitative restriction on trade in goods. This section discusses: (1) the definition and types of quantitative restriction on trade in goods; (2) the rules on quantitative restrictions; and (3) the administration of quantitative restrictions.[6]

2.1   Definition and Types

A quantitative restriction on trade in goods, also referred to as a 'QR', is a measure that *limits the quantity* of a product that may be imported or exported. A typical example of a quantitative restriction is a measure allowing the importation of a maximum of 1,000 tonnes of cocoa powder a year or a measure allowing the importation of a maximum of 450 tractors a year. While usually based on the number of units, weight or volume, quantitative restrictions may also be based on value, for example a limit on the importation of flowers to the value of €12 million per year.

There are different types of quantitative restriction: (1) a *prohibition*, or ban, on the importation or exportation of a product; such a prohibition may be absolute or conditional, i.e. only applicable when certain defined conditions are *not* fulfilled; (2) an import or export *quota*, i.e. a measure, as the examples given above, indicating the quantity that may be imported or exported; a quota can be a global quota, a global quota allocated among countries or a bilateral quota; (3) import or export *licensing*, as further discussed below;[7] and (4) *other* quantitative restrictions, such as a quantitative restriction made effective through State trading operations; a mixing regulation; a minimum price, triggering a quantitative restriction; and a voluntary export restraint.[8]

Confusingly perhaps, a tariff (rate) quota, or 'TRQ', is *not* a quota in the strict sense of the term; it is *not* a quantitative restriction.[9] A tariff quota is a quantity, which can be imported at a certain duty. The panel in *US – Line Pipe (2002)* stated that a tariff quota involves the 'application of a higher tariff rate to

---

5   See below, p. 972.
6   This section concludes with a short note on special and differential treatment regarding quantitative restrictions on trade in goods.
7   See below, p. 495.
8   For an illustrative list of quantitative restrictions, see Council for Trade in Goods, *Decision on Notification Procedures for Quantitative Restrictions*, adopted on 22 June 2012, G/L/59/Rev.1, dated 22 June 2012, Annex 2.
9   See Panel Report, *EEC – Bananas II (1994)*, paras. 138–9. Note that this GATT panel report was not adopted.

imported goods after a specific quantity of the item has entered the country at a lower prevailing rate'.[10] Any quantity above the quota is subject to a higher duty.[11] For example, a Member may allow the importation of 5,000 tractors at 10 per cent *ad valorem* and any tractor imported above this quantity at 30 per cent *ad valorem*. Tariff quotas are not quantitative restrictions since they do not directly prohibit or restrict the quantity of imports. They only subject the imports to varying duties. The European Communities' intricate import regime for bananas, at issue in *EC – Bananas III (1997)* and subsequent *EC – Bananas III* disputes, provided for tariff quotas. Under this regime, the European Communities initially granted, for example, duty-free access to 90,000 tonnes of non-traditional ACP bananas; the out-of-quota tariff rate for these same bananas was 693 ECU per tonne. In general, tariff quotas are widely used with regard to agricultural products.[12] However, they are also sometimes used for non-agricultural products.

WTO Members are required to notify the WTO Secretariat of any quantitative restrictions which they maintain, and of any changes in these restrictions, as and when they occur.[13] Such notifications must contain and/indicate: (1) a general description of the restriction; (2) the type of restriction; (3) the relevant tariff line code; (4) a detailed product description; (5) the WTO justification for the measure concerned; (6) the national legal basis for the restriction; and (7) information on the administration of the restriction and, where relevant, an explanation of the modification of a previously notified restriction.[14] With this information, the WTO Secretariat maintains a QR database, which Members and the general public may consult.[15]

Questions and Assignments 7.1

What is a quantitative restriction? Discuss the different types of quantitative restriction. Are tariff quotas quantitative restrictions or quotas? Why?

2.2 Rules on Quantitative Restrictions

The GATT 1994 and other multilateral agreements on trade in goods set out specific rules on quantitative restrictions. This sub-section discusses in turn: (1) the general prohibition on quantitative restrictions set out in Article XI of the GATT 1994; (2) the rationale behind the marked difference in the GATT rules on

---

10 Panel Report, *US – Line Pipe (2002)*, para. 7.18.

11 To imports within the quota, the 'in quota duty' applies; to imports over and above the quota, the higher 'out of quota duty' applies.

12 The frequent use of tariff quotas with regard to agricultural products is a result of the 'tariffication' exercise under which quantitative restrictions on trade in agricultural products were 'translated' into tariffs and in particular 'tariff quotas'. See below, p. 489.

13 See Council for Trade in Goods, *Decision on Notification Procedures for Quantitative Restrictions*, G/L/59/Rev.1, dated 3 July 2012, para. 1.

14 See *ibid.*, para. 2. For an example of such notification, see a notification by Australia, G/MA/QR/N/AUS/1, dated 30 October 2012.

15 See www.wto.org/english/res_e/statis_e/statis_e.htm.

customs duties and quantitative restrictions; (3) the rules on quantitative restrictions on specific products, in particular agricultural products and textiles; and (4) the rules on voluntary export restraints (VERs).

2.2.1   General Prohibition on Quantitative Restrictions

Article XI:1 of the GATT 1994, entitled 'General Elimination of Quantitative Restrictions', sets out a general prohibition on quantitative restrictions, whether on imports or exports. As the panel in *Turkey – Textiles (1999)* stated:

> The prohibition on the use of quantitative restrictions forms one of the cornerstones of the GATT system.[16]

Article XI:1 provides, in relevant part:

> No prohibitions or restrictions other than duties, taxes or other charges, whether made effective through quotas, import or export licences or other measures, shall be instituted or maintained by any [Member] on the importation of any product of the territory of any other [Member] or on the exportation or sale for export of any product destined for the territory of any other [Member].

The panel in *Japan – Semi-Conductors (1988)* noted that the wording of Article XI:1 is *comprehensive* as:

> it applied to *all measures* instituted or maintained by a contracting party *prohibiting or restricting* the importation, exportation or sale for export of products *other than* measures that take the form of duties, taxes or other charges.[17]

As an illustration of the broad scope of the prohibition on quantitative restrictions, consider that Article XI was found to apply to: export quotas;[18] minimum import price requirements;[19] minimum export price requirements;[20] a discretionary and non-automatic licensing system;[21] trade balancing requirements;[22] and restrictions on ports of entry.[23]

Unlike other GATT provisions, Article XI refers not to laws or regulations but more broadly to *measures*. A measure instituted or maintained by a Member, which restricts imports or exports, is covered by Article XI, *irrespective* of the legal status of the measure.[24] In *Japan – Semi-Conductors (1988)*, the panel thus ruled that *non-mandatory* measures of the Japanese Government, restricting

---

16 Panel Report, *Turkey – Textiles (1999)*, para. 9.63.
17 Panel Report, *Japan – Semi-Conductors (1988)*, para. 104. Emphasis added. See also Panel Report, *India – Quantitative Restrictions (1999)*, para. 5.129. The panel in this case further noted that: 'the scope of the term "restriction" is also broad, as seen in its ordinary meaning, which is "a limitation on actions, a limiting condition or regulation"'.
18 See *China – Raw Materials (2012)*.
19 See *EEC – Minimum Import Prices (1978)*. Note that, in this case, the minimum import price requirement was enforced with an import certificate and a security lodgment measure.
20 See *Japan – Semi-Conductors (1988)*; and *China – Raw Materials (2012)*.
21 See *India – Quantitative Restrictions (1999)*; and *China – Raw Materials (2012)*.
22 See *India – Autos (2002)*.
23 See *Colombia – Ports of Entry (2009)*.
24 See Panel Report, *Japan – Semi-Conductors (1988)*, para. 106.

the export of certain semi-conductors at below-cost price, were nevertheless 'restrictions' within the meaning of Article XI:1.[25]

Note that, in addition, quantitative restrictions which do not *actually* restrict or impede trade are nevertheless prohibited under Article XI:1 of the GATT 1994.[26] The panel in *EEC – Oilseeds I (1990)* ruled in this respect:

> [T]he Contracting Parties have consistently interpreted the basic provisions of the General Agreement on restrictive trade measures as provisions establishing conditions of competition. Thus they decided that an import quota constitutes an import restriction within the meaning of Article XI:1 whether or not it actually impeded imports.[27]

On the other hand, the panel in *EEC – Minimum Import Prices (1978)* found that automatic import licensing does not constitute a restriction of the type meant to fall within the scope of application of Article XI:1.[28]

The broad scope of application of Article XI:1 was confirmed by the panels in *India – Quantitative Restrictions (1999)* and *India – Autos (2002)*. The panel in the latter dispute explicitly addressed the question whether Article XI also covered situations where products are technically allowed into the market without an express formal quantitative restriction, but yet subject to certain conditions which create a disincentive to import.[29] The panel responded to this question as follows:

> On a plain reading, it is clear that a 'restriction' need not be a blanket prohibition or a precise numerical limit. Indeed, the term 'restriction' cannot mean merely 'prohibitions' on importation, since Article XI:1 expressly covers both 'prohibition or restriction'. Furthermore, the Panel considers that the expression 'limiting condition' used by the *India – Quantitative Restrictions* panel to define the term 'restriction' and which this Panel endorses, is helpful in identifying the scope of the notion in the context of the facts before it. That phrase suggests the need to identify not merely a condition placed on importation, but a condition that is limiting, i.e. that has a limiting effect. In the context of Article XI, that limiting effect must be on importation itself.[30]

The panel in *Dominican Republic – Import and Sale of Cigarettes (2005)* further clarified the scope of application of Article XI:1 by stating:

> Not every measure affecting the opportunities for entering the market would be covered by Article XI, but only those measures that constitute a prohibition or a restriction on the

---

25 *Ibid.*, paras. 104–17. The panel considered that, in order to determine whether the *non-mandatory* measures were measures falling within the scope of Article XI, it needed to be satisfied on two essential criteria: (1) there were reasonable grounds to believe that sufficient incentives or disincentives existed for non-mandatory measures to take effect; and (2) the operation of the measures was essentially dependent on government action or intervention. The panel considered that, if these two criteria were met, the measures would be operating in a manner equivalent to mandatory requirements such that the difference between the measures and mandatory requirements was only one of form and not one of substance.

26 Such non-biting quotas, i.e. quotas above current levels of trade, cause increased transaction costs and create uncertainties, which could affect investment plans. See Panel Report, *Japan – Leather (US II) (1984)*, para. 55.

27 Panel Report, *EEC – Oilseeds I (1990)*, para. 150.

28 See Panel Report, *EEC – Minimum Import Prices (1978)*, para. 4.1.

29 See Panel Report, *India – Autos (2002)*, para. 7.269.

30 *Ibid.*, para. 7.270.

importation of products, i.e. those measures which affect the opportunities for importation itself.[31]

In *Brazil – Retreaded Tyres (2007)*, the European Communities claimed, *inter alia*, that the imposition of fines on the importation, marketing, transportation, storage, keeping and warehousing of imported retreaded tyres was inconsistent with Article XI:1 of the GATT 1994.[32] In addressing this claim, the panel considered whether these fines, imposed by Brazil as an enforcement measure of the import prohibition, constituted a restriction on importation within the meaning of Article XI:1. The panel reached the following conclusion:

> [W]hat is important in considering whether a measure falls within the types of measures covered by Article XI:1 is the nature of the measure. In the present case, we note that the fines as a whole, including that on marketing, have the effect of penalizing the act of 'importing' retreaded tyres by subjecting retreaded tyres already imported and existing in the Brazilian internal market to the prohibitively expensive rate of fines. To that extent, we consider that the fact that the fines are not administered at the border does not alter their nature as a restriction on importation within the meaning of Article XI:1.[33]

Article XI:1 of the GATT 1994 does not only prohibit *de jure* quantitative restrictions; restrictions of a *de facto* nature are also prohibited under Article XI:1. The scope of quantitative restrictions within the meaning of Article XI:1 is thus not limited to measures that set an explicit numerical ceiling. Rather, measures which have in fact that effect are also quantitative restrictions within the meaning of Article XI:1. In *Argentina – Hides and Leather (2001)*, the issue arose whether Argentina violated Article XI:1 by authorising the presence of domestic tanners' representatives in the customs inspection procedures for hides destined for export operations. According to the European Communities, the complainant in this case, Argentina, imposed a *de facto* restriction on the exportation of hides inconsistent with Article XI:1. The panel ruled:

> There can be no doubt, in our view, that the disciplines of Article XI:1 extend to restrictions of a *de facto* nature.[34]

However, the panel concluded with respect to the Argentinian regulation providing for the presence of the domestic tanners' representatives in the customs inspection procedures that there was insufficient evidence that this regulation actually operated as an export restriction inconsistent with Article XI:1 of the GATT 1994.[35] According to the panel, there was 'no persuasive explanation

---

31 Panel Report, *Dominican Republic – Import and Sale of Cigarettes (2005)*, para. 7.261.
32 See Panel Report, *Brazil – Retreaded Tyres (2007)*, para. 7.361. This finding was not appealed.
33 *Ibid.*, para. 7.372. The panel noted in addition that: 'the level of the fines – R$ 400 per unit, which significantly exceeds the average prices of domestically produced retreaded tyres for passenger cars (R$ 100–280) – is significant enough to have a restrictive effect on importation.' See *ibid.*
34 Panel Report, *Argentina – Hides and Leather (2001)*, para. 11.17. In support of this finding, the panel referred to the Panel Report in *Japan – Semi-Conductors (1988)*, paras. 105–9. For findings on *de facto* quantitative restrictions, see also *Colombia – Ports of Entry (2009)*, *US – Poultry (China) (2010)* and *China – Raw Materials (2012)*.
35 See Panel Report, *Argentina – Hides and Leather (2001)*, para. 11.55.

of precisely how the measure at issue causes or contributes to the low level of exports'.[36] Taking a different approach, the panel in *Colombia – Ports of Entry (2009)* stated, however, that:

> to the extent Panama were able to demonstrate a violation of Article XI:1 based on the measure's design, structure, and architecture, the Panel is of the view that it would not be necessary to consider trade volumes or a causal link between the measure and its effects on trade volumes.[37]

In *China – Raw Materials (2012)*, the panel found that the minimum export price requirement on exporters of bauxite, coke, fluorspar, magnesium, silicon carbide, yellow phosphorus and zinc was a quantitative restriction on exports, inconsistent with Article XI:1 of the GATT 1994.[38]

Finally, with regard to the controversial issue whether Article XI:1 covers only border measures or also measures concerning, for example, the sale, offering for sale, transportation, distribution and use of products after they have been imported, please refer to the discussion on the respective scopes of Articles III and XI of the GATT 1994 in Chapter 5 of this book.[39]

While it is explicitly referred to as a 'general prohibition', the prohibition on quantitative restrictions set out in Article XI:1 of the GATT 1994 is not without exceptions. The many and broad exceptions discussed in Chapters 8 and 9 of this book, as well as the special and differential treatment of developing-country Members referred to later in this chapter, are most important in this respect.[40] In addition, note that Article XI exempts certain measures from the scope of application of prohibition on quantitative restrictions.[41] Note in particular Article XI:2(a) which allows for export prohibitions or restrictions temporarily applied to prevent or relieve critical shortages of foodstuffs or other products essential to the exporting Member. In *China – Raw Materials (2012)* the Appellate Body clarified the meaning of the terms 'temporarily applied', 'essential products' and 'prevent or relieve critical shortages' as used in Article XI:2(a).[42]

To date, Members have been found to have acted inconsistently with the prohibition on quantitative restrictions of Article XI:1 of the GATT 1994 in twelve disputes.[43]

---

36 *Ibid.*, para. 11.21.   37 Panel Report, *Colombia – Ports of Entry (2009)*, para. 7.252.
38 See Panel Reports, *China – Raw Materials (2012)*, para. 8.20.
39 See above, pp. 252 and 403.   40 See below, pp. 545, 607 and 497.
41 See Appellate Body Reports, *China – Raw Materials (2012)*, para. 334.
42 See Appellate Body Reports, *China – Raw Materials (2012)*, paras. 318–28. The Appellate Body in this case upheld the finding of the panel that refractory-grade bauxite is 'essential' to China, but that China had not demonstrated that its export quota on refractory-grade bauxite is 'temporarily applied' within the meaning of Article XI:2(a) to either prevent or relieve a 'critical shortage'. See *ibid.*, para. 344.
43 See *Canada – Periodicals (1997)*; *US – Shrimp (1998)*; *India – Quantitative Restrictions (1999)*; *Turkey – Textiles (1999)*; *Korea – Various Measures on Beef (2001)*; *Argentina – Hides and Leather (2001)*; *US – Shrimp (Article 21.5 – Malaysia) (2001)*; *India – Autos (2002)*; *Brazil – Retreaded Tyres (2007)*; *Colombia – Ports of Entry (2009)*; *US – Poultry (China) (2010)*; and *China – Raw Materials (2012)*.

Are quantitative restrictions allowed under the GATT 1994? To which measures does Article XI:1 of the GATT 1994 apply? Does Article XI:1 apply to border measures only? Is the scope of application of Article XI:1 limited to mandatory measures? Is a quantitative restriction which does not actually impede trade inconsistent with Article XI:1? Give an example of a *de facto* quantitative restriction. When is such a restriction consistent with Article XI:1? Can a WTO Member in times of national or international food shortages prohibit the export of foodstuffs?

2.2.2 Quantitative Restrictions and Customs Duties

As already noted in Chapter 6, the WTO has a clear preference for customs duties over quantitative restrictions, and this preference is reflected in the relevant provisions of the GATT 1994.[44] In comparing customs duties with quantitative restrictions, the panel in *Turkey – Textiles (1999)* noted:

> A basic principle of the GATT system is that tariffs are the preferred and acceptable form of protection ... The prohibition against quantitative restrictions is a reflection that tariffs are GATT's border protection 'of choice'.[45]

The reasons for this preference are both economic and political in nature. First, customs duties are more transparent. The economic impact of customs duties on imported products, i.e. how much more expensive imported products are as a result of customs duties, is immediately clear. Quantitative restrictions also increase the price of the imported products. As supply of the imported product is limited, the price increases. However, it is not immediately clear by how much quantitative restrictions increase the price of imported products. As it is less obvious what the negative impact of quantitative restrictions is on prices (paid by consumers and companies using imports), those affected are less likely to mobilise against these measures, and special interest groups are more likely to be able to convince governments to adopt them.

Secondly, and related to the first reason, it is considered easier to negotiate, in successive rounds of negotiations, the gradual reduction of customs duties than it is to negotiate the elimination (or liberalisation) of quantitative restrictions.

Thirdly, while the price increase resulting from customs duties goes to the government as revenue, the price increase resulting from quantitative restrictions ordinarily benefits the importers. The importers will be able to sell at higher prices because of the limits on the supply of the product. This 'extra profit' is commonly referred to as the 'quota rent', and, unless a quota is auctioned (which is seldom done), no part of this quota rent goes to the government.

Fourthly, the administration of quantitative restrictions is more open to corruption than the administration of customs duties. This is because quantitative restrictions, and, in particular, quotas, are usually administered through an

44 See above, p. 426.   45 Panel Report, *Turkey – Textiles (1999)*, para. 9.63.

import-licensing system; import-licensing procedures are often not transparent, and decisions by government officials to award an import licence not necessarily based on the general interest.[46]

Finally, and arguably most importantly, quantitative restrictions impose absolute limits on imports, while customs duties do not. While customs duties are surmountable (at least, if they are not set at prohibitively high levels), quantitative restrictions cannot be surmounted. If a foreign producer is sufficiently more efficient than a domestic producer, the customs duty will not prevent imported products from competing with domestic products. By contrast, once the limit of a quantitative restriction is reached, no more products can be imported. Even the most efficient foreign producer cannot 'overcome' the quantitative restriction. Above the quota, domestic products have no competition from imported products.[47]

2.2.3   Rules on Quantitative Restrictions on Specific Products

Under the GATT 1947, the prohibition against quantitative restrictions was often *not* respected. The panel in *Turkey – Textiles (1999)* noted:

> From early in the GATT, in sectors such as agriculture, quantitative restrictions were maintained and even increased ... In the sector of textiles and clothing, quantitative restrictions were maintained under the Multifibre Agreement [*sic*] ... Certain contracting parties were even of the view that quantitative restrictions had gradually been tolerated and accepted as negotiable and that Article XI could not be, and had never been considered to be, a provision prohibiting such restrictions irrespective of the circumstances specific to each case.[48]

However, the overall detrimental effect of these quantitative restrictions in the sectors of agriculture and textiles was generally recognised. Therefore, their elimination was high on the agenda of the Uruguay Round negotiations, and the *Agreement on Agriculture* and the *Agreement on Textiles and Clothing* (resulting from these negotiations) contain specific rules regarding the elimination of quantitative restrictions.

The *Agreement on Agriculture* provides that quantitative import restrictions and voluntary export restraints, *inter alia*, must be converted into tariffs and that no new restrictions of this kind can be adopted. Article 4.2 of the *Agreement on Agriculture* states:

> Members shall not maintain, resort to, or revert to any measures of the kind which have been required to be converted into ordinary customs duties, except as otherwise provided for in Article 5 and Annex 5.

---

46 On import-licensing procedures, see below, p. 495.
47 See also Panel Report, *Turkey – Textiles (1999)*, para. 9.63.
48 *Ibid.*, para. 9.64. Note that the argument of certain Contracting Parties that Article XI could not be a provision prohibiting quantitative restrictions irrespective of the circumstances in which they were imposed, in a specific case, was explicitly rejected by the panel in *EEC – Import Restrictions (1983)*.

In footnote 1 to this provision, the measures which had to be converted into tariffs (or tariff quotas) were identified as: quantitative import restrictions, variable import levies, minimum import prices, discretionary import licensing, non-tariff measures maintained through State trading enterprises, voluntary export restraints, and similar border measures other than ordinary customs duties.[49] The process of converting these non-tariff measures into tariffs is commonly referred to as the 'tariffication process'. As this process provided for the replacement of non-tariff measures with a tariff which afforded *an equivalent level of protection*, many of the tariffs resulting from the 'tariffication process' are very high.[50] However, by introducing a system of *tariff quotas*, it was possible to guarantee: (1) that the quantities imported before Article 4.2 of the *Agreement on Agriculture* took effect could continue to be imported; and (2) that some new quantities were subject to tariffs that were not prohibitive. Under this system of tariff quotas, lower tariffs applied to specified quantities (in-quota quantities), while higher (often prohibitive) tariffs applied to quantities that exceed the quota (over-quota quantities).[51]

With respect to the relationship between Article 4.2 of the *Agreement on Agriculture* and Article XI of the GATT 1994, the panel in *Korea – Various Measures on Beef (2001)* stated that:

when dealing with measures relating to agricultural products which should have been converted into tariffs or tariff-quotas, a violation of Article XI of GATT ... would necessarily constitute a violation of Article 4.2 of the *Agreement on Agriculture* and its footnote.[52]

As mentioned above, trade in textiles and clothing also largely 'escaped' from the GATT 1947 rules and disciplines, and in particular the prohibition of Article XI on quantitative restrictions. Under the *Multifibre Arrangement* (MFA), in effect from 1974, developed and developing countries, respectively importing and exporting textiles, entered into bilateral agreements requiring the exporting developing countries to limit their exports of certain categories of textiles and clothing. In 1995, the main importing countries had eighty-one such restraint agreements with exporting countries, comprising over a thousand individual quotas.[53] The MFA, which was negotiated within the framework of the GATT, provided a 'legal cover' for the GATT-inconsistency of these quotas.[54] The *Agreement on Textiles and Clothing* (ATC) negotiated during the Uruguay Round

---

49 Note that measures maintained under balance-of-payments provisions or under other general, non-agriculture-specific provisions of the GATT 1994 or of the other multilateral agreements on trade in goods did *not* need to be converted into tariffs.

50 The customs duties resulting from the 'tariffication process' concern, on average, one-fifth of the total number of agricultural tariff lines in the national customs tariffs of developed-country Members.

51 On the reduction of customs duties on agricultural products agreed on during the Uruguay Round negotiations, see above, pp. 437–8.

52 Panel Report, *Korea – Various Measures on Beef (2001)*, para. 7.62.

53 In addition, there were also a number of non-MFA agreements or unilateral measures restricting the imports of textiles and clothing. See *Business Guide to the World Trading System*, 2nd edn (International Trade Centre/Commonwealth Secretariat, 1999), 164.

54 *Ibid.*, 165.

sought to address this situation and contained specific rules for quantitative restrictions on textiles and clothing. The panel in *US – Underwear (1997)* stated:

[T]he overall purpose of the ATC is to integrate the textiles and clothing sector into GATT 1994. Article 1 of the ATC makes this point clear. To this effect, the ATC requires notification of all existing quantitative restrictions (Article 2 of the ATC) and provides that they will have to be terminated by the year 2004 (Article 9 of the ATC).[55]

The ten-year-long 'integration process', provided for in the ATC, was to be carried out in four stages, ending on 31 December 2004. At each stage, products amounting to a certain minimum percentage of the volume of a Member's 1990 imports of textiles and clothing were made fully subject to the disciplines of the GATT 1994, including the prohibition on quantitative restrictions of Article XI.[56] Moreover, the level of the remaining quantitative restrictions was to be increased annually.[57]

While the integration process of the ATC was successfully completed by the end of 2004 and quantitative restrictions on textiles terminated, the benefits of this return to GATT discipline have been unevenly spread. A number of smaller, textile-producing developing-country Members, such as Mauritius, Lesotho and Costa Rica, which before 2005 had enjoyed guaranteed quota access, encountered serious adjustment problems as their textile exports could not compete with the textile exports of the large textile-producing developing-country Members, such as Bangladesh, Brazil, India, and especially China.[58] When it was suggested that the WTO should address the problems of small textile-producing developing-country Members adversely affected by the elimination of quotas, China, Brazil, India and Hong Kong objected to the inclusion of this issue on the agenda of the Council for Trade in Goods.[59] As reported in *Bridges Weekly Trade News Digest* in June 2005:

The Chinese responded forcefully against the idea of continued work in the Goods Council on textiles, noting that the quota system, which expired with the Agreement on Textiles and Clothing on 1 January 2005, discriminated against China and hurt the Chinese people. The WTO's job, argued China, was to promote trade competition, not to stabilise market prices. Indian diplomats also said that their country opposed special measures for particular industries.[60]

---

55 Panel Report, *US – Underwear (1997)*, para. 7.19.
56 See Articles 2.6 and 2.7 of the ATC. Note, however, that this integration process applied to *all* textile products listed in the ATC, including products on which there were no quantitative restrictions. This allowed the United States and the European Communities, during the first stages, to 'integrate' mainly products on which there were *no* quantitative restrictions into the GATT 1994. To the discontent and disappointment of the textile-exporting Members, the two major importing Members, the European Union and the United States, could at least initially meet their obligations under the ATC without significantly removing quantitative restrictions. They removed most of their quantitative restrictions only in the fourth and last stage of the integration process, ending on 1 January 2005.
57 E.g. the quotas were increased by 25 per cent per year from 1998 to 2001. See Articles 2.13 and 2.14 of the ATC.
58 See F. Williams, 'China and India Gain from End of Quotas', *Financial Times*, 25 October 2005.
59 See *Bridges Weekly Trade News Digest*, 18 May 2005.
60 *Bridges Weekly Trade News Digest*, 22 June 2005.

2.2.4 Voluntary Export Restraints

Voluntary export restraints (VERs) are actions taken by exporting countries involving a *self-imposed* quantitative restriction of exports. VERs are taken either
unilaterally or under the terms of an agreement or arrangement between two
or more countries. As the term indicates, in theory, VERs are entered into on a
voluntary basis, i.e. the exporting country voluntarily limits the volume of its
exports. However, in reality, the voluntary nature of VERs is usually a fiction. A
1983 GATT report observed:

> It appeared ... that exporting countries which accepted so-called 'grey-area' actions did so
> primarily because ... they felt that they had little choice and that the alternative was, or
> would have been, unilateral action in the form of quantitative restrictions, harassment by
> anti-dumping investigations, countervailing action ... involving greater harm to their ex-
> ports in terms of quantity or price.[61]

Under the GATT 1947, the legality of voluntary export restraints was a much-
debated issue. With the entry into force of the *WTO Agreement*, this issue has
been definitively decided. The WTO *Agreement on Safeguards* specifically prohibits voluntary export restraints.[62] Article 11.1(b) of this Agreement provides:

> [A] Member shall not seek, take or maintain any voluntary export restraints, orderly mar-
> keting arrangements or any other similar measures on the export or the import side.[63]

Article 11.1(b) of the *Agreement on Safeguards* furthermore required that any
such measure existing in 1995 had to be phased out (or brought into compliance
with the *Agreement on Safeguards*) before the end of 1999.

2.3 Administration of Quantitative Restrictions

Article XI:1 of the GATT 1994 prohibits quantitative restrictions. There are,
however, as noted above and discussed elsewhere in this book, many exceptions
to this prohibition of Article XI:1.[64] Article XIII of the GATT 1994 bears testimony to this by setting out rules on the *administration* of quantitative restrictions. This sub-section addresses: (1) the rule of non-discrimination; (2) the rules
on the distribution of trade; and (3) the rules on import-licensing procedures.

While tariff quotas are not quantitative restrictions, pursuant to Article XIII:5
of the GATT 1994, the rules on the administration of quantitative restrictions set
out in Article XIII, and discussed in this sub-section, also apply to the administration of tariff quotas. In fact, many of the disputes on Article XIII are related

---

61 Report of the Chairman of the Safeguards Committee, BISD 30S/216, 218.
62 For a detailed discussion of the *Agreement on Safeguards*, see below, p. 608. Also, Article 4.2, read together
   with footnote 1, of the *Agreement on Agriculture* contains a prohibition of voluntary export restraints.
63 Footnote 4 to this provision contains an illustrative list of 'similar measures', including export moderation,
   export-price or import-price monitoring systems, export or import surveillance, compulsory import cartels
   and discretionary export or import-licensing schemes, any of which afford protection.
64 See above, p. 484; and, *inter alia*, below, pp. 538 and 548.

to the administration of tariff quotas.[65] This sub-section therefore includes some examples of tariff quotas applied by the European Union.

2.3.1   Rule of Non-Discrimination

Article XIII:1 of the GATT 1994 provides that quantitative restrictions, when applied, should be administered in a non-discriminatory manner. Article XIII:1 states:

> No prohibition or restriction shall be applied by any [Member] on the importation of any product of the territory of any other [Member] or on the exportation of any product destined for the territory of any other [Member], unless the importation of the like product of all third countries or the exportation of the like product to all third countries is *similarly prohibited or restricted*.[66]

What Article XIII:1 requires is that, if a Member imposes a quantitative restriction on products to or from another Member, products to or from all other countries are 'similarly prohibited or restricted'. This requirement of Article XIII:1 is an MFN-like obligation. As the Appellate Body noted in *EC – Bananas III (1997)*, the essence of the non-discrimination obligations of Articles I:1 *and* XIII of the GATT 1994 is that:

> like products should be treated equally, irrespective of their origin.[67]

The GATT panel in *EEC – Apples (Chile I) (1980)* found that the European Communities had acted inconsistently with the non-discrimination obligation of Article XIII:1. The importation of apples from Argentina, Australia, New Zealand and South Africa into the European Communities had been restricted through voluntary restraint agreements negotiated and concluded with these countries. The European Communities tried to agree on a similar voluntary restraint agreement with Chile but the negotiations failed. The European Communities subsequently adopted measures restricting the importation of Chilean apples to approximately 42,000 tonnes a year. The panel in *EEC – Apples (Chile I) (1980)* found that the measure applied to apple imports from Chile were *not* a restriction *similar* to the voluntary restraint agreements negotiated with the other apple-exporting countries and therefore was inconsistent with Article XIII:1. The panel came to this conclusion primarily on the basis that: (1) there was a difference in transparency between the two types of action; (2) there was a difference in the administration of the restrictions, the one being an import restriction, the other an export restraint; and (3) the import restriction was unilateral and mandatory while the other was voluntary and negotiated.[68]

---

65 See e.g. the controversial administration of the tariff quotas under the EC's import regime for bananas at issue in *EC – Bananas III (1997)*, or for poultry at issue in *EC – Poultry (1998)*. See also the tariff quotas at issue in *US – Line Pipe (2002)*.

66 Emphasis added.   67 Appellate Body Report, *EC – Bananas III (1997)*, para. 190.

68 See Panel Report, *EEC – Apples (Chile I) (1980)*, para. 4.11.

2.3.2   Rules on the Distribution of Trade

If quantitative restrictions, other than a prohibition or ban, are applied on the importation of a product, the question arises how the trade that is still allowed will be distributed among the different Members exporting that product. The chapeau of Article XIII:2 of the GATT 1994 provides in this respect:

In applying import restrictions to any product, [Members] shall aim at a distribution of trade in such product approaching as closely as possible the shares which the various [Members] might be expected to obtain in the absence of such restrictions.[69]

In *EC – Bananas III (1997)*, the Appellate Body found the reallocation of non-utilised tariff quotas only among those countries that concluded the *Banana Framework Agreement* with the European Communities to be inconsistent with Article XIII:2, as the reallocation failed to approximate, in the administration of tariff quotas, the relative trade flows which would exist in the absence of the tariff quotas.[70] The panel in *US – Line Pipe (2002)* found:

There is nothing in the record before the Panel to suggest that the line pipe measure was based in any way on historical trade patterns in line pipe, or that the United States otherwise 'aim[ed] at a distribution of trade … approaching as closely as possible the shares which the various Members might be expected to obtain in the absence of' the line pipe measure. Instead, as noted by Korea, 'the in-quota import volume originating from Korea, the largest supplier historically to the US market, was reduced to the same level as the smallest – or even then non-existent – suppliers to the US market (9,000 short tons)'. For this reason, we find that the line pipe measure is inconsistent with the general rule contained in the chapeau of Article XIII:2.[71]

Furthermore, Article XIII:2 sets out a number of requirements to be met when imposing quantitative restrictions. Pursuant to Article XIII:2(a) and (b), when imposing a quantitative restriction, a quota – whether global or allocated among the supplying countries – is preferred to quantitative restrictions applied through import licences or permits without a quota. In cases in which a quota is allocated among supplying countries, Article XIII:2(d) provides:

[T]he [Member] applying the restrictions may seek agreement with respect to the allocation of shares in the quota with all other [Members] having a substantial interest in supplying the product concerned.

However, when this method of allocating the shares in the quota 'is not reasonably practicable', i.e. when no agreement can be reached with *all* the Members having a substantial interest, the Member applying the quota:

shall allot to [Members] having a substantial interest in supplying the product shares based upon the proportions, supplied by such [Members] during a previous representative period,

---

69 Note that the panel in *US – Line Pipe (2002)* stated that the chapeau of Article XIII:2 contains 'a general rule, and not merely a statement of principle'. See Panel Report, *US – Line Pipe (2002)*, footnote 64.
70 See Appellate Body Report, *EC – Bananas III (1997)*, para. 163.
71 Panel Report, *US – Line Pipe (2002)*, para. 7.55.

of the total quantity or value of imports of the product, due account being taken of any special factors which may have affected or may be affecting the trade in the product.

In other words, if no agreement can be reached, the quota must be allocated among the Members having a substantial interest on the basis of their share of the trade during a previous representative period. It is normal GATT practice to use a three-year period prior to the imposition of the quota as the 'representative period'.[72] Quotas allocated among supplying countries *must* be allocated among *all* Members having a *substantial interest* in supplying the product.[73] There is no additional obligation to allocate a part of the quota to Members *without* a substantial interest in supplying the product concerned. While the requirement of Article XIII:2(d) is not expressed as an exception to the basic non-discrimination requirement of Article XIII:1, it may be regarded, to the extent that its practical application is inconsistent with it, as a *lex specialis*.[74] It allows for the discrimination between Members with and Members without a substantial interest in supplying the product at issue.

In *EC – Bananas III (1997)*, the panel addressed the question of whether quota shares or tariff quota shares (as they were in this case) *can* also be allocated to Members that do not have a substantial interest in supplying the product at issue. According to the panel, quota shares and tariff quota shares *can* be allocated to Members with minor market shares. The panel ruled:

[W]e note that the first sentence of Article XIII:2(d) refers to allocation of a quota 'among supplying countries'. This could be read to imply that an allocation may also be made to Members that do not have a substantial interest in supplying the product.[75]

However, if a Member wishes to allocate quota shares or tariff quota shares to some Members with minor market shares, then such shares must be allocated to *all* such Members. If not, imports from such Members would not be 'similarly restricted' as required by Article XIII:1 of the GATT 1994.[76] Moreover, the same method as was used to allocate the shares to the Members having a substantial interest in supplying the product would have to be used. Otherwise, again, the non-discrimination obligation of Article XIII:1 would not be met.[77] If a Member wishes to allocate a part of the quota or tariff quota to Members with minor market shares, then this is best done by providing – next to country-specific quota shares for Members with a substantial interest – for an 'others' category for all Members not having a substantial interest in supplying the product.[78] The

---

72 See Panel Report, *EEC – Apples (Chile I) (1980)*, para. 4.16; and Panel Report, *EEC – Dessert Apples (1989)*, para. 12.22.

73 As discussed above, a share of 10 per cent of the market of the Member applying the quota has generally been considered to be a 'significant share' of the market, required to claim a 'substantial interest'. See above, p. 451.

74 See Panel Reports, *EC – Bananas III (1997)*, para. 7.75.

75 *Ibid.*, para. 7.73.   76 See above, p. 317.   77 See *ibid.*

78 The alternative is to allocate to all supplying countries, including Members with minor market shares, country-specific tariff quota shares. This method, however, is more likely to lead to a long-term freezing of market shares and a less competitive market. See also Panel Reports, *EC – Bananas III (1997)*, para. 7.76.

use of an 'others' category is consistent with the object and purpose of Article XIII (as expressed in the chapeau of Article XIII:2) to achieve a distribution of trade as close as possible to that which would have been the distribution of trade in the absence of the quantitative restriction.[79] The panel in *EC – Bananas III (1997)* noted:

When a significant share of a tariff quota is assigned to 'others', the import market will evolve with a minimum amount of distortion. Members not having a substantial supplying interest will be able, if sufficiently competitive, to gain market share in the 'others' category and possibly achieve 'substantial supplying interest' status ... New entrants will be able to compete in the market, and likewise have an opportunity to gain 'substantial supplying interest' status.[80]

Questions and Assignments 7.3

How should quantitative restrictions be administered? Are the rules set out in Article XIII also applicable to the administration of measures other than quantitative restrictions? If the importation of a product is subject to a quota, how then should the trade that is still allowed be distributed among the different Members exporting that product? Can a Member applying a quota, or tariff quota, allocate part of that quota, or tariff quota, to Members with minor market shares? If so, how is this done best? Why?

2.3.3   Import-Licensing Procedures

Quotas and tariff quotas are usually administered through import-licensing procedures. Article 1.1 of the *Agreement on Import Licensing Procedures*, commonly referred to as the *Import Licensing Agreement*, defines import-licensing procedures as:

administrative procedures ... requiring the submission of an application or other documentation (other than that required for customs purposes) to the relevant administrative body as a prior condition for importation into the customs territory of the importing Member.[81]

A trader who wishes to import a product that is subject to a quota or tariff quota must apply for an import licence, i.e. a permit to import. Whether this import licence will be granted depends on whether the quota is already filled or not, and on whether the trader meets the requirements for an import licence.[82] Economists agree that a first-come, first-served distribution rule for import licences is the most economically efficient licensing method.[83] However, import-licensing

---

79 See *ibid.*, para. 7.76.   80 *Ibid.*, para. 7.76.

81 While Article 1.1 of the *Import Licensing Agreement* does not explicitly state that import-licensing procedures for tariff quotas are import-licensing procedures within the meaning of Article 1.1, the Appellate Body in *EC – Bananas III (1997)* ruled that a careful reading of that provision 'leads inescapably to that conclusion'. As the Appellate Body noted, import-licensing procedures for tariff quotas require 'the submission of an application' for import licences as 'a prior condition for importation' of a product at the lower in-quota tariff rate. See Appellate Body Report, *EC – Bananas III (1997)*, para. 193.

82 This would be an example of non-automatic import licensing. As discussed below, there is also automatic import licensing, but this would not occur with respect to the importation of a product that is subject to a quota or tariff quota. See below, p. 484.

83 See e.g. P. Lindert and T. Pugel, International Economics, 10th edn (McGraw Hill, 1996).

rules and procedures are often much more complex, as was illustrated by the import-licensing system for bananas at issue in *EC – Bananas III (1997)*.[84]

One of the most important rules of the *Import Licensing Agreement* is set out in Article 1.3, which reads:

> The rules for import licensing procedures shall be neutral in application and administered in a fair and equitable manner.

As emphasised by the Appellate Body in *EC – Bananas III (1997)*, the requirements of Article 1.3 do not concern the licensing rules *per se*, but concern the *application* and *administration* of these rules.[85]

Moreover, Article 1.4 of the *Import Licensing Agreement* requires that the rules and all information concerning procedures for the submission of applications for import licences must be published in such a manner as to enable Members and traders to become acquainted with them.[86] In no event shall such a publication be later than the date on which the licence requirement becomes effective.[87] In *EC – Poultry (1998)*, Brazil argued that frequent changes to the EC licensing rules and procedures regarding the poultry tariff quota made it difficult for Members and traders to become familiar with the rules, contrary to the provisions of Article 1.4 and other provisions of the *Import Licensing Agreement*. The panel rejected this complaint as follows:

> We note that the transparency requirement under the cited provisions is limited to publication of rules and other information. While we have sympathy for Brazil regarding the difficulties caused by the frequent changes to the rules, we find that changes in rules *per se* do not constitute a violation of Articles 1.4, 3.3, 3.5(b), 3.5(c) or 3.5(d).[88]

Articles 1.7 and 1.8 of the *Import Licensing Agreement* require that, in the administration and application of licensing rules, minor documentation errors or minor variations in value should not matter. For example, an application for an import licence shall not be refused for minor documentation errors, which do not alter basic data contained therein.[89]

The *Import Licensing Agreement* distinguishes between automatic and non-automatic import licensing. *Automatic import licensing* is defined as import licensing where approval of the application is granted *in all cases*.[90] Automatic import licensing may be maintained to collect statistical and other information on imports. Article 2.2 of the *Import Licensing Agreement* requires that

---

84 See Panel Reports, *EC – Bananas III (1997)*, paras. 7.142–7.273.
85 See Appellate Body Report, *EC – Bananas III (1997)*, paras. 197–8. See also Panel Report, *Korea – Various Measures on Beef (2001)*, paras. 784–5; and Panel Report, *EC – Poultry (1998)*, para. 254.
86 The rules and information concerned include rules and information on the eligibility of persons, firms and institutions to make such applications and the administrative body(ies) to be approached.
87 See *ibid*. Whenever practicable, the publication shall take place twenty-one days prior to the effective date. Note that any exceptions, derogations or changes in or from the rules concerning licensing procedures or the list of products subject to import licensing shall also be published in the same manner and within the same period. See *ibid*.
88 Panel Report, *EC – Poultry (1998)*, para. 246.
89 See Article 1.7 of the *Import Licensing Agreement*.   90 See *ibid.*, Article 2.1.

automatic import-licensing procedures shall not be administered in such a manner as to have 'restricting effects on imports subject to automatic licensing'.[91] *Non-automatic import licensing* is import licensing where approval is *not* granted in all cases. Import-licensing procedures for quotas and tariff quotas are by definition non-automatic import-licensing procedures. However, non-automatic import licences are also used by countries for many other reasons. Note, for example, that Saudi Arabia requires non-automatic import licences for certain 'distillation equipment' due to the fact that the latter has been used to produce alcoholic beverages in the past. Since alcohol is generally prohibited in Saudi Arabia, it has decided therefore to establish an import-licence requirement for certain distillation equipment.[92] With regard to non-automatic import licensing, Article 3.2 of the *Import Licensing Agreement* requires that:

Non-automatic licensing shall not have trade-restrictive or distortive effects on imports additional to those caused by the imposition of the restriction.

Other requirements relating to non-automatic import licensing concern: (1) the non-discrimination among applicants for import licences;[93] (2) the obligation to give reasons for refusing an application;[94] (3) the right of appeal or review of the decisions on applications;[95] (4) time-limits for processing applications;[96] (5) the validity of import licences;[97] and (6) the desirability of issuing licences for products in economic quantities.[98]

Questions and Assignments 7.4

What are import-licensing procedures and how do they relate to quotas and tariff quotas? How are import-licensing rules to be applied and administered? What is the difference between automatic and non-automatic import licensing? Are they subject to different requirements?

2.4 Special and Differential Treatment

The GATT 1994 provides for special and differential treatment of developing-country Members regarding the rules on quantitative restrictions discussed above. Article XVIII of the GATT 1994 allows developing-country Members to impose quantitative restrictions for balance-of-payments reasons under less demanding conditions than apply for developed-country Members under Article XII of the GATT 1994. For a discussion of this special and differential treatment, please refer to Chapter 9 of this book.[99]

---

91 On situations in which automatic licensing procedures shall *be deemed* to have trade-restricting effects, see Article 2.2 of the *Import Licensing Agreement*.
92 See Working Party Report on the Accession of the Kingdom of Saudi Arabia to the WTO, WT/ACC/SAU/61, dated November 2005, para. 149.
93 See Article 3.5(e) of the *Import Licensing Agreement*.
94 See *ibid.*   95 See *ibid.*   96 See *ibid.*, Article 3.5(f).
97 See *ibid.*, Article 3.5(g).   98 See *ibid.*, Article 3.5(h).
99 See below, p. 639.

3   OTHER NON-TARIFF BARRIERS ON TRADE IN GOODS

In addition to customs duties and other duties and charges (i.e. tariff barriers), and quantitative restrictions (i.e. the first sub-category of non-tariff barriers), trade in goods may also be impeded by 'other non-tariff barriers'. As the term indicates, this is a *residual* category of measures, actions or omissions, which restrict, to various degrees and in different ways, market access for goods.[100] The category of 'other non-tariff barriers' includes, *inter alia*, technical barriers to trade, sanitary and phytosanitary measures, customs formalities and procedures, and government procurement laws and practices. Also, the unfair and arbitrary application of trade measures may constitute an important barrier to trade. However, not only action but also omission, and in particular the failure to inform about the applicable trade laws, regulations and procedures, promptly and accurately, may constitute a formidable barrier to trade.

This section addresses in turn the following 'other non-tariff barriers' to trade in goods: (1) lack of transparency; (2) unfair and arbitrary application of trade measures; (3) customs formalities and procedures; (4) government procurement laws and practices; and (5) other measures or actions, such as preshipment inspection, marks of origin, and measures relating to transit shipments. As mentioned above, and due to their importance and detailed nature, the rules on technical barriers to trade and sanitary and phytosanitary measures are discussed, separately, in Chapters 13 and 14 of this book respectively.[101]

3.1   Lack of Transparency

As discussed above, lack of information, uncertainty or confusion with respect to the trade laws, regulations and procedures applicable in actual or potential export markets is an important barrier to trade. Therefore, WTO law provides for rules and procedures to ensure a high level of transparency of its Members' trade laws, regulations and procedures. There are four kinds of relevant WTO rules and procedures: (1) the *publication* requirement; (2) the *notification* requirement; (3) the requirement to establish *enquiry points*; and (4) the trade policy *review* process.

Article X of the GATT 1994, entitled 'Publication and Administration of Trade Regulations', requires in its first paragraph that Members *publish* their laws, regulations, judicial decisions, administrative rulings of general application and international agreements relating to trade matters. Article X:1 does not prescribe in any detail how these laws, regulations, etc. have to be published, but it does

---

100 See e.g. *Table of Contents of the Inventory of Non-Tariff Measures*, Note by the Secretariat, TN/MA/S/5/Rev.1, dated 28 November 2003.
101 See below, pp. 851 and 896.

state that they have to be published: (1) 'promptly'; and (2) 'in such a manner as to enable governments and traders to become acquainted with them'.[102] The panel in *EC – IT Products (2010)* noted that:

> Article X:1 addresses the due process notion of notice by requiring publication that is prompt and that ensures those who need to be aware of certain laws, regulations, judicial decisions and administrative rulings of general application can become acquainted with them.[103]

With regard to the 'promptness' requirement, the panel in *EC – IT Products (2010)* considered that:

> the meaning of prompt is not an absolute concept, i.e. a pre-set period of time applicable in all cases. Rather, an assessment of whether a measure has been published 'promptly', that is 'quickly' and 'without undue delay', necessarily requires a case-by-case assessment.[104]

In this case, the panel found that publication in the EU's *Official Journal* eight months after the measures were made effective was not 'prompt'. However, the panel noted that the measures were posted on an EU website prior to the date that they were made effective. The panel found that the latter publication was 'prompt' but that it was not 'in such a manner as to enable governments and traders to become acquainted' with the measures at issue.[105]

With regard to the concept of 'administrative ruling of general application', note that, to the extent that an administrative ruling is addressed to a specific company or applied to a specific shipment, it cannot be qualified as an administrative ruling of general application. However, to the extent that an administrative ruling affects an unidentified number of economic operators, it can be qualified as a ruling of general application. The fact that a measure is country-specific does not preclude the possibility of it being an administrative ruling of general application.[106] In *EC – IT Products (2010)*, the question arose whether a CNEN (i.e. an explanatory note to the EU's Customs Nomenclature) could be considered to be a measure to which Article X:1 applied. The panel found that:

> the instruments covered by Article X:1 range from imperative rules of conduct to the exercise of influence or an authoritative pronouncement by certain authoritative bodies. Accordingly, we consider that the coverage of Article X:1 extends to instruments with a degree of authoritativeness issued by certain legislative, administrative or judicial bodies. This does not mean, however, that they have to be 'binding' under domestic law. Hence, the

---

102 Note that these requirements do not explicitly apply to the publication of the international agreements, but it may be assumed that they also apply in this context. Moreover, note that Article X:1 does not require Members to disclose confidential information which would impede law enforcement or otherwise be contrary to the public interest or which would prejudice the legitimate commercial interests of particular enterprises, public or private. See Article X:1, last sentence, of the GATT 1994. See also Panel Report, *Thailand – Cigarettes (Philippines) (2011)*, para. 7.819.
103 Panel Report *EC – IT Products (2010)*, para. 7.1015.
104 *Ibid.*, para. 7.1074.   105 See *ibid.*, para. 7.1088.
106 See Appellate Body Report, *US – Underwear (1997)*, 29. See also Appellate Body Report, *EC – Poultry (1998)*, paras. 111–13. Note that the panel in *Japan – Film (1998)* stated that: 'it stands to reason that inasmuch as the Article X:1 requirement applies to all administrative rulings of general application, it also should extend to administrative rulings in individual cases where such rulings establish or revise principles or criteria applicable in future cases.' See Panel Report, *Japan – Film (1998)*, para. 10.388.

fact that CNENs are not legally binding under EC law does not preclude them from being contemplated by the terms 'laws, regulations, judicial decisions [or] administrative rulings' under Article X:1.[107]

The panel in *Thailand – Cigarettes (Philippines) (2011)* found that the explanation given by the Thai Excise Department of the methodology for calculating the minimum retail sales prices (MRSPs) for imported and domestic cigarettes applied 'prospectively and generally' to all potential sales of cigarettes. Therefore, the panel considered that this methodology for determining the MRSPs to be a measure to which Article X:1 applied.[108]

In addition to Article X:1, Article X:2 of the GATT 1994 also concerns the publication of trade measures of general application. Article X:2 provides:

No measure of general application taken by any [Member] effecting an advance in a rate of duty or other charge on imports under an established and uniform practice, or imposing a new or more burdensome requirement, restriction or prohibition on imports, or on the transfer of payments therefor, shall be enforced before such measure has been officially published.

Pursuant to Article X:2, Members may not enforce measures of general application, imposing new or higher barriers to trade, *before* they are officially published.[109] Such trade measures will only take effect *after* official publication.[110] With respect to the rationale of Article X:2, the Appellate Body noted in *US – Underwear (1997)*:

Article X:2, *General Agreement*, may be seen to embody a principle of fundamental importance – that of promoting full disclosure of governmental acts affecting Members and private persons and enterprises, whether of domestic or foreign nationality. The relevant policy principle is widely known as the principle of transparency and has obviously due process dimensions. The essential implication is that Members and other persons affected, or likely to be affected, by governmental measures imposing restraints, requirements and other burdens, should have a reasonable opportunity to acquire authentic information about such measures and accordingly to protect and adjust their activities or alternatively to seek modification of such measures.[111]

Note that the GATT 1994 and other WTO agreements also require Members to publish, or give public notice of, certain *specific* trade measures of general application.[112]

---

107 Panel Report, *EC – IT Products (2010)*, para. 7.1027.

108 Panel Report, *Thailand – Cigarettes (Philippines) (2011)*, para. 7.779. Note that the panel in *China – Raw Materials (2012)* found that China's failure to set a quota amount was a measure to which Article XI:1 applied. See Panel Reports, *China – Raw Materials (2012)*, para. 7.803.

109 The panel in *EC – IT Products (2011)* ruled that even a *single* instance of enforcement before the official publication could amount to a violation of Article X:2. See Panel Report, *EC – IT Products (2011)*, para. 7.1129. Note that Article X:1 refers to 'publication', while Article X:2 refers to 'official publication'.

110 Note that, with respect to the issue of the retroactive effect of trade measures, the Appellate Body ruled in *US – Underwear (1997)* that Article X:2 does not speak to, and hence does not resolve, the permissibility of giving retroactive effect to trade-restrictive measures. Where no authority exists to give retroactive effect to a trade-restrictive measure, that deficiency is not cured by publishing the measure some time before its actual application. See Appellate Body Report, *US – Underwear (1997)*, 29.

111 *Ibid.*

112 See e.g. Article XIII:3 of the GATT 1994 (concerning quotas and tariff quotas) and Article 2.11 of the *TBT Agreement* (concerning technical regulations). See below, p. 884.

As noted above, WTO law also provides for a *notification* requirement. Almost all WTO agreements require Members to notify the WTO of measures or actions covered by these agreements. A typical example of such a notification requirement is found in Article 12.6 of the *Agreement on Safeguards*, which states:

> Members shall notify promptly the Committee on Safeguards of their laws, regulations and administrative procedures relating to safeguard measures as well as any modifications made to them.[113]

A number of WTO agreements also provide for the possibility for a Member to notify measures or actions of other Members, which the latter failed to notify.[114] The 1993 *Decision on Notification Procedures* lists in an annex the many measures and actions Members must notify to the WTO.[115] To improve the operation of the notification requirements under almost all WTO agreements, and thereby contribute to the transparency of Members' trade policies and measures, a *central registry of notifications* has been established under the responsibility of the WTO Secretariat. This central registry records the measures notified and the information provided by Members with respect to the purpose of the measure, its trade coverage and the requirement under which it has been notified. The central registry cross-references its records of notifications by Members and their obligations.[116] Information in the central registry regarding individual notifications is made available, on request, to any Member entitled to receive the notification concerned. The central registry informs each Member annually of the regular notification obligations to which that Member will be expected to respond in the course of the following year. It must be noted that many Members, and especially developing-country Members, fail to comply with one or more of their notification requirements. Often this failure is due to a lack of administrative capacity and WTO expertise within the relevant ministries of the Members concerned.[117]

In addition to a publication requirement and a notification requirement, some WTO agreements also require Members to establish national *enquiry points* where further information and relevant documents on certain trade laws and regulations can be obtained by other Members or interested parties. This is, for example, the case with regard to technical barriers to trade and SPS measures, as discussed in Chapters 13 and 14 of this book respectively.[118]

---

113 See also below, p. 622.
114 See e.g. Article 12.8 of the *Agreement on Safeguards*. Such notifications are often referred to as 'cross notifications' or 'reverse notifications'.
115 *Decision on Notification Procedures*, adopted by the Trade Negotiations Committee on 15 December 1993 and annexed to the Final Act Embodying the Results of the Uruguay Round of Multilateral Trade Negotiations.
116 See *ibid.*, 388.
117 On technical assistance in this respect to developing-country Members, see above, p. 101. Note that the failure of Members to comply with their notification requirements may also be due to the lack of an incentive for doing so, or of a sanction for not doing so.
118 See below, pp. 884 and 936.

Finally, the transparency of Members' trade policies, legislation and procedures is also advanced considerably by the periodic trade policy reviews under the *Trade Policy Review Mechanism*. This mechanism is discussed in detail in Chapter 2 of this book.[119]

Questions and Assignments 7.5

Why is the lack of transparency with respect to a country's trade laws, regulations and other measures of general application, a formidable barrier to trade in goods? How does WTO law seek to ensure transparency with respect to its Members' trade measures of general application?

3.2   Unfair and Arbitrary Application of Trade Measures

It is clear that the unfair and arbitrary application of national trade measures, and the degree of uncertainty and unpredictability this generates for other Members and traders, constitutes a significant barrier to trade – in the same way as the lack of transparency discussed above. To ensure minimum standards for transparency and procedural fairness in the administration of national trade measures,[120] Article X:3 of the GATT 1994 provides for: (1) a requirement of uniform, impartial and reasonable administration of national trade measures; and (2) a requirement for procedures for the objective and impartial review of the administration of national customs rules.

The first of these two requirements is set out in Article X:3(a) of the GATT 1994, which provides:

Each [Member] shall administer in a uniform, impartial and reasonable manner all its laws, regulations, decisions and rulings of the kind described in paragraph 1 of this Article.

The panel in *Thailand – Cigarettes (Philippines) (2011)* ruled that to establish a violation of Article X:3(a):

a complaining party must therefore show that the responding Member *administers* the legal instruments of the kind described in Article X:1 in a manner that is *non-uniform, partial* and/or *unreasonable* ... The obligations of uniformity, impartiality and reasonableness are legally independent and the WTO Members are obliged to comply with all three requirements. This means that ... a violation of any of the three obligations will lead to a violation of the obligations under Article X:3(a).[121]

As the words of Article X:3(a) clearly indicate, the requirements of 'uniformity, impartiality and reasonableness' do not apply to the laws, regulations, decisions and rulings *themselves*, but rather to the *administration* of those laws, regulations, decisions and rulings.[122] To the extent that these measures themselves are

---

119 See above, p. 95.
120 See Appellate Body Report, *US – Shrimp (1998)*, para. 183.
121 Panel Report, *Thailand – Cigarettes (Philippines) (2011)*, paras. 7.866–7.867.
122 See Appellate Body Report, *EC – Bananas III (1997)*, para. 200. See also Panel Report, *EC – Poultry (1998)*; and Panel Report, *US – Corrosion-Resistant Steel Sunset Review (2004)*.

discriminatory, they may be found inconsistent with, for example, Articles I:1, III:2 or III:4 of the GATT 1994.[123] However, as the Appellate Body clarified in *EC – Selected Customs Matters (2006)*, it is possible to challenge under Article X:3(a) the substantive content of a legal instrument that regulates the administration of a law, regulation, decision or ruling falling under Article X:1.[124] The Appellate Body stated:

Under Article X:3(a), a distinction must be made between the legal instrument being administered and the legal instrument that regulates the application or implementation of that instrument. While the substantive content of the legal instrument being administered is not challengeable under Article X:3(a), we see no reason why a legal instrument that regulates the application or implementation of that instrument cannot be examined under Article X:3(a) if it is alleged to lead to a lack of uniform, impartial, or reasonable administration of that legal instrument.[125]

Under Article X:3(a), one can thus challenge: (1) the manner in which legal instruments of the kind falling under Article X:1 are applied or implemented in particular cases; and (2) legal instruments that regulate such application or implementation. Note that also administrative processes leading to administrative decisions have been found to fall within the scope of application of Article X:3(a).[126]

   With regard to the requirement that national trade rules be applied in a uniform manner (the requirement of 'uniform administration'), the panel in *US – Stainless Steel (Korea) (2001)* stated:

[T]he requirement of uniform administration of laws and regulations must be understood to mean uniformity of treatment in respect of persons similarly situated; it cannot be understood to require identical results where relevant facts differ.[127]

Furthermore, the Appellate Body ruled in *EC – Selected Customs Matters (2006)* that:

Article X:3(a) of the GATT 1994 does not contemplate uniformity of administrative processes. In other words, non-uniformity or differences in administrative processes do not, by themselves, constitute a violation of Article X:3(a) ... [U]nder Article X:3(a), it is the application of a legal instrument ... that is required to be uniform, but not the processes leading to administrative decisions, or the tools that might be used in the exercise of administration.[128]

Note that, in *China – Raw Materials (2012)*, the panel found that a system under which export quotas were allocated by thirty-two local governmental entities which were not provided with any guidelines for the allocation of such export quotas, posed a very real risk to the interests of relevant parties such

---

123 See above, pp. 320, 356 and 382.
124 See Appellate Body Report, *EC – Selected Customs Matters (2006)*, para. 200. See also Panel Report, *Argentina – Hides and Leather (2001)*, paras. 11.71–11.72.
125 Appellate Body Report, *EC – Selected Customs Matters (2006)*, para. 200.
126 See Panel Report, *Thailand – Cigarettes (Philippines) (2011)*, para. 7.873.
127 Panel Report, *US – Stainless Steel (Korea) (2001)*, para. 6.51.
128 Appellate Body Report, *EC – Selected Customs Matters (2006)*, para. 224.

that this necessarily leads to 'non-uniform' administration inconsistently with Article X:3(a).[129]

With respect to the requirement that national trade rules be applied in an impartial manner (the requirement of 'impartial administration'), the panel in *Thailand – Cigarettes (Philippines) (2011)* addressed the question whether the features of the administrative process at issue, namely, the fact that certain Thai government officials in charge of customs and tax determinations also serve on the board of directors of the Thai Tobacco Monopoly to which these customs and tax determinations applied, leads to a lack of 'impartial administration'.[130] The panel started out by ruling that:

[b]ased on the ordinary meaning ... *impartial* administration would appear to mean the application or implementation of the relevant laws and regulations in a fair, unbiased and unprejudiced manner.[131]

After considering in detail the evidence submitted by the complainant, the Philippines, the panel concluded that:

unless it can be shown that these determinations are made because of the very presence of the government officials serving also as [Thai Tobacco Monopoly] directors, we are not in a position to find that the appointment of dual function officials led to a partial administration of customs and tax rules.[132]

With respect to the requirement that national trade rules be applied in a reasonable manner (the requirement of 'reasonable administration'), the panel in *Argentina – Hides and Leather (2001)* found that:

a process aimed at assuring the proper classification of products, but which inherently contains the possibility of revealing confidential business information, is an unreasonable manner of administering the laws, regulations and rules identified in Article X:1 and therefore is inconsistent with Article X:3(a).[133]

Note that, in *Dominican Republic – Import and Sale of Cigarettes (2005)*, the panel found that the Dominican Republic had applied the provisions regarding

---

129 See Panel Reports, *China – Raw Materials (2012)*, para. 7.752. Note that the Appellate Body declared this finding moot and of no legal effect because the panel made this finding regarding a claim not properly identified in the panel request. See Appellate Body Reports, *China – Raw Materials (2012)*, para. 235.

130 See Panel Report, *Thailand – Cigarettes (Philippines) (2011)*, para. 7.898.

131 *Ibid.*, para. 7.899.

132 *Ibid.*, para. 7.904. A similar situation arose in *Argentina – Hides and Leather (2001)*. At issue in that case was an Argentinian regulation providing for the participation of representatives of the domestic tanners' association, ADICMA, in the customs inspection procedures for hides destined for export operations. The representatives of ADICMA 'assisted' Argentina's customs authorities in the application and enforcement of the rules on customs classification, valuation and export duties. The panel in that case ruled that the Argentinian measure was inconsistent with the 'requirement of impartiality' of Article X:3(a). The panel noted that adequate safeguards could remedy this situation. However, such safeguards were, according to the panel, not in place. See Panel Report, *Argentina – Hides and Leather (2001)*, paras. 11.99–11.101. In *China – Raw Materials (2012)*, the panel examined the claim that the involvement of the China Chamber of Commerce of Metals, Minerals and Chemicals Importers and Exporters (CCCMC) in administering the export quotas on various raw materials constituted partial administration inconsistent with Article X:3(a). The panel concluded that, given the specific circumstances, it did not. See Panel Reports, *China – Raw Materials (2012)*, para. 7.785.

133 Panel Report, *Argentina – Hides and Leather (2001)*, para. 11.94.

the determination of the tax base for the imposition of tax on cigarettes in an unreasonable manner. According to the panel:

[t]he fact that the Dominican Republic authorities did not support its decisions regarding the determination of the tax base for imported cigarettes by resorting to the rules in force at the time and that they decided to disregard retail selling prices of imported cigarettes, is not 'in accordance with reason', 'having sound judgement', 'sensible', 'within the limits of reason', nor 'articulate'.[134]

The panel in *Thailand – Cigarettes (Philippines) (2011)* examined whether the delays in appeals of customs valuation determinations constituted 'unreasonable administration' of the Thai customs laws. The panel found that, although the 'requirement of reasonable administration' of Article X:3(a) does not set a specific time-limit for administrative review process, the delays at issue (the appeals process took over seven years) resulted in the administration of the Thai customs law in an unreasonable manner and were inconsistent with Article X:3(a).[135] In *China – Raw Materials (2012)*, the panel found that a system under which export quotas were allocated by thirty-two local governmental entities which were not provided with any guidelines for the allocation of such export quotas, posed a very real risk to the interests of relevant parties such that this necessarily leads to 'unreasonable' administration inconsistent with Article X:3(a).[136]

To conclude on Article X:3(a) of the GATT 1994, four more observations of a general nature must be made. First, the panel in *Argentina – Hides and Leather (2001)* clarified the nature of the obligation under Article X:3(a) by distinguishing between transparency between WTO Members and transparency with respect to individual traders. According to that panel, unlike for other rules under the GATT 1994, for Article X:3(a):

the test generally will not be whether there has been discriminatory treatment in favour of exports to one Member relative to another. Indeed, the focus is on the treatment accorded by government authorities to the *traders* in question.[137]

Secondly, the same panel in *Argentina – Hides and Leather (2001)* ruled that, while a showing of trade damage is not required, Article X:3(a) requires an examination of the real effect that a measure might have on traders operating in the commercial world. The assessment of a violation of Article X:3(a) can therefore involve an examination of whether there is a possible impact on the competitive situation due to alleged partiality, unreasonableness or lack of uniformity in the application of a law, regulation, decision or ruling.[138]

---

134 Panel Report, *Dominican Republic – Import and Sale of Cigarettes (2005)*, para. 7.388.
135 See Panel Report, *Thailand – Cigarettes (Philippines) (2011)*, para. 7.969.
136 See Panel Reports, *China – Raw Materials (2012)*, para. 7.746. Note that the Appellate Body declared this finding moot and of no legal effect because the panel made this finding regarding a claim not properly identified in the panel request. See Appellate Body Reports, *China – Raw Materials (2012)*, para. 235.
137 See Panel Report, *Argentina – Hides and Leather (2001)*, para. 11.76. Emphasis added.
138 See *ibid.*, para. 11.77.

Thirdly, as the panel in *US – Hot-Rolled Steel (2001)* ruled, for a finding of violation of Article X:3(a), a Member's actions would have to have 'a significant impact on the overall administration of the law, and not simply on the outcome in the single case in question'.[139]

Fourthly, the Appellate Body in *US – Oil Country Tubular Goods Sunset Reviews (2004)* cautioned WTO Members on bringing a case under Article X:3(a):

We observe, first, that allegations that the conduct of a WTO Member is biased or unreasonable are serious under any circumstances. Such allegations should not be brought lightly, or in a subsidiary fashion.[140]

The requirements of uniform, impartial and reasonable administration of national trade measures are also reflected in WTO agreements other than the GATT 1994. Article 1.3 of the *Import Licensing Agreement*, for example, provides:

The rules for import licensing procedures shall be neutral in application and administered in a fair and equitable manner.[141]

The Appellate Body ruled in *EC – Bananas III (1997)* that Article 1.3 of the *Import Licensing Agreement* and Article X:3(a) of the GATT 1994 have 'identical coverage'.[142] In disputes involving the administration of import-licensing procedures, Article 1.3 of the *Import Licensing Agreement* should be applied *first* since the *Import Licensing Agreement* deals specifically, and in detail, with the administration of import-licensing procedures.[143]

Apart from the requirements of Article X:3(a) that national trade measures be administered in a uniform, impartial and reasonable manner, Article X:3 contains – as noted above – a second rule to ensure transparency and procedural fairness in the administration of trade measures, namely, the requirement of procedures for the *objective and impartial review*, and possible correction, of the administration of national customs rules. Article X:3(b) of the GATT 1994 provides:

Each [Member] shall maintain, or institute as soon as practicable, judicial, arbitral or administrative tribunals or procedures for the purpose, *inter alia*, of the prompt review and correction of administrative action relating to customs matters.

In *EC – Selected Customs Matters (2006)*, the panel reflected on the function of Article X:3(b) as follows:

[A] due process theme underlies Article X of the GATT 1994. In the Panel's view, this theme suggests that an aim of the review provided for under Article X:3(b) of the GATT 1994 is to ensure that a trader who has been adversely affected by a decision of an administrative

---

139 Panel Report, *US – Hot-Rolled Steel (2001)*, para. 7.268.
140 Appellate Body Report, *US – Oil Country Tubular Goods Sunset Reviews (2004)*, para. 217. See also Panel Report, *Thailand – Cigarettes (Philippines) (2011)*, para. 7.874.
141 See also above, p. 495.
142 Appellate Body Report, *EC – Bananas III*, para. 203. The Appellate Body noted the difference in wording between Article 1.3 of the *Import Licensing Agreement* and Article X:3(a) of the GATT 1994, but considered that 'the two phrases are, for all practical purposes, interchangeable'.
143 See *ibid.*, para. 204.

agency has the ability to have that adverse decision reviewed by a tribunal or procedure that is independent from the agency that originally took the adverse decision.[144]

Article X:3(b) does not prescribe one particular type of review or correction. It refers very broadly to 'judicial, arbitral or administrative tribunals or procedures'. Members thus have a significant degree of discretion in complying with the obligation under Article X:3(b). However, Article X:3(b) does explicitly require that the 'tribunals or procedures' be *independent* of the agencies entrusted with administrative enforcement[145] and Article X:3(c) calls for the review of the 'tribunals or procedures' to be 'objective and impartial.'[146] Furthermore, Article X:3(b) requires that the review or correction be 'prompt'. As discussed above, the panel in *Thailand – Cigarettes (Philippines) (2011)* was confronted with a situation in which there were excessive delays in the administrative appeals process; this process took over seven years and was the prerequisite step necessary to reach the Thai Tax Court. The panel ruled that Thailand had 'failed to maintain an independent tribunal for the *prompt* review of customs value determinations inconsistently with Article X:3(b)'.[147]

Note that Article X:3(b) refers to 'administrative action relating to customs matters', i.e. the administration of *customs rules*, and *not* to the administration of the broader category of 'laws, regulations, decisions and rulings relating to trade matters' or, in short, the administration of *trade rules*.[148] In *Thailand – Cigarettes (Philippines) (2011)*, the Appellate Body agreed with the panel in that case that 'administrative action relating to customs matters' encompasses 'a wide range of acts applying legal instruments that have a rational relationship with customs matters'.[149]

Questions and Assignments 7.6

Does Article X:3(a) of the GATT 1994 require that laws, regulations, decisions and rulings relating to trade in goods are 'uniform, impartial and reasonable'? Inspired by the case law to date, give a few examples of inconsistency with Article X:3(a). Does Article X:3(b) require Members to provide for independent judicial review of all government legislation and measures relating to trade in goods? Does the obligation under Article X:3(b) differ from the obligation under Article VI:2 of the GATS?

3.3 Customs Formalities and Procedures

Another important type of 'other non-tariff barrier' to trade in goods are customs formalities and procedures, i.e. administrative barriers to trade. The losses

---

144 Panel Report, *EC – Selected Customs Matters (2006)*, para. 7.536.
145 The decisions of the 'tribunals or procedures' concerned must be implemented by the administrative agencies, unless the decisions are appealed. See Article X:3(b).
146 For situations in which the procedures are not fully or formally independent of the agencies entrusted with administrative enforcement, see Article X:3(c) of the GATT 1994.
147 Panel Report, *Thailand – Cigarettes (Philippines) (2011)*, para. 7.1015.
148 See in this respect the 'parallel' and broader obligation under Article VI:2 of the GATS, discussed below, p. 533.
149 Appellate Body Report, *Thailand – Cigarettes (Philippines) (2011)*, para. 202.

that traders suffer through delays at borders, complicated and/or unnecessary documentation requirements and lack of automation of customs procedures are estimated to exceed, in many cases, the costs of customs duties. In a speech at the World Customs Organization in June 2011, WTO Director-General Pascal Lamy noted:

For OECD countries it currently takes on average about four separate documents and clearing the goods in an average of ten days at an average cost of about $1,100 per container. By contrast, in sub-Saharan Africa almost double the number of documents are required and goods take from 32 days (for exports) to 38 days (for imports) to clear at an average cost per container of between $2,000 (for exports) and $2,500 (for imports). The overall world champion at trade facilitation is Singapore, where four documents are required and goods are cleared in, at most, five days at an average cost of around $456 per container. At the other end of the scale are many of the low-income developing countries, in particular the landlocked developing countries, whose trade-processing costs can mushroom as a result of the effort required to move goods in transit by road or rail through their neighbours to their nearest international port. According to recent research, every extra day required to ready goods for import or export decreases trade by around 4%.[150]

Article VIII:1(c) of the GATT 1994 states:

The [Members] ... recognize the need for minimizing the incidence and complexity of import and export formalities and for decreasing and simplifying import and export documentation requirements.

Nevertheless, WTO law currently contains few rules on customs formalities and procedures aimed at mitigating their adverse impact on trade. Article VIII:2 requires Members, in very general terms, to 'review' the operation of their laws and regulations in light of the acknowledged need for: (1) minimising the incidence and complexity of customs formalities; and (2) decreasing and simplifying documentation requirements. Article VIII:3 of the GATT 1994 furthermore requires penalties for breaches of customs regulations and procedural requirements to be *proportional*. Members may not impose substantial penalties for minor breaches of customs regulations or procedural requirements.

In view of the paucity of substantive WTO rules with respect to customs formalities and procedures, the 1996 Singapore Ministerial Conference directed the Council for Trade in Goods 'to undertake exploratory and analytical work ... on the simplification of trade procedures in order to assess the scope for WTO rules in this area'.[151] The negotiations on simplification of trade procedures, commonly referred to as 'trade facilitation', are currently part of the Doha Round negotiations.[152] The negotiations on 'trade facilitation' aim at clarifying and

---

150 Speech at the World Customs Organization in Brussels on 24 June 2011, www.wto.org/english/news_e/
     sppl_e/sppl197_e.htm.
151 Ministerial Conference, *Singapore Ministerial Declaration*, adopted 13 December 1996, WT/MIN(96)/DEC,
     para. 21.
152 See Ministerial Conference, *Doha Ministerial Declaration*, adopted 14 November 2001, WT/MIN(01)/DEC/1,
     para. 27; and General Council, *Doha Work Programme*, Decision adopted on 1 August 2004, WT/L/579,
     dated 2 August 2004, para. 1(g). By the latter decision, WTO Members agreed to add negotiations on 'trade
     facilitation' to the agenda of the Doha Round. See also above, p. 89.

improving the relevant provisions of the GATT 1994, and in particular Article VIII thereof.[153] These negotiations also aim to enhance technical assistance and capacity building in this area. It is important to note that, for the first time in GATT/WTO negotiations, an explicit link is made between the adoption of new WTO obligations *and* the technical assistance, which developing-country Members in particular will need to implement new obligations. At present, the cost of moving trade worldwide is, according to the WTO Secretariat, roughly 10 per cent of the value of trade.[154] By cutting red tape at the border, standardising customs procedures, improving customs 'productivity' and limiting the scope for corruption, a WTO agreement on 'trade facilitation' could bring down this cost to 5 per cent.[155]

Questions and Assignments 7.7

Are customs procedures and formalities significant barriers to trade? Are there any *specific* WTO rules on customs procedures and formalities? Discuss the 'trade facilitation' negotiations conducted since 2004 in the context of the Doha Round.

3.4 Government Procurement Laws and Practices

National laws and/or practices relating to the procurement of goods by a government for its own use are often significant barriers to trade. Under such laws or practices, governments frequently buy domestic products rather than imported products. It is undisputed that a government can most effectively ensure 'best value for money' by purchasing goods (and services) through an open and non-discriminatory procurement process. However, governments often use public procurement to support the domestic industry or to promote employment. As discussed above, the national treatment obligation of Article III:4 of the GATT 1994 does not apply to government procurement laws and practices.[156] As government procurement typically represents between 15 and 20 per cent of GDP,[157] it is clear that the absence of this and other multilateral disciplines represents a significant gap in the multilateral trading system and leaves a considerable source of barriers to trade unaddressed.

The plurilateral WTO *Agreement on Government Procurement* provides for some disciplines with respect to government procurement of goods as well as

---

153 Also on the agenda of the 'trade facilitation' negotiations are Article V (Freedom of Transit) (see below, p. 512); and Article X (Publication and Administration of Trade Regulations) (see above, p. 498).

154 See speech of WTO Director-General Pascal Lamy at the meeting of ACP Ministers of Trade in Brussels on 24 October 2012, www.wto.org/english/news_e/sppl_e/sppl256_e.htm.

155 See *ibid.* For an overview of the current state of play of the 'trade facilitation' negotiations, see Negotiating Group on Trade Facilitation, *Draft Consolidated Negotiation Text* (revision), TN/TF/W/165/Rev.13, dated 24 October 2012.

156 See Article III:8(a) of the GATT 1994; and above, p. 386.

157 The total size of the government procurement sector was estimated by the OECD to be in the range of 15–20 per cent of GDP across OECD and non-OECD economies. See R. Anderson, P. Pelletier, K. Osei-Lah and A. Müller, Assessing the Value of Future Accessions to the WTO Agreement on Government Procurement (GPA), Staff Working Paper ERSD-2011–15 (WTO, 2011), 9.

services. However, it does so only for the forty-two Members that are currently a party to this Agreement.[158] The *Agreement on Government Procurement* applies to the laws, regulations, procedures and practices regarding procurement by those government bodies which a party has listed in Appendix I to the Agreement.[159] Furthermore, for the Agreement to apply, the government procurement contract must be worth more than a specified threshold value.[160] The key discipline provided for in the plurilateral *Agreement on Government Procurement* is non-discrimination. Article III:1(a) of the *Agreement on Government Procurement* sets out a national treatment obligation; Article III:1(b) sets out an MFN treatment obligation.[161] Furthermore, in order to ensure that these non-discrimination obligations are abided by, the Agreement also provides for rules to ensure that laws, regulations, procedures and practices regarding government procurement are transparent.[162] On 15 December 2011, the parties to the Agreement agreed in principle on a revision thereof.[163] This revision aims at making the provisions of the Agreement more user-friendly and adapting them to recent developments in government procurement practices (such as the use of electronic tools in the procurement process). The revised Agreement also includes more explicit special and differential treatment provisions, so as to facilitate developing-country Members to become a party to the Agreement. Most importantly, however, the revised Agreement provides for a significantly extended coverage. The WTO Secretariat has estimated the gains in market access as a result of the extended coverage of the Agreement are between US$80 and 100 billion annually.[164] These gains result from lower thresholds and additions of new entities and sectors to the parties' lists in Appendix I to the Agreement. On 30 March 2012, the revised *Agreement on Government Procurement* was formally adopted.[165]

It deserves to be stressed again that the *Agreement on Government Procurement* discussed above is a *plurilateral* agreement, which applies to only

---

158 The parties to the *Agreement on Government Procurement* currently are: Armenia, Canada, Chinese Taipei, the European Union and its twenty-seven Member States, Hong Kong China, Iceland, Israel, Japan, Liechtenstein, the Netherlands with respect to Aruba, Norway, Singapore, South Korea, Switzerland and the United States. Accession negotiations are under way with, *inter alia*, China, New Zealand and Ukraine.

159 See, in this respect, Panel Report, *Korea – Procurement (2000)*, in which the question arose whether the Korean Airport Construction Authority, the Korean Airports Authority and the Inchon International Airport Corporation were within the scope of Korea's list of 'central government entities' as specified in Korea's Schedule in Appendix I to the *Agreement on Government Procurement*.

160 See Article I:4 of the *Agreement on Government Procurement*. In Appendix I to the Agreement, each party specifies relevant thresholds.

161 Note that these non-discrimination obligations *only apply* between the parties to the Agreement.

162 See Articles VII to XVI of the *Agreement on Government Procurement*.

163 See Ministerial-Level Meeting of the Committee on Government Procurement on 15 December 2011, *Decision on the Outcomes of the Negotiations under Article XXIV:7 of the Agreement on Government Procurement*, GPA/112, dated 16 December 2011.

164 See www.wto.org/english/tratop_e/gproc_e/negotiations_e.htm.

165 See Committee on Government Procurement, *Adoption of the Results of the Negotiations under Article XXIV:7 of the Agreement on Government Procurement, Following Their Verification and Review, as Required by the Ministerial Decision of 15 December 2011 (GPA/112), Paragraph 5*, GPA/113, dated 2 April 2012. The revised Agreement will enter into force thirty days after two-thirds of the parties have deposited their instruments of acceptance.

forty-two Members, none of which is a developing-country Member.[166] In the 2001 Doha Ministerial Declaration, Members expressly recognised the case for a *multilateral* agreement on transparency in government procurement.[167] However, in the years that followed, they failed to agree on the modalities of the negotiations on such a multilateral agreement, and transparency on government procurement was thus never included in the Doha Round agenda.[168] Many developing-country Members were concerned about their ability to engage 'successfully' in such negotiations and to implement the new international commitments resulting from these negotiations.

Questions and Assignments 7.8

Why is the plurilateral *Agreement on Government Procurement* an important agreement? What are the basic disciplines set out in this Agreement? Did the 2012 revision bring about significant changes to the Agreement? Can the ministry of defence of the country of which you are a national discriminate against army boots from other WTO Members when buying 100,000 pairs of boots?

3.5 Other Measures and Actions

In addition to technical barriers to trade and SPS measures, the lack of transparency, unfair and arbitrary application of trade rules, customs formalities and procedures, and government procurement laws and practices, the category of 'other non-tariff barriers' to trade in goods also includes many other measures or actions, or the lack thereof. This section briefly addresses the following 'other non-tariff barriers': (1) preshipment inspection; (2) marks of origin; (3) measures relating to transit shipments; (4) operations of State trading enterprises; (5) trade-related investment measures; and (6) exchange controls or exchange restrictions.

Preshipment inspection is the practice of employing private companies to check the price, quantity, quality and/or the customs classification of goods *before* their shipment to the importing country.[169] Preshipment inspection is primarily used by developing-country Members to prevent commercial fraud and evasion of customs duties. Preshipment inspection is used to compensate for inadequacies in national customs administrations. While certainly beneficial, the problem with preshipment inspection is that it may give rise to unnecessary delays or unequal treatment, and thus constitute a barrier to trade. The WTO *Agreement on Preshipment Inspection* sets out obligations for both importing

---

166 China is likely to be the first developing-country Member to become a party to the *Agreement on Government Procurement*.

167 Ministerial Conference, *Doha Ministerial Declaration*, adopted 14 November 2001, WT/MIN(01)/DEC/1, para. 26. A first step in this direction was taken at the 1996 Singapore Ministerial Conference. See Ministerial Conference, *Singapore Ministerial Declaration*, adopted 13 December 1996, WT/MIN(96)/DEC, para. 21.

168 See General Council, *Doha Work Programme*, Decision adopted on 1 August 2004, WT/L/579, dated 2 August 2004, para. 1(g).

169 See Article 1 of the *Agreement on Preshipment Inspection*.

Members using preshipment inspection and the exporting Members on whose territory the inspection is carried out.

The importing Members using preshipment inspection must ensure, *inter alia*, that: (1) preshipment inspection activities are carried out in a non-discriminatory manner;[170] (2) preshipment inspection activities are carried out in a transparent manner;[171] (3) the companies carrying out the inspection respect the confidentiality of business information received in the course of the preshipment inspection;[172] and (4) the companies carrying out the inspection avoid unreasonable delays in the inspection of shipments.[173]

The exporting Members on whose territory the preshipment inspection is carried out must ensure non-discrimination and transparency with regard to their laws and regulations relating to preshipment inspection activities.[174] The *Agreement on Preshipment Inspection* also provides for rules on procedures for independent review of disputes between the companies carrying out the inspection and the exporters.[175]

With respect to *marks of origin* 'attached' to imported goods, Article IX:2 of the GATT 1994 states:

> The [Members] recognize that, in adopting and enforcing laws and regulations relating to marks of origin, the difficulties and inconveniences which such measures may cause to the commerce and industry of exporting countries should be *reduced to a minimum*, due regard being had to the necessity of protecting consumers against fraudulent or misleading indications.[176]

Note that marking requirements are, of course, subject to all relevant WTO rules and disciplines, such as the MFN treatment obligation.[177]

With respect to measures concerning *traffic in transit*, Article V of the GATT 1994, entitled 'Freedom of Transit', sets out a number of obligations on Members not to impede this traffic. Traffic in transit is the traffic of goods from country A to country C, through the territory of country B. It is clear that any restriction or impediment that country B would impose on the transit of the goods concerned would constitute a barrier to trade. Article V:2 of the GATT 1994 provides:

> There shall be freedom of transit through the territory of each [Member], via the routes most convenient for international transit, for traffic in transit to or from the territory of other [Members]. No distinction shall be made which is based on the flag of vessels, the place of origin, departure, entry, exit or destination, or on any circumstances relating to the ownership of goods, of vessels or of other means of transport.

> Traffic in transit shall not be subject to any unnecessary delays or restrictions and shall be exempt from customs duties and from all transit duties or other charges

---

170 See *ibid.*, Articles 2.1 and 2.2.   171 See *ibid.*, Articles 2.5 to 2.8.
172 See *ibid.*, Articles 2.9 to 2.13.   173 See *ibid.*, Articles 2.15 to 2.19.
174 See *ibid.*, Articles 3.1 and 3.2. These Members must also provide to user Members, if requested, technical assistance directed towards the achievement of the objectives of this Agreement on mutually agreed terms. See *ibid.*, Article 3.3.
175 See *ibid.*, Article 4.   176 Emphasis added.   177 See Article IX:1 of the GATT 1994.

imposed in respect of transit, except charges for transportation or those commensurate with administrative expenses entailed by transit or with the cost of services rendered.[178] All charges, regulations and formalities in connection with transit shall be reasonable and be subject to the MFN treatment obligation.[179]

Furthermore, the *operations of State trading enterprises* can be a significant barrier to trade in goods. State trading enterprises are:

[g]overnmental and non-governmental enterprises, including marketing boards, which have been granted exclusive or special rights or privileges, including statutory or constitutional powers, in the exercise of which they influence through their purchases or sales the level or direction of imports or exports.[180]

The WTO does not prohibit the establishment or maintenance of State trading enterprises. However, Article XVII of the GATT 1994 requires that: (1) State trading enterprises act in accordance with the MFN treatment obligation and other basic obligations under the GATT 1994;[181] and (2) only commercial considerations should guide their decisions on purchases and sales for import and export. To increase transparency regarding the use of State trading, Members must notify their State trading enterprises to the WTO annually.

Trade-related investment measures can also be barriers to trade when these measures take the form of direct or indirect quantitative restrictions on imports or exports. For example, a foreign car manufacturer may be allowed to establish a production plant in a country but only if it uses in the production of the cars steel produced in that country.[182] Article 2.1 of the *TRIMS Agreement* states in relevant part:

Without prejudice to other rights and obligations under GATT 1994, no Member shall apply any TRIM that is inconsistent with the provisions of ... Article XI of GATT 1994.

Finally, *exchange controls* or *exchange restrictions* may make it difficult, if not impossible, for an importer to pay for imports or for an exporter to be paid for exports. If so, these measures constitute a significant impediment to trade. Article XV:9 of the GATT 1994 stipulates in this regard that the GATT 1994 does not preclude Members to use exchange controls or exchange restrictions that are in accordance with: (1) the *Articles of Agreement* of the IMF; or (2) a Member's special exchange arrangement with the WTO. Nothing in the GATT 1994 precludes restrictions or controls on imports or exports the sole effect of which is to make effective such exchange controls or exchange restrictions.

Questions and Assignments 7.9

Explain how preshipment inspection, marks of origin, measures relating to traffic in transit, and the operations of State trading enterprises can constitute barriers to trade in goods. Does WTO law regulate these types of other non-tariff barriers? If so, how?

---

178 See Article V:3 of the GATT 1994.   179 See Article V:4 and 5 of the GATT 1994.
180 *WTO Understanding on the Interpretation of Article XVII*, para. 1.
181 See Articles II:1 and XI of the GATT 1994, as discussed above, pp. 335 and 483.
182 For an illustrative list of trade-related investment measures in the form of quantitative restrictions, see
     TRIMS Agreement, Annex, para. 2.

4 MARKET ACCESS BARRIERS TO TRADE IN SERVICES

This chapter on non-tariff barriers to trade has dealt thus far with non-tariff barriers to trade in *goods*. The remainder of the chapter discusses non-tariff barriers to trade in services. As already discussed, the production and consumption of services are a principal economic activity in virtually all countries, developed and developing, alike. Financial, telecommunication and transport services are the backbone of a modern economy, and economic development and prosperity are dependent on the availability and efficiency of these and other services.[183] Services play a central role in the world economy. They represent 71 per cent of world GDP.[184] However, the importance of services in the world economy is *not* reflected (yet) in their share of world trade. In 2011, trade in services amounted to merely 18.6 per cent of world trade, the smallest such share since 1990.[185]

As discussed in Chapter 6 and in the introduction to this chapter, trade in services is, unlike trade in goods, not subject to tariff barriers.[186] Trade in services, however, faces many non-tariff barriers. The production and consumption of services are subject to a vast range of internal regulations. Barriers to trade in services are primarily the result of these internal regulations. Examples of such internal regulations that may constitute barriers to trade in services are: (1) a restriction on the number of drugstores allowed within a geographical area; (2) an obligation for all practising lawyers to be a member of the local bar association; (3) sanitation standards for restaurants; (4) technical safety requirements for oil-drilling companies; (5) a requirement that all professional services be offered in the national language; (6) professional qualification requirements for accountants; and (7) a prohibition for banks to sell life insurance.

WTO law, and the GATS in particular, provides for rules and disciplines on barriers to trade in services. Note, however, that, as explained below, most internal regulation of services does not constitute a GATS-inconsistent barrier to trade in services.[187] The production and consumption of services are often subject to internal regulation for good reason, including the protection of consumers and the protection of public health and safety. The Preamble to the GATS explicitly recognises:

> the right of Members to regulate, and to introduce new regulations on, the supply of services within their territories in order to meet national policy objectives.

It is important to stress that the objective of the GATS is *not* the *deregulation* of services. In fact, the liberalisation of some services sectors, such as

---

183 See WTO Secretariat, Market Access: Unfinished Business, Special Studies Series 6 (WTO, 2001), 98.
184 See World Bank, *Services, Etc., Value Added (% of GDP)*, http://data.worldbank.org/indicator/NV.SRV. TETC.ZS.
185 See WTO Secretariat, Press Release of 12 April 2012, www.wto.org/english/news_e/pres12_e/pr658_e.htm.
186 See above, pp. 419 and 480. As discussed, tariff barriers to trade in services *currently* do not exist. However, such barriers *can* exist. See, for example, the 'bit tax'.
187 See below, pp. 515–518.

telecommunications, may require *increased* regulation in order to ensure quality of service or competition in the market.

With regard to non-tariff barriers to trade in services, the GATS distinguishes between, on the one hand, market access barriers, and, on the other hand, other barriers to trade in services. This section addresses the GATS rules on market access barriers and discusses in turn: (1) the definition and types of market access barriers; (2) rules on market access barriers; (3) negotiations on market access; (4) Schedules of Specific Commitments; and (5) modification and withdrawal of commitments. The next section in this chapter deals with the GATS rules on other barriers to trade in services.[188]

4.1   Definition and Types of Market Access Barriers

The GATS does not explicitly define the concept of 'market access barriers'. However, Article XVI:2(a) to (f) of the GATS provide an *exhaustive* list of such measures.[189] This list comprises six types of market access barrier. Five of the six types are quantitative restrictions on: (1) the number of service suppliers; (2) the value of the service transactions; (3) the number of service operations: (4) the number of legal persons employed by a service supplier; and (5) the amount of foreign capital invested in service suppliers.[190] One type of market access barrier is of a different nature. It is a limitation on the kind of legal entity or joint venture through which services may be supplied.[191]

These market access barriers can be discriminatory *or* non-discriminatory with respect to foreign services or service suppliers. For example, a restriction on the broadcasting time available for foreign movies is obviously a *discriminatory* market access barrier, while a licence for a fast food restaurant subject to an economic needs test based on population density is a *non-discriminatory* market access barrier.[192] Article XVI:2 covers both discriminatory *and* non-discriminatory market access barriers.

---

188   Recall that Chapter 4 of this book discusses the scope of application of the GATS. See above, pp. 335–45.
189   The panel in *US – Gambling (2005)* confirmed that the list of Article XVI:2 is exhaustive. It came to this conclusion based on the text of the provision, its context and the 1993 Scheduling Guidelines. See Panel Report, *US – Gambling (2005)*, paras. 6.293–6.298. Antigua appealed this finding. The Appellate Body, however, chose not to deal with this issue. See Appellate Body Report, *US – Gambling (2005)*, para. 256. The panel in *China – Publications and Audiovisual Products (2010)* reiterated that the list of Article XVI:2 is exhaustive. See also Panel Report, *China – Publications and Audiovisual Products (2010)*, para. 7.1353.
190   See Article XVI:2(a) to (d) and (f) of the GATS. As the Appellate Body noted in *US – Gambling (2005)*, the focus of Article XVI:2 is on quantitative restrictions. See Appellate Body Report, *US – Gambling (2005)*, para. 225.
191   See Article XVI:2(e) of the GATS.
192   See *Guidelines for the Scheduling of Specific Commitments under the General Agreement on Trade in Services (GATS)*, adopted by the Council for Trade in Services on 23 March 2001, S/L/92, dated 28 March 2001, para. 12. As stated in an explanatory note, these Guidelines were based on two documents which were produced and circulated during the Uruguay Round negotiations: MTN.GNS/W/164, *Scheduling of Initial Commitments in Trade in Services: Explanatory Note*, dated 3 September 1993; and MTN.GNS/W/164, Add.1, *Scheduling of Initial Commitments in Trade in Services: Explanatory Note, Addendum*, dated 30 November 1993. See *ibid.*, footnote 1.

Note that, when a market access barrier takes the form of a quantitative re-striction referred to in sub-paragraphs (a) to (d), this restriction can be expressed numerically, *or* through the criteria specified in these provisions, such as an economic needs test. It is important to note, however, that these criteria do *not* relate to: (1) the quality of the service supplied; or (2) the ability of the supplier to supply the service (i.e. technical standards or qualification of the supplier).[193] A requirement, for example, that services be offered in the national language or a requirement for engineers to have specific professional qualifications may impede trade in services but is *not* a market access barrier within the meaning of Article XVI:2 of the GATS.

Also note that the quantitative restrictions specified in sub-paragraphs (a) to (d) refer to *maximum* limitations. Minimum requirements such as those com-mon to licensing criteria (for example, minimum capital requirements for the establishment of a corporate entity) do not fall within the scope of Article XVI of the GATS.[194]

In *US – Gambling (2005)*, the panel found that, by maintaining measures that *prohibit* the supply of certain services, the United States effectively lim-ited to zero the service suppliers and service operations relating to that serv-ice. According to the panel, such a zero quota constituted a limitation 'on the number of service suppliers ... in the form of numerical quotas' within the meaning of Article XVI:2(a) and a limitation 'on the total number of service operations ... in the form of quotas' within the meaning of Article XVI:2(c).[195] On appeal, the United States argued that the panel had ignored the fact that Article XVI:2(a) and (c) refer to measures in the *form* of numerical quotas and not to measures having the *effect* of numerical quotas. According to the United States, the measures concerned were not market access barriers within the meaning of Article XVI:2. The Appellate Body disagreed with the United States and upheld the relevant findings of the panel.[196] The Appellate Body noted that the words 'in the form of' must not be interpreted as 'prescribing a rigid mechanical formula'.[197] According to the Appellate Body, a measure equiva-lent to a zero quota is a market access barrier within the meaning of Article XVI:2.[198] An example of such limitation would be a nationality requirement for suppliers of services.[199]

The panel in *Mexico – Telecoms (2004)* noted that none of the six types of market access barrier of Article XVI:2 relates to *temporal* limitations on the

---

193 *Guidelines for the Scheduling of Specific Commitments under the General Agreement on Trade in Services (GATS)*, S/L/92, dated 28 March 2001, para. 8.
194 See *ibid.*, para. 11.   195 See Panel Report, *US – Gambling (2005)*, para. 6.332.
196 See Appellate Body Report, *US – Gambling (2005)*, para. 250.
197 *Ibid.*, para. 232. It is the numerical or quantitative nature of the limitation that matters, not the form of the limitation.
198 See *ibid.*, paras. 238 and 251.
199 Note that the Appellate Body ruled in *US – Gambling (2005)* that 'it is neither necessary nor appropriate for us to draw, in the abstract, the line between quantitative and qualitative measures'. See Appellate Body Report, *US – Gambling (2005)*, para. 250.

supply of a service. According to the panel, this suggests that temporal limitations cannot constitute market access barriers within the meaning of Article
XVI:2.[200]

4.2 Rules on Market Access Barriers

The GATS does not provide for a general prohibition on the market access barriers discussed in the above paragraphs. Whether a Member may maintain or
adopt these market access barriers with regard to a specific service depends on
whether, and if so to what extent, that Member has, in its Services Schedule,
made market access commitments with regard to that service or the relevant
services sector. This is commonly referred to as the 'positive list' or 'bottom-up'
approach to the liberalisation of trade in services. Article XVI of the GATS, entitled 'Market Access', provides, in paragraph 1:

> With respect to market access through the modes of supply identified in Article I, each
> Member shall accord services and service suppliers of any other Member *treatment no less
> favourable* than that provided for under the terms, limitations and conditions agreed and
> specified in its Schedule.[201]

Furthermore, the chapeau of Article XVI:2 of the GATS states:

> In sectors where market-access commitments are undertaken, the measures which a Member
> shall not maintain or adopt either on the basis of a regional subdivision or on the basis of
> its entire territory, unless otherwise specified in its Schedule, are defined as ...

Paragraphs (a) to (f) of Article XVI:2 then provide for the list of market access barriers discussed above. In other words, when a Member has undertaken a market
access commitment in a services sector, it may not maintain or adopt any of the
listed market access barriers with regard to trade in services in that sector, unless
otherwise specified in its Services Schedule. A Member can specify in its Schedule
that it maintains, or reserves the right to adopt, certain market access barriers.

  When a Member makes a market access commitment, it *binds* the level of
market access specified in its Schedule (see Article XVI:1) and agrees not to impose any market access barrier that would restrict access to the market beyond
the level specified (see Article XVI:2).[202] In *US – Gambling (2005)*, the United States had inscribed the term 'none' in its Schedule with respect to market
access limitations for 'other recreational services (excluding sporting)', which

---

200 See Panel Report, *Mexico – Telecoms (2004)*, para. 7.358. For example, a measure that makes the supply
     of a service subject to a permit which would not be granted until the corresponding regulations are issued
     would not be a market access barrier within the meaning of Article XVI:2.
201 Emphasis added. The panel in *China – Publications and Audiovisual Products (2010)* stated that, under
     Article XVI, a Member is free to maintain a market access regime less restrictive than that set out in its
     Schedule.
202 On the relationship between Article XVI:1 and XVI:2, the panel in *China – Publications and Audiovisual
     Products (2010)* stated that Article XVI:2 was 'more specific' as it describes the measures that a Member
     must not adopt. See Panel Report, *China – Publications and Audiovisual Products (2010)*, para. 7.1353.

was interpreted to include gambling and betting services.[203] Both the panel and the Appellate Body confirmed that this means that the United States has committed itself to providing *full* market access in that services sector.[204]

To date, Members have been found to have acted inconsistently with the prohibition on market access barriers of Article XVI of the GATS in three disputes.[205]

Questions and Assignments 7.10

Are the following measures inconsistent with Article XVI of the GATS: a governmental measure prohibiting the broadcasting of American and Australian television soaps; a law limiting the number of foreign workers employed by construction companies; a law requiring that only plumbers speaking the national language may do repairs in private households; a law stating that foreign banks may not hold more than 49 per cent of the capital of domestic banks; a government measure limiting the number of pubs to one for every 5,000 people? What must you know in order to answer this question?

4.3   Negotiations on Market Access for Services

Article XIX of the GATS, entitled 'Negotiation of Specific Commitments', states, in its first paragraph:

In pursuance of the objectives of this Agreement, Members shall enter into successive rounds of negotiations ... with a view to achieving a progressively higher level of liberalization.

The GATS thus aims at achieving *progressively* higher levels of liberalisation of trade in services through *successive* rounds of negotiations. The Uruguay Round negotiations on the liberalisation of trade in services were only a first step in what will definitely be a long process of progressive liberalisation. The negotiations on 'specific commitments' under Article XIX concern not only market access commitments but also national treatment commitments, discussed in Chapter 6.[206] While the focus in this sub-section is on the negotiations on market access, it must be kept in mind that the rules discussed in this sub-section equally apply to the negotiations on national treatment. This sub-section addresses in turn: (1) the basic rules governing Article XIX negotiations; and (2) the organisation of Article XIX negotiations.

4.3.1   Basic Rules Governing Article XIX Negotiations

With regard to the negotiations on the progressive liberalisation of trade in services, Article XIX:1 provides:

203 See below, pp. 527–8.
204 See Panel Report, *US – Gambling (2005)*, paras. 6.267–6.279; and Appellate Body Report, *US – Gambling (2005)*, paras. 214–15.
205 See *US – Gambling (2005)*; *China – Publications and Audiovisual Products (2009)*; and *China – Electronic Payment Services (2012)*.
206 See above, p. 462.

Such negotiations shall be directed to the reduction or elimination of the adverse effects on trade in services of measures as a means of providing effective market access. This process shall take place with a view to promoting the interests of all participants on a mutually advantageous basis and to securing an overall balance of rights and obligations.

The objective of the negotiations is thus to provide effective *market access* for services. In Article XIX negotiations, Members strive for a 'mutually advantageous' outcome, i.e. 'reciprocity'. The main approach to negotiations on the liberalisation of services is a request-and-offer approach.[207] At the initial stage of negotiations, Members first make requests for the liberalisation of trade in specific services.[208] The exchange of requests, as a process, is mainly bilateral, but may also be plurilateral.[209] It is simply a process of letters being addressed from the requesting participants to their negotiating partners.[210] After Members participating in the negotiations have made requests, they submit offers.[211] A Member submits an offer in response to all the requests that it has received, but does not necessarily have to address each element contained in those requests in its offer.[212] Unlike a request, which is usually presented in the form of a letter, an offer is normally presented in the form of a draft schedule of commitments.[213] While requests are addressed bilaterally (or plurilaterally) to negotiating partners, offers are circulated multilaterally.[214] Offers are to be open to consultations and negotiation by all negotiating partners; not only to those who have made requests to the Member concerned but also any other participant in the negotiations.[215] In fact, offers are a signal of the real start of the advanced stage of bilateral negotiations, i.e. when negotiators come to Geneva to hold many bilateral talks with various different delegations. The submission of offers may also trigger the submission of further requests and then the process continues and becomes a succession of requests and offers.[216]

---

207 See *Guidelines and Procedures for the Negotiations on Trade in Services*, adopted by the Special Session of the Council for Trade in Services on 28 March 2001, S/L/93, dated 29 March 2001, para. 11. On approaches to tariff negotiations, see above, pp. 431–3.

208 There are possibly four types of content in a request, which are not mutually exclusive: (i) the addition of new services sectors; (ii) the removal of existing limitations or the introduction of bindings in modes which have so far been unbound; (iii) the undertaking of additional commitments under Article XVIII; and (iv) the termination of MFN exemptions. See *Technical Aspects of Requests and Offers*, Summary of Presentation by the WTO Secretariat at the WTO Seminar on the GATS, 20 February 2002, 1, www.wto.org/english/tratop_e/serv_e/requests_offers_approach_e.doc. For further clarification, see below, p. 520.

209 See *Guidelines and Procedures for the Negotiations on Trade in Services*, adopted by the Special Session of the Council for Trade in Services on 28 March 2001, S/L/93, dated 29 March 2001, para. 11; and Ministerial Conference, *Ministerial Declaration*, adopted on 18 December 2005, WT/MIN(05)/DEC, dated 22 December 2005, Annex C, para. 7.

210 See *ibid.*

211 In terms of content, offers normally address the same four types referred to in footnote 207 above.

212 See *Technical Aspects of Requests and Offers*, Summary of Presentation by the WTO Secretariat at the WTO Seminar on the GATS, 20 February 2002, 3, www.wto.org/english/tratop_e/serv_e/requests_offers_approach_e.doc.

213 See *ibid.*

214 See *ibid.* The multilateral circulation is useful not only from a transparency point of view but also from a functional point of view since, in an offer, a participant is actually responding to *all* the requests that it has received.

215 See *ibid.*   216 See *ibid.*

Article XIX:2 of the GATS explicitly requires that the process of liberalisation of trade in services takes place with due respect for: (1) national policy objectives; and (2) the level of development of individual Members, both overall and in individual sectors. Article XIX:2 further provides specifically with respect to the position of developing-country Members in the negotiations on the liberalisation of trade in services that:

[t]here shall be appropriate flexibility for individual developing-country Members for opening fewer sectors, liberalizing fewer types of transactions, progressively extending market access in line with their development situation and, when making access to their markets available to foreign service suppliers, attaching to such access conditions aimed at achieving the objectives referred to in Article IV.

It is thus accepted that developing-country Members undertake fewer and more limited market access commitments than developed-country Members. 'Full reciprocity' is not required from developing-country Members. These Members are only expected to undertake market access commitments commensurate with their level of development.

4.3.2   Organisation of Article XIX Negotiations

As provided in Article XIX:3 of the GATS, for each round of multilateral negotiations on the liberalisation of trade in services, negotiating guidelines and procedures shall be established. For the current negotiations, initiated pursuant to Article XIX:1 of the GATS in January 2000 and now conducted in the context of the Doha Round negotiations,[217] the *Guidelines and Procedures for the Negotiations on Trade in Services* were adopted on 28 March 2001 by the Council for Trade in Services.[218]

Members have been exchanging bilateral initial requests since June 2002, and, as of the end of June 2008, WTO Members had submitted seventy-one initial offers and thirty-one revised offers.[219] However, from early on, there was – and there currently still is – widespread disappointment regarding the progress made in the negotiations. In April 2004, the Chair of the Special Session of the Council for Trade in Services reported to the Trade Negotiations Committee as follows:

[T]here was a feeling among Members that … far too few offers had been submitted and that the minimalist character of many of these offers was disappointing.[220]

In its Decision of 1 August 2004 on the *Doha Work Programme*, the General Council reaffirmed the Members' commitment to make progress in the services

---

217 Ministerial Conference, *Doha Ministerial Declaration*, adopted 14 November 2001, WT/MIN(01)/DEC/1, dated 20 November 2001, para. 15.

218 Council for Trade in Services, *Guidelines and Procedures for the Negotiations on Trade in Services*, S/L/93, dated 29 March 2001. Note that, while the negotiations focus on market access, they also cover three other major areas, namely, internal regulation, GATS rules, and the implementation of LDC modalities.

219 As of April 2011, this was still the number of initial and revised offers submitted. See www.wto.org/english/tratop_e/serv_e/market_access_negs_e.htm. On the request-and-offer approach to the negotiations on trade in services, see above, p. 519.

220 Council for Trade in Services, *Report by the Chairman to the Trade Negotiations Committee*, TN/S/15, dated 14 April 2004, para. 5.

negotiations;[221] and, in December 2005, the Ministerial Conference, at its meeting in Hong Kong, called on Members to intensify the negotiations with a view to expanding coverage of commitments and improving their quality. The Ministerial Conference provided in Annex C to the Hong Kong Ministerial Declaration more detailed negotiating objectives to guide Members.[222] The Ministerial Conference also agreed that least-developed-country Members were not expected to undertake new services commitments. As provided for in Annex C to the Hong Kong Ministerial Declaration, Members tried out, as from March 2006, a new approach to the negotiations, namely, the plurilateral request approach. Under this approach, a group of Members requesting market access started negotiations with targeted Members on the basis of a *collective* request. However, this and other efforts to produce a breakthrough in the market access negotiations were to little avail. In his 2011 report to the Trade Negotiation Committee, the Chair of the Special Session of the Council for Trade in Services described the state of play of the negotiations as follows:

Members agree that much more work is needed to conclude the market access negotiations, although their views differ on the current state of play ... Some Members have expressed concern over the state of the market access negotiations, indicating that no progress has occurred since the 2010 stocktaking, and little or none since the July 2008 Signalling Conference. They stated that the remaining gaps between offers or signals and bilateral and plurilateral requests or applied regimes were still substantial, and that they had difficulty in obtaining clarity from recipient Members about real difficulties faced in meeting requests. They expressed the need for an ambitious outcome from the services negotiations ... The status of the market access negotiations was viewed in a different light by others. For some Members, there was an imbalance in the market access negotiations, resulting from developing country flexibilities not being taken into account in other Members' requests, and sectors of export interest not being fully reflected in their offers ... For several Members, there were plurilateral requests and recent proposals that embodied a level of ambition going beyond that agreed in Annex C of the Hong Kong Ministerial Declaration.[223]

In short, the negotiations on market access for services are, as the Doha Round negotiations in general, deadlocked. On the one hand, there are Members, mainly developed-country Members, for which the market access offers currently on the table are insufficient. On the other hand, there are Members, primarily developing-country Members, for which the requests for market access go too far.[224] As noted in Chapter 2 of this book – and indicative of the impasse reached in the Doha Round negotiations on market access for services – there are at present talks – outside the Doha Round negotiations – on an ambitious liberalisation

---

221 See General Council, *Doha Work Programme*, Decision adopted on 1 August 2004, WT/L/579, dated 2 August 2004, para. 1(e).
222 Ministerial Conference, *Ministerial Declaration*, adopted on 18 December 2005, WT/MIN(05)/DEC, dated 22 December 2005.
223 Council for Trade in Services, Special Session, *Negotiations on Trade in Services*, Report by the Chairman, Ambassador Fernando de Mateo, to the Trade Negotiations Committee, TN/S/36, dated 21 April 2011, paras. 4–6.
224 Note that some of these developing-country Members, and in particular Brazil, have linked their willingness to accept far-reaching requests for market access to a successful conclusion of the negotiations on the liberalisation of trade in agricultural products.

of trade in services, building upon but going far beyond the existing GATS.[225] These negotiations among a group of about 20 developed- and developing-country Members include the European Union and the United States, but not Brazil, China or India. The latter Members have warned of the consequences for the multilateral trading system of adopting a plurilateral approach to negotiations on the liberalisation of trade in services.[226]

Questions and Assignments 7.11

What is the objective of the Article XIX negotiations? How are these negotiations conducted? How is the special situation of developing-country Members taken into consideration in these negotiations? Discuss the progress on the further liberalisation of trade in services, and in particular with regard to market access commitments, made to date in the context of the Doha Round negotiations.

4.4   Schedules of Specific Commitments

The results of negotiations on market access for services are set out in Schedules of Specific Commitments, commonly referred to as 'Services Schedules'. This is what was done in 1994 with the results of the Uruguay Round negotiations on market access for services. This sub-section discusses: (1) the contents and structure of Services Schedules; (2) the interpretation of Services Schedules; and (3) the market access commitments agreed to in the Uruguay Round Services Schedules.

4.4.1   Contents and Structure of Services Schedules

The Services Schedules set out the terms of market access for services agreed to in the context of market access negotiations. In addition to the terms of market access, Services Schedules also set out the terms of national treatment, discussed in Chapter 5 of this book, and the terms of additional commitments, discussed later in this chapter.[227] Each Member has a Services Schedule. In fact, each Member *must* have a Services Schedule, albeit that there is no minimum requirement as to the scope or depth of the commitments set out in that Schedule. All Services Schedules are annexed to the GATS and form an integral part thereof.[228] All Services Schedules are available on the WTO website.[229] The online WTO Services Database gives information on all commitments undertaken by all Members, and can be used to establish the commitments of a particular Member with regard to a specific services sector or sub-sector, or to compare services commitments across Members.[230]

---

225 See above, p. 93.
226 See *Bridges Weekly Trade News Digest*, 4 April 2012, 11 July 2012 and 26 September 2012. Other Members involved include Australia, Canada, Colombia, Costa Rica, Hong Kong China, Israel, Japan, Mexico, New Zealand, Norway, Pakistan, Panama, Peru, South Korea, Switzerland, Chinese Taipei and Turkey.
227 See above, p. 404, and below, p. 534.   228 Article XX:3 of the GATS.
229 See www.wto.org/english/tratop_e/serv_e/serv_commitments_e.htm.
230 See http://tsdb.wto.org/wto/WTOHomepublic.htm. Be aware that the Consolidated Services Schedule of the European Union and its Member States (S/C/W/273, dated 9 October 2006), resulting from the enlargement

Services Schedules have two parts: (1) a part containing the *horizontal commitments*; and (2) a part containing the *sectoral commitments*. Horizontal commitments apply to all sectors included in the Schedule. Schedules include horizontal commitments to *avoid repeating* in relation to each sector contained in the Schedule the same information regarding limitations, conditions or qualifications of commitments.[231] Horizontal commitment often concern two modes of supply in particular, namely, supply through commercial presence (mode 3) and supply through the presence of natural persons (mode 4).[232] For example, with regard to mode 4 supply of all services scheduled, the Services Schedule of the European Union and its Member States stipulates:

Unbound except for measures concerning the entry into and temporary stay within a Member State, without requiring compliance with an economic needs test, of the following categories of natural persons providing services ...[233]

Unlike horizontal commitments, sectoral commitments (or sector-specific commitments) are, as the term indicates, commitments made regarding specific services sectors or sub-sectors. For scheduling commitments, WTO Members distinguish twelve broad services sectors: business services; communication services; construction and related engineering services; distribution services; educational services; environmental services; financial services; health-related and social services; tourism and travel-related services; recreational, cultural and sporting services; transport services; and other services not included elsewhere. These twelve broad services sectors are further divided into more than 150 sub-sectors.[234] For example, the 'business services' sector includes: professional services (including, for example, legal services, accounting, architectural services, engineering services, and medical and dental services); computer and related services; research and development services; real estate services; rental/leasing services without operators; and other business services (including, for example, building cleaning services and publishing). The 'communication services' sector includes: postal services; courier services; telecommunications services (including, for example, voice telephone services, electronic mail, voice mail and electronic data interchange); and audiovisual services (including, for example, motion picture and video tape production and distribution services, radio and television services and sound recording). This WTO classification of

---

of the European Union, is not included in the searchable database of commitments (as it had not yet entered into force at the time of establishing this database).

231 Horizontal commitments are found at the beginning of a schedule. The concept of 'horizontal commitments' may be misleading since 'horizontal commitments' are often, in fact, horizontal limitations, i.e. limitations applicable to all commitments. Only with regard to mode 4 supply of services, horizontal commitments are frequently positive undertakings.

232 On the four modes of supply of services (cross-border supply, consumption abroad, supply through commercial presence and supply through the presence of natural persons), see above, p. 339.

233 GATS/SC/31, dated 15 April 1994, 7–10.

234 Note that, if a market access commitment is given in a particular sector, that commitment applies to the whole of that sector, including all of its sub-sectors (unless of course a sub-sector is specifically excluded or a different regime is specified for it). See Panel Report, *US – Gambling (2005)*, para. 6.290.

services sectors, set out in the Services Sectoral Classification List of the WTO Secretariat, also referred to as 'document W/120',[235] is based on the provisional Central Product Classification (CPC) of the United Nations. In the Secretariat's List, each sector is identified by the corresponding CPC number. The CPC gives a detailed explanation of the services covered by each of the sectors and sub-sectors.[236] Note that a specific service cannot fall within two different sectors or sub-sectors. The sectors and sub-sectors are mutually exclusive.[237] In scheduling their commitments, most Members follow the WTO's Services Sectoral Classification List. Thus, most Schedules have the same structure. A services sector or sub-sector is of course only included in a Member's Services Schedule if that Member undertakes commitments in that sector or sub-sector.

Services Schedules have four columns: (1) a first column identifying the services sector or sub-sector which is the subject of the commitment; (2) a second column containing the terms, limitations and conditions on market access; (3) a third column containing the conditions and qualifications on national treatment; and (4) a fourth column for undertakings relating to additional commitments. With regard to market access commitments, Members indicate, in the second column of their Schedule, the presence or absence of limitations on market access. They do so for each services sector scheduled and with regard to each of the four modes of supply: cross-border supply (mode 1); consumption abroad (mode 2); supply through commercial presence (mode 3); and supply through presence of natural persons (mode 4).

For each market access commitment with respect to each mode of supply, four different situations can occur:[238]

(1) First situation: *full commitment*, i.e. the situation in which a Member does not seek in any way to limit market access in a given sector and mode of supply through market access barriers within the meaning of Article XVI:2. A Member in this situation records in the second column of its Schedule the word 'none'.[239]

(2) Second situation: *commitment with limitations*, i.e. the situation in which a Member wants to limit market access in a given sector and mode of supply

---

235 See MTN.GNS/W/120, dated 10 July 1991.
236 A breakdown of the CPC, including explanatory notes for each sub-sector, is contained in the UN Provisional Central Product Classification, http://unstats.un.org/unsd/cr/registry/regcst.asp?Cl=16&Lg=1. To determine the coverage of the services sectors and sub-sectors of the WTO Services Sectoral Classification List, the detailed explanation of the CPC system can be used. Entries in Schedules often include CPC numbers.
237 See Appellate Body Report, *US – Gambling (2005)*, para. 180. See also Panel Report, *China – Electronic Payment Services (2012)*, para. 7.531.
238 See Council for Trade in Services, *Guidelines for the Scheduling of Specific Commitments under the General Agreement on Trade in Services* (GATS), adopted on 23 March 2001, S/L/92, dated 28 March 2001.
239 Note, however, that any relevant limitation listed in the 'horizontal commitments' part of the Schedule also applies. See above, p. 523.

through market access barriers within the meaning of Article XVI:2. A Member in this situation describes in the second column of its Schedule the market access barrier(s) that is/are maintained.[240]

(3) Third situation: *no commitment*, i.e. the situation in which a Member wants to remain free in a given sector and mode of supply to introduce or maintain market access barriers within the meaning of Article XVI:2. A Member in this situation records in the second column of its Schedule the word 'unbound'.[241]

(4) Fourth situation: *no commitment technically feasible*, i.e. the situation in which a particular mode of supply is not technically possible, such as the cross-border supply of hair-dressing services. A Member in this situation records in the second column of its Schedule 'unbound*'.[242]

As discussed in Chapter 5 of this book, and as is evident from the excerpt from the Services Schedule of Brazil shown in Figure 7.1, national treatment commitments and limitations thereof are inscribed in the third column of the Schedules in the same way as market access commitments and limitations thereof are inscribed. It is possible that a measure is both a market access barrier prohibited under Article XVI:2 and a measure inconsistent with the national treatment obligation of Article XVII. For this type of situation, Article XX:2 of the GATS provides that:

[m]easures inconsistent with both Articles XVI and XVII shall be inscribed in the column relating to Article XVI. In this case the inscription will be considered to provide a condition or qualification to Article XVII as well.

As the panel in *China – Publications and Audiovisual Products (2010)* stated:

If a limitation affects *both* market access and national treatment then, by a convention set out in Article XX:2 of the GATS (avoiding the need to repeat an inscription), it is to be inscribed *only* in the market access column.[243]

In *China – Electronic Payment Services (2012)*, China had with regard to mode 1 of the sub-sector at issue inscribed in the national treatment column of its Schedule 'None', while in the market access column it had inscribed 'Unbound'. The United States contended that China had made a full national treatment commitment with regard to mode 1 of the sub-sector at issue. China contested

240 Two main possibilities can be envisaged in such a situation: the first is the binding of an existing situation ('standstill'); the second is the binding of a more liberal situation where some, but not all, of the access barriers inconsistent with Article XVI:2 will be removed ('rollback').
241 Note that this situation will only occur when a Member made a commitment in a sector with respect to at least one mode of supply. Where all modes of supply are 'unbound', and no additional commitments have been undertaken in the sector, the sector should not appear in the Schedule.
242 The asterisk refers to a footnote which states: 'Unbound due to lack of technical feasibility'.
243 Panel Report, *China – Publications and Audiovisual Products (2010)*, para. 7.921.

Sector or sub-sector	Limitations on market access	Limitations on national treatment	Additional commitments
e) Engineering Services			
Advisory and consultative engineering services (CPC 86721)	1. Unbound 2. Unbound 3. Same conditions as in Architectural services 4. Unbound except as indicated in the horizontal section	1. Unbound 2. Unbound 3. None 4. Unbound except as indicated in the horizontal section	
Industrial engineering (CPC 86725)	1. Unbound 2. Unbound 3. Same conditions as in Architectural services 4. Unbound except as indicated in the horizontal section	1. Unbound 2. Unbound 3. None 4. Unbound except as indicated in the horizontal section	
Engineering design (CPC 86722, CPC 86723, CPC 86724)	1. Unbound 2. Unbound 3. Same conditions as in Architectural services 4. Unbound except as indicated in the horizontal section	1. Unbound 2. Unbound 3. None 4. Unbound except as indicated in the horizontal section	
Other engineering services (CPC 86729)	1. Unbound 2. Unbound 3. Same conditions as in Architectural services 4. Unbound except as indicated in the horizontal section	1. Unbound 2. Unbound 3. None 4. Unbound except as indicated in the horizontal section	

Figure 7.1 Excerpt from the Schedule of Specific Commitments of Brazil (engineering services)

this, arguing that measures described in Article XVI:2 cannot simultaneously be subject to Article XVII. The panel in this case ruled:

> By inscribing 'Unbound' under market access, China reserves the right to maintain any type of measure within the six categories falling under Article XVI:2, regardless of its inscription in the national treatment column.[244]

The panel added that its interpretation, however, also gave meaning to the term 'None' in the national treatment column, because:

> [d]ue to the inscription of 'None', China must grant national treatment with respect to any of the measures at issue that are not inconsistent with Article XVI:2. China's national treatment commitment could thus have practical application should China, for example, choose to allow in practice the supply of services from the territory of other WTO Members into its market, despite the fact that it has not undertaken any market access commitments in subsectors (a) to (f) of its Schedule.[245]

---

244 Panel Report, *China – Electronic Payment Services (2012)*, para. 7.663.
245 *Ibid.*

The panel in *China – Electronic Payment Services (2012)* emphasised that it did *not* find that either Article XVI or Article XVII is substantively subordinate to the other.[246] The panel stated:

We find simply that Article XX:2 establishes a certain scheduling primacy for entries in the market access column, in that a WTO Member not wishing to make any commitment under Article XVI, discriminatory or non-discriminatory, may do so by inscribing the term 'Unbound' in the market access column of its schedule.[247]

Questions and Assignments 7.12

What is the difference between horizontal and sectoral commitments? What is the function of the WTO's Services Sectoral Classification List? Examine the Services Schedules of the European Union and its Member States, the United States, Brazil, China and India, and draw conclusions as to the extent of market access commitments in the legal services sub-sector and audiovisual services sub-sector. Find out whether Mexico, Indonesia and South Africa, as well as the WTO Member of which you are a national, have made market access commitments in the engineering services sub-sector.

4.4.2   Interpretation of Services Schedules

Just as Goods Schedules are an integral part of the GATT 1994, Services Schedules are an integral part of the GATS.[248] Article XX:3 of the GATS states:

Schedules of specific commitments shall be annexed to this Agreement and shall form an integral part thereof.

The issue of interpretation of Services Schedules arose in *US – Gambling (2005)*. In this case, the panel had to interpret the Services Schedule of the United States. The question was:

whether the US Schedule includes specific commitments on gambling and betting services notwithstanding the fact that the words 'gambling and betting services' do not appear in the US Schedule.[249]

The United States had inscribed 'other recreational services (except sporting)' in its Schedule, and had recorded *no* limitations on market access in mode 1 (cross-border supply of services). It argued, however, that the term 'sporting' includes gambling and betting and that gambling and betting services were therefore excluded from its specific commitments. The panel in this case, however, first noted – referring to the Appellate Body's finding regarding tariff concessions in *EC – Computer Equipment (1998)* – that scheduled commitments 'are reciprocal and result from mutually advantageous negotiations between importing and exporting Members'.[250] The panel then noted:

The United States has repeated several times in these proceedings that it did not intend to schedule a commitment for gambling and betting services. This may well be true, given

246 See *ibid.*, para. 7.664.   247 *Ibid.*
248 On the interpretation of Goods Schedules, see above, p. 439.
249 Panel Report, *US – Gambling (2005)*, para. 6.41.
250 Appellate Body Report, *EC – Computer Equipment (1998)*, para. 84. See also above, p. 444.

that the legislation at issue in this dispute predates by decades, not only the GATS itself, but even the notion of 'trade in services' as embodied therein. We have, therefore, some sympathy with the United States' point in this regard. However, the scope of a specific commitment cannot depend upon what a Member intended or did not intend to do at the time of the negotiations.[251]

What matters, according to the panel, is the *common* intent of all negotiating parties. To determine this common intent with regard to the specific commitment at issue in this case, the panel applied – as did the Appellate Body in *EC – Computer Equipment (1998)* – the rules of interpretation set out in Articles 31 and 32 of the *Vienna Convention on the Law of Treaties*.[252] On appeal, the Appellate Body agreed with the panel's reliance on the rules of interpretation of the *Vienna Convention* to ascertain the meaning of the Services Schedule of the United States.[253] As the panel, the Appellate Body found that the United States' Services Schedule includes specific commitments on gambling and betting services.[254]

As the Appellate Body held in *US – Gambling (2005)*, other Members' Schedules could be relevant context for the interpretation of a particular Schedule, since all Schedules are an integral part of the GATS.[255] Furthermore, there are three specific documents dealing with the classification of services that may be useful in assisting the interpretation of a Services Schedule, namely: (1) the 1991 UN *Provisional Central Product Classification* (CPC); (2) the GATT Secretariat's Services Sectoral Classification List (document W/120); and (3) the 1993 Guidelines for the Scheduling of Specific Commitments under the GATS.[256]

Finally, note that, in *China – Publication and Audiovisual Products (2009)*, China contended on appeal that the panel had erred in interpreting its Services Schedule entry 'Sound recording distribution services' according to the contemporary meaning of the words it contains, i.e. also covering the *electronic* distribution of sound recordings. According to China, the principle of progressive liberalisation does not allow for the expansion of the scope of the commitments of a WTO Member by interpreting the terms used in the Schedule based on the meaning of those terms at the time of interpretation.[257] Disagreeing with China, the Appellate Body ruled:

---

251 Panel Report, *US – Gambling (2005)*, para. 6.136.
252 See Appellate Body Report, *EC – Computer Equipment (1998)*, para. 84.
253 See Appellate Body Report, *US – Gambling (2005)*, para. 160. See also Panel Report, *China – Publications and Audiovisual Products (2010)*, para. 7.922.
254 See Appellate Body Report, *US – Gambling (2005)*, para. 213. Although coming to the same conclusion as the panel, the Appellate Body applied the *Vienna Convention* rules of interpretation differently than the panel did. See Appellate Body Report, *US – Gambling (2005)*, para. 197.
255 See Appellate Body Report, *US – Gambling (2005)*, para. 182. As the Appellate Body noted, each Schedule has, however, 'its own intrinsic logic'. See *ibid*.
256 See Panel Report, *China – Publications and Audiovisual Products (2010)*, para. 7.923; and Appellate Body Report, *US – Gambling (2005)*, paras. 196–7. With regard to the 1993 Guidelines for the Scheduling and document W/120, the Appellate Body ruled in *US – Gambling (2005)*, that these instruments constituted 'supplementary means of interpretation' under Article 32 of the *Vienna Convention*. See *ibid*. On this point, the Appellate Body reversed the panel, which considered these instruments to be 'context' under Article 31.2 of the *Vienna Convention*. See also above, p. 189, footnote 173, and p. 193.
257 See Appellate Body Report, *China – Publications and Audiovisual Products (2009)*, para. 390.

we consider that the terms used in China's GATS Schedule ('sound recording' and 'distribution') are sufficiently generic that what they apply to may change over time.[258]

4.4.3   Market Access Commitments Agreed to in the Uruguay Round Services Schedules

The market access commitments agreed to during the Uruguay Round negotiations on the liberalisation of trade in services are, in general, modest. On average, WTO Members have only undertaken market access commitments on about twenty-five sub-sectors, i.e. 15 per cent of the total.[259] Only one-third of the Members have undertaken commitments on more than sixty-one sub-sectors.[260] Furthermore, the market access commitments rarely go beyond the *status quo*, i.e. they bind the degree of market access already existing. The value of these bindings, also referred to as 'standstill bindings', is that they give traders and investors a degree of security and predictability with respect to market access in the services sectors of interest to them.

In a number of important sectors, such as financial services, telecommunications and maritime transport, and with respect to the movement of natural persons, the Uruguay Round negotiators were unable to complete the market access negotiations, and the GATS made provision for further negotiations. These further negotiations led in 1997 to agreements providing for significant market access commitments in the sectors of basic telecommunications and financial services.[261] Further negotiations on market access for maritime transport failed, while further negotiations on the movement of natural persons were completed in July 1995 with very modest results. To the dissatisfaction of developing-country Members, the agreement reached on the movement of natural persons was largely confined to business visitors (to establish business contacts or negotiate contracts) and intra-corporate transfers of managers and technical staff.

Thus far, tourism has been the services sector in which most market access commitments have been made, followed by financial and business services. In the health and education sectors, Members have made the fewest market access commitments, but few commitments were also made in the sector of distribution services. On the whole, developed-country Members have made market access commitments with regard to nearly all sectors, except health and education. Note, however, that, for example, the European Union, Canada and Switzerland made no commitments with regard to audiovisual services.[262]

Market access commitments with respect to 'consumption abroad' (mode 2) are much less subject to limitations than market access commitments with respect

---

258 *Ibid.*, para. 396. See also above, p. 408.
259 See WTO Secretariat, *Market Access: Unfinished Business*, Special Studies Series 6 (WTO, 2001), 104.
260 See *ibid.*   261 See above, pp. 86–7.
262 See WTO Secretariat, *Market Access: Unfinished Business*, Special Studies Series 6 (WTO, 2001), 104.

to other modes of supply of services.[263] Presumably, governments feel less of a need to restrict their nationals' consumption of services abroad or consider it impracticable to enforce such restrictions.[264] Market access commitments with respect to 'supply through the presence of natural persons' (mode 4), however, are usually subject to broad limitations.[265] Members, developed and developing alike, are clearly hesitant to undertake any commitments involving the entry of natural persons onto their territory. They are unwilling to expose their labour markets to competition from foreign workers.

Questions and Assignments 7.13

Discuss the extent of market access commitments for trade in services agreed to in the context of the WTO thus far.

4.5   Modification or Withdrawal of Commitments

As is the case with tariff concessions for goods, market access commitments for services can also be modified or withdrawn.[266] According to Article XXI of the GATS, a Member may modify or withdraw any commitment in its Schedule, at any time after three years have elapsed from the date on which that commitment entered into force.[267] A Member wishing to 'unbind' a commitment must first notify its intention to do so to the Council for Trade in Services. Subsequently, it must – if so requested – enter into negotiations with a view to reaching agreement on any necessary compensatory adjustment. The purpose of these negotiations on compensatory adjustment is to maintain a general level of mutually advantageous commitments not less favourable to trade than that provided for in the Schedule. If no agreement on compensatory adjustment can be reached between the modifying Member and any affected Member, the affected Member(s) may refer the matter to arbitration.[268] Recall that this possibility to refer to arbitration is not specifically provided for in the context of the modification or withdrawal of tariff concessions.[269] If no arbitration is requested, the modifying Member is free to implement the intended modification or withdrawal.[270] If arbitration is requested, however, the modifying Member may not modify or withdraw its commitment until it has made compensatory

---

263 On the relative importance of each of the four modes of supply in the total world services trade, see above, p. 339 footnote 95.

264 See WTO Secretariat, *Market Access: Unfinished Business*, Special Studies Series 6 (WTO, 2001), 105.

265 Also note that the Annex on Movement of Natural Persons excludes from the scope of the GATS measures regarding citizenship and permanent residency, and visas.

266 For the details of the relevant procedure, see *Procedures for the Implementation of Article XXI of the General Agreement on Trade in Services (GATS) (Modification of Schedules)*, adopted on 19 July 1999, S/L/80, dated 29 October 1999. On the modification or withdrawal of tariff concessions, see above, p. 530.

267 In certain exceptional circumstances, the period of three years is reduced to one year. See Article X of the GATS.

268 See Article XXI:3(a) of the GATS. Any affected Member that wishes to enforce a right that it may have to compensation must participate in the arbitration. See *ibid.*

269 See above, p. 530.   270 See Article XXI:3(b) of the GATS.

adjustments in conformity with the findings of the arbitration.[271] In case the modifying Member does not comply with the findings of the arbitration, any affected Member that participated in the arbitration may modify or withdraw *substantially equivalent benefits* in conformity with those findings.[272] Note that any compensatory adjustment made by the Member 'unbinding' a commitment must be made on an MFN basis. However, the modification or withdrawal of substantially equivalent benefits by the affected Member(s) in case of non-compliance with the arbitration findings may be implemented solely with respect to the modifying Member.[273]

After an Article 21.5 panel had established in March 2007 that the United States had failed to comply with the recommendations and rulings of the DSB in *US – Gambling (2005)*,[274] the United States announced in May 2007 that it would not comply with these recommendations and rulings, but was modifying its market access commitments in the sub-sector of 'recreational services', the services sub-sector at issue in *US – Gambling (2005)*. Reportedly, seven other WTO Members joined Antigua in notifying their intent to seek compensation from the United States. The United States reached agreement on compensatory adjustment with Australia, Canada, the European Union and Japan, by making additional market access commitments in the sub-sectors of postal services, research and development services, technical testing services, and warehousing. However, with Antigua, no agreement on compensatory adjustment was reached. In early 2008, Antigua referred this matter to arbitration pursuant to Article XXI:3(a).

Questions and Assignments 7.14

Can market access commitments for services be modified or withdrawn? If so, how? How does this differ from the modification or withdrawal of tariff concessions?

5   OTHER BARRIERS TO TRADE IN SERVICES

In addition to the market access barriers, discussed above, trade in services can also be impeded by a wide array of other barriers. With regard to a number of these other barriers, WTO law, and in particular the GATS, provides for specific

271 See Article XXI:4(a) of the GATS.   272 See Article XXI:4(b) of the GATS.
273 See Article XXI:2(b) of the GATS (for the compensatory adjustment) and Article XXI:4(b) of the GATS (for the modification or withdrawal of substantially equivalent benefits).
274 See Panel Report, *US – Gambling (Article 21.5) (2007)*. Subsequently, in June 2007, Antigua requested the DSB to authorise the taking of retaliatory measures up to an amount of US$3.443 billion. See WT/DS285/22, dated 22 June 2007. On 21 December 2007, the Arbitrator under Article 22.6 of the DSU determined that the annual level of nullification or impairment of benefits accruing to Antigua is US$21 million. The Arbitrator also found that suspension of commitments or other obligations under the GATS was not practicable and effective for Antigua and that circumstances were serious enough to permit 'cross-retaliation' under various sections of the *TRIPS Agreement*. See WT/DS285/ARB, dated 21 December 2007. On 24 April 2012, Antigua informed the DSB that the United States was still not in compliance with the recommendations and rulings of the DSB, and that it had notified the United States of its wish to seek recourse to the good offices of the WTO Director-General in finding a mediated solution to this dispute. On 28 January 2013, the DSB granted Antigua authorisation to suspend commitments and other obligations including under the *TRIPS Agreement*.

rules. Some of these rules have general application.[275] Other rules apply only in services sectors with regard to which specific market access commitments were made.[276] This section discusses in turn the following other barriers to trade in services: (1) lack of transparency; (2) unfair or arbitrary application of measures affecting trade in services; (3) licensing and qualification requirements and technical standards; (4) lack of recognition of diplomas and professional certificates; (5) government procurement; and (6) other measures and actions.

5.1 Lack of Transparency

For trade in services, as much as for trade in goods discussed above, lack of information, uncertainty and confusion with respect to the relevant laws and regulations applicable in actual or potential foreign markets are formidable barriers to trade. Effective market access for services is impossible without transparency regarding the laws and regulations affecting the services concerned. Service suppliers must have accurate information concerning the rules with which they must comply.

As Article X of the GATT 1994 does with regard to trade in goods, Article III of the GATS requires with regard to trade in services that Members *publish* all measures of general application affecting trade in services.[277] Publication must take place promptly, and at the latest by the time the measure enters into force.[278] Since the end of 1997, each Member has been required to establish one or more *enquiry points* to provide information on laws and regulations affecting trade in services.[279] Members have an obligation to respond promptly to all requests by any other Member for specific information on any of its measures of general application.[280] For the benefit of developing-country Members, developed-country Members have a special obligation to establish 'contact points' to facilitate the access of service suppliers from developing-country Members to information of special interest to them.[281] Article III of the GATS also requires a Member to *notify* the Council for Trade in Services of any new, or any changes to, laws, regulations or administrative guidelines which significantly affect trade in sectors where that Member has made specific commitments. Members must

---

275 For example, the requirement that Members maintain or institute as soon as practicable judicial, arbitral or administrative tribunals for the prompt review of decisions affecting trade in services. See Article VI:2(a) of the GATS, and below, p. 533.

276 For example, the requirement to administer measures affecting trade in services in a reasonable, objective and impartial manner. See Article VI:1 of the GATS, and below, p. 533.

277 Where publication is not practicable, the information must be made otherwise publicly available (see Article III:2 of the GATS). The publication requirement exists also for measures affecting trade in services with regard to which a Member has not made specific commitments.

278 See Article III:1 of the GATS. This obligation can be waived in emergency situations. This publication obligation also applies to international agreements pertaining to or affecting trade in services to which a Member is a signatory.

279 See Article III:4 of the GATS.   280 See *ibid.*

281 See Article IV:2 of the GATS. Such information includes information on registration, recognition and obtaining of professional qualifications; and the availability of services technologies.

do so at least once a year.[282] Note that the transparency of Members' measures affecting trade in services is also advanced by the trade policy reviews under the *Trade Policy Review Mechanism*.[283]

5.2 Unfair and Arbitrary Application of Trade Measures

In sectors where specific commitments are undertaken, Article VI:1 of the GATS requires a Member to ensure:

> that all measures of general application affecting trade in services are administered in a reasonable, objective and impartial manner.

This obligation is the counterpart to Article X:3(a) of the GATT 1994, discussed above, for trade in services.[284]

In all services sectors, including those in which no specific commitments are undertaken, Article VI:2(a) of the GATS requires Members to maintain procedures which allow service suppliers to challenge administrative decisions affecting them. These procedures may be administrative or judicial but must be objective and impartial. Moreover, they must provide for prompt review and, where necessary, appropriate remedies.[285]

Where authorisation is required for the supply of a service on which a commitment has been made, the competent authorities of a Member must, within a reasonable period of time, inform the applicant of the decision concerning the application.[286]

5.3 Licensing and Qualification Requirements and Technical Standards

As discussed above, trade in services is primarily impeded or restricted by internal regulations. For scheduled services, certain internal regulations may constitute market access barriers within the meaning of Article XVI:2 of the GATS and, as discussed above, are prohibited unless otherwise specified in the Schedule.[287] However, most internal regulations do not constitute market access barriers within the meaning of Article XVI:2.[288] Apart from the rules concerning transparency and the rules on unfair and arbitrary application, discussed above, the GATS currently only provides for a few other disciplines applicable to internal regulations which do not constitute market access barriers. The most

---

282 See Article III:3 of the GATS. Members are not required, however, to supply confidential information. See Article III*bis* of the GATS.
283 See above, p. 95.   284 See above, p. 502.   285 See Article VI:2(a) of the GATS.
286 See Article VI:3 of the GATS.   287 See above, p. 517.
288 The panel in *US – Gambling (2005)* stated: 'Under Article VI and Article XVI, measures are either of the type covered by the disciplines of Article XVI or are internal regulations relating to qualification requirements and procedures, technical standards and licensing requirements subject to the specific provisions of Article VI. Thus, Articles VI:4 and VI:5 on the one hand and XVI on the other hand are mutually exclusive.' Panel Report, *US – Gambling (2005)*, para. 6.305.

important of these disciplines concerns licensing requirements, qualification requirements, and technical standards. Article VI:5(a) of the GATS states:

> In sectors in which a Member has undertaken specific commitments ... the Member shall
> not apply licensing and qualification requirements and technical standards that nullify or
> impair such specific commitments in a manner which:
>
> i. does not comply with the criteria outlined in sub-paragraphs 4(a), (b) or (c); and
> ii. could not reasonably have been expected of that Member at the time the specific com-
>   mitments in those sectors were made.

According to the criteria of Article VI:4(a), (b) and (c) to which the above provision refers, licensing requirements, qualification requirements and technical
standards relating to services sectors in which specific commitments are undertaken must: (1) be based on objective and transparent criteria such as competence and the ability to supply the service; (2) not be more burdensome than
necessary to ensure the quality of the service; and (3) in the case of licensing
procedures, not be, in themselves, a restriction on the supply of the service. If
licensing requirements, qualification requirements or technical standards relating to services sectors, in which specific commitments are undertaken, do not
meet these criteria *and*, furthermore, nullify or impair the specific commitments
undertaken in a manner which could not reasonably have been expected at the
time the commitments were made, the Member acts inconsistently with its obligations under Article VI:5(a) of the GATS.[289] The Member must then amend the
licensing requirement, qualification requirement or technical standard at issue.

Note that Article VI:4 of the GATS gives the Council for Trade in Services a
broad and ambitious mandate to develop the multilateral disciplines necessary
to ensure that licensing requirements, qualification requirements and procedures
and technical standards do not constitute *unnecessary barriers* to trade in services. To date, such disciplines have only been successfully developed with regard
to accountancy.[290]

Note also that Article XVIII, entitled 'Additional Commitments', provides:

> Members may negotiate commitments with respect to measures affecting trade in services
> not subject to scheduling under Articles XVI or XVII, including those regarding qualifica-
> tions, standards or licensing matters. Such commitments shall be inscribed in a Member's
> Schedule.

Members may therefore make commitments with respect to measures which are
neither market access barriers (Article XVI) nor inconsistent with the national
treatment obligation (Article XVII). These additional commitments are recorded

289 In determining whether a Member is in conformity with the obligation under Article VI:5(a), account shall
    be taken of international standards of relevant international organisations applied by that Member. See
    Article VII:5(b) of the GATS.
290 See Council for Trade in Services, *Disciplines on Domestic Regulation in the Accountancy Sector*, adopted on
    14 December 1998, S/L/64, dated 17 December 1998. While adopted in 1998, these disciplines are not yet in
    force.

in the fourth column of a Member's Schedule.[291] In practice, such commitments are uncommon in most services sectors. However, with regard to basic telecommunication services, many Members took additional commitments regarding transparency, licensing, competition and universal service in the telecommunication sector. They did so by inserting in the fourth column of their Schedule any or all of the provisions of the *Reference Paper on Basic Telecommunications* containing pro-competitive regulatory principles.[292]

5.4 Government Procurement Laws and Practices

As discussed above in the context of trade in goods, government procurement laws and practices often constitute significant barriers to trade as governments give preferences to domestic services or service suppliers over foreign services or service suppliers. The GATS, like the GATT 1994 with regard to government procurement of goods, does not set forth any multilateral disciplines on the procurement of services for governmental purposes. Article XIII:1 of the GATS provides:

> Articles II, XVI and XVII shall not apply to laws, regulations or requirements governing the procurement by governmental agencies of services purchased for governmental purposes and not with a view to commercial resale or with a view to use in the supply of services for commercial sale.

The general MFN treatment obligation (of Article II) and specific commitments on market access and national treatment (of Articles XVI and XVII respectively) do not, generally speaking, apply to laws, regulations or requirements governing government procurement of services. However, Article XIII:2 provides for multilateral negotiations on government procurement of services, which are currently taking place as part of the Doha Round of negotiations.

Note that the plurilateral WTO *Agreement on Government Procurement*, discussed above, applies not only to government procurement of goods but also to government procurement of services. The plurilateral disciplines set forth in that Agreement also apply to laws and regulations on the government procurement of services.[293]

5.5 Other Measures and Actions

In addition to lack of transparency, unfair or arbitrary application of measures affecting trade in services, licensing and qualification requirements, technical standards and government procurement laws and practices, trade in services is impeded by a number of other measures and actions. This section briefly

291 See above, p. 526.
292 Such additional commitments were at issue in *Mexico – Telecoms (2004)*.
293 See above, p. 509.

addresses the following: (1) lack of recognition of foreign diplomas and professional certificates; (2) monopolies and exclusive service providers; and (3) international payments and transfers.

Foreign service suppliers, such as doctors, engineers, nurses, lawyers or accountants, will usually have obtained their *diplomas and professional certificates* in their country of origin and will not have diplomas or professional certificates of other countries in which they may wish to be active. Members are required to provide for adequate procedures, in sectors where specific commitments regarding professional services are undertaken, to verify the competence of professionals from any other Member.[294] However, it is clear that, even with these procedures, having only a foreign diploma or professional certificate may constitute an important impediment for persons to supply services in other Members. While WTO law does not require that Members recognise foreign diplomas or professional certificates, it encourages and facilitates their recognition. As discussed in Chapter 4 of this book, the GATS does so by allowing Members to deviate, under certain conditions, from the basic MFN treatment obligation of Article II of the GATS.[295] Article VII:1 of the GATS provides in relevant part:

[A] Member may recognize the education or experience obtained, requirements met, or licences or certifications granted in *a particular country*.[296]

Pursuant to Article VII:1, such recognition: (1) may be achieved through harmonisation *or* otherwise; and (2) may be based upon an agreement with the country concerned *or* may be accorded autonomously. However, the recognition must be based on objective criteria, and may not discriminate among Members where similar conditions prevail. As discussed in Chapter 4, Members who are parties to recognition agreements are required to afford adequate opportunity for other interested Members to negotiate their accession to such agreements or negotiate comparable agreements with them. If recognition is accorded on an autonomous basis, the Member concerned must give adequate opportunity for any other Member concerned to demonstrate that qualifications acquired in its territory should be recognised. Members must notify the Council for Trade in Services of all existing recognition measures.[297] In the long term, Members aim at adopting common standards for the recognition of diplomas and professional qualifications. A first effort in this respect has been the *Guidelines for Mutual Recognition Agreements or Arrangements in the Accountancy Sector*, agreed upon by the Council for Trade in Services in May 1997.[298]

While *monopolies* or *exclusive service suppliers* can obviously impede trade in services, WTO law does not prohibit them. It is common for governments to

---

294 See Article VI:6 of the GATS.   295 See above, p. 345.   296 Emphasis added.

297 See Article VII:4 of the GATS. They must also inform the Council of the opening of negotiations on a recognition agreement in order to give any other Member the opportunity to indicate an interest in participating in the negotiations.

298 See S/L/38, dated 28 May 1997. Negotiations on these guidelines were conducted in the WTO Working Party on Professional Services. See WPPS/W/12/Rev.1, dated 20 May 1997.

grant entities an exclusive right to supply certain services, such as rail transport, telecommunications, sanitation, etc. However, pursuant to Article VIII:1 of the GATS, a Member must ensure that:

> any monopoly supplier of a service in its territory does not, in the supply of the monopoly service in the relevant market, act in a manner inconsistent with that Member's obligations under Article II and specific commitments.

A Member must also ensure that, when a monopoly supplier competes in the supply of a service outside the scope of its monopoly rights, the Member does not abuse its monopoly position inconsistent with its commitments regarding that service.[299] These obligations also apply with regard to exclusive service suppliers, subject to the conditions set out in Article VIII:5.[300] Business practices, other than monopolies, may also hinder competition and thereby restrict trade in services. Article IX of the GATS requires Members, at the request of any other Member, to enter into consultations with a view to eliminating such practices.

It is obvious that restrictions on *international transfers and payments for services* can constitute a barrier to trade in services. Article XI:1 of the GATS requires Members not to apply any restriction on international transfers and payments related to services covered by specific commitments. However, Article XI:2 allows the use of exchange controls or exchange restrictions in certain situations, such as serious balance-of-payments difficulties within the meaning of Article XII, or when such exchange actions are requested by the IMF.

Questions and Assignments 7.15

Briefly describe the GATS rules on transparency and the unfair and arbitrary application of measures affecting trade in services. Does the GATS lay down rules with respect to internal regulation other than market access barriers? Are there any GATS rules regarding the recognition of diplomas and professional qualifications? Are there any WTO rules on government procurement of services?

6   SUMMARY

Market access for goods and services from other countries can be, and frequently is, impeded or restricted in various ways. There are two main categories of barriers to market access: tariff barriers, discussed in Chapter 6; and non-tariff barriers, the focus of this chapter. While tariff barriers have been systematically reduced since the late 1940s as a result of successive rounds of tariff negotiations, non-tariff barriers have in recent decades gradually become an ever more

---

299 See Article VIII:2 of the GATS.

300 The panel in *China – Electronic Payment Services (2012)* distinguished 'monopoly suppliers' from 'exclusive service suppliers'. See Panel Report, *China – Electronic Payment Services (2012)*, paras. 7.585–7.587.

prominent instrument of protection. The non-tariff barriers discussed in this chapter include: (1) quantitative restrictions on trade in goods: (2) 'other non-tariff barriers' on trade in goods; (3) market access barriers to trade in services; and (4) other barriers to trade in services. Note, however, that this chapter does not deal with technical barriers to trade, and sanitary and phytosanitary measures. The rules on these 'other non-tariff barriers' are discussed in Chapters 13 and 14 of this book respectively. This chapter does not deal either with non-tariff barriers to trade resulting from the lack of effective protection of intellectual property rights. The WTO rules addressing these barriers are dealt with in Chapter 15 of this book.

A quantitative restriction on trade in goods is a measure which *limits the quantity* of a product that may be imported or exported. Quantitative restrictions take many forms, including bans, quotas and import or export licences. Article XI:1 of the GATT 1994 sets out a general prohibition on quantitative restrictions, whether on imports or exports. Unlike other GATT provisions, Article XI refers not to laws or regulations but more broadly to measures. A measure instituted or maintained by a Member, which restricts imports or exports, is covered by Article XI, *irrespective* of the legal status of the measure. Furthermore, quantitative restrictions which do not *actually* impede trade are nevertheless prohibited under Article XI:1 of the GATT 1994. Also note that restrictions of a *de facto* nature are also prohibited under Article XI:1 of the GATT 1994.

While quantitative restrictions are, as a rule, prohibited, there are many exceptions to this prohibition. Article XIII of the GATT 1994 sets out rules on the *administration* of these GATT-consistent quantitative restrictions. Article XIII:1 of the GATT 1994 provides that quantitative restrictions, when applied, should be administered in a non-discriminatory manner. According to Article XIII:2 of the GATT 1994, the distribution of trade still allowed should be as close as possible to what would have been the distribution of trade in the absence of the quantitative restriction. Furthermore, Article XIII:2 sets out a number of requirements to be met when imposing quotas. Article XIII:2(d) provides that, if no agreement can be reached with all Members having a substantial interest in supplying the product concerned, the quota must be allocated among these Members on the basis of their share of the trade during a previous representative period. Note that the rules set out in Article XIII also apply to tariff rate quotas, even though the latter are not considered to be quantitative restrictions.

Quotas and tariff quotas are usually administered through import-licensing procedures. A trader who wishes to import a product that is subject to a quota or tariff quota must apply for an import licence, i.e. a permit to import. The *Import Licensing Agreement* sets out rules on import licensing. The most important of these rules, set out in Article 1.3, is that the rules for import-licensing procedures shall be neutral in application and administered in a fair and equitable manner.

Trade in goods is also impeded by 'other non-tariff barriers', including: lack of transparency; unfair and arbitrary application of trade laws and regulations; customs formalities and procedures; and government procurement laws and practices. Lack of information, uncertainty or confusion with respect to the trade laws, regulations and procedures applicable in actual or potential export markets is an important barrier to trade in goods. To ensure a high level of *transparency* of its Members' trade laws, regulations and procedures, WTO law requires their publication and notification, as well as the establishment of enquiry points. The *unfair and arbitrary application* of national trade measures, and the degree of uncertainty and unpredictability this generates for other Members and traders, also constitutes a significant barrier to trade in goods. Therefore, WTO law provides for: (1) a requirement of uniform, impartial and reasonable administration of national trade rules; and (2) a requirement of procedures for the objective and impartial review of the administration of national customs rules. The losses that traders suffer through delays at borders and complicated and/or unnecessary documentation requirements and other *customs procedures and formalities* are estimated to exceed the costs of tariffs in many cases. However, WTO law currently contains few rules on customs formalities and procedures aimed at mitigating their adverse impact on trade. The ongoing Doha Round negotiations on trade facilitation may result in more disciplines on customs procedures and formalities. National laws and/or practices relating to the procurement of goods by a government for its own use are often significant barriers to trade. Under such laws or practices, governments frequently buy domestic products rather than imported products. The plurilateral WTO *Agreement on Government Procurement* provides for some disciplines with respect to government procurement. However, it does so only for the forty-two Members that are currently a party to this Agreement.

As with trade in goods, trade in services is also often subject to restrictions in the form of non-tariff barriers. The production and consumption of services are subject to a vast range of internal regulations. Barriers to trade in services primarily result from these internal regulations. WTO law, and the GATS in particular, provides for rules and disciplines on barriers to trade in services. A distinction must be made between: (1) market access barriers; and (2) other barriers to trade in services.

Article XVI:2 of the GATS contains an *exhaustive* list of *market access barriers*. This list comprises six types of market access barriers: five of these types are quantitative restrictions (sub-paragraphs (a) to (d) and (f)); and one type is a limitation on the kind of legal entity or joint venture through which services may be supplied (sub-paragraph (e)). These market access barriers can be discriminatory *or* non-discriminatory with regard to foreign services or service suppliers. Four of the five types of quantitative restrictions referred to in Article

XVI:2 can be expressed numerically, or through the criteria specified in these provisions, such as an economic needs test. It is important, however, that these criteria do not relate to: (1) the quality of the service supplied; or (2) the ability of the supplier to supply the service (i.e. technical standards or qualification of the supplier). The GATS does not provide for a general prohibition of market access barriers. Whether a Member may maintain or adopt market access barriers with regard to a specific service depends on whether, and if so to what extent, that Member has made market access commitments with regard to the relevant services sector in its Schedule of Specific Commitments, i.e. its Services Schedule. When a Member makes a market access commitment, it binds the level of market access specified in its Services Schedule (see Article XVI:1) and agrees not to impose any market access barrier that would restrict access to the market beyond the level specified (see Article XVI:2).

To achieve *progressively* higher levels of liberalisation of trade in services, the GATS provides for *successive* rounds of negotiations on further market access and national treatment commitments. The approach to negotiations on the liberalisation of services is a request-and-offer approach. It is accepted that developing-country Members undertake fewer and more limited market access commitments than developed-country Members. The terms, limitations and conditions on *market access* agreed to in the negotiations are set out in the second column of the Services Schedules. Each Member has a Services Schedule, and these Schedules, all annexed to the GATS, form an integral part thereof, and are to be interpreted accordingly. Like tariff concessions for goods, market access commitments for services can also be modified or withdrawn. To do so, the procedure set out in Article XXI of the GATS must be followed.

In addition to market access barriers, trade in services can also be impeded by a wide array of other barriers. With regard to a number of these other barriers, WTO law, and in particular the GATS, provides for specific rules. The GATS requires the prompt *publication* of all measures of general application affecting trade in services. It also requires Members to establish *enquiry points* to provide information on laws and regulations affecting trade in services. Furthermore, the GATS requires Members to ensure that all measures of general application affecting trade in services with regard to which specific commitments were made are administered in a *reasonable, objective and impartial* manner. As noted above, trade in services is primarily impeded or restricted by internal regulation. Most internal regulations do not constitute market access barriers within the meaning of Article XVI:2. Apart from the rules concerning transparency and the rules on unfair and arbitrary application, the GATS currently only provides for a few other disciplines applicable to internal regulations which do not constitute market access barriers. The most important of these disciplines concerns licensing requirements, qualification requirements, and technical standards. These requirements and standards must: (1) be based on objective and transparent criteria such as competence and the ability to supply the service; (2) not be more burdensome than necessary to ensure the quality of the service; and (3) in the case of licensing procedures, not be, in themselves, a restriction on the supply of the service. Finally, note that the GATS encourages and facilitates the recognition of diplomas and professional certificates of foreign service suppliers.

Exercise 7: Shoe Ease

Shoe Comfort Inc. is a footwear manufacturer from Small Rapids, Newland. Shoe Comfort produces a very successful model of men's shoes under the name of Shoe Ease. In recent years, these cheap but well-made and trendy shoes have become very popular among young people in the European Union. The European Union, and (within the EU) Italy, Spain and Portugal in particular, have a long tradition in shoe-making and were once the world's biggest shoe producers. Now, the EU's shoe industry is struggling and employment in this industry is falling dramatically.

Fearing the further demise of its once great shoe industry, the European Union decides to limit the importation of men's shoes to 100 million pairs per year. This quota is divided among China (60 million pairs), Vietnam (20 million pairs) and others (20 million pairs). Last year, Newland exported as many shoes to the European Union as did Vietnam. While the quota of 100 million pairs per year was published in the EU's *Official Journal*, the allocation of this quota was made public on the website of the Directorate General for Trade of the European Commission, and this was done so three working days before the quota took effect. Foreign footwear manufacturers, such as Shoe Comfort, must apply for an import licence. Import licences are granted by the newly established EU Shoe Import Board, on which also the representatives of the EU shoe industry sit. Importers can appeal decisions by the EU Shoe Import Board, but such appeals can only be brought to the EU Trade Commissioner. The European Union not only imposes a quota on shoes, it also requires that all shoes be imported through the port of Valletta, Malta. No reason was given for this requirement.

Several EU Member States have regulations in place requiring government departments and the armed forces to buy European shoes only. Also, all shoe-repair work must be done by European companies.

Undeterred by the import quota and the other measures referred to above (which, it is confident, will soon be withdrawn), Shoe Comfort wants to set up its own chain of Shoe Ease shops in Europe. However, it is informed by the Spanish Ministerio de Economía y Competitividad that under the 'Ley de Protección de Pequeños Comerciantes' (the 'Small Shopkeepers Protection Act') of 1976, the number of shoe retail shops in a specific area is limited on the basis of an economic needs test. Moreover, under the 'Ley de Identidad Cultural' (the

'*Cultural Identity Act*') of 1998, all retail shopkeepers in Spain must have Spanish nationality and speak Spanish.

A subsidiary company of Shoe Comfort, BuyItNow, has acquired significant expertise in advertising Shoe Ease shoes and intends to offer advertising services to European shoe retailers, either via the Internet or by sending its experts to Europe. The French authorities, however, inform BuyItNow that only persons holding European professional qualifications, or qualifications recognised as equivalent, can supply advertising services in France. While the Government of Newland has tried to get the diplomas and professional certificates awarded in Newland recognised by the European Union, such efforts have been to no avail to date.

You are Shoe Comfort's young (but brilliant) in-house international trade lawyer working at the corporate headquarters in Small Rapids, Newland. You have been asked to prepare a legal brief on the WTO consistency of the trade barriers referred to above.

8 General and Security Exceptions

CONTENTS

1 INTRODUCTION

The promotion and protection of public health, consumer safety, the environment, employment, economic development and national security are *core* tasks of governments. Often, trade liberalisation and the resulting availability of better and cheaper products and services facilitate the promotion and protection of these and other societal values and interests. Through trade, environmentally friendly products or life-saving medicines, that would not be available otherwise, become available to consumers and patients respectively. At a more general level, trade generates the degree of economic activity and economic welfare that enables governments effectively to promote and protect the societal values and interests referred to above.

In order to protect and promote these societal values and interests, however, governments also adopt legislation or take measures that, inadvertently or deliberately, constitute barriers to trade. Members may be, politically and/or economically, 'compelled' to adopt legislation or measures, which are inconsistent with rules of WTO law and, in particular, with the rules on non-discrimination and the rules on market access, discussed in Chapters 4, 5, 6 and 7 of this book. Trade liberalisation, market access and non-discrimination rules may conflict with other important societal values and interests. WTO law recognises this and, therefore, provides for a set of rules to reconcile trade liberalisation, market access and non-discrimination rules with the need to protect and promote other societal values and interests. As the 2004 Sutherland Report noted:

> Neither the WTO nor the GATT was ever an unrestrained free trade charter. In fact, both were and are intended to provide a structured and functionally effective way to harness the value of open trade to principle and fairness. In so doing they offer the security and predictability of market access advantages that are sought by traders and investors. But the rules provide checks and balances including mechanisms that reflect political realism as well as free trade doctrine. It is not that the WTO disallows market protection, only that it sets some strict disciplines under which governments may choose to respond to special interests.[1]

This chapter and the next two chapters, Chapters 9 and 10, address the wide-ranging *exceptions* to the basic WTO rules, allowing Members to adopt trade-restrictive legislation and measures that pursue the promotion and protection of other societal values and interests. This chapter deals with the 'general exceptions' as well as the 'security exceptions'. Chapter 9 deals with the 'economic emergency exceptions';[2] and Chapter 10 discusses the 'regional trade exceptions'.[3] These exceptions differ in scope and nature. Some allow deviation from all GATT or GATS obligations; others allow deviation from specific obligations only; some are of indefinite duration; others temporary. However, while different in scope and nature, all the exceptions have something in common: they allow Members, under specific conditions, to adopt and maintain legislation and measures that promote or protect other important societal values and interests,

---

1 Report by the Consultative Board to the Director-General Supachai Panitchpakdi, The Future of the WTO: Addressing Institutional Challenges in the New Millennium ('Sutherland Report') (WTO, 2004), para. 39. Emphasis omitted.
2 See below, pp. 606–47.
3 As explained above, WTO law provisions providing for special and differential treatment of developing-country Members and least-developed-country Members are not discussed in a separate chapter of this book, but are discussed together with the rules from which they allow deviation. See above, pp. 648–72.

even though this legislation or these measures are inconsistent with substantive disciplines imposed by the GATT 1994 or the GATS. These exceptions clearly allow Members, under specific conditions, to give *priority* to certain societal values and interests *over* trade liberalisation, market access and/or non-discrimination rules.

This chapter focuses on the most widely available of the exceptions, namely, the 'general exceptions' and the 'security exceptions'. This chapter discusses in turn: (1) the 'general exceptions under the GATT 1994'; (2) the 'general exceptions under the GATS'; and (3) the 'security exceptions' under the GATT 1994 and the GATS.[4]

2 GENERAL EXCEPTIONS UNDER THE GATT 1994

Article XX of the GATT 1994, entitled 'General Exceptions', states:

Subject to the requirement that such measures are not applied in a manner which would constitute a means of arbitrary or unjustifiable discrimination between countries where the same conditions prevail, or a disguised restriction on international trade, nothing in this Agreement shall be construed to prevent the adoption or enforcement by any [Member] of measures:

(a) necessary to protect public morals;
(b) necessary to protect human, animal or plant life or health;
(c) ...
(d) necessary to secure compliance with laws or regulations which are not inconsistent with the provisions of this Agreement, including those relating to customs enforcement, the enforcement of monopolies operated under paragraph 4 of Article II and Article XVII, the protection of patents, trade marks and copyrights, and the prevention of deceptive practices;
(e) relating to the products of prison labour;
(f) imposed for the protection of national treasures of artistic, historic or archaeological value;
(g) relating to the conservation of exhaustible natural resources if such measures are made effective in conjunction with restrictions on domestic production or consumption ...

Note that paragraphs (c), (h), (i) and (j) of Article XX are not included in the quote above. These paragraphs relate to trade in gold and silver (see paragraph (c)); obligations under international commodities agreements (see paragraph (h)); efforts to ensure essential quantities of materials to a domestic processing

---

4 Note that other agreements contain 'exceptions' or 'flexibilities' addressing the same concerns. They are discussed, together with those agreements, in other parts of this book. Consider, for example, the 'flexibility' in Article 2.1 of the *TBT Agreement* or the exceptions in Articles 8 and 31 of the *TRIPS Agreement*. See below, pp. 863, 955 and 994, respectively.

industry (see paragraph (i)); and the acquisition or distribution of products in general or local short supply (see paragraph (j)). To date, these paragraphs have been of less importance in international trade law and practice. Therefore, they are not discussed in this chapter.

2.1   Key Features of Article XX of the GATT 1994

This sub-section discusses the key features of Article XX of the GATT 1994 and addresses first the nature and function of Article XX, and then its scope of application.

2.1.1   Nature and Function of Article XX

The panel in *US – Section 337 Tariff Act (1989)* noted with respect to the nature and function of Article XX:

> that Article XX is entitled 'General Exceptions' and that the central phrase in the introductory clause reads: 'nothing in this Agreement shall be construed to prevent the adoption or enforcement ... of measures ... '. Article XX(d) thus provides for a limited and conditional exception from obligations under other provisions. The Panel therefore concluded that Article XX(d) applies only to measures inconsistent with another provision of the General Agreement, and that, consequently, the application of Section 337 has to be examined first in the light of Article III:4. If any inconsistencies with Article III:4 were found, the Panel would then examine whether they could be justified under Article XX(d).[5]

Article XX is relevant, and will be invoked by a Member, *only* when a measure of that Member has been found to be inconsistent with another GATT provision. In such a case, Article XX will be invoked to justify the GATT-inconsistent measure. As the panel in *US – Section 337 Tariff Act (1989)* noted, the central phrase in the first sentence of Article XX is that 'nothing in this Agreement shall be construed to prevent the adoption or enforcement by any [Member] of measures ...'. Measures satisfying the conditions set out in Article XX are thus permitted, even if they are inconsistent with other provisions of the GATT 1994. As noted by the panel in *US – Section 337 Tariff Act (1989)*, Article XX provides, however, for *limited and conditional exceptions* from obligations under other GATT provisions. The exceptions are 'limited' as the list of exceptions in Article XX is exhaustive. The exceptions are 'conditional' in that Article XX only provides for justification of an otherwise GATT-inconsistent measure when the conditions set out in Article XX – and discussed in detail below – are fulfilled. While Article XX allows Members to adopt or maintain measures promoting or protecting other important societal values, it provides an exception to, or limitation of, affirmative commitments under the GATT 1994. In this light, it is not surprising that Article XX has played a prominent role in many GATT and WTO disputes.

---

5 Panel Report, *US – Section 337 Tariff Act (1989)*, para. 5.9.

It could be argued that it is an accepted principle of interpretation that exceptions are to be interpreted narrowly (*singularia non sunt extendenda*) and that Article XX should, therefore, be interpreted narrowly. However, the Appellate Body does not seem to have adopted this approach. Instead, it has followed in *US – Gasoline (1996)* and *US – Shrimp (1998)* an approach which seeks to balance the affirmative commitments and the exceptions. It stated with regard to Article XX(g), the exception at issue in those cases, the following:

The context of Article XX(g) includes the provisions of the rest of the *General Agreement*, including in particular Articles I, III and XI; conversely, the context of Articles I and III and XI includes Article XX. Accordingly, the phrase 'relating to the conservation of exhaustible natural resources' may not be read so expansively as seriously to subvert the purpose and object of Article III:4. Nor may Article III:4 be given so broad a reach as effectively to emasculate Article XX(g) and the policies and interests it embodies. The relationship between the affirmative commitments set out in, e.g. Articles I, III and XI, and the policies and interests embodied in the 'General Exceptions' listed in Article XX, can be given meaning within the framework of the *General Agreement* and its object and purpose by a treaty interpreter only on a case-to-case basis, by careful scrutiny of the factual and legal context in a given dispute, without disregarding the words actually used by the WTO Members themselves to express their intent and purpose.[6]

This does not reflect a restrictive interpretation by the Appellate Body of the exceptions of Article XX of the GATT 1994. Rather, the Appellate Body strikes a *balance* between, on the one hand, trade liberalisation, market access and non-discrimination rules and, on the other hand, other societal values and interests. Article XX is in essence a *balancing* provision.

With regard to the nature and function of Article XX, finally note that the Appellate Body stated in *Thailand – Cigarettes (Philippines) (2011)* that:

[i]t is true that, in examining a specific measure, a panel may be called upon to analyze a substantive obligation and an affirmative defence, and to apply both to that measure. It is also true that such an exercise will require a panel to find and apply a 'line of equilibrium' between a substantive obligation and an exception. Yet this does not render that panel's analyses of the obligation and the exception a single and integrated one. On the contrary, an analysis of whether a measure infringes an obligation necessarily precedes, and is distinct from, the 'further and separate' assessment of whether such measure is otherwise justified.[7]

In this case, Thailand argued that the Appellate Body should also reverse its finding of inconsistency with Article III:4 of the GATT 1994 after, and because, it had found that the panel erred in its analysis of Thailand's Article XX(d) defence. The Appellate Body refused to do so because the Article III:4 analysis and the Article XX(d) analysis are distinct and separate.

---

6 Appellate Body Report, *US – Gasoline (1996)*, 18.
7 Appellate Body Report, *Thailand – Cigarettes (Philippines) (2011)*, para. 173.

2.1.2   Scope of Application of Article XX

As noted above, some exceptions discussed in this and the next chapters allow deviation from all GATT or GATS obligations, while other exceptions allow deviation from specific obligations only. Article XX allows, under specific conditions, deviation from *all* GATT obligations. In other words, Article XX may justify inconsistency with *any* of the GATT obligations, be it Article I:1 (MFN treatment), Article II:1 (tariff concessions), Articles III:2 and III:4 (national treatment), Article XI:1 (quantitative restrictions) or any other obligation under the GATT 1994. As discussed above, Article XX states that '*nothing* in this Agreement shall be construed to prevent the adoption or enforcement by any [Member] of measures ...'.[8] In this sense, the scope of application of Article XX is broad.

The question has arisen whether Article XX may also justify inconsistency with obligations set out in WTO agreements other than the GATT 1994. In *China – Publications and Audiovisual Products (2010)*, China invoked Article XX(a) in order to justify measures that the panel found to be inconsistent with China's trading rights commitments under its Accession Protocol.[9] China invoked Article XX, relying upon the introductory clause of paragraph 5.1 of its Accession Protocol, which reads:

Without prejudice to China's right to regulate trade in a manner consistent with the WTO Agreement ...

The panel in this case stated that:

China's invocation of Article XX(a) presents complex legal issues. We observe in this respect that Article XX contains the phrase 'nothing in this Agreement', with the term 'Agreement' referring to the GATT 1994, not other agreements like the Accession Protocol. The issue therefore arises whether Article XX can be directly invoked as a defence to a breach of China's trading rights commitments under the Accession Protocol, which appears to be China's position, or whether Article XX could be invoked only as a defence to a breach of a GATT 1994 obligation.[10]

However, rather than resolving the issue whether China could invoke Article XX, the panel decided to proceed on the assumption that Article XX was available to China, and to examine first whether the measures found to be inconsistent with China's Accession Protocol satisfied the requirements of Article XX.[11] This examination led the panel to the conclusion that the measures concerned could not be justified under Article XX. The panel in *China – Publications and Audiovisual Products (2010)* thus never ruled on the availability of Article XX.[12] However, unlike the panel, the Appellate Body did address this issue.[13] According to the

---

8 Emphasis added.
9 Appellate Body Report, *China – Publications and Audiovisual Products (2010)*, para. 205.
10 Panel Report, *China – Publications and Audiovisual Products (2010)*, para. 7.743.
11 See *ibid.*, para. 7.745.   12 See *ibid.*, para. 8.2(a)(ii).
13 While recognising that reliance upon an assumption *arguendo* is a legal technique that an adjudicator may use in order to enhance simplicity and efficiency in decision-making, the Appellate Body criticised the panel's reliance on this technique with respect to the availability of Article XX of the GATT 1994 in this case. See Appellate Body Report, *China – Publications and Audiovisual Products (2010)*, para. 215.

Appellate Body, the phrase 'China's right to regulate trade' in paragraph 5.1 of China's Accession Protocol is a reference to its power to subject international commerce to regulation. This power may not be impaired by China's obligation to grant the right to trade, *provided that* China regulates trade 'in a manner consistent with the WTO Agreement'.[14] The Appellate Body observed that:

> the reference to China's power to regulate trade 'in a manner consistent with the WTO Agreement' seems to us to encompass both China's power to take regulatory action provided that its measures satisfy prescribed WTO disciplines and meet specified conditions (for example, an SPS measure that conforms to the *SPS Agreement*) and China's power to take regulatory action that derogates from WTO obligations that would otherwise constrain China's exercise of such power – that is, to relevant exceptions.[15]

The Appellate Body subsequently considered that the measures that China sought to justify have 'a clearly discernible, objective link to China's regulation of trade in the relevant products'.[16] In light of this relationship between, on the one hand, the measures that are inconsistent with China's trading rights commitments, and, on the other hand, China's regulation of trade in the relevant products, the Appellate Body found that China could rely upon the introductory clause of paragraph 5.1 of its Accession Protocol and that, therefore, in this particular case, Article XX was available to justify measures inconsistent with China's Accession Protocol, i.e. inconsistent with a WTO agreement other than the GATT 1994.[17]

The question of whether Article XX is available to justify measures inconsistent with WTO agreements other than the GATT 1994 arose again in *China – Raw Materials (2012)*, when China sought to justify under Article XX(g) export duties found to be inconsistent with the obligations under paragraph 11.3 of its Accession Protocol.[18] Paragraph 11.3 requires China to eliminate export duties unless such duties are 'specifically provided for in Annex 6' to China's Accession Protocol. Annex 6 in turn provides for maximum export duty levels on eighty-four listed products. The Note to Annex 6 clarifies that the maximum rates set out in Annex 6 'will not be exceeded'. After careful examination of paragraph 11.3 and related provisions of China's Accession Protocol, the Appellate Body upheld the panel in this case, which had concluded that paragraph 11.3 does not make available to China the exceptions under Article XX of the GATT 1994.[19] In coming to this conclusion, the Appellate Body noted, *inter alia*, that there is no language in paragraph 11.3 similar to that found in paragraph 5.1 of China's Accession Protocol, namely, 'without prejudice to China's right to regulate trade in a manner consistent with the WTO Agreement'.[20] As discussed above, it was the latter language which made the Appellate Body decide in *China – Publications and Audiovisual Products (2010)* that Article XX was available as a defence

14 See Appellate Body Report, *China – Publications and Audiovisual Products (2010)*, para. 221.
15 *Ibid.*, para. 228. See also *ibid.*, para. 223.   16 *Ibid.*, para. 233.   17 See *ibid.*
18 On the inconsistency of export duties with para. 11.3 of China's Accession Protocol, see above, p. 472.
19 See Appellate Body Reports, *China – Raw Materials (2012)*, para. 307.
20 See *ibid.*, para. 304.

550 General and Security Exceptions

in that particular case.[21] In *China – Raw Materials (2012)*, the Appellate Body upheld the panel's finding that, in the case at hand, Article XX was *not* available to justify measures inconsistent with China's Accession Protocol.[22]

In *China – Raw Materials (2012)*, the panel and the Appellate Body noted that WTO Members have, on occasion, incorporated, by cross-reference, the provisions of Article XX of the GATT 1994 into other covered agreements.[23] By way of example, they referred to Article 3 of the *TRIMs Agreement*, which states that '[a]ll exceptions under GATT 1994 shall apply, as appropriate, to the provisions of this Agreement'. In such instances, the availability of Article XX to justify measures inconsistent with obligations under WTO agreements other than the GATT 1994 is of course a non-issue.

Apart from the question whether Article XX may apply to measures inconsistent with WTO agreements other than the GATT 1994, also other questions regarding the scope of application have arisen. With regard to the *kind* of measure that can be justified under Article XX, the panel in *US – Shrimp (1998)* ruled that Article XX could not justify measures that 'undermine the WTO multilateral trading system'.[24] The measure at issue in *US – Shrimp (1998)* was a US measure, which required India, Pakistan, Thailand and Malaysia to harvest shrimp in the manner set out in US law if they wanted to import this shrimp into the United States. The panel found that a measure of a Member 'conditioning access to its market for a given product upon the adoption by the exporting Member of certain policies' would undermine the multilateral trading system.[25] On appeal, however, the Appellate Body categorically rejected this panel's finding on the scope of measures that Article XX can justify. The Appellate Body held that:

conditioning access to a Member's domestic market on whether exporting Members comply with, or adopt, a policy or policies unilaterally prescribed by the importing Member may, to some degree, be a common aspect of measures falling within the scope of one or another of the exceptions (a) to (j) of Article XX. Paragraphs (a) to (j) comprise measures that are recognized as *exceptions to substantive obligations* established in the GATT 1994, because the domestic policies embodied in such measures have been recognized as important and legitimate in character. It is not necessary to assume that requiring from exporting countries compliance with, or adoption of, certain policies (although covered in principle by one or another of the exceptions) prescribed by the importing country, renders a measure *a priori* incapable of justification under Article XX. Such an interpretation renders most, if not all, of the specific exceptions of Article XX inutile, a result abhorrent to the principles of interpretation we are bound to apply.[26]

---

21 See above, p. 549.
22 See Appellate Body Reports, *China – Raw Materials (2012)*, para. 307. Note, however, that Article XX of the GATT 1994 was available in *China – Raw Materials (2012)* with regard to the export restrictions, inconsistent with Article XI:1 of the GATT 1994, also at issue in that case. See above, p. 486.
23 See Appellate Body Reports, *China – Raw Materials (2012)*, para. 303. See also Panel Reports, *China – Raw Materials (2012)*, para. 7.153.
24 Panel Report, *US – Shrimp (1998)*, para. 7.44.   25 *Ibid.*, para. 7.45.
26 Appellate Body Report, *US – Shrimp (1998)*, para. 121.

Measures requiring that exporting countries comply with, or adopt, certain policies prescribed by the importing country are, in fact, typical of the measures that
Article XX *can* justify. They are definitely not *a priori* excluded from the scope
of application of Article XX.

Another question relating to the scope of application of Article XX is whether
Article XX can also justify measures that protect, or purport to protect, a societal value or interest outside the territorial jurisdiction of the Member taking the measure – for example an import prohibition imposed by Richland on
aluminium from Newland that is produced at very low cost but in a manner
detrimental to the environment in Newland. To date, the Appellate Body has
yet to rule whether such measures that protect, or purport to protect, a societal
value or interest outside the territorial jurisdiction of the Member taking the
measure, can be justified under Article XX. There is no *explicit* jurisdictional
limitation in Article XX. However, is there an *implied* jurisdictional limitation,
so that Article XX cannot be invoked to protect non-economic values *outside*
the territorial jurisdiction of the Member concerned? In *US – Shrimp (1998)*, a
case involving an import ban on shrimp harvested through methods resulting
in the incidental killing of sea turtles, the Appellate Body noted that sea turtles
migrate to or traverse waters subject to the jurisdiction of the United States, and
subsequently stated:

> We do not pass upon the question of whether there is an implied jurisdictional limitation
> in Article XX(g), and if so, the nature or extent of that limitation. We note only that in the
> specific circumstances of the case before us, there is a sufficient nexus between the migra-
> tory and endangered marine populations involved and the United States for purposes of
> Article XX(g).[27]

While the position of the Appellate Body on the question of the extra-territorial
application of Article XX is still undetermined, the panel in *EC – Tariff Preferences (2004)* found that:

> the policy reflected in the Drug Arrangements is not one designed for the purpose of pro-
> tecting human life or health *in the European Communities* and, therefore, the Drug Arrange-
> ments are not a measure for the purpose of protecting human life or health under Article
> XX(b) of GATT 1994.[28]

Questions and Assignments 8.1

When can a Member invoke Article XX of the GATT 1994? Which societal values are
covered by Article XX? Give at least two examples of non-economic, societal values that

27 *Ibid.*, para. 133.
28 Panel Report, *EC – Tariff Preferences (2004)*, para. 7.210. Emphasis added. The panel in *US – Tuna (1994)*
    noted, in an unadopted report, that it could not be said that the GATT proscribed in an absolute manner
    measures that related to things or actions outside the territorial jurisdiction of the party taking the measure.
    See Panel Report, *US – Tuna (1994)*, para. 5.16. The panel stated that: '[it] could see no valid reason support-
    ing the conclusion that the provisions of Article XX(g) apply only to policies related to the conservation of
    exhaustible natural resources located within the territory of the contracting party invoking the provision.' See
    ibid., para. 5.20. The panel therefore found that the policy to conserve dolphins in the eastern tropical Pacific
    Ocean, which the United States pursued within its jurisdiction over its nationals and vessels, fell within the
    range of policies covered by Article XX(g).

are *not* explicitly referred to in Article XX. Does Article XX provide for an exhaustive list of grounds of exception? If so, what are the advantages and the disadvantages of such a closed-list approach? Can Article XX be invoked to justify measures inconsistent with WTO agreements other than the GATT 1994? What did the Appellate Body rule in *US – Shrimp (1998)* regarding the kinds of measure that may be justified under Article XX? Would a measure by the European Union to protect the biodiversity of tropical forests in Africa fall within the scope of application of Article XX?

2.2   Two-Tier Test Under Article XX of the GATT 1994

Article XX sets out a two-tier test for determining whether a measure, otherwise inconsistent with GATT obligations, can be justified. In *US – Gasoline (1996)*, the Appellate Body stated:

> In order that the justifying protection of Article XX may be extended to it, the measure at issue must not only come under one or another of the particular exceptions – paragraphs (a) to (j) – listed under Article XX; it must also satisfy the requirements imposed by the opening clauses of Article XX. The analysis is, in other words, two-tiered: first, provisional justification by reason of characterization of the measure under Article XX(g); second, further appraisal of the same measure under the introductory clauses of Article XX.[29]

Thus, for a GATT-inconsistent measure to be justified under Article XX, it must meet: (1) the requirements of one of the exceptions listed in paragraphs (a) to (j) of Article XX; and (2) the requirements of the introductory clauses, commonly referred to as the 'chapeau', of Article XX. The Appellate Body further clarified, in *US – Shrimp (1998)*, that, to determine whether a measure can be justified under Article XX, one must always examine, first, whether this measure can be provisionally justified under one of the specific exceptions listed in paragraphs (a) to (j) of Article XX; and, if so, whether the application of this measure meets the requirements of the chapeau of Article XX.[30] Hence, an analysis under Article XX first focuses on the measure at issue itself and then on the application of that measure. This distinction between the two elements of the Article XX test is well illustrated by the panel in *Brazil – Retreaded Tyres (2007)*:

> [In its analysis under Article XX(b)] [t]he Panel will *not* … examine … the manner in which the measure is implemented *in practice*, including any elements extraneous to the measure itself that could affect its ability to perform its function … or consider situations in which the ban does *not* apply … These elements will, however, be relevant to later parts of the Panel's assessment, especially under the chapeau of Article XX, where the focus will be, by contrast, primarily on the manner in which the measure is applied.[31]

---

29 Appellate Body Report, *US – Gasoline (1996)*, 22. See also Appellate Body Report, *Brazil – Retreaded Tyres (2007)*, para. 139.
30 See Appellate Body Report, *US – Shrimp (1998)*, paras. 119–20.
31 Panel Report, *Brazil – Retreaded Tyres (2007)*, para. 7.107. Emphasis added.

To date, WTO Members have been successful only wise GATT-inconsistent measures under Article XX of important, however, to make two observations in this respec otherwise GATT-inconsistent measures adopted to promote or values, which were initially found non-justifiable under Article X sequently modified (rather than withdrawn) in accordance with the DS mendations and rulings, and were *not* further challenged. Secondly, M adopt or maintain very many otherwise GATT-inconsistent measures to pron or protect societal values, which clearly meet the requirements of Article XX These measures seldom go to WTO dispute settlement. Therefore, the limited success Members have had in invoking Article XX does *not* indicate that Article XX plays only a marginal role in allowing WTO Members to adopt or maintain otherwise GATT-inconsistent measures to promote or protect societal values. Rather, the opposite is true.

The following sub-sections will first discuss the specific exceptions and their requirements provided for in paragraphs (a) to (j) of Article XX, before analysing the requirements of the chapeau of Article XX.

Questions and Assignments 8.2

What are the main elements of the Article XX test? Does the sequence in which these elements of the Article XX test are examined matter?

2.3   Specific Exceptions Under Article XX of the GATT 1994

Article XX sets out, in paragraphs (a) to (j), specific grounds of justification for measures, which are otherwise inconsistent with provisions of the GATT 1994. These grounds of justification relate to the protection of societal values such as human, animal or plant life or health, exhaustible natural resources, national treasures of artistic, historic or archaeological value, and public morals.[33] Comparing the terms used in the different paragraphs of Article XX, the Appellate Body stated in *US – Gasoline (1996)*:

In enumerating the various categories of governmental acts, laws or regulations which WTO Members may carry out or promulgate in pursuit of differing legitimate state policies or

---

32 See *US – Shrimp (Article 21.5 – Malaysia) (2001)*. Article XX of the GATT 1994 was invoked, but 'unsuccessfully' or 'incorrectly' so, in *US – Gasoline (1996)*; *US – Shrimp (1998)*; *EC – Asbestos (2001)*; *Argentina – Hides and Leather (2001)*; *Canada – Wheat Exports and Grain Imports (2004)*; *EC – Tariff Preferences (2004)*; *Dominican Republic – Import and Sale of Cigarettes (2005)*; *EC – Trademarks and Geographical Indications (Australia) (2005)*; *EC – Trademarks and Geographical Indications (US) (2005)*; *Mexico – Taxes on Soft Drinks (2006)*; *Brazil – Retreaded Tyres (2007)*; *US – Customs Bond Directive (2008)*; *US – Shrimp (Thailand) (2008)*; *China – Auto-Parts (2009)*; *Colombia – Ports of Entry (2009)*; *US – Poultry (China) (2010)*; *China – Publications and Audiovisual Products (2010)*; *Thailand – Cigarettes (Philippines) (2011)*; and *China – Raw Materials (2012)*. Note with regard to *EC – Asbestos (2001)* that the Appellate Body found that there was *no* inconsistency with the GATT 1994 that needed to be justified under Article XX. See above, p. 382, footnote 165.

33 As noted above, the list of grounds of justification contained in Article XX of the GATT 1994 is exhaustive. See above, p. 545.

f trade liberalization, Article XX uses different terms in respect
ssary' – in paragraphs (a), (b) and (d); 'essential' – in paragraph
phs (c), (e) and (g); 'for the protection of' – in paragraph (f); 'in
h (h); and 'involving' – in paragraph (i).

to suppose that the WTO Members intended to require, in re-
egory, the same kind or degree of connection or relationship
ppraisal and the state interest or policy sought to be promoted

Article XX contain different requirements regarding the
measure at issue and the societal value pursued. Some
essary' for the protection or promotion of the societal
value they pursue (e.g. the protection of life and health of humans, animals and
plants), while for other measures it suffices that they 'relate to' the societal value
they pursue (e.g. the conservation of exhaustible natural resources). Therefore,
the grounds of justification, and the accompanying requirements provided for
in Article XX, will be examined separately. This sub-section focuses first and
foremost on these grounds of justification, which have been most frequently
invoked in GATT and WTO dispute settlement.

2.3.1   Article XX(b)

Article XX(b) concerns measures which are 'necessary to protect human, animal
or plant life or health'. It sets out a two-tier test to determine whether a measure
is *provisionally* justified under this provision. A GATT-inconsistent measure is
provisionally justified under Article XX(b) if: (1) the policy objective pursued by
the measure is the protection of the life or health of humans, animals or plants;
and (2) the measure is necessary to fulfil that policy objective.[35]

The first element of this test under Article XX(b) is relatively easy to apply
and has not given rise to major interpretative problems. To determine whether
the policy objective pursued by a measure, panels and the Appellate Body have
examined the design and structure of the measure. Overall, they have shown
a significant degree of deference in accepting that the policy objective of a
measure was to protect life or health of humans, animals or plants. The wide
range of measures that has been considered to pursue this policy objective
includes measures to reduce the smoking of cigarettes,[36] measures to reduce air
pollution,[37] and measures to reduce risks arising for the accumulation of waste
tyres.[38] In *Brazil – Retreaded Tyres (2007)*, for example, Brazil submitted with
regard to its import ban on retreaded tyres that:

---

34 Appellate Body Report, *US – Gasoline (1996)*, 17–18.
35 See Panel Report, *US – Gasoline (1996)*, para. 6.20. For a more recent application of this test, see Panel
   Report, *EC – Tariff Preferences (2004)*, paras. 7.179 and 7.199; Panel Report, *Brazil – Retreaded Tyres (2007)*,
   paras. 7.40–7.41; and Panel Reports, *China – Raw Materials (2012)*, paras. 7.479–7.480.
36 See *Thailand – Cigarettes (1990)*.   37 See *US – Gasoline (1996)*.
38 See *Brazil – Retreaded Tyres (2007)*.

ote
mbers
CB recom-
X, were sub-
protect societal
First, many of the
he GATT 1994.[32] It is
once in justifying other-

the accumulation of waste tyres creates a risk of mosquito-borne diseases such as dengue and yellow fever ... because waste tyres create perfect breeding grounds for disease carrying mosquitoes and that these diseases are also spread through interstate transportation of waste tyres for disposal operations ... [The] accumulation of waste tyres [also] creates a risk of tyre fires and toxic leaching ...

... [M]osquito-borne diseases also pose health risks to animals. Numerous toxic chemicals and heavy metals contained in pyrolytic oil released from tyre fires harm animal and plant life and health, and hazardous substances contained in toxic plumes emitted from tyre fires harm not only humans but also animals.[39]

The panel accepted Brazil's arguments, and concluded that:

Brazil's policy of reducing exposure to the risks to human, animal or plant life or health arising from the accumulation of waste tyres falls within the range of policies covered by Article XX(b).[40]

In *China – Raw Materials (2012)*, China submitted with regard to the export restrictions on certain raw materials at issue in this case that these export restrictions were:

part of a comprehensive environmental protection framework whose objectives are pollution reduction for the protection of health of the Chinese population.[41]

However, the respondents in this case, the European Union, the United States and Mexico, argued that China's export restrictions were not designed to address the health risks associated with environmental pollution, and that China's invocation of environmental and health concerns was 'merely a post hoc rationalization developed solely for purposes of this dispute'.[42] The panel found that China was unable to substantiate that the export restrictions at issue 'were part of a comprehensive programme maintained in order to reduce pollution', and thus cast serious doubts over whether the policy objective pursued by the export restriction was the protection of life or health of humans, animals or plants.[43]

As Article XX(b) covers measures designed for the protection of 'human, animal or plant life or health', it covers public health policy measures as well as environmental policy measures. However, as the panel noted in *Brazil – Retreaded Tyres (2007)*, a party Article XX(b) with regard to environmental policy measures 'has to establish the existence not just of risks to "the environment" generally, but specifically of risks to animal or plant life or health'.[44] For this reason, not all environmental policy measures would fall within the scope of application of Article XX(b) of the GATT 1994.[45]

---

39 Panel Report, *Brazil – Retreaded Tyres (2007)*, paras. 7.53 and 7.84.
40 *Ibid.*, para. 7.102. This issue was not appealed.
41 Panel Reports, *China – Raw Materials (2012)*, para. 7.498.
42 *Ibid.*, para. 7.499.   43 *Ibid.*, para. 7.516.
44 Panel Report, *Brazil – Retreaded Tyres (2007)*, para. 7.46.
45 Note that Article XX(g) of the GATT 1994 is concerned with measures relating to the conservation of exhaustible natural resources. See below, pp. 560–5.

The second element of the test under Article XX(b), the 'necessity' requirement, is more complex than the first element. The interpretation and application of the 'necessity' requirement has evolved considerably over the years. It is not the ambition of this sub-section to give a full account of this evolution. Rather, this sub-section focuses on those cases which best reflect the current interpretation and application of the 'necessity' requirement of Article XX(b). In fact, the current case law on the 'necessity' requirement was introduced by an Appellate Body report relating to the 'necessity' requirement, not in the context of Article XX(b), but in the context of Article XX(d), namely, the Appellate Body report in *Korea – Various Measures on Beef (2001)*, discussed in the next sub-section.[46] The first case in which the Appellate Body applied in the context of Article XX(b) this new approach to the 'necessity' requirement was *Brazil – Retreaded Tyres (2007)*. In its report in this case, the Appellate Body summed up how the 'necessity' requirement of Article XX(b) is currently interpreted and applied, as follows:

[I]n order to determine whether a measure is 'necessary' within the meaning of Article XX(b) of the GATT 1994, a panel must consider the relevant factors, particularly the importance of the interests or values at stake, the extent of the contribution to the achievement of the measure's objective, and its trade restrictiveness. If this analysis yields a preliminary conclusion that the measure is necessary, this result must be confirmed by comparing the measure with possible alternatives, which may be less trade restrictive while providing an equivalent contribution to the achievement of the objective. This comparison should be carried out in the light of the importance of the interests or values at stake. It is through this process that a panel determines whether a measure is necessary.[47]

The Appellate Body emphasised that the 'weighing and balancing' required to determine whether a measure is 'necessary' is a '*holistic operation* that involves putting all the variables of the equation together and evaluating them in relation to each other after having examined them individually, in order to reach an overall judgement'.[48]

To understand the current case law on the 'necessity' requirement of Article XX(b), it is important, however, to consider the Appellate Body's findings in *EC – Asbestos (2001)* relating to Article XX(b). While the Appellate Body had found that the measure at issue in this case – a French ban on asbestos and asbestos products – was not inconsistent with Article III:4 of the GATT 1994 and the panel's findings relating to Article XX(b) were therefore moot, the Appellate Body nevertheless addressed *some* of the issues that arise when determining whether an otherwise GATT-inconsistent measure is justified under Article XX(b). The Appellate Body made in *EC – Asbestos (2001)* four findings in this respect which deserve to be mentioned as they are important in understanding the current state of the law as set out in *Brazil – Retreaded Tyres (2007)*.

---

46 See below, 564.
47 Appellate Body Report, *Brazil – Retreaded Tyres (2007)*, para. 178. The Appellate Body referred in this regard to its report in *US – Gambling (2005)*, para. 307.
48 Appellate Body Report, *Brazil – Retreaded Tyres (2007)*, para. 182. Emphasis added.

First, according to the Appellate Body, the more important the societal value pursued by the measure at issue (e.g. human life and health) and the more this measure contributes to the protection or promotion of this value, the more easily the measure at issue may be considered to be 'necessary'.[49] In *EC – Asbestos (2001)*, the societal value pursued by the measure was the preservation of human life and health through the elimination, or reduction, of the well-known, and life-threatening, health risks posed by asbestos fibres. The Appellate Body observed with regard to this value that it is 'both vital and important in the highest degree'.[50] In *EC – Asbestos (2001)*, the Appellate Body did not explicitly refer to the third factor in the 'weighing and balancing' process now applied to determine whether an otherwise GATT-inconsistent measure is 'necessary', namely, the restrictive impact of the measure at issue on international trade. However, in *Brazil – Retreaded Tyres (2007)*, the Appellate Body clearly suggested with regard to this factor that the more restrictive the impact of the measure at issue is on international trade, the more difficult it is to consider that measure 'necessary'.[51]

Secondly, with regard to the existence of less trade-restrictive alternative measures, Canada asserted before the Appellate Body in *EC – Asbestos (2001)* that the panel had erred in finding that 'controlled use' of asbestos and asbestos products is not a reasonably available alternative to the import ban on asbestos. According to Canada, an alternative measure is only excluded as a 'reasonably available' alternative if implementation of that measure is 'impossible'. The Appellate Body stated that, in determining whether a suggested alternative measure is 'reasonably available', several factors must be taken into account, *alongside* the difficulty of implementation. It subsequently referred to its earlier report in *Korea – Various Measures on Beef (2001)* (concerning the 'necessity' requirement under Article XX(d), discussed in the next section)[52] and noted with regard to the determination of 'necessity' under Article XX(b):

> We indicated in *Korea – Beef* that one aspect of the 'weighing and balancing process ... comprehended in the determination of whether a WTO-consistent alternative measure' is reasonably available is the extent to which the alternative measure 'contributes to the realization of the end pursued'.[53]

Canada, the complainant in *EC – Asbestos (2001)*, had asserted that 'controlled use' of asbestos and asbestos products represented a 'reasonably available' measure that would serve the same end as the ban on asbestos and asbestos products. The issue for the Appellate Body was, therefore, whether France could reasonably be expected to employ 'controlled use' practices to achieve its chosen level of health protection – a halt in the spread of asbestos-related health risks. The Appellate Body concluded that this was not the case. It reasoned as follows:

---

49 Appellate Body Report, *EC – Asbestos (2001)*, para. 172.
50 *Ibid.*   51 See Appellate Body Report, *Brazil – Retreaded Tyres (2007)*, para. 150.
52 See below, 564.   53 Appellate Body Report, *EC – Asbestos (2001)*, para. 172.

In our view, France could not reasonably be expected to employ *any* alternative measure if that measure would involve a continuation of the very risk that the Decree seeks to 'halt'. Such an alternative measure would, in effect, prevent France from achieving its chosen level of health protection. On the basis of the scientific evidence before it, the Panel found that, in general, the efficacy of 'controlled use' remains to be demonstrated. Moreover, even in cases where 'controlled use' practices are applied 'with greater certainty', the scientific evidence suggests that the level of exposure can, in some circumstances, still be high enough for there to be a 'significant residual risk of developing asbestos-related diseases' ... 'Controlled use' would, thus, not be an alternative measure that would achieve the end sought by France.[54]

In *Brazil – Retreaded Tyres (2007)*, the Appellate Body confirmed that a Member cannot reasonably be expected to employ an alternative measure if that measure does not allow it to achieve its desired level of protection with respect to the policy objective pursued. The Appellate Body also recalled in *Brazil – Retreaded Tyres (2007)* its finding in *US – Gambling (2005)* (concerning the 'necessity' requirement under Article XIV(a) of the GATS, discussed later in this chapter)[55] that:

[a]n alternative measure may be found not to be 'reasonably available' ... where it is merely theoretical in nature, for instance, where the responding Member is not capable of taking it, or where the measure imposes an undue burden on that Member, such as prohibitive costs or substantial technical difficulties.[56]

Thirdly, the Appellate Body ruled in *EC – Asbestos (2001)* that it is for WTO Members to determine the *level* of protection of health or the environment they consider appropriate.[57] Other Members cannot challenge the level of protection chosen; they can only argue that the measure at issue is not 'necessary' to achieve that level of protection.[58]

Fourthly, quoting from its case law on the *SPS Agreement*, the Appellate Body in *EC – Asbestos (2001)* ruled that:

responsible and representative governments may act in good faith on the basis of what, at a given time, may be a divergent opinion coming from qualified and respected sources. In justifying a measure under Article XX(b) of the GATT 1994, a Member may also rely, in good faith, on scientific sources which, at that time, may represent a divergent, but qualified and respected, opinion. A Member is not obliged, in setting health policy, automatically to

---

54 *Ibid.*, para. 174.   55 See below, pp. 585–90.

56 Appellate Body Report, *Brazil – Retreaded Tyres (2007)*, para. 156, citing Appellate Body Report, *US – Gambling (2005)*, para. 308. In *Brazil – Retreaded Tyres (2007)*, the Appellate Body found that the alternative measures proposed by the European Communities were either already part of the strategy implemented by Brazil to deal with waste tyres, did not achieve the level of protection chosen by Brazil, or were costly and required advanced technologies and know-how not readily available on a large scale. Therefore, they could not be regarded as 'reasonably available' alternatives to the import ban. See Appellate Body Report, *Brazil – Retreaded Tyres (2007)*, paras. 172–5.

57 See Appellate Body Report, *EC – Asbestos (2001)*, para. 168. This finding is in line with the case law under the *SPS Agreement*: see below, pp. 894–950. See also Panel Report, *Brazil – Retreaded Tyres (2007)*, para. 7.108.

58 As France did in *EC – Asbestos (2001)*, a WTO Member can choose a zero-risk level. This means that there will be few, if any, measures other than a full ban that will achieve this level of protection. Also note that the panel in *US – Gasoline (1996)* ruled that it is not the necessity of the policy objective but the necessity of the disputed measure to *achieve* that objective which is at issue. See Panel Report, *US – Gasoline (1996)*, para. 6.22.

follow what, at a given time, may constitute a majority scientific opinion. Therefore, a panel need not, necessarily, reach a decision under Article XX(b) of the GATT 1994 on the basis of the 'preponderant' weight of the evidence.[59]

With regard to the contribution to the achievement of the value or policy objective pursued, the Appellate Body ruled in *Brazil – Retreaded Tyres (2007)* that a measure contributes to the achievement of the objective 'when there is a genuine relationship of ends and means between the objective pursued and the measure at issue'.[60] The Appellate Body furthermore held in *Brazil – Retreaded Tyres (2007)* that a measure must bring about a *material* contribution to the achievement of its objective; and that whether a measure brings about such contribution can be demonstrated either by evidence that the measure: (1) has already resulted in a material contribution; or (2) is apt to produce a material contribution.[61]

On the question of which party bears the burden of proof with regard to the existence of a reasonably available alternative measure, the Appellate Body in *Brazil – Retreaded Tyres (2007)* recalled its finding in *US – Gambling (2005)* (concerning the 'necessity' requirement under Article XIV(a) of the GATS).[62] Applying the same allocation of the burden of proof as in the latter case, the Appellate Body stated:

It rests upon the complaining Member to *identify* possible alternatives to the measure at issue that the responding Member could have taken. As the Appellate Body indicated in *US – Gambling*, while the responding Member must show that a measure is necessary, it does not have to 'show, in the first instance, that there are *no* reasonably available alternatives to achieve its objectives'.[63]

A noteworthy example of recent case law on the 'necessity' requirement of Article XX(b) are the reports of the panel in *China – Raw Materials (2012)*.[64] The panel examined in turn: (1) whether the objectives of the export restrictions were the protection of health and the environment;[65] (2) whether the export restrictions at issue already made, or were apt to produce, a material contribution

---

59 Appellate Body Report, *EC – Asbestos (2001)*, para. 178 (emphasis added), quoting from Appellate Body Report, *EC – Hormones (1999)*, para. 194, footnote 48. For a discussion of this SPS case law, see below, pp. 894–950.
60 Appellate Body Report, *Brazil – Retreaded Tyres (2007)*. In this case, the Appellate Body rejected the European Communities' argument that the contribution of the measure at issue to the achievement of its objective must be quantified by a panel. It held instead that either a quantitative or a qualitative evaluation is permissible. What is required is 'a genuine relationship of ends and means between the objective pursued and the measure at issue'.
61 See *ibid.*, para. 151.
62 See Appellate Body Report, *US – Gambling (2005)*, paras. 309–11, discussed below, p. 589.
63 Appellate Body Report, *Brazil – Retreaded Tyres (2007)*, para. 156. Emphasis added.
64 On the availability of Article XX to justify export restrictions inconsistent with Article XI:1 of the GATT 1994, as opposed to the unavailability of Article XX to justify export duties inconsistent with China's Accession Protocol, see above, p. 549.
65 Note that the panel did not examine the importance of the policy objective pursued. It noted that, in the Appellate Body Report in *Brazil – Retreaded Tyres (2007)*, it was stated that 'few interests are more "vital" and "important" than protecting human beings from health risks, and that protecting the environment is no less important'. See Panel Reports, *China – Raw Materials (2012)*, para. 7.482. As discussed above, the panel subsequently cast serious doubt over whether the policy objective pursued by the export restrictions at issue was the protection of life or health of humans, animals or plants. See above, p. 555.

to the achievement of the policy objective pursued; (3) what was the impact of the export restrictions on trade; and (4) whether there were WTO-consistent or less trade-restrictive alternative measures that could be used in lieu of applying export restrictions. The panel concluded that China had not demonstrated that the export restrictions at issue were 'necessary' within the meaning of Article XX(b).[66] China did not appeal this finding of the panel.

Questions and Assignments 8.3

What are the constituent elements of the test under Article XX(b) of the GATT 1994? When is a measure 'necessary' within the meaning of Article XX(b)? What factors are to be taken into account in determining whether there is a 'reasonably available alternative' within the meaning of the case law on Article XX(b)? Is it appropriate for panels or the Appellate Body to come to conclusions on the relative importance of societal values pursued by Members (e.g. religious purity or piety *versus* human health)? Must a Member invoking Article XX(b) justify the *level* of protection of public health or the environment it has chosen to pursue? Can a Member consider a measure to be 'necessary' to protect public health or the environment when the prevailing view among scientists is that there is no risk to public health or the environment? Briefly describe the measures at issue in *EC – Asbestos (2001)*, *Brazil – Retreaded Tyres (2007)* and *China – Raw Materials (2012)* and explain how the panel or the Appellate Body concluded that these measures were or were not provisionally justified under Article XX(b). Who has the burden of proof to establish that there is or is not an alternative measure that is reasonably available under the 'necessity' requirement of Article XX(b) of the GATT 1994?

2.3.2 Article XX(d)

As mentioned above, Article XX(d) concerns and can justify measures:

necessary to secure compliance with laws or regulations which are not inconsistent with the provisions of this Agreement, including those relating to customs enforcement, the enforcement of monopolies operated under paragraph 4 of Article II and Article XVII, the protection of patents, trade marks and copyrights, and the prevention of deceptive practices.

Article XX(d) sets out a two-tier test for the provisional justification of otherwise GATT-inconsistent measures.[67] In *Korea – Various Measures on Beef (2001)*, a dispute concerning a regulation on retail sales of both domestic and imported beef products (the dual retail system), allegedly designed to secure compliance with a consumer protection law, the Appellate Body ruled:

For a measure, otherwise inconsistent with GATT 1994, to be justified provisionally under paragraph (d) of Article XX, two elements must be shown. First, the measure must be one designed to 'secure compliance' with laws or regulations that are not themselves inconsistent with some provision of the GATT 1994. Second, the measure must be 'necessary' to

---

66 See Panel Reports, *China – Raw Materials (2012)*, para. 7.615. The panel found – assuming *arguendo* that Article XX was available to justify export duties inconsistent with China's Accession Protocol – that China had not demonstrated that these export duties were 'necessary' within the meaning of Article XX(b). See Panel Reports, *China – Raw Materials (2012)*, para. 7.616.

67 Note that the panel in *Canada – Wheat Exports and Grain Imports (2004)* applied a three-tier test. See below, footnote 69.

secure such compliance. A Member who invokes Article XX(d) as a justification has the burden of demonstrating that these two requirements are met.[68]

Thus, for a GATT-inconsistent measure to be provisionally justified under Article XX(d) the measure: (1) must be *designed* to secure compliance with national law, such as customs law or intellectual property law, which, itself, is not GATT-inconsistent; and (2) must be *necessary* to secure such compliance.[69]

With respect to the first element of the Article XX(d) test, namely, that the measure must be 'designed to secure compliance' with GATT-consistent laws or regulations, note that the panel in *US – Gasoline (1996)* found that:

maintenance of discrimination between imported and domestic gasoline contrary to Article III:4 under the baseline establishment methods did not 'secure compliance' with the baseline system. These methods were not an enforcement mechanism. They were simply rules for determining the individual baselines. As such, they were not the type of measures with which Article XX(d) was concerned.[70]

Two more recent cases, *EC – Trademarks and Geographical Indications (2005)*[71] and *Mexico – Taxes on Soft Drinks (2006)*, provide us with further insights into the first element of the Article XX(d) test. In *Mexico – Taxes on Soft Drinks (2006)*, the Appellate Body was called upon to clarify the meaning of the phrase 'to secure compliance with laws or regulations'. Mexico had argued before the panel that the measures at issue in this case were necessary to secure compliance 'by the United States with the United States' obligations under the NAFTA, an international agreement that is a law not inconsistent with the provisions of the GATT 1994'.[72] The panel, however, found that 'the phrase "to secure compliance" in Article XX(d) does not apply to measures taken by a Member in order to induce another Member to comply with obligations owed to it under a non-WTO treaty'.[73] In considering Mexico's appeal of this panel finding, the Appellate Body started with an analysis of the terms 'laws or regulations' of Article XX(d).[74] According to the Appellate Body:

[t]he terms 'laws or regulations' are generally used to refer to domestic laws or regulations. As Mexico and the United States note, previous GATT and WTO disputes in which Article

---

68 Appellate Body Report, *Korea – Various Measures on Beef (2001)*, para. 157. See also Panel Report, *US – Gasoline (1996)*, para. 6.31.

69 As mentioned above, the panel in *Canada – Wheat Exports and Grain Imports (2004)* applied a *three*-tier test. According to the panel, for a GATT-inconsistent measure to be provisionally justified under Article XX(d): (a) the measure for which justification is claimed must secure compliance with other laws or regulations; (b) those other laws or regulations must not be inconsistent with the provisions of the GATT 1994; and (c) the measure for which justification is claimed must be necessary to secure compliance with those other laws or regulations. See Panel Report, *Canada – Wheat Exports and Grain Imports (2004)*, para. 6.218.

70 Panel Report, *US – Gasoline (1996)*, para. 6.33. The panel referred in a footnote to Panel Report, *EEC – Parts and Components (1990)*, paras. 5.12–5.18. See also Panel Report, *Canada – Periodicals (1997)*, para. 5.11, where the panel held that Tariff Code 9958, prohibiting the import of certain periodicals, could not be justified under Article XX(d) as the import prohibition was not necessary to 'secure compliance' with the Canadian Income Tax Act.

71 Counting *EC – Trademarks and Geographical Indications (Australia) (2005)* and *EC – Trademarks and Geographical Indications (US) (2005)* as one case.

72 Panel Report, *Mexico – Taxes on Soft Drinks (2006)*, para. 8.162.

73 See *ibid.*, para. 8.181.

74 See Appellate Body Report, *Mexico – Taxes on Soft Drinks (2006)*, paras. 68–9.

XX(d) has been invoked as a defence have involved domestic measures. Neither disputes that the expression 'laws or regulations' encompasses the rules adopted by a WTO Member's legislative or executive branches of government. We agree with the United States that one does not immediately think about international law when confronted with the term 'laws' in the plural ... In our view, the terms 'laws or regulations' refer to rules that form part of the domestic legal system of a WTO Member. Thus the 'laws or regulations' with which the Member invoking Article XX(d) may seek to secure compliance do not include obligations of *another* WTO Member under an international agreement.[75]

The Appellate Body made it clear that 'laws or regulations' refer to domestic rules, and not the obligations of another WTO Member under an international agreement. This conclusion is strengthened by the illustrative list of 'laws or regulations' in Article XX(d).[76] The Appellate Body further referred to the context of Article XX(d) and to other provisions of the GATT 1994. It noted that, where international laws or agreements are meant to be covered by the relevant GATT rules, explicit reference is made to them.[77] Where international law is a part of domestic law, whether through implementation or through direct effect,[78] the Appellate Body recognised that it falls within the ambit of the terms 'laws or regulations' as used in Article XX(d). However, this is only the case for international obligations of the WTO Member concerned. International obligations of *other* WTO Members, such as, in this case, obligations of the United States under the NAFTA, are *not* covered by the terms 'laws or regulations' of Article XX(d) of the GATT 1994.[79]

The Appellate Body then turned in *Mexico – Taxes on Soft Drinks (2006)* to the phrase 'to secure compliance'. According to the Appellate Body, this phrase 'speak[s] to the types of measures that a WTO Member can seek to justify under Article XX(d)' and 'relate[s] to the design of the measures sought to be justified'.[80] The panel had argued that there was uncertainty regarding the effectiveness of the tax measures, and that it was therefore not convinced that these measures were meant 'to secure compliance'. The Appellate Body, however, did not agree with this reasoning:

In our view, a measure can be said to be designed 'to secure compliance' even if the measure cannot be guaranteed to achieve its result with absolute certainty. Nor do we consider that the 'use of coercion' is a necessary component of a measure designed 'to secure compliance'. Rather, Article XX(d) requires that the design of the measure *contribute* 'to secur[ing]' compliance with laws or regulations which are not inconsistent with the provisions of the GATT 1994.[81]

The fact that the tax measures at issue in *Mexico – Taxes on Soft Drinks (2006)* were designed 'to secure compliance' did not alter the general conclusion of the

---

75 *Ibid.*, para. 69.   76 *Ibid.*, para. 70.   77 See *ibid.*, para. 71.
78 See *ibid.*, footnote 148 to para. 69.
79 The Appellate Body noted that an interpretation of 'laws or regulations', which would comprise international obligations (including WTO obligations), is not in accordance with WTO law for two other reasons, discussed in Appellate Body Report, *Mexico – Taxes on Soft Drinks (2006)*, paras. 77 and 78.
80 *Ibid.*, para. 72.
81 *Ibid.*, para. 74. Emphasis added. See also Panel Report, *EEC – Parts and Components (1990)*, paras. 5.14–5.18, where the Panel held that 'to secure compliance' means 'to enforce obligations under laws and regulations' rather than 'to ensure the attainment of the objectives of the laws and regulations'.

Appellate Body that Article XX(d) was not applicable in that case. As explained above, international obligations of other WTO Members, such as the United States' obligations under the NAFTA, do not fall within the scope of the terms 'laws or regulations' with which Article XX(d) measures must be designed to secure compliance.

In *EC – Trademarks and Geographical Indications (2005)*, the European Communities had invoked the exception of Article XX(d) to justify the otherwise GATT-inconsistent measures at issue in this case, contending that these measures were employed to secure compliance with EU legislation, namely, EC Council Regulation (EEC) No. 2081/92 of 14 July 1992 on the protection of geographical indications and designations of origin for agricultural products and foodstuffs. The panel noted that the terms 'laws or regulations' in Article XX(d) are qualified by the phrase 'not inconsistent with the provisions of this Agreement'.[82] In other words, the 'laws or regulations' referred to in Article XX(d) have to be GATT-consistent. However, the panel found EC Council Regulation (EEC) No. 2081/92 to be inconsistent with the GATT 1994,[83] and therefore not to qualify as a 'law or regulation' within the meaning of Article XX(d).[84] Similarly, in *Thailand – Cigarettes (Philippines) (2011)*, the panel rejected an Article XX(d) defence by Thailand that the measures at issue were necessary to secure compliance with Thai tax laws, because the panel had already found that these laws were WTO-inconsistent.[85] This latter finding was reversed on appeal but for a different reason.[86]

With respect to the second element of the Article XX(d) test, the 'necessity' requirement, it was – as already noted above – in the context of a case involving Article XX(d) that the current approach to the interpretation and application of the 'necessity' requirement was introduced by the Appellate Body. The case in question was *Korea – Various Measures on Beef (2001)*. In its report in this case, the Appellate Body first noted that:

[w]e believe that, as used in the context of Article XX(d), the reach of the word 'necessary' is not limited to that which is 'indispensable' or 'of absolute necessity' or 'inevitable'. Measures which are indispensable or of absolute necessity or inevitable to secure compliance certainly fulfil the requirements of Article XX(d). But other measures, too, may fall within the ambit of this exception. As used in Article XX(d), the term 'necessary' refers, in our view, to a range of degrees of necessity. At one end of this continuum lies 'necessary' understood as 'indispensable'; at the other end, is 'necessary' taken to mean as 'making a contribution to'. We consider that a 'necessary' measure is, in this continuum, located significantly closer to the pole of 'indispensable' than to the opposite pole of simply 'making a contribution to'.[87]

---

82 See Panel Report, *EC – Trademarks and Geographical Indications (Australia) (2005)*, para. 7.331; and Panel Report, *EC – Trademarks and Geographical Indications (US) (2005)*, para. 7.296.
83 *Ibid.*, para. 7.332; and *ibid.*, para. 7.297.   84 *Ibid.*, para. 7.332; and *ibid.*, para. 7.297.
85 See Panel Report, *Thailand – Cigarettes (Philippines) (2011)*, para. 7.758.
86 See Appellate Body Report, *Thailand – Cigarettes (Philippines) (2011)*, para. 171. The Appellate Body was 'compelled' to reverse this panel finding because the panel made an obvious error in the relevant paragraph of its report by referring to the wrong Thai legislation.
87 Appellate Body Report, *Korea – Various Measures on Beef (2001)*, para. 161.

The Appellate Body subsequently stated:

> It seems to us that a treaty interpreter assessing a measure claimed to be necessary to secure compliance of a WTO-consistent law or regulation may, in appropriate cases, take into account the relative importance of the common interests or values that the law or regulation to be enforced is intended to protect. The more vital or important those common interests or values are, the easier it would be to accept as 'necessary' a measure designed as an enforcement instrument.
>
> There are other aspects of the enforcement measure to be considered in evaluating that measure as 'necessary'. One is the extent to which the measure contributes to the realization of the end pursued, the securing of compliance with the law or regulation at issue. The greater the contribution, the more easily a measure might be considered to be 'necessary'. Another aspect is the extent to which the compliance measure produces restrictive effects on international commerce, that is, in respect of a measure inconsistent with Article III:4, restrictive effects *on imported goods*. A measure with a relatively slight impact upon imported products might more easily be considered as 'necessary' than a measure with intense or broader restrictive effects.[88]

The Appellate Body thus came to the following conclusion in *Korea – Various Measures on Beef (2001)* concerning the 'necessity' requirement of Article XX(d):

> In sum, determination of whether a measure, which is not 'indispensable', may nevertheless be 'necessary' within the contemplation of Article XX(d), involves in every case a process of weighing and balancing a series of factors which prominently include the contribution made by the compliance measure to the enforcement of the law or regulation at issue, the importance of the common interests or values protected by that law or regulation, and the accompanying impact of the law or regulation on imports or exports.[89]

In brief, an evaluation of whether a measure is 'necessary', as required by the second element of the test under Article XX(d), involves, in every case, the weighing and balancing of factors such as: (1) the relative importance of the common interests or values protected (or intended to be protected) by the law or regulation compliance with which it is to be secured; (2) the extent to which the measure contributes to the securing of compliance with the law or regulation at issue; and (3) the extent to which the compliance measure produces restrictive effects on international trade. As noted by the Appellate Body in *Korea – Various Measures on Beef (2001)*, the process of weighing and balancing these factors:

> is comprehended in the determination of whether a WTO-consistent alternative measure which the Member concerned could 'reasonably be expected to employ' is available, or whether a less WTO-inconsistent measure is 'reasonably available'.[90]

---

88 *Ibid.*, paras. 162–3. In *ibid.*, para. 165, the Appellate Body cited Panel Report, *US – Section 337 Tariff Act (1989)*, para. 5.26.

89 Appellate Body Report, *Korea – Various Measures on Beef (2001)*, para. 164.

90 *Ibid.*, para. 166. In *Canada – Wheat Exports and Grain Imports (2004)*, the panel stated, with reference to the Appellate Body reports in *EC – Asbestos (2001)* and *Korea – Various Measures on Beef (2001)*, that in order to establish whether an alternative measure was reasonably available the relevant factors to consider are: (1) the extent to which the alternative measure contributes to the achievement of the policy objective; (2) the difficulty of implementing the alternative measure; and (3) the impact of the alternative measure on international trade. See Panel Report, *Canada – Wheat Exports and Grain Imports (2004)*, para. 6.226.

Note that the panels in *Canada – Wheat Exports and Grain Imports (2004)*, *Dominican Republic – Import and Sale of Cigarettes (2005)*, *EC – Trademarks and Geographical Indications (2005)*, *US – Shrimp (Thailand) (2008)* and *Colombia – Ports of Entry (2009)* have applied the 'necessity' requirement of Article XX(d) as interpreted and clarified by the Appellate Body in *Korea – Various Measures on Beef (2001)*.[91] Also note that the Appellate Body's ruling in this case on the 'necessity' requirement of Article XX(d) formed the basis of the Appellate Body's later rulings on the 'necessity' requirement of Article XIV(a) of the GATS (in *US – Gambling (2005)*) and Article XX(b) of the GATT 1994 (in *Brazil – Retreaded Tyres (2007)*). However, this case law on the 'necessity' requirement did not cease to evolve.[92]

Questions and Assignments 8.4

What are the constituent elements of the test under Article XX(d) of the GATT 1994? When does a measure 'secure compliance' within the meaning of Article XX(d)? How does one establish whether a measure is 'necessary' within the meaning of Article XX(d)? Explain why the Appellate Body concluded that the measures at issue in *Korea – Various Measures on Beef (2001)*, *EC – Trademarks and Geographical Indications (2005)* and *Mexico – Taxes on Soft Drinks (2006)* were not provisionally justified under Article XX(d).

2.3.3   Article XX(g)

Article XX(g) concerns measures relating to the conservation of exhaustible natural resources. Like Article XX(b), it addresses measures that depart from core GATT rules for environmental protection purposes. Article XX(g) sets out a three-tier test requiring that a measure: (1) relate to the 'conservation of exhaustible natural resources'; (2) 'relate to' the conservation of exhaustible natural resources; and (3) be 'made effective in conjunction with' restrictions on domestic production or consumption.

With respect to the first element of the test under Article XX(g), namely, that the measure must relate to the 'conservation of exhaustible natural resources', the Appellate Body, in *US – Shrimp (1998)*, adopted a broad, 'evolutionary' interpretation of the concept of 'exhaustible natural resources'. In this case, the complainants had taken the position that Article XX(g) was limited to the conservation of 'mineral' or 'non-living' natural resources. Their principal argument was rooted in the notion that 'living' natural resources are 'renewable' and therefore cannot be 'exhaustible' natural resources. The Appellate Body disagreed. It noted:

---

91 See Panel Report, *Canada – Wheat Exports and Grain Imports (2004)*, paras. 6.222–6.248; Panel Report, *Dominican Republic – Import and Sale of Cigarettes (2005)*, paras. 7.205–7.209, 7.212–7.215 and 7.217–7.232; Panel Report, *EC – Trademarks and Geographical Indications (Australia) (2005)*, paras. 7.333–7.341; and Panel Report, *EC – Trademarks and Geographical Indications (US) (2005)*, paras. 7.298–7.306 and 7.449–7.462.

92 With regard to Article XX(b) of the GATT 1994, see above, pp. 556–60. With regard to Article XX(a) of the GATT 1994 and Article XIV(a) of the GATS, see below, pp. 569–72 and 585–90.

We do not believe that 'exhaustible' natural resources and 'renewable' natural resources are mutually exclusive. One lesson that modern biological sciences teach us is that living species, though in principle, capable of reproduction and, in that sense, 'renewable', are in certain circumstances indeed susceptible of depletion, exhaustion and extinction, frequently because of human activities. Living resources are just as 'finite' as petroleum, iron ore and other non-living resources.[93]

The Appellate Body further noted with regard to the appropriate interpretation of the concept of 'exhaustible natural resources':

The words of Article XX(g), 'exhaustible natural resources', were actually crafted more than 50 years ago. They must be read by a treaty interpreter in the light of contemporary concerns of the community of nations about the protection and conservation of the environment. While Article XX was not modified in the Uruguay Round, the preamble attached to the *WTO Agreement* shows that the signatories to that Agreement were, in 1994, fully aware of the importance and legitimacy of environmental protection as a goal of national and international policy. The preamble of the *WTO Agreement* – which informs not only the GATT 1994, but also the other covered agreements – explicitly acknowledges 'the objective of *sustainable development*'.

... From the perspective embodied in the preamble of the *WTO Agreement*, we note that the generic term of 'natural resources' in Article XX(g) is not 'static' in its content or reference but is rather 'by definition, evolutionary'. It is, therefore, pertinent to note that modern international conventions and declarations make frequent references to natural resources as embracing both living and non-living resources.[94]

The Appellate Body thus concluded on the scope of the concept of 'exhaustible natural resources' that 'measures to conserve exhaustible natural resources, whether *living* or *non-living*, may fall within Article XX(g)'.[95]

With respect to the second element of the test under Article XX(g), namely, that the measure must be a measure 'relating to' the conservation of exhaustible natural resources, the Appellate Body stated in *US – Shrimp (1998)* with regard to the measure in dispute, Section 609 of Public Law 101-162 Relating to the Protection of Sea Turtles in Shrimp Trawl Fishing Operations:

In its general design and structure ... Section 609 is not a simple, blanket prohibition of the importation of shrimp imposed without regard to the consequences (or lack thereof) of the mode of harvesting employed upon the incidental capture and mortality of sea turtles. Focusing on the design of the measure here at stake, it appears to us that Section 609, *cum* implementing guidelines, is not disproportionately wide in its scope and reach in relation to the policy objective of protection and conservation of sea turtle species. *The means are, in principle, reasonably related to the ends*. The means and ends relationship between Section 609 and the legitimate policy of conserving an exhaustible, and, in fact, endangered species, is observably a close and real one.[96]

---

93 Appellate Body Report, *US – Shrimp (1998)*, para. 128.   94 *Ibid.*, paras. 129 and 130.
95 *Ibid.*, para. 131. Note that, in coming to this conclusion, the Appellate Body also referred to 'recent acknowledgement by the international community of the importance of concerted bilateral or multilateral action to protect living natural resources'. See *ibid*. The Appellate Body also noted that already the panels in *US – Canada Tuna (1982)*, at para. 4.9, and *Canada – Herring and Salmon (1988)*, at para. 4.4, had found fish to be an 'exhaustible' natural resource. See *ibid*.
96 Appellate Body Report, *US – Shrimp (1998)*, para. 141. Emphasis added.

Thus, according to the Appellate Body in *US – Shrimp (1998)*, Article XX(g) requires 'a close and real' relationship between the measure and the policy objective. The means employed, i.e. the measure, must be *reasonably* related to the end pursued, i.e. the conservation of an exhaustible natural resource. A measure may *not* be *disproportionately wide* in its scope or reach in relation to the policy objective pursued. In *China – Raw Materials (2012)*, the Appellate Body, referring to its report in *US – Shrimp (1998)* stated that:

> [i]n order to fall within the ambit of [Article XX(g)], a measure must 'relat[e] to the conservation of exhaustible natural resources'. The term 'relat[e] to' is defined as 'hav[ing] some connection with, be[ing] connected to'. The Appellate Body has found that, for a measure to relate to conservation in the sense of Article XX(g), there must be 'a close and genuine relationship of ends and means'.[97]

The third element of the test under Article XX(g), namely, that the measure at issue is 'made effective in conjunction with', has been interpreted and applied by the Appellate Body in *US – Gasoline (1996)* as follows:

> [T]he clause 'if such measures are made effective in conjunction with restrictions on domestic product[ion] or consumption' is appropriately read as a requirement that the measures concerned impose restrictions, not just in respect of imported gasoline but also with respect to domestic gasoline. The clause is a requirement of *even-handedness* in the imposition of restrictions, in the name of conservation, upon the production or consumption of exhaustible natural resources.[98]

Basically, the third element of the Article XX(g) test is a requirement of 'even-handedness' in the imposition of restrictions on imported and domestic products. Article XX(g) does *not* require imported and domestic products to be treated identically; it merely requires that they are treated in an 'even-handed' manner. The Appellate Body in *US – Gasoline (1996)* stated in this respect:

> There is, of course, no textual basis for requiring identical treatment of domestic and imported products. Indeed, where there is identity of treatment – constituting real, not merely formal, equality of treatment – it is difficult to see how inconsistency with Article III:4 would have arisen in the first place.[99]

Applying the 'even-handedness' requirement to the baseline establishment rules, the measure at issue in *US – Gasoline (1996)*, the Appellate Body found that 'restrictions on the consumption or depletion of clean air by regulating the domestic production of "dirty" gasoline' were established 'jointly with corresponding restrictions with respect to imported gasoline'.[100] The baseline establishment rules at issue in *US – Gasoline (1996)* thus met the 'made effective in conjunction with' requirement.

In *US – Shrimp (1998)*, the Appellate Body confirmed its approach to the third element of the Article XX(g) test. It found in that case that the record

---

97 Appellate Body Reports, *China – Raw Materials (2012)*, para. 355.
98 Appellate Body Report, *US – Gasoline (1996)*, 20–1.
99 *Ibid.*, 21.   100 *Ibid.*

reflected that the United States had – through earlier regulations[101] – taken measures applicable to US shrimp trawl vessels to prevent the incidental killing of sea turtles. Because of these regulations imposing 'restrictions on domestic production', the import ban at issue in this case met the 'even-handedness' requirement of the third element of the Article XX(g) test.[102]

A noteworthy example of recent case law on Article XX(g) are the reports of the panel in *China – Raw Materials (2012)*.[103] The panel found in turn that: (1) China had not met its burden of proving that its export quota on refractory-grade bauxite 'relate to the conservation' of refractory-grade bauxite; (2) China had not demonstrated that its 2009 export restrictions were made effective in conjunction with domestic restrictions designed to limit production or consumption in the present; and (3) China had not demonstrated that its domestic measures aimed at restricting production or consumption impose at present an even-handed burden on foreign and domestic consumers. The panel thus concluded that China had not demonstrated that its export quota on refractory-grade bauxite was justified pursuant to Article XX(g) of the GATT 1994.[104] China did not appeal these findings of the panel, except on one point. On appeal, the Appellate Body found that the panel erred in interpreting the phrase 'made effective in conjunction with' to require a separate showing that the purpose of the measure at issue must be to make effective restrictions on domestic production or consumption.[105] What is required is that the measure at issue 'work[s] together with restrictions on domestic production or consumption, which operate so as to conserve an exhaustible natural resource'.[106]

It is of interest to note that, in *China – Raw Materials (2012)*, China argued, and the panel agreed, that, consistently with Article 31.3(c) of the *Vienna Convention on the Law of Treaties*, the interpretation of Article XX(g) should 'take into account' the principle of sovereignty over natural resources. In the panel's view, however, Article XX(g) has been interpreted and applied in a manner that respects WTO Members' sovereign rights over their own natural resources.[107]

Questions and Assignments 8.5

What are the constituent elements of the test under Article XX(g) of the GATT 1994? How has the Appellate Body interpreted the concept of 'exhaustible natural resources'? Pursuant to Article XX(g), what kind of relationship must exist between the measure at issue and the environmental conservation policy objective pursued? When does a Member meet the requirement of Article XX(g) that 'measures are made effective in conjunction with

---

101 I.e. regulations pursuant to the US *Endangered Species Act*, issued in 1987 and fully effective in 1990.
102 See Appellate Body Report, *US – Shrimp (1998)*, para. 144.
103 On the availability of Article XX to justify export restrictions inconsistent with Article XI:1 of the GATT 1994, as opposed to the unavailability of Article XX to justify export duties inconsistent with China's Accession Protocol, see above, p. 549.
104 See Panel Reports, *China – Raw Materials (2012)*, para. 7.467.
105 See Appellate Body Reports, *China – Raw Materials (2012)*, para. 361.
106 See *ibid.*, para. 360.
107 See Panel Reports, *China – Raw Materials (2012)*, para. 7.381. See also below, p. 582.

restrictions on domestic production or consumption'? Must a Member impose identical conservation measures on imported and domestic products? Briefly describe the measures at issue in *US – Gasoline (1996)* and *US – Shrimp (1998)* and explain why the Appellate Body concluded that these measures were provisionally justified under Article XX(g). Why did the panel come to the opposite conclusion in *China – Raw Materials (2012)*?

2.3.4   Other Paragraphs of Article XX

Among the other exceptions provided for in Article XX of the GATT 1994, note in particular Article XX(a), which concerns measures necessary for the protection of public morals. WTO case law on Article XX(a) is still limited. Article XX(a) was referred to in *US – Tuna (Mexico) (1991)* and *US – Malt Beverages (1992)*, but in neither case did the panel examine the relevance of this provision.[108] In *US – Tuna (Mexico) (1991)*, Australia, a third party in this case, suggested that the measure at issue could be justified, under Article XX(a) of the GATT 1947, as a measure against inhumane treatment of animals.[109] The panel in *China – Publications and Audiovisual Products (2010)* was the first panel to interpret and apply Article XX(a). The measures at issue in that case concerned restrictions on trading and distribution of publications and audiovisual products in China. These measures provided for a content-review mechanism and a system for the selection of importation entities which played an essential role in the content review of imported publications and audiovisual products. Only 'approved' importation entities were authorised to import publications and audiovisual products. China invoked Article XX(a) to justify certain of these otherwise GATT-inconsistent restrictions on trading and distribution of publications and audiovisual products. According to China, these restrictions could be justified under Article XX(a) because 'the system of selecting importation entities undertaking content review is, as a whole, necessary to protect public morals'.[110]

For a GATT-inconsistent measure to be provisionally justified under Article XX(a), the measure must be: (1) *designed* to protect public morals (meaning that the policy objective pursued by the measure is the protection of morals); and (2) *necessary* to fulfil that policy objective. With regard to the term 'public morals', the panel in *China – Audiovisual Products (2010)* adopted the interpretation given to this term in the context of Article XIV(a) of the GATS by the panel in *US – Gambling (2005)*.[111] As discussed below, the panel in *US – Gambling (2005)* found, in brief, that: (1) the term 'public morals' denotes standards of right and wrong conduct maintained by or on behalf of a community or nation; (2) the

---

108 See Panel Report, *US – Tuna (Mexico) (1991)*, para. 4.4; and Panel Report, *US – Malt Beverages (1992)*, paras. 3.126 and 5.70.
109 See Panel Report, *US – Tuna (Mexico) (1991)*, para. 4.4.
110 Panel Report, *China – Publications and Audiovisual Products (2010)*, para. 7.727.
111 See *ibid.*, para. 7.759. The panel's interpretation of 'public morals' in *US – Gambling (2005)* was left undisturbed by the Appellate Body.

content of the concept of 'public morals' can vary from Member to Member, depending upon a range of factors, including prevailing social, cultural, ethical and religious values; and (3) Members should be given some scope to define and apply for themselves the concept of 'public morals' in their respective territories, according to their own systems and scales of values.[112] In line with this deferential interpretation of the concept of 'public morals', the panel in *China – Publications and Audiovisual Products (2010)* proceeded with its analysis on the *assumption* that:

> each of the prohibited types of content listed in China's measures is such that, if it were brought into China as part of a physical product, it could have a negative impact on 'public morals' in China within the meaning of Article XX(a) of the GATT 1994.[113]

With regard to the second element of the Article XX(a) test, namely, the 'necessity' requirement, the panel in *China – Publications and Audiovisual Products (2010)* first recalled that it is the measures at issue (i.e. the restrictions on trading and distribution), and not the policy objective pursued (i.e. the content review and the protection of 'public morals'), that must be 'necessary'.[114] Subsequently, the panel engaged in the examination of the 'necessity' of the measures at issue. Very much in line with the case law on the 'necessity' requirement of Article XX(b) and (d) of the GATT 1994, the panel: (1) identified the importance of the objective pursued;[115] (2) identified, for each of the measures at issue, the contribution made to the achievement of the protection of 'public morals'; and (3) identified the restrictive impact on international trade of each of the measures at issue.[116] The panel then 'weighed and balanced' these three factors, and came to the conclusion with regard to some of the measures at issue that they were *not* necessary to protect public morals,[117] while with regard to other measures it concluded that – absent reasonably available, less trade-restrictive alternative measures – these measures could be characterised as 'necessary'.[118] For the latter measures, the panel subsequently analysed the alternative measures proposed by the United States and came to the conclusion that, because at least one less trade-restrictive alternative measure was available, the measures at issue were *not* 'necessary' to protect public morals.[119] On appeal, the Appellate Body upheld most of the panel's intermediate findings and upheld the panel's conclusion

---

112 See below, p. 586.

113 Panel Report, *China – Publications and Audiovisual Products (2010)*, para. 7.763. Note that this finding by the panel was not appealed and that it was therefore not addressed by the Appellate Body.

114 See *ibid.*, para. 7.789. The panel referred in this respect to the Appellate Body Report, *US – Gasoline (1996)*, 20, discussed above, pp. 553–4.

115 The panel considered that the protection of 'public morals' ranks among the most important values or interests pursued by Members (see Panel Report, *China – Publications and Audiovisual Products (2010)*, para. 7.817), and that China has adopted a high level of protection of 'public morals' within its territory (see *ibid.*, para. 7.828).

116 The panel considered both the restrictive effect on imports and the restrictive effect on those wishing to engage in importing. See *ibid.*, para. 7.788.

117 See e.g. *ibid.*, paras. 7.848 and 7.868.

118 See e.g. *ibid.*, paras. 7.828 and 7.836.

119 See *ibid.*, para. 7.909. This alternative measure proposed by the United States was a measure under which the Chinese government would be given the sole responsibility for the conduct of the content review.

that the measures at issue were *not* 'necessary' to protect public morals.[120] The Appellate Body observed:

> The less restrictive the effects of the measure, the more likely it is to be characterized as 'necessary'. Consequently, if a Member chooses to adopt a very restrictive measure, it will have to ensure that the measure is carefully designed so that the other elements to be taken into account in weighing and balancing the factors relevant to an assessment of the 'necessity' of the measure will 'outweigh' such restrictive effect.[121]

While Article XX(a) has only been invoked once in dispute settlement proceedings to date, it is frequently 'used' (explicitly or otherwise) by Members to impose import bans or restrictions on a wide array of products. Bangladesh, for example, invokes Article XX(a) to justify an import ban on horror comics, obscene and subversive literature and 'maps, charts and geographical globes which indicate the territory of Bangladesh but do not do so in accordance with the maps published by the Department of Survey, Government of the People's Republic of Bangladesh'.[122] From the Report of the Working Party on the Accession of Saudi Arabia, it appears that this Member, which acceded to the WTO in December 2005, invokes Article XX(a) of the GATT 1994 to ban the importation of the Holy Quran; alcoholic beverages and intoxicants of all kinds; all types of machines, equipment and tools for gambling or games of chance; live swine, meat, fat, hair, blood, guts, limbs and all other products of swine; dogs (other than hunting dogs, guard dogs or guide dogs for the blind); mummified animals; and all foodstuffs containing animal blood in their manufacturing.[123]

Article XX(e) of the GATT 1994 concerns measures 'relating to' the products of prison labour. On the basis of Article XX(e), Members can, for example, ban the importation of goods that have been produced by prisoners. Article XX(e) is currently of little importance, and there is no case law under this paragraph to date. It has been suggested, however, that this could change if an evolutionary interpretation of the concept of 'products of prison labour' would allow this concept to include products produced in conditions of slave labour or conditions contrary to the most fundamental labour standards.[124]

Finally, Article XX(f) concerns measures 'imposed for' the protection of national treasures of artistic, historic or archaeological value. It allows Members to adopt or maintain otherwise GATT-inconsistent measures for the protection of national treasures. Note that Article XX(f) does not require that these measures are 'necessary' for, but merely that they are 'imposed for', the protection of

---

120 See Appellate Body Report, *China – Publications and Audiovisual Products (2010)*, paras. 336–7.
121 *Ibid.*, para. 310.
122 See Report by the Secretariat, *Trade Policy Review: Bangladesh*, WT/TPR/S/168, dated 9 August 2006, Appendix, Table AIII.3.
123 See Report of the Working Party on the Accession of the Kingdom of Saudi Arabia to the World Trade Organization, WT/ACC/SAU/61, dated 1 November 2005, Annex F, List of Banned Products.
124 See Gabrielle Marceau, 'Trade and Labour', in D. Bethlehem, D. McRae, R. Neufeld and I. Van Damme, *International Trade Law* (Oxford University Press, 2009), 549–52. For an example of evolutionary interpretation, see the findings of the Appellate Body on the concept of 'exhaustible natural resources' in *US – Shrimp (1998)*, discussed above, pp. 565–6.

national treasures. There is no case law on Article XX(f) to date. If the concept of 'national treasures of artistic value' could be given a broad meaning to include also 'endangered' cultural goods, Article XX(f) may be useful to justify import and export restrictions or bans imposed for the protection and promotion of cultural identity and/or diversity.

Questions and Assignments 8.6

What are the constituent elements of the tests under Article XX(a) and Article XX(f) of the GATT 1994? Can an otherwise GATT-inconsistent ban on products of child labour be found provisionally justified under Article XX? Can an import ban on books containing hate speech against an ethnic minority meet the requirements of Article XX(a)? Does the WTO allow Members to take measures restricting trade in cultural goods to protect their cultural identity?

2.4   Chapeau of Article XX of the GATT 1994

As discussed above, Article XX sets out a two-tier test for determining whether a measure, otherwise inconsistent with GATT obligations, can be justified. First, a measure must meet the requirements of one of the particular exceptions listed in the paragraphs of Article XX. Secondly, the application of that measure must meet the requirements of the chapeau of Article XX. The legal requirements imposed by the chapeau of Article XX of the GATT 1994 have been highly relevant in dispute settlement practice. Several of the most controversial decisions by panels and the Appellate Body have turned on these requirements. The chapeau of Article XX, with regard to measures provisionally justified under one of the paragraphs of Article XX, imposes:

the requirement that such measures are not applied in a manner which would constitute a means of arbitrary or unjustifiable discrimination between countries where the same conditions prevail, or a disguised restriction on international trade.

2.4.1   Object and Purpose of the Chapeau of Article XX

With respect to the object and purpose of the chapeau of Article XX, the Appellate Body ruled in *US – Gasoline (1996)*:

The chapeau by its express terms addresses, not so much the questioned measure or its specific contents as such, but rather the manner in which that measure is applied ... The chapeau is animated by the principle that while the exceptions of Article XX may be invoked as a matter of legal right, they should not be so applied as to frustrate or defeat the legal obligations of the holder of the right under the substantive rules of the *General Agreement*. If those exceptions are not to be abused or misused, in other words, the measures falling within the particular exceptions must be applied reasonably, with due regard both to the legal duties of the party claiming the exception and the legal rights of the other parties concerned.[125]

---

125 Appellate Body Report, *US – Gasoline (1996)*, 22. In a footnote, the Appellate Body referred to Panel Report, *US – Spring Assemblies (1983)*, para. 56.

Further, in *US – Shrimp (1998)*, the Appellate Body stated with regard to the chapeau:

[W]e consider that it embodies the recognition on the part of WTO Members of the need to maintain a balance of rights and obligations between the right of a Member to invoke one or another of the exceptions of Article XX, specified in paragraphs (a) to (j), on the one hand, and the substantive rights of the other Members under the GATT 1994, on the other hand. Exercise by one Member of its right to invoke an exception, such as Article XX(g), if abused or misused, will, to that extent, erode or render naught the substantive treaty rights in, for example, Article XI:1, of other Members. Similarly, because the GATT 1994 itself makes available the exceptions of Article XX, in recognition of the legitimate nature of the policies and interests there embodied, the right to invoke one of those exceptions is not to be rendered illusory.[126]

In short, the object and purpose of the chapeau of Article XX is to avoid that provisionally justified measures are *applied* in such a way as would constitute a misuse or an abuse of the exceptions of Article XX.[127] According to the Appellate Body, a balance must be struck between the *right* of a Member to invoke an exception under Article XX and the substantive rights of the other Members under the GATT 1994. The chapeau was inserted at the head of the list of 'General Exceptions' in Article XX to ensure that this balance is struck and to prevent abuse. The Appellate Body held in *US – Shrimp (1998)*:

In our view, the language of the chapeau makes clear that each of the exceptions in paragraphs (a) to (j) of Article XX is a *limited and conditional* exception from the substantive obligations contained in the other provisions of the GATT 1994, that is to say, the ultimate availability of the exception is subject to the compliance by the invoking Member with the requirements of the chapeau.[128]

According to the Appellate Body, the chapeau of Article XX is an expression of the principle of good faith, a general principle of law as well as a general principle of international law, which controls the exercise of rights by States. As the Appellate Body held:

One application of this general principle, the application widely known as the doctrine of *abus de droit*, prohibits the abusive exercise of a state's rights and enjoins that, whenever the assertion of a right 'impinges on the field covered by [a] treaty obligation, it must be exercised *bona fide*, that is to say, reasonably'. An abusive exercise by a Member of its own treaty right thus results in a breach of the treaty rights of the other Members, and, as well, a violation of the treaty obligation of the Member so acting.[129]

In light of the above, the Appellate Body came to the following conclusion in *US – Shrimp (1998)* with respect to the interpretation and application of the chapeau:

---

126 Appellate Body Report, *US – Shrimp (1998)*, para. 156. In a footnote, to the following paragraph, the Appellate Body referred to Panel Report, *US – Section 337 Tariff Act (1989)*, para. 5.9.

127 In *Brazil – Retreaded Tyres (2007)*, the Appellate Body emphasised that the 'focus of the chapeau, by its express terms, is on the application of a measure already found to be inconsistent with an obligation of the GATT 1994 but falling within one of the paragraphs of Article XX'. See Appellate Body Report, *Brazil – Retreaded Tyres (2007)*, para. 215.

128 Appellate Body Report, *US – Shrimp (1998)*, para. 157.

129 *Ibid.*, para. 158. See also Appellate Body Report, *Brazil – Retreaded Tyres (2007)*, paras. 215 and 224.

The task of interpreting and applying the chapeau is, hence, essentially the delicate one of locating and marking out a line of equilibrium between the right of a Member to invoke an exception under Article XX and the rights of the other Members under varying substantive provisions (e.g. Article XI) of the GATT 1994, so that neither of the competing rights will cancel out the other and thereby distort and nullify or impair the balance of rights and obligations constructed by the Members themselves in that Agreement. The location of the line of equilibrium, as expressed in the chapeau, is not fixed and unchanging; the line moves as the kind and the shape of the measures at stake vary and as the facts making up specific cases differ.[130]

In short, the interpretation and application of the chapeau in a particular case is a search for the appropriate *line of equilibrium* between, on the one hand, the right of Members to adopt and maintain trade-restrictive legislation and measures that pursue certain legitimate societal values or interests and, on the other hand, the right of other Members to trade. The search for this line of equilibrium is guided by the requirements set out in the chapeau that the application of the trade-restrictive measure may not constitute: (1) 'a means of arbitrary or unjustifiable discrimination between countries where the same conditions prevail'; or (2) 'a disguised restriction on international trade'. The following sub-sections examine these requirements of the chapeau in more detail.

2.4.2   Arbitrary or Unjustifiable Discrimination

For a measure to be justified under Article XX, the application of that measure, pursuant to the chapeau of Article XX, may *not* constitute 'a means of arbitrary or unjustifiable discrimination between countries where the same conditions prevail'. In *US – Gasoline (1996)*, the Appellate Body found that the 'discrimination' at issue in the chapeau of Article XX must necessarily be different from the discrimination addressed in other provisions of the GATT 1994, such as Articles I and III. The Appellate Body stated:

> The enterprise of applying Article XX would clearly be an unprofitable one if it involved no more than applying the standard used in finding that the [measure at issue] [was] inconsistent with Article III:4 ... The provisions of the chapeau cannot logically refer to the same standard(s) by which a violation of a substantive rule has been determined to have occurred.[131]

As the Appellate Body noted, the chapeau of Article XX does not prohibit discrimination *per se*, but rather *arbitrary* and *unjustifiable* discrimination.[132]

In *US – Shrimp (1998)*, the Appellate Body found that three elements must exist for 'arbitrary or unjustifiable discrimination' to be established: (1) the application of the measure at issue must result in *discrimination*; (2) this discrimination must be *arbitrary* or *unjustifiable* in character; and (3) this discrimination

---

130   Appellate Body Report, *US – Shrimp (1998)*, para. 159. This was reiterated in Appellate Body Report, *Brazil – Retreaded Tyres (2007)*, para. 224.
131   Appellate Body Report, *US – Gasoline (1996)*, 23.   132   See *ibid*.

must occur *between countries where the same conditions prevail*.[133] The Appellate Body further elaborated on the concept of 'discrimination' within the meaning of the chapeau of Article XX, and stated:

It may be quite acceptable for a government, in adopting and implementing a domestic policy, to adopt a single standard applicable to all its citizens throughout that country. However, it is not acceptable, in international trade relations, for one WTO Member to use an economic embargo to *require* other Members to adopt essentially the same comprehensive regulatory program, to achieve a certain policy goal, as that in force within that Member's territory, *without* taking into consideration different conditions which may occur in the territories of those other Members.

We believe that discrimination results not only when countries in which the same conditions prevail are differently treated, but also when the application of the measure at issue does not allow for any inquiry into the appropriateness of the regulatory program for the conditions prevailing in those exporting countries.[134]

The Appellate Body came to the conclusion in *US – Shrimp (1998)* that the application of the measure at issue constituted '*arbitrary* discrimination' as follows:

Section 609, in its application, imposes a single, rigid and unbending requirement that countries applying for certification … adopt a comprehensive regulatory program that is essentially the same as the United States' program, without inquiring into the appropriateness of that program for the conditions prevailing in the exporting countries. Furthermore, there is little or no flexibility in how officials make the determination for certification pursuant to these provisions. In our view, this rigidity and inflexibility also constitute 'arbitrary discrimination' within the meaning of the chapeau.[135]

The Appellate Body thus decided that discrimination may result when the same measure is applied to countries where different conditions prevail. When a measure is applied without any regard for the difference in conditions between countries and this measure is applied in a rigid and inflexible manner, the application of the measure may constitute 'arbitrary discrimination' within the meaning of the chapeau of Article XX.

To implement the recommendations and rulings in *US – Shrimp (1998)*, the United States modified the measure at issue in this case. Malaysia challenged the WTO-consistency of the implementing measure in an Article 21.5 proceeding.[136] The panel in *US – Shrimp (Article 21.5 – Malaysia) (2001)* concluded that, unlike the original US measure, the implementing measure was justified under Article XX and thus WTO-consistent. In the appeal from this panel report, the Appellate Body held:

In our view, there is an important difference between conditioning market access on the adoption of essentially the same programme, and conditioning market access on the

---

133 Appellate Body Report, *US – Shrimp (1998)*, para. 150. See also Panel Report, *EC – Tariff Preferences (2004)*, paras. 7.225–7.235; and Panel Report, *Brazil – Retreaded Tyres (2007)*, paras. 7.226–7.251.
134 Appellate Body Report, *US – Shrimp (1998)*, paras. 164–5.
135 *Ibid.*, para. 177.   136 On proceedings under Article 21.5 of the DSU, see above, pp. 293–5.

adoption of a programme *comparable in effectiveness*. Authorizing an importing Member to condition market access on exporting Members putting in place regulatory programmes *comparable in effectiveness* to that of the importing Member gives sufficient latitude to the exporting Member with respect to the programme it may adopt to achieve the level of effectiveness required. It allows the exporting Member to adopt a regulatory programme that is suitable to the specific conditions prevailing in its territory. As we see it, the Panel correctly reasoned and concluded that conditioning market access on the adoption of a programme *comparable in effectiveness*, allows for sufficient flexibility in the application of the measure so as to avoid 'arbitrary or unjustifiable discrimination'.[137]

Note that the Appellate Body thus seemed to introduce into the chapeau of Article XX an 'embryonic' and 'soft' requirement on Members to recognise the equivalence of foreign measures comparable in effectiveness.[138] The Appellate Body found in *US – Shrimp (Article 21.5 – Malaysia) (2001)* that the revised US measure at issue in the implementation dispute was sufficiently flexible to meet the standards of the chapeau.[139] The Appellate Body added:

[A] measure should be designed in such a manner that there is sufficient flexibility to take into account the specific conditions prevailing in *any* exporting Member, including, of course, Malaysia. Yet this is not the same as saying that there must be specific provisions in the measure aimed at addressing specifically the particular conditions prevailing in *every individual* exporting Member. Article XX of the GATT 1994 does not require a Member to anticipate and provide explicitly for the specific conditions prevailing and evolving in *every individual* Member.[140]

Pursuant to the chapeau of Article XX, the application of measures provisionally justified under one of the paragraphs of Article XX may not only not constitute 'arbitrary discrimination', it may also not constitute '*unjustifiable* discrimination'. In *US – Gasoline (1996)*, the Appellate Body concluded that the measure at issue constituted 'unjustifiable discrimination' for the following reasons:

We have above located two omissions on the part of the United States: to explore adequately means, including in particular cooperation with the governments of Venezuela and Brazil, of mitigating the administrative problems relied on as justification by the United States for rejecting individual baselines for foreign refiners; and to count the costs for foreign refiners that would result from the imposition of statutory baselines. In our view, these two omissions go well beyond what was necessary for the Panel to determine that a violation of Article III:4 had occurred in the first place. The resulting discrimination must have been *foreseen*, and was *not merely inadvertent or unavoidable*. In the light of the foregoing, our conclusion is that the baseline establishment rules in the Gasoline Rule, in their application, constitute 'unjustifiable discrimination'.[141]

Note that the Appellate Body emphasised the *deliberate* nature of the discrimination, i.e. discrimination that is foreseen and not merely inadvertent or

---

137 Appellate Body Report, *US – Shrimp (Article 21.5 – Malaysia) (2001)*, para. 144.
138 See also G. Marceau and J. Trachtmann, 'A Map of the World Trade Organization Law of Domestic Regulations of Goods', in G. A. Bermann and P. C. Mavroidis (eds.), Trade and Human Health and Safety (Cambridge University Press, 2006), 9–76, at 42.
139 See Appellate Body Report, *US – Shrimp (Article 21.5 – Malaysia) (2001)*, paras. 145–8.
140 *Ibid.*, para. 149.
141 Appellate Body Report, *US – Gasoline (1996)*, 28–29. Emphasis added.

unavoidable. Likewise, the panel in *Argentina – Hides and Leather (2001)* found that the application of the measure at issue resulted in unjustifiable discrimination as several alternative measures were available, which rendered the measure *not unavoidable*.[142]

The Appellate Body in *US – Shrimp (1998)* also addressed the question of whether the application of the measure at issue constituted an 'unjustifiable discrimination' within the meaning of the chapeau. The Appellate Body noted the following:

> Another aspect of the application of Section 609 that bears heavily in any appraisal of justifiable or unjustifiable discrimination is the failure of the United States to engage the appellees, as well as other Members exporting shrimp to the United States, in serious, across-the-board negotiations with the objective of concluding bilateral or multilateral agreements for the protection and conservation of sea turtles, before enforcing the import prohibition against the shrimp exports of those other Members.[143]

The Appellate Body made three observations in this respect.[144] First, the Congress of the United States expressly recognised in enacting Section 609 the importance of securing international agreements for the protection and conservation of the sea turtle species. Secondly, the protection and conservation of highly migratory species of sea turtle, i.e. the very policy objective of the measure, demands concerted and cooperative efforts on the part of the many countries whose waters are traversed in the course of recurrent sea turtle migrations. The need for, and the appropriateness of, such efforts are recognised in the WTO Agreement itself, as well as in a significant number of other international instruments and declarations. Thirdly, the United States negotiated and concluded the *Inter-American Convention for the Protection and Conservation of Sea Turtles*. The existence of this regional agreement provided convincing demonstration that an alternative course of action was reasonably open to the United States for securing the legitimate policy goal of its measure, a course of action other than the unilateral and non-consensual procedures of the import prohibition under Section 609. However, the record did not show that serious efforts were made by the United States to negotiate similar agreements with any other country or group of countries.[145] The Appellate Body therefore concluded:

> Clearly, the United States negotiated seriously with some, but not with other Members (including the appellees), that export shrimp to the United States. The effect is plainly discriminatory and, in our view, unjustifiable. The unjustifiable nature of this discrimination emerges clearly when we consider the cumulative effects of the failure of the United States

---

142 See Panel Report, *Argentina – Hides and Leather (2001)*, paras. 11.324–11.330.
143 Appellate Body Report, *US – Shrimp (1998)*, para. 166.
144 See *ibid.*, paras. 167–9.
145 The record also did not show that the United States attempted to have recourse to such international mechanisms that exist to achieve cooperative efforts to protect and conserve sea turtles before imposing the import ban. The United States, for example, did not make any attempt to raise the issue of sea turtle mortality due to shrimp trawling in the CITES Standing Committee as a subject requiring concerted action by States.

to pursue negotiations for establishing consensual means of protection and conservation of the living marine resources here involved.[146]

The extent to which a Member has to seek a multilateral solution to a problem before it may make use of unilateral measures was one of the main issues in *US – Shrimp (Article 21.5 – Malaysia) (2001)*. The Appellate Body made it clear that, in order to meet the requirement of the chapeau of Article XX, the Member needs to make serious efforts, in good faith, to negotiate a multilateral solution before resorting to unilateral measures.[147] Failure to make such efforts may lead to the conclusion that the discrimination is 'unjustifiable'.[148]

The panel in *Brazil – Retreaded Tyres (2007)* considered that the Appellate Body reports in *US – Gasoline (1996)*, *US – Shrimp (1998)* and *US – Shrimp (Article 21.5 – Malaysia) (2001)*, all discussed above, provided useful illustrations on what might render discrimination 'arbitrary' or 'unjustifiable' within the meaning of the chapeau of Article XX.[149] However, the panel continued:

We do not assume ... that exactly the same elements will necessarily be determinative in every situation ... We recall in this regard the Appellate Body's observation, in its ruling in *US – Shrimp*, that the 'location of the line of equilibrium [between the right of a Member to invoke an exception under Article XX and the rights of the other Members under varying substantive provisions], as expressed in the chapeau, is not fixed and unchanging; the line moves as the kind and the shape of the measures at stake vary and as the facts making up specific cases differ.'[150]

In *Brazil – Retreaded Tyres (2007)*, the panel had determined that discrimination arose in the application of the measure at issue, an import ban on retreaded tyres, from two sources: discrimination arising from the exemption from the import ban of imports of remoulded tyres originating in MERCOSUR countries (the 'MERCOSUR exemption'); and discrimination arising from the importation of used tyres under court injunctions.[151]

With regard to the application of the import ban, in conjunction with imports of remoulded tyres under the MERCOSUR exemption, the panel found that this application constituted neither arbitrary nor unjustifiable discrimination,[152] as the MERCOSUR exemption was granted to MERCOSUR countries pursuant to a ruling by the MERCOSUR Tribunal finding an import ban on remoulded tyres inconsistent with MERCOSUR rules.[153] The panel thus ruled that:

146 Appellate Body Report, *US – Shrimp (1998)*, para. 172.
147 See Appellate Body Report, *US – Shrimp (Article 21.5 – Malaysia) (2001)*, paras. 115–34.
148 In *US – Shrimp (1998)*, the Appellate Body also found that the application of the US measures resulted in differential treatment among various countries desiring certification: for example, by granting different countries different phasing-in periods to comply with the US requirements, and concluded that this differential treatment also constituted 'unjustifiable discrimination'. See Appellate Body Report, *US – Shrimp (1998)*, paras. 173–5.
149 See Panel Report, *Brazil – Retreaded Tyres (2007)*, para. 7.261.
150 *Ibid.*, para. 7.262.   151 See *ibid.*, para. 7.251.   152 See *ibid.*, para. 7.289.
153 See *ibid.*, para. 7.270. As noted by both the panel and the Appellate Body, Brazil could have sought to justify before the MERCOSUR Tribunal the challenged Import Ban on the grounds of human, animal and plant health under Article 50(d) of the Treaty of Montevideo, but that Brazil, however, decided not to do so. See Appellate Body Report, *Brazil – Retreaded Tyres (2007)*, para. 234.

the discrimination resulting from the MERCOSUR exemption cannot, in our view, be said to be 'capricious' or 'random'. To that extent, the measure at issue is not being applied in a manner that would constitute *arbitrary* discrimination.[154]

The panel considered that if imports of remoulded tyres under the MERCOSUR exemption were to take place in such amounts that the achievement of the objective of the import ban would be significantly undermined, the application of the import ban, in conjunction with the exemption, would constitute a means of *unjustifiable* discrimination.[155] The panel found, however, the levels of imports 'not to have been significant'[156] and thus concluded that the operation of the MERCOSUR exemption had not resulted in the measure being applied in a manner that would constitute *unjustifiable* discrimination.[157]

Similarly, with regard to the application of the import ban, in conjunction with imports of used tyres under court injunctions, the panel found that this application did not constitute *arbitrary* discrimination because the discrimination was not the result of 'capricious' or 'random' action (but the result of court injunctions).[158] However, the panel concluded that the application of the import ban, in conjunction with imports of used tyres under court injunctions, constituted *unjustifiable* discrimination because the imports of used tyres under court injunctions had taken place 'in significant amounts', undermining Brazil's stated policy objective.[159]

On appeal, the Appellate Body, referring to its analysis of whether the application of a measure results in arbitrary or unjustifiable discrimination in *US – Gasoline (1996)*, *US – Shrimp (1998)* and *US – Shrimp (Article 21.5 – Malaysia) (2001)*, noted that:

[a]nalyzing whether discrimination is arbitrary or unjustifiable usually involves an analysis that relates primarily to *the cause or the rationale* of the discrimination.[160]

The Appellate Body thus rejected the panel's interpretation of the term 'unjustifiable' as it did not depend on the *cause* or *rationale* of the discrimination but, instead, 'focused exclusively on the assessment of the *effects* of the discrimination'.[161] According to the Appellate Body, an abuse of the Article XX exceptions – contrary to the purpose of the chapeau – exists when the reasons given for discrimination 'bear no rational connection to the objective falling within the purview of a paragraph of Article XX, or would go against that objective'.[162] Therefore, whether discrimination is 'arbitrary or unjustifiable' should be assessed in light of the *objective* of the measure.[163] The Appellate Body then had to assess whether the explanation provided by Brazil, namely, that it had introduced the MERCOSUR exemption to comply with a ruling issued by the MERCOSUR

---

154 Panel Report, *Brazil – Retreaded Tyres (2007)*, para. 7.281.   155 See *ibid.*, para. 7.287.
156 *Ibid.*, para. 7.288.   157 See *ibid.*, para. 7.289.
158 See *ibid.*, para. 7.294.   159 See *ibid.*, paras. 7.303 and 7.306.
160 Appellate Body Report, *Brazil – Retreaded Tyres (2007)*, para. 225. Emphasis added.
161 *Ibid.*, para. 229.   162 *Ibid.*, para. 227.   163 See *ibid.*

Tribunal, was 'acceptable as a justification for discrimination between MERCO-SUR countries and non-MERCOSUR countries in relation to retreaded tyres'.[164] The Appellate Body stated:

[W]e have difficulty understanding how discrimination might be viewed as complying with the chapeau of Article XX when the alleged rationale for discriminating does not relate to the pursuit of or would go against the objective that was provisionally found to justify a measure under a paragraph of Article XX.

... [T]he ruling issued by the MERCOSUR arbitral tribunal is not an acceptable rationale for the discrimination, because it bears no relationship to the legitimate objective pursued by the Import Ban that falls within the purview of Article XX(b), and even goes against this objective, to however small a degree. Accordingly, we are of the view that the MERCOSUR exemption has resulted in the Import Ban being applied in a manner that constitutes arbitrary or unjustifiable discrimination.[165]

While the Appellate Body agreed with the panel that Brazil's decision was not 'capricious' or 'random', since decisions to implement rulings of judicial or qua-si-judicial bodies cannot be characterised as such, it noted that 'discrimination can result from a rational decision or behaviour, and still be "arbitrary or un-justifiable", because it is explained by a rationale that bears no relationship to the objective of a measure provisionally justified under one of the paragraphs of Article XX, or goes against that objective'.[166] The Appellate Body made a similar finding with regard to the imports of tyres under court injunctions.[167]

In brief, the application of a provisionally justified measure will constitute 'arbitrary or unjustifiable' discrimination when the *discrimination arising in the application* of the provisionally justified measure is explained by a rationale that bears no relation to the objective of the measure or even goes against that objective. As the Appellate Body held in *Brazil – Retreaded Tyres (2007)*, whether discrimination is arbitrary or unjustifiable depends on the cause or rationale of the discrimination, *not* on the effects of the discrimination (as the panel had held). The rationale of the discrimination must be assessed in light of the contribution of the discrimination to achieving the legitimate objective provisionally found to justify the measure at issue.

2.4.3 Disguised Restriction on International Trade

With respect to the requirement that the application of the measure at issue does not constitute a 'disguised restriction on international trade', the Appellate Body stated in *US – Gasoline (1996)*:

'Arbitrary discrimination', 'unjustifiable discrimination' and 'disguised restriction' on international trade may, accordingly, be read side-by-side; they impart meaning to one another. It is clear to us that 'disguised restriction' includes disguised *discrimination* in international trade. It is equally clear that *concealed or unannounced* restriction or discrimination in international trade does *not* exhaust the meaning of 'disguised restriction'. We consider that 'disguised restriction', whatever else it covers, may properly be read as embracing

---

164 *Ibid.*   165 *Ibid.*, paras. 227–8.   166 *Ibid.*, para. 232.   167 See *ibid.*, paras. 246–7.

restrictions amounting to arbitrary or unjustifiable discrimination in international trade taken under the guise of a measure formally within the terms of an exception listed in Article XX.[168]

According to the Appellate Body in *US – Gasoline (1996)*:

the kinds of considerations pertinent in deciding whether the application of a particular measure amounts to 'arbitrary or unjustifiable discrimination', may also be taken into account in determining the presence of a 'disguised restriction' on international trade. The fundamental theme is to be found in the purpose and object of avoiding abuse or illegitimate use of the exceptions to substantive rules available in Article XX.[169]

The panel in *EC – Asbestos (2001)* further clarified the requirement of the chapeau that the application of the measure at issue does not constitute a 'disguised restriction on international trade' as follows:

[A] restriction which formally meets the requirements of Article XX(b) will constitute an abuse if such compliance is in fact only a disguise to conceal the pursuit of trade-restrictive objectives. However, as the Appellate Body acknowledged in *Japan – Alcoholic Beverages*, the aim of a measure may not be easily ascertained. Nevertheless, we note that, in the same case, the Appellate Body suggested that the protective application of a measure can most often be discerned from its design, architecture and revealing structure.[170]

Questions and Assignments 8.7

What is the object and purpose of the chapeau of Article XX? When is discrimination 'arbitrary or unjustifiable' within the meaning of Article XX? What is 'a disguised restriction on international trade' within the meaning of the chapeau of Article XX? Briefly describe the measures at issue in *US – Gasoline (1996)*, *US – Shrimp (1998)* and *Brazil – Retreaded Tyres (2007)* and discuss why the Appellate Body found that these measures did not meet the requirements of the chapeau of Article XX. Why and to what extent must a Member who wishes to invoke Article XX to justify an otherwise GATT-inconsistent measure seek a multilateral solution to the problem the measure addresses? What does the Appellate Body Report in *Brazil – Retreaded Tyres (2007)* add to our understanding of the concepts of arbitrary and unjustifiable discrimination within the meaning of the chapeau of Article XX of the GATT 1994?

2.5   Policy Space for Members to Protect Other Societal Values

In two prominent WTO disputes involving the protection of the environment, *US – Gasoline (1996)* and *US – Shrimp (1998)*, the measures at issue were found to be provisionally justified under Article XX(g), but the application of the measures failed to satisfy the requirements of the chapeau of Article XX. The public perception of the Appellate Body reports in these disputes has been negative and unsympathetic. In particular, there is a widely held view among

---

168 Appellate Body Report, *US – Gasoline (1996)*, 25.   169 *Ibid.*
170 Panel Report, *EC – Asbestos (2001)*, para. 8.236. In a footnote, the panel noted that '[a]lthough this approach was developed in relation to Article III:4 of the GATT 1994, we see no reason why it should not be applicable in other circumstances where it is necessary to determine whether a measure is being applied for protective purposes'. *Ibid.*, footnote 199.

environmental activists that the WTO undermines necessary environmental legislation. It is noteworthy that the Appellate Body (with foresight but only with
relative success) added a paragraph to the end of both its report in *US – Gasoline
(1996)* and its report in *US – Shrimp (1998)*. In these paragraphs, the Appellate Body explained in straightforward language the policy space for Members
to enact environmental legislation and the limited nature of its rulings in both
cases. In *US – Shrimp (1998)*, the Appellate Body concluded with the following
observation:

> In reaching these conclusions, we wish to underscore what we have *not* decided in this
> appeal. We have *not* decided that the protection and preservation of the environment is
> of no significance to the Members of the WTO. Clearly, it is. We have *not* decided that the
> sovereign nations that are Members of the WTO cannot adopt effective measures to protect
> endangered species, such as sea turtles. Clearly, they can and should. And we have *not*
> decided that sovereign states should not act together bilaterally, plurilaterally or multilater-
> ally, either within the WTO or in other international fora, to protect endangered species or
> to otherwise protect the environment. Clearly, they should and do.
>
> What we *have* decided in this appeal is simply this: although the measure of the United
> States in dispute in this appeal serves an environmental objective that is recognized as
> legitimate under paragraph (g) of Article XX of the GATT 1994, this measure has been
> applied by the United States in a manner which constitutes arbitrary and unjustifiable
> discrimination between Members of the WTO, contrary to the requirements of the chapeau
> of Article XX ... As we emphasized in *United States – Gasoline*, WTO Members are free
> to adopt their own policies aimed at protecting the environment as long as, in so doing,
> they fulfill their obligations and respect the rights of other Members under the *WTO
> Agreement*.[171]

In the same vein, the panel in *China – Raw Materials (2012)* observed the following:

> [T]he ability to enter into international agreements – such as the WTO Agreement – is a
> quintessential example of the exercise of sovereignty. In joining the WTO, China obtained
> significant commercial and institutional benefits, including with respect to its natural re-
> sources. It also committed to abide by WTO rights and obligations.
>
> Exercising its sovereignty over its own natural resources while respecting the require-
> ments of Article XX(g) that China committed to respect, is an efficient way for China to
> pursue its own social and economic development.[172]

Questions and Assignments 8.8

How much policy space does the GATT 1994 leave WTO Members to define and pursue
environmental or public health policy objectives? Do you consider the environmentalist
criticism of the decisions in *US – Gasoline (1996)* and *US – Shrimp (1998)* justified?
How does the sovereignty of WTO Members relate to their obligations under the WTO
agreements?

---

171 Appellate Body Report, *US – Shrimp (1998)*, paras. 185–6. For a similar statement, see Appellate Body
Report, *US – Gasoline (1996)*, 29–30.
172 Panel Reports, *China – Raw Materials (2012)*, paras. 7.382–7.383. On the principle of sovereignty over natural resources and its relevance for the interpretation of Article XX(g) of the GATT 1994, see above, p. 582.

3 GENERAL EXCEPTIONS UNDER THE GATS

Like the GATT 1994, the GATS also provides for a 'general exceptions' provision allowing Members to deviate, under certain conditions, from obligations and commitments under the GATS. Article XIV of the GATS provides, in relevant part:

Subject to the requirement that such measures are not applied in a manner which would constitute a means of arbitrary or unjustifiable discrimination between countries where like conditions prevail, or a disguised restriction on trade in services, nothing in this Agreement shall be construed to prevent the adoption or enforcement by any Member of measures:

(a) necessary to protect public morals or to maintain public order;

(b) necessary to protect human, animal or plant life or health;

(c) necessary to secure compliance with laws or regulations which are not inconsistent with the provisions of this Agreement including those relating to:

  (i) the prevention of deceptive and fraudulent practices or to deal with the effects of a default on services contracts;

  (ii) the protection of the privacy of individuals in relation to the processing and dissemination of personal data and the protection of confidentiality of individual records and accounts;

  (iii) safety;

(d) inconsistent with Article XVII, provided that the difference in treatment is aimed at ensuring the equitable or effective imposition or collection of direct taxes in respect of services or service suppliers of other Members;

(e) inconsistent with Article II, provided that the difference in treatment is the result of an agreement on the avoidance of double taxation or provisions on the avoidance of double taxation in any other international agreement or arrangement by which the Member is bound.

The similarities between Article XX of the GATT 1994 and Article XIV of the GATS are striking. However, there are also differences. An obvious difference is that some of the justifications in Article XIV of the GATS, such as the maintenance of public order, the protection of safety and privacy, and the equitable and effective imposition or collection of direct taxes, do not appear (at least not explicitly) in Article XX of the GATT 1994. Likewise, other grounds in Article XX of the GATT 1994, such as the protection of national treasures of artistic value, are not included in Article XIV of the GATS. Nevertheless, because of the similarity in architecture and in core concepts, Article XX of the GATT and its jurisprudence provide us with a basis to interpret Article XIV of the GATS. In the first case that dealt with Article XIV of the GATS, *US – Gambling (2005)*, the Appellate Body stated:

Article XIV of the GATS sets out the general exceptions from obligations under that Agreement in the same manner as does Article XX of the GATT 1994. Both of these provisions affirm the right of Members to pursue objectives identified in the paragraphs of these provisions even if, in doing so, Members act inconsistently with obligations set out in other provisions of the respective agreements, provided that all of the conditions set out therein are satisfied. Similar language is used in both provisions, notably the term 'necessary' and the requirements set out in their respective chapeaux. Accordingly, like the Panel, we find previous decisions under Article XX of the GATT 1994 relevant for our analysis under Article XIV of the GATS.[173]

3.1   Two-Tier Test Under Article XIV of the GATS

As with Article XX of the GATT 1994, Article XIV of the GATS sets out a two-tier test for determining whether a measure, otherwise inconsistent with GATS obligations, can be justified. As the Appellate Body in *US – Gambling (2005)* stated:

> Article XIV of the GATS, like Article XX of the GATT 1994, contemplates a 'two-tier analysis' of a measure that a Member seeks to justify under that provision. A panel should first determine whether the challenged measure falls within the scope of one of the paragraphs of Article XIV. This requires that the challenged measure address the particular interest specified in that paragraph and that there be a sufficient nexus between the measure and the interest protected. The required nexus – or 'degree of connection' – between the measure and the interest is specified in the language of the paragraphs themselves, through the use of terms such as 'relating to' and 'necessary to'. Where the challenged measure has been found to fall within one of the paragraphs of Article XIV, a panel should then consider whether that measure satisfies the requirements of the chapeau of Article XIV.[174]

Thus, to determine whether a measure can be justified under Article XIV of the GATS, it must be examined, first, whether this measure can provisionally be justified under one of the specific exceptions of paragraphs (a) to (e) of Article XIV; and, if so, second, whether the application of this measure meets the requirements of the chapeau of Article XIV.

To date, Article XIV of the GATS has been invoked in dispute settlement proceedings only once, and unsuccessfully, to justify a measure otherwise GATS-inconsistent.[175]

This sub-section, first, discusses the specific exceptions provided for in Article XIV, and, secondly, analyses the requirements of the chapeau of Article XIV.

Questions and Assignments 8.9

What are the main elements of the Article XIV test? Explain why the interpretation of Article XX of the GATT is relevant for the analysis of Article XIV of the GATS. Give some examples of similarities and differences between Article XX of the GATT and Article XIV of the GATS.

3.2   Specific Exceptions Under Article XIV of the GATS

Article XIV of the GATS sets out, in paragraphs (a) to (e), specific grounds of justification for measures, which are otherwise inconsistent with the GATS. These

---

173 Appellate Body Report, *US – Gambling (2005)*, para. 291.   174 *Ibid.*, para. 292.
175 See *US – Gambling (2005)*. Article XIV of the GATS was not invoked in *China – Publications and Audiovisual Products (2010)* or *China – Electronic Payment Services (2012)*.

grounds of justification relate, *inter alia*, to: (1) the protection of public morals; (2) the maintenance of public order; (3) the protection of human, animal or plant life or health; (4) the prevention of deceptive and fraudulent practices; (5) the protection of the privacy of individuals; (6) the protection of safety; and (7) the equitable or effective imposition or collection of direct taxes.[176]

As the Appellate Body noted in *US – Gambling (2005)*, the paragraphs of Article XIV of the GATS contain different requirements regarding the relationship between the measure at issue and the policy objective pursued. For a measure to be provisionally justified under the exceptions listed in paragraphs (a), (b) and (c) of Article XIV, that measure must be *necessary* to achieve the policy objective pursued. No such requirement of necessity exists under paragraphs (d) and (e). To date, there is case law only on the exceptions under paragraphs (a) and (c) of Article XIV.

3.2.1   Article XIV(a)

Article XIV(a) of the GATS deals with measures which are 'necessary to protect public morals or to maintain public order'. Article XIV(a) sets out a two-tier test to determine whether a measure is *provisionally* justified under this provision. The Member invoking Article XIV(a) must establish that: (1) the policy objective pursued by the measure at issue is the protection of public morals or the maintenance of public order; and (2) the measure is necessary to fulfil that policy objective.

With regard to the first element of this two-tier test, note that the panel in *US – Gambling (2005)* dealt extensively with the interpretation and application of this element. Antigua and Barbuda challenged the GATS-consistency of a number of US federal and state laws, including the Wire Act, the Travel Act and the Illegal Gambling Business Act, which prohibit the remote supply of gambling and betting services, including Internet gambling.[177] The United States, *inter alia*, argued that the measures at issue could be justified under Article XIV(a) of the GATS, as necessary to protect public morals and maintain public order. With regard to the meaning of the concepts of 'public morals' and 'public order', the panel in *US – Gambling (2005)* found that it:

can vary in time and space, depending upon a range of factors, including prevailing social, cultural, ethical and religious values. Further, the Appellate Body has stated on several occasions that Members, in applying similar societal concepts, have the right to determine the level of protection that they consider appropriate. Although these Appellate Body statements were made in the context of Article XX of the GATT 1994, it is our view that such statements are also valid with respect to the protection of public morals and public order under Article [XIV] of the GATS.[178]

---

176   Note that the grounds of justification in Article XIV of the GATS do not include a ground equivalent to Article XX(g) of the GATT 1994, relating to the conservation of exhaustible natural resources. See also above, pp. 565–8.

177   Hereinafter referred to as 'Antigua'.

178   Panel Report, *US – Gambling (2005)*, para. 6.461.

According to the panel:

Members should be given some scope to define and apply for themselves the concepts of 'public morals' and 'public order' in their respective territories, according to their own systems and scales of values.[179]

To determine the ordinary meanings of 'public morals' and 'public order', the panel turned to the *Shorter Oxford English Dictionary*, and found that the term 'public' is defined therein as: 'Of or pertaining to the people as a whole; belonging to, affecting, or concerning the community or nation.' The panel thus ruled that a measure that is sought to be justified under Article XIV(a) must be aimed at 'protecting the interests of the people within a community or a nation as a whole'.[180] The term 'morals' was defined by the panel, referring to the *Shorter Oxford English Dictionary*, as: 'habits of life with regard to right and wrong conduct'. The panel ruled that the term 'public morals' denotes:

standards of right and wrong conduct maintained by or on behalf of a community or nation.[181]

Finally, with regard to the term 'order', the panel noted that the dictionary definition that appears to be relevant in the context of Article XIV(a) reads as follows:

A condition in which the laws regulating the public conduct of members of a community are maintained and observed; the rule of law or constituted authority; absence of violence or violent crimes.[182]

The panel subsequently noted that footnote 5 to Article XIV(a) of the GATS states with regard to the 'public order' exception that it:

may be invoked only where a genuine and sufficiently serious threat is posed to one of the fundamental interests of society.

The panel thus concluded that the dictionary definition of the term 'order', read together with footnote 5, suggests that 'public order' refers to:

the preservation of the fundamental interests of a society, as reflected in public policy and law. These fundamental interests can relate, *inter alia*, to standards of law, security and morality.[183]

While 'public morals' and 'public order' are two different concepts, the panel in *US – Gambling (2005)* considered that overlap may nevertheless exist as those concepts 'seek to protect largely similar values'.[184] The Appellate Body left the panel's interpretation of the concepts of 'public morals' and 'public order', as well as the panel's application of the first element of the test under Article XIV(a), undisturbed.[185]

---

179 *Ibid.*   180 *Ibid.*, para. 6.463.   181 *Ibid.*, para. 6.465.
182 *Ibid.*, para. 6.466.   183 *Ibid.*, para. 6.467.   184 *Ibid.*, para. 6.468.
185 See Appellate Body Report, *US – Gambling (2005)*, paras. 296–9. The Appellate Body merely clarified the function of footnote 5 to Article XIV(a). According to the Appellate Body, this footnote does *not* require a separate and explicit finding that its standard is met. See Appellate Body Report, *US – Gambling (2005)*, para. 298.

The United States had argued that Internet gambling posed threats with regard to organised crime, money laundering and fraud; risks to children; and risks to health due to the possible development of an addiction to gambling.[186] The panel had no difficulty in finding that these concerns fell within the scope of 'public morals' and 'public order' as meant in Article XIV(a) and that the Wire Act, the Travel Act and the Illegal Gambling Business Act, the measures at issue, were measures to protect 'public morals or public order'.[187]

The second element of the test under Article XIV(a) of the GATS concerns the 'necessity' requirement. As both the panel and the Appellate Body in *US – Gambling (2005)* explicitly recognised, the extensive case law on the 'necessity' requirement of Article XX(b) and (d) of the GATT 1994 – discussed at length above – is very relevant for the interpretation and application of the 'necessity' requirement of Article XIV of the GATS.[188] On the basis of this Article XX GATT case law, the panel stated that, in determining whether a measure is 'necessary' within the meaning of Article XIV(a) of the GATS, it must assess the following factors:

(a) the importance of the interests or values that the challenged measure is intended to protect. (With respect to this requirement, the Appellate Body has suggested that, if the value or interest pursued is considered important, it is more likely that the measure is 'necessary'.)
(b) the extent to which the challenged measure contributes to the realization of the end pursued by that measure. (In relation to this requirement, the Appellate Body has suggested that the greater the extent to which the measure contributes to the end pursued, the more likely that the measure is 'necessary'.)
(c) the trade impact of the challenged measure. (With regard to this requirement, the Appellate Body has said that, if the measure has a relatively slight trade impact, the more likely that the measure is 'necessary'. The Appellate Body has also indicated that whether a reasonably available WTO-consistent alternative measure exists must be taken into consideration in applying this requirement.)[189]

With regard to the first of these factors, the panel found that the interests and values protected by the Wire Act, the Travel Act and the Illegal Gambling Business Act[190] can be characterised as 'vital and important in the highest degree'.[191] With regard to the second factor, the panel found that all three Acts contribute,

---

186 See Panel Report, *US – Gambling (2005)*, para. 6.479.
187 See *ibid.*, para. 6.487. The Appellate Body upheld the panel's findings, but did not discuss them substantively. See Appellate Body Report, *US – Gambling (2005)*, para. 299.
188 See above, pp. 556–65.
189 Panel Report, *US – Gambling (2005)*, para. 6.477. Note that one could debate whether this is a fully correct rendition of the case law on the 'necessity' requirement of Article XX(b) and (d) of the GATT 1994. See above, pp. 558–9.
190 Namely, to protect society against the threat of money laundering, organised crime, fraud and risks to children (i.e. under-age gambling) and health (i.e. pathological gambling).
191 Panel Report, *US – Gambling (2005)*, para. 6.492. The panel noted that this characterisation is similar to the characterisation of the protection of human life and health against a life-threatening health risk by the Appellate Body in *EC – Asbestos (2001)*. See Appellate Body Report, *EC – Asbestos (2001)*, para. 172.

at least to some extent, to addressing the concerns pertaining to money laundering, organised crime, fraud, under-age gambling and pathological gambling.[192]
With regard to the third factor, the panel noted that:

> [A] key element of the application of the 'necessity' test of Article XIV in this dispute is
> whether the United States has explored and exhausted reasonably available WTO-consistent
> alternatives to the US prohibition on the remote supply of gambling and betting services
> that would ensure the same level of protection.[193]

However, the panel found that the United States, in rejecting Antigua's invitation to engage in bilateral or multilateral consultations, failed to pursue a good
faith course of action to explore the possibility of finding a reasonably available WTO-consistent alternative.[194] Having assessed each of the three factors,
the panel then 'weighed and balanced' those factors and concluded that the
measures at issue were *not* 'necessary' within the meaning of Article XIV(a) of
the GATS.[195]

   On appeal, the Appellate Body stated that the weighing and balancing process
to determine whether a measure is 'necessary' to maintain public order or protect public morals within the meaning of Article XIV(a) of the GATS begins with:

> an assessment of the 'relative importance' of the interests or values furthered by the chal-
> lenged measure. Having ascertained the importance of the particular interests at stake, a
> panel should then turn to the other factors that are to be 'weighed and balanced'. The Ap-
> pellate Body has pointed to two factors that, in most cases, will be relevant to a panel's
> determination of the 'necessity' of a measure, although not necessarily exhaustive of factors
> that might be considered. One factor is the contribution of the measure to the realization of
> the ends pursued by it; the other factor is the restrictive impact of the measure on interna-
> tional commerce.[196]

Next, having assessed each of these factors:

> [a] comparison between the challenged measure and possible alternatives should then be
> undertaken, and the results of such comparison should be considered in the light of the
> importance of the interests at issue. It is on the basis of this 'weighing and balancing' and
> comparison of measures, taking into account the interests or values at stake, that a panel
> determines whether a measure is 'necessary' or, alternatively, whether another, WTO-con-
> sistent measure is 'reasonably available'.[197]

With respect to the availability and the nature of an 'alternative measure', the
Appellate Body noted:

> An alternative measure may be found not to be 'reasonably available', however, where it is
> merely theoretical in nature, for instance, where the responding Member is not capable of
> taking it, or where the measure imposes an undue burden on that Member, such as prohibi-
> tive costs or substantial technical difficulties. Moreover, a 'reasonably available' alternative

192 See Panel Report, *US – Gambling (2005)*, para. 6.494.
193 *Ibid.*, para. 6.528.   194 See *ibid.*, para. 6.531.   195 See *ibid.*, para. 6.535.
196 Appellate Body Report, *US – Gambling (2005)*, para. 306.
197 *Ibid.*, para. 307.

measure must be a measure that would preserve for the responding Member its right to achieve its desired level of protection with respect to the objective pursued under paragraph (a) of Article XIV.[198]

As to the question of who bears the burden of proof to establish the existence of a reasonably available 'alternative measure', the Appellate Body noted that:

it is not the responding party's burden to show, in the first instance, that there are *no* reasonably available alternatives to achieve its objectives. In particular, a responding party need not identify the universe of less trade-restrictive alternative measures and then show that none of those measures achieves the desired objective. The WTO agreements do not contemplate such an impracticable and, indeed, often impossible burden.

Rather, it is for a responding party to make a *prima facie* case that its measure is 'necessary' by putting forward evidence and arguments that enable a panel to assess the challenged measure in the light of the relevant factors to be 'weighed and balanced' in a given case. The responding party may, in so doing, point out why alternative measures would not achieve the same objectives as the challenged measure, but it is under no obligation to do so in order to establish, in the first instance, that its measure is 'necessary'.

If, however, the complaining party raises a WTO-consistent alternative measure that, in its view, the responding party should have taken, the responding party will be required to demonstrate why its challenged measure nevertheless remains 'necessary' in the light of that alternative or, in other words, why the proposed alternative is not, in fact, 'reasonably available'.[199]

As discussed above, the panel had concluded that the United States had not established that its measures were 'necessary' because, in rejecting Antigua's invitation to engage in bilateral or multilateral consultations, it had failed to explore and exhaust reasonably available WTO-consistent alternatives to the measures at issue.[200] According to the Appellate Body, the panel's 'necessity' analysis was flawed because it did *not* focus on an alternative measure that was reasonably available to the United States to achieve the stated objectives.[201] Engaging in consultations with Antigua was not an appropriate alternative for the panel to consider *because* consultations are 'by definition a process, the results of which are uncertain and therefore not capable of comparison with the measures at issue in this case'.[202]

Having reversed the panel's conclusion on 'necessity', the Appellate Body then examined for itself whether the measures at issue, the Wire Act, the Travel Act and the Illegal Gambling Business Act, were 'necessary' within the meaning of Article XIV(a) of the GATS.[203] The Appellate Body agreed with the United States that the 'sole basis' for the panel's conclusion that the measures were not necessary was its finding relating to the requirement of consultations with Antigua.[204]

---

198 *Ibid.*, para. 308.   199 *Ibid.*, paras. 309–11.
200 See Panel Report, *US – Gambling (2005)*, para. 6.531. For a summary by the Appellate Body of the key findings of the panel, see Appellate Body Report, *US – Gambling (2005)*, para. 315.
201 See Appellate Body Report, *US – Gambling (2005)*, para. 317.
202 *Ibid.*   203 See *ibid.*, paras. 322–7.
204 The Appellate Body noted that the panel had acknowledged that it would have found that the United States had made its *prima facie* case that its measures were 'necessary' if the United States had not refused to accept Antigua's invitation to consult. See *ibid.*, para. 325.

As the Appellate Body had found that the panel had erred in finding that consultations with Antigua constituted a measure reasonably available to the United States,[205] and as Antigua had raised no other 'alternative measure', the Appellate Body concluded as follows:

> In our opinion, therefore, the record before us reveals no reasonably available alternative measure proposed by Antigua or examined by the Panel that would establish that the three federal statutes are not 'necessary' within the meaning of Article XIV(a). Because the United States made its *prima facie* case of 'necessity', and Antigua failed to identify a reasonably available alternative measure, we conclude that the United States demonstrated that its statutes are 'necessary', and therefore justified, under paragraph (a) of Article XIV.[206]

Thus, according to the Appellate Body, the measures at issue in *US – Gambling (2005)*, which prohibit the remote supply of gambling and betting services, including Internet gambling, are 'necessary' for the maintenance of public order and the protection of public morals within the meaning of Article XIV of the GATS.

Questions and Assignments 8.10

What are the constituent elements of the test under Article XIV(a) of the GATS? How did the panel in *US – Gambling (2005)* interpret the concepts of 'public morals' and 'public order'? Did the Appellate Body agree with this interpretation? Give some examples of 'public morals'. When is a measure 'necessary' within the meaning of Article XIV(a)? When can an 'alternative measure' be found not to be 'reasonably available'? Does the responding party have to prove that there is no reasonably available alternative measure? Why did the Appellate Body in *US – Gambling (2005)* reverse the panel's finding on the 'necessity' requirement under Article XIV(a) of the GATS?

3.2.2 Article XIV(c)

As mentioned above, Article XIV(c) can justify otherwise GATS-inconsistent measures which are necessary to secure compliance with laws or regulations which are not inconsistent with the provisions of the GATS. Article XIV(c) gives three broad *examples* of such laws or regulations, namely, those relating to: (1) the prevention of deceptive and fraudulent practices or to deal with the effects of a default on services contracts; (2) the protection of the privacy of individuals in relation to the processing and dissemination of personal data and the protection of confidentiality of individual records and accounts; and (3) safety. As the panel in *US – Gambling (2005)* noted, this list in Article XIV(c) of possible laws and regulations is not exhaustive.[207]

As held by the panel in *US – Gambling (2005)*, Article XIV(c) of the GATS sets out a three-tier test to determine whether a measure is *provisionally* justified under Article XIV(c). The Member invoking Article XIV(c) must establish that:

---

205 See *ibid.*, para. 317.   206 *Ibid.*, para. 326.
207 See Panel Report, *US – Gambling (2005)*, para. 6.540.

(1) the measure at issue is *designed* to secure compliance with national laws or regulations; (2) those national laws and regulations are *not inconsistent* with the *WTO Agreement*; and (3) the measure at issue is *necessary* to secure compliance with those national laws and regulations.[208]

For the interpretation and application of the first two elements of the test under Article XIV(c) of the GATS, the panel in *US – Gambling (2005)* referred back to the case law on Article XX(d) of the GATT 1994, discussed above.[209] In view of the similarity of Article XIV(c) of the GATS with Article XX(d) of the GATT 1994, this case law is, according to the panel in *US – Gambling (2005)*, most relevant. Consequently, the panel noted that measures for which justification is sought must enforce 'obligations' contained in the laws and regulations rather than 'merely ensure attainment of the objectives of those laws and regulations'.[210] In addition, the panel stated that a measure does not have to be designed exclusively to secure compliance; it is sufficient that 'securing compliance' is part of the reason to put the measure into place.[211]

The third element under the Article XIV(c) test concerns the 'necessity' requirement. The analysis required to determine whether a measure is necessary under Article XIV(c) of the GATS is essentially the same as the analysis required under Article XIV(a) of the GATS, discussed above. The panel in *US – Gambling (2005)* applied the same analysis, but, in doing so, it quite logically made the same mistake that the Appellate Body subsequently identified in the panel's Article XIV(a) analysis.[212] The Appellate Body thus also reversed the panel's conclusion on the 'necessity' requirement under Article XIV(c).[213]

Questions and Assignments 8.11

What are the constituent elements of the test under Article XIV(c) of the GATS? What does the necessity test under Article XIV(c) entail?

3.2.3   Other Paragraphs of Article XIV

With regard to the remaining paragraphs of Article XIV of the GATS, a distinction must be drawn between paragraph (b), which requires that the measure be *necessary* to achieve the policy objective pursued, and paragraphs (d) and (e), which do not impose such a 'necessity' requirement.

---

208 See *ibid.*, para. 6.536.
209 See *ibid.*, paras. 6.536–6.540. With regard to the case law on Article XX(d) of the GATT 1994, see above, pp. 560–5.
210 Panel Report, *US – Gambling (2005)*, para. 6.538. See also Panel Report, *EEC – Parts and Components (1990)*, paras. 5.14–5.18.
211 See Panel Report, *US – Gambling (2005)*, para. 6.539. See also Panel Report, *Korea – Various Measures on Beef (2001)*, para. 658.
212 The panel considered that the measures at issue were not 'necessary' because, in failing to engage in consultations with Antigua, the United States failed to explore and exhaust all reasonably available alternative measures. See above, p. 589.
213 See Appellate Body Report, *US – Gambling (2005)*, para. 336. Note that the Appellate Body did not consider it necessary to complete the legal analysis and determine whether the measures at issue were justified under Article XIV(c) since it had already found that the measures were justified under Article XIV(a). See Appellate Body Report, *US – Gambling (2005)*, para. 337.

Paragraph (b) relates to measures 'necessary to protect human, animal or plant life or health'. Hence, for an otherwise GATS-inconsistent measure to be *provisionally* justified under Article XIV(b): (1) the policy objective pursued by the measure must be the protection of life or health of humans, animals or plants; and (2) the measure must be necessary to fulfil that policy objective. To date, there has been no case law on the requirements set out by Article XIV(b). However, as regards the 'necessity' test, it may be assumed that the interpretation of the necessity requirement under Article XIV(a) and (c) of the GATS and the extensive case law on the necessity requirement of Article XX(b) and (d) of the GATT 1994 are relevant.[214]

With regard to Article XIV(d) and (e) of the GATS, it must be noted that the scope of these provisions is rather narrow. The grounds of justification set out in these provisions *only* justify inconsistency with the national treatment obligation of Article XVII of the GATS *or* the MFN treatment obligation of Article II of the GATS. With regard to measures relating to direct taxation, Article XIV(d) of the GATS allows Members to adopt or enforce measures which are inconsistent with the national treatment obligation of Article XVII:

provided that the difference in treatment is aimed at ensuring the equitable or effective imposition or collection of direct taxes in respect of services or service suppliers of other Members.[215]

Footnote 6 to Article XIV(d) contains a non-exhaustive list of measures that are aimed at ensuring the equitable or effective imposition or collection of direct taxes. This list includes measures taken by a Member under its taxation system which apply: (1) to non-residents in order to ensure the imposition or collection of taxes in the Member's territory; or (2) to non-residents or residents to prevent the avoidance or evasion of taxes.

Article XIV(e) of the GATS allows a Member to adopt or enforce measures which are inconsistent with the MFN treatment obligation of Article II:

provided that the difference in treatment is the result of an agreement on the avoidance of double taxation or provisions on the avoidance of double taxation in any other international agreement or arrangement by which the Member is bound.

Note that Article XIV of the GATS does not contain a counterpart to Article XX(g) of the GATT relating to the conservation of natural resources. In this regard, the 1993 Uruguay Round *Decision on Trade in Services and the Environment* notes that, 'since measures necessary to protect the environment typically have as their objective the protection of human, animal or plant life or health, it is not clear that there is a need to provide for more than is contained' in Article XIV(b). The Decision contemplates that the Committee on Trade and Environment should examine and report 'whether any modification of Article XIV' is required to take into account the 'relationship between services trade and the

214 See above, pp. 585–91 and pp. 554–65.   215 Article XIV(d) of the GATS.

environment, including sustainable development'. No such modification of Article XIV of the GATS has occurred.

Questions and Assignments 8.12

Discuss the measures relating to direct taxes which Members are allowed to take under Article XIV of the GATS. Can a measure which is inconsistent with Article XVI of the GATS (market access) be provisionally justified under Article XIV (d) and (e) thereof?

3.3 Chapeau of Article XIV of the GATS

As discussed above, Article XIV of the GATS sets out a two-tier test for determining whether a measure, otherwise inconsistent with GATS obligations, can be justified. Under this test, once it has been established that the measure at issue meets the requirements of one of the particular exceptions of paragraphs (a) to (e), it must be examined whether the measure meets the requirements of the chapeau of Article XIV. The chapeau of Article XIV requires that the *application* of the measure at issue does not constitute: (1) 'arbitrary or unjustifiable discrimination between countries where the same conditions prevail'; or (2) 'a disguised restriction on trade in services'.

Note that the language of the chapeau of Article XIV of the GATS is quite similar to that of the chapeau of Article XX of the GATT 1994. Therefore, many lessons can be drawn from the extensive case law on the application of the chapeau of Article XX, discussed in detail above.[216] The panel in *US – Gambling (2005)* looked at this case law and concluded:

To sum up these interpretive principles, the chapeau of Article XX of the GATT 1994 addresses not so much a challenged measure or its specific content, but rather the manner in which that measure is applied, with a view to ensuring that the exceptions of Article XX are not abused. In order to do so, the chapeau of Article XX identifies three standards which may be invoked in relation to the same facts: arbitrary discrimination, unjustifiable discrimination and disguised restriction on trade. In our view, these principles would also be applicable in relation to Article XIV of the GATS.[217]

Moreover, the panel stated that, in determining whether the application of the measures at issue constitutes 'arbitrary and unjustifiable discrimination' or a 'disguised restriction on trade':

the *absence of consistency* in this regard may lead to a conclusion that the measures in question are applied in a manner that constitutes 'arbitrary and unjustifiable discrimination between countries where like conditions prevail' and/or a 'disguised restriction on trade'.[218]

In the course of its examination of the requirements of the chapeau of Article XIV of the GATS, the panel found that the United States had not prosecuted

---

216 See above, pp. 572–81.
217 Panel Report, *US – Gambling (2005)*, para. 6.581. The Appellate Body confirmed the importance of Article XX of the GATT 1994 for the interpretation of Article XIV of the GATS in *US – Gambling (2005)*, as explained above, pp. 585 and 587.
218 Panel Report, *US – Gambling (2005)*, para. 6.584. Emphasis added.

certain domestic remote suppliers of gambling services and that the US Inter-state Horseracing Act was 'ambiguous' as to whether or not it permitted certain types of remote betting on horse racing within the United States.[219] On the basis of these two findings indicating a lack of consistency in the application of the prohibition on the remote supply of gambling and betting services, the panel in *US – Gambling (2005)* concluded that:

> the United States has not demonstrated that it does not apply its prohibition on the re-mote supply of wagering services for horse racing in a manner that [constitutes] 'arbitrary and unjustifiable discrimination between countries where like conditions prevail' and/or a 'disguised restriction on trade' in accordance with the requirements of the chapeau of Article XIV.[220]

On appeal, the United States argued that the 'consistency' standard applied by the panel is not adequate for a complete examination under the requirements of the chapeau of Article XIV.[221] The Appellate Body, however, dismissed this argument of the United States and upheld the panel's 'consistency' standard.[222]

Questions and Assignments 8.13

In what way does the chapeau of Article XIV of the GATS differ from the chapeau of Article XX of the GATT 1994? What is the object and purpose of the chapeau of Article XIV of the GATS?

4   SECURITY EXCEPTIONS UNDER THE GATT 1994 AND THE GATS

In addition to the 'general exceptions' contained in Article XX of the GATT 1994 and Article XIV of the GATS, WTO law also provides for exceptions relating to national and international security. This section discusses, first, the security exceptions of Article XXI of the GATT 1994 and, secondly, the security exceptions of Article XIV*bis* of the GATS.[223]

---

219 On the failure to prosecute certain domestic remote suppliers of gambling services, see Panel Report, *US – Gambling (2005)*, para. 6.588. On the US Interstate Horseracing Act, see Panel Report, *US – Gambling (2005)*, para. 6.599.

220 Panel Report, *US – Gambling (2005)*, para. 6.608.

221 According to the United States, the panel assessed only whether the United States treats domestic service suppliers differently from foreign service suppliers. The United States considered such an assessment to be inadequate, because the chapeau of Article XIV of the GATS also requires a determination of whether differential treatment, or discrimination, is 'arbitrary' or 'unjustifiable'.

222 Appellate Body Report, *US – Gambling (2005)*, paras. 348–51. Note, however, that, while the Appellate Body agreed with the panel's approach to the examination of the chapeau of Article XIV of the GATS, it eventually upheld only the panel's finding of 'inconsistency' with regard to the Interstate Horseracing Act. The Appellate Body reversed the panel's finding of 'inconsistency' based on the alleged non-prosecution of certain domestic remote suppliers of gambling services (because the three Acts at issue, on their face, do *not* discriminate between US and foreign suppliers of remote gambling services *and* the evidence of the alleged non-enforcement of the three Acts was 'inconclusive'). See Appellate Body Report, *US – Gambling (2005)*, paras. 352–7, 358–66 and 368–9.

223 Note that also other WTO agreements, such as the *TBT Agreement*, contain provisions relating to measures taken in the context of national security policies. See e.g. Article 2.2 of the *TBT Agreement*. See below, pp. 874–5.

4.1 Article XXI of the GATT 1994

Article XXI of the GATT 1994, entitled 'Security Exceptions', states:

Nothing in this Agreement shall be construed

(a) to require any [Member] to furnish any information the disclosure of which it considers contrary to its essential security interests; or
(b) to prevent any [Member] from taking any action which it considers necessary for the protection of its essential security interests

   (i)   relating to fissionable materials or the materials from which they are derived;
   (ii) relating to the traffic in arms, ammunition and implements of war and to such traffic in other goods and materials as is carried on directly or indirectly for the purpose of supplying a military establishment;
   (iii) taken in time of war or other emergency in international relations; or

(c) to prevent any [Member] from taking any action in pursuance of its obligations under the United Nations Charter for the maintenance of international peace and security.

Unlike Article XX, Article XXI has, to date, not played a significant role in the practice of dispute settlement under the GATT 1947 or the WTO. Article XXI has been invoked in only a few disputes.[224] Nevertheless, this provision is not without importance. WTO Members do, on occasion, take trade-restrictive measures, either unilaterally or multilaterally, against other Members as a means to achieve national or international security. Members taking such measures will seek justification for these measures under Article XXI. As will be discussed, there are significant structural and interpretative differences between Article XX and Article XXI.

4.1.1 Article XXI(a) and (b)

Traditionally, in international relations, national security takes precedence over the benefits of trade. This may be the case in three types of situation. First, States may consider it necessary to restrict trade in order to protect strategic domestic production capabilities from import competition. The judgment as to which production capabilities deserve to be qualified as strategically important differs among countries and is, to a great extent, political. Some Members argue that industries equipping the military, industries producing staple foods and industries producing gasoline or other energy productions are of 'strategic' importance. Secondly, States may wish to use trade sanctions, as an instrument of foreign policy, against other States, which either violate international law

---

224 Article XXI of the GATT was of relevance in *US – Export Restrictions (Czechoslovakia) (1949)*, *US – Sugar Quota (1984)*, *US – Nicaraguan Trade (1986)* and *US – Cuban Liberty and Democratic Solidarity Act (Helms–Burton Act) (1996)*. Note also that, in December 1991, the European Communities notified the GATT Contracting Parties of the measures it took in respect of Yugoslavia, and indicated that such measures were taken under Article XXI of the GATT. See Communication from the European Communities, *Trade Measures Taken by the European Communities against the Socialist Federal Republic of Yugoslavia*, GATT Document L/6948, 2 December 1991.

or pursue policies considered to be unacceptable or undesirable. Thirdly, States may want to prohibit the export of arms or other products of military use to countries with which they do not have friendly relations. Note that GATT provisions, other than Article XXI, may allow Members leeway, for example, to preserve national industries of strategic importance. WTO Members can, subject to limitations, provide protection through import tariffs, production subsidies and government procurement practices. In some situations, however, Article XXI can be useful to provide justification for otherwise GATT-inconsistent measures.

Article XXI(a) allows a Member to withhold information that it would normally be required to supply when 'it considers' disclosure of that information 'contrary to its essential security interests'. Some Members have interpreted this provision broadly. In this regard, note the following statement by the United States from 1949:

> The United States does consider it contrary to its security interest – and to the security interest of other friendly countries – to reveal the names of the commodities that it considers to be most strategic.[225]

Article XXI(b) allows a Member to adopt or maintain certain measures which that Member considers necessary for the protection of its essential security interests. The categories of measure concerned are broadly defined in sub-paragraphs (i), (ii) and (iii) of Article XXI(b) as: (1) measures relating to fissionable materials; (2) measures relating to trade in arms or in other materials, directly or indirectly, for military use; and (3) measures taken in time of war or other emergency in international relations. In view of the wording of Article XXI(b), and in particular the use of the terms 'action which it *considers* necessary' (emphasis added), the question arises whether the exceptions of this paragraph are 'justiciable', i.e. whether the application of these exceptions can usefully be reviewed by panels and the Appellate Body. Indeed, Article XXI(b) gives a Member very broad discretion to take national security measures which it 'considers necessary' for the protection of its essential security interests. However, it is imperative that a certain degree of 'judicial review' be maintained; otherwise the provision would be prone to abuse without redress.[226] At a minimum, panels and the Appellate Body should conduct an examination as to whether the explanation provided by the Member concerned is reasonable or whether the measure constitutes an apparent abuse. With regard to avoiding abuse of the exceptions listed in Article XXI(b), and more generally the exceptions listed in Article XXI as a whole, it must be noted that, unlike Article XX of the GATT 1994, Article XXI does not have a chapeau to prevent misuse or abuse of the exceptions contained therein.[227]

The exceptions of Article XXI(b) have been invoked in a few GATT disputes and have been discussed on a few other occasions before the establishment of

225 GATT/CP.3/38, 9.
226 See the panel's statement in *US – Nicaraguan Trade (1986)*, in *GATT Activities 1986*, 58–9.
227 On the function of the chapeau of Article XX of the GATT 1994, see above, pp. 572–81.

the WTO. For instance, in one of the very first panel reports, the panel report in *US – Export Restrictions (Czechoslovakia) (1949)*, it was stated that:

every country must be the judge in the last resort on questions relating to its own security. On the other hand, every Contracting Party should be cautious not to take any step which might have the effect of undermining the General Agreement.[228]

In 1982, in the context of the armed conflict between the United Kingdom and Argentina over the Falkland Islands/Islas Malvinas, the European Economic Community and its Member States as well as Canada and Australia applied trade restrictions against imports from Argentina. In a 'reaction' to these actions, the GATT CONTRACTING PARTIES adopted a Ministerial Declaration, which stated that:

the contracting parties undertake, individually and jointly ... to abstain from taking restrictive trade measures, for reasons of a non-economic character, *not consistent* with the General Agreement.[229]

At the time, the GATT CONTRACTING PARTIES also adopted the following *Decision Concerning Article XXI of the General Agreement*:

Considering that the exceptions envisaged in Article XXI of the General Agreement constitute an important element for safeguarding the rights of contracting parties when they consider that reasons of security are involved; *Noting* that recourse to Article XXI could constitute, in certain circumstances, an element of disruption and uncertainty for international trade and affect benefits accruing to contracting parties under the General Agreement; *Recognizing* that in taking action in terms of the exceptions provided in Article XXI of the General Agreement, contracting parties should take into consideration the interests of third parties which may be affected; That until such time as the Contracting Parties may decide to make a formal interpretation of Article XXI it is appropriate to set procedural guidelines for its application;

The Contracting Parties *decide* that:

1. Subject to the exception in Article XXI:a, contracting parties should be informed to the fullest extent possible of trade measures taken under Article XXI.
2. When action is taken under Article XXI, all contracting parties affected by such action retain their full rights under the General Agreement.
3. The Council may be requested to give further consideration to this matter in due course.[230]

In 1985, the United States imposed a trade embargo on Nicaragua.[231] The United States was strongly opposed to the communist Sandinistas who were in power in Nicaragua at that time. Nicaragua argued that the trade embargo imposed by the United States was inconsistent with Articles I, II, V, XI and XIII and Part IV

---

228 Panel Report, *US – Export Restrictions (Czechoslovakia) (1949)*, GATT/CP.3/SR.22, Corr.1.
229 L/5424, adopted on 29 November 1982, 29S/9, 3. Emphasis added.
230 L/5426, adopted on 2 December 1982, 29S/23.
231 Note that, in 1983, Nicaragua's share of the total US sugar import quota was already substantially reduced. The US stated before the panel examining this measure that 'it was neither invoking any exceptions under the provisions of the General Agreement nor intending to defend its actions in GATT terms' (see Panel Report, *US – Sugar Quota (1984)*, para. 3.10). The panel found that the US had acted inconsistently with Article XIII of the GATT 1947. See Panel Report, *US – Sugar Quota (1984)*.

of the GATT and could not be justified – as the United States argued – under Article XXI. Nicaragua requested the establishment of a panel. According to the United States, however, Article XXI left it to each Contracting Party to judge what action it considered necessary for the protection of its essential security interests.[232] A panel was established in this case but the terms of reference of this panel stated that the panel could not examine or judge the validity or motivation for the invocation of Article XXI by the United States. In its report, the panel therefore concluded that:

> as it was not authorized to examine the justification for the United States' invocation of [Article XXI], it could find the United States neither to be complying with its obligations under the General Agreement nor to be failing to carry out its obligations under that Agreement.[233]

To date, the exceptions of Article XXI have not been invoked in any case before a WTO panel or the Appellate Body. Note, however, that, in the *US – Cuban Liberty and Democratic Solidarity Act* dispute in 1996 between the European Communities and the United States, commonly referred to as *US – Helms–Burton Act* dispute, the United States informed the WTO that it would not participate in the panel proceedings since it was of the opinion that the Helms–Burton Act was not within the scope of application of WTO law and, therefore, not within the jurisdiction of the panel. The Helms–Burton Act permits US nationals to bring legal action in US courts against foreign companies that deal or traffic in US property confiscated by the Cuban government. The European Communities contended that this and other measures provided for under the Helms–Burton Act were inconsistent with the obligations of the United States under Articles I, III, V, XI and XIII of the GATT 1994.[234] According to the United States, however, this dispute concerned diplomatic and *security issues* and 'was not fundamentally a trade matter' and, therefore, not a WTO matter.[235] Few Members shared this opinion.[236]

Questions and Assignments 8.14

Which measures, otherwise GATT-inconsistent, can be justified under Article XXI(a) and (b) of the GATT 1994? Why is 'judicial review' by panels and the Appellate Body of the invocation by Members of the exceptions of Article XXI(b) problematic? Is such review desirable and, if so, to what extent? Give an example of a measure that could be justified under Article XXI(b) of the GATT 1994.

---

232 See *Analytical Index: Guide to GATT Law and Practice* (WTO, 1995), 601, 603 and 604.

233 Panel Report, *US – Nicaraguan Trade (1986)*, L/6053, dated 13 October 1986, para. 5.3. This report was never adopted.

234 See Request for Consultations, *US – The Cuban Liberty and Democratic Solidarity Act (Helms–Burton Act)*, WT/DS38/1, dated 13 May 1996.

235 WT/DSB/M/24, dated 16 October 1996, 7. At the request of the European Communities, the panel proceedings were suspended to allow for further negotiations to reach a mutually agreed solution to this dispute. No such solution has ever been explicitly agreed on but the United States has never applied the most controversial aspects of the Helms–Burton Act.

236 See WT/DSB/M/24, dated 16 October 1996, 8–9. On the Helms–Burton Act dispute, see also above, p. 595.

4.1.2 Article XXI(c)

Article XXI(c) of the GATT 1994 allows WTO Members to take actions in pursuance of their obligations under the United Nations Charter for the maintenance of international peace and security. This means that Members may depart from their GATT obligations in order to implement economic sanctions imposed by the United Nations. Article 41 of the *UN Charter* empowers the Security Council to impose economic sanctions, once it has determined the existence of any threat to the peace, breach of the peace or act of aggression. Such Security Council decisions to apply economic sanctions are binding on UN Members according to Article 25 of the *UN Charter*. Hence, Article XXI(c) enables WTO Members to honour their commitments under the *UN Charter*.[237]

At first glance, the issue of 'justiciability', discussed above with regard to Article XXI(b), appears less problematic for the exception provided in Article XXI(c), given that this provision does not refer to what the Member invoking the exception 'considers' to be necessary. The basis for the departure from GATT obligations must be an obligation under the UN Charter, and a panel can assess the question of whether there is such an obligation.

Questions and Assignments 8.15

Which measures, otherwise GATT-inconsistent, can be justified under Article XXI(c) of the GATT 1994? Give an example of a measure that could be justified under Article XXI(c) of the GATT 1994.

4.2 Article XIV*bis* of the GATS

Article XIV*bis* of the GATS, entitled 'Security Exceptions', allows Members to adopt and enforce measures, in the interest of national or international security, otherwise inconsistent with GATS obligations. The language of this provision is virtually identical to Article XXI of the GATT 1994.[238] Like Article XXI of the GATT 1994, Article XIV*bis* of the GATS is not without importance. On occasion, WTO Members take unilateral or multilateral measures affecting the trade in services of other Members, as a means to achieve national or international security. Members taking such measures can seek justification for these measures under Article XIV*bis*. To date, Article XIV*bis* of the GATS has never been invoked in dispute settlement proceedings. However, in terms of 'justiciability',

---

237 Article XXI(c) of the GATT 1994 gives effect to the rule of conflict contained in Article 103 of the *UN Charter*, pursuant to which in the event of a conflict between obligations under the *UN Charter* and obligations under any other international agreement, the obligations under the *UN Charter* shall prevail.

238 Note that the second paragraph of Article XIV*bis* of the GATS provides for a requirement to inform the Council for Trade in Services, to the fullest extent possible, of measures taken under paragraphs 1(b) and (c) of Article XIV*bis*. Article XIV*bis*:2 of the GATS reflects the *Decision Concerning Article XXI of the General Agreement* of the GATT Contracting Parties of 2 December 1982. See above, p. 597.

Article XIV*bis*, and in particular paragraph 2 thereof, is likely to be as problematic as Article XXI(b), discussed above.[239]

Questions and Assignments 8.16

Give two examples of a measure affecting trade in services which would require justification under Article XIV*bis* of the GATS.

5   SUMMARY

Trade liberalisation, market access and non-discrimination rules may conflict with other important societal values and interests, such as the promotion and protection of public health, consumer safety, the environment, employment, economic development and national security. WTO law provides for rules to reconcile trade liberalisation, market access and non-discrimination rules, on the one hand, with these other important societal values and interests, on the other hand. These rules can take the form of wide-ranging *exceptions*, allowing Members, under specific conditions, to adopt or maintain legislation and measures that protect other important societal values and interests, even though this legislation or these measures are in conflict with substantive disciplines imposed by the GATT 1994 or the GATS. These exceptions clearly allow Members, under specific conditions, to give *priority* to certain societal values and interests *over* trade liberalisation, market access and/or non-discrimination rules. This chapter discusses the 'general exceptions' and the 'security exceptions' under the GATT 1994 and the GATS. The next two chapters, Chapters 9 and 10, focus on other exceptions.

The most widely available of the exceptions 'reconciling' trade liberalisation, market access and non-discrimination rules with other societal values and interests are the 'general exceptions' of Article XX of the GATT 1994 and Article XIV of the GATS. In determining whether a measure which is otherwise GATT-inconsistent can be justified under Article XX of the GATT 1994, one must always examine: first, whether this measure can be *provisionally* justified under one of the specific exceptions under paragraphs (a) to (j) of Article XX; and, if so, secondly, whether the application of this measure meets the requirements of the chapeau of Article XX.

Article XX(b) concerns otherwise GATT-inconsistent measures allegedly adopted or maintained for the protection of public health or the environment. For such a measure to be provisionally justified under Article XX(b): (1) the policy *objective* pursued by the measure must be the protection of the life or health

239 See above, pp. 596–8.

of humans, animals or plants; and (2) the measure must be *necessary* to fulfil that policy objective. In deciding whether a measure is necessary, the following factors must be 'weighed and balanced': (a) the *importance* of the societal value pursued by the measure at issue; (b) the *impact* of the measure at issue on trade; and (c) the *extent* to which the measure at issue contributes to the protection or promotion of that value. It is clear that the more important the societal value pursued by the measure at issue, the more this measure contributes to the protection or promotion of this value, and the less restrictive its impact is on international trade, the more easily the measure may be considered to be 'necessary'. If this analysis yields a preliminary conclusion that the measure is necessary, this result must be confirmed by comparing the measure at issue with possible alternative measures, which may be WTO-consistent or less trade-restrictive but provide an equivalent contribution to the achievement of the measure's objective. A measure can only be considered 'necessary' if there is no reasonably available alternative measure that achieves the policy objective of, and is WTO-consistent or less trade-restrictive than, the measure at issue.

Article XX(d) concerns otherwise GATT-inconsistent measures allegedly adopted or maintained to secure compliance with national legislation. For such a measure to be provisionally justified under Article XX(d): (1) the measure must be designed to *secure compliance* with national law – such as customs law, consumer protection law or intellectual property law – which is in itself not GATT-inconsistent; and (2) the measure must be *necessary* to secure compliance. The 'necessity' requirement in Article XX(d) is interpreted in the same way as in Article XX(b).

Article XX(g) concerns otherwise GATT-inconsistent measures allegedly adopted or maintained for the conservation of exhaustible natural resources. For such a measure to be provisionally justified under Article XX(g): (1) the measure must relate to the '*conservation of exhaustible natural resources*'; (2) the measure must '*relate to*' the conservation of exhaustible natural resources; and (3) the measure must be '*made effective in conjunction with*' restrictions on domestic production or consumption. The concept of 'exhaustible natural resources' has been interpreted in a broad, evolutionary manner to include also living resources and, in particular, endangered species. A measure 'relates to' the conservation of exhaustible natural resources when the relationship between the means, i.e. the measure, and the end, i.e. the conservation of exhaustible resources, is real and close, and the measure is not disproportionately wide in its scope or reach in relation to the policy objective pursued. Finally, the requirement that the measure must be 'made effective in conjunction with restrictions on domestic production or consumption' is, in essence, a requirement of 'even-handedness' in the imposition of restrictions on imported and domestic products.

Measures provisionally justified under one of the exceptions of Article XX(a) to (j) must subsequently meet the requirements of the chapeau of Article XX. The object and purpose of the chapeau is to avoid the *application* of the measures provisionally justified could constitute a misuse or abuse of the exceptions of Article XX. The interpretation and application of the chapeau in a particular case is a search for the appropriate *line of equilibrium* between, on the one hand, the right of Members to adopt and maintain trade-restrictive measures that pursue certain legitimate societal values, and, on the other hand, the right of other Members to trade. The search for this line of equilibrium is guided by the requirements set out in the chapeau that the *application* of the trade-restrictive measure may not constitute: (1) *arbitrary* or *unjustifiable discrimination* between countries where the same conditions prevail; or (2) a *disguised restriction* on international trade.

Discrimination has been found to be 'arbitrary' when a measure is applied without any regard for the difference in conditions between countries and the measure is applied in a rigid and inflexible manner. Discrimination has been found to be 'unjustifiable' when the discrimination 'was not merely inadvertent or unavoidable'. Unjustifiable discrimination exists when a Member fails to make serious, good faith efforts to negotiate a multilateral solution before resorting to the unilateral, discriminatory measure for which justification is sought. Moreover, discrimination is arbitary or unjustifiable when the reasons given for the discrimination bear no rational connection to the policy objective of the provisional measure or would go against that objective. A measure, which is provisionally justified under Article XX, will be considered to constitute a 'disguised restriction on international trade' if compliance with such measure is in fact only a disguise to conceal the pursuit of trade-restrictive objectives.

Although Article XX provides for *exceptions* to basic GATT rules and disciplines, the Appellate Body has *not* given a narrow interpretation to Article XX. Instead, it has insisted that a balance must be struck between, on the one hand, trade liberalisation, market access and non-discrimination rules, and, on the other hand, the other societal values referred to in Article XX. The Appellate Body has repeatedly emphasised that WTO Members are free to adopt their own policies and measures aimed at protecting or promoting other societal values, such as public health or the environment, as long as, in so doing, they fulfil their obligations, and respect the rights of other Members, under the *WTO Agreement*. Note that, if the conditions discussed above are fulfilled, Article XX can justify inconsistencies with *any* of the GATT provisions. However, Article XX can *only* justify inconsistencies with GATT provisions (or provisions in other agreements that refer to or incorporate Article XX).

As is the case for Article XX of the GATT 1994, Article XIV of the GATS sets out a two-tier test for determining whether a measure affecting trade in services, otherwise inconsistent with GATS obligations and commitments, can be justified under that provision. To determine whether a measure can be justified under Article XIV of the GATS, one must always examine: first, whether this measure can be provisionally justified under one of the specific exceptions under paragraphs (a) to (e) of Article XIV; and, if so, secondly, whether the application of this measure meets the requirements of the chapeau of Article XIV. The similarities between Article XX of the GATT 1994 and Article XIV of the GATS are striking. However, there are also differences. The specific grounds of justification for measures which are otherwise inconsistent with provisions of the GATS are set out in Article XIV(a) to (e) of the GATS. In the case law to date, there has been particular attention given to Article XIV(a) of the GATS, which concerns otherwise GATS-inconsistent measures that are 'necessary to protect public morals or to maintain public order'. To provisionally justify a measure under Article XIV(a), a Member must establish that: (1) the policy objective pursued by the measure at issue is the protection of *public morals* or the maintenance of *public order*; and (2) the measure is *necessary* to fulfil that policy objective. To be provisionally justified under the exceptions listed in Article XIV(a) as well as in Article XIV(b) and (c), a measure must be *necessary* to achieve the policy objective pursued. In this respect, the extensive case law on the 'necessity' requirement of Article XX(b) and (d) of the GATT 1994 has been held to be relevant. No requirement of 'necessity' exists under paragraphs (d) and (e) of Article XIV. Just as with the chapeau of Article XX of the GATT 1994, the chapeau of Article XIV of the GATS requires that the *application* of the measure at issue does not constitute: (1) a means of *arbitrary or unjustifiable discrimination* between countries where the same conditions prevail; or (2) a *disguised restriction* on trade in services.

In addition to the 'general exceptions' contained in Article XX of the GATT 1994 and Article XIV of the GATS, the GATT 1994 and the GATS provide for exceptions relating to national and international security. WTO Members take, on occasion, either unilaterally or multilaterally, trade-restrictive measures against other Members as a means to achieve national or international security. Members taking such measures may seek justification for these measures under Article XXI of the GATT 1994 or Article XIV*bis* of the GATS. Article XXI(b) of the GATT 1994 allows a Member to adopt or maintain: (1) measures relating to fissionable materials; (2) measures relating to trade in arms or in other materials, directly or indirectly, for military use; and (3) measures taken in time of war or other emergency in international relations. A Member may take such measures if and when that Member *considers* these measures to be necessary for the protection of its essential security interests. Article XIV*bis* of the GATS is virtually identical to Article XXI(b) of the GATT 1994. The 'justiciability' of these exceptions is not clear. Article XXI(c) of the GATT 1994 and Article XIV*bis* (c) of the GATS are much less problematic in this respect as they allow WTO Members to take trade and economic sanctions in compliance with UN Security Council decisions related to the maintenance of international peace and security.

Exercise 8: Tetra Pack Containers

Last year, Newland adopted legislation, commonly referred to as the '*Tetra Pack Act*', which requires that all non-alcoholic beverages be sold in Tetra Pack containers. Until last year, non-alcoholic beverages were often sold in glass bottles. According to Newland, the recycling of Tetra Pack containers is more eco-friendly than the recycling of glass bottles (since no water and no detergents are used). Moreover, the use of Tetra Pack containers, rather than glass bottles, will reduce the use of silica, which is, according to Newland, a mineral in ever-shorter supply. Newland also argues that the mandatory use of Tetra Pack containers for non-alcoholic beverages will help consumers to differentiate between alcoholic beverages and non-alcoholic beverages and thus help to avoid consumer fraud, as defined in Newland's Consumer Protection Act of 2010. Newland backs up these various justifications for its *Tetra Pack Act* with scientific studies, but the conclusions of few of these studies reflect the majority view in the scientific community. The *Tetra Pack Act* also prohibits the advertising for, and the distribution of, non-alcoholic beverages in glass bottles. Newland argues that such prohibition is necessary to protect public morals and maintain public order, until last year.

Richland was the main exporter of non-alcoholic beverages in glass bottles to Newland. It was, therefore, much affected by Newland's *Tetra Pack Act*. Richland is of the opinion that Newland introduced this legislation primarily to support its emerging packaging industry. In Richland's opinion, there is no serious scientific basis for Newland's requirement to use Tetra Pack containers, and the level of environmental protection set by Newland is exaggeratedly high. Richland also points out that alcoholic beverages, and in particular wine, of which Newland is an important producer and exporter, can be sold in glass bottles as well as Tetra Pack containers. Moreover, for the next ten years, fruit juice produced in least-developed countries will not be subject to the packaging requirements of the *Tetra Pack Act* in order to give producers of countries sufficient time to adapt to the new requirements. Richland notes that Newland rejected without much ado Richland's invitation to start multilateral negotiations on a gradual reduction of the use of glass bottles for non-alcoholic beverages. Also, the *Tetra Pack Act* prohibition on advertising and distribution – two services sectors with respect to which Newland has made market access and national treatment commitments – hits Richland badly, as its advertising and distribution companies were very active in Newland.

Richland has requested consultations with Newland on the WTO-consistency of the *Tetra Pack Act*. You are part of a team of young trade officials instructed to prepare a legal brief in support of the position of Richland. Your task is to write the part of this brief dealing with Newland's possible justifications for its *Tetra Pack Act* under Article XX of the GATT 1994 and Article XIV of the GATS.

9 Economic Emergency Exceptions

CONTENTS

1   INTRODUCTION

As mentioned in Chapter 8, apart from the 'general exceptions' and the 'security exceptions', discussed in that chapter, WTO law also provides for 'economic emergency exceptions'. These exceptions allow Members to adopt two types of measures, otherwise WTO-inconsistent, namely, 'safeguard measures' and 'balance-of-payments measures'. This chapter deals in turn with: (1) safeguard measures under the GATT 1994 and the *Agreement on Safeguards*; (2) safeguard measures under other WTO agreements; and (3) balance-of-payments measures under the GATT 1994 and the GATS.

2   SAFEGUARD MEASURES UNDER THE GATT 1994 AND THE *AGREEMENT ON SAFEGUARDS*

The most important and most frequently used of the measures discussed in this chapter are the safeguard measures under the GATT 1994 and the *Agreement on Safeguards*. These safeguard measures may be adopted where a surge in imports causes, or threatens to cause, serious injury to the domestic industry. The possibility to restrict trade in such situations is a 'safety valve' which has always been, and still is, provided for in most trade agreements, including the *WTO Agreement*. It reflects the political reality that trade liberalisation may be difficult to sustain if and when it creates unexpected and severe economic hardship for certain sectors of a country's economy, especially import-competing industries. Safeguard measures temporarily restrict import competition to allow the domestic industry time to adjust to new economic realities. Their application does not depend upon 'unfair' trade actions, as is the case with anti-dumping or countervailing measures.[1] Safeguard measures are applied to 'fair trade', that is, trade occurring under normal competitive conditions and in accordance with WTO law. The Appellate Body therefore noted in *Argentina – Footwear (EC) (2000)* that:

> the import restrictions that are imposed on products of exporting Members when a safeguard action is taken must be seen ... as *extraordinary*. And, when construing the prerequisites for taking such actions, their extraordinary nature must be taken into account.[2]

In *US – Line Pipe (2002)*, the Appellate Body stated that 'part of the *raison d'être*' of safeguard measures is:

> unquestionably, that of giving a WTO Member the possibility, as trade is liberalized, of resorting to an effective remedy in an extraordinary emergency situation that, in the judgment of that Member, makes it necessary to protect a domestic industry temporarily.[3]

The Appellate Body further stated that there is:

> a natural tension between, on the one hand, defining the appropriate and legitimate scope of the right to apply safeguard measures and, on the other hand, ensuring that safeguard measures are not applied against 'fair trade' beyond what is necessary to provide extraordinary and temporary relief. A WTO Member seeking to apply a safeguard measure will argue, correctly, that the *right* to apply such measures must be respected in order to maintain the *domestic* momentum and motivation for ongoing trade liberalization. In turn, a WTO Member whose trade is affected by a safeguard measure will argue, correctly, that the *application* of such measures must be limited in order to maintain the *multilateral* integrity of ongoing trade concessions. The balance struck by the WTO Members in reconciling this natural tension relating to safeguard measures is found in the provisions of the *Agreement on Safeguards*.[4]

---

1 See below, pp. 677–8 and 814–15.
2 Appellate Body Report, *Argentina – Footwear (EC) (2000)*, para. 94. Emphasis added.
3 Appellate Body Report, *US – Line Pipe (2002)*, para. 82.   4 *Ibid.*, para. 83.

Article XIX of the GATT 1994 and the provisions of the *Agreement on Safe-guards* set out the rules according to which Members may take safeguard meas-ures. Article XIX of the GATT 1994, entitled 'Emergency Action on Imports of Particular Products', provides, in paragraph 1(a):

> If, as a result of unforeseen developments and of the effect of the obligations incurred by a [Member] under this Agreement, including tariff concessions, any product is being imported into the territory of that [Member] in such increased quantities and under such conditions as to cause or threaten serious injury to domestic producers in that territory of like or directly competitive products, the [Member] shall be free ... to suspend the obligation in whole or in part or to withdraw or modify the concession.

Under Article XIX of the GATT 1947, which was, in all respects, identical to Article XIX of the GATT 1994, some 150 safeguard measures were officially notified to the Contracting Parties. However, Contracting Parties often resorted to measures other than safeguard measures to address situations in which im-ports caused particular economic hardship. These 'other' measures included vol-untary export restraints (VERs), voluntary restraint arrangements (VRAs) and orderly marketing arrangements (OMAs), as discussed above.[5] Unlike safeguard measures, these other measures did not involve compensation, and were applied selectively to the main exporting countries.[6] This explained the 'popularity' of VERs, VRAs and OMAs. The *Agreement on Safeguards* was negotiated during the Uruguay Round because of the need to clarify and reinforce the disciplines of Article XIX of the GATT, re-establish multilateral control over safeguard meas-ures and eliminate measures, such as VERs, VRAs and OMAs, that escaped such control. The *Agreement on Safeguards* now prohibits these 'other' measures and requires that all safeguard measures comply with Article XIX of the GATT 1994 and the detailed disciplines of the *Agreement on Safeguards* discussed below.

The *Agreement on Safeguards*, which is part of Annex 1A to the *WTO Agree-ment*, confirms and clarifies the provisions of Article XIX of the GATT 1994 but also provides for new rules. The *Agreement on Safeguards* sets out: (1) the substantive requirements that must be met in order to apply a safeguard measure (Articles 2 and 4); (2) the (national and international) procedural requirements that must be met by a Member applying a safeguard measure (Articles 3 and 12); and (3) the characteristics of, and conditions relating to, a safeguard measure (Articles 5 to 9). On the relationship between the provisions of the *Agreement on Safeguards* and Article XIX of the GATT 1994, the Appellate Body in *Korea – Dairy (2000)* ruled, on the basis of Articles 1 and 11.1(a) of the *Agreement on Safeguards*, that:

---

5   See above, p. 491.
6   For a discussion on the requirement of compensation and the difficulty of applying safeguard measures selectively, see below, pp. 625–7 and 630–1.

any safeguard measure imposed after the entry into force of the *WTO Agreement* must comply with the provisions of *both* the *Agreement on Safeguards* and Article XIX of the GATT 1994.[7]

As the Appellate Body noted in *Argentina – Footwear (EC) (2000)*, nothing in the *WTO Agreement* suggests the intention by the Uruguay Round negotiators to subsume the requirements of Article XIX of the GATT 1994 *within* the *Agreement on Safeguards* and thus to render those requirements no longer applicable.[8] As discussed below, this is of particular importance for the requirement that the surge in imports be the result of 'unforeseen developments'.[9] This requirement is included in Article XIX of the GATT 1994 but not in the more detailed *Agreement on Safeguards*. Nevertheless, this requirement is in the Appellate Body's view fully applicable. Article XIX of the GATT 1994 and the *Agreement on Safeguards* apply *cumulatively*.[10]

Since the establishment of the WTO in 1995 until 30 April 2012, 234 initiations of safeguard measure investigations were reported to the WTO. Approximately half of these investigations resulted in the actual imposition of safeguard measures. India has been the most frequent user of safeguard measures with a total of twenty-eight reported initiations since 1995. Indonesia follows with eighteen initiations, and then Jordan and Turkey with sixteen initiations each. The United States has also been a significant user, with ten initiations since 1995.[11] Moreover, the 2002 US safeguard measures on steel were some of the largest ever imposed in terms of magnitude.[12] In contrast, the European Union has initiated only five investigations since 1995, thus appearing to avoid using safeguard measures if possible. Since the WTO's establishment, an average of approximately thirteen safeguard measure investigations have been initiated per year up to the end of April 2012. New initiations peaked at thirty-four in 2002, with ten initiations in 2008, twenty-five initiations in 2009, twenty initiations in 2010, and eleven initiations in 2011, respectively.[13]

---

7 Appellate Body Report, *Korea – Dairy (2000)*, para. 77.

8 See Appellate Body Report, *Argentina – Footwear (EC) (2000)*, para. 83. The Appellate Body therefore rejected the panel's finding that those requirements of Article XIX of the GATT 1994 which are not reflected in the *Agreement on Safeguards* were superseded by the requirements of the latter.

9 See below, pp. 614–15.

10 Note, however, that this does not prevent a panel or the Appellate Body from exercising judicial economy with respect to a claim of violation of Article XIX where it has found that the measure at issue is inconsistent with the *Agreement on Safeguards*. On the exercise of judicial economy, see above, pp. 222–4.

11 This number is based on the notifications of WTO Members under Article 12.1 of the *Agreement on Safeguards* from 29 March 1995 to 30 April 2012. See www.wto.org/english/tratop_e/safeg_e/SG-Initiations_By_Reporting_Member.pdf.

12 On 5 March 2002, the United States imposed safeguard measures on imports of a range of steel products in the form of additional duties ranging from 8, 13, 15 and up to 30 per cent as well as a tariff quota for a three-year period beginning on 20 March 2002.

13 See www.wto.org/english/tratop_e/safeg_e/SG-Initiations_By_Reporting_Member.pdf, visited 8 February 2013.

To date, 118 final safeguard measures have been imposed by Members.[14] The number of disputes relating to safeguard measures is not insignificant but overall still fairly moderate. To date, there have been forty-five disputes relating to Article XIX of the GATT and the *Agreement on Safeguards*.[15] In only ten of these disputes were panel reports issued, of which six were appealed.[16] Issues related to specific safeguard mechanisms have also arisen in three disputes related to safeguard mechanisms under the *Agreement on Textiles and Clothing*,[17] two disputes related to the *Agreement on Agriculture*,[18] and to specific safeguards under China's Protocol of Accession.[19]

To date, WTO Members have been found to have acted inconsistently with Article XIX of the GATT 1994 and/or the *Agreement on Safeguards* in nine disputes.[20]

Questions and Assignments 9.1

What is the rationale behind the 'economic emergency exception' provided for in Article XIX of the GATT 1994 and the *Agreement on Safeguards*? In your opinion, are safeguard measures applied to fair *or* unfair trade? Does the 'nature' of the trade to which safeguard measures are applied affect the interpretation of the requirements for the application of safeguard measures? Why was the *Agreement on Safeguards* negotiated in the context of the Uruguay Round? Why did GATT Contracting Parties prefer voluntary export restraints (and other similar measures) over safeguard measures? How does the *Agreement on Safeguards* relate to Article XIX of the GATT 1994?

2.1   Requirements for the Use of Safeguard Measures

Article 2.1 of the *Agreement on Safeguards* provides:

A Member may apply a safeguard measure to a product only if that Member has determined, pursuant to the provisions set out below, that such product is being imported into its

---

14 This number is based on the notifications of WTO Members under Article 12.1 of the *Agreement on Safeguards* from 29 March 1995 to 30 April 2012. See www.wto.org/english/tratop_e/safeg_e/SG-Measures_By_Reporting_Member.pdf.

15 By December 2012, there had been forty-five complaints under the *Agreement on Safeguards*: see www.worldtradelaw.net/dsc/database/agreementcount.asp.

16 See Appellate Body Reports in *Korea – Dairy (2000)*; *Argentina – Footwear (EC) (2000)*; *US – Wheat Gluten (2001)*; *US – Lamb (2001)*; *US – Line Pipe (2002)*; and *US – Steel Safeguards (2003)*. See also www.worldtradelaw.net/dsc/database/safeguards.asp.

17 See Appellate Body Reports in *US – Underwear (Costa Rica) (1997)*; *US – Wool Shirts and Blouses from India (1997)*; and *US – Cotton Yarn (Pakistan) (2001)*.

18 See Appellate Body Reports in *EC – Poultry (1998)*; *Chile – Price Band System (2002)*; and *Chile – Price Band System (Article 21.5 – Argentina) (2007)*.

19 For example, the dispute concerning a product-specific safeguard measure on *Certain Passenger Vehicle and Light Truck Tires from China* under Section 16 of the Protocol on the Accession of the People's Republic of China to the WTO (WT/L/432). Both the panel and the Appellate Body found the safeguard measures at issue to be consistent with Chapter 16 of China's Protocol of Accession.

20 See www.worldtradelaw.net/dsc/database/safeguards.asp, accessed 27 February 2013. These include: *Argentina – Footwear (EC) (2000)*; *Korea – Dairy (2000)*; *US – Wheat Gluten (2001)*; *US – Lamb (2001)*; *US – Line Pipe (2002)*; *Argentina – Preserved Peaches (2003)*; *US – Steel Safeguards (2003)*; and *Dominican Republic – Safeguard Measures (2012)*. In *Chile – Price Band System (2002)*, inconsistency with the *Agreement on Agriculture* was found; *China – Tyres (2011)* involved transitional safeguards under China's Protocol of Accession, but no finding of inconsistency was made.

territory in such increased quantities, absolute or relative to domestic production, and under such conditions as to cause or threaten to cause serious injury to the domestic industry that produces like or directly competitive products.

Article XIX:1(a) of the GATT 1994, which – as explained above – applies together with the *Agreement on Safeguards*, provides for the same requirements for the application of safeguard measures as Article 2.1, but, in addition, requires that the increase in imports occurs:

as a result of unforeseen developments and of the effect of the obligations incurred by a [Member] under this Agreement.

In short, Members may apply safeguard measures only when three requirements are met. These requirements are: (1) the 'increased imports' requirement (including the 'unforeseen developments' requirement); (2) the 'serious injury' requirement; and (3) the 'causation' requirement. This section examines each of these requirements in turn.

2.1.1 'Increased Imports' Requirement

Article 2.1 of the *Agreement on Safeguards* explicitly states that the increase in imports can be: (1) an *absolute* increase (i.e. an increase by tonnes or units of the imported products) *or* (2) a *relative* increase (i.e. an increase of imports relative to domestic production, for example even if imports and domestic production decreased, imports decreased less than domestic production).[21] This, however, leaves unanswered the question as to how much, and over what time span, imports must have increased. In *Argentina – Footwear (EC) (2000)*, the Appellate Body clarified the 'increased imports' requirement.

[T]he increase in imports must have been recent enough, sudden enough, sharp enough, and significant enough, both quantitatively and qualitatively, to cause or threaten to cause 'serious injury'.[22]

In *US – Steel Safeguards (2003)*, the Appellate Body reaffirmed these parameters for the interpretation of the 'increased imports' requirement. According to the Appellate Body, the 'increased imports' requirement demands the presence of the following four elements: (1) recent increase; (2) sudden increase; (3) sharp increase; and (4) significant increase. However, the Appellate Body also held that there is no absolute standard as to *how* sudden, recent and significant the increase in imports must be.[23] Thus this test requires a *concrete* evaluation on a case-by-case basis. The result of the test does not depend on the proof of the mere existence of the conditions, but on the extent and intensity of their manifestations.[24] That is why the Appellate Body held in *US – Steel Safeguards*

---

21 See Appellate Body Report, *US – Steel Safeguards (2003)*, para. 390.
22 Appellate Body Report, *Argentina – Footwear (EC) (2000)*, para. 131.
23 See Appellate Body Report, *US – Steel Safeguards (2003)*, paras. 350 and 358.
24 For a detailed discussion, see *ibid.*, paras. 352–60.

(2003) that a demonstration of '*any* increase' in imports is not sufficient to establish 'increased imports' under the *Agreement on Safeguards*.[25] According to the Appellate Body:

[t]he question whether 'such increased quantities' of imports will suffice as 'increased imports' to justify the application of a safeguard measure is a question that can be answered only in the light of 'such conditions' under which those imports occur. The relevant importance of these elements varies from case to case.[26]

If the increase in imports is not recent, sudden and sharp, there will be no economic *emergency* situation justifying the application of a safeguard measure. Furthermore, the *rate* of the increase (e.g. an increase by 30 per cent) as well as the *amount* of the increase (e.g. an increase by 10,000 units) must be considered.[27] In addition, the import *trends* during the entire investigation period must be considered. It does not suffice to compare the level of imports at the beginning of the investigation period with the imports at the end and to conclude that there is an increase in imports within the meaning of the *Agreement on Safeguards*.[28] The analysis of the import trends during the investigation period must also show an increase in imports. However, recall that the increase in imports must be sudden and recent. Therefore, the investigation period should include the *recent past*. Thus, it is not appropriate to examine the import trends over an investigation period that ends some time before the safeguard determination is made.[29] Moreover, the period of investigation must, of course, be sufficiently long to allow appropriate conclusions to be drawn regarding the state of the domestic industry.[30]

Furthermore, while the competent authorities must consider the data for the entire investigation period,[31] more weight is to be given in the assessment to the data relating to the most recent past within the investigation period. In *US – Steel Safeguards (2003)*, the Appellate Body held that the United States made an error by failing to address the decrease in imports that had occurred at the very end of the investigation period.[32]

Consider the examples in Figures 9.1 and 9.2 concerning the imports of chocolate in Member A during the investigation period of 2011–13. In both examples,

---

25 See *ibid.*, para. 355.   26 *Ibid.*, para. 351.
27 See Article 4.2(a) of the *Agreement on Safeguards*.
28 See Appellate Body Report, *Argentina – Footwear (EC) (2000)*, para. 129.
29 See *ibid.*, para. 130.
30 See Appellate Body Report, *US – Lamb (2001)*, para. 138.
31 In *US – Lamb (2001)*, the Appellate Body noted that, 'in conducting their evaluation under Article 4.2(a), competent authorities cannot rely *exclusively* on data from the most recent past, but must assess that data in the context of the data for the entire investigative period'. See Appellate Body Report, *US – Lamb (2001)*, para. 138. See also Appellate Body Report, *Argentina – Footwear (EC) (2000)*, para. 129. The panel in *Argentina – Preserved Peaches (2003)* stated that, '[i]ndeed, detecting an increase in only part of the period is synonymous with isolating the data for that part from the data corresponding to the entire period'. See Panel Report, *Argentina – Preserved Peaches (2003)*, para. 7.67.
32 See Appellate Body Report, *US – Steel Safeguards (2003)*, para. 388.

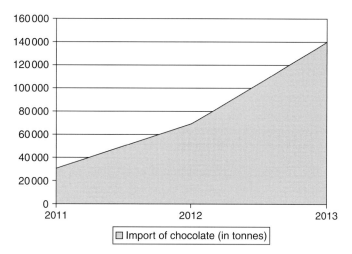

Figure 9.1 'Increased imports' requirement: example 1

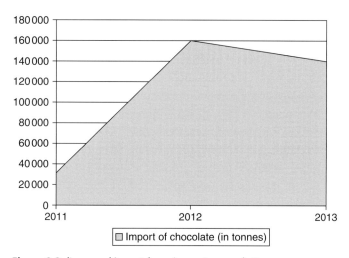

Figure 9.2 'Increased imports' requirement: example 2

there is an increase in imports in the investigation period. The rate of increase as well as the amount of increase is quite significant. In both examples, imports increased from 30,000 tonnes to 140,000 tonnes, representing an increase of more than 460 per cent during the investigation period. However, a different picture emerges if one looks at the import trends. The example in Figure 9.1 is a clear case of a recent, sudden and sharp increase in imports within the meaning of the *Agreement on Safeguards*. It is doubtful whether that same conclusion can be reached with respect to the example in Figure 9.2.[33]

33 It may also be possible to conclude that there is an increase in imports in the example in Figure 9.2, within the meaning of the *Agreement on Safeguards*, if it can be shown that the decline in 2013 was of a temporary and incidental nature.

Pursuant to Article XIX:1 of the GATT 1994, the increase in imports must occur as a result of 'unforeseen developments' and as a result of the effect of obligations incurred under the GATT 1994, including tariff concessions. According to the Working Party in *US – Fur Felt Hats (1951)*, 'unforeseen developments' are:

> developments occurring after the negotiation of the relevant tariff concession which it would not be reasonable to expect that the negotiators of the country making the concession could and should have foreseen at the time when the concession was negotiated.[34]

In 1951, the Working Party held that the fact that hat styles had changed did not constitute an 'unforeseen development'. However, the degree to which the change in fashion affected the competitive situation could not, according to the Working Party, reasonable have been foreseen by the US authorities in 1947.

As discussed above, despite a challenge to the continuing existence of the 'unforeseen developments' requirement under the renovated multilateral safeguards framework of the WTO, this requirement is still 'alive'.[35] Therefore, 'any safeguard measure imposed after the entry into force of the WTO Agreement must comply with the provisions of both the Agreement on Safeguards and Article XIX of the GATT 1994'.[36] In 2000, the Appellate Body ruled in *Korea – Dairy (2000)* that 'unforeseen developments' means unexpected developments.[37] Note that, before imposing a safeguard measure, the Member concerned must demonstrate, as a matter of fact, that the increase in imports is indeed the result of unforeseen, i.e. unexpected, developments.[38] The requirement to demonstrate the causal relationship between the measure taken and an 'unforeseen development' is independent of factual proof of increase in imports. As stated by the panel in *Argentina – Preserved Peaches (2003)*:

> [I]ncrease in imports and the unforeseen developments must be two distinct elements. A statement that the increase in imports, or the way in which they were being imported, was unforeseen, does not constitute a demonstration as a matter of fact of the existence of unforeseen *developments*.[39]

In *US – Steel Safeguards (2003)*, the Appellate Body held that, when an importing Member wishes to apply safeguard measures on imports of several products, it

---

34 Working Party Report, *US – Fur Felt Hats (1951)*, para. 9.   35 See above, p. 609.
36 Appellate Body Report, *Argentina – Footwear (EC) (2000)*, para. 84.
37 See Appellate Body Report, *Korea – Dairy (2000)*, para. 84.
38 See *ibid.*, para. 85. See also Appellate Body Report, *Argentina – Footwear (EC) (2000)*, para. 92.
39 Panel Report, *Argentina – Preserved Peaches (2003)*, para. 7.24. There seems to be a difference of opinion regarding the link between the 'unforeseen developments' and the 'increase in imports'. The panel in *Argentina – Preserved Peaches (2003)* expressly disagreed with the Appellate Body in *Argentina – Footwear (EC) (2000)* that the unforeseen development could itself be the increased quantities of imports. The contradiction appears to pertain to *what* may qualify as an unforeseen development – whether such development ought to be a factor *other than* the increased imports, though *necessarily resulting* in such increased imports, or whether the increased imports could have themselves been unforeseen (*ibid.*, para. 7.24). Note, however, that the Appellate Body itself interpreted the sentence in question, 'the increased quantities of imports should have been "unforeseen" or "unexpected"', appearing in *Argentina – Footwear (EC) (2000)*, para. 131, as 'referring to the fact that the increased imports must, under Article XIX:1(a), *result* from "unforeseen developments"'. See also Appellate Body Report, *US – Steel Safeguards (2003)*, para. 350.

is not sufficient for the competent authority merely to demonstrate that 'unforeseen developments' resulted in increased imports of a *broad category of products* that includes the specific products on which the safeguard measure is imposed.[40] According to the Appellate Body, the competent authorities are required to demonstrate that the unforeseen developments have resulted in increased imports for the *specific products* that are subject to the safeguard measures.[41]

Also in *US – Steel Safeguards (2003)*, the Appellate Body held that the competent authority of the importing Member imposing a safeguard measure must demonstrate in its published report, *through a reasoned and adequate explanation* and a *reasoned conclusion*, that unforeseen developments resulted in increased imports.[42] The panel in *US – Steel Safeguards (2003)* ruled with respect to the determination of 'unforeseen circumstances':

> The nature of the facts, including their complexity, will dictate the extent to which the relationship between the unforeseen developments and increased imports causing injury needs to be explained. The timing of the explanation [relating to unforeseen developments], its extent and its quality are all factors that can affect whether [that] explanation is reasoned and adequate.[43]

On appeal, the Appellate Body upheld this finding.[44] The Appellate Body pointed out that, since a panel may not conduct a *de novo* review of the evidence before the competent authority, it is the *explanation* given by the competent authority for its determination that enables a panel to determine whether there has been compliance with the substantive requirements for the imposition of a safeguard measure.[45]

Questions and Assignments 9.2

What constitutes 'increased imports' within the meaning of the *Agreement on Safeguards*? Do imports that have increased steadily over a period of five years from 10 per cent to 60 per cent of domestic consumption, while decreasing in absolute terms, meet the 'increased imports' requirement of Article 2.1 of the *Agreement on Safeguards*? In your opinion, what could be 'unforeseen developments' within the meaning of Article XIX:1 of the GATT 1994?

2.1.2 'Serious Injury' Requirement

A second main substantive requirement for the application of a safeguard measure on imports of a product is the existence of serious injury or threat thereof to the domestic industry producing like or directly competitive products. Article 4.1 of the *Agreement on Safeguards* defines 'serious injury' as 'a significant overall

---

40 See Appellate Body Report, *US – Steel Safeguards (2003)*, para. 319.   41 See *ibid*.
42 See *ibid*., paras. 273, 289–91 and 297. The panel in *Argentina – Preserved Peaches (2003)*, forcefully asserted that '[a] mere phrase in a conclusion, without supporting analysis of the existence of unforeseen developments, is not a substitute for a demonstration of fact'. See Panel Report, *Argentina – Preserved Peaches (2003)*, para. 7.33.
43 Panel Reports, *US – Steel Safeguards (2003)*, para. 10.115.
44 See Appellate Body Report, *US – Steel Safeguards (2003)*, paras. 293–6.
45 See *ibid*., paras. 298–9 and 301–3. On the standard of review applicable under the *Agreement on Safeguards*, see also *US – Lamb (2001)*, paras. 103 and 106–7.

impairment in the position of a domestic industry'. The Appellate Body has recognised the standard of 'serious injury' to be 'very high' and 'exacting'.[46] It is stricter than the standard of 'material injury' of the *Anti-Dumping Agreement* and the *SCM Agreement*.[47] Since safeguard measures, unlike anti-dumping and countervailing duties, are applied to 'fair' trade, it is not surprising that the threshold for applying these measures is higher.

Article 4.1(c) of the *Agreement on Safeguards* defines a 'domestic industry' as:

the producers as a whole of the like or directly competitive products operating within the territory of a Member, or those whose collective output of the like or directly competitive products constitutes a major proportion of the total domestic production of those products.

Article 4.1(c) lays down two criteria to define the 'domestic industry' in a particular case. The first criterion relates to the products at issue; the second criterion relates to the number and the representative nature of the producers of these products.

As to the first criterion, note that the domestic industry is composed of producers making products that are 'like or directly competitive' to the imported products. As the Appellate Body noted in *US – Lamb (2001)*, the definition of 'domestic industry':

focuses exclusively on the producers of a very specific group of products. Producers of products that are *not* 'like or directly competitive products' do not, according to the text of the treaty, form part of the domestic industry.[48]

Therefore, in order to determine what constitutes the 'domestic industry', in a particular case, one must first identify the domestic products which are 'like or directly competitive' to the imported products. The producers of those products will make up the 'domestic industry'. The concepts of 'like products' and 'directly competitive products' are not defined in the *Agreement on Safeguards*, and there is little relevant case law as of yet on the meaning of these concepts as used in the *Agreement on Safeguards*. However, there is a significant body of case law on the meaning of these concepts as used in the GATT 1994.[49] While the Appellate Body has ruled that the concept of 'like products' may have different meanings in the different contexts in which it is used, this case law – discussed in detail above – is definitely of relevance here. It follows from this case law that the determination of whether products are 'like products' or 'directly competitive products' is, fundamentally, a determination about the nature and extent of the competitive relationship between these products. The factors that must be considered in determining 'likeness' or 'direct competitiveness' include, among others, the following: (1) physical characteristics of the products; (2) end-use;

---

46 See Appellate Body Report, *US – Lamb (2001)*, para. 124; and Appellate Body Report, *US – Wheat Gluten (2001)*, para. 149.

47 See below, pp. 699–706 and 781–4.

48 See Appellate Body Report, *US – Lamb (2001)*, para. 84.   49 See above, pp. 360–8 and 372–8.

(3) consumer habits and preferences regarding the products; and (4) customs classification of the products. In *US – Lamb (2001)*, one of the few safeguard cases in which the issue of 'like products' and 'directly competitive products' was addressed, the Appellate Body held that:

> if an input product and an end-product are not 'like or directly competitive', then it is irrelevant, under the *Agreement on Safeguards*, that there is a continuous line of production between an input product and an end-product.[50]

Consequently, production structures (for example, from lambs to lamb meat) are not relevant in determining whether products are 'like' or 'directly competitive' (and thus do not make lambs and meat products 'like products'). The Appellate Body explained in *US – Lamb (2001)* that the 'focus must, therefore, be on the identification of the *products*, and their "like or directly competitive" relationship, and not on the *processes* by which those products are produced'.[51]

As mentioned above, the second criterion to define the 'domestic industry' in a particular case relates to the number and the representative nature of the producers of the 'like or directly competitive' products. The 'domestic industry' for the purposes of the *Agreement on Safeguards* is: (1) the totality of the domestic producers; or (2) at least a major proportion thereof. There is no general explanation of what constitutes 'a major proportion' of the domestic producers. What is required to meet this condition will depend on the specific circumstances of a case and will most likely differ from case to case.[52]

Once the domestic industry has been identified, one can examine whether this domestic industry has suffered 'serious injury'. To this end, Article 4.2(a) of the *Agreement on Safeguards* requires an evaluation of 'all relevant factors of an objective and quantifiable nature having a bearing on the situation of that industry'. These so-called 'injury factors' include: (1) the rate and amount of the increase in imports, of the product concerned, in absolute and relative terms; (2) the share of the domestic market taken by increased imports; and (3) changes in the level of sales, production, productivity, capacity utilisation, profits and losses, and employment.[53] This list of injury factors is not exhaustive. *All* factors having a bearing on the situation of the domestic industry can and must be examined.[54] The examination of the factors expressly mentioned is, however, a

---

50 See Appellate Body Report, *US – Lamb (2001)*, para. 90. According to the Appellate Body, '[w]hen input and end-product are not "like" or "directly competitive", then it is irrelevant ... that there is a continuous line of production between an input product and an end-product, that the input product represents a high proportion of the value of the end-product, that there is no use for the input product other than as an input for the particular end-product, or that there is a substantial coincidence of economic interests between the producers of these products'. *Ibid.*

51 See *ibid.*, para. 94.

52 This issue also arises in the context of anti-dumping measures and countervailing measures: see above, pp. 697–8 and 780–1.

53 See Article 4.2(a) of the *Agreement on Safeguards*.

54 See Appellate Body Report, *Argentina – Footwear (EC) (2000)*, para. 136; Appellate Body Report, *US – Wheat Gluten (2001)*, para. 55; and Appellate Body Report, *US – Lamb (2001)*, para. 103. Failure to consider a relevant factor, in full or in part, amounts to a violation of Article 4.2(a) of the *Agreement on Safeguards*.

minimum requirement.[55] Domestic authorities do not have a duty to investigate *all* other possible injury factors. However, if the domestic authority considers a factor, other than a factor raised by one of the interested parties, to be relevant, it must be investigated.[56]

It is not sufficient for competent authorities applying safeguard measures to examine all relevant injury factors. The authorities are also required to give a reasoned and adequate explanation of how the facts support their conclusion that the domestic industry is suffering 'serious injury'.[57] As discussed above, the standard of 'serious injury' in Article 4.1(a) is 'very high' and 'exacting'.[58] To find 'serious injury', it is not necessary that all injury factors show that the domestic industry is under threat.[59] In a situation where employment and capacity utilisation in an industry are declining but profitability remains positive, it may nevertheless be possible to conclude that 'serious injury' exists provided that a reasoned and adequate explanation is given in the determination.

As noted above, a safeguard measure can be applied not only in case of 'serious injury' but also in case of a 'threat of serious injury'. A 'threat of serious injury' is defined as 'serious injury that is clearly imminent'.[60] The concept of 'clearly imminent' was clarified by the Appellate Body in *US – Lamb (2001)*. 'Imminent' implies that the anticipated 'serious injury' must be on the verge of occurring; 'clearly' indicates that there must be a very high degree of likelihood that the threat will materialise in the very near future.[61] In this regard, there is a duty to 'assess' the data from the most recent past against the overall trends during the entire investigating period in an injury analysis,[62] very similar to the

---

55 These principles with regard to Article 4.2(a) now seem to be well established in dispute settlement practice. See Appellate Body Report, *US – Wheat Gluten (2001)*, para. 55.

56 See Appellate Body Report, *US – Wheat Gluten (2001)*, paras. 55–6.

57 See Appellate Body Report, *US – Lamb (2001)*, para. 103. This is usually referred to as the *substantive* aspect of the examination of the injury factors. See also Panel Report, *Argentina – Preserved Peaches (2003)*, paras. 7.102–7.117.

58 See above, p. 616; and Appellate Body Report, *US – Lamb (2001)*, para. 124; and Appellate Body Report, *US – Wheat Gluten (2001)*, para. 149.

59 See Appellate Body Report, *US – Lamb (2001)*, para. 144. However, competent authorities must have a *sufficient* factual basis to allow them to draw reasoned and adequate conclusions concerning the situation of the 'domestic industry'. The need for such a sufficient factual basis, in turn, implies that the data examined, concerning the relevant factors, must be *representative* of the 'domestic industry'. See Appellate Body Report, *US – Lamb (2001)*, para. 131.

60 Article 4.1(b) of the *Agreement on Safeguards*.

61 See Appellate Body Report, *US – Lamb (2001)*, para. 125. Note that an independent fact-based assessment of the 'high degree of likelihood' is necessary and that mere acknowledgment of possibility is not sufficient. See Panel Report, *Argentina – Preserved Peaches (2003)*, para. 7.122.

62 See Appellate Body Report, *US – Lamb (2001)*, para. 138. Data relating to the most recent past will provide competent authorities 'with an essential, and, usually, the most reliable, basis for a determination of a threat of serious injury. The likely state of the domestic industry in the very near future can best be gauged from data from the most recent past.' However, 'although data from the most recent past has special importance, competent authorities should not consider such data in isolation from the data pertaining to the entire period of investigation. The real significance of the short-term trends in the most recent data, evident at the end of the period of investigation, may only emerge when those short-term trends are assessed in the light of the longer-term trends in the data for the whole period of investigation.' See Appellate Body Report, *US – Lamb (2001)*, paras. 137–8.

duty in an 'increased imports' determination under Article 2.1.[63] For a finding of 'threat of serious injury', Article 4.1(b) of the *Agreement on Safeguards* also requires that this determination must 'be based on facts and not merely on allegation, conjecture or remote possibility'.

The relationship between 'serious injury' and a 'threat of serious injury' was considered in *US – Line Pipe (2002)*. The question was whether a domestic authority could make an alternative finding of 'serious injury *or* [a] threat of serious injury', without a discrete finding as to which of these was, in fact, the reason for the imposition of the safeguard measure. Reversing the panel finding, the Appellate Body held:

> [A]s the right [to impose a safeguard] exists if there is a finding by the competent authorities of a 'threat of serious injury' or – something *beyond* – 'serious injury', then it seems to us that it is irrelevant, *in determining whether the right exists*, if there is 'serious injury' or only [a] 'threat of serious injury' – so long as there is a determination that there is *at least* a 'threat'.[64]

Questions and Assignments 9.3

How do you define in a particular case the 'domestic industry' within the meaning of Article 4.1(c) of the *Agreement on Safeguards*? Do producers of cars and producers of light trucks belong to the same 'domestic industry'? Do mills and bakeries belong to the same domestic industry? What is 'serious injury' to the domestic industry? What is a 'threat of serious injury'? How must domestic authorities determine whether there is serious injury (or a threat thereof) to the domestic industry?

2.1.3 'Causation' Requirement

The third substantive requirement for the application of a safeguard measure to the imports of a product is the 'causation' requirement. Article 4.2(b) of the *Agreement on Safeguards* provides:

> The determination referred to in subparagraph (a) shall not be made unless this investigation demonstrates, on the basis of objective evidence, the existence of the causal link between increased imports of the product concerned and serious injury or a threat thereof. When factors other than increased imports are causing injury to the domestic industry at the same time, such injury shall not be attributed to increased imports.

The test for establishing causation is twofold: (1) a demonstration of the causal link between the 'increased imports' and the 'serious injury' or threat thereof

---

63 See Panel Report, *Chile – Price Band System (2002)*, footnote 714 to para. 7.153. In fact, the panel in that case affirmed this duty as applying *mutatis mutandis* to Article 2.1 and Article 4.1(b), read together with Article 4.2(a). The panel ruled that, where a pre-existing measure like a Price Band System is in place, leading to significantly increasing tariffs, it is not proper for a competent authority to argue *a contrario* in a safeguards investigation that the removal or reduction of such a measure would lead to lower net duties on the imported product, thereby causing injury. See *ibid.*, para. 7.172.

64 Appellate Body Report, *US – Line Pipe (2002)*, para. 170. In the same report, the Appellate Body explained that, in 'terms of the rising continuum of an injurious condition of a domestic industry that ascends from a "threat of serious injury" up to "serious injury", we see "serious injury" – because it is something *beyond* a "threat" – as necessarily *including* the concept of a "threat" and *exceeding* the presence of a "threat"'. *Ibid.*

(the 'causal link' element);[65] and (2) an identification of any injury caused by factors other than the increased imports and the non-attribution of this injury to these imports (the 'non-attribution' element).[66]

With respect to the 'causal link' element, a 'genuine and substantial relationship of cause and effect' has to exist between increased imports and serious injury to the domestic industry (or threat thereof).[67] The Appellate Body has ruled in *US – Wheat Gluten (2001)* that it is not necessary to show that increased imports *alone* must be capable of causing serious injury:

> [T]he need to distinguish between the facts caused by increased imports and the facts caused by other factors does *not* necessarily imply ... that increased imports *on their own* must be capable of causing serious injury nor that injury caused by other factors must be *excluded* from the determination of serious injury.[68]

To the contrary, the language of Article 4.2(b), as a whole, suggests that 'the causal link' between increased imports and serious injury may exist, even though other factors are also contributing, 'at the same time', to the situation of the domestic industry.[69]

With respect to the 'non-attribution' element, the Appellate Body found in *US – Wheat Gluten (2001)* that Article 4.2(b) presupposes, 'as a first step in the competent authorities' examination of causation', that the injurious effects caused to the domestic industry by increased imports 'are *distinguished from* the injurious effects caused by other factors'.[70] The competent authorities can then, as a second step in their examination, attribute to increased imports, on the one hand, and, by implication, to other relevant factors, on the other hand, 'injury' caused by all of these different factors, including increased imports. By virtue of this two-stage process, the competent authorities comply with Article 4.2(b) by ensuring that any injury to the domestic industry that was *actually* caused by factors other than increased imports is not 'attributed' to increased imports and is, therefore, not treated as if it were injury caused by increased imports, when it is not. In this way, the competent authorities can determine, as a final step, whether 'the causal link' exists between 'increased imports and serious injury, and whether this causal link involves a genuine and substantial relationship of cause and effect between these two elements, as required by the *Agreement on Safeguards*'.[71] When a number of Members raised questions about this ruling, the Appellate Body further explained in *US – Lamb (2001)*:

---

65 With respect to the phrase in Article 2.1, 'imported ... under such conditions', the panel in *US – Wheat Gluten (2001)* noted: 'We are of the view that the phrase "under such conditions" does not impose a separate analytical requirement in addition to the analysis of increased imports, serious injury and causation. Rather, this phrase refers to the *substance* of the causation analysis that must be performed under Article 4.2(a) and (b) SA.' See Panel Report, *US – Wheat Gluten (2001)*, para. 8.108.

66 See e.g. Appellate Body Report, *US – Line Pipe (2002)*, para. 215.

67 Appellate Body Report, *US – Wheat Gluten (2001)*, para. 69.

68 *Ibid.*, para. 70. The Appellate Body thus reversed the panel's finding that the imports, *in and of themselves*, must have caused the serious injury. See Panel Report, *US – Wheat Gluten (2001)*, paras. 8.90–8.154.

69 Appellate Body Report, *US – Wheat Gluten (2001)*, para. 67.

70 *Ibid.*, para. 69.   71 *Ibid.*

In a situation where *several factors* are causing injury 'at the same time', a final determination about the injurious effects caused by *increased imports* can only be made if the injurious effects caused by all the different causal factors are distinguished and separated. Otherwise, any conclusion based exclusively on an assessment of only one of the causal factors – increased imports – rests on an uncertain foundation, because it *assumes* that the other causal factors are *not* causing the injury which has been ascribed to increased imports. The non-attribution language in Article 4.2(b) precludes such an assumption and, instead, requires that the competent authorities assess appropriately the injurious effects of the other factors, so that those effects may be disentangled from the injurious effects of the increased imports. In this way, the final determination rests, properly, on the genuine and substantial relationship of cause and effect between increased imports and serious injury.[72]

Domestic authorities therefore have to separate and distinguish the injurious effects of 'other factors' from the injurious effects of the increased imports. They have to give a reasoned and adequate explanation of the nature and the extent of the injurious effects of the other factors, as distinguished from the injurious effects of the increased imports.[73]

Finally, it is clear that, when a competent authority's report neither demonstrates the threshold of 'increased imports' under Article 2.1, nor satisfies the requirement of the existence of 'serious injury' or 'threat thereof' under Article 4.2(b), *a fortiori*, no causal link between these two elements can exist.[74]

Questions and Assignments 9.4

What does the 'causation requirement' of Article 4.2(b) of the *Agreement on Safeguards* entail? If a domestic industry suffers serious injury as a result of a mix of factors, including increased imports and changes in consumer preferences, may a domestic authority still conclude that the 'causation requirement' of Article 4.2(b) of the *Agreement on Safeguards* is met? How must domestic authorities determine whether the 'causation requirement' of Article 4.2(b) of the *Agreement on Safeguards* is met?

2.2 Domestic Procedures and Notification and Consultation Requirements

The *Agreement on Safeguards* sets out the procedural requirements that domestic authorities, wishing to impose safeguard measures, must meet.[75] Most importantly, Article 3 of the *Agreement on Safeguards* permits a Member to apply a safeguard measure only following an investigation by the competent

---

72 Appellate Body Report, *US – Lamb (2001)*, para. 179. See also Appellate Body Report, *US – Wheat Gluten (2001)*, paras. 67–9.
73 See Appellate Body Report, *US – Line Pipe (2002)*, paras. 213, 215 and 217. The mere assertion that injury caused by other factors has not been attributed to increased imports is definitely not sufficient to meet the requirement of Article 4.2(b) of the *Agreement on Safeguards*. As the Appellate Body noted in *US – Steel Safeguards (2003)*: 'In order to provide such a reasoned and adequate explanation, the competent authority *must explain how it ensured that it did not attribute* the injurious effects of factors other than included imports ... to the imports included in the measure' (emphasis added): Appellate Body Report, *US – Steel Safeguards (2003)*, para. 452. See also Appellate Body Report, *US – Hot-Rolled Steel (2001)*, paras. 226 and 230.
74 See Panel Report, *Chile – Price Band System (2002)*, para. 7.176, relying on Appellate Body Report, *Argentina – Footwear (EC) (2000)*, para. 145.
75 These procedural obligations are set out in Articles 3, 6 and 12 of the *Agreement on Safeguards*.

authorities of that Member pursuant to procedures previously established and made public.[76] The competent domestic authorities must also publish a report setting forth their findings and reasoned conclusions reached on all pertinent issues of fact and law.[77] Failure to do so results in a formal defect in the safeguard measure. Moreover, if the report of the competent domestic authorities does not address the issues arising under Article 2 (increased imports) and/or Article 4 (serious injury), this failure amounts to a failure to show that the requirements of Articles 2 and 4 were met and results in a finding of breach of Article 2 and/or Article 4.

The *Agreement on Safeguards* also imposes obligations on Members to notify the WTO Committee on Safeguards of matters relating to safeguard measures and to consult with other Members on such measures. Article 12.1 of the *Agreement on Safeguards* requires 'immediate' notification by Members to the WTO Committee on Safeguards whenever an investigation is initiated, a finding of serious injury or threat of serious injury caused by increased imports is made or where a decision is taken to apply or extend a safeguard measure.[78]

As to when a notification is necessary in the case of 'taking a decision to apply or extend a safeguard measure', the Appellate Body held in *US – Wheat Gluten (2001)* that notification needs to be given *only* after a decision has been taken and not when a decision is *proposed to be taken*.[79] However, it also noted that the meaning of the term '*immediate*' implies a 'degree of urgency'[80] and observed that the 'relevant triggering event' is the 'taking' of a decision. Article 12.1(c) is thus focused upon a 'decision' that 'has *occurred*, or has been taken', not on when that 'decision has been *given effect*'.[81]

Article 12.2 of the *Agreement on Safeguards* provides that a Member making a finding of serious injury or threat thereof, or taking a decision to apply or extend a safeguard, should provide 'all pertinent information' to the WTO Committee on Safeguards. The pertinent information to be provided includes

76 See Article 3.1 of the *Agreement on Safeguards*. Note that this investigation must include reasonable public notice to all interested parties and public hearings or other appropriate means by which importers, exporters and other interested parties could present evidence, and their views, *inter alia*, as to whether or not the application of a safeguard measure would be in the public interest. These procedural 'due process rights' of the parties to a safeguard investigation are set out in Article 3.1 of the *Agreement on Safeguards*.
77 See Article 3.1 of the *Agreement on Safeguards*. See also Appellate Body Report, *US – Lamb (2001)*, para. 76; and Appellate Body Report, *US – Steel Safeguards (2003)*, paras. 286–8. As to publication of confidential information, see Panel Report, *US – Wheat Gluten (2001)*, paras. 8.13–8.26. It is impermissible to adduce evidence of consideration of relevant information in a document that is not made available *publicly*: see Panel Report, *Chile – Price Band System (2002)*, para. 7.128.
78 See Panel Report, *US – Wheat Gluten (2001)*, paras. 8.185–8.207. The use of the term 'immediately' indicates a certain degree of urgency of the notification. See Appellate Body Report, *US – Wheat Gluten (2001)*, para. 105. The panel in *Korea – Dairy (2000)* noted that the requirement to notify 'immediately' does not mean notifying 'as soon as practically possible'. See Panel Report, *Korea – Dairy (2000)*, para. 7.134. The degree of urgency that is required by the duty to notify immediately is assessed on a case-by-case basis. This degree of urgency will depend on administrative difficulties, the character of the information and the need to translate documents (if any). In any case, the time taken for notification should be kept to the bare minimum. See Appellate Body Report, *US – Wheat Gluten (2001)*, paras. 105–6.
79 See Appellate Body Report, *US – Wheat Gluten (2001)*, paras. 119–25, reversing the panel's interpretation.
80 See *ibid.*, para. 105.   81 *Ibid.*, para. 120.

a mandatory minimum list,[82] comprising: evidence of serious injury or threat thereof due to increased imports; precise description of the product involved and the proposed measure; proposed date of introduction; expected duration; and a timetable for progressive liberalisation. The 'evidence of serious injury' to be demonstrated is evidence that would satisfy the requirements of Article 4.2(a), and not merely what the applying Member considers sufficient.[83]

Under Article 12.3 of the *Agreement on Safeguards*, the Member applying or extending a measure shall provide *adequate opportunity* for prior consultations with Members affected by the measure, for the purpose of reviewing the information provided, exchanging views and, most importantly, to facilitate reaching an understanding on the substantially equivalent levels of concessions to be maintained under Article 8.1. As the Appellate Body explained in *US – Wheat Gluten (2001)*, 'adequate opportunity' means that the exporting Member should be provided with sufficient *information* and *time* to allow a *meaningful exchange* on the issues identified.[84] In *US – Line Pipe (2002)*, the Appellate Body stated that the final measure applied ought to be one that is substantially the same as the proposed measure covered during the prior consultations:

[W]here ... the proposed measure 'differed substantially' from the measure that was later applied, and not as a consequence of 'prior consultations', we fail to see how meaningful 'prior consultations' could have occurred, as required by Article 12.3.[85]

It is to be noted that a violation of Article 12.3 automatically triggers a violation of Article 8.1 of the *Agreement on Safeguards*. As the Appellate Body ruled in *US – Wheat Gluten (2001)*:

In view of this explicit link between Articles 8.1 and 12.3 of the *Agreement on Safeguards*, a Member cannot ... 'endeavour to maintain' an adequate balance of concessions unless it has, as a first step, provided an adequate opportunity for prior consultations on a proposed measure.[86]

Questions and Assignments 9.5

Discuss the main procedural requirements under the *Agreement on Safeguards* that a Member imposing a safeguard measure must meet.

2.3 Characteristics of Safeguard Measures

Safeguard measures are measures, otherwise inconsistent with Articles II or XI of the GATT 1994, which are justified under the economic emergency exception

---

82 See Appellate Body Report, *Korea – Dairy (2000)*, para. 107. Additional information may be requested by the Council for Trade in Goods or the Committee on Safeguards in terms of Article 12.2 of the *Agreement on Safeguards*.

83 See Appellate Body Report, *Korea – Dairy (2000)*, para. 108, reversing the panel's interpretation.

84 See Appellate Body Report, *US – Wheat Gluten (2001)*, para. 136.

85 Appellate Body Report, *US – Line Pipe (2002)*, para. 104. See also Appellate Body Report, *US – Wheat Gluten (2001)*, para. 137.

86 Appellate Body Report, *US – Wheat Gluten (2001)*, para. 146.

provided for in Article XIX of the GATT 1994 and the *Agreement on Safeguards*. The purpose of a safeguard measure is to give 'breathing space' to a domestic industry to adapt itself to the new market situation by temporarily restricting imports. Safeguard measures therefore typically take the form of: (1) customs duties above the binding (inconsistent with Article II:1 of the GATT 1994); or (2) quantitative restrictions (inconsistent with Article XI of the GATT 1994).[87] Safeguard measures can also take other forms, because, unlike anti-dumping measures and countervailing measures, discussed above, safeguard measures are not limited to particular types of measures.[88] This does not mean, however, that safeguard measures are not subject to strict requirements. In general terms, Article 5.1, first sentence, of the *Agreement on Safeguards* provides:

A Member shall apply safeguard measures only to the extent necessary to prevent or remedy serious injury or to facilitate adjustment ... Members should choose measures most suitable for the achievement of these objectives.[89]

The *Agreement on Safeguards* sets out specific requirements with respect to: (1) the duration of safeguard measures; (2) the non-discriminatory application of safeguard measures; (3) the extent of safeguard measures; (4) the compensation of affected exporting Members; and (5) provisional safeguard measures. This section discusses each of these specific requirements regarding safeguard measures in turn.

2.3.1   Duration of Safeguard Measures

Safeguard measures are, by nature, *temporary* measures. Article 7.1 of the *Agreement on Safeguards* provides that safeguard measures may only be applied:

for such period of time as may be necessary to prevent or remedy serious injury and to facilitate adjustment.[90]

In fact, the initial period of application of a definitive safeguard measure must not exceed four years.[91] Furthermore, a safeguard measure exceeding one year must be progressively liberalised,[92] and, if the measure exceeds three years, the Member applying the measure must carry out a mid-term review to establish whether the measure still meets the requirements discussed below.[93] Extension of a safeguard measure beyond four years is possible but only if: (1) the safeguard measure continues to be necessary to prevent or remedy serious

---

87   On customs duties above the binding and on quantitative restrictions, see above, pp. 472 and 487–8.

88   See above, pp. 676–7 and 747–8.

89   Also Article XIX:1 of the GATT 1994 states that Members 'shall be free' to take safeguard measures 'to the extent and for such time as may be necessary to prevent or remedy such injury'.

90   Article 7.1, first sentence, of the *Agreement on Safeguards*.

91   See Article 7.1 of the *Agreement on Safeguards*. Pursuant to Article 6, the duration of a provisional safeguard measure, if applied, is included in this maximum period of four years.

92   See Article 7.4 of the *Agreement on Safeguards*.

93   See Article 7.3 of the *Agreement on Safeguards*. As a result of the review, the Member must, if appropriate, withdraw the safeguard measure or increase the rate of liberalisation of trade.

injury to the domestic industry;[94] and (2) there is evidence that the domestic industry is adjusting.[95] In no case, however, may the duration of a safeguard measure exceed eight years.[96] Once the import of a product has been subjected to a safeguard measure, this product cannot be subjected to such a measure again for a period of time equal to the duration of the safeguard measure that was previously applied.[97] In other words, if a Member applies a safeguard measure on imports of trucks for a period of eight years, it cannot apply any safeguard measure on imports of these trucks during the eight years following the termination of the first measure. In this way, the *Agreement on Safeguards* prevents a situation where the temporary character of safeguards is circumvented by the repeated application of safeguard measures on the imports of the same product.

Note that Article 9.2 of the *Agreement on Safeguards* allows developing-country Members to apply a safeguard measure for up to ten years, instead of eight. Developing-country Members may also apply a *new* safeguard measure on the same product sooner than developed-country Members.[98]

Questions and Assignments 9.6

For how long may a safeguard measure be applied? Can a safeguard measure be extended? What is the maximum duration of a safeguard measure? How does Article 7.5 of the *Agreement on Safeguards* ensure that the provision on the maximum duration of safeguard measures is not circumvented? In what way do the rules on the duration of safeguard measures applied by developing-country Members differ from the rules on the duration of safeguard measures applied by other Members?

2.3.2 Non-Discriminatory Application of Safeguard Measures

Article 2.2 of the *Agreement on Safeguards* provides:

> Safeguard measures shall be applied to a product being imported irrespective of its source.

Under the GATT 1947, there was much disagreement as to whether safeguard measures could be applied on a selective basis, that is, only against certain supplying countries and not against others. The *Agreement on Safeguards* has put an end to that debate by clearly requiring that safeguard measures be applied on an MFN basis, that is without discrimination between supplying Members. If

---

94 Note that, when the initial measure is itself not in compliance with Articles 2, 3, 4 or 5 of the *Agreement on Safeguards*, any extension of such measure by definition is tainted by inconsistency as well. See Panel Report, *Chile – Price Band System (2002)*, para. 7.198.

95 See Article 7.2 of the *Agreement on Safeguards*. A safeguard measure that is extended may never be more restrictive than it was at the end of the initial period. See Panel Report, *Argentina – Footwear (EC) (2000)*, paras. 8.303–8.304.

96 See Article 7.3 of the *Agreement on Safeguards*.

97 See Article 7.5 of the *Agreement on Safeguards*. However, the minimum period during which a safeguard measure cannot be applied again is two years. An exception to this rule, allowing for the application of safeguard measures of short duration (i.e. a maximum of 180 days), is provided for in Article 7.6 of the *Agreement on Safeguards*.

98 See Article 9.2 of the *Agreement on Safeguards*.

the computer industry of Member A suffers serious injury as a result of a sudden surge of imports of laptops from Member B, Member A may be entitled to take a safeguard measure, for example, in the form of a quota on laptops, however, this measure will have to be applied to the importation of all 'like or directly competitive' laptops, whether from Member B or from other exporting countries. The 'selective' application of safeguard measures is, in principle, prohibited.

In a number of disputes, the question arose whether a Member can exclude products from Members that are its partners in a free trade area or a customs union from the application of a safeguard measure. As also discussed in Chapter 10 of this book, in *Argentina – Footwear (EC) (2000)*, the Appellate Body ruled that, if a WTO Member has imposed a measure after conducting an investigation on imports from *all* sources, it is also required under Article 2.2 of the *Agreement on Safeguards* to apply such a measure to all sources, including partners in a free trade area.[99] It reaffirmed in *US – Wheat Gluten (2001)* that, in 'the usual course', the imports included in the determinations made under Articles 2.1 and 4.2 should correspond to the imports included in the application of the measure, under Article 2.2.[100] This has been referred to as the principle of 'parallelism'. In *US – Line Pipe (2002)* and in *US – Steel Safeguards (2002)*, the Appellate Body explained that the principle of 'parallelism' is derived from the parallel language used in the first and second paragraphs of Article 2 of the *Agreement on Safeguards*.[101]

The *Agreement on Safeguards* provides for two exceptions to the prohibition of 'selective' application of safeguard measures. These exceptions are set out in Article 5.2(b) and Article 9.1 of the *Agreement on Safeguards*. Article 5.2(b) allows the selective application of safeguard measures taken in the form of quotas allocated among supplying countries if, apart from other requirements:

clear demonstration is provided to the Committee [on Safeguards] that ... imports from certain Members have increased in disproportionate percentage in relation to the total increase of imports of the product.[102]

Article 9.1 of the *Agreement on Safeguards* contains an exception from the prohibition of selective application for the benefit of developing-country Members. Article 9.1 states:

Safeguard measures shall not be applied against a product originating in a developing country Member as long as its share of imports of the product concerned in the importing Member does not exceed 3 per cent, provided that developing country Members with less than 3 per cent import share collectively account for not more than 9 per cent of total imports of the product concerned.

---

99 See Appellate Body Report, *Argentina – Footwear (EC) (2000)*, para. 112; Appellate Body Report, *US – Wheat Gluten (2001)*, para. 96; Appellate Body Report, *US – Line Pipe (2002)*, para. 181; and Appellate Body Report, *US – Steel Safeguards (2003)*, para. 441. See also below, pp. 657–8.

100 Appellate Body Report, *US – Wheat Gluten (2001)*, para. 96.

101 For a further discussion of the concept of parallelism, see below, pp. 657–8.

102 For the other requirements, see Article 5.2(b) of the *Agreement on Safeguards*.

The Appellate Body held in *US – Line Pipe (2002)* that Article 9.1 does not contain an obligation to provide a specific list of developing-country Members that are included or excluded from the safeguard measure.[103] In *US – Line Pipe (2002)*, the United States had set, for each country without any differentiation, a quantitative allocation of 9,000 tonnes for imports free from supplementary duties. These 9,000 tonnes represented 2.7 per cent of its overall imports. The United States argued that, since the safeguard measure would reduce the level of imports, it was 'expected' that any country which breached its quota-free import threshold of 9,000 tons would also breach the 3 per cent *de minimis* level set in Article 9.1. The Appellate Body rejected this argument and held that the United States had not taken all reasonable steps to ensure that imports from developing-country Members above the US threshold level, but still below the *de minimis* level, would be excluded from the application of the safeguard measure.[104] Therefore, this mechanism was inconsistent with Article 9.1 of the *Agreement on Safeguards*.[105]

The panel in *Dominican Republic – Safeguard Measures (2012)* interpreted the obligation to exclude from the application of the safeguard those imports from developing-country Members that meet the requirements laid down in Article 9.1. The panel found that such developing-country imports must be excluded from application even when those imports were taken into account in the substantive injury and causation analysis of the investigation.[106] The panel found that the Dominican Republic did not act inconsistently with the *Agreement on Safeguards* and the principle of 'parallelism' by not conducting a new analysis excluding imports from those developing countries that the Dominican Republic had excluded from the scope of application of the safeguard measure by virtue of Article 9.1, in order to determine the existence of an increase in imports, serious injury and causation in respect of imports from non-excluded countries only.[107]

Questions and Assignments 9.7

Member A imposes a safeguard measure on the importation of bicycles following a 200 per cent increase in imports from Member B. The safeguard measure takes the form of a quota to be allocated among the supplying Members. The shares of imports of bicycles are currently as follows: Member B, 70 per cent; Member C, 20 per cent; Member D, 7 per cent; and Members E and F each 1.5 per cent. Note that Members D, E and F are developing-country Members. Which bicycles should be subject to the safeguard measure – bicycles originating in Member B, C, D, E and/or F? Is your answer different if Member A takes a safeguard measure in the form of an increased customs duty or a tariff quota on bicycles?

---

103 See Appellate Body Report, *US – Line Pipe (2002)*, para. 128.
104 See *ibid.*, paras. 120–33.   105 See *ibid.*, para. 133.
106 See Panel Report, *Dominican Republic – Safeguard Measures (2012)*, paras. 7.367–7.392.
107 *Ibid.*

2.3.3   Safeguard Measures Commensurate with the Extent of Necessity

As mentioned above, Article 5.1 of the *Agreement on Safeguards* provides that a safeguard shall apply only to the extent necessary to prevent or remedy serious injury and to facilitate adjustment. Article 5.1 also provides that, where the safeguard measure takes the form of a quantitative restriction and such a measure reduces the quantity of imports to a level less than the average imports in the last three representative years, a 'clear justification' to that effect is necessary.

A safeguard measure may not seek to address injury caused by factors other than *increased imports*. In *US – Line Pipe (2002)*, the Appellate Body held that, although the term 'serious injury' has the same meaning in Articles 4.2 and 5 of the *Agreement on Safeguards*,[108] safeguard measures may only be applied to the extent that they address the serious injury (or threat thereof) attributable to *increased imports*.[109] As the Appellate Body noted in *US – Line Pipe (2001)*, the object and purpose of both Article XIX of the GATT 1994 and the *Agreement on Safeguards* support the conclusion that safeguard measures should be applied so as to address only the consequences of *imports* and, therefore:

the limited objective of Article 5.1, first sentence, is limited by the consequences of *imports*.[110]

Explaining the nature of the requirement in Article 5.1, the Appellate Body in *Korea – Dairy (2000)* held that there is an '*obligation* on a Member applying a safeguard measure to ensure that the measure applied is commensurate with the goals of preventing or remedying serious injury or facilitating adjustment'.[111] This obligation applies regardless of the particular form a safeguard measure might take.[112] However, the Appellate Body disagreed with the panel in this case that Members are always required '*to explain* how they considered the facts before them and why they concluded, *at the time of the decision*, that the measure to be applied was necessary to remedy the serious injury and facilitate the adjustment of the industry'.[113] Instead, the Appellate Body held that Article 5.1, second sentence, requires 'clear justification' only for safeguard measures taking the form of a quantitative restriction that reduces the quantity of imports below the average of imports in the last three representative years for which statistics are available.[114] The Appellate Body reiterated this view in *US – Line Pipe (2002)*. It stated:

---

108 The US argued that, since the Appellate Body had held in *US – Wheat Gluten (2001)* that in the determination of 'serious injury' under Article 4.2 of the *Agreement on Safeguards*, injury caused by factors other than increased imports need not be excluded, safeguard measures may be applied to address the 'entirety' of serious injury. See Appellate Body Report, *US – Line Pipe (2002)*, paras. 242–3.

109 Appellate Body Report, *US – Line Pipe (2002)*, paras. 242–62.   110 *Ibid.*, para. 258.

111 Appellate Body Report, *Korea – Dairy (2000)*, para. 96. The panel in *Chile – Price Band System (2002)* held that the word 'ensure' means that there must be a 'rational connection' between the measure imposed and the objective of preventing or remedying serious injury or facilitating adjustment. See Panel Report, *Chile – Price Band System (2002)*, para. 7.183.

112 See Appellate Body Report, *Korea – Dairy (2000)*, para. 96.

113 Panel Report, *Korea – Dairy (2000)*, para. 7.109.

114 See Appellate Body Report, *Korea – Dairy (2000)*, para. 98.

Article 5.1 imposes a general substantive obligation, namely, to apply safeguard measures only to the permissible extent, and also a particular procedural obligation, namely, to provide a clear justification in the specific case of quantitative restrictions reducing the volume of imports below the average of imports in the last three representative years. Article 5.1 does not establish a general procedural obligation to demonstrate compliance with Article 5.1, first sentence, at the time a measure is applied.[115]

However, the Appellate Body clarified that this does not imply that, in cases not covered by Article 5.1, second sentence, 'the measure may be devoid of justification or that the multilateral verification of the consistency of the measure with the *Agreement on Safeguards* is impeded'.[116] Instead, several obligations in the *Agreement on Safeguards*, including those requiring Members to separate and distinguish the injurious effects of factors other than increased imports (Article 4.2(b)) and to include a detailed analysis in the report of their findings and reasoned conclusions (Articles 3.1 and 4.2(c)):

should have the incidental effect of providing sufficient "justification" for a measure and ... should also provide a benchmark against which the permissible extent of the measure should be determined.[117]

The Appellate Body found support for this interpretation in the non-attribution language found in the second sentence of Article 4.2(b),[118] which is 'a benchmark for ensuring that only an appropriate share of the overall injury is attributed to increased imports'.[119] This, in turn, 'informs the permissible extent to which the safeguard measure may be applied pursuant to Article 5.1, first sentence'.[120] For the Appellate Body it would be:

illogical to require an investigating authority to ensure that the 'causal link' between increased imports and serious injury not be based on the share of injury attributed to factors other than increased imports while, at the same time, permitting a Member to apply a safeguard measure addressing injury caused by all factors.[121]

In cases where the safeguard measure takes the form of a quota allocated among supplying countries, Article 5.2(a) of the *Agreement on Safeguards* provides for rules on the allocation of the share of the quota. These rules are similar to the rules of Article XIII of the GATT 1994 on the 'non-discriminatory administration of quantitative restrictions', discussed above.[122]

---

115 Appellate Body Report, *US – Line Pipe (2002)*, para. 234.
116 *Ibid.*, para. 236.   117 *Ibid.*
118 The Appellate Body recalled that the non-attribution requirement seeks, 'in situations where several factors cause injury at the same time, to prevent investigating authorities from inferring the required "causal link" between increased imports and serious injury or threat thereof on the basis of the injurious effects caused by factors other than increased imports'. See Appellate Body Report, *US – Line Pipe (2002)*, para. 252.
119 *Ibid.*   120 *Ibid.*   121 *Ibid.*
122 See above, p. 492. Note, however, that Members may deviate from these rules as provided for in Article 5.2(b) of the *Agreement on Safeguards*, discussed above, p. 626. Also note that, unlike Article XIII of the GATT 1994, Article 5.1, second sentence, and Article 5.2(a) do not apply to tariff quotas. See Panel Report, *US – Line Pipe (2002)*, para. 7.75.

Questions and Assignments 9.8

What is the appropriate extent of a safeguard measure? Is a Member obliged to demonstrate in the context of a safeguards investigation that the safeguard measure concerned is 'commensurate with the extent of necessity'?

2.3.4   Compensation of Affected Exporting Members

As noted above, a safeguard measure is a measure that restricts *fair* trade from other Members.[123] A safeguard measure disturbs the balance of rights and obligations to the detriment of the affected exporting Members. Therefore, the *Agreement on Safeguards* requires that a Member taking a safeguard measure agree with the affected exporting Members on appropriate *compensation* so as to restore the balance of rights and obligations. Article 8.1 of the *Agreement on Safeguards* provides:

> A Member proposing to apply a safeguard measure or seeking an extension of a safeguard measure shall endeavour to maintain a substantially equivalent level of concessions and other obligations ... between it and the exporting Members which would be affected by such a measure ... To achieve this objective, the Members concerned may agree on any adequate means of trade compensation for the adverse effects of the measure on their trade.

The objective of appropriate compensation is to be achieved by following the consultation procedures established under Article 12.3 of the *Agreement on Safeguards*. When a Member fails to consult affected Members in accordance with Article 12.3, it also violates Article 8.1.[124] If an agreement on compensation is not reached within thirty days, Article 8.2 of the *Agreement on Safeguards* provides that the affected exporting Members are free:

> to suspend ... the application of substantially equivalent concessions or other obligations under GATT 1994, to the trade of the Member applying the safeguard measure.[125]

However, affected exporting Members cannot always exercise this right of suspension. As set out in Article 8.3 of the *Agreement on Safeguards*, this right of suspension shall not be exercised during the first three years that a safeguard measure is in effect in cases where: (1) the safeguard measure has been taken as a result of an absolute increase in imports; and (2) the safeguard measure conforms to the provisions of the *Agreement on Safeguards*. In *US – Steel Safeguards (2003)*, the United States arguably did not provide an adequate opportunity for consultations on compensation prior to the imposition of its safeguard measures because it implemented the measures only fifteen days after its notification of

---

123 See above, pp. 606–10.

124 See Appellate Body Reports, *US – Wheat Gluten (2001)*, paras. 144–6; and *US – Line Pipe (2002)*, paras. 114–19. Both Articles 8.1 and 12.3 make an explicit reference to each other and are thus automatically linked. See also above, p. 623.

125 The right of suspension of 'substantially equivalent concessions' is conditional upon the notification of the proposed suspension measure to the Council for Trade in Goods and the absence of disapproval by the Goods Council. As the Council for Trade in Goods takes decisions by consensus, disapproval is *de facto* excluded.

the measures.[126] Although this issue was not raised before the panel, several affected Members, including the European Union, Japan, China, Switzerland and Norway notified, as required by Article 12.5 of the *Agreement on Safeguards*, their intention to suspend concessions of an equivalent amount against the United States.[127] In September 2002, the United States notified a reduction of the range of steel products subject to its safeguard measures.[128] After the adoption of the panel and Appellate Body reports that found its steel safeguards measures WTO-inconsistent, the United States withdrew these measures and the suspensions that other Members had threatend to impose were not implemented.[129]

Questions and Assignments 9.9

Why must a Member applying a safeguard measure try to reach an agreement on compensation? Do exporting Members, adversely affected by a safeguard measure, have a right to suspend, in 'retaliation', equivalent concessions or other obligations? If so, are there any limitations to this right?

2.3.5 Provisional Safeguard Measures

Article 6 of the *Agreement on Safeguards* allows Members to take provisional safeguard measures in 'critical circumstances'. Critical circumstances are defined as circumstances 'where delay would cause damage which it would be difficult to repair'. Before taking provisional safeguard measures, the competent domestic authorities must make a preliminary determination that there is clear evidence that the increased imports have caused or are threatening to cause serious injury.[130] Provisional measures may be applied only for a maximum of 200 days and can only take the form of tariff increases.[131] If the competent authorities conclude, after a full-fledged investigation, that the conditions for imposing a safeguard measure are not fulfilled, the provisional measure shall lapse and duties collected must be refunded.[132]

---

126 Y. S. Lee, 'Test of Multilateralism in International Trade: US Steel Safeguards', bepress Legal Series Paper 253, 2004, 42.

127 See G/SG/43 and Suppl.1, G/SG/44 and Suppl.1, G/SG/45, G/SG/46, G/SG/47, all dated May 2002. For example, the European Communities notified the adoption of Council Regulation (EC) No. 1031/2002 of 13 June 2002 establishing additional customs duties on imports of certain products originating in the United States of America, OJ 2002, L157, 8. The regulation notes that the safeguard measure applied to 'certain flat steel products' was not taken in response to an *absolute increase* in imports and therefore that a part of the Community's concessions corresponding to the safeguard measure that was not taken as a result of an absolute increase of imports and representing an amount of applicable duties of €379 million might be subject to additional duties as from 18 June 2002. However, the Community indicated that it would decide whether to apply additional duties in light of decisions by the United States on economically meaningful product exclusions and on the presentation of an acceptable offer on trade compensation. Similarly, Japan notified the adoption of the Cabinet Order concerning the Suspension of Concessions to Certain Steel Products Originating in the United States of America (Cabinet Order No. 212, proclaimed by publication in the Official Gazette on 17 June 2002) on 14 June 2002, which became effective on 18 June 2002, upon the expiration of thirty days from the day on which written notice of the suspension was received by the CTG.

128 G/SG/N/10/USA/6/Suppl.7, G/SG/N/11/USA/5/Suppl.7, dated September 2002.

129 G/SG/N/10/USA/6/Suppl.8, dated 12 December 2003.

130 On these requirements for the application of provisional safeguard measures, see above, pp. 615–19.

131 Extension is not possible and the duration of the provisional safeguard measure will be counted when calculating the duration of the definitive safeguard measure. See above, pp. 624–5.

132 See Article 6 of the *Agreement on Safeguards*.

In view of the maximum duration of provisional safeguard measures, the average length of WTO dispute settlement proceedings and the prospective nature of WTO remedies, it may be difficult to challenge such measures effectively in practice. In *Dominican Republic – Safeguard Measures (2012)*, the panel considered it unnecessary to make specific findings on the provisional measure which had expired and been replaced by the definitive measure at the time of the establishment of the panel, because the complainants' principal claims in respect of the expired provisional measure were the same claims made in respect of the definitive measure.[133]

Questions and Assignments 9.10

When can a Member take a provisional safeguard measure? Why does Article 6 of the *Agreement on Safeguards* provide that provisional safeguard measures can only take the form of tariff increases?

3   SAFEGUARD MEASURES UNDER OTHER WTO AGREEMENTS

Next to safeguard measures under the GATT 1994 and the *Agreement on Safeguards*, WTO law also provides for safeguard measures under other WTO agreements. This section deals in turn with: (1) safeguard measures under the *Agreement on Agriculture*; and (2) safeguard measures under the *Protocol on the Accession of the People's Republic of China*.[134] This section also discusses the absence of safeguard measures under the GATS.

3.1   Safeguard Measures Under the *Agreement on Agriculture*

The *Agreement on Agriculture* provides for 'special safeguards' that a Member may take in relation to the products that have been 'tariffied' (i.e. converted from certain non-tariff barriers into tariffs) and that have been designated in that Member's Schedule with the symbol 'SSG'.[135] As the Appellate Body explained in *Chile – Price Band System (Article 21.5 – Argentina) (2007)*, the provisions of Article 5 of the *Agreement on Agriculture* establish the conditions in which a Member may have recourse to such a special safeguard, set out rules on the form and duration of such safeguard measures, and establish certain transparency requirements that attach to their use. According to the Appellate Body in that case:

One circumstance in which a qualifying Member may be authorized to adopt a special safeguard is when the price of imports of a relevant agricultural product falls below a specified

---

133 See Panel Report, *Dominican Republic – Safeguard Measures (2012)*, para. 7.22.
134 Note that the transitional textile safeguard measures under the *Agreement on Textiles and Clothing* are no longer available because that Agreement has expired. See above, p. 130. Safeguard measures under the now defunct *Agreement on Textiles and Clothing* were subject to WTO dispute settlement in *US – Underwear (Costa Rica) (1997)*; *US – Wool Shirts and Blouses from India (1997)*; and *US – Cotton Yarn (Pakistan) (2001)*.
135 On 'tariffication', see above, p. 489. 'SSG' stands for 'special safeguards'.

trigger price. However, pursuant to Article 5, a special safeguard can be imposed only on those agricultural products for which measures within the meaning of footnote 1 were converted into ordinary customs duties and for which a Member has reserved in its Schedule of Concessions a right to resort to these safeguards.[136]

Under Article 5, a special safeguard can be imposed when the *volume* of imports of an agricultural product during any year *exceeds* a specific trigger level,[137] *or*, where the *import price* of such product, determined on the basis of its c.i.f. import price, falls *below* a trigger price which is equal to the average 1986–8 reference price for the product.[138] With regard to special safeguards based on *prices*, the Appellate Body held in *EC – Poultry (1998)* that the import price to be considered against the trigger price is merely the c.i.f. price and that it does not include ordinary customs duties that became payable on the imports.[139] Under Article 5.1(b), therefore, the price at which 'the product may enter the customs territory of the Member granting the concession, as determined on the basis of the c.i.f. import price' is the c.i.f. import price alone and not the c.i.f. import price *plus* applicable duties. The method of calculation of these trigger levels and prices is specified in paragraphs 4 and 5 of Article 5, respectively. The amount of additional duty that may be imposed on a product is determined in accordance with these provisions. The Appellate Body held in *EC – Poultry (1998)* that, under Article 5.5, the comparison of the c.i.f. price with the trigger price can only be on a *shipment-by-shipment basis*. The practice of the European Communities to determine the import price on the basis of a fixed standard 'representative price' therefore was impermissible.[140] Note that, in order to impose special safeguards, there is no need to demonstrate injury to the domestic industry/agricultural sector. Note also that special safeguard measures can only take the form of additional duties on the products concerned.[141]

As discussed in Chapter 7 of this book, Article 4.2 of the *Agreement on Agriculture* states:

Members shall not maintain, resort to, or revert to any measures of the kind which have been required to be converted into ordinary customs duties, except as otherwise provided for in Article 5 and Annex 5.[142]

---

136 Appellate Body Report, *Chile – Price Band System (Article 21.5 – Argentina) (2007)*, para. 173.
137 See Article 5.1(a) of the *Agreement on Agriculture*. The trigger level relates to existing market access opportunity as set out in Article 5.4. Note that, as a general rule, safeguards of this kind will expire by the end of the given year. See Article 5.4 of the *Agreement on Agriculture*.
138 See *ibid.*, Article 5.1(b) of *Agreement on Agriculture*. According to the footnote to the provision, this will in general be the average c.i.f. per unit value of the product. Sub-paragraphs (a) and (b) of Article 5.1 cannot be applied concurrently.
139 See Appellate Body Report, *EC – Poultry (1998)*, paras. 144–6. Note that the panel's interpretation in this regard was reversed.
140 See *ibid.*, paras. 159–71.
141 On the relationship between the *Agreement on Agriculture*, on the one hand, and the *Agreement on Safeguards* and the GATT 1994, on the other hand, note Article 5.8 and Article 21.1 of the *Agreement on Agriculture*.
142 See above, pp. 488–9.

The Appellate Body addressed the relationship between Articles 4.2 and 5 of the *Agreement on Agriculture* in *Chile – Price Band System (2002)*. The Appellate Body argued that:

the existence of a market access exemption in the form of a special safeguard provision under Article 5 implies that Article 4.2 should *not* be interpreted in a way that permits Members to maintain measures that a Member would not be permitted to maintain *but for* Article 5, and, much less, measures that are even more trade-distorting than special safeguards. In particular, if Article 4.2 were interpreted in a way that allowed Members to maintain measures that operate in a way similar to a special safeguard within the meaning of Article 5 – but without respecting the conditions set out in that provision for invoking such measures – it would be difficult to see how proper meaning and effect could be given to those conditions set forth in Article 5.[143]

According to the Appellate Body in *Chile – Price Band System (Article 21.5 – Argentina) (2007)*:

the existence of an exemption from the market access requirements in the form of a special safeguard under Article 5 suggests that this provision ... was the narrowly circumscribed vehicle to be used by those Members who reserved their rights to do so in order to derogate from the requirements of Article 4.2.[144]

3.2 Safeguard Measures Under China's Accession Protocol

Section 16 of the *Protocol on the Accession of the People's Republic of China*, commonly referred to as China's Accession Protocol, provides for a *transitional product-specific safeguard mechanism*.[145] Paragraph 16.1 of China's Accession Protocol sets out the general conditions for the application of a special safeguard measure under this mechanism.[146] It states:

---

143 Appellate Body Report, *Chile – Price Band System (2002)*, para. 217.
144 Appellate Body Report, *Chile – Price Band System (Article 21.5 – Argentina) (2007)*, para. 174.
145 It should be noted that many trading partners enacted relevant regulations in order to implement para. 16 of the Protocol on the Accession of China. The EU published Council Regulation No. 427/2003 on 8 March 2003. See Council Regulation No. 427/2003 on a transitional product-specific safeguard mechanism for imports originating in the People's Republic of China and amending Regulation No. 519/94 on common rules for imports from certain third countries. The product-specific safeguard mechanism is implemented in US law through Sections 421–423 of the United States Trade Act of 1974 (Public Law No. 93-618, 3 January 1975, 88 Stat. 1978, as amended (codified in *United States Code*, Title 19, Section 2451, Chapter 12), as amended), commonly referred to as 'Section 421' (added as Public Law No. 106-286, 10 October 2000, 114 Stat. 882 (codified in *United States Code*, Title 19, Section 2451)). Section 421 of the Trade Act of 1974 regulates market disruption investigations, and Section 422 regulates trade diversion investigation, available at www.usitc.gov/trade_remedy/731_ad_701_cvd/investigations/completed/index.htm, visited on 13 February 2013.
146 Note that, in addition to the transitional product-specific safeguard mechanism provided for in para. 16 of China's Accession Protocol, an additional safeguards regime, applicable to textiles and clothing, was established in para. 242 of the Report of the Working Party on the Accession of China. Under this provision, if a Member believed that Chinese textiles or clothing imports were, due to market disruption, threatening to impede the orderly development of trade in these products, it could request consultations with China. Upon receipt of the consultations request, China would hold its shipments in the relevant textile categories to a level no greater than 7.5 per cent (or 6 per cent for wool categories) above the amount entered during the first twelve months of the most recent fourteen months preceding the month of the request for consultations. This regime was applicable until 31 December 2008.

In cases where products of Chinese origin are being imported into the territory of any WTO Member in such increased quantities or under such conditions as to cause or threaten to cause *market disruption* to the domestic producers of like or directly competitive products, the WTO Member so affected may request consultations with China with a view to seeking a mutually satisfactory solution.[147]

A core condition for the application of a product-specific transitional safeguard is 'market disruption'. Paragraph 16.4 of China's Accession Protocol provides that market disruption is deemed to exist whenever imports of a product, that is like or directly competitive with a product produced by the domestic industry, are increasing rapidly, either absolutely or relatively, so as to be a significant cause of material injury, or threat of material injury to the domestic industry.[148] The injury threshold provided for in paragraph 16.4 requires a showing of 'material injury', rather than 'serious injury' (such as in Article 2.1 of the *Agreement on Safeguards* as discussed above). Such lower injury threshold thus implies that a lower degree of injurious effects caused by rapidly increasing imports to the domestic industry needs to be shown. In addition, paragraph 16.4 of China's Accession Protocol also sets out a distinct causation standard. Paragraph 16.4 requires that rapidly increasing imports be a 'significant cause' of material injury to the domestic industry. The term 'significant' qualifies 'the causal relationship or nexus that must be found to exist between rapidly increasing imports and material injury to the domestic industry. This nexus must be such that 'rapidly increasing imports make an "important" or "notable" contribution in bringing about material injury to the domestic industry.'[149] The threshold for the application of special safeguard measures under China's Accession Protocol is lower than that for general safeguard measures under the *Agreement on Safeguards*. However, this deviation from the general safeguard regime is limited in time. Pursuant to paragraph 16.9 of China's Accession Protocol, the special safeguard mechanism expires at the end of 2013. In view of the expiration of this special safeguard mechanism, this book does not further discuss the Appellate Body's interpretation of paragraph 16 of the Protocol in *US – Tyres (2011)*.

3.3 Safeguard Measures Under the GATS

Article X of the GATS calls for multilateral negotiations on the question of emergency safeguard measures relating to trade in services. After more than eighteen years of negotiations, WTO Members still hold diverging views on the question of an emergency safeguard mechanism (ESM) under the GATS. Divergences remain on basic issues such as the structure, desirability, necessity and feasibility of such a services ESM.

---

147 Emphasis added.   148 See para. 16.4 of China's Accession Protocol.
149 See Appellate Body Report, *US – Tyres (2011)*, para. 176.

Members who oppose or are sceptical about an ESM for trade in services (virtually all OECD countries and a few developing-country Members) are not convinced that an ESM is desirable, considering: (1) the flexibility that Members have in scheduling commitments under the GATS; and (2) the risk that an ESM might undermine the stability of existing commitments. Those Members also doubt how a services ESM would work in practice, and point to the scarcity of reliable trade and production data in many sectors and the technical complexities associated with the multi-modal structure of the GATS. For example, under mode 3 ('commercial presence') and mode 4 ('presence of natural persons'), how – and to what extent – would an ESM restrict service output of service suppliers of foreign origin that are established juridical persons (but owned or controlled by another Member) or resident citizens of foreign origin in the Member that seeks to impose safeguard measures under such a mechanism?

Members who support the creation of a services ESM argue that the availability of safeguards in the event of unforeseeable market disruptions is necessary in order to convince domestic constituents to accept the undertaking of access commitments in services. These Members also argue that the availability of an ESM 'safety valve' would encourage Members to enter into more far-reaching commitments in services negotiations. In their view, abuse could be avoided through strict procedural disciplines, and data problems should not be exaggerated, given the existence of professional associations, regulators and licensing bodies that compile relevant information in many sectors.[150]

4   BALANCE-OF-PAYMENTS MEASURES UNDER THE GATT 1994 AND THE GATS

In addition to safeguard measures, the 'economic emergency exceptions' discussed in this chapter, also allow Members to adopt 'balance-of-payments measures', commonly referred to as 'BoP measures'. This section first addresses BoP measures under the GATT 1994, and then briefly refers to BoP measures under the GATS.

4.1   Balance-of-Payments Measures Under the GATT 1994

The rules regarding BoP measures under the GATT 1994 are set out in Articles XII and XVIII:B of the GATT 1994. The BoP exception for trade in goods is further elaborated in the *Understanding on Balance of Payments Provisions of the*

---

150   See Annual Report of the Working Party on GATS Rules to the Council for Trade in Services 2012, S/WOPGR/23, dated 29 November 2012; and Annual Report of the Working Party on GATS Rules to the Council for Trade in Services 2011, S/WPGR/22, dated 10 November 2011.

GATT 1994 (the '*Understanding on BoP Provisions*'), which is part of the GATT 1994. The rules set out in these provisions allow Members to adopt measures, that would be otherwise GATT-inconsistent, to safeguard their external financial position and to protect their balance of payments. The outflow of money from a country can indeed be limited, in a fairly simple and effective manner, by imposing trade-restrictive measures on imports into the country. In the past, the BoP measures were quite frequent. In today's world of floating exchange rates, BoP problems may be resolved by other means than trade restrictions. Nevertheless, BoP measures are still of some importance. Developing-country Members, in particular, continue to use these measures. In times of rapid economic development, countries often experience severe pressure on their monetary reserves. However, important users in the 1980s and 1990s of trade restrictions for BoP purposes, such as India and Nigeria, no longer use such measures.[151]

Article XII of the GATT 1994, entitled 'Restrictions to Safeguard the Balance of Payments', states, in its first paragraph:

Notwithstanding the provisions of paragraph 1 of Article XI, any [Member], in order to safeguard its external financial position and its balance of payments, may restrict the quantity or value of merchandise permitted to be imported, subject to the provisions of the following paragraphs of this Article.

Article XVIII of the GATT 1994, entitled 'Governmental Assistance to Economic Development', provides in paragraph 4(a) as follows:

[A Member], the economy of which can only support low standards of living and is in the early stages of development, shall be free to deviate temporarily from the provisions of the other Articles of this Agreement, as provided in Sections A, B and C of this Article.

Section B of Article XVIII (i.e. paragraphs 8 to 12 of Article XVIII) provides for a special BoP exception for developing-country Members. Article XVIII:9 states, in relevant part:

In order to safeguard its external financial position and to ensure a level of reserves adequate for the implementation of its programme of economic development, a [Member] coming within the scope of paragraph 4(*a*) of this Article may, subject to the provisions of paragraphs 10 to 12, control the general level of its imports by restricting the quantity or value of merchandise permitted to be imported; *Provided* that ...

Under Article XII, the purpose of a Member's BoP measure is 'to safeguard its external financial position and its balance of payments'. Under Article XVIII:B, the purpose of a BoP measure taken by a developing-country Member is also 'to safeguard its external financial position' but, in addition, 'to ensure a level of reserves adequate for the implementation of its programme of economic

---

151 On India, see Report by the Secretariat, *Trade Policy Review: India*, WT/TPR/S/182, dated 18 April 2007, para. 58. On Nigeria, see A. Oyejide, O. Ogunkola and A. Bankole, 'Nigeria: Import Prohibition as a Trade Policy', in P. Gallagher, P. Low and A. Stoler (eds.), Managing the Challenges of WTO Participation, 45 Case Studies (Cambridge University Press, 2005), 444–5.

development'. This section examines: (1) the nature of measures that may be taken for BoP purposes; (2) the requirements for taking such measures; and (3) relevant procedural issues.

4.1.1 Nature of Balance-of-Payments Measures

Articles XII and XVIII:B of the GATT 1994 only allow quantitative restrictions to be used to address BoP problems. They did originally not allow for tariff measures.[152] However, it was common practice under the GATT 1947 for Contracting Parties to take BoP action in the form of tariff or tariff-like measures, such as import surcharges. In 1979, the use of such measures was formally authorised in the *Declaration on Trade Measures Taken for Balance of Payments Purposes* (the '*1979 Declaration*').[153] The 1994 *Understanding on BoP Provisions* goes much further and commits WTO Members to give preference to price-based BoP measures. Paragraph 2 of the *Understanding on BoP Provisions* states:

> Members confirm their commitment to give preference to those measures which have the least disruptive effect on trade. Such measures (referred to in this Understanding as 'price-based measures') shall be understood to include import surcharges, import deposit requirements or other equivalent trade measures with an impact on the price of imported goods. It is understood that, notwithstanding the provisions of Article II, price-based measures taken for balance-of-payments purposes may be applied by a Member in excess of the duties inscribed in the Schedule of that Member ...

If a Member decides to apply a price-based BoP measure, it must indicate the amount by which the price-based measure exceeds the bound duty clearly and separately.[154]

While, under Article XII, quantitative restrictions were initially the only form of BoP measures allowed, paragraph 3 of the *Understanding on BoP Provisions* now reads:

> Members shall seek to avoid the imposition of new quantitative restrictions for balance-of-payments purposes unless, because of a critical balance-of-payments situation, price-based measures cannot arrest a sharp deterioration in the external payments position.

If a Member applies a quantitative restriction as a BoP measure, it must provide justification as to the reasons why price-based measures are not an adequate instrument to deal with the BoP situation.[155] Pursuant to the *Understanding on BoP Provisions*, not more than one type of restrictive import measure, taken for BoP purposes, may be applied on the same product.[156] A combination of

---

152 Note that this rule is inconsistent with the general GATT preference for using tariffs instead of quantitative restrictions. See above, pp. 487–8.

153 Adopted on 28 November 1979, BISD 26S/205–9. Note that this Declaration is still applicable law.

154 See *Understanding on BoP Provisions*, para. 2. For this purpose, the notification procedure, discussed below, must be followed.

155 See *ibid.*, para. 3. Note that Members applying quantitative restrictions as BoP measures must also indicate in successive consultations the progress made in significantly reducing the incidence and restrictive effect of such measures (*ibid.*).

156 See *ibid.*

price-based measures and quantitative restrictions on the same product is therefore prohibited.

4.1.2   Requirements for the Use of Balance-of-Payments Measures

BoP measures, whether in the form of price-based measures or quantitative restrictions, are often inconsistent with the obligations under Articles II or XI of the GATT 1994. Therefore, they may only be applied when strict requirements are met.

First, BoP measures may *not exceed what is necessary* to address the BoP problem at hand. Article XII:2 of the GATT 1994 states that BoP measures adopted by a Member:

shall not exceed those necessary: i. to forestall the imminent threat of, or to stop, a serious decline in its monetary reserves, or ii. in the case of a [Member] with very low monetary reserves, to achieve a reasonable rate of increase in its reserves.

Article XVIII:9 of the GATT 1994 requires that BoP measures adopted by a developing-country Member:

shall not exceed those necessary: a. to forestall the threat of, or to stop, a serious decline in its monetary reserves, or b. in the case of a [Member] with inadequate monetary reserves, to achieve a reasonable rate of increase in its reserves.

Note that developing-country Members may adopt BoP measures to forestall a *threat* of a serious decline in monetary reserves, while other Members are only permitted to forestall an *imminent threat* of such decline. Also, developing-country Members with *inadequate* monetary reserves may also adopt BoP measures to achieve a reasonable rate of *increase* in their reserves while other Members may do so only when they have *very low* monetary reserves. In *India – Quantitative Restrictions (1999)*, the panel distinguished the requirements for taking BoP measures under Article XVIII from the requirements applicable under Article XII, and noted:

These provisions reflect an acknowledgement of the specific needs of developing countries in relation to measures taken for balance-of-payments purposes.[157]

At its Doha Session in November 2001, the WTO Ministerial Conference explicitly affirmed that Article XVIII is a special and differential treatment provision for developing-country Members and that recourse to it should be *less onerous* than to Article XII.[158]

The determination of what constitutes a serious decline of monetary reserves or an (imminent) threat thereof, or the determination of what constitutes very low or inadequate monetary reserves, is primarily left to the IMF. The WTO

---

157   Panel Report, *India – Quantitative Restrictions (1999)*, para. 5.155.
158   See Ministerial Conference, *Ministerial Decision on Implementation-Related Issues and Concerns*, adopted on 14 November 2001, WT/MIN(01)/17, dated 20 November 2001, para. 1.1.

consults the IMF on these matters, and Article XV:2 of the GATT 1994 states, in relevant part:

The [WTO] in reaching [its] final decision in cases involving the criteria set forth in paragraph 2(*a*) of Article XII or in paragraph 9 of Article XVIII, shall accept the determination of the [IMF] as to what constitutes a serious decline in the [Member's] monetary reserves, a very low level of its monetary reserves or a reasonable rate of increase in its monetary reserves, and as to the financial aspects of other matters covered in consultation in such cases.

Note that, in *India – Quantitative Restrictions (1999)*, the IMF reported that India's reserves as of 21 November 1997 were US$25.1 billion and that an adequate level of reserves at that date would have been US$16 billion. The IMF had also reported that India did not face a serious decline of its monetary reserves or a threat thereof.[159] To a large extent, the panel's conclusions in this case were based on these IMF findings.

Secondly, BoP measures must *avoid unnecessary damage* to the commercial and economic interests of other Members.[160] BoP measures may be discriminatory with respect to products (i.e. apply to some products and not to others), but *not* with respect to countries (i.e. apply to some countries and not to others). Note that the *Understanding on BoP Provisions* requires that Members administer BoP measures in a transparent manner. The authorities of the importing Member must therefore provide adequate justification as to the criteria used to determine which products are subject to the BoP measure.[161]

Thirdly, BoP measures are *temporary measures*. Members applying BoP measures must announce publicly, as soon as possible, time-schedules for the removal of these measures.[162] Referring to the conditions for their adoption (such as 'a serious decline in monetary reserves' or 'inadequate monetary reserves'), Article XII:2(b) of the GATT 1994 states:

[Members] applying restrictions under sub-paragraph (*a*) of this paragraph shall progressively relax them as such conditions improve, maintaining them only to the extent that the conditions specified in that sub-paragraph still justify their application. They shall eliminate the restrictions when conditions would no longer justify their institution or maintenance under that sub-paragraph.

As the external financial situation improves, the BoP measures must be relaxed; when the external financial situation has returned to 'normal', the BoP measures

---

159 See Panel Report, *India – Quantitative Restrictions (1999)*, paras. 5.174 and 5.177.
160 See Articles XII:3(c)(i) and XVIII:10 of the GATT 1994.
161 In the case of certain 'essential products', a Member may exclude or limit the application of surcharges applied across the board or other measures applied for BoP purposes. The concept of 'essential products' shall be understood to mean products which meet basic consumption needs or which contribute to the Member's effort to improve its BoP situation, such as capital goods or inputs needed for production. See Articles XII:3 and XVIII:10 of the GATT 1994; and *Understanding on BoP Provisions*, para. 4.
162 See *ibid.*, para. 1.

must be eliminated.[163] Article XVIII:11 of the GATT 1994 provides for similar obligations with respect to the elimination or relaxation of BoP measures adopted by developing-country Members. However, Article XVIII:11 adds the proviso:

that no [Member] shall be required to withdraw or modify restrictions on the ground that a change in its development policy would render unnecessary the restrictions which it is applying under this Section.

In *India – Quantitative Restrictions (1999)*, the Appellate Body upheld the panel's finding that India could manage its BoP situation using macroeconomic policy instruments alone, without maintaining quantitative restrictions. India appealed this finding, arguing that the panel required India to change its development policy. The Appellate Body, however, ruled:

[W]e are of the opinion that the use of macroeconomic policy instruments is not related to any particular development policy, but is resorted to by all Members regardless of the type of development policy they pursue.[164]

The Appellate Body clarified the meaning of the proviso of Article XVIII:11 by stating:

We believe that structural measures are different from macroeconomic instruments with respect to their relationship to development policy. If India were asked to implement agricultural reform or to scale back reservations on certain products for small-scale units as indispensable policy changes in order to overcome its balance-of-payments difficulties, such a requirement would probably have involved a change in India's development policy.[165]

Questions and Assignments 9.11

When is a Member allowed to adopt a balance-of-payments measure? What form may such a measure take? With which obligations of the GATT 1994 may a balance-of-payments measure be inconsistent: the obligations under Article I, Article II or Article XI? When must a Member eliminate or relax the balance-of-payments measures it applies?

4.1.3 Procedural Issues

BoP measures are reviewed by the WTO to determine their consistency with the GATT 1994. This review is conducted by the Committee on Balance-of-Payments Restrictions (the 'BoP Committee'). The procedures applicable to this review are set out in the *Understanding on BoP Provisions*.[166] A Member shall notify the

---

163 For BoP measures of developing-country Members, however, note that, if the elimination or relaxation of the BoP measures would produce immediately or very quickly the conditions justifying the adoption or intensification of BoP measures, the BoP measures 'may be maintained'. See Note *Ad* Article XVIII; and Appellate Body Report, *India – Quantitative Restrictions (1999)*, paras. 117–20.
164 Appellate Body Report, *India – Quantitative Restrictions (1999)*, para. 126.
165 *Ibid.*, para. 128.
166 As *Understanding on BoP Provisions*, para. 5, states, the BoP Committee shall follow the procedures for consultations on BoP restrictions approved on 28 April 1970 (BISD 18S/48–53) (the 'full consultation procedures'), subject to the provisions set out in the *Understanding*. Consultations may be held under the 'simplified consultation procedures' approved on 19 December 1972 (BISD 20S/47–9) in the case of least-developed-country Members or in the case of developing-country Members in certain situations. See *ibid.*, para. 8.

introduction of, or any changes in the application of, a BoP measure to the General Council.[167] A Member applying new restrictions or raising the general level of its existing restrictions must enter into consultation with the BoP Committee within four months of the adoption of such measures.[168] If the Member concerned fails to request a consultation, the Chair of the BoP Committee shall invite that Member to hold such a consultation. Any Member may request that notifications on BoP measures are reviewed by the BoP Committee.[169] Furthermore, all BoP measures are subject to *periodic* review in the BoP Committee.[170] For instance, Bangladesh has been subject to GATT/WTO consultations since 1973 for the import bans and restrictions it employs on certain products for BoP purposes.[171] The last consultations took place in October 2002 and November 2004. In February 2004, Bangladesh notified the BoP Committee that it had withdrawn restrictions in seven categories, maintaining import restrictions only on four categories of products: chicks, eggs, cartons and common salt.[172] Bangladesh subsequently notified the removal of restrictions on cartons as from July 2005 and common salt as from 31 December 2008.[173] In 2007, Bangladesh submitted a document to the BoP Committee, providing information with regard to its economic situation and pointing out that its last BoP restrictions would be removed by 31 December 2008. However, it stated:

It is to be mentioned that more than three million people are involved in the production, distribution and marketing of eggs, chicks and salt. They are mainly small poor farmers, women and youth. They totally depend on these items for their livelihood. If the import restrictions on these items are withdrawn, it is apprehended that these poorer sections of the population will suffer enormously. Yet, the Government of Bangladesh is highly committed to maintain its commitments with the WTO. It has therefore decided to withdraw BOP restrictions under GATT Article XVIII:B on the remaining items from 31 December 2008 in consistence with the decision of the Committee on BOPs. It is expected that the next one year and eight months will provide a breathing time to these sections of population to adjust themselves with the new competitive environment.[174]

The BoP Committee reports on its consultations to the General Council. Pursuant to paragraph 13 of the *Understanding on BoP Provisions*, the BoP Committee shall endeavour to include in its conclusions 'proposals for recommendations aimed at promoting the implementation of Articles XII and XVIII:B, the 1979 Declaration and this Understanding'. In those cases in which a time-schedule has been presented for the removal of BoP measures, the General

---

167 See *ibid.*, para. 9. Every year, each Member shall make available to the WTO Secretariat a consolidated notification on all aspects of the BoP measures applied. *Ibid.*

168 See *ibid.*, para. 6. Note that the Member adopting BoP measures may request that a consultation be held under Articles XII:4(a) or XVIII:12(a) of the GATT 1994 as appropriate. *Ibid.* On the course of the consultation process and the role of the WTO Secretariat, see *ibid.*, paras. 11 and 12.

169 See *ibid.*, para. 10.

170 See *ibid.*, para. 7, which refers in this respect to Articles XII:4(b) and XVIII:12(b) of the GATT 1994.

171 See Report by the Secretariat, *Trade Policy Review: Bangladesh*, WT/TPR/S/168, dated 9 August 2006, 55.

172 See WT/BOP/N/62, dated 18 February 2004.

173 See WT/BOP/N/63, dated 9 September 2005; and WT/BOP/N/64, dated 20 April 2007.

174 See WT/BOP/G/14, dated 2 May 2007, para. 16.

Council may recommend that, in adhering to such a time-schedule, a Member shall be deemed to be in compliance with its GATT 1994 obligations. Whenever the General Council has made specific recommendations, the rights and obligations of Members shall be assessed in light of such recommendations. In the absence of specific proposals for recommendations by the General Council, the Committee's conclusions should record the different views expressed in the Committee.[175]

Since its establishment in 1995, the BoP Committee has reviewed many BoP measures notified by Members. In most cases, the Members concerned made commitments to eliminate or relax the BoP measures under review and these commitments satisfied the BoP Committee. In other cases, Members were unable to agree within the BoP Committee on a timeframe for the relaxation and/or elimination of the BoP measures under review.

In *India – Quantitative Restrictions (1999)*, India argued that it had the right to maintain BoP measures until the BoP Committee or the General Council ordered it to eliminate or relax these measures. The panel rejected this argument. It noted that the obligation of Article XVIII:11 to eliminate or relax BoP measures:

is not conditioned on any BOP Committee or General Council decision. If we were to interpret Article XVIII:11 to be so conditioned, we would be adding terms to Article XVIII:11 that it does not contain.[176]

In *India – Quantitative Restrictions (1999)*, India also argued that WTO dispute settlement panels have no authority to examine Members' justifications of BoP measures.[177] India based its position on the second sentence of footnote 1 to the *Understanding on BoP Provisions*, which reads:

The provisions of Articles XXII and XXIII of GATT 1994 as elaborated and applied by the Dispute Settlement Understanding may be invoked with respect to any matters arising from the application of restrictive import measures taken for balance-of-payments purposes.

India interpreted this footnote to mean that the WTO dispute settlement system may be invoked in respect of matters relating to the specific use or purpose of a BoP measure or to the manner in which a BoP measure is applied in a particular case, but not with respect to the question of the BoP *justification* of these measures. More generally, India argued for the existence of a 'principle of institutional balance' that requires panels to refrain from reviewing the justification of BoP restrictions under Article XVIII:B. Such review was entrusted to the BoP Committee and the General Council, the political organs of the WTO. Thus

---

175 Note also the powers given to the Ministerial Conference in Articles XII:4(c), (d) and (f) and XVIII:12(c), (d) and (f) of the GATT 1994. These powers have never been used.
176 Panel Report, *India – Quantitative Restrictions (1999)*, para. 5.79.
177 See also above, p. 644.

panels and the Appellate Body, the 'judicial' organs of the WTO, must refrain from such review. The Appellate Body rejected India's arguments and stated:

> Any doubts that may have existed in the past as to whether the dispute settlement procedures under Article XXIII were available for disputes relating to balance-of-payments restrictions have been removed by the second sentence of footnote 1 to the *BOP Understanding* ...

> [I]n light of footnote 1 to the *BOP Understanding*, a dispute relating to the justification of balance-of-payments restrictions is clearly within the scope of matters to which the dispute settlement provisions of Article XXIII of the GATT 1994, as elaborated and applied by the DSU, are applicable.[178]

The fact that panels are competent to review the justification of BoP measures does *not* make the competence of the BoP Committee and the General Council, discussed above, redundant. In *India – Quantitative Restrictions (1999)*, the Appellate Body ruled:

> We are cognisant of the competence of the BOP Committee and the General Council with respect to balance-of-payments restrictions under Article XVIII:12 of the GATT 1994 and the *BOP Understanding*. However, we see no conflict between that competence and the competence of panels. Moreover, we are convinced that, in considering the justification of balance-of-payments restrictions, panels should take into account the deliberations and conclusions of the BOP Committee, as did the panel in *Korea – Beef*.[179]

The Appellate Body agreed with the panel that the BoP Committee and panels have different functions, and that the BoP Committee procedures and the dispute settlement procedures differ in nature, scope, timing and type of outcome.[180]

In recent years, the use of BoP measures and notifications to the BoP Committee have become rare. In 2009, the BoP Committee reviewed notifications of BoP measures taken by Ecuador and by Ukraine. Ecuador agreed to replace most of the quantitative restrictions with price-based measures and to modify progressively the level and scope of the measures as its BoP situation improved. Ukraine notified the introduction of an import surcharge on imports of certain products for BoP purposes. The BoP Committee concluded that the measures taken by Ukraine were not justified by its BoP situation and had not been applied in a manner consistent with the requirements of Article XII of the GATT 1994 and the BoP Understanding. On 8 September 2009, Ukraine notified the Committee that the measures in question had been discontinued on the previous day.[181] In 2010, the BoP Committee met to hear reports from Ecuador on its phasing out of all surcharges introduced as BoP safeguards, and Ecuador removed all measures

---

178   Appellate Body Report, *India – Quantitative Restrictions (1999)*, paras. 87 and 95.
179   *Ibid.*, para. 103.
180   See *ibid.*, paras. 5.90 and 5.114.
181   Annual Report of the BoP Committee for 2009 (WT/BOP/R/96), dated 30 October 2009. Ecuador's notification is contained in WTO document WT/BOP/N/65; and Ukraine's notification is in WTO document WT/BOP/N/65.

taken for BoP purposes on 23 July 2010.[182] In 2011, the BoP Committee held its final review under China's Transitional Review Mechanism according to paragraph 18 of China's Protocol of Accession.[183] No activities were reported by the BoP Committee in 2012.[184]

Questions and Assignments 9.12

What is the role of the BoP Committee? Find out whether South Africa or Brazil currently maintain balance-of-payments measures. Can a panel review the balance-of-payments justification of the measure before or during the review of the GATT-consistency of this measure by the BoP Committee?

4.2   Balance-of-Payments Measures Under the GATS

Article XII:1 of the GATS, entitled 'Restrictions to Safeguard the Balance of Payments', provides, in its first sentence:

In the event of serious balance-of-payments and external financial difficulties or threat thereof, a Member may adopt or maintain restrictions on trade in services on which it has undertaken specific commitments, including on payments or transfers for transactions related to such commitments.

Article XII:1, second sentence, of the GATS recognises that particular pressures on the balance of payments situation of a Member in the process of economic development or economic transition may necessitate the use of restrictions to maintain, *inter alia*, a level of financial reserves adequate for the implementation of its programme of economic development or economic transition.

In situations of *serious* BoP and external financial difficulties or a threat thereof, Members may adopt or maintain BoP measures that restrict trade in services in a GATS-inconsistent manner. However, as explicitly provided in Article XII:2 of the GATS, these BoP measures shall: (1) not discriminate among Members; (2) be consistent with the *Articles of Agreement of the IMF*; (3) avoid unnecessary damage to the commercial, economic and financial interests of any other Member; (4) not exceed those necessary to deal with the circumstances described in Article XII:1, quoted above; and (5) be temporary and phased out progressively as the situation described in Article XII:1 improves. Any BoP measure restricting trade in services, or any changes thereto, must be promptly notified to the General Council.[185] Members adopting or changing BoP measures must consult with the BoP Committee promptly.[186] Just as with BoP measures restricting trade in goods, BoP measures restricting trade in services are the subject of

---

182 Annual Report of the BoP Committee for 2010 (WT/BOP/R/101), dated 2 November 2010. For Ecuador's notification, see WTO document WT/BOP/N/75. Reports of the BoP Committee meetings are contained in WTO documents WT/BOP/R/98, WT/BOP/R/99 and WT/BOP/R/100.
183 Annual Report of the BoP Committee for 2011 (WT/BOP/R/104), dated 24 October 2011.
184 Annual Report of the BoP Committee for 2012 (WT/BOP/R/105), dated 2 November 2012.
185 See Article XII:4 of the GATS.   186 See Article XII:5(c) of the GATS.

periodic consultations. The consultations with the BoP Committee shall address the compliance of BoP measures with the requirements of Article XII:2, in particular the progressive phasing out of restrictions.[187] The IMF also plays a central role with regard to BoP measures restricting trade in services in the consultations on the GATS-consistency of BoP measures.[188]

Questions and Assignments 9.13

When are measures that restrict trade in services, in a manner that is inconsistent with other GATS provisions justified under Article XII of the GATS?

5   SUMMARY

WTO law provides for 'economic emergency exceptions'. These exceptions, set out primarily in Article XIX of the GATT 1994 and the *Agreement on Safeguards*, allow Members to adopt measures that are otherwise WTO-inconsistent in situations where a surge in imports causes, or threatens to cause, serious injury to the domestic industry. The otherwise WTO-inconsistent measures taken in economic emergency situations are referred to as *safeguard measures*. Safeguard measures temporarily restrict imports to give the domestic industry concerned time for structural adjustment to new economic realities. Safeguard measures typically take the form of customs duties exceeding tariff bindings or quantitative restrictions. Safeguard measures must be limited in time and applied in a non-discriminatory manner to all sources of supply. Moreover, a Member applying a safeguard measure must seek to compensate other Members affected by the measure. Safeguard measures may only be applied when three requirements are met: (1) the 'increased imports' requirement; (2) the 'serious injury or threat thereof' requirement; and (3) the 'causation' requirement.

The 'increase in imports' must be recent, sudden, sharp and significant. 'Serious injury' exists when there is a significant overall impairment in the position of a domestic industry. A 'threat of serious injury' exists when serious injury is clearly imminent. The relevant domestic industry is the industry (or at least a major proportion of the domestic producers) producing like or directly competitive products. To determine whether there is, in fact, serious injury or a threat thereof to a domestic industry, all relevant factors of an objective and quantifiable nature having a bearing on the situation of that industry must be considered. The test for establishing 'causation' is twofold: (1) a demonstration of the causal

---

187 See Article XII:5(d) of the GATS.

188 See Article XII:5(e) of the GATS. All findings of statistical and other facts presented by the IMF relating to foreign exchange, monetary reserves and balance of payments shall be accepted and the conclusions of the BoP Committee shall be based on the assessment by the IMF of the balance of payments and the external financial situation of the consulting Member.

link between the 'increased imports' and the 'serious injury or threat thereof' (the 'causal link' sub-requirement); and (2) an identification of any injury caused by factors other than the increased imports and the non-attribution of this injury to the increased imports (the 'non-attribution' sub-requirement).

WTO law also provides for 'balance-of-payments exceptions', set out in Articles XII and XVIII:B of the GATT 1994 (elaborated in the *Understanding on BoP Provisions*) and Article XII of the GATS. These exceptions allow Members to adopt measures, otherwise inconsistent with Articles II and XI of the GATT 1994 or Article XVI of the GATS, to safeguard their external financial position and to protect their balance of payments. BoP measures restricting trade in goods can take the form of quantitative restrictions *or* tariff-like, i.e. price-based, measures (such as import surcharges). The latter type of BoP measure is preferred. Generally speaking, BoP measures must not exceed what is necessary to safeguard the external financial situation (in terms of decline of its monetary reserves or the level of its monetary reserves). The requirements for BoP measures taken by developing-country Members (see Article XVIII:B) are less stringent than those for BoP measures taken by other Members (see Article XII).

Exercise 9: Glass Producers in Dire Straits

TrueBleu and Verras, the two largest manufacturers of glass bottles in Richland, are experiencing severe economic problems. Over the last two years, they saw their combined share of the market in Richland for glass bottles drop from 60 per cent to 30 per cent and they had to lay off almost half of their workforce. Since 2001, the import of glass bottles into Richland has doubled every year. Most of these imports come from Richland, the home of the world's most efficient manufacturers Sunland, a developing-country Member of the WTO and of glass bottles. To prevent further job losses at TrueBleu and Verras and to give both companies some 'breathing space' to allow them to modernise their production, the Government of Richland decided last month to limit the import of glass bottles from Sunland to 1999 levels. It should be noted that the problems of Richland's manufacturers of glass bottles are due not only to import competition but also to the fact that in recent times beer drinkers in Richland seem to prefer their beer in aluminium cans rather than glass bottles.

Sunland has requested consultations with Richland on the import restriction of glass bottles. You are a lawyer with the Geneva-based Advisory Centre on WTO Law (ACWL). Newland, a member of the ACWL, has requested the ACWL to advise and assist its ambassador to the WTO in the upcoming consultations. In preparation for these discussions, you have been asked to write a legal brief in support of the position of Sunland.

10 Regional Trade Exceptions

CONTENTS

1 INTRODUCTION

In addition to the 'general and security exceptions' and the 'economic emergency exceptions' discussed in Chapters 8 and 9 respectively, WTO law also provides for 'regional trade exceptions'. These exceptions allow Members to adopt measures that would otherwise be WTO-inconsistent, when they are in the pursuit of economic integration among a group of WTO Members. While, in the past, the term 'regional trade exceptions' as well as the term 'regional trade agreements' (RTAs) described well the reality they referred to, in recent years these terms have given rise to some confusion. In the past, the term 'regional trade agreements' was used to refer to the economic integration efforts between adjacent countries or countries in the same region. Good examples of such *regional* economic integration efforts are the *North American Free Trade Agreement*, the *Southern Common Market (MERCOSUR) Agreement* and the *ASEAN Free Trade Area (AFTA) Agreement*.[1] To the extent that these and other *regional* economic integration efforts involved GATT 1994 or GATS-inconsistent measures, these measures could – under specific conditions – be justified under the *regional* trade exceptions of the GATT 1994 and the GATS. In recent years, however, the countries involved in economic integration efforts are often countries or groups of countries from *different regions*. Consider, for example, the *European Union–South Korea Free Trade Agreement*, the *United States–Colombia Trade Promotion Agreement* and the *India–MERCOSUR Preferential Trade Agreement*.[2] Instead of referring to these agreements as 'regional trade agreements', they are often referred to as 'preferential trade agreements' (PTAs). The WTO *World Trade Report 2011* stated:

One half of the PTAs currently in force are not strictly 'regional'. The advent of cross-regional PTAs has been particularly pronounced in the last decade. The trend towards a broader geographical scope of PTAs is even more pronounced for those PTAs that are currently under negotiation or have recently been signed (but are not yet in force). Practically all of these are of the cross-regional type.[3]

However, as WTO Members and the WTO Secretariat continue to use the term 'regional trade agreements',[4] this book also continues to use this term, and discusses in this chapter the 'regional trade exceptions', even though the word 'regional' is almost a misnomer because such economic integration agreements often no longer have the traditional geographical connotation. The 'regional trade exceptions' are set out in Article XXIV and the Enabling Clause of the GATT 1994, and Article V of the GATS.[5] This chapter addresses: (1) the proliferation of regional trade agreements and their impact on the multilateral trading system; (2) regional trade exceptions under the GATT 1994; and (3) regional trade exceptions under the GATS.

---

1 For further details on these agreements, see below, pp. 650–5.
2 Also consider e.g. the *China–Costa Rica Free Trade Agreement*, the *Australia–Chile Free Trade Agreement*, the *Peru–Japan Economic Partnership Agreement*, the *Japan–Switzerland Free Trade and Economic Partnership Agreement* and the Economic Partnership Agreements (EPAs) between the European Union and groups of African, Caribbean and Pacific (ACP) States, such as the CARIFORUM States or the ECOWAS States.
3 World Trade Report 2011, The WTO and Preferential Trade Agreements: From Co-existence to Coherence (WTO, 2011), 6.
4 See e.g. www.wto.org/english/tratop_e/region_e/rta_pta_e.htm. Also note that the WTO Secretariat uses the term 'preferential trade *arrangements*' (PTAs) to refer to *unilateral* trade preferences. They include Generalized System of Preferences schemes (under which developed countries grant preferential tariffs to imports from developing countries). Information on PTAs notified to the WTO is available in the PTA Database, at http://ptadb.wto.org/?lang=1. See above, p. 649.
5 The economic integration exception for trade in goods is elaborated on further in the *Understanding on the Interpretation of Article XXIV of the GATT 1994* (the '*Understanding on Article XXIV*'), which forms part of the GATT 1994.

2   PROLIFERATION OF REGIONAL TRADE AGREEMENTS

Regional trade agreements have proliferated since the early 1990s, and have become an indelible feature of the international trading landscape. In February 2013, there were 237 regional trade agreements in force between WTO Members.[6] The share of world trade between parties to regional trade agreements has increased along with the proliferation of these agreements. It is estimated that, currently, half of world trade occurs among parties to regional trade agreements. However, it is important to note that only a portion of that trade actually takes place under the preferential conditions that in theory apply to the trade between parties to regional trade agreements.[7]

Well-known examples of regional trade agreements, establishing either a customs union or a free trade area, are the European Union (EU),[8] the European Free Trade Association (EFTA),[9] the European Economic Area (EEA),[10] the North American Free Trade Agreement (NAFTA),[11] the ASEAN (Association of Southeast Asian Nations) Free Trade Area (AFTA),[12] the Southern Common Market (MERCOSUR),[13] the Andean Community,[14] the Common Market of the Caribbean (CARICOM),[15] the Australia–New Zealand Closer Economic Relations Agreement (ANZCERTA),[16] the Southern African Development Community (SADC),[17] the Economic Community of West African States (ECOWAS)[18] and the Common Market of Eastern and Southern Africa (COMESA).[19] Negotiations on many other regional trade agreements, such as the Trans-Pacific Partnership (TPP)

---

6   See http://rtais.wto.org/UI/publicsummarytable.aspx.

7   World Trade Report 2011, *The WTO and Preferential Trade Agreements: From Co-existence to Coherence* (WTO, 2011), 72.

8   The European Union comprises Austria, Belgium, Bulgaria, Cyprus, Czech Republic, Denmark, Estonia, Finland, France, Germany, Greece, Hungary, Ireland, Italy, Latvia, Lithuania, Luxembourg, Malta, Netherlands, Poland, Portugal, Romania, Slovak Republic, Slovenia, Spain, Sweden, the United Kingdom and – as of 1 July 2013 – Croatia. Note that the European Union is of course more than a customs union, but at its core it is, *inter alia*, a customs union.

9   A free-trade agreement between Iceland, Liechtenstein, Norway and Switzerland.

10   A customs union and economic integration agreement between Iceland, Liechtenstein and Norway.

11   A free trade agreement and economic integration agreement between Canada, Mexico and the United States.

12   A free trade agreement between Brunei Darussalam, Cambodia, Indonesia, Laos, Malaysia, Myanmar, Philippines, Singapore, Thailand, and Vietnam.

13   A customs union and economic integration agreement between Argentina, Brazil, Paraguay (temporarily suspended), Uruguay and Venezuela.

14   A customs union between Bolivia, Colombia, Ecuador and Peru.

15   A customs union and economic integration agreement between Antigua and Barbuda, Bahamas, Barbados, Belize, Dominica, Grenada, Guyana, Haiti, Jamaica, Montserrat, Saint Kitts and Nevis, Saint Lucia, Saint Vincent and the Grenadines, Suriname and Trinidad and Tobago.

16   A free trade agreement and economic integration agreement between Australia and New Zealand.

17   A free trade agreement between Angola, Botswana, the Democratic Republic of Congo, Lesotho, Madagascar, Malawi, Mauritius, Mozambique, Namibia, the Seychelles, South Africa, Swaziland, Tanzania, Zambia and Zimbabwe.

18   A customs union between Benin, Burkina Faso, Cape Verde, Côte d'Ivoire, Gambia, Ghana, Guinea, Guinea-Bissau, Liberia, Mali, Niger, Nigeria, Senegal, Sierra Leone and Togo.

19   A customs union between Burundi, Comoros, the Democratic Republic of Congo, Djibouti, Egypt, Eritrea, Ethiopia, Kenya, Libya, Madagascar, Malawi, Mauritius, Rwanda, the Seychelles, Sudan, Swaziland, Uganda, Zambia and Zimbabwe.

Agreement,[20] are currently ongoing. In February 2013, the European Union and the United States formally announced the decision to launch negotiations for a trans-Atlantic trade and investment agreement. These negotiations are envisioned to cover market access, issues relating to TBT and SPS measures, government procurement and environmental and labour issues.[21]

A WTO Member is, on average, a party to thirteen regional trade agreements.[22] In 2013, only one WTO Member, namely, Mongolia, was not a party to any regional trade agreement.[23]

The key characteristic of regional trade agreements is that the parties to such agreements offer each other more favourable treatment in trade matters than they offer other trading partners. To the extent that these other trading partners, which are denied the same treatment, are WTO Members, such discriminatory treatment is – as discussed in Chapter 4 – inconsistent with the MFN treatment obligation, one of the basic principles of WTO law. Yet, both the GATT 1994 and the GATS allow, under certain conditions, regional trade agreements establishing customs unions or free trade areas. As is stated in Article XXIV:4 of the GATT 1994:

The [Members] recognize the desirability of increasing freedom of trade by the development, through voluntary agreements, of closer integration between the economies of the countries parties to such agreements.

WTO law recognises the advantages of economic integration and trade liberalisation even when these efforts involve only some of its Members. At a regional level, it may be possible to achieve a degree of trade liberalisation which may be out of reach at the global level. It has been argued that trade liberalisation will occur more quickly if it is pursued within regional trading blocs, and that trade liberalisation achieved at a regional level may serve as a *stepping stone* for trade liberalisation at the multilateral level at a later time. Also, regional trade liberalisation may create significant economic growth within the region concerned, which can, in turn, generate more trade with the rest of the world. It is not clear, however, whether regional trade agreements *divert* rather than *create* trade. In this connection, economic studies of customs unions and free trade areas have revealed that the trade-creation effects may often be smaller than the trade-diversion effects as trade between the participants replaces trade between the participants and non-participants. The economic theory which explains the potential dangers of regional trade agreements focuses on a trade creation/trade diversion dichotomy:

20 As of December 2012, the TPP negotiations involved Australia, Brunei Darussalam, Chile, Canada, Malaysia, Mexico, New Zealand, Peru, Singapore, the United States and Vietnam.
21 *Bridges Weekly Trade News Digest*, 13 February 2013.
22 World Trade Report 2011, *The WTO and Preferential Trade Agreements: From Co-existence to Coherence* (WTO, 2011), 72.
23 Mongolia was not party to any regional trade agreement. See www.wto.org/english/tratop_e/region_e/ summary_e.xls, visited on 27 February 2013.

[P]referential trade opening allows some domestic production to be replaced by imports from more efficient firms located in preference-receiving countries, leading to welfare gains (trade creation). At the same time [regional trade agreements] may reduce imports from more efficient non-member countries, implying a welfare loss (trade diversions). The net welfare effect of [regional trade agreements] depends on the relative magnitude of these opposing trends.[24]

On whether regional trade agreements may be stepping stones for later multilateral trade liberalisation, the 2004 Sutherland Report noted:

There is ... real reason to doubt assertions that the pursuit of multiple PTAs will enhance, rather than undermine, the attractiveness of multilateral trade liberalization.[25]

However, apart from economic reasons, countries may also have political reasons to pursue deeper economic integration and trade liberalisation with some other countries. The example *par excellence* here is the European Union, which, through economic integration of, and trade liberalisation between, its Member States sought to create, and was successful in creating, 'an ever closer union' among the peoples of Europe to avoid the recurrence of war. The establishment of MERCOSUR, a customs union originally between Argentina, Brazil, Paraguay and Uruguay,[26] was motivated by the wish to buttress democracy in these countries. Furthermore, preferential trade agreements can also serve to reinforce the participation of their member countries in the WTO, particularly in the case of the developing countries. A case study on the role of the COMESA and SADC membership of Zambia and Mauritius in supporting and facilitating the participation of these countries in the WTO revealed that:

[while] RTA Membership had little *direct* impact so far on the preparation and conduct of the WTO negotiations ... regional groupings can play a much needed role in the WTO preparations through indirect means ... By raising awareness, by training, by providing a platform for the exchange of views and information, and by stimulating trade capacity building initiatives, COMESA and the SADC have contributed to a better preparation of their member countries on trade issues, which have had positive spillovers on their participation [in] the WTO.[27]

WTO law should not stand in the way of such processes. However, a balance must be struck between the interests of countries pursuing closer economic integration among a select group of countries and the interests of countries excluded from that group. The *Understanding on Article XXIV of the GATT 1994* states in its Preamble:

---

24 World Trade Report 2011, *The WTO and Preferential Trade Agreements: From Co-existence to Coherence* (WTO, 2011), 9.
25 Report by the Consultative Board to the Director-General Supachai Panitchpakdi, *The Future of the WTO: Addressing Institutional Challenges in the New Millennium* (WTO, 2004), para. 85.
26 Note that Venezuela joined MERCOSUR as a full member on 31 July 2012.
27 S. Bilal and S. Szepesi, 'How Regional Economic Communities Can Facilitate Participation in the WTO: The Experience of Mauritius and Zambia', in P. Gallagher, P. Low and A. Stoler (eds.), *Managing the Challenges of WTO Participation: 45 Case Studies* (Cambridge University Press, 2005), 389–90.

[T]he purpose of [regional trade] agreements should be to facilitate trade between the constituent territories and not to raise barriers to the trade of other Members with such territories ... [I]n their formation or enlargement the parties to them should to the greatest possible extent avoid creating adverse effects on the trade of other Members.

WTO rules on regional trade agreements are designed to ensure that these agreements create more trade than they divert. In the context of the Doha Round, Members are negotiating with the aim of further clarifying and improving the current rules applying to regional trade agreements.[28] While negotiations on the clarification and improvement of the substantive rules on regional trade agreements have not been successful to date, Members have been successful in agreeing in December 2006 on a new transparency mechanism, the Transparency Mechanism for Regional Trade Agreements (the 'RTA Transparency Mechanism').[29] This transparency mechanism provides for early announcement of negotiations towards a preferential trade agreement, as well as of newly signed preferential trade agreements. It sets out detailed notification requirements for parties to preferential trade agreements, to allow Members to have a clearer picture of the rapidly growing 'spaghetti bowl' of overlapping preferential trade agreements. The RTA Transparency Mechanism also establishes a procedure for the consideration of regional trade agreements on the basis of a factual presentation by the WTO Secretariat in either the WTO Committee on Regional Trade Agreements (CRTA) or the Committee on Trade and Development (CTD).[30] The RTA Transparency Mechanism also mandates the WTO Secretariat to maintain an updated electronic database on individual preferential trade agreements.[31] This database, which can be accessed through the WTO's website, was launched in January 2009, and contains useful facts and figures on preferential trade agreements which have been notified to the WTO.[32]

In times of no or slow progress in multilateral trade liberalisation in WTO negotiations, regional trade liberalisation has often been advocated as an alternative. Note, however, that such efforts may aggravate the lack of progress at the multilateral level.[33] Moreover, such efforts are likely to leave out many of the world's poorest countries.[34] As Jagdish Bhagwati noted:

28 See Ministerial Conference, *Doha Ministerial Declaration*, adopted on 14 November 2001, WT/MIN(01)/DEC/1, dated 20 November 2001, para. 29.

29 General Council, *Transparency Mechanism for Regional Trade Agreements*, Decision adopted on 14 December 2006, WT/L/671, dated 18 December 2006. It must be noted that the new mechanism is implemented on a provisional basis, to be reviewed and replaced by a permanent mechanism as part of the overall results of the Doha Round. In 2012, a total of three early announcements were received from Members, two for RTAs under negotiation and one for newly signed RTAs. To date, thirty-five early announcements of RTAs have been made. See WT/REG/12, dated 26 November 2012.

30 The Committee on Regional Trade Agreements implements the transparency mechanism for RTAs falling under Article XXIV of the GATT 1994 and Article V of the GATS, and the Committee on Trade and Development does so for RTAs falling under para. 2(c) of the Enabling Clause. See *Decision on the Transparency Mechanism*, WT/L/671, para. 18.

31 See *Decision on the Transparency Mechanism*, WT/L/671, para. 21.

32 See the RTA Database, at http://rtais.wto.org/UI/PublicMaintainRTAHome.aspx.

33 See above, p. 93 and footnote 90 therein.

34 For a critical view on RTAs, see e.g. Report by the Consultative Board to the Director-General Supachai Panitchpakdi, *The Future of the WTO: Addressing Institutional Challenges in the New Millennium* (WTO, 2004), paras. 75–87.

Everyone loses out but the poor countries suffer the most because their companies are least prepared to deal with the confusion.[35]

Moreover, Bhagwati observed that:

where a significant power such as the US or the European Union is involved in an agreement, it almost always sneaks in reverse preferences – and trade-unrelated issues such as patent protection and labour standards – that exact a heavy cost on developing countries.[36]

Nonetheless, the debate on regionalism is gradually shifting away from a discussion of costs and benefits to a discussion on how to achieve coherence between multilateralism and regionalism. Pascal Lamy, Director-General of the WTO, noted the following in 2012:

It is therefore important that we look at how to manage the relationship between preferential trade agreements and the multilateral trading system in ways that support world trade. The starting assumption being that preferential trade agreements are not going to disappear any time soon.

One suggestion is to continue to negotiate and construct a multilateral framework that responds to those needs manifested in preferential agreements that can be met through a multilateral approach. This could include revisiting the existing rules on preferential trade arrangements such as those in Article XXIV of GATT.

Some have also argued for a process that builds gradually towards a better understanding among WTO members of preferential trade agreements, what motivates them, and how they are both similar and different. This would be not so much a negotiation as a conversation in the first instance, of the kind that could possibly be carried out under the Transparency Mechanism recently established as a forum for notifying and discussing PTAs. The ultimate objective of this exercise would be to build on those elements of commonality in preferential trade agreements that could be multilateralized on a non-discriminatory basis. As our publication 'World Trade Report 2011' indicated, it is about 'coherence' rather than just 'coexistence'.[37]

The WTO's *World Trade Report 2011* focused on the coherence between the regional and multilateral trade regimes. The report, *inter alia*, identified a number of different approaches which have been proposed for improving coherence between regional trade agreements and the multilateral trading system. These include:

accelerating multilateral trade opening; fixing the deficiencies in the WTO legal framework; adopting a softer approach as a complement to the existing legal framework; multilateralizing regionalism (extending preferential arrangements in a non-discriminatory manner to additional parties). These approaches are not mutually exclusive. They all aim at making sure that [regional trade agreements] contribute to trade co-operation and opening in a non-discriminatory manner.[38]

---

35 J. Bhagwati, 'A Costly Pursuit of Free Trade', *Financial Times*, 6 March 2001.
36 *Ibid.*
37 P. Lamy, 'The Multilateral Trading System and Regional Economic Co-operation', Speech of the Director-General at the University of International Business and Economics, Beijing, 20 September 2012, at www.wto.org/english/news_e/sppl_e/sppl246_e.htm.
38 World Trade Report 2011, *The WTO and Preferential Trade Agreements: From Co-existence to Coherence* (WTO, 2011), 15.

Questions and Assignments 10.1

Name three regional trade agreements other than those referred to above. From a WTO law perspective, what is the problem with regional trade agreements? Why does WTO law, under certain conditions, allow for regional trade agreements?

3   REGIONAL TRADE EXCEPTIONS UNDER THE GATT 1994

The chapeau of Article XXIV:5 of the GATT 1994 provides, in relevant part:

[T]he provisions of this Agreement shall not prevent ... the formation of a customs union or of a free-trade area or the adoption of an interim agreement necessary for the formation of a customs union or of a free-trade area.

In examining this provision in *Turkey – Textiles (1999)*, the Appellate Body noted:

We read this to mean that the provisions of the GATT 1994 *shall not make impossible* the formation of a customs union. Thus, the chapeau makes it clear that Article XXIV may, under certain conditions, justify the adoption of a measure which is inconsistent with certain other GATT provisions, and may be invoked as a possible 'defence' to a finding of inconsistency.[39]

There are two conditions that must be met in order to justify under Article XXIV a measure which is otherwise GATT-inconsistent. As the Appellate Body stated in *Turkey – Textiles (1999)*:

First, the party claiming the benefit of this defence must demonstrate that the measure at issue is introduced upon the formation of a customs union that fully meets the requirements of sub-paragraphs 8(a) and 5(a) of Article XXIV. And, second, that party must demonstrate that the formation of that customs union would be prevented if it were not allowed to introduce the measure at issue.[40]

There is therefore a two-tier test to determine whether a measure, otherwise inconsistent with the GATT 1994, can be justified under Article XXIV. Such measure is justified: (1) if the measure is introduced upon the formation of a customs union, a free trade area or an interim agreement that meets all the requirements set out in WTO law; and (2) if the formation of the customs union or free trade area would be prevented, if the introduction of the measure concerned were not allowed. This section discusses these conditions, first, with regard to a measure adopted in the context of a customs union, secondly, with regard to a measure adopted in the context of a free trade area, and, finally, with regard to a measure adopted under an interim agreement. This section also discusses, *in fine*, special rules for developing-country Members' regional trade agreements as well as general procedural issues.

---

39 Appellate Body Report, *Turkey – Textiles (1999)*, para. 45.
40 *Ibid.*, para. 58. See also Appellate Body Report, *Argentina – Footwear (EC) (2000)*, para. 109.

Questions and Assignments 10.2

In general terms, what is the test to determine whether a measure which is otherwise inconsistent with the GATT 1994 is justified under Article XXIV?

3.1   Exceptions Relating to Customs Unions

As noted above, a measure which is otherwise GATT-inconsistent is justified
under Article XXIV of the GATT 1994: (1) if that measure is introduced upon the
formation of a customs union that meets the requirements of Article XXIV:8(a)
and Article XXIV:5(a); and (2) if the formation of that customs union would be
prevented if the introduction of the measure concerned were not allowed. The
Appellate Body noted in *Turkey – Textiles (1999)* that it is necessary to establish
that both conditions are fulfilled and that it may not always be possible to determine whether the second condition is met 'without *first* determining whether
there *is* a customs union'.[41] Therefore, this section explores the definition of
a 'customs union' before addressing the conditions that need to be fulfilled to
justify a measure that would otherwise be GATT-inconsistent.

3.1.1   Definition of a 'Customs Union'

A 'customs union' is defined in Article XXIV:8(a) of the GATT 1994 as follows:

A customs union shall be understood to mean the substitution of a single customs territory
for two or more customs territories so that

i.   duties and other restrictive regulations of commerce (except, where necessary, those
     permitted under Articles XI, XII, XIII, XIV, XV and XX) are eliminated with respect to
     substantially all the trade between the constituent territories of the union or at least with
     respect to substantially all the trade in products originating in such territories, and
ii. ... *substantially the same* duties and other regulations of commerce are applied by each
     of the members of the union to the trade of territories not included in the union.[42]

To satisfy the definition of a 'customs union', Article XXIV:8(a) establishes:
(1) a standard for the *internal trade* between constituent members (under sub-
paragraph (i)); and (2) a standard for the *trade* of constituent members *with third
countries* (under sub-paragraph (ii)).

    With respect to the first standard, i.e. the standard for the *internal trade* be-
tween the constituent members of a customs union, Article XXIV:8(a) requires
that members of a customs union eliminate 'duties and other restrictive regulations of commerce' with respect to 'substantially all the trade' between them.
As the Appellate Body noted in *Turkey – Textiles (1999)*, WTO Members have
never reached an agreement on the interpretation of the term 'substantially' all
in this provision.[43] According to the Appellate Body, it is clear that 'substantially

41 Appellate Body Report, *Turkey – Textiles (1999)*, para. 59. Emphasis on 'first' added.
42 Emphasis added.
43 See Appellate Body Report, *Turkey – Textiles (1999)*, para. 48.

all the trade' is not the same as *all* the trade, and also that 'substantially all the trade' is something considerably more than merely *some* of the trade.[44] It should also be noted that members of a customs union may maintain, where necessary, certain restrictive regulations of commerce in their internal trade that are permitted under Articles XI to XV and under Article XX of the GATT 1994.[45] The Appellate Body in *Turkey – Textiles (1999)* therefore agreed with the panel in that case that Article XXIV:8(a)(i), which sets out the standard for the *internal trade* between members of a customs union, offers 'some flexibility' to the constituent members of a customs union when liberalising their internal trade barriers. However, the Appellate Body cautioned that this degree of 'flexibility' is limited by the requirement that 'duties and other restrictive regulations of commerce' be 'eliminated'.

As discussed in Chapter 9 of this book, in *Argentina – Footwear (EC) (2000)*, the question arose whether Article XXIV:8(a)(i) prohibited Argentina, as a member of MERCOSUR, from imposing safeguard measures on other MERCOSUR countries.[46] While imports from all sources had been taken into account in the investigation at issue, Argentina imposed the safeguards measure at issue only on non-MERCOSUR countries. The Appellate Body considered that Article XXIV:8(a)(i) did not prohibit the imposition of safeguard measures on other MERCOSUR countries. In light of the specific circumstances of this case, the Appellate Body even opined that Argentina *should* have applied the safeguard measures also to other MERCOSUR countries. The Appellate Body ruled:

> [W]e find that Argentina's investigation, which evaluated whether serious injury or the threat thereof was caused by imports from *all* sources, could only lead to the imposition of safeguard measures on imports from *all* sources. Therefore, we conclude that Argentina's investigation, in this case, cannot serve as a basis for excluding imports from other MERCOSUR member States from the application of the safeguard measures.[47]

The Appellate Body found again in *US – Wheat Gluten (2001)* that, in 'the usual course', the imports included in a safeguards investigation should correspond to the imports included in the application of the measure.[48] This has been referred to as the principle of 'parallelism'. In *US – Line Pipe (2002)* and in *US – Steel Safeguards (2003)*, the Appellate Body explained that the principle of 'parallelism' derives from the parallel language used in the first and second paragraphs of Article 2 of the *Agreement on Safeguards*.[49] In *US – Wheat Gluten (2001)* and *US – Line Pipe (2002)*, the competent US authorities took imports from all sources into consideration in the investigation, but excluded

---

44 See *ibid.*
45 See Article XXIV:8(a)(i) of the GATT 1994. For a discussion on Articles XI and XIII, see above, pp. 482–91 and 492–498; and Article XX, see above, pp. 546–82.
46 See above, p. 607.
47 Appellate Body Report, *Argentina – Footwear (EC) (2000)*, para. 113.
48 Appellate Body Report, *US – Wheat Gluten (2001)*, para. 96.
49 For a further discussion of the concept of parallelism, see above, p. 626.

imports from other NAFTA countries from the application of the safeguards measure. In *US – Steel Safeguards (2003)*, the competent authority of the United States considered *all imports* in its injury investigation, but ultimately did not apply the safeguard measures to imports from Canada, Israel, Jordan and Mexico.[50]

With respect to the second standard, i.e. the standard for the trade of constituent members *with third countries*, Article XXIV:8(a)(ii) of the GATT 1994 requires that the constituent members of a customs union apply 'substantially the same' duties and other regulations of commerce to trade with third countries. The constituent members of a customs union are therefore required to apply a common external trade regime, relating to both duties and other regulations of commerce. As the Appellate Body noted in *Turkey – Textiles (1999)*, it is *not* required that each constituent member of a customs union applies the *same* duties and other regulations of commerce as other constituent members with respect to trade with third countries. Article XXIV:8(a)(ii) requires that *substantially the same* duties and other regulations of commerce shall be applied.[51] Also, the phrase 'substantially the same' offers a certain degree of 'flexibility' to the constituent members of a customs union in 'the creation of a common commercial policy'. However, the Appellate Body cautioned that this 'flexibility' is limited. Something closely approximating 'sameness' is definitely required.[52]

A customs union under Article XXIV must, however, not only meet the requirements of Article XXIV:8(a). It must also meet the requirement of Article XXIV:5(a). This provision states:

> [W]ith respect to a customs union ... the duties and other regulations of commerce imposed at the institution of any such union ... in respect of trade with [Members] not parties to such union ... shall not on the whole be higher or more restrictive than the general incidence of the duties and regulations of commerce applicable in the constituent territories prior to the formation of such union ... as the case may be.

The precise meaning of the requirement that the duties and other regulations of commerce, applicable after the formation of the customs union, are, *on the whole*, not higher or more restrictive than the *general incidence* of the duties and other regulations of commerce applicable prior to the formation of the customs union, has been controversial. Paragraph 2 of the *Understanding on Article XXIV* has sought to clarify this requirement. With respect to duties, paragraph 2 requires that the evaluation under Article XXIV:5(a) of the *general incidence of the duties* applied before and after the formation of a customs union:

---

50 See Appellate Body Report, *US – Steel Safeguards (2003)*, paras. 440–4.
51 See Appellate Body Report, *Turkey – Textiles (1999)*, para. 49. The Appellate Body agreed with the panel in *Turkey – Textiles (1999)* that the expression 'substantially the same duties and other regulations of commerce are applied by each of the Members of the [customs] union' would appear to encompass both quantitative and qualitative elements, the quantitative aspect being emphasised more in relation to duties. See Panel Report, *Turkey – Textiles (1999)*, para. 9.148.
52 Appellate Body Report, *Turkey – Textiles (1999)*, para. 50.

shall ... be based upon an overall assessment of weighted average tariff rates and of customs duties collected.[53]

As noted by the Appellate Body in *Turkey – Textiles (1999)*, under the GATT 1947, the GATT Contracting Parties held divergent views as to whether in applying the test of Article XXIV:5(a), the *bound* rates of duty or the *applied* rates of duty should be considered. This issue has been resolved by paragraph 2 of the *Understanding on Article XXIV*, which clearly states that the *applied* rate of duty must be used.[54]

With respect to 'other regulations of commerce', paragraph 2 of the *Understanding on Article XXIV* recognises that it may be difficult to evaluate whether the general incidence of the 'other regulations of commerce' after the formation of the customs union is more restrictive than before its formation. Paragraph 2 recognises, in particular, that the quantification and aggregation of regulations of commerce other than duties may be difficult. Therefore, paragraph 2 of the *Understanding on Article XXIV* provides:

[F]or the purpose of the overall assessment of the incidence of other regulations of commerce ... the examination of individual measures, regulations, products covered and trade flows affected may be required.

The test for assessing whether a specific customs union meets the requirements of Article XXIV:5(a) is, in essence, an *economic* test, i.e. a test of the extent of trade restriction before and after the formation of the customs union.[55]

If, in the formation of a customs union, a constituent member must increase a bound duty (because the duty of the customs union is higher than the bound duty applied by that Member before the formation of the customs union), Article XXIV:6 of the GATT 1994 requires that the procedure for modification of schedules, set out in Article XXVIII of the GATT 1994, be applied.[56] This procedure for the withdrawal or modification of previously bound tariff concessions must be followed with a view to achieving mutually satisfactory compensatory adjustment.[57] Article XXIV:6 further stipulates, however, that:

[i]n providing for compensatory adjustment, due account shall be taken of the compensation already afforded by the reduction brought about in the corresponding duty of the other constituents of the union.

If the reduction in the previously applied duty of other constituent members of the customs union is not sufficient to provide the necessary compensatory

---

53 This assessment shall be based on import statistics for a previous representative period to be supplied by the customs union, on a tariff-line basis and in values and quantities, broken down by WTO country of origin. The WTO Secretariat shall compute the weighted average tariff rates and customs duties collected in accordance with the methodology used in the assessment of tariff offers in the Uruguay Round. For this purpose, the duties and charges to be taken into consideration shall be the applied rates of duty. See para. 2 of the *Understanding on Article XXIV*.
54 See Appellate Body Report, *Turkey – Textiles (1999)*, para. 53.
55 See *ibid.*, para. 55.   56 See above, pp. 449–52.
57 See *Understanding on Article XXIV*, para. 5.

adjustment, the customs union must offer compensation.[58] This compensation may take the form of reductions of duties on other tariff lines. If no agreement on compensatory adjustment can be reached, the customs union shall nevertheless be free to modify or withdraw the concessions at issue; and the affected WTO Members shall then be free to withdraw substantially equivalent concessions in accordance with Article XXVIII.[59]

3.1.2   Conditions for the Justification of GATT-Inconsistency

As noted at the beginning of this section, a measure that would otherwise be GATT-inconsistent, can be justified under Article XXIV of the GATT 1994 when two conditions are fulfilled. The first condition – that the measure must be introduced upon the formation of a customs union that meets the requirements of Article XXIV:8(a) and Article XXIV:5(a) – is discussed in detail above. The second condition requires that, absent the introduction of the measure concerned, the formation of a customs union would be prevented.

In *Turkey – Textiles (1999)*, the measures at issue were quantitative restrictions on textiles and clothing from India. Turkey did not deny that these quantitative restrictions were inconsistent with its obligations under Articles XI and XIII of the GATT 1994 and Article 2.4 of the *Agreement on Textiles and Clothing*. However, according to Turkey, these quantitative restrictions were justified under Article XXIV. Turkey argued that, unless it was allowed to introduce quantitative restrictions on textiles and clothing from India, Turkey would be prevented from forming a customs union with the European Communities.[60] Turkey asserted that, had it not introduced the quantitative restrictions on textiles and clothing products from India that were at issue, the European Communities would have excluded these products from free trade within the EC–Turkey customs union. According to Turkey, the European Communities would have done so in order to prevent the circumvention of the EC's quantitative restrictions on textiles and clothing from India by importing them into the European Communities via Turkey. Turkey's exports of these products accounted for 40 per cent of Turkey's total exports to the European Communities. Therefore, Turkey expressed strong doubts as to whether the requirement of Article XXIV:8(a)(i) that duties and other restrictive regulations of commerce be eliminated with respect to 'substantially all trade' between Turkey and the European Communities could be met if 40 per cent of Turkey's total exports to the European Communities were excluded.[61] The Appellate Body rejected this argument. It ruled:

---

58 Note that the GATT 1994 does not require a WTO Member, benefiting from a reduction of duties upon the formation of a customs union, to provide compensatory adjustment. See *Understanding on Article XXIV*, para. 6.

59 See *Understanding on Article XXIV*, para. 5; and see above, pp. 449–52 (451 in particular).

60 See Appellate Body Report, *Turkey – Textiles (1999)*, para. 61.

61 For this summary of Turkey's argument, see *ibid.*, para. 61.

We agree with the Panel that had Turkey not adopted the same quantitative restrictions that are applied by the European Communities, this would not have prevented Turkey and the European Communities from meeting the requirements of sub-paragraph 8(a)(i) of Article XXIV, and consequently from forming a customs union. We recall our conclusion that the terms of sub-paragraph 8(a)(i) offer some – though limited – flexibility to the constituent members of a customs union when liberalizing their internal trade. As the panel observed, there are other alternatives available to Turkey and the European Communities to prevent any possible diversion of trade, while at the same time meeting the requirements of sub-paragraph 8(a)(i). For example, Turkey could adopt rules of origin for textile and clothing products that would allow the European Communities to distinguish between those textile and clothing products originating in Turkey, which would enjoy free access to the European Communities under the terms of the customs union, *and* those textile and clothing products originating in third countries, including India.[62]

Questions and Assignments 10.3

What requirements must a 'customs union', within the meaning of Article XXIV of the GATT 1994, meet? What is the meaning of the concepts of 'substantially all trade' and 'substantially the same' in Article XXIV:8(a)? How does the *Understanding on Article XXIV* clarify the requirements that a 'customs union', within the meaning of Article XXIV, must meet? What did the panel and the Appellate Body rule in *Turkey – Textiles (1999)* with respect to the question of whether the regional trade arrangement between Turkey and the European Communities is, in fact, a 'customs union' which meets the requirements of paragraphs 8(a) and 5(a) of Article XXIV? How did the Appellate Body come to the conclusion in *Turkey – Textiles (1999)* that the quantitative restriction at issue in that case could not be justified under Article XXIV of the GATT 1994?

3.2 Exceptions Relating to Free Trade Areas

As noted above, a measure which is otherwise GATT-inconsistent is justified under Article XXIV of the GATT 1994: (1) if that measure is introduced upon the formation of a free trade area that meets the requirements of Article XXIV:8(b) and Article XXIV:5(b); and (2) if the formation of that free trade area would be made impossible if the introduction of the measure concerned were not allowed. This section explores, first, the definition of a 'free trade area', before, secondly, addressing the conditions that need to be met in order to justify a measure that would otherwise be GATT-inconsistent.

3.2.1 Definition of a 'Free Trade Area'

A 'free trade area' is defined in Article XXIV:8(b) of the GATT 1994 as follows:

A free-trade area shall be understood to mean a group of two or more customs territories in which the duties and other restrictive regulations of commerce (except, where necessary,

---

62 *Ibid.*, para. 62. The Appellate Body also noted that Decision 1/95 of the EC–Turkey Association Council specifically provided for the possibility of applying a system of certificates of origin. Rather than making use of this possibility, Turkey had adopted quantitative restrictions on imports of textiles and clothing from India.

those permitted under Articles XI, XII, XIII, XIV, XV and XX) are eliminated *on substantially all the trade* between the constituent territories in products originating in such territories.[63]

In contrast to the definition of a 'customs union', discussed above, the definition of a 'free trade area' establishes only a standard for the *internal trade* between constituent members. There is no standard, i.e. there are no requirements, for the trade of constituent members *with third countries*. The standard for the *internal trade* between constituent members of a free trade area – namely, the elimination of duties and other restrictive regulations of commerce on substantially all trade between constituent members – is identical to the standard for the internal trade between constituent members of a customs union. The case law discussed and observations made in the previous section on 'customs unions' are therefore also relevant for free trade areas.

A free trade area under Article XXIV, however, does not only have to meet the requirements of Article XXIV:8(b). It must also meet the requirement of Article XXIV:5(b). This provision states:

[W]ith respect to a free-trade area ... the duties and other regulations of commerce maintained in each of the constituent territories and applicable at the formation of such free-trade area ... to the trade of [Members] not included in such area ... shall not be higher or more restrictive than the corresponding duties and other regulations of commerce existing in the same constituent territories prior to the formation of the free-trade area.

Article XXIV:5(b) therefore requires that the duties and other regulations of commerce applied by a member of a free trade area to trade with third countries *after* the formation of the free trade area must *not be higher or more restrictive* than the duties and other regulations of commerce applied by that member *before* the formation of the free trade area. Establishing that this is indeed the case is much less problematic than establishing whether the requirements of Article XXIV:5(a) with respect to customs unions are met.[64]

3.2.2 Conditions for the Justification of GATT-Inconsistency

As noted at the beginning of this section, for a measure, otherwise GATT-inconsistent, to be justified under Article XXIV of the GATT 1994, that measure must be of such a nature that, if the introduction of the measure concerned were not allowed, the formation of a free trade area would be prevented. There is no relevant WTO case law on this point as yet.

Questions and Assignments 10.4

What requirements must a 'free trade area' within the meaning of Article XXIV of the GATT 1994 meet? How does a 'free trade area' differ from a 'customs union'? When are otherwise GATT-inconsistent measures justified under Article XXIV of the GATT 1994?

63 Emphasis added.   64 See above, pp. 658–9.

3.3   Interim Agreements

Measures that are otherwise GATT-inconsistent may be justified under Article XXIV if they are taken in the context of interim agreements leading to the formation of customs unions and free trade areas meeting the requirements discussed in the two previous sections.[65] This is a recognition of the fact that customs unions and free trade areas will not, and cannot, be established overnight. Nevertheless, although most customs unions and free trade areas have been – at least in part – implemented in stages, only a few have expressly been notified as 'interim agreements'.[66] In this regard, as of 7 February 2013, only fourteen interim agreements have been notified to the WTO and are currently in force. Thus, the number of interim agreements is much lower than one might expect.

Article XXIV:5(c) of the GATT 1994 requires with respect to interim agreements:

> [A]ny interim agreement ... shall include a plan and schedule for the formation of such a customs union or of such a free-trade area within a reasonable length of time.

Not surprisingly, the vague requirement that the customs union or free trade area be established 'within a reasonable length of time' was quite controversial under the GATT 1947. The *Understanding on Article XXIV* therefore provides that this reasonable period of time should not exceed ten years except in exceptional circumstances.[67] It remains an open question whether existing interim arrangements actually result in the formation of a free-trade area or customs union within this ten-year time-limit.

Questions and Assignments 10.5

Why does Article XXIV of the GATT 1994 provide rules for interim agreements leading to the formation of a customs union or free trade area? When may measures, otherwise GATT-inconsistent, be justified under Article XXIV as measures taken in the context of an interim agreement leading to the establishment of a customs union or a free trade area?

3.4   Special and Differential Treatment of Developing-Country Members

The Decision of the GATT Contracting Parties of 28 November 1979 on *Differential and More Favourable Treatment, Reciprocity and Fuller Participation of Developing Countries*, commonly referred to as the 'Enabling Clause',[68] provides, in relevant part:

1. Notwithstanding the provisions of Article I of the General Agreement, [Members] may accord differential and more favourable treatment to developing countries, without according such treatment to other [Members].
2. The provisions of paragraph 1 apply to the following:

---

65 See above, p. 660.   66 See WT/REG/W/37, para. 47.   67 See *Understanding on Article XXIV*, para. 3.
68 On the Enabling Clause of the GATT 1994, see also above, pp. 330–5, and below, pp. 668–71.

3. ...
4. Regional or global arrangements entered into amongst less-developed [Members] for the
    mutual reduction or elimination of tariffs and, in accordance with criteria or conditions
    which may be prescribed by the [Ministerial Conference], for the mutual reduction or
    elimination of non-tariff measures, on products imported from one another.[69]

The Enabling Clause is now part of the GATT 1994.[70] It allows preferential arrangements *among developing-country Members* in derogation from the MFN
treatment obligation of Article I of the GATT 1994. The conditions that regional
trade agreements under the Enabling Clause must meet are less demanding and
less specific than those set out in Article XXIV of the GATT 1994. Thus, there
are no substantive requirements under the Enabling Clause which approximate
the substantive requirements – discussed above – of Article XXIV. In fact, paragraph 3 of the Enabling Clause 'merely' requires that:

[a]ny differential and more favourable treatment provided under this clause:

a. shall be designed to facilitate and promote the trade of developing countries and not to
    raise barriers to or create undue difficulties for the trade of any other [Members].

...

As of 7 February 2013, thirty-six regional trade agreements had been noti-
fied to the WTO under the Enabling Clause.[71] These include: (1) the Cartagena
Agreement Establishing the Andean Community; (2) the Treaty Establishing the
Common Market for Eastern and Southern Africa ('COMESA'); (3) the Treaty Es-
tablishing the Common Market of the South (MERCOSUR); and (4) the Common
Effective Preferential Tariffs Scheme for the ASEAN Free Trade Area (AFTA).

Questions and Assignments 10.6

Does Article XXIV of the GATT 1994 apply to regional trade agreements between developing-
country Members? What requirements apply to these agreements?

4 REGIONAL TRADE EXCEPTIONS UNDER THE GATS

Article V of the GATS, entitled 'Economic Integration', is the counterpart of Article
XXIV of the GATT 1994 for trade in services. Article V:1 of the GATS provides:

---

69 See BISD 26S/203.
70 See paragraph 1(b)(iv) of the GATT 1994. See also above, p. 330 (subsequently 331–335).
71 The text of the Enabling Clause suggests that the parties to a preferential agreement that is notified under the
   Enabling Clause must be developing countries. This may seem obvious but this has given rise to some controversy due to the fact that in WTO law the concept of developing country is not defined and a Member 'self-
   selects' itself as a 'developing-country Member'. See above, p. 331 (subsequently 332–335). For example, the
   Gulf Co-operation Council Agreement was initially notified under Article XXIV of the GATT 1994, but, before
   the CRTA could examine it, the parties rescinded the notification under Article XXIV and sought to notify the
   Gulf Co-operation Council Agreement under the Enabling Clause for review by the CTD. Other WTO Members
   questioned the change of course. The incentive to notify an RTA under the Enabling Clause rather than under
   Article XXIV of the GATT 1994 is that there are no substantive requirements for RTAs under the Enabling
   Clause that are similarly stringent as the requirements of Articles XXIV:8 and XXIV:5 of the GATT 1994.

This Agreement shall not prevent any of its Members from being a party to or entering into an agreement liberalizing trade in services between or among the parties to such an agreement, provided that such an agreement:

a. has substantial sectoral coverage,[72] and
b. provides for the absence or elimination of substantially all discrimination, in the sense of Article XVII, between or among the parties, in the sectors covered under subparagraph (a), through:

    i.   elimination of existing discriminatory measures, and/or
    ii. prohibition of new or more discriminatory measures,

    either at the entry into force of that agreement or on the basis of a reasonable time-frame, except for measures permitted under Articles XI, XII, XIV and XIV*bis*.

Article V:4 of the GATS states:

Any agreement referred to in paragraph 1 shall be designed to facilitate trade between the parties to the agreement and shall not in respect of any member outside the agreement raise the overall level of barriers to trade in services within the respective sectors or subsectors compared to the level applicable prior to such an agreement.

4.1 Requirements for Economic Integration Agreements

The panel in *Canada – Autos (2000)* noted that:

Article V provides legal coverage for measures taken pursuant to economic integration agreements, which would otherwise be inconsistent with the MFN obligation in Article II.[73]

It follows from Article V:1 that a measure which is otherwise GATS-inconsistent can be justified under Article V: (1) if the measure is introduced as part of an agreement liberalising trade in services that meets all the requirements set out in Article V:1(a) (the 'substantial sectoral coverage' requirement), Article V:1(b) (the 'substantially all discrimination' requirement) and Article V:4 (the 'barriers to trade' requirement); and (2) if WTO Members would be prevented from entering into such an agreement liberalising trade in services, if the measure concerned were not allowed (see the chapeau of Article V:1). This section, further, discusses primarily the requirements that an economic integration agreement pursuant to Articles V:1(a), V:1(b) and V:4 of the GATS must meet.

4.1.1 'Substantial Sectoral Coverage' Requirement

Pursuant to Article V:1(a) of the GATS, an economic integration agreement must have 'substantial sectoral coverage' of the trade in services among the parties to the agreement. The footnote to the provision states that 'substantial sectoral coverage' should be 'understood in terms of the number of sectors, volume of

---

72 The original footnote 1 in the quote reads: 'This condition is understood in terms of number of sectors, volume of trade affected and modes of supply. In order to meet this condition, agreements should not provide for the *a priori* exclusion of any mode of supply.'
73 Panel Report, *Canada – Autos (2000)*, para. 10.271.

trade affected and modes of supply'.[74] The footnote also provides that an economic integration agreement may not *a priori* exclude any of the four modes of supply. In particular, no economic integration agreement should *a priori* exclude investment or labour mobility in the sense of modes 3 and 4. Members disagree on whether one or more services sectors can be excluded from an economic integration agreement, but the use of the wording 'number of sectors' in the footnote to paragraph 1(a) seems to indicate that not all sectors must be covered under an economic integration agreement to meet the 'substantial sectoral coverage' test. However, it is clear that the number of exclusions must be limited. As the panel in *Canada – Autos (2000)* stated:

> the purpose of Article V is to allow for ambitious liberalization to take place at a regional level, while at the same time guarding against undermining the MFN obligation by engaging in *minor preferential arrangements*.[75]

4.1.2 'Substantially All Discrimination' Requirement

Article V:1(b) of the GATS requires that an economic integration agreement should provide for 'the absence or elimination of substantially all discrimination'.[76] As Article V:1(b) does not require the absence or elimination of *all* discrimination, but rather the absence or elimination of *substantially all* discrimination, the question arises as to what extent discriminatory measures should be allowed to exist in an economic integration agreement.[77] The scope of such permissible discriminatory measures is, of course, circumscribed by the scope of the list of exceptions in Article V:1(b). This list explicitly includes exceptions permitted under Articles XI, XII, XIV and XIV*bis* of the GATS, but it is unclear whether this list is exhaustive. The scope of permissible discriminatory measures is also affected by the meaning given to the 'and/or' wording in Article V:1(b) linking provisions (i) and (ii). Some Members are of the opinion that the 'or' allows the parties to an economic integration agreement to choose between provisions (i) and (ii), that is, the elimination of existing discriminatory measures, or, alternatively, the introduction of a standstill. A party could therefore choose only to refrain from adding new measures or from making existing measures more restrictive, rather than having to eliminate existing measures. Other Members have rejected this interpretation. They argue that, considering that Article V:1(b) aims to deal with

---

74 It is not clear whether the parameters to be examined in determining the conformity with an economic integration agreement with Article V of the GATS are limited to the parameters listed in the footnote, or whether other considerations may also be taken into account.

75 Panel Report, *Canada – Autos (2000)*, para. 10.271. Emphasis added.

76 Note that Article V:2 of the GATS states that the evaluation of an agreement's consistency with Article V:1(b) may also take into account its relationship with 'a wider process of economic integration or trade liberalization' among the parties to the agreement. A 'wider process of economic integration' refers to a process of economic integration involving the elimination of barriers to trade not only in services but also in goods.

77 Note that Article V:6 of the GATS provides that a third-party supplier, legally recognised as a juridical person by a party to an economic integration agreement, is entitled to equivalent treatment granted within the economic integration area, provided that it engages in 'substantive business operations' in the territory of the parties to that agreement.

'substantially all discrimination', it would be appropriate to interpret the 'and/or' wording in such a way that both (i) and (ii) are found to be applicable. Thus, it is argued that paragraphs (i) and (ii) are *options* to be judged as appropriate against the circumstances of the service sector being considered, *not* as *alternatives* to be freely chosen by the parties to the economic integration agreement.[78]

The panel in *Canada – Autos (2000)* noted with respect to the obligation under Article V:1(b):

> Although the requirement of Article V:1(b) is to provide non-discrimination in the sense of Article XVII (National Treatment), we consider that once it is fulfilled it would also ensure non-discrimination between all service suppliers of other parties to the economic integration agreement. It is our view that the object and purpose of this provision is to eliminate all discrimination among services and service suppliers of parties to an economic integration agreement, including discrimination between the suppliers of other parties to an economic integration agreement.[79]

According to the panel, it would be inconsistent with Article V:1(b) if a party to an economic integration agreement were to extend more favourable treatment to the service suppliers of one party than it does to the service suppliers of another party to that agreement.[80] In other words, the obligation under Article V:1(b) also has an MFN treatment dimension.

The concept of 'a reasonable time-frame' in Article V:1(b) is not defined or clarified in any way in the GATS. On the basis of Article XXIV:5(c) of the GATT 1994 and paragraph 3 of the *Understanding on Article XXIV* concerning the similar concept of 'a reasonable length of time', it would be reasonable to assume that, in defining the 'reasonable time-frame' of Article V:1(b), a ten-year limit would be used as a general starting point.

4.1.3 'Barriers to Trade' Requirement

Article V:4 requires that an economic integration agreement must be designed to facilitate trade between the parties to the agreement and must *not*, in respect of any WTO Member that is not a party to the agreement, *raise* the overall level of *barriers* to trade in services within the respective sectors or sub-sectors as compared to the level applicable prior to such an agreement. The absence of detailed data on trade in services and differences in regulatory mechanisms between Members makes it difficult to evaluate the level of barriers in effect before the establishment of an economic integration agreement. A possible approach to the application of this 'barriers to trade' requirement would be to require that an economic integration agreement reduce neither the level, nor the growth, of trade in any sector or sub-sector below a historical trend.[81]

---

78 See Committee on Regional Trade Agreements, *Examination of the North American Free Trade Agreements*, Note on the Meeting of 24 February 1997, WT/REG4/M/4, dated 16 April 1997.

79 Panel Report, *Canada – Autos (2000)*, para. 10.270.   80 *Ibid.*

81 Changes in the volume of trade could be judged by data on domestic economic activities if data on trade in services is unavailable.

4.2   Labour Markets Integration Agreements

Article V*bis* of the GATS entitled 'Labour Markets Integration Agreements', deals with a specific form of economic integration agreement which establishes full integration of labour markets between or among the parties to such an agreement. Such agreements give the nationals of the parties free access to each other's labour markets. Usually, these agreements also include provisions concerning conditions of pay, other conditions of employment and social benefits. Article V*bis* provides that the GATS shall not prevent any WTO Member from being a party to such an agreement provided that the agreement: (1) exempts citizens of parties to the agreement from requirements concerning residency and work permits; and (2) is notified to the Council for Trade in Services.

4.3   Special and Differential Treatment of Developing-Country Members

With regard to economic integration agreements to which developing countries are parties, Article V:3(a) of the GATS provides for flexibility regarding the conditions set out in Article V:1, quoted and discussed above. This flexibility is to be granted 'in accordance with the level of development of the countries concerned, both overall and in individual sectors and subsectors'. Article V:3(b) of the GATS provides that, in the case of an economic integration agreement involving only developing countries, 'more favourable treatment may be granted to juridical persons owned or controlled by natural persons of the parties to such an agreement'.[82]

Questions and Assignments 10.7

When is a measure, which is otherwise GATS-inconsistent, justified under Article V of the GATS? Give two examples of economic integration agreements not already mentioned above. When must a party to an economic integration agreement initiate the procedure for the modification of schedules and compensatory adjustment set forth in Article XXI of the GATS? What are labour markets integration agreements?

5   INSTITUTIONAL AND PROCEDURAL MATTERS

Customs unions and free trade areas, as well as interim agreements leading to the formation of such a union or area, are reviewed by the WTO to determine their consistency with the GATT 1994 (including the Enabling Clause). Economic integration agreements covering trade in services are also reviewed by the WTO to determine their consistency with the GATS. The final section of this chapter discusses the notification obligations of WTO members in respect of their

---

82 Article V:3(b) applies notwithstanding Article V:6 of the GATS, referred to above at page 666, footnote 77.

regional trade agreements, as well as the WTO's institutional framework for the review of such agreements.

Article XXIV of the GATT, the Enabling Clause, and Article V of the GATS each require WTO Members to notify regional trade agreements to the WTO. Article XXIV:7(a) of the GATT and Article V:7(a) of the GATS require WTO Members to 'promptly' notify their participation in regional trade agreements concerning trade in goods, and trade in services, respectively. Moreover, paragraph 4(b) of the Enabling Clause calls for the notification of regional trade agreements in which developing countries are involved.

As discussed above, while Doha Round negotiations on the clarification and improvement of the substantive rules on regional trade agreements have not been successful to date, WTO Members have been successful in agreeing in December 2006 on the Transparency Mechanism for Regional Trade Agreements (the 'RTA Transparency Mechanism').[83] The RTA Transparency Mechanism clarifies and strengthens the notification obligations of WTO Members and introduces new procedures to enhance the transparency of regional trade agreements. The rationale for the introduction of the RTA Transparency Mechanism in relation to the notification of regional trade agreements has been explained as follows:

> The obligation for notification [had] not been complied with in a systematic manner by WTO Members: for instance, while the wording of GATT Article XXIV suggests that [a regional trade agreement] should be notified before the entry into force of the [regional trade agreement], notifications are generally received after the entry into force, in some cases months or even years after. There is no provision in WTO rules for counter-notification, i.e. for a third party to notify on behalf of other WTO Members. The [RTA Transparency Mechanism] tightens up existing provisions on notification by stipulating in paragraph 3 that notification is to take place 'as early as possible ... no later than directly following the parties' ratification of the [regional trade agreement] or any party's decision on application of the relevant part of an agreement, and before the application of preferential treatment between the parties'. By requiring notification to take place before the application of preferential treatment, WTO Members will be informed about new [regional trade agreements] before their implementation, thus promoting transparency.[84]

WTO Members deciding to enter into a customs union, free trade area or an interim agreement must notify this intention to the Council for Trade in Goods.[85] In contrast, WTO Members deciding to enter into an economic integration agreement, i.e. a regional trade agreement concerning trade in services, must notify this intention to the Council for Trade in Services.[86] Customs unions, free trade areas, interim agreements and agreements between developing countries under

---

83 See General Council, *Transparency Mechanism for Regional Trade Agreements*, Decision adopted on 14 December 2006, WT/L/671, dated 18 December 2006. See also above, p. 653.

84 J. Crawford, 'A New Transparency Mechanism for Regional Trade Agreements', *Singapore Yearbook of International Law*, 2007, 138.

85 See Article XXIV:7(a) of the GATT 1994. For example, on 27 September 2006, the European Communities notified the Treaty of Accession of Bulgaria and Romania to the European Union. See WT/REG220/N/1, dated 2 October 2006.

86 See Article V:7 of the GATS.

the Enabling Clause are notified to the Council for Trade in Goods, while economic integration agreements in services are notified to the Council for Trade
in Services. The Committee on Regional Trade Agreements (CRTA) considers
regional trade agreements that are notified under Article XXIV of the GATT and
Article V of the GATS, while the Committee on Trade and Development (CTD)
considers agreements between developing countries which are notified under
the Enabling Clause.[87] The CRTA and CTD report to the Council for Trade in
Goods in respect of regional trade agreements notified under Article XXIV of the
GATT and agreements between developing countries notified under the Enabling
Clause. The Council for Trade in Goods then makes a recommendation to Members concerning the GATT-consistency of these agreements.[88] The examination
of the GATT-consistency is, as was stated by the panel in *Turkey – Textiles
(1999)*, 'a very complex undertaking' requiring consideration by the CRTA 'from
the economic, legal and political perspectives of different Members, of the numerous facets of a regional trade agreement'.[89] The CRTA has thus far considered
seventy-six regional trade agreements within the meaning of Article XXIV of
the GATT 1994, but, to date, has adopted only seventeen reports on the GATT-
consistency of a customs union, free trade area or interim agreement. The CTD
has considered only four agreements under the Enabling Clause, and has adopted
one report on the consistency of an RTA with the Enabling Clause.

It has been suggested that in view of the existence of the committee process of
reviewing the GATT-consistency of customs unions, free trade areas and interim
agreements, WTO dispute settlement panels (and the Appellate Body) would not
have jurisdiction to decide on the GATT-consistency of such unions, areas or
agreements. In *Turkey – Textiles (1999)*, the Appellate Body effectively rejected
this view.[90]

Customs unions and constituents of free trade areas must report periodically (i.e. every two years) to the Council for Trade in Goods.[91] Any significant
changes to the agreements establishing customs unions or free trade agreements
should be reported as they occur.[92] In accordance with paragraph 14 of the RTA
Transparency Mechanism, WTO Members are required to notify any changes
affecting the implementation of a regional trade agreement as soon as possible.

---

87 On the terms of reference of the CRTA, see WT/L/127.
88 See *Understanding on Article XXIV*, para. 7.
89 Panel Report, *Turkey – Textiles (1999)*, para. 9.52.
90 Appellate Body Report, *Turkey – Textiles (1999)*, para. 60. Although the Appellate Body was not called
    upon to address this issue, it explicitly referred to its conclusions on a 'similar' issue in *India – Quantitative
    Restrictions (1999)*, paras. 87 and 95. See above, p. 644. Furthermore, note para. 12 of the *Understanding
    on Article XXIV*, which states: 'The provisions of Articles XXII and XXIII of GATT 1994 as elaborated and
    applied by the Dispute Settlement Understanding may be invoked with respect to any matters arising from
    the application of those provisions of Article XXIV relating to customs unions, free-trade areas or interim
    agreements leading to the formation of a customs union or free-trade area.'
91 See *Understanding on Article XXIV*, para. 11.
92 See *ibid*. These reporting requirements are not applicable to regional trade agreements among developing-
    country Members.

With regard to economic integration agreements notified under Article V of the GATS, the CRTA examines such agreements (or enlargement or modification thereof) and reports back on their GATS-consistency.[93] The Council for Trade in Services may make such recommendations as it deems appropriate. To date, 108 economic integration agreements have been notified to the CRTA, including: (1) the North American Free Trade Agreement;[94] (2) the Australia–New Zealand Closer Economic Relations Trade Agreement;[95] (3) the Free Trade Agreement between Chile and Mexico;[96] and (4) the Treaty of Accession of the Czech Republic, Estonia, Cyprus, Latvia, Lithuania, Hungary, Malta, Poland, Slovenia and the Slovak Republic to the European Union. Article V:5 of the GATS requires a party to an economic integration agreement to provide at least ninety days' advance notice of any modification or withdrawal of a specific commitment that would give rise to an inconsistency with the terms and conditions set out in its Schedule. In such situations, that party must initiate the procedure for the modification of Schedules and the compensatory adjustment set forth in Article XXI of the GATS.

Questions and Assignments 10.8

Has the examination of the GATT/GATS-consistency of customs unions, free trade areas, economic integration agreements and interim agreements by the CRTA been 'successful'? In your opinion, should panels have jurisdiction to assess the GATT-consistency of customs unions, free trade areas, economic integration agreements and interim agreements?

6 SUMMARY

Besides the 'general exceptions', the 'security exceptions' and the 'economic emergency exceptions', WTO law also provides for 'regional trade exceptions'. These exceptions allow Members to adopt measures which are otherwise WTO-inconsistent but taken in the context of (regional) economic integration. The regional trade exceptions are set out in Article XXIV of the GATT 1994 (elaborated in the *Understanding on Article XXIV*), in the Enabling Clause of the GATT 1994, and Article V of the GATS. WTO law recognises the advantages of economic integration and trade liberalisation even when these efforts involve only some of its Members. A measure which is otherwise inconsistent with the GATT 1994 can be justified under Article XXIV of the GATT 1994: (1) if the measure is introduced upon the formation of a customs union, a free trade area or an interim agreement that meets all the requirements set out in Article XXIV:8 and

---

93 See http://rtais.wto.org/UI/publicsummarytable.aspx.   94 See S/C/M/3, paras. 27 and 28.
95 See S/C/M/14, Section E.
96 See S/C/M/52, Section C

Article XIV:5 of the GATT 1994; and (2) if the formation of the customs union or free trade area would be prevented if the introduction of the measure concerned were not allowed. A measure which is otherwise GATS-inconsistent can be justified under Article V of the GATS: (1) if the measure is introduced as part of an agreement liberalising trade in services that meets all the requirements set out in Article V:1(a), Article V:1(b) and Article V:4 of the GATS; and (2) if WTO Members would be prevented from being a party to an agreement liberalising trade in services if the measure concerned were not allowed. Regional trade agreements among developing-country Members are subject to less onerous requirements pursuant to the Enabling Clause of the GATT 1994 and Article V:3 of the GATS.

Exercise 10: Stepping Stone or Stumbling Block?

Select two recently concluded free trade agreements and examine their consistency with WTO law. Assess to what extent these agreements may, in the longer run, strengthen or weaken the multilateral trading system.

11 Dumping

CONTENTS

1 INTRODUCTION

While professing support for trade liberalisation, trade policy-makers often insist that international trade should be 'fair'. 'Unfair' trade comes in many forms and guises. Unfair trade practices may include cartel agreements, price fixing and the abuse of a dominant position on the market.[1] WTO law, at present, does not provide for rules on these and many other particular forms of unfair trade. This absence of rules partly reflects a lack of agreement on what are 'fair' and 'unfair' trade practices. WTO law provide for detailed rules with respect to dumping and certain types of subsidisation – two specific trade practices commonly considered to be 'unfair'. While these two practices, and in particular subsidisation, may be considered unfair, Members differ in opinion as to what extent these trade practices are truly 'unfair'. This difference in opinion among Members reflects differences in their societies in general and their economic systems in particular.

The basic idea underlying WTO rules on 'unfair' trade practices, such as dumping and subsidisation, is that the response of importing countries at least partially 'offsets' the negative effects of the unfair practices, and may even have punitive effects that inhibit such practices in the future. A commonly expressed goal of 'trade remedy' measures, such as anti-dumping or countervailing measures,[2] is to 'level the playing field', that is, international competition should occur based upon a set of rules agreed upon by all participants. In contrast, others consider 'price discrimination' (i.e. price differentiation) between the markets of the exporting and importing countries (as long as the sales price exceeds variable costs) as actually beneficial to national or global welfare. Another concern raised with regard to price discrimination is that large and economically powerful firms could use their market leverage to drive small firms out of business, thus reducing competition; in turn, these predatory firms can then raise their prices and reap monopoly profits.[3] Finally, it has also been argued that international dumping depends on import barriers of the exporting country that make reintroducing of the dumped product into the home market difficult, if not impossible, and thus unfair.

---

1 The concept of 'unfair trade' is also commonly used to refer to trade on terms and conditions which are disadvantageous for developing countries in general and small companies, workers and farmers in these countries in particular.

2 On the concept of 'trade remedies', see above, p. 38.

3 J. Jackson, *The World Trading System: Law and Policy of International Economic Relations*, 2nd edn (MIT Press, 1997), 253–4. J. Viner noted that, 'in the absence of a world-wide monopoly, the dumping concern will have to share with rival concerns in its own country or in the other foreign countries the benefit accruing from the destruction of the native industry in the country dumped on'. However, there are 'sufficient instances of trusts and combinations, many of them international in their membership or affiliations, that are within reach of world-wide quasi-monopolistic control of their industry, to make the danger of predatory competition a real one even if this reasoning is unqualifiedly accepted'. See J. Viner, *Dumping: A Problem in International Trade* (1969), 120.

The next chapter, Chapter 12, deals with WTO rules on subsidies. This chapter examines WTO rules on dumping. It successively discusses the following: (1) basic elements of WTO law on dumping; (2) the determination of dumping; (3) the determination of injury to the domestic industry; (4) the determination of a causal link between the dumping and the injury; (5) the manner in which anti-dumping investigations must be conducted; (6) anti-dumping measures; (7) institutional and procedural provisions, including the standard of review applicable under the *Anti-Dumping Agreement*; and (8) special and differential treatment of developing-country Members.

2 BASIC ELEMENTS OF WTO LAW ON DUMPING

Before entering into a more detailed, and often technical, discussion of the rules on dumping and anti-dumping measures, this section first addresses the following in general terms: (1) the history of WTO law on dumping; (2) the concept of 'dumping'; (3) WTO treatment of dumping; (4) the response to injurious dumping; and (5) current use of anti-dumping measures.

2.1 History of the Law on Dumping

WTO law on dumping and anti-dumping measures is set out in Article VI of the GATT 1994 and in the WTO *Agreement on Implementation of Article VI of the GATT 1994*, commonly referred to as the *Anti-Dumping Agreement*. When the GATT was negotiated in 1947, participants initially failed to agree on whether a provision allowing countries to impose anti-dumping measures in response to dumping should even be included.[4] However, largely at the insistence of the United States, Article VI was included to provide a basic framework as to how countries could respond to dumping.[5] In the years following its negotiation, Article VI alone proved to be inadequate in addressing the anti-dumping measures. Its language was particularly vague and was therefore interpreted and applied in an inconsistent manner.[6] Many GATT Contracting Parties began to feel that other Contracting Parties were applying anti-dumping laws in a manner that effectively raised new barriers to trade.[7] The inadequacies of Article VI dictated that it would have to be fleshed out in further agreements. This was achieved,

---

4 The United Kingdom and others argued that national anti-dumping laws were a hindrance to free trade and that the GATT should actually prohibit the imposition of anti-dumping duties. See B. Blonigen and T. Prusa, *Antidumping* (July 2001), NBER Working Paper No. W8398, http://papers.ssrn.com/sol3/papers.cfm?abstract_id=278031.
5 The United States was one of the few countries at this time with anti-dumping legislation in place.
6 See M. Trebilcock and R. Howse, *The Regulation of International Trade*, 3rd edn (Routledge, 2005), 233.
7 See J. Jackson, The World Trading System: Law and Policy of International Economic Relations, 2nd edn (MIT Press, 1997), 256.

in 1967 by the Kennedy Round *Anti-Dumping Code*, which was replaced by the Tokyo Round *Anti-Dumping Code* in 1979. However, in spite of the clarification and elaboration of Article VI by the Tokyo Round *Anti-Dumping Code*, even more criticism of the anti-dumping regime emerged in the 1980s. At that time, there was a genuine proliferation of anti-dumping activity, with developed countries being the dominant users of the regime and developing countries a significant target.[8] Not surprisingly, therefore, the anti-dumping regime was one of the most controversial issues placed on the agenda of the Uruguay Round negotiations. The positions taken by the participants in the negotiations varied greatly. Some participants wanted to facilitate the use of anti-dumping measures (i.e. the United States and the European Communities), while others wanted to impose stricter disciplines (i.e. Japan, Korea and Hong Kong, China). At the end of the Uruguay Round, a compromise was reached that was ultimately reflected in the WTO *Anti-Dumping Agreement* and which, together with Article VI of the GATT 1994, sets out the current rules on dumping and anti-dumping measures. As will be noted in this chapter, the conflicting, and sometimes even opposing, interests that existed in the negotiations resulted in provisions with ambiguous language. Some of these provisions have been 'clarified' by case law, while others still await clarification.

In the Doha Ministerial Declaration of November 2001, WTO Members agreed to place anti-dumping rules on the agenda of the Doha Round negotiations:

> In the light of experience and of the increasing application of these instruments by Members, we agree to negotiations aimed at clarifying and improving disciplines under the Agreements on Implementation of Article VI of the GATT 1994 and on Subsidies and Countervailing Measures, while preserving the basic concepts, principles and effectiveness of these Agreements and their instruments and objectives, and taking into account the needs of developing and least-developed participants.[9]

In April 2011, the Chair of the Negotiating Group on Rules circulated among WTO Members a Revised Draft Consolidated Chair Text of the *Anti-Dumping Agreement*, reflecting the state of play of the negotiations.[10] From this Text, it is clear that the Membership was still deeply divided on what changes to the *Anti-Dumping Agreement* should be made, if any.

2.2   Concept of 'Dumping'

'Dumping' is a situation of *international price discrimination* involving the price and cost of a product in the exporting country in relation to its price in the importing country. Article VI of the GATT 1994 and Article 2.1 of the

---

8 Between July 1980 and June 1988, nearly 1,200 anti-dumping actions were initiated. See M. Trebilcock and R. Howse, *The Regulation of International Trade*, 2nd edn (Routledge, 1999), 166.

9 Ministerial Conference, *Doha Ministerial Declaration*, WT/MIN(01)/DEC/1, dated 20 November 2001, para. 28.

10 Negotiating Group on Rules, Communication from the Chairman, TN/RL/W/254, 21 April 2011.

Anti-Dumping Agreement define dumping as the introduction of a product into the commerce of another country at less than its 'normal value'.[11] Thus, a product can be considered 'dumped' where the export price of that product is less than its normal value, that is, the comparable price, in the ordinary course of trade, for the 'like product' destined for consumption in the exporting country.[12]

2.3 WTO Treatment of Dumping

WTO law does *not* prohibit dumping. In fact, since prices of products are ordinarily set by private companies, 'dumping' in and of itself is *not* regulated by WTO law. As discussed above, WTO law in general only imposes obligations on, and regulates the measures and actions of, WTO Members in response to dumping. It does not directly regulate the actions of private companies. However, as dumping may cause injury to the domestic industry of the importing country, Article VI of the GATT 1994 states, in relevant part, that:

> [t]he [Members] recognize that dumping ... is to be *condemned* if it causes or threatens material injury to an established industry in the territory of a [Member] or materially retards the establishment of a domestic industry.[13]

Consequently, Article VI of the GATT 1994 and the *Anti-Dumping Agreement* provide a framework of substantive and procedural rules governing how a Member may counteract or 'remedy' dumping, through the imposition of 'anti-dumping' measures.

It is not mandatory for a WTO Member to enact anti-dumping legislation or to have in place a system for conducting anti-dumping investigations and imposing anti-dumping measures. However, if a Member makes the policy choice to have the option of imposing anti-dumping measures, Article 1 of the *Anti-Dumping Agreement* specifies that:

> [a]n anti-dumping measure shall be applied only under the circumstances provided for in Article VI of GATT 1994 and pursuant to investigations initiated and conducted in accordance with the provisions of this Agreement. The following provisions govern the application of Article VI of GATT 1994 in so far as action is taken under anti-dumping legislation or regulations.

Pursuant to Article VI of the GATT 1994 and the *Anti-Dumping Agreement*, WTO Members are entitled to impose anti-dumping measures if, after an investigation initiated and conducted in accordance with the Agreement, on the basis of pre-existing legislation that has been properly notified to the WTO, a determination is

---

11 Note that the Appellate Body in *US – Zeroing (Japan) (2007)* stated that Article 2.1 of the *Anti-Dumping Agreement* and Article VI:1 of the GATT 1994 are 'definitional provisions' and do not impose independent obligations. See Appellate Body Report, *US – Zeroing (Japan) (2007)*, para. 140.

12 See Article 2.1 of the *Anti-Dumping Agreement*. For a more detailed analysis of the concept of dumping, see below, pp. 682–4.

13 Emphasis added.

made that: (1) there is dumping; (2) the domestic industry producing the like product in the importing country is suffering injury (or threat thereof); and (3) there is
a causal link between the dumping and the injury. Later sections of this chapter
discuss in detail the concepts of 'dumping', 'injury', and 'causal link'.[14]

2.4 Response to Injurious Dumping

In response to injurious dumping, Members may take anti-dumping measures.
However, Article VI, and in particular Article VI:2, read in conjunction with the
Anti-Dumping Agreement, limits the permissible responses to dumping to: (1)
provisional measures; (2) price undertakings; and (3) definitive anti-dumping
duties.[15] Article 18.1 of the *Anti-Dumping Agreement* provides:

> No specific action against dumping of exports from another Member can be taken except in
> accordance with the provisions of GATT 1994, as interpreted by this Agreement.[16]

In *US – 1916 Act (2000)*, the Appellate Body ruled that any 'specific action
against dumping', i.e. action that is taken in response to situations presenting
the constituent elements of 'dumping', can only take the form of the measures
referred to in Article VI:2 of the GATT 1994.[17] The US legislation at issue in
US – 1916 Act (2000) provided for civil and criminal proceedings and penalties
for conduct which presented the constituent elements of dumping. Since these
civil and criminal actions are not among the permissible responses to dumping
listed in Article VI:2, the Appellate Body upheld the finding of the panel in this
case that the 1916 Act was inconsistent with Article VI:2, as interpreted by the
Anti-Dumping Agreement.[18]

In *US – Offset Act (Byrd Amendment) (2003)*, the measure at issue was the
United States Continued Dumping and Subsidy Offset Act of 2000 (CDSOA).[19]
This Act provided, in relevant part, that United States Customs shall *distribute*
duties assessed pursuant to an anti-dumping duty order to 'affected domestic
producers' for 'qualifying expenditures'.[20] Recalling its ruling in *US – 1916 Act
(2000)* that Article VI:2, read in conjunction with the *Anti-Dumping Agreement*,
limits the permissible responses to dumping to definitive anti-dumping duties,

---

14 See below, pp. 682–4, 699 and 708–9, respectively.
15 See Appellate Body Report, *US – 1916 Act (2000)*, para. 137.
16 Footnote 24 to this provision reads: 'This is not intended to preclude action under other relevant provisions
of GATT 1994, as appropriate.'
17 See Appellate Body Report, *US – 1916 Act (2000)*, para. 137. On the concept of 'specific action against
dumping', see Appellate Body Report, *US – 1916 Act (2000)*, para. 126. In *US – Offset Act (Byrd Amendment) (2003)*, the Appellate Body found that a measure is a 'specific action against dumping' when that
measure is inextricably linked to, or has a strong correlation with, a determination of dumping. See Appellate
Body, *US – Offset Act (Byrd Amendment) (2003)*, para. 239. See also Panel Report, *Mexico – Anti-Dumping
Measures on Rice (2005)*, para. 7.278.
18 See Appellate Body Report, *US – 1916 Act (2000)*, para. 137.
19 The CDSOA amends Title VII of the US Tariff Act of 1930 by adding a new Section 754 entitled 'Continued
Dumping and Subsidy Offset' and is often referred to as the 'Byrd Amendment'.
20 See Appellate Body Report, *US – Offset Act (Byrd Amendment) (2003)*, para. 12.

provisional measures and price undertakings,[21] the Appellate Body concluded in *US – Offset Act (Byrd Amendment) (2003)*:

> As CDSOA offset payments are not definitive anti-dumping duties, provisional measures or price undertakings, we conclude, in the light of our finding in *US – 1916 Act*, that the CDSOA is not 'in accordance with the provisions of the GATT 1994, as interpreted by' the *Anti-Dumping Agreement*. It follows that the CDSOA is inconsistent with Article 18.1 of that Agreement.[22]

2.5 Current Use of Anti-Dumping Measures

During the period from July 2011 to July 2012, twenty-three Members initiated a total of 200 anti-dumping investigations.[23] This indicates that the number of investigations is on the rise, having already reached a high level in the preceding period from July 2010 to July 2011, when twenty-two Members initiated 169 anti-dumping investigations.[24] In the period July 2011 to July 2012, seventeen Members imposed a total of 105 new anti-dumping measures against exports from other countries or customs territories, whereas, in the period July 2010 to July 2011, twenty Members imposed the same total number of 105 new anti-dumping measures.[25]

The overall use of anti-dumping measures fluctuates from year to year. In the period since the establishment of the WTO, the number of anti-dumping measures taken by Members has been on average 153 per year.[26] From January 1995 to December 2011, India was the most frequent user of the anti-dumping instrument, with a total of 478 measures. The United States was second, with 305 measures and the European Union was third with 282.[27] In the period from July 2011 to July 2012, India imposed the most new measures (twenty-eight), followed by Brazil (twenty), Pakistan and the European Union (nine each), China and Ukraine (six each) and the United States (five).[28] In the preceding year, the period from July 2010 to July 2011, most anti-dumping measures were imposed by India (twenty), Argentina (seventeen), the United States (fifteen), China (eleven), the European Union (eight), Indonesia (seven), Brazil (six) and Pakistan (five).[29] These figures make clear that the days when anti-dumping measures were taken almost exclusively by developed-country Members have passed. Developing-country

21 See below, pp. 723–4.
22 Appellate Body Report, *US – Offset Act (Byrd Amendment) (2003)*, para. 265. See also Panel Report, *Mexico – Anti-Dumping Measures on Rice (2005)*, para. 7.278. In the latter case, the measure at issue was fines imposed on importers of products on which anti-dumping investigations were under way.
23 Report (2012) of the Committee on Anti-Dumping Practices, G/L/1006, dated 25 October 2012; and Report (2012) of the Committee on Anti-Dumping Practices: Corrigendum, G/L/1006/Corr.1, dated 31 October 2012.
24 See Report (2011) of the Committee on Anti-Dumping Practices, G/L/966, dated 26 October 2011.
25 See *ibid.*
26 Note that, in the final years of the GATT, this number was considerably higher.
27 See www.wto.org/english/tratop_e/adp_e/AD_MeasuresByRepMem.pdf.
28 Report (2012) of the Committee on Anti-Dumping Practices, G/L/1006, dated 25 October 2012; and Report (2012) of the Committee on Anti-Dumping Practices: Corrigendum, G/L/1006/Corr.1, dated 31 October 2012.
29 Report (2011) of the Committee on Anti-Dumping Practices, WT/G/L/966, 26 October 2011.

Members have 'discovered' this trade policy instrument and some have become avid users. In addition, some Members who acceded to the WTO in the last decade have begun using anti-dumping measures quite frequently.

Furthermore, contrary to a widespread misconception, anti-dumping measures are not only used against developing-country Members; indeed, they are used frequently against both developed Members and developing-country Members. China has been by far the biggest target of anti-dumping measures, with 630 such measures being taken between January 1995 and December 2011, followed by Chinese Taipei (140) and the United States being the target of 136 such measures.[30] In the period from July 2011 to July 2012, most anti-dumping measures were imposed against China (twenty-nine), the United States (ten), the European Union, Thailand and Chinese Taipei (six each). In the preceding period from July 2010 to July 2011, anti-dumping measures were imposed against mainly China (forty-six), Indonesia and Brazil (six each), Malaysia and Thailand (five each) and the United States, Chinese Taipei and Korea (four each). Of the 2,601 anti-dumping measures imposed by Members since 1995, forty-two were the subject of WTO dispute settlement. To date, Members have been found to have acted inconsistently with their obligations under Article VI of the GATT 1994 and the *Anti-Dumping Agreement* in thirty-nine disputes.[31]

Anti-dumping law is one of the most controversial and politically sensitive areas of WTO law. WTO Members are often put under severe pressure by domestic producers to impose anti-dumping measures on particular products, and by foreign producers and domestic users of such products *not* to impose such measures. Consider the full-page advertisement of ANCI, the National Association of Italian Shoe Factories, published, *inter alia*, in the *Financial Times* in 2006, and shown in Figure 11.1.

The 2006 discussion on the imposition of anti-dumping measures on shoes exemplifies the highly controversial and political character of anti-dumping cases. *Bridges Weekly* reported on this 'shoe-spat' as follows:

After months of contentious discussions, EU member states narrowly voted on 4 October to slap anti-dumping duties on shoes imported from China and Vietnam ... The decision had badly split EU members. Mediterranean states, led by Italy, generally supported the

---

30 See www.wto.org/english/tratop_e/adp_e/AD_MeasuresByRepMem.pdf.
31 See *US – DRAMs (1999)*; *Guatemala – Cement II (2000)*; *Mexico – Corn Syrup (2000)*; *US – 1916 Act (2000)*; *Argentina – Ceramic Tiles (2001)*; *US – Hot-Rolled Steel (2001)*; *EC – Bed Linen (2001)*; *Thailand – H-Beams (2001)*; *US – Stainless Steel (Korea) (2001)*; *Egypt – Steel Rebar (2002)*; *US – Steel Plate (2002)*; *Argentina – Poultry Anti-Dumping Duties (2003)*; *US – Offset Act (Byrd Amendment) (2003)*; *EC – Tube or Pipe Fittings (2003)*; *EC – Bed Linen (Article 21.5 – India) (2003)*; *US – Softwood Lumber V (2004)*; *US – Softwood Lumber VI (2004)*; *US – Oil Country Tubular Goods Sunset Reviews (2004)*; *Korea – Certain Paper (2005)*; *Mexico – Anti-Dumping Measures on Rice (2005)*; *US – Anti-Dumping Measures on Oil Country Tubular Goods (2005)*; *US – Zeroing (EC) (2006)*; *US – Zeroing (Japan) (2007)*; *US – Shrimp (Ecuador) (2007)*; *Mexico – Steel Pipes and Tubes (2007)*; *EC – Salmon (Norway) (2008)*; *US – Shrimp (Thailand) (2008)*; *US – Customs Bond Directive (2008)*; *US – Stainless Steel (Mexico) (2008)*; *US – Continued Zeroing (2009)*; *US – Anti-Dumping Measures on PET Bags (2010)*; *US – Orange Juice (Brazil) (2011)*; *US – Shrimp (Viet Nam) (2011)*; *US – Zeroing (Korea) (2011)*; *EC – Fasteners (China) (2011)*; *US – Shrimp and Sawblades (2012)*; *EU – Footwear (China) (2012)*; and *China – GOES (2012)*.

Appeal to Commissioner Peter Mandelson

Here are the reasons for implementing antidumping measures on leather foot-wear imported from China and Vietnam.

Imports of footwear from China to EU25:

* 2002–2003: +19%; 2004: +39%
* first 10 months 2005: +300%; leather footwear no longer subject to quo-tas; average prices: –25%

Leather footwear is being imported at a price that is lower than the cost of the raw materials. The European footwear industry gives work directly or through suppliers to over 600,000 people. More than 75,000 jobs were lost in 2005. Thousands of footwear firms are going out of business in Italy and across Europe, and tens of thousands of workers are losing their jobs. In extreme situations, the reactions must be firm, bold and swift.

Mr Mandelson, yours is a very delicate role. The EU has an interest in defend-ing those who produce real wealth and create jobs in Europe.

The antidumping process has but one purpose: to defend manufacturing. Six months have gone by since it was officially proposed, and it is time to con-clude the procedures. All types of leather footwear must be covered by the measure, including STAF, Special Technology Athletic Footwear, which is made throughout Europe.

The Italian and European footwear manufacturers are not afraid of competi-tion, but we are defenceless against those who practise dumping in order to sell their products. The state of the industry is getting worse day by day, and we cannot wait any longer. These are the criteria on which you should base your decisions. We trust that your intervention will be bold and swift.

Figure 11.1 Advertisement of the National Association of Italian Shoe Factories (ANCI)

measures, in the face of active opposition from the Scandinavian countries and Germany. The UK was another of the 12 countries that voted against the new tariffs – just one short of the majority that would have been necessary to block them. On 7 October, the EU started imposing extra duties of 16.5 per cent on leather shoes from China, and 10 per cent on those from Vietnam. These replace higher provisional duties that had been in place since April. Under a compromise brokered by France, they will remain in force for two years, though the European Commission had originally sought five. Brussels claims that there is 'compelling evidence of serious state intervention' in the footwear sector in China and Vietnam – in the form of cheap finance, tax holidays, favourable land rental and electricity rates, and the like – which allow them to 'dump' goods on the EU market at unfairly low prices.[32]

---

32 *Bridges Weekly Trade News Digest*, 11 October 2006. See also A. Bounds, 'Deal Ends EU Impasse on Asian Shoe Tariffs', *Financial Times*, 5 October 2006.

However, the Federation of European Sporting Goods Retail Associations and the Federation of European Sporting Goods Industries noted with regard to the use of anti-dumping measures:

[W]e fail to see how duties would serve Europe's interest, given that they will raise prices for consumers and add costs and barriers for retailers, while benefiting no one.

Anti-dumping policy cannot be used to offer once-protected European sectors respite from global competition. It would be extremely damaging for Europe's relations with China as well as a bad signal to other European sectors facing global competition if anti-dumping became a protectionist tool rather than a targeted measure founded on strict legal and economic criteria.[33]

Furthermore, the use of anti-dumping measures is increasingly at odds with contemporary tendencies of outsourcing, one of the characteristics of the globalised economy. Peter Mandelson, EU Trade Commissioner at the time, noted in this respect:

[A]nti-dumping tariffs and quotas could harm Europe's own manufacturers, which have increasingly outsourced the production of shoes, textiles, lightbulbs and other goods, aiming to maintain a competitive edge against cheaper Asian rivals ... While Europe should tackle unfair trade, globalisation means the definitions of what is European-made have become blurred ... If producing cheaply in China helps generate profits and jobs in Europe, how should we treat these companies when disputes over unfair trading arise?'[34]

Questions and Assignments 11.1

Has the WTO *Anti-Dumping Agreement* set aside and replaced Article VI of the GATT 1947? What is 'dumping' in simple terms? Is all dumping to be 'condemned'? Why does WTO law not prohibit dumping? What is the essence of the WTO rules on dumping? Is it mandatory for WTO Members to enact anti-dumping legislation? To which measures do Article VI of the GATT 1994 and the *Anti-Dumping Agreement* apply? What forms can an anti-dumping measure take? Is it WTO-consistent for a measure against dumping to take the form of civil and criminal proceedings and penalties? Discuss the relevant case law in this respect. How has the use of anti-dumping measures evolved over the years? Does the use of anti-dumping measures make political and/or economic sense?

3 DETERMINATION OF DUMPING

As discussed above, Article VI:1 of the GATT 1994 and Article 2.1 of the *Anti-Dumping Agreement* define 'dumping' as the introduction of a product into the commerce of another country at less than its 'normal value'. In other words, 'dumping' exists where the 'normal value' of the product exceeds the 'export price'. This section explains: (1) how the 'normal value' of the product concerned is determined; (2) how the relevant 'export price' is determined; (3) how

---

33 W. Haizmann and H. Widmann, 'Letters to the Editor: Anti-Dumping Not the Right EU Step in Chinese Shoe Trade', *Financial Times*, 6 February 2006.
34 A. Bounds, 'Mandelson Warns Over Extra Taxes on Asian Imports', *Financial Times*, 4 September 2007.

the existence of dumping is determined; and (4) how the 'dumping margin' is calculated.

Ordinarily, dumping is discerned through a price-to-price comparison of the 'normal value' with the 'export price'. However, the *Anti-Dumping Agreement* envisages circumstances in which such a straightforward price-to-price comparison may not be possible or appropriate, and, therefore, provides for alternative methods for determining the existence of dumping in such cases.

Before engaging in this discussion of how to determine the existence of dumping, it is important to recall that only dumping causing injury is to be condemned and potentially subject to anti-dumping measures under Article VI of the GATT 1994 and the *Anti-Dumping Agreement*. However, the injurious effect that 'dumping' may have on a Member's domestic industry is not relevant in determining whether there is 'dumping'. Injury to the domestic industry is not a constituent element of 'dumping'.[35] In addition, the intent of the persons engaging in 'dumping' is irrelevant in the determination of whether dumping exists.[36]

The Appellate Body has emphasised repeatedly that the definitions of the terms 'dumping', as well as 'dumped imports', have the same meaning in all provisions of the Agreement and for all types of anti-dumping proceedings, including original investigations, new shipper reviews, and periodic reviews.[37] In each case, they relate to a *product* because it is the product that is introduced into the commerce of another country at less than its normal value in that country.[38] Thus, the margin of dumping is also defined in relation to a 'product'. The Appellate Body noted in *US – Zeroing (Japan) (2007)* and *US – Stainless Steel (Mexico) (2008)* that: (1) the concepts of 'dumping' and 'margins of dumping' pertain to a 'product' and are related to an exporter or foreign producer;[39] and (2) 'dumping' and 'dumping margins' must be determined in respect of each known exporter or foreign producer examined.[40] The Appellate Body further

---

35 See Appellate Body Report, *US – 1916 Act (2000)*, para. 107.   36 See *ibid*.

37 For a discussion on these various types of proceedings, see below, pp. 712–23, 727 and 728–32. Note that 'periodic' reviews are also referred to as 'administrative' reviews.

38 See Appellate Body Report, *US – Zeroing (Japan) (2007)*, para. 109, referring to Article 2.1, regarding original investigations. See Appellate Body Report, *US – Stainless Steel (Mexico) (2008)*, para. 84, referring to Article 9.3, regarding periodic reviews; and Appellate Body Report, *US – Corrosion-Resistant Steel Sunset Review (2004)*, para. 109, referring to Article 11.3, regarding sunset reviews. See also Appellate Body Report, *US – Continued Zeroing (2009)*, para. 280. The Appellate Body noted that the concepts of 'dumping', 'injury' and 'margin of dumping' are interlinked and, therefore, should be considered and interpreted in a coherent and consistent manner for all parts of the *Anti-Dumping Agreement*. Appellate Body Report, *US – Zeroing (Japan) (2007)*, para. 114; Appellate Body Report, *US – Stainless Steel (Mexico) (2008)*, para. 94.

39 According to the Appellate Body, '[d]umping arises from the pricing practices of exporters as both normal values and export prices reflect their pricing strategies in home and foreign markets. These margins of dumping have to be calculated on an exporter-wide rather than on a transaction-specific basis. The fact that "dumping" and "margin of dumping" are exporter-specific concepts under the *Anti-Dumping Agreement* is not altered by the fact that the export price may be the result of negotiation between the importer and the exporter. Nor is it altered by the fact that it is the importer that incurs the liability to pay anti-dumping duties.' See Appellate Body Report, *US – Stainless Steel (Mexico) (2008)*, para. 95. For a more detailed discussion on 'zeroing', see below, pp. 689–96.

40 The Appellate Body also emphasised that anti-dumping duties can be levied only in an amount not exceeding the margin of dumping established for each exporter or foreign producer. See Appellate Body Report, *US – Zeroing (Japan) (2007)*, paras. 111–14; and Appellate Body Report, *US – Stainless Steel (Mexico) (2008)*, para. 94.

clarified that a 'proper determination as to whether an exporter is dumping or not can only be made on the basis of an examination of the exporter's pricing behaviour as reflected in all its transactions over a period of time'.[41]

3.1 'Normal Value'

Article 2.1 of the *Anti-Dumping Agreement* defines the 'normal value' of a product as:

[t]he comparable price, in the ordinary course of trade, for the like product when destined for consumption in the exporting country.

In other words, the 'normal value' is the price of the like product in the home market of the exporter or producer. According to the Appellate Body in *US – Hot-Rolled Steel (2001)*, the text of Article 2.1 expressly imposes four conditions on domestic sales transactions so that they may be used to determine 'normal value': (1) the sale must be 'in the ordinary course of trade'; (2) the sale must be of the 'like product'; (3) the product must be 'destined for consumption in the exporting country'; and (4) the price must be 'comparable'.[42]

The first of the four conditions that sales transactions must fulfil so that they may be used to determine the 'normal value' is that the sale must be 'in the ordinary course of trade'. The decision as to whether sales in the domestic market of the exporting Member are made 'in the ordinary course of trade' can be a complex one. There are many situations that *may* form a reason to determine that transactions were not made 'in the ordinary course of trade', such as sales to affiliated parties; aberrationally high-priced sales, or abnormally low-priced sales; or sales below cost.[43] Sales not made in the ordinary course of trade may be *disregarded* in determining normal value, which would then be determined on the basis of the remaining sales.[44] As the Appellate Body stated in *US – Hot-Rolled Steel (2001)*:

Article 2.1 requires investigating authorities to exclude sales not made 'in the ordinary course of trade', from the calculation of normal value, precisely to ensure that normal value is, indeed, the 'normal' price of the like product, in the home market of the exporter.[45]

As the Appellate Body found in *US – Hot-Rolled Steel (2001)*, the *Anti-Dumping Agreement* affords WTO Members discretion to determine how to ensure that

41 Appellate Body Report, *US – Stainless Steel (Mexico) (2008)*, para. 98.
42 See Appellate Body Report, *US – Hot-Rolled Steel (2001)*, para. 165. Other provisions in the *Anti-Dumping Agreement*, such as Article 2.4, discussed below, permit the domestic investigating authorities to take account of considerations that may not be expressly identified in Article 2.1, such as the identity of the seller in a particular sales transaction.
43 See Article 2.2.1 of the *Anti-Dumping Agreement*. Note that pricing below cost alone is not sufficient. Such sales must be made over an extended period of time, in substantial quantities, and at prices that do not provide for the recovery of costs within a reasonable period of time. With regard to the second of these criteria, see Panel Report, *EC – Salmon (Norway) (2008)*, paras. 7.231–7.279.
44 See Appellate Body Report, *US – Hot-Rolled Steel (2001)*, para. 139. However, where the exclusion of such below-cost sales results in a level of sales that is too low to permit a proper comparison with export price, an alternative method of calculation may be used.
45 *Ibid.*, para. 140.

normal value is not distorted through the inclusion of sales that are not 'in the ordinary course of trade'. However, the Appellate Body noted at the same time that this discretion is not without limits. The Appellate Body ruled:

> In particular, the discretion must be exercised in an *even-handed* way that is fair to all parties affected by an anti-dumping investigation. If a Member elects to adopt general rules to prevent distortion of normal value through sales between affiliates, those rules must reflect, even-handedly, the fact that both high and low-priced sales between affiliates might not be 'in the ordinary course of trade'.[46]

The second of the four conditions that sales transactions have to meet so that they may be used to determine the 'normal value' is that the sale must be of the 'like product'. The determination of what constitutes a 'like product' involves, first examining the imported product or products that is or are alleged to be dumped and, secondly, establishing the product that is 'like'. Article 2.6 of the *Anti-Dumping Agreement* defines the 'like product' as:

> [a] product which is identical, i.e. alike in all respects to the product under consideration, or in the absence of such a product, another product which, although not alike in all respects, has characteristics closely resembling those of the product under consideration.[47]

A 'like product' is thus an identical product or a product with a close resemblance to the product under consideration.[48]

The third and fourth conditions provided for in Article 2.1 that sales transactions must meet, so that they may be used to determine the 'normal value', are that the product must be 'destined for consumption in the exporting country' *and* that the price must be 'comparable'. With respect to the latter condition, note that Article 2.4 of tne *Anti-Dumping Agreement* requires that a 'fair comparison' be made between export price and normal value. This comparison 'shall be made at the same level of trade, normally at the ex-factory level'. As the Appellate Body stated in *US – Hot-Rolled Steel (2007)*, in making a 'fair comparison:

> Article 2.4 mandates that due account be taken of 'differences which affect price comparability', such as differences in the 'levels of trade' at which normal value and the export price are calculated.[49]

The *Anti-Dumping Agreement* acknowledges that in certain circumstances consideration of the domestic price in the exporting country does not produce an appropriate 'normal value' for the purposes of comparison with the export price. Such circumstances may arise when there are no sales of the like product

---

46 *Ibid.*, para. 148.
47 Article 2.6 explicitly states that this definition applies 'throughout this Agreement', i.e. throughout the *Anti-Dumping Agreement*. See also Panel Report, *Korea – Certain Paper (2005)*, para. 7.272, as discussed below, p. 705.
48 Compare with the concept of 'like products' as used in the GATT 1994 (see above, pp. 325–9, 360–8, and 386–94) and in the *SCM Agreement*, especially Article 15.1 and footnote 46 to that Agreement (see below, p. 780). See also Appellate Body Report, *EC and certain member States – Large Civil Aircraft (2011)*, para. 1118. See also Panel Report, *EC – Salmon (Norway) (2008)*, para. 7.52.
49 Appellate Body Report, *US – Hot-Rolled Steel*, para. 167.

in the 'ordinary course of trade' in the domestic market of the exporting country; or when, because of the low volume of sales in that market, such sales do
not permit a proper comparison.[50] The *Anti-Dumping Agreement* also recognises that the domestic price in the exporting country market may not constitute
an appropriate normal value for the purposes of comparison with the export
price because of 'a particular market situation', but does not offer any criteria
to assist domestic investigating authorities in determining whether such a particular market situation exists.[51] The second Supplementary Provision to Article
VI:1 of the GATT 1994 (to which Article 2.7 of the *Anti-Dumping Agreement*
also refers) acknowledges that a straightforward comparison with the home
market price may not always be appropriate in the case of imports from a
country which has a complete or substantially complete monopoly of its trade
and where all domestic prices are fixed by the State, often referred to as a 'non-
market economy'.

Where the domestic price in the exporting country market may not represent
an appropriate normal value for the purposes of comparison with the export
price, Article 2.2 of the *Anti-Dumping Agreement* provides that an importing
Member may select one of two alternative methods for determining an appropriate normal value for comparison with the export price: (1) using a third-country
price as the normal value; or (2) constructing the normal value. No preference or
hierarchy between these alternatives is expressed in the Agreement. First, Article
2.2 of the *Anti-Dumping Agreement* permits the determination of 'normal value'
through consideration of the comparable price of the like product when exported
to an 'appropriate' third country, provided that this price is representative. Note,
however, that the Agreement does not define criteria for determining whether a
third country is 'appropriate'. Secondly, Article 2.2 of the *Anti-Dumping Agreement* permits a Member to construct the normal value on the basis of:

[t]he cost of production in the country of origin plus a reasonable amount for administrative, selling and general costs and for profits.

The amounts for administrative, selling and general costs and for profits shall be
based on actual data pertaining to production and sales in the ordinary course
of trade of the like product by the exporter or producer under investigation.[52]

---

50 Footnote 2 to Article 2.2 of the *Anti-Dumping Agreement* provides that the volume of sales in the domestic
    market of the exporting country shall normally be considered 'sufficient' for the purposes of calculating
    normal value if such sales constitute 5 per cent or more of the sales of the like product under consideration to
    the importing Member.
51 A panel established under the Tokyo Round *Anti-Dumping Code*, when considering a similar provision in that
    Code, found that the combined circumstance created by hyper-inflation and a frozen exchange rate in Brazil
    did not constitute such a particular market situation and therefore did not render home market prices an
    inappropriate basis for calculating normal value. See Panel Report, *EEC – Cotton Yarn (1995)*, para. 479.
52 Article 2.2.2 of the *Anti-Dumping Agreement*. If the amounts for administrative, selling and general costs
    and for profits cannot be determined in this way, they may be determined in one of the three ways discussed
    in Article 2.2.2(i) to (iii) of the *Anti-Dumping Agreement*. On the interpretation and application of these
    provisions, see Panel Report, *EC – Bed Linen (2001)*, paras. 6.59–6.562; and Appellate Body Report, *EC – Bed
    Linen (2001)*, paras. 74–83.

Questions and Assignments 11.2

What is the 'normal value' of a product within the meaning of Article 2.1 of the *Anti-Dumping Agreement*? What are the four conditions that sales transactions must fulfil in order to be used to determine the 'normal value'? What is the 'ordinary course of trade' and why is it important? What is a 'like product' within the meaning of the *Anti-Dumping Agreement*? What differences may, according to Article 2.4 of the *Anti-Dumping Agreement*, affect the price comparability and what should be done about this? Under what circumstances does consideration of the domestic price in the exporting country market not produce an appropriate normal value? In such cases, how can the 'normal value' be determined?

3.2 'Export Price'

The export price is ordinarily based on the transaction price at which the producer in the exporting country sells the product to an importer in the importing country. However, the *Anti-Dumping Agreement* recognises that the transaction price may not be an appropriate export price. For example, there may be no export price where the transaction involves an internal transfer or barter. Additionally, an association or a compensatory arrangement between the exporter and the importer or a third party may affect the transaction price. Article 2.3 of the *Anti-Dumping Agreement* therefore provides for an alternative method to calculate, or 'construct', an appropriate export price. The 'constructed export price' is based on the price at which the product is first sold to an independent buyer. Where it is not possible to construct the export price on this basis, the investigating authorities may determine a reasonable basis on which to calculate the export price.

Questions and Assignments 11.3

How is the 'export price' normally determined? When is the transaction price at which the producer in the exporting country sells to the importer in the importing country not an appropriate export price? In such a case, how is the export price to be determined?

3.3 Comparison of the 'Export Price' with the 'Normal Value'

To determine whether dumping, as defined above, exists, the export price is compared with the normal value. This section discusses in turn: (1) the 'fair comparison' requirement of Article 2.4 of the *Anti-Dumping Agreement*; and (2) the calculation of the dumping margin.

3.3.1 'Fair Comparison' Requirement

Article 2.4 of the *Anti-Dumping Agreement* provides in relevant part:

> A fair comparison shall be made between the export price and the normal value. This comparison shall be made at the same level of trade, normally at the ex-factory level, and in respect of sales made at as nearly as possible the same time.

In order to ensure a fair comparison between the export price and normal value, Article 2.4 of the *Anti-Dumping Agreement* requires that adjustments be made to the normal value, the export price, or both. Thus, Article 2.4 requires that:

[d]ue allowance shall be made in each case, on its merits, for differences which affect price comparability, including differences in conditions and terms of sale, taxation, levels of trade, quantities, physical characteristics, and any other differences which are also demonstrated to affect price comparability.[53]

As the reference to 'any other differences' indicates, this provision does not exhaustively identify differences that may affect price comparability. What is identified in Article 2.4 is a difference 'in conditions and terms of sale', which refers to considerations such as, for example, transport costs or credit terms associated with particular transactions involving the product concerned. In *US – Stainless Steel (Korea) (2001)*, the question arose as to whether differences resulting from the unforeseen bankruptcy of a customer and consequent failure to pay for certain sales fell within 'differences in the conditions and terms of sale' for which due allowance is to be made. The panel in that case stated that:

[t]he requirement to make due allowance for differences that affect price comparability is intended to neutralise differences in a transaction that an exporter could be expected to have reflected in his pricing.[54]

The panel therefore found that an unanticipated failure of a customer to pay for certain sales cannot be considered to be a 'difference in conditions and terms of sale', requiring adjustment to the export price, the normal value or both, to ensure price comparability.[55] In *US – Hot-Rolled Steel (2001)*, the United States used downstream sales prices to make a comparison without making any allowances. The Appellate Body ruled in this case that:

Article 2.4 of the *Anti-Dumping Agreement* requires that appropriate 'allowances' be made to any downstream sales prices which are used to calculate normal value in order to ensure a 'fair comparison' between export price and normal value. If those proper 'allowances' were not, in fact, made in this case, the comparison made by [the US Department of Commerce] between export price and normal value was, by definition, not 'fair', and not consistent with Article 2.4 of the *Anti-Dumping Agreement*.[56]

The Appellate Body also recalled that Article 2.4 requires that allowances are made not only for the differences explicitly mentioned in that Article (i.e. differences in conditions and terms of sale, taxation, levels of trade, etc.) but for *any other differences* which are also demonstrated to affect price comparability.[57] The panel in *US – Softwood Lumber V (2004)*, agreeing with the panel in *EC – Tube or Pipe Fittings (2003)*, found that:

[t]he requirement to make due allowance for such differences, in each case on its merits, means that the authority must *at least* evaluate identified differences – in this case,

---

53 Footnote 7 to the *Anti-Dumping Agreement* notes that: 'It is understood that some of the above factors may overlap, and authorities shall ensure that they do not duplicate adjustments that have been already made under this provision.'

54 Panel Report, *US – Stainless Steel (Korea) (2001)*, para. 6.77.   55 See *ibid*.

56 Appellate Body Report, *US – Hot-Rolled Steel (2001)*, para. 176.   57 *Ibid.*, para. 177.

differences in dimension – with a view to determining whether or not an adjustment is required to ensure a fair comparison between normal value and export price under Article 2.4, and make an adjustment where it determines this to be necessary on the basis of its evaluation. We consider that Article 2.4 does *not* require that an adjustment be made automatically in all cases where a difference is found to exist, but only where – based on the merits of the case – that difference is demonstrated to affect price comparability.[58]

In *US – Zeroing (EC) (2006)*, the Appellate Body stated:

> Article 2.4 also applies *a contrario*: this sentence implies that allowances should not be made for differences that do not affect price comparability.[59]

Where the export price is constructed, Article 2.4 of the *Anti-Dumping Agreement* contains special rules regarding adjustments. An allowance should be made for costs, including duties and taxes, incurred *between* the importation of the product and its resale to the first independent purchaser, as well as for profits.[60] Where the comparison of the 'normal value' with the export price requires conversion of currency, Article 2.4.1 of the *Anti-Dumping Agreement* provides specific rules governing that conversion.[61]

The question of making a *fair* comparison between the 'normal value' and the 'export price' is often one of the most contentious aspects of an anti-dumping investigation, as there will always be adjustments that arguably should be made. Frequently, the extent of the adjustments allowed will have an important impact on the outcome of the anti-dumping investigation. Note that, while it is incumbent upon the investigating authorities to ensure a fair comparison, the interested parties must substantiate their assertions concerning the need for adjustments as constructively as possible.[62]

In a number of disputes, the question arose whether 'zeroing' is inconsistent with the fair comparison requirement in Article 2.4.[63] The Appellate Body agreed

---

58 Panel Report, *US – Softwood Lumber V (2004)*, para. 7.165. See also Panel Report, *EC – Tube or Pipe Fittings (2003)*, para. 7.157.

59 Appellate Body Report, *US – Zeroing (EC) (2006)*, para. 156.

60 On the non-mandatory nature of these adjustments, see Panel Report, *US – Stainless Steel (Mexico) (2008)*, para. 6.93.

61 On the interpretation of this provision, see Panel Report, *US – Stainless Steel (Mexico) (2008)*, paras. 6.11–6.12. The panel in that case concluded that it was inconsistent with Article 2.4.1 of the *Anti-Dumping Agreement* to undertake currency conversions in instances where the prices being compared were in the same currency. On the currency conversion rules of Article 2.4.1 of the *Anti-Dumping Agreement*, see also Panel Report, *EC – Tube or Pipe Fittings (2003)*, paras. 7.198–7.199.

62 See Panel Report, *US – Softwood Lumber V (2004)*, para. 7.158.

63 The concept of 'zeroing' relates to the determination of margins of dumping. When export prices and normal value are compared for purposes of calculating dumping margins (according to various methodologies such as weighted average to weighted average or transaction to transaction or weighted average normal value to individual export price transactions), the comparison results can be 'negative' or 'positive': i.e. when export prices are below normal value, the comparison result is 'positive'; when export price exceeds normal value, the comparison result is 'negative'. In calculating the dumping margin, the United States used to take into account only the positive comparison results (when export price was below normal value); however, it did not take into account negative comparison results (when export price exceeded normal value). Instead, it assigned these comparison results the value 'zero' (this practice was referred to as 'zeroing'); in other words, when the practice of zeroing is applied, positive comparison results are not 'offset' against negative comparison results between export price and normal value. For a further discussion of the concept of 'zeroing', see below, pp. 692–6.

with the panel in *US – Zeroing (EC) (2006)*, first, that the 'fair comparison' language in the first sentence of Article 2.4 creates an independent obligation, and, secondly, that the scope of this obligation is not exhausted by the general subject-matter expressly addressed by paragraph 4 (that is to say, price comparability) and thus applies in original investigations and periodic reviews as well.[64] The Appellate Body stated in *US – Softwood Lumber V (Article 21.5 – Canada) (2005)* that the subsequent paragraphs of that Article (e.g. Article 2.4.2 spelling out comparison methodologies for calculating margins of dumping are '[s]ubject to the provisions governing fair comparison') are expressly made subject to the requirements of Article 2.4.[65] It noted that the term 'fair' is generally understood to connote 'impartiality, even-handedness, or lack of bias', and that the use of zeroing was 'difficult to reconcile with the[se] notions'.[66] The Appellate Body found that:

[t]he use of zeroing under the transaction-to-transaction comparison methodology artificially inflates the magnitude of dumping, resulting in higher margins of dumping and making a positive determination of dumping more likely. This way of calculating cannot be described as impartial, even-handed, or unbiased. For this reason, we do not consider that the calculation of 'margins of dumping', on the basis of a transaction-to-transaction comparison that uses zeroing, satisfies the 'fair comparison' requirement within the meaning of Article 2.4 of the *Anti-Dumping Agreement*.[67]

The Appellate Body further ruled that the use of zeroing in periodic reviews (Article 9.3), new shipper reviews (Article 9.5) and the reliance in sunset reviews on 'zeroed' margins of dumping in likelihood-of-continuation or recurrence-of-dumping determinations are also inconsistent with the fair comparison requirement found in Article 2.4 of the *Anti-Dumping Agreement*.[68]

Questions and Assignments 11.4

Which differences may affect price comparability and may therefore require adjustment of the 'export price', the 'normal value', or both? How can price comparability be ensured?

3.3.2 Calculation of the Margin of Dumping

The margin of dumping is the difference between the export price and the 'normal value'. This would appear simple enough. However, the methodology to be applied when calculating the difference between the export price and the 'normal value' may raise difficult and controversial issues.

---

64 Appellate Body Report, *US – Zeroing (EC) (2006)*, para. 146.
65 Appellate Body Report, *US – Softwood Lumber V (Article 21.5 – Canada) (2005)*, para. 132.
66 *Ibid.*, paras. 138–42, referring to the use of zeroing in the transaction-to-transaction comparison methodology. See also Appellate Body Report, *US – Zeroing (Japan) (2007)*, para. 146.
67 Appellate Body Report, *US – Softwood Lumber V (Article 21.5 – Canada) (2005)*, para. 142; Appellate Body Report, *US – Zeroing (Japan) (2007)*, para. 146.
68 See Appellate Body Report, *US – Zeroing (Japan) (2007)*, paras. 168–9; and Appellate Body Report, *US – Corrosion-Resistant Steel Sunset Review (2004)*, para. 127.

As already noted above, the Appellate Body has clarified repeatedly that a number of provisions in the *Anti-Dumping Agreement* require a determination of dumping by reference to an exporter and to a 'product under consideration'.[69] This is because dumping arises from the pricing behaviour of individual exporters or foreign producers. The context found in various provisions of the *Anti-Dumping Agreement* confirms that dumping and margins of dumping are concepts that are exporter-specific and not importer-specific.[70] Margins are established accordingly for each exporter or foreign producer on the basis of a comparison between normal value and export prices, both of which relate to the pricing behaviour of that exporter or foreign producer. In order to assess properly the pricing behaviour of an individual exporter or foreign producer, and to determine whether the exporter or foreign producer is, in fact, dumping the product under investigation and, if so, by which margin, it is necessary to take into account the prices of all the export transactions of that exporter or foreign producer.[71]

As provided in Article 2.4.2, first sentence, of the *Anti-Dumping Agreement*, the calculation of the dumping margin *generally* requires either the *comparison of the weighted average* 'normal value' to the weighted average of prices of all comparable export transactions; or a *transaction-to-transaction comparison* of 'normal value' and export price.[72] However, as provided in Article 2.4.2, second sentence, a comparison of the weighted average normal value to export prices in individual transactions may occur if: (1) there is 'targeted dumping' (i.e. a pattern of export prices differing significantly among different purchasers, regions or time periods); and (2) the investigating authorities provide an explanation as

---

69 See Appellate Body Report, *US – Zeroing (Japan) (2007)*, para. 111; Appellate Body Report, *US – Stainless Steel (Mexico) (2008)*, para. 89; and Appellate Body Report, *US – Continued Zeroing (2009)*, para. 283. See also above, pp. 682–7.

70 See Appellate Body Report, *US – Stainless Steel (Mexico) (2008)*, para. 87. In this report, the Appellate Body relied upon the context found in Articles 2.1, 2.2, 2.3, 5.2(ii), 5.8, 6.1.1, 6.7, 6.10 and 9.5 of the *Anti-Dumping Agreement*. The Appellate Body concluded that '[t]here is nothing in Articles 5.8, 6.10, and 9.5 of the *Anti-Dumping Agreement* to suggest that it is permissible to interpret the term "margin of dumping" under those provisions as referring to multiple "dumping margins" occurring at the level of individual importers. Instead, these provisions reinforce the notion that a single margin of dumping is to be established for each individual exporter investigated.' See Appellate Body Report, *US – Stainless Steel (Mexico) (2008)*, para. 89.

71 According to the Appellate Body, other provisions of the *Anti-Dumping Agreement* also make it clear that 'dumping' and 'margins of dumping' relate to the exporter or foreign producer. For example, a 'plain reading' of Article 5.8 indicates that the term 'margin of dumping' as used in that provision refers to a single margin. Article 6.10 requires, 'as a rule', that investigating authorities determine 'an individual margin of dumping for each known exporter or producer'. Similarly, Article 9.4 of the *Anti-Dumping Agreement* refers to situations where anti-dumping duties are applied to exporters or foreign producers not examined individually in an investigation, and provides that such duties shall not exceed 'the weighted average margin of dumping established with respect to the selected exporters'. In addition, Article 9.5 indicates that the purpose of new shipper reviews is to determine 'individual margins of dumping for any exporters or producers in the exporting country in question who have not exported the product' and refers to a 'determination of dumping in respect of such producers or exporters'. See Appellate Body Report, *US – Zeroing (Japan) (2007)*, para. 112; Appellate Body Report, *US – Stainless Steel (Mexico) (2008)*, para. 89; and Appellate Body Report, *US – Continued Zeroing (2009)*, para. 283.

72 Article 2.4.2 provides that these two methodologies 'shall normally' be used by investigating authorities to establish margins of dumping.

to why such differences cannot be taken into account appropriately in weighted-average-to-weighted-average or transaction-to-transaction comparisons.[73] As the Appellate Body noted in *US – Softwood Lumber V (Article 21.5 – Canada) (2005)*:

[t]he methodology in the second sentence of Article 2.4.2 is an exception. Article 2.4.2 clearly provides that investigating authorities 'shall normally' use one of the two methodologies set out in the first sentence of that provision.[74]

Significant questions have arisen with regard to the calculation of margins of dumping under Article 2.4.2. Specifically, the practice of 'zeroing' has been challenged many times in anti-dumping disputes. The practice of zeroing was explained by the Appellate Body in *EC – Bed Linen (2001)* as follows:

[F]irst, the European Communities identified with respect to the product under investigation – cotton-type bed linen – a certain number of different 'models' or 'types' of that product. Next, the European Communities calculated, for each of these models, a *weighted average* normal value and a *weighted average* export price. Then, the European Communities compared the weighted average normal value with the weighted average export price for each model. For some models, normal value was *higher* than export price; by subtracting export price from normal value for these models, the European Communities established a '*positive* dumping margin' for each model. For other models, normal value was *lower* than export price; by subtracting export price from normal value for these other models, the European Communities established a '*negative* dumping margin' for each model. Thus, there is a 'positive dumping margin' where there *is* dumping, and a 'negative dumping margin' where there *is not*. The 'positives' and 'negatives' of the amounts in this calculation are an indication of precisely *how much* the export price is above or below the normal value. Having made this calculation, the European Communities then added up the amounts it had calculated as 'dumping margins' for each model of the product in order to determine an *overall* dumping margin for the product *as a whole*. However, in doing so, the European Communities treated any 'negative dumping margin' as zero – hence the use of the word 'zeroing'. Then, finally, having added up the 'positive dumping margins' and the zeroes, the European Communities divided this sum by the cumulative total value of all the export transactions involving all types and models of that product. In this way, the European Communities obtained an overall margin of dumping for the product under investigation.[75]

The effect of zeroing, as the Appellate Body noted in *US – Corrosion-Resistant Steel Sunset Review (2004)*, is that, apart from artificially inflating the dumping margin for the product as a whole, it may turn a negative margin of dumping into a positive margin, introducing what the Appellate Body referred to as an 'inherent bias'.[76] Examining this practice of the European Communities under Article 2.4.2 of the *Anti-Dumping Agreement*, the Appellate Body in *EC – Bed Linen (2001)* stated:

---

73 See Appellate Body Report, *US – Zeroing (Japan) (2007)*, para. 118.
74 Appellate Body Report, *US – Softwood Lumber V (Article 21.5 – Canada) (2005)*, para. 97; and Appellate Body Report, *US – Zeroing (Japan) (2007)*, para. 123.
75 Appellate Body Report, *EC – Bed Linen (2001)*, para. 47.
76 See Appellate Body Report, *US – Corrosion-Resistant Steel Sunset Review (2004)*, para. 135. See also *ibid.*, paras. 127–8 and 130.

We see nothing in Article 2.4.2 or in any other provision of the *Anti-Dumping Agreement* that provides for the establishment of 'the existence of margins of dumping' for *types* or *models* of the product under investigation; to the contrary, all references to the establishment of 'the existence of margins of dumping' are references to the *product* that is the subject of the investigation ... Whatever the method used to calculate the margins of dumping, in our view, these margins must be, and can only be, established for the *product* under investigation as a whole.[77]

The Appellate Body in *EC – Bed Linen (2001)* thus held that the practice where an investigating authority does not offset the difference between the export price and the normal value in cases where the export price is *above* the normal value, and treats the difference as 'zero', is incompatible with Article 2.4.2 of the *Anti-Dumping Agreement*. The conclusions of the Appellate Body in that case focused on the first method for calculating the dumping margin set out in Article 2.4.2, first sentence, namely, the weighted-average-to-weighted-average method, and thus related to so-called 'model zeroing'. The United States adopted a similar practice of margin determination, which was at issue in *US – Softwood Lumber V (2004)*. Again, the Appellate Body held that:

[i]f an investigating authority has chosen to undertake multiple comparisons, the investigating authority necessarily has to take into account the results of *all* those comparisons in order to establish margins of dumping for the product as a whole under Article 2.4.2.[78]

The Appellate Body in *US – Zeroing (EC) (2006)*, in *US – Zeroing (Japan) (2007)* and in *US – Stainless Steel (Mexico) (2008)* again expressed its view that:

[t]here is no justification for 'taking into account the "results" of only some multiple comparisons in the process of calculating margins of dumping, while disregarding other "results"'.[79]

In fact, the consistency of this line of reasoning was pertinently highlighted by the panel in *US – Shrimp (Ecuador) (2007)*, which stated:

[I]n our view, there is now a consistent line of Appellate Body Reports, from *EC – Bed Linen* to *US – Zeroing (EC)* that holds that 'zeroing' in the context of the weighted average-to-weighted average methodology in original investigations ... is inconsistent with Article 2.4.2.[80]

---

77 Appellate Body Report, *EC – Bed Linen (2001)*, para. 53.
78 Appellate Body Report, *US – Softwood Lumber V (2004)*, para. 98. The Appellate Body explained that zeroing 'means, *in effect*, that at least in the case of *some* export transactions, the export prices are treated as if they were less than what they actually are. Zeroing, therefore, does not take into account the *entirety* of the prices of *some* export transactions, namely, the prices of export transactions in those sub-groups in which the weighted average normal value is less than the weighted average export price. Zeroing thus inflates the margin of dumping for the product as a whole.' See *ibid.*, para. 101. In *US – Softwood Lumber V (Article 21.5 – Canada) (2005)*, the Appellate Body again found nothing in the *Anti-Dumping Agreement* that would prohibit an investigating authority from dividing the product under investigation into product types or models of 'comparable' transactions. However, this did not permit zeroing in aggregating results of comparisons at the sub-group level by disregarding those where weighted average normal values are below weighted average export prices. See Appellate Body Report, *US – Softwood Lumber V (Article 21.5 – Canada) (2005)*, paras. 87–94.
79 Appellate Body Report, *US – Zeroing (EC) (2006)*, para. 126, citing Appellate Body Report, *US – Softwood Lumber V (2004)*, para. 98. See also Appellate Body Report, *US – Zeroing (Japan) (2007)*, paras. 125–8.
80 Panel Report, *US – Shrimp (Ecuador) (2007)*, para. 7.40.

It is now well-established case law that – as discussed above – zeroing also amounts to a violation of the 'fair comparison' requirement set out in Article 2.4.[81] An inflated margin of dumping, that violates Article 2.4.2, cannot qualify as being the result of a 'fair' comparison under Article 2.4. As noted by the Appellate Body in *US – Softwood Lumber V (Article 21.5 – Canada) (2005)*:

> Article 2.4.2 begins with the phrase '[s]ubject to the provisions governing fair comparison in paragraph 4'. Thus, the application of the comparison methodologies set out in Article 2.4.2 of the *Anti-Dumping Agreement*, including the transaction-to-transaction methodology ... is expressly made subject to the 'fair comparison' requirement set out in Article 2.4.[82]

A new question arose in *US – Softwood Lumber V (Article 21.5 – Canada) (2005)*, namely, the legality of zeroing when the second methodology for calculating the dumping margin is used, as set out in Article 2.4.2, first sentence, that is, the transaction-to-transaction methodology. The Appellate Body found in this case that the practice of zeroing in the transaction-to-transaction methodology was equally impermissible under Article 2.4.2 and Article 2.4. This was reiterated in the following appeal, when, in *US – Zeroing (Japan) (2007)*, the Appellate Body reversed the findings of the panel which had found that the United States had not acted inconsistently by maintaining zeroing procedures in respect of weighted-average-to-weighted-average and/or transaction-to-transaction methodologies to calculate margins of dumping.[83]

The current state of the law is that, in the case of the calculation of the dumping margin by a weighted-average-to-weighted-average comparison, or by a transaction-to-transaction comparison, the *entirety of the prices* for all comparable transactions involving the product that is the subject of the investigation must be included in the calculation of the dumping margin. The practice of zeroing has been rejected by the Appellate Body whenever it ruled on it. It has been reported that:

> [s]ome trade observers who oppose zeroing as a form of unfair protectionism have described the Appellate Body's rulings as a contribution to free trade that would have been difficult to achieve in negotiations. Talks on changing WTO anti-dumping rules have faltered alongside other issues in the Doha Round, with the US particularly reluctant to accept reforms that would have made it harder to impose extra duties.[84]

Appeals to date have not yet involved the use of zeroing in the circumstances of the third methodology mentioned in Article 2.4.2, second sentence, that is,

---

81 See above, pp. 687–90.
82 Appellate Body Report, *US – Softwood Lumber V (Article 21.5 – Canada) (2005)*, para. 132. See also Appellate Body Report, *US – Zeroing (EC) (2006)*, para. 146, for a similar argument on the pervasiveness of the 'fair comparison' requirement in Article 2.4 and its role in the interpretation of Article 2.4.2.
83 Appellate Body Report, *US – Softwood Lumber V (Article 21.5 – Canada) (2005)*, paras. 89 and 93. Appellate Body Report, *US – Zeroing (Japan) (2007)*, paras. 129 and 138. In this report, the Appellate Body found that the zeroing prohibition also applies to other stages of anti-dumping procedures, such as periodic reviews and new shipper reviews.
84 *Bridges Weekly Trade News Digest*, 17 January 2007.

when dumping margins are calculated on the basis of comparisons of weighted-average normal value with individual export transactions.[85]

The question of whether zeroing is permissible in periodic reviews surfaced in *US – Zeroing (EC) (2006), US – Zeroing (Japan) (2007)* and *US – Stainless Steel (Mexico) (2008).*[86] The panels in *US – Zeroing (EC) (2006)* and *US – Zeroing (Japan) (2007)* had found that simple zeroing was not in contravention of Article 2.4.2 and therefore also not inconsistent with Article 9.3.[87] However, the Appellate Body determined that zeroing in periodic reviews is inconsistent with Article 9.3.[88] The Appellate Body concluded in *US – Continued Zeroing (2009)* as regards zeroing in periodic reviews:

We fail to see a textual or contextual basis in the GATT 1994 or the *Anti-Dumping Agreement* for treating transactions that occur above normal value as 'dumped', for purposes of determining the existence and magnitude of dumping in the original investigation, and as 'non-dumped', for purposes of assessing the final liability for payment of anti-dumping duties in a periodic review. If, as a consequence of zeroing, the results of certain comparisons are disregarded only for purposes of assessing final liability for payment of anti-dumping duties in a periodic review, a mismatch is created between the product considered 'dumped' in the original investigation and the product for which anti-dumping duties are collected. This is not consonant with the need for consistent treatment of a product at the various stages of anti-dumping duty proceedings.[89]

In respect of sunset reviews, the Appellate Body noted in *US – Corrosion-Resistant Steel Sunset Review (2004)*:

[W]e see no obligation under Article 11.3 for investigating authorities to calculate or rely on dumping margins in determining the likelihood of continuation or recurrence of dumping.

---

85 The Appellate Body explained in *US – Zeroing (Japan) (2007)* that: 'the second sentence of Article 2.4.2 provides an asymmetrical comparison methodology to address a pattern of "targeted" dumping found among certain purchasers, in certain regions, or during certain time periods. By its terms, this methodology may be used if two conditions are met: first, that the investigating authorities "find a pattern of export prices which differ significantly among different purchasers, regions or time periods"; and secondly, that an "explanation" be provided as to why such differences in export prices cannot be taken into account appropriately by the use of either of the two *symmetrical* comparison methodologies set out in the first sentence of Article 2.4.2 ... The asymmetrical methodology in the second sentence is clearly an exception to the comparison methodologies which normally are to be used.' See Appellate Body Report, *US – Zeroing (Japan)*, para. 131. In *US – Softwood Lumber (Article 21.5 – Canada) (2005)*, the Appellate Body noted that the 'permissibility of zeroing under the weighted average-to-transaction comparison methodology provided in the second sentence of Article 2.4.2 is not before us in this appeal, nor have we examined it in previous cases'. See Appellate Body Report, *US – Softwood Lumber (Article 21.5 – Canada) (2005)*, para. 98; see also Appellate Body Report, *US – Zeroing (Japan) (2007)*, para. 136. The Appellate Body noted in *US – Stainless Steel (Mexico) (2008)* that it had 'so far not ruled on the question of whether or not zeroing is permissible under the comparison methodology in the second sentence of Article 2.4.2'. See Appellate Body Report, *US – Stainless Steel (Mexico) (2008)*, para. 127.

86 On the concept of 'periodic review', also referred to as 'administrative review', see below, pp. 728–32.

87 Panel Report, *US – Zeroing (EC) (2006)*, para. 8.1(d). Note that the panel differentiated between 'model zeroing' and 'simple zeroing': 'model zeroing' was found to be inconsistent with Article 2.4.2, first sentence, while 'simple zeroing' was not found to be inconsistent with that Article. In the panel's view, therefore, simple zeroing was also not inconsistent with Article 9.3. Note that, in this case, the Appellate Body explicitly refrained from endorsing the panel's interpretation on this point. See Appellate Body Report, *US – Zeroing (EC) (2006)*, para. 164.

88 Appellate Body Report, *US – Zeroing (Japan) (2007)*, para. 156. See also Appellate Body Report, *US – Stainless Steel (Mexico) (2008)*, para. 133.

89 See Appellate Body Report, *US – Continued Zeroing (2009)*, para. 285. Appellate Body Report, *US – Stainless Steel (Mexico) (2008)*, para. 106.

constitutes a major proportion of the total domestic production, it follows that the higher the proportion, the more producers will be included, and the less likely the injury determination conducted on this basis would be distorted.[99]

The domestic industry may presumably consist of one *or* multiple producers. The panel in *EC – Bed Linen (2001)* stated:

> Article 4.1 of the [*Anti-Dumping*] *Agreement* defines the domestic industry in terms of 'domestic producers' in the plural. Yet we consider it indisputable that a single domestic producer may constitute the domestic industry under the [*Anti-Dumping*] *Agreement*, and that the provisions concerning domestic industry under Article 4 continue to apply in such a factual situation.[100]

Article 4.1 of the *Anti-Dumping Agreement* recognises that it may not be appropriate to include *all* producers of the like product in the domestic industry when producers are 'related' to the exporters or importers or are themselves importers of the allegedly dumped product.[101] Related producers may not entirely share the interests of purely domestic producers. A producer is deemed to be 'related' to exporters or importers only if: (1) one of them directly or indirectly controls the other; or both of them are directly or indirectly controlled by a third person; or together they directly or indirectly control a third person; and (2) there are grounds for believing or suspecting that the effect of the relationship is such as to cause the producer concerned to behave differently from non-related producers.[102]

The panel in *EC – Salmon (Norway) (2008)* made it clear that the text of Article 4.1 of the *Anti-Dumping Agreement* does not support the notion that there is any other circumstance in which the domestic industry can be interpreted, from the outset, as not including certain categories of producers of the like product, other than those set out in Article 4.1(i).[103] Note that, in limited circumstances, a *regional industry*, instead of the total domestic industry, may be defined as the basis for the injury analysis.[104]

Questions and Assignments 11.6

What is the 'domestic industry' within the meaning of Article 4 of the *Anti-Dumping Agreement*? Must the 'domestic industry' consist of all producers, or at least those

---

99 *Ibid.*, para. 414. The Appellate Body explained that, in 'the special case of a fragmented industry with numerous producers, the practical constraints on an authority's ability to obtain information may mean that what constitutes "a major proportion" may be lower than what is ordinarily permissible in a less fragmented industry'. The Appellate Body, however, added as a cautionary note that 'a domestic industry defined on the basis of a proportion that is low, or defined through a process that involves active exclusion of certain domestic producers, is likely to be more susceptible to a finding of inconsistency under Article 4.1 of the *Anti-Dumping Agreement*'. See *ibid.*, para. 419.

100 Panel Report, *EC – Bed Linen (2001)*, para. 6.72.

101 See Article 4.1(i) of the *Anti-Dumping Agreement*.

102 See footnote 11 to the *Anti-Dumping Agreement*. Note that one is deemed to control another 'when the former is legally or operationally in a position to exercise restraint or direction over the latter'.

103 See Panel Report, *EC – Salmon (Norway) (2008)*, para. 7.112.

104 See Article 4.1(ii) of the *Anti-Dumping Agreement*. On the application of anti-dumping measures in that case, see Article 4.2 of the *Anti-Dumping Agreement*.

producers representing more than 50 per cent of the domestic production? Which producers, established in a Member, may be excluded from the relevant 'domestic industry' of that Member?

4.2 'Injury'

An affirmative determination of injury to the domestic industry is a fundamental pre-condition for the imposition of anti-dumping measures, along with a determination of the causal link between the dumped imports and injury. The *Anti-Dumping Agreement* defines 'injury' to mean one of three things: (1) material injury to a domestic industry; (2) threat of material injury to a domestic industry; or (3) material retardation of the establishment of a domestic industry.[105] The following sub-sections will discuss in turn what 'material injury', 'threat of material injury' and 'material retardation' mean and how a domestic investigating authority establishes their existence.

However, before engaging in this discussion, it is appropriate to make a general observation on the architecture of Article 3 of the *Anti-Dumping Agreement*, entitled 'Determination of Injury'. As the title suggests, this Article deals with the determination of injury (or threat thereof), but it also deals with the requirement to demonstrate a causal link between the dumping and the injury, a requirement discussed in the next section of this chapter.[106] As the Appellate Body noted in *Thailand – H-Beams (2001)*, and most recently reiterated in *China – GOES (2012)*, the first paragraph of Article 3 is an 'overarching provision' on the determination of injury and causation, while the subsequent paragraphs of Article 3 stipulate, in detail, an investigating authority's obligations in determining the injury to the domestic industry caused by dumping.[107] The Appellate Body stated in *China – GOES (2012)* that the paragraphs of Article 3, together, provide 'an investigating authority with the relevant framework and disciplines for conducting an injury and causation analysis'.[108] According to the Appellate Body, these provisions contemplate 'a logical progression of inquiry leading to an investigating authority's ultimate injury and causation determination'.[109]

---

105 See footnote 9 to Article 3 of the *Anti-Dumping Agreement*. Note that the *Anti-Dumping Agreement*, like the *SCM Agreement*, requires *material* injury or threat thereof, rather than *serious* injury as required under the *Agreement on Safeguards*. See above, pp. 615–19. The Appellate Body in *US – Lamb (2001)* noted that the standard of 'serious injury' is higher than that of 'material injury'. See Appellate Body Report, *US – Lamb (2001)*, para. 124.
106 See below, pp. 708–12.
107 See Appellate Body Report, *Thailand – H-Beams (2001)*, para. 106; and Appellate Body Report, *China – GOES (2012)*, para. 128.
108 Appellate Body Report, *China – GOES (2012)*, paras. 126–8.
109 *Ibid.* This inquiry entails a consideration of the volume of dumped imports and their price effects, and requires an examination of the impact of such imports on the domestic industry as revealed by a number of economic factors. These various elements are then linked through a causation analysis between dumped imports and the injury to the domestic industry, taking into account all factors that are being considered and evaluated.

4.2.1 Material Injury

Article 3.1 of the *Anti-Dumping Agreement* requires that a determination of injury to the domestic industry:

[b]e based on positive evidence and involve an objective examination of both (*a*) the volume of dumped imports and the effect of the dumped imports on prices in the domestic market for like products, and (*b*) the consequent impact of these imports on domestic producers of such products.

As noted above, the Appellate Body referred in *Thailand – H-Beams (2001)*, and most recently again in *China – GOES (2012)*, to Article 3.1 as an 'overarching provision' that sets forth a Member's fundamental, substantive obligations with respect to the determination of injury.[110] Article 3.1 informs the more detailed obligations in succeeding paragraphs. These obligations concern: (1) the determination of the volume of dumped imports, and their effect on prices (Article 3.2); (2) investigations of imports from more than one country (Article 3.3); (3) the impact of dumped imports on the domestic industry (Article 3.4); (4) the causal link between dumped imports and injury (Article 3.5); (5) the assessment of the domestic production of the like product (Article 3.6); and (6) the determination of the threat of material injury (Articles 3.7 and 3.8). As the Appellate Body emphasised in *Thailand – H-Beams (2001)*, the focus of Article 3 is thus on *substantive* obligations that a Member must fulfil in making an injury determination.[111]

In *US – Hot-Rolled Steel (2001)*, the Appellate Body held that the thrust of the investigating authorities' obligation under Article 3.1, lies in the requirement that they: (1) base their determination on 'positive evidence'; and (2) conduct an 'objective examination'. According to the Appellate Body, the concept of 'positive evidence' relates to the quality of the evidence that authorities may rely on in making a determination. It focuses on the facts underpinning and justifying the injury determination. The word 'positive' means that the evidence must be of an affirmative, objective and verifiable character, and that it must be credible.[112] The concept of 'objective examination' aims at a different aspect of the investigating authorities' determination. It is concerned with the investigation process itself. The word 'objective', which qualifies the word 'examination', indicates essentially that the 'examination' process must conform to the dictates of the basic principles of good faith and fundamental fairness.[113] In short, an 'objective examination' requires that the domestic industry, and the effects of dumped imports, be investigated in an unbiased manner, without favouring the interests of any interested party, or group of interested parties, in the investigation.[114] If an examination is to be 'objective', the identification, investigation

---

110 Appellate Body Report, *Thailand – H-Beams (2001)*, para. 106; and Appellate Body Report, *China – GOES (2012)*, para. 126.
111 See Appellate Body Report, *Thailand – H-Beams (2001)*, para. 106.
112 See Appellate Body Report, *US – Hot-Rolled Steel (2001)*, para. 192.
113 See *ibid.*, para. 193.   114 See *ibid.*

and evaluation of the relevant factors must be *even-handed*. Thus, investigating authorities are not entitled to conduct their investigation in such a way that it becomes more likely that, because of the fact-finding or evaluation process, they will determine that the domestic industry is injured.[115] In *Mexico – Anti-Dumping Measures on Rice (2005)*, the panel found that Mexico's investigating authority had acted inconsistently with Article 3.1 of the *Anti-Dumping Agreement* for three reasons: (1) because it chose to base its determination of injury on a period of investigation which ended more than fifteen months before the initiation of the investigation; (2) because it excluded six months of data from each year of the investigation period; and (3) because it used assumptions in its evaluation of export volumes and price effects.[116] The Appellate Body upheld the panel's findings of inconsistency. It stated that:

> [b]ecause the conditions to impose an anti-dumping duty are to be assessed with respect to the current situation, the determination of whether injury exists should be based on data that provide indications of the situation prevailing when the investigation takes place.[117]

The panel in *Mexico – Steel Pipes and Tubes (2007)* stated that the data considered by the investigating authority should include, to the extent practicable, the most recent information possible, 'taking into account the inevitable delay caused by the need for an investigation, as well as any practical problems of data collection in a particular case'.[118] As the Appellate Body stated in *Mexico – Anti-Dumping Measures on Rice (2005)*:

> Articles 3.1 and 3.2 do not prescribe a methodology that must be followed by an investigating authority in conducting an injury analysis. Consequently, an investigating authority enjoys a certain discretion in adopting a methodology to guide its injury analysis. Within the bounds of this discretion, it may be expected that an investigating authority might have to rely on reasonable assumptions or draw inferences. In doing so, however, the investigating authority must ensure that its determinations are based on 'positive evidence' ... An investigating authority that uses a methodology premised on unsubstantiated assumptions does not conduct an examination based on positive evidence. An assumption is not properly substantiated when the investigating authority does not explain why it would be appropriate to use it in the analysis.[119]

As noted above, Article 3.1 requires that a determination of injury to the domestic market must involve an examination of both: (1) the volume of dumped imports and the effect of the dumped imports on prices in the domestic market for like products (first requirement); and (2) the consequent impact of these imports on domestic producers of such products (second requirement). With regard to the

---

115 See *ibid.*, para. 196. Note that the Appellate Body in *US – Hot-Rolled Steel (2001)* ruled that an examination of only certain parts of a domestic industry does not ensure a proper evaluation of the state of the domestic industry as a whole, and does not, therefore, satisfy the requirements of 'objectiv[ity]' in Article 3.1 of the *Anti-Dumping Agreement*. See Appellate Body Report, *US – Hot-Rolled Steel (2001)*, para. 206.

116 See Panel Report, *Mexico – Anti-Dumping Measures on Rice (2005)*, paras. 7.53–7.65, 7.74–7.87 and 7.96–7.116. See also Panel Report, *Mexico – Steel Pipes and Tubes (2007)*, paras. 7.211 *et seq.*

117 Appellate Body Report, *Mexico – Anti-Dumping Measures on Rice (2005)*, para. 165.

118 Panel Report, *Mexico – Steel Pipes and Tubes (2007)*, para. 7.228.

119 Appellate Body Report, *Mexico – Anti-Dumping Measures on Rice (2005)*, paras. 204–5.

first requirement, the Appellate Body in *EC – Bed Linen (Article 21.5 – India) (2003)* made clear that imports from those *exporters* who were not found to be dumping may *not* be included in the volume of dumped imports from a country:

It is clear from the text of Article 3.1 that investigating authorities must ensure that a 'determination of injury' is made on the basis of 'positive evidence' and an 'objective examination' of the volume and effect of imports that *are dumped* – and to the exclusion of the volume and effect of imports that *are not dumped*. It is clear from the text of Article 3.2 that investigating authorities must consider whether there has been a significant increase in *dumped* imports, and that they must examine the effect of *dumped* imports on prices resulting from price undercutting, price depression, or price suppression.[120]

Having considered also Article 3.5 of the *Anti-Dumping Agreement*, the Appellate Body concluded:

None of these provisions of the *Anti-Dumping Agreement* can be construed to suggest that Members may include in the volume of *dumped* imports the imports from producers that are *not* found to be dumping.[121]

With regard to the first requirement, that is, an examination of the volume of dumped imports and the effect of the dumped imports on prices in the domestic market for like products, note also that the injury inquiry focuses on developments in the domestic market of the importing Member. Article 3.2, first sentence, requires the investigating authorities:

[t]o *consider* whether there has been a *significant increase* in the dumped imports, either in absolute terms or relative to production or consumption, in the domestic market.[122]

Article 3.2, second sentence, requires the investigating authorities:

[t]o *consider* whether there has been *significant price undercutting* by the dumped imports as compared with the price of a like product of the importing Member, or whether the effect is otherwise to *depress prices to a significant degree* or *prevent price increases*, which would otherwise have occurred, to a significant degree.[123]

China argued in *China – GOES (2012)*, that Article 3.2 merely requires an investigating authority to *consider* whether the domestic prices are depressed or

---

120 Appellate Body Report, *EC – Bed Linen (Article 21.5 – India) (2003)*, para. 111.

121 Appellate Body Report, *EC – Bed Linen (Article 21.5 – India) (2003)*, para. 112. In *Argentina – Poultry Anti-Dumping Duties (2003)*, Brazil claimed that Argentina violated Article 3 of the *Anti-Dumping Agreement* because it had in its injury determination included the imports from two companies which had been found not to have dumped. Referring to the Appellate Body Report in *EC – Bed Linen (Article 21.5 – India) (2003)*, the panel found that the term 'dumped imports' excludes imports from producers/exporters found in the course of the investigation not to have dumped and that the imports from those should thus have been 'excluded outright' from the injury analysis. See Panel Report, *Argentina – Poultry Anti-Dumping Duties (2003)*, paras. 7.303–7.306.

122 Emphasis added.

123 Emphasis added. The panel in *EC – Tube or Pipe Fittings (2003)* found that there is no requirement under Article 3.2 of the *Anti-Dumping Agreement* to 'establish one single margin of undercutting on the basis of an examination of every transaction involving the product concerned and the like product'. However, the investigating authorities must, of course, conduct an unbiased and even-handed price undercutting analysis. The panel concluded that the EC's methodology for an injury determination – a zeroing methodology that offsets 'undercutting prices' with 'overcutting prices' – does not contravene Articles 3.1 and 3.2 to the extent that the application of this methodology reflects the full impact of price undercutting on the domestic industry. See Panel Report, *EC – Tube or Pipe Fittings (2003)*, paras. 7.276 and 7.279.

suppressed. Article 3.2 did not call for a consideration of the relationship between dumped imports and domestic prices. According to China, interpreting Article 3.2 as requiring a consideration of the relationship between dumped imports and domestic prices would result in *duplicating* the causation analysis under Article 3.5.[124]

The Appellate Body began its analysis in *China – GOES (2012)* by noting that the use of the word 'consider' in Article 3.2 obliges a decision-maker to 'take something into account' in reaching a decision. According to the Appellate Body, the word 'consider' does:

> [n]ot impose an obligation on an investigating authority to make *a definitive determination* on the volume of subject imports and the effect of such imports on domestic prices. Nonetheless, an authority's *consideration* of the volume of subject imports and their price effects ... is also subject to the overarching principles ... that it be based on positive evidence and involve an objective examination. In other words, the fact that no definitive determination is required does not diminish the rigour that is required of the inquiry' under Article 3.2 ... which includes 'whether the effect of' the subject imports is to depress prices or prevent price increases to a significant degree.[125]

With regard to the inquiry set out in Article 3.2, second sentence, the Appellate Body ruled in *China – GOES (2012)* that this provision postulates an inquiry as to the 'effect' of dumped imports on domestic prices, and each inquiry links the dumped imports with the prices of the like domestic products.[126] The Appellate Body noted that, with respect to significant price undercutting, Article 3.2, second sentence, expressly establishes 'a link between the price of [dumped] imports and that of like domestic products, by requiring that a comparison be made between the two'.[127]

With respect to price depression or price suppression,[128] the Appellate Body observed that Article 3.2, second sentence, expressly links also these market phenomena with dumped imports. Article 3.2 contemplates an inquiry into the relationship between two variables, namely, dumped imports and domestic prices. More specifically, an investigating authority is required to consider whether a first variable – that is, dumped imports – has '*explanatory force for the occurrence of*' significant depression or suppression of a second variable – that is, domestic prices.[129] Moreover, as the Appellate Body stated

---

124 On the causation analysis, see below, pp. 708–12.

125 Appellate Body Report, *China – GOES (2012)*, paras. 130–1, referring to, *inter alia*, Panel Report, *Thailand – H-Beams (2001)*, para. 7.161; and Panel Report, *Korea – Certain Paper (2005)*, para. 7.253. The Appellate Body in *China – GOES (2012)* finally stated that an investigating authority's *consideration* under Article 3.2 'must be reflected in relevant documentation, such as an authority's final determination, so as to allow an interested party to verify whether the authority indeed *considered* such factors'. See *ibid.*

126 Appellate Body Report, *China – GOES (2012)*, para. 135.   127 *Ibid.*, para. 136.

128 Article 3.2, second sentence, refers to 'prevent[ing] price increases, which would otherwise have occurred'. This market phenomenon is commonly referred to as 'price suppression'.

129 Appellate Body Report, *China – GOES (2012)*, para. 136. Emphasis added. The inquiries set out in the second sentence of Article 3.2 are separated by the words 'or' and 'otherwise'. This indicates that the elements relevant to the consideration of significant price undercutting may differ from those relevant to the consideration of significant price depression and suppression. Thus, even if prices of dumped imports do not significantly undercut those of like domestic products, dumped imports could still have a price-depressing or price-suppressing effect on domestic prices. See *ibid.*, para. 137.

in *China – GOES (2012)*, given that Article 3.2 contemplates an inquiry into the relationship between dumped imports and domestic prices, it is *not* sufficient for an investigating authority to confine its consideration to what is happening to domestic prices for purposes of considering significant price depression or suppression. Rather, an investigating authority is required to examine domestic prices in conjunction with dumped imports in order to understand whether dumped imports have '*explanatory force for the occurrence of*' significant depression or suppression of domestic prices.[130] According to the Appellate Body, this interpretation is reinforced by the very concepts of price depression and price suppression. With regard to price depression, it explained that price depression refers to a situation in which prices are pushed down, or reduced, *by something*. An examination of price depression, by definition, calls for more than a simple observation of a price *decline*, and also encompasses an analysis of *what* is pushing down the prices. With regard to price suppression, the Appellate Body observed that Article 3.2 requires the investigating authority to consider 'whether the effect of' dumped imports is '[to] prevent price increases, *which otherwise would have occurred*, to a significant degree'. Accordingly, price suppression cannot be properly examined without a consideration of whether, in the absence of dumped imports, prices 'otherwise would have' increased. The concepts of both price depression and price suppression thus implicate an analysis concerning the question of what brings about such price phenomena.[131] Interpreting Article 3.2 as requiring a consideration of the relationship between dumped imports and domestic prices does *not* result in a duplication of the causation analysis under Article 3.5. Rather, Article 3.5, on the one hand, and Article 3.2, on the other hand, posit different inquiries. The Appellate Body explained that:

[t]he analysis pursuant to Article 3.5 ... concerns the causal relationship between [*dumped*] *imports* and *injury* to the domestic industry. In contrast, the analysis under Article 3.2 ... concerns the relationship between [dumped] imports and a different variable, that is, *domestic prices*. An understanding of the latter relationship serves as a basis for the injury and causation analysis under Article 3.5 ... In addition, Article 3.5 ... require[s] an investigating authority to demonstrate that [dumped] imports are causing injury 'through the effects of [dumping ...]', as set forth in Article 3.2 ... as well as in Article 3.4 ... Thus, the examination under Article 3.5 ... encompasses 'all relevant evidence' before the authority, including the volume of [dumped] imports and their price effects [listed under Article 3.2], as well as all relevant economic factors concerning the state of the domestic industry [listed in Article 3.4]. The examination under Article 3.5, by definition, covers a broader scope than the scope of the elements considered in relation to price depression and suppression under Article 3.2.[132]

As indicated in the quote above, apart from Article 3.2, also Article 3.4 of the *Anti-Dumping Agreement* plays an important role in setting out how an investigating authority must determine injury. Article 3.4 states:

---

130 *Ibid.*, para. 138. Emphasis added.   131 *Ibid.*, para. 141.   132 *Ibid.*, para. 147.

The examination of the impact of the dumped imports on the domestic industry concerned shall include an evaluation of all relevant economic factors and indices having a bearing on the state of the industry ...

Article 3.4 then lists the following relevant economic factors or indicators that must be evaluated: (1) factors and indices having a bearing on the state of the industry (such as an actual or potential decline in sales, profits, output, market share, productivity, return on investments, or utilisation of capacity); (2) factors affecting the domestic prices; (3) the magnitude of the margin of dumping; and (4) actual or potential negative effects on cash flow, inventories, employment, wages, growth, ability to raise capital, or investments. Article 3.4 explicitly states that this list is not exhaustive. It also stresses that one or more of these factors or indices, no matter how pronounced, will not necessarily give decisive guidance as to the existence of injury to the domestic industry or lack thereof.

While not exhaustive, it is widely accepted that the list of factors in Article 3.4 is a *mandatory* minimum, and that investigating authorities must therefore collect and analyse data relating to each of these individual enumerated factors.[133] In addition, investigating authorities must also collect and analyse data relating to *any other relevant factors* that may have a bearing on the state of a domestic industry in a particular case.[134] Putting the obligation of Article 3.4 in context and clarifying what exactly is expected from an investigating authority, the panel in *Korea – Certain Paper (2005)* considered:

[t]hat the [investigating authority's] obligation to evaluate all relevant economic factors under Article 3.4 shall be read in conjunction with the overarching obligation to carry out an 'objective examination' on the basis of 'positive evidence' as set out under Article 3.1. Therefore, the obligation to analyse the mandatory list of fifteen factors under Article 3.4 is not a mere 'checklist obligation' consisting of a mechanical exercise to make sure that each listed factor has somehow been addressed by the [investigating authority]. We recognize that the relevance of each one of these injury factors may vary from one case to the other. The fact remains, however, that Article 3.4 requires the [investigating authority] to carry out a reasoned analysis of the state of the industry. This analysis cannot be limited to a mere identification of the 'relevance or irrelevance' of each factor, but rather must be based on a thorough evaluation of the state of the industry. The analysis must explain in a satisfactory way why the evaluation of the injury factors set out under Article 3.4 lead[s] to the determination of material injury, including an explanation of why factors which would seem to lead in the other direction do not, overall, undermine the conclusion of material injury.[135]

133 See Panel Report, *Thailand – H-Beams (2001)*, paras. 7.224–7.225, as upheld by Appellate Body Report, *Thailand – H-Beams (2001)*, para. 125. See also Panel Report, *Argentina – Poultry Anti-Dumping Duties (2003)*, para. 7.314.

134 See Panel Report, *Thailand – H-Beams (2001)*, para. 7.225; and Appellate Body Report, *US – Hot-Rolled Steel (2001)*, para. 195.

135 Panel Report, *Korea – Certain Paper (2005)*, para. 7.272. As the Appellate Body noted in *EC – Tube or Pipe Fittings (2003)*, the obligation of Article 3.4 to evaluate all listed factors is *distinct* from the manner in which the evaluation is to be set out in the published documents. According to the Appellate Body, '[b]y its terms, [Article 3.4] does not address the manner in which the results of this evaluation are to be set out, nor the type of evidence that may be produced before a panel for the purpose of demonstrating that this evaluation was indeed conducted. The provision simply requires Members to include an evaluation of all relevant economic factors in its examination of the impact of the dumped imports.' See Appellate Body Report, *EC – Tube or Pipe Fittings (2003)*, para. 131.

In *China – GOES (2012)*, the Appellate Body emphasised that Article 3.4 requires an investigating authority to examine the *impact of dumped imports* on the domestic industry. According to the Appellate Body, Article 3.4 does not merely require an examination of the state of the domestic industry, but 'contemplate[s] that an investigating authority must derive an understanding of *the impact of* [dumped] imports on the basis of such an examination'.[136] The Appellate Body noted:

> Consequently, Article 3.4 ... [is] concerned with the relationship between [dumped] imports and the state of the domestic industry, and this relationship is analytically akin to the type of link contemplated by the term 'the effect of' under Article 3.2 ... In other words, Article 3.4 ... require[s] an examination of the 'explanatory force of [dumped] imports for the state of the domestic industry' ... [S]uch an interpretation does not duplicate the relevant obligations in Article 3.5 ... [because] the inquiry set forth in Article 3.2 ... and the examination required under Article 3.4 ... are necessary in order to answer the ultimate question in Article 3.5 ... as to whether [dumped] imports are causing injury to the domestic industry.[137]

Moreover, as the Appellate Body explained in *China – GOES (2012)*, an investigating authority is required to *examine* the impact of dumped imports on the domestic industry pursuant to Article 3.4. An investigating authority is *not* required to *demonstrate* that dumped imports are causing injury to the domestic industry. Rather, the latter analysis is specifically mandated by Article 3.5, as discussed in section 11.4.3 of this chapter.[138]

Questions and Assignments 11.7

What does the term 'injury' in the *Anti-Dumping Agreement* mean? What is the thrust of the investigating authorities' obligation under Article 3 of the *Anti-Dumping Agreement*? What is 'positive evidence' and an 'objective examination' within the meaning of Article 3.1 of the *Anti-Dumping Agreement*? Can the total volume of dumped imports legally include imports from exporters that were not found to be dumping? Does the use of the word 'consider' in Article 3.2 suggest that the obligation under this provision is a soft, inconsequential obligation? Does Article 3.2 require an investigating authority to consider the relationship between dumped imports and domestic prices? If so, does Article 3.2 duplicate the causation requirement set out in Article 3.5? Why not? What is the role and importance of the list of economic factors contained in Article 3.4?

4.2.2   Threat of Material Injury

As discussed above, the term 'injury' in the *Anti-Dumping Agreement* refers not only to material injury but also to the threat of material injury. Article 3.7 of the *Anti-Dumping Agreement* relates to the determination of a threat of material injury. It provides:

> A determination of a threat of material injury shall be based on facts and not merely on allegation, conjecture or remote possibility. The change in circumstances which would create a situation in which the dumping would cause injury must be clearly foreseen and imminent.

136 Appellate Body Report, *China – GOES (2012)*, para. 149.   137 *Ibid.*
138 See Appellate Body Report, *China – GOES (2012)*, para. 150. See below, pp. 708–12.

Article 3.7 further provides that, in making a determination regarding the existence of a threat of material injury, the investigating authorities should consider, *inter alia*, factors such as: (1) a significant rate of increase of dumped imports into the domestic market indicating the likelihood of substantially increased importation; (2) sufficient freely disposable, or an imminent substantial increase in, capacity of the exporter indicating the likelihood of substantially increased dumped exports to the importing Member's market, taking into account the availability of other export markets to absorb any additional exports; (3) whether imports are entering at prices that will have a significant depressing or suppressing effect on domestic prices, and would be likely to increase demand for further imports; and (4) inventories of the product being investigated.[139] However, no one of these factors alone can necessarily give decisive guidance. The totality of the factors considered must lead to the conclusion that further dumped exports are imminent and that, unless protective action is taken, material injury would occur.[140] As the panel in *US – Softwood Lumber VI (2004)* concluded:

> What is critical, however, is that it be clear from the determination that the investigating authority has evaluated how the future will be different from the immediate past, such that the situation of no present material injury will change in the imminent future to a situation of material injury, in the absence of measures.[141]

The panel in *Mexico – Corn Syrup (2000)* stated that it is clear that, in making a determination regarding the threat of material injury, investigating authorities must conclude that *material injury would occur* in the absence of an antidumping measure. However, a determination that material injury would occur cannot be made solely on the basis of a consideration of the factors listed in Article 3.7. The panel in *Mexico – Corn Syrup (2000)* ruled that:

> [c]onsideration of the Article 3.4 factors in examining the consequent impact of imports is required in a case involving threat of injury in order to make a determination consistent with the requirements of Articles 3.1 and 3.7.[142]

---

139 Note that the panel in *US – Softwood Lumber VI (2004)* found that consideration of the factors set out in Articles 3.7 and 15.7 of the *Anti-Dumping Agreement* 'must go beyond a mere recitation of the facts in question, and put them into context'. The panel did, however, consider that 'the investigating authorities are not required by Articles 3.7 and 15.7 to make an explicit "finding" or "determination" with respect to the factors considered'. See Panel Report, *US – Softwood Lumber VI (2004)*, para. 7.67.

140 See Article 3.7 of the *Anti-Dumping Agreement*.

141 Panel Report, *US – Softwood Lumber VI (2004)*, para. 7.58. In *US – Softwood Lumber VI (Article 21.5 – Canada) (2006)*, the Appellate Body implied that a 'high standard ... applies to a threat of injury determination ... [T]he reasoning set out by an investigating authority making a determination of threat of injury must clearly disclose the assumptions and extrapolations that were made, on the basis of the record evidence, regarding future occurrences. Nor are the panel's statements inconsistent with the requirements that the reasoning of the investigating authority demonstrate that such assumptions and extrapolations were based on positive evidence and not merely on allegation, conjecture, or remote possibility; and show a high degree of likelihood that projected occurrences will occur.' See Appellate Body Report, *US – Softwood Lumber VI (Article 21.5 – Canada) (2006)*, para. 109.

142 Panel Report, *Mexico – Corn Syrup (2000)*, para. 7.127. The panel in this case further stated that the language of Article 3.7 itself recognised that factors in addition to those set out in that provision would be relevant for a threat of injury determination. *Ibid.*, para. 7.124. See also Panel Report, *US – Softwood Lumber VI (2004)*, para. 7.105.

The Appellate Body ruled in *Mexico – Corn Syrup (Article 21.5 – US) (2001)* that:

In determining the existence of a *threat* of material injury, the investigating authorities will necessarily have to make assumptions relating to 'the occurrence of future events' since such *future* events 'can never be definitively proven by facts'. Notwithstanding this intrinsic uncertainty, a 'proper establishment' of facts in a determination of threat of material injury must be based on events that, although they have not yet occurred, must be 'clearly foreseen and imminent', in accordance with Article 3.7 of the *Anti-Dumping Agreement*.[143]

Not surprisingly, Article 3.8 of the *Anti-Dumping Agreement* requires that the application of anti-dumping measures shall be considered and decided with 'special care' where a determination of threat of material injury is involved. While Article 3.8 offers no further guidance as to the meaning of 'special care', it is clear that this provision cautions against the 'automatic' imposition of measures in such cases.[144]

Questions and Assignments 11.8

When does a 'threat of material injury' within the meaning of Article 3.7 of the *Anti-Dumping Agreement* exist? Which factors should investigating authorities consider in order to establish a 'threat of material injury'?

4.2.3   Determination of Material Retardation

Beyond specifying that the term 'injury' as used in the *Anti-Dumping Agreement* also includes 'material retardation', the Agreement contains no further explicit language pertaining to this concept. Some guidance may perhaps be derived from the 1967 *Anti-Dumping Code*,[145] which refers to the retardation of the establishment of a new industry, and indicates that a finding must be based on 'convincing evidence' that such a new industry is actually forthcoming. Examples of such evidence include plans for an industry being at an advanced stage, a factory under construction or new capital equipment already having been ordered.

5   DEMONSTRATION OF A CAUSAL LINK

As already noted above, Article 3.5 of the *Anti-Dumping Agreement* requires the demonstration of a *causal link* between the dumped imports *and* the injury to

---

143 Appellate Body Report, *Mexico – Corn Syrup (Article 21.5 – US) (2001)*, para. 85.
144 See Panel Report, *US – Softwood Lumber VI (2004)*, para. 7.33. See also the concern of the Appellate Body regarding statements of the panel in *US – Softwood Lumber VI (Article 21.5 – Canada) (2006)*, which seemed to imply 'a greater likelihood of panels upholding a *threat* of injury determination, as compared to a determination of *current* material injury, when those determinations rest on the same level of evidence'. See Appellate Body Report, *US – Softwood Lumber VI (Article 21.5 – Canada) (2006)*, para. 110.
145 See above, pp. 675–6.

the domestic industry. Article 3.5 also contains a *'non-attribution' requirement*. According to this requirement, investigating authorities must examine any known factors other than the dumped imports that are injuring the domestic industry at the same time *and* they must not attribute the injury caused by these other factors to the dumped imports. It is important to note that the *Anti-Dumping Agreement* does *not* require that the dumped imports are the *sole cause* of the injury to the domestic industry.[146] The *Anti-Dumping Agreement* requires that the dumped imports be a genuine and substantial cause of material injury and that other causes of injury not be attributed to the dumped imports.

5.1   Relevant Factors

Article 3.5 of the *Anti-Dumping Agreement* identifies several factors which 'may be relevant' in demonstrating a causal link between dumped imports and injury *and* in ensuring non-attribution to the dumped imports of injury being caused by other factors. These factors include: (1) the volume and prices of imports not sold at dumping prices; (2) contraction in demand or changes in the patterns of consumption; (3) trade-restrictive practices of and competition between the foreign and domestic producers; (4) developments in technology; and (5) the export performance and productivity of the domestic industry. However, Article 3.5 does not *require* examination of any particular factors nor does it *give clear guidance* on the manner in which the investigating authorities should evaluate relevant evidence in order to establish the causal link *and* to ensure non-attribution to the dumped imports of injury being caused by other factors. As the Appellate Body ruled in *US – Hot-Rolled Steel (2001)*:

[P]rovided that an investigating authority does not attribute the injuries of other causal factors to dumped imports, it is free to choose the methodology it will use in examining the 'causal relationship' between dumped imports and injury.[147]

The panel in *Thailand – H-Beams (2001)* made clear its view that, in contrast to the mandatory list of factors in Article 3.4, the list of factors in Article 3.5 was merely *illustrative*. Thus, while the listed factors in Article 3.5 might be relevant in many cases, and while the list contains useful guidance as to the kinds of factors other than imports that might cause injury to the domestic industry, the specific list in Article 3.5 is not itself mandatory.[148]

---

146 Note that this was the requirement under Article 3 of the Kennedy Round *Anti-Dumping Code*, BISD 15S/74. As discussed above, the Kennedy Round *Anti-Dumping Code* was superseded by the Tokyo Round *Anti-Dumping Code* in which this requirement was already dropped.

147 Appellate Body Report, *US – Hot-Rolled Steel (2001)*, paras. 224 and 226. See also Appellate Body Report, *EC – Tube or Pipe Fittings (2003)*, para. 189.

148 See Panel Report, *Thailand – H-Beams (2001)*, para. 7.274.

5.2 'Non-Attribution' Requirement

The Appellate Body in *US – Hot-Rolled Steel (2001)* clarified the 'non-attribution' requirement of Article 3.5 of the *Anti-Dumping Agreement* as follows:

The non-attribution language in Article 3.5 of the *Anti-Dumping Agreement* applies solely in situations where dumped imports and other known factors are causing injury to the domestic industry *at the same time*. In order that investigating authorities, applying Article 3.5, are able to ensure that the injurious effects of the other known factors are not 'attributed' to dumped imports, they must appropriately assess the injurious effects of those other factors. Logically, such an assessment must involve separating and distinguishing the injurious effects of the other factors from the injurious effects of the dumped imports. If the injurious effects of the dumped imports are not appropriately separated and distinguished from the injurious effects of the other factors, the authorities will be unable to conclude that the injury they ascribe to dumped imports is actually caused by those imports, rather than by the other factors. Thus, in the absence of such separation and distinction of the different injurious effects, the investigating authorities would have no rational basis to conclude that the dumped imports are indeed causing the injury which, under the *Anti-Dumping Agreement*, justifies the imposition of anti-dumping duties.[149]

In short, in order to comply with the 'non-attribution' requirement of Article 3.5, investigating authorities must make an appropriate *assessment* of the injury caused to the domestic industry by the other known factors, and they must *separate and distinguish* the injurious effects of the dumped imports from the injurious effects of those other factors.[150] In order for this obligation to be triggered, the Appellate Body noted in *EC – Tube or Pipe Fittings (2003)* that Article 3.5 requires that the factor at issue: (1) be 'known' to the investigating authority; (2) be a factor 'other than dumped imports'; and (3) be injuring the domestic industry at the same time as the dumped imports.[151] The *Anti-Dumping Agreement* does not expressly state how such factors should become 'known' to the investigating authority, or if and in what manner they must be raised by interested parties, in order to qualify as 'known'.[152]

---

149 Appellate Body Report, *US – Hot-Rolled Steel (2001)*, para. 223.

150 See Panel Report, *EC – Salmon (Norway) (2008)*, paras. 7.660 and 7.668–7.669. According to the panel in *US – Norwegian Salmon AD (1994)*, a separate identification of the injurious effects of causal factors other than dumped imports was not required under the GATT 1947. See Panel Report, *US – Norwegian Salmon AD (1994)*, para. 550. The GATT 1947 and the Tokyo Round *Anti-Dumping Code* did not contain a provision akin to Article 3.5 of the WTO *Anti-Dumping Agreement*, which expressly requires that injury caused by any other known factors is not attributed to dumped imports.

151 Appellate Body Report, *EC – Tube or Pipe Fittings (2003)*, para. 175. In that report, as it later noted, the Appellate Body 'found that there was no reason for the investigating authority to undertake the analysis of whether the alleged "other factor" had any *effect* on the domestic industry under Article 3.5 because the alleged "other factor" "had effectively been found *not* to exist". In other words, [the Appellate Body] did not rule that minimal (or not significant) factors need not be considered by the competent authorities in conducting non-attribution analyses. Rather, we ruled that only factors that have been found to exist need be taken into account in the non-attribution analysis.' See Appellate Body Report, *US – Steel Safeguards (2003)*, para. 491.

152 See Appellate Body Report, *EC – Tube or Pipe Fittings (2003)*, para. 176. The Appellate Body added to this: 'In our view, a factor is either "known" to the investigating authority, or it is not "known"; it cannot be "known" in one stage of the investigation and unknown in a subsequent stage.' *Ibid.*, para. 178.

In interpreting the 'non-attribution' requirement of Article 3.5, the Appellate Body in *US – Hot-Rolled Steel (2001)* recognised that the different causal factors operating on a domestic industry may interact, and their effects may well be interrelated, such that they produce a *combined* effect on the domestic industry. Therefore, it may not be easy, as a practical matter, to separate and distinguish the injurious effects of different causal factors. However, although not easy, this is the function of the 'non-attribution' requirement.[153]

5.3 Cumulation

A cumulative analysis is the consideration of the effects of dumped imports from more than one country in determining whether dumped imports are causing injury to the domestic industry. As such an analysis will necessarily increase the volume of imports whose impact is being considered, it will clearly augment the possibility of an affirmative injury determination. A controversial topic during the Uruguay Round negotiations, the conditions for cumulative analysis of the effects of imports from more than one country are now set forth in Article 3.3 of the *Anti-Dumping Agreement*. Cumulation is *not mandatory* under any circumstances but is *permitted*, be it only under the conditions set forth in Article 3.3.

Pursuant to Article 3.3 of the *Anti-Dumping Agreement*, an investigating authority may cumulatively assess the effects of imports if it determines that: (1) the margin of dumping established in relation to the imports from each country is more than *de minimis* (as defined in Article 5.8) and the volume of imports from each country is not negligible; and (2) a cumulative assessment of the effects of the imports is appropriate in light of the conditions of competition between the imported products and the conditions of competition between the imported products and the like domestic product.[154] In *EC – Tube or Pipe Fittings (2003)*, the Appellate Body stated that:

The text of Article 3.3 expressly identifies three conditions that must be satisfied before an investigating authority is permitted under the *Anti-Dumping Agreement* to assess

---

153 According to the Appellate Body, '[i]f the injurious effects of the dumped imports and the other known factors remain lumped together and indistinguishable, there is simply no means of knowing whether injury ascribed to dumped imports was, in reality, caused by other factors. Article 3.5, therefore, requires investigating authorities to undertake the process of assessing appropriately, and separating and distinguishing, the injurious effects of dumped imports from those of other known causal factors.' See Appellate Body Report, *US – Hot-Rolled Steel (2001)*, para. 228; and Appellate Body Report, *EC – Tube or Pipe Fittings (2003)*, para. 190. In the latter appeal, however, the Appellate Body did not find that an examination of *collective* effects is necessarily required by the non-attribution language of the *Anti-Dumping Agreement*. The Appellate Body stated: 'In particular, we are of the view that Article 3.5 does not compel, *in every case*, an assessment of the *collective* effects of other causal factors, because such an assessment is not always necessary to conclude that injuries ascribed to dumped imports are actually caused by those imports and not by other factors.' See Appellate Body Report, *EC – Tube or Pipe Fittings (2003)*, para. 191. See also Appellate Body Report, *US – Softwood Lumber VI (Article 21.5 – Canada) (2006)*, para. 154.
154 See Appellate Body Report, *EC – Bed Linen (Article 21.5 – India) (2003)*, para. 145; Appellate Body Report, *EC – Tube and Pipe Fittings (2003)*, para. 110; Appellate Body Report, *US – Oil Country Tubular Goods Sunset Reviews (2004)*, para. 300.

cumulatively the effects of imports from several countries ... By the terms of Article 3.3, it is 'only if' the above conditions are established that an investigating authority 'may' make a cumulative assessment of the effects of dumped imports from several countries.[155]

The Appellate Body further noted in *EC – Tube or Pipe Fittings (2003)*:

A cumulative analysis logically is premised on a recognition that the domestic industry faces the impact of the 'dumped imports' as a whole and that it may be injured by the total impact of the dumped imports, even though those imports originate from various countries ... In our view, therefore, by expressly providing for cumulation in Article 3.3 of the *Anti-Dumping Agreement*, the negotiators appear to have recognized that a domestic industry confronted with dumped imports originating from several countries may be injured by the cumulated effects of those imports, and that those effects may not be adequately taken into account in a country-specific analysis of the injurious effects of dumped imports.[156]

Questions and Assignments 11.9

Does the *Anti-Dumping Agreement* require that the dumped imports are the principal cause of the injury to the domestic industry? What does the 'non-attribution' requirement of Article 3.5 entail? What is the purpose or relevance of the list of economic factors contained in Article 3.5 of the *Anti-Dumping Agreement*? Why must an investigating authority 'separate and distinguish' the injurious effects of dumped imports from those of other known causal factors of the injury? What is a cumulative analysis within the meaning of Article 3.3 of the *Anti-Dumping Agreement*? Are investigating authorities permitted to apply such analysis?

6   ANTI-DUMPING INVESTIGATION

The *Anti-Dumping Agreement* sets out, in considerable detail, how investigating authorities of WTO Members have to initiate and conduct an anti-dumping investigation. This section addresses in turn: (1) the initiation of an anti-dumping investigation; and (2) the conduct of an investigation.

6.1   Initiation of an Investigation

Article 5 of the *Anti-Dumping Agreement* contains numerous requirements concerning the initiation of an anti-dumping investigation. The domestic investigating authorities can instigate an investigation on their own initiative. However,

---

155 Appellate Body Report, *EC – Tube or Pipe Fittings (2003)*, para. 109. Note that, with regard to the third requirement, the Appellate Body ruled that: 'cumulation must be appropriate in the light of the conditions of competition: (i) between the imported products; and (ii) between the imported products and the like domestic product.' See *ibid*.

156 *Ibid*., para. 116. According to the Appellate Body, '[i]f, for example, the dumped imports from some countries are low in volume or are declining, an exclusively country-specific analysis may not identify the causal relationship between the dumped imports from those countries and the injury suffered by the domestic industry. The outcome may then be that, because imports from such countries could not *individually* be identified as causing injury, the dumped imports from these countries would not be subject to anti-dumping duties, even though they are in fact causing injury.' See *ibid*.

the *Anti-Dumping Agreement* specifies that investigations must *generally* be initiated on the basis of a written application submitted 'by or on behalf of' a domestic industry as defined in Article 4 of the *Anti-Dumping Agreement*.[157] Sufficient support for the application must therefore exist among domestic producers to warrant initiation.[158] The *Anti-Dumping Agreement* contains guidance relating to the required contents of the initiation request, including: (1) evidence of dumping; (2) evidence of injury to the domestic industry; and (3) evidence of a causal link between the dumped imports and the injury to the domestic industry. As the panel in *Mexico – Corn Syrup (2000)* stated and the panel in *Thailand – H-Beams (2001)* affirmed:

Article 5.2 does not require an application to contain analysis, but rather to contain information, in the sense of evidence, in support of allegations.[159]

The application must contain information that is 'reasonably available' to the applicant in accordance with Article 5.2.[160] Simple assertion, unsubstantiated by relevant evidence, cannot be considered to meet the requirements of this provision.[161] In considering the nature and extent of the information that must be provided in an application pursuant to Article 5.2(iv), the panel in *Mexico – Corn Syrup (2000)* stated:

Obviously, the quantity and quality of the information provided by the applicant need not be such as would be required in order to make a preliminary or final determination of injury. Moreover, the applicant need only provide such information as is 'reasonably available' to it with respect to the relevant factors. Since information regarding the factors and indices set out in Article 3.4 concerns the state of the domestic industry and its operations, such information would generally be available to applicants. Nevertheless, we note that an application which is consistent with the requirements of Article 5.2 will not necessarily contain sufficient evidence to justify initiation under Article 5.3.[162]

Article 5.3 of the *Anti-Dumping Agreement* requires that the investigating authorities examine the accuracy and adequacy of the evidence provided in the application to determine whether there is sufficient evidence to justify the

---

157 In *US – 1916 Act (Japan) (2000)*, the panel found a violation of Articles 4 and 5 of the *Anti-Dumping Agreement* because the 1916 Act did not require 'a minimum representation of a US industry in applications for the initiation of proceedings under the 1916 Act'. See Panel Report, *US – 1916 Act (Japan) (2000)*, paras. 6.255–6.261. See also Panel Report, *US – 1916 Act (EC) (2000)*, paras. 6.212–6.214.

158 An application is considered to have been made 'by or on behalf of the domestic industry' if it is supported by those domestic producers whose collective output makes up over 50 per cent of the total production of the like product produced by that portion of the domestic industry expressing support for or opposition to the application, *and* the domestic producers supporting the application account for at least 25 per cent of total domestic production of the like product. See Article 5.4 of the *Anti-Dumping Agreement*.

159 Panel Report, *Thailand – H-Beams (2001)*, para. 7.75, citing Panel Report, *Mexico – Corn Syrup (2000)*, para. 7.76.

160 As the panel in *US – Softwood Lumber V (2004)* found, this provision is not intended to require an applicant to submit *all* information that is reasonably available to it. The 'reasonably available' language is intended to avoid putting an undue burden on the applicant to submit information which is *not* reasonably available to it. See Panel Report, *US – Softwood Lumber V (2004)*, para. 7.54.

161 See Panel Report, *US – Softwood Lumber V (2004)*, para. 7.52.

162 Panel Report, *Mexico – Corn Syrup (2000)*, para. 7.74.

initiation of the investigation.[163] Statements and assertions unsubstantiated by any evidence cannot constitute sufficient evidence within the meaning of Article 5.3 of the *Anti-Dumping Agreement*.[164] However, in determining whether there is sufficient evidence to initiate an investigation, an investigating authority is not limited to the information contained in the application. The panel in *Guatemala – Cement II (2000)* noted:

> We have expressed the view that Articles 5.2 and 5.3 contain different obligations. One of the consequences of this difference in obligations is that investigating authorities need not content themselves with the information provided in the application but may gather information on their own in order to meet the standard of sufficient evidence for initiation in Article 5.3.[165]

With respect to the nature and extent of the evidence required to initiate an anti-dumping investigation, the panel in *Guatemala – Cement II (2000)* ruled:

> We do not of course mean to suggest that an investigating authority must have before it at the time it initiates an investigation evidence of dumping within the meaning of Article 2 of the quantity and quality that would be necessary to support a preliminary or final determination. An anti-dumping investigation is a process where certainty on the existence of all the elements necessary in order to adopt a measure is reached gradually as the investigation moves forward. However, the evidence must be such that an unbiased and objective investigating authority could determine that there was sufficient evidence of dumping within the meaning of Article 2 to justify initiation of an investigation.[166]

The same is true for the evidence on injury to the domestic industry and the causal link between dumped imports and injury.[167]

Article 5.5 of the *Anti-Dumping Agreement* requires that the investigating authorities 'avoid, unless a decision has been made to initiate an investigation, any publicizing of the application for the initiation of an investigation'. However, 'after receipt of a properly documented application and before proceeding to initiate an investigation, the authorities shall notify the government of the exporting Member concerned'.[168] There are also public notice requirements

---

163 The panel in *Mexico – Steel Pipes and Tubes (2007)* found that, although there is no express reference to evidence of 'dumping' or 'injury' or 'causation' in Article 5.3 of the *Anti-Dumping Agreement*, reading Article 5.3 in the context of Article 5.2 makes clear that the evidence to which Article 5.3 refers is the evidence in the application concerning dumping, injury and causation. See Panel Report, *Mexico – Steel Pipes and Tubes (2007)*, para. 7.21.

164 See Panel Report, *Argentina – Poultry Anti-Dumping Duties (2003)*, para. 7.60. See also Panel Report, *US – Softwood Lumber V (2004)*, para. 7.79; and Panel Report, *Mexico – Steel Pipes and Tubes (2007)*, para. 7.24.

165 Panel Report, *Guatemala – Cement II (2000)*, para. 8.62. See also Panel Report, *US – Softwood Lumber V (2004)*, para. 7.75.

166 Panel Report, *Guatemala – Cement II (2000)*, para. 8.35. See also Panel Report, *US – Softwood Lumber V (2004)*, para. 7.84; and Panel Report, *Mexico – Steel Pipes and Tubes (2007)*, para. 7.22.

167 Where an investigation is self-initiated by the authorities, the authorities may proceed only if they have sufficient evidence of dumping, injury and a causal link to justify the initiation of the investigation. See Article 5.6 of the *Anti-Dumping Agreement*.

168 See Article 5.5 of the *Anti-Dumping Agreement*. Several panels (*Guatemala – Cement I (1998)*; *Guatemala – Cement II (2000)*; *US – 1916 Act (EC) (2000)*; and *Thailand – H-Beams (2001)*) have considered the nature and extent of the obligation imposed by Article 5.5. See also *Recommendation Concerning the Timing of the Notification under Article 5.5*, adopted by the Committee on Anti-Dumping Practices on 29 October 1998, G/ADP/5, dated 3 November 1998.

concerning the initiation of an investigation in Article 12.1 of the *Anti-Dumping Agreement*.[169]

An application to initiate an anti-dumping investigation shall be rejected, and an investigation shall be terminated *promptly*, as soon as the investigating authorities are satisfied that there is not enough evidence either of dumping or of injury.[170] Moreover, in order to ensure that an unwarranted investigation is not continued, Article 5.8 provides for prompt termination of investigations in the event that: (1) the margin of dumping is *de minimis* (i.e. less than 2 per cent of the export price); and (2) the volume of imports from each country is *negligible* (i.e. normally less than 3 per cent of imports of the like product in the importing Member, unless countries accounting for less than 3 per cent *individually* account *collectively* for more than 7 per cent of imports of the like product in the importing Member).[171]

6.2   Conduct of the Investigation

Article 6 of the *Anti-Dumping Agreement* contains detailed rules concerning the process of the investigation, including evidentiary, informational and procedural elements. The Appellate Body in *EC – Tube or Pipe Fittings (2003)* stated:

> [W]e wish to underscore the importance of the obligations contained in Article 6 of the *Anti-Dumping Agreement*. This Article 'establishes a framework of procedural and due process obligations'. Its provisions 'set out evidentiary rules that apply *throughout* the course of the anti-dumping investigation, and provide also for due process rights that are enjoyed by "interested parties" *throughout* such an investigation'.[172]

Article 6.1 requires that all interested parties in an anti-dumping investigation be given *notice* of the information which the authorities require as well as ample *opportunity to present* in writing all evidence which parties consider relevant in respect of the investigation.[173] Domestic producers can control the timing of the submission of a request for initiation of an anti-dumping investigation

---

169 See below, pp. 721–3.

170 See Article 5.8 of the *Anti-Dumping Agreement*. See e.g. Panel Report, *Mexico – Steel Pipes and Tubes*, para. 7.61; Panel Report, *Mexico – Corn Syrup (2000)*, para. 7.99; Panel Report, *Guatemala – Cement II (2000)*, para. 8.75; Panel Report, *Argentina – Poultry Anti-Dumping Duties (2003)*, para. 7.112; and Appellate Body Report, *Mexico – Anti-Dumping Measures on Rice (2005)*, para. 208.

171 See Appellate Body Report, *Mexico – Anti-Dumping Measures on Rice (2005)*, paras. 217 *et seq.* and 305 *et seq.*

172 Appellate Body Report, *EC – Tube or Pipe Fittings (2003)*, para. 138.

173 On the requirement to give notice, see Panel Report, *Egypt – Steel Rebar (2002)*, para. 7.96; and Appellate Body Report, *Mexico – Anti-Dumping Measures on Rice (2005)*, para. 251. On the requirement to give ample opportunity to present evidence, see Panel Report, *Guatemala – Cement II (2002)*, paras. 8.119, 8.178 and 8.237–8.239; Panel Report, *US – Corrosion-Resistant Steel Sunset Review (2004)*, paras. 6.257–6.263; Panel Report, *US – Oil Country Tubular Goods Sunset Reviews (2004)*, paras. 7.107–7.128; Appellate Body Report, *US – Oil Country Tubular Goods Sunset Reviews (2004)*, para. 241; and Panel Report, *US – Oil Country Tubular Goods Sunset Reviews (Article 21.5 – Argentina) (2007)*, paras. 7.109–7.120. In *US – Oil Country Tubular Goods Sunset Reviews (2004)*, the Appellate Body emphasised that 'disregarding a respondent's evidence ... is incompatible with the respondent's right, under Article 6.1, to present evidence that it considers relevant in respect of the sunset review'. See Appellate Body Report, *US – Oil Country Tubular Goods Sunset Reviews (2004)*, para. 246.

as it is their complaint that triggers the authority's investigative process. The complaining producers therefore have an opportunity to gather the evidence necessary to support their complaint in advance. The responding parties, on the other hand, typically receive no notice until the initiation of the investigation. In practice, investigating authorities typically send interested parties 'questionnaires' in which they identify the information that they require in order to conduct the investigation.[174] Article 6.1.1 protects exporters and foreign producers by requiring investigating authorities to provide them with at least thirty days to reply to 'questionnaires', and by allowing that extensions should be granted whenever practicable, upon cause shown.[175] This indicates that the specific due process interest of exporters and foreign producers to be afforded an ample opportunity to respond has been expressly provided.[176] Article 6.2 also requires that interested parties be given 'a full opportunity for the defence of [their] interests'.[177] Finally, the proper interpretation of Article 6.1.1 must also take into considerations the interests of investigating authorities in controlling the investigative process and bringing investigations to a close within a stipulated period of time.[178]

Pursuant to Article 6.6 of the *Anti-Dumping Agreement*, an investigating authority must *generally* satisfy itself as to the accuracy of the information supplied by interested parties upon which its determinations are based.[179] The investigating authority will often verify the information supplied by on-site visits to review the records of the companies involved.[180] In this regard, the panel in *US – DRAMs (1999)* stated the following in support of its position that the text of Article 6.6 does *not* explicitly *require* verification of all information relied upon:

Article 6.6 simply requires Members to 'satisfy themselves as to the accuracy of the information'. In our view, Members could 'satisfy themselves as to the accuracy of the information' in a number of ways without proceeding to some type of formal verification,

---

174 The 'questionnaires' referred to in Article 6.1.1 are a particular type of document containing substantial requests for information, distributed early in an investigation, and through which the investigating authority solicits a substantial amount of information relating to the key aspects of the investigation that is to be conducted by the authority (that is, on dumping, injury, and causation). Appellate Body Report, *EC – Fasteners (2011)*, paras. 612–13.

175 Article 6.1 sets 'flexible' thirty-day minimum time-limits for submissions and responses to questionnaires from all interested parties. See Appellate Body Report, *US – Hot-Rolled Steel (2001)*, paras. 73–5, where the Appellate Body stated that pursuant to Article 6.1.1 investigating authorities may impose time-limits for questionnaire responses, that these time-limits are not necessarily absolute and immutable and that in appropriate circumstances these time-limits must be extended.

176 In *US – Oil Country Tubular Goods Sunset Reviews (2004)*, the Appellate Body stated: 'the "ample" and "full" opportunities guaranteed by Articles 6.1 and 6.2, respectively, cannot extend indefinitely and must, at some point, legitimately cease to exist ... Where the continued granting of opportunities to present evidence and attend hearings would impinge on an investigating authority's ability to "control the conduct" of its inquiry and to "carry out the multiple steps" required to reach a timely completion of the sunset review, a respondent will have reached the limit of the "ample" and "full" opportunities provided for in Articles 6.1 and 6.2.' See Appellate Body Report, *US – Oil Country Tubular Goods Sunset Reviews (2004)*, para. 242.

177 Appellate Body Report, *US – Oil Country Tubular Goods Sunset Reviews (2004)*, para. 246.

178 Appellate Body Report, *EC – Fasteners (2011)*, paras. 610–11.

179 See Panel Report, *Guatemala – Cement II (2000)*, paras. 8.173–8.174.

180 See Annex I to the *Anti-Dumping Agreement* on 'Procedures for on-the-spot investigations pursuant to paragraph 7 of Article 6'.

including for example reliance on the reputation of the original source of the information. Indeed, we consider that anti-dumping investigations would become totally unmanageable if investigating authorities were required to actually verify the accuracy of all information relied on.[181]

To ensure the transparency of the anti-dumping investigation and proceedings, the investigating authorities must, according to Article 6.4 of the *Anti-Dumping Agreement*, provide timely opportunities for all interested parties to see all non-confidential information that is relevant to the presentation of *their* cases and used by the investigating authority.[182] Article 6.4 thus applies to a broad range of information that is used by an investigating authority in carrying out a required step in an anti-dumping investigation.[183] One of the stated objectives of the disclosure of information under Article 6.4 is to allow interested parties 'to prepare presentations on the basis of this information'.[184] Note, however, that an investigating authority's reasoning or internal deliberation is not subject to the obligation under Article 6.4.[185] Also note that Article 6.5 of the *Anti-Dumping Agreement* requires that investigating authorities preserve the confidentiality of sensitive business information relating to the exporting firms and the domestic industry involved in the investigation.[186] The investigating authority must review whether a party requesting confidential treatment of information shows 'good cause' for such treatment.[187] As the Appellate Body stated in *EC – Fasteners (2011)*, the 'good cause' alleged must constitute a reason sufficient to justify the withholding of information both from the public and from the other parties interested in the investigation, who would otherwise have a right to view

---

181 Panel Report, *US – DRAMs (1999)*, para. 6.78. The panel in *US – DRAMs (1999)* questioned, for example, 'whether investigating authorities should be required to verify import statistics from a different government office' and 'whether investigating authorities should be required to verify "official" exchange rates obtained from a central bank'. See *ibid.*, para. 6.78, footnote 513.

182 Article 6.4 of the *Anti-Dumping Agreement* defines what information is 'relevant' for the purposes of this provision. See e.g. Appellate Body Report, *EC – Fasteners (2011)*, para. 480.

183 Indeed, the broad range of information subject to the obligation under Article 6.4 may take various forms, including data submitted by the interested parties, and information that has been processed, organised, or summarised by the investigating authority. See Appellate Body Report, *EC – Fasteners (2011)*, para. 480.

184 See Appellate Body Report, *EC – Tube and Pipe Fittings (2003)*, para. 149. Article 6.2 confirms that access to all such information is important because, without such information, the interested parties may not have 'a full opportunity for the defence of their interests'. See *ibid.* As the Appellate Body explained in *EC – Fasteners (2011)*, the 'information' relevant to the presentation of an interested party's case can be a broader concept than the 'essential facts' within the meaning of Article 6.9 relied on by the authority, or they may overlap. See Appellate Body Report, *EC – Fasteners (2011)*, para. 483.

185 See *ibid.*, para. 480.

186 Article 6.5 of the *Anti-Dumping Agreement* protects information which is by its nature confidential (i.e. information of which the disclosure would, for example, be of significant competitive advantage to a competitor or would have a significantly adverse effect upon a person supplying the information) or information which has been supplied on a confidential basis by the parties to the investigation. However, regardless of the type of confidential information, good cause must be shown in order to qualify for confidential treatment. See Panel Report, *Guatemala – Cement II (2000)*, paras. 8.219–8.221; and Panel Report, *Korea – Certain Paper (2005)*, paras. 7.334–7.335.

187 See Panel Report, *Mexico – Steel Pipes and Tubes (2007)*, para. 7.382. As the Appellate Body stated in *EC – Fasteners (2011)*, the requirement to show 'good cause' for confidential treatment applies to both information that is 'by nature' confidential and that which is provided to the investigating authority 'on a confidential basis'. See Appellate Body Report, *EC – Fasteners (2011)*, para. 536.

this information.[188] When investigating authorities grant confidential treatment, they shall require interested parties to furnish non-confidential summaries in sufficient detail to permit a reasonable understanding of the substance of the information submitted in confidence.[189] All interested parties enjoy certain rights to participate in the proceedings and to make presentations.[190] In addition, investigating authorities must provide opportunities for industrial users of the product under investigation and for representative consumer organisations, in cases where the product is commonly sold at the retail level, to provide information which is relevant to the investigation regarding dumping, injury and causation.[191]

Hardly surprisingly, under the *Anti-Dumping Agreement* it is preferred that investigating authorities base their determinations on 'first-hand information'. The Agreement does not, however, allow any party to hold an investigating authority hostage by not providing the necessary information, and thus provides that 'second-best information' from secondary sources may be used in certain well-defined circumstances.[192] Article 6.8 of, and Annex II to, the *Anti-Dumping Agreement* identify the circumstances in which investigating authorities may overcome a lack of information, in the responses of the interested parties, by using 'facts' which are otherwise 'available' to the investigating authorities, i.e. the 'best information available'.[193] As the Appellate Body noted in *Mexico – Anti-Dumping Measures on Rice (2007)*:

[W]e understand that an investigating authority in an anti-dumping investigation may rely on the facts available to calculate margins for a respondent that failed to provide some or all of the necessary information requested by the agency. In so doing, however, the agency must first have made the respondent aware that it may be subject to a margin calculated on the basis of the facts available because of the respondent's failure to provide necessary information. Furthermore, assuming a respondent acted to the best of its ability, an agency must generally use, in the first instance, the information the respondent did provide, if any.[194]

---

188   See Appellate Body Report, *EC – Fasteners (2011)*, para. 538. A wide range of reasons could constitute 'good cause' justifying confidential treatment of information. For example, an advantage being bestowed on a competitor, or inflicting an adverse effect on the submitting party or the party from which it was acquired, may constitute 'good cause' which could justify the non-disclosure of confidential information. See *ibid.* Thus, 'the risk of a potential consequence [must be demonstrated], the avoidance of which is important enough to warrant the non-disclosure of the information'. Appellate Body Report, *EC – Fasteners (2011)*, paras. 537–40.

189   See Article 6.5.1 of the *Anti-Dumping Agreement*. See also Appellate Body Report, *EC – Fasteners (2011)*, para. 542. In exceptional circumstances, parties may indicate that such information is not susceptible of summary. In such exceptional circumstances, a statement of the reasons why summarisation is not possible must be provided. See Appellate Body Report, *EC – Fasteners (2011)*, paras. 535 and 543–4.

190   Article 6.13 of the *Anti-Dumping Agreement* requires investigating authorities to take due account of the difficulties interested parties, in particular small companies, may experience in supplying information. Investigating authorities must provide interested parties with any assistance practicable.

191   See Article 6.12 of the *Anti-Dumping Agreement*.

192   See Panel Report, *Mexico – Anti-Dumping Measures on Rice (2005)*, para. 7.238.

193   If the producer submits information meeting the requirements of Annex II, para. 3, no use may be made of 'best information available' under Article 6.8. See Panel Report, *EC – Salmon (Norway) (2008)*, paras. 7.371–7.372.

194   Appellate Body Report, *Mexico – Anti-Dumping Measures on Rice (2005)*, para. 288.

Moreover, in *US – Hot-Rolled Steel (2001)*, the Appellate Body held:

According to Article 6.8, where the interested parties do not 'significantly impede' the investigation, recourse may be had to facts available only if an interested party fails to submit necessary information 'within a reasonable period'. Thus, if information is, in fact, supplied 'within a reasonable period', the investigating authorities cannot use facts available, but must use the information submitted by the interested party.[195]

In *EC – Fasteners (2011)*, the Appellate Body reaffirmed its ruling in *US – Hot-Rolled Steel (2001)*, and added that what is a reasonable period in one set of circumstances may prove to be less than reasonable in different circumstances. What is 'reasonable' must be defined on a case-by-case basis, in light of the specific circumstances of each investigation.[196]

Paragraph 7 of Annex II to the *Anti-Dumping Agreement* indicates that a lack of 'cooperation' by an interested party may, by virtue of the use made of facts available, lead to a result that is 'less favourable' to the interested party than would have been the case had that interested party cooperated. In *US – Hot-Rolled Steel (2001)*, the Appellate Body cautioned, however, that investigating authorities should not arrive at a 'less favourable' outcome simply because an interested party fails to furnish requested information if, in fact, the interested party has 'cooperated' with the investigating authorities. Parties may very well 'cooperate' to a high degree, even though the requested information is, ultimately, not obtained.[197] The Appellate Body noted:

In order to complete their investigations, investigating authorities are entitled to expect a very significant degree of effort – to the 'best of their abilities' – from investigated exporters. At the same time, however, the investigating authorities are not entitled to insist upon *absolute* standards or impose *unreasonable* burdens upon those exporters.[198]

It is the common practice of WTO Members to conduct an anti-dumping investigation using data from a fixed 'period of investigation' which precedes the date of initiation of an investigation. The *Anti-Dumping Agreement* refers to the concept of a 'period of investigation', and the use of such a period appears to be implicit in several provisions of the Agreement.[199] As discussed above, the panel

195 Appellate Body Report, *US – Hot-Rolled Steel (2001)*, para. 77. See also Panel Report, *Guatemala – Cement II (2000)*, para. 8.255, in which the panel found that recourse to the 'best information available' was not warranted because the exporter had *not* impeded the investigation. See also Panel Report, *US – Steel Plate (2002)*, para. 7.55; Panel Report *Egypt – Steel Rebar (2002)*, para. 7.147; Panel Report, *Argentina – Poultry Anti-Dumping Duties (2003)*, para. 7.187; Panel Report, *Korea – Certain Paper (2005)*, para. 7.75; and Appellate Body Report *Mexico – Anti-Dumping Measures on Rice (2005)*, para. 259.
196 Appellate Body Report, *US – Hot-Rolled Steel (2001)*, para. 84. In considering whether information is submitted within a reasonable period of time, 'investigating authorities should consider, in the context of a particular case, factors such as: (i) the nature and quantity of the information submitted; (ii) the difficulties encountered by an investigated exporter in obtaining the information; (iii) the verifiability of the information and the ease with which it can be used by the investigating authorities in making their determination; (iv) whether other interested parties are likely to be prejudiced if the information is used; (v) whether acceptance of the information would compromise the ability of the investigating authorities to conduct the investigation expeditiously; and (vi) the numbers of days by which the investigated exporter missed the applicable time-limit.' See Appellate Body Report, *US – Hot-Rolled Steel (2001)*, para. 85.
197 See Appellate Body Report, *US – Hot-Rolled Steel (2001)*, para. 99.
198 *Ibid.*, para. 102.   199 For example, Articles 2.4.2 and 2.2.1 of the *Anti-Dumping Agreement*.

in *Mexico – Anti-Dumping Measures on Rice (2007)* concluded that, by choosing to base its determination of injury on a period of investigation that ended more than fifteen months before the initiation of the investigation, Mexico acted inconsistently with the obligation in Article 3.1 of the *Anti-Dumping Agreement* to make a determination of injury an objective examination of positive evidence.[200]

The Appellate Body in *EC – Tube or Pipe Fittings (2003)* agreed with the panel in that case that:

> [d]iscretionary selection of data from a period of time within [a period of investigation] ... would defeat the objectives underlying investigating authorities' reliance on [such a period]. As the Panel correctly noted, the [period of investigation] 'form[s] the basis for an objective and unbiased determination by the investigating authority'.[201]

The Appellate Body further noted:

> [W]e understand a [period of investigation] to provide data collected over a sustained period of time, which period can allow the investigating authority to make a dumping determination that is less likely to be subject to market fluctuations or other vagaries that may distort a proper evaluation. We agree with the Panel that the standardized reliance on a [period of investigation], although not fixed in duration by the *Anti-Dumping Agreement*, assures the investigating authority and exporters of 'a consistent and reasonable methodology for determining present dumping', which anti-dumping duties are intended to offset.[202]

The WTO Committee on Anti-Dumping Practices has adopted a *Recommendation Concerning the Periods of Data Collection for Anti-Dumping Investigations*.[203] Pursuant to this Recommendation, the period of data collection for *dumping investigations* normally should not exceed twelve months and, in any case, be no less than six months, ending as close to the date of initiation as is practicable. Furthermore, the period of data collection for *injury investigations* normally should be at least three years, unless a party from whom data is being gathered has existed for a shorter period, and should include the entirety of the period of data collection for the dumping investigation.[204]

Finally, note with regard to the conduct of an anti-dumping investigation that Article 5.10 of the *Anti-Dumping Agreement* specifies that such investigation must be completed within one year, and in no case be more than eighteen months, after initiation.

Questions and Assignments 11.10

How is an anti-dumping investigation initiated? On what basis does an investigating authority decide to initiate an investigation? How does the *Anti-Dumping Agreement* ensure that unwarranted investigations are not continued? What is the 'period of investigation' in

---

200 See Panel Report, *Mexico – Anti-Dumping Measures on Rice (2005)*, para. 7.65. See also above, p. 700–1.
201 Appellate Body Report, *EC – Tube or Pipe Fittings (2003)*, para. 80.
202 *Ibid.*
203 G/ADP/6, adopted by the Committee on Anti-Dumping Practices on 5 May 2000.
204 While it reflects the common practice of Members, the Recommendation does not have binding effect. See E. Vermulst, The WTO Anti-Dumping Agreement: A Commentary (Oxford University Press, 2006), 82–3.

anti-dumping investigations? Can or should the period of investigation differ from case to case depending on the facts? How are interested parties involved in an anti-dumping investigation? Are there any specific rules on the involvement of consumer organisations? When may investigating authorities make use of 'best information available' within the meaning of Article 6.8 of, and Annex II to, the *Anti-Dumping Agreement*? Is it recommendable for an interested party not to cooperate with the investigating authorities in the context of an anti-dumping investigation? Within what timeframe must investigating authorities complete an anti-dumping investigation?

6.3 Public Notice and Judicial Review

Article 6.9 and Article 12 of the *Anti-Dumping Agreement* both concern the transparency of the anti-dumping investigations and the conclusions reached. Both provisions require notice to be given to interested parties and/or the general public.

Article 6.9 of the *Anti-Dumping Agreement* requires investigating authorities, before a final determination is made, to inform all interested parties of the 'essential facts under consideration' which form the basis for the decision whether to apply definitive measures.[205] 'Essential facts' refer to those facts that are significant in the process of reaching a decision as to whether or not to apply definitive measures. Such facts are those that are salient for a decision to apply definitive measures, as well as those that are salient for a contrary outcome. An authority must disclose such facts, in a coherent way, so as to permit an interested party to understand the basis for the decision whether or not to apply definitive measures.[206] As the Appellate Body stated in *China – GOES (2012)*, disclosing the essential facts under consideration pursuant to Article 6.9 is paramount for ensuring the ability of the parties concerned to defend their interests and, therefore, such disclosure should take place in sufficient time for the parties to do so.[207]

Article 12 of the *Anti-Dumping Agreement* contains detailed requirements for public notice by investigating authorities of: (1) the initiation of an investigation (see Article 12.1.1); (2) a preliminary determination (see Article 12.2.1); (3) a final determination (see Article 12.2.2); and (4) a price undertaking (see Article 12.2.2). While the disclosure of 'essential facts' under Article 6.9 must take place *before* a final determination is made, the obligation to give public

---

205 As to the type of information that must be disclosed, Article 6.9 covers 'facts under consideration' in the course of such investigations 'before a final determination is made'. These are facts on the record that may be taken into account by an authority in reaching a decision as to whether or not to apply definitive anti-dumping duties. Article 6.9 does not require the disclosure of *all* the facts that are before an authority but, instead, those that are 'essential', i.e. facts that are significant, important, or salient. See Appellate Body Report, *China – GOES (2012)*, para. 240.

206 As discussed above, in order to apply definitive measures at the conclusion of an anti-dumping investigation, an investigating authority must find dumping, injury to the domestic industry and a causal link between dumping and injury. What constitutes an 'essential fact' must therefore be understood in light of the content of the findings needed to satisfy the substantive obligations with respect to the imposition of definitive measures under the *Anti-Dumping Agreement*, as well as the factual circumstances of each case.

207 See Appellate Body Report, *China – GOES (2012)*, para. 240.

notice of the conclusion of an investigation within the meaning of Article 12.2.2, for example, is triggered *once there is* an affirmative determination providing for the imposition of definitive duties.[208] The purpose of this public notice requirement set out in Article 12 is to increase the transparency of the determinations made by the investigating authorities and to encourage solid and thorough reasoning substantiating such determinations. The public notice of a final determination, for example, *must* set forth, or otherwise make available through a separate report, in sufficient detail, the findings and conclusions reached on all issues of fact and law considered material by the investigating authorities.[209] In particular, the notice or report *must* contain: (1) the names of the suppliers, or, when this is impracticable, the supplying countries involved; (2) a description of the product which is sufficient for customs purposes; (3) the margins of dumping established and a full explanation of the reasons for the methodology used in the establishment and comparison of the export price and the normal value under Article 2; (4) considerations relevant to the injury determination as set out in Article 3; and (5) the main reasons leading to the determination.[210] The Appellate Body explained in *China – GOES (2012)*, with regard to 'matters of fact', that Article 12.2.2 does not require authorities to disclose *all* the factual information that is before them, but rather those facts that allow an understanding of the factual basis that led to the imposition of final measures. The inclusion of this information should therefore give a reasoned account of the factual support for an authority's decision to impose final measures. Furthermore, the notice or report *must* set out the reasons for the acceptance or rejection of relevant legal arguments or claims made by the exporters and importers.[211] The consistency of notices or reports with the requirements of Article 12.2 of the *Anti-Dumping Agreement* at issue in many disputes.[212] In *EC – Tube or Pipe Fittings (2003)*, for example, the panel found that the European Communities acted inconsistently with Articles 12.2 and 12.2.2 of the *Anti-Dumping Agreement*:

[i]n that it is not directly discernible from the published Provisional or Definitive Determination that the European Communities addressed or explained the lack of significance of certain listed Article 3.4 factors.[213]

---

208 See Article 12.2.2 in conjunction with Article 12.2.1 of the *Anti-Dumping Agreement*.

209 See Article 12.2.2 of the *Anti-Dumping Agreement*. Note, however, that Article 12.2.2 does require that due regard be paid to the requirement to protect confidential information.

210 See Article 12.2.2 in conjunction with Article 12.2.1 of the *Anti-Dumping Agreement*. As discussed above, the imposition of final anti-dumping duties requires that an authority finds dumping, injury to the domestic industry, and a causal link between dumping and injury. Therefore, what constitutes 'relevant information on the matters of fact' is to be understood in light of the content of the findings needed to satisfy the substantive requirements with respect to the imposition of final measures under the *Anti-Dumping Agreement*, as well as the factual circumstances of each case. See Appellate Body Report, *China – GOES (2012)*, paras. 256–7.

211 Article 12.2.2 of the *Anti-Dumping Agreement*.

212 See Panel Report, *EC – Tube or Pipe Fittings (2003)*, para. 7.435.

213 Appellate Body Report, *China – GOES (2012)*, para. 258. With respect to the form in which the relevant information must be disclosed, Article 12.2.2 allows authorities to decide whether to include the information in the public notice itself or otherwise make it available through a separate report. See also *ibid.*, para. 259.

In *China – GOES (2012)*, the Appellate Body took the view that Article 12.2.2 captures the principle that those parties whose interests are affected by the imposition of final anti-dumping duties are entitled to know, as a matter of fairness and due process, the facts, law and reasons that have led to the imposition of such duties. The Appellate Body stated in that case:

> The obligation of disclosure under Article 12.2.2 is framed by the requirement of 'relevance', which entails the disclosure of the matrix of facts, law and reasons that logically fit together to render the decision to impose final measures. By requiring the disclosure of 'all relevant information' regarding these categories of information, the provision seeks to guarantee that interested parties are able to pursue judicial review of a final determination as provided in Article 13 of the *Anti-Dumping Agreement*.[214]

As provided for in Article 13, entitled 'Judicial Review', each Member whose national legislation contains provisions on anti-dumping measures must maintain judicial, arbitral or administrative tribunals or procedures to ensure *inter alia*, the prompt review of administrative actions relating to final determinations and reviews of determinations. Such tribunals or procedures must be independent of the authorities responsible for the determination or review in question.[215]

7 ANTI-DUMPING MEASURES

The *Anti-Dumping Agreement* provides for three kinds of anti-dumping measures: (1) provisional measures; (2) price undertakings; and (3) definitive anti-dumping duties. This section discusses the rules on the imposition of each of these measures. It also addresses the issues of the duration, termination and review of definitive anti-dumping duties.

7.1 Imposition of Provisional Anti-Dumping Measures

Article 7 of the *Anti-Dumping Agreement* contains rules relating to the imposition of provisional measures. Before applying a provisional anti-dumping measure, investigating authorities must make a *preliminary* affirmative determination of dumping, injury and causation.[216] Furthermore, the investigating authorities must judge that such a measure is *necessary* to prevent injury being caused during the investigation. A provisional measure cannot be applied earlier than sixty days following the initiation of the investigation.[217] Provisional measures may take the form of a provisional duty or, preferably, a security, by cash deposit or bond, equal to the amount of the preliminarily determined margin of dumping.[218]

---

214 See Article 13 of the *Anti-Dumping Agreement*.   215 See *ibid.*, Article 7.1(ii).
216 See *ibid.*, Article 7.1(iii).   217 See *ibid.*, Article 7.3.   218 See *ibid.*, Article 7.2.

With regard to the time period for application of the provisional measure, Article 7.4 of the *Anti-Dumping Agreement* states that it:

[s]hall be limited to as short a period as possible, not exceeding four months or, on decision of the authorities concerned, upon request by exporters representing a significant percentage of the trade involved, to a period not exceeding six months.

Where the Member applies the 'lesser duty rule' in its administration of anti-dumping duties, the period of provisional application is generally six months, with the possibility of extension to nine months upon request of the exporters.[219]

7.2   Price Undertakings

Article 8 of the *Anti-Dumping Agreement* provides for the option of offering and accepting price undertakings as an alternative to the imposition of anti-dumping duties. Undertakings to revise prices or cease exports at the dumped price may be entered into only after the investigating authorities have made an *affirmative preliminary determination* of dumping, injury and causation. Such undertakings are voluntary on the part of both exporters and investigating authorities.[220] An exporter may request that the investigation be continued after the acceptance of an undertaking. The undertaking would then automatically lapse in the event of a negative final determination of dumping, injury or causation.[221]

Questions and Assignments 11.11

When can provisional anti-dumping measures be imposed according to the *Anti-Dumping Agreement*? What form can these provisional measures take? For how long can provisional anti-dumping measures be applied? What are price undertakings within the meaning of Article 8 of the *Anti-Dumping Agreement*? When can such price undertakings be agreed on?

7.3   Imposition and Collection of Anti-Dumping Duties

Article 9 of the *Anti-Dumping Agreement* governs the imposition and collection of anti-dumping duties. This provision establishes the general principle that 'it is desirable' that, even where all the requirements for imposition of duties have been fulfilled, the imposition of anti-dumping duties remains *optional*. Article 9 also contains the so-called 'lesser duty rule', under which 'it is desirable' that

---

219 On the 'lesser duty rule', see below, pp. 724–5. On the question of the allowable duration of a provisional measure, see Panel Report, *Mexico – Corn Syrup (2000)*, paras. 7.182–7.183.

220 Exporters and investigating authorities may enter into price undertakings over the opposition of the domestic industry. See Panel Report, *US – Offset Act (Byrd Amendment) (2003)*, paras. 7.79 *et seq.*

221 Article 8.6 of the *Anti-Dumping Agreement* sets out consequences of violation of an undertaking.

the duty imposed be *less* than the margin of dumping *if* such lesser duty would be *adequate* to remove the injury to the domestic industry.[222]

Article 9.2 of the *Anti-Dumping Agreement* requires Members to collect anti-dumping duties on a *non-discriminatory* basis on imports from 'all sources' found to be dumped and causing injury.[223] The MFN treatment obligation thus applies to the collection of anti-dumping duties.[224] The competent national authorities should name the supplier or suppliers of the products affected by the anti-dumping duty. However, if several suppliers from the same country are involved, and it is impracticable to name all these suppliers, the authorities may just name the supplying country concerned. If several suppliers from more than one country are involved, the authorities may either name all the suppliers involved or, if this is impracticable, all the supplying countries involved.[225]

Pursuant to Article 9.3 of the *Anti-Dumping Agreement*, the anti-dumping duty collected *shall not exceed* the dumping margin. As the Appellate Body stated in *US – Zeroing (Japan) (2007)*:

Under any system of duty collection, the margin of dumping established in accordance with Article 2 operates as a ceiling for the amount of anti-dumping duties that could be collected in respect of the sales made by an exporter. To the extent that duties are paid by an importer, it is open to that importer to claim a refund if such a ceiling is exceeded. Similarly, under its retrospective system of duty collection, the United States is free to assess duty liability on a transaction-specific basis, but the total amount of anti-dumping duties that are levied must not exceed the exporters' or foreign producers' margins of dumping.[226]

The Agreement lays down the 'margin of dumping' as the *ceiling* for collection of duties regardless of whether the duties are assessed 'retrospectively' or 'prospectively'.[227] In case the ceiling is exceeded, the Agreement provides for a refund obligation.[228]

---

222 The European Union applies the 'lesser duty rule'; the United States usually does not. See P. F. J. Macrory, 'The Anti-Dumping Agreement', in P. Macrory, A. Appleton and M. Plummer (eds.), *The World Trade Organization: Legal, Economic and Political Analysis* (Springer, 2005), 519.

223 See Article 9.2 of the *Anti-Dumping Agreement*. Note, however, that the anti-dumping duty will not be applied to imports from sources in respect of which a price undertaking is in force.

224 See above, pp. 36–7; 321–3. The Appellate Body noted in *EC – Fasteners (2011)* that the term 'all sources', as used in Article 9.2, 'refers to individual exporters or producers and not to the country as a whole'. See Appellate Body Report, *EC – Fasteners (2011)*, para. 338.

225 See Article 9.2 of the *Anti-Dumping Agreement*.

226 Appellate Body Report, *US – Zeroing (Japan) (2007)*, para. 162.

227 *Ibid.*, para. 163. See also Appellate Body Report, *US – Stainless Steel (Mexico) (2008)*, paras. 102, 114 and 133; Appellate Body Report, *US – Zeroing (EC) (2006)*, para. 131; and Appellate Body Report, *US – Softwood Lumber V (Article 21.5 – Canada) (2006)*, para. 108. Which mechanism for duty assessment a Member opts to use will depend on whether the Member collects the anti-dumping duties on a prospective basis (i.e. where a Member collects the duty at the time of importation – as is the case for the European Union) or on a retrospective basis (i.e. where a Member calculates a specific amount of anti-dumping duty to be paid only after permitting importation and collecting an estimated duty – as the United States does). See further Articles 9.3.1 and 9.3.2 of the *Anti-Dumping Agreement*. As the Appellate Body has repeatedly ruled, the *Anti-Dumping Agreement* is neutral as between different systems for levy and collection of anti-dumping duties. See Appellate Body Report, *US – Zeroing (Japan) (2007)*, para. 156.

228 See Appellate Body Report, *US – Zeroing (Japan) (2007)*, para. 163.

When anti-dumping duties are imposed, pursuant to Article 6.10 of the *Anti-Dumping Agreement*, the investigating authorities must, 'as a rule', calculate a dumping margin for each known exporter or producer of the product under investigation. However, Article 6.10 recognises that this may not always be possible.[229] As set out in the second sentence of Article 6.10, it may not be possible to determine individual dumping margins in cases where the number of exporters, producers, importers or types of products is so large as to make such determinations impracticable. In such cases, the authorities may deviate from the obligation to determine individual anti-dumping margins for all known exporters or producers, and may limit their examination either: (1) to a reasonable number of interested parties or products by using samples, which are statistically valid; or (2) to the largest percentage of the volume of exports from the country in question that can reasonably be investigated. This limited examination is generally referred to as 'sampling'.[230] When 'sampling' is used, the anti-dumping duty imposed on exporters or producers not examined individually is calculated – in accordance with the first sentence of Article 9.4 of the *Anti-Dumping Agreement* – on the basis of the *weighted average dumping margin* actually established for individually investigated exporters or producers, commonly referred to as the 'all others' rate.[231] However, the investigating authorities: (1) must not include in this weighted average calculation any dumping margins that are *de minimis*, zero or based on the 'facts available'; and (2) must calculate an individual margin for any exporter or producer who provides the necessary information during the course of the investigation.[232] With respect to the 'all others' rate applied to sources not examined individually, the Appellate Body stated in *US – Hot-Rolled Steel (2001)*:

Article 9.4 does not prescribe any method that WTO Members must use to establish the 'all others' rate that is actually applied to exporters or producers that are not investigated. Rather, Article 9.4 simply identifies a maximum limit, or ceiling, which investigating authorities '*shall not exceed*' in establishing an 'all others' rate.[233]

229 This will be the case when the number of exporters, producers, importers or types of products concerned is considerable. The Appellate Body noted, in *EC – Fasteners (2011)*, that the obligation in Article 6.10 (see the use of the word 'shall') is qualified by the use of the term 'as a rule'. The use of this term indicates that the obligation in Article 6.10 is not absolute, and foreshadows the possibility of exceptions. The Appellate Body added, however, that, while the term 'as a rule' should be read as modifying the obligation to determine individual margins, it does not render it a mere preference. Otherwise, the use of 'shall' in the first sentence would be deprived of its ordinary meaning. See Appellate Body Report, *EC – Fasteners (2011)*, para. 317.

230 Even where a statistically valid sample is not used but the second alternative for limiting the examination is applied, such examination is commonly referred to as 'sampling'. See Appellate Body Report, *EC – Fasteners (2011)*, para. 318. 'Sampling' is the only exception to the determination of individual dumping margins that is expressly provided for in Article 6.10. See *ibid*.

231 Note, in this context, Panel Report, *Korea – Certain Paper (2005)*, para. 7.171.

232 See Article 9.4 of the *Anti-Dumping Agreement*. Also, when a dumping margin was calculated, even if only to a very limited extent, on the basis of 'facts available' pursuant to Article 6.8 of the *Anti-Dumping Agreement*, this dumping margin may not be used to calculate the 'all others' rate. See Appellate Body Report, *US – Hot-Rolled Steel (2001)*, paras. 122–3.

233 Appellate Body Report, *US – Hot-Rolled Steel (2011)*, para. 116. Article 9.4 of the *Anti-Dumping Agreement* seeks to prevent exporters who were not asked to cooperate in the investigation from being prejudiced by gaps or shortcomings in the information supplied by the investigated exporters. See *ibid*., para. 123. The Appellate Body explained that this *lacuna* arises because, while Article 9.4 *prohibits* the use of certain margins in the calculation of the ceiling for the 'all others' rate, it does not expressly address the issue of *how* that

With respect to the individual margin of dumping for producers or exporters who were not sources of imports considered during the period of investigation, commonly referred to as 'new shippers', Article 9.5 of the *Anti-Dumping Agreement* provides that:

[t]he authorities shall promptly carry out a review for the purpose of determining individual margins of dumping.

The investigating authorities must therefore conduct an expedited review to determine a specific margin of dumping for exports from such 'new shippers'. No anti-dumping duties may be levied on imports from such exporters or producers while the review is being carried out.[234]

Article 10 of the *Anti-Dumping Agreement* establishes the general principle that both provisional and definitive duties may be applied only as of the date on which the preliminary or final determinations of dumping, injury and causation have been made.[235] *Retroactive application* of anti-dumping duties is thus, in principle, prohibited. However, Article 10 contains rules for the retroactive application of anti-dumping duties in specific circumstances. According to Article 10.2, where the imposition of the anti-dumping duty is based on a determination of material injury – as opposed to a threat thereof, or material retardation – the duties may be collected as of the date of imposition of the provisional measures.[236] If provisional duties were collected in an amount exceeding the amount of the final duty or if the imposition of duties is based on a finding of threat of material injury or of material retardation, a refund of provisional duties is necessary.[237] Article 10.6 also permits retroactive application of final anti-dumping duties in exceptional circumstances. These exceptional circumstances involve: (1) a history of dumping which caused injury; *or* a situation in which the importer was, or should have been, aware that the exporter practises injurious dumping; and (2) the injury is caused by massive dumped imports in a short time which is likely to undermine the remedial effect of the definitive anti-dumping duty (this may be the case because of a rapid and massive build-up of stocks of the imported product).[238] In these circumstances, Article 10.6 permits *retroactive*

---

ceiling should be calculated in the event that *all* margins are to be *excluded* from the calculation, under the prohibitions in Article 9.4. See Appellate Body Report, *US – Hot-Rolled Steel (2001)*, para. 126.

234 See Article 9.5 of the *Anti-Dumping Agreement*. The authorities may, however, withhold appraisal and/or request guarantees to ensure that, if necessary, anti-dumping duties can be levied retroactively to the date of the initiation of the review. See also Appellate Body Report, *Mexico – Anti-Dumping Measures on Rice (2005)*, paras. 323–4. Finally, the Appellate Body found zeroing in calculating dumping margins for new shippers to be inconsistent with Article 9.5 of the *Anti-Dumping Agreement*. See Appellate Body Report, *US – Zeroing (Japan) (2007)*, para. 165.

235 See Article 10.1 of the *Anti-Dumping Agreement*.

236 Also, in the case of a final determination of a threat of injury, where the effect of the dumped imports would, in the absence of the provisional measures, have led to a determination of injury, the anti-dumping duties may be applied retroactively for the period for which provisional measures, if any, have been applied. See Article 10.2 of the *Anti-Dumping Agreement*.

237 See Article 10.3 of the *Anti-Dumping Agreement*. Note, however, that, if the final anti-dumping duty is higher than the provisional duty, the difference may *not* be collected.

238 See Article 10.6 of the *Anti-Dumping Agreement*.

application of final duties to a date not earlier than ninety days prior to the application of provisional measures.[239]

Questions and Assignments 11.12

What is the 'lesser duty rule' of Article 9 of the *Anti-Dumping Agreement*? Are Members required to collect anti-dumping duties on imports from all sources and all exporters and producers found to be dumped and causing injury? Will the competent authority have to name the supplier or suppliers of the products affected by the anti-dumping duty *or* will it simply name the supplying country concerned? Does it matter for the imposition and collection of anti-dumping duties whether the duties are assessed 'retrospectively' or 'prospectively'? Must investigating authorities calculate a dumping margin for each exporter or producer (i.e. each source) of the dumped product? What is the maximum amount of anti-dumping duty that may, pursuant to Article 9.4 of the *Anti-Dumping Agreement*, be imposed on sources not investigated individually? Can anti-dumping duties be applied retroactively? Can anti-dumping duties be levied prior to the date of initiation of an anti-dumping investigation?

7.4 Duration, Termination and Review of Anti-Dumping Duties

Responding to the concern of some Members that some countries were leaving anti-dumping duties in place indefinitely, Article 11 of the *Anti-Dumping Agreement* establishes rules governing the duration of anti-dumping duties and a requirement for the periodic review of any continuing necessity for the imposition of anti-dumping duties. With respect to the duration of anti-dumping duties, Article 11.1 of the *Anti-Dumping Agreement* provides:

An anti-dumping duty shall remain in force only as long as and to the extent necessary to counteract dumping which is causing injury.[240]

The Appellate Body considered in *US – Anti-Dumping Measures on Oil Country Tubular Goods (2005)* that:

Article 11.1 of the Agreement establishes an overarching principle for 'duration' and 'review' of anti-dumping duties in force ... This principle applies during the entire life of an anti-dumping duty. If, at any point in time, it is demonstrated that no injury is being caused to the domestic industry by the dumped imports, the rationale for the continuation of the duty would cease.[241]

With respect to the periodic review of anti-dumping duties applied, Article 11.2, first sentence, requires the investigating authorities to:

---

239 Note that Article 10.7 of the *Anti-Dumping Agreement* provides that: 'The authorities may, after initiating an investigation, take such measures ... *as may be necessary to collect* anti-dumping duties retroactively, as provided for in paragraph 6 ...' (emphasis added). Once the authorities have 'sufficient evidence' that the conditions of Article 10.6 are satisfied, they may take the conservatory or precautionary measures provided for in Article 10.7. On what constitutes 'sufficient evidence', and other issues relating to Articles 10.6 and 10.7, see Panel Report, *US – Hot-Rolled Steel (2001)*, paras. 7.143–7.144; and Panel Report, *Mexico – Corn Syrup (2000)*, paras. 7.190–7.191.

240 Article 11.2, last sentence, provides: 'If as a result of the review under [paragraph 2] the authorities determine that the anti-dumping duty is no longer warranted, it shall be terminated immediately.'

241 Appellate Body Report, *US – Anti-Dumping Measures on Oil Country Tubular Goods (2005)*, para. 115. See also Appellate Body Report, *US – Stainless Steel (Mexico) (2008)*, para. 93.

review the need for the continued imposition of the duty, where warranted, on their own initiative or, provided that a reasonable period of time has elapsed since the imposition of the definitive anti-dumping duty, upon request by any interested party which submits positive information substantiating the need for a review.[242]

The Appellate Body in *Mexico – Anti-Dumping Measures on Rice (2005)* found that:

Article 11.2 *requires* an agency to conduct a review, *inter alia*, at the request of an interested party, and to terminate the anti-dumping duty where the agency determines that the duty 'is no longer warranted'. The interested party has the right to request the authority to examine whether the continued imposition of the duty is necessary to offset dumping, whether the injury would be likely to continue or recur if the duty were removed or varied, or both. Article 11.2 conditions this obligation on (i) the passage of a reasonable period of time since imposition of the definitive duty; and (ii) the submission by the interested party of 'positive information' substantiating the need for a review. As the Panel correctly observed, this latter condition may be satisfied in a particular case with information not related to export volumes. Where the conditions in Article 11.2 have been met, the plain words of the provision make it clear that the agency has no discretion to refuse to complete a review, including consideration of whether the duty should be terminated in the light of the results of the review.[243]

The second sentence of Article 11.2 requires investigating authorities to examine whether the 'continued imposition' of the duty is necessary to offset dumping. The panel in *US – DRAMs (1999)* interpreted the second sentence as follows:

The word 'continued' covers a temporal relationship between past and future. In our view, the word 'continued' would be redundant if the investigating authority were restricted to considering only whether the duty was necessary to offset *present* dumping. Thus, the inclusion of the word 'continued' signifies that the investigating authority is entitled to examine whether imposition of the duty may be applied henceforth to offset dumping.[244]

Furthermore, with regard to injury, Article 11.2, second sentence, provides for a review of 'whether the injury would be likely to continue or recur if the duty were removed or varied'. The panel in *US – DRAMs (1999)* stated in this respect that:

[i]n conducting an Article 11.2 injury review, an investigating authority may examine the causal link between injury and dumped imports. If, in the context of a review of such a causal link, the only injury under examination is injury that may recur following revocation (i.e. future rather than present injury), an investigating authority must necessarily be examining whether that future injury would be caused by dumping with a commensurately prospective timeframe. To do so, the investigating authority would first need to have established a status regarding the prospects of dumping. For these reasons, we do not agree that Article 11.2 precludes *a priori* the justification of continued imposition of anti-dumping duties when there is no present dumping.

---

242 The determination of whether or not good and sufficient grounds exist for the self-initiation of a review necessarily depends upon the factual situation in a given case and will vary from case to case. See Panel Report, *EC – Tube or Pipe Fittings (2003)*, para. 7.115. Where an interested party requests a review, the need for the continued imposition of the duty must be demonstrable on the basis of the evidence adduced. See Panel Report, *US – DRAMs (2007)*, para. 6.42.

243 Appellate Body Report, *Mexico – Anti-Dumping Measures on Rice (2005)*, para. 314.

244 Panel Report, *US – DRAMs (1999)*, para. 6.27.

In addition, we note that there is nothing in the text of Article 11.2 of the [Anti-Dumping] Agreement that explicitly limits a Member to a 'present' analysis, and forecloses a prospective analysis, when conducting an Article 11.2 review.[245]

In other words, Article 11.2 does not preclude *a priori* continued imposition of anti-dumping duties in the *absence* of present dumping. However, it may also be clear from the plain meaning of the text of Article 11.2 that the continued imposition must still satisfy the 'necessity' standard, even where the need for the continued imposition of an anti-dumping duty is tied to the *recurrence* of dumping.[246]

Pursuant to Article 11.3 (the so-called 'sunset clause'), any definitive anti-dumping duty shall be *terminated* on a date not later than *five years* from its imposition,[247] *unless* the authorities determine, in a review initiated before that date, that the expiry of the duty 'would be likely to lead to continuation or recurrence of dumping and injury'.[248] Such a review is commonly referred to as a 'sunset review'. It can be initiated: (1) at the initiative of the investigating authorities; or (2) upon a duly substantiated request made by or on behalf of the domestic industry.[249] Any such review shall be carried out expeditiously and shall normally be concluded within twelve months of the date of initiation of the review.[250] In *US – Oil Country Tubular Goods Sunset Reviews (2004)*, the Appellate Body noted:

[A] decision not to terminate an anti-dumping duty must be based on determinations of likelihood of continuation or recurrence of dumping and likelihood of continuation or recurrence of injury.[251]

In *US – Corrosion-Resistant Steel Sunset Review (2004)*, the Appellate Body explained the difference between original investigations and sunset reviews:

In an original anti-dumping investigation, investigating authorities must determine whether *dumping exists* during the period of investigation. In contrast, in a sunset review of an

---

245 See *ibid.*, paras. 6.28–6.29.

246 See *ibid.*, para. 6.43. Note also that the panel in *US – DRAMs (1999)* found that, with regard to injury, an absence of dumping during the preceding three years and six months is not in and of itself indicative of the likely state of the relevant domestic industry if the duty were removed or varied. Likewise, with regard to causality, an absence of dumping during the preceding three years and six months is not in and of itself indicative of causal factors other than the absence of dumping. See *ibid.*, para. 6.59.

247 Or, alternatively, from the date of the most recent review under Article 11.2, if that review has covered both dumping and injury, or the date of the most recent review under Article 11.3.

248 The duty may remain in force pending the outcome of such a review. See Article 11.3 of the *Anti-Dumping Agreement*.

249 See *ibid.*

250 See *ibid.*, Article 11.4. The provisions of Article 6 of the *Anti-Dumping Agreement* regarding evidence and procedure shall apply to any review carried out under Article 11.

251 Appellate Body Report, *US – Oil Country Tubular Goods Sunset Reviews (2004)*, para. 323. In *US – Corrosion-Resistant Steel Sunset Review (2004)*, the Appellate Body agreed with the panel that Article 11.3 does not expressly prescribe any specific methodology for investigating authorities to use in making a likelihood determination in a sunset review. Nor does Article 11.3 identify any particular factors that authorities must take into account in making such a determination. Thus, Article 11.3 neither explicitly requires authorities in a sunset review to calculate fresh dumping margins, nor explicitly prohibits them from relying on dumping margins calculated in the past. This silence in the text of Article 11.3 suggests that no obligation is imposed on investigating authorities to calculate or rely on dumping margins in a sunset review. See Appellate Body Report, *US – Corrosion-Resistant Steel Sunset Review (2004)*, para. 123.

anti-dumping duty, investigating authorities must determine whether the expiry of the duty that was imposed at the conclusion of an original investigation would be *likely to lead to continuation or recurrence of dumping.*[252]

In *US – Corrosion-Resistant Steel Sunset Review (2004)*, the Appellate Body furthermore explained the structure and content of the sunset review provisions:

Article 11.3 imposes a temporal limitation on the maintenance of anti-dumping duties. It lays down a mandatory rule with an exception. Specifically, Members are required to terminate an anti-dumping duty within five years of its imposition '*unless*' the following conditions are satisfied: first, that a review be initiated before the expiry of five years from the date of the imposition of the duty; second, that in the review the authorities determine that the expiry of the duty would be likely to lead to continuation or recurrence of *dumping*; and third, that in the review the authorities determine that the expiry of the duty would be likely to lead to continuation or recurrence of *injury*. If any one of these conditions is not satisfied, the duty must be terminated.[253]

The panel in *US – DRAMs (1999)* observed with regard to the termination of a definitive anti-dumping duty five years from its imposition that:

[s]uch termination is conditional. First, the terms of Article 11.3 itself lay down that this should occur unless the authorities determine that the expiry would be 'likely to lead to continuation or recurrence of dumping and injury'. Where there is a determination that both are likely, the duty may remain in force, and the five year clock is reset to start again from that point. Second, Article 11.3 provides also for another situation whereby this five year period can be otherwise effectively extended, viz in a situation where a review under paragraph 2 covering both dumping and injury has taken place. If, for instance, such a review took place at the four year point, it could effectively extend the sunset review until 9 years from the original determination. In the first case, we note that the provisions of Article 11.3 explicitly [condition] the prolongation of the five year period on a finding that there is *likelihood* of dumping and injury continuing or recurring. In the second case, where there is reference to review under Article 11.2, there is no such explicit reference.[254]

However, since both instances of review (i.e. review and sunset review) have the same practical effect of prolonging the application of anti-dumping duties beyond five years, the panel in *US – DRAMs (1999)* argued that the investigating authorities are entitled to apply the same test concerning the likelihood of recurrence or the continuation of dumping for both Article 11.2 and Article 11.3 reviews.

Moreover, in *US – Anti-Dumping Measures on Oil Country Tubular Goods (2005)*, the Appellate Body found in the context of sunset reviews that Article 11.3 does not require investigating authorities to establish the existence of a 'causal link' between likely dumping and likely injury, but that:

[i]nstead, by its terms, Article 11.3 requires investigating authorities to determine whether the *expiry of the duty* would be likely to lead to *continuation or recurrence of dumping and*

---

252 Appellate Body Report, *US – Corrosion-Resistant Steel Sunset Review (2004)*, para. 107.
253 Appellate Body Report, *US – Corrosion-Resistant Steel Sunset Review (2004)*, para. 104; Appellate Body Report, *US – Oil Country Tubular Goods Sunset Reviews (Article 21.5 – Argentina) (2007)*, para. 163.
254 Panel Report, *US – DRAMs (1999)*, para. 6.48, footnote 494.

injury. Thus, in order to continue the duty, there must be a nexus between the 'expiry of the duty', on the one hand, and 'continuation or recurrence of dumping and injury', on the other hand, such that the former 'would be likely to lead to' the latter. This nexus must be clearly demonstrated.[255]

Finally, the Appellate Body described the standard of review applicable in assessing sunset reviews in *US – Corrosion-Resistant Steel Sunset Review (2004)* as follows:

> This language in Article 11.3 makes clear that it envisages a process combining *both* investigatory and adjudicatory aspects. In other words, Article 11.3 assigns an active rather than a passive decision-making role to the authorities. The words 'review' and 'determine' in Article 11.3 suggest that authorities conducting a sunset review must act with an appropriate degree of diligence and arrive at a reasoned conclusion on the basis of information gathered as part of a process of reconsideration and examination. In view of the use of the word 'likely' in Article 11.3, an affirmative likelihood determination may be made only if the evidence demonstrates that dumping would be probable if the duty were terminated – and not simply if the evidence suggests that such a result might be possible or plausible.[256]

In addition, as the Appellate Body has explained, a sunset review determination must be made on the basis of a 'rigorous examination'[257] leading to 'reasoned and adequate conclusions',[258] and must be supported by 'positive evidence' and a 'sufficient factual basis'.[259]

Questions and Assignments 11.13

How long can an anti-dumping duty remain in force? When, and on whose initiative, will the domestic investigating authorities review the continued need for the imposition of an anti-dumping duty? On what basis will the investigating authorities decide on the continued need for the imposition of an anti-dumping duty? What is a 'sunset review'? Describe two ways in which the imposition of an anti-dumping duty can be prolonged beyond the period of five years provided for in Article 11.3 of the *Anti-Dumping Agreement*.

7.5 Problem of Circumvention of Anti-Dumping Duties

As explained above, anti-dumping duties are typically levied on a specific product of a specific exporter or producer from a specific country. An exporter or producer may try to change the characteristics of the product concerned so that it no longer corresponds to the characteristics of the product subject to an anti-dumping duty. An exporter or producer also may move part of its assembly or manufacturing operations to the importing country or to a third country so that

255 Appellate Body Report, *US – Anti-Dumping Measures on Oil Country Tubular Goods (2005)*, para. 108.
256 Appellate Body Report, *US – Corrosion-Resistant Steel Sunset Review (2004)*, para. 111. Although the panel did not elaborate with respect to the meaning of 'likely', or expressly state that 'likely' means 'probable', the Appellate Body concluded that nothing in the Panel Report suggested that the panel was of the view that 'likely' does not mean 'probable', or that 'likely' means 'anything less than probable'. Appellate Body Report, *US – Oil Country Tubular Goods Sunset Reviews (2004)*, para. 309.
257 Appellate Body Report, *US – Corrosion-Resistant Steel Sunset Review (2004)*, para. 113.
258 *Ibid.*, para. 114 (quoting Panel Report, *US – Corrosion-Resistant Steel Sunset Review (2004)*, para. 7.271).
259 *Ibid.*

the product arguably no longer originates in the country an anti-dumping duty was imposed. In short, the exporter or producer may attempt to avoid or 'circumvent' the anti-dumping duties. Members have different ways of approaching this problem and the question as to what extent the 'new' products may continue to be subject to the existing anti-dumping duties.[260] The problem of circumvention and anti-circumvention measures was on the agenda of the Uruguay Round but no agreement on specific rules was reached. The matter was referred to the WTO Committee on Anti-Dumping Practices for resolution.[261]

8   INSTITUTIONAL AND PROCEDURAL PROVISIONS OF THE *ANTI-DUMPING AGREEMENT*

As with most WTO agreements, the *Anti-Dumping Agreement* also contains a few institutional and procedural provisions. This section discusses in turn: (1) the Anti-Dumping Committee; and (2) dispute settlement regarding rights and obligations under the *Anti-Dumping Agreement*.

8.1   The Committee on Anti-Dumping Practices

The Committee on Anti-Dumping Practices, commonly referred to as the Anti-Dumping Committee, is composed of representatives of each Member. It met twice in 2012. According to Article 16.1, the Committee carries out the responsibilities assigned to it under the Agreement. It reviews Members' notifications of any changes of laws and regulations relevant to the Agreement and in the administration of such laws and regulations pursuant to Article 18.5. The Committee conducts an annual review of the implementation and operation of the Agreement as foreseen by Article 18.6 and informs the Council for Trade in Goods of developments. Article 16.4 requires Members to report all preliminary or definitive anti-dumping actions taken. They also have to submit, on a half-yearly basis, reports on any anti-dumping actions taken within the preceding six months. In accordance with Article 16.5, each Member has to notify the Committee which of its authorities are competent to initiate and conduct investigations and domestic procedures governing such investigations. Article 16.2 authorises the Anti-Dumping Committee to establish subsidiary bodies (such as the working groups on implementation and anti-circumvention). Pursuant to

---

260 The rules of the European Communities on anti-circumvention were found inconsistent with Article III:2 of the GATT 1947 because they provided for an internal tax not applied to like products of EC origin and were found to be inconsistent with Article III:4 of the GATT 1947 because they made the grant of an advantage dependent on an undertaking to limit the use of Japanese parts or materials. See GATT Panel Report, *EEC – Parts and Components*, paras. 5.9 and 5.21.
261 See the Uruguay Round *Decision on Anti-Circumvention*.

Article 16.3, the Committee and its subsidiary bodies may consult with and seek information from any source.

8.2 Dispute Settlement

As noted above, the rights and obligations under the *Anti-Dumping Agreement* have given rise to a significant number of disputes.[262] Pursuant to Article 17.1 of the *Anti-Dumping Agreement*, disputes between Members on the consistency of anti-dumping measures with the obligations under the Agreement are subject to the general rules on WTO dispute settlement contained in the Dispute Settlement Understanding (DSU), *except as otherwise provided*. This section discusses the special or additional dispute settlement rules and procedures provided for in Article 17 of the *Anti-Dumping Agreement*. This section addresses: (1) the standard of review under Article 17.6; and (2) other special or additional rules and procedures set out in Articles 17.4, 17.5 and 17.7.

8.2.1 Standard of Review

As discussed in Chapter 3 of this book, Article 11 of the DSU sets forth the appropriate standard of review for panels, the 'objective assessment' standard.[263] Article 17.6 of the *Anti-Dumping Agreement*, however, provides for two special rules with regard to the standard of review that applies to panels hearing disputes concerning anti-dumping measures.

The first of these special rules on the standard of review is found in Article 17.6(i) of the *Anti-Dumping Agreement*, which states:

[I]n its assessment of the facts of the matter, the panel shall determine whether the authorities' establishment of the facts was proper and whether their evaluation of those facts was unbiased and objective. If the establishment of the facts was proper and the evaluation was unbiased and objective, even though the panel might have reached a different conclusion, the evaluation shall not be overturned.

In this context, the Appellate Body emphasised that it is 'important to bear in mind the different roles of panels and investigating authorities'.[264] Investigating authorities are charged with making factual determinations relevant to their overall determination of dumping and injury, while the 'task of panels is simply to review the investigating authorities' "establishment" and "evaluation" of the facts'.[265] The Appellate Body further explained that Article 17.6(i) requires a panel not to engage in a 'new and independent fact-finding exercise',[266] or to conduct a *de novo* review of the evidence before an investigating authority.[267]

262 See above, p. 680.   263 See above, pp. 219–20.
264 Appellate Body Report, *US – Hot-Rolled Steel (2001)*, para. 55.   265 *Ibid.*
266 Appellate Body Report, *Mexico – Corn Syrup (Article 21.5 – US) (2001)*, para. 84.
267 See Panel Report, *US – Steel Plate (2002)*, para. 7.6; and Panel Report, *Egypt – Steel Rebar (2002)*, paras. 7.8 and 7.14.

Rather, the mandate of the panel is confined to examining whether the evaluation of the evidence by the investigating authority was 'unbiased and objective'.[268] In doing so, a panel should consider all information, *both* confidential and non-confidential, that was *before* the investigating authority.[269] Read together with Article 11 of the DSU, panels operating under the mandate of Article 17.6(i) of the *Anti-Dumping Agreement* should make an *objective* review of the investigating authority's establishment and evaluation of facts.[270] In interpreting Article 17.6(i), the Appellate Body largely assimilated the standard of review under that special provision to the general standard of review found in Article 11 of the DSU. In *US – Hot-Rolled Steel (2001)*, the Appellate Body noted that Article 17.6(i):

> [r]eflects closely the obligation imposed on panels under Article 11 of the DSU to make an '*objective assessment* of the *facts*'. Thus the text of both provisions requires panels to 'assess' the facts and this, in our view, clearly necessitates an active review or examination of the pertinent facts ... [I]t is inconceivable that Article 17.6(i) should require anything other than that panels make an *objective* 'assessment of the facts of the matter'. In this respect, we see no 'conflict' between Article 17.6(i) of the *Anti-Dumping Agreement* and Article 11 of the DSU.[271]

The second special rule on the standard of review is set out in Article 17.6(ii) of the *Anti-Dumping Agreement*, which states:

> [T]he panel shall interpret the relevant provisions of the Agreement in accordance with customary rules of interpretation of public international law. Where the panel finds that a relevant provision of the Agreement admits of more than one permissible interpretation, the panel shall find the authorities' measure to be in conformity with the Agreement if it rests upon one of those permissible interpretations.[272]

Not surprisingly, the first sentence of Article 17.6(ii) requires panels to 'interpret the relevant provisions of the Agreement in accordance with customary rules of interpretation of public international law'. However, the second sentence of Article 17.6(ii) then continues with one of the most controversial rules of the *Anti-Dumping Agreement*.[273] According to the second sentence of Article 17.6(ii), '[w]here the panel finds that a relevant provision ... admits of more than one

---

268 See Panel Report, *Mexico – Corn Syrup (2000)*, para. 7.94; Panel Report, *Guatemala – Cement II (2000)*, para. 8.19; Panel Report, *Thailand – H-Beams (2001)*, para. 7.51; Panel Report, *US – Stainless Steel (Mexico) (2008)*, para. 6.3; and Panel Report, *US – Hot-Rolled Steel (2001)*, para. 7.26.

269 See Appellate Body Report, *Thailand – H-Beams (2001)*, paras. 113–20. See also Panel Report, *EC – Tube or Pipe Fittings (2003)*, para. 7.45.

270 See Appellate Body Report, *US – Hot-Rolled Steel (2001)*, paras. 55 and 62; Panel Report, *US – Steel Plate (2002)*, para. 7.5; Appellate Body Report, *Mexico – Corn Syrup (Article 21.5 – US) (2001)*, para. 130; and Panel Report, *Korea – Certain Paper (2005)*, paras. 6.1–6.3.

271 Appellate Body Report, *US – Hot-Rolled Steel (2001)*, para. 55.

272 See Article 17.6(ii) of the *Anti-Dumping Agreement*. See e.g. Panel Report, *US – Softwood Lumber V (Article 21.5 – Canada) (2005)*, para. 5.66. The panel in this case found that two permissible interpretations existed, and therefore accepted the respondent's interpretation. However, the Appellate Body reversed the finding that two interpretations were permissible within the meaning of Article 17.6(ii). See Appellate Body Report, *US – Softwood Lumber V (Article 21.5 – Canada) (2005)*, para. 123.

273 In several anti-dumping dispute settlement proceedings, the question arose whether, on the basis of the second sentence of Article 17.6(ii), zeroing in the calculation of dumping margins can be found to be one of the permissible interpretations of the relevant substantive provisions of the *Anti-Dumping Agreement*.

permissible interpretation, the panel shall find the authorities' measure to be in conformity with the Agreement if it rests upon one of the permissible interpretations'. The Appellate Body acknowledged in *US – Hot-Rolled Steel (2001)* that:

[t]he *second* sentence of Article 17.6(ii) *presupposes* that application of the rules of treaty interpretation in Articles 31 and 32 of the *Vienna Convention* could give rise to, at least, two interpretations of some provisions of the *Anti-Dumping Agreement*, which, under that Convention, would both be '*permissible* interpretations'.[274]

The Appellate Body subsequently observed in *US – Continued Zeroing (2009)*:

Article 17.6(ii) contemplates a sequential analysis. The first step requires a panel to apply the customary rules of interpretation to the treaty to see what is yielded by a conscientious application of such rules including those codified in the *Vienna Convention*. Only *after* engaging this exercise will a panel be able to determine whether the second sentence of Article 17.6(ii) applies. The structure and logic of Article 17.6(ii) therefore do not permit a panel to determine first whether an interpretation is permissible under the second sentence and then to seek validation of that permissibility by recourse to the first sentence.[275]

In the same case, the Appellate Body further stated that the second sentence of Article 16.7(ii):

[c]annot be interpreted in a way that would render it redundant, or that derogates from the customary rules of interpretation of public international law … [T]he second sentence allows for the possibility that the application of the rules of the *Vienna Convention* may give rise to an interpretative range and, if it does, an interpretation falling within that range is permissible and must be given effect by holding the measure to be in conformity with the covered agreement.[276]

According to the Appellate Body, the rules and principles of the *Vienna Convention* cannot, however, contemplate interpretations with mutually contradictory results.[277] As the Appellate Body explained, the enterprise of interpretation is intended to ascertain the proper meaning of a provision – one that fits harmoniously with the terms, context and object and purpose of the treaty. The purpose of such an exercise is therefore to narrow the range of interpretations, not to generate conflicting, competing interpretations.[278] According to the Appellate Body, it would be a subversion of the interpretative disciplines of the *Vienna Convention* if application of those disciplines yielded contradiction instead of coherence and harmony among all relevant treaty provisions.[279] The Appellate Body then concluded by observing:

Moreover, a permissible interpretation for purposes of the second sentence of Article 17.6(ii) is not the result of an inquiry that asks whether a provision of domestic law is 'necessarily excluded' by the application of the *Vienna Convention*. Such an approach subverts the hierarchy between the treaty and municipal law. It is the proper interpretation of a covered agreement that is the enterprise with which Article 17.6(ii) is engaged, not whether the treaty can be interpreted consistently with a particular Member's municipal law or with

---

274 Appellate Body Report, *US – Hot-Rolled Steel (2001)*, para. 59.
275 Appellate Body Report, *US – Continued Zeroing (2009)*, para. 271.
276 *Ibid.*, para. 272.   277 See *ibid.*, para. 273.   278 See *ibid.*   279 See *ibid.*

municipal laws of Members as they existed at the time of the conclusion of the relevant treaty.[280]

In applying this interpretation of Article 17.6(ii) to the relevant provisions of the *Anti-Dumping Agreement*, the Appellate Body in *US – Continued Zeroing (2009)* ultimately found that the United States' practice of 'zeroing' did not rest upon a 'permissible interpretation' of any provision of the *Anti-Dumping Agreement*.[281]

Questions and Assignments 11.14

Do you agree with the Appellate Body's interpretation of Article 17.6(ii) of the *Anti-Dumping Agreement*? Can you identify a provision of that Agreement that would admit of more than one permissible interpretation under the Appellate Body's test? What would be the implications if the Appellate Body had found that zeroing as well as a prohibition of zeroing are permissible interpretations of the relevant provisions of the *Anti-Dumping Agreement*?

8.2.2   Other Special or Additional Rules and Procedures

As noted above, further special and additional rules and procedures, set out in Articles 17.4, 17.5 and 17.7, apply to disputes under the *Anti-Dumping Agreement*. If consultations failed to achieve a mutually agreed solution and if final action has been taken by anti-dumping authorities, according to Article 17.4, the matter may be referred to the Dispute Settlement Body (DSB). When a provisional measure has a significant impact and is alleged to be contrary to the requirements relating to provisional measures under Article 7, such measure may also be referred to the DSB. At the request of the complaining party, the DSB shall, as provided for by Article 17.5, establish a panel to examine the matter, (i) based on a written statement indicating how a Member considers that a benefit accruing to it, directly or indirectly, under the Agreement has been nullified or impaired, and (ii) on the basis of the facts made available to the investigating authorities in conformity with appropriate domestic procedures. Article 17.7 requires that confidential information provided to the panel not be disclosed without formal authorisation from the person, body or authority providing such information. In the absence of such authorisation to disclose, a non-confidential summary shall be provided.

9   SPECIAL AND DIFFERENTIAL TREATMENT FOR DEVELOPING-COUNTRY MEMBERS

As with many other WTO agreements, the *Anti-Dumping Agreement* contains a provision relating to special and differential treatment for developing-country Members. Article 15 of the *Anti-Dumping Agreement* states:

280 *Ibid.*   281 See above, pp. 689–96.

It is recognized that special regard must be given by developed country Members to the special situation of developing country Members when considering the application of anti-dumping measures under this Agreement. Possibilities of constructive remedies provided for by this Agreement shall be explored before applying anti-dumping duties where they would affect the essential interests of developing country Members.

The panel in *EC – Tube or Pipe Fittings (2003)* characterised Article 15 as follows:

[T]here is no requirement for any specific outcome set out in the first sentence of Article 15. We are furthermore of the view that, even assuming that the first sentence of Article 15 imposes a general obligation on Members, it clearly contains no operational language de-lineating the precise extent or nature of that obligation or requiring a developed country Member to undertake any specific action. The second sentence serves to provide operational indications as to the nature of the specific action required. Fulfilment of the obligations in the second sentence of Article 15 would therefore necessarily, in our view, constitute fulfil-ment of any general obligation that might arguably be contained in the first sentence.[282]

Examining the nature of the obligation contained in the second sentence of Article 15, the panel in *EC – Bed Linen (2001)* interpreted the term 'explore' as follows:

In our view, while the exact parameters of the term are difficult to establish, the concept of 'explore' clearly does not imply any particular outcome. We recall that Article 15 does not require that 'constructive remedies' must be explored, but rather that the 'possibilities' of such remedies must be explored, which further suggests that the exploration may conclude that no possibilities exist, or that no constructive remedies are possible, in the particular circumstances of a given case.

While Article 15 clearly does not impose an obligation to actually provide or accept any constructive remedy that may be identified and/or offered, according to the panel in *EC – Bed Linen (2001)*, Article 15 does, however, impose an ob-ligation to actively consider, with an open mind, the possibility of such a remedy prior to imposition of an anti-dumping measure that would affect the essential interests of a developing country.[283] For example, a developed-country Member that fails to acknowledge the willingness of a developing-country Member to enter into a price undertaking would fail to 'explore constructive remedies' and act inconsistently with Article 15.

With respect to the meaning of the phrase 'constructive remedies provided for by this Agreement' in the second sentence of Article 15, the panel in *EC – Bed Linen (2001)* rejected the argument that a 'constructive remedy' might be a deci-sion not to impose anti-dumping duties at all. The panel stated that:

Article 15 refers to 'remedies' in respect of injurious dumping. A decision not to impose an anti-dumping duty, while clearly within the authority of a Member under Article 9.1 of the [Anti-Dumping] Agreement, is not a 'remedy' of any type, constructive or otherwise.[284]

---

282 Panel Report, *EC – Tube or Pipe Fittings (2003)*, para. 7.68. On the meaning of the first sentence of Article 15, see also Panel Report, *US – Steel Plate (2002)*, para. 7.110.

283 See Panel Report, *EC – Bed Linen (2001)*, paras. 6.233 and 6.238. See also Panel Report, *EC – Tube or Pipe Fittings (2003)*, para. 7.72.

284 Panel Report, *EC – Bed Linen (2001)*, para. 6.228.

Addressing what the phrase 'constructive remedies provided for by this Agreement' might encompass, the panel in *EC – Bed Linen (2001)* stated:

The Agreement provides for the imposition of anti-dumping duties, either in the full amount of the dumping margin, or desirably, in a lesser amount, or the acceptance of price undertakings, as a means of resolving an anti-dumping investigation resulting in a final affirmative determination of dumping, injury, and causal link. Thus, in our view, imposition of a lesser duty, or a price undertaking would constitute 'constructive remedies' within the meaning of Article 15. We come to no conclusions as to what other actions might in addition be considered to constitute 'constructive remedies' under Article 15, as none have been proposed to us.[285]

The panel in *EC – Bed Linen (2001)* understood the phrase 'before applying anti-dumping duties' to mean before the application of definitive (as opposed to provisional) anti-dumping measures, at the end of the investigative process.[286]

At the Doha Ministerial Conference in November 2001, WTO Members recognised the following in relation to Article 15 of the *Anti-Dumping Agreement*:

[W]hile Article 15 ... is a mandatory provision, the modalities for its application would benefit from clarification. Accordingly, the Committee on Anti-Dumping Practices is instructed, through its working group on implementation, to examine this issue and to draw up appropriate recommendations within twelve months on how to operationalize this provision.[287]

Questions and Assignments 11.15

What does the 'special and differential treatment' provision of Article 15 of the *Anti-Dumping Agreement* require from developed-country Members?

10   SUMMARY

WTO law provides for detailed rules with respect to dumping and subsidisation – two specific practices commonly considered to be unfair trade practices. This chapter deals with dumping. 'Dumping' is the bringing of a product onto the market of another country at a price less than the normal value of that product. In WTO law, dumping is not prohibited. However, WTO Members are allowed to take measures to protect their domestic industry from the injurious effects of dumping. Pursuant to Article VI of the GATT 1994 and the *Anti-Dumping Agreement*, WTO Members are entitled to impose anti-dumping measures if three conditions are fulfilled.

The first condition for the imposition of an anti-dumping measure is that dumping exists. Dumping is generally determined through a price-to-price comparison

285 *Ibid.*, para. 6.229. See also Panel Report, *EC – Tube or Pipe Fittings (2003)*, paras. 7.71–7.72.
286 See Panel Report, *EC – Bed Linen (2001)*, paras. 6.231–6.232.
287 Ministerial Conference, *Decision on Implementation-Related Issues and Concerns of 14 November 2001*, WT/MIN(01)/17, dated 20 November 2001, para. 7.2.

of the 'normal value' with the 'export price'. The 'normal value' is the price of the like product in the domestic market of the exporter or producer. Where this price in the exporting country market is not an 'appropriate' normal value, an importing Member may determine the normal value by: (1) using the export price to an appropriate third country as the normal value; or (2) constructing the normal value. The export price is ordinarily based on the transaction price at which the producer in the exporting country sells the product to an importer in the importing country. Where the transaction price is not an 'appropriate' export price, the importing Member may calculate, or 'construct', an export price. In order to ensure a fair comparison between the export price and normal value, the *Anti-Dumping Agreement* requires that adjustments be made to either the normal value, the export price, or both. The dumping margin is the difference between the export price and the 'normal value'. The calculation of the dumping margin *generally* requires *either* a comparison of the weighted average 'normal value' to the weighted average of prices of all comparable export transactions; *or* a transaction-to-transaction comparison of 'normal value' and export price. However, in particular circumstances, a comparison of the weighted average normal value to export prices in individual transactions may be used.

The second condition for the imposition of an anti-dumping measure is that the domestic industry producing the like product in the importing country must be suffering injury. The *Anti-Dumping Agreement* defines 'injury' to mean one of three things: (1) material injury to a domestic industry; (2) the threat of material injury to a domestic industry; or (3) material retardation of the establishment of a domestic industry. The *Anti-Dumping Agreement* defines the 'domestic industry' generally as 'the domestic producers as a whole of the like products or ... those of them whose collective output of the products constitutes a major proportion of the total domestic production of those products'. The *Anti-Dumping Agreement* requires that a determination of injury to the domestic industry be based on positive evidence and involve an objective examination of both: (1) the volume of dumped imports and the effect of the dumped imports on prices in the domestic market for like products; and (2) the consequent impact of these imports on domestic producers of such products. A determination of a threat of material injury shall be based on facts and not merely on allegation, conjecture or remote possibility. A threat of material injury exists when a change in circumstances, creating a situation in which the dumping would cause injury, is clearly foreseen and imminent.

The third and last condition for the imposition of an anti-dumping measure is that there is a causal link between the dumped imports *and* the injury to the domestic industry. According to the '*non-attribution*' requirement, investigating authorities must examine any known factors, other than the dumped imports, that are injuring the domestic industry at the same time and must not attribute the injury caused by these other factors to the dumped imports.

The *Anti-Dumping Agreement* contains detailed rules on the initiation of an anti-dumping investigation, the process of the investigation (including evidentiary issues) and requirements for public notice. The main objectives of these procedural rules are to ensure that: (1) the investigations are conducted in a transparent manner; (2) all interested parties have the opportunity to defend their interests; and (3) the investigating authorities adequately explain the basis for their determinations.

The *Anti-Dumping Agreement* provides for three kinds of anti-dumping measure: (1) provisional anti-dumping measures; (2) price undertakings; and (3) definitive anti-dumping duties. To apply a provisional anti-dumping measure, investigating authorities must make a *preliminary* affirmative determination of dumping, injury and causation. Furthermore, the investigating authorities must judge that such a measure is *necessary* to prevent injury being caused during the investigation. The *Anti-Dumping Agreement* provides for an alternative to the imposition of anti-dumping duties by affording exporters the possibility to offer, and investigating authorities the possibility to accept, price undertakings. These voluntary undertakings to revise prices or cease exports at the dumped price may be entered into only after the investigating authorities have made an affirmative preliminary determination of dumping, injury and causation. Where a definitive determination is made of the existence of dumping, injury and causation, a definitive anti-dumping duty may be imposed. The amount of the anti-dumping duty *may not exceed* the dumping margin, although it may be a lesser amount. Members are required to collect duties, on a *non-discriminatory* basis, on imports from each known exporter or producer found to be dumping and causing injury. When anti-dumping duties are imposed, the investigating authorities must, in principle, calculate a dumping margin for each exporter. However, the *Anti-Dumping Agreement* recognises that this may not always be possible. When it is not possible to calculate a dumping margin for each exporter, the investigating authorities may limit the number of exporters considered individually. The anti-dumping duty imposed on uninvestigated exporters is based on the weighted average dumping margin actually established for individually investigated exporters.

An anti-dumping duty shall remain in force only as long as and to the extent necessary to counteract dumping which is causing injury. The need for the continued imposition of an anti-dumping duty must be reviewed periodically by the competent authorities, where warranted, on their own initiative or upon a request by any interested party. In any case, any definitive anti-dumping duty shall be *terminated* at a date not later than *five years* from its imposition, *unless* the authorities determine – in the context of a sunset review – that the expiry of the duty 'would be likely to lead to continuation or recurrence of dumping and injury'. As with many other WTO agreements, the *Anti-Dumping Agreement* contains a provision relating to special and differential treatment for developing-country Members. Article 15 of the *Anti-Dumping Agreement* requires developed-country Members to explore 'possibilities of constructive remedies' provided for by the *Anti-Dumping Agreement* before applying anti-dumping duties, where such duties would affect the essential interests of developing-country Members.

Finally, the *Anti-Dumping Agreement* provides for two special rules with regard to the standard of review that applies to disputes concerning anti-dumping measures taken by national investigating authorities. The first rule relates to the objective, proper and unbiased assessment of the facts, and the second rule provides for the possibility that a provision of the Agreement may admit of more than one permissible interpretation.

Exercise 11: Dirty Play, but by Whom?

Newland has three important manufacturers of furniture: AEKI, Schoeder and Style-Mark. Together, they represent 70 per cent of the domestic furniture industry. Many small manufacturers make up the rest of the industry. Over the last few years, all manufacturers of furniture in Newland have been exporting an ever increasing part of their production to Richland, as the trendy but cheap furniture from Newland is quite popular with consumers in Richland.

The furniture industry in Richland is not happy with this development. The market share of the domestic furniture manufacturers has steadily decreased over recent years and many of the smaller manufacturers are going out of business. The six major furniture manufacturers, which together represent about 56 per cent of total furniture production in Richland, want to take action against the imports of furniture from Newland. They request the Government of Richland to impose anti-dumping on the furniture imported from Newland or to take any other action that would reduce the flow of furniture from Newland. They are convinced that the furniture from Newland is sold on the market of Richland at prices far below the cost of production. They claim that this is the case in particular for bedroom furniture produced by AEKI and StyleMark. However, upon reflection, Ikelea, one of the six Richland furniture manufacturers, loses interest in the initiation of an anti-dumping investigation. Ikelea has a joint venture with Newland manufacturer StyleMark that operates in a third country.

Alarmed by reports in the *Financial Times* on the calls of the Richland furniture industry for action against imports of furniture from Newland, the Government of Newland turns to the Advisory Centre on WTO Law (ACWL) for legal advice on whether, and under what conditions, Richland may, consistent with WTO law, impose anti-dumping duties or take any other action. Newland also wants to know what procedures WTO law prescribes for the imposition of anti-dumping duties. Should Richland be allowed to impose such duties, Newland wants to know: (1) whether duties may be imposed on all furniture imported from Newland; (2) the maximum level of duties that may be applied; and (3) the maximum length of time duties may be imposed.

The Executive Director of the ACWL has instructed you, a junior lawyer at the Centre, to prepare a presentation for a group of Newland trade officials and representatives of the Newland furniture industry addressing the concerns and queries put forward by the Government of Newland.

Subsidies

CONTENTS

1 INTRODUCTION

In addition to rules on dumping and anti-dumping measures, WTO law also includes rules on another practice that may or may not be considered unfair, namely, subsidisation. Subsidies are a very sensitive matter in international trade relations. On the one hand, subsidies are evidently used by governments to pursue and promote important and fully legitimate objectives of economic and social policy. On the other hand, subsidies may have adverse effects on the interests of trading partners whose industry may suffer, in its domestic or export markets, from unfair competition with subsidised products. Disputes about subsidies, and in particular subsidies to 'strategic economic sectors', have been prominent on the GATT/WTO agenda. Most noteworthy are the *EC and certain member States – Large Civil Aircraft (2011)* and *US – Large Civil Aircraft (2nd complaint) (2012)* disputes. Agricultural subsidies promoting production and export of commodities such as cotton or sugar have also triggered much WTO litigation.

As mentioned in Chapter 1, subsidies are subject to an intricate set of rules.[1] Some subsidies, such as export and import subsidies, are, as a rule, prohibited, while other subsidies are not prohibited but must be 'actionable' and withdrawn (or their adverse effects removed) when they cause adverse effects to the interests of other Members. Furthermore, if a subsidy causes or threatens to cause material injury to the domestic industry of a Member, that Member is authorised to impose countervailing duties on the subsidised products to offset the subsidisation.

This chapter examines the WTO rules on subsidies and subsidised trade. It discusses: (1) basic elements of WTO law on subsidies and subsidised trade; (2) subsidies covered by the *SCM Agreement*; (3) prohibited subsidies; (4) actionable subsidies; (5) countervailing investigation; (6) countervailing measures; (7) institutional and procedural provisions; and (8) special and differential treatment of developing-country Members.

---

1 See above, pp. 35–9, 44.

2   BASIC ELEMENTS OF WTO LAW ON SUBSIDIES AND SUBSIDISED TRADE

Before entering into a more detailed, and often technical, discussion of the rules on subsidies and countervailing measures, this section addresses in general terms: (1) the history of the law on subsidies and subsidised trade; (2) the concept of 'subsidies'; (3) WTO treatment of subsidies; (4) the response to injurious subsidised trade; and (5) the current use of subsidies and countervailing duties.

2.1   History of the Law on Subsidies and Subsidised Trade

The WTO rules on subsidies and subsidised trade are set out in Articles VI and XVI of the GATT 1994 but also, and more importantly, in the WTO *Agreement on Subsidies and Countervailing Measures*, commonly referred to as the *SCM Agreement*. The GATT 1947 did not contain clear and comprehensive rules on subsidies. In fact, Article XVI of the GATT 1947, entitled 'Subsidies', did not even define the concept of 'subsidies'. Moreover, with regard to subsidies in general, Article XVI merely provided that Contracting Parties to the GATT should notify subsidies that have an effect on trade and should be prepared to discuss limiting such subsidies if they cause serious damage to the interests of other Contracting Parties.[2] With regard to export subsidies, Article XVI provided that Contracting Parties were to 'seek to avoid' using subsidies on exports of primary products.[3] In 1962, Article XVI was amended to add a provision prohibiting Contracting Parties from granting export subsidies to non-primary products which would reduce the sales price on the export market below the sales price on the domestic market.[4] Note, however, that this amendment did not apply to developing countries. In addition, Article VI of the GATT 1947, which dealt with measures taken to offset any subsidy granted to an imported product (i.e. countervailing duties), did not provide for clear and comprehensive rules. In order to elaborate on the GATT rules on subsidies and countervailing duties and to provide greater uniformity and certainty in their implementation, the GATT Contracting Parties, during the Tokyo Round (1973–9), negotiated and concluded the *Agreement on Interpretation and Application of Articles VI, XVI and XXIII of the General Agreement*, commonly referred to as the Tokyo Round *Subsidies Code*.[5] No more than twenty-five Contracting Parties accepted this plurilateral agreement.[6] The *Subsidies Code* certainly did not bring the degree of clarification and elaboration

---

2   See Article XVI:1 of the GATT 1947.
3   See Article XVI:3, first sentence, of the GATT 1947. Contracting Parties 'should not' give a subsidy which results in the exporting country gaining 'more than an equitable share of world export trade in that product'. See Article XVI:3, second sentence, of the GATT 1947.
4   See Article XVI:4 of the GATT 1947, as amended.
5   See BISD 26S/56.
6   Both the United States and the European Community accepted the Tokyo Round *Subsidies Code*.

of the rules on subsidies and countervailing duties sought by some of the Contracting Parties. During the 1980s, the lack of clear rules on subsidies and countervailing duties led to many disputes between the GATT Contracting Parties. It was therefore not surprising that the 1986 Punta del Este Ministerial Declaration on the Uruguay Round instructed the negotiators to review Articles VI and XVI of the GATT 1947 as well as the Tokyo Round *Subsidies Code*:

with the objective of improving GATT disciplines relating to all subsidies and countervailing measures that affect international trade.[7]

The Uruguay Round negotiations eventually resulted in the *SCM Agreement*, which forms part of Annex 1A to the *WTO Agreement*. The multilateral rules on subsidies and subsidised trade are now set out in Articles VI and XVI of the GATT 1994 and, most importantly, in the *SCM Agreement*. With respect to the object and purpose of this Agreement, the panel in *Brazil – Aircraft (1999)* stated that:

[t]he object and purpose of the SCM Agreement is to impose multilateral disciplines on subsidies which distort international trade.[8]

The panel in *Canada – Aircraft (1999)* further clarified that:

[t]he object and purpose of the SCM Agreement could more appropriately be summarised as the establishment of multilateral disciplines 'on the premise that some forms of government intervention distort international trade [or] have the potential to distort [international trade]'.[9]

2.2 Concept of 'Subsidy'

The *SCM Agreement* contains, for the first time in the GATT/WTO context, a detailed and comprehensive definition of the concept of 'subsidy'. As the panel in *US – FSC (2000)* stated:

the inclusion of this detailed and comprehensive definition of the term 'subsidy' is generally considered to represent one of the most important achievements of the Uruguay Round in the area of subsidy disciplines.[10]

Broadly speaking, Article 1.1 of the *SCM Agreement* defines a subsidy as a financial contribution by a government or public body, which confers a benefit.[11] Furthermore, Article 1.2 of the *SCM Agreement* provides that the WTO rules on subsidies and subsidised trade only apply to 'specific' subsidies, i.e. subsidies granted to an enterprise or industry, or a group of enterprises or industries. The concepts of 'subsidy' and 'specificity' are examined in detail below.[12]

---

7 BISD 33S/25.   8 Panel Report, *Brazil – Aircraft (1999)*, para. 7.26.
9 Panel Report, *Canada – Aircraft (1999)*, para. 9.119.
10 Panel Report, *US – FSC (2000)*, para. 7.80.
11 On this definition and its constituent elements, see below, pp. 750–70 . See also Panel Report, *US – Export Restraints (2001)*, paras. 8.22–8.24.
12 See below, pp. 764–70 (specificity).

2.3   WTO Treatment of Subsidies

As discussed in Chapter 11 of this book, dumping *per se* is not prohibited. However, WTO law permits the imposition of anti-dumping measures if dumping
causes injury. The WTO law on subsidies is different. Article XVI of the GATT
1994 and Articles 3 to 9 of the *SCM Agreement* impose disciplines on the use of
subsidies.[13] Certain subsidies are prohibited, and many other subsidies, at least
when they are *specific*, rather than generally available, may be challenged when
they cause adverse effects to the interests of other Members.[14] WTO law distinguishes between prohibited subsidies, actionable subsidies and non-actionable
subsidies.[15] Each of these kinds of subsidy has its own substantive and procedural rules. Moreover, subsidies on agricultural products are subject to specific
rules set out in the *Agreement on Agriculture.*

2.4   Response to Injurious Subsidised Trade

As discussed in Chapter 11 of this book, Members may respond to injurious
dumping by imposing anti-dumping duties on dumped products. Similarly,
Members may, pursuant to Article VI of the GATT 1994 and Articles 10 to 23 of
the *SCM Agreement*, respond to subsidised trade which causes injury to the domestic industry producing the like product by imposing countervailing duties on
subsidised imports. These countervailing duties are to offset the subsidisation.
However, comparable to the anti-dumping measures discussed above, countervailing duties may only be imposed when the relevant investigating authority
properly establishes that there are subsidised imports, that there is injury to a
domestic industry and that there is a causal link between the subsidised imports
and the injury. As with the conduct of anti-dumping investigations, the conduct
of countervailing investigations is subject to relatively strict procedural requirements. Note that the substantive and procedural rules on the imposition and
maintenance of countervailing measures are similar to (albeit somewhat less
detailed than) the equivalent rules on anti-dumping measures.

2.5   Current Use of Subsidies and Countervailing Duties

With regard to the use of subsidies, note that Members have notified to the
WTO Secretariat thousands of subsidy measures.[16] The number of notifications

---

13 On the relationship between Article XVI of the GATT 1994 and the provisions of the *SCM Agreement*, note
   that the obligations and procedures set out in Article XVI of the GATT 1994 must be read and applied
   together with the *SCM Agreement*. As the Appellate Body concluded in *Brazil – Desiccated Coconut (1997)*,
   Article XVI of the GATT 1994 cannot be invoked independently from the *SCM Agreement*. See Appellate
   Body Report, *Brazil – Desiccated Coconut (1997)*, 182–3.
14 See Part III on Actionable Subsidies and Part V on Countervailing Measures of the *SCM Agreement*.
15 Note, however, that, in accordance with Article 31 of the *SCM Agreement*, Part IV on 'Non-Actionable Subsidies' expired five years after the entry into force of the Agreement. See also below, p. 813.
16 On the notification of subsidies and countervailing measures, see below, pp. 832–4.

reflects the widespread use of subsidies by Members in pursuit of economic, social and other policy objectives. By way of example, consider the Brazilian support programme for projects that contribute to the consolidation of the domestic pharmaceutical industry, notified in 2012;[17] the Belgian (Flemish) subsidy programme to encourage employers to hire older (age fifty and over) jobseekers, notified by the European Union in 2011;[18] the Chinese programme providing for preferential tax treatment to HIV/AIDS medicine, notified in 2011;[19] Indian preferential tax policies for certain companies, notified in 2011;[20] and the US programme providing for government-backed loan guarantees to the US commercial fishing sector for the construction, reconstruction, replacement and, under certain circumstances, the purchase of fishing vessels, notified in 2011.[21]

With regard to the use of countervailing duties, note that, in the period 1995–2012, Members imposed a total of 167 countervailing measures, while they initiated 279 countervailing investigations.[22] The most frequent users of this trade policy instrument were the United States (seventy-three), the European Union (thirty) and Canada (seventeen).[23] Countervailing measures were primarily imposed on imports from China (thirty-four) and India (thirty-one), and on imports of base metals and articles (seventy-six).[24] In the twelve-month period from 1 January 2011 to 31 December 2011, nine countervailing measures were notified: three by the United States, two each by China and the European Union, and one each by Canada and Australia. This was a reduction over the previous twelve-month period, in which nineteen countervailing measures were notified: ten by the United States, two by Peru, three by the European Union, two by China and one each by Canada and Australia.[25] On 30 June 2011, a total of eighty countervailing measures (definitive duties and price undertakings) were in force, of which fifty were maintained by the United States, eleven by the European Communities and nine by Canada.[26] According to the 2012 Report of the SCM Committee, on 30 June 2012 eighty-two notified countervailing measures were in force (definitive duties and price undertakings) of which fifty were maintained by the United States, ten by the European Union and eleven by Canada.[27]

Questions and Assignments 12.1

Briefly discuss the origins of the *SCM Agreement*. What is the object and purpose of the *SCM Agreement*? Explain briefly how WTO law regulates subsidisation and the response

---

17 See G/SCM/N/220/BRA, dated 10 January 2012, 3.
18 See G/SCM/N/220/EEC/Add.2, dated 8 December 2011, 39.
19 See G/SCM/N/155/CHN, G/SCM/N/186/CHN, dated 21 October 2011, 107.
20 See G/SCM/N/155/IND, G/SCM/N/123/IND, dated 29 October 2010, 1.
21 See G/SCM/N/220/USA, dated 19 October 2011, 37.
22 See www.wto.org/english/tratop_e/scm_e/scm_e.htm.
23 See *ibid*. In the period 1995–2012, Brazil imposed seven and Mexico eight countervailing measures.
24 See *ibid*. Note that few countervailing measures were imposed on machinery and electrical equipment (ten), textiles and articles (eight) or vehicles, airplanes and vessels (one).
25 See *ibid*.   26 See WTO Secretariat, *WTO Annual Report 2012*, 48.
27 See Report (2012) of the Committee on Subsidies and Countervailing duties (G/L/1005), dated 25 October 2012, Annex F, 16–17.

to injurious subsidised trade. Compare the current use of countervailing duties with that of anti-dumping duties.

3 SUBSIDIES COVERED BY THE *SCM AGREEMENT*

Article 1.1 of the *SCM Agreement* provides, in relevant part:

For the purpose of this Agreement, a subsidy shall be deemed to exist if:

(a) (1) there is a financial contribution by a government or any public body within the territory of a Member ... or
(a) (2) there is any form of income or price support in the sense of Article XVI of GATT 1994 and
(b) a benefit is thereby conferred.

Article 1.2 of the *SCM Agreement* further provides:

A subsidy as defined in paragraph 1 shall be subject to the provisions of Part II or shall be subject to the provisions of Part III or V only if such a subsidy is specific in accordance with the provisions of Article 2.

The Appellate Body stated in *US – FSC (1999)* that Article 1.1 sets forth the general definition of the term 'subsidy' which applies 'for the purpose of this Agreement'. This definition, therefore, applies wherever the word 'subsidy' occurs throughout the *SCM Agreement* and conditions the application of the provisions of that Agreement regarding *prohibited* subsidies in Part II, *actionable* subsidies in Part III, *non-actionable* subsidies in Part IV (now defunct) and countervailing measures in Part V.[28]

This section first examines the three constituent elements of the concept of 'subsidy': (1) a *financial contribution*; (2) a financial contribution *by a government or any public body*; and (3) a financial contribution *conferring a benefit*. Subsequently, this section discusses the concept of 'specificity'.

3.1 Financial Contribution

For a measure to be a subsidy within the meaning of Article 1.1 of the *SCM Agreement*, that measure must constitute a 'financial contribution' *or* take the form of income or price support in the sense of Article XVI of the GATT 1994. Article 1.1 provides for an exhaustive list of types of financial contribution. This list includes: (1) direct transfers of funds, such as grants, loans and equity infusions;[29] (2) potential direct transfers of funds or liabilities, such as loan guarantees;[30] (3) government revenue, otherwise due, that is foregone or not

---

28 Appellate Body Report, *US – FSC (2000)*, para. 93.
29 See Article 1.1(a)(1)(i) of the *SCM Agreement*.   30 See *ibid*.

collected;[31] (4) the provision by a government of goods or services other than general infrastructure;[32] (5) the purchase by a government of goods;[33] and (6) government payments to a funding mechanism or through a private body.[34] The Appellate Body found in *US – Softwood Lumber IV (2004)*:

> A wide range of transactions falls within the meaning of 'financial contribution' in Article 1.1(a)(1). According to paragraphs (i) and (ii) of Article 1.1(a)(1), a financial contribution may be made through a direct transfer of funds by a government, or the foregoing of government revenue that is otherwise due. Paragraph (iii) of Article 1.1(a)(1) recognizes that, in addition to such monetary contributions, a contribution having financial value can also be made *in kind* through governments providing goods or services, or through government purchases. Paragraph (iv) of Article 1.1(a)(1) recognizes that paragraphs (i)–(iii) could be circumvented by a government making payments to a funding mechanism or through entrusting or directing a private body to make a financial contribution. It accordingly specifies that these kinds of actions are financial contributions as well. This range of government measures capable of providing subsidies is broadened still further by the concept of 'income or price support' in paragraph (2) of Article 1.1(a).[35]

While the list in Article 1.1 of types of financial contribution is *exhaustive*, the concept of 'financial contribution' is broad. This section will discuss in turn these various types of financial contribution.

3.1.1   Direct Transfers of Funds

The Appellate Body observed in *Japan – DRAMs (Korea) (2007)* that the words 'grants, loans, and equity infusion' in Article 1.1(a)(1)(i) are preceded by the abbreviation 'e.g.', which indicates that grants, loans, and equity infusion are cited *examples* of transactions falling within the scope of Article 1.1(a)(1)(i). Therefore, transactions that are similar to those expressly listed, such as an interest rate reduction, debt forgiveness or the extension of a loan maturity, are also covered by the provision.'[36] The Appellate Body noted in *Japan – DRAMs (Korea) (2007)* that:

> [t]he term 'funds' encompasses not only 'money' but also financial resources and other financial claims more generally ... We are unable to agree that direct transfers of funds, as contemplated in Article 1.1(a)(1)(i), are confined to situations where there is an incremental flow of funds to the recipient that enhances the net worth of the recipient. Therefore, the Panel did not err in finding that the [Japanese investigating authorities] properly characterized the modification of the terms of pre-existing loans in the present case as a direct transfer of funds.[37]

---

31 See Article 1.1(a)(1)(ii) of the *SCM Agreement*.
32 See Article 1.1(a)(1)(iii) of the *SCM Agreement*.
33 See *ibid*.
34 See Article 1.1(a)(1)(iv) of the *SCM Agreement*.
35 Appellate Body Report, *US – Softwood Lumber IV (2004)*, para. 52.
36 See Appellate Body Report, *Japan – DRAMs (Korea) (2007)*, para. 251. As the Appellate Body noted: 'In all of these cases, the financial position of the borrower is improved and therefore there is a direct transfer of funds within the meaning of Article 1.1(a)(1)(i).' See *ibid*. See also e.g. Panel Report, *Korea – Commercial Vessels (2005)*, para. 7.31.
37 Appellate Body Report, *Japan – DRAMs (Korea) (2007)*, para. 250.

In *US – Large Civil Aircraft (2nd complaint) (2012)*, the Appellate Body confirmed and further clarified its earlier case law by stating:

Subparagraph (i) of Article 1.1(a)(1) identifies, as one type of financial contribution, a government practice involving 'a direct transfer of funds'. It indicates action involving the conveyance of funds from the government to the recipient ... The direct transfer of funds in subparagraph (i) therefore captures conduct on the part of the government by which money, financial resources, and/or financial claims are made available to a recipient.

Article 1.1(a)(1)(i) lists in brackets examples of direct transfers of funds ('e.g. grants, loans, and equity infusion') ... These examples, which are illustrative, do not exhaust the class of conduct captured by subparagraph (i). The inclusion of specific examples nevertheless provides an indication of the types of transactions intended to be covered by the more general reference to 'direct transfer of funds'.[38]

For the Appellate Body, it was 'clear from the examples in subparagraph (i) that a direct transfer of funds will normally involve financing by the government to the recipient. In some instances, as in the case of grants, the conveyance of funds will not involve a reciprocal obligation on the part of the recipient. In other cases, such as loans and equity infusions, the recipient assumes obligations to the government in exchange for the funds provided.'[39] Thus, the Appellate Body concluded that the 'provision of funding may amount to a donation or may involve reciprocal rights and obligations'.[40]

A financial contribution exists not only when a direct transfer of funds or a potential direct transfer of funds has actually been effectuated. Pursuant to Article 1.1(a)(1)(i), it is sufficient that there is a 'government practice' involving the transfer of funds. The panel in *Brazil – Aircraft (1999)* noted in this respect:

If subsidies were deemed to exist only once a direct or potential direct transfer of funds had actually been effectuated, the Agreement would be rendered totally ineffective and even the typical WTO remedy (i.e. the cessation of the violation) would not be possible.[41]

3.1.2 Government Revenue, Otherwise Due, that is Foregone

As provided in Article 1.1(a)(1)(ii), government revenue, otherwise due, that is foregone or not collected is also a financial contribution within the meaning of Article 1.1. In *US – FSC (2000)*, the Appellate Body held:

In our view, the '*foregoing*' of revenue '*otherwise* due' implies that less revenue has been raised by the government than would have been raised in a different situation, or, that is, 'otherwise'. Moreover, the word 'foregone' suggests that the government has given up an entitlement to raise revenue that it could 'otherwise' have raised. This cannot, however, be an entitlement in the abstract, because governments, in theory, could tax *all* revenues. There must, therefore, be some defined, normative benchmark against which a comparison can be made between the revenue actually raised and the revenue that would have been raised 'otherwise'. We, therefore, agree with the Panel that the term 'otherwise due' implies some

---

38 Appellate Body Report, *US – Large Civil Aircraft (2nd complaint) (2012)*, paras. 614–15.
39 See *ibid.*, para. 617.   40 *Ibid.*, para. 617.
41 Panel Report, *Brazil – Aircraft (1999)*, para. 7.13.

kind of comparison between the revenues due under the contested measure and revenues that would be due in some other situation. We also agree with the Panel that the basis of comparison must be the tax rules applied by the Member in question ... A Member, in principle, has the sovereign authority to tax any particular categories of revenue it wishes. It is also free *not* to tax any particular categories of revenues. But, in both instances, the Member must respect its WTO obligations. What is 'otherwise due', therefore, depends on the rules of taxation that each Member, by its own choice, establishes for itself.[42]

The term 'otherwise', as used in 'government revenue, otherwise due, that was foregone', refers to a normative benchmark as established by the tax rules applied by the Member concerned.[43] The panel in *US – FSC (2000)* explained that the term 'otherwise due' refers to the situation that would prevail *but for* the measure at issue.[44] In *US – Large Civil Aircraft (2nd complaint) (2012)*, the Appellate Body addressed the question of whether the reduction in the Washington State business-and-occupation tax rate applicable to commercial aircraft and component manufacturers constitutes the foregoing of revenue *otherwise due* within the meaning of Article 1.1(a)(1)(ii).[45] The Appellate Body explained that:

[a] panel must be aware of the limitations inherent in identifying and comparing a general rule of taxation, and an exception from that rule. For instance, we noted that it could be misleading to identify a benchmark within a domestic tax regime solely by reference to historical tax rates. By that measure, the fact that commercial aircraft and component manufacturers were *previously* subject to higher tax rates would not in itself be determinative of what the benchmark is at the time of the challenge ...

We have also noted that it could be misleading to compare rates applicable to a general category of income with rates applicable to a subcategory of that income, without considering whether the scope of the 'exceptions' undermines the existence of a 'general rule' ... This reflects consideration by the Panel as to the relative tax treatment of other taxpayers engaged in the same broad category of business activities as commercial aircraft manufacturers.[46]

The Appellate Body concluded in *US – Large Civil Aircraft (2nd complaint) (2012)* that it was satisfied the panel had a proper basis for selecting as the benchmark the tax treatment generally applicable in Washington State to

---

42 Appellate Body Report, *US – FSC (2000)*, para. 90.

43 The Appellate Body in *US – FSC (Article 21.5 – EC) (2002)* clarified that Article 1.1(a)(1)(ii) does not require panels to identify a general rule of taxation and exceptions to that general rule, but rather they should compare the domestic fiscal treatment of 'legitimately' comparable income 'to determine whether the contested measure involves the foregoing of revenue that is '"otherwise due"'. See Appellate Body Report, *US – FSC (Article 21.5 – EC) (2002)*, para. 91.

44 See Panel Report, *US – FSC (2000)*, para. 7.45. Note, however, that the Appellate Body stated that, although the panel's 'but for' test works in this case, it may not work in other cases. The Appellate Body had 'certain abiding reservations' about applying any legal standard, such as this 'but for' test, in place of the actual treaty language. See Appellate Body Report, *US – FSC (2000)*, para. 91.

45 Appellate Body Report, *US – Large Civil Aircraft (2nd complaint) (2012)*, paras. 801–31. The Appellate Body noted that, 'in identifying a general rule and exception relationship ... a panel might artificially create a rule and an exception where no such distinction exists. In addition, an approach that focuses too narrowly on the change effected by a tax measure could result in a finding that government revenue otherwise due has been foregone anytime the tax rate applicable to a recipient is lowered ... Moreover, we note that a domestic tax system may be so replete with exceptions that the rate applicable to the general category of income in fact no longer represents the "general rule" but, rather, the "exception".' Appellate Body Report, *US – Large Civil Aircraft (2nd complaint) (2012)*, para. 815.

46 *Ibid.*, paras. 823–4.

businesses engaged in manufacturing, wholesaling, and retailing activities. In addition, the Appellate Body considered that the panel properly concluded that a comparison of these general tax rates to the lower tax rate that was applied to the gross income of commercial aircraft and component manufacturers indicated the foregoing of government revenue otherwise due within the meaning of Article 1.1(a)(1)(ii) of the *SCM Agreement*.[47]

3.1.3 Provision or Purchase by a Government

Article 1.1(a)(1)(iii) covers financial contributions where 'a government provides goods or services other than general infrastructure, or purchases goods'. According to the Appellate Body in *US – Softwood Lumber IV (2004)*, sub-paragraph (iii) contemplates two distinct types of transaction:

> The first is where a government provides goods or services other than general infrastructure. Such transactions have the potential to lower artificially the cost of producing a product by providing, to an enterprise, inputs having a financial value. The second type of transaction falling within [subparagraph (iii)] is where a government purchases goods from an enterprise. This type of transaction has the potential to increase artificially the revenues gained from selling the product.[48]

With regard to the 'provision of goods' within the meaning of Article 1.1(a)(1)(iii), first sub-clause, the Appellate Body stated in *US – Softwood Lumber IV (2004)* that:

> [t]he concept of 'making available' or 'putting at the disposal of' ... requires there to be a reasonably proximate relationship between the action of the government providing the good or service on the one hand, and the use or enjoyment of the good or service by the recipient on the other. Indeed, a government must have some control over the *availability* of a specific thing being 'made available'.[49]

The panel in *US – Softwood Lumber III (2002)* found that the Canadian provincial stumpage programme at issue in that case constituted a 'financial contribution', as the programme, under which harvesting companies were allowed by the government to cut trees, amounted to the 'supply' by the government of a particular good, namely, standing timber.[50]

With regard to the 'purchase of goods' within the meaning of Article 1.1(a)(1)(iii), second sub-clause, the Appellate Body stated in *US – Large Civil Aircraft (2nd complaint) (2012)* that:

> [t]he goods are provided *to* the government by the recipient, in contrast to the first sub-clause of that paragraph, where the goods are provided *by* the government.[51]

As to the difference between the first and second sub-clauses of Article 1.1 (a)(1)(iii), the Appellate Body noted that: (1) the second sub-clause uses the term

47 See *ibid.*, para. 825.
48 Appellate Body Report, *US – Softwood Lumber IV (2004)*, para. 53.   49 *Ibid.*, para. 71.
50 See Panel Report, *US – Softwood Lumber III (2002)*, para. 7.30.
51 Appellate Body Report, *US – Large Civil Aircraft (2nd complaint) (2012)*, para. 619.

'purchase', which is usually understood to mean that the person or entity providing the goods will receive some consideration in return; (2) in contrast to the first sub-clause that addresses the provision of goods *and services*, the second sub-clause refers only to purchases of 'goods', and not of 'services'.[52] While 'government purchase of services' is excluded from the scope of sub-paragraph (iii), the question has arisen whether such purchase measures could fall within the scope of sub-paragraph (i), discussed above. According to the panel in *US – Large Civil Aircraft (2nd complaint) (2012)*, the omission of the term 'services' from the second sub-clause of sub-paragraph (iii) is an indication that the drafters of the *SCM Agreement* did not intend measures constituting government purchases of services to be covered as financial contributions under sub-paragraph (i). The Appellate Body did not rule on this interpretative issue, as it was not relevant for purposes of resolving the dispute before it, and it:

[d]eclare[d] the Panel's interpretation that 'transactions properly characterized as purchases of services are excluded from the scope of Article 1.1(a)(1)(i) of the SCM Agreement' to be moot and of no legal effect.[53]

The Appellate Body found instead that the payments and access to facilities, equipment and employees provided to Boeing pursuant to the NASA procurement contracts and Department of Defense assistance instruments at issue constituted 'direct transfers of funds' and the 'provision of goods or services', and were therefore financial contributions covered by Article 1.1(a)(1)(i) and (iii) of the *SCM Agreement*.[54]

As noted above, Article 1.1(a)(1)(iii) covers financial contributions through the government provision of goods or services, *other than general infrastructure*. Excluded from the scope of sub-paragraph (iii) is therefore the provision of general infrastructure. The term 'general infrastructure' has been defined by the panel in *EC and certain member States – Large Civil Aircraft (2011)* as:

[i]nfrastructure that is not provided to or for the advantage of only a single entity or limited group of entities, but rather is available to all or nearly all entities.[55]

52 See *ibid.*   53 *Ibid.*, paras. 619–20.
54 *Ibid.*, paras. 550–625. The Appellate Body found that the NASA procurement contracts and Department of Defense assistance instruments at issue 'are most appropriately characterized as being akin to a species of joint venture and that these joint venture arrangements between NASA/[Department of Defense] and Boeing have characteristics analogous to equity infusions, one of the examples of financial contribution included in Article 1.1(a)(1)(i) of the *SCM Agreement*'. Under the 'respective joint ventures ... both NASA and the [Department of Defense] provided payments to Boeing to undertake the research. These payments constitute a direct transfer of funds within the meaning of Article 1.1(a)(1)(i). In addition, Boeing was given access to NASA facilities, equipment, and employees and to [Department of Defense] facilities, which constitute the provision of goods or services within the meaning of Article 1.1(a)(1)(iii) of the *SCM Agreement*.' See *ibid.*, para. 624.
55 Panel Report, *EC and certain member States – Large Civil Aircraft (2011)*, para. 7.1063. For the panel, 'the existence of limitations on access to or use of infrastructure, whether *de jure* or *de facto*, is highly relevant in determining whether that infrastructure is "general infrastructure"'. However, other considerations were also relevant 'such as the circumstances surrounding the creation of the infrastructure in question, consideration of the type of infrastructure, conditions and circumstances of the provision of the infrastructure, the recipients or beneficiaries of the infrastructure, and the legal regime applicable to such infrastructure, including the terms and conditions of access to and/or limitations on use of the infrastructure'. See Panel Report, *EC and certain member States – Large Civil Aircraft (2011)*, paras. 7.1037 and 7.1039.

The provision of infrastructure that is not 'general' falls within the scope of sub-paragraph (iii). With regard to this infrastructure, the Appellate Body noted in *EC and certain member States – Large Civil Aircraft (2011)* that the panel erred in its interpretation and application of sub-paragraph (iii) by failing to recognise that the relevant transaction for purposes of its analysis under sub-paragraph (iii) was the *provision* of goods or services in the form of infrastructure to Airbus, not the *creation* of that infrastructure.[56] The Appellate Body emphasised that, 'when a good or service has not been *provided* by a government, there cannot be a financial contribution cognizable under Article 1.1(a)(1)(iii)'.[57]

3.1.4 Payments to a Funding Mechanism or Through a Private Body

Article 1.1(a)(1)(iv) refers to financial contributions where a 'government makes payments to a funding mechanism, or entrusts or directs a private body to carry out one or more of the type of functions' illustrated in subparagraphs (i) to (iii), which would normally be vested in the government and the practice, in no real sense, differs from practices normally followed by governments. In defining 'government payments in a funding mechanism or entrustment or direction of a private body' within the meaning of subparagraph (iv) of Article 1.1(a)(1), the Appellate Body recalled in *US – Countervailing Duty Investigation on DRAMs (2005)* that the *SCM Agreement* reflects a 'delicate balance between the Members that sought to impose more disciplines on the use of subsidies and those that sought to impose more disciplines on the application of countervailing measures'.[58] It noted that this balance must be borne in mind in interpreting subparagraph (iv):

[w]hich allows Members to apply countervailing measures to products in situations where a government uses a private body as a proxy to provide a financial contribution ... At the same time, the interpretation of paragraph (iv) cannot be so broad so as to allow Members to apply countervailing measures to products whenever a government is merely exercising its general regulatory powers.[59]

According to the Appellate Body, sub-paragraph (iv) is, in essence, an anti-circumvention provision.[60] In *US – Countervailing Duty Investigation on DRAMs (2005)*, the Appellate Body ruled:

[P]ursuant to paragraph (iv), 'entrustment' occurs where a government gives responsibility to a private body, and 'direction' refers to situations where the government exercises its authority over a private body. In both instances, the government uses a private body as proxy to effectuate one of the types of financial contributions listed in [sub]paragraphs (i) through (iii).[61]

---

56 See Appellate Body Report, *EC and certain member States – Large Civil Aircraft (2011)*, para. 966.
57 See *ibid.*, para. 964.
58 Appellate Body Report, *US – Countervailing Duty Investigation on DRAMs (2005)*, para. 115.
59 *Ibid.*   60 See *ibid.*, para. 113.
61 See *ibid.*, para. 116.

The Appellate Body recognised that it may be difficult to identify precisely, in the abstract, the types of government actions that constitute entrustment or direction and those that do not. The terms 'entrusts' and 'directs' are not limited to acts of 'delegation' and 'command'. The particular label used to describe the governmental action is not necessarily dispositive. Indeed, in some circumstances, 'guidance' by a government can constitute direction. However, in most cases, one would expect entrustment or direction of a private body to 'involve some form of *threat* or *inducement*, which could, in turn, serve as evidence of entrustment or direction'.[62]

3.1.5   Income and Price Support

Article 1.1(a)(2) refers to 'any form of income or price support in the sense of Article XVI of GATT 1994', which may also qualify as a subsidy if it confers a benefit to a specific enterprise or industry. The panel in *China – GOES (2012)* addressed the meaning of 'any form of … price support', and observed that the phrase is broad and, on its face, could be read to include any government measure that has the effect of raising prices within a market. However, reading the term 'price support' in context, the panel found that this term only captures government measures that set or target a given price; it does not capture every government measure that has an incidental and random effect on price.[63] This more narrow interpretation is appropriate because, under Article 1.1(a)(1)(i)–(iv), the existence of each of the four types of financial contribution is determined by reference to the action of the government concerned, rather than by reference to the effects of the measure on a market.[64] Reading the term 'price support' in this context, the panel concluded that:

[i]t does not include all government intervention that may have an effect on prices, such as tariffs and quantitative restrictions. In particular, it is not clear that Article 1.1(a)(2) was intended to capture all manner of government measures that do not otherwise constitute a financial contribution, but may have an indirect effect on a market, including on prices. The concept of 'price support' also acts as a gateway to the SCM Agreement, and it is our view that its focus is on the nature of government action, rather than upon the effects of such action. Consequently, the concept of 'price support' has a more narrow meaning than suggested by the applicants, and includes direct government intervention in the market with the design to fix the price of a good at a particular level, for example, through purchase of surplus production when price is set above equilibrium.[65]

Questions and Assignments 12.2

Give five examples of 'financial contributions' within the meaning of Article 1.1 of the *SCM Agreement*. When does the non-taxation of income constitute a 'financial contribution'? Is debt forgiveness a 'financial contribution' and, if so, why? When is government provision of infrastructure excluded from the scope of sub-paragraph (iii) of Article 1.1(a)(1) of the *SCM Agreement*? Is government purchase of a service a 'financial contribution'? Is a temporary waiver of environmental standards for a company in financial and economic difficulty

---

62 *Ibid.* Emphasis added.   63 See Panel Report, *China – GOES (2012)*, para. 7.84.
64 See *ibid.*, para. 7.85.   65 *Ibid.*

a 'financial contribution'? Is any government measure that lowers the price of products a 'price support' measure within the meaning of Article 1.1(a)(2) of the *SCM Agreement*?

3.2   Financial Contribution by a Government

For a financial contribution to be a subsidy within the meaning of Article 1.1 of the *SCM Agreement*, the financial contribution must be made by a government or a public body, including regional and local authorities as well as State-owned companies. The Appellate Body interpreted the meaning of the term 'public body' in Article 1.1(a)(1) in *US – Anti-Dumping and Countervailing Duties (China) (2011)*. It reversed the panel's finding in that case that the term means 'any entity controlled by a government' and found instead that the term 'public body' in the context of Article 1.1(a)(1) covers only those entities that possess, exercise or are vested with governmental authority.[66] The Appellate Body started its interpretation of the term 'public body' by pointing out that:

[t]he dictionary definitions suggest a rather broad range of potential meanings of the term 'public body', which encompasses a variety of entities, including both entities that are vested with or exercise governmental authority and entities belonging to the community or nation.[67]

The Appellate Body subsequently noted that the term 'government' is used twice in the chapeau of Article 1.1(a)(1). It appears, first, within the phrase 'a government or any public body' (i.e. government in the narrow sense), and, secondly, it appears within a parenthetical phrase specifying that, for purposes of the *SCM Agreement*, this word refers collectively to 'a government or any public body' (i.e. government in the collective sense).[68] The Appellate Body then turned to the question of what essential characteristics an entity must share with government in the narrow sense in order to be a public body and, thus, part of government in the collective sense. In *Canada – Dairy (1999)*, the Appellate Body found that the essence of government is that it enjoys the effective power to regulate, control or supervise individuals, or otherwise restrain their conduct, through the exercise of lawful authority.[69] The Appellate Body further found that this meaning is derived, in part, from the functions performed by a government and, in part, from the government having the powers and authority to perform those functions.[70] From this, the Appellate Body concluded in *US – Anti-Dumping and Countervailing Duties (China) (2011)* that:

[t]he performance of governmental functions, or the fact of being vested with, and exercising, the authority to perform such functions are core commonalities between government and public body.[71]

66 See Appellate Body Report, *US – Anti-Dumping and Countervailing Duties (2011)*, paras. 290 and 322.
67 *Ibid.*, para. 285.   68 See *ibid.*, para. 286.
69 See Appellate Body Report, *Canada – Dairy (1999)*, para. 97.   70 See *ibid.*
71 Appellate Body Report, *US – Anti-Dumping and Countervailing Duties (China) (2011)*, para. 290.

The Appellate Body found contextual support for its interpretation of 'public body' in Article 1.1(a)(1)(iv), discussed above. The Appellate Body noted that:

[p]ursuant to subparagraph (iv), a public body may exercise its authority in order to compel or command a private body, or govern a private body's actions (direction), and may be responsibility for certain tasks to a private body (entrustment). As we see it, for a public body to be able to exercise its authority over a private body (direction), a public body must itself possess such authority, or ability to compel or command. Similarly, in order to be able to give responsibility to a private body (entrustment), it must itself be vested with such responsibility. If a public body did not itself dispose of the relevant authority or responsibility, it could not effectively control or govern the actions of a private body or delegate such responsibility to a private body. This, in turn, suggests that the requisite attributes to be able to entrust or direct a private body, namely, authority in the case of direction and responsibility in the case of entrustment, are common characteristics of both government in the narrow sense and a public body.[72]

The Appellate Body recognised that, while a public body within the meaning of Article 1.1(a)(1) must be an entity that possesses, exercises or is vested with governmental authority, the precise contours and characteristics of a public body are bound to differ from entity to entity, State to State, and case to case.[73] The Appellate Body considered that:

[p]anels or investigating authorities confronted with the question of whether conduct falling within the scope of Article 1.1(a)(1) is that of a public body will be in a position to answer that question only by conducting a proper evaluation of the core features of the entity concerned, and its relationship with government in the narrow sense.[74]

As the Appellate Body noted, in some cases, 'such as when a statute or other legal instrument expressly vests authority in the entity concerned, determining that such entity is a public body may be a straightforward exercise'.[75] However, in others, the picture may be more mixed, and the challenge more complex. The same entity may possess certain features suggesting it is a public body, and others that suggest that it is a private body.[76] According to the Appellate Body, the absence of an express statutory delegation of authority does not necessarily preclude a determination that a particular entity is a public body.[77] As the Appellate Body stated:

What matters is *whether* an entity is vested with authority to exercise governmental functions, rather than *how* that is achieved. There are many different ways in which government in the narrow sense could provide entities with authority. Accordingly, different types of evidence may be relevant to showing that such authority has been bestowed on a particular

---

72 *Ibid.*, para. 294.   73 See *ibid.*, para. 317.   74 *Ibid.*   75 *Ibid.*, para. 318.

76 See *ibid.* In this context, the Appellate Body referred to comments by the panel in *US – Countervailing Duty Investigation on DRAMs (2005).* See Panel Report, *US – Countervailing Duty Investigation on DRAMs (2005),* footnote 29 to para. 7.8. While the Appellate Body did not agree with 'that panel's implication that the particular evidence to which it referred – evidence of government ownership – could be decisive, [the Appellate Body considered] ... that the analysis of whether the conduct of a particular entity is conduct of the government or a public body or conduct of a private body is indeed multi-faceted and that an entity may display characteristics pointing into different directions'. See Appellate Body Report, *US – Anti-Dumping and Countervailing Duties (China) (2011),* footnote 230.

77 See Appellate Body Report, *US – Anti-Dumping and Countervailing Duties (China) (2011),* para. 318.

entity. Evidence that an entity is, in fact, exercising governmental functions may serve as evidence that it possesses or has been vested with governmental authority, particularly where such evidence points to a sustained and systematic practice.[78]

Evidence that a government exercises *meaningful control* over an entity and its conduct *may serve*, in certain circumstances, *as evidence* that the relevant entity possesses governmental authority and exercises such authority in the performance of governmental functions.[79] The Appellate Body emphasised that:

[t]he mere fact that a government is the majority shareholder of an entity does not demonstrate that the government exercises meaningful control over the conduct of that entity, much less that the government has bestowed it with governmental authority. In some instances, however, where the evidence shows that the formal indicia of government control are manifold, and there is also evidence that such control has been exercised in a meaningful way, then such evidence may permit an inference that the entity concerned is exercising governmental authority.[80]

Questions and Assignments 12.3

Can a financial contribution by a local authority or a private body be a 'subsidy' within the meaning of Article 1.1 of the *SCM Agreement*? What is a 'public body' within the meaning of Article 1.1 of the *SCM Agreement*? How can one distinguish between private and public bodies for the purpose of Article 1.1 of the *SCM Agreement*? Why is this distinction important? Is financial assistance given by an NGO to cotton growers in African countries a 'financial contribution by a government'?

3.3 Financial Contribution Conferring a Benefit

A financial contribution by a government or a public body is a subsidy within the meaning of Article 1.1 of the *SCM Agreement* only if the financial contribution *confers a benefit*. If a government gives a sum of money to a company, it seems clear that this financial contribution would generally confer a benefit. However, it may be less clear whether a government loan to that same company, the purchase of goods or services by the government from the company or an equity infusion by the government in the company confer a benefit. In *Canada – Aircraft (1999)*, Canada argued that 'cost to government' is one way of conceiving of 'benefit'. The Appellate Body rejected this argumentation as follows:

A 'benefit' does not exist in the abstract, but must be received and enjoyed by a beneficiary or a recipient. Logically, a 'benefit' can be said to arise only if a person, natural or legal, or a group of persons, has in fact received something. The term 'benefit', therefore, implies that there must be a recipient. This provides textual support for the view that the focus of the inquiry under Article 1.1(b) of the *SCM Agreement* should be on the recipient and not on the granting authority. The ordinary meaning of the word 'confer', as used in Article 1.1(b), bears this out. 'Confer' means, *inter alia*, 'give', 'grant' or 'bestow'. The use of the past participle 'conferred' in the passive form, in conjunction with the word 'thereby', naturally calls for an inquiry into *what was conferred on the recipient*.[81]

78 *Ibid.*   79 See *ibid.*   80 *Ibid.*
81 Appellate Body Report, *Canada – Aircraft (1999)*, para. 154.

This reading of the term 'benefit' is confirmed by Article 14 of the *SCM Agreement*, which sets forth guidelines for calculating the amount of a subsidy in terms of 'the benefit *to the recipient*'.[82] The guidelines set forth in Article 14 apply to the calculation of the 'benefit *to the recipient* conferred pursuant to paragraph 1 of Article 1'.[83] In *Canada – Aircraft (1999)*, the Appellate Body further held with regard to the term 'benefit' that:

[t]he word 'benefit', as used in Article 1.1(b), implies some kind of comparison. This must be so, for there can be no 'benefit' to the recipient unless the 'financial contribution' makes the recipient 'better off' than it would otherwise have been, absent that contribution. In our view, the marketplace provides an appropriate basis for comparison in determining whether a 'benefit' has been 'conferred', because the trade-distorting potential of a 'financial contribution' can be identified by determining whether the recipient has received a 'financial contribution' on terms more favourable than those available to the recipient in the market.[84]

In *US – Large Civil Aircraft (2nd complaint) (2012)*, the Appellate Body found that the payments and access to facilities, equipment and employees provided under the NASA procurement contracts and Department of Defense assistance instruments at issue conferred on Boeing a benefit within the meaning of Article 1.1(b).[85] In reaching this finding, the Appellate Body confirmed its earlier case law and stated that:

[t]he determination of 'benefit' under Article 1.1(b) of the *SCM Agreement* seeks to identify whether the financial contribution has made 'the recipient "better off" than it would otherwise have been, absent that contribution'.[86]

This interpretation of 'benefit' within the meaning of Article 1.1(b) is confirmed by Article 14 of the *SCM Agreement*. Pursuant to Article 14(a), a government provision of equity capital shall not be considered as conferring a benefit when the investment decision can be regarded as consistent with the usual investment practice of private investors. Pursuant to Article 14(b), governmental loans shall not be considered as conferring a benefit, unless (and to the extent that) there is a difference between the amount that the firm receiving the loan pays on the government loan and the amount the firm would pay on a comparable commercial loan which the firm could actually obtain on the market. Pursuant to Article 14(c), the same benchmark applies for loan guarantees. Pursuant to Article 14(d), the provision of goods or services or the purchase of goods by a government shall not be considered as conferring a benefit unless the provision is made for less than adequate remuneration, or the purchase is made for more than adequate remuneration. As Article 14(d) states, the adequacy of the

---

82 See *ibid.*, para. 155. The reference to 'benefit to the recipient' in Article 14 also implies that the word 'benefit', as used in Article 1.1, is concerned with the 'benefit to the recipient' and not with the 'cost to government'. Although Article 14 explicitly states that its guidelines apply '[f]or the purposes of Part V' of the *SCM Agreement*, which relates to 'countervailing measures', the Appellate Body was of the opinion that Article 14, nonetheless, constitutes a relevant context for the interpretation of 'benefit' in Article 1.1(b).

83 See *ibid.*   84 *Ibid.*, para. 157.

85 Appellate Body Report, *US – Large Civil Aircraft (2nd complaint) (2012)*, paras. 626–66.

86 *Ibid.*, para. 662.

remuneration shall be determined in relation to prevailing market conditions for the good or service in question in the country of provision or purchase (including price, quality, availability, marketability, transportation and other conditions of purchase or sale).

In brief, a 'benefit' arises if the recipient has received a 'financial contribution' on terms more favourable than those available to any recipient in the market.[87] The Appellate Body recognised in *Japan – DRAMs (Korea) (2007)* that it may be difficult to find a proper *undistorted* market benchmark. It noted:

> The terms of a financial transaction must be assessed against the terms that would result from unconstrained exchange in the relevant market. The relevant market may be more or less developed; it may be made up of many or few participants. By way of example, there are now well-established markets in many economies for distressed debt, and a variety of financial instruments are traded on these markets. In some instances, the market may be more rudimentary. In other instances, it may be difficult to establish the relevant market and its results. But these informational constraints do not alter the basic framework from which the analysis should proceed. We also do not consider that there are different standards applicable to inside and to outside investors. There is but one standard – the market standard – according to which rational investors act.[88]

In *US – Large Civil Aircraft (2nd complaint) (2012)*, the Appellate Body had difficulties with the panel's reasoning regarding the market benchmark with respect to both the NASA procurement contracts and the Department of Defense assistance instruments:

> [T]he Panel stated its view that 'no commercial entity, i.e. no private entity acting pursuant to commercial considerations, would provide payments (and access to its facilities and personnel) to another commercial entity on the condition that the other entity perform R&D activities principally for the benefit and use of that other entity' ... The Panel's finding as to the behaviour of a market actor was based exclusively on the Panel's own view of how a commercial actor would behave and its inferences as to what a rational investor would do.
>
> It is possible that the Panel believed that its view represented common sense, or its own conception of economic rationality ... We do not believe that panels can base determinations as to what would occur in the marketplace only on their own intuition of what rational economic actors would do ... More importantly, we are of the view that a panel should test its intuitions empirically, especially where the parties have submitted evidence as to how market actors behave.[89]

With regard to 'benefit' within the meaning of Article 1.1(b) of the *SCM Agreement*, two specific issues have arisen in the case law to date that deserve special attention: (1) the issue of 'pass-through' of benefit; and (2) the issue of 'extinction' of benefit. With regard to the issue of 'pass-through' of benefit, the Appellate Body explained in *US – Softwood Lumber IV (2005)* that:

---

87 See also Panel Report, *US – Lead and Bismuth II (2000)*, para. 6.66; Panel Report *Canada – Aircraft (1999)*, para. 9.112; Appellate Body Report, *Canada – Aircraft (1999)*, para. 157; Panel Report, *Canada – Aircraft Credits and Guarantees (2002)*, paras. 7.67 and 7.144; Panel Report, *EC – Countervailing Measures on DRAM Chips (2005)*, para. 7.176; Panel Report, *Japan – DRAMs (Korea) (2007)*, para. 7.256.

88 Appellate Body Report, *Japan – DRAMs (Korea) (2007)*, para. 172.

89 Appellate Body Report, *US – Large Civil Aircraft (2nd complaint) (2012)*, paras. 642–3.

[w]here a subsidy is conferred on input products, and the countervailing duty is imposed on processed products, the initial recipient of the subsidy and the producer of the eventually countervailed product, may not be the same. In such a case, there is a direct recipient of the benefit – the producer of the input product. When the input is subsequently processed, the producer of the processed product is an indirect recipient of the benefit – provided it can be established that the benefit flowing from the input subsidy is passed through, at least in part, to the processed product. Where the input producers and producers of the processed products operate at arm's length, the pass-through of input subsidy benefits from the direct recipients to the indirect recipients downstream cannot simply be presumed; it must be established by the investigating authority.[90]

With regard to the issue of 'extinction' of benefit, the Appellate Body found in *US – Lead and Bismuth (2000)* and *US – Countervailing Measures on Certain EC Products (2003)* that benefits provided to the State-owned firm, which was subsequently *privatised* through transactions conducted *at arm's length* and *for fair market value*, could be treated as having been 'extinguished', and therefore not passed to the new private owners.[91] In *US – Countervailing Measures on Certain EC Products (2003)*, the Appellate Body specifically stated that '[p]rivatizations at arm's length and for fair market value *may* result in extinguishing the benefit' and that 'there is a *rebuttable* presumption that a benefit ceases to exist after such a privatization'.[92] As the Appellate Body emphasised, it depends, however, on the facts of each case whether a 'benefit' derived from pre-privatisation financial contributions is extinguished following privatisation at arm's length and for fair market value.[93] The issue of 'extinction' of benefit also arose in *EC and certain member States – Large Civil Aircraft (2011)*, albeit that the sales transactions in that case did not amount to a full privatisation of a previously State-owned company. In *EC and certain member States – Large Civil Aircraft (2011)*, the issue was whether sales of shares between private entities, and sales conducted in the context of partial privatisations, eliminate all or part of past subsidies, when these sales are at arm's length and for fair market value.[94] The Appellate Body discussed this issue at length, but 'no common view emerged'.[95] Eventually, the Appellate Body reversed the panel's reasoning and findings concerning this issue, because the panel had failed to assess: (1) whether each of the sales was on arm's-length terms and for fair market value; and (2) to what extent the sales involved a transfer in ownership and control to new owners.[96]

Questions and Assignments 12.4

Why is 'cost to government' an invalid method of conceiving of 'benefit' within the meaning of Article 1.1(b) of the *SCM Agreement*? When does a financial contribution confer a

---

90 Appellate Body Report, *US – Softwood Lumber IV (2004)*, para. 143.
91 See Appellate Body Report, *US – Lead and Bismuth (2000)*, para. 68; and Appellate Body Report, *US – Countervailing Measures on Certain EC Products (2003)*, para. 127.
92 *Ibid.* Emphasis added.   93 See *ibid.*
94 See Appellate Body Report, *EC and certain member States – Large Civil Aircraft (2011)*, para. 724.
95 See *ibid.*, para. 725. As set out in the report, each Member of the Division took a different view. See *ibid.*
96 See *ibid.*, para. 733.

benefit? When is a government loan or an equity infusion or the purchase of goods by the government a subsidy within the meaning of Article 1.1 of the *SCM Agreement*? Where an input producer and a producer of the processed products operate at arm's length, does the benefit from a financial contribution granted to the input producer pass through to the producer of the processed products? Do the sales of shares between private entities and sales conducted in the context of partial privatisations extinguish all or part of past benefits, when these sales are at arm's length and for fair market value?

3.4 Requirement of 'Specificity' of the Subsidy

The WTO rules on subsidies do not apply to all 'financial contributions by a government that confer a benefit'. In other words, these rules do not apply to all subsidies. They apply only to *specific* subsidies. Article 1.2 of the *SCM Agreement*, quoted above, states:

A subsidy as defined in paragraph 1 shall be subject to the provisions of Part II or shall be subject to the provisions of Part III or V only if such a subsidy is specific in accordance with the provisions of Article 2.

Article 2 of the *SCM Agreement* distinguishes between four types of specificity: (1) *enterprise specificity*, i.e. a situation in which a government targets a particular company or companies for subsidisation;[97] (2) *industry specificity*, i.e. a situation in which a government targets a particular sector or sectors for subsidisation;[98] (3) *regional specificity*, i.e. a situation in which a government targets producers in specified parts of its territory for subsidisation;[99] and (4) the *specificity of prohibited subsidies*, i.e. a situation in which a government targets export goods or goods using domestic inputs for subsidisation.[100] For a subsidy to fall within the scope of application of the *SCM Agreement*, it has to be *specific* in one of the above four ways. A subsidy that is widely available within an economy is presumed not to distort the allocation of resources within that economy and, therefore, does not fall within the scope of the *SCM Agreement*.

The Appellate Body interpreted Article 2 of the *SCM Agreement* in *US – Anti-Dumping and Countervailing Duties (China) (2011)*, in *EC and certain member States – Large Civil Aircraft (2011)* and in *US – Large Civil Aircraft (2nd complaint) (2012)*. The Appellate Body noted that the chapeau of Article 2.1 frames the central inquiry as to whether a subsidy is specific to 'certain enterprises'. In such an examination, the 'principles' set out in sub-paragraphs (a) to (c) of Article 2.1 'shall apply'. The use of the term 'principles' – instead of, for instance, 'rules' – suggests that the sub-paragraphs:

[a]re to be considered within an analytical framework that recognizes and accords appropriate weight to each principle. Consequently, the application of one of the subparagraphs of

---

97 See Article 2.1 of the *SCM Agreement*. See below, pp. 764–9.
98 See *ibid.*
99 See Article 2.2 of the *SCM Agreement*. See below, p. 769.
100 See Article 2.3 of the *SCM Agreement*. See below, p. 769.

Article 2.1 may not by itself be determinative in arriving at a conclusion that a particular subsidy is or is not specific.[101]

The chapeau establishes that the term 'certain enterprises' refers to 'an enterprise or industry or group of enterprises or industries'. Turning to the nouns qualified by 'certain' and 'group', the Appellate Body considered that 'enterprise' may be defined as '[a] business firm, a company', whereas 'industry' signifies '[a] particular form or branch of productive labour; a trade, a manufacture'.[102] In *US – Anti-Dumping and Countervailing Duties (China) (2011)*, the Appellate Body noted with approval the statement by the panel in *US – Upland Cotton (2004)* that: (1) an industry, or group of 'industries', may be generally referred to by the type of products they produce; (2) the concept of an 'industry' relates to producers of certain products; and (3) the breadth of this concept of 'industry' may depend on several factors in a given case.[103] The panel in *US – Upland Cotton (2004)* explained that:

> [a]t some point that is not made precise in the text of the agreement, and which may modulate according to the particular circumstances of a given case, a subsidy would cease to be specific because it is sufficiently broadly available throughout an economy as not to benefit a particular limited group of producers of certain products. The plain words of Article 2.1 indicate that specificity is a general concept, and the breadth or narrowness of specificity is not susceptible to rigid quantitative definition. Whether a subsidy is specific can only be assessed on a case-by-case basis.[104]

According to the Appellate Body in *US – Anti-Dumping and Countervailing Duties (China) (2011)*, the term 'certain enterprises': (1) refers to a single enterprise or industry or a class of enterprises or industries that are known and particularised'; and (2) this concept involves 'a certain amount of indeterminacy at the edges', such that any determination of whether a number of enterprises or industries constitute 'certain enterprises' can only be made on a case-by-case basis.[105]

As mentioned above, Article 2.1 of the *SCM Agreement* sets out in subparagraphs (a), (b) and (c) 'principles' to determine specificity. The Appellate Body stated in *US – Anti-Dumping and Countervailing Duties (China) (2011)* that:

> [a] proper understanding of specificity under Article 2.1 must allow for the *concurrent application* of these principles to the various legal and factual aspects of a subsidy in any given case.[106]

---

101 Appellate Body Report, *US – Anti-Dumping and Countervailing Duties (China) (2011)*, para. 366.
102 *Ibid.*, para. 373.
103 See Panel Report, *US – Upland Cotton (2004)*, para. 7.1142.
104 *Ibid.* The same panel also considered that 'specificity' extends to a group of industries because the words 'certain enterprises' are defined broadly in the opening terms of Article 2.1, as an enterprise or industry or group of enterprises or industries. See *ibid.*, para. 7.1140.
105 See Appellate Body Report, *US – Anti-Dumping and Countervailing Duties (China) (2011)*, para. 373, referring to Panel Report, *US – Upland Cotton (2004)*, para. 7.1142.
106 Appellate Body Report, *US – Anti-Dumping and Countervailing Duties (China) (2011)*, para. 371.

As already noted, the application of one of the principles 'may not by itself be determinative in arriving at a conclusion that a particular subsidy is or is not specific'.[107] This section further discusses in turn the three principles to determine specificity.

With regard to Article 2.1(a) of the *SCM Agreement*, the Appellate Body held in *US – Anti-Dumping and Countervailing Duties (China) (2011)* that:

Article 2.1(a) establishes that a subsidy is specific if the granting authority, or the legislation pursuant to which the granting authority operates, *explicitly* limits access to that subsidy to eligible enterprises or industries.[108]

The word 'explicitly' qualifies the phrase 'limits access to a subsidy to certain enterprises'. The Appellate Body, therefore, considered that:

[a] subsidy is specific under Article 2.1(a) if the limitation on access to the subsidy to certain enterprises is express, unambiguous, or clear from the content of the relevant instrument, and not merely 'implied' or 'suggested'.[109]

In *Japan – DRAMs (Korea) (2007)*, the panel addressed the concern that, if an investigating authority were to focus on *individual payments* made under a subsidy programme, rather than on the *programme per se*, it would always find 'specificity'. The panel noted that:

[i]f an investigating authority were to focus on an individual transaction, and that transaction flowed from a generally available support programme whose normal operation would generally result in financial contributions on pre-determined terms (that are therefore not tailored to the recipient company), that individual transaction would not, in our view, become 'specific' in the meaning of Article 2.1 simply because it was provided to a specific company. An individual transaction would be 'specific', though, if it resulted from a framework programme whose normal operation (1) does not generally result in financial contributions, and (2) does not pre-determine the terms on which any resultant financial contributions might be provided, but rather requires (a) conscious decisions as to whether or not to provide the financial contribution (to one applicant or another), and (b) conscious decisions as to how the terms of the financial contribution should be tailored to the needs of the recipient company.[110]

In *US – Large Civil Aircraft (2nd complaint) (2012)*, the Appellate Body noted that:

Article 2.1(a) refers to limitations on access to 'a subsidy'. Although the use of this term in the singular might suggest a limited conception, we note that, if construed too narrowly, any individual subsidy transaction would be, by definition, specific to the recipient. Other context in Article 2.1 suggests a potentially broader framework within which to examine specificity.[111]

The Appellate Body considered that, although the subsidy is the starting point of the specificity inquiry under Article 2.1(a), the scope of this inquiry is broader

---

107 *Ibid.*, para. 366.   108 *Ibid.*, para. 372.   109 *Ibid.*
110 Panel Report, *Japan – DRAMs (Korea) (2007)*, para. 7.374.
111 Appellate Body Report, *US – Large Civil Aircraft (2nd complaint) (2012)*, para. 749.

in the sense that it must examine the legislation pursuant to which the granting authority operates, or the express acts of the granting authority.[112] As the Appellate Body noted in *US – Large Civil Aircraft (2nd complaint) (2012)*:

Members may design the legal framework for the distribution of subsidies in many ways. However, the choice of the legal framework by the respondent cannot predetermine the outcome of the specificity analysis.[113]

According to the Appellate Body, determining whether multiple subsidies are part of the same 'subsidy' is not always a clear-cut exercise and may require careful scrutiny of the relevant legislation (set out in one *or* several instruments) or of the pronouncements of the granting authority(ies).[114] Another factor that may be considered is whether there is an 'overarching purpose behind the subsidies', albeit that this overarching purpose must be something more concrete than a vague policy of providing assistance or promoting economic growth.[115] As the Appellate Body explained:

Once the proper subsidy scheme is identified, then the question is whether that subsidy is explicitly limited to 'certain enterprises', defined in the chapeau of Article 2.1 as 'an enterprise or industry or group of enterprises or industries'. To be clear, such examination must seek to discern from the legislation and/or the express acts of the granting authority(ies) which enterprises are eligible to receive the subsidy and which are not. This inquiry focuses not only on whether the subsidy was provided to the particular recipients identified in the complaint, but focuses also on all enterprises or industries eligible to receive that same subsidy. Thus, even where a complaining Member has focused its complaint on the grant of a subsidy to one or more enterprises or industries, the inquiry may have to extend beyond the complaint to determine what other enterprises or industries also have access to that same subsidy under that subsidy scheme.[116]

While Article 2.1(a) sets out when 'specificity' exists, Article 2.1(b) of the *SCM Agreement* sets out that 'specificity' shall *not* exist if the granting authority, or the legislation pursuant to which the granting authority operates, establishes *objective* criteria or conditions governing the eligibility for, and the amount of, the subsidy, provided that: (1) eligibility is automatic; (2) such criteria or conditions are strictly adhered to; and (3) the criteria or conditions are clearly spelled out in an official document so as to be capable of verification.[117] In the footnote to Article 2.1(b), 'objective criteria and conditions' are defined as:

[c]riteria or conditions which are neutral, which do not favour certain enterprises over others, and which are economic in nature and horizontal in application.

While Article 2.1(a) describes limitations on eligibility that favour certain enterprises, Article 2.1(b) describes criteria or conditions that guard against selective eligibility. A critical common feature of these provisions, however, is that they both situate the analysis for assessing any limitations on *eligibility* in the

---

112 See *ibid.*, para. 750.   113 *Ibid.*   114 See *ibid.*, para. 752.
115 See *ibid.*   116 *Ibid.*, para. 753.
117 Appellate Body Report, *US – Anti-Dumping and Countervailing Duties (China) (2011)*, para. 367.

particular legal instrument or government conduct effecting such limitations. In *US – Anti-Dumping and Countervailing Duties (China) (2011)*, the Appellate Body noted that:

> Article 2.1(a) thus focuses not on whether a subsidy has been granted to certain enterprises, but on whether *access* to that subsidy has been explicitly limited. This suggests that the focus of the inquiry is on whether certain enterprises are eligible for the subsidy, not on whether they in fact receive it. Similarly, Article 2.1(b) points the inquiry towards 'objective criteria or conditions governing the eligibility for, and the amount of, a subsidy'.[118]

According to the Appellate Body in *US – Anti-Dumping and Countervailing Duties (China) (2011)*, where the eligibility requirements of a measure present some indications pointing to sub-paragraph (a) and certain others pointing to sub-paragraph (b), the specificity analysis must accord appropriate consideration to both principles.[119]

A third principle for determining specificity is set out in Article 2.1(c) of the *SCM Agreement*. The introductory sentence of Article 2.1(c) establishes that, 'notwithstanding any appearance of non-specificity' resulting from the application of Article 2.1(a) and (b), a subsidy may nevertheless be found to be *de facto* specific. The reference in Article 2.1(c) to 'any appearance of non-specificity' resulting from the application of Article 2.1(a) and (b) suggests that the conduct or instruments of a granting authority may not clearly satisfy the eligibility requirements of Article 2.1(a) or (b), but may nevertheless give rise to specificity 'in fact'. In such circumstances, the consideration of 'other factors', namely, those listed in Article 2.1(c), is warranted in order to determine whether the subsidy at issue is *de facto* specific.

The factors listed in Article 2.1(c) are: (1) the use of a subsidy programme by a limited number of certain enterprises; (2) the predominant use of a subsidy programme by certain enterprises; (3) the granting of disproportionately large subsidies to certain enterprises; and (4) the manner in which discretion has been exercised by the granting authority in the decision to grant a subsidy, including the frequency with which applications for a subsidy are refused or approved and the reasons for such decisions are of particular relevance in this context.[120] In determining whether a subsidy is *de facto* specific, account shall be taken of: (1) the extent of diversification of economic activities within the jurisdiction of the granting authority: and (2) the length of time during which the subsidy programme has been in operation.[121] In *US – Large Civil Aircraft (2nd complaint) (2012)*, the Appellate Body addressed the meaning of 'the granting of disproportionately large amounts of subsidy to certain enterprises' in Article 2.1(c). It noted that:

---

118 *Ibid.*, para. 368.   119 *Ibid.*, para. 369. Emphasis added.

120 See Article 2.1(c) of, and footnote 3 to, the *SCM Agreement*. See Panel Report, *EC – Countervailing Measures on DRAM Chips (2005)*, para. 7.226. See also Panel Report, *US – Softwood Lumber IV (2005)*, para. 7.123, on the fact that there is no obligation on the investigating authorities to examine the 'other factors' referred to in Article 2.1(c) of the *SCM Agreement*. Article 2.1(c) states that these factors 'may' be considered.

121 See Article 2.1(c) of the *SCM Agreement*. See Panel Report, *US – Softwood Lumber IV (2004)*, para. 7.124.

Article 2.1(c) does not offer clear guidance as to how to measure whether certain enterprises are 'grant[ed] disproportionately large amounts of subsidy'. The language ... indicates that the first task is to identify the 'amounts of subsidy' granted. Second, an assessment must be made as to whether the amounts of subsidy are 'disproportionately large'. This term suggests that disproportionality is a relational concept that requires an assessment as to whether the amounts of subsidy are out of proportion, or relatively too large. When viewed against the analytical framework set out above regarding Article 2.1(c), this factor requires a panel to determine whether the actual allocation of the 'amounts of subsidy' to certain enterprises is too large relative to what the allocation would have been if the subsidy were administered in accordance with the conditions for eligibility for that subsidy as assessed under Article 2.1(a) and (b). In our view, where the granting of the subsidy indicates a disparity between the expected distribution of that subsidy, as determined by the conditions of eligibility, and its actual distribution, a panel will be required to examine the reasons for that disparity so as ultimately to determine whether there has been a granting of disproportionately large amounts of subsidy to certain enterprises.[122]

As mentioned above, the *SCM Agreement* distinguishes between four types of specificity: enterprise specificity, industry specificity, regional specificity and the specificity of prohibited subsidies. Article 2.1 of the *SCM Agreement*, discussed at length in this section, concerns both enterprise specificity and industry specificity. Regional specificity is dealt with in Article 2.2 of the *SCM Agreement*, which provides that:

[a] subsidy which is limited to certain enterprises located within a designated geographical region within the jurisdiction of the granting authority shall be specific.

The panel in *EC and certain member States – Large Civil Aircraft (2011)* addressed the question whether a subsidy granted by a regional authority must, to be specific within the meaning of Article 2.2, not only be limited to a designated region within the territory of the granting authority, but must in addition be limited to only a sub-set of enterprises within that region. The panel concluded that Article 2.2 is properly understood to provide that a subsidy available in a designated region within the territory of the granting authority is specific, even if it is available to all enterprises in that designated region.[123] Finally, pursuant to Article 2.3 of the *SCM Agreement*, any *de jure* or *de facto* export-contingent subsidies or import substitution subsidies falling under the provisions of Article 3, i.e. any prohibited subsidy, shall be deemed to be specific.[124]

Questions and Assignments 12.5

Do the rules of the *SCM Agreement* apply to all 'financial contributions by the government that confer a benefit'? Discuss the various types of 'specificity' within the meaning

---

122 Appellate Body Report, *US – Large Civil Aircraft (2nd complaint) (2012)*, para. 879.
123 Panel Report, *EC and certain member States – Large Civil Aircraft (2011)*, para. 7.1223. The panel in *US – Anti-Dumping and Countervailing Duties (China) (2011)* reached the same conclusion. This panel stated that the term 'certain enterprises' in Article 2.2 'refers to those enterprises located within, as opposed to outside, the designated geographical region in question, with no further limitation within the region being required'. See Panel Report, *US – Anti-Dumping and Countervailing Duties (China) (2010)*, para. 9.135.
124 On prohibited subsidies, see below, pp. 770–8.

of Article 2.1 of the *SCM Agreement*. Can it be determined whether a subsidy is specific or not by applying one only of the sub-paragraphs of Article 2.1? In determining 'specificity', should one look at individual subsidy payments or individual subsidy transactions made under a subsidy programme, rather than at the programme *per se*? When is a subsidy not specific? Does the *SCM Agreement* apply also to *de facto* specific subsidies? How is a *de facto* specific subsidy identified?

4   PROHIBITED SUBSIDIES

The *SCM Agreement* distinguishes between prohibited subsidies, actionable subsidies and non-actionable subsidies.[125] This section will discuss the rules relating to prohibited subsidies. Article 3 of the *SCM Agreement*, entitled 'Prohibition', states, in its first paragraph:

Except as provided in the Agreement on Agriculture, the following subsidies, within the meaning of Article 1, shall be prohibited:

a. subsidies contingent, in law or in fact, whether solely or as one of several conditions, upon export performance, including those illustrated in Annex I;
b. subsidies contingent, whether solely or as one of several conditions, upon the use of domestic over imported products.

In short, WTO Members may not grant or maintain: (1) export subsidies; or (2) import substitution subsidies.[126] These subsidies, which are often referred to as 'red light' subsidies, are prohibited because they aim to affect trade and are most likely to cause adverse effects to other Members.

4.1   Export Subsidies

As defined in Article 3.1(a) of the *SCM Agreement*, quoted above, export subsidies are subsidies contingent upon export performance. Annex I to the *SCM Agreement* contains an 'Illustrative List of Export Subsidies'. This non-exhaustive list includes eleven types of export subsidy, including, *inter alia*: (1) direct export subsidies; (2) export retention schemes which involve a bonus on exports; (3) export-related exemption, remission or deferral of direct taxes and social welfare charges; (4) excess exemption or remission, in respect of the production and distribution of exported products, of indirect taxes in excess of those levied in respect of the production and distribution of like products when sold domestically; (5) provision of goods or services for use in the production of exported goods on terms more favourable than those for the production of goods for domestic consumption; and (6) provision of certain forms of export

---

125 Note, however, that, since 1 January 2000, the category of 'non-actionable subsidies' only contains non-specific subsidies, to which the *SCM Agreement* does not apply. See above, p. 748, footnote 15, and below, p. 813.
126 See Article 3.2 of the *SCM Agreement*.

financing extended at rates below those which the government actually had to pay for the funds (subject to certain considerations).

Article 3.1(a) of the *SCM Agreement* prohibits subsidies *contingent* upon export performance. The meaning of 'contingent' in this provision is 'conditional' or 'dependent for its existence on something else'.[127] Thus, for a subsidy to be an export subsidy, the Appellate Body ruled in *US – FSC (Article 21.5 – EC) (2002)* that 'the grant of the subsidy must be conditional or dependent upon export performance'.[128] In *US – Upland Cotton (2005)*, the Appellate Body emphasised that:

'[a] relationship of conditionality or dependence', namely that the granting of a subsidy should be 'tied to' the export performance, lies at the 'very heart' of the legal standard in Article 3.1(a) of the *SCM Agreement*.[129]

Article 3.1(a) prohibits both subsidies that are contingent *de jure* and subsidies that are contingent *de facto* on exports. In *Canada – Aircraft (1999)*, the Appellate Body stated:

The Uruguay Round negotiators have, through the prohibition against export subsidies that are contingent *in fact* upon export performance, sought to prevent circumvention of the prohibition against subsidies contingent *in law* upon export performance.[130]

Pursuant to footnote 4 to the *SCM Agreement*, a subsidy is contingent *de facto* upon export performance:

[w]hen the facts demonstrate that the granting of a subsidy, without having been made legally contingent upon export performance, is in fact tied to actual or anticipated exportation or export earnings. The mere fact that a subsidy is granted to enterprises which export shall not for that reason alone be considered to be an export subsidy within the meaning of this provision.

While the legal standard expressed by the term 'contingent' is the same for both *de jure* and *de facto* contingency, there is an important difference in what evidence may be employed to demonstrate that a subsidy is export contingent.[131] *De jure* export contingency can be demonstrated on the basis of the words of the relevant legislation, regulation or other legal instrument.[132] In *Canada – Autos (2000)*, the Appellate Body held:

The simplest, and hence, perhaps, the uncommon, case is one in which the condition of exportation is set out expressly, in so many words, on the face of the law, regulation or other legal instrument. We believe, however, that a subsidy is also properly held to be

---

127 See Appellate Body Report, *Canada – Aircraft (1999)*, para. 166. See also Panel Report, *Australia – Automotive Leather II (1999)*, para. 9.55.
128 Appellate Body Report, *US – FSC (Article 21.5 – EC) (2002)*, para. 111.
129 Appellate Body Report, *US – Upland Cotton (2005)*, para. 572.
130 Appellate Body Report, *Canada – Aircraft (1999)*, para. 167.
131 See *ibid*.
132 See e.g. Appellate Body Report, *Canada – Autos (2000)*, para. 100; and Appellate Body Report, *US – Upland Cotton (2005)*, para. 572.

de jure export contingent where the condition to export is clearly, though implicitly, in the instrument comprising the measure.[133]

According to the Appellate Body, for a subsidy to be *de jure* export contingent, the underlying law, regulation or other legal instrument does *not* have to provide *expressis verbis* that the subsidy is available only upon the fulfilment of the condition of export performance.[134] The *de jure* export contingency can also 'be derived by necessary implication from the words actually used in the measure'.[135]

With respect to *de facto* export contingency, footnote 4 to the *SCM Agreement* states that the standard of 'in fact' contingency is met if the facts demonstrate that the subsidy is 'in fact tied to actual or anticipated exportation or export earnings'.[136] *De facto* export contingency is much more difficult to demonstrate than *de jure* export contingency. The Appellate Body stated in *Canada – Aircraft (1999)* that satisfaction of the standard for determining *de facto* export contingency set out in footnote 4 requires proof of three different substantive elements: (1) the '*granting* of a subsidy'; (2) 'is ... *tied to* ...'; and (3) 'actual or anticipated exportation or export earnings'.[137] According to the Appellate Body in *Canada – Aircraft (1999)*, *de facto* export contingency must be inferred from the *total* configuration of the facts constituting and surrounding the granting of the subsidy.[138] None of these facts on its own is likely to be decisive. In combination, however, they may lead to the conclusion that there is *de facto* export contingency in a given case.

The panel in *Australia – Automotive Leather II (1999)* considered that, in certain circumstances, a Member's awareness that its domestic market is too small to absorb domestic production of a subsidised product may indicate that the subsidy is granted on the condition that it be exported.[139] However, a subsidy to an export-oriented company is not *per se* an export subsidy. The second sentence of footnote 4 precludes a panel from making a finding of *de facto* export contingency for the sole reason that the subsidy is 'granted to enterprises which export'.[140] The export orientation of a recipient may be taken into account but it will be only one among several facts which are considered and cannot be the only fact supporting a finding of *de facto* export contingency.[141] The Appellate Body further cautioned in *Canada – Aircraft (1999)* that the term 'tied to' should

---

133 Appellate Body Report, *Canada – Autos (2000)*, para. 100. See also Appellate Body Report, *US – FSC (Article 21.5 – EC) (2002)*, para. 117.
134 See *ibid.*   135 *Ibid.*
136 Panel Report, *Australia – Automotive Leather II (1999)*, para. 9.55. The panel in this case noted that the ordinary meaning of 'tied to' is 'restrain or constrain to or from an action; limit or restrict as to behaviour, location, conditions, etc.'. See *ibid.* For a further discussion of the term 'tied to', see Appellate Body Report, *Canada – Aircraft (1999)*, para. 171.
137 See Appellate Body Report, *Canada – Aircraft (1999)*, para. 169.   138 See *ibid.*
139 See Panel Report, *Australia – Automotive Leather II (1999)*, para. 9.67.
140 Appellate Body Report, *Canada – Aircraft (1999)*, para. 173.
141 Appellate Body Report, *Canada – Aircraft (Article 21.5 – Brazil) (2000)*, paras. 48 and 51. See footnote 4, second sentence, to the *SCM Agreement*; and Panel Report, *Australia – Automotive Leather II (1999)*, paras. 9.56 and 9.66. The panel also noted that 'consideration of the level of a particular company's exports' is not precluded. See Panel Report, *Australia – Automotive Leather II (1999)*, para. 9.57.

not be equated with a 'but for' test, in the sense of simply examining whether the subsidy would have been granted 'but for' the anticipated exportation or export earnings.[142]

The Appellate Body clarified the test for determining whether a subsidy is *de facto* contingent upon export performance in *EC and certain member States – Large Civil Aircraft (2011)*. It emphasised that the existence of *de facto* export contingency 'must be *inferred* from the total configuration of the facts constituting and surrounding the granting of the subsidy',[143] which may include the following factors: (1) the design and structure of the measure granting the subsidy; (2) the modalities of operation set out in such a measure; and (3) the relevant factual circumstances surrounding the granting of the subsidy that provide the context for understanding the measure's design, structure, and modalities of operation. It further explained:

[W]here relevant evidence exists, the assessment could be based on a comparison between, on the one hand, the ratio of *anticipated* export and domestic sales of the subsidized product that would come about in consequence of the granting of the subsidy, and, on the other hand, the situation in the absence of the subsidy. The situation in the absence of the subsidy may be understood on the basis of historical sales of the same product by the recipient in the domestic and export markets before the subsidy was granted. In the event that there are no historical data untainted by the subsidy, or the subsidized product is a new product for which no historical data exists, the comparison could be made with the performance that a profit-maximizing firm would hypothetically be expected to achieve in the export and domestic markets in the absence of the subsidy. Where the evidence shows, all other things being equal, that the granting of the subsidy provides an incentive to skew anticipated sales towards exports, in comparison with the historical performance of the recipient or the hypothetical performance of a profit-maximizing firm in the absence of the subsidy, this would be an indication that the granting of the subsidy is in fact tied to anticipated exportation within the meaning of Article 3.1(a) and footnote 4 of the *SCM Agreement*.[144]

The Appellate Body ruled in *EC and certain member States – Large Civil Aircraft (2011)* that the standard for determining whether the granting of a subsidy is 'in fact tied to ... anticipated exportation' within the meaning of Article 3.1(a) and footnote 4 is an objective standard:

[t]o be established on the basis of the total configuration of facts constituting and surrounding the granting of the subsidy, including the design, structure, and modalities of operation

---

142 Appellate Body Report, *Canada – Aircraft (1999)*, para. 171.
143 Appellate Body Report, *EC and certain member States – Large Civil Aircraft (2011)*, para. 1046.
144 *Ibid.*, para. 1047. It gave the following numerical example to illustrate when the granting of a subsidy may, or may not, be geared to induce promotion of future export performance by a recipient: 'Assume that a subsidy is designed to allow a recipient to increase its future production by five units. Assume further that the existing ratio of the recipient's export sales to domestic sales, at the time the subsidy is granted, is 2:3. The granting of the subsidy will *not* be tied to anticipated exportation if, all other things being equal, the anticipated ratio of export sales to domestic sales is not greater than the existing ratio. In other words, if, under the measure granting the subsidy, the recipient would not be expected to export more than two of the additional five units to be produced, then this is indicative of the absence of a tie. By contrast, the granting of the subsidy would be tied to anticipated exportation if, all other things being equal, the recipient is expected to export at least three of the five additional units to be produced. In other words, the subsidy is designed in such a way that it is expected to skew the recipient's future sales in favour of export sales, even though the recipient may also be expected to increase its domestic sales.' See Appellate Body Report, *EC and certain member States – Large Civil Aircraft (2011)*, para. 1048.

of the measure granting the subsidy. Indeed, the conditional relationship between the granting of the subsidy and export performance must be objectively observable on the basis of such evidence in order for the subsidy to be geared to induce the promotion of future export performance by the recipient.[145]

Given that the standard for *de facto* export contingency is an *objective* standard, this standard cannot be satisfied by relying on the subjective motivation of the granting government to promote the future export performance of the recipient. However, as noted by the Appellate Body, 'objectively reviewable expressions of a government's policy objectives for granting a subsidy' may constitute relevant evidence in an inquiry into whether a subsidy is geared to induce the promotion of future export performance by the recipient.[146] Similarly, for the Appellate Body, the standard for *de facto* export contingency does not require a panel to ascertain a government's reason(s) for granting a subsidy:

> The government's reason for granting a subsidy only explains *why* the subsidy is granted. It does not necessarily answer the question as to *what* the government did, in terms of the design, structure, and modalities of operation of the subsidy, in order to induce the promotion of future export performance by the recipient. Indeed, whether the granting of a subsidy is conditional on future export performance must be determined by assessing *the subsidy itself*, in the light of the relevant factual circumstances, rather than by reference to the granting authority's reasons for the measure. This is not to say, however, that evidence regarding the policy reasons of a subsidy is necessarily excluded from the inquiry into whether a subsidy is geared to induce the promotion of future export performance by the recipient.[147]

The Appellate Body summarised in *EC and certain member States – Large Civil Aircraft (2011)* its test for *de facto* export contingency as follows:

> We find that the [*de facto*] conditionality between the granting of a subsidy and anticipated exportation can be established where the granting of the subsidy is geared to induce the promotion of future export performance of the recipient. The standard for *de facto* export contingency under Article 3.1(a) and footnote 4 of the SCM Agreement would be met when the subsidy is granted so as to provide an incentive to the recipient to export in a way that is not simply reflective of the conditions of supply and demand in the domestic and export markets undistorted by the granting of the subsidy.[148]

To illustrate the scope of the prohibition on export subsidies, note that panels and/or the Appellate Body found *inter alia* the following measures to be prohibited export subsidies: (1) payments by the Government of Brazil, related to the export of regional aircraft, which cover, at most, the difference between the interest charges contracted with the buyer and the cost to the financing party of raising the required funds; these payments were made under the interest rate equalisation component of the 'PROEX', an export financing programme (see *Brazil – Aircraft (1999)*); (2) grants for a total of A$30 million and a loan of A$25 million (on 'non-commercial' terms) provided by the Australian government to Howe, the only producer and exporter of automotive leather in

---

145 *Ibid.*, para. 1051.   146 *Ibid.*   147 *Ibid.*, para. 1052.   148 *Ibid.*, para. 1102.

Australia (see *Australia – Automotive Leather II (1999)*); and (3) the exemption from US income tax of a portion of export-related income of 'foreign sales corporations' (FSCs), i.e. foreign corporations in charge of specific activities with respect to the sale or lease of goods produced in the United States for export outside the United States (see *US – FSC (2000)*). Note that the Appellate Body was unable to come to a conclusion in *EC and certain member States – Large Civil Aircraft (2011)* as to whether – under its newly clarified test of *de facto* export contingency discussed above – the 'Launch Aid/Member State Financing' subsidies at issue amounted to prohibited export subsidies, because a panel's factual findings and undisputed facts on the record did not provide a sufficient basis to do so.

Questions and Assignments 12.6

Which subsidies are 'prohibited' under the *SCM Agreement*? Define an export subsidy. Give three examples of an export subsidy. When is a subsidy *de jure* contingent on export performance? Is a subsidy that is *de facto* export contingent an export subsidy? How is *de facto* export contingency demonstrated? What makes a subsidy 'geared to induce the promotion of future export performance' by the recipient? What kind of evidence would be useful or required in order to demonstrate that a subsidy creates such an incentive?

4.2 Import Substitution Subsidies

In addition to export subsidies, the category of prohibited subsidies also includes import substitution subsidies. As defined in Article 3.1(b) of the *SCM Agreement*, quoted above, import substitution subsidies are subsidies contingent upon the use of domestic over imported goods.[149] The Appellate Body in *Canada – Autos (2000)* noted that the phrase 'contingent … upon the use of domestic over imported goods' is unclear as to whether Article 3.1(b) covers both subsidies contingent 'in law' and subsidies contingent 'in fact' upon the use of domestic over imported goods.[150] Unlike in Article 3.1(a), the words 'in law or in fact' are absent from Article 3.1(b). However, according to the Appellate Body, this does not necessarily mean that Article 3.1(b) extends to *de jure* contingency only.[151] The Appellate Body held:

[W]e believe that a finding that Article 3.1(b) extends only to contingency 'in law' upon the use of domestic over imported goods would be contrary to the object and purpose of the *SCM Agreement* because it would make circumvention of obligations by Members too easy.[152]

In *US – Upland Cotton (2005)*, the Panel (and the Appellate Body on appeal) concluded that the subsidies at issue in that case, namely, payments to domestic users of US upland cotton, were subsidies contingent upon the use of domestic

---

149 'Import substitution subsidies' are also referred to as 'local content subsidies'.
150 See Appellate Body Report, *Canada – Autos (2000)*, para. 139.
151 See *ibid.*, para. 141.   152 *Ibid.*, para. 142.

over imported goods and were, therefore, inconsistent with Article 3.1(b) of the *SCM Agreement.*[153]

Questions and Assignments 12.7

Define an import substitution subsidy. How does the import substitution concept relate to the national treatment obligation in Article III of the GATT 1994? Is a subsidy that is *de facto* contingent on import substitution a prohibited subsidy?

4.3 Multilateral Remedies for Prohibited Subsidies

The multilateral remedies for prohibited subsidies, be they export subsidies or import substitution subsidies, are set out in Article 4 of the *SCM Agreement*. Pursuant to Article 4.1, consultations may be requested with any Member believed to be granting or maintaining a prohibited subsidy. Such a request for consultations shall include a 'statement of available evidence with regard to the existence and nature of the subsidy in question'.[154] If such consultations fail to resolve the dispute, the dispute may be referred to a dispute settlement panel, and then to the Appellate Body, for adjudication. The rules applicable to consultations and adjudication are primarily those of the DSU, discussed in detail in Chapter 3 of this book.[155] However, Article 4 of the *SCM Agreement* sets out a number of 'special or additional rules and procedures', which prevail over the DSU rules in cases of conflict.[156] The most notable difference between the rules and procedures of Article 4 of the *SCM Agreement* and the DSU rules and procedures relates to timeframes. The timeframes under Article 4 are half as long as the timeframes provided for under the DSU.[157] For example, the timeframe for 'ordinary' panel proceedings is six months from the date of composition of the panel;[158] under Article 4 of the *SCM Agreement*, the time-limit for panel proceedings concerning prohibited subsidies is three months. Note also that a panel established for a 'prohibited subsidy' dispute may ask a Permanent Group

---

153 See Panel Report, *US – Upland Cotton (2005)*, paras. 7.1088 and 7.1097–7.1098; and Appellate Body Report, *US – Upland Cotton (2005)*, para. 552. In the same case, the Appellate Body recalled 'that the introductory language of Article 3.1 of the *SCM Agreement* clarifies that this provision applies "[e]xcept as provided in the Agreement on Agriculture"', but also held that import substitution subsidies on agricultural products are not exempt from the prohibition in Article 3.1(b) of the *SCM Agreement* by virtue of Article 6.3 of, or Annex 3, paragraph 7, to, the *Agreement on Agriculture*. Thus, in providing domestic support that is consistent with the *Agreement on Agriculture*, WTO Members 'must be mindful of the prohibition in Article 3.1(b) of the *SCM Agreement* on the provision of subsidies that are contingent on the use of domestic over imported goods'. Appellate Body Report, *US – Upland Cotton (2005)*, para. 541, 545–6 and 550.

154 Article 4.2 of the *SCM Agreement*. On the interpretation of Article 4.2, see Panel Report, *Canada – Aircraft (1999)*; Panel Report, *Australia – Automotive Leather II (1999)*; Panel Report, *US – FSC (2000)* and Appellate Body Report, *US – FSC (2000)*; Panel Report, *US – Upland Cotton (2004)* and Appellate Body Report, *US – Upland Cotton (2005)*; see also Annex V on 'Procedures for Developing Information Concerning Serious Prejudice'.

155 See above, pp. 269–74.   156 See below, pp. 776–8.

157 Note, however, that parties can, and commonly do, agree on an extension of these special timeframes. See Article 4.12 of the *SCM Agreement*. Also, when a complainant brings claims under both the *SCM Agreement* and other WTO agreements, the shorter timeframes under the *SCM Agreement* do not apply.

158 See Article 12.8 of the DSU. See also above, pp. 246–50.

of Experts (PGE) whether the measure at issue is a prohibited subsidy.[159] The determination of the PGE is binding on the panel. To date, panels have not yet made use of this possibility.

If a panel finds a measure to be a prohibited subsidy, Article 4.7 of the *SCM Agreement* states that:

[t]he panel shall recommend that the subsidizing Member withdraw the subsidy without delay. In this regard, the panel shall specify in its recommendation the time-period within which the measure must be withdrawn.

On several occasions, panels and the Appellate Body have emphasised that prohibited subsidies must therefore be withdrawn *without delay*, and the time period within which the subsidy must be withdrawn is to be specified by the panel.[160] As the Appellate Body clarified in *Brazil – Aircraft (Article 21.5 – Canada) (2000)*, withdrawal of the prohibited subsidy involves the removal of the subsidy.[161] The panel in *Australia – Automotive Leather II (Article 21.5 – US) (2000)* concluded that the obligation to withdraw the prohibited subsidy, in that case, could only be met by repayment of the subsidy received. As discussed in Chapter 3 of this book, in general, remedies for breaches of WTO law are only prospective, but, according to the panel in *Australia – Automotive Leather II (Article 21.5 – US) (2000)*, the obligation under Article 4.7 to withdraw the prohibited subsidy requires the company that received a non-recurrent prohibited subsidy to repay that subsidy to the subsidising Member.[162] The panel in *Australia – Automotive Leather II (Article 21.5 – US) (2000)* reasoned as follows:

We believe it is incumbent upon us to interpret 'withdraw the subsidy' so as to give it effective meaning. A finding that the term 'withdraw the subsidy' may not encompass repayment would give rise to serious questions regarding the efficacy of the remedy in prohibited subsidy cases involving one-time subsidies paid in the past whose retention is not contingent upon future export performance.[163]

This ruling of that panel was heavily criticised by WTO Members because of its retroactive character.[164] To date, no other panel has made a similar ruling.[165]

Panels in 'prohibited subsidy' disputes specify the time period within which the prohibited subsidy must be withdrawn, i.e. they specify what is meant by

---

159 See Article 4.5 of the *SCM Agreement*. See also above, pp. 129–30.
160 See Appellate Body Report, *US – FSC (Article 21.5 – EC II) (2006)*, para. 82.
161 See Appellate Body Report, *Brazil – Aircraft (Article 21.5 – Canada) (2000)*, para. 45.
162 See also above, pp. 204–5.
163 Panel Report, *Australia – Automotive Leather II (Article 21.5 – US) (2000)*, para. 6.35.
164 See Dispute Settlement Body, *Minutes of the DSB Meeting of 11 February 2000*, WT/DSB/M/75. See also above, p. 205, footnote 259. Note that the United States, the original complainant in this dispute, had *not* requested the repayment of the export subsidy at issue.
165 Note that the panels in *Canada – Aircraft (Article 21.5 – Brazil) (2000)* and *Brazil – Aircraft (Article 21.5 – Canada) (2000)* did not rule on the repayment of subsidies because repayment had not been requested by the complainants and the panels considered that their findings should be restricted to the scope of the disagreement between the parties. See Panel Report, *Canada – Aircraft (Article 21.5 – Brazil) (2000)*, para. 5.48; and Panel Report, *Brazil – Aircraft (Article 21.5 – Canada) (2000)*, footnote 17.

'withdraw without delay' as required by Article 4.7 of the *SCM Agreement*.[166] Note by way of example the conclusion reached by the panel in *Korea – Commercial Vessels (2005)*:

> Taking into account the procedures that may be required to implement our recommendation on the one hand, and the requirement that Korea withdraw its subsidies 'without delay' on the other, we recommend that Korea withdraw the individual APRG and PSL subsidies within 90 days.[167]

To date, several panels have specified a period of three months for the withdrawal of a prohibited subsidy. In *US – FSC (2000)*, however, the panel specified a period of more than a year to allow the United States to adopt the necessary fiscal legislation.[168] In *Brazil – Aircraft (Article 21.5 – Canada) (2000)*, the Appellate Body stated that 'the obligation to withdraw prohibited subsidies "without delay" is unaffected by contractual obligations that a Member itself may have assumed under municipal law'.[169] Similarly, in *US – FSC (Article 21.5 – EC) (2002)*, the Appellate Body clarified that there is 'no basis' for extending the time period prescribed in Article 4.7 for withdrawal: (1) to protect the contractual interests of private parties; or (2) to ensure an orderly transition to the regime of the new measure.[170]

If in an Article 21.5 proceeding the measure taken to comply with the Article 4.7 recommendation in the original proceedings is found not to achieve full withdrawal of the prohibited subsidy – either because it leaves the entirety or part of the original prohibited subsidy in place, or because it replaces that subsidy with another prohibited subsidy – the implementing Member continues to be under the obligation to achieve full withdrawal of the subsidy.[171]

If a recommendation to withdraw a prohibited subsidy is not followed within the time period set by the panel, the DSB must, upon the request of the original complainant(s) and by reverse consensus, authorise 'appropriate countermeasures' pursuant to Article 4.10 of the *SCM Agreement*. In 'prohibited subsidies' disputes, these 'appropriate countermeasures' replace the suspension of concessions or other obligations, i.e. retaliation measures, available under the DSU in case of non-implementation in WTO disputes under covered agreements other than the *SCM Agreement*.[172] 'Appropriate countermeasures' and 'retaliation measures' may differ in that the level of 'appropriate countermeasures' could be the amount of the prohibited subsidy rather than the level of any trade effects or the nullification or impairment that has been caused.[173]

---

166 On the general rules of Article 21.3 of the DSU concerning the 'reasonable period of time for implementation', see above, pp. 195–200.
167 Panel Report, *Korea – Commercial Vessels (2005)*, para. 8.5.
168 See Panel Report, *US – FSC (2000)*, para. 8.8.
169 Appellate Body Report, *Brazil – Aircraft (Article 21.5 – Canada) (2000)*, paras. 45–6.
170 See Appellate Body Report, *US – FSC (Article 21.5 – EC) (2002)*, paras. 229–30.
171 Appellate Body Report, *US – FSC (Article 21.5 – EC II) (2006)*, para. 82.
172 See above, pp. 776–8.
173 The arbitrators in *Brazil – Aircraft (Article 22.6 – Brazil) (2000)* accepted the view of the parties that the term 'countermeasures', as used in these provisions, includes suspension of concessions or other obligations. Furthermore, the arbitrators concluded that, when dealing with a prohibited export subsidy, an amount of

Questions and Assignments 12.8

Questions and Assignments 12.8

What happens when a panel finds that a subsidy granted by a Member is an export or import substitution subsidy within the meaning of Article 3 of the *SCM Agreement*?

5   ACTIONABLE SUBSIDIES

Unlike export subsidies and import substitution subsidies, most subsidies are not prohibited but are 'actionable', i.e. they are subject to challenge in the event that they cause adverse effects on the interests of another Member. To the extent that these subsidies do not cause adverse effects, or the adverse effects are removed, they cannot, or can no longer, be challenged successfully. The chapeau of Article 5 of the *SCM Agreement* provides:

No Member should cause, through the use of any subsidy referred to in paragraphs 1 and 2 of Article 1, adverse effects to the interests of other Members.

Paragraphs (a) to (c) of Article 5 distinguish between three types of 'adverse effects' on the interests of other Members: (1) *injury* to the domestic industry of another Member (Article 5(a)); (2) *nullification or impairment* of benefits accruing directly or indirectly to other Members under the GATT 1994 (Article 5(b)); and (3) *serious prejudice*, including a threat thereof, to the interests of another Member (Article 5(c)). This section discusses in turn these three types of 'adverse effects'.

5.1   Subsidies Causing Injury

Subsidies have adverse effects on the interests of other Members within the meaning of Article 5(a) of the *SCM Agreement* – and are therefore 'actionable' – when the subsidised imports cause injury to the domestic industry producing the like product.[174] This sub-section examines, in turn, the concepts of (1) 'like

countermeasures that corresponds to the total amount of the subsidy is appropriate. See Decision by the Arbitrator, *Brazil – Aircraft (Article 22.6 – Brazil) (2000)*, paras. 3.28, 3.29 and 3.33–3.40 and 3.44. According to the arbitrators in *US – FSC (Article 22.6 – US) (2002)*, it would be 'consistent with the reading of the plain meaning of the concept of countermeasure to say that it can be directed either at countering the measure at issue (in this case, at effectively neutralizing the export subsidy with respect to all countries affected by it) or at counteracting its effects on the affected party, or both'. See Decision by the Arbitrators, *US – FSC (Article 22.6 – US) (2002)*, para. 5.6. See however, the Decision by the Arbitrator, *US – Upland Cotton (Article 22.6 – Brazil) (2009)*. The arbitrators in that arbitration noted the difference between the use of the term 'countermeasures' in Article 4.10 of the *SCM Agreement* and the terms of Article 22 of the DSU, which refers to the 'suspension of concessions or other obligations'. However, they understood the term 'countermeasures' not to designate anything other than a temporary suspension of certain obligations. The arbitrators were not convinced that the use of the term 'countermeasures' necessarily connotes, in and of itself, an intention to refer to retaliatory action that 'goes beyond the mere rebalancing of trade interests' between the parties to the dispute. See Decision by the Arbitrator, *US – Upland Cotton (Article 22.6 – Brazil) (2009)*, paras. 4.34–4.43.

174 In *EC and certain member States – Large Civil Aircraft (2011)*, the panel explained that it would interpret 'injury to the domestic industry' in Article 5(a) harmoniously with the provisions of Article 15 governing countervailing duty investigations. Since, in an 'adverse effects' case, it was essentially fulfilling the role of an investigating authority in a countervailing or anti-dumping duty investigation, the panel decided to base its examination and determination of the various injury elements as required by the more specific provisions of Article 15. See Panel Report, *EC and certain member States – Large Civil Aircraft (2011)*, paras. 7.2068 and 7.2080.

product', (2) 'domestic industry', (3) 'injury' and (4) 'causation' as they apply in Part III of the *SCM Agreement* on actionable subsidies.[175]

5.1.1 Like Product

The concept of 'like product' is defined in footnote 46 to the *SCM Agreement* as:

[a] product which is identical, i.e. alike in all respects to the product under consideration, or in the absence of such a product, another product which, although not alike in all respects, has characteristics closely resembling those of the product under consideration.[176]

When compared to the definitions of 'like products' resulting from the case law on Articles I and III of the GATT 1994 or the definition of 'like products' in the *Agreement on Safeguards*, the definition in the *SCM Agreement* seems narrower in scope. The approach to establishing 'likeness' under the *SCM Agreement* is, however, in fact similar to the approach under the GATT 1994.[177] In *Indonesia – Autos (1998)*, the panel found:

Although we are required in this dispute to interpret the term 'like product' in conformity with the specific definition provided in the SCM Agreement, we believe that useful guidance can nevertheless be derived from prior analysis of 'like product' issues under other provisions of the WTO Agreement.[178]

The provisions of the *WTO Agreement* referred to are, of course, Articles I:1, III:2 and III:4 of the GATT 1994. In establishing 'likeness', the same elements (physical characteristics as well as end-uses, consumer habits and preferences and tariff classification) will be of importance. As the panel in *Indonesia – Autos (1998)* ruled, the term 'characteristics closely resembling' includes but is not limited to physical characteristics; the SCM Agreement does not preclude looking at criteria other than physical characteristics, where relevant to the like product analysis.[179]

5.1.2 Domestic Industry

The definition of 'domestic industry' in the *SCM Agreement* is quite similar to the definition of that concept in the *Anti-Dumping Agreement*.[180] Article 16.1 of the *SCM Agreement* defines the 'domestic industry' as:

---

175 Note that footnote 11 to the *SCM Agreement* stipulates that the term 'injury to the domestic industry' is used in Article 5(a) in the same sense as it is used in Part V of that Agreement. They are addressed here together, although it may be important to note that considerations may differ under certain provisions of Part III and Part V of the Agreement. See below, pp. 802–14.

176 Note that this definition applies throughout the *SCM Agreement* and not merely in the context of the determination of material injury. It also applies, for example, in the context of the serious prejudice determination of Article 6 of the *SCM Agreement*. See below, pp. 785–6.

177 For the determination of 'likeness' under Articles I:1, III:2 and III:4 of the GATT 1994, see above, pp. 327–8, 360–81 and 386–94.

178 Panel Report, *Indonesia – Autos (1998)*, para. 14.174.   179 See *ibid.*, para. 14.173.

180 See above, pp. 696–8. With regard to the definition of 'domestic industry' under the *Anti-Dumping Agreement*, consider, in particular, the Appellate Body's interpretation of that term in *EC – Fasteners (China) (2011)*. See Appellate Body Report, *EC – Fasteners (China) (2011)*, para. 411.

[t]he domestic producers as a whole of the like products or ... those of them whose collective output of the products constitutes a major proportion of the total domestic production of those products.

There are two exceptions to this definition of 'domestic industry'. First, domestic *producers that are related* to exporters or importers or which themselves import the subsidised products may be excluded from the relevant 'domestic industry'.[181] Secondly, in exceptional circumstances, the territory of a Member may be divided into *two or more competitive markets* and the producers within each market may be regarded as a separate industry. A regional industry then constitutes the relevant 'domestic industry'.[182]

5.1.3   Injury

The concept of 'injury' to a domestic industry in the *SCM Agreement* covers: (1) material injury to a domestic industry;[183] (2) a threat of material injury to a domestic industry; and (3) material retardation of the establishment of a domestic industry.[184]

The determination of 'injury' to the domestic industry must, pursuant to Article 15.1 of the *SCM Agreement*, be based on positive evidence and involve an objective examination of, *first*, the volume of the subsidised imports and the effect of the subsidised imports on prices in the domestic market for like products, and, *secondly*, the consequent impact of these imports on the domestic producers of such products.[185] With regard to the *first* element of the examination under Article 15.1 of the *SCM Agreement*, Article 15.2 thereof provides that, with respect to the volume of the subsidised imports, it must be examined whether there has been a *significant increase* of the subsidised imports.[186] With respect to the effect of the subsidised imports on prices, it must be examined whether there has been a *significant price undercutting* by the subsidised imports, or whether these imports otherwise *depress or suppress prices to a significant degree*.[187] As discussed in Chapter 11 of this book, the Appellate Body interpreted in *China – GOES (2012)* the requirements of Article 15.2 of the *SCM Agreement* and the identical requirements of Article 3.2 of the *Anti-Dumping Agreement*. According to the Appellate Body, Article 15.2 contemplates an inquiry into the relationship

---

181   See Article 16.1 of the *SCM Agreement*.

182   See Article 16.2 of the *SCM Agreement*.

183   Note that the *SCM Agreement*, like the *Anti-Dumping Agreement*, requires *material* injury, or a threat thereof, rather than *serious* injury as required under the *Agreement on Safeguards*. As already mentioned, the Appellate Body in *US – Lamb (2001)* noted that the standard of 'serious injury' is higher than that of 'material injury'. See above, pp. 616–19.

184   See footnote 45 to the *SCM Agreement*.

185   Note in this regard that the panel in *US – Softwood Lumber VI (2004)* recalled the definitions of the Appellate Body with respect to 'positive evidence' and 'objective examination' under the *Anti-Dumping Agreement* (as in *US – Hot-Rolled Steel (2001)*). See Panel Report, *US – Softwood Lumber VI (2004)*, para. 7.28, referring to Appellate Body Report, *US – Hot-Rolled Steel (2001)*, paras. 192–3.

186   This increase may be an increase in absolute terms or relative to production or consumption in the importing country.

187   Note that to 'suppress' prices is to prevent price increases that would otherwise occur.

between two variables, namely, subsidised imports and domestic prices. More specifically, an investigating authority is required to consider whether a first variable – that is, dumped imports – has '*explanatory force for the occurrence of*' significant depression or suppression of a second variable – that is, domestic prices.[188] For a further discussion of the requirements of Article 15.2 of the *SCM Agreement*, please refer to the discussion of the *Anti-Dumping Agreement* in Chapter 11.[189]

With regard to the *second* element of the examination under Article 15.1 of the *SCM Agreement*, Article 15.4 thereof requires that the examination of the consequent impact of the subsidised imports on the domestic industry must include an evaluation of all *relevant economic factors and indices* having a bearing on the state of the industry. Article 15.4 lists the following specific factors: (1) an actual and potential decline in the output, sales, market share, profits, productivity, return on investments or utilisation of capacity; (2) factors affecting domestic prices; and (3) actual and potential negative effects on cash flow, inventories, employment, wages, growth or the ability to raise capital or investments. The examination of all factors on this list is mandatory in each case.[190] However, this list is not exhaustive and *other* relevant factors must also be considered. Furthermore, note that no single factor, or combination of factors, listed in Article 15.4 necessarily gives decisive guidance.[191] In *China – GOES (2012)*, the Appellate Body emphasised that Article 15.4 also requires an examination of the *impact of subsidised imports* on the domestic industry. In other words, Article 15.4 does not merely require an examination of the state of the domestic industry, but contemplates that an understanding of *the impact* of subsidised imports be derived on the basis of such an examination.[192]

As indicated above, the concept of 'injury' to a domestic industry in the *SCM Agreement* covers not only 'material injury' but also 'threat of material injury'. The determination of a 'threat of material injury' must be based on facts and not merely on allegations, conjecture or remote possibility.[193] For there to be a 'threat of material injury', the change in circumstances which would create a situation in which the subsidy would cause injury must be clearly foreseen and imminent.[194] Article 15.7 lists a number of factors to be considered in making a determination regarding the existence of a 'threat of material injury'. This non-exhaustive list of factors includes, *inter alia*: (1) the nature of the subsidy

---

188   Appellate Body Report, *China – GOES (2012)*, paras. 136–7. It is necessary to examine domestic prices in conjunction with subsidised imports in order to understand whether subsidised imports have '*explanatory force for the occurrence of*' significant depression or suppression of domestic prices. Appellate Body Report, *China – GOES (2012)*, para. 136. Emphasis added.

189   See above, pp. 700–6.

190   The existence of an obligation to examine all the factors of the Article 15.4 list can be established by analogy to panel and Appellate Body reports interpreting similar provisions in the *Anti-Dumping Agreement* and the *Agreement on Safeguards*. See above, pp. 704–6 (AD Agreement), 618–620 (Safeguards Agreement).

191   See Article 15.4, last sentence, of the *SCM Agreement*.

192   Appellate Body Report, *China – GOES (2012)*, para. 149.

193   See Article 15.7 of the *SCM Agreement*.

194   Article 15.7, second sentence, of the *SCM Agreement*.

and the trade effects likely to arise from it; (2) a significant rate of increase of subsidised imports; and (3) whether imports are entering at prices that will have a significant depressing or suppressing effect on domestic prices.[195] Article 15.7 does not prescribe a specific methodology for determining the rate of increase in imports or for the examination of the price effects of dumped/subsidised imports.[196] The factors listed in Article 15.7 must all be considered.[197] Moreover, any other relevant factor must also be considered in order to establish whether further subsidised imports are imminent and whether, unless protective action is taken, material injury would occur.[198] In addition, as in the case of dumping, Article 15.8 requires 'special care' when considering and deciding on situations of 'threat of material injury'.[199] Therefore, there is definitely no *lower* standard of care and explanation on the grounds that a determination of 'threat of injury' rather than a determination of current material injury is to be made. To the contrary, the reasoning underlying a determination of 'threat of injury' must clearly disclose the assumptions and extrapolations that were made, on the basis of the positive record evidence, regarding future occurrences and not merely on allegation, conjecture or remote possibility; and show a high degree of likelihood that projected occurrences will materialise.[200]

Pursuant to Article 15.3 of the *SCM Agreement*, when the subsidised imports originate in several countries and several countries are therefore subject to the anti-subsidy investigations, the effects of the subsidised imports may be assessed *cumulatively* for the purpose of establishing injury to the domestic industry. It is quite common for WTO Members to make a cumulative assessment of the effects of subsidised imports. However, pursuant to Article 15.3 of the *SCM Agreement*, such cumulative assessment is allowed only when: (1) the amount of subsidisation is more than *de minimis* (i.e. more than or equal to 1 per cent *ad valorem*);[201] (2) the volume of the imports of each country is not negligible; and (3) the cumulative assessment of the effects of the imports is appropriate in light of the conditions of

---

195 See the factors mentioned in Article 15.7(i), (ii) and (iv) of the *SCM Agreement*.

196 Regardless of the methodology followed, the Appellate Body clarified that what must be examined is: (i) the trends in the prices at which 'imports are entering'; (ii) the 'effect' of those prices on 'domestic prices'; and (iii) the 'demand for further imports'. Discerning the 'effect' of prices of imports on domestic prices necessarily calls for an analysis of the interaction between the two. Otherwise, the links between the prices of imports and the depressing or suppressing effect on domestic prices, and the consequent likelihood of a 'demand for further imports', may not be properly established. See Appellate Body Report, *US – Softwood Lumber VI (Article 21.5 – Canada) (2006)*, para. 151.

197 See, by analogy, Panel Report, *Mexico – Corn Syrup (2000)*, para. 7.133, which concerned an identical provision in the *Anti-Dumping Agreement*. See above, pp. 707–8.

198 See Article 15.7, last sentence, of the *SCM Agreement*. Note that the panel in *US – Softwood Lumber VI (2004)* stated that a threat of injury determination is made against the background of an evaluation of the condition of the industry in light of the Article 15.4 factors. Once such an analysis has been carried out in the context of an investigation of material injury, however, the panel found that none of the relevant provisions of Article 15 require a second analysis of the injury factors in cases involving a threat of material injury. See Panel Report, *US – Softwood Lumber VI (2004)*, paras. 7.97–7.112.

199 See Panel Report, *US – Softwood Lumber VI (2004)*, para. 7.33.

200 Appellate Body Report, *US – Softwood Lumber VI (Article 21.5 – Canada) (2006)*, paras. 107 and 109.

201 See Article 11.9 of the *SCM Agreement*. The amount of the subsidy is considered *de minimis* if the subsidy is less than 1 per cent of the value of the subsidised product.

competition between products imported from different countries and the conditions of competition between the imported products and the like domestic products.

5.1.4 Causation

Finally, Article 15.5 of the *SCM Agreement* spells out the requirement to establish the existence of a *causal link* between subsidised imports and injury to the domestic industry. The first sentence of Article 15.5 requires that 'the subsidized imports are, through the effects of subsidies, causing injury' to the domestic industry. The second sentence emphasises that the demonstration of the causal relationship between the subsidised imports and the injury shall be based on all relevant evidence. In both sentences, the subject to which the phrase 'are causing injury' applies, or in respect of which 'a causal relationship' is to be established, is 'the subsidized imports'.[202]

The injury suffered by the domestic industry may be caused not only by the subsidised imports. Other factors may also cause injury to the domestic industry, including: (1) the volumes and prices of non-subsidised imports of the product in question; (2) a contraction in demand or changes in the patterns of consumption; (3) trade-restrictive practices of, and competition between, the foreign and domestic producers; (4) developments in technology; and (5) the export performance and productivity of the domestic industry. As set out in Article 15.5, third sentence, the injury caused by these other factors may *not be attributed* to the subsidised imports.[203]

In sum, the demonstration of the causal relationship envisaged in the first two sentences of Article 15.5 is to be carried out by following the analysis set forth in Articles 15.2 and 15.4 for examining the 'effects' of the subsidised imports. Accordingly, such an examination will comprise the following elements: (1) whether there has been a significant increase in subsidised imports; (2) the effect of the subsidised imports on prices; and (3) the consequent impact of the subsidised imports on the domestic industry.[204] The Appellate Body found that the phrase 'the subsidized imports are, through the effects of subsidies, causing injury' in Article 15.5 does not impose an additional requirement to make two distinct types of examinations into (1) the 'effects of the subsidies' as distinguished from (2) the effects of 'the subsidised imports' on a case-by-case basis.[205] The 'non-attribution' requirement contained in the third sentence of Article 15.5 is concerned with answering that the injurious effects of any known factors *other than subsidised imports* are not attributed to the subsidised imports.[206]

Questions and Assignments 12.9

When is a subsidy 'actionable' under the *SCM Agreement*? What are 'like products' in the context of the *SCM Agreement*? What is the relevant 'domestic industry' in the context of

---

202 Appellate Body Report, *Japan – DRAMs (Korea) (2007)*, para. 262.   203 *Ibid.*, para. 267.
204 See *ibid.*, para. 263.   205 See *ibid.*, paras. 264 and 277.   206 See *ibid.*, para. 267.

the *SCM Agreement*? What does the concept of 'injury', within the meaning of Article 15 of the *SCM Agreement*, cover? How is 'injury' to the domestic industry established? When is there a 'threat of material injury'? May the effects of subsidised imports from different countries be assessed *cumulatively* for the purpose of establishing injury to the domestic industry? Is the existence of a causal link between the subsidised imports and the injury to the domestic industry required? If so, how must this link be established? Explain the non-attribution requirement provided for in Article 15.5 of the *SCM Agreement*.

5.2   Subsidies Causing Nullification or Impairment

Subsidies have adverse effects on the interests of other Members within the meaning of Article 5(b) of the *SCM Agreement* – and are therefore 'actionable' – also when the subsidised imports cause the nullification or impairment of benefits accruing directly or indirectly to other Members under the GATT 1994. This may be the case, in particular, with respect to the benefits from tariff concessions bound under Article II:1 of the GATT 1994. Subsidisation may undercut improved market access resulting from a tariff concession.[207]

5.3   Subsidies Causing Serious Prejudice

Subsidies have adverse effects on the interests of other Members within the meaning of Article 5(c) of the *SCM Agreement* – and are therefore 'actionable' – when the subsidised imports cause serious prejudice to the interests of another Member. Pursuant to Article 6.3 of the *SCM Agreement*, 'serious prejudice' *may* arise where a subsidy has one or more of the following effects: (1) the subsidy displaces or impedes imports of a like product of another Member into the market of the subsidising Member (Article 6.3(a)); (2) the subsidy displaces or impedes the export of a like product of another Member from a third country market (Article 6.3(b)); (3) the subsidy results in a significant price undercutting by the subsidised product in comparison to the like product of another Member in the same market, or significant price suppression, price depression or lost sales in the same market (Article 6.3(c)); or (4) the subsidy leads to an increase in the world market share of the subsidising Member in a particular primary product or commodity in comparison to the average share it had during the previous

---

207   The existence of nullification or impairment is established in accordance with the practice of the application of Article XXIII of the GATT 1994. See footnote 12 of the *SCM Agreement*. However, in *US – Offset Act (Byrd Amendment) (2003)*, Mexico, one of the complainants, had argued that, since the panel had already found that the CDSOA was inconsistent with, *inter alia*, Articles 11.4 and 32.1, there was, pursuant to Article 3.8 of the DSU, a presumption of nullification or impairment. According to Mexico, this nullification or impairment was sufficient to demonstrate nullification or impairment for the purpose of Article 5(b) of the *SCM Agreement*. The panel rejected this argument and stated that, for the purpose of Article 5(b) of the *SCM Agreement*, Mexico must show that the *use* of the subsidy caused nullification or impairment. See Panel Report, *US – Offset Act (Byrd Amendment) (2003)*, para. 7.119. The panel subsequently referred to the panel report in *Japan – Film (1998)* on the three elements that must be established in order to uphold a claim of nullification or impairment. See above, p. 174.

period of three years (Article 6.3(d)).[208] If a complaining Member can show that a subsidy has any of these effects, then 'serious prejudice' may be found to exist. On the other hand, if the subsidising Member can show that subsidies do not result in any of these effects, these subsidies will *not* be found to cause serious prejudice.[209]

The concepts of 'serious prejudice' and 'injury' to a particular domestic industry are different and distinct concepts. The panel in *Korea – Commercial Vessels (2005)* explained that the concept of serious prejudice is concerned with negative effects on a Member's trade interests in respect of a product, such as lost import or export volume or market share, or adverse price effects, or a combination thereof, in various product and geographic markets.[210]

Both Article 5(c) and Article 6.3 of the *SCM Agreement* refer to 'serious prejudice'. In *US – Upland Cotton (2005)*, the question arose whether a finding of 'significant price suppression' under Article 6.3(c) is conclusive in establishing 'serious prejudice' under Article 5(c). The panel concluded that a detrimental impact on a complaining Member's production of, and/or trade in, the product concerned under Article 6.3 may fall within the concept of 'prejudice' in Article 5(c) of the *SCM Agreement*. In the particular facts and circumstances of *US – Upland Cotton (2005)*, the panel arrived at the conclusion that 'significant price suppression' under Article 6.3 amounted to 'serious prejudice' within the meaning of Article 5(c) of the *SCM Agreement*.[211] The panel in *US – Upland Cotton (Article 21.5 – Brazil) (2008)* concurred that, once the conditions set forth in Article 6.3(a)–(d) are fulfilled, there is a sufficient basis for a finding of serious prejudice within the meaning of Article 5(c).

To assess whether there is 'serious prejudice' within the meaning of Articles 5(c) and 6 of the *SCM Agreement*, it is necessary to determine: (1) what the relevant 'geographical market' and 'product market' is; (2) whether there is 'displacement' or 'impedance' of imports or exports; (3) whether there is 'price undercutting', 'price suppression', 'price depression' or 'lost sales'; (4) whether the price undercutting, price suppression, price depression or lost sales are 'significant'; (5) whether there is an 'increase in world market share'; (6) whether there is 'threat of serious prejudice'; and/or (7) whether the market phenomena referred to above are 'the effect of' the challenged subsidies (i.e. causal link and non-attribution). This section deals with each of these issues in turn. In conclusion this section also addresses a number of other issues relevant to the analysis of the effects on subsidies, including: (1) the temporal scope of Articles 5 and 6

---

208 Note that Article 6.1 of the *SCM Agreement* listed several situations in which subsidies are *deemed* to cause 'serious prejudice'. However, this provision lapsed on 31 December 1999. See Article 31 of the *SCM Agreement*.
209 Article 6.2 of the *SCM Agreement*.
210 Panel Report, *Korea – Commercial Vessels (2005)*, para. 7.578.
211 Panel Report, *US – Upland Cotton (2004)*, paras. 7.1392–7.1395. See also Panel Report, *Indonesia – Autos (1998)*, paras. 14.254–14.255.

of the *SCM Agreement*; (2) the pass-through of subsidies; (3) the effect of subsidies over time; (4) the collective analysis of the effects of subsidies; and (5) Annex V on Procedures for Developing Information Concerning Serious Prejudice.

5.3.1   The Relevant Geographic and Product Market

The question of the relevant geographic and product market for the assessment of serious prejudice claims under Article 6.3 of the *SCM Agreement* arose in *US – Upland Cotton (2005)*, *US – Upland Cotton (Article 21.5 – Brazil) (2008)*, *EC and certain member States – Large Civil Aircraft (2011)* and *US – Large Civil Aircraft (2nd complaint) (2012)*. Article 6.3(c) of the *SCM Agreement* addresses the situation where 'the effect of the subsidy is ... significant price suppression ... in the same *market*'. Aside from the qualification that it must be 'the same' market, Article 6.3(c) imposes no explicit *geographical* limitation on the scope of the relevant market. According to the Appellate Body in *US – Upland Cotton (2005)*:

> This contrasts with the other paragraphs of Article 6.3: paragraph (a) restricts the relevant market to 'the market of the subsidizing Member'; paragraph (b) restricts the relevant market to 'a third country market'; and paragraph (d) refers specifically to the 'world market share' ... [T]his difference may indicate that the drafters did not intend to confine, *a priori*, the market examined under Article 6.3(c) to any particular area. Thus, the ordinary meaning of the word 'market' in Article 6.3(c), when read in the context of the other paragraphs of Article 6.3, neither requires nor excludes the possibility of a national market or a world market.[212]

The phrase 'in the same market' in Article 6.3(c) 'applies to all four situations covered in that provision, namely, "significant price undercutting", "significant price suppression, price depression [and] lost sales"'.[213] In *US – Upland Cotton (2005)*, the term 'market' was defined as 'a place ... with a demand for a commodity or service'; 'a geographical area of demand for commodities or services'; 'the area of economic activity in which buyers and sellers come together and the forces of supply and demand affect prices'.[214] The Appellate Body noted, however, that this 'does not, of itself, impose any limitation on the "geographical area" that makes up any given market. Nor does it indicate that a "world market" cannot exist for a given product.' The 'degree to which a market is limited by geography will depend on the product itself and its ability to be traded across distances'.[215] The Appellate Body concluded that:

> [t]wo products would be in the same market if they were engaged in actual or potential competition in that market. Thus, two products may be 'in the same market' even if they

212 Appellate Body Report, *US – Upland Cotton (2005)*, para. 406.
213 In *US – Upland Cotton (2005)*, the Appellate Body was of the view that the phrase 'in the same market' suggests that the subsidised product in question (US upland cotton in this case) and the relevant product of the complaining Member (Brazilian upland cotton) must be 'in the same market'. See Appellate Body Report, *US – Upland Cotton (2005)*, para. 407.
214 Panel Report, *US – Upland Cotton (2004)*, para. 7.1236.
215 Appellate Body Report, *US – Upland Cotton (2005)*, para. 405. See also Panel Report, *Korea – Commercial Vessels (2005)*, paras. 7.562–7.566.

are not necessarily sold at the same time and in the same place or country ... The scope of the 'market', for determining the area of competition between two products, may depend on several factors such as the nature of the product, the homogeneity of the conditions of competition, and transport costs. This market for a particular product could well be a 'world market'.[216]

With regard to the relevant 'market price' for making a finding on the price phenomena listed in Article 6.3(c), in *US – Upland Cotton (2005)*, the question arose whether it was sufficient for the panel to analyse the price of upland cotton in general in the world market or whether an analysis of the price of Brazilian upland cotton in the world market was required in order to make a finding of significant price suppression with respect to that price. The Appellate Body agreed with the panel that:

'[d]evelopments in the world upland cotton price would inevitably affect prices' wherever Brazilian and United States upland cotton compete, 'due to the nature of the world prices in question and the nature of the world upland cotton market, and the relative proportion of that market enjoyed by the United States and Brazil'. It was not necessary, in these circumstances, for the Panel to proceed to a separate analysis of the prices of Brazilian upland cotton in the world market.[217]

In contrast to the words 'same market' that appear in Article 6.3(c), Article 6.3(a) refers to the 'market of the subsidizing Member', and Article 6.3(b) refers to a 'third country market'. Despite this wording, the Appellate Body found in *EC and certain member States – Large Civil Aircraft (2011)* that under Articles 6.3(a) and (b) an assessment of the competitive relationship between products in the market is nevertheless required in order to determine 'whether such products form part of the same market' and 'whether and to what extent one product may displace another'.[218] Thus, while the Appellate Body accepted that 'a complaining Member may identify a subsidized product and the like product by reference to footnote 46, the products thereby identified must be analysed under the discipline of the product market so as to be able to determine whether displacement is occurring'.[219] Ordinarily, the subsidised product and the like product will form part of a larger product market. But it may be the case that a complainant chooses to define the subsidised and like products so broadly that it is necessary to analyse these products in different product markets. This will be necessary so as to analyse further the real competitive interactions that are taking place, and thereby determine whether displacement is occurring.[220]

---

216 See Appellate Body Report, *US – Upland Cotton (2005)*, para. 408. The Appellate Body agreed with the panel that 'the fact that a world market exists for one product does not necessarily mean that such a market exists for every product'. See *ibid*. Thus the determination of the relevant market under Article 6.3(c) of the *SCM Agreement* depends on the subsidised product in question. If a world market exists for the product in question, Article 6.3(c) does not exclude the possibility of this 'world market' being the 'same market' for the purposes of a significant price suppression analysis under that Article. See *ibid*.
217 Appellate Body Report, *US – Upland Cotton (2005)*, para. 417.
218 Appellate Body Report, *EC and certain member States – Large Civil Aircraft (2011)*, para. 1119.
219 *Ibid*.   220 *Ibid*.

In making these observations in *EC and certain member States – Large Civil Aircraft (2011)*, the Appellate Body relied on the fundamental economic proposition that:

[a] market comprises only those products that exercise competitive constraint on each other. This is the case when the relevant products are substitutable.

Although physical characteristics, end-uses and consumer preferences may assist in deciding whether two products are in the same market, the Appellate Body cautioned that these likeness criteria should *not* be treated as exclusive factors in deciding whether those products are sufficiently substitutable so as to create competitive constraints on each other.[221] The Appellate Body explained that:

[d]emand-side substitutability – that is, when two products are considered substitutable by consumers – is an indispensable, but not the only relevant, criterion to consider when assessing whether two products are in a single market. Rather, a consideration of substitutability on the supply side may also be required. For example, evidence on whether a supplier can switch its production at limited or prohibitive cost from one product to another in a short period of time may also inform the question of whether two products are in a single market.[222]

In respect of the relevant product market to be examined for the purposes of displacement and impedance under Article 6.3(a) and (b), the Appellate Body concluded in *EC and certain member States – Large Civil Aircraft (2011)* that it is likely to vary from case to case depending upon the particular factual circumstances, including the nature of the products at issue, as well as demand-side and supply-side factors. The Appellate Body noted:

In some cases, the entire product range offered by the complainant may compete with the range of products of the respondent that is allegedly subsidized. In other cases, an assessment ... may reveal the existence of multiple product markets in which particular products of the complaining Member compete with particular subsidized products of the respondent. However, it is important to note that whether or not a broad or narrow range of products benefit from subsidization says little about whether all these products compete in the same market. Indeed, products benefiting from subsidies may compete in very different markets.[223]

On the basis of these considerations, the Appellate Body observed in *EC and certain member States – Large Civil Aircraft (2011)* that there is 'both a geographic and product market component to the assessment of displacement'[224] and, by implication, impedance.[225] In principle, the manner in which the geographic dimension of a market is determined will depend on a number of factors. As explained by the Appellate Body in *EC and certain member States – Large Civil Aircraft (2011)* and *US – Large Civil Aircraft (2nd complaint) (2012)*:

[I]n some cases, the geographic market may extend to cover the entire country concerned; in others, an analysis of the conditions of competition for sales of the product in question

---

221 See *ibid.*, para. 1120.   222 *Ibid.*, para. 1121.   223 *Ibid.*, para. 1123.
224 *Ibid.*, para. 1168.   225 See *ibid.*, footnote 2466 to para. 1119.

may provide an appropriate foundation for a finding that a geographic market exists *within* that area, for example, a region. There may also be cases where the geographic dimension of a particular market exceeds national boundaries or could be the world market.[226]

A plain reading of Article 6.3(b), however, reveals that a finding of displacement or impedance under that provision is to be limited to the territory of the third country at issue. The Appellate Body recognised that findings of displacement and impedance under Article 6.3(b) are to be made only with respect to the territory of the third country involved, even though, from an economic perspective, the geographic market may not be national in scope. The Appellate Body concluded that:

[e]ven in cases where the geographic dimension of a particular market exceeds national boundaries or is worldwide, a panel faced with a claim under Article 6.3(b) should 'focus the analysis of displacement and impedance on the territory of the ... third countries involved'.[227]

5.3.2 Displacement or Impedance of Imports or Exports

As noted above, pursuant to Article 6.3(a) and (b) of the *SCM Agreement*, 'serious prejudice' may arise where a subsidy results in the 'displacement' or 'impedance' of imports or exports of like products of another Member. The Appellate Body interpreted the concepts of 'displacement' and 'impedance' in *EC and certain member States – Large Civil Aircraft (2011)* and in *US – Large Civil Aircraft (2nd complaint) (2012)*. Displacement refers to an 'economic mechanism in which exports of a like product are replaced by the sales of the subsidized product'.[228] The concept connotes 'a substitution effect between the subsidized product and the like product of the complaining Member'. In the context of Article 6.3(a), this means that the effect of the subsidy is that imports of a like product of the complaining Member are substituted by the subsidised product. Under Article 6.3(b), displacement arises where exports of the like product of the complaining Member are substituted in a third country market by exports of the subsidised product.[229] According to the Appellate Body:

The existence of displacement depends upon there being a competitive relationship between these two sets of products in that market and, when this is the case, certain behaviour such as '[a]ggressive pricing' may 'lead to displacement of exports ... in [that] particular market'.[230]

---

226 *Ibid.*, para. 1117 (original emphasis); and Appellate Body Report, *US – Large Civil Aircraft (2nd complaint) (2012)*, para. 1076. Where the geographical size of the market is smaller in scope than the entire territory of the third-country Member concerned, the wording of Article 6.3(b) suggests that a panel will nonetheless have to ensure that any finding reached relates to that territory as a whole, and explain why this is so. *Ibid.*
227 Appellate Body Report, *US – Large Civil Aircraft (2nd complaint) (2012)*, para. 1076. See also Appellate Body Report, *EC and certain member States – Large Civil Aircraft (2011)*, para. 1117.
228 *Ibid.*, para. 1071; and *ibid.*, para. 1119.
229 See *ibid.*, para. 1160.
230 Appellate Body Report, *US – Large Civil Aircraft (2nd complaint) (2012)*, para. 1071. See also Appellate Body Report, *EC and certain member States – Large Civil Aircraft (2011)*, para. 1119.

An analysis of displacement should assess whether this phenomenon is discernible by examining trends in data relating to export volumes and market shares over an appropriately representative period.[231]

With regard to 'impedance', the Appellate Body considered in *US – Large Civil Aircraft (2nd complaint)* that this concept:

[m]ay involve a broader range of situations than displacement and arises both in 'situations where the exports or imports of the like product of the complaining Member would have expanded had they not been "obstructed" or "hindered" by the subsidized product', as well as when such exports or imports 'did not materialize at all because production was held back by the subsidized product'.[232]

While there may be some overlap between the concepts, 'displacement' and 'impedance' are therefore not interchangeable concepts.[233]

5.3.3   Price Undercutting, Price Suppression, Price Depression and Lost Sales

Article 6.3(c) of the *SCM Agreement* states that serious prejudice may arise where a subsidy results in a significant price undercutting by the subsidised product in comparison to the like product of another Member in the same market, or significant price suppression, price depression or lost sales in the same market. This section discusses in turn the 'market phenomena' referred to in Article 6.3(c), and in particular price suppression, price depression and lost sales.

The concepts of 'price suppression' and 'price depression' were interpreted in *US – Upland Cotton (2005)*, in *US – Upland Cotton (Article 21.5 – Brazil) (2008)*, in *EC and certain member States – Large Civil Aircraft (2011)* and in *US – Large Civil Aircraft (2nd complaint) (2012)*. 'Price suppression' refers to the situation where prices either are prevented or inhibited from rising (i.e. they do not increase when they otherwise would have) or they do actually increase, but the increase is less than it otherwise would have been. 'Price depression' refers to the situation where prices are pressed down, or reduced.[234] The Appellate Body, however, recognised in *US – Upland Cotton (2005)* that the situation where prices are prevented or inhibited from rising (i.e. 'price suppression') and the situation where prices are pressed down, or reduced (i.e. 'price depression') may overlap.[235] There are nevertheless important differences between these two

---

231 See Appellate Body Report, *EC and certain member States – Large Civil Aircraft (2011)*, paras. 1165, 1166 and 1170; and Appellate Body Report, *US – Large Civil Aircraft (2nd complaint) (2012)*, para. 1071.

232 Appellate Body Report, *US – Large Civil Aircraft (2nd complaint) (2012)*, para. 1071. See also Appellate Body Report, *EC and certain member States – Large Civil Aircraft (2011)*, para. 1161. While the Appellate Body was not required to consider the meaning of impedance in that appeal, it nevertheless considered that this concept (which is found within the same provision of the *SCM Agreement*) serves as relevant context for a better understanding of displacement.

233 Appellate Body Report, *US – Large Civil Aircraft (2nd complaint) (2012)*, para. 1071.

234 Panel Report, *US – Upland Cotton (2005)*, para. 7.1277; and Appellate Body Report, *US – Upland Cotton (2005)*, para. 423. The Panel described the assessment of 'price suppression' under Article 6.3(c) as an examination of 'whether these prices were suppressed, that is, lower than they would have been without the United States subsidies in respect of upland cotton'. See Panel Report, *US – Upland Cotton (2005)*, para. 7.1288. See also Appellate Body Report, *US – Large Civil Aircraft (2nd complaint) (2012)*, paras. 1091–2.

235 Appellate Body Report, *US – Upland Cotton (2005)*, para. 424.

market phenomena. As the Appellate Body observed in *US – Upland Cotton (Article 21.5 – Brazil) (2008)*, while 'price depression' is a directly observable phenomenon, 'price suppression' is not. 'Price suppression' exists where prices are less than they would otherwise have been, as a result of the subsidies.[236] The Appellate Body explained:

The identification of price suppression, therefore, presupposes a comparison of an observable factual situation (prices) with a counterfactual situation (what prices would have been) where one has to determine whether, in the absence of the subsidies (or some other controlling phenomenon), prices would have increased or would have increased more than they actually did.[237]

Thus, the Appellate Body considered in *US – Upland Cotton (Article 21.5 – Brazil) (2008)* that a counterfactual analysis is an 'inescapable part' of analysing the effect of a subsidy under Article 6.3(c) of the *SCM Agreement*.[238] It recalled in *US – Large Civil Aircraft (2nd complaint) (2012)* that price suppression is concerned with 'whether prices are less than they would otherwise have been in consequence of ... the subsidies' and that, for this reason, 'a counterfactual analysis is likely to be of particular utility for panels faced with claims that subsidies have caused price suppression'.[239]

With regard to the market phenomenon of 'lost sales', the Appellate Body stated in *EC and certain member States – Large Civil Aircraft (2011)* that a 'lost sale' is one that a supplier 'failed to obtain'.[240] The concept of 'lost sales' was understood in *EC and certain member States – Large Civil Aircraft (2011)* and *US – Large Civil Aircraft (2nd complaint) (2012)* as 'relational', entailing consideration of 'the behaviour of both the subsidized firm(s), which must have won the sales, and the competing firm(s), which allegedly lost the sales', due to the effect of the subsidy.[241] Sales can be lost 'in the same market', within the meaning of Article 6.3(c), only if the subsidised product and the like product compete in the same product market. The Appellate Body noted in *EC and certain member States – Large Civil Aircraft (2011)* that:

[it] will sometimes be necessary to look beyond individual sales campaigns fully to understand the competitive dynamics that are at play in a particular market. Thus, an approach in which sales are aggregated by supplier or by customer, or on a country-wide or global basis, rather than examined individually, is also permissible.[242]

Understood in this way, the Appellate Body recognised that there may be some overlap between the concepts of displacement, impedance and lost sales.[243]

5.3.4 The Meaning of 'Significant'

When price undercutting, price depression, price suppression or lost sales occurs, it must reach the degree or level of 'significance' contemplated by Article 6.3(c).

236 Appellate Body Report, *US – Upland Cotton (Article 21.5 – Brazil) (2008)*, para. 351.
237 *Ibid.*   238 *Ibid.*
239 Appellate Body Report, *US – Large Civil Aircraft (2nd complaint) (2012)*, paras. 1091–2.
240 Appellate Body Report, *EC and certain member States – Large Civil Aircraft (2011)*, para. 1214.
241 *Ibid.*   242 *Ibid.*, para. 1217.   243 See *ibid.*, para. 1218.

The panel in *US – Upland Cotton (2005)* found that the word 'significant' means 'important, notable or consequential'.[244] As the Appellate Body explained in *US – Upland Cotton (Article 21.5 – Brazil) (2008)*, the fact that the price suppression must be 'significant' does not mean, however, that a panel examining various factors that support a finding of significant price suppression:

[m]ust make a determination precisely quantifying the effects of each factor. A factor that itself is not 'significant' may, together with other factors (whether individually shown to be of a significant degree or not), establish 'significant price suppression'. What needs to be significant is the degree of price suppression, not necessarily the degree of each factor used as an indicator for establishing its existence. Nor does each factor necessarily have to be capable of demonstrating, to the same extent, significant price suppression.[245]

The Appellate Body concluded that the panel in *US – Upland Cotton (2008) (Article 21.5 – Brazil)* did not have to determine 'the precise degree of market insulation, which is but one factor in the Panel's overall analysis.'[246] The panel *US – Upland Cotton (2005)* had based its conclusion not only on a 'given level of numerical significance', it also relied on the structure, design, and operation of the payments at issue as well as market structure and product homogeneity.[247] The text of Article 6.3(c) does not set forth any specific guidance or methodology for establishing the existence of *significant* price suppression. The Appellate Body considered in *US – Upland Cotton (2005)* that there 'may well be different ways to make this determination'.[248] In *US – Upland Cotton (2005)*, the panel examined the following factors in determining whether *significant* price suppression occurred: (1) the relative magnitude of US production and exports in the world upland cotton market; (2) general price trends; and (3) the nature of the subsidies at issue, and in particular whether or not the nature of these subsidies is such as to have discernible price-suppressive effects.[249] The panel in *US – Upland Cotton (2005)* also noted that:

[w]hat may be significant in a market for upland cotton would [not] necessarily also be applicable or relevant to a market for a very different product ... [F]or a basic and widely traded commodity, such as upland cotton, a relatively small decrease or suppression of prices could be significant because, for example, profit margins may ordinarily be narrow, product homogeneity means that sales are price sensitive or because of the sheer size of the market in terms of the amount of revenue involved in large volumes traded on the markets experiencing the price suppression.[250]

In the absence of explicit guidance in the text of Article 6.3(c), the Appellate Body found in *US – Upland Cotton (2005)*:

[n]o reason to reject the relevance of these factors for the Panel's assessment in the present case. An assessment of 'general price trends' is clearly relevant to significant price

---

244 See Panel Report, *US – Upland Cotton (2005)*, para. 7.1325; and Appellate Body Report, *US – Upland Cotton (2005)*, para. 426.
245 Appellate Body Report, *US – Upland Cotton (Article 21.5 – Brazil) (2008)*, para. 416.
246 *Ibid.*, paras. 416–18.   247 Panel Report, *US – Upland Cotton (2005)*, paras. 7.1329–7.1330.
248 Appellate Body Report, *US – Upland Cotton (2005)*, para. 427.
249 See Panel Report, *US – Upland Cotton (2005)*, para. 7.1332.   250 *Ibid.*, para. 7.1330.

suppression (although, as the Panel itself recognized, price trends alone are not conclusive). The two other factors – the nature of the subsidies and the relative magnitude of the United States' production and exports of upland cotton – are also relevant for this assessment.[251]

An assessment of whether subsidy amounts are significant should not necessarily be limited to a mere inquiry into *what* those amounts are, either in absolute or per-unit terms:

Rather, such an analysis may be situated within a larger inquiry that could, for instance, entail viewing these amounts against considerations such as the size of the market as a whole, the size of the subsidy recipient, the per-unit price of the subsidized product, the price elasticity of demand, and, depending on the market structure, the extent to which a subsidy recipient is able to set its own prices in the market, and the extent to which rivals are able or prompted to react to each other's pricing within that market structure.[252]

In sum, it is not only the *absolute* amounts of subsidies that may be of relevance; also, the *relative* significance of subsidies and, in particular, whether the challenged subsidies were of a size that, when considered in relation to product values or prices, could produce market effects amounting to serious prejudice may have to be taken into account.

With regard to 'price undercutting', the panel in *Indonesia – Autos (1998)* stated that the inclusion of the qualifier 'significant' in Article 6.3(c) 'presumably was intended to ensure that margins of undercutting so small that they could not meaningfully affect suppliers of the imported product whose price was being undercut are not considered to give rise to serious prejudice'.[253] With regard to 'lost sales', the Appellate Body has noted that, just as when it is used to qualify 'price suppression' and 'price depression', 'this term means "important, notable or consequential", and has both quantitative and qualitative dimensions'.[254]

5.3.5 Increase in World Market Share

Article 6.3(d) of the *SCM Agreement* states that serious prejudice may arise where a subsidy leads to an increase in the world market share of the subsidising Member in a particular primary product or commodity in comparison to the average share it had during the previous period of three years.[255] The panel in *US – Upland Cotton (2005)* found that 'world market share' did not refer to either a Member's share of the world market for *exports* as argued by Brazil, nor did it refer to all *consumption* by a Member as contended by the United States;

251 Appellate Body Report, *US – Upland Cotton (2005)*, para. 434.
252 Appellate Body Report, *US – Large Civil Aircraft (2nd complaint) (2012)*, para. 1193; Appellate Body Report, *US – Upland Cotton (2005)*, para. 468; and Appellate Body Report, *US – Upland Cotton (Article 21.5 – Brazil) (2008)*, para. 362.
253 Panel Report, *Indonesia – Autos (1998)*, para. 14.254.
254 Appellate Body Report, *US – Large Civil Aircraft (2nd complaint) (2012)*, para. 1052; Appellate Body Report, *EC and certain member States – Large Civil Aircraft (2011)*, para. 1218. See also Appellate Body Report, *US – Upland Cotton (2005)*, para. 426, referring to Panel Report, *US – Upland Cotton (2005)*, para. 7.1326.
255 Note that Article 6.3(d) refers to 'world *market* share', whereas Article XVI of the GATT 1994 refers to subsidies resulting in a more than equitable share of world *export trade* in the product in question.

rather, the panel found that the phrase referred to the 'share of the world market supplied by the subsidizing member of the product concerned'.[256] Because Brazil had failed to establish a *prima facie* case due to its erroneous legal interpretation of the phrase at issue,[257] and because its appeal was conditional, the Appellate Body considered it 'unnecessary' to develop an interpretation of the term 'world market share' in Article 6.3(d) for purposes of resolving the dispute.[258]

5.3.6 Threat of Serious Prejudice

Footnote 13 to Article 5(c) clarifies that:

> [t]he term 'serious prejudice to the interests of another Member' is used in [the SCM] Agreement in the same sense as it is used in paragraph 1 of Article XVI of [the] GATT 1994, and *includes threat of serious prejudice*.[259]

A claim of present serious prejudice may relate to a different situation than a claim of *threat* of serious prejudice. The Appellate Body explained in *US – Upland Cotton (Article 21.5 – Brazil) (2008)* that 'a claim of *present* serious prejudice relates to the existence of prejudice in the past, and present, and that may continue in the future. By contrast, a claim of *threat* of serious prejudice relates to prejudice that does not yet exist, but is imminent such that it will materialize in the near future. Therefore, a threat of serious prejudice claim does not necessarily capture and provide a remedy with respect to the same scenario as a claim of present serious prejudice.'[260]

In *EC and certain member States – Large Civil Aircraft (2011)*, the Appellate Body noted that neither sub-paragraph (a) nor (b) of Article 6.3 expressly refer to 'threat of displacement'.[261] Nevertheless, the introductory paragraph of Article 6.3 states that 'serious prejudice in the sense of paragraph (c) of Article 5 may arise' where there is one of the market phenomena described in the sub-paragraphs, including (a) and (b). Footnote 13 in turn clarifies that serious prejudice 'includes threat of serious prejudice'. The Appellate Body found relevant guidance for the interpretation of that concept in Article 15.7 even though the latter concerns 'threat of *material injury*'.[262] Thus, it considered it reasonable to require that the determination of threat of serious prejudice 'be based on facts and not merely on allegation, conjecture or remote possibility' and that '[t]he change in circumstances' that would create a situation in which the subsidy would cause displacement 'must be clearly foreseen and imminent'.[263]

---

256 Panel Report, *US – Upland Cotton (2005)*, para. 7.1464.   257 See *ibid.*, para. 7.1465.

258 See Appellate Body Report, *US – Upland Cotton (2005)*, paras. 505–7 and 511.

259 Emphasis added.

260 Appellate Body Report, *US – Upland Cotton (Article 21.5 – Brazil) (2008)*, para. 244. The Appellate Body further noted that a 'distinction between injury and threat of injury also exists in the context of countervailing duty measures. Once a determination of present material injury is made, a Member may impose countervailing duties on future imports without any obligation to demonstrate a threat of material injury.' See *ibid.*

261 Appellate Body Report, *EC and certain member States – Large Civil Aircraft (2011)*, para. 1171.

262 *Ibid.* (original emphasis).   263 See Article 15.7 of the *SCM Agreement*.

5.3.7   Causation and Non-Attribution

As Article 6.3 of the *SCM Agreement* states, serious prejudice may arise where *the effect of the subsidy* is one or more of the market phenomena, listed in paragraphs (a) to (d) of Article 6.3 and discussed above. The Appellate Body noted in *US – Upland Cotton (2005)* that the ordinary meaning of the noun 'effect' is '[s]omething ... caused or produced; a result, a consequence'.[264] It agreed therefore with the panel that:

[t]he text of the treaty requires the establishment of a causal link between the subsidy and the significant price suppression.[265]

In *US – Upland Cotton (Article 21.5 – Brazil) (2008)*, the Appellate Body observed that:

[w]hile the term 'cause' focuses on the factors that may trigger a certain event, the term 'effect of' focuses on the results of that event. The effect – price suppression – must result from a chain of causation that is linked to the impugned subsidy.[266]

Thus, in respect of all forms of serious prejudice under Part III of the *SCM Agreement*, the complainant must demonstrate not only the existence of the relevant subsidies and of the adverse effects to its interests, but also that the subsidies at issue have *caused* such effects.[267] In all serious prejudice cases under Articles 5(c) and 6.3, the Appellate Body has consistently described the causal link required as 'a genuine and substantial relationship of cause and effect'. While it gave its guidance concerning the assessment of causation in the cotton disputes in the context of significant price suppression under Article 6.3(c), the Appellate Body noted in *EC and certain member States – Large Civil Aircraft (2011)* that the language of Article 6.3(a) and (b) expresses the causation requirement in very similar terms to those used in Article 6.3(c). The Appellate Body therefore saw no reason why the standard for causation and non-attribution should be different under Article 6.3(a) and (b) than under Article 6.3(c).[268] The Appellate Body further explained in *US – Large Civil Aircraft (2nd complaint) (2012)* that, in order to find that the subsidy is a genuine and substantial cause, a panel need not determine it to be the *sole* cause of that effect, or even that it is the *only* substantial cause of that effect.[269]

Questions related to the causal link between challenged subsidies and the market phenomena listed in Article 6.3 of the *SCM Agreement* have been at the centre of all disputes under Part III of the *SCM Agreement*. In *US – Upland Cotton (2005)*, *US – Upland Cotton (Article 21.5 – Brazil) (2008)*, *EC and certain member States – Large Civil Aircraft (2011)* and *US – Large Civil Aircraft (2nd*

---

264 Appellate Body Report, *US – Upland Cotton (2005)*, para. 435.
265 *Ibid.*, quoting Panel Report, *US – Upland Cotton (2005)*, para. 7.1341.
266 Appellate Body Report, *US – Upland Cotton (Article 21.5 – Brazil) (2008)*, para. 372.
267 See Appellate Body Report, *US – Large Civil Aircraft (2nd complaint) (2012)*, para. 913.
268 See Appellate Body Report, *EC and certain member States – Large Civil Aircraft (2011)*, para. 1232.
269 See Appellate Body Report, *US – Large Civil Aircraft (2nd complaint) (2012)*, para. 914.

complaint) (2012), the Appellate Body has discussed issues such as: (1) the order of analysis; (2) the methodologies and elements relevant for establishing causation; (3) the role of counterfactual analysis; and (4) the non-attribution of effects of other factors.

First, with regard to the *order of analysis*, the question that arises is whether the examination of the effect of the subsidy – i.e. whether the effect of the subsidy is one or more of the market phenomena of Article 6.3(a)–(d) – that can, or perhaps even should, take a 'three-step approach' or a 'unitary approach'. Under the 'three-step approach', one would examine, first, whether one of the market phenomena exists, i.e. whether there is displacement, impedance, price undercutting, price suppression, price depression or lost sales; secondly, whether these market phenomena are of a level or degree that is 'significant'; and, thirdly and finally, whether the market phenomena are the 'effect' of challenged subsidies, i.e. whether a causal relationship exists between the subsidies and the market phenomena. Under the 'unitary approach', one would address these three questions together and conduct *one* all-encompassing examination.

Article 6.3(c) is silent as to which approach is to be followed in assessing whether the effect of a subsidy is serious prejudice. In *US – Upland Cotton (2005)*, the Appellate Body considered that the provision does not 'preclude the approach taken by the Panel to examine first whether significant price suppression exists and then, if it is found to exist, to proceed further to examine whether the significant price suppression is the effect of the subsidy'.[270] The Appellate Body saw no legal error in this two-step approach,[271] but stated that one might contend that, 'having decided to separate its analysis of significant price suppression from its analysis of the effects of the challenged subsidies, the Panel's price suppression analysis should have addressed prices without reference to the subsidies and their effects'.[272] That would be the logic of a two-step approach. However, according to the Appellate Body, an analysis of price suppression without reference to the subsidies and their effect may be problematic. The Appellate Body noted that:

[t]he ordinary meaning of the transitive verb 'suppress' implies the existence of a subject (the challenged subsidies) and an object (in this case, prices in the world market for upland cotton). This suggests that it would be difficult to make a judgment on significant price *suppression* without taking into account the effect of the subsidies. The Panel's definition of price suppression ... reflects this problem; it includes the notion that prices 'do not increase when they *otherwise* would have' or 'they do actually increase, but the increase is less than it *otherwise* would have been'. The word 'otherwise' in this context refers to the hypothetical situation in which the challenged subsidies are absent. Therefore, the fact that the Panel may have addressed some of the same or similar factors in its reasoning as to significant price suppression and its reasoning as to 'effects' is not necessarily wrong.[273]

---

270 Appellate Body Report, *US – Upland Cotton (2005)*, para. 431.
271 See *ibid*.   272 *Ibid*., para. 432.   273 *Ibid*., para. 433.

In *US – Upland Cotton (Article 21.5 – Brazil) (2008)*, the panel adopted a 'unitary approach' and decided not to separate the three analytical steps of (1) whether there was price suppression in the world market for upland cotton, (2) whether this price suppression was significant, and (3) whether a causal relationship existed between this significant price suppression and the subsidies. On appeal, the Appellate Body, referring to its observations in *US – Upland Cotton (2005)*, quoted above, stated that:

[t]he Panel's 'unitary analysis', at least in respect of identifying price suppression and its causes, has a sound conceptual foundation.[274]

The Appellate Body consequently endorsed a 'unitary approach' to analysing whether significant price suppression was the effect of the challenged subsidies. The Appellate Body noted that

[i]n undertaking a unitary analysis, the Panel considered both quantitative and qualitative elements in its assessment. It made a quantitative assessment of significance by evaluating the magnitude of the subsidies, the gap between United States upland cotton producers' revenues and costs of production, the United States' share of world production and exports, and the economic simulations; and it made a qualitative assessment by evaluating the structure, design, and operation of the subsidies.[275]

Note, however, that the Appellate Body cautioned that the adoption of a unitary approach did 'not absolve the Panel from clearly explaining its position on the question of "significance"'.[276]

Secondly, with regard to the *methodologies and elements* relevant for establishing whether market phenomena listed in Article 6.3 are the effect of the challenged subsidies, it is important to bear in mind that, in an Article 6.3 analysis, a panel is the *first trier of facts*, and not a reviewer of factual determinations made by a domestic investigating authority.[277] It is therefore the panel's responsibility to gather and analyse relevant factual data and information in assessing claims under Article 6.3(c) in order to arrive at reasoned conclusions.[278] Panels and the Appellate Body have recognised the relevance of a number of factors for an assessment of serious prejudice, such as: (1) the nature of the subsidy; (2) the way in which the subsidy operates; (3) the extent to which the subsidy is provided in respect of a particular product or products; (4) conditions in the market; and (5) the conceptual distance between the activities of the subsidy recipient and the products in respect of which price suppression/price depression is alleged.[279] With regard to the correlation between the subsidies and suppressed prices, the Appellate Body noted in *US – Upland Cotton (2005)* that:

[o]ne would normally expect a discernible correlation between significantly suppressed prices and the challenged subsidies if the effect of these subsidies is significant price suppression.[280]

---

274 Appellate Body Report, *US – Upland Cotton (Article 21.5 – Brazil) (2008)*, para. 354.
275 *Ibid.*, para. 361.   276 *Ibid.*   277 See Appellate Body Report, *US – Upland Cotton (2005)*, para. 458.
278 See *ibid.*, para. 458.   279 See Panel Report, *Korea – Commercial Vessels (2005)*, para. 7.560.
280 Appellate Body Report, *US – Upland Cotton (2005)*, para. 451.

While correlation is an important factor, the Appellate Body cautioned that 'mere correlation' between payment of subsidies and significantly suppressed prices would be 'insufficient, without more, to prove that the effect of the subsidies is significant price suppression'.[281] Note, however, that, in *US – Upland Cotton (Article 21.5 – Brazil) (2008)*, the Appellate Body found that the difficulty in discerning a temporal coincidence between the US subsidies, the increase in US exports, and the drop in market prices did not necessarily undermine the panel's finding on market insulation.[282] With regard to the magnitude of subsidies and benefit, the text of Article 6.3(c) does not state explicitly that a panel needs to quantify the amount of the challenged subsidy. However, in *US – Upland Cotton (2005)*, the Appellate Body found the magnitude of the subsidy to be an important factor in assessing whether 'the effect of the subsidy is ... significant price suppression', and ultimately serious prejudice.[283] Still, the magnitude of a subsidy is 'only one of the factors that may be relevant to the determination of the effects of a challenged subsidy'.[284] A panel needs to assess the effect of the subsidy 'taking into account all relevant factors'.[285] In the same case, the Appellate Body considered that 'the definitions of a specific subsidy in Articles 1 and 2 do not expressly require the quantification of the "benefit" conferred by the subsidy on any particular product'.[286] The Appellate Body summed up in *US – Upland Cotton (2005)* that Article 6.3(c), read in its context, suggests that:

[a] panel should have regard to the magnitude of the challenged subsidy and its relationship to prices of the product in the relevant market when analyzing whether the effect of a subsidy is significant price suppression. In many cases, it may be difficult to decide this question in the absence of such an assessment. Nevertheless, this does not mean that Article 6.3(c) imposes an obligation on panels to quantify precisely the amount of a subsidy benefiting the product at issue in every case. A precise, definitive quantification of the subsidy is not required.[287]

In addition, the Appellate Body recalled in *US – Upland Cotton (Article 21.5 – Brazil) (2008)* that the panel had 'linked the probative value of the magnitude of the subsidies, for purposes of the analysis of significant price suppression, to its findings on the structure, design, and operation of the subsidies and on the gap between costs of production and market revenues of United States upland cotton producers'.[288]

---

281 *Ibid.*
282 While the share of US production and exports was not increasing, this did not undermine the panel's finding (i.e. that the subsidies shielded US cotton producers from world market price fluctuations), which was based also on market insulation factors, such as their mandatory and price-contingent nature and their revenue-stabilizing effect. See Appellate Body Report, *US – Upland Cotton (Article 21.5 – Brazil) (2008)*, para. 414.
283 Appellate Body Report, *US – Upland Cotton (2005)*, para. 461. The Appellate Body stated that a 'large subsidy that is closely linked to prices of the relevant product is likely to have a greater impact on prices than a small subsidy that is less closely linked to prices. All other things being equal, the smaller the subsidy for a given product, the smaller the degree to which it will affect the costs or revenue of the recipient, and the smaller its likely impact on the prices charged by the recipient for the product.' See *ibid.*
284 Appellate Body Report, *US – Upland Cotton (2005)*, para. 461.
285 *Ibid.*   286 *Ibid.*, para. 462.   287 *Ibid.*, para. 467.
288 Appellate Body Report, *US – Upland Cotton (Article 21.5 – Brazil) (2008)*, para. 443.

The Appellate Body explained in *US – Upland Cotton (Article 21.5 – Brazil) (2008)* that the analysis should focus on the effects of the subsidies on production levels by examining whether there was more production than there otherwise would have been as a result of the payments. For the Appellate Body, 'it is the marginal production attributable to the payments that matters'.[289] It stated that, 'given the focus on production and price effects, an analysis of price suppression would normally include a quantitative component. There is some inherent difficulty in quantifying the effects of subsidies', because the increase in prices, absent the subsidies, cannot be directly observed. The Appellate Body suggested that '[o]ne way to undertake the analysis is to use economic modelling or other quantitative techniques. These techniques can be used to estimate whether there are higher levels of production resulting from the subsidies and, in turn, the price effects of that production. Economic modelling and other quantitative techniques provide a framework to analyse the relationship between subsidies, other factors, and price movements.'[290]

Thirdly, with regard to the role of counterfactual analysis, panels and the Appellate Body have emphasised repeatedly the relevance and importance of counterfactual analysis in determining whether market phenomena, such as price suppression, are the effect of the challenged subsidies. Already in *Korea – Commercial Vessels (2005)*, the panel stated that establishing a causal relationship between the *subsidy* and the significant price suppression or price depression implies looking at a *counterfactual situation*, i.e. 'trying to determine what prices would have been in the absence of the subsidy'. In the case of alleged price depression, 'whether in the absence of the subsidies prices for ships would not have declined, or would have declined by less than was in fact the case'. For price suppression, the question would be whether, 'in the absence of the subsidies, ship prices would have increased, or would have increased by more than was in fact the case'.[291]

The Appellate Body noted in *US – Upland Cotton (2005)* that Part III of the *SCM Agreement* leaves panels with 'a certain degree of discretion in selecting an appropriate methodology for determining whether the "effect" of a subsidy is significant price suppression under Article 6.3(c)'.[292] In *US – Upland Cotton (Article 21.5 – Brazil) (2008)*, the Appellate Body recalled that a price-suppression analysis is *counterfactual* in nature. This required consideration of what prices would have been absent the subsidies, and thus a counterfactual analysis is an 'inescapable part' of analysing the effect of a subsidy under Article

---

289 *Ibid.*, para. 355. According to the Appellate Body, if there were to be increased upland cotton production, the analysis would then focus on whether that increase in supply had effects on prices in the world market. All else being equal, the marginal production attributable to the subsidy would be expected to have an effect on world prices, particularly if the subsidy is provided in a country with a meaningful share of world output. See *ibid.*

290 *Ibid.*, para. 356.

291 Panel Report, *Korea – Commercial Vessels (2005)*, paras. 7.604 and 7.612–7.615.

292 Appellate Body Report, *US – Upland Cotton (2005)*, para. 436.

6.3(c).[293] In consequence, it was for the panel to determine whether the world price of upland cotton would have been higher in the absence of the subsidies (that is, *but for* the subsidies).[294] In some circumstances, a determination that the market phenomena captured by Article 6.3 would not have occurred 'but for' the challenged subsidies will suffice to establish causation:

This is because, in some circumstances, the 'but for' analysis will show that the subsidy is both a necessary cause of the market phenomenon *and* a substantial cause. It is not required that the 'but for' analysis establish that the challenged subsidies are a sufficient cause of the market phenomenon provided that it shows a genuine and substantial relationship of cause and effect. However, there are circumstances in which a 'but for' approach does not suffice. For example, where a necessary cause is too remote and other intervening causes substantially account for the market phenomenon.[295]

In *EC and certain member States – Large Civil Aircraft (2011)*, the Appellate Body explained that counterfactual analysis provides an adjudicator with a useful analytical framework to isolate and properly identify the effects of the challenged subsidies:

In general terms, the counterfactual analysis entails comparing the actual market situation that is before the adjudicator with the market situation that would have existed in the absence of the challenged subsidies. This requires the adjudicator to undertake a modelling exercise as to what the market would look like in the absence of the subsidies. Such an exercise is a necessary part of the counterfactual approach. As with other factual assessments, panels clearly have a margin of discretion in conducting the counterfactual analysis.[296]

The Appellate Body reiterated in *US – Large Civil Aircraft (2nd complaint) (2012)* that 'a counterfactual analysis is likely to be of particular utility for panels faced with claims that subsidies have caused price suppression'.[297] As with the other market phenomena in Article 6.3, the 'lost sales must be the "effect" of the challenged subsidy', and counterfactual analysis is a useful and appropriate approach to assessing whether this is so. According to the Appellate Body in *EC and certain member States – Large Civil Aircraft (2011)*:

[t]his would involve a comparison of the sales actually made by the competing firm(s) of the complaining Member with a counterfactual scenario in which the firm(s) of the respondent

---

293 The Appellate Body explained that the identification of price suppression presupposes a comparison of an observable factual situation (prices) with a counterfactual situation (what prices would have been) where one has to determine whether, in the absence of the subsidies (or some other controlling phenomenon), prices would have increased or would have increased more than they actually did. Price depression, by contrast, can be directly observed, in that falling prices are observable. The determination of whether such falling prices are the effect of the subsidies will require consideration of what prices would have been absent the subsidies. See Appellate Body Report, *US – Upland Cotton (Article 21.5 – Brazil) (2008)*, para. 351. See also above, pp. 791–804.
294 See *ibid.*, para. 370.
295 Appellate Body Report, *EC and certain member States – Large Civil Aircraft (2011)*, para. 1233. According to the Appellate Body, this example underscored the importance of carrying out a proper non-attribution analysis. See *ibid.*
296 *Ibid.*, para. 1110. See Appellate Body Report, *US – Upland Cotton (Article 21.5 – Brazil) (2008)*, para. 357.
297 See Appellate Body Report, *US – Large Civil Aircraft (2nd complaint) (2012)*, paras. 1091–2.

Member would not have received the challenged subsidies. There would be lost sales where the counterfactual scenario shows that sales won by the subsidized firm(s) of the respondent Member would have been made instead by the competing firm(s) of the complaining Member, thus revealing the effect of the challenged subsidies.[298]

Fourthly, with regard to the non-attribution of effects of other factors, note that Articles 5 and 6.3 of the *SCM Agreement* do not contain the more elaborate and precise causation and non-attribution language found in Part V of the *SCM Agreement*, which relates to the imposition of countervailing duties, and requires, *inter alia*, an examination of 'any known factors other than the subsidized imports which at the same time are injuring the domestic industry'.[299] The Appellate Body noted in *US – Upland Cotton (2005)* that the absence of such express non-attribution requirements in Part III suggests that:

[a] panel has a certain degree of discretion in selecting an appropriate methodology for determining whether the 'effect' of a subsidy is significant price suppression under Article 6.3(c).[300]

Nevertheless, it is necessary to ensure that the effects of other factors on prices are not improperly attributed to the challenged subsidies.[301] Therefore, the Appellate Body did:

[n]ot find fault with the Panel's approach of 'examin[ing] whether or not "the effect of the subsidy" is the significant price suppression which [it had] found to exist in the same world market' and separately 'consider[ing] the role of other alleged causal factors in the record before [it] which may affect [the] analysis of the causal link between the United States subsidies and the significant price suppression'.[302]

At the same time, the Appellate Body cautioned in *US – Upland Cotton (2005)* that its interpretations of the provisions relating to causation and non-attribution of the *Agreement on Safeguards* and the *Anti-Dumping Agreement*, as well as the provisions of Part V of the *SCM Agreement*:

[r]elate to a determination of 'injury' rather than 'serious prejudice', and they apply in different contexts and with different purposes. Therefore, they must not be automatically transposed into Part III of the *SCM Agreement*. Nevertheless, they may suggest ways of assessing whether the effect of a subsidy is significant price suppression rather than it being the effect of other factors.[303]

In *US – Upland Cotton (Article 21.5 – Brazil) (2008)*, the Appellate Body noted that the compliance panel had taken a different approach to causation and

---

298 Appellate Body Report, *EC and certain member States – Large Civil Aircraft (2011)*, para. 1216.
299 Article 15.5 of the *SCM Agreement*. See above, p. 784.
300 Appellate Body Report, *US – Upland Cotton (2005)*, para. 436.
301 See *ibid.*, para. 437. The Appellate Body reasoned that, pursuant to 'Article 6.3(c) of the *SCM Agreement*, "[s]erious prejudice in the sense of paragraph (c) of Article 5 may arise" when "the effect of *the subsidy* is ... significant price suppression" ... If the significant price suppression found in the world market for upland cotton were caused by factors other than the challenged subsidies, then that price suppression would not be "the effect of" the challenged subsidies in the sense of Article 6.3(c).' See *ibid.* (original emphasis).
302 *Ibid.*, para. 437.   303 *Ibid.*, para. 438.

non-attribution than that taken by the original panel. In the original proceedings, the panel examined whether or not 'the effect of the subsidy' is significant price suppression which it had found to exist 'in the same world market'. The original panel then separately considered the role of other alleged causal factors in the record before it, which may have affected the analysis of the causal link between the US subsidies and the significant price suppression. The Article 21.5 'compliance' panel adopted a 'but for' approach to the question of whether the effect of the challenged subsidies to upland cotton producers is significant price suppression within the meaning of Article 6.3(c). In the view of the compliance panel, having adopted a 'but for' approach, it was not necessary to undertake 'a comprehensive evaluation of factors affecting the world market price for upland cotton'.[304] The Appellate Body recalled in *US – Upland Cotton (Article 21.5 – Brazil) (2008)* that 'a panel has a certain degree of discretion in selecting an appropriate methodology' and 'Articles 5(c) and 6.3(c) of the *SCM Agreement* do not exclude, therefore, that a panel could examine causation based on a "but for" approach'. The panel's choice, in *US – Upland Cotton (Article 21.5 – Brazil) (2008)*, 'of a "but for" approach reflects [that] a price suppression analysis is counterfactual in nature'[305] and 'is consistent with the definition of price suppression endorsed by the Appellate Body in the original proceedings, insofar as the counterfactual determination of whether price suppression exists cannot be separated from the analysis of the effects of the subsidies'.[306] However, the Appellate Body chided the Article 21.5 compliance panel for not clearly articulating the standard implicated in its 'but for' approach. It stated that:

[a] subsidy may be necessary, but not sufficient, to bring about price suppression. Understood in this way, the 'but for' test may be too undemanding. By contrast, the 'but for' test would be too rigorous if it required the subsidy to be the only cause of the price suppression. Instead, the 'but for' test should determine that price suppression is the effect of the subsidy and that there is a 'genuine and substantial relationship of cause and effect'.[307]

While the panel was required 'to have ensured that the effects of other factors on prices did not dilute the "genuine and substantial" link between the subsidies and the price suppression', in view of the discretion enjoyed by panels in choosing the methodology used for its Article 6.3 analysis:

[i]t would not have been improper for the Panel to have assessed the effect of other factors as part of its counterfactual analysis, rather than conducting a separate analysis of non-attribution.[308]

On the basis of that understanding, the Appellate Body found the panel's 'but for' standard 'permissible under Article 6.3(c) of the *SCM Agreement*, and consistent with the panel's counterfactual analysis of price suppression'.[309]

---

304 Appellate Body Report, *US – Upland Cotton (Article 21.5 – Brazil) (2008)*, para. 369.
305 *Ibid.*, para. 370. In consequence, the panel had to determine whether the world price of upland cotton would have been higher in the absence of the subsidies (that is, *but for* the subsidies). See *ibid.*
306 *Ibid.*, para. 371.   307 *Ibid.*, para. 374.   308 *Ibid.*, para. 375.   309 See *ibid.*

The Appellate Body recognised the need for a non-attribution analysis also in *US – Large Civil Aircraft (2nd complaint) (2012)*. It noted that a panel will often be confronted with multiple factors that may have contributed, to varying degrees, to the adverse effect. In some circumstances, factors other than the subsidy at issue have caused a particular market effect. Yet the mere presence of other causes that contribute to a particular market effect does not, in itself, preclude the subsidy from being found to be a 'genuine and substantial' cause of that effect. Thus, the Appellate Body explained in *US – Large Civil Aircraft (2nd complaint) (2012)* that:

[a]s part of its assessment of the causal nexus between the subsidy at issue and the effect(s) that it is alleged to have had, a panel must seek to understand the interactions between the subsidy at issue and the various other causal factors, and make an assessment of their connections to, as well as the relative importance of the subsidy and of the other factors in bringing about, the relevant effects ... A panel must, however, take care to ensure that it does not attribute the effects of those other causal factors to the subsidies at issue, and that the other causal factors do not dilute the causal link between those subsidies and the alleged adverse effects such that it is not possible to characterize that link as a genuine and substantial relationship of cause and effect.[310]

Thus, the subsidy at issue may be found to exhibit the requisite causal link notwithstanding the existence of other causes that contribute to producing the relevant market phenomena if, having given proper consideration to all other relevant contributing factors and their effects, the panel is satisfied that the contribution of the subsidy has been demonstrated to rise to that of a *genuine and substantial cause*.[311]

Questions and Assignments 12.10

When will a subsidy be found to cause 'serious prejudice' within the meaning of Article 6 of the *SCM Agreement*? What are the relevant 'geographical market' and 'product market' in the context of Article 6 of the *SCM Agreement*? When does 'displacement' or 'impedance' of imports or exports within the meaning of Article 6.3(a) and (b) of the *SCM Agreement* exist? What is 'price undercutting', 'price suppression', 'price depression' or 'lost sales' within the meaning of Article 6.3(c) of the *SCM Agreement*? When is price undercutting, price suppression, price depression or lost sales 'significant' as required by Article 6.3(c)? What is meant by an 'increase in world market share' in Article 6.3(d) of the *SCM Agreement*? Does the concept of 'serious prejudice' also include 'threat of serious prejudice'? Why? How does one assess whether there is 'threat of serious prejudice'? How can it be established whether the market phenomena referred to in Article 6.3 of the *SCM Agreement* are 'the effect of' the challenged subsidies? Is a non-attribution analysis required in the context of Article 6.3 of the *SCM Agreement*? Can a WTO Member bring a claim that *another* Member has suffered serious prejudice?

310 Appellate Body Report, *US – Large Civil Aircraft (2nd complaint) (2012)*, para. 914. See also Appellate Body Report, *US – Upland Cotton (2005)*, para. 437; Appellate Body Report, *US – Upland Cotton (Article 21.5 – Brazil) (2008)*, para. 375; Appellate Body Report, *EC and certain member States – Large Civil Aircraft (2011)*, paras. 1232 and 1376.
311 Appellate Body Report, *US – Large Civil Aircraft (2nd complaint) (2012)*, para. 914.

5.3.8 Other Issues Relevant to the Analysis of the Effects of Subsidies

In addition to the issues relating to 'serious prejudice' discussed so far in this section, there are a number of other issues relevant to the analysis of the effects of subsidies that deserve to be discussed, including: (1) the temporal scope of Article 5 of the *SCM Agreement*; (2) the pass-through of subsidies; (3) the effect of subsidies over time; (4) the collective analysis of the effects of subsidies; and (5) Annex V on Procedures for Developing Information Concerning Serious Prejudice.

First, with regard to the *temporal scope* of Article 5 of the *SCM Agreement*, the Appellate Body rejected in *EC and certain member States – Large Civil Aircraft (2011)* the European Communities' request to exclude from the temporal scope of the dispute subsidies granted prior to 1 January 1995, when the *SCM Agreement* entered into force. The Appellate Body found that Article 5 addresses:

[a] 'situation' that consists of causing, through the use of any subsidy, adverse effects to the interests of another Member.[312]

According to the Appellate Body, it is this 'situation' which 'is to be construed consistently with the non-retroactivity principle reflected in Article 28 of the *Vienna Convention*'.[313] The relevant question for purposes of determining the temporal scope of Article 5 is whether the causing of adverse effects has 'ceased to exist' or continues as a 'situation'.[314] The Appellate Body consequently disagreed with the proposition that, by virtue of Article 28 of the *Vienna Convention*, no obligation arising from Article 5 of the *SCM Agreement* is to be imposed on a Member in respect of subsidies granted or brought into existence prior to 1 January 1995.[315] A pre-1995 subsidy may fall within the scope of Article 5 of the *SCM Agreement* because of its possible nexus to the continuing situation of causing, through the use of this subsidy, adverse effects to which Article 5 applies.[316]

Secondly, with regard to the *pass-through of subsidies*, recall the discussion earlier in this chapter on 'pass-through' in the context of the determination of 'benefit', an essential element of any subsidy.[317] As noted there, the Appellate Body found in *US – Softwood Lumber IV (2004)* that 'it cannot be presumed that a "subsidy" ... provided to a producer of an input "passes through" to the producer of the processed product'.[318] However, in *US – Upland Cotton (2005)*, the Appellate Body observed that its reasoning regarding pass-through in *US – Softwood Lumber IV (2004)* did not focus on the requirements for establishing

312 Appellate Body Report, *EC and certain member States – Large Civil Aircraft (2011)*, para. 686.
313 *Ibid.*   314 See *ibid.*   315 See *ibid.*
316 See *ibid.* Note, however, that, in reaching this conclusion, the Appellate Body was '*not* saying that the causing of adverse effects, through the use of pre-1995 subsidies, can necessarily be characterized as a "continuing" situation ... [R]ather ... [it found] that a challenge to pre-1995 subsidies is not *precluded* under the terms of the *SCM Agreement.*' See *ibid.* (original emphasis).
317 See above, pp. 762–3.
318 Appellate Body Report, *US – Softwood Lumber IV (2004)*, paras. 140–2.

serious prejudice under Articles 5(c) and 6.3(c) of Part III, but rather on the existence of a subsidy and the conduct of countervailing duty investigations pursuant to Part V of the *SCM Agreement*.[319] Specifically with regard to the establishment of serious prejudice, the Appellate Body ruled in *US – Upland Cotton (2005)* that the need for a 'pass-through' analysis under Part V is 'not critical' for an assessment of significant price suppression under Article 6.3(c) in Part III.[320] Nevertheless, the Appellate Body acknowledged that:

[t]he 'subsidized product' must be properly identified for purposes of significant price suppression under Article 6.3(c) of the *SCM Agreement*. And if the challenged payments do not, in fact, subsidize that product, this may undermine the conclusion that the effect of the subsidy is significant suppression of prices of that product in the relevant market.[321]

The Appellate Body found that the facts in *EC and certain member States – Large Civil Aircraft (2011)* did not give rise to a requirement to conduct an analysis of whether the benefit of subsidies provided to the Airbus Industrie consortium *passed through* to Airbus SAS. First, there was no suggestion that 'subsidies were provided to a different "input product" that was separate or distinct from a downstream "subsidized product", as was the case in *US – Softwood Lumber IV*.[322] Secondly, although it did not exclude that there may be other circumstances, including ones involving the restructuring of companies in which the receipt of a subsidy by a predecessor company may not mean that it is enjoyed by a successor company, it recalled the panel's finding that, 'despite the changes to their "legal organization", the "economic realities" of production of Airbus LCA [large civil aircraft] demonstrated that the Airbus Industrie consortium ... and Airbus SAS were the "same producer" of LCA'.[323] Finally, the Appellate Body concluded, therefore, that it was 'not faced with a situation where predecessor and successor companies are unrelated and operate at arm's length and where a "pass-through" analysis might therefore be required'.[324]

Thirdly, with regard to the *effect of subsidies over time*, the question that arises is whether the effect of a subsidy may continue beyond the year in which it is paid. In *US – Upland Cotton (2005)*, the parties disagreed on whether the effect of a 'recurring' subsidy may continue beyond the year in which it was paid. The Appellate Body noted that there is:

[n]othing in the text of Article 6.3(c) that excludes *a priori* the possibility that the effect of a 'recurring' subsidy may continue after the year in which it is paid.[325]

---

319 See Appellate Body Report, *US – Upland Cotton (2005)*, para. 471.
320 See *ibid.*, para. 472.   321 *Ibid.*
322 Appellate Body Report, *EC and certain member States – Large Civil Aircraft (2011)*, para. 775.
323 *Ibid.* The Appellate Body referred to Panel Report, *EC and certain member States – Large Civil Aircraft (2011)*, para. 7.199.
324 Appellate Body Report, *EC and certain member States – Large Civil Aircraft (2011)*, para. 776. The Appellate Body did not consider that 'the relationship between the predecessor companies and Airbus SAS is one that can be characterized as a relationship between unrelated companies operating at "arm's length". Instead, the companies and Airbus SAS were related, at least to some extent, through common ownership.' See *ibid.*
325 Appellate Body Report, *US – Upland Cotton (2005)*, para. 476.

The Appellate Body further observed that also the context of Article 6.3(c), and in particular Article 6.2 and 6.4, did *not* support the view that 'the effect of a subsidy is immediate, short-lived, or limited to one year, regardless of whether or not it is paid every year'.[326] To the contrary, the Appellate Body considered that one might expect a time lag between the provision of the subsidy and the resulting effect.[327] Consequently, the Appellate Body found that the 'proposition that, if subsidies are paid annually, their effects are also necessarily extinguished annually' cannot stand.[328]

In *EC and certain member States – Large Civil Aircraft (2011)*, the Appellate Body found that Articles 5 and 6 do not require that a complainant demonstrate that a benefit 'continues' or is 'present' during the reference period for purposes of an adverse effects analysis.[329] The Appellate Body emphasised, however, in *EC and certain member States – Large Civil Aircraft (2011)*, that:

[e]ffects of a subsidy will ordinarily dissipate over time and will end at some point after the subsidy has expired. Indeed, as with a subsidy that has a finite life and materializes over time, so too do the effects of a subsidy accrue and diminish over time.[330]

Therefore, a panel is required to consider whether the 'life of a subsidy' has ended, for example, by reason of the 'amortization of the subsidy over the relevant period or because the subsidy was removed from the recipient'.[331] Moreover, the Appellate Body emphasised that 'the effects of a subsidy will generally diminish and come to an end with the passage of time'.[332]

Fourthly, with regard to the *collective analysis of the effects of subsidies*, it should be noted that a 'serious prejudice' analysis of multiple subsidies may be integrated to the extent appropriate in the light of the facts and circumstances of a given case. As the panel in *US – Upland Cotton (2005)* found, while due attention must be paid to each subsidy at issue as it relates to the subsidised product, the reference in Article 6.3 to 'the effect of the subsidy' in the singular does not mean that price suppression analysis 'must clinically isolate each individual subsidy and its effects'.[333] Accordingly, Article 6.3 permits an *integrated* examination of the effects of any subsidies when these subsidies have a sufficient nexus with the subsidised product and the particular effects-related variable under examination. The panel in *US – Upland Cotton (2005)* concluded that:

[t]o the extent a sufficient nexus with [the subsidised product and the particular effects-related variable under examination] exists among the subsidies at issue so that their effects manifest themselves collectively, we believe that we may legitimately treat them as a 'subsidy' and group them and their effects together.[334]

---

326 *Ibid.*, para. 477. The Appellate Body refers to Article 6.2 of the *SCM Agreement* in para. 477, and to Article 6.4 in para. 478.
327 See *ibid.*, para. 477.   328 *Ibid.*, para. 482.
329 See Appellate Body Report, *EC and certain member States – Large Civil Aircraft (2011)*, para. 715.
330 *Ibid.*, para. 713.   331 *Ibid.*, para. 1236.   332 *Ibid.* See also *ibid.*, para. 714.
333 Panel Report, *US – Upland Cotton (2005)*, para. 7.1192.   334 *Ibid.*

In *EC and certain member States – Large Civil Aircraft (2011)*, the panel under-took what it called an '*aggregated*' analysis of the effects of the subsidies. It first examined the effects of Launch Aid/Member State Financing subsidies (LA/MSF) on Airbus' ability to launch particular models of large civil aircraft, and then sought to determine whether other non-LA/MSF subsidies had similar effects.[335] On the basis of a separate and quite limited assessment of the collective effect of measures comprised under each group of non-LA/MSF subsidies, the panel concluded that the effect of LA/MSF was 'complemented and supplemented' by the effects of other specific non-LA/MSF subsidies it found to exist in this dispute.[336] The Appellate Body was of the view that the panel had *not* conducted an 'aggregated' effects analysis, but had rather examined whether the effects of these non-LA/MSF subsidies 'complemented and supplemented' the effects of LA/MSF subsidies. According to the Appellate Body, the panel had established a 'genuine and substantial relationship of cause and effect' between the LA/MSF measures, the launch and marketing of each of Airbus models of LCA, and the displacement and lost sales of Boeing LCA during the reference period. According to the Appellate Body, the panel had further concluded that, 'insofar as the three sets of non-LA/MSF subsidies "complemented and supplemented" the "product effect" of LA/MSF, these subsidies "had the same effect on Airbus' ability to launch the LCA it launched at the time that it did".'[337] The Appellate Body ruled that the panel's approach 'is permissible under Article 6.3 ... provided that a *genuine* causal link between the non-LA/MSF subsidies and the market phenomena alleged under Article 6.3 is established'.[338] The Appellate Body furthermore ruled that:

[o]nce the Panel determined that LA/MSF subsidies were a substantial cause of the observed displacement and lost sales, it was not necessary to establish that non-LA/MSF subsidies were also substantial causes of the same phenomena ... Rather, it was conceivable that non-LA/MSF subsidies complemented or supplemented the effects of LA/MSF subsidies.[339]

The Appellate Body thus concluded in *EC and certain member States – Large Civil Aircraft (2011)* that Articles 5(c) and 6.3 do not preclude an affirmative finding that non-LA/MSF subsidies cause adverse effects where they 'complement and supplement' the effects of LA/MSF subsidies that have been found to be a substantial and genuine cause of adverse effects.[340] Finally, note that, in *US – Large Civil Aircraft (2nd complaint) (2012)*, the Appellate Body observed that two distinct means of undertaking a *collective* assessment of the effects of multiple subsidies have been used, namely, 'aggregation' and 'cumulation'. First, '*aggregation*' referred to an *ex ante* decision taken by a panel to undertake

---

335 The non-LA/MSF subsidies comprised three groups: (1) equity infusions; (2) infrastructure measures; and (3) research & technology development subsidies.
336 Panel Report, *EC and certain member States – Large Civil Aircraft (2011)*, para. 7.1956.
337 Appellate Body Report, *EC and certain member States – Large Civil Aircraft (2011)*, para. 1377.
338 *Ibid.*, para. 1378 (emphasis added).   339 *Ibid.*   340 *Ibid.*

a single analysis of the effects of multiple subsidies whose structure, design and operation are similar and thereby to assess in an integrated causation analysis the collective effects of such subsidy measures (this was the approach employed by the panel in *US – Upland Cotton (2005)*).[341] Secondly, '*cumulation*' referred to an examination undertaken by a panel *after* it has found that at least one subsidy has caused adverse effects as to whether the effects of other subsidies complement and supplement those adverse effects (this was the approach employed by the panel in *EC and certain member States – Large Civil Aircraft (2011)*).[342]

In sum, Articles 5(c) and 6.3 do not require that a serious prejudice analysis 'clinically isolate each individual subsidy and its effects'.[343] The way in which a panel structures its evaluation of a claim that multiple subsidies have caused serious prejudice will necessarily vary from case to case. Relevant circumstances that will bear upon the appropriateness of a panel's approach include the design, structure and operation of the subsidies at issue, the alleged market phenomena, and the extent to which the subsidies are provided in relation to a particular product or products.[344] A panel must also take account of the manner in which the claimant presents its case, and the extent to which it claims that multiple subsidies have similar effects on the same product, or that the effects of multiple subsidies manifest themselves collectively in the relevant market. A panel enjoys a 'degree of methodological latitude' in selecting its approach to analysing the collective effects of multiple subsidies for purposes of assessing causation. However, the Appellate Body emphasised in *US – Large Civil Aircraft (2nd complaint) (2012)* that 'a panel is never absolved from having to establish

341 According to the Appellate Body, a panel may group together subsidy measures that are sufficiently similar in their design, structure and operation in order to ascertain their aggregated effects in an integrated causation analysis and determine whether there is a genuine and substantial causal relationship between these multiple subsidies, taken together, and the relevant market phenomena identified in Article 6.3. In such circumstances, the panel is not required to find that each subsidy measure is, individually, a genuine and substantial cause of the relevant phenomenon. Nor is it required to assess the relative contribution of each subsidy within the group to the resulting effects. When such an analysis is appropriate in light of the design, structure and operation of multiple subsidies, a panel may also add together the *amounts* of the subsidies as part of its analysis of the collective effects of that group of subsidies. Whether such an analysis is appropriate will depend upon the particular features of the subsidies at issue and the case presented by the complainant. The causal mechanism through which a subsidy produces effects is one criterion that will be relevant to the issue of whether aggregation is appropriate in any given instance. See Appellate Body Report, *US – Large Civil Aircraft (2nd complaint) (2012)*, para. 1285.
342 The Appellate Body noted in *US – Large Civil Aircraft (2nd complaint) (2012)* that, in the alternative, a panel may begin by analysing the effects of a *single* subsidy, or an *aggregated* group of subsidies, in order to determine whether it constitutes a genuine and substantial cause of adverse effects. Having reached that conclusion, a panel may then assess whether *other* subsidies – either individually or in aggregated groups – have a *genuine* causal connection to the same effects, and complement and supplement the effects of the *first* subsidy (or group of subsidies) that was found, alone, to be a *genuine* and *substantial* cause of the alleged market phenomena. The other subsidies have to be a 'genuine' cause, but they need not, in themselves, amount to a 'substantial' cause in order for their effects to be combined with those of the first subsidy or group of subsidies that, alone, has been found to be a genuine and substantial cause of the adverse effects. See Appellate Body Report, *US – Large Civil Aircraft (2nd complaint) (2012)*, para. 1287.
343 Panel Report, *US – Upland Cotton (2005)*, para. 7.1192. See also Panel Report, *Indonesia – Autos (1998)*, para. 14.206; and Panel Report, *Korea – Commercial Vessels (2005)*, para. 7.616.
344 Appellate Body Report, *EC and certain member States – Large Civil Aircraft (2011)*, para. 1376 (referring to Panel Report, *US – Upland Cotton (2005)*, para. 7.1194; and Panel Report, *Korea – Commercial Vessels (2005)*, para. 7.560).

a "genuine and substantial relationship of cause and effect"[345] between the impugned subsidies and the alleged market phenomena under Article 6.3, or from assessing whether such causal link is diluted by the effects of other factors.'[346] Moreover, a panel must take care not to segment unduly its analysis such that, when confronted with multiple subsidy measures, it considers the effects of each on an individual basis only, and, as a result of such an atomised approach, finds that no subsidy alone is a substantial cause of the relevant adverse effects.[347]

Fifthly, the existence of serious prejudice must be determined on the basis of the information submitted to, or obtained by, the panel. If a Member fails to cooperate in the information-gathering process, the panel may rely on the 'best information available', and it may draw adverse inferences from the lack of co-operation.[348] Specific procedures for developing information on serious prejudice are set out in Annex V to the *SCM Agreement* on the *Procedures for Developing Information Concerning Serious Prejudice*. The Appellate Body ruled in *US – Large Civil Aircraft (2nd complaint) (2012)* that the initiation of an Annex V procedure occurs *automatically* when there is a request for initiation of such a procedure at the time that the DSB establishes a panel, even if the respondent or another Member would object in the DSB.[349] The Appellate Body reasoned that:

[t]he first sentence of paragraph 2 of Annex V, along with other provisions of Annex V, refers directly to the establishment of a panel pursuant to Article 7.4 of the *SCM Agreement*. Provided that a request for initiation of an Annex V procedure has been made, the DSB's initiation of such a procedure is a procedural incident of the establishment of a panel in serious prejudice cases. The function assigned to the DSB under paragraph 2 of Annex V is executory in nature, and is automatically discharged by it once the two specified conditions precedent are satisfied.[350]

The Appellate Body said that an interpretation of Annex V:2 that 'would enable a single WTO Member to frustrate the important role that an information-gathering procedure plays in serious prejudice disputes by preventing the DSB from initiating such a procedure would be at odds with WTO Members' clear intention to promote the early and targeted collection of information pertinent to the parties' subsequent presentation of their cases to the panel'.[351] As the Appellate Body explained:

---

345 Appellate Body Report, *US – Large Civil Aircraft (2nd complaint) (2012)*, para. 1284 (referring to Appellate Body Report, *US – Upland Cotton (Article 21.5 – Brazil) (2008)*, para. 368 (quoting Appellate Body Report, *US – Upland Cotton (2005)*, para. 438)).

346 Appellate Body Report, *US – Large Civil Aircraft (2nd complaint) (2012)*, para. 1284 (referring to Appellate Body Report, *US – Upland Cotton (Article 21.5 – Brazil) (2008)*, para. 375).

347 Appellate Body Report, *US – Large Civil Aircraft (2nd complaint) (2012)*, para. 1284.

348 See Annex V, paras. 6 and 7, to the *SCM Agreement*.

349 Appellate Body Report, *US – Large Civil Aircraft (2nd complaint) (2012)*, paras. 480–549. The Appellate Body considered that the Panel had erred in rejecting various requests made by the European Communities regarding the information-gathering procedure under Annex V to the *SCM Agreement*.

350 Appellate Body Report, *US – Large Civil Aircraft (2nd complaint) (2012)*, para. 532.

351 *Ibid.*, para. 533. It would also be contrary to the obligation to cooperate in the collection of information in serious prejudice disputes imposed on all Members under Annex V:1 to and Article 6.6 of the *SCM Agreement*. See *ibid.*

The initiation and conduct of Annex V procedures have important consequences for the ability of parties to a dispute to present their case, and for panels and the Appellate Body to fulfil their respective roles in complex serious prejudice disputes under the *SCM Agreement*. Annex V procedures are key to affording parties early access to critical information, which may in turn serve as the foundation upon which those parties will construct their arguments and seek to satisfy their evidentiary burden. Moreover, the initiation and conduct of such procedures are key to the ability of panels to make findings of fact that have a sufficient evidentiary basis or to draw negative inferences from instances of non-cooperation.[352]

Questions and Assignments 12.11

What is the temporal scope of Articles 5 and 6 of the *SCM Agreement*? Explain the concept of pass-through of subsidies. Does the effect of subsidies dissipate over time? Is a 'collective analysis' of the effects of subsidies allowed? Discuss the relevance of Annex V of the *SCM Agreement* in subsidy disputes.

5.4 Multilateral Remedies for Actionable Subsidies

The multilateral remedies for actionable subsidies are set out in Article 7 of the *SCM Agreement*. Like the remedies for prohibited subsidies, the remedies for actionable subsidies also differ from the remedies generally provided for in the DSU. Compared with the remedies against prohibited subsidies, however, the timeframes are longer and the Permanent Group of Experts is not involved.[353] If a panel concludes that a subsidy causes adverse effects to the interests of another Member (be it injury, nullification or impairment, or serious prejudice), the subsidising Member must:

[t]ake appropriate steps to remove the adverse effect or ... withdraw the subsidy.[354]

In *US – Upland Cotton (2005)*, the Appellate Body noted that Article 7.8 provides that:

[w]here it has been determined that 'any subsidy has *resulted* in adverse effects to the interests of another Member', the subsidizing Member must 'take appropriate steps *to remove the adverse effects* or ... withdraw the subsidy'. The use of the word 'resulted' suggests that there could be a time-lag between the payment of a subsidy and any consequential adverse effects. If expired measures underlying past payments could not be challenged in WTO dispute settlement proceedings, it would be difficult to seek a remedy for such adverse effects. Further – in contrast to Articles 3.7 and 19.1 of the DSU – the remedies under Article 7.8 of the *SCM Agreement* for adverse effects of a subsidy are (i) the withdrawal of the subsidy *or* (ii) the removal of adverse effects. Removal of adverse effects through actions other than the withdrawal of a subsidy could not occur if the expiration of a measure would automatically exclude it from a panel's terms of reference.[355]

352 See *ibid.*
353 Several of the timeframes provided for under Article 7 are, however, still shorter than the 'ordinary' timeframes provided for in the DSU. For example, the timeframe for the panel proceedings is four months. See Article 7.5 of the *SCM Agreement*. For the 'normal' timeframes, see above, pp. 776–8.
354 Article 7.8 of the *SCM Agreement*.
355 Appellate Body Report, *US – Upland Cotton (2005)*, para. 273 (emphasis added).

Further elaborating on the implementing Member's obligation to withdraw the subsidy or remove adverse effects under Article 7.8, the Appellate Body ruled in *US – Upland Cotton (Article 21.5 – Brazil) (2008)*:

Article 7.8 is one of the 'special or additional rules and procedures on dispute settlement contained in the covered agreements' ... which prevail over the general DSU rules and procedures to the extent that there is a difference between them. As we see it, Article 7.8 specifies the actions that the respondent Member must take when a subsidy granted or maintained by that Member is found to have resulted in adverse effects to the interests of another Member ... Pursuant to Article 7.8, the implementing Member has two options to come into compliance. The implementing Member: (i) shall take appropriate steps to remove the adverse effects; or (ii) shall withdraw the subsidy. The use of the terms 'shall take' and 'shall withdraw' indicate that compliance with Article 7.8 of the SCM Agreement will usually involve some action by the respondent Member. This affirmative action would be directed at effecting the withdrawal of the subsidy or the removal of its adverse effects. A Member would normally not be able to abstain from taking any action on the assumption that the subsidy will expire or that the adverse effects of the subsidy will dissipate on their own.[356]

As to the question in relation to which subsidies the implementing Member must take steps to remove the adverse effects or withdraw the subsidy, the Appellate Body ruled in *US – Upland Cotton (Article 21.5 – Brazil) (2008)* that it did:

[n]ot see the obligation in Article 7.8 as being limited to subsidies granted in the past. Article 7.8 expressly refers to a Member 'granting or maintaining such subsidy'.[357]

According to the Appellate Body, this means that, in the case of recurring annual payments, the obligation in Article 7.8 would extend to payments 'maintained' by the respondent Member beyond the time period examined by the panel for purposes of determining the existence of serious prejudice, as long as those payments continue to have adverse effects.[358]

As noted, an implementing Member has under Article 7.8 of the *SCM Agreement* the choice between: (1) removing the adverse effects; or (2) withdrawing the subsidy. In *US – Upland Cotton (Article 21.5 – Brazil) (2008)*, the Appellate Body noted that the availability of this choice is 'arguably a consequence of the fact that actionable subsidies are not prohibited *per se*; rather, they are actionable to the extent they cause adverse effects.' The Appellate Body emphasised, however, that the fact that the implementing Member may choose to remove the adverse effects, rather than withdraw the subsidy:

[c]annot be read as allowing a Member to continue to cause adverse effects by maintaining the subsidies that were found to have resulted in adverse effects.[359]

---

356 Appellate Body Report, *US – Upland Cotton (Article 21.5 – Brazil) (2008)*, paras. 235–6. A Member would not comply with the obligation in Article 7.8 to withdraw the subsidy 'if it leaves an actionable subsidy in place, either entirely or partially, or replaces that subsidy with another actionable subsidy'. Appellate Body Report, *US – Upland Cotton (Article 21.5 – Brazil) (2008)*, para. 238.
357 *Ibid.*, para. 237.
358 See *ibid*. Otherwise, the adverse effects of subsequent payments would simply replace the adverse effects that the implementing Member was under an obligation to remove. See *ibid*.
359 *Ibid.*, para. 238.

The subsidising Member must withdraw the subsidy or remove adverse effects within six months from the adoption of the report by the DSB.[360] Instead of withdrawing the subsidy at issue or removing its adverse effects, the subsidising Member may also agree with the complaining Member on compensation.[361] If an Article 21.5 'compliance' proceeding results in a finding that the subsidy has not been withdrawn, or its adverse effects have not been removed, within six months from the adoption of the report, or no agreement on compensation is reached, the DSB must, at the request of the complaining Member and by reverse consensus, grant authorisation to the complaining Member to take countermeasures. These countermeasures must be commensurate with the degree and nature of the adverse effects of the subsidies granted.[362]

Questions and Assignments 12.12

What happens when a panel finds that a subsidy granted by a Member causes adverse effects to the interests of other Members? What does the obligation to take appropriate steps to remove adverse effects entail in the case of subsidies granted in the 1990s and 2000s and found to have caused adverse effects? How do the rules of remedies provided for in Article 7.8 of the *SCM Agreement* apply to recurring subsidies? What are the differences between the remedies under Article 7.8 and under Article 4.7 for prohibited subsidies?

5.5   Non-Actionable Subsidies

As already mentioned, in addition to prohibited subsidies and actionable subsidies, the *SCM Agreement* identifies a third category of subsidies: non-actionable subsidies.[363] This group of subsidies now only includes non-specific subsidies, to which, as discussed above, the disciplines of the *SCM Agreement* do not apply.[364] Until 31 December 1999, this category of non-actionable subsidies also included certain types of specific subsidies listed in Article 8.2 of the *SCM Agreement*, such as certain narrowly defined regional subsidies, environmental subsidies and research and development subsidies. At present, these subsidies, provided that they are specific, are actionable.[365]

6   COUNTERVAILING MEASURES

Prohibited subsidies and actionable subsidies which cause injury to the domestic industry can be challenged directly in WTO dispute settlement, or, in the

---

360 See Article 7.9 of the *SCM Agreement*.
361 See *ibid*. Note that, in this specific context, compensation is a permanent alternative for bringing the measure into consistency with WTO law. This is not the case under the DSU. See above, p. 200.
362 Article 7.9 of the *SCM Agreement*. The contrast between 'appropriate countermeasures' in Article 4.10 and 'countermeasures ... commensurate with the degree and nature of the adverse effects' was emphasised in Decision by the Arbitrators in *Brazil – Aircraft (Article 22.6 – Brazil) (2000)*, para. 3.49, and Decision by the Arbitrators in *US – FSC (Article 22.6 – US) (2002)*, paras. 4.24–4.26.
363 See above, p. 813.   364 See above, p. 770, footnote 125.   365 See Article 31 of the *SCM Agreement*.

alternative, they can be offset by the application of a countervailing measure.[366] A Member whose domestic industry is injured by subsidised imports has the choice between: (1) challenging the subsidy concerned *multilaterally*, pursuant to Article 4 or 7 of the *SCM Agreement*, as discussed in detail above;[367] or (2) *unilaterally* imposing countervailing duties on the subsidised imports, following an investigation procedure before a domestic investigating authority conducted pursuant to the procedural requirements set out in Part V of the *SCM Agreement*. A countervailing duty is defined in Article VI of the GATT 1994 and footnote 36 to the *SCM Agreement* as:

[a] special duty levied for the purpose of offsetting ... any subsidy bestowed, directly, or indirectly, upon the manufacture, production or export of any merchandise.

Article 10 of the *SCM Agreement* provides with respect to countervailing duties:

Members shall take all necessary steps to ensure that the imposition of a countervailing duty on any product of the territory of any Member imported into the territory of another Member is in accordance with the provisions of Article VI of GATT 1994 and the terms of this Agreement. Countervailing duties may only be imposed pursuant to investigations initiated and conducted in accordance with the provisions of this Agreement and the Agreement on Agriculture.

This section examines: (1) under what conditions countervailing duties may be imposed on subsidised imports; (2) how the investigations leading up to the imposition of countervailing duties should be conducted; and (3) how countervailing duties must be applied.

6.1   Conditions for the Imposition of Countervailing Duties

It follows from Article VI of the GATT 1994 and Articles 10 and 32.1 of the *SCM Agreement* that WTO Members may impose countervailing duties when three conditions are fulfilled, namely: (1) there are *subsidised imports*, i.e. imports of products from producers who benefited or benefit from specific subsidies within the meaning of Articles 1, 2 and 14 of the *SCM Agreement*; (2) there is *injury* to the domestic industry of the like products within the meaning of Articles 15 and 16 of the *SCM Agreement*; and (3) there is a *causal link* between the subsidised imports and the injury to the domestic industry *and* injury caused by other factors is *not attributed* to the subsidised imports. The discussion in the previous sections of this chapter on 'specific subsidies', 'injury' and 'causal link and non-attribution' is, *mutatis mutandis*, also relevant for the three conditions for the imposition of countervailing duties.[368] On each of these conditions, please refer to the discussion above.

---

366 A countervailing measure is also sometimes referred to as an 'anti-subsidy measure'.
367 See above, pp. 776–9 (multilateral remedies for prohibited subsidies) 811–813 (multilateral remedies for actionable subsidies).
368 On 'specific subsidies', see above, pp. 764–9; on 'injury', see above, pp. 781–4; and on 'causal link and non-attribution', see above, pp. 784–5.

Questions and Assignments 12.13

When may a Member impose countervailing duties under the terms of the *SCM Agreement*? Compare the conditions for imposing countervailing duties on subsidised imports to the conditions for a successful multilateral challenge of subsidies pursuant to Article 4 or 7 of the *SCM Agreement*.

6.2   Conduct of Countervailing Investigations

The *SCM Agreement* provides for detailed procedural requirements regarding the initiation and conduct of a countervailing investigation by the competent authorities of the Member imposing the countervailing duties on the subsidised imports. These requirements are set out in Articles 11 to 13 of the *SCM Agreement*. The main objectives of these requirements are to ensure that: (1) the investigations are conducted in a transparent manner; (2) all interested parties have the opportunity to defend their interests; and (3) the investigating authorities adequately explain the basis for their determinations.

The Appellate Body and panels have interpreted these requirements in a number of disputes. Note that the procedural requirements for countervailing investigations set out in the *SCM Agreement* are very similar to the procedural requirements for anti-dumping investigations set out in the *Anti-Dumping Agreement* and discussed in Chapter 11.[369] This is true, in particular, for that part of the investigation dealing with injury and the general notification and explanation requirements. The remaining parts of the investigation, not dealing with injury, have of course a somewhat different substantive focus. In a countervailing investigation, the focus is on establishing the extent to which countervailable subsidies are granted and the assessment of the amount of such subsidisation, while, in an anti-dumping investigation, the focus is on the determination of a dumping margin. The obligations under the *SCM Agreement* to examine whether a *causal link* exists between the subsidised imports and the injury to the domestic industry *and* whether injury caused by other factors is *not attributed* to the subsidised imports are similar to the causation and non-attribution rules under the *Anti-Dumping Agreement*.

6.2.1   Initiation of an Investigation

A countervailing investigation normally starts with the submission of a so-called application, i.e. a written complaint that injurious subsidisation is taking place. This application is submitted by, or on behalf of, the domestic industry allegedly injured by the subsidised imports.[370] A countervailing investigation shall not be initiated unless the investigating authorities have determined, on the basis of an examination of the degree of support for, or opposition to, the application, that the application has been made 'by or on behalf of' the domestic industry. Pursuant

---

369 See above, pp. 712–23 (investigation and other procedural steps).   370 See Article 11.1 of the *SCM Agreement*.

to Article 11.2 of the *SCM Agreement*, the application must contain sufficient evidence of the existence of: (1) a subsidy and, if possible, its amount; (2) injury to the domestic industry; and (3) a causal link between the subsidised imports and the alleged injury.[371] Simple assertion, unsubstantiated by relevant evidence, is not considered to meet the requirement of 'sufficient evidence' under Article 11.2 of the *SCM Agreement*. Pursuant to Article 11.3 of the *SCM Agreement*, an investigating authority has an obligation to determine whether there is 'sufficient evidence' to justify initiation of an investigation. Part of this determination must involve an assessment of the accuracy and adequacy of the evidence furnished.[372] Although definitive proof of the existence and nature of a subsidy, injury and a causal link is not necessary for the purposes of justifying initiation under Article 11.3, adequate evidence, providing a sufficient indication of the existence of these elements, is required.[373] The panel in *China – GOES (2012)* stated that, in making the determination of whether there is sufficient evidence for initiation:

[t]he investigating authority is balancing two competing interests, namely the interest of the domestic industry 'in securing the initiation of an investigation' and the interest of respondents in ensuring that 'investigations are not initiated on the basis of frivolous or unfounded suits'.[374]

As mentioned above, the application for the initiation of a countervailing investigation is submitted by, or on behalf of, the domestic industry allegedly injured by the subsidised imports. As is set out in Article 11.4 of the *SCM Agreement*, the application shall be considered to have been made 'by or on behalf of the domestic industry' if it is supported by those domestic producers whose collective output constitutes more than 50 per cent of the total production of the like product produced by that portion of the domestic industry expressing either support for *or* opposition to the application. However, no investigation shall be initiated when domestic producers expressly supporting the application account for less than 25 per cent of total production of the like product produced by the domestic industry. Article 11.4 does not provide that an investigating authority examine the motives of domestic producers that elect to support an investigation. As the Appellate Body explained in *US – Offset Act (Byrd Amendment) (2003)*:

The use of the terms 'expressing support' and 'expressly supporting' clarify that Article ... 11.4 require[s] only that authorities 'determine' that support has been 'expressed' by a sufficient number of domestic producers. Thus ... 'examination' of the 'degree' of support, and not the 'nature' of support is required. In other words, it is the 'quantity', rather than the 'quality', of support that is the issue.[375]

371 Article 11.2 of the *SCM Agreement* sets out in significant detail the information the application must contain.
372 See Article 11.3 of the *SCM Agreement*. Note, however, that Article 11.3 of the *SCM Agreement* does not specify how this examination is to be carried out. Note also that 'sufficient evidence' is, of course, not the same as 'full proof'; it is clearly a lower standard.
373 See Panel Report, *China – GOES (2012)*, para. 7.55.
374 *Ibid.*, para. 7.54. See also Panel Report, *US – Offset Act (Byrd Amendment) (2003)*, para. 7.61. For the interpretation of Article 5.3 of the *Anti-Dumping Agreement* which provides for largely similar obligations, see Panel Report, *Guatemala – Cement I (1998)*, para. 7.52.
375 Appellate Body Report, *US – Offset Act (Byrd Amendment) (2003)*, para. 283.

In special circumstances, investigating authorities may also decide to initiate countervailing investigations of their own accord.[376] However, they may only do so when they have sufficient evidence of the existence of a subsidy, injury and causal link to justify the initiation of an investigation.

If the investigating authorities concerned find that there is not sufficient evidence of either subsidisation or injury to justify proceeding with the case, they must reject the application for the initiation of an investigation, or, if the investigation has already been initiated, promptly terminate that investigation.[377] There shall be immediate termination in cases where the amount of a subsidy is *de minimis* (i.e. less than 1 per cent *ad valorem*), or where the volume of subsidised imports, actual or potential, or the injury, is negligible.[378] The nature of the *de minimis* rule set forth in Article 11.9 was explored by the Appellate Body in *US – Carbon Steel (2002)*. According to the panel in *US – Carbon Steel (2002)*, the *de minimis* requirement establishes a certain threshold, below which subsidisation is always non-injurious.[379] The Appellate Body disagreed and clarified:

> To us, there is nothing in Article 11.9 to suggest that its *de minimis* standard was intended to create a special category of '*non-injurious*' subsidization, or that it reflects a concept that subsidization at less than a *de minimis* threshold *can never* cause injury. For us, the *de minimis* standard in Article 11.9 does no more than lay down an agreed rule that if *de minimis* subsidization is found to exist in an original investigation, authorities are obliged to terminate their investigation, with the result that no countervailing duty can be imposed in such cases.[380]

In *Mexico – Anti-Dumping Measures on Rice (2005)*, the Appellate Body further ruled that, when a company has been found not to have received countervailable subsidies above *de minimis* levels during the original period of investigation, it necessarily follows from Article 11.9 of the *SCM Agreement* that such companies can no longer be made subject to administrative and changed circumstances reviews.[381]

6.2.2 Conduct of the Investigation

When the investigating authorities decide to initiate an investigation, be it at the request of the domestic industry or of their own accord, several procedural obligations must be respected in order to provide adequate protection for those potentially affected by such an investigation. First, a public notice of the initiation must be issued,[382] and, as soon as the investigation is initiated,[383] the

---

376 See Article 11.6 of the *SCM Agreement*.   377 See Article 11.9 of the *SCM Agreement*.

378 See *ibid*.   379 See Panel Report, *US – Carbon Steel (2002)*, para. 8.79.

380 Appellate Body Report, *US – Carbon Steel (2002)*, para. 83 (original emphasis).

381 Appellate Body Report, *Mexico – Anti-Dumping Measures on Rice (2005)*, para. 305.

382 See Article 22.1 of the *SCM Agreement*. Article 22.2 sets out the information which this public notice must contain.

383 Note that, before the investigation is actually initiated, the investigating authorities must invite the subsidising Member for consultations. Such consultations will continue throughout the investigation. See Articles 13.1 and 13.2 of the *SCM Agreement*.

application for the initiation of an investigation must be made available to the known exporters of the subsidised products and the exporting Member.[384] Secondly, interested Members and all interested parties in the investigation, including, of course, the exporter(s) of the subsidised products and the domestic producer(s) of the like product,[385] must be given: (1) notice of the information which the authorities require; and (2) ample opportunity to present in writing all evidence which they consider relevant.[386] Thirdly, Members and interested parties must then be given at least thirty days to reply to the questionnaire they receive from the investigating authorities.[387] In *Mexico – Anti-Dumping Measures on Rice (2005)*, the Appellate Body made clear that the thirty-day period must be accorded to *all* exporters and foreign producers receiving a questionnaire, to be counted from the date of receipt of the questionnaire.[388] The Appellate Body furthermore made clear that it interprets the thirty-day period strictly: a period of twenty-eight working days following the date of publication of the initiating resolution does not suffice.[389] Fourthly, the investigating authorities must provide opportunities for industrial users of the product under investigation, and for representative consumer organisations in cases where the product is commonly sold at the retail level, to provide information.[390] Fifthly, all interested parties must be invited to participate in the hearings held by the investigating authorities.[391] Sixthly, the investigating authorities are obliged to make all information that is not confidential available to all interested Members and interested parties.[392] However, any information the disclosure of which would be of significant competitive advantage to a competitor or would have significant adverse effects on those supplying the information (i.e. any confidential information or other information which is provided on a confidential basis) must, where good cause is shown, be treated as confidential by the investigating authorities.[393] Such confidential information may only be disclosed with the specific permission of the party submitting it.[394] Finally, throughout an

---

384 See Article 12.1.3 of the *SCM Agreement*. The application shall also be made available, upon request, to other interested parties involved.

385 For a definition of 'interested parties', see Article 12.9 of the *SCM Agreement*. Note that domestic or foreign parties other than those mentioned above may also be considered to be 'interested parties'.

386 See Article 12.1 of the *SCM Agreement*.

387 See Article 12.1.1 of the *SCM Agreement*. Where cause is shown, a thirty-day extension period should be granted whenever practicable.

388 See Appellate Body Report, *Mexico – Anti-Dumping Measures on Rice (2005)*, para. 280.

389 See *ibid.*, para. 283.   390 See Article 12.10 of the *SCM Agreement*.

391 See Article 12.2 of the *SCM Agreement*. Note, however, that any decision of the investigating authorities can only be based on such information and arguments as were on the written record of these authorities. Therefore, information provided orally must also be submitted in writing.

392 See Article 12.3 of the *SCM Agreement*.

393 See Article 12.4 of the *SCM Agreement*.

394 See *ibid.* Investigating authorities may, however, be asked to provide non-confidential summaries in sufficient detail to provide a reasonable understanding of the substance of the information submitted in confidence. See Article 12.4.1 of the *SCM Agreement*. See also Appellate Body Report, *EC – Fasteners (2011)*, paras. 535–44 and 549; and Panel Report, *US – Oil Country Tubular Goods Sunset Reviews (Article 21.5 – Argentina) (2007)*, para. 7.135 for the interpretation of Article 6.5 of the *Anti-Dumping Agreement* which provides for largely similar obligations in respect of the protection of confidential information and the provision of non-confidential summaries.

investigation, the investigating authorities must satisfy themselves as to the accuracy of the information supplied by interested Members or interested parties upon which their findings are based.[395]

When investigating authorities, in spite of their best efforts, fail to obtain all relevant information, they may take decisions on the basis of the 'best information available'. Article 12.7 of the *SCM Agreement* provides:

[I]n cases in which any interested Member or interested party refuses access to, or otherwise does not provide, necessary information within a reasonable period or significantly impedes the investigation, preliminary and final determinations, affirmative or negative, may be made on the basis of the facts available.

According to the Appellate Body in *Mexico – Anti-Dumping Measures on Rice (2005)*, Article 12.7 is intended to ensure that the failure of an interested party to provide necessary information does not hinder an agency's investigation. Thus, the provision permits the use of facts on record solely for the purpose of replacing information that may be missing, in order to arrive at an accurate subsidisation or injury determination.[396] In the same appeal, the Appellate Body drew a comparison with Article 6.8 of the *Anti-Dumping Agreement*, which also 'permits an investigating authority, under certain circumstances, to fill in gaps in the information necessary to arrive at a conclusion as to subsidization (or dumping) and injury'.[397] While the Appellate Body recognised that Article 6.8 of the *Anti-Dumping Agreement* contains far more detailed rules as regards the use of 'facts available' by an investigating authority, it considered that:

[i]t would be anomalous if Article 12.7 of the *SCM Agreement* were to permit the use of 'facts available' in countervailing duty investigations in a manner markedly different from that in anti-dumping investigations.[398]

Hence, according to the Appellate Body, similar limitations apply under Article 12.7 of the *SCM Agreement* (as apply under Article 6.8 of the *Anti-Dumping Agreement*). It held that:

[r]ecourse to facts available does not permit an investigating authority to use any information in whatever way it chooses. First, such recourse is not a licence to rely on only part of the evidence provided. To the extent possible, an investigating authority using the 'facts available' in a countervailing duty investigation must take into account all the substantiated facts provided by an interested party, even if those facts may not constitute the complete information requested of that party. Secondly, the 'facts available' to the agency are generally limited to those that may reasonably replace the information that an interested party failed to provide. In certain circumstances, this may include information from secondary sources.[399]

---

395 Article 12.5 of the *SCM Agreement*.
396 See Appellate Body Report, *Mexico – Anti-Dumping Measures on Rice (2005)*, para. 293. Similarly, the panel in *EC – Countervailing Measures on DRAM Chips (2005)* considered that Article 12.7 of the *SCM Agreement* 'identifies the circumstances in which investigating authorities may overcome a lack of information, in the response of the interested parties, by using "facts" which are otherwise "available" to the investigating authority'. See Panel Report, *EC – Countervailing Measures on DRAM Chips (2005)*, para. 7.245.
397 Appellate Body Report, *Mexico – Anti-Dumping Measures on Rice (2005)*, para. 291.
398 *Ibid.*, para. 295.   399 *Ibid.*, para. 294.

While the possibility for investigating authorities to use 'facts available' is important to avoid investigations being frustrated and deadlocked because of the lack of cooperation from an interested party holding the relevant information, this possibility may evidently also potentially give rise to abuse on the part of investigating authorities. To ensure due process in the countervailing investigation, Article 12.8 of the *SCM Agreement* requires that:

[t]he authorities shall, before a final determination is made, inform all interested Members and interested parties of the essential facts under consideration which form the basis for the decision whether to apply definitive measures. Such disclosure should take place in sufficient time for the parties to defend their interests.

As to the type of information that must be disclosed, the provision covers 'those facts on the record that may be taken into account by an authority in reaching a decision as to whether or not to apply' definitive countervailing duties.[400] Unlike Article 22.5, which governs the disclosure of matters of fact and law and reasons at the conclusion of the countervailing duty investigations, Article 12.8 concerns the disclosure of 'facts' in the course of such investigations 'before a final determination is made'. According to the Appellate Body in *China – GOES (2012)*, Article 12.8:

[d]oes not require the disclosure of *all* the facts that are before an authority but, instead, those that are 'essential'; a word that carries a connotation of significant, important, or salient. In considering which facts are 'essential' ... such facts are, first, those that 'form the basis for the decision whether to apply definitive measures' and, second, those that ensure the ability of interested parties to defend their interests.[401]

In other words, Article 12.8 requires authorities to inform interested parties of those facts that are significant in the process of reaching a decision as to whether or not to apply definitive measures. Such facts are those that are salient for a decision to apply definitive measures, as well as those that are salient for a contrary outcome. As the Appellate Body also found in *China – GOES (2012)*, an investigating authority must 'disclose such facts, *in a coherent way*, so as to permit an interested party to understand the basis for the decision whether or not to apply definitive measures' because disclosing the essential facts under consideration pursuant to Article 12.8 is 'paramount for ensuring the ability of the parties concerned to defend their interests'.[402]

Note that Articles 12.7 and 12.8 of the *SCM Agreement* refer to 'interested parties'. Article 12.9 of the *SCM Agreement* provides in this respect:

For the purposes of this Agreement, 'interested parties' shall include:

(i) an exporter or foreign producer or the importer of a product subject to investigation, or a trade or business association a majority of the members of which are producers, exporters or importers of such product; and

---

400 Appellate Body Report, *China – GOES (2012)*, para. 240.
401 *Ibid.* (original emphasis).   402 *Ibid.* (emphasis added).

(ii) a producer of the like product in the importing Member or a trade and business association a majority of the members of which produce the like product in the territory of the
importing Member.

This list shall not preclude Members from allowing domestic or foreign parties other than
those mentioned above to be included as interested parties.

In *Japan – DRAMs (Korea) (2007)*, the panel and the Appellate Body addressed
the question whether the inclusion of a party as an 'interested party' in an investigation requires a prior determination that that party has an interest in the
outcome of an investigation.[403] Korea had argued that such a requirement was
implied in the language of Article 12.9.[404] The panel disagreed and found that
Article 12.9 does not provide an exhaustive list as to which parties 'can be taken
to be "interested parties"'.[405] The Appellate Body in *Japan – DRAMs (Korea)
(2007)* stated that, while it agreed with Korea that:

[t]he entities specified in subparagraphs (i) and (ii) – which are all involved in the production, export, or import of the product under investigation, or in the production of the like
product in the importing country – are likely to 'have an interest in the outcome of the
proceeding', but [it found] nothing in Article 12.9 to suggest that interested parties are
restricted to entities of this kind under the residual clause of Article 12.9. Although the
term 'interested party' by definition suggests that the party must have an interest related
to the investigation, the mere fact that the lists in subparagraphs (i) and (ii) comprise
entities that may be directly interested in the outcome of the investigation does not imply that parties that may have other forms of interest pertinent to the investigation are
excluded.[406]

The last sentence of Article 12.9 provides that Members are not precluded from
allowing domestic or foreign parties other than those listed in sub-paragraphs (i)
and (ii) to be included as interested parties. This does not mean, however, that
investigating authorities enjoy an unfettered discretion in designating entities
as interested parties regardless of the relevance of such entities to the conduct of
an objective investigation. At the same time, an investigating authority needs to
have some discretion to include as interested parties entities that are relevant for
conducting an objective investigation and for obtaining information or evidence
relevant to the investigation at hand. Nonetheless, the Appellate Body stressed
that, in designating entities as interested parties, an investigating authority must
be mindful of the burden that such designation may entail for other interested
parties.[407]

Investigations must normally be concluded within one year,[408] and in no case
should an investigation take longer than eighteen months.[409]

403 See Appellate Body Report, *Japan – DRAMs (Korea) (2007)*, para. 237.
404 See *ibid.*, para. 238.
405 See Panel Report, *Japan – DRAMs (Korea) (2007)*, para. 7.388.
406 Appellate Body Report, *Japan – DRAMs (Korea) (2007)*, paras. 238–9.
407 See *ibid.*, para. 242.
408 See Article 11.11 of the *SCM Agreement*.
409 See *ibid.*

6.2.3   Public Notice and Judicial Review

In order to increase the transparency of decisions taken by investigating authorities and to encourage solid and thorough reasoning supporting such decisions, Article 22 of the *SCM Agreement* contains detailed requirements for public notice by investigating authorities of decisions on the initiation of an investigation, provisional countervailing measures, voluntary undertakings or definitive countervailing duties. For example, under Article 22.5 of the *SCM Agreement*, the public notice issued when the investigating authorities decide to impose a definitive countervailing duty *must* set forth, or otherwise make available through a separate report, all relevant information on the matters of fact, law and reasons which have led to the imposition of the countervailing duty.[410] In particular, the notice or report *must* contain: (1) the names of the suppliers or, when this is impracticable, the supplying countries involved; (2) a description of the product which is sufficient for customs purposes; (3) the amount of subsidy established and the basis on which the existence of a subsidy has been determined; (4) considerations relevant to the injury determination as set out in Article 15; and (5) the main reasons leading to the determination.[411] Furthermore, the notice or report *must* set out the reasons for the acceptance or rejection of relevant arguments or claims made by interested Members and by the exporters and importers.[412] In *China – GOES (2012)*, the Appellate Body found with regard to the requirement to disclose 'relevant information on the matters of fact' that Article 22.5 does not require authorities to disclose *all* the factual information that is before them, but rather those facts that allow an understanding of the factual basis that led to the imposition of final measures.[413] According to the Appellate Body, what constitutes 'relevant information on the matters of fact' is to be understood in light of the content of the findings needed to satisfy the substantive requirements for the imposition of definitive measures under the *SCM Agreement*, as well as the factual circumstances of each case.[414] The Appellate Body in *China – GOES (2012)* stated with regard to the 'public notice' requirement under Article 22.5 of the *SCM Agreement* that:

[Article 22.5] capture[s] the principle that those parties whose interests are affected by the imposition of final ... countervailing duties are entitled to know, as a matter of fairness and due process, the facts, law and reasons that have led to the imposition of such duties. The

---

410 See Article 22.5 of the *SCM Agreement*. Note, however, that Article 22.5 requires that due regard be paid to the requirement for the protection of confidential information.

411 See Article 22.5 of the *SCM Agreement*, referring to Article 22.4 thereof.

412 See Article 22.5 of the *SCM Agreement*.

413 See Appellate Body Report, *China – GOES (2012)*, para. 256. The inclusion of this information should therefore give a reasoned account of the factual support for an authority's decision to impose definitive measures. See *ibid.*

414 The imposition of final countervailing duties requires that an investigating authority finds subsidisation, injury to the domestic industry, and a causal link between subsidisation and injury. See Appellate Body Report, *China – GOES (2012)*, para. 257.

obligation of disclosure under [Article 22.5] is framed by the requirement of 'relevance', which entails the disclosure of the matrix of facts, law and reasons that logically fit together to render the decision to impose final measures ... [Article 22.5] seeks to guarantee that interested parties are able to pursue judicial review of a final determination as provided in ... Article 23.[415]

As provided for in Article 23 of the *SCM Agreement*, entitled 'Judicial Review', each Member whose national legislation contains provisions on countervailing measures must maintain judicial, arbitral or administrative tribunals or procedures for the purpose of, *inter alia*, the prompt review of administrative actions relating to definitive determinations and reviews of determinations. Such tribunals or procedures must be independent from the authorities responsible for the determination or review in question, and must provide all interested parties who participated in the administrative proceeding, and are affected directly and individually by the administrative actions, with access to review.[416]

Questions and Assignments 12.14

Describe the key features of a countervailing investigation. What is the main objective of the procedural requirements set out in Articles 11 to 13 of the *SCM Agreement*? How is a countervailing investigation initiated? When are investigating authorities obliged to terminate a countervailing investigation immediately? How does the *SCM Agreement* ensure that all interested parties get an opportunity to be heard in a countervailing investigation? What does the 'disclosure' requirement under Article 12.8 of the *SCM Agreement* entail and how does this requirement differ from the 'public notice' requirement set out in Article 22.5 of the *SCM Agreement*? Who is an 'interested party' within the meaning of Article 12.7 of the *SCM Agreement*? Discuss how confidential information is treated in a countervailing investigation. Are investigating authorities permitted to base their conclusions on the 'best information available'? Why is the public notice requirement of Article 22 of the *SCM Agreement* important? What must the public notice, issued when the investigating authorities decide to impose a definitive countervailing duty, contain, or otherwise make available through a separate report? What does Article 23 of the *SCM Agreement* require from Members?

6.3   Application of Countervailing Measures

The *SCM Agreement* provides for three types of countervailing measure: (1) provisional countervailing measures; (2) voluntary undertakings; and (3) definitive countervailing duties. This section discusses in turn these three types of countervailing measure.

6.3.1   Imposition of Provisional Countervailing Measures

After making a preliminary determination that a subsidy is causing or threatening to cause injury to a domestic industry, an importing Member can impose *provisional countervailing measures* on the subsidised imports if the authorities judge such measures necessary to prevent injury being caused during the

---

415 *Ibid.*, para. 258.   416 See Article 23 of the *SCM Agreement*.

investigation.[417] Provisional countervailing measures may take the form of provisional countervailing duties guaranteed by cash deposits or bonds equal to the amount of the provisionally calculated amount of subsidisation.[418] However, such provisional countervailing measures cannot be applied earlier than sixty days from the date of initiation of the investigation. Furthermore, their application must be limited to as short a period as possible and in no case may they be applied for more than four months.[419] In *US – Softwood Lumber III (2002)*, the panel found that the United States had violated Articles 17.3 and 17.4 of the *SCM Agreement* because it had imposed provisional countervailing measures on imports of softwood lumber prior to the lapse of the sixty-day period after the date of initiation and had exceeded the four-month maximum length by three months.[420]

6.3.2   Voluntary Undertakings

Investigations may be suspended or terminated without the imposition of provisional measures or countervailing duties upon receipt of satisfactory *voluntary undertakings* under which: (1) the government of the exporting Member agrees to eliminate or limit the subsidy or to take other measures concerning its effects; or (2) the exporter agrees to revise its prices so that the investigating authorities are satisfied that the injurious effect of the subsidy is eliminated.[421] Note that, pursuant to Article 18.2 of the *SCM Agreement*, undertakings may not be sought or accepted unless the investigating authorities have made a preliminary affirmative determination of subsidisation and injury caused by such subsidisation. In case of undertakings from exporters, the consent of the exporting Member must be obtained. Article 18.4 of the *SCM Agreement* provides that, if an undertaking is accepted, the investigation of subsidisation and injury shall nevertheless be completed if the exporting Member so desires or the importing Member so decides.[422]

6.3.3   Imposition and Collection of Countervailing Duties

Members may impose *definitive countervailing duties* only after making a final determination that: (1) a countervailable subsidy exists; and (2) the subsidised imports cause, or threaten to cause, injury to the domestic industry.[423] Note that Article 32.1 of the *SCM Agreement* states:

No specific action against a subsidy of another Member can be taken except in accordance with the provisions of GATT 1994, as interpreted by this Agreement.[424]

417 See Article 17 of the *SCM Agreement*.   418 See Article 17.2 of the *SCM Agreement*.
419 See Articles 17.3 and 17.4 of the *SCM Agreement*.
420 See Panel Report, *US – Softwood Lumber III (2002)*, para. 7.101.
421 See Article 18.1 of the *SCM Agreement*.
422 Article 18.6 of the *SCM Agreement* sets out the consequences of a violation of an undertaking.
423 See Article 19.1 of the *SCM Agreement*.
424 The Appellate Body established in *US – Offset Act (Byrd Amendment) (2003)* the following test to determine whether a measure constitutes 'a specific action': '[A] measure that may be taken only when the constituent

In *US – Offset Act (Byrd Amendment) (2003)*, the Appellate Body ruled that it follows from this provision that the response to a countervailable subsidy must be in one of the *four* forms provided for in provisions of the GATT 1994 or the *SCM Agreement*.[425] As discussed above, the GATT 1994 and the *SCM Agreement* provide four responses to a countervailable subsidy: definitive countervailing duties; provisional measures; price undertakings; and multilaterally sanctioned countermeasures under the dispute settlement system. No other response to subsidisation is permitted. In *US – Offset Act (Byrd Amendment) (2003)*, the measure at issue was the US Continued Dumping and Subsidy Offset Act of 2000 (CDSOA).[426] This Act provided, in relevant part, that the United States Customs shall *distribute* duties assessed pursuant to a countervailing duty order to 'affected domestic producers' for 'qualifying expenditures'.[427] According to the Appellate Body, in applying Article 32.1 of the *SCM Agreement* to the measure at issue in this case, it was necessary:

[t]o assess whether the design and structure of a measure is such that the measure is 'opposed to', has an adverse bearing on, or, more specifically, has the effect of dissuading ... the practice of subsidization, or creates an incentive to terminate such practice.[428]

In the Appellate Body's view, the CDSOA has exactly those effects because of its design and structure.[429] However, a measure cannot 'be against' a subsidy simply because it facilitates or induces the exercise of rights that are WTO-consistent.[430] The Appellate Body concluded:

As the CDSOA does not correspond to any of the responses to subsidization envisaged by the GATT 1994 and the *SCM Agreement*, we conclude that it is not in accordance with the provisions of the GATT 1994, as interpreted by the *SCM Agreement*, and that, therefore, the CDSOA is inconsistent with Article 32.1 of the *SCM Agreement*.[431]

The panel in *Mexico – Anti-Dumping Measures on Rice (2005)* held that the provision in a Mexican regulation imposing fines on importers importing products subject to countervailing duty investigations was a form of 'specific action' against a subsidy, that fines were not provided for in the GATT 1994 or the *SCM Agreement*, and that the fines at issue were thus inconsistent with Article 32.1 of the *SCM Agreement*.[432] However, the panel in *EC – Commercial Vessels (2005)*

---

elements of ... a subsidy are present, is a "specific action" in response to ... subsidization within the meaning of Article 32.1 of the *SCM Agreement*. In other words, the measure must be inextricably linked to, or have a strong correlation with, the constituent elements of dumping or of a subsidy. Such link or correlation may ... be derived from the text of the measure itself.' See Appellate Body Report, *US – Offset Act (Byrd Amendment) (2003)*, para. 239.

425 *Ibid.*, para. 269.   426 See *ibid.*, paras. 11–14.   427 See *ibid.*, para. 14.   428 *Ibid.*, para. 254.

429 See *ibid.*, para. 254. The Appellate Body further explained that 'in order to determine whether the CDSOA is "against" ... subsidization, it was not necessary, nor relevant, for the Panel to examine the conditions of competition under which domestic products and ... subsidized imports compete, and to assess the impact of the measure on the competitive relationship between them. An analysis of the term "against", in our view, is more appropriately centred on the design and structure of the measure; such an analysis does not mandate an economic assessment of the implications of the measure on the conditions of competition under which domestic product and ... subsidized imports compete.' See *ibid.*, para. 257.

430 *Ibid.*, para. 258.   431 *Ibid.*, para. 273.

432 See Panel Report, *Mexico – Anti-Dumping Measures on Rice (2005)*, para. 7.278.

ruled that a European regulation on shipbuilding constituted a form of 'specific action', but as it was not directed 'against' a subsidy, Article 32.1 of the *SCM Agreement* was not violated.[433]

With respect to the amount of the countervailing duty imposed on subsidised imports, Article 19.4 of the *SCM Agreement* provides:

No countervailing duty shall be levied on any imported product in excess of the amount of the subsidy found to exist, calculated in terms of subsidization per unit of the subsidized and exported product.

Thus, Article 19.4 'places a quantitative ceiling on the amount of a countervailing duty which may not exceed the amount of subsidization'.[434] Moreover, if the amount of the injury caused is less than the amount of the subsidy, the definitive countervailing duty should *preferably* be limited to the amount necessary to counteract the injury caused.[435] This is commonly referred to as the 'lesser duty' rule.[436] As discussed above, Members have a margin of discretion in deciding on the method used to calculate the amount of the subsidy.[437] The Appellate Body's reference in *US – Softwood Lumber IV (2004)* to calculation of countervailing duty rates on a per unit basis under Article 19.4 supports the interpretation that an investigating authority is permitted to calculate the total amount and the rate of subsidisation on an aggregate basis.[438]

In *Japan – DRAMs (Korea) (2007)*, the issue was raised whether subsidisation must be 'found to exist' – as is stated in Article 19.4 of the *SCM Agreement* – at the time of imposition of the countervailing duty, or whether a determination that a subsidy was 'found to exist' during some prior period suffices.[439] The panel found that 'countervailing duties may only be imposed if there is present subsidization at the time of duty imposition'.[440] According to the panel, this does not, however, exclude the possibility that an investigating authority may rely on previous data.[441] As the panel observed, the situation during the period

---

433 See Panel Report, *EC – Commercial Vessels (2005)*, para. 7.143.
434 Appellate Body Report, *US – Anti-Dumping and Countervailing Duties (China) (2011)*, para. 554.
435 See Article 19.2 of the *SCM Agreement*. Moreover, a Member may even decide to abstain from imposing countervailing duties altogether. See also Article 19.2 of the *SCM Agreement*.
436 See above, pp. 724–5.
437 As explained in more detail above, Article 14 of the *SCM Agreement* requires: first, that the method used shall be provided for in national legislation or implementing regulations; secondly, that the application of the method to each particular case shall be transparent and adequately explained; and, thirdly, that the method must be consistent with the guidelines set out in Article 14(a)–(d).
438 Appellate Body Report, *US – Softwood Lumber IV (2004)*, para. 153.
439 See Panel Report, *Japan – DRAMs (Korea) (2007)*, para. 7.351.
440 *Ibid.*, para. 7.355.
441 The panel in *Japan – DRAMs (Korea) (2007)* held that: '[C]ountervailing duties may be imposed on the basis of the investigating authority's review of a past period of investigation. We are not suggesting that an investigating authority is somehow required to conduct a new investigation at the time of imposition, in order to confirm the continued existence of the subsidization found to exist during the period of investigation. That would defeat the very purpose of using periods of investigation in the first place.' See Panel Report, *Japan – DRAMs (Korea) (2007)*, para. 7.356.

of investigation may serve as a proxy for the situation prevailing at the time of imposition. However, in the case of non-recurring subsidies, if the review of the period of investigation indicates that the subsidy will no longer exist at the time of imposition, the fact that subsidisation existed during the period of investigation will not be sufficient to demonstrate 'current' subsidisation at the time of imposition.[442] On appeal, the Appellate Body noted in this regard that, by its terms, Article 19.4 refers to a subsidy 'found to exist',[443] and that it saw:

[n]o requirement in Article 19.4 for an investigating authority to conduct a new investigation or to 'update' the determination at the time of imposition of a countervailing duty in order to confirm the continued existence of the subsidy. However, in the case of a non-recurring subsidy, a countervailing duty cannot be imposed if the investigating authority has made a finding in the course of its investigation as to the duration of the subsidy and, according to that finding, the subsidy is no longer in existence at the time that the Member makes a final determination to impose a countervailing duty.[444]

This is because, in such a situation, the countervailing duty, if imposed, would be in excess of the amount of subsidy found to exist, contrary to the provisions of Article 19.4.

Countervailing duties must be collected on a non-discriminatory basis. Article 19.3 of the *SCM Agreement* states:

When a countervailing duty is imposed in respect of any product, such countervailing duty shall be levied, in the appropriate amounts in each case, on a non-discriminatory basis on imports of such product from all sources found to be subsidized and causing injury.[445]

Thus, the provision contains: (1) a requirement that countervailing duties be levied in the appropriate amounts in each case; and (2) a requirement that these duties be levied on a non-discriminatory basis on imports of such product from all sources found to be subsidised and causing injury, except for imports from sources that have renounced the relevant subsidies or from which undertakings have been accepted.[446] While a Member imposing countervailing duties has to levy such duties 'on a non-discriminatory basis', this does not mean that the 'appropriate' amount of the countervailing duty imposed will necessarily be the same for each individual exporter. An exporter or producer who was examined individually and has cooperated in the investigation will normally be levied an individual countervailing duty. Note that any exporter whose exports are subject to a definitive countervailing duty but who was not actually investigated is entitled to an expedited review so that the investigating authorities can

---

442 See *ibid.*, para. 7.357.

443 See Appellate Body Report, *Japan – DRAMs (Korea) (2007)*, para. 210.   444 *Ibid.*

445 As discussed above, the MFN treatment obligation applies to countervailing duties. See above, p. 322. The MFN treatment obligation also applies to anti-dumping duties. See above, p. 725. Note that countervailing duties shall not be applied to imports from sources which have renounced any subsidies in question or sources from which undertakings have been accepted. See Article 19.3 of the *SCM Agreement*.

446 See Appellate Body Report, *US – Anti-Dumping and Countervailing Duties (China) (2011)*, para. 552.

promptly establish an individual countervailing duty rate for that exporter.[447] Moreover, the Appellate Body stressed that:

[c]ountry-wide or company-specific countervailing duty rates may be imposed under Part V of the *SCM Agreement* only *after* the investigating authority has determined the existence of subsidization, injury to the domestic industry, and a causal link between them. In other words, the fact that Article 19 permits the imposition of countervailing duties on imports from producers or exporters not investigated individually, does not exonerate a Member from the obligation to determine the total amount of subsidy and the countervailing duty rate consistently with the provisions of the *SCM Agreement* and Article VI of the GATT 1994.[448]

A final comment regarding Article 19.3 of the *SCM Agreement* concerns the issue of 'double-counting' or 'double-remedies', i.e. a situation in which duties are imposed against the same imports from non-market economies – and allegedly for the same injury – under both the *Anti-Dumping Agreement* and the *SCM Agreement*. In *US – Anti-Dumping and Countervailing Duties (China) (2011)*, the Appellate Body found that Article 19.3 is of relevance to this issue. The Appellate Body held that, under Article 19.3:

[t]he appropriateness of the amount of countervailing duties cannot be determined without having regard to anti-dumping duties imposed on the same product to offset the same subsidization. The amount of a countervailing duty cannot be 'appropriate' in situations where that duty represents the full amount of the subsidy and where anti-dumping duties, calculated at least to some extent on the basis of the same subsidization, are imposed concurrently to remove the same injury to the domestic industry. Dumping margins calculated based on an NME [non-market economy] methodology are, for the reasons explained above, likely to include some component that is attributable to subsidization.[449]

The Appellate Body concluded that the imposition of double remedies, that is, offsetting the same subsidisation twice by the concurrent imposition of anti-dumping duties calculated on the basis of a non-market economy methodology and countervailing duties, is inconsistent with Article 19.3 of the *SCM Agreement*.[450]

---

447 See Article 19.3 of the *SCM Agreement*. This does not apply to exporters for whom no individual countervailing duty was established due to their refusal to cooperate with the investigating authorities. As the Appellate Body stated in *US – Anti-Dumping and Countervailing Duties (China) (2011)*, '[I]t would not be appropriate for an importing Member to levy countervailing duties on imports from sources that have renounced relevant subsidies, or on imports from sources whose price undertakings have been accepted. Similarly, because the requirement that the duty be levied in "appropriate amounts" implies a certain tailoring of the amounts according to circumstances, this suggests that the requirement that the duty be imposed on a non-discriminatory basis on imports from all subsidized sources should not be read in an overly formalistic or rigid manner. The second sentence of Article 19.3 provides a specific example of circumstances in which it is permissible not to differentiate amongst individual exporters, as well as of when and how differentiated treatment in the establishment of a countervailing duty rate is required.' See Appellate Body Report, *US – Anti-Dumping and Countervailing Duties (China) (2011)*, para. 553.

448 Appellate Body Report, *US – Softwood Lumber IV (2004)*, para. 154 (original emphasis).

449 Appellate Body Report, *US – Anti-Dumping and Countervailing Duties (China) (2011)*, para. 582. In the same report, the Appellate Body noted that 'Article 19.4 makes clear that the amount that could be "appropriate" cannot be more than the amount of the subsidy'. It also noted that Article 19.2 'states that it is "desirable" that "duty should be less than the total amount of the subsidy if such lesser duty would be adequate to remove the injury". Article 19.2 thus encourages such authorities to link the actual amount of the countervailing duty to the injury to be removed.' See Appellate Body Report, *US – Anti-Dumping and Countervailing Duties (China) (2011)*, paras. 556–7.

450 Appellate Body Report, *US – Anti-Dumping and Countervailing Duties (China) (2011)*, para. 583.

Pursuant to Article 20.1 of the *SCM Agreement*, countervailing duties, in principle, may not be applied retroactively, i.e. they may only be applied to products imported after the decision to impose countervailing duties entered into force.[451] As set out in Article 20.5 of the *SCM Agreement*, where a final determination is negative, any cash deposit made during the period of the application of provisional measures shall be refunded and any bonds released in an expeditious manner.[452]

6.3.4 Duration, Termination and Review of Countervailing Duties

With respect to the period of imposition of countervailing duties, Article 21.1 of the *SCM Agreement* states as a rule:

> A countervailing duty shall remain in force only as long as and to the extent necessary to counteract subsidization which is causing injury.

The Appellate Body held in *US – Carbon Steel (2002)* that it considered Article 21.1 of the *SCM Agreement* to be:

> [a] general rule that, after the imposition of a countervailing duty, the continued application of that duty is subject to certain disciplines. These disciplines relate to the *duration* of the countervailing duty ('only as long as ... necessary'), its *magnitude* ('only ... to the extent necessary'), and its *purpose* ('to counteract subsidization which is causing injury'). Thus, the general rule of Article 21.1 underlines the requirement for periodic review of countervailing duties and highlights the factors that must inform such reviews.[453]

Upon a request from an interested party or upon their own initiative where warranted, the investigating authorities shall review the need for the continued application of the duty.[454] Interested parties may request such review once a reasonable period has elapsed since the imposition of the definitive countervailing duty. The interested parties requesting a review must submit positive information substantiating the need for a review.[455] During the review, the investigating authorities examine at the request of the interested party: (1) whether the continued imposition of the duty is necessary to offset subsidisation; and/or (2) whether injury would be likely to continue or recur if the duty were removed

---

451 Note, however, that the retroactive application of countervailing duties is permitted in specific circumstances. See Articles 20.2 and 20.6 of the *SCM Agreement*.

452 However, if the definitive countervailing duty is higher than the amount guaranteed by the cash deposit or bond, the difference shall not be collected. See Article 20.3 of the *SCM Agreement*.

453 Appellate Body Report, *US – Carbon Steel (2002)*, para. 70 (original emphasis).

454 See Article 21.2 of the *SCM Agreement*. Such periodic reviews can be initiated upon the initiative of the investigating authorities or, provided that a reasonable period of time has elapsed since the imposition of the definitive countervailing duty, upon request by any interested party which submits positive information substantiating the need for such a review. Interested parties have the right to request the authorities to examine whether the continued imposition of the duty is necessary to offset subsidisation, whether the injury would be likely to continue or recur if the duty were removed or varied, or both. See also Appellate Body Report, *US – Lead and Bismuth II (2000)*, para. 53. See also Panel Report, *US – Softwood Lumber III (2002)*, para. 7.151. The panel in this case noted that Article 21.2 does *not* impose an obligation to establish an annual periodic review procedure as was undertaken by the United States in its retrospective duty assessment system.

455 See Article 21.2 of the *SCM Agreement*.

or varied.[456] The Appellate Body in *Mexico – Anti-Dumping Measures on Rice (2005)* found that Members are not allowed to condition the right of interested parties to a review upon requirements other than those set out in Article 21.2 of the *SCM Agreement*.[457]

In *US – Lead and Bismuth II (2000)*, the Appellate Body noted with regard to the determination an investigating authority must make in an Article 21.2 review:

> On the basis of its assessment of the information presented to it by interested parties, as well as of other evidence before it relating to the period of review, the investigating authority must determine whether there is a continuing need for the application of countervailing duties. The investigating authority is not free to ignore such information. If it were free to ignore this information, the review mechanism under Article 21.2 would have no purpose.[458]

As to the question whether the existence of a 'benefit' in an Article 21.2 review, the Appellate Body held in *US – Lead and Bismuth II (2000)*:

> We do not agree with the Panel's implied view that, in the context of an administrative review under Article 21.2, an investigating authority must *always* establish the existence of a 'benefit' during the period of review *in the same way as* an investigating authority must establish a 'benefit' in an original investigation ... In an original investigation, the investigating authority must establish that *all* conditions set out in the *SCM Agreement* for the imposition of countervailing duties are fulfilled. In an administrative review, however, the investigating authority must address those issues which have been raised before it by the interested parties or, in the case of an investigation conducted on its own initiative, those issues which warranted the examination.[459]

The Appellate Body hence draws a distinction between the original investigation which is concerned with the initial imposition of a countervailing duty *and* the review procedure of Article 21.2.[460]

If the investigating authorities, such a review, reach the conclusion that continued imposition of the countervailing duty is no longer necessary it shall be

---

456   See *ibid*. The review must be conducted pursuant to the same procedural rules as those that applied to the original investigation. See Article 21.4 of the *SCM Agreement*.

457   See Appellate Body Report, *Mexico – Anti-Dumping Measures on Rice (2005)*, para. 314.

458   Appellate Body Report, *US – Lead and Bismuth II (2000)*, para. 61.

459   *Ibid*., paras. 62–3.

460   The extent of the obligations of the investigating authorities in the context of a review procedure was clarified by the Appellate Body in *US – Countervailing Measures on Certain EC Products (2003)*. The measure at issue in this case was an administrative practice employed by the United States in review procedures following a change in ownership. The Appellate Body examined the consistency of this practice, referred to as the 'same person' method, with Article 21.2 and found that: 'under the "same person" method, when the [US Department of Commerce] determines that no new legal person is created as a result of privatization, the [US Department of Commerce] will conclude from this determination, *without any further analysis*, and irrespective of the price paid by the new owners for the newly privatized enterprise, that the newly privatized enterprise continues to receive the benefit of a previous financial contribution. This approach is contrary to the obligation in Article 21.2 of the *SCM Agreement* that the investigating authority must take into account in an administrative review "positive information substantiating the need for a review".' For this reason, the Appellate Body held the 'same person method' to be as such inconsistent with Article 21.2. See Appellate Body Report, *US – Countervailing Measures on Certain EC Products (2003)*, para. 146.

terminated immediately.[461] Should the investigating authorities conclude that the countervailing duty remains warranted, it will continue to apply, albeit possibly at a reduced level.

Article 21.3 of the *SCM Agreement* provides for a so-called 'sunset' clause according to which all definitive countervailing duties must be terminated, at the latest, five years after their imposition or latest review. However, where the investigating authorities determine that the lapse of the countervailing duty would be likely to lead to continuation or recurrence of subsidisation and injury, the duty will not be terminated.[462] Investigating authorities make that determination in the context of a review that is commonly referred to as a 'sunset review'. A sunset review may be initiated by the investigating authorities at their own initiative *or* upon a duly substantiated request made by, or on behalf of, the domestic industry.[463] The Appellate Body explained in *US – Carbon Steel (2002)* that Article 21.3 differs from Article 21.2, discussed above, in that the latter identifies certain circumstances in which investigating authorities are under an *obligation* to review ('shall review') whether the continued imposition of the countervailing duty is necessary. In contrast, the principal obligation in Article 21.3 is not, *per se*, to conduct a review, but rather to *terminate* a countervailing duty *unless* a specific determination is made in a review that the continued imposition is necessary.[464]

The provisions of Article 12 of the *SCM Agreement*, setting out rules on the collection of evidence, transparency, due process and procedure with regard to original investigations, also apply to sunset reviews.[465] Sunset reviews shall be carried out expeditiously and shall normally be concluded within twelve months of their initiation.[466]

Questions and Assignments 12.15

Discuss briefly the three types of countervailing measure. In what circumstances can a Member impose a provisional countervailing measure? When can a Member impose a definitive countervailing duty? Is a Member allowed to impose a countervailing duty in excess of the subsidy found to exist? Is a Member allowed to impose a countervailing duty in excess of the amount necessary to counteract the injury caused? Discuss whether the MFN treatment obligation applies to countervailing duties. Can countervailing duties be applied retroactively? What is

---

461 See Article 21.2 of the *SCM Agreement*.
462 See Article 21.3 of the *SCM Agreement*.
463 See Article 21 of the *SCM Agreement*. Note that a request for a sunset review must be made within a reasonable period of time prior to the expiry of the countervailing duties and that investigating authorities must initiate the review before that expiration date. Note also that Article 21.3, unlike Article 11.9, does not impose a *de minimis* standard for the initiation of a sunset review. The Appellate Body held in *US – Carbon Steel (2002)* that the *de minimis* requirement of Article 11.9 is also *not implied* in Article 21.3. See Appellate Body Report, *US – Carbon Steel (2002)*, para. 92. See also above, p. 831. With regard to sunset reviews initiated by investigating authorities on their own initiative, the Appellate Body held in *US – Carbon Steel (2002)* that there are no evidentiary standards for self-initiation of sunset reviews. See Appellate Body Report, *US – Carbon Steel (2002)*, para. 112.
464 See Appellate Body Report, *US – Carbon Steel (2002)*, para. 108.
465 See Article 21.4 of the *SCM Agreement*.
466 See *ibid*. During a sunset review, the countervailing duties may remain in force. See Article 21.3 of the *SCM Agreement*.

the maximum duration of a countervailing duty? What is the objective and rationale of the review procedure of Article 21.2 of the *SCM Agreement*? What is a 'sunset review' within the meaning of Article 21.3 of the *SCM Agreement*?

6.4 Countervailing Duties or Countermeasures

Note that the provisions relating to prohibited and actionable subsidies, discussed above, may be invoked, and relied upon, *in parallel with* the provisions relating to countervailing duties. However, with regard to the effects of a particular subsidy, only *one* form of remedy (either a countervailing duty *or* a countermeasure) may be applied.[467]

Questions and Assignments 12.16
Can countervailing duties and countermeasures be applied simultaneously with regard to the same instance of subsidisation?

7 INSTITUTIONAL AND PROCEDURAL PROVISIONS

Like most other WTO agreements, the *SCM Agreement* contains a few institutional and procedural provisions. This section discusses, in particular, Article 24, which establishes the WTO Subsidies Committee, and Article 25, which provides for transparency and notification requirements. This section also refers to Articles 4 and 7, which deal with dispute settlement regarding prohibited and actionable subsidies, as discussed above.

7.1 Transparency and Notification Requirements

Transparency is essential for the effective operation of the *SCM Agreement*. Article 25 requires that Members notify all specific subsidies by 30 June of each year. Currently, there is an understanding in the Subsidies Committee that emphasis should be placed on new and full subsidy notifications being submitted every two years, while updating notifications in the interim years is de-emphasised. As of October 2012, thirty-eight Members[468] had submitted their 2011 new and full notifications indicating that they provided specific subsidies within the meaning of the *SCM Agreement*. Fifteen Members had notified that they provided no notifiable specific subsidies. Sixty-three Members did not submit any notification.[469]

---

467 See footnote 35 to the *SCM Agreement*.
468 For this purpose, the European Communities and the Member States of the European Union were counted as a single Member.
469 The 2011 notifications may be found in document series G/SCM/N/220. See also *Report (2012) of the Committee on Subsidies and Countervailing Measures*, G/L/1005, dated 25 October 2012, p. 6.

7.2   Subsidies Committee

The Committee on Subsidies and Countervailing Measures, commonly referred to as the Subsidies Committee, is composed of representatives from each WTO Member. Pursuant to Article 24.1 of the *SCM Agreement*, the Committee shall meet not less than twice a year. It carries out the responsibilities assigned to it under the *SCM Agreement*. It shall afford Members the opportunity to consult on any matter relating to the operation of the agreement or the furtherance of its objectives. Article 25.9 of the *SCM Agreement* entitles a Member that considers that requested information has not been provided at all or not with sufficient detail, to bring the matter before the Committee. The same may occur under Article 25.10 if a measure having the effects of a subsidy has not been properly notified by a Member. Article 25.11 provides that Members shall report without delay to the Subsidies Committee all preliminary or final actions taken with respect to countervailing duties as well as submit semi-annual reports on any countervailing duty actions taken within the preceding six months. Pursuant to Article 26 of the *SCM Agreement*, such notifications and reports shall be kept under surveillance at meetings of the Subsidies Committee. Finally, Article 25.12 requires each Member to notify the Committee which of its authorities are competent to initiate and conduct countervailing investigations and its domestic procedures governing the initiation and conduct of such investigations.

According to Articles 24.2 and 24.3 of the *SCM Agreement*, the Subsidies Committee may set up subsidiary bodies, including the Permanent Group of Experts (PGE), which is composed of five independent persons highly qualified in the fields of subsidies and trade relations. The PGE may be requested to assist panels, in accordance with Article 24.3, or may be consulted by any Member and may give confidential advisory opinions on the existence and nature of any subsidy pursuant to Article 24.4. The Subsidies Committee or its advisory bodies may, as foreseen in Article 24.5, consult with and seek information from any source.[470]

7.3   Dispute Settlement

The provisions of the DSU apply also to consultations and the settlement of disputes relating to subsidies and countervailing measures. As explained above, accelerated procedures and specific remedies apply to prohibited and actionable subsidies in accordance with Articles 4 and 7 of the *SCM Agreement*, respectively.[471] For example, a number of the time periods provided for in the DSU for particular procedural steps or compliance are halved for prohibited subsidies

---

470 On the Permanent Group of Experts (PGE), see also above, pp. 129–30, 776–7.
471 See above, pp. 776–7 and 811–13.

and shortened for actionable subsidies that have been found to cause adverse effects such as injury or serious prejudice.

8 SPECIAL AND DIFFERENTIAL TREATMENT FOR DEVELOPING-COUNTRY MEMBERS

Subsidies can play an important role in the economic development pro-grammes of developing-country Members. Article 27 of the *SCM Agreement* recognises this and provides for some rules and disciplines for developing-country Members that are less strict than the general rules and disciplines. Pursuant to Article 27, the prohibition on export subsidies under Article 3 of the *SCM Agreement* does not apply to least-developed countries and to coun-tries with a per capita annual income of less than US$1,000.[472] The remedies available against these export subsidies are those available against actionable subsidies as set out in Article 7 of the *SCM Agreement*.[473] Furthermore, certain subsidies which are normally actionable are not actionable when granted by developing-country Members in the context of privatisation programmes. This is the case, for example, for direct forgiveness of debts and subsidies to cover social costs.[474]

With respect to countervailing duties, Article 27.2 of the *SCM Agreement* provides that any countervailing investigation of a product originating in a developing-country Member must be terminated as soon as the investigating authorities determine that: (1) the overall level of subsidies granted to the prod-uct in question does not exceed 2 per cent *ad valorem*; or (2) the volume of the subsidised imports represents less than 4 per cent of the total imports of the like product of the importing Member. Note, however, that the latter rule does not apply when the imports from developing-country Members whose individual shares of total imports represent less than 4 per cent, collectively account for

---

472 See Article 27.2 of the *SCM Agreement*. Note that, until 2003, the prohibition of export subsidies also did not apply to other developing-country Members even though these Members had to phase out export subsidies progressively. Their export subsidies could not be increased and had to be phased out even before 2003 if their use was inconsistent with their development needs. See Article 27.4 of the *SCM Agreement* and the panel and Appellate Body reports in *Brazil – Aircraft (1999)*. The Subsidies Committee was authorised to extend the period of non-application of the prohibition of export subsidies in Article 3 under certain conditions and/or in certain countries beyond 2003. Accordingly, in 2002, the Subsidies Committee granted extensions of the transition period for exemption from the prohibition of export subsidies with respect to a number of programmes of twenty-one developing-country Members. These extensions were time-bound and programme-specific. They were granted on the basis of Article 27.4, in most cases in conjunction with pro-cedures (G/SCM/39) adopted by Ministers at the Doha Ministerial Conference and/or paragraph 10.6 of the *Doha Decision on Implementation Issues* (WT/MIN(01)/17). The Subsidies Committee authorised some further extensions in 2003. Note that the prohibition of import substitution subsidies applies to least-developed-country Members since 2003 and to other developing-country Members since 2000. See Article 27.3 of the *SCM Agreement*.
473 See above, pp. 811–13.
474 See Article 27.13 of the *SCM Agreement*. Note also the limitation in Article 27.9 of the *SCM Agreement* on remedies for actionable subsidies granted by developing countries.

more than 9 per cent of the total imports of the like product of the importing Member.[475]

Questions and Assignments 12.17

To what extent does the *SCM Agreement* provide special and differential treatment for developing-country Members?

9   AGRICULTURAL SUBSIDIES UNDER THE *AGREEMENT ON AGRICULTURE*

Agricultural subsidies have traditionally been, and continue to be, a very contentious issue in international trade. Agricultural subsidies were a central issue during the Uruguay Round and are currently one of the major stumbling blocks in the Doha Development Round.[476] Agricultural export subsidies and domestic agricultural support measures are indispensable instruments of agricultural policies of a number of developed-country Members. At the same time, the trade interests and the economic development of many other Members are severely affected by these agricultural subsidies. Developing countries in particular are seriously harmed by the effects of agricultural subsidies of developed countries. *The Economist* noted in 2004 with regard to the EC's sugar subsidies:

> Subsidising sugar producers is not just economically stupid, it is morally indefensible, too. For Europe's subsidies are not merely a quaint way to keep a few farmers in business. They cause so much sugar to be produced that the stuff is exported to poor countries, hurting farmers who might otherwise earn a living by growing it themselves – and perhaps even exporting it to Europe ... Brazil loses around $500 m a year, and Thailand about $151 m, even though these two countries are the most efficient sugar producers in the world. Even less efficient, and poorer, African countries lose out. Mozambique will lose $38 m in 2004 – as much as it spends on agriculture and rural development. The costs to Ethiopia equal the sums it spends on HIV/AIDS programmes.[477]

The subsidies paid by the US government to cotton farmers were successfully challenged by Brazil in several WTO dispute settlement proceedings. When the United States was found to have failed to comply fully with the DSB's rulings, Brazil obtained authorisation from the DSB to take retaliatory measures against imports of US goods and US intellectual property rights up to amount determined by an arbitrator.[478] In order to avoid this retaliation, the United States negotiated a compensatory settlement with Brazil. A commentator polemicised:

> What could be more outrageous than the hefty subsidies the US government lavishes on rich American cotton farmers? How about the hefty subsidies the US government is about to

---

475 See Article 27.10 of the *SCM Agreement*.
476 On the negotiations on agricultural trade in the context of the Doha Round, see above, p. 81, footnote 26 and 89.
477 'Oh, Sweet Reason', *The Economist*, 15 April 2004.
478 On retaliation, see above, pp. 200–3.

start lavishing on rich Brazilian cotton farmers? If that sounds implausible or insane, well, welcome to US agricultural policy, where the implausible and the insane are the routine. Our perplexing $147.3 million-a-year handout to Brazilian agribusiness, part of a last-minute deal to head off an arcane trade dispute, barely even qualified as news ... If you're perplexed, here's the short explanation: We're shoveling our taxpayer dollars to Brazilian farmers to make sure we can keep shoveling our taxpayer dollars to American farmers – which is, after all, the overriding purpose of US agricultural policy. Basically, we're paying off foreigners to let us maintain our ludicrous *status quo*.

By encouraging Americans to plant cotton even when prices are low, [US cotton subsidies] promote overproduction and further depress prices. An Oxfam study found that removing them entirely would boost world prices about 10%, which would be especially helpful to the 20,000 subsistence cotton growers in Africa.[479]

Nevertheless, *The Economist* reported in 2012:

Government support for agriculture in the mostly rich countries of the OECD amounted to $252 billion in 2011, or 19% of total farm receipts. Although there is a move away from support linked directly to production, it is still about half of the total. The general trend is downwards: compared with the second half of the 1990s subsidies fell in all countries. But levels of support vary widely. In Norway, Switzerland and Japan, more than half of gross farm receipts in 2009–11 came from support policies; for producers in Australia, Chile and New Zealand, it was less than 5%.[480]

The particular sensitivities of agricultural subsidies explain why the disciplines of the *SCM Agreement* do not apply *in full* to agricultural subsidies. The *Agreement on Agriculture* provides for special rules on agricultural subsidies and, in case of conflict, these special rules prevail over the rules of the *SCM Agreement*. Article 21.1 of the *Agreement on Agriculture* states in this respect:

The provisions of GATT 1994 and of other Multilateral Trade Agreements in Annex 1A to the WTO Agreement shall apply subject to the provisions of this Agreement.

In *US – Upland Cotton (2005)*, the Appellate Body has interpreted Article 21.1 to mean that the provisions of the GATT 1994 and of other Multilateral Trade Agreements in Annex 1A apply, 'except to the extent that the *Agreement on Agriculture* contains specific provisions dealing specifically with the same matter'.[481]

---

479 M. Grunwald, 'Why the US Is Also Giving Brazilians Farm Subsidies', *Time*, 9 April 2010. See
    www.time.com/time/nation/article/0,8599,1978963,00.html.
480 See 'Economic and Financial Indicators: Agricultural Subsidies', *The Economist*, 22 September 2012. See:
    www.economist.com/node/21563323.
481 See Appellate Body Report, *US – Upland Cotton (2005)*, para. 532, referring to Appellate Body Report,
    EC – Bananas III (1997), para. 155; and Appellate Body Report, *Chile – Price Band System (2002)*,
    para. 186. The Appellate Body agreed with the panel in *US – Upland Cotton (2005)* that Article 21.1
    could apply in the three situations, namely: (1) where, for example, the domestic support provisions of
    the *Agreement on Agriculture* would prevail in the event that an explicit carve-out or exemption from the
    prohibition of import substitution subsidies in Article 3.1(b) of the *SCM Agreement* existed in the *text* of
    the *Agreement on Agriculture*; (2) where it would be impossible for a Member to comply with its domestic
    support obligations under the *Agreement on Agriculture* and the Article 3.1(b) prohibition simultane-
    ously; or (3) where the text of the *Agreement on Agriculture* explicitly authorises a measure that, in the
    absence of such authorisation, would be prohibited by Article 3.1(b) of the *SCM Agreement*. According
    to the Appellate Body, there could, however, be situations other than those identified by the panel where
    Article 21.1 of the *Agreement on Agriculture* may be applicable. See Appellate Body Report, *US – Upland
    Cotton (2005)*, para. 532.

This section briefly discusses the special rules of the *Agreement on Agriculture* regarding: (1) agricultural export subsidies; and (2) domestic agricultural support measures.[482]

Questions and Assignments 12.18

Do the rules of the *SCM Agreement* apply to agricultural subsidies? In your opinion, should WTO law provide special rules on agricultural subsidies?

9.1   Agricultural Export Subsidies

The prohibition on export subsidies, provided for in Article 3 of the *SCM Agreement* and discussed in detail above, applies to agricultural export subsidies *except* as provided otherwise in the *Agreement on Agriculture*. The relationship between the *SCM Agreement* and the *Agreement on Agriculture* is defined, in part, by Article 3.1 of the *SCM Agreement*, which states that the export subsidies and import substitution subsidies are prohibited '[e]*xcept* as provided in the Agreement on Agriculture'.[483] This clause indicates that the WTO-consistency of an export subsidy for agricultural products has to be examined, in the first place, under the *Agreement on Agriculture*.[484]

In *US – FSC (2000)*, the Appellate Body found that the *Agreement on Agriculture* and the *SCM Agreement* use exactly the same words to define 'export subsidies' and that, although there are differences between the disciplines established under the two agreements, those differences do not, according to the Appellate Body, 'affect the common substantive requirements relating to export contingency'.[485] The Appellate Body thus concluded that it is appropriate to apply the interpretation of export contingency adopted under the *SCM Agreement* to the interpretation of export contingency under the *Agreement on Agriculture*.[486]

While export subsidies on non-agricultural products are prohibited, with respect to export subsidies on agricultural products a distinction must be made between export subsidies on: (1) agricultural products that are specified in Section II of Part IV of a Member's GATT Schedule of Concessions; and (2) agricultural products that are not specified in that section.[487] With respect to agricultural products *not* specified in the relevant section of their Schedule, Members shall not

---

482 The third pillar of the *Agreement on Agriculture* relating to WTO Members' market access commitments is discussed in Chapter 6 (on tariff barriers) and Chapter 7 (on non-tariff barriers) of this book. See above, pp. 438–9 and 517–27.

483 Emphasis added.

484 See Appellate Body Report, *Canada – Dairy (Article 21.5 – New Zealand and US) (2001)*, paras. 123–4.

485 Appellate Body Report, *US – FSC (2000)*, para. 141. See also Panel Report, *US – Upland Cotton (2005)*, para. 7.754.

486 See Appellate Body Report, *US – FSC (2000)*, para. 141. See also Appellate Body Report, *US – Upland Cotton (2005)*, para. 571.

487 Note that the term 'export subsidy commitments' covers commitments and obligations relating to *both* scheduled and unscheduled agricultural products.

provide any export subsidies.[488] With respect to the agricultural products specified in the relevant section of their Schedule, Members have agreed – pursuant
to Article 9 of the *Agreement on Agriculture* – to subject all export subsidies,
defined in paragraphs (a) to (f) of Article 9.1, to reduction commitments.[489]
Article 9.1 sets forth a list of practices that, by definition, involve export subsidies: (1) direct export subsidies (including payments-in-kind) by governments
or their agencies contingent on export performance (Article 9.1(a));[490] (2) sales
of non-commercial stocks of agricultural products for export at prices lower
than comparable prices for such goods on the domestic market (Article 9.1(b));
(3) payments on agricultural exports financed by virtue of governmental action,
whether or not a charge on the public account is involved (Article 9.1(c));[491] (4)
cost reduction measures such as subsidies to reduce the cost of marketing goods
for export (Article 9.1(d));[492] (5) internal transport subsidies applying to exports
only, provided or mandated by the government, on terms more favourable than

---

488 See Article 3.3 of the *Agreement on Agriculture*. Under the second clause of Article 3.3, Members have
     committed *not* to provide *any* export subsidies, listed in Article 9.1, with respect to *unscheduled* agricultural
     products. This clause clearly also involves 'export subsidy commitments' within the meaning of Article 10.1.
     See Appellate Body Report, *US – FSC (2000)*, para. 146.

489 See Article 3.3 of the *Agreement on Agriculture*. Under the first clause of Article 3.3, Members have made a
     commitment that 'they will not "provide export subsidies listed in paragraph 1 of Article 9 in respect of the
     agricultural products or groups of products specified in Section II of Part IV of its Schedule in excess of the
     budgetary outlay and quantity commitments levels specified therein"'. See Appellate Body Report, *US – FSC
     (2000)*, para. 145.

490 See Appellate Body Report, *US – Upland Cotton (2005)*, para. 582. On the term 'payments' in the term
     'payments-in-kind', and the distinction between the economic transfer effected and the analysis of the
     benefit thereby conferred, see Appellate Body Report, *Canada – Dairy (1999)*, para. 87. On the meaning of
     the terms 'government' and 'government agency', as well as the relevance of 'functions performed by the
     government', the 'power and authority' to perform those functions 'vested in an agency' and the 'degree of
     discretion in the exercise of such functions', see Appellate Body Report, *Canada – Dairy (1999)*, para. 97.
     The Appellate Body discussed the appropriate benchmark for 'payments-in-kind' in Appellate Body Report,
     Canada – Dairy (Article 21.5 – New Zealand and US) (2001), paras. 73–6. The benchmarks discussed by the
     Appellate Body included the world market price versus domestic prices or also total cost of production. See
     Appellate Body Report, *Canada – Dairy (Article 21.5 – New Zealand and US) (2001)*, paras. 83–8.

491 Note that Article 9.1(c) describes an unusual form of export subsidy in that 'payments' can be made and
     funded by private parties, and not just by the government. The Appellate Body further noted that '"pay-
     ments" need not be funded from government resources, provided they are "financed by virtue of govern-
     mental action". Article 9.1(c), therefore, contemplates that "payments" may be made and funded by private
     parties, without the type of governmental involvement ordinarily associated with a subsidy.' See Appellate
     Body Report, *Canada – Dairy (Article 21.5 – New Zealand and US II) (2003)*, para. 87. The Appellate Body
     in *EC – Export Subsidies on Sugar (2005)* stated that: '[A] "payment", within the meaning of Article 9.1(c)
     certainly occurs when one entity transfers economic resources to another entity ... This, however, does not
     imply that the term "payment" necessarily requires, in each and every case, the presence of two distinct
     entities.' See Appellate Body Report, *EC – Export Subsidies on Sugar (2005)*, paras. 263–4. Regarding the
     meaning of the term 'financed', payments do not have to be funded from government resources because
     Article 9.1(c) contemplates that payments can be financed by virtue of governmental action *whether or not*
     a charge on the public account is involved. See Appellate Body Report, *Canada – Dairy (Article 21.5 – New
     Zealand and US) (2001)*, para. 114. The words 'by virtue of' indicate the need to demonstrate a 'link' or
     'nexus' between the 'governmental action' at issue and the 'financing of the payments' as a result of that
     action. Where a government does not fund the payment itself, it must play a sufficiently important part
     in the process through which a private party funds payments, such that the requisite nexus exists between
     governmental action and financing. See Appellate Body Report, *Canada – Dairy (Article 21.5 – New Zea-
     land and US II) (2003)*, paras. 131–3; and Appellate Body Report, *EC – Export Subsidies on Sugar (2005)*,
     para. 237. The Appellate Body ruled in *Canada – Dairy (Article 21.5 – New Zealand and US) (2001)* 'that
     "payments" will be an export subsidy "only when they are financed by virtue of governmental action"'. See
     Appellate Body Report, *Canada – Dairy (Article 21.5 – New Zealand and US) (2001)*, paras. 97 and 112.

492 This can include upgrading and handling costs and the costs of international freight. See Appellate Body
     Report, *US – FSC (2000)*, paras. 130–1.

for domestic shipments (Article 9.1(e)); and (6) subsidies on agricultural products contingent on their incorporation into exported products (Article 9.1(f)). As the Appellate Body found in *EC – Export Subsidies on Sugar (2005)*, a measure falling within the list in Article 9.1:

[i]s deemed to be an export subsidy within the meaning of Article 1(e) of the *Agreement on Agriculture* ... Article 9.1(c) requires no independent enquiry into the existence of a 'benefit'.[493]

Also note that Article 1(e) defines 'export subsidies' as:

[s]ubsidies contingent upon export performance, including the export subsidies listed in Article 9 of this Agreement.

The use of the word 'including' suggests that the term 'export subsidies' should be interpreted broadly and that the list of export subsidies in Article 9 is not exhaustive.[494]

Export subsidy commitments in a Member's Schedule must be expressed in terms of both budgetary outlay *and* quantity commitment levels.[495] The drafters of the *Agreement on Agriculture* recognised the need to limit both budgetary outlays and quantities in order to restrain subsidised exports. The Appellate Body explained in *EC – Export Subsidies on Sugar (2005)* that:

[a] commitment on budgetary outlay alone provides little predictability on export quantities, while a commitment on quantity alone could lead to subsidized exports taking place that would otherwise have not taken place but for the budgetary support.[496]

This is especially so given that the *Agreement on Agriculture* has initiated a reform process in an environment of high levels of export subsidies taking the form of budgetary outlays and quantities. As set out in the relevant section of their Schedule, developed-country Members agreed to reduce the export subsidies on these products by an average of 36 per cent by value (budgetary outlay) and 21 per cent by volume (subsidised quantities). Developing-country Members agreed to reduce the export subsidies by an average of 24 per cent by value and 14 per cent by volume. Members may *not* provide listed export subsidies *in excess of* the budgetary outlay and quantitative commitment levels specified in their Schedules.[497] As the Appellate Body ruled in *EC – Export Subsidies on Sugar (2005)*, Article 3.1 thus requires with regard to export subsidies:

[a] Member to limit its subsidization to the budgetary outlay and quantity reduction commitments specified in its Schedule in accordance with the provisions of the *Agreement on Agriculture*.[498]

---

493 Appellate Body Report, *EC – Export Subsidies on Sugar (2005)*, para. 269.
494 See Appellate Body Report, *US – Upland Cotton (2005)*, para. 615.
495 See Article 3.3 (as well as Article 9.2).
496 Appellate Body Report, *EC – Export Subsidies on Sugar (2005)*, para. 197.
497 See *ibid.* See also Article 8 of the *Agreement on Agriculture*, which states that a Member must undertake not to provide export subsidies otherwise than in conformity with the Agreement and with commitments as specified in that Member's Schedule. See also Appellate Body Report, *EC – Export Subsidies on Sugar (2005)*, paras. 209 and 216.
498 *Ibid.*, para. 209.

In other words, as the Appellate Body already noted in *US – FSC (2000)*, as regards *scheduled* products, when the specific reduction commitment levels have been reached, the *limited authorisation* to provide export subsidies as listed in Article 9.1 is transformed, effectively, into a *prohibition* against the provision of further subsidies.[499] A finding of inconsistency with Article 3.3 of the *Agreement on Agriculture* cannot be made unless the Member concerned has provided export subsidies *listed in Article 9.1*.[500]

Pursuant to Article 10.1 of the *Agreement on Agriculture*, Members shall *not* apply export subsidies that are not listed in Article 9.1 of the *Agreement on Agriculture* in a manner that results in or threatens to lead to circumvention of export subsidy commitments.[501] This effectively prohibits any other export subsidies.

With regard to international food aid, the Appellate Body stated in *US – Upland Cotton (2005)* that such aid is covered by the second clause of Article 10.1 to the extent that it is a 'non-commercial transaction', which should 'not be used to circumvent' a Member's export subsidy commitments. Article 10.4 provides specific disciplines that may be relied on to determine whether international food aid is being 'used to circumvent' a WTO Member's export subsidy commitments. Therefore, WTO Members are free to grant as much food aid as they wish, provided that they do so consistently with Articles 10.1 and 10.4 of the *Agreement on Agriculture*.[502]

With regard to export credit guarantees, export credits and insurance programmes, the Appellate Body noted in *US – Upland Cotton (2005)* that:

> [a]lthough Article 10.2 commits WTO Members to work toward the development of internationally agreed disciplines on export credit guarantees, export credits and insurance programs, it is in Article 10.1 that [it found] the disciplines that currently apply to export subsidies not listed in Article 9.1.[503]

Even though an export credit guarantee may not necessarily include a subsidy component, there is nothing inherent about export credit guarantees that precludes such measures from falling within the definition of a subsidy. The Appellate Body did not believe that Article 10.2 of the *Agreement on Agriculture*

---

499 See Appellate Body Report, *US – FSC (2000)*, para. 152.
500 See *ibid.*, para. 132.
501 Thus it is not necessary to show actual circumvention: a threat or likelihood of circumvention is also prohibited. See Appellate Body Report, *US – Upland Cotton (2005)*, paras. 616 and 704. See also Appellate Body Report, *US – FSC (2000)*, para. 148. According to the Appellate Body, '[it] is clear from the opening clause of Article 10.1 that this provision is residual in character to Article 9.1 ... If a measure is an export subsidy listed in Article 9.1, it cannot simultaneously be an export subsidy under Article 10.1.' See Appellate Body Report, *Canada – Dairy (Article 21.5 – New Zealand and US) (2001)*, para. 121.
502 See Appellate Body Report, *US – Upland Cotton (2005)*, para. 619.
503 *Ibid.*, para. 615. The Appellate Body explained that, under 'Article 10.2, WTO Members have taken on two distinct commitments in respect of these three types of measures: (i) to work toward the development of internationally agreed disciplines to govern their provision; and (ii) after agreement on such disciplines, to provide them only in conformity therewith ... This means that "after" international disciplines have been agreed upon, Members shall provide export credit guarantees, export credits and insurance programs only in conformity with those agreed disciplines.' See *ibid.*, para. 607.

exempts export credit guarantees, export credits and insurance programmes from the export subsidy disciplines in the *Agreement on Agriculture*.[504] However, the Appellate Body cautioned that this does not mean that export credit guarantees, export credits and insurance programmes will necessarily constitute export subsidies for purposes of the *Agreement on Agriculture*. Export credit guarantees are subject to the export subsidy disciplines only to the extent that such measures include an export subsidy component.[505]

Article 10.3 of the *Agreement on Agriculture* pursues the aim of preventing circumvention of export subsidy commitments by providing special rules on the reversal of burden of proof where a Member exports an agricultural product in quantities that exceed its reduction commitment level; in such a situation, a WTO Member is treated as if it has granted WTO-*inconsistent* export subsidies for the excess quantities, unless the Member presents adequate evidence to 'establish' the contrary.[506] This special rule for proof of export subsidies applies in certain disputes under Articles 3, 8, 9 and 10 of the *Agreement on Agriculture*.[507] By contrast, as discussed in Chapter 3 of this book, under the usual allocation of the burden of proof, a responding Member's measure will be considered to be WTO-consistent, until the complaining Member has presented sufficient evidence to prove the contrary.[508]

In *Canada – Dairy (Article 21.5 – New Zealand and US) (2001)*, the Appellate Body noted that it is possible that the economic effects of WTO-consistent domestic support in favour of producers may 'spill over' to provide certain benefits to export production.[509] In this respect, it considered:

[i]t would erode the distinction between the domestic support and export subsidies disciplines of the *Agreement on Agriculture* if WTO-consistent domestic support measures were automatically characterized as export subsidies because they produced spill-over economic benefits for export production.[510]

504 *Ibid.* Note that one Appellate Body member dissented from that interpretation, explaining in a separate opinion that neither Article 9 nor 10 covered and prohibited export credit guarantees. *Ibid.*, paras. 631–41. For the majority, such an interpretation would have led to a situation where 'WTO Members are free to "circumvent" their export subsidy commitments through the use of export credit guarantees, export credits and insurance programs until internationally agreed disciplines are developed, whenever that may be ... Indeed, such an interpretation would *undermine* the objective of preventing circumvention of export subsidy commitments, which is central to the *Agreement on Agriculture*.' See *ibid.*, para. 617.
505 See *ibid.*, para. 626.   506 See *ibid.*, para. 616.
507 The Appellate Body held in *US – Upland Cotton (2005)* that this reversal of the burden of proof does not apply to *unscheduled* products (for which no export subsidies at all may be maintained) because this would in effect mean that 'any export of unscheduled products is presumed to be subsidized'. See Appellate Body Report, *US – Upland Cotton (2005)*, para. 652 (original emphasis).
508 See above, pp. 257–61. See also Appellate Body Report, *Canada – Dairy (Article 21.5 – New Zealand and US II) (2003)*, paras. 66 and 68. The Appellate Body clarified in *Canada – Dairy (Article 21.5 – New Zealand and US II) (2003)* that there are *two* separate parts to a claim alleging illegal agricultural export subsidies in respect of products for which reduction commitments have been scheduled. 'First, the responding Member must have exported an agricultural product in quantities exceeding its quantity commitment level ... The second part of the claim is ... that the responding Member must have granted export subsidies with respect to quantities exceeding the quantity commitment level. There is, in other words, a *quantitative* aspect and an *export subsidization* aspect to the claim.' See Appellate Body Report, *Canada – Dairy (Article 21.5 – New Zealand and US II) (2003)*, para. 70 (original emphasis).
509 See Appellate Body Report, *Canada – Dairy (Article 21.5 – New Zealand and US) (2001)*, paras. 89–90.
510 *Ibid.*

However, the Appellate Body also considered that this distinction 'would also be eroded if a WTO Member were entitled to use domestic support, without limit, to provide support for exports of agricultural products'.[511] Consequently, if domestic support could be used, without limit, to provide support for exports, it would undermine the benefits intended to accrue through a WTO Member's export subsidy commitments.[512]

9.2 Domestic Agricultural Support Measures

With respect to domestic agricultural support measures, Members have agreed – pursuant to Article 6 of the *Agreement on Agriculture* – to reduce the level of support. Developed-country Members agreed to reduce between 1995 and 2000 their 'aggregate measurement of support', or 'AMS', by 20 per cent.[513] Developing-country Members agreed to reduce their AMS by 13.3 per cent in the period 1995–2004.[514] The commitments of Members on the reduction of domestic agricultural support measures are set out in Part IV of their GATT Schedule of Concessions. Pursuant to Article 6.3 of the *Agreement on Agriculture*, Members may *not* provide domestic support *in excess of* the commitment levels specified in their Schedules. As the Appellate Body noted in *US – Upland Cotton (2005)*, Article 6.3:

[e]stablishes only a *quantitative* limitation on the amount of domestic support that a WTO Member can provide in a given year. The quantitative limitation in Article 6.3 applies generally to all domestic support measures that are included in a WTO Member's AMS.[515]

Recall that, under Article 3.1(b) of the *SCM Agreement*, 'subsidies contingent … upon the use of domestic over imported goods' are prohibited.[516] This raises the question as to the WTO-consistency of *agricultural* import substitution subsidies. In *US – Upland Cotton (2005)*, the Appellate Body answered this question as follows:

Article 6.3 does not authorize subsidies that are contingent on the use of domestic over imported goods. It only provides that a WTO Member shall be considered to be in compliance with its domestic support *reduction commitments* if its Current Total AMS does not exceed that Member's annual or final bound commitment level specified in its Schedule. It does not say that compliance with Article 6.3 of the *Agreement on Agriculture* insulates the subsidy from the prohibition in Article 3.1(b).[517]

---

511 *Ibid.*, para. 91.   512 See *ibid.*
513 On the calculation of the AMS, see Annex 3 to the *Agreement on Agriculture*.
514 See Article 15.2 of the *Agreement on Agriculture*. Least-developed-country Members are not required to undertake reduction commitments. See *ibid.*
515 Appellate Body Report, *US – Upland Cotton (2005)*, para. 544.
516 See above, pp. 775–6.
517 Appellate Body Report, *US – Upland Cotton (2005)*, para. 545. In the same case, the Appellate Body recalled 'that the introductory language of Article 3.1 of the *SCM Agreement* clarifies that this provision applies "[e]xcept as provided in the Agreement on Agriculture"'. Nevertheless, the Appellate Body concluded that import substitution subsidies on agricultural products are not exempt from the prohibition in Article 3.1(b) of the *SCM Agreement* by virtue of Annex 3, paragraph 7, as 'measures directed at agricultural processors that shall be included in the aggregate measurement of support calculation'. Nor does Article 6.3 (which provides that a WTO Member shall be considered in compliance with its domestic support commitment level specified in its Schedule) 'insulate a subsidy from the prohibition in Article 3.1(b) of the *SCM Agreement*'. Thus, in providing domestic support that is consistent with the *Agreement on Agriculture*, WTO Members

Domestic agricultural support measures that do not have the effect of providing price support to producers are, under certain conditions, exempt from the reduction commitments. These exempted domestic support measures are commonly referred to as 'green box' and 'blue box' measures.[518] 'Green box' measures include support for agricultural research and infrastructure, training and advisory services, domestic food aid and environmental programmes.[519] 'Blue box' subsidies include certain developing-country subsidies designed to encourage agricultural production, certain *de minimis* subsidies, and certain direct payments aimed at limiting agricultural production.[520] The conditions which these subsidies must fulfil to be exempted from the reduction commitments are set out in the *Agreement on Agriculture* in Annex 2 (for 'green box' subsidies) and in Articles 6.2, 6.4 and 6.5 (for 'blue box' subsidies). With regard to 'green box' subsidies, Annex 2, entitled 'Domestic Support: The Basis for Exemption from the Reduction Commitments', lays down in paragraph 1 a 'fundamental requirement' for 'green box' measures. 'Green box' subsidies must have 'no, or at most minimal, trade-distorting effects or effects on production'. Accordingly, 'green box' measures must conform to the basic criteria stated in that provision, *plus* the 'policy-specific criteria and conditions' set out in the remaining paragraphs of Annex 2, including those in paragraph 6. The specific paragraphs of Annex 2 deal with: (1) payments for general services; (2) public stockholding for food security purposes; (3) domestic food aid; (4) direct payments to producers; (5) decoupled income support; (6) governmental financial participation in income insurance and income safety-net programmes; (7) payments for relief in natural disasters; (8) structural adjustment assistance provided through producer or resource retirement programmes, or through investment aids; (9) payments under environmental programmes; and (10) payments under regional assistance programmes.

In *US – Upland Cotton (2005)*, the Appellate Body interpreted 'decoupled income support' within the meaning of paragraph 6 of Annex 2.[521] The paragraph applies to one type of 'direct payments' to producers that may benefit from exemption from reduction commitments.[522] The Appellate Body found that

---

'must be mindful of the prohibition in Article 3.1(b) of the *SCM Agreement* on the provision of subsidies that are contingent on the use of domestic over imported goods'. Appellate Body Report, *US – Upland Cotton (2005)*, paras. 541, 545–6 and 550.

518 Note that domestic support measures that are subject to reduction commitments are commonly referred to as 'amber box' subsidies.

519 See Annex 2 to the *Agreement on Agriculture*. Article 7 provides that Members must ensure that any 'green box' subsidies are maintained in conformity with the criteria set out in Annex 2, which justify their exemption from reduction commitments.

520 See Article 6 of the *Agreement on Agriculture*.

521 See Appellate Body Report, *US – Upland Cotton (2005)*, paras. 321–5.

522 Paragraph 6(a) sets forth that eligibility for payments under a decoupled income support program must be determined by reference to certain 'clearly defined criteria' in a 'defined and fixed base period'. Paragraph 6(b) requires the severing of any link between the *amount of payments* under such a program and the *type or volume of production* undertaken by recipients of payments under that program in any year after the base period. Paragraphs 6(c) and 6(d) serve to require that payments are also decoupled from *prices* and *factors of production employed* after the base period. Paragraph 6(e) makes it clear that '[n]o production shall be required in order to receive ... payments' under a decoupled income support program. See Appellate Body Report, *US – Upland Cotton (2005)*, para. 321.

'[d]ecoupling of payments from production under paragraph 6(b) can only be ensured if the payments are not related to, or based upon, either a positive requirement to produce certain crops or a negative requirement not to produce certain crops or a combination of both positive and negative requirements on production of crops'. The Appellate Body concluded that the measures at issue (production flexibility contract payments and direct payments)[523] did not qualify for the 'green box' exemption from the domestic support disciplines under the *Agreement on Agriculture*.[524]

9.3   The 'Peace' Clause

Until the end of the nine-year implementation period,[525] agricultural export subsidies that conformed fully to the requirements of the *Agreement on Agriculture*, and domestic agricultural support that was within commitment levels and fulfilled certain other conditions, benefited from the 'due restraint' or 'peace' clause of Article 13 of the *Agreement on Agriculture*.[526] Pursuant to Article 13, the consistency of many agricultural subsidies with the *SCM Agreement* could not be challenged. Furthermore, 'green box' subsidies could not be offset by countervailing duties.[527] Since 2004, when the implementation period expired, however, the 'peace' clause no longer applies. The consistency of agricultural subsidies with the *SCM Agreement* can be challenged and countervailing duties be imposed on 'green box' subsidies. As mentioned above, in case of conflict between the rules of the *SCM Agreement* and those of the *Agreement on Agriculture*, the rules of the *Agreement on Agriculture* prevail.

Questions and Assignments 12.19

Are agricultural export subsidies prohibited under the *Agreement on Agriculture*? Are developing-country Members more or less 'affected' by the WTO's disciplines on agricultural export subsidies? Is international food aid prohibited under the *Agreement on Agriculture* or the *SCM Agreement*? Can Members grant agricultural export credit guarantees

523 Production flexibility contract payments and direct payments do 'not concern a measure *requiring* producers to grow certain crops in order to receive payments; it also does not concern a measure with complete planting *flexibility* that provides payments without regard whatsoever to the crops that are grown. Indeed, it does not concern a measure that requires the production of any crop at all; nor does it involve a measure that totally *prohibits* the growing of any crops as a condition for payments.' See Appellate Body Report, *US – Upland Cotton (2005)*, para. 322.

524 See *ibid.*, para. 342.

525 This period began in 1995. By virtue of Article 1(i) of the *Agreement on Agriculture*, the term 'year' refers to the calendar, financial or marketing year specified in the Schedule relating to that Member.

526 With respect to the requirements to be fulfilled for agricultural export subsidies, see Articles 9, 10 and 11 of the *Agreement on Agriculture*; for 'amber box' subsidies, see Article 7 (not in excess of the reduction commitments); for 'green box' subsidies, see Annex 2; and for 'blue box' subsidies, see Article 6.

527 In *US – Upland Cotton (2005)*, Brazil challenged US domestic subsidies on cotton during the implementation period in which Article 13 applied. The Appellate Body upheld the panel's finding that those measures were not entitled to the exemption provided by the peace clause from actions under Article XVI:1 of the GATT 1994 and Articles 5 and 6 of the *SCM Agreement*. This was due to the fact that the US subsidies did not meet the requirement in Article 13(b)(ii) that non-green box domestic support measures must not 'grant support to a specific commodity in excess of that decided during the 1992 marketing year', if such measures are to enjoy exemption. See Appellate Body Report, *US – Upland Cotton (2005)*, paras. 391–4.

or agricultural export credits? Do the normal rules on burden of proof apply in disputes regarding agricultural export subsidies? What are the obligations of Members with respect to domestic agricultural support measures? What are 'amber box', 'green box' and 'blue box' measures? What is or was the 'peace' clause and to what extent is this clause still relevant now?

10 SUMMARY

WTO law provides for detailed rules with respect to subsidies as well as counter-vailing measures, i.e. measures taken against injurious subsidisation. The *SCM Agreement* defines a subsidy as a financial contribution by a government or public body which confers a benefit. Both the *SCM Agreement* and the case law work out and clarify each element of this definition. Furthermore, the *SCM Agreement* provides that the WTO rules on subsidies and countervailing measures only apply to 'specific' subsidies. Article XVI of the GATT 1994 and Parts II, III and IV of the *SCM Agreement* deal with the WTO treatment of subsidies. The WTO treatment of subsidies is different from the treatment of dumping. Under WTO law, certain subsidies are prohibited, and many other subsidies may be challenged as WTO-inconsistent when they cause adverse effects to the interests of other Members. Article VI of the GATT 1994 and Part V of the *SCM Agreement* concern the manner in which WTO Members may respond to subsidised trade which causes injury to the domestic industry. Members may, in these situations, impose countervailing duties on the subsidised imports to offset the subsidisation.

The *SCM Agreement* distinguishes between prohibited subsidies and action-able subsidies. The prohibited subsidies are: (1) export subsidies; and (2) import substitution subsidies. Export subsidies are subsidies contingent upon export performance. Annex I of the *SCM Agreement* contains an 'Illustrative List of Export Subsidies'. Import substitution subsidies are subsidies contingent upon the use of domestic over imported goods. Both export subsidies and import sub-stitution subsidies are prohibited regardless of whether the subsidy is contingent *de jure* or *de facto* upon exportation or the use of domestic over imported goods. The rules applicable to consultations and adjudication concerning allegedly pro-hibited subsidies are primarily those of the DSU. However, the timeframes under Article 4 of the *SCM Agreement* are half as long as the timeframes provided for under the DSU. Moreover, if a panel finds a measure to be a prohibited subsidy, that subsidy must be withdrawn, i.e. removed, without delay. If a compliance panel finds that a recommendation for withdrawal has not been followed within the time period set by the panel in original proceedings, the DSB must, upon the request of the original complainant(s) and by reverse consensus, authorise 'appropriate countermeasures'.

Unlike export subsidies and import substitution subsidies, most subsidies are not prohibited but are 'actionable', i.e. they are subject to challenge in the event that they cause adverse effects to the interests of another Member. There are three main types of 'adverse effects' to the interests of other Members: (1) *injury* to the domestic industry of another Member; (2) *nullification or impairment* of benefits accruing directly or indirectly to other Members under the GATT 1994; and (3) *serious prejudice*, including a threat thereof, to the interests of another Member.

The concept of 'injury' to a domestic industry covers: material injury, i.e. genuine injury, to a domestic industry; a threat of material injury to a domestic industry; and material retardation of the establishment of a domestic industry. The definition of 'domestic industry' in the *SCM Agreement* is quite similar to the definition of this concept in the *Anti-Dumping Agreement*. There is also a high degree of similarity between the concepts of 'material injury' and the 'threat of material injury' in the *Anti-Dumping Agreement* and the *SCM Agreement*. Note that it must be demonstrated that the subsidised imports are causing injury to the domestic industry (the 'causal link' requirement) and that injury caused by other factors may not be attributed to the subsidised imports (the 'non-attribution' requirement).

The adverse effects of subsidies on the interests of other Members can also take the form of 'serious prejudice'. 'Serious prejudice' *may arise* where a subsidy has one or more of the effects described in the *SCM Agreement*, including the displacement or impedance of imports of another Member into the market of the subsidising Member or third country markets. Other forms of serious prejudice are significant price undercutting by the subsidised product as compared to the like product of another Member in the same market, significant price suppression, significant price depression or significant lost sales in the same market (provided that the relevant product and geographic markets have been determined properly). Finally, serious prejudice may also arise where subsidisation has the effect of a disproportionate increase in the world market share of the subsidising Member. A demonstration that these volume or price phenomena are the 'effect' of the challenged subsidies must include establishing the existence of a causal link between the subsidy and the serious prejudice phenomena as well as ensuring that effects caused by other factors are not attributed to the subsidised imports. Members and panels enjoy a margin of discretion in structuring the analysis of serious prejudice phenomena, in choosing appropriate methodologies, parameters and tools for analysing causation/non-attribution analysis. If a complaining Member can show that a subsidy has any of the effects listed in the *SCM Agreement*, serious prejudice may be found to exist. Note that the concept of 'serious prejudice' includes a 'threat of serious prejudice', i.e. a situation in which the serious prejudice is clearly foreseen and imminent.

As is the case with multilateral remedies for prohibited subsidies, the multilateral remedies for actionable subsidies are principally, but not entirely, the remedies for breach of WTO law provided for in the DSU. If a panel concludes that a subsidy causes adverse effects to the interests of another Member (be it injury, nullification or impairment, or serious prejudice), the subsidising Member must take appropriate steps to remove the adverse effect or withdraw the subsidy. The subsidising Member must do so within six months from the adoption of the report by the DSB. Instead of withdrawing the subsidy at issue or removing its adverse effects, the subsidising Member can also agree with the complaining Member on compensation. If a compliance panel concludes that, within six months from the adoption of the report, the subsidy has not been withdrawn, its adverse effects have not been removed or no agreement on compensation is reached, the DSB shall, at the request of the complaining Member and by reverse consensus, grant authorisation to that Member to take countermeasures commensurate with the degree and nature of the adverse effects of the subsidy.

Prohibited and actionable subsidies which cause injury to the domestic industry can, apart from being challenged multilaterally, also be offset by the application of a countervailing duty. WTO Members may impose countervailing duties when three conditions are fulfilled: (1) there are *subsidised imports*, i.e. imports of products from producers who benefited from specific subsidies; (2) there is *injury* to the domestic industry; and (3) there is a *causal link* between the subsidised imports and the injury to the domestic industry *and* injury caused by other factors is *not attributed* to the subsidised imports. The *SCM Agreement* provides for detailed procedural requirements regarding the initiation and conduct of a countervailing investigation by the competent authorities of the Member imposing the countervailing duties on the subsidised imports. Note that the procedural requirements for countervailing investigations set out in the *SCM Agreement* are largely the same as the procedural requirements for anti-dumping investigations set out in the *Anti-Dumping Agreement*. The main objectives of these requirements are also the same. The *SCM Agreement* provides for three types of countervailing measure: (1) provisional countervailing measures; (2) voluntary undertakings; and (3) definitive countervailing duties.

After making a preliminary determination that a subsidy is causing or threatening to cause injury to a domestic industry, an importing Member can impose *provisional countervailing measures* on the subsidised imports. Investigations may be suspended or terminated without the imposition of provisional measures or countervailing duties upon receipt of satisfactory *voluntary undertakings* under which: (1) the government of the exporting Member agrees to eliminate or limit the subsidy or take other measures concerning its effects; or (2) the exporter agrees to revise its prices so that the investigating authorities are satisfied that the injurious effect of the subsidy is eliminated.

Members may impose *definitive countervailing duties* only after they have made a final determination that a countervailable subsidy exists; and that the subsidy causes, or threatens to cause, injury to the domestic industry. The amount of a countervailing duty must never exceed the amount of the subsidy. Moreover, if the amount of the injury caused is less than the amount of the subsidy, the definitive countervailing duty should preferably be limited to the amount necessary to counteract the injury caused. Countervailing duties must be collected on a non-discriminatory basis. Note that any exporter whose exports are subject to a definitive countervailing duty but who was not investigated individually is entitled to an expedited review so that the investigating authorities promptly establish an individual countervailing duty rate for that exporter. Countervailing duties may not be applied retroactively, except in certain specific circumstances. A countervailing duty shall remain in force only as long as and to the extent necessary to counteract subsidisation which is causing injury. Upon their own initiative or upon a request from an interested party, the investigating authorities shall review the need for the continued imposition of the duty. All definitive countervailing duties must be terminated, at the latest, five years after their imposition or the latest review. However, where the investigating authorities determine – in the context of a sunset review – that the expiry of the countervailing duty would be likely to lead to a continuation or recurrence of subsidisation and injury, the duty will not be terminated. Note that countervailing duties and countermeasures cannot be applied simultaneously with regard to the same instance of subsidisation.

The *Agreement on Agriculture* provides for special rules on agricultural export subsidies and domestic agricultural support measures. In case of conflict, these special rules prevail over the rules of the *SCM Agreement*. Export subsidies on agricultural products not specified in Section II of Part IV of a Member's GATT Schedule of Concessions are prohibited under the terms of the *Agreement on Agriculture*. Export subsidies on agricultural products specified in Section II of Part IV of a Member's GATT Schedule of Concessions and listed in Article 9.1 of the *Agreement on Agriculture* are not prohibited but are subject to reduction commitments. Members may *not* provide these export subsidies *in excess of* the budgetary outlay and quantitative commitment levels specified in the Schedule. Also with respect to domestic agricultural support measures, Members have agreed to reduce the level of support. Members may *not* provide domestic support *in excess of* the commitment levels specified in their Schedules. However, domestic agricultural support measures that do not have the effect of providing price support to producers (i.e. 'green box' and 'blue box' subsidies) are exempt from the reduction commitments.

Subsidies can play an important role in the economic development programmes of developing-country Members. Article 27 of the *SCM Agreement*, therefore, provides some rules and disciplines for developing-country Members that are less strict than the general rules on subsidies of the *SCM Agreement*.

Exercise 12: Airbus Replay

The materials for this exercise consist of the Appellate Body Report in *EC and certain member States – Large Civil Aircraft (2011)*. In this exercise, there are three roles: the European Union, the United States and the Appellate Body. You will be assigned one of these roles. Those who will be assigned the role of the European Union or the United States should familiarise themselves with, and should present, the legal arguments made by the European Union or the United States during the Appellate Body proceedings in this dispute. Those who will be assigned the role of the Appellate Body should familiarise themselves with, and should present, the rulings of the Appellate Body on the many issues raised on appeal in this dispute. Please address each of the issues in the case in turn.

13 Technical Barriers to Trade

CONTENTS

1   INTRODUCTION

As discussed in Chapters 6 and 7 of this book, the importance of tariffs and quantitative restrictions as barriers to trade in goods has gradually decreased over time. While continued vigilance and further liberalisation efforts regarding these traditional barriers to trade are certainly called for, *regulatory measures* for trade in goods raise now a more pressing challenge for the multilateral trading system.[1] As discussed in Chapter 7, such regulatory measures can take the form of technical barriers to trade. This chapter deals with the WTO rules applicable to technical barriers to trade (TBT). The next chapter, Chapter 14, will deal with the different WTO rules applicable to sanitary and phytosanitary (SPS) measures, which pose challenges to international trade similar to technical barriers to trade.

The WTO rules applicable to technical barriers to trade and those applicable to SPS measures have in common that they go *beyond* the general rules applicable to non-tariff barriers, as set out in the GATT 1994. As discussed in Chapters 4, 5 and 7, these general rules focus on eliminating the negative trade effects of non-tariff measures, primarily by prohibiting them (as is the case for quantitative restrictions) or by ensuring their non-discriminatory application (as is the case for internal tax and regulatory measures).[2] However, the rules applicable to technical barriers to trade, as set out in the *TBT Agreement*, and the rules applicable to SPS measures, as set out in the *SPS Agreement*, go *further* in addressing non-tariff barriers to trade by *also* promoting regulatory harmonisation.[3] The relevant rules of the *TBT Agreement* and the *SPS Agreement* encourage Members to harmonise their national TBT and SPS measures around standards set by the relevant international standard-setting bodies.

Technical barriers to trade, the subject-matter of this chapter, are omnipresent in modern society. Television sets, toys, cosmetics, medical equipment, fertilisers, meat and cheese are all subject to requirements relating to their (intrinsic and extrinsic) characteristics and the manner in which they are produced. The objective of these requirements may be – and often is – the protection of life or health, the protection of the environment, the protection of consumers, the prevention of deceptive practices, or protection or promotion of many other legitimate societal values or interests. These requirements may be mandatory, set and enforced by governments. More often, however, these requirements are rules laid down by national standardising bodies, which are not mandatory but are nevertheless generally adopted in business transactions in a given country. In both cases, these requirements may constitute formidable barriers to trade, even where they are not applied in a discriminatory manner. This is so because the divergence in the regulatory requirements imposed in different countries increases the cost and difficulty of gaining market access for exporters. Television sets and cheese made according to the requirements of Newland may be banned from, or difficult to market in, Richland when the requirements of Richland relating

---

1 For a general discussion, see *World Trade Report 2012, Trade and Public Policies: A Closer Look at Non-Tariff Measures in the 21st Century* (World Trade Organization, 2012), 34–224, available at www.wto.org/english/res_e/publications_e/wtr12_e.htm.

2 See above, pp. 317–21 (MFN treatment), 356–9 (internal tax), 383–6 (regulatory measures) and 481–498 (quantitative restrictions).

3 As discussed in Chapter 15 of this book, the rules set out in the *TRIPS Agreement* also promote regulatory harmonisation around international standards. However, unlike the *TBT Agreement* and the *SPS Agreement*, the *TRIPS Agreement* lays down mandatory *minimum standards* of intellectual property protection and enforcement. See below, pp. 972 (fn. 90) and in particular pages 1002–1005.

to the characteristics or the manner of production are different. Furthermore, procedures used to verify whether a product meets certain mandatory or voluntary requirements may obstruct trade.

It is beyond dispute that technical barriers to trade play an important role in fulfilling multiple societal needs, such as those mentioned above. However, technical barriers to trade can also be a means of hidden protectionism. As noted in the *World Trade Report 2005*:

[i]n a world of reduced tariff protection and multilateral trade rules that limit the ability of governments arbitrarily to increase taxes and quantitative restrictions on trade, it is not surprising that they are sometimes tempted to use other means to restrict imports. This is a perennial issue in international trade relations.[4]

To date, WTO Members have been found to have acted inconsistently with their obligations under the *TBT Agreement* in four disputes.[5]

This chapter consecutively addresses: (1) the scope of application of the *TBT Agreement*; (2) the substantive provisions of the *TBT Agreement*; and (3) the institutional and procedural provisions of the *TBT Agreement*.

2 SCOPE OF APPLICATION OF THE *TBT AGREEMENT*

With respect to the scope of application of the *TBT Agreement*, this section distinguishes between: (1) the measures to which the *TBT Agreement* applies; (2) the entities covered by the Agreement: and (3) the *temporal* scope of application of the Agreement. This section also addresses the relationship between the *TBT Agreement* and other agreements on trade in goods, such as the *SPS Agreement*, the *Agreement on Government Procurement* and the GATT 1994.

2.1 Measures to Which the *TBT Agreement* Applies

The rules of the *TBT Agreement* apply to: (1) technical regulations; (2) standards; and (3) conformity assessment procedures. As the Appellate Body stated in *EC – Asbestos (2001)*, the *TBT Agreement* thus applies to a 'limited class of measures'.[6] The three types of measures to which the *TBT Agreement* applies are defined in Annex 1 of the *TBT Agreement*.

In Annex 1.1, a *technical regulation* is defined as a:

[d]ocument which lays down product characteristics or their related processes and production methods, including the applicable administrative provisions, with which compliance

---

4 *World Trade Report 2005: Exploring the Links between Trade, Standards and the WTO* (World Trade Organization, 2007), 29.
5 See *EC – Sardines (2002)*; *US – Clove Cigarettes (2012)*; *US – Tuna II (Mexico) (2012)*; and *US – COOL (2012)*. With regard to *EC – Asbestos (2001)*, see below, pp. 855–6.
6 Appellate Body Report, *EC – Asbestos (2001)*, para. 80.

is mandatory. It may also include or deal exclusively with terminology, symbols, packaging, marking or labelling requirements as they apply to a product, process or production method.

For example, a law requiring that batteries be rechargeable or a law requiring that wine be sold in green glass bottles is a technical regulation within the meaning of the *TBT Agreement*. The rules specifically applicable to technical regulations are set out in Articles 2 and 3 of the *TBT Agreement*.

Annex 1.2 of the *TBT Agreement* defines a *standard* as a:

[d]ocument approved by a recognized body, that provides, for common and repeated use, rules, guidelines or characteristics for products or related processes and production methods, with which compliance is not mandatory. It may also include or deal exclusively with terminology, symbols, packaging, marking or labelling requirements as they apply to a product, process or production method.

Contrary to technical regulations, standards are of a voluntary nature, meaning that compliance is not mandatory. The voluntary standards set by, for example, SACS (the State Administration of China for Standardization) or CEN (the European Committee for Standardization),[7] such as standards for building materials, mobile phones or electrical toothbrushes, are 'standards' within the meaning of the *TBT Agreement*. While only products complying with the standards would be eligible to be certified by the relevant body and/or bear its mark or logo, compliance with these standards is not mandatory. Companies comply with these voluntary standards for various reasons, ranging from the wish to be responsive to consumer concerns to practical considerations of compatibility of products. However, often companies have little choice but to comply with these voluntary standards as non-adherence would *in practice* make it much more difficult (if not impossible) to sell their products. It is therefore important that these voluntary standards are also subject to international disciplines under the *TBT Agreement*. As discussed below, the distinction between a mandatory 'technical regulation' and a non-mandatory 'standard' is not always clear-cut.[8] The rules specifically applicable to standards are set out in Article 4 of and Annex 3 to the *TBT Agreement*. Annex 3 contains the Code of Good Practice for the Preparation, Adopting and Application of Standards.

Note that the definition of both a 'technical regulation' and a 'standard' refers to 'a document'. As a 'document' is defined quite broadly as 'something written, inscribed, etc., which furnishes evidence or information upon any subject', the Appellate Body stated in *US – Tuna II (Mexico) (2012)* that 'the use of the term "document" could therefore cover a broad range of instruments or apply to a variety of measures'.[9]

---

7 Note that the SACS is a central government body, while the CEN is a non-governmental body. On the application of the *TBT Agreement* on standards set by non-governmental bodies, see below, p. 889.
8 See below, pp. 858–9.
9 Appellate Body Report, *US – Tuna II (Mexico) (2012)*, para. 185.

In addition to technical regulations and standards, conformity assessment procedures also fall within the scope of application of the *TBT Agreement*. Conformity assessment procedures are defined in Annex 1.3 to the *TBT Agreement* as:

> [a]ny procedure used, directly or indirectly, to determine that relevant requirements in technical regulations or standards are fulfilled.

Examples of conformity assessment procedures include procedures for sampling, testing and inspection. The rules specifically applicable to conformity assessment procedures are set out in Articles 5, 6, 7, 8 and 9 of the *TBT Agreement*.

The *TBT Agreement* applies to technical regulations, standards and conformity assessment procedures relating to: (1) products (including industrial and agricultural products); and (2) processes and production methods (PPMs).[10] It is the subject of much debate, however, whether the processes and production methods to which the *TBT Agreement* applies include so-called *non-product-related processes and production methods* (NPR-PPMs). This term is commonly used to refer to processes and production methods that do not affect the characteristics of the final product put on the market. An example of a technical regulation relating to an NPR-PPM would be the prohibition of the use of environmentally unfriendly sources of energy, or the use of child labour, in the production of a product. During the negotiations on the *TBT Agreement*, there was much discussion on whether technical regulations, standards or conformity assessment procedures relating to NPR-PPMs should be included in the scope of the Agreement. However, the negotiators seem to have failed to reach agreement on this issue.[11] The definitions in Annex 1, quoted above, could be read to indicate that technical regulations, standards and conformity assessment procedures relating to NPR-PPMs do *not* fall within the scope of application of the *TBT Agreement*. The definition of 'technical regulation' in Annex 1.1 refers in its first sentence to 'product characteristics or their *related* processes and production methods'; and the definition of 'standard' in Annex 1.2 refers in its first sentence to 'characteristics for products or *related* processes and production methods'.[12] However, note that the explanatory note to Annex 1.2 states that the *TBT Agreement* deals with 'technical regulations, standards and conformity assessment procedures related to products or processes and production methods'. There is thus debate about whether technical regulations, standards or conformity assessment procedures relating to NPR-PPMs fall within the scope of application of the *TBT*

---

10 See Article 1.3 and the explanatory note to Annex 1, para. 2, of the *TBT Agreement*. Note that the *TBT Agreement* does not apply to technical regulations, standards and conformity assessment procedures that deal with services.

11 See Committee on Technical Barriers to Trade, *Negotiating History of the Coverage of the Agreement on Technical Barriers to Trade with regard to Labelling Requirements, Voluntary Standards and Processes and Production Methods Unrelated to Product Characteristics*, Note by the Secretariat, G/TBT/W/11, dated 29 August 1995. See also Committee on Trade and Environment, *Report (1996) of the Committee on Trade and Environment*, WT/CTE/1, dated 12 November 1996, paras. 55–81.

12 Emphasis added.

Agreement. However, with regard to some types of measures, the definitions of Annexes 1.1 and 1.2 give more guidance. According to the last sentence of both definitions, technical regulations and standards include measures that are concerned with 'terminology, symbols, packaging, marking or labelling requirements *as they apply to a product, process or production method*'.[13] Note the absence of the adjective 'related'. It could therefore be argued that, for example, labelling requirements relating to NPR-PPMs are technical barriers to trade within the meaning of Annex 1 to the *TBT Agreement*, and thus fall within the scope of application of the *TBT Agreement*. The measures at issue in both *US – Tuna II (Mexico) (2012)* and *US – COOL (2012)* were labelling requirements relating to NPR-PPMs. In neither case did the respondent, the United States, argue that these measures did not fall within the scope of application of the *TBT Agreement*.

There have been six disputes to date in which panels and/or the Appellate Body have had occasion to examine whether the measure at issue was a 'technical regulation'.

In *EC – Asbestos (2001)*, the measure at issue consisted of, on the one hand, a general ban on asbestos and asbestos-containing products and, on the other hand, some exceptions referring to situations in which asbestos-containing products would be allowed. The panel concluded that the ban itself was *not* a technical regulation, whereas the exceptions to the ban *were*.[14] On appeal, the Appellate Body first firmly rejected the panel's approach of considering separately the ban and the exceptions to the ban. According to the Appellate Body, the 'proper legal character' of the measure cannot be determined unless the measure is looked at as a whole, including both the prohibitive and the permissive elements that are part of it.[15] The Appellate Body then examined whether the measure at issue, considered as a whole, was a technical regulation within the meaning of the *TBT Agreement*. On the basis of the definition of a 'technical regulation' of Annex 1.1, quoted above, the Appellate Body set out a number of considerations for determining whether a measure is a technical regulation.

First, for a measure to be a 'technical regulation', it must 'lay down' – i.e. set forth, stipulate or provide – 'product characteristics'. With respect to the term 'characteristics', the Appellate Body noted:

[T]he 'characteristics' of a product include, in our view, any objectively definable 'features', 'qualities', 'attributes', or other 'distinguishing mark' of a product. Such 'characteristics' might relate, *inter alia*, to a product's composition, size, shape, colour, texture, hardness, tensile strength, flammability, conductivity, density, or viscosity.[16]

The Appellate Body further noted that, in the second sentence of the definition of a 'technical regulation' in Annex 1.1, the *TBT Agreement* itself gives certain

---

13 Emphasis added.
14 See Panel Report, *EC – Asbestos (2001)*, paras. 8.71–8.72.
15 See Appellate Body Report, *EC – Asbestos (2001)*, para. 64.   16 *Ibid.*, para. 67.

examples of 'product characteristics', namely: 'terminology, symbols, packaging, marking or labelling requirements'. These examples, according to the Appellate Body, indicate that:

'product characteristics' include, not only features and qualities *intrinsic* to the product itself, but also related *extrinsic* 'characteristics', such as the means of identification, the presentation and the appearance of a product.[17]

The Appellate Body also noted that pursuant to the definition in Annex 1.1, a 'technical regulation' may be confined to laying down *only* one or a few product characteristics. In other words, it is not required that a 'technical regulation' lays down the characteristics of a product in a comprehensive manner.

Secondly, a 'technical regulation' lays down product characteristics or their related PPMs 'with which compliance is mandatory'. According to the Appellate Body in *EC – Asbestos (2001)*, it follows that:

with respect to products, a 'technical regulation' has the effect of *prescribing* or *imposing* one or more 'characteristics' – 'features', 'qualities', 'attributes', or other 'distinguishing mark'.[18]

The Appellate Body further noted that product characteristics may be prescribed or imposed in either a *positive* or a *negative* form. For example, the regulation may provide, positively, that products *must possess* certain characteristics, or the regulation may require, negatively, that products *must not possess* certain characteristics.[19] In both cases, the result is the same: the regulation lays down certain 'characteristics' with which compliance is mandatory.[20]

Thirdly, the Appellate Body in *EC – Asbestos (2001)* held that a 'technical regulation' must 'be applicable to an *identifiable* product, or group of products'.[21] Unlike the panel, the Appellate Body did not consider that a 'technical regulation' must apply to 'given' products, which are actually named, identified or specified in the regulation. Nothing in the text of the *TBT Agreement* suggests that the products concerned need be named or otherwise *expressly* identified in a 'technical regulation'. The Appellate Body noted that:

there may be perfectly sound administrative reasons for formulating a 'technical regulation' in a way that does *not* expressly identify products by name, but simply makes them identifiable – for instance, through the 'characteristic' that is the subject of regulation.[22]

On the basis of the above three considerations, the Appellate Body concluded that the measure at issue in *EC – Asbestos (2001)* constituted a 'technical regulation' under the *TBT Agreement*.[23]

---

17 *Ibid.*, para. 67. Emphasis added.   18 *Ibid.*, para. 68.
19 See *ibid.*, para. 69. The prohibition of all asbestos-containing products at issue in *EC – Asbestos (2001)* was a measure which effectively prescribed – albeit negatively – certain objective characteristics for all products.
20 See *ibid.*   21 *Ibid.*, para. 70.
22 *Ibid.*, para. 70. While the products to which the prohibition applied could not be determined from the terms of the measure itself, the Appellate Body considered that the products covered by the measure are *identifiable*: all products must be asbestos-free; any products containing asbestos are prohibited. See *ibid.*, para. 72.
23 *Ibid.*, para. 75. Note that the Appellate Body observed that, if this measure consisted *only* of a prohibition on asbestos, it might not constitute a 'technical regulation'. However, the Appellate Body considered that

Confirming its ruling in *EC – Asbestos (2001)*, the Appellate Body in *EC – Sardines (2002)* established a three-tier test for determining whether a measure is a 'technical regulation' under the *TBT Agreement*:

- the measure must apply to an *identifiable* product or group of products;
- the measure must lay down *product characteristics*; and
- compliance with the product characteristics laid down in the measure must be *mandatory*.[24]

Applying this test in *EC – Sardines (2002)*, the Appellate Body further clarified its reasoning in *EC – Asbestos (2001)*. The measure at issue in *EC – Sardines (2002)* was an EC regulation setting out a number of prescriptions for the sale of 'preserved sardines', including a requirement that a product sold under the name 'preserved sardines' contained only one species of sardines (namely, the *Sardina pilchardus Walbaum*), to the exclusion of other species (such as the *Sardinops sagax*). With regard to the first element of its three-tier test, the Appellate Body held that a measure, which does not expressly identify the products to which it applies, could still be applicable to identifiable products (as required by the first element of the test).[25] The tool that the Appellate Body used to determine whether, in this case, *Sardinops sagax* was an identifiable product was an examination of the way the EC Regulation was enforced. As the enforcement of the EC Regulation had led to a prohibition against labelling *Sardinops sagax* as 'preserved sardines', this product was considered to be 'identifiable'.[26]

With regard to the second element of the three-tier test, the question arose as to whether a 'naming' rule, such as the rule that only *Sardina pilchardus* could be named 'preserved sardines', laid down product characteristics. The Appellate Body held in this respect that product characteristics include means of identification and that, therefore, the naming rule at issue definitely met the requirement of the second element of the test.[27] As the European Communities did not contest that compliance with the Regulation at issue was mandatory, the Appellate Body found that the third element of the three-tier test was also met, and the measure was therefore a 'technical regulation' for purposes of the *TBT Agreement*.[28]

In *EC – Trademarks and Geographical Indications (Australia) (2005)*, the panel applied the Appellate Body's three-tier test in order to assess whether (1) a requirement that the country of origin must be indicated clearly on the product label, and (2) inspection structures for the registration of individual geographical indications (GIs), qualified as technical regulations. First, with regard to the labelling requirement, the panel concluded that this requirement was a 'technical

---

'an integral and essential aspect of the measure' is the regulation of *products containing asbestos fibres*. In effect, the measure provides that *all* products must *not* contain asbestos fibres. See *ibid.*, para. 72. Moreover, the Appellate Body noted that, through the exceptions to the prohibition, the measure at issue set out the 'applicable administrative provisions, with which compliance is mandatory' for products with certain objective 'characteristics'. See *ibid.*, para. 74.

24 *See* Appellate Body Report, *EC – Sardines (2002)*, para. 176.   25 See *ibid.*, para. 180.
26 See *ibid.*, para. 184.   27 See *ibid.*, paras. 190–1.   28 See *ibid.*, paras. 194–5.

regulation' within the meaning of Annex 1.1 to the *TBT Agreement*.[29] The panel noted that '[t]he issue is not whether the content of the label refers to a product characteristic; the label on a product *is* a product characteristic'.[30] Secondly, with regard to the inspection structures, Australia had argued that these inspection structures qualified as a 'technical regulation'. The panel disagreed. The panel appeared to consider that the inspection structures were 'conformity assessment procedures', and, since they were 'conformity assessment procedures', they could not be 'technical regulations' at the same time.[31]

In *US – Clove Cigarettes (2012)*, which concerned a US ban on clove cigarettes and other flavoured cigarettes, with the exception of menthol cigarettes, and in *US – COOL (2012)*, which concerned a US measure imposing a requirement on retailers selling beef and pork to label those products with their country of origin,[32] the question of whether the core measures at issue were 'technical regulations' was not disputed between the parties.[33] However, in *US – Tuna II (Mexico) (2012)*, which concerned a measure establishing the conditions for use of a 'dolphin-safe' label on tuna products, the correct characterisation of the measure at issue was a central element of the dispute.[34] According to the respondent, the United States, the measure at issue was a 'standard' and not a 'technical regulation'. The panel disagreed. According to the panel, the measure at issue was a 'technical regulation'.[35] On appeal, the United States did not challenge the panel's findings regarding the first and second element of the test set out above. However, it did challenge the panel's finding regarding the third element of the test, namely, that compliance with the measure at issue was mandatory. In challenging this finding, the United States argued, in particular, that compliance with a labelling requirement is 'mandatory' within the meaning of

---

29 Panel Report, *EC – Trademarks and Geographical Indications (Australia) (2005)*, para. 7.449.

30 See *ibid*. The panel furthermore held that the labelling requirement at issue was a mandatory requirement because products with a geographical indication identical to a Community-protected name that do not satisfy this labelling requirement must *not* be marketed in the European Communities using that geographical indication. See *ibid.*, para. 7.456. Compare with *US – Tuna II (Mexico) (2012)* below, pp. 858–9.

31 See *ibid.*, para. 7.514. The panel noted that the terms 'technical regulations' and 'standards' are themselves part of the definition of the term 'conformity assessment procedures'. According to the panel, this suggests that 'technical regulations' and 'conformity assessment procedures' are not only distinct from one another, but mutually exclusive. As the panel argued, '[w]hilst a single measure can combine both a technical regulation and a procedure to assess conformity with that technical regulation, it would be an odd result if a conformity assessment procedure could fall within the definition of a technical regulation as well'. *Ibid.*

32 Note that, under the US measure at issue, the 'country of origin' of beef or pork is defined not as a function of the country in which the last substantial transformation to the beef or pork took place, but as a function of the country or countries in which the production steps (birth, raising and slaughter), involving the animals from which the beef and pork is derived, took place.

33 In *US – COOL (2012)*, the United States did argue that a second measure at issue, the Vilsack letter, was not a 'technical regulation'. The panel agreed with the United States after finding that the Vilsack letter was not 'mandatory within the meaning of Annex 1.1'. See Panel Reports, *US – COOL (2012)*, paras. 7.194–7.196.

34 Eligibility for a 'dolphin-safe' label depended upon certain documentary evidence that varied depending on the area where the tuna contained in the tuna product was harvested and the type of vessel and fishing method by which it was harvested.

35 Note, however, the separate opinion of one of the panellists, see Panel Report, *US – Tuna II (Mexico) (2012)*, paras. 7.146–7.188. The dissenting panellist was of the opinion that the measure at issue, the 'dolphin-safe' labelling scheme, was not a technical regulation because it was not a mandatory scheme as the tuna could be put on the market without the label. See *ibid.*

Annex 1.1 only 'if there is also a requirement to use the label in order to place the product for sale on the market'.[36] Since tuna products could be sold on the US market with *or* without a 'dolphin-safe' label, the labelling requirement was, according to the United States, not 'mandatory'. The Appellate Body disagreed. The Appellate Body pointed out that a labelling requirement, i.e. a provision that sets out conditions to be fulfilled in order to use a particular label, can be a 'technical regulation' *or* a 'standard'.[37] According to the Appellate Body, the mere fact that a labelling requirement does not require the use of a particular label in order to place a product for sale on the market, does not preclude that this labelling requirement is a 'technical regulation'.[38] The Appellate Body considered that a determination of whether a particular measure constitutes a 'technical regulation' or a 'standard' must be made in light of the features of the measure and the circumstances of the case.[39] Such exercise may involve considering: (1) whether the measure consists of a law or a regulation enacted by a WTO Member; (2) whether it prescribes or prohibits particular conduct; (3) whether it sets out specific requirements that constitute the sole means of addressing a particular matter; and (4) the nature of the matter addressed by the measure.[40] After careful examination of the measure at issue in *US – Tuna II (Mexico) (2012)*, the Appellate Body concluded:

In this case, we note that the US measure is composed of legislative and regulatory acts of the US federal authorities and includes administrative provisions. In addition, the measure at issue sets out a single and legally mandated definition of a 'dolphin-safe' tuna product and disallows the use of other labels on tuna products that do not satisfy this definition. In doing so, the US measure prescribes in a broad and exhaustive manner the conditions that apply for making any assertion on a tuna product as to its 'dolphin-safety', regardless of the manner in which that statement is made. As a consequence, the US measure covers the entire field of what 'dolphin-safe' means in relation to tuna products. For these reasons, we *find* that the Panel did not err in characterizing the measure at issue as a 'technical regulation' within the meaning of Annex 1.1 to the *TBT Agreement*.[41]

Questions and Assignments 13.1

What types of measure fall within the scope of application of the *TBT Agreement*? What are the criteria to determine whether a measure is a 'technical regulation' for the purposes of the *TBT Agreement*? Explain these criteria. What is the main difference between a technical regulation and a standard for the purposes of the *TBT Agreement*? Why can an inspection procedure not be a 'technical regulation' as defined in the *TBT Agreement*? Is a labelling requirement a 'technical regulation' or a 'standard'? In that context, does it matter whether a labelling requirement does or does not require the use of a particular label in order to place a product for sale on the market?

---

36 United States' appellant's submission, para. 32 (as referred to in Appellate Body Report, *US – Tuna II (Mexico) (2012)*, para. 196).
37 See *ibid.*, para. 187.   38 See *ibid.*, para. 196.
39 See *ibid.*, para. 190.   40 See *ibid.*, para. 188.
41 *Ibid.*, para. 199. Note that, having found that the measure at issue constituted a 'technical regulation', Mexico's alternative argument that the US measure is *de facto* mandatory did not need to be addressed by the Appellate Body.

2.2 Entities Covered by the *TBT Agreement*

The *TBT Agreement* is mainly addressed to *central government* bodies. However, it explicitly aims to extend its application to other bodies involved in the
preparation, adoption and application of technical regulations, standards and/or
conformity assessment procedures. These other bodies covered by the *TBT Agreement* are local government bodies and non-governmental bodies. *Local government* bodies are all bodies of government other than central government, such
as provinces or municipalities. They include any organ subject to the 'control of
such a government in respect of the activity in question'.[42] *Non-governmental*
bodies in the context of the *TBT Agreement* are very broadly defined as bodies other than central government or local government bodies.[43] These non-
governmental bodies include, for example, ABNT (the Associação Brasileira de
Normas Técnicas), ANSI (the American National Standards Institute) and CEN
(the European Committee for Standardization).[44]

Pursuant to Article 3 (with regard to technical regulations), Annex 3.B (with
regard to standards) and Articles 7 and 8 (with regard to conformity assessment
procedures), the *TBT Agreement* extends its application to local government and
non-governmental bodies, by imposing, on WTO Members, the obligation: (1)
to take 'such reasonable measures as may be available to them' to ensure compliance with the *TBT Agreement* by local government and non-governmental
bodies; and (2) to refrain from taking measures that could encourage actions
by these bodies that are inconsistent with the provisions of the *TBT Agreement*.

This obligation may be of particular importance in light of the increasing impact on international trade of 'private sector standards', i.e. standards adopted
by NGOs such as the Forest Stewardship Council (FSC) (which sets standards for
sustainable forest management),[45] or standards adopted by commercial enterprises such as Tesco, the multinational grocery and general merchandise retailer
(which sets and applies, *inter alia*, minimum labour standards to its suppliers in
China, India and Bangladesh). The proliferation of these 'private sector standards' is of significant concern to producers in developing-country Members.[46]
As noted above, 'non-governmental bodies' are very broadly defined in Annex
1.8, as bodies other than central government or local government bodies. There
is, however, much debate on whether NGOs and commercial enterprises are
'non-governmental bodies' within the meaning of Article 3, Annex 3.B and
Article 8 of the *TBT Agreement*.

---

42 Annex 1.7 of the *TBT Agreement*.   43 See Annex 1.8 to the *TBT Agreement*.
44 Note that CEN, together with ETSI (the European Telecommunications Standards Institute) and CENELEC (the
     European Committee for Electrotechnical Standardisation) are officially recognised by the European Union as
     a European standardising body.
45 Other examples of such NGOs adopting 'private sector standards' are *GlobalGAP* (which sets standards for
     production processes of agricultural products trade), and the *Fairtrade Foundation* (which sets standards for
     socially responsible production and trade).
46 For a further discussion on 'private sector standards' in the context of the *SPS Agreement*, see below, p. 901.

2.3 Temporal Scope of Application of the *TBT Agreement*

In *EC – Sardines (2002)*, the issue arose whether the *TBT Agreement* applies to technical regulations which were already in force on 1 January 1995, i.e. the date on which the *TBT Agreement* entered into force. In deciding this issue, the panel and Appellate Body referred to Article 28 of the *Vienna Convention on the Law of Treaties*, which states that:

[u]nless a different intention appears from the treaty or is otherwise established, its provisions do not bind a party in relation to any act or fact which took place or any situation which ceased to exist before the date of the entry into force of the treaty with respect to that party.

Applying this basic provision of treaty law, both the panel and the Appellate Body held that the EC regulation at issue, although adopted prior to 1 January 1995, was still in force and thus could not be considered as a 'situation which has ceased to exist'.[47] Therefore, it can be concluded that the *TBT Agreement* applies to technical regulations, which, although adopted prior to 1995, are still in force.

Questions and Assignments 13.2

What institutions or bodies are covered by the rules of the *TBT Agreement*? Why are the rules of the *TBT Agreement* not limited to central government bodies? What are 'private sector standards'? Are 'private sector standards' subject to the disciplines of the *TBT Agreement*? Does the *TBT Agreement* apply to a technical regulation adopted before this Agreement entered into force?

2.4 Relationship with other WTO Agreements

This section examines, first, the relationship of the *TBT Agreement* with the *SPS Agreement* and the *Agreement on Government Procurement*, and then on its relationship with the GATT 1994.

2.4.1 The SPS Agreement and the Agreement on Government Procurement

As mentioned above, the scope of application of the *TBT Agreement* is determined by the type of measure. The *TBT Agreement* applies, in principle, to technical regulations, standards and conformity assessment procedures as defined in Annex 1 thereof. However, to avoid overlap with other WTO agreements, the scope of application of the *TBT Agreement* has been limited in favour of two other WTO agreements: the *SPS Agreement* and the *Agreement on Government Procurement*. Generally speaking, the applicability of either of these agreements to a measure excludes the applicability of the *TBT Agreement*. However, in specific cases, the situation may not be so clear-cut.

---

47 See Panel Report, *EC – Sardines (2002)*, para. 7.60; and Appellate Body Report, *EC – Sardines (2002)*, para. 216.

Pursuant to Article 1.4 of the *TBT Agreement*, purchasing specifications related to the production or consumption of governmental bodies do not fall within the scope of application of the *TBT Agreement* as they are dealt with in the *Agreement on Government Procurement*. Note, however, that the *Agreement on Government Procurement* is a plurilateral agreement; the disciplines set out in this agreement do not apply to most WTO Members.[48]

Pursuant to Article 1.5 of the *TBT Agreement*, sanitary and phytosanitary measures are excluded from the scope of application of the *TBT Agreement*, even if they take the form of technical regulations, standards or conformity assessment procedures. Sanitary and phytosanitary measures are subject to the distinct disciplines of the *SPS Agreement*, discussed in Chapter 14 of this book.[49] It is the *purpose* of the measure that qualifies it as a sanitary or phytosanitary measure. In *EC – Hormones (1998)*, the United States and Canada claimed, *inter alia*, that the measures at issue were inconsistent with the *TBT Agreement*. Referring to Article 1.5 of the *TBT Agreement*, the panel found, however, that, since these measures were SPS measures, the *TBT Agreement* did not apply in the *EC – Hormones (1998)* dispute.[50] However, note that the panel in *EC – Approval and Marketing of Biotech Products (2006)* recognised that a single measure can have more than one purpose: one that falls within the definition of an SPS measure *and* one that does not. The panel thus held that, assuming that the measure at issue falls within the definition of a technical regulation, to the extent that the measure is applied for a non-SPS purpose, it is a measure to which the disciplines of the *TBT Agreement* apply.[51]

2.4.2   The GATT 1994

The relationship between the GATT 1994 and the *TBT Agreement* is of a different nature and is not characterised by mutual exclusivity. The panel in *EC – Asbestos (2001)* held that, in a case where both the GATT 1994 and the *TBT Agreement* appear to apply to a given measure, a panel must first examine whether the measure at issue is consistent with the *TBT Agreement* since this agreement deals 'specifically and in detail' with technical barriers to trade.[52] However, should a panel find a measure to be consistent with the *TBT Agreement*, it must still examine whether the measure is also consistent with the GATT 1994.[53] Under the *TBT* Agreement, there is – unlike under the *SPS Agreement* – no presumption of GATT-consistency when a technical barrier to trade is found to be consistent with the *TBT Agreement*.[54]

---

48 See above, pp. 509–11.   49 See below, pp. 896–903.
50 See Panel Report, *EC – Hormones (US) (1998)*, para. 8.29; and Panel Report, *EC – Hormones (Canada) (1998)*, para. 8.32.
51 See Panel Reports, *EC – Approval and Marketing of Biotech Products (2006)*, para. 7.167.
52 See Panel Report, *EC – Asbestos (2001)*, para. 8.16. See on this point more generally, Appellate Body Report, *EC – Bananas III (1997)*, para. 204. See also Panel Report, *EC – Sardines (2002)*, paras. 7.14–7.19.
53 It is understood that, if a panel should find that a measure is inconsistent with the *TBT Agreement*, it may exercise judicial economy with regard to a claim that this measure is also inconsistent with the GATT 1994. On the exercise of judicial economy, see above, pp. 222–4.
54 On the presumption of GATT-consistency under Article 2.4 of the *SPS Agreement*, see below, p. 903.

Note, in general, that the relationship between the GATT 1994 and the other multilateral agreements on trade in goods (including the *TBT Agreement*) is governed by the *General Interpretative Note to Annex 1A* of the *WTO Agreement*. This Note provides that, in case of conflict between a provision of the GATT 1994 and a provision of another multilateral agreement on trade in goods, the latter will prevail to the extent of the conflict.[55]

Questions and Assignments 13.3

Can the *SPS Agreement* and the *TBT Agreement* apply to the same measure? Can the *TBT Agreement* and the GATT 1994 apply to the same measure? How would a panel deal with such a situation?

3 SUBSTANTIVE PROVISIONS OF THE *TBT AGREEMENT*

The substantive provisions of the *TBT Agreement* contain several obligations that are also found in the GATT 1994, such as: the most-favoured-nation (MFN) treatment obligation, the national treatment obligation and the obligation to refrain from creating unnecessary obstacles to international trade. In *EC – Asbestos (2001)*, the Appellate Body observed that the *TBT Agreement* intends to further the objectives of the GATT 1994. However, it immediately noted that the *TBT Agreement* does so through a specialised legal regime, containing *different* and *additional* obligations to those emanating from the GATT 1994.[56] This section will address the following obligations under the *TBT Agreement*: (1) the MFN treatment and national treatment obligations; (2) the obligation to refrain from creating unnecessary obstacles to international trade; (3) the obligation to base technical barriers to trade on international standards; and (4) other obligations, including obligations relating to mutual recognition and transparency.

3.1 MFN Treatment and National Treatment Obligations

With respect to technical regulations, Article 2.1 of the *TBT Agreement* provides that:

Members shall ensure that in respect of technical regulations, products imported from the territory of any Member shall be accorded treatment no less favourable than that accorded to like products of national origin and to like products originating in any other country.

Technical regulations are thus subject to a national treatment obligation and the MFN treatment obligation. Pursuant to Annex 3.D to and Article 5.1.1 of the *TBT Agreement*, these obligations also apply to standards and conformity assessment

---

55 For a discussion on the relationship between the GATT 1994 and other multilateral agreements on trade in goods, see above, pp. 42–5.

56 See Appellate Body Report, *EC – Asbestos (2001)*, para. 80. Therefore, caution needs to be used when transposing the interpretation given to these obligations under the GATT 1994 to the similar provisions in the *TBT Agreement*. See also below, pp. 863–73.

procedures respectively. Thus, a requirement that furniture from Brazil must be made from sustainable wood (i.e. wood from sustainably managed forests), while there is no such requirement for furniture from African countries, would constitute a violation of the MFN treatment obligation set out in Article 2.1 of the *TBT Agreement*. Requiring accurate testing for the presence of GMOs in corn imported from the United States, while such verification is not required for corn from Australia, would constitute a violation of the MFN treatment obligation set out in Article 5.1.1 of the *TBT Agreement*. A requirement that imported furniture is fire-resistant, while no such requirement exists for domestically produced furniture, would constitute a violation of the national treatment obligation set out in Article 2.1 of the *TBT Agreement*.

The Appellate Body first interpreted the national treatment obligation of Article 2.1 of the *TBT Agreement* in *US – Clove Cigarettes (2012)* and further clarified this obligation in *US – Tuna II (Mexico) (2012)* and *US – COOL (2012)*. In *US – Tuna II (Mexico) (2012)*, the Appellate Body also addressed the MFN treatment obligation of Article 2.1.

In *US – Clove Cigarettes (2012)*, the Appellate Body ruled that:

[f]or a violation of the national treatment obligation in Article 2.1 to be established, three elements must be satisfied: (i) the measure at issue must be a technical regulation; (ii) the imported and domestic products at issue must be like products; and (iii) the treatment accorded to imported products must be less favourable than that accorded to like domestic products.[57]

Article 2.1 of the *TBT Agreement* thus sets out a three-tier test of consistency with the national treatment obligation. This test of consistency requires the examination of:

- whether the measure at issue is a '*technical regulation*' within the meaning of Annex 1.1;
- whether the imported and domestic products at issue are '*like products*'; and
- whether the imported products are accorded '*treatment no less favourable*' than like domestic products.

As the Appellate Body found in *US – Tuna II (Mexico) (2012)*, Article 2.1 of the *TBT Agreement* sets out a largely similar test of consistency with the MFN treatment obligation. Under the third element of the test, however, instead of examining whether the imported products are accorded 'treatment no less favourable' than like domestic products, a panel must examine whether products imported from one WTO Member are accorded 'treatment no less favourable' than like products originating in any other country.[58] As noted above, standards and conformity assessment procedures are also subject to an MFN treatment and the national treatment obligation under the *TBT Agreement*.[59] It is reasonable to

---

57 Appellate Body Report, *US – Clove Cigarettes (2012)*, para. 87.
58 See Appellate Body Report, *US – Tuna II (Mexico) (2012)*, para. 202.
59 See above, pp. 863–5.

expect that, *mutatis mutandis*, a similar test of consistency with the MFN treatment obligation and the national treatment obligation will apply with regard to standards and conformity assessment procedures.

Below, each element of the three-tier test of consistency with the national treatment and MFN treatment obligations under Article 2.1 of the *TBT Agreement* will be discussed in turn.[60] Before engaging in this discussion, it is useful to note the following. For a proper understanding of this test of consistency, and in particular the third element of the test ('treatment no less favourable'), it is important to keep in mind that the *TBT Agreement* does not contain a provision, such as Article XX of the GATT 1994, which could justify measures found to be inconsistent with the MFN-treatment obligation or the national treatment obligation of Article 2.1.[61]

To date, WTO Members have been found to have acted inconsistently with the national treatment obligation of Article 2.1 in three disputes.[62] In one dispute, a WTO Member was found to have acted inconsistently with the MFN treatment obligation of Article 2.1.[63]

Questions and Assignments 13.4

What are the constituent elements of the national treatment test of Article 2.1 of the *TBT Agreement*? How does this test differ from the MFN treatment test of Article 2.1?

3.1.1 'Technical Regulations'

With regard to this first element of the test of consistency with the non-discrimination obligations of Article 2.1 of the *TBT Agreement*, namely, whether the measure at issue is a 'technical regulation', refer to the discussion above on the scope of application of the *TBT Agreement*.[64]

3.1.2 'Like Products'

The second element of the test of consistency with the non-discrimination obligations of Article 2.1 relates to the question of whether the imported and domestic products concerned (for the national treatment obligation) or the imported products originating in different countries concerned (for the MFN treatment obligation) are 'like'. As the non-discrimination obligations under the GATT 1994 discussed in Chapters 4 and 5 of this book, the non-discrimination obligations of Article 2.1 only apply to 'like products'. Therefore, for the application of these non-discrimination obligations, it is also important to be able to determine whether, for example, a sports utility vehicle (SUV) is 'like' a family car; orange juice is 'like' tomato juice; a laptop is 'like' a tablet computer; pork is 'like' beef; or whisky is 'like' brandy.

---

60 See below, pp. 865–72. 61 See below, pp. 869-70.
62 See *US – Clove Cigarettes (2012)*; *US – Tuna II (Mexico) (2012)*; and *US – COOL (2012)*.
63 See *US – Tuna II (Mexico) (2012)*. 64 See above, pp. 852–63.

As discussed above in Chapter 5, the determination of 'likeness' under Article III of the GATT 1994 is a determination about the nature and extent of a competitive relationship between and among products. The panel in *US – Clove Cigarettes (2012)* held that the text and context of the *TBT Agreement* supported an interpretation of the concept of 'likeness' in Article 2.1 of the *TBT Agreement* that focused on the objectives and purposes of the technical regulation, rather than on the competitive relationship between and among the products. The panel adopted a purpose-based approach to the determination of 'likeness', rather than a competition-based approach. The panel found that, in the circumstances of this case, in the determination of 'likeness' under Article 2.1 the weighing of the evidence relating to the 'likeness' criteria (physical characteristics, end-uses, consumers' tastes and habits, and customs classification) should be influenced by the fact that the measure at issue was a technical regulation having the immediate purpose of regulating flavoured cigarettes for public health reasons.[65] The Appellate Body rejected the panel's purpose-based approach to the determination of 'likeness' under Article 2.1.[66] The Appellate Body considered in *US – Clove Cigarettes (2012)* that:

the concept of 'like products' serves to define the scope of products that should be compared to establish whether less favourable treatment is being accorded to imported products. If products that are in a sufficiently strong competitive relationship to be considered like are excluded from the group of like products on the basis of a measure's regulatory purposes, such products would not be compared in order to ascertain whether less favourable treatment has been accorded to imported products. This would inevitably distort the less favourable treatment comparison, as it would refer to a 'marketplace' that would include some like products, but not others.[67]

While it rejected the panel's purpose-based approach to the determination of 'likeness', the Appellate Body noted, however, that:

regulatory concerns underlying a measure, such as the health risks associated with a given product, may be relevant to an analysis of the 'likeness' criteria under Article III:4 of the GATT 1994, as well as under Article 2.1 of the *TBT Agreement*, to the extent they have an impact on the competitive relationship between and among the products concerned.[68]

The Appellate Body in *US – Clove Cigarettes (2012)* unmistakably opted for a competition-based approach to the determination of 'likeness' under Article 2.1.

---

65 See Panel Report, *US – Clove Cigarettes (2012)*, para. 7.119.

66 See Appellate Body Report, *US – Clove Cigarettes (2012)*, para. 112. The Appellate Body noted in this context that measures often pursue a multiplicity of objectives, which are not always easily discernible. The Appellate Body also noted that the panel's purpose-based approach to the determination of 'likeness' does not, necessarily, leave more regulatory autonomy for Members, because it almost invariably puts panels into the position of having to determine which of the various objectives purportedly pursued by Members are more important, or which of these objectives should prevail in determining 'likeness' in the event of conflicting objectives. See Appellate Body Report, *US – Clove Cigarettes (2012)*, paras. 113–15.

67 *Ibid.*, para. 116.

68 *Ibid.*, para. 119. See also *ibid.*, paras. 120 and 156. The Appellate Body explicitly referred to its approach to the determination of 'likeness' in *EC – Hormones (1998)*.

It stated that the determination of 'likeness' under Article 2.1 of the *TBT Agreement* is, as under Article III:4 of the GATT 1994:

a determination about the nature and extent of a competitive relationship between and among the products at issue.[69]

As noted above, the panel considered in its determination of 'likeness' the 'likeness' criteria already discussed in Chapters 4 and 5 in the context of the non-discrimination obligations of the GATT 1994. The United States did not appeal the panel's findings regarding 'physical characteristics' or 'customs classification'. It did appeal the panel's findings regarding 'end-uses' and 'consumers' tastes and habits'. While the Appellate Body disagreed with certain aspects of the panel's analysis, it did agree with the panel that the 'likeness' criteria it examined supported its overall conclusion that clove cigarettes and menthol cigarettes are 'like' products within the meaning of Article 2.1 of the *TBT Agreement*.[70]

In *US – Clove Cigarettes (2012)*, the Appellate Body also noted that, while the products identified by the complainant are the starting point of a panel's 'likeness' analysis, a panel is not limited to those products specifically identified by the complainant when it determines the scope of like imported and domestic products. The Appellate Body held that:

Article 2.1 requires panels to assess objectively, on the basis of the nature and extent of the competitive relationship between the products in the market of the regulating Member, the universe of domestic products that are like the products imported from the complaining Member.[71]

Questions and Assignments 13.5

How should a panel determine whether a sports utility vehicle (SUV) is 'like' a family car within the meaning of Article 2.1 of the *TBT Agreement*? In determining the 'likeness' of these two products, what is the relevance of the regulatory concerns underlying the technical regulation concerned? If, in a particular market, SUVs and family cars would be 'like' products within the meaning of Article III:4 of the GATT, would they then also be 'like' products within the meaning of Article 2.1 of the *TBT Agreement*?

3.1.3 'Treatment no Less Favourable'

The third and last element of the test of consistency with the non-discrimination obligations of Article 2.1 of the *TBT Agreement* relates to the question of whether the measure at issue accords 'treatment no less favourable'. As discussed below, the fact that a measure distinguishes between 'like products' does not suffice to conclude that this measure is inconsistent with Article 2.1.[72] To establish inconsistency with Article 2.1, a panel must examine whether or not

---

69 Appellate Body Report, *US – Clove Cigarettes (2012)*, para. 120. See also *ibid.*, para. 156. For the relevant case law under Article III:4 of the GATT 1994, see above, pp. 383–94.

70 *Ibid.*, para. 160.

71 See *ibid.*, para. 192. Note, however, that this does not absolve the complainant from making a *prima facie* case of violation of Article 2.1. See *ibid.*

72 See below, pp. 869–72.

imported products are accorded 'treatment no less favourable' than like products imported from other countries (the MFN treatment obligation) or like domestic products (national treatment obligation).

As discussed in Chapter 5 of this book in the context of national treatment under the GATT 1994, there is well-established case law on the term 'treatment no less favourable' in Article III:4 of the GATT 1994. Recall that the Appellate Body ruled in *Korea – Various Measures on Beef (2001)* that:

[w]hether or not imported products are treated 'less favourably' than like domestic products should be assessed ... by examining whether a measure modifies the *conditions of competition* in the relevant market to the detriment of imported products.[73]

According to this case law regarding Article III:4, the term 'treatment no less favourable' prohibits WTO Members from modifying the conditions of competition in the marketplace to the detriment of the group of imported products *vis-à-vis* the group of domestic like products.[74] According to this same case law, Article III:4 prohibits both *de jure* and *de facto* less favourable treatment.[75] While the Appellate Body was mindful that the term 'treatment no less favourable' in Article 2.1 of the *TBT Agreement* is to be interpreted in the light of the specific context provided by the *TBT Agreement*, the Appellate Body nonetheless considered in *US – Clove Cigarettes (2012)* the case law on the term 'treatment no less favourable' in Article III:4 of the GATT 1994 to be 'instructive' in assessing the meaning of the term 'treatment no less favourable' in Article 2.1.[76] Inspired by the case law regarding Article III:4, the Appellate Body ruled in *US – Clove Cigarettes (2012)* that the 'treatment no less favourable' requirement of Article 2.1 prohibited both *de jure* and *de facto* discrimination against imported products, and that:

a panel examining a claim of violation under Article 2.1 should seek to ascertain whether the technical regulation at issue modifies the conditions of competition in the market of the regulating Member to the detriment of the group of imported products *vis-à-vis* the group of like domestic products.[77]

However, while a detrimental impact on the competitive conditions in the relevant market may be sufficient to establish a violation of Article III:4 of the GATT 1994, the Appellate Body unequivocally stated in *US – Clove Cigarettes (2012)* that the existence of such detrimental impact is *not sufficient* to establish a violation of Article 2.1 of the *TBT Agreement*. The Appellate Body ruled that:

where the technical regulation at issue does not *de jure* discriminate against imports, the existence of a detrimental impact on competitive opportunities for the group of imported

---

73 Appellate Body Report, *Korea – Various Measures on Beef (2001)*, para. 137.
74 See above, pp. 395–402.   75 See above, pp. 399–402.
76 See Appellate Body Report, *US – Clove Cigarettes (2012)*, para. 180. More generally, the Appellate Body found that '[t]he very similar formulation of the provisions, and the overlap in their scope of application in respect of technical regulations, confirm that Article III:4 of the GATT 1994 is relevant context for the interpretation of the national treatment obligation of Article 2.1 of the TBT Agreement'. See *ibid.*, para. 100.
77 Appellate Body Report, *US – Clove Cigarettes (2012)*, para. 179.

vis-à-vis the group of domestic like products is not dispositive of less favourable treatment under Article 2.1.[78]

According to the Appellate Body, a panel must in such cases of *de facto* discrimination:

further analyze whether the detrimental impact on imports stems exclusively from a legitimate regulatory distinction rather than reflecting discrimination against the group of imported products.[79]

To determine whether the detrimental impact stems exclusively from a legitimate regulatory distinction rather than reflecting discrimination, a panel must:

carefully scrutinize the particular circumstances of the case, that is, the design, architecture, revealing structure, operation, and application of the technical regulation at issue, and, in particular, whether that technical regulation is even-handed, in order to determine whether it discriminates against the group of imported products.[80]

The Appellate Body came to this understanding of the meaning of the term 'treatment no less favourable' in Article 2.1 on the basis of its context and the object and purpose of the *TBT Agreement*. With regard to the context of the term 'treatment no less favourable', the Appellate Body referred to Annex 1.1,[81] Article 2.2[82] and the sixth recital of the Preamble[83] to the *TBT Agreement*. The Appellate Body emphasised, in particular, that, while the *TBT Agreement* does not contain a general exceptions clause similar to Article XX of the GATT 1994,[84] the WTO Members recognise in the sixth recital of the Preamble to the *TBT Agreement* that 'no country should be prevented from taking measures necessary' to pursue policy objectives such as the protection of public health, the protection of the environment and the protection of the consumer. As the sixth recital of the Preamble states, countries should not be prevented from taking such measures 'subject to the requirement that [these measures] are not applied in a manner which would constitute a means of arbitrary or unjustifiable discrimination between countries where the same conditions prevail or a disguised restriction on international trade, and are otherwise in accordance with the provisions of this Agreement'. With regard to the object and purpose of the *TBT Agreement*, the Appellate Body noted that the object and purpose of the *TBT Agreement* is to strike a balance between, on the one hand, the objective of trade liberalisation and, on the other hand, a Member's right to regulate.[85] Thus, the Appellate Body interpreted the 'treatment no less favourable' requirement of Article 2.1 as:

prohibiting both *de jure* and *de facto* discrimination against imported products, while at the same time permitting detrimental impact on competitive opportunities for imports that stems exclusively from legitimate regulatory distinctions.[86]

---

78 *Ibid.*, para. 182. See also *ibid.*, para. 215.   79 *Ibid.*, para. 182. See also *ibid.*, para. 215.
80 *Ibid.*   81 See *ibid.*, para. 169.   82 See *ibid.*, paras. 170–1.
83 See *ibid.*, paras. 172–3.   84 See *ibid.*, para. 101.
85 See *ibid.*, para. 174. See also *ibid.*, paras. 94 and 95.   86 *Ibid.*, para. 175.

As discussed in Chapter 5 of this book, the national treatment obligation of Article III:4 of the GATT 1994 does not require Members to accord no less favourable treatment to *each and every* imported product as compared to *each and every* domestic like product. Recall that regulatory distinctions between like products are not inconsistent with the national treatment obligation of Article III:4 as long as the treatment accorded to the *group* of imported products is no less favourable than the treatment accorded to the *group* of like domestic products.[87] In *US – Clove Cigarettes (2012)*, the Appellate Body ruled that the same is true for the national treatment obligation of Article 2.1 of the *TBT Agreement.*[88]

In *US – Clove Cigarettes (2012)*, the Appellate Body held that the design, architecture, revealing structure, operation and application of the measure at issue (a US ban on clove cigarettes and other flavoured cigarettes, with the exception of menthol cigarettes) strongly suggested that the detrimental impact on competitive opportunities for clove cigarettes reflects discrimination against the group of like products imported from Indonesia. Note that the 'vast majority' of clove cigarettes consumed in the United States came from Indonesia, while almost all menthol cigarettes consumed in the United States were produced in the United States.[89] Moreover, the Appellate Body was not persuaded that the detrimental impact of the measure at issue on competitive opportunities for imported clove cigarettes stemmed from a legitimate regulatory distinction.[90] The Appellate Body ultimately upheld, albeit for different reasons, the panel's finding that, by exempting menthol cigarettes from the ban on flavoured cigarettes, the measure at issue accorded to clove cigarettes imported from Indonesia less favourable treatment than that accorded to domestic like products, and was, therefore, inconsistent with the national treatment obligation of Article 2.1 of the *TBT Agreement.*[91]

In *US – Tuna II (Mexico) (2012)* and *US – COOL (2012)*, the Appellate Body built on, and further clarified, the interpretation of the term 'treatment no less favourable' of Article 2.1 set out in *US – Clove Cigarettes (2012)*.

As discussed in Chapter 5 of this book in the context of the national treatment requirement of Article III:4 of the GATT 1994, there must be a *genuine relationship* between the measure at issue and the detrimental impact on competitive opportunities for imported products for the measure at issue to be found to modify the conditions of competition to the detriment of imported products.[92] In *US – Tuna II (Mexico) (2012)*, the Appellate Body considered that in the context of the national treatment obligation of Article 2.1 of the *TBT Agreement* the same

87 See above, p. 396.
88 See Appellate Body Report, *US – Clove Cigarettes (2012)*, para. 193.
89 See *ibid.*, para. 224.   90 See *ibid.*, para. 225.
91 Note that the Appellate Body expressly stated that it was not saying that a Member cannot adopt measures to pursue legitimate health objectives such as curbing and preventing youth smoking. The Appellate Body stated: 'In particular, we are not saying that the United States cannot ban clove cigarettes: however, if it chooses to do so, this has to be done consistently with the TBT Agreement.' See *ibid.*, para. 236.
92 See above, pp. 396–400.

genuine relationship must exist between the technical regulation at issue and the detrimental impact on the competitive opportunities for imported products.[93]

In *US – COOL (2012)*, the Appellate Body repeated that a *de facto* detrimental impact on imports may not be inconsistent with Article 2.1 when such impact stems exclusively from a legitimate regulatory distinction. It clarified what this means by stating:

> [W]here a regulatory distinction is not designed and applied in an even-handed manner – because, for example, it is designed or applied in a manner that constitutes a means of arbitrary or unjustifiable discrimination – that distinction cannot be considered 'legitimate' and thus the detrimental impact will reflect discrimination prohibited under Article 2.1.[94]

In *US – Clove Cigarettes (2012)*, the Appellate Body already ruled that, in a case of *de facto* less favourable treatment, a panel must take into consideration 'the totality of facts and circumstances before it'.[95] In *US – COOL (2012)*, the Appellate Body added that:

> such an examination must take account of all the relevant features of the market, which may include the particular characteristics of the industry at issue, the relative market shares in a given industry, consumer preferences, and historical trade patterns.[96]

In *US – Tuna II (Mexico) (2012)*, the Appellate Body held, with regard to the measure at issue (a measure establishing the conditions for use of a 'dolphin-safe' label on tuna products) that the United States had not demonstrated that the difference in labelling conditions for tuna products containing tuna caught by setting on dolphins in the Eastern Tropical Pacific, on the one hand, and for tuna products containing tuna caught by other fishing methods outside the Eastern Tropical Pacific, on the other hand, is 'calibrated' to the risks to dolphins arising from different fishing methods in different areas of the ocean.[97] The Appellate Body was not persuaded that the United States had demonstrated that the measure at issue is 'even-handed' in the relevant aspects. According to the Appellate Body, the United States had not demonstrated that the detrimental impact of the measure at issue on Mexican tuna products stemmed exclusively from a legitimate regulatory distinction.[98]

In *US – COOL (2012)*, the Appellate Body held that informational requirements imposed on upstream producers and processors by the measure at issue (a US measure imposing a requirement on retailers selling beef and pork to label

---

93 See Appellate Body Report, *US – Tuna II (Mexico) (2012)*, footnote 457 to para. 214. See also Appellate Body Reports, *US – COOL (2012)*, para. 270.

94 Appellate Body Report, *US – COOL (2012)*, para. 271.

95 Appellate Body Report, *US – Clove Cigarettes (2012)*, para. 206.

96 Appellate Body Reports, *US – COOL (2012)*, para. 269.

97 See Appellate Body Report, *US – Tuna II (Mexico) (2012)*, para. 297.

98 See *ibid.* In isolation, these findings by the Appellate Body may be incorrectly read as suggesting that the burden was on the United States to demonstrate that the measure at issue was *not* inconsistent with Article 2.1. This is not so. The burden of proof is on the complainant, *in casu* Mexico. Mexico had, however, made a *prima facie* case that the measure at issue was inconsistent with Article 2.1, and the Appellate Body noted that the United States failed to rebut this *prima facie* case. See *ibid.*, para. 216. See also Appellate Body Report, *US – COOL (2012)*, para. 272.

those products with their country of origin) were *disproportionate* as compared to the level of information communicated to consumers through the retail labels. According to the Appellate Body, nothing in the panel's findings or on the panel record explained or supplied a rational basis for the 'disconnect' between the informational requirements imposed on upstream producers and processors and the level of information communicated to consumers. The Appellate Body, therefore, considered that the manner in which the measure at issue sought to provide information to consumers on origin was arbitrary, and that the disproportionate burden on upstream producers and processors was unjustifiable.[99]

Questions and Assignments 13.6

How should a panel establish whether or not a measure accords 'treatment no less favourable' within the meaning of Article 2.1 of the *TBT Agreement*? In this context, how relevant is the case law on the term 'treatment no less favourable' under Article III:4 of the GATT 1994? If a measure is found to accord treatment less favourable to imported products within the meaning of Article III:4 of the GATT 1994, does that same measure then also accord treatment less favourable to imported products within the meaning of Article 2.1 of the *TBT Agreement*? How can a panel establish whether the detrimental impact on the competitive opportunities of imported products stems exclusively from a legitimate regulatory distinction? Briefly discuss why the Appellate Body concluded that the measures at issue in *US – Clove Cigarettes (2012)*, *US – Tuna II (Mexico) (2012)* and *US – COOL (2012)* accorded treatment less favourable to imported products.

3.2 Obligation to Refrain from Creating Unnecessary Obstacles to International Trade

The first sentence of Article 2.2 of the *TBT Agreement* provides that, with respect to technical regulations:

Members shall ensure that technical regulations are not prepared, adopted or applied with a view to or with the effect of creating unnecessary obstacles to international trade.

With respect to standards and conformity assessment procedures, Annex 3.E and Article 5.1.2 of the *TBT Agreement* provide for the same obligation that such measures shall not be 'prepared, adopted or applied with the view to, or the effect of, creating unnecessary obstacles to trade'.[100]

The first sentence of Article 2.2 is followed by a second sentence, which reads:

For this purpose, technical regulations shall not be more trade-restrictive than necessary to fulfil a legitimate objective, taking account of the risks non-fulfilment would create.[101]

With regard to the relationship between the first and second sentences of Article 2.2, the Appellate Body observed that both the first and second sentences of Article 2.2 reflect the notion of 'necessity'. In the first sentence, this is through

---

99 See Appellate Body Reports, *US – COOL (2012)*, paras. 347–9.

100 Annex 3.E to the *TBT Agreement*. With respect to conformity assessment procedures, the implementation of this obligation is further specified in Articles 5.2.2, 5.2.3, 5.2.6 and 5.2.7 of the *TBT Agreement*.

101 For conformity assessment procedures, a similar provision is contained in Article 5.1.2, second sentence, of the *TBT Agreement*.

the reference to '*unnecessary* obstacles to international trade'; in the second sentence through the reference to 'not ... more trade restrictive than *necessary*'.[102] The Appellate Body also observed that these sentences are linked by the term '[f] or this purpose' and it found that this suggests that the second sentence qualifies the terms of the first sentence and elaborates on the scope and the meaning of the obligation contained in the first sentence.[103]

The third sentence of Article 2.2 enumerates several of the 'legitimate objectives' to which the second sentence refers. This list of legitimate objectives includes: (1) national security; (2) the prevention of deceptive practices; (3) the protection of human health and safety, animal or plant life or health; and (4) the protection of the environment.

Finally, the fourth sentence of Article 2.2 refers back to the final clause of the second sentence, namely, 'taking account of the risks non-fulfilment would create'. The fourth sentence states that, in assessing such risks, it is relevant to consider, *inter alia*: (1) available scientific information; (2) related processing technology; or (3) intended end-uses of products.

Article 2.2 sets out a three-tier test of consistency. There are three main questions which must be answered to determine whether or not a technical regulation is consistent with Article 2.2, namely:

- whether the measure at issue is '*trade-restrictive*':
- whether the measure at issue *fulfils a legitimate objective*; and
- whether the measure at issue is '*not more trade-restrictive than necessary*' to fulfil a legitimate objective, taking account of the risks non-fulfilment would create.

Below, each element of this three-tier test of consistency will be discussed in turn.

To date, no WTO Member has been found to have acted inconsistently with Article 2.2 of the *TBT Agreement*.[104]

Questions and Assignments 13.7

What are the constituent elements of the test of consistency with Article 2.2 of the *TBT Agreement*? How does the second sentence of Article 2.2 relate to the first sentence of this provision? What is the function of the third and fourth sentence of Article 2.2?

3.2.1 'Trade-Restrictive'

The first element of the test of consistency with Article 2.2 of the *TBT Agreement* relates to the question of whether the measure at issue is 'trade-restrictive'. In *US – Tuna II (Mexico) (2012)*, the Appellate Body defined 'trade-restrictive'

---

102 See Appellate Body Report, *US – Tuna II (Mexico) (2012)*, para. 318. See also Appellate Body Reports, *US – COOL (2012)*, para. 374.
103 See Appellate Body Report, *US – Tuna II (Mexico) (2012)*, para. 318.
104 The panel in *US – COOL (2012)* had found that the United States acted inconsistently with Article 2.2. The Appellate Body, however, found that the panel had erred in its interpretation and application of Article 2.2 and thus reversed the panel's finding of inconsistency, but was unable to complete the legal analysis.

to mean 'having a limiting effect on trade'.[105] It is clear that the mere fact that a measure is 'trade-restrictive' does not make that measure inconsistent with Article 2.2. In fact, the reference in the first sentence of Article 2.2 to 'unnecessary obstacles to international trade' implies that *some* trade-restrictiveness is allowed.[106] It is, however, equally clear from the text of Article 2.2 that measures that are not trade-restrictive cannot be inconsistent with Article 2.2. A measure that is *not* trade-restrictive can never be *more* trade-restrictive than necessary. In this sense, the trade-restrictiveness of the measure at issue is a threshold issue. It is unlikely that there will be many disputes in which the trade-restrictiveness *as such* of the measure at issue is contested between the parties. It is more likely that disagreement relating to the trade-restrictiveness relates to the *degree* of trade-restrictiveness. The degree of trade-restrictiveness is important in both the 'relational analysis' and the 'comparative analysis' under the third element of the test of consistency discussed below.[107]

3.2.2   Fulfilling a Legitimate Objective

The second element of the test of consistency with Article 2.2 of the *TBT Agreement* relates to the question of whether the measure at issue fulfils a legitimate objective. This question raises a number of intermediate questions, such as: (1) how to establish the objective pursued by the measure at issue; (2) which objectives are 'legitimate objectives' within the meaning of Article 2.2; (3) when a measure 'fulfil[s]' a legitimate objective; and (4) how to establish whether, and if so, to what extent, the measure at issue fulfils the legitimate objective pursued. Below, each of these intermediate questions will be addressed in turn.

With regard to the first intermediate question, namely, how to establish the objective pursued by the measure at issue, the Appellate Body ruled in *US – Tuna II (Mexico) (2012)* – in line with an earlier ruling relating to Article XIV of the GATS[108] – that a panel is *not* bound by a Member's characterisation of the objectives it pursues through the measure. While a panel may well take a Member's characterisation of the objectives as a starting point, it must independently and objectively assess the objective or objectives pursued. In doing so, a panel may take into account the text of statutes, the legislative history and other evidence regarding the structure and operation of the measure.[109]

With regard to the second intermediate question, namely, which objectives are 'legitimate objectives' within the meaning of Article 2.2, the Appellate Body observed in *US – Tuna II (Mexico) (2012)* that the dictionary meaning of the term

---

105 See Appellate Body Report, *US – Tuna II (Mexico) (2012)*, para. 319.
106 See *ibid.* What is prohibited under Article 2.2 are restrictions on international trade which exceed what is necessary to fulfil a legitimate objective. See below, pp. 876–7.
107 See below, pp. 876–8.   108 See above, pp. 585–90.
109 See Appellate Body Report, *US – Tuna II (Mexico) (2012)*, para. 314. See also Appellate Body Reports, *US – COOL (2012)*, para. 395.

'legitimate objective' is an aim or target that is lawful, justifiable or proper.[110] As already noted above, the third sentence of Article 2.2 lists specific examples of such 'legitimate objectives', namely: (1) national security; (2) the prevention of deceptive practices; (3) the protection of human health and safety, animal or plant life or health; and (4) the protection of the environment.[111] However, as indicated by the words '*inter alia*' at the beginning of the list, this is *not* an exhaustive list of legitimate policy objectives.[112] It is an open question which other policy objectives may be considered to be legitimate within the meaning of Article 2.2 of the *TBT Agreement*. Are animal welfare or fair labour practices '*legitimate* objectives' within the meaning of Article 2.2? As the Appellate Body stated in *US – Tuna II (Mexico) (2012)*, the objectives expressly listed provide an illustration and reference point for other objectives that may be considered 'legitimate'.[113] Also, the objectives recognised in the sixth and seventh recitals of the Preamble to the *TBT Agreement* as well as objectives reflected in the provisions of other WTO agreements may provide guidance for, or may inform, the analysis of what might be considered to be a legitimate objective under Article 2.2.[114] In *US – COOL (2012)*, the Appellate Body considered the provision of information to consumers on origin to be a 'legitimate objective'. The Appellate Body reasoned that this objective bears some relationship to the objective of the prevention of deceptive practices reflected in both Article 2.2 itself and Article XX(d) of the GATT 1994, and that the objective of providing information to consumers on origin is also found in Article IX of the GATT 1994.[115] Whether objectives not reflected in the WTO agreements may nevertheless be 'legitimate objectives' for the purpose of Article 2.2 is a question which is likely to give rise to some debate. It is, however, important to note in this regard that it is for the complainant to prove that an objective is *not* legitimate within the meaning of Article 2.2. The respondent does not have to prove that an objective is legitimate.[116]

With regard to the third intermediate question, namely, when does a measure 'fulfil' a legitimate objective, or, in other words, what does 'fulfil' mean in this context, the Appellate Body observed in *US – Tuna II (Mexico) (2012)* that the word 'fulfil' is defined in the dictionary as 'provide *fully* with what is wished for'.[117] The Appellate Body recognised that, read in isolation, the word 'fulfil' appears to describe complete achievement of something. However, the Appellate Body considered that, in Article 2.2, the word 'fulfil' is used in the phrase 'to fulfil a legitimate objective', and that it is inherent in the notion of an 'objective'

---

110 See Appellate Body Report, *US – Tuna II (Mexico) (2012)*, para. 313.   111 See above, p. 873.

112 Recall that the list of legitimate policy objectives of Article XX of the GATT 1994 is an *exhaustive* list. See above, p. 545.

113 See Appellate Body Report, *US – Tuna II (Mexico) (2012)*, para. 313. See also Appellate Body Reports, *US – COOL (2012)*, para. 444.

114 See Appellate Body Report, *US – Tuna II (Mexico) (2012)*, para. 313.

115 See Appellate Body Reports, *US – COOL (2012)*, para. 445.

116 See *ibid.*, para. 449.

117 Appellate Body Report, *US – Tuna II (Mexico) (2012)*, para. 315. Emphasis added.

that it may be pursued and achieved to a greater or lesser degree.[118] The Appellate Body thus ruled that:

we consider that the question of whether a technical regulation 'fulfils' an objective is concerned with the *degree of contribution* that the technical regulation makes toward the achievement of the legitimate objective.[119]

That degree of contribution toward the achievement of the legitimate objective is of significant importance in both the 'relational analysis' and the 'comparative analysis' under the third element of the test of consistency discussed below.[120]

With regard to the fourth and last intermediate question, namely, how to establish whether, and, if so, to what extent, the measure at issue fulfils the legitimate objective pursued, the Appellate Body noted in *US – Tuna II (Mexico) (2012)* that the degree of fulfilment of the objective pursued, i.e. the degree of contribution towards the achievement of the objective, may be discerned from the design, structure and operation of the technical regulation, *as well as* from evidence relating to the application of the measure.[121] As in the context of Article XX of the GATT 1994 and Article XIV of the GATS,[122] a panel must also in the context of Article 2.2 of the *TBT Agreement* assess the contribution to the legitimate objective *actually achieved* by the measure at issue, not the contribution that is intended to be achieved.[123]

Questions and Assignments 13.8

Is the protection of cultural identity a 'legitimate objective' within the meaning of Article 2.2 of the *TBT Agreement*? What does the word 'fulfil' mean in the context of Article 2.2? Is the level of achievement of the legitimate objective which a Member considers appropriate relevant in the context of Article 2.2?

3.2.3 'Not More Trade-Restrictive than Necessary'

The third and last element of the test of consistency with Article 2.2 of the *TBT Agreement* relates to the question of whether the measure at issue is '*not more trade-restrictive than necessary*' to fulfil a legitimate objective, taking account of the risks non-fulfilment would create. As discussed in Chapter 8 of this book, in the context of Article XX of the GATT 1994 and Article XIV of the GATS, it is the measure at issue, which is assessed for 'necessity'.[124] As is clear from

---

118   See *ibid.* Note that the panel in *US – COOL (2012)* wrongly considered it necessary for the measure at issue to have 'fulfilled' the objective completely (or at least to have satisfied some minimum level of fulfilment) to be consistent with Article 2.2.

119   Appellate Body Report, *US – Tuna II (Mexico) (2012)*, para. 315. Emphasis added.

120   See below, p. 877.

121   See Appellate Body Report, *US – Tuna II (Mexico) (2012)*, para. 317.

122   See above, p. 874.

123   See Appellate Body Report, *US – Tuna II (Mexico) (2012)*, para. 317. See also Appellate Body Reports, *US – COOL (2012)*, paras. 373 and 390.

124   See e.g. Panel Report, *China – Audiovisual Products (2010)*, para. 7.789, referring to Appellate Body Report, *US – Gasoline (1996)*, 20, see above below, p. 921.

the text of Article 2.2, in the context of this provision, it is not the measure but the *trade-restrictiveness* of the measure, which is assessed for 'necessity'.[125] In *US – Tuna II (Mexico) (2012)*, the Appellate Body found that in the assessment of whether a technical regulation is 'not more trade-restrictive than necessary' within the meaning of Article 2.2 of the *TBT Agreement*:

a panel should begin by considering factors that include: (i) the degree of contribution made by the measure to the legitimate objective at issue; (ii) the trade-restrictiveness of the measure; and (iii) the nature of the risks at issue and the gravity of consequences that would arise from non-fulfilment of the objective(s) pursued by the Member through the measure.[126]

The Appellate Body referred to this analysis as a 'relational analysis' of the factors referred to above.[127] The Appellate Body immediately added, however, that, *in most cases*:

a comparison of the challenged measure and possible alternative measures should be undertaken.[128]

In other words, in addition to a 'relational analysis', *in most cases* also a 'comparative analysis' should be undertaken to establish whether a technical regulation is 'more trade-restrictive than necessary'.[129] In the context of such 'comparative analysis', it may be relevant to consider in particular: (1) whether the proposed alternative measure is less trade-restrictive; (2) whether it would make an equivalent contribution to the relevant legitimate objective, taking account of the risks non-fulfilment would create; and (3) whether it is reasonably available.[130] As the Appellate Body noted in a footnote, the 'comparative' analysis is similar to the 'weighing and balancing' to establish 'necessity' in the context of Article XX of the GATT 1994 and Article XIV of the GATS, discussed in Chapter 8 of this book.[131]

   With respect to the requirement to consider 'the risks non-fulfilment would create', the Appellate Body explained in *US – Tuna II (Mexico) (2012)* that the comparison of the measure at issue with a possible alternative measure should be made:

in the light of the nature of the risks at issue and the gravity of the consequences that would arise from non-fulfilment of the legitimate objective.[132]

It is clear that, for example, the risks non-fulfilment of the objective of preventing deceptive practices create are less grave than the risks non-fulfilment of the

---

125 See Appellate Body Report, *US – Tuna II (Mexico) (2012)*, para. 319.
126 *Ibid.*, para. 322.   127 See *ibid.*, para. 318.
128 *Ibid.*, para. 322. The Appellate Body identified two instances where a comparison of the challenged measure and possible alternative measures may not be required, namely: (1) when the measure at issue is not trade-restrictive; and (2) when the measure makes *no* contribution to the achievement of the legitimate objective. See *ibid.*, footnote 647 to para. 322.
129 *Ibid.*, para. 320.   130 See *ibid.*, para. 322.
131 See *ibid.*, footnote 645 to para. 320. For the discussion of 'weighing and balancing' to establish 'necessity' in the context of Article XX of the GATT 1994 and Article XIV of the GATS, see above, pp. 556–65 and 585–8.
132 Appellate Body Report, *US – Tuna II (Mexico) (2012)*, para. 321. As the Appellate Body noted, this suggests a 'further element of weighing and balancing' in the analysis of Article 2.2.

objective of protecting human health create. As mentioned above, the fourth sentence of Article 2.2 states that, in assessing the risks non-fulfilment would create, it is relevant to consider, *inter alia*: (1) available scientific information; (2) related processing technology; or (3) intended end-uses of products.[133]

A technical regulation, which is found to be not more trade-restrictive than necessary within the meaning of Article 2.2, will not necessarily remain so in the future. Article 2.3 of the *TBT Agreement* provides that:

> Technical regulations shall not be maintained if the circumstances or objectives giving rise to their adoption no longer exist or if the changed circumstances or objectives can be addressed in a less trade-restrictive manner.

WTO Members must therefore continually assess whether their technical regulations are not more trade-restrictive than necessary.[134]

Questions and Assignments 13.9

How should a panel assess whether the measure at issue is or is not 'more trade-restrictive than necessary' to fulfil the legitimate objective pursued? Explain the difference between the 'relational analysis' and the 'comparative analysis'. When will a 'comparative analysis' not be called for? Is the case law on the assessment of 'necessity' under Article XX of the GATT 1994 and Article XIV of the GATS of relevance in the context of an assessment of 'necessity' under Article 2.2 of the *TBT Agreement*?

3.3   Obligation to Base Technical Barriers to Trade on International Standards

The harmonisation of national technical regulations, standards and conformity assessment procedures around international standards greatly facilitates the conduct of international trade. Harmonisation around international standards diminishes the trade-restrictive effect of technical barriers to trade by minimising the variety of requirements that exporters have to meet in their different export markets.

Thus, the *TBT Agreement* requires Members to base their technical regulations, standards and conformity assessment procedures on international standards. Article 2.4 of the *TBT Agreement* provides in relevant part:

> Where technical regulations are required and relevant international standards exist or their completion is imminent, Members shall use them, or the relevant parts of them, as a basis for their technical regulations.

However, Article 2.4 further provides that Members do not have to use international standards as a basis when:

> such international standards or relevant parts would be an ineffective or inappropriate means for the fulfilment of the legitimate objectives pursued, for instance because of fundamental climatic or geographical factors or fundamental technological problems.

---

133 See above, p. 873.
134 With regard to conformity assessment procedures, see Article 5.2.7 of the *TBT Agreement*.

With respect to standards and conformity assessment procedures, Annex 3.F and Article 5.4 of the *TBT Agreement* respectively provide for the same or a similar obligation that such measures shall use international standards or international guides or recommendations as a basis.

Article 2.4 of the *TBT Agreement* sets out a three-tier test of consistency. There are three main questions, which must be answered to determine whether or not a technical regulation is consistent with Article 2.4, namely:

- whether there exists a *relevant international standard*:
- whether the relevant international standard is '*used as a basis*' for the technical regulation at issue; and
- whether the relevant international standard is an *effective and appropriate* means for the fulfilment of the legitimate objectives pursued.

Below, each element of this three-tier test of consistency will be discussed in turn. To date, WTO Members have been found to have acted inconsistently with Article 2.4 of the *TBT Agreement* in one dispute.[135]

3.3.1 Relevant international standard

The first element of the test of consistency with Article 2.4 of the *TBT Agreement* relates to the question of whether there exists a 'relevant international standard' or its completion is imminent. This question raises a number of intermediate questions, such as: (1) When is a standard an 'international' standard? (2) What is an international standardising body? (3) When is an international standard a 'relevant' international standard? (4) How must an international standard be adopted? Below, each of these intermediate questions will be addressed in turn.

With regard to the first intermediate question, namely, *when is a standard an 'international' standard*, the Appellate Body found in *US – Tuna II (Mexico) (2012)* that it is primarily the characteristics of the entity approving a standard that makes a standard an 'international' standard.[136] The subject-matter of a standard is not material to the determination of whether a standard is 'international'. A standard is an international standard if it is approved by an international standardising body.[137]

This brings us to the second intermediate question, namely, *what is an 'international standardising body'*. First, note that a 'body' is a broader concept than an 'organisation'. As the Appellate Body found in *US – Tuna II (Mexico) (2012)*, a 'body' is a 'legal or administrative entity that has specific tasks and composition', whereas an 'organisation' is a 'body that is based on the membership of other bodies or individuals and has an established constitution and its own administration'.[138] It follows that international standardising bodies

135 See *EC – Sardines (2002)*.
136 See *Appellate Body Report, US – Tuna II (Mexico) (2012)*, para. 353.
137 See *ibid.*, para. 356.   138 Appellate Body Report, *US – Tuna II (Mexico) (2012)*, para. 355.

may be, but need not necessarily be, international organisations.[139] Secondly, pursuant to a TBT Committee decision of November 2000, for a standardising body to be an 'international standardising body' within the meaning of Article 2.4, its membership 'should be open on a non-discriminatory basis to relevant bodies of at least all WTO Members'.[140] In *US – Tuna II (Mexico) (2012)*, the Appellate Body ruled that provisions for accession that *de jure* or *de facto* disadvantage some WTO Members or their relevant bodies as compared to other Members or their bodies 'would tend to indicate that a body is not an "international" standardising body'.[141] The Appellate Body further held that it is not sufficient for the body to be open, or have been open, at a particular point in time; the body must be 'open at every stage of standards development'.[142] As to the question whether a body is 'open' if WTO Members, or their relevant bodies, can only accede pursuant to an invitation, the Appellate Body replied that such a body could be considered 'open' if the invitation 'occurred automatically once a Member or its relevant body has expressed interest in joining' the body concerned.[143]

For an international body to be an 'international standardising body', such body must have 'recognized activities in standardization'. According to the Appellate Body in *US – Tuna II (Mexico) (2012)*, 'evidence of recognition by WTO Members as well as evidence of recognition by national standardizing bodies would be relevant' in this respect.[144] Moreover, the Appellate Body found that, for an international body to be an 'international standardising body', such body does not need to be, or have been, involved in the development of more than one standard.[145] Also, an 'international standardising body' does not need to have 'standardisation as its principal function'.[146] However, at a minimum, WTO Members must be aware, or have reason to expect, that the international body is engaged in standardising activities.[147]

With regard to the third intermediate question, namely, *when is an international standard a 'relevant' international standard*, the panel in *EC – Sardines (2002)* found that the international standard 'Codex Stan 94', developed by an international food-standard-setting body, the Codex Alimentarius Commission, and the EC's technical regulation at issue both covered the same product (*Sardina pilchardus*). They both also included similar types of requirements as regards this product, such as those relating to labelling, presentation and

---

139 See *ibid.*, para. 356.
140 TBT Committee Decision on *Principles for the Development of International Standards, Guides and Recommendations with Relation to Articles 2, 5, and Annex 3 to the Agreement*, in WTO document G/TBT/1/Rev.10, dated 9 June 2011, pp. 46–8, para. 6.
141 See Appellate Body Report, *US – Tuna II (Mexico) (2012)*, para. 375.
142 See *ibid.*, para. 374.   143 *Ibid.*, para. 386.
144 *Ibid.*, para. 363. Also, to the extent that a standardising body complies with the principles and procedures of the TBT Decision of November 2000, referred to above in footnote 140, it would be easier to find that the body has 'recognized activities in standardization'. See *ibid.*, para. 376.
145 See *ibid.*, para. 360.   146 *Ibid.*, para. 362.   147 See *ibid.*

packing medium. The panel, therefore, concluded that the Codex Stan 94 was a *relevant* international standard for the EC's technical regulation at issue.[148]

With regard to the fourth and last intermediate question, namely, *how must an international standard be adopted*, the Appellate Body ruled in *EC – Sardines (2002)* that it is not required that an international standard within the meaning of Article 2.4 is adopted *by consensus* in the relevant international standardising body.[149] Note, however, that the Appellate Body stated in *US – Tuna II (Mexico) (2012)*:

> Since the United States' appeal is limited to the characteristics of the entity approving an 'international' standard, we do not need to address in this appeal the question of whether in order to constitute an 'international standard', a standard must also be 'based on consensus'.[150]

3.3.2 'Used as a Basis'

The second element of the test of consistency with Article 2.4 of the *TBT Agreement* relates to the question of whether the relevant international standard is *'used as a basis'* for the technical regulation at issue. In line with the case law on the meaning of the term 'based on' in Article 3.2 of the *SPS Agreement*, discussed in Chapter 14 of this book,[151] the panel in *EC – Sardines (2002)* concluded that the requirement to 'use as a basis' imposes the obligation to 'employ or apply' the international standard as 'the principal constituent or fundamental principle for the purpose of enacting the technical regulation'.[152] According to the Appellate Body in *EC – Sardines (2002)*, this comes down to an analysis of 'whether there is a contradiction between Codex Stan 94 and the EC regulation'.[153]

3.3.3 Ineffective or inappropriate means

The third and last element of the test of consistency with Article 2.4 of the *TBT Agreement* relates to the question of whether the relevant international standard is an *'ineffective or inappropriate means'* for the fulfilment of the legitimate objectives pursued. As indicated above, the relevant international standard must not be used as a basis for the technical regulation at issue *when* that standard constitutes an inappropriate or ineffective means to achieve the legitimate

---

148 See Panel Report, *EC – Sardines (2002)*, paras. 7.69–7.70. The finding was upheld by the Appellate Body. See Appellate Body Report, *EC – Sardines (2002)*, para. 233.

149 See Appellate Body Report, *EC – Sardines (2002)*, paras. 222–3. The Appellate Body came to this conclusion because the Explanatory Note to Annex 1.2 to the *TBT Agreement* states that the *TBT Agreement* covers also documents that are *not* based on consensus. See, however, paras. 8 and 9 of the TBT Committee Decision of November 2000, referred to above in footnote 140.

150 Appellate Body Report, *US – Tuna II (Mexico) (2012)*, para. 353.

151 See below, pp. 910–13 (912 in particular).

152 Panel Report, *EC – Sardines (2002)*, para. 7.110. On the meaning of 'based on' in the *SPS Agreement*, see below, pp. 911–12 and 919–20.

153 Appellate Body Report, *EC – Sardines (2002)*, para. 249. The Appellate Body thus concluded in *EC – Sardines (2002)* that the EC technical regulation at issue was not based on Codex Stan 94 because the former contradicted the latter.

objective pursued. The question to be answered here raises a number of intermediate questions, such as: (1) whether a legitimate objective is pursued; (2) how
to assess the ineffectiveness and inappropriateness of the international standard; and (3) who has the burden of proof with regard to the ineffectiveness or
inappropriateness of the relevant international standard. Below, each of these
intermediate questions will be addressed in turn.

With regard to the first intermediate question, namely, *whether a legitimate
objective is pursued*, please refer to the discussion in the context of Article 2.2 of
the *TBT Agreement* on the determination of the objective(s) pursued by a technical regulation, and on the concept of 'legitimate objective'.[154]

With regard to the second intermediate question, namely, *how to assess the
ineffectiveness and inappropriateness of the international standard*, the panel
observed in *EC – Sardines (2002)* that the difference between effectiveness and
appropriateness is that:

[t]he question of effectiveness bears upon the *results* of the means employed, whereas the
question of appropriateness relates more to the *nature* of the means employed.[155]

In other words, the international standard is *effective* if it has the capacity to
accomplish the objective(s) pursued, and it is *appropriate* if it is suitable for the
fulfilment thereof.[156] Note that the panel in *US – COOL (2012)* found that Codex
Stan 1-1985 did not have the capacity of accomplishing the objective of providing information about the countries in which an animal was born, raised and
slaughtered, because this international standard conferred origin exclusively on
the country of slaughter or another substantial transformation (such as processing). The panel concluded that Codex Stan 1-1985 was neither an effective nor
an appropriate means to fulfil the legitimate objective of the technical regulation
at issue.[157] Recall that Article 2.4 itself states that an international standard may
be ineffective or inappropriate because of 'fundamental climatic or geographical
factors or fundamental technological problems.' Note in this respect also Article
12.2 of the *TBT Agreement*, which provides for relevant special and differential
treatment for developing-country Members, and which is discussed below.[158]

With regard to the third and last intermediate question, namely, who has the
burden of proof with regard to the ineffectiveness or inappropriateness of the
relevant international standard, the Appellate Body in *EC – Sardines (2002)*
ruled that it is for the complainant to demonstrate that the international standard in question is both an effective and an appropriate means to fulfil the legitimate objective.[159]

---

154 See above, p. 874.   155 Panel Report, *EC – Sardines (2002)*, para. 7.116.
156 See Appellate Body Report, *EC – Sardines (2002)*, para. 288.
157 See Panel Reports, *US – COOL (2012)*, para. 7.735.   158 See below, p. 886.
159 See Appellate Body Report, *EC – Sardines (2002)*, paras. 274–5 and 287. Given the conceptual similarities
between Articles 3.1 and 3.3 of the *SPS Agreement*, and Article 2.4 of the *TBT Agreement*, the Appellate Body held that its findings in *EC – Hormones (1998)* regarding the burden of proof under the former

Finally, note that – as provided for in Article 2.5 of the *TBT Agreement* – a technical regulation which is adopted with a view to achieving a legitimate objective explicitly enumerated in Article 2.2 and is in accordance with a relevant international standard, shall be *presumed* not to create an unnecessary obstacle to trade. Such technical regulation shall thus be presumed to be consistent with Article 2.2.[160]

Questions and Assignments 13.10

Do WTO Members have to use relevant international standards as a basis for their technical regulations? If so, when is this requirement satisfied? What is an 'international' standard and when is it 'relevant' within the meaning of Article 2.4 of the *TBT Agreement*? Under what circumstances may Members adopt or maintain a technical regulation that is not based on an existing international standard? Is it for the complainant to prove that the international standard is 'effective' and 'appropriate', or for the respondent to show that the international standard is 'ineffective' or 'inappropriate'? In your opinion, is the harmonisation of national technical regulations and national standards around international standards a useful exercise?

3.4   Other Substantive Provisions

Apart from the substantive provisions discussed in the previous sub-sections, the *TBT Agreement* also contains a number of other substantive provisions, which deserve to be mentioned. This sub-section briefly examines the substantive provisions of the *TBT Agreement* relating to: (1) equivalence and mutual recognition; (2) product requirements in terms of performance; (3) transparency and notification; and (4) special and differential treatment for developing-country Members.

3.4.1   Equivalence and Mutual Recognition

Article 2.7 of the *TBT Agreement* provides:

Members shall give positive consideration to accepting as equivalent technical regulations of other Members, even if these regulations differ from their own, provided they are satisfied that these regulations adequately fulfil the objectives of their own regulations.

The *TBT Agreement* thus requires WTO Members to *consider* accepting, as equivalent, the technical regulations of other Members. However, they must do so only if the foreign technical regulations *adequately* fulfil the legitimate objectives pursued by their own technical regulations.

With regard to conformity assessment procedures, Article 6.1 of the *TBT Agreement* requires Members to ensure, whenever possible, that results of such

---

provisions were 'equally apposite' for the case at hand. It accordingly found that, 'as with Articles 3.1 and 3.3 of the SPS Agreement, there is no "general rule–exception" relationship between the first and the second parts of Article 2.4'. See *ibid.*, paras. 274–5.

160   See above, pp. 872–8.

procedures by other Members, are accepted even if their conformity assessment procedures differ, as long as they provide an assurance of conformity with the domestic technical regulations or standards.

3.4.2 Product Requirements in Terms of Performance

With respect to technical regulations, Article 2.8 of the *TBT Agreement* provides:

Wherever appropriate, Members shall specify technical regulations based on product requirements in terms of performance rather than design or descriptive characteristics.

The *TBT Agreement* thus prefers Members to adopt technical regulations on the basis of product requirements in terms of performance. With regard to standards, Annex 3.I of the *TBT Agreement* provides for the same preference for standards based on product requirements in terms of performance. Performance-based requirements are typically less prescriptive than requirements based on product characteristics. Note, however, that the obligation of Article 2.8 applies only when 'appropriate'.

3.4.3 Transparency and Notification

When no relevant international standard exists or when a proposed technical regulation is not in accordance with a relevant international standard and the proposed technical regulation may have a significant effect on trade of other Members, Article 2.9 of the *TBT Agreement* imposes on WTO Members detailed transparency and notification requirements. Members are, *inter alia*, required to notify other Members through the WTO Secretariat of the proposed technical regulation.[161] Such notification must be done at an early stage of the process, when amendments to the proposed technical regulation can still be made and comments can be taken into account.

When a technical regulation is adopted to address an *urgent* problem of safety, health, environmental protection or national security, a Member may set aside the notification (and consultation) requirements set out in Article 2.9 of the *TBT Agreement*. However, in such instances, Members are subject to certain notification (and consultation) obligations *after* the adoption of the technical regulation.[162]

Article 2.11 of the *TBT Agreement* requires that all adopted technical regulations are published promptly or otherwise made available in such a manner as to enable interested parties in other Members to become acquainted with them. Except when a technical regulation addresses an *urgent* problem, technical regulations may not enter into force immediately after publication. Article 2.12 of the *TBT Agreement* provides in relevant part:

Members shall allow a reasonable interval between the publication of technical regulations and their entry into force in order to allow time for producers in exporting Members

161 Article 2.9.2 of the *TBT Agreement*.   162 See Article 2.10 of the *TBT Agreement*.

to adapt their products or methods of production to the requirements of the importing Member.

Such a reasonable interval between the publication and the entry into force of a technical regulation is particularly important for producers in exporting developing-country Members. This interest is reflected in paragraph 5.2 of the Doha Ministerial Decision on *Implementation-Related Issues and Concerns* of 14 November 2001, which provides:

> Subject to the conditions specified in paragraph 12 of Article 2 of the Agreement on Technical Barriers to Trade, the phrase 'reasonable interval' shall be understood to mean normally a period of not less than 6 months, except when this would be ineffective in fulfilling the legitimate objectives pursued.[163]

In *US – Clove Cigarettes (2012)*, the Appellate Body ruled that Article 2.12 of the *TBT Agreement*, as clarified by paragraph 5.2 of the Doha Ministerial Decision, imposes an obligation on importing Members to provide a 'reasonable interval' of not less than six months between the publication and entry into force of a technical regulation. However, an importing Member may depart from this obligation if this interval 'would be ineffective to fulfil the legitimate objectives pursued' by the technical regulation.[164] In *US – Clove Cigarettes (2012)*, the interval between the publication of the technical regulation at issue and its entry into force was three months. The Appellate Body found that Indonesia, the complainant, had made a *prima facie* case of inconsistency by establishing that there was no interval of at least six months between the publication and the entry into force of the technical regulation at issue;[165] and that the United States, the respondent, failed to rebut this *prima facie* case of inconsistency, since it did not show that allowing a period of not less than six months would have been ineffective to fulfil the legitimate objective of the technical regulation at issue.[166] The Appellate Body thus concluded that the United States had acted inconsistently with Article 2.12 of the *TBT Agreement*.[167]

The *TBT Agreement* contains similar transparency and notification provisions with regard to standards and conformity assessment procedures.[168] As an additional requirement for standards, the Code of Good Practice of the *TBT Agreement* requires standardising bodies to publish, at least every six months, their work programme and report on the progress regarding the preparation and adoption of standards.[169]

Furthermore, Article 10 of the *TBT Agreement* requires each Member to establish an enquiry point which will answer inquiries of other Members and which

---

163 Ministerial Conference, Decision of 14 November 2001 on *Implementation-Related Issues and Concerns*, WT/MIN(01)/17, dated 20 November 2001, para. 5.2. On the legal status of this decision, see above, p. 189.
164 See Appellate Body Report, *US – Clove Cigarettes (2012)*, para. 275.
165 See *ibid.*, para. 291.   166 See *ibid.*, para. 295.   167 See *ibid.*, para. 297.
168 See Annex 3.L, M, N and O to the *TBT Agreement* (for standards) and Articles 5.6, 5.7, 5.8 and 5.9 of the *TBT Agreement* (for conformity assessment procedures).
169 See Annex 3.J to the *TBT Agreement*.

will provide relevant documentation related to adopted technical regulations, standards and conformity assessment procedures.[170]

The WTO Secretariat maintains a publicly available database of all information provided by WTO Members in relation to technical regulations, standards and conformity assessment procedures. This database, the *Technical Barriers to Trade Information Management System* (TBT IMS), greatly enhances the implementation of the transparency provisions of the *TBT Agreement*.[171] As of 6 October 2012, this database contained over 15,600 notifications relating to technical barriers to trade.

3.4.4 Special and Differential Treatment

The *TBT Agreement* explicitly recognises the difficulties that developing-country Members may face in implementing their obligations under the *TBT Agreement*. Therefore, Members shall, pursuant to Article 12.1 of the *TBT Agreement*, 'provide differential and more favourable treatment' to developing-country Members, and shall, pursuant to Articles 12.2 and 12.3, 'take into account [their] special development, financial and trade needs' in the implementation of the *TBT Agreement* as well as in the preparation and application of technical regulations, standards and conformity assessment procedures. In accordance with Article 12.8 of the *TBT Agreement*, the TBT Committee may grant, upon request, time-limited exceptions, in whole or in part, from obligations under the *TBT Agreement*. In addition, pursuant to Article 12.4 of the *TBT Agreement*, developing-country Members do not have to base their technical regulations, standards or conformity assessment procedures on international standards, if the international standards are not appropriate to their development or financial and trade needs. Finally, Article 12.6 of the *TBT Agreement* requires that Members shall take 'such reasonable measures as available to them' to ensure that the international standardising bodies, upon the request of developing-country Members, examine the possibility of developing international standards concerning products of special interest to developing-country Members.

In *US – Clove Cigarettes (2012)* and *US – COOL (2012)*, the developing-country complainants, Indonesia and Mexico respectively, argued that the respondent, the United States, had acted inconsistently with its obligation under Article 12.3 of the *TBT Agreement* by failing to take into account the complainant's special development, financial and trade needs when preparing and applying the measures at issue. With respect to the obligation set out in Article 12.3, both panels referred to, and agreed with, the findings of the panel in *EC – Approval and Marketing of Biotech Products (2006)*, which concerned a very

---

170 A full list of national enquiry points is contained in Committee on Technical Barriers to Trade, *Note by the Secretariat on National Enquiry Points*, G/TBT/ENQ/38/Rev.1, dated 8 July 2011.

171 See http://tbtims.wto.org.

similar provision in the *SPS Agreement*, namely, Article 10.1 thereof.[172] The panel in *US – COOL (2012)* noted:

[W]e do not consider that the United States had an explicit obligation, enforceable in WTO dispute settlement, to reach out and collect Mexico's views during the preparation and application of the COOL measure. The United States is merely required under Article 12.3 to 'take account of [Mexico's] special development, financial and trade needs' 'in the preparation and application of [the COOL measure]'. This means giving active and meaningful consideration to such needs.[173]

According to the panel, Mexico had not demonstrated that the United States failed to do this.[174] The panel in *US – Clove Cigarettes (2012)* came to the same conclusion with regard to Indonesia's claim.[175] These findings by the panels in *US – Clove Cigarettes (2012)* and *US – COOL (2012)* illustrate well the limited 'value' which at least some of the special and differential treatment provisions of Article 12 of the *TBT Agreement* have for developing-country Members.

Questions and Assignments 13.11

Under what circumstances are Members *obliged* to consider other Members' technical regulations as equivalent? Should technical regulations be based on product requirements in terms of performance rather than design or descriptive characteristics? If so, why? When and how are Members required to notify their proposed technical regulations or conformity assessment procedures? In what ways does the *TBT Agreement* provide for special and differential treatment of developing-country Members?

4   INSTITUTIONAL AND PROCEDURAL PROVISIONS OF THE *TBT AGREEMENT*

In addition to the substantive provisions discussed above, the *TBT Agreement* also contains a number of institutional and procedural provisions. This section deals briefly with the provisions on: (1) the TBT Committee; (2) dispute settlement; and (3) technical assistance to developing-country Members.

4.1   TBT Committee

The *TBT Agreement* establishes a Committee on Technical Barriers to Trade, commonly referred to as the 'TBT Committee'.[176] This Committee is composed of representatives of all WTO Members and meets when necessary.[177] In 2012, the TBT Committee held two regular meetings.[178] The function of the TBT Committee

---

172 See below, pp. 939–40.   173 Panel Reports, *US – COOL (2012)*, para. 7.790.
174 See *ibid.*, paras. 7.791–7.799.
175 See Panel Report, *US – Clove Cigarettes*, paras. 7.634–7.648.
176 See Article 13.1 of the *TBT Agreement*.
177 Pursuant to Article 13.1 of the *TBT Agreement*, the TBT Committee has to meet *at least* once a year.
178 See Committee on Technical Barriers to Trade, *Report (2012)*, G/L/1017, dated 30 November 2012.

is to provide Members with a forum for consultations regarding any matters pertaining to the operation or objectives of the *TBT Agreement*. In particular, the TBT Committee has functioned as a forum to discuss so-called 'specific trade concerns' with regard to proposed draft measures notified to the TBT Committee or the implementation of existing measures. At the TBT Committee meeting of 10 and 11 November 2011, for example, Members discussed thirteen new and forty-three previously raised specific trade concerns.[179] The new specific trade concerns discussed at this meeting included, for example: (1) the Draft Decree Amending Provisions for Drinks with Caffeine (draft measure of Mexico; concern raised by the EU); (2) a ruling of the European Court of Justice with respect to honey containing pollen from genetically modified maize (measure of the European Union; concern raised by Argentina); and (3) Technical Guidelines for the Implementation of the Adoption and Supervision of Indonesian National Standards for Obligatory Toy Safety (measure of Indonesia; concern raised by the United States).[180] The WTO Secretariat compiles information about the status of specific trade concerns raised by Members in the TBT Committee.[181]

The TBT Committee also undertakes an annual review of the implementation and operation of the *TBT Agreement* (annual review).[182] Moreover, at the end of every three-year period, the TBT Committee undertakes an in-depth review of the operation of the Agreement (triennial review), at which time it may recommend amendments to the *TBT Agreement* if this is considered necessary 'to ensure mutual economic advantage and balance of rights and obligations'.[183]

While not as 'productive' as the SPS Committee, discussed in Chapter 14 of this book, the TBT Committee has adopted a number of decisions and recommendations. These decisions and recommendations include, for example, the 2000 Decision on *Principles for the Development of International Standards, Guides and Recommendations with relation to Articles 2, 5 and Annex 3 of the Agreement*.[184] As discussed above, the Appellate Body ruled in *US – Tuna II (Mexico) (2012)* with regard to this TBT Committee Decision that:

[it] can be considered as a 'subsequent agreement' within the meaning of Article 31(3)(a) of the *Vienna Convention*. The extent to which this Decision will inform the interpretation and application of a term or provision of the *TBT Agreement* in a specific case, however, will depend on the degree to which it 'bears specifically' on the interpretation and application of the respective term or provision. [185]

---

179 See Committee on Technical Barriers to Trade, *Minutes of the Meeting of 10–11 November 2011*, G/TBT/M/55, dated 9 February 2012, 2-60.

180 See *ibid.*, 2–14.

181 The G/TBT/GEN/74/ – series of documents contain an overview of the specific trade concerns raised since 1995. Alternatively, one can consult the Technical Barriers to Trade Information Management System (TBT IMS): see http://tbtims.wto.org.

182 See Article 15.3 of the *TBT Agreement*.   183 See Article 15.4 of the *TBT Agreement*.

184 See G/TBT/9, 13 November 2000, para. 20 and Annex 4. The most recent compilation of the decisions and recommendations adopted by the TBT Committee can be found in G/TBT/1/Rev.10, dated 9 June 2011.

185 Appellate Body Report, *US – Tuna II (Mexico) (2012)*, para. 372. See also above, p. 54.

4.2   Dispute Settlement

Consultations and the settlement of disputes with respect to any matter affecting the operation of the *TBT Agreement* shall follow the provisions of Articles XXII and XXIII of the GATT 1994 as elaborated on and applied by the DSU.[186] The *TBT Agreement* contains a few 'special or additional rules and procedures' set out in Articles 14.2, 14.3, 14.4 of and Annex 2 to the *TBT Agreement*.[187] Pursuant to Article 14.2 of the *TBT Agreement*, a panel, charged with the settlement of a dispute under the *TBT Agreement*, may establish, at the request of one of the parties to the dispute or at its own initiative, a *technical expert group* to assist the panel in questions of a technical nature.[188] Note, however, that, in *EC – Asbestos (2001)*, the panel decided to consult experts on an individual basis, rather than establishing a technical expert group.[189]

As mentioned above, not only central government bodies but also local government and non-governmental entities may adopt and apply technical regulations, standards and conformity assessment procedures. Articles 3, 4, 7, 8 and 9 of the *TBT Agreement* impose certain obligations on Members with regard to the conduct of these local government and non-governmental entities.[190] Article 14.4 of the *TBT Agreement* provides:

> The dispute settlement provisions set out above can be invoked in cases where a Member considers that another Member has not achieved satisfactory results under Articles 3, 4, 7, 8 and 9 and its trade interests are significantly affected. In this respect, such results shall be equivalent to those as if the body in question were a Member.

4.3   Technical Assistance

Pursuant to Article 11 of the *TBT Agreement*, Members shall, upon request, advise or provide technical assistance to requesting Members, in particular to developing-country Members. The advice and technical assistance referred to in Article 11 primarily concern assistance in establishing institutions or legal frameworks dealing with the preparation of technical regulations and standards and the development of conformity assessment procedures. In addition, requested Members shall, *inter alia*, assist the requesting Member to meet technical regulations of the requested Members; and assist the requesting Member to participate in the work of international standardisation bodies. In the provision

---

186 See Article 14.1 of the *TBT Agreement*. For a discussion of the WTO dispute settlement system, see above, pp. 156–311 (chapter on dispute settlement).

187 See Appendix 2 to the DSU.

188 As stated in Article 14.3, a technical expert group is governed by the procedures set out in Annex 2 to the *TBT Agreement*. The panel in question shall define the composition, terms of reference and working procedures of the expert group it has established. The members of a technical expert group shall be persons of professional standing and of relevant experience and shall not include citizens or government officials of a Member that is party to the dispute.

189 See Panel Report, *EC – Asbestos (2001)*, paras. 8.10–8.11.

190 See above, p. 860.

of advice or technical assistance under Article 11, priority must be given to the needs of least-developed-country Members.[191]

Questions and Assignments 13.12

What are the most important functions of the TBT Committee? What special rules are in place to deal with the fact that panels may be faced with difficult technical issues in disputes relating to the *TBT Agreement*? What is special about Article 14.4 of the *TBT Agreement*? Are Members *obliged* to provide technical assistance to developing-country Members under the *TBT Agreement*? What form does this technical assistance take?

5 SUMMARY

While continued vigilance and further liberalisation efforts regarding traditional barriers to trade (customs duties and quantitative restrictions) are certainly called for, *regulatory measures* for trade in goods now raise a more pressing challenge for the multilateral trading system. As discussed in Chapter 7, many such regulatory measures are 'technical barriers to trade'. This chapter deals with the WTO rules applicable to these measures. The next chapter, Chapter 14, will deal with the different WTO rules applicable to sanitary and phytosanitary (SPS) measures, which poses to international trade challenges similar to technical barriers to trade.

The WTO rules applicable to technical barriers to trade, as set out in the *TBT Agreement*, go *beyond* the general rules applicable to non-tariff barriers, as set out in the GATT 1994. They go *further* in addressing non-tariff barriers to trade by *also* promoting regulatory harmonisation around international standards.

The rules of the *TBT Agreement* apply to technical regulations, standards and conformity assessment procedures relating to products and (related) processes and production methods (PPMs). A measure is a 'technical regulation' within the meaning of the *TBT Agreement* if: (1) the measure applies to an identifiable product or group of products; (2) the measure lays down product characteristics; and (3) compliance with the product characteristics laid down in the measure is mandatory. A standard differs from a technical requirement in that compliance with a standard is not mandatory.

Although the *TBT Agreement* is mainly addressed to central government bodies, it extends its application also to local government and non-governmental standardising bodies. WTO Members must: (1) take 'such reasonable measures as may be available to them' in order to ensure compliance with the *TBT Agreement* by local government and non-governmental standardising bodies; and (2) refrain from taking measures that could encourage actions by these bodies that are inconsistent with the provisions of the *TBT Agreement*.

191 See Article 11.8 of the *TBT Agreement*.

With regard to the relationship between the *TBT Agreement* and other WTO agreements, note that, generally speaking, the applicability of the *SPS Agreement* or the *Agreement on Government Procurement* to a specific measure excludes the applicability of the *TBT Agreement* to that measure. However, the *TBT Agreement* and the GATT 1994 can both be applicable to a specific measure.

The *TBT Agreement* requires that, in respect of technical barriers to trade, Members accord national treatment and MFN treatment to imported products. With regard to technical regulations, Article 2.1 of the *TBT Agreement* sets out a three-tier test of consistency with the national treatment obligation and the MFN treatment obligation. This test of consistency requires the examination of: (1) whether the measure at issue is a '*technical regulation*' within the meaning of Annex 1.1; (2) whether the imported and domestic products (for the national treatment obligation) or the imported products originating in different countries (for the MFN treatment obligation) are '*like products*'; and (3) whether the imported products at issue are accorded '*treatment no less favourable*' than like domestic products or than like imported products originating in other countries.

The *TBT Agreement* also requires that technical barriers to trade do not create unnecessary obstacles to international trade. With regard to technical regulations, Article 2.2 of the *TBT Agreement* sets out a three-tier test of consistency. This test of consistency requires the examination of: (1) whether the technical regulation at issue is '*trade-restrictive*'; (2) whether the technical regulation at issue *fulfils a legitimate objective*; and (3) whether the technical regulation at issue is '*not more trade-restrictive than necessary*' to fulfil a legitimate objective, taking account of the risks non-fulfilment would create.

The *TBT Agreement* requires that, in principle, Members use international standards as a basis for their technical barriers to trade. With regard to technical regulations, Article 2.4 of the *TBT Agreement* sets out a *three-tier test of consistency*. This test of consistency requires the examination of: (1) whether there exists a *relevant international standard*; (2) whether the relevant international standard is '*used as a basis*' for the technical regulation at issue; and (3) whether the relevant international standard is an *effective or appropriate means* for the fulfilment of the legitimate objectives pursued.

In addition to these core, substantive obligations, the *TBT Agreement* furthermore requires WTO Members *to consider* accepting, as equivalent, the technical regulations of other Members if they are satisfied that the foreign technical regulations *adequately* fulfil the legitimate objectives pursued by their own technical regulations. The *TBT Agreement* also subjects Members to a number of detailed transparency and notification obligations and provides for special and differential treatment for developing-country Members.

Exercise 13: Safe Cars

Since 2008, Nana Motors, Newland's largest car manufacturer, has been manufactur-ing and selling the 'Tato', a four-passenger, rear-engined city car. In January 2012, the cheapest Tato costed around €2,000. The Tato is currently without any doubt the cheapest car in the world. While until recently sales of the Tato were almost exclusively on Newland's domestic market and exports were small, Nana Motors is convinced that there is also a market for its Tato in other countries, and in particular in Richland. It has therefore developed an export version of the Tato, the 'Tato Plus'. Upgraded to meet, *inter alia*, Richland's safety and emission standards (as applicable in January 2010), the Tato Plus is more expensive, heavier and less fuel efficient than the standard Tato, but, at around €3,000 (retail price in January 2012), it is still priced well below the price of other city cars such as the 'Taif 500' (a front-engined city car), produced by Taif Inc. of Richland, which sells at around €6,000 (retail price in January 2012).

In response to the rapidly increasing sales of the Tato on the market of Richland, Taif turned to the Government of Richland for 'help'. According to Taif, any further increase in imports of the cheap Tato would do great damage to Richland's car in-dustry and give rise to massive unemployment among car workers in Richland. The Richland Trade Union Confederation (RTUC) immediately joined Taif's call for decisive government action.

Referring to its obligations under the WTO agreements, the Government of Rich-land rejected a proposal to impose an additional €200 specific customs duty per car on city cars. It also refused to impose a special crisis tax of 20 per cent (to be added to the VAT) on rear-engined city cars. Likewise, the Government of Richland refused to deny Nana Motors permission to establish a chain of car dealerships to sell the Tato in Richland.

After years of debate and consultations with interested parties both at home and abroad, the Parliament of Richland adopted in May 2011 an amendment to its car safety legislation requiring that rear-engined city cars, such as the Tato Plus, be equipped with side airbags (in addition to frontal airbags). Note that front-engined city cars (such as the Taif 500) do not have to be equipped with side airbags. The Tato Plus has no side airbags but could at a cost of €300 per car be equipped with such air-bags. In justification of the requirement of side airbags for rear-engined city cars, it is argued that rear-engined cars (as opposed to front-engined cars) pose a greater risk to the safety of their driver and passengers. As already mentioned above, crash tests and other scientific evidence confirm that front-engined cars are safer than rear-engined cars (at least in case of a head-on collision (which is a relatively rare event)). A recent survey showed that people in Richland generally consider front-engined cars to be much safer than rear-engined cars, although that does not seem to stop them from buying rear-engined cars. Nana Motors questions whether the increased safety, if any, resulting from side airbags is proportionate to the significant additional cost (i.e. 10 per cent of the price of the car) imposed on rear-engined city cars. The side airbag requirement entered into force two months after its publication in the Official Gazette of Richland. Note that rear-engined city cars produced in, and imported from, Rockland will be exempted from the side airbag requirement for a period of two years. This should allow RockCar SA, Rockland's struggling manufacturer of city cars, to adapt to this new requirement. Under the terms of the Richland–Rockland Free Trade Agreement, such grace period of two years is mandatory.

Contemporaneous with the adoption of the amendment to Richland's car safety legislation, the Richland Committee for Standardisation, a non-governmental standardising body approved a new standard, Standard No. 412 on 'Side Impact Protection – Rear-Engined City Cars'. This standard specifies performance requirements for protection of occupants of city cars in side impact crashes. The purpose of this standard is to reduce the risk of serious and fatal injury to occupants of rear-engined city cars. While Standard No. 412 is not mandatory, Nana Motors is very concerned about this standard, as the Tato Plus would currently not meet performance requirements set out therein. Nana Motors points out that the performance requirements set out in Standard No. 412 are much higher than the performance requirements set out in the standard approved by the International Car Manufacturers' Association (ICMA) in 1970.

Recently, the Members of Parliament of Richland's New Freedom Party, which is closely associated with the Richland Trade Union Confederation (RTUC), have proposed draft legislation for the introduction of a quality label that domestic and foreign car manufacturers would be allowed to use on cars produced in countries which (unlike Newland) enforce the minimum labour standards set out in the relevant ILO Conventions.

The CEO of Nana Motors has requested a meeting with Newland's Minister of Trade to discuss possible action by Newland against Richland in the context of the WTO. You are a senior lawyer working at the Ministry of Trade of Newland and you have been instructed to write a note for the Minister on the consistency with the obligations of the *TBT Agreement* of the measures, set out above, affecting the interests of Nana Motors. Time allowing, you will also consider the consistency of these measures with the obligations of the GATT 1994.

14 Sanitary and Phytosanitary Measures

CONTENTS

1 INTRODUCTION

This chapter deals with the WTO rules applicable to sanitary and phytosanitary measures, commonly referred to as 'SPS measures'. Generally speaking, SPS measures are measures aimed at the protection of human, animal or plant life or health from certain specified risks. As mentioned in Chapter 13, SPS measures often take the form of technical barriers to trade but are subject to a different set of WTO rules.[1]

---

1 See above, p. 851.

The negotiators of the WTO agreements considered that these measures merited special attention for two reasons: first, because the preservation of domestic regulatory autonomy was, and still is, considered of particular importance where health risks are at issue; and, secondly, because of the close link between SPS measures and agricultural trade, a sector that is notoriously difficult to liberalise. As a result, SPS measures are dealt with in a separate agreement, the *Agreement on the Application of Sanitary and Phytosanitary Measures*, commonly referred to as the *SPS Agreement*. This Agreement provides for rights and obligations, which, although broadly similar, differ in certain key respects from those provided in the GATT 1994 and the *TBT Agreement*.[2]

WTO Members frequently adopt SPS measures to protect humans and animals from food safety risks, or to protect humans, animals and plants from risks arising from pests and diseases. However, countries exporting food and agricultural products, as well as international organisations, have observed that in recent years SPS measures are increasingly used as instruments of 'trade protectionism'. W. Barnes reported in the *Financial Times* in April 2006:

Stringent, often excessively strict, hygiene standards are increasingly being used by rich countries to block food imports from developing economies, according to researchers in Thailand, India and Australia ... The recent bird flu scare was manna for Western safety officials, said a trade negotiator at the Thai commerce ministry. 'The rich food importers are getting better and better at manufacturing safety hazards – real and imagined', the official said ... A World Bank study found that trade in cereals and nuts would increase by $12bn if all 15 importing countries [referring to the fifteen EU Member States at the time of the study] adopted the international Codex standards for aflatoxin contamination, which is produced by a cancer-linked mould, than if they all abided by tougher EU requirements. Some safety measures appear exotic. Australia demands that imported chicken flesh be heated to 70 degrees Celsius for 143 minutes, creating 'poultry soup' according to one exporter.[3]

Similarly, the following report by A. Beattie in the *Financial Times* in July 2007 illustrates well the tension between regulations to address health concerns and trade in food and agricultural products:

The spat between the US and China over contaminated food exports highlights a rapidly spreading battle line in the world economy: the use of product standards to regulate, and some would say stifle, international trade. Such 'non-tariff barriers', particularly food standards, are frequently both more important and harder to eliminate than simple tariffs. Arguments frequently descend into a mire of competing scientific claims about safety and risk in which trade negotiators – let alone ministers and the general public – risk drowning in complexity. And while consumers' patriotic desire to protect domestic farmers or manufacturers requires some degree of altruism, given the higher prices this entails, fears of

---

2 As explained further below, while the GATT 1994 may also apply to SPS measures, Article 1.5 of the *TBT Agreement* expressly provides that the provisions of that Agreement do not apply to sanitary and phytosanitary measures as defined in the *SPS Agreement*. See below, pp. 862 and 902–3. See also above, pp. 861–2.

3 W. Barnes, 'Food Safety Fears "Used as Excuse to Ban Imports"', *Financial Times*, 6 April 2006.

being poisoned by foreign food appeal directly to their self-interest ... As the global trade in processed and perishable food grows faster than that for traditional commodities, there appears every likelihood that standards rather than tariffs will be the greater barrier to such goods' unimpeded journey around the world economy.[4]

The rules contained in the *SPS Agreement* reflect an attempt to balance the sometimes-conflicting interests of the protection of health against SPS risks and the liberalisation of trade in food and agricultural products.

To date, WTO Members have been found to have acted inconsistently with their obligations under the *SPS Agreement* in nine disputes.[5]

This chapter deals with: (1) the scope of application of the *SPS Agreement*; (2) the substantive provisions of the *SPS Agreement*; and (3) the institutional and procedural provisions of the *SPS Agreement*.

2 SCOPE OF APPLICATION OF THE *SPS AGREEMENT*

With regard to the scope of application of the *SPS Agreement*, this section distinguishes between: (1) the measures to which the *SPS Agreement* applies; (2) the entities covered by the Agreement; and (3) the temporal scope of application of the Agreement. This section will also address the relationship between the *SPS Agreement* and other agreements on trade in goods, such as the *TBT Agreement* and the GATT 1994.

2.1 Measures to which the *SPS Agreement* Applies

The disciplines of the *SPS Agreement* do not cover all measures for the protection of human, plant or animal life or health but, rather, apply to an explicitly circumscribed set of measures. The substantive scope of application of the *SPS Agreement* is set out in Article 1.1, which provides, in relevant part:

This Agreement applies to all sanitary and phytosanitary measures which may, directly or indirectly, affect international trade.

Thus, for a measure to be subject to the *SPS Agreement*, it must be: (1) a sanitary or phytosanitary measure; and (2) a measure that may affect international trade.

A sanitary or phytosanitary measure, or 'SPS measure', is defined in paragraph 1 of Annex A to the *SPS Agreement* as:

---

4 A. Beattie, 'Food Safety Clash Tells of Trade Battles Ahead', *Financial Times*, 31 July 2007.
5 See *EC – Hormones (1998)*; *Australia – Salmon (1998)*; *Japan – Agricultural Products II (1999)*; *Australia – Salmon (Article 21.5 – Canada) (2000)*; *Japan – Apples (2003)*; *Japan – Apples (Article 21.5 – US) (2005)*; *EC – Approval and Marketing of Biotech Products (2006)*; *US – Poultry (China) (2010)*; and *Australia – Apples (2010)*. Note that, in *US/Canada – Continued Suspension (2008)*, the Appellate Body reversed the panel's findings of inconsistency with the *SPS Agreement* and was unable to complete the legal analysis.

Any measure applied:

(a) to protect animal or plant life or health within the territory of the Member from risks arising from the entry, establishment or spread of pests, diseases, disease-carrying organisms or disease-causing organisms;

(b) to protect human or animal life or health within the territory of the Member from risks arising from additives, contaminants, toxins or disease-causing organisms in foods, beverages or feedstuffs;

(c) to protect human life or health within the territory of the Member from risks arising from diseases carried by animals, plants or products thereof, or from the entry, establishment or spread of pests; or

(d) to prevent or limit other damage within the territory of the Member from the entry, establishment or spread of pests.

Sanitary or phytosanitary measures include all relevant laws, decrees, regulations, requirements and procedures including, *inter alia*, end product criteria; processes and production methods; testing, inspection, certification and approval procedures; quarantine treatments including relevant requirements associated with the transport of animals or plants, or with the materials necessary for their survival during transport; provisions on relevant statistical methods, sampling procedures and methods of risk assessment; and packaging and labelling requirements directly related to food safety.

As pointed out by the Appellate Body in *Australia – Apples (2010)*, the fundamental element of this definition relates to the *purpose* or *intention* of the measure, which 'is to be ascertained on the basis of objective considerations'.[6] The Appellate Body held that the purpose of a measure:

must be ascertained not only from the objectives of the measure as expressed by the responding party, but also from the text and structure of the relevant measure, its surrounding regulatory context, and the way in which it is designed and applied.[7]

In broad terms, an 'SPS measure' is one that: (1) *aims at* the protection of human or animal life or health from food-borne risks; or (2) *aims at* the protection of human, animal or plant life or health from risks from pests or diseases; or (3) *aims at* the prevention or limitation of other damage from risks from pests.

In *EC – Approval and Marketing of Biotech Products (2006)*, involving a complaint by the United States, Canada and Argentina against the European Communities with respect to measures relating to biotech products (i.e. genetically modified organisms or GMOs), the panel had to determine whether the contested measures, namely: (1) the *de facto* moratorium on new approvals of biotech products by the European Communities; (2) certain measures of the European Communities affecting the approval of specific biotech products; and (3) the bans on biotech products in place in six EU Member States, were 'SPS measures' within the meaning of Annex A(1) of the *SPS Agreement*, quoted above.[8] The panel interpreted the purposes enumerated in sub-paragraphs (a)

---

6 Appellate Body Report, *Australia – Apples (2010)*, para. 172.   7 *Ibid.*, para. 173.

8 Note that the bans on biotech products in place in six EU Member States related to varieties of biotech products that had already been approved at the European level. These bans are also referred to as 'safeguard measures'.

to (d) of Annex A(1) very broadly and found that almost all the objectives of the challenged European approval legislation, as well as those of the EU Member States' bans, fell within the scope of Annex A(1)(a)–(d). Only with regard to the EC Regulation on novel foods and novel food ingredients did the panel find that two of the three purposes of that Regulation were outside the scope of sub-paragraphs (a) to (d).[9] To the extent that the Regulation pursued those two purposes, it was held not to be an SPS measure. To the extent that the Regulation sought to ensure that novel foods did not present health risks to consumers, however, the panel considered it to be an SPS measure falling within Annex A(1)(b).

It is interesting to note that the panel in *EC – Approval and Marketing of Biotech Products (2006)* disagreed with the European Communities' argument that the *SPS Agreement* was not intended to cover risks to the environment in general. Instead, the panel interpreted 'other damage' in sub-paragraph (d) to include not only economic damage or damage to property, but also damage to the environment (other than to the life or health of plants or animals) encompassing adverse effects on biodiversity, population dynamics of species or biogeochemical cycles.[10] The residual category of 'other damage' referred to in sub-paragraph (d) is potentially very broad.

In *Australia – Apples (2010)*, the Appellate Body found that, as indicated by the words 'include' and 'all relevant', the first part of the sentence in the final paragraph of Annex A(1), quoted above, provides an 'illustrative and expansive'[11] list of instruments which may be SPS measures. According to the Appellate Body, the word 'relevant' refers back to the 'list of specific purposes that are the defining characteristic of every SPS measure',[12] and is key to a proper understanding of what an SPS measure within the meaning of Annex A(1) is.[13] Similarly, the use of the words 'including, *inter alia*' in the second part of that sentence to introduce the list of instruments 'emphasizes that the list is only indicative'.[14] The Appellate Body held:

The list thus serves to illustrate, through a set of concrete examples, the different types of measures that, when they exhibit the appropriate nexus to one of the specified purposes,

9   According to the panel, to the extent that the Regulation seeks to achieve the second and the third of its three purposes, namely, to ensure that novel foods do not mislead the consumer, and that they are not nutritionally disadvantageous for the consumer, it is not a measure applied for one of the purposes mentioned in Annex A(1) and is therefore not an SPS measure (and could be a measure falling within the scope of application of the *TBT Agreement*). See Panel Reports, *EC – Approval and Marketing of Biotech Products (2006)*, paras. 7.415–7.416. See also above, p. 862.

10 See *ibid.*, paras. 7.197–7.211.

11 Appellate Body Report, *Australia – Apples (2010)*, para. 175. Note that it is the list of instruments in the final paragraph of Annex A(1) that is 'illustrative and expansive', *not* the list of purposes in Annex A(1)(a)–(d).

12 Appellate Body Report, *Australia – Apples (2010)*, para. 175.

13 The Appellate Body found in *Australia – Apples (2010)*: 'measures of a type not expressly listed may nevertheless constitute SPS measures when they are "relevant", that is, when they are "applied" for a purpose that corresponds to one of those listed in subparagraphs (a) through (d). Conversely, the fact that an instrument is of a type listed in the last sentence of Annex A(1) is not, in itself, sufficient to bring such an instrument within the ambit of the *SPS Agreement*.' *Ibid.*

14 *Ibid.*, para. 176.

will constitute SPS measures and, accordingly, be subject to the disciplines set out in the SPS Agreement.[15]

The broad range of possible types of measures that may fall within the definition of an 'SPS measure' once they have one of the purposes listed in Annex A(1)(a)–(d) is illustrated by the *US – Poultry (China) (2010)* dispute, where the measure at issue was a provision in a US appropriations bill that prohibited the use of funds under the relevant bill to establish or implement a rule allowing Chinese poultry products to be imported into the US. This restriction was imposed due to concerns arising from serious incidents of food contamination and the high incidence of the H5N1 virus in China together with the weakness of its government controls which undermined confidence that poultry imports from China would be H5N1-free. Thus, despite the fact that the measure, an appropriations restriction, was not of a nature normally associated with SPS measures, the fact that it aimed to protect human and animal life and health from risks posed by contaminated poultry products from China and was of a type described in the second part of Annex A(1) (a law), led the panel to conclude that it fell within the definition of an 'SPS measure'.[16]

Thus, once a measure is objectively determined to aim at one of the purposes listed in Annex A(1)(a)–(d) of the *SPS Agreement*, and is of a type covered by the open, illustrative list in the final paragraph of Annex A(1), it falls within the definition of an 'SPS measure'.

Note that the definitions in Annex A(1) refer specifically to the protection of human, animal or plant life or health or the prevention of other damage 'within the territory of the Member', thus excluding measures aimed at extraterritorial health protection from the scope of application of the *SPS Agreement*.

---

15 *Ibid.*, para. 176. Note that the panel in *EC – Approval and Marketing of Biotech Products (2006)* had a fundamentally different interpretation of the definition of 'SPS measures'. The panel in that case held on the basis of a textual analysis of the first sentence in the final paragraph of Annex A(1), quoted above, that the definition of 'SPS measures' had three separate elements: (1) the *purpose* of the measure, as enumerated in sub-paragraphs (a) to (d); (2) the *form* of the measure, namely, 'laws, decrees [and] regulations'; and (3) the *nature* of the measure, namely, 'requirements and procedures'. See Panel Reports, *EC – Approval and Marketing of Biotech Products (2006)*, para. 7.149. The panel found that two of the measures at issue, namely: (1) the *de facto* moratorium on new approvals of biotech products by the European Communities; and (2) certain measures of the European Communities affecting the approval of specific biotech products, did not have the 'nature' of SPS measures as they were neither 'requirements' nor 'procedures' and thus fell outside the scope of the *SPS Agreement*. See Panel Reports, *EC – Approval and Marketing of Biotech Products (2006)*, paras. 7.1338–7.1378, 7.1690–7.1697, 7.1701–7.1704 and 7.1711–7.1712. However, first the panel in *Australia – Apples (2010)* and then the panel in *US – Poultry (China) (2010)* both rejected this interpretation of the definition of 'SPS measures' for having no clear basis in the text of Annex A(1). See Panel Report, *Australia – Apples (2010)*, para. 7.153; and Panel Report, *US – Poultry (China) (2010)*, paras. 7.100–7.101. The Appellate Body in *Australia – Apples (2010)* made no reference to the interpretation of the definition of 'SPS measures' in the panel reports in *EC – Approval and Marketing of Biotech Products (2006)*, and clearly interpreted this definition differently.
16 Panel Report, *US – Poultry (China) (2010)*, paras. 7.119–7.120. In this regard, the panel stated, '[a]lthough, Section 727 is an appropriations bill, it is Congress' way of exerting control over the activities of an Executive Branch agency responsible for implementing substantive laws and regulations on SPS matters. Thus the fact that it is an appropriations bill does not exclude it from the scope of the types of SPS measures set forth in the second part of Annex A(1).'

As noted above, a further requirement for the application of the *SPS Agreement* according to Article 1.1 is that the measure at issue must be a measure that 'may directly or indirectly affect international trade'. This requirement is easy to fulfil, as any measure that applies to imports can be said to affect international trade. Moreover, as pointed out by the panel in *EC – Approval and Marketing of Biotech Products (2006)*, Article 1.1 only requires that the measure *may* affect international trade. Thus, 'it is not necessary to demonstrate that an SPS measure has an actual effect on trade'.[17] Hygiene requirements for street food vendors are arguably an example of an SPS measure that does not fall within the scope of application of the *SPS Agreement* because such a measure does not – actually or potentially – affect international trade.

When a measure is an SPS measure *and* affects international trade, actually or potentially, that measure falls within the substantive scope of application of the *SPS Agreement*.[18]

2.2 Entities Covered by the *SPS Agreement*

SPS measures are often measures adopted and implemented by the central government bodies of a WTO Member. Members are fully responsible for the observance of the *SPS Agreement* by their central government bodies. However, the adoption and implementation of SPS measures are not only in the hands of central government bodies. They may also be in the hands of other bodies, such as regulatory agencies, regional bodies, sub-federal governments and non-governmental bodies.[19] With regard to these other bodies, Article 13 of the *SPS Agreement* provides:

Members shall formulate and implement positive measures and mechanisms in support of the observance of the provisions of this Agreement by other than central government bodies. Members shall take such reasonable measures as may be available to them to ensure that non-governmental entities within their territories, as well as regional bodies in which relevant entities within their territories are members, comply with the relevant provisions of this Agreement.[20]

Moreover, Article 13 of the *SPS Agreement* states that WTO Members may not rely on non-governmental bodies to implement their SPS measures *unless* these bodies comply with the *SPS Agreement*.

---

17 Panel Reports, *EC – Approval and Marketing of Biotech Products (2006)*, para. 7.435.
18 As the panel in *EC – Hormones (1998)* noted, there are no additional requirements for the applicability of the *SPS Agreement*. In particular, and contrary to what the European Communities argued in that case, the *SPS Agreement* contains no requirement of a prior violation of a provision of the GATT 1994. See Panel Report, *EC – Hormones (Canada) (1998)*, para. 8.39; and Panel Report, *EC – Hormones (US) (1998)*, para. 8.36.
19 Note that, in *Australia – Salmon (Article 21.5 – Canada) (2000)*, the measures at issue were measures taken by the Government of Tasmania, an Australian state. See Panel Report, *Australia – Salmon (Article 21.5 – Canada) (2000)*, para. 7.13.
20 Pursuant to Article 13 of the *SPS Agreement*, Members shall also abstain from taking measures which have the effect, directly or indirectly, of requiring or encouraging such regional or non-governmental entities, or local governmental bodies, to act in a manner inconsistent with the provisions of the *SPS Agreement*.

In recent years, the obligations enshrined in Article 13 of the *SPS Agreement* have become of particular significance with regard to SPS-related private sector standards.[21] While these standards have the potential to boost international trade, they can also be – and increasingly are – burdensome for small suppliers. Since 2005, when St Vincent and the Grenadines first raised concerns regarding the impact of EurepGAP standards imposed by supermarket chains on banana exports to the UK, this issue of private sector standards has been a regular item on the agenda of SPS Committee meetings.[22] It remains a much-debated question to what extent WTO Members should and/or could take responsibility for the WTO-compatibility of standards adopted by NGOs such as GlobalGAP (the successor of EurepGAP), adopted by trade associations, such as the British Retail Consortium, or adopted by commercial enterprises such as McDonald's, the world's largest chain of fast food restaurants.[23]

2.3 Temporal Scope of Application of the *SPS Agreement*

In *EC – Hormones (1998)*, the European Communities, the respondent in that case, raised the question whether the *SPS Agreement* is applicable to SPS measures adopted and/or applied before the Agreement entered into force. The Appellate Body answered this question as follows:

> If the negotiators had wanted to exempt the very large group of SPS measures in existence on 1 January 1995 from the disciplines of provisions as important as Articles 5.1 and 5.5, it appears reasonable to us to expect that they would have said so explicitly. Articles 5.1 and 5.5 do not distinguish between SPS measures adopted before 1 January 1995 and measures adopted since; the relevant implication is that they are intended to be applicable to both.[24]

Thus, the *SPS Agreement* applies pre-1995 SPS measures, to the extent of course that these measures are still in force.

Questions and Assignments 14.1

What requirements must be met for the *SPS Agreement* to apply to a specific measure? Would a ban on the use of lead in children's playground equipment be regarded as an SPS measure? Would an SPS measure adopted by a local regulatory agency be covered

---

21 For a definition of 'private sector standards', see the draft definition proposed by the WTO Secretariat on the basis of discussions in the SPS Committee. See G/SPS/W/265/Rev.1, 26 June 2012. According to this draft definition, 'SPS-related private sector standards are market requirements which are [developed and/or] applied by [private] [non-governmental] entities, which may directly or indirectly affect international trade, and which relate to' one of the objectives set out in sub-paragraphs (a) to (d) of Annex A(1) to the *SPS Agreement* (square brackets in the original). A non-governmental entity is any entity that does not possess, exercise, or is not vested with governmental authority. Non-governmental entities are private entities, including private sector bodies, companies, industrial organisations, and private standard-setting bodies.

22 An *ad hoc* working group was established in 2008 to consider the issue, and to date five actions have been adopted. See Committee on Sanitary and Phytosanitary Measures, *Decision of the Committee on Actions regarding SPS-Related Private Standards*, G/SPS/55, dated 6 April 2011.

23 This question also arises in the context of the *TBT Agreement*. For a discussion of the applicability of the *TBT Agreement* on private sector standards, see above, p. 860.

24 Appellate Body Report, *EC – Hormones (1998)*, para. 128.

by the rules of the *SPS Agreement*? If so, against whom could the complaining Member institute a challenge? In your opinion, should WTO Members be responsible for the WTO-compatibility of SPS-related private sector standards? Give five examples of 'real life' SPS measures.

2.4   Relationship with Other WTO Agreements

The *SPS Agreement* is not the only WTO agreement of relevance to measures for the protection of human, animal or plant life or health. The GATT 1994 and the *TBT Agreement* obviously also contain rules applicable to such measures. Within their respective spheres of application, all three agreements are relevant in determining the WTO-consistency of health measures. It is therefore necessary to examine the relationship between the *SPS Agreement* and the other relevant WTO agreements.

2.4.1   The TBT Agreement

The *TBT Agreement*, as discussed in Chapter 13 of this book, applies to technical regulations, standards and conformity assessment procedures in general. Clearly, SPS measures often take the form of technical regulations, standards or conformity assessment procedures. However, as already discussed above and as explicitly set out in Article 1.5 of the *TBT Agreement*, the *TBT Agreement* does not apply to SPS measures.[25] When a measure is an 'SPS measure', as defined in Annex A(1) to the *SPS Agreement*, the *SPS Agreement* applies to the exclusion of the *TBT Agreement*, even if the measure would otherwise be considered a 'technical regulation, standard or conformity assessment procedure' for purposes of the *TBT Agreement*. The relationship between the *SPS Agreement* and the *TBT Agreement* can thus be described as one of mutual exclusivity. However, as discussed above,[26] the panel in *EC – Approval and Marketing of Biotech Products (2006)* noted that a single measure or requirement may be imposed for a purpose that falls within the definition of an SPS measure as well as for a purpose not covered by this definition. It held that:

> to the extent the requirement in the consolidated law is applied for one of the purposes enumerated in Annex A(1), it may be properly viewed as a measure which falls to be assessed under the *SPS Agreement*; to the extent it is applied for a purpose which is not covered by Annex A(1), it may be viewed as a separate measure which falls to be assessed under a WTO agreement other than the *SPS Agreement*. It is important to stress, however, that our view is premised on the circumstance that the requirement at issue could be split up into two separate requirements which would be identical to the requirement at issue, and which would have an autonomous *raison d'être*, i.e., a different purpose which would provide an independent basis for imposing the requirement.[27]

---

25 See above, p. 862.   26 See above, p. 862.
27 Panel Reports, *EC – Approval and Marketing of Biotech Products (2006)*, para. 7.165.

According to the panel, such a requirement would simultaneously be an SPS measure and a 'non-SPS measure'. As Article 1.5 of the *TBT Agreement* does not apply to non-SPS measures, if the requirement falls within the definition of a 'technical regulation' as defined in Annex 1.1 of the *TBT Agreement*, it is to be assessed under the *TBT Agreement* 'to the extent it embodies a non-SPS measure'.[28]

2.4.2 The GATT 1994

Contrary to the situation with respect to the *TBT Agreement*, no relationship of mutual exclusivity exists between the *SPS Agreement* and the GATT 1994. It is therefore possible for a measure to be subject to the GATT disciplines as well as those of the *SPS Agreement*. However, Article 2.4 of the *SPS Agreement* states:

> Sanitary or phytosanitary measures which conform to the relevant provisions of this Agreement shall be presumed to be in accordance with the obligations of the Members under the provisions of GATT 1994 which relate to the use of sanitary or phytosanitary measures, in particular the provisions of Article XX(b).

Article 2.4 thus provides for a (rebuttable) presumption of GATT 1994 consistency of all measures that are in conformity with the *SPS Agreement*. The opposite is not the case. Measures that are in conformity with the GATT 1994 cannot be presumed to be consistent with the *SPS Agreement*, as the latter Agreement also provides for obligations that clearly do not exist under the GATT 1994.[29]

Questions and Assignments 14.2

Is it possible for both the *SPS Agreement* and the *TBT Agreement* to apply to one and the same measure? If a complainant argues that a particular measure is inconsistent with both the *SPS Agreement* and the GATT 1994, how should a panel proceed?

3 SUBSTANTIVE PROVISIONS OF THE *SPS AGREEMENT*

This section deals with the substantive provisions of the *SPS Agreement*. It first discusses the basic principles of the *SPS Agreement* provided for in Article 2 of the *SPS Agreement*. Subsequently, this section discusses the goal of harmonisation; the obligations relating to risk assessment; the obligations relating to risk management; and provisional SPS measures and the precautionary principle. This section concludes with a brief discussion of some other substantive provisions, such as the provisions relating to the recognition of equivalence, transparency, and special and differential treatment of developing-country Members.

---

28 *Ibid.*, para. 7.167. Although the Regulation on novel foods was found to be both an SPS measure and a non-SPS measure, the panel exercised judicial economy with regard to the claims of Canada and Argentina under the *TBT Agreement*. See *ibid.*, paras. 7.2524 and 7.2527, and paras. 7.3412–7.3413.

29 E.g. the obligations set out in Articles 5.1 and 5.5 of the *SPS Agreement*. See below, pp. 908 and 909–10.

3.1   Basic Principles

The basic principles of the *SPS Agreement* are set out in Article 2, entitled 'Basic rights and obligations'.[30] These basic principles reflect the underlying aim of balancing the need to increase market access for food and agricultural products, on the one hand, with the recognition of the sovereign right of governments to take measures to protect human, animal and plant life and health in their territories, on the other.

This section discusses the following basic principles of the *SPS Agreement*: (1) the sovereign right of WTO Members to take SPS measures; (2) the obligation to take or maintain only SPS measures *necessary* to protect human, animal or plant life or health (the 'necessity requirement'); (3) the obligation to take or maintain only SPS measures based on scientific principles and on sufficient scientific evidence (the 'scientific disciplines'); and (4) the obligation not to adopt or maintain SPS measures that arbitrarily or unjustifiably discriminate or constitute a disguised restriction on trade (the 'non-discrimination' requirement).

3.1.1   Right to Take SPS Measures

It is significant that the *SPS Agreement*, in Article 2.1, expressly recognises the *right* of Members to take SPS measures necessary for the protection of human, animal or plant life or health. This differs from the position of health measures under GATT rules, where discriminatory measures or quantitative restrictions for health protection purposes are in principle prohibited; justification for such measures must be found under Article XX(b) of the GATT 1994. This difference has important implications for the burden of proof in dispute settlement proceedings.[31] Under the GATT 1994, a Member imposing a discriminatory health measure or one that constitutes a quantitative restriction bears the burden of proving that it complies with the requirements of the Article XX(b) exception. In contrast, under the *SPS Agreement*, the complaining Member must show that the measure is inconsistent with the rules of the *SPS Agreement*.

The right to take SPS measures is, however, not unlimited but is subject to the disciplines contained in the rest of the *SPS Agreement*. The basic disciplines are set out in Articles 2.2 and 2.3, and are further elaborated upon in other provisions of the *SPS Agreement*. These provisions incorporate the existing GATT rules applicable to health measures *and* introduce new requirements for the use of SPS measures.

3.1.2   'Only to the Extent Necessary'

As set forth in Article 2.2 of the *SPS Agreement*, the sovereign right of Members to take SPS measures is, first of all, limited by the requirement that:

---

30 The panel in *US – Poultry (China) (2010)* noted that the title of Article 2 leads to the conclusion that the provisions of this Article inform all of the *SPS Agreement*. See Panel Report, *US – Poultry (China) (2010)*, para. 7.142.
31 See above, pp. 257–61.

any sanitary or phytosanitary measure [be] applied only to the extent necessary to protect human, animal or plant life and health.

Although this general necessity requirement in Article 2.2 has not yet been subject to interpretation in dispute settlement, the related, and more specific, requirement set forth in Article 5.6 has been interpreted, as explained below.[32] As the Appellate Body has suggested, a violation of Article 5.6 may also imply a violation of Article 2.2.[33]

Questions and Assignments 14.3

What is the most significant implication of the principle that WTO Members have the right to adopt and maintain SPS measures? How does the treatment of health measures under the *SPS Agreement* differ from that under Article XX(b) of the GATT? Do you agree that the 'necessity' requirement of Article 2.2 of the *SPS Agreement* reflects the 'necessity' requirement of Article XX(b) of the GATT 1994? Are complainants likely to argue a violation of the 'necessity' requirement of Article 2.2 of the *SPS Agreement*?

3.1.3 Scientific Basis for SPS Measures

Article 2.2 of the *SPS Agreement* also introduces new scientific disciplines for the use and maintenance of SPS measures. It requires that:

any sanitary or phytosanitary measure ... [be] based on scientific principles and ... not [be] maintained without sufficient scientific evidence, except as provided for in paragraph 7 of Article 5.

These requirements introduce science as the touchstone against which SPS measures will be judged. These scientific requirements are further elaborated on in Article 5.1, which provides that SPS measures must be based on a risk assessment.[34] With regard to these scientific disciplines, the Appellate Body held in *EC – Hormones (1998)*:

The requirements of a risk assessment under Article 5.1, as well as of 'sufficient scientific evidence' under Article 2.2, are essential for the maintenance of the delicate and carefully negotiated balance in the *SPS Agreement* between the shared, but sometimes competing, interests of promoting international trade and of protecting the life and health of human beings.[35]

The panel in *Japan – Apples (2003)* was the first to consider the meaning of the terms 'scientific' and 'evidence' in Article 2.2.[36] It held that for evidence to be 'scientific' it must be gathered through scientific methods[37] and it favoured

---

32 See below, pp. 923–6.
33 In *Australia – Salmon (1998)*, the Appellate Body stated that '[t]he establishment or maintenance of an SPS measure which implies or reflects a higher level of protection than the appropriate level of protection determined by an importing Member, could constitute a violation of the necessity requirement of Article 2.2'. Appellate Body Report, *Australia – Salmon (1998)*, footnote 166 to para. 213. See also Appellate Body Report, *Australia – Apples (2010)*, paras. 340 and 346–7.
34 See below, pp. 914–20.
35 Appellate Body Report, *EC – Hormones (1998)*, para. 177.
36 See Panel Report, *Japan – Apples (2003)*, paras. 8.91–8.98.
37 *Ibid.*, para. 8.92.

relying on scientifically produced evidence rather than purely circumstantial evidence.[38] With regard to the term 'evidence', the panel held:

> Negotiators could have used the term 'information', as in Article 5.7, if they considered that any material could be used. By using the term 'scientific evidence', Article 2.2 excludes in essence not only insufficiently substantiated information, but also such things as a non-demonstrated hypothesis.[39]

The panel noted that it would consider both direct and indirect scientific evidence, although their probative value would differ.[40]

The issue of what is meant by '*sufficient* scientific evidence' was addressed for the first time in *Japan – Agricultural Products II (1999)*. In that case, the Appellate Body held that this requires a *rational relationship* between the SPS measure and the scientific evidence. The Appellate Body ruled as follows:

> [W]e agree with the Panel that the obligation in Article 2.2 that an SPS measure not be maintained without sufficient scientific evidence requires that there be a rational or objective relationship between the SPS measure and the scientific evidence. Whether there is a rational relationship between an SPS measure and the scientific evidence is to be determined on a case-by-case basis and will depend upon the particular circumstances of the case, including the characteristics of the measure at issue and the quality and quantity of the scientific evidence.[41]

It is thus clear that panels have some discretion in determining whether a 'rational relationship' between the measure and the scientific evidence exists, in light of the particular circumstances of each case. It would seem that where reputable scientific support for a measure exists, the requirement of 'sufficient scientific evidence' would be met. Moreover, in *EC – Hormones (1998)*, the Appellate Body noted that, in determining whether sufficient scientific evidence exists, panels should:

> bear in mind that responsible, representative governments commonly act from perspectives of prudence and precaution where risks of irreversible, e.g. life-terminating, damage to human health are concerned.[42]

It therefore seems that the more serious the risks to life or health, the less demanding the requirement of 'sufficient scientific evidence'. The panel in *Japan – Apples (2003)* further elaborated on the 'rational relationship' test by introducing a proportionality criterion into Article 2.2 of the *SPS Agreement*. It found, based on the evidence before it, that the risk of transmission of fire blight through the importation of apple fruit was negligible,[43] and contrasted this with the rigorous requirements of the measure at issue. It found the measure at issue to be clearly disproportionate to the risk and thus a violation of Article 2.2.[44]

---

38 *Ibid.*, para. 8.95.   39 *Ibid.*, para. 8.93.   40 See *ibid.*, para. 8.98.
41 Appellate Body Report, *Japan – Agricultural Products II (1999)*, para. 84.
42 Appellate Body Report, *EC – Hormones (1998)*, para. 124.
43 See Panel Report, *Japan – Apples (2003)*, para. 8.169.
44 See *ibid.*, para. 8.198.

The Appellate Body did not take issue with this proportionality test.[45] More re-cently, the panel in *US – Poultry (China) (2010)* found that, for the SPS measure at issue to be maintained with sufficient scientific evidence:

the scientific evidence must bear a rational relationship to the measure, be sufficient to demonstrate the existence of the risk which the measure is supposed to address, and be of the kind necessary for a risk assessment.[46]

Pursuant to Article 2.2 of the *SPS Agreement*, SPS measures must not be main-tained without sufficient scientific evidence, *except* as provided for under Article 5.7. This provision, discussed in more detail below, deals with a situation in which scientific evidence is lacking.[47] Governments are sometimes faced with situations where they need to act to prevent a possible risk despite insufficient scientific data regarding the existence and likelihood of the risk. Article 2.2 takes account of this fact by expressly referring to Article 5.7, which allows for provisional SPS measures to be taken. The relationship between Articles 2.2 and 5.7 was set out by the Appellate Body in *Japan – Agricultural Products II (1999)* as follows:

[I]t is clear that Article 5.7 of the *SPS Agreement*, to which Article 2.2 explicitly refers, is part of the context of the latter provision and should be considered in the interpretation of the obligation not to maintain an SPS measure without sufficient scientific evidence. Article 5.7 allows Members to adopt provisional SPS measures '[i]n cases where relevant scientific evidence is insufficient' and certain other requirements are fulfilled. Article 5.7 operates as a *qualified* exemption from the obligation under Article 2.2 not to maintain SPS measures without sufficient scientific evidence.[48]

As the Appellate Body itself recognised in that dispute, the existence of Arti-cle 5.7 thus argues against an 'overly broad and flexible interpretation' of the requirement in Article 2.2 that SPS measures not be maintained without suffi-cient scientific evidence.[49] In *EC – Approval and Marketing of Biotech Products (2006)*, the relationship between Article 5.7 and the scientific obligations con-tained in Article 2.2 (and Article 5.1) was again at issue. The European Commu-nities argued that 'Article 5.7 is not an exception to Article 2.2 in the sense that it could be invoked as an affirmative defence to a claim of violation under Arti-cle 2.2'.[50] Rather, it averred that 'Article 5.7 establishes an autonomous right of the importing Member'.[51] The panel agreed with the European Communities in

---

45 Appellate Body Report, *Japan – Apples (2003)*, para. 163. The panel also found that, in order to be sufficient, the scientific evidence must confirm the existence of the risk that the measure is supposed to address. *Ibid.*, para. 8.104. See also Panel Report, *Japan – Apples (Article 21.5 – US) (2005)*, paras. 8.45 and 8.71.
46 Panel Report, *US – Poultry (China) (2010)*, para. 7.200.
47 See below.
48 Appellate Body Report, *Japan – Agricultural Products II (1999)*, para. 80.
49 See *ibid.*
50 Panel Reports, *EC – Approval and Marketing of Biotech Products (2006)*, para. 7.2962.
51 *Ibid.* The argument of the European Communities was based on an analogy with the relationship between Articles 3.1 and 3.3 of the *SPS Agreement*, as set out by the Appellate Body in *EC – Hormones (1998)*, para. 104. See *ibid.*

this regard,[52] and therefore considered that a measure falling under Article 5.7 is excluded from the scope of application of the scientific disciplines in Article 2.2.[53] In *US/Canada – Continued Suspension (2008)*, the Appellate Body confirmed this interpretation of the relationship between Articles 2.2 and 5.7.[54] The practical implication of this interpretation is that the complaining party bears the burden of proof with respect to Article 5.7. In other words, to be successful in claiming that an SPS measure is inconsistent with Article 2.2, a complainant may also have to show that the measure does *not* fall under Article 5.7.[55]

It should also be borne in mind that – as mentioned above – the basic scientific disciplines contained in Article 2.2 are further elaborated in Article 5.1 of the *SPS Agreement*, which requires – as discussed below – that SPS measures be based on a risk assessment, taking into account certain factors.[56] A violation of Article 5.1 will necessarily imply a violation of Article 2.2, but the opposite is not true as Article 2.2 is broader than Article 5.1.[57]

Questions and Assignments 14.4

What are the 'scientific disciplines' set forth in Article 2.2 of the *SPS Agreement*? When is a measure maintained 'without sufficient scientific evidence'? Are Members ever allowed to maintain SPS measures for which there is insufficient scientific evidence? What is the relationship between Article 2.2 and Article 5.7 of the *SPS Agreement*? What is the implication of this relationship for the burden of proof?

3.1.4 No Arbitrary or Unjustifiable Discrimination ...

A third basic limitation on a Member's right to impose SPS measures can be found in Article 2.3 of the *SPS Agreement*. Article 2.3 reflects the basic GATT non-discrimination obligations of national treatment and most-favoured-nation treatment, and its language replicates part of the chapeau of Article XX of the GATT 1994.[58] Article 2.3 provides:

---

52 See Panel Reports, *EC – Approval and Marketing of Biotech Products (2006)*, paras. 7.2969 and 7.2976. Note that the panel refers not only to the scientific obligations set out in Article 2.2 but also those set out in Article 5.1 of the SPS Agreement, discussed below at pp. 915–19. While this is contrary to the finding of the panel in *Japan – Apples (2003)*, which held that the burden of proof under Article 5.7 is on the respondent, the panel in *EC – Approval and Marketing of Biotech Products (2006)* understood the Appellate Body in the former case as implicitly expressing its reservations with regard to this allocation of the burden of proof. In coming to its interpretation of the relationship between Articles 2.2 and 5.7, the panel relied on the test used by the Appellate Body in *EC – Tariff Preferences (2004)*. See Panel Reports, *EC – Approval and Marketing of Biotech Products (2006)*, para. 7.2985, citing Appellate Body Report, *EC – Tariff Preferences (2004)*, para. 88.

53 See Panel Reports, *EC – Approval and Marketing of Biotech Products (2006)*, para. 7.2969.

54 See Appellate Body Reports, *US/Canada – Continued Suspension (2008)*, para. 674.

55 For a detailed discussion of these requirements of Article 5.7 of the *SPS Agreement*, see below, pp. 927–32.

56 See below, pp. 914–20; and Appellate Body Report, *EC – Hormones (1998)*, para. 180. Note that the requirement in Article 5.1 is itself elaborated in Articles 5.2 and 5.3 of the *SPS Agreement*. As the panel in *Australia – Salmon (1998)* noted, Articles 5.2 and 5.3 qualify the way in which a risk assessment has to be carried out; they do not qualify the substantive obligation set out in Article 5.1. See Panel Report, *Australia – Salmon (1998)*, para. 8.57.

57 See Appellate Body Report, *Australia – Salmon (1998)*, para. 137.

58 See *ibid.*, para. 251. For a detailed discussion of Articles I and III of the GATT 1994, see above, pp. 317–30 and 350–56; for a discussion of the chapeau of Article XX of the GATT 1994, see above, pp. 572–81.

Members shall ensure that their sanitary and phytosanitary measures do not arbitrarily or unjustifiably discriminate between Members where identical or similar conditions prevail, including between their own territory and that of other Members. Sanitary and phytosanitary measures shall not be applied in a manner which would constitute a disguised restriction on international trade.

Article 2.3 was at issue in *Australia – Salmon (Article 21.5 – Canada) (2000)*, where Canada claimed that Australia violated this provision by imposing import requirements on particular types of fish (salmonids) imported from Canada but providing no internal control measures on the movement of dead fish within Australia. The panel identified three cumulative requirements that must be met for a violation of Article 2.3 of the *SPS Agreement* to be established, namely, that: (1) the measure discriminates between the territories of Members other than the Member imposing the measure, or between the territory of the Member imposing the measure and another Member; (2) the discrimination is arbitrary or unjustifiable; and (3) identical or similar conditions prevail in the territory of the Members compared.[59]

Further, the panel in *Australia – Salmon (Article 21.5 – Canada) (2000)* noted that discrimination in the sense of the first element of Article 2.3 includes discrimination between *different* products (in this case, salmonids from Canada and Australian fish including non-salmonids).[60] This differs significantly from the non-discrimination rules of the GATT (and the *TBT Agreement*) that apply only to 'like' or 'directly competitive or substitutable' products.[61] Article 2.3 recognises that it is the similarity of the risks, rather than the similarity of the products, that matters. Thus, when dissimilar products pose the same or similar health risks, they should be treated in the same way. For example, different animals may be carriers of foot-and-mouth disease and should thus be subject to similar measures where this risk is present. This broad prohibition on discriminatory treatment is tempered by the other two elements that must be established before a violation of Article 2.3 can be found. Thus, if the discriminatory treatment is not arbitrary or unjustifiable, or if conditions in the Members compared are not similar or identical, Article 2.3 is not violated. In this regard, the panel in *Australia – Salmon (Article 21.5 – Canada) (2000)* was not convinced that 'identical or similar' conditions prevailed in Australia and Canada, as there was a substantial difference in the disease status of these two Members.[62]

The basic discipline in Article 2.3 finds reflection in the more specific prohibition in Article 5.5 on arbitrary or unjustifiable distinctions in the levels of protection chosen by a Member in different situations, where these distinctions

---

59 See Panel Report, *Australia – Salmon (Article 21.5 – Canada) (2000)*, para. 7.111.
60 *Ibid.*, para. 7.112.
61 See above, pp. 317–30 (for Article I of the GATT 1994); pp. 327–8, 350–6 and 410–11 (for Article III of the GATT 1994); and pp. 865–72 (for Article 2.1 of the *TBT Agreement*).
62 See Panel Report, *Australia – Salmon (Article 21.5 – Canada) (2000)*, para. 7.113.

lead to discrimination or disguised restrictions on trade.[63] A violation of Article 5.5 will necessarily imply a violation of Article 2.3, but the opposite is not true as Article 2.3 is broader than Article 5.5.[64]

Questions and Assignments 14.5

What are the criteria for a violation of Article 2.3 of the *SPS Agreement*? What significant difference is there between the obligation contained in Article 2.3 and the non-discrimination rules of the GATT 1994?

3.2 Goal of Harmonisation

Due to the different factors that regulators take into account when enacting SPS measures (national consumer preferences, industry interests, geographic and climatic conditions, etc.), there are large differences in SPS measures from one country to another. The resulting wide variety of SPS measures that producers face in their different export markets has a negative impact on market access for their products, as they may have to adjust products to many different SPS measures.[65] The *SPS Agreement* addresses this problem in Article 3 by encouraging, but not obliging, Members to harmonise their SPS measures around international standards.[66] In *US/Canada – Continued Suspension (2008)*, the Appellate Body noted:

> As the preamble of the *SPS Agreement* recognizes, one of the primary objectives of the *SPS Agreement* is to 'further the use of harmonized sanitary and phytosanitary measures between Members, on the basis of international standards, guidelines and recommendations developed by the relevant international organizations'. This objective finds reflection in Article 3 of the *SPS Agreement*, which encourages the harmonization of SPS measures on the basis of international standards, while at the same time recognizing the WTO Members' right to determine their appropriate level of protection. [67]

Under Article 3 of the *SPS Agreement*, Members have three *autonomous options* with regard to international standards, each with its own consequences. Members may choose to: (1) *base* their SPS measures on international standards according to Article 3.1; (2) *conform* their SPS measures to international standards under Article 3.2; or (3) impose SPS measures resulting in a *higher level* of protection than would be achieved by the relevant international standard in terms of Article 3.3.

As the Appellate Body already made clear in *EC – Hormones (1998)*, these options are equally available options and there is no rule–exception relationship

---

63 See below, pp. 921–6.
64 See Appellate Body Report, *Australia – Salmon (1998)*, para. 252; and Panel Report, *Australia – Salmon (Article 21.5 – Canada) (2000)*, para. 8.160.
65 See also above, pp. 933–8.
66 Article 3 refers to 'international standards, guidelines or recommendations'. For reasons of convenience, the term 'international standards' will be used in this chapter to refer to 'international standards, guidelines or recommendations'.
67 Appellate Body Reports, *US/Canada – Continued Suspension (2008)*, para. 692.

between them.[68] Thus a Member is not penalised for choosing the Article 3.3 alternative. The three options will now be examined in more detail.

The first option is set out in Article 3.1 of the *SPS Agreement*. Article 3.1 obliges Members to base their SPS measures on international standards where they exist, except as provided for in Article 3.3. The 'international standards' to which Article 3.1 refers are standards set by international organisations, such as the Codex Alimentarius Commission with respect to food safety, the World Organisation for Animal Health (formerly called the International Office of Epizootics (OIE)) for animal health, and the Secretariat of the International Plant Protection Convention (IPPC) with respect to plant health.[69]

Where a relevant international standard exists, Members must – according to Article 3.1 – base their SPS measures thereon. With respect to the meaning of the 'based on' requirement, the Appellate Body made the following observations in *EC – Hormones (1998)*:

> To read Article 3.1 as requiring Members to harmonize their SPS measures *by conforming those measures with international standards*, guidelines and recommendations, *in the here and now*, is, in effect, to vest such international standards, guidelines and recommendations (which are by the terms of the Codex *recommendatory* in form and nature) with *obligatory* force and effect. The Panel's interpretation of Article 3.1 would, in other words, transform those standards, guidelines and recommendations into binding *norms*. But, as already noted, the *SPS Agreement* itself sets out no indication of any intent on the part of the Members to do so. We cannot lightly assume that sovereign states intended to impose upon themselves the more onerous, rather than the less burdensome, obligation by mandating *conformity* or *compliance with* such standards, guidelines and recommendations. To sustain such an assumption and to warrant such a far-reaching interpretation, treaty language far more specific and compelling than that found in Article 3 of the *SPS Agreement* would be necessary.[70]

Thus, the non-binding standards set by the international standard-setting organisations do not become binding by virtue of the *SPS Agreement*. According to the Appellate Body in *EC – Hormones (1998)*, a measure that is 'based on' an international standard is one that 'stands' or 'is founded', or 'built' upon or 'supported', by the international standard. An SPS measure, which is 'based on' an international standard, need not 'conform to' that standard, since not all of the elements of that standard have to be incorporated into the measure.[71]

---

68 See *ibid.*, para. 104.
69 See Annex A, para. 3(a), (b) and (c) of the *SPS Agreement*. For matters not covered by the three organisations mentioned, see Annex A, para. 3(d) of the *SPS Agreement*. Note that the panel in *EC – Hormones (1998)* found that it only needs to establish whether an international standard exists; there is no need to establish for example whether these standards were adopted by consensus or by a wide or narrow majority, or whether they were adopted before or after the entry into force of the *SPS Agreement*. See Panel Report, *EC – Hormones (Canada) (1998)*, para. 8.72; and Panel Report, *EC – Hormones (US) (1998)*, para. 8.69. Pursuant to Article 3.4 of the *SPS Agreement*, Members have an obligation to participate in the work of the Codex Alimentarius Commission and the other organisations to the extent that their resources permit and to promote the development and periodic review of international standards.
70 Appellate Body Report, *EC – Hormones (1998)*, para. 165.
71 *Ibid.*, para. 163.

When a WTO Member maintains that its SPS measure is 'based on' an international standard, another WTO Member challenging such measure under Article 3.1 will bear the burden of proving that this is not the case. Such measure does not, however, benefit from any presumption of consistency.[72]

The *second* option available to Members under Article 3.2 of the *SPS Agreement* is to 'conform' their SPS measures to the relevant international standard. To 'conform to' is more demanding than to 'base on'. In *EC – Hormones (1998)*, the Appellate Body interpreted this requirement as follows:

> Such a measure would embody the international standard completely and, for practical purposes, converts it into a municipal standard.[73]

Article 3.2 provides that SPS measures, which 'conform to' international standards, are presumed to be consistent with the *SPS Agreement* and the GATT 1994. This presumption of consistency is rebuttable.[74] However, the presumption of consistency is designed to create an *incentive* for Members to conform their SPS measures to international standards, rather than to base them on those standards.[75] Clearly, the burden of proof lies on the complaining party to demonstrate a violation of the *SPS Agreement*, under both the Article 3.1 option and the Article 3.2 option. However, the burden is heavier in the latter case as the complaining party has to overcome the presumption of consistency. Members conforming their SPS measures to international standards make these measures less vulnerable to challenges under the *SPS Agreement* and the GATT. Hence, there is an *incentive* for Members to opt for conforming their standards to international standards. As the Appellate Body noted in *US/Canada – Continued Suspension (2008)*:

> International standards are given a prominent role under the *SPS Agreement*, particularly in furthering the objective of promoting the harmonization of sanitary and phytosanitary standards between WTO Members. This is to be achieved by encouraging WTO Members to base their SPS measures on international standards, guidelines or recommendations, where they exist. There is a rebuttable presumption that SPS measures that conform to international standards, guidelines or recommendations are 'necessary to protect human, animal or plant life or health, and ... [are] consistent with the relevant provisions of this Agreement and of GATT 1994'.[76]

The third option that Members may choose, with respect to international standards, is to deviate from the relevant international standard by choosing a measure resulting in a higher level of protection than that achieved by the international standard. This option, provided for in Article 3.3 of the *SPS Agreement*, is important as it reflects the recognition of the right of Members to choose the

---

72 *Ibid.*, para. 171. As discussed below, an SPS measure benefits from a presumption of consistency when it conforms to the international standard. See below, pp. 912–13.

73 *Ibid.*, para. 170.

74 See *ibid.* See also Appellate Body Reports, *US/Canada – Continued Suspension (2008)*, para. 532.

75 See Appellate Body Report, *EC – Hormones (1998)*, para. 102.

76 Appellate Body Reports, *US/Canada – Continued Suspension (2008)*, para. 532.

level of protection they deem appropriate in their territories. In respect of this option, the Appellate Body in *EC – Hormones (1998)* held that:

> [t]his right of a Member to establish its own level of sanitary protection under Article 3.3 of the *SPS Agreement* is an autonomous right and *not* an 'exception' from a 'general obligation' under Article 3.1.[77]

This right to choose measures that deviate from international standards is not an 'absolute or unqualified right', as confirmed by the Appellate Body in *EC – Hormones (1998)*.[78] Two *alternative* conditions are laid down in Article 3.3, namely, that: (1) either there must be a scientific justification for the SPS measure (defined in a footnote as a scientific examination and evaluation in accordance with the rules of the *SPS Agreement*); or (2) the measure must be a result of the level of protection chosen by the Member in accordance with Articles 5.1 to 5.8. The difference between these two conditions is not clear and the Appellate Body noted, in *EC – Hormones (1998)*, that 'Article 3.3 is evidently not a model of clarity in drafting and communication'.[79] What is clear, however, is that under both alternative conditions a risk assessment in terms of Article 5.1 is required.[80] Therefore, the Appellate Body held *in EC – Hormones (1998)* that, given that the European Communities had established for itself a level of protection higher than that implied in the relevant Codex standards, it was bound to comply with the requirements established in Article 5.1.[81] In *US/Canada – Continued Suspension (2008)*, the Appellate Body clarified that:

> [w]hile use of international standards is encouraged, the *SPS Agreement* recognizes the right of WTO Members to introduce or maintain an SPS measure which results in a higher level of protection than would be achieved by measures based on such international standards.[82]

Where a Member exercises its right to adopt an SPS measure that results in a higher level of protection, that right 'is qualified in that the SPS measure must comply with the other requirements of the *SPS Agreement*, including the requirement to perform a risk assessment.'[83] However, the Appellate Body found in *EC – Hormones (1998)*, and confirmed in *US/Canada – Continued Suspension (2008)*, that the adoption of an SPS measure that does not conform to an international standard and results in a higher level of protection does not give rise to a more exacting burden of proof under the *SPS Agreement*.[84]

---

77 *Ibid.*, para. 172. Furthermore, in *US/Canada – Continued Suspension (2008)*, the Appellate Body noted that the adoption of an SPS measure that results in a higher level of protection 'does not give rise to a more exacting burden of proof under the SPS Agreement'. See Appellate Body Reports, *US/Canada – Continued Suspension (2008)*, para. 532.
78 See Appellate Body Report, *EC – Hormones (1998)*, para. 173.
79 *Ibid.*, para. 175.   80 *Ibid.*   81 *Ibid.*, para. 176.
82 Appellate Body Reports, *US/Canada – Continued Suspension (2008)*, para. 532.
83 *Ibid.*
84 See Appellate Body Report, *EC – Hormones (1998)*, para. 102; and Appellate Body Reports, *US/Canada – Continued Suspension (2008)*, para. 532.

Questions and Assignments 14.6

What three options do Members have with regard to international standards? When is an SPS measure 'based on' an international standard? When does an SPS measure 'conform to' an international standard? Is the right of Members to adopt or maintain measures that deviate from international standards an 'absolute and unqualified right'? Explain. Are Members in any way penalised or rewarded for choosing one of the three options provided for in Article 3 of the *SPS Agreement*? Does the *SPS Agreement* also address the situation in which a WTO Member deviates from the relevant international standard by choosing a measure resulting in a *lower* level of protection than that recommended and achieved by the international standard?

3.3 Obligations Relating to Risk Assessment

The national regulatory process by means of which SPS measures are imposed typically involves *risk analysis*. For the purposes of the *SPS Agreement*, two elements of risk analysis are relevant, namely, risk assessment and risk management. The term 'risk assessment' refers to the scientific process of identifying the existence of a risk and establishing the likelihood that the risk may actually materialise according to the measures that could be applied to address the risk. 'Risk management', by contrast, is the policy-based process of determining the level of protection a country wants to ensure in its territory and choosing the measure that will be used to achieve that level of protection. Risk management decision-making takes into account not only the scientific results of the risk assessment, but also considerations relating to societal values such as consumer preferences, industry interests, relative costs, etc. The distinction between these two elements of the risk analysis process is not absolute. Non-scientific considerations do play some part in risk assessment, and scientific considerations inform risk management. However, the distinction is a useful tool in understanding the regulatory process.

The risk assessment/risk management distinction is *implicitly* taken into account in those disciplines of the *SPS Agreement* that relate to the risk analysis process contained in Article 5.[85] Articles 5.1 and 5.2 establish disciplines for the risk assessments on which SPS measures must be based, whereas a Member's choice of the appropriate level of protection – an aspect of risk management – is regulated by Articles 5.4 and 5.5. The selection of a measure to achieve this level of protection – another aspect of risk management – is subject to Article 5.6.

---

85 In *EC – Hormones (1998)*, the Appellate Body noted that the *SPS Agreement* does not expressly use the term 'risk management', and it rejected the rigid distinction drawn by the panel between 'risk assessment' and 'risk management' for 'having no textual basis'. See *ibid.*, para. 181. In *US/Canada – Continued Suspension (2008)*, the Appellate Body found that the panel in that case made the same error of drawing a rigid distinction between 'risk assessment' and 'risk management'. See Appellate Body Reports, *US/Canada – Continued Suspension (2008)*, paras. 541–2. This does not mean, however, that it would be incorrect to use the term 'risk management'. It is undeniable that the *SPS Agreement* deals in different ways with the obligations of Members with regard to risk assessment and their obligations applicable to what is commonly referred to as risk management.

3.3.1   Risk Assessment

Article 5.1 of the *SPS Agreement* states:

> Members shall ensure that their sanitary or phytosanitary measures are based on an assessment, as appropriate to the circumstances, of the risks to human, animal or plant life or health, taking into account risk assessment techniques developed by the relevant international organizations.

Article 5.1 thus obliges Members to base their SPS measures on a risk assessment as appropriate to the circumstances. As noted by the panel in *EC – Approval and Marketing of Biotech Products (2006)*, two distinct issues must be addressed to determine whether there is a violation of Article 5.1, (1) whether there is a 'risk assessment' within the meaning of the *SPS Agreement*; and (2) whether the SPS measure at issue is 'based on' this risk assessment.[86]

A 'risk assessment' is defined in paragraph 4 of Annex A to the *SPS Agreement* as follows:

> The evaluation of the likelihood of entry, establishment or spread of a pest or disease, within the territory of an importing Member according to the sanitary or phytosanitary measures which might be applied, and of the associated potential biological and economic consequences; *or* the evaluation of the potential for adverse effects on human or animal health arising from the presence of additives, contaminants, toxins or disease-causing organisms in food, beverages or feedstuffs.[87]

Thus, there are *two* types of risk assessment, each with different requirements. The type of risk assessment required in a given case will depend on the objective of the SPS measure at issue. The first type of risk assessment is applicable to SPS measures aimed at risks from pests or diseases; the second to SPS measures aimed at food-borne risks.

The first type of risk assessment involves not only an assessment of the risk of entry, establishment or spread of a pest or disease, but also an assessment of the risk of the associated potential biological and economic consequences.[88] Such a risk assessment must: (1) *identify the pests or diseases* whose entry, establishment or spread a Member wants to prevent, as well as the *potential biological and economic consequences* associated with the entry, establishment or spread of such pests/diseases; (2) *evaluate the likelihood* of entry, establishment or spread of these pests or diseases and the associated biological and economic consequences; and (3) evaluate the likelihood of entry, establishment or spread of these pests or diseases *according to the SPS measures that might be applied.*[89]

The second type of risk assessment, which applies to food-borne risks, must: (1) *identify the adverse effects* on human or animal health (if any) arising from

---

86 See Panel Reports, *EC – Approval and Marketing of Biotech Products (2006)*, para. 7.3019.
87 Emphasis added.
88 See Panel Report, *Australia – Salmon (1998)*, para. 8.72.
89 This three-pronged test was first set out by the panel, and endorsed by the Appellate Body, in *Australia – Salmon (1998)*. See Appellate Body Report, *Australia – Salmon (1998)*, para. 121.

the additive, contaminant, toxin or disease-causing organism in food/beverages/feedstuffs; and (2) if such adverse health effects exist, *evaluate the potential* for such adverse effects to occur.[90]

There are three important differences between these two types of risk assessment. First, the requirements for the second type of risk assessment do not include an evaluation of associated biological and economic consequences. Secondly, while the first type of risk assessment requires an evaluation of the 'likelihood' that the risk might materialise, the second type requires only an evaluation of the 'potential' for adverse effects. The word 'likelihood' used with regard to the first type of risk assessment was held to imply a higher degree of potentiality than the word 'potential' used with regard to the second type.[91] Thirdly, a risk assessment of the first type must evaluate likelihood according to the SPS measures 'which might be applied'. A risk assessment of this type may not be limited to an examination of the measure already in place but other possible alternatives must also be evaluated.[92]

It would appear that the differences between the two types of risk assessment are intended to set less strict requirements for those risk assessments where risks to human health are more likely to be at issue, namely, when dealing with food safety issues rather than when the risk relates to animal or plant pests or diseases.

Furthermore, eight general observations can be made with respect to the requirements for risk assessments, as identified by the Appellate Body in its case law. First, a risk assessment must show proof of an actual risk, not just a theoretical uncertainty.[93] Secondly, a risk assessment does not require the risk assessed to be quantified (i.e. expressed numerically). The risk may be expressed either quantitatively or qualitatively.[94] Thirdly, a risk assessment may go beyond controlled laboratory conditions and take account of the actual potential for adverse effects in the 'real world where people live and work and die'.[95] Fourthly, the risk assessment must be specific to the particular type of risk at issue in the

---

90 This two-pronged test can be deduced from Panel Report, *EC – Hormones (Canada)*, para. 8.101; and Panel Report, *EC – Hormones (US) (1998)*, para. 8.98, as modified by the Appellate Body (Appellate Body Report, *EC – Hormones (1998)*, paras. 184–6).

91 See Appellate Body Report, *Australia – Salmon (1998)*, para. 123 (with regard to the first type of risk assessment); Appellate Body Report, *EC – Hormones (1998)*, para. 184; and Appellate Body Reports, *US/Canada – Continued Suspension (2008)*, para. 569 (with regard to the second type of risk assessment).

92 See Panel Report, *Japan – Apples (2003)*, para. 8.283. As the Appellate Body noted in this case, 'a risk assessment should not be distorted by preconceived views on the nature and the content of the measure to be taken; nor should it develop into an exercise tailored to and carried out for the purpose of justifying decisions *ex post facto*'. See Appellate Body Report, *Japan – Apples (2003)*, para. 208.

93 See Appellate Body Report, *EC – Hormones (1998)*, para. 186. See also Appellate Body Reports, *US/Canada – Continued Suspension (2008)*, para. 569.

94 See Appellate Body Report, *EC – Hormones (1998)*, para. 186; Appellate Body Report, *Australia – Salmon (1998)*, paras. 124–5; and Appellate Body Reports, *US/Canada – Continued Suspension (2008)*, para. 569. Note, however, that the panel in *Australia – Apples (2010)* observed that a quantitative method should only be used when reliable specific numeric data are available. In the absence of such data, a quantitative method may be misleading. See Panel Report, *Australia – Apples (2010)*, para. 7.441.

95 See Appellate Body Report, *EC – Hormones (1998)*, para. 187. See also below, p. 918.

case and not merely show a general risk of harm.[96] Fifthly, Article 5.1 does not oblige Members to carry out their own risk assessments. Instead, they may rely on risk assessments carried out by other Members or an international organisation.[97] Sixthly, the phrase 'as appropriate to the circumstances' in Article 5.1 does not alleviate the obligation of Members to base their SPS measures on a risk assessment, but relates to the way such risk assessment is carried out.[98] Seventhly, the phrase 'taking into account risk assessment techniques developed by the relevant international organisations' in Article 5.1 does not mean that a risk assessment must be based on or conform to such techniques, nor does it mean that compliance with such techniques alone suffices to show that the risk assessment is consistent with the requirements under the *SPS Agreement*.[99] However, reference by the risk assessor to such techniques 'is useful ... should a dispute arise in relation to the risk assessment'.[100] Eighthly, since Article 5.1 is to be read together with Article 2.2, which requires that SPS measures not be 'maintained' without sufficient scientific evidence, the evolution of the scientific evidence since the completion of the risk assessment must also be considered as 'this may be an indication that the risk assessment should be reviewed or a new assessment undertaken'.[101]

Although the *SPS Agreement* does not lay down any methodology of risk assessment to be followed by Members, other than to require them to take account of risk assessment techniques developed by international organisations, it does specify certain factors that Members must take into account in their risk assessments. Article 5.2 of the *SPS Agreement* lists certain scientific and technical factors that Members must consider when assessing risks. These are:

[A]vailable scientific evidence; relevant processes and production methods; relevant inspection, sampling and testing methods; prevalence of specific diseases or pests; existence of pest- or disease-free areas; relevant ecological and environmental conditions; and quarantine or other treatment.[102]

96 See Appellate Body Report, *EC – Hormones (1998)*, para. 200. In *Japan – Apples*, the Appellate Body agreed with the panel that a risk assessment must be specific not only to the harm at issue but also to the agent that causes the harm (in that case, the product that transmitted the disease). See Appellate Body Report, *Japan – Apples (2003)*, para. 204.
97 See Appellate Body Report, *EC – Hormones (1998)*, para. 190.
98 See Panel Report, *Australia – Salmon (1998)*, para. 8.57. See also Appellate Body Reports, *US/Canada – Continued Suspension (2008)*, para. 562; and Appellate Body Report, *Australia – Apples (2010)*, paras. 237 and 244.
99 See Appellate Body Report, *Australia – Apples (2010)*, para. 246.
100 *Ibid.*
101 Panel Report, *Japan – Apples (2003)*, para. 7.12. In a similar vein, in *EC – Approval and Marketing of Biotech Products (2006)*, the panel held that, as circumstances may change (for example, new scientific evidence may affect the relevance or validity of a risk assessment on which a measure is based), a panel must determine whether, on the date of its establishment, the measure at issue was based on an assessment of risks which was appropriate to the circumstances existing *at that time*. See Panel Reports, *EC – Approval and Marketing of Biotech Products (2006)*, paras. 7.3033–7.3034.
102 Note that, in *EC – Hormones (1998)*, the Appellate Body held that this list in Article 5.2 is not a closed list. See Appellate Body Report, *EC – Hormones (1998)*, para. 187. See also Appellate Body Report, *Australia – Apples (2010)*, para. 207.

In *Australia – Apples (2010)*, the Appellate Body ruled:

Article 5.2 requires a risk assessor to take into account the available scientific evidence, together with other factors. Whether a risk assessor has taken into account the available scientific evidence in accordance with Article 5.2 of the SPS Agreement and whether its risk assessment is a proper risk assessment within the meaning of Article 5.1 and Annex A(4) must be determined by assessing the relationship between the conclusions of the risk assessor and the relevant available scientific evidence.[103]

As already observed above, a risk assessment for the purposes of the *SPS Agreement* is *not* purely scientific (in the sense of laboratory science) but includes a consideration of real-world factors that affect risk, such as climatic conditions, control mechanisms, etc. The Appellate Body in *EC – Hormones (1998)* rejected the panel's finding that the risks relating to control and detection of failure to observe good veterinary practices must be excluded from risk assessments as they are non-scientific and thus outside the scope of Article 5.2.[104] In *US/Canada – Continued Suspension (2008)*, the Appellate Body confirmed the relevance of such risks. It recalled that the Codex Alimentarius draws a distinction between 'risk assessment' and 'risk management' and that the Codex defines 'risk management' as:

the process, *distinct from risk assessment*, of weighing policy alternatives ... considering risk assessment and other factors relevant for the health protection of consumers and for the promotion of fair trade practices, and, if needed, selecting appropriate prevention and control options.[105]

While the Appellate Body has not provided a clear demarcation of the factors that may be considered in a 'risk assessment', the Appellate Body held in *EC – Hormones (1998)*, and reaffirmed in *US/Canada – Continued Suspension (2008)*, that the list of factors provided in Article 5.2 is not a closed list and, in particular, that the risks arising from the abuse or misuse and difficulties of control in the administration of hormones may be considered in the context of a risk assessment.[106] The Appellate Body added in *US/Canada – Continued Suspension (2008)* that:

Where a WTO Member has taken such risks into account, they must be considered by a panel reviewing that Member's risk assessment. Any suggestion that such risks cannot form part of a risk assessment would constitute legal error.[107]

Moreover, the Appellate Body has made certain observations about the relationship between the risk assessment and the 'appropriate level of protection', a

---

103 Appellate Body Report, *Australia – Apples (2010)*, para. 208.
104 Appellate Body Report, *EC – Hormones (1998)*, para. 187. However, the Appellate Body qualified its finding by noting that it does not imply that risks related to problems of control *always* need to be evaluated in a risk assessment. The necessity to evaluate such risks depends on the circumstances of each case. See *ibid.*, para. 206.
105 Appellate Body Reports, *US/Canada – Continued Suspension (2008)*, para. 535.
106 See Appellate Body Report, *EC – Hormones (1998)*, paras. 187 and 206; and Appellate Body Reports, *US/Canada – Continued Suspension (2008)*, para. 535.
107 Appellate Body Reports, *US/Canada – Continued Suspension (2008)*, para. 545.

concept discussed below.[108] In *US/Canada – Continued Suspension (2008)*, the Appellate Body stated:

> The risk assessment cannot be entirely isolated from the appropriate level of protection. There may be circumstances in which the appropriate level of protection chosen by a Member affects the scope or method of the risk assessment. This may be the case where a WTO Member decides not to adopt an SPS measure based on an international standard because it seeks to achieve a higher level of protection. In such a situation, the fact that the WTO Member has chosen to set a higher level of protection may require it to perform certain research as part of its risk assessment that is different from the parameters considered and the research carried out in the risk assessment underlying the international standard.[109]

Finally, with regard to risk assessments concerning animal or plant life or health, Article 5.3 of the *SPS Agreement* requires Members to take into account the following relevant economic factors: (1) the potential damage in terms of loss of production or sales; (2) the costs of control or eradication in the territory of the importing Member; and (3) the relative cost-effectiveness of alternative approaches to limiting risks.[110] There is no requirement to take such economic factors into account in risk assessments concerning human life or health.

3.3.2 Based on a Risk Assessment

As noted above, Article 5.1 of the *SPS Agreement* requires that SPS measures be 'based on' a risk assessment. The meaning of 'based on' was clarified in *EC – Hormones (1998)*. The Appellate Body in that case rejected the panel's finding that the risk assessment must be shown to have been 'taken into account' by the Member in imposing the SPS measure and that the SPS measure must 'conform' to the risk assessment.[111] Instead, the Appellate Body held that, for an SPS measure to be 'based on' a risk assessment, there must be a 'rational relationship' between the measure and the risk assessment, and the risk assessment must 'reasonably support' the measure.[112]

The Appellate Body has also ruled that it is permissible for an SPS measure to be based on a divergent or minority view rather than mainstream scientific opinion. In *EC – Hormones (1998)*, it stated:

> The risk assessment could set out both the prevailing view representing the 'mainstream' of scientific opinion, as well as the opinions of scientists taking a divergent view. Article 5.1 does not require that the risk assessment must necessarily embody only the view of

---

108 See below, pp. 921–6.

109 Appellate Body Reports, *US/Canada – Continued Suspension (2008)*, para. 534.

110 Note that Article 5.3 of the *SPS Agreement* also requires that these economic factors are taken into account in the choice of SPS measures for the protection of the life and health of animals and plants. See below, p. 923.

111 See Appellate Body Report, *EC – Hormones (1998)*, paras. 189–94.

112 *Ibid.*, para. 193. In *EC – Approval and Marketing of Biotech Products (2006)*, the panel held that there existed no apparent rational relationship between the bans on biotech products imposed by six EU Member States, and the relevant risk assessments, which found no evidence that the biotech products concerned present any greater risk to human health or the environment than their conventional (non-biotech) counterparts. See e.g. Panel Reports, *EC – Approval and Marketing of Biotech Products (2006)*, paras. 7.3085–7.3089 (with regard to Austria's ban on T25 maize).

a majority of the relevant scientific community ... In most cases, responsible and representative governments tend to base their legislative and administrative measures on 'mainstream' scientific opinion. In other cases, equally responsible and representative governments may act in good faith on the basis of what, at a given time, may be a divergent opinion coming from *qualified and respected sources*. By itself, this does not necessarily signal the absence of a reasonable relationship between the SPS measure and the risk assessment, especially where the risk involved is life-threatening in character and is perceived to constitute a clear and imminent threat to public health and safety. Determination of the presence or absence of that relationship can only be done on a case-to-case basis, after account is taken of all considerations rationally bearing upon the issue of potential adverse health effects.[113]

The Appellate Body confirmed in *US/Canada – Continued Suspension (2008)* that the 'scientific basis need not reflect the majority view within the scientific community but may reflect divergent or minority views', and clarified the nature of the divergent or minority view on which an SPS measure can be based as follows:

Having identified the scientific basis underlying the SPS measure, the panel must then verify that the scientific basis comes from a respected and qualified source. Although the scientific basis need not represent the majority view within the scientific community, it must nevertheless have the necessary scientific and methodological rigour to be considered reputable science. In other words, while the correctness of the views need not have been accepted by the broader scientific community, the views must be considered to be legitimate science according to the standards of the relevant scientific community.[114]

Questions and Assignments 14.7

Explain the distinction between risk assessment and risk management. How is this distinction reflected in the *SPS Agreement*? What are the main differences between the two types of risk assessment defined in Annex A, paragraph 4, of the *SPS Agreement*? What do you think is the reason for these differences? When is an SPS measure 'based on' a risk assessment? Can an SPS measure, which is not 'based on' mainstream scientific opinion, be consistent with Article 5.1 of the *SPS Agreement*? Must a WTO Member adopting an SPS measure necessarily conduct a risk assessment?

3.4   Obligations Relating to Risk Management

Risk management, as explained above, entails policy decision-making regarding: (1) the level of protection that a country wants to secure in its territory; and (2) the measure it will use to achieve this level of protection. These choices are 'based on' both scientific evidence and societal value judgments. The *SPS Agreement* gives national regulators substantial latitude in making risk management decisions, but there are certain non-scientific disciplines in place to ensure that the adverse trade effects of these decisions are limited as much as possible.

---

113 Appellate Body Report, *EC – Hormones (1998)*, para. 194. Emphasis added.
114 Appellate Body Reports, *US/Canada – Continued Suspension (2008)*, para. 591.

3.4.1   Appropriate Level of Protection

Risk management involves, in the first place, a decision on the 'appropriate level of protection', defined in paragraph 5 of Annex A to the *SPS Agreement* as:

The level of protection *deemed appropriate by the Member* establishing a sanitary or phytosanitary measure to protect human, animal or plant life or health within its territory.[115]

Thus, there is a clear recognition that it is the *prerogative* of the Member imposing the SPS measure to choose the level of protection of human, animal or plant life or health it will ensure in its territory.[116] Once the existence of a risk has been established by means of a risk assessment, a Member is free to choose even a zero-risk level of protection.[117]

Two provisions in the *SPS Agreement* deal with the choice of an appropriate level of protection. First, Article 5.4 provides that 'Members should ... take into account the objective of minimising negative trade effects' when choosing their level of protection. The word 'should' suggests that this provision is merely hortative. Indeed, obliging Members to choose the least trade-restrictive level of protection would seem to go against the underlying principle of the *SPS Agreement* that it is the prerogative of each Member to determine the level of protection it deems appropriate in its territory. The Appellate Body has, nonetheless, stated that Article 5.4 is one of the disciplines that a WTO Member *must respect* when it sets its appropriate level of protection with regard to a particular risk.[118] Note, however, that the obligation under Article 5.4 is not to '[minimise] negative trade effects', but to 'take into account the objective of minimising negative trade effects'.

The second discipline with regard to the appropriate level of protection is contained in Article 5.5, which provides in relevant part:

With the objective of achieving consistency in the application of the concept of appropriate level of sanitary or phytosanitary protection against risks to human life or health, or to animal and plant life or health, each Member shall avoid arbitrary or unjustifiable distinctions in the levels it considers to be appropriate in different situations, if such distinctions result in discrimination or a disguised restriction on international trade.

The Article 5.5 discipline consists of two elements, namely: (1) the *goal* of achieving consistency in the application of the concept of appropriate level of sanitary or phytosanitary protection;[119] and (2) the *legal obligation* to avoid

---

115 Emphasis added. In *Australia – Apples (2010)*, the Appellate Body referred to the 'appropriate level of protection' also as the 'acceptable level of risk'. See Appellate Body Report, *Australia – Apples (2010)*, para. 405.

116 See Appellate Body Report, *Australia – Salmon (1998)*, para. 199; and Appellate Body Reports, *US/Canada – Continued Suspension (2008)*, para. 523.

117 See Appellate Body Report, *Australia – Salmon (1998)*, para. 125.

118 See Appellate Body Reports, *US/Canada – Continued Suspension (2008)*, footnote 1088.

119 In *EC – Hormones (1998)*, the Appellate Body agreed with the panel that no legal obligation of consistency in levels of protection exists, but that consistency in levels of protection is only a goal for the future. See Appellate Body Report, *EC – Hormones (1998)*, para. 213.

arbitrary or unjustifiable distinctions in the levels of protection deemed appropriate in different situations, *if* these distinctions lead to discrimination or disguised restrictions on trade.

In *EC – Hormones (1998)*, the Appellate Body recognised that countries establish their levels of protection *ad hoc* as risks arise. Absolute consistency in levels of protection is neither realistic nor required by Article 5.5 of the *SPS Agreement*.[120] To establish whether an SPS measure is inconsistent with Article 5.5, three questions need to be answered:

- whether the Member concerned has set *different levels of protection* in different situations;
- whether these different levels of protection show *arbitrary or unjustifiable differences* in their treatment of different situations; and
- whether these arbitrary or unjustifiable differences lead to *discrimination or disguised restrictions* on trade.[121]

With regard to the *first element* of this three-tier test, it is obvious that not all risks can be treated the same. Thus, according to the Appellate Body in *EC – Hormones (1998)*, the 'different situations' referred to in Article 5.5 of the *SPS Agreement* must be *comparable* situations, that is, they must have some common element or elements.[122] For example, a common element would be the fact that the spread of the same disease is at issue, or that identical biological or economic consequences could result.[123] A difference in the levels of protection applied in the comparable situations must then be shown. With regard to the *second element* of the test of consistency with Article 5.5, it is necessary to examine whether reasons exist to justify the differences in levels of protection in order to determine whether these differences are 'arbitrary or unjustifiable'.[124] In *Australia – Salmon (1998)*, the Appellate Body found that distinctions in the level of protection can be said to be arbitrary or unjustifiable where the risk is at least equally high between the different situations at issue.[125] With regard to the *third element* of the Article 5.5 test, the Appellate Body stated in *EC – Hormones (1998)* that this is the most important of the elements of this three-tier test.[126] Whether the arbitrary or unjustifiable distinctions in levels of protection lead to 'discrimination or disguised restrictions on trade' can be determined by means of three 'warning signals' identified in the case law. Such 'warning signals' are not conclusive in their own right but, taken together and with other factors,

---

120 *Ibid.*, para. 213.

121 See *ibid.*, para. 214, reiterated in Appellate Body Report, *Australia – Salmon (1998)*, para. 140. Note, however, that the panel in *Australia – Apples (2010)*, due to the 'specific circumstances' of the case, departed from a strict application of this three-tier test. See Panel Report, *Australia – Apples (2010)*, para. 7.985.

122 Appellate Body Report, *EC – Hormones (1998)*, para. 217.

123 See Appellate Body Report, *Australia – Salmon (1998)*, para. 146.

124 For a discussion of the meaning of the terms 'unjustifiable' and 'arbitrary' as used in the chapeau of Article XX of the GATT 1994 and Article XIV of the GATS, see above, pp. 578–9 and 602. See also Panel Report, *US – Poultry (2010)*, paras. 7.260–7.261.

125 See Appellate Body Report, *Australia – Salmon (1998)*, para. 158.

126 See Appellate Body Report, *EC – Hormones (1998)*, para. 240.

they may support a finding that arbitrary or unjustifiable distinctions in levels of protection lead to 'discrimination or disguised restrictions on trade'.[127] The 'warning signals' that may indicate that the measure is a disguised restriction on trade are: (1) the arbitrary character of the differences in the levels of protection; (2) the existence of substantial differences in the levels of protection; and (3) the absence of scientific justification for the differences.[128]

In June 2000, the SPS Committee drew up guidelines for the implementation of Article 5.5.[129] The guidelines, resulting from a series of consultations in the SPS Committee, reflect the clarifications emerging from the case law on Article 5.5, including the use of the three 'warning signals'.

3.4.2 'Not More Trade-Restrictive than Required'

In addition to the disciplines regarding the choice of an appropriate level of protection, the *SPS Agreement* contains rules regarding the choice of an SPS measure to achieve the chosen level of protection.

The first such rule is Article 5.3 of the *SPS Agreement*, which lists certain economic criteria, such as damage in terms of loss of production or sales that Members must consider in their choice of SPS measures.[130] This rule, however, only applies to SPS measures for the protection of the life and health of animals and plants.[131]

The second and much more important rule on the choice of measure is contained in Article 5.6 of the *SPS Agreement*, which provides:

> Without prejudice to paragraph 2 of Article 3, when establishing or maintaining sanitary or phytosanitary measures to achieve the appropriate level of sanitary or phytosanitary protection, Members shall ensure that such measures are not more trade-restrictive than required to achieve their appropriate level of sanitary or phytosanitary protection, taking into account technical and economic feasibility.

In a footnote to Article 5.6, it is stated:

> For purposes of paragraph 6 of Article 5, a measure is not more trade-restrictive than required unless there is another measure, reasonably available taking into account technical and economic feasibility, that achieves the appropriate level of sanitary or phytosanitary protection and is significantly less restrictive to trade.

On the basis of this footnote, the panel in *Australia – Salmon (1998)* identified a three-tier test, which was later upheld by the Appellate Body. Pursuant to this

---

127 See Panel Report, *Australia – Salmon (1998)*, paras. 8.149–8.151, as approved by the Appellate Body. See Appellate Body Report, *Australia – Salmon (1998)*, paras. 162, 164 and 166. The first two warning signals were also relied upon in Appellate Body Report, *EC – Hormones (1998)*, paras. 215 and 240.

128 See *ibid*. The absence of scientific justification can be clear from earlier findings of a violation of Articles 2.2 and 5.1.

129 These guidelines are contained in Committee on Sanitary and Phytosanitary Measures, *Guidelines to Further the Practical Implementation of Article 5.5*, G/SPS/15, dated 18 June 2000.

130 Note that Article 5.3 of the *SPS Agreement* also requires that these economic factors are taken into account in the assessment of risks to the life and health of animals and plants. See above, p. 923.

131 See also above, p. 919, footnote 110.

test, an SPS measure is more trade-restrictive than required (and thus inconsistent with Article 5.6) *only* if there is an alternative SPS measure which: (1) is reasonably available, taking into account technical and economic feasibility; (2) achieves the Member's appropriate level of protection; and (3) is significantly less trade-restrictive than the contested measure.[132] Only when all three of these cumulative requirements are satisfied will an SPS measure be inconsistent with Article 5.6.[133]

In *Australia – Apples (2010)*, the Appellate Body identified the general function of Article 5.6 as follows:

> The function of Article 5.6 is to ensure that SPS measures are not more trade restrictive than necessary to achieve a Member's appropriate level of protection. Compliance with this requirement is tested through a comparison of the measure at issue to possible alternative measures. Such alternatives, however, are mere conceptual tools for the purpose of the Article 5.6 analysis. A demonstration that an alternative measure meets the relevant Member's appropriate level of protection, is reasonably available, and is significantly less trade restrictive than the existing measure suffices to prove that the measure at issue is more trade restrictive than necessary. Yet this does not imply that the importing Member must adopt that alternative measure or that the alternative measure is the only option that would achieve the desired level of protection.[134]

To determine whether the first element of the test under Article 5.6 of the *SPS Agreement* is met, namely, *whether an alternative measure is reasonably available*, a panel will look at the facts of the case, including the characteristics of the SPS measure actually applied, as well as the alternative measures considered in the risk assessment, in order to determine which of the latter measures is a feasible alternative.[135] It is important to emphasise that it is the complainant, and not the panel or the panel's scientific experts, which must identify the alternative measure or measures, which is or are reasonably available.[136]

To determine whether the second element of this test is met, namely, *whether an alternative measure achieves the importing Member's appropriate level of protection*, it is necessary: (1) to identify what is the importing Member's appropriate level of protection; (2) to determine the level of protection that would be achieved by the complainant's proposed alternative measure; and (3) to determine whether the level of protection that would be achieved by the alternative measure would satisfy the importing Member's appropriate level of protection.[137] In *Australia – Apples (2010)*, the Appellate Body held that:

132 See Panel Report, *Australia – Salmon (1998)*, para. 95; and Appellate Body Report, *Australia – Salmon (1998)*, para. 194. Also note that the Appellate Body ruled in *Australia – Apples (2010)* that the obligations set out in Article 5.1 and Article 5.6 are distinct and legally independent of each other and that a complainant is free to challenge the consistency of a measure with Article 5.6 without, at the same time, alleging a violation of Article 5.1. See Appellate Body Report, *Australia – Apples (2010)*, para. 354.
133 See Appellate Body Report, *Australia – Salmon (1998)*, para. 194, reiterated in Appellate Body Report, *Japan – Agricultural Products II (1999)*, para. 95.
134 Appellate Body Report, *Australia – Apples (2010)*, para. 363.
135 See Panel Report, *Australia – Salmon (1998)*, para. 8.171; and Panel Report, *Australia – Salmon (Article 21.5 – Canada) (2000)*, paras. 7.146–7.149.
136 See *Japan – Agricultural Products II (1999)*, paras. 124–5. See also below, pp. 924–6.
137 Appellate Body Report, *Australia – Apples (2010)*, para. 368.

a panel must identify both the level of protection that the importing
its appropriate level, and the level of protection that would be achieve
tive measure put forth by the complainant. Thereupon the panel will be ab
requisite comparison between the level of protection that would be achieved b
native measure and the importing Member's appropriate level of protection. If the
protection achieved by the proposed alternative meets or exceeds the appropriate le
protection, then (assuming that the other two conditions in Article 5.6 are met) the impo
ing Member's SPS measure is more trade restrictive than necessary to achieve its desired
level of protection.[138]

In *Australia – Salmon (1998)*, the Appellate Body rejected the panel's finding
that the appropriate level of protection can be implied from the level of protection that is afforded by the SPS measure imposed. The Appellate Body emphasised that the choice of a level of protection is the prerogative of the Member
concerned.[139] Further, it held:

The 'appropriate level of protection' established by a Member and the 'SPS measure' have to
be clearly distinguished. They are not one and the same thing. The first is an *objective*, the
second is an *instrument* chosen to attain or implement that objective.

It can be deduced from the provisions of the *SPS Agreement* that the determination by
a Member of the 'appropriate level of protection' logically precedes the establishment or
decision on maintenance of an 'SPS measure'.[140]

There are, however, cases where Members do not expressly determine their appropriate level of protection, or do so with insufficient clarity so that it becomes impossible to apply Article 5.6.[141] The Appellate Body in *Australia – Salmon (1998)*
recognised this, and thus read into paragraph 3 of Annex B and Articles 4.1,
5.4 and 5.6 an implicit obligation on Members to determine their appropriate
levels of protection.[142] This was further explained as follows in *Australia –
Apples (2010)*:

While there is no obligation to set the appropriate level of protection in quantitative terms,
a Member is not free to establish its level with such vagueness or equivocation as to render
impossible the application of the relevant disciplines of the *SPS Agreement*, including the
obligation set out in Article 5.6.[143]

The Appellate Body has also explained, in *Australia – Salmon (1998)*, that,
when a Member does not comply with its obligation to identify its appropriate
level of protection, that level may be deduced from the SPS measure actually
applied:

[I]n cases where a Member does not determine its appropriate level of protection, or does
so with insufficient precision, the appropriate level of protection may be established by
panels on the basis of the level of protection reflected in the SPS measure actually applied.

138 *Ibid.*, para. 344.
139 Appellate Body Report, *Australia – Salmon (1998)*, para. 199; and Appellate Body Reports, *US/Canada –
Continued Suspension (2008)*, para. 523. See also above, pp. 921–3.
140 Appellate Body Report, *Australia – Salmon (1998)*, paras. 200–1.
141 The same problem may arise under Article 5.5 of the *SPS Agreement*.
142 See Appellate Body Report, *Australia – Salmon (1998)*, paras. 205–7.
143 Appellate Body Report, *Australia – Apples (2010)*, para. 343.

r's failure to comply with the implicit obligation to determine its appro-
:tion – with sufficient precision – would allow it to escape from its obli-
greement and, in particular, its obligations under Articles 5.5 and 5.6.[144]

t element of the test under Article 5.6 of the *SPS Agreement*,
alternative measure is significantly less trade-restrictive, was
h the original panel and the Article 21.5 panel in *Australia –*
id by the panel in *Japan – Agricultural Products II (1999)*.[145]
iese cases that the issue relates to whether market access would
mproved if an alternative measure were imposed.

Questions and Assignments 14.8

What obligation does Article 5.5 impose on Members? Does it include the obligation to
ensure consistency in the level of SPS protection maintained in comparable situations?
Discuss the three-tier test under Article 5.5 as established in the case law. Are Members
required to adopt and maintain the least-trade-restrictive appropriate levels of sanitary
protection? Are Members required to adopt and maintain the least-trade-restrictive SPS
measure? How does one establish that the SPS measure at issue is more trade-restrictive
than required?

3.5 Provisional Measures and the Precautionary Principle

While the *SPS Agreement* requires that SPS measures be 'based on' science and
uses science as the touchstone against which SPS measures will be judged, it
is obvious that science does not have clear and unambiguous answers to all
regulatory questions. Situations may arise where there is, in fact, insufficient
scientific evidence regarding the existence and extent of the relevant risk but
where governments consider they need to act promptly and take measures to
avoid possible harm. Thus, governments act with precaution without waiting for
the collection of sufficient scientific information to assess the risks conclusively.
This is commonly referred to as acting in accordance with the 'precautionary
principle', or the 'precautionary approach'. Considerable difference of opinion
exists between Members regarding the role that precaution should play in the
regulatory process, and the European Union and the United States often find
themselves on opposite sides in this debate. It is indisputable that precaution is
an inherent part of risk regulation, particularly in the area of health and environment. What is disputed, however, is whether precaution should be taken into
account in risk assessment or whether it only comes into play in risk management decisions.[146] It is therefore important to establish to what extent the *SPS
Agreement* allows for precaution to play a role in Members' SPS regulation.

---

144 Appellate Body Report, *Australia – Salmon (1998)*, para. 207.
145 See Panel Report, *Australia – Salmon (1998)*, para. 8.182; Panel Report, *Australia – Salmon (Article 21.5 –
Canada) (2000)*, paras. 7.150–7.153; Panel Report, *Japan – Agricultural Products II (1999)*, paras. 8.79,
8.89, 8.95–8.96 and 8.103–8.104.
146 There is also a difference of opinion as to whether precaution has emerged as a 'principle' in international
law, or whether it is a mere 'approach' followed by countries.

Article 5.7 of the *SPS Agreement* provides for the possibility to take – under certain conditions – provisional SPS measures where scientific evidence is insufficient. As already discussed above, the Appellate Body stated in *Japan – Agricultural Products II (1999)* that:

Article 5.7 operates as a *qualified* exemption from the obligation under Article 2.2 not to maintain SPS measures without sufficient scientific evidence.[147]

Article 5.7 could thus be regarded as a particular formulation of the precautionary principle. As held by the Appellate Body in *US/Canada – Continued Suspension (2008)*, Article 5.7 provides:

[a] temporary 'safety valve' in situations where some evidence of risk exists but not enough to complete a full risk assessment, thus making it impossible to meet the rigorous standards set by Articles 2.2 and 5.1.[148]

Article 5.7 provides:

In cases where relevant scientific evidence is insufficient, a Member may provisionally adopt sanitary or phytosanitary measures on the basis of available pertinent information, including that from the relevant international organizations as well as from sanitary or phytosanitary measures applied by other Members. In such circumstances, Members shall seek to obtain the additional information necessary for a more objective assessment of risk and review the sanitary or phytosanitary measure accordingly within a reasonable period of time.

From this provision, four cumulative requirements for provisional measures were identified by the panel, and confirmed by the Appellate Body, in *Japan – Agricultural Products II (1999)* and *US/Canada – Continued Suspension (2008)*, namely, that the measure must: (1) be imposed in respect of a situation where relevant scientific evidence is insufficient; (2) be adopted on the basis of available pertinent information; (3) not be maintained unless the Member seeks to obtain the additional information necessary for a more objective assessment of risk; and (4) be reviewed accordingly within a reasonable period of time.[149]

According to the Appellate Body in *US/Canada – Continued Suspension (2008)*, the four conditions set out above must be interpreted keeping in mind that the precautionary principle finds reflection in Article 5.7.[150] In *Japan – Apples (2003)*, the panel addressed the *first* requirement. It held that the existence of a situation where 'relevant scientific evidence is insufficient' cannot merely be implied from a finding that the measure is maintained 'without sufficient scientific evidence' under Article 2.2.[151] It held:

Article 5.7 refers to 'relevant scientific evidence' which implies that the body of material that might be considered includes not only evidence supporting Japan's position, but also evidence supporting other views.[152]

---

147 Appellate Body Report, *Japan – Agricultural Products II (1999)*, para. 80. See above, pp. 905–8.
148 Appellate Body Reports, *US/Canada – Continued Suspension (2008)*, para. 678.
149 See Panel Report, *Japan – Agricultural Products II (1999)*, para. 8.54; Appellate Body Report, *Japan – Agricultural Products II (1999)*, para. 89; and Appellate Body Reports, *US/Canada – Continued Suspension (2008)*, para. 676.
150 Appellate Body Reports, *US/Canada – Continued Suspension (2008)*, para. 680.
151 Panel Report, *Japan – Apples (2003)*, para. 8.215.   152 *Ibid.*, para. 8.216.

Since a wealth of scientific evidence was submitted in that case by both the parties and the panel experts, the panel found that it was indisputable that a large amount of relevant scientific evidence was available. It held:

The current 'situation', where scientific studies as well as practical experience have accumulated for the past 200 years, is clearly not the type of situation Article 5.7 was intended to address. Article 5.7 was obviously designed to be invoked in situations where little, or no, reliable evidence was available on the subject-matter at issue.[153]

On appeal, Japan challenged the panel's finding that Article 5.7 is intended only to address situations where little, or no, reliable evidence was available on the subject-matter at issue. According to Japan, Article 5.7 covers not only situations of 'new uncertainty' (where a new risk is identified) but also 'unresolved uncertainty' (where considerable scientific evidence exists on the risk but uncertainty still remains). The Appellate Body, however, upheld the panel's finding, pointing out that Article 5.7:

is triggered not by the existence of scientific uncertainty, but rather by the insufficiency of scientific evidence.[154]

Thus the concept of *insufficiency* of scientific evidence and the concept of scientific *uncertainty* are not interchangeable. Further, the Appellate Body identified a contextual link between the first requirement of Article 5.7 and the obligation to perform a risk assessment in Article 5.1. Thus, relevant scientific evidence will be 'insufficient' within the meaning of Article 5.7 if it:

does not allow, in qualitative or quantitative terms, the performance of an adequate assessment of risks as required under Article 5.1.[155]

According to the Appellate Body in *Japan – Apples (2003)*, the factual findings of the panel showed that the scientific evidence available *did* permit the performance of a risk assessment under Article 5.1 and the relevant scientific evidence was thus not insufficient within the meaning of Article 5.7. This analysis of the first requirement of Article 5.7 in *Japan – Apples (2003)* is important. It clarifies the role of Article 5.7, establishing that it is there to address situations where there is a true lack of sufficient scientific evidence regarding the risk at issue, either due to the small amount of evidence on new risks, or due to the fact that accumulated evidence is inconclusive or unreliable. In either case, the insufficiency of the evidence must be such as to make the performance of an adequate risk assessment impossible. Thus, Article 5.7 cannot be used to justify measures that are adopted in disregard of reliable scientific evidence.[156]

---

153   *Ibid.*, para. 8.215.
154   Appellate Body Report, *Japan – Apples (2003)*, para. 184. Moreover, it noted that the panel's finding referred to the availability of *reliable* evidence, and thus did not exclude cases 'where the available evidence is more than minimal in quantity, but has not led to reliable or conclusive results'. *Ibid.*, para. 185.
155   *Ibid.*, para. 179.
156   When an international standard (presumably based on a risk assessment) exists, a complainant may argue that the existence of such standard indicates that there is not insufficient evidence to conduct a risk

The first requirement of Article 5.7 of the *SPS Agreement* was again at issue in *EC – Approval and Marketing of Biotech Products (2006)*. The European Communities argued that, because the bans on biotech products imposed by certain of its Member States are by nature provisional, it is by reference to the rules in Article 5.7, not the rules in Article 5.1, that these bans must be assessed.[157] The panel examined this argument in light of the first sentence of Article 5.7. It found:

> The first sentence follows a classic 'if – then' logic: if a certain condition is met (*in casu*, insufficiency of relevant scientific evidence), a particular right is conferred (*in casu*, the right provisionally to adopt an SPS measure based on available pertinent information). Thus, it is clear that Article 5.7 is applicable whenever the relevant condition is met, that is to say, in every case where relevant scientific evidence is insufficient. The provisional adoption of an SPS measure is not a condition for the applicability of Article 5.7. Rather, the provisional adoption of an SPS measure is permitted by the first sentence of Article 5.7.[158]

Therefore, the trigger for applicability of Article 5.7 is the insufficiency of the scientific evidence, not the provisional nature of the measure at issue.[159]

In *US/Canada – Continued Suspension (2008)*, the Appellate Body further clarified that 'the existence of scientific controversy in itself is not enough to conclude that the relevant scientific evidence is "insufficient"',[160] since Article 5.1 allows Members to base their SPS measures on divergent or minority views from a respected or qualified source. In such cases, it is possible to perform a risk assessment that meets the requirements of Article 5.1. Instead, the Appellate Body emphasised that:

> Article 5.7 is concerned with situations where deficiencies in the body of scientific evidence do not allow a WTO Member to arrive at a sufficiently objective conclusion in relation to risk.[161]

In *US/Canada – Continued Suspension (2008)*, the Appellate Body made two further observations on the 'insufficiency' of scientific evidence, namely, that: (1) the possibility of conducting further scientific investigation (which is in fact always possible) does not, by itself, mean that the relevant scientific evidence is or becomes 'insufficient' within the meaning of Article 5.7;[162] and (2) for existing scientific evidence to become 'insufficient' within the meaning of Article 5.7, no paradigmatic shift in the scientific knowledge is required; it is enough that 'new scientific developments call into question whether the body of scientific evidence still permits of a sufficiently objective assessment

---

assessment and that therefore recourse to Article 5.7 is not possible. However, the existence of an international standard is not dispositive as to the question of the sufficiency of the scientific evidence, and may be rebutted. See Appellate Body Reports, *US/Canada – Continued Suspension (2008)*, para. 696.

157 See Panel Reports, *EC – Approval and Marketing of Biotech Products (2006)*, paras. 7.2930–7.2933.
158 *Ibid.*, para. 7.2939.
159 Further, the panel pointed out that the insufficiency of the evidence must be determined by reference to the time the relevant provisional SPS measure was adopted. See *ibid.*, para. 7.3253.
160 Appellate Body Reports, *US/Canada – Continued Suspension (2008)*, para. 677.
161 *Ibid.*   162 See *ibid.*, para. 702.

of risk'.[163] The Appellate Body noted that 'science continuously evolves', and thought it was:

useful to think of the degree of change as a spectrum. On one extreme of this spectrum lies the incremental advance of science. Where these scientific advances are at the margins, they would not support the conclusion that previously sufficient evidence has become insufficient. At the other extreme lie the more radical scientific changes that lead to a paradigm shift. Such radical change is not frequent. Limiting the application of Article 5.7 to situations where scientific advances lead to a paradigm shift would be too inflexible an approach. WTO Members should be permitted to take a provisional measure where new evidence from a qualified and respected source puts into question the relationship between the pre-existing body of scientific evidence and the conclusions regarding the risks.[164]

Accordingly, the Appellate Body rejected the panel's notion that 'there must be a *critical mass* of new evidence and/or information that calls into question the fundamental precepts of previous knowledge and evidence so as to make relevant, previously sufficient, evidence now insufficient' because this could be understood as requiring that the new scientific evidence lead to a paradigm shift, an approach that the Appellate Body found too inflexible.[165]

Finally, note with regard to the insufficiency of the scientific evidence that the Appellate Body disagreed with the European Communities' argument in *US/Canada – Continued Suspension (2008)* that SPS measures either are 'based on' a risk assessment under Article 5.1, or otherwise the relevant scientific evidence will be 'insufficient' within the meaning of Article 5.7, so that provisional SPS measures may be justified. The Appellate Body explained:

There may be situations where the relevant scientific evidence is sufficient to perform a risk assessment, a WTO Member performs such a risk assessment, but does not adopt an SPS measure either because the risk assessment did not confirm the risk, or the risk identified did not exceed that Member's chosen level of protection. Also, there may be situations where there is no pertinent scientific information available indicating a risk such that an SPS measure would be unwarranted even on a provisional basis.[166]

The second requirement of Article 5.7 of the *SPS Agreement*, namely, that provisional measures must be adopted on the basis of available pertinent information, was addressed for the first time in the *US/Canada – Continued Suspension (2008)* cases. The Appellate Body held that this refers to situations where 'there is some evidentiary basis indicating the possible existence of a risk, but not enough to permit the performance of a risk assessment'.[167] It further held that a 'rational and objective relationship' between the information concerning a risk and the provisional SPS measure is required.[168]

As the Appellate Body found in *US/Canada – Continued Suspension (2008)*, the third and fourth requirements of Article 5.7 of the *SPS Agreement* relate to

163 *Ibid.*, para. 725.   164 *Ibid.*, para. 703.
165 *Ibid.*, para. 705, referring to Panel Report, *US – Continued Suspension (2008)*, para. 7.648; and Panel Report, *US/Canada – Continued Suspension (2008)*, para. 7.626. See also Appellate Body Reports, *US/Canada – Continued Suspension (2008)*, para. 725.
166 Appellate Body Reports, *US/Canada – Continued Suspension (2008)*, para. 681.
167 *Ibid.*, para. 678.   168 *Ibid.*

the *maintenance* of SPS measures taken under Article 5.7 and highlight their provisional nature.[169]

The third requirement of Article 5.7 of the *SPS Agreement* obliges Members to seek to obtain the additional information necessary for a more objective risk assessment. This requirement was clarified by the Appellate Body in *Japan – Agricultural Products II (1999)* and *US/Canada – Continued Suspension (2008)* in three respects, namely: (1) the insufficiency of scientific evidence 'is not a perennial state, but a transitory one'; as of the adoption of the provisional measure, a WTO Member 'must make best efforts to remedy the insufficiency'; (2) Article 5.7 does not specify what actual results must be achieved; the obligation is to 'seek to obtain' additional information; and (3) the information sought must be germane to conducting a risk assessment within the meaning of Article 5.1.[170]

The fourth requirement of Article 5.7 of the *SPS Agreement*, namely, to review the provisional SPS measure within a reasonable period of time, is another reflection of the time-limited nature of such measures under the *SPS Agreement*. However, as scientific uncertainty may sometimes persist for extended periods of time, artificially linking the requirement of review to a fixed time-limit was avoided in the *SPS Agreement*. Instead, Article 5.7 refers to a 'reasonable period of time'. As the Appellate Body stated in *Japan – Agricultural Products II (1999)*, what constitutes a 'reasonable period of time' depends on the specific circumstances of each case, including the difficulty of obtaining the additional information necessary for the review *and* the characteristics of the provisional SPS measure.[171]

The question has arisen whether Article 5.7 of the *SPS Agreement* exhausts the relevance of the precautionary principle for purposes of the *SPS Agreement*. In *EC – Hormones (1998)*, the European Communities tried to rely on the precautionary principle as a rule of customary international law, or at least a general principle of law applicable to the interpretation of the scientific disciplines in the *SPS Agreement*. The Appellate Body expressed doubts as to whether the precautionary principle had developed into a principle of general or customary international law, but considered that it was 'unnecessary, and probably imprudent', to take a position on this important, but abstract, question.[172] The Appellate Body did postulate, however, that Article 5.7 does not exhaust the relevance of the precautionary principle in the *SPS Agreement*. This principle is also reflected in the sixth paragraph of the Preamble and Article 3.3 of the *SPS Agreement*. Both these provisions deal with the right of Members to set their own level of protection, even if this level is higher than that reflected in

---

169 See *ibid.*, para. 679. See also already Appellate Body Report, *Japan – Apples (2003)*, footnote 318 to para. 176.

170 See Appellate Body Report, *Japan – Agricultural Products II (1999)*, para. 92; and Appellate Body Reports, *US/Canada – Continued Suspension (2008)*, para. 679.

171 See Appellate Body Report, *Japan – Agricultural Products II (1999)*, para. 93.

172 See Appellate Body Report, *EC – Hormones (1998)*, para. 123. On this question, see also Panel Reports, *EC – Approval and Marketing of Biotech Products (2006)*, paras. 7.88–7.89.

international standards.[173] Note, however, that the Appellate Body held in *EC – Hormones (1998)* that the precautionary principle (presumably regardless of its status under international law) cannot override the explicit requirements of the *SPS Agreement*, and in particular Articles 5.1 and 5.2 thereof.[174] The practical effect of this ruling is to limit the relevance of the precautionary principle under the *SPS Agreement* to the situation covered by Article 5.7. The precautionary principle can thus *not* be relied upon to add flexibility to the scientific disciplines in Articles 2.2 and 5.1 of the *SPS Agreement*. However, as the Appellate Body held in *US/Canada – Continued Suspension (2008)* and as discussed above, Article 5.7 'must be interpreted keeping in mind that the precautionary principle finds reflection in this provision'.[175]

Another question that has arisen relates to the relationship between Article 5.7 and Article 5.1 of the *SPS Agreement*. In *EC – Approval and Marketing of Biotech Products (2006)*, the European Communities argued before the panel that the bans on biotech products imposed by certain of its Member States fell to be assessed under Article 5.7, to the exclusion of Article 5.1, because 'Article 5.7 is not an exception from a general obligation under Article 5.1, but an autonomous right'.[176] In addressing this argument, the panel in *EC – Approval and Marketing of Biotech Products (2006)* reasoned as follows:

> 'In cases where relevant scientific evidence is insufficient', it is impossible, under the Appellate Body's interpretation of that phrase, for Members to meet the obligation to base their SPS measures on a risk assessment as defined in Annex A(4). We find it unreasonable to assume that Members would accept, even in principle, an obligation with which they cannot comply. In our view, the phrase '[i]n cases where relevant scientific evidence is insufficient' should, therefore, be taken to suggest that the obligation in Article 5.1 is not applicable to measures falling within the scope of Article 5.7.[177]

Thus, the relationship between Articles 5.7 and 5.1 can be said to be one of exclusion, rather than exception.[178]

Questions and Assignments 14.9

How does the *SPS Agreement* provide for situations where scientific evidence is insufficient? What requirements must Members meet in order to be able to take measures in such situations? Does Article 5.7 of the *SPS Agreement* allow Members to take provisional SPS measures in situations of scientific uncertainty? Can the precautionary principle override the explicit provisions of the *SPS Agreement*? Does Article 5.7 of the *SPS Agreement* exhaust the relevance of the precautionary principle for the *SPS Agreement*? Can the precautionary principle be relied on to add flexibility to the scientific disciplines of the *SPS Agreement*? If not, why?

---

173 See above, pp. 910–14.
174 See Appellate Body Report, *EC – Hormones (1998)*, para. 124.
175 Appellate Body Reports, *US/Canada – Continued Suspension (2008)*, para. 680.
176 Panel Reports, *EC – Approval and Marketing of Biotech Products (2006)*, para. 7.2984.
177 *Ibid.*, para. 7.2995.
178 It follows from this that a Member challenging the consistency of an SPS measure with Article 5.1 bears the burden of proving that the measure is inconsistent with at least one of the cumulative requirements of

3.6   Other Substantive Provisions

In addition to the basic substantive provisions discussed in the previous sections, the *SPS Agreement* also contains a number of other substantive provisions, which deserve to be mentioned. This section briefly examines the substantive provisions of the *SPS Agreement* relating to: (1) recognition of equivalence; (2) adaptation to regional conditions; (3) control, inspection and approval procedures; (4) transparency and notification; and (5) special and differential treatment for developing-country Members.

3.6.1   Recognition of Equivalence

Due to differences between Members with regard to local climatic and geographical conditions, consumer preferences and technical and financial resources, it may sometimes be difficult, or even undesirable, to harmonise SPS measures. In such cases, the resulting variety of SPS measures can substantially hinder trade. Such negative effects can be limited if importing Members recognise that it is possible for different measures to achieve the same level of protection (i.e. be equally effective in reducing risk) and are willing to allow imports of products that comply with different, but equally effective, SPS measures. For this reason, Article 4 of the *SPS Agreement* sets out certain obligations for Members with regard to the recognition of equivalence.

Article 4.1 of the *SPS Agreement* obliges Members to accept different SPS measures as equivalent if the exporting Member objectively demonstrates to the importing Member that its measures achieve the latter's appropriate level of protection. The exporting Member is to provide appropriate science-based and technical information to the importing Member, as well as reasonable access, upon request, to the importing Member for inspection, testing and other relevant procedures for the recognition of equivalence.[179] In addition, Article 4.2 obliges Members, when requested, to enter into consultations with the aim of concluding agreements on the recognition of equivalence.

Problems with the implementation of Article 4 of the *SPS Agreement* led the SPS Committee to engage in discussions on equivalence. These discussions resulted in the adoption, in October 2001, of the 'Decision on Equivalence'.[180] This Decision sets out binding guidelines for any Member requesting the recognition of equivalence and for the importing Member to whom such request is addressed. After the adoption of the Decision on Equivalence, the SPS Committee undertook a work programme to clarify and further elaborate certain provisions

Article 5.7. As discussed earlier, the same holds true when a Member challenges the consistency of an SPS measure with Article 2.2 of the *SPS Agreement*. See above, pp. 907–8.

179 See Committee on Sanitary and Phytosanitary Measures, *Decision on the Implementation of Article 4 of the Agreement on the Application of Sanitary and Phytosanitary Measures. Revision*, G/SPS/19/Rev.2, dated 23 July 2004, para. 4.

180 See Committee on Sanitary and Phytosanitary Measures, *Decision on the Implementation of Article 4 of the Agreement on the Application of Sanitary and Phytosanitary Measures*, G/SPS/19, dated 24 October 2001.

of that Decision. This led, in July 2004, to the adoption of the current version of the Decision.[181]

3.6.2   Adaptation to Regional Conditions

Although traditionally an importing country applies its SPS measures to an exporting country as a whole, differences in sanitary and phytosanitary conditions *within* exporting countries often exist. In particular, pest and disease prevalence is independent of national boundaries and can differ within a specific country, due to variations in climate, environment, geographic conditions and regulatory systems in place to control or eradicate pests or diseases. The adaptation of SPS measures to the conditions prevailing in the region of origin of the product may thus be highly desirable. Failure to adapt SPS measures to regional conditions is 'unfair' and leads to excessively trade-restrictive SPS measures.

For this reason, Article 6 of the *SPS Agreement* obliges Members to ensure that their SPS measures are adapted to the sanitary and phytosanitary *characteristics* of the region of origin and destination of the product. These characteristics must be determined with reference to, *inter alia*: (1) the level of pest or disease prevalence; (2) the existence of eradication or control programmes; and (3) guidelines developed by international organisations.

Article 6.2 of the *SPS Agreement* specifically obliges Members to recognise the concepts of pest-free and disease-free areas and areas of low pest and disease prevalence. It is for the exporting Member to provide the necessary evidence that regions in its territory are pest-free or disease-free or have low pest or disease prevalence. For this purpose, the importing Member is entitled to reasonable access to carry out inspection, testing and other relevant procedures.[182]

In May 2008, the TBT Committee adopted a decision on non-binding guidelines for implementing Article 6 of the *SPS Agreement*, commonly referred to as the Regionalisation Decision.[183]

Questions and Assignments 14.10

When are Members obliged to accept the SPS measures of other Members as equivalent? Compare Article 4 of the *SPS Agreement* with Article 2.7 of the *TBT Agreement*. Find the actual text of the Decision on Equivalence and discuss the reasons for its adoption. Can non-compliance with the Decision on Equivalence be the basis for a dispute settlement complaint? Must SPS measures be adapted to regional conditions? How is the existence of pest-free or disease-free areas within countries taken into account by the *SPS Agreement*?

---

181   See Committee on Sanitary and Phytosanitary Measures, *Decision on the Implementation of Article 4 of the Agreement on the Application of Sanitary and Phytosanitary Measures. Revision*, G/SPS/19/Rev.2, dated 23 July 2004. On the legal status of this Decision, see above, pp. 941–2.

182   See Article 6.3 of the *SPS Agreement*.

183   See Committee on Sanitary and Phytosanitary Measures, *Guidelines to Further the Practical Implementation of Article 6 of the Agreement on the Application of Sanitary and Phytosanitary Measures*, G/SPS/48, dated 16 May 2008.

3.6.3   Control, Inspection and Approval Procedures

In order to ensure that their SPS requirements are complied with, countries usually have control, inspection and approval procedures in place.[184] If these procedures are complex, lengthy or costly, they may restrict market access. To avoid this, Article 8 of the *SPS Agreement* obliges Members to comply with the disciplines contained in Annex C as well as other provisions of the *SPS Agreement* in the operation of their control, inspection and approval procedures. The disciplines in Annex C aim to ensure that procedures are not more lengthy and burdensome than is reasonable and necessary and do not discriminate against imports.

Paragraph 1 of Annex C provides, *inter alia*:

Members shall ensure, with respect to any procedure to check and ensure the fulfilment of sanitary or phytosanitary measures, that:

(a) such procedures are undertaken and completed without undue delay and in no less favourable manner for imported products than for like domestic products;

...

(c) information requirements are limited to what is necessary for appropriate control, inspection and approval procedures, including for approval of the use of additives or for the establishment of tolerances for contaminants in food, beverages or feedstuffs;

...

With regard to the 'without undue delay' requirement of Annex C(1)(a), the Appellate Body ruled in *Australia – Apples (2010)*:

Annex C(1)(a) requires Members to ensure that relevant procedures are undertaken and completed with appropriate dispatch, that is, that they do not involve periods of time that are unwarranted, or otherwise excessive, disproportionate or unjustifiable. Whether a relevant procedure has been unduly delayed is, therefore, not an assessment that can be done in the abstract, but one which requires a case-by-case analysis as to the reasons for the alleged failure to act with appropriate dispatch, and whether such reasons are justifiable.[185]

Earlier, the panel in *EC – Approval and Marketing of Biotech Products (2006)* had already interpreted the 'without undue delay' requirement of Annex C(1)(a) in the same manner. The panel in that case examined and rejected the European Communities' arguments that the delays were justified by the perceived inadequacy of its existing legislation and the prudent and precautionary approach it applied due to the fact that the relevant science was evolving and in a state of flux.[186] What matters for purposes of the 'without undue delay' requirement of

---

184 Note that, in the context of the *TBT Agreement* these measures are referred to as 'conformity assessment procedures'. See above, p. 854.

185 Appellate Body Report, *Australia – Apples (2010)*, para. 437.

186 See Panel Reports, *EC – Approval and Marketing of Biotech Products (2006)*, paras. 7.1511–7.1530. The panel pointed out that the core obligation of Annex C(1)(a) is for Members to come to a substantive decision. This decision need not give 'a straight yes or no answer to applicants'. Instead, a Member, for example, may reject an application subject to later review, or give a time-limited approval.

Annex C(1)(a) is not the length of the delay, but rather whether there is a legitimate reason or justification for it.

With regard to the 'in no less favourable manner' requirement of Annex C(1)(a), the panel in *EC – Approval and Marketing of Biotech Products (2006)* found that, in order to establish a violation of this requirement of Annex C(1)(a), it is necessary to establish:

(i) that imported products have been treated in a 'less favourable manner' than domestic products in respect of the undertaking and completion of approval procedures, and (ii) that the imported products which are alleged to have been treated less favourably are 'like' the domestic products which are alleged to have been treated more favourably.[187]

On the first element of this test, the panel noted that it clearly lays down a national treatment obligation, and it therefore considered it useful to look to case law on Article III:4 of the GATT 1994 for appropriate interpretative guidance.[188]

Finally, with regard to the requirements set out in Annex C(1)(c), the panel in *EC – Approval and Marketing of Biotech Products (2006)* observed that this provision contains 'five separate, but related, obligations to be observed by Members in the operation of approval procedures'.[189] These obligations relate to: (1) the publication or communication to applicants of the processing period of each procedure; (2) the examination of the completeness of the documentation and the communication to applicants of deficiencies; (3) the transmission of the results of the procedure; (4) the processing of applications which have deficiencies; and (5) the provision of information about the stage of a procedure and the provision of an explanation of any delay.[190] However, the panel in this case rejected the claims of inconsistency with Annex C(1)(c) as the complainants had not brought sufficient evidence to show a violation of these obligations.[191]

3.6.4 Transparency and Notification

Lack of transparency with regard to SPS measures may constitute a significant barrier to market access since it increases the cost and difficulty for exporters in determining what requirements their products must comply with on their export markets.[192] This issue is addressed in Article 7 of the *SPS Agreement*, which obliges Members to notify changes in their SPS measures and to provide information on their SPS measures according to Annex B to the *SPS Agreement*. Annex B contains multiple, detailed rules on: (1) the publication of adopted SPS measures; (2) national enquiry points; and (3) the prior notification of proposed

187 *Ibid.*, para. 7.2400.
188 See *ibid.*, para. 7.2401. On the case law on Article III:4 of the GATT 1994, see above, pp. 321–8, 355–62, and 382–403.
189 *Ibid.*, para. 7.1574.   190 See *ibid.*
191 See *ibid.*, paras. 7.1585–7.1602 (with regard to the United States' claim in respect of the general *de facto* moratorium) and paras. 7.2439–7.2472 (with regard to the claims of the United States and Argentina in respect of the product-specific measures).
192 For a general discussion of the lack of transparency as a trade barrier, see above, pp. 532–3.

SPS measures that differ from international standards, to allow time for comments from other Members.

With regard to the 'publication' requirement of Annex B(1), the Appellate Body in *Japan – Agricultural Products II (1999)* found that the object and purpose of Annex B(1) is:

'to enable interested Members to become acquainted with' the sanitary and phytosanitary regulations adopted or maintained by other Members and thus to enhance transparency regarding these measures. In our opinion, the scope of application of the publication requirement of paragraph 1 of Annex B should be interpreted in the light of the object and purpose of this provision.[193]

In *Japan – Agricultural Products II (1999)*, the Appellate Body upheld the panel's finding that Japan had violated the 'publication' requirement of Annex B(1) to and Article 7 of the *SPS Agreement*. It was undisputed that Japan's varietal testing requirement was generally applicable, and that it had not been published. The Appellate Body agreed with the panel that the actual impact of the varietal testing requirement on exporting countries was such that it had 'a character similar to laws, decrees and ordinances', i.e. the instruments with regard to which Annex B(1) explicitly imposes a 'publication' requirement.[194]

With regard to the 'prior notification' requirements of Annex B(5) and (7), the panel in *Japan – Apples (2003)* had to determine whether the relevant changes of the SPS measure at issue constituted changes which were subject to the 'prior notification' requirement because they 'may have a significant effect on trade of other Members', as the chapeau to Annex B(5) states. The panel considered that:

the most important factor in this regard is whether the change affects the conditions of market access for the product concerned, that is, would the exported product (apple fruit from the United States in this case) still be permitted to enter Japan if they complied with the prescription contained in the previous regulations. If this is not the case, then we must consider whether the change could be considered to potentially have a *significant* effect on trade of other Members. In this regard, it would be relevant to consider whether the change has resulted in any increase in production, packaging and sales costs, such as more onerous treatment requirements or more time-consuming administrative formalities.[195]

As the United States, the complainant in this case, had not presented arguments regarding in what respects the SPS measure at issue departed from the previous one, the panel found that the United States had failed to make a *prima facie* case and accordingly rejected the US claim.[196]

In order to promote the implementation of the transparency obligations, the SPS Committee in 2002 adopted recommended notification procedures, which were revised in 2008.[197] As of 30 September 2011, 102 out of then 153 Members

---

193 Appellate Body Report, *Japan – Agricultural Products II (1999)*, para. 106.
194 See *ibid.*, paras. 107–8. Footnote 5 to Annex B(1) of the *SPS Agreement* refers to 'laws, decrees and ordinances'.
195 Panel Report, *Japan – Apples (2003)*, para. 8.314.   196 *Ibid.*, paras. 8.324 and 8.326.
197 See Committee on Sanitary and Phytosanitary Measures, *Recommended Procedures for Implementing the Transparency Obligations of the SPS Agreement (Article 7), Revision*, G/SPS/7/Rev.3, dated 20 June 2008.

(or 67 per cent) had submitted at least one notification to the WTO.[198] While the number of notifications circulated by Members has increased significantly in recent years,[199] the failure to notify (or notify correctly) new, or changes to, SPS measures is still a frequently raised concern at meetings of the SPS Committee.[200] In response, in 2011, the WTO Secretariat launched a new online SPS Notification Submission System. During 2011, 1,388 notifications were submitted, bringing the total number of notifications since the entry into force of the *SPS Agreement* in 1995 to 13,644.[201] To assist Members in the formidable task of managing the flow of information regarding notified SPS measures, in 2007, the WTO Secretariat launched the SPS Information Management System, which has since remained available on a dedicated website.[202]

In addition to the 'publication' and 'prior notification' requirements discussed above, Annex B also provides for an 'enquiry point' requirement. Annex B(3) and (4) of the *SPS Agreement* oblige WTO Members to create the necessary infrastructure to carry out their transparency obligations by establishing a National Notification Authority, responsible for the implementation of notification procedures, and an 'Enquiry Point', responsible for answering all reasonable questions and providing relevant documents upon request.[203]

Finally, note that Article 5.8 of the *SPS Agreement* also contains an important obligation for the promotion of transparency. It obliges Members to provide information, upon request, regarding the reasons for their SPS measures where such measures are not 'based on' international standards or no relevant international standards exist. A Member, which has reason to believe that such an SPS measure does or could potentially restrain its exports, may request information under Article 5.8 of the *SPS Agreement* from the Member adopting or maintaining the SPS measure.

Questions and Assignments 14.11

What are the key obligations under the *SPS Agreement* with respect to control, inspection and approval procedures? What notification obligations do Members have under the *SPS Agreement*? In your opinion, why are transparency and notification obligations with respect to SPS measures important?

---

198 See Committee on Sanitary and Phytosanitary Measures, Note by the Secretariat, *Overview Regarding the Level of Implementation of the Transparency Provisions of the SPS Agreement*, G/SPS/GEN/804/Rev.4, dated 13 October 2011, para. 15. Members, which had not submitted any notification, included nineteen developing countries, twenty-one least-developed countries, and one developed country.

199 In 2006, 1,157 notifications were submitted, a considerable increase as compared to 2005, when 850 notifications were made. See WTO Secretariat, *Annual Report 2007*, 29.

200 See Committee on Sanitary and Phytosanitary Measures, Note by the Secretariat, *Specific Trade Concerns*, G/SPS/GEN/204/Rev.12, dated 2 March 2012.

201 See WTO Secretariat, *WTO Annual Report 2012*, 46.

202 See http://spsims.wto.org. The SPS Information Management System also contains information on national notification authorities and enquiry points.

203 The WTO Secretariat regularly updates and circulates lists of these authorities, under official document numbers G/SPS/NNA/– and G/SPS/ENQ/–.

3.6.5   Special and Differential Treatment

The *SPS Agreement* provides for special and differential treatment of developing-country Members, both by other Members and by the SPS Committee, in order to take account of the difficulties they face in implementing the *SPS Agreement* and complying with SPS measures on their export markets. These provisions aim to give additional flexibility to developing-country Members.

Article 10.1 of the *SPS Agreement* provides:

> In the preparation and application of sanitary or phytosanitary measures, Members shall take account of the special needs of developing country Members, and in particular of the least-developed country Members.

This provision was relied upon for the first time by Argentina in *EC – Approval and Marketing of Biotech Products (2006)*. Argentina claimed that the general *de facto* moratorium on the approval of biotech products maintained by the European Communities had important implications for Argentina's economic development, due to its strong dependence on agricultural exports and its position as the world's second-largest producer, and leading developing-country producer, of biotech products. It further pointed to its great interest in the integrated European market. Therefore, Argentina argued that the European Communities was obliged, under Article 10.1 of the *SPS Agreement*, to take into account Argentina's special needs in the preparation and application of its SPS measure. Argentina emphasised the mandatory nature of Article 10.1 and claimed that it requires more than mere attention to developing-country problems. Instead, Article 10.1 requires 'positive action', in this case 'preferential market access' for developing-country products or implementation of the Member's obligations in a manner that is 'beneficial, or less detrimental, to the interests of developing country Members'.[204] According to Argentina, the European Communities had failed to comply with this obligation. The panel in this case interpreted Article 10.1 in keeping with previous case law on special and differential treatment provisions in other WTO agreements.[205] It held that the obligation to 'take account' of developing-country needs merely requires Members 'to consider' the needs of developing countries. This obligation, according to the panel, does not prescribe a particular result to be achieved, and notably does not provide that the importing Member must invariably accord special and differential treatment where a measure may lead to a decrease, or slower increase, in developing-country imports.[206] Indeed, the panel considered it conceivable that the European Communities did take account of Argentina's needs, but at the same time took account of other legitimate interests (such as those of its consumers and environment) and gave priority to the latter.[207] After examining the arguments

---

204 See *ibid.*, para. 7.1607.   205 See above, pp. 737–9, 834–5 and 1010–11.
206 See Panel Reports, *EC – Approval and Marketing of Biotech Products (2006)*, para. 7.1620.
207 See *ibid.*, para. 7.1621.

made by Argentina in this regard, the panel found that Argentina had not met its burden of proof for showing a violation of Article 10.1.[208]

Article 10.2 of the *SPS Agreement* provides:

Where the appropriate level of sanitary or phytosanitary protection allows scope for the phased introduction of new sanitary or phytosanitary measures, longer time-frames for compliance should be accorded on products of interest to developing country Members so as to maintain opportunities for their exports.

This provision encourages, but does not oblige, Members to grant developing countries a longer period for compliance with new SPS measures. In the 2001 Doha Ministerial Decision on *Implementation-Related Issues and Concerns*, this longer period was specified as normally not less than six months.[209] The Doha Decision further provides that, if longer periods for compliance are not possible and a Member identifies specific problems with the measure, the importing Member must enter into consultations with a view to reaching a mutually satisfactory solution that continues to achieve its appropriate level of protection.[210]

Article 10.3 of the *SPS Agreement* allows the SPS Committee to grant developing-country Members, upon request, specified, time-limited 'exceptions' from some or all of their obligations, taking account of their financial, trade and development needs. These 'exceptions' are – as is explicitly stated in Article 10.3 – aimed at 'ensuring that developing country Members are able to comply with the provisions of this Agreement'.

Finally, Article 10.4 of the *SPS Agreement* provides that Members should encourage and facilitate the participation of developing countries in the relevant international organisations. This provision does not contain any binding obligation but is purely hortatory.

As discussed above, the Doha Ministerial Declaration mandates, as part of the Doha Round negotiations, a review of the special and differential treatment provisions in the WTO agreements, in order to make them more precise, effective and operational.[211] The proposals concerning Articles 9 and 10 of the *SPS Agreement* made in this context are still under consideration.[212] Note, however, that, in October 2009, the SPS Committee adopted a procedure to enhance the transparency of special and differential treatment of developing-country Members.[213]

---

208 See *ibid.*, paras. 7.1623–7.1625. Note, however, that the panel explicitly stated that, in coming to this conclusion, it was *not* suggesting that there is a duty on developing countries specifically to request that their needs as developing countries be considered. See *ibid.*, para. 7.1625.

209 See Ministerial Conference, Doha Decision on *Implementation-Related Issues and Concerns*, WT/MIN(01)/17, dated 14 November 2001, para. 3.1.

210 See *ibid.*, para. 3.1.

211 Ministerial Conference, *Doha Ministerial Declaration*, WT/MIN(01)/DEC/1, dated 20 November 2001, para. 44.

212 For the relevant proposals, see Committee on Sanitary and Phytosanitary Measures, *Report on Proposals for Special and Differential Treatment*, G/SPS/35, dated 7 July 2005, para. 41. This report noted that some Members are concerned that modification of Articles 9 or 10 could change the balance of rights and obligations established by the *SPS Agreement*.

213 See Committee on Sanitary and Phytosanitary Measures, Decision by the Committee on *Procedure to Enhance Transparency of Special and Differential Treatment in Favour of Developing Country Members*, G/SPS/33/Rev.1, dated 18 December 2009.

Questions and Assignments 14.12

What options are available to a developing-country Member which is unable to meet its obligations under the *SPS Agreement*? Can a developing country insist on being given a longer time period for compliance with other Members' new SPS measures? Has any change been brought about in this respect by the Doha *Decision on Implementation*?

4   INSTITUTIONAL AND PROCEDURAL PROVISIONS OF THE *SPS AGREEMENT*

In addition to the substantive provisions discussed above, the *SPS Agreement* also contains a number of institutional and procedural provisions. This section deals with the provisions on: (1) the SPS Committee; (2) dispute settlement; and (3) technical assistance to developing-country Members.

4.1   SPS Committee

The Committee on Sanitary and Phytosanitary Measures, commonly referred to as the 'SPS Committee', is established under Article 12.1 of the *SPS Agreement* with a mandate to carry out the functions necessary for the implementation of the *SPS Agreement* and the furtherance of its objectives. The SPS Committee is composed of representatives of all WTO Members and takes decisions by consensus. It meets at least three times a year.[214] In 2012, it held four formal meetings.[215]

The SPS Committee has three main tasks. First, pursuant to Article 12.2 of the *SPS Agreement*, it is a forum for consultations and must encourage and facilitate consultations or negotiations between Members on SPS issues. Often SPS disputes can be resolved through such consultations without resort to dispute settlement. At each meeting of the SPS Committee, Members raise and discuss specific trade concerns with regard to the SPS measures of other Members. By the end of 2011, 328 specific trade concerns had been raised, of which 173 were raised by developing-country Members and three by least-developed-country Members.[216] In all but one year since 2008, developing-country Members raised significantly more concerns than developed-country Members.[217] Of the 328 trade concerns raised in the SPS Committee by the end of 2011, ninety-five

---

214 See WTO Secretariat, *Annual Report 2007*, 28.

215 Committee on Sanitary and Phytosanitary Measures, Minutes of the Meetings of 27–28 March, 10–11 July and 18–19 October 2012, G/SPS/R/66, G/SPS/R/67 and G/SPS/R/69. See also G/SPS/R/68.

216 The WTO Secretariat maintains an annually updated list, summarising specific trade concerns brought to the Committee's attention since 1995. See e.g. Committee on Sanitary and Phytosanitary Measures, *Specific Trade Concerns*, Note by the Secretariat, G/SPS/GEN/204/Rev.12, dated 2 March 2012. For the number of concerns raised, see para. 4.

217 See *ibid*., para. 3, Figure 3B.

trade concerns have been reported resolved and eighteen partially resolved.[218] The specific trade concerns discussed in the SPS Committee in 2011 included restrictions relating to bird flu and 'mad cow' disease; maximum levels of pesticide residues in various products; restrictions regarding food and animal feed additives; as well as some pest-specific concerns relevant for food safety.[219] In addition to specific trade concerns, the SPS Committee also discusses general issues relating to the implementation of the *SPS Agreement*. More than any other WTO committee, the SPS Committee has been successful in translating such discussions into decisions. In this respect, note in particular the Decision on Equivalence of 2001, as last revised in 2004.[220]

Secondly, pursuant to Article 12.2 of the *SPS Agreement*, the SPS Committee must encourage the use of international standards by Members. In this respect, the SPS Committee is obliged, pursuant to Article 12.3 of the *SPS Agreement*, to maintain close contact with the international standard-setting organisations, and must, pursuant to Article 12.4 of the *SPS Agreement*, develop a procedure for monitoring the process of international harmonisation.[221]

Thirdly, pursuant to Article 12.7 of the *SPS Agreement*, the SPS Committee is obliged to undertake a review of the operation and implementation of the *SPS Agreement* three years after its entry into force and as necessary thereafter. Where appropriate, it may propose amendments to the *SPS Agreement* to the Council for Trade in Goods. The first review was completed in 1999 and no amendments were proposed. In the 2001 Doha Ministerial Decision on *Implementation-Related Issues and Concerns*, the SPS Committee was instructed to conduct subsequent reviews at least once every four years.[222] The third review was completed in March 2010, resulting in a report with multiple recommendations for further action on SPS issues by Members and the SPS Committee.[223]

218 See *ibid.*, para. 4. Note that other trade concerns may have been resolved without the SPS Committee being informed of this.

219 Committee on Sanitary and Phytosanitary Measures, *Report (2011) on the Activities of the Committee on Sanitary and Phytosanitary Measures*, G/L/969, dated 27 October 2011, para. 3.

220 See Decision on the *Implementation of Article 4 of the Agreement on the Application of Sanitary and Phytosanitary Measures*, of 2001 and revised in 2004, G/SPS/19, dated 24 October 2001; and Decision on the *Implementation of Article 4 of the Agreement on the Application of Sanitary and Phytosanitary Measures. Revision*, G/SPS/19/Rev.2, dated 23 July 2004, para. 4. For a discussion on the Decision on Equivalence, see above, pp. 933–4. Other decisions by the SPS Committee include: *Guidelines to Further the Practical Implementation of Article 6 of the Agreement on the Application of Sanitary and Phytosanitary Measures*, G/SPS/48, dated 16 May 2008 (see above, pp. 894–6); *Decision on a Procedure to Enhance Transparency of Special and Differential Treatment in Favour of Developing Country Members*, G/SPS/33/Rev.1, dated 18 December 2009 (see above, pp. 939–41); and *Decision of the Committee on Actions regarding SPS-Related Private Standards*, G/SPS/55, dated 6 April 2011 (see above, p. 901, footnote 22).

221 Such a procedure was developed in 1997 (see G/SPS/11) on a provisional basis, in terms of which the SPS Committee draws up annual reports regarding the use of existing standards, the need for new standards and work on the adoption of such standards. This provisional procedure was revised in October 2004 (see G/SPS/GEN/11/Rev.1) and extended indefinitely in 2006 (see G/SPS/40).

222 Ministerial Conference, *Doha Decision on Implementation-Related Issues and Concerns*, WT/MIN(01)/17, dated 14 November 2001.

223 Committee on Sanitary and Phytosanitary Measures, *Review of the Operation and Implementation of the SPS Agreement*, G/SPS/53, dated 3 May 2010.

4.2 Dispute Settlement

Pursuant to Article 11.1 of the *SPS Agreement*, the provisions of Articles XXII and XXIII of the GATT 1994 as elaborated by the DSU apply to consultations and the settlement of disputes under the *SPS Agreement*, except as otherwise provided. To date, two specific issues relating to the settlement of SPS disputes have generated much debate: (1) the issue of the selection and the role of scientific experts consulted by panels; and (2) the issue of the standard of review to be applied by panels when reviewing the SPS-consistency of SPS measures.

4.2.1 Scientific Experts

Article 11.2 of the *SPS Agreement* authorises panels to consult experts to help them to deal with the complex issues of scientific fact that arise in SPS disputes.[224] These experts are chosen by the panel in consultation with the parties. Panels may also set up advisory technical expert groups or consult relevant international organisations. They may do so at the request of either party to the dispute or on their own initiative. In all SPS disputes to date, panels have consulted individual experts to help them to understand the complex issues of scientific fact that arose in these disputes. Experts are to act as an 'interface' between the scientific evidence and the panel, to allow the latter to perform its task as the trier of fact. The selection and the use made of experts was very controversial in *US/Canada – Continued Suspension (2008)*. In that case, the Appellate Body noted the central role that scientific experts, and their opinions, may play in a panel's review of the SPS measure at issue, especially in cases involving highly complex scientific issues.[225] Experts consulted by a panel can have a decisive role in such cases.[226] The independence and impartiality of these scientific experts consulted by a panel is therefore of great importance. The Appellate Body recognised that panels are often faced with practical difficulties in selecting experts who have the required level of expertise and to whose selection the parties do not object.[227] However, as the Appellate Body observed, the practical difficulties that a panel may encounter in selecting experts cannot displace the need to ensure their independence and impartiality and thus to guarantee that the consultations with the experts respect the parties' due process rights.[228] In *US/Canada – Continued Suspension (2008)*, the Appellate Body considered that:

there was an objective basis to conclude that the institutional affiliation with JECFA of Drs Boisseau and Boobis, and their participation in JECFA's evaluations of the six hormones at

---

224 As discussed in Chapter 3 of this book, Article 13 of the DSU generally authorises panels to seek information and technical advice from any individual or body, and to seek information from any source, consult experts or request advisory reports. This provision also applies to disputes under the *SPS Agreement*. See above, p. 225.

225 See Appellate Body Reports, *US/Canada – Continued Suspension (2008)*, para. 436.

226 See *ibid.*, para. 480.   227 See *ibid.*   228 See *ibid.*

issue, was likely to affect or give rise to justifiable doubts as to their independence or impartiality given that the evaluations conducted by JECFA lie at the heart of the controversy between the parties.[229]

According to the Appellate Body, the appointment of and consultations with Drs Boisseau and Boobis compromised the adjudicative independence and impartiality of the panel.[230]

With regard to the use of scientific experts by panels, recall that the Appellate Body in *Japan – Agricultural Products II (1999)* found that, while a panel has broad authority to consult experts to help it to understand and evaluate the evidence submitted and the arguments made by the parties, a panel may not – with the help of its experts – make the case for one or the other party.[231] Similarly, in *Australia – Apples (2010)*, the Appellate Body cautioned that:

> whether or not an alternative measure's level of risk achieves a Member's appropriate level of protection is a question of legal characterization, the answer to which will determine the consistency or inconsistency of a Member's measure with its obligation under Article 5.6. Answering this question is not a task that can be delegated to scientific experts.[232]

4.2.2 Standard of Review

The second issue relating to the settlement of SPS disputes that has generated much debate is the issue of the standard of review to be applied by panels when reviewing the SPS-consistency of SPS measures.[233] In *US/Canada – Continued Suspension (2008)*, the Appellate Body held with regard to the standard of review to be applied by a panel when it assesses under Article 5.1 of the *SPS Agreement* whether an SPS measure is 'based on' a risk assessment:

> It is the WTO Member's task to perform the risk assessment. The panel's task is to review that risk assessment. Where a panel goes beyond this limited mandate and acts as a risk assessor, it would be substituting its own scientific judgement for that of the risk assessor and making a *de novo* review and, consequently, would exceed its functions under Article 11 of the DSU.[234]

According to the Appellate Body, the review power of a panel is not to determine whether the risk assessment undertaken by a WTO Member is correct, but rather to determine whether that risk assessment 'is supported by coherent reasoning and respectable scientific evidence and is, in this sense, objectively justifiable'.[235] A panel reviewing the consistency of an SPS measure with Article 5.1 of the *SPS Agreement* must: (1) identify the scientific basis upon which the SPS

229 *Ibid.*, para. 481. 'JECFA' stands for 'Joint FAO/WHO Expert Committee on Food Additives', which is an international expert scientific committee that is administered jointly by the Food and Agriculture Organization of the United Nations (FAO) and the World Health Organization (WHO).
230 See *ibid.*
231 See Appellate Body Report, *Japan – Agricultural Products II (1999)*, para. 129. See above, p. 227.
232 Appellate Body Report, *Australia – Apples (2010)*, para. 384.
233 For a general discussion on the standard of review of panels, see above, pp. 219–22.
234 Appellate Body Reports, *US/Canada – Continued Suspension (2008)*, para. 590.
235 *Ibid.*

945 Institutional and Procedural Provisions of the *SPS Agreement*

measure was adopted; (2) verify that the scientific basis comes from a respected and qualified source; (3) review whether the particular conclusions drawn by the Member assessing the risk find sufficient support in the scientific evidence relied upon, or, in other words, assess whether the reasoning articulated on the basis of the scientific evidence is objective and coherent; and (4) determine whether the results of the risk assessment 'sufficiently warrant' the SPS measure at issue.[236] It is important in this context to keep in mind that the scientific basis cited as warranting the SPS measure at issue need not reflect the majority view of the scientific community. As discussed above, SPS measures can be based on a divergent or minority view rather than mainstream scientific opinion, provided that it 'comes from a qualified and respected source', and has 'the necessary scientific and methodological rigour to be considered reputable science'.[237]

In *Australia – Apples (2010)*, the Appellate Body further clarified the standard of review applicable under Article 5.1 of the *SPS Agreement*. The Appellate Body distinguished two aspects of a panel's scrutiny of a risk assessment: (1) scrutiny of the underlying scientific basis; and (2) scrutiny of the reasoning of the risk assessor based upon such underlying science. With respect to the first aspect, the Appellate Body saw the panel's role as limited to reviewing whether the scientific basis constitutes 'legitimate science according to the standards of the relevant scientific community'.[238] However, the Appellate Body considered that the second aspect of a panel's review was somewhat less deferential and that it involved an 'assessment of whether the reasoning of the risk assessor is objective and coherent, that is, whether the conclusions find sufficient support in the scientific evidence relied upon'.[239] The Appellate Body disagreed with the view that 'a panel should assess the reasoning and conclusions reached by a risk assessor and the scientific evidence relied upon in the same way', and pointed out that:

a distinction should be drawn between, on the one hand, the scientific evidence relied upon by the risk assessor and, on the other hand, the reasoning employed and the conclusions reached by the risk assessor on the basis of that scientific evidence.[240]

The Appellate Body stated in *Australia – Apples (2010)* that the more deferential standard of review applicable to the underlying scientific evidence was explained by the fact that 'a panel is not well suited to conduct scientific research and assessments itself'. In contrast, the Appellate Body affirmed that, without substituting its judgment for that of the risk assessor, a panel must be

---

236 See *ibid.*, para. 591.
237 See *ibid.* Note that, in *Australia – Apples (2010)*, the Appellate Body stated that: 'in *US/Canada – Continued Suspension*, [it] did not set out a series of steps that a panel must *mechanically* follow in the evaluation of a risk assessment under Article 5.1 of the *SPS Agreement*.' See Appellate Body Report, *Australia – Apples (2010)*, para. 219. Emphasis added.
238 See Appellate Body Report, *Australia – Apples (2010)*, para. 215 (referring to Appellate Body Reports, *US/Canada – Continued Suspension (2008)*, para. 591).
239 Appellate Body Report, *Australia – Apples (2010)*, para. 215.
240 *Ibid.*, para. 224.

able to review the reasoning of the risk assessor, because this reasoning plays an important role in revealing whether or not the requisite rational or objective relationship between the reasoning and scientific evidence exists.[241]

In *Australia – Apples (2010)*, the Appellate Body also made clear that the standard of review to be applied by a panel assessing a claim under Article 5.6 of the *SPS Agreement* differs from, and is less deferential than, the standard of review to be employed when assessing a claim under Article 5.1:

> Caution not to conduct a *de novo* review is appropriate where a panel reviews a risk assessment conducted by the importing Member's authorities in the context of Article 5.1. However, the situation is different in the context of an Article 5.6 claim. The legal question under Article 5.6 is not whether the authorities of the importing Member have, in conducting the risk assessment, acted in accordance with the obligations of the *SPS Agreement*. Rather, the legal question is whether the importing Member could have adopted a less trade-restrictive measure. This requires the panel itself to objectively assess, *inter alia*, whether the alternative measure proposed by the complainant would achieve the importing Member's appropriate level of protection.[242]

4.3   Technical Assistance

Due to the financial and human resource constraints encountered by developing-country Members, they are often in need of technical assistance in various areas of relevance to the *SPS Agreement*. Technical assistance encompasses not only information to enhance understanding of the disciplines of the *SPS Agreement* and practical training on its operation, but also the provision of soft infrastructure (training of technical and scientific personnel and the development of national regulatory frameworks) as well as hard infrastructure (laboratories, equipment, veterinary services and the establishment of pest- or disease-free areas).[243]

Technical assistance is dealt with in Article 9 of the *SPS Agreement*.[244] In terms of Article 9.1, Members 'agree to facilitate' the provision of technical assistance to other Members, especially developing countries, either bilaterally or through international organisations. Such technical assistance may take various forms and may aim, *inter alia*, at helping developing countries to comply with SPS measures on their export markets. Article 9.2 deals with the situation where a Member's SPS measure requires substantial investments from an exporting developing-country Member and obliges the importing Member to 'consider providing' technical assistance to allow the developing country to maintain or increase its market opportunities for the relevant product. These provisions are in the nature of 'best-endeavour' obligations and are thus difficult to enforce.

---

241 *Ibid.*, para. 225.   242 *Ibid.*, para. 356.
243 This typology of technical assistance was drawn up by the WTO Secretariat. See Committee on Sanitary and Phytosanitary Measures, *Technical Assistance Typology*, Note by the Secretariat, G/SPS/GEN/206, dated 18 October 2000.
244 For a discussion on trade-related technical assistance in general, see above, pp. 101–4.

The 2001 Doha Ministerial Decision on *Implementation-Related Issues and Concerns* urges Members to provide 'to the extent possible' technical and financial assistance to least-developed-country Members to help them respond to SPS measures that may affect their trade and to assist them to implement the *SPS Agreement*.[245]

As a result of an initiative taken at the 2001 Doha Ministerial Conference, the WTO established in 2002 together with the World Bank, the Food and Agricultural Organization (FAO), the World Health Organization (WHO) and the World Organization for Animal Health (OIE), the Standards and Trade Development Facility (STDF). The STDF acts as a coordinating and financing mechanism and aims to assist developing countries to establish and implement SPS standards, in order to improve their human, animal and plant health status and their ability to gain or maintain access to markets.[246]

Questions and Assignments 14.13

What are the main tasks of the SPS Committee? How does the *SPS Agreement* deal with the fact that panels are often faced with complex scientific issues in disputes under the *SPS Agreement*? Why did the Appellate Body in *US/Canada – Continued Suspension (2008)* consider that the appointment of and consultations with Drs Boisseau and Boobis constituted a legal error on the part of the panel? How should a panel assess whether an SPS measure is 'based on' a risk assessment as required by Article 5.1 of the *SPS Agreement*? Does the standard of review applied by a panel in this context differ from the standard applied in other disputes? Can Members be obliged to provide technical assistance to developing countries under the *SPS Agreement*? What forms could technical assistance take?

5 SUMMARY

The *SPS Agreement* applies to SPS measures that may affect international trade. Whether a measure is an 'SPS measure' depends on its purpose or aim. In broad terms, an 'SPS measure' is a measure that: (1) aims at the protection of human or animal life or health from food-borne risks; or (2) aims at the protection of human, animal or plant life or health from risks from pests or diseases. The adoption and implementation of SPS measures is sometimes in the hands of bodies other than the central government, such as regulatory agencies, regional bodies, subfederal governments and non-governmental bodies. The *SPS Agreement* takes this into account by providing that Members must enact and implement positive measures to ensure the observance of its rules by bodies other than central government bodies. With regard to the relationship between the *SPS Agreement* and other WTO agreements, note that, to the extent a measure is an 'SPS measure' as

---

245 See Ministerial Conference, *Doha Decision on Implementation-Related Issues and Concerns*, WT/MIN(01)/17, dated 14 November 2001, para. 3.6.
246 See www.standardsfacility.org.

defined in Annex A to the *SPS Agreement*, the *SPS Agreement* applies to the exclusion of the *TBT Agreement*. No such relationship of mutual exclusivity exists between the *SPS Agreement* and the GATT 1994. However, the *SPS Agreement* contains a presumption of consistency with the relevant provisions of the GATT 1994 for all measures that are in conformity with the *SPS Agreement*.

The *SPS Agreement* explicitly acknowledges the sovereign right of WTO Members to take SPS measures (Article 2.1). At the same time, however, the *SPS Agreement* subjects Members to a number of obligations regarding their SPS measures. These obligations include: (1) the obligation to take or maintain only SPS measures *necessary* to protect human, animal or plant life or health (Article 2.2); (2) the obligation to take or maintain only SPS measures 'based on' scientific principles and on sufficient scientific evidence (Article 2.2); and (3) the obligation not to adopt or maintain SPS measures that arbitrarily or unjustifiably discriminate or constitute a disguised restriction on trade (Article 2.3). Moreover, the *SPS Agreement* encourages the harmonisation of SPS measures around international standards by imposing an obligation to base SPS measures on international standards, except if there is scientific justification for deviation from these standards (Article 3).

The obligations set out in Articles 2.2 and 2.3 of the *SPS Agreement* are further specified and elaborated on in a number of other provisions containing substantive obligations relating to risk assessment *and* risk management. With regard to risk assessment, the *SPS Agreement* primarily requires that SPS measures be 'based on' a risk assessment (Article 5.1), as defined in Annex A(4). The latter provides for two types of risk assessment: one for risks from pests and diseases; one for risks from food and feed. With regard to risk management, the *SPS Agreement* primarily requires Members to: (1) avoid arbitrary or unjustifiable distinctions in the levels of protection deemed appropriate in different situations, if these distinctions lead to discrimination or disguised restrictions on trade (Article 5.5); and (2) ensure that SPS measures are not more trade-restrictive than required to achieve their appropriate level of protection (Article 5.6). Where scientific evidence is insufficient for the conduct of a risk assessment, the *SPS Agreement* allows Members to take – under certain conditions – provisional SPS measures which are not based on a risk assessment (Article 5.7). The *SPS Agreement* thus contains a specific formulation of what is often referred to as the precautionary principle. The *SPS Agreement* also provides for substantive provisions relating to: (1) the recognition of equivalence of SPS measures of other Members; (2) the obligation to adapt SPS measures to regional conditions in other Members; (3) SPS-related control, inspection and approval procedures; (4) transparency and notification obligations regarding SPS measures; and (5) special and differential treatment of developing-country Members.

Members consult regarding any matters pertaining to the operation or objectives of the *SPS Agreement* in the SPS Committee. This Committee is composed of all WTO Members and meets several times a year. The WTO dispute settlement rules and procedures, discussed in Chapter 3, apply to disputes concerning the *SPS Agreement*. However, in the context of SPS disputes, specific questions have arisen regarding the standard of review to be applied by panels as well as the appointment and use made of scientific experts by panels. Acknowledging the difficulties developing-country Members may face in implementing the obligations under the *SPS Agreement*, Members have agreed 'to facilitate' the provision of technical assistance to Members in need.

Exercise 14: Healthy Fruit

Richland has enacted legislation, requiring that all fruit marketed and sold in Richland be organically grown and packaged in biodegradable materials made from natural fibres. According to Richland, all pesticides and fertilisers used in conventional fruit farming have a harmful effect on human health in the long term. In addition, Richland asserts that non-biodegradable packaging is a major source of pollution and constitutes a serious environmental problem in its territory.

Newland, whose main agricultural export is fruit, is hard hit by this regulation.[247] Its main export market is Richland, whose health-conscious inhabitants eat a lot of fruit. Due to the high incidence of fruit flies and the inhospitable soil in Newland, its fruit farmers use chemical pesticides and fertilisers in their orchards, but ensure that the residues of these chemicals do not exceed the maximum residue limits set by the Codex Alimentarius Commission. Fruit flies and poor soil, as well as the lack of technical know-how and financial resources, make it virtually impossible for Newland's fruit farmers to switch to organic farming. In addition, while Newland exporters use recyclable packaging for their fruit, biodegradable packaging is too costly for them.

Tutti Frutti, Newland's largest fruit exporter, approaches the Newland government to request that this matter be brought before the WTO dispute settlement system. It claims that Richland's legislation should have been notified under the *SPS Agreement* and a reasonable adaptation period should have been provided. It also argues that the prohibition on all fertilisers and pesticides exceeds the Codex Alimentarius Commission standards, which instead set maximum residue levels (MRLs) for particular harmful substances in pesticides and fertilisers. It further points out that there is no scientific evidence that pesticide or fertiliser residues below the Codex MRLs have harmful effects on health. The long-term effects of small quantities of these chemicals

247 Recall from previous exercises that Newland is a developing-country Member of the WTO, while Richland is a developed-country Member.

have never been established. Further, it notes that vegetable imports into Richland are not required to be organically grown. With regard to Richland's packaging requirements, Tutti Frutti claims that they are more trade-restrictive than necessary, as simply requiring recyclable packaging would eliminate the risk to the environment.

A recent, albeit controversial, study by scientists of the University of Utopia concluded that bio-degradable plastic packaging 'contaminates' food products and thus adversely affects human health. In light of the consumer fears and the growing demand for alternative packaging triggered by this study, Rich-Mart, Richland's biggest supermarket chain, decided that it will only sell fruit in (biodegradable) paper packaging. Since Tutti Frutti's fruit is transported over long distances, it has no choice but to package its fruit in plastic. Tutti Frutti is therefore very concerned about Rich-Mart's decision. In its opinion, this decision cannot be justified on grounds of health protection.

In response to Tutti Frutti's call for help, the Government of Newland decides that – rather than resorting to WTO dispute settlement – it will raise the issues referred to above at the next meeting of the SPS Committee. You are the legal advisor to Newland's representative on the SPS Committee. You have been asked to brief this representative in preparation for the meeting on any issues that can be addressed under the *SPS Agreement*.

15 Intellectual Property Rights

CONTENTS

1   INTRODUCTION

The *Agreement on Trade-Related Aspects of Intellectual Property Rights* (the '*TRIPS Agreement*') is arguably the most innovative of the WTO agreements. While references to intellectual property (IP) rights were included in the GATT 1947,[1] the *TRIPS Agreement*, for the first time, establishes and imposes a positive regulatory obligation on Members to ensure a minimum level of protection and enforcement of IP rights in their territories.

Part I of the *TRIPS Agreement* contains general provisions and basic principles that apply to all the IP rights falling within its coverage. Part II is subdivided into eight sections, each dealing with a different area of IP protection. Part III sets out the obligations of Members with regard to enforcement of IP rights. The remainder of the *TRIPS Agreement* addresses issues relating to the acquisition and maintenance of IP rights, and contains institutional and procedural provisions.

This chapter provides an overview of the *TRIPS Agreement* and focuses on: (1) origins and objectives; (2) scope of application; (3) basic principles; (4) substantive protection provided to selected IP rights; (5) rules on enforcement of IP rights; (6) rules on acquisition of IP rights; (7) institutional and procedural provisions; and (8) rules providing for special and differential treatment of developing-country Members.

2   THE ORIGINS AND OBJECTIVES OF THE *TRIPS AGREEMENT*

Intellectual property, broadly speaking, refers to the legal rights that result from intellectual activity in the artistic, literary, scientific or industrial fields.[2] When this intellectual activity leads to the creation of something new and innovative, many countries recognise and protect the right of the author or inventor in his or her creation, in order to reward and stimulate creative endeavour. Many countries have rules in place for the protection and enforcement of IP rights. IP rights, it should be noted, confer *negative* rights, i.e. the right to exclude others from the use of the protected subject-matter for a particular period of time. They

---

1 Articles XX(d), IX, XII:3(c)(iii) and XVIII:10 of the GATT refer to intellectual property rights. In addition, other GATT provisions lay down general rules that are also applicable to trade-related aspects of intellectual property rights, for example the national treatment and most-favoured-nation obligations and the prohibition on quantitative restrictions. See Negotiating Group on Trade-Related Aspects of Intellectual Property Rights, Including Trade in Counterfeit Goods, Note by the Secretariat, *GATT Provisions Bearing on Trade-Related Aspects of Intellectual Property Rights*, MTN.GNG/NG11/W/6, dated 22 May 1987, para. 2. On the relationship between the GATT 1994 and the *TRIPS Agreement*, see the General Interpretative Note to Annex 1A of the *WTO Agreement*, discussed above, at pp. 44–5.

2 See *WIPO Intellectual Property Handbook: Policy, Law and Use* (WIPO, 2004), 3, available at www.wipo.int/about-ip/en/iprm/index.html, visited on 15 February 2013.

do not confer positive rights, such as the right to produce or market the product embodying the IP right.

Trade and intellectual property protection are closely connected. The achievements in trade liberalisation through WTO disciplines on and removal of trade barriers, discussed in previous chapters, can be greatly undermined if IP rights related to the traded goods or services are not respected in the export market or in the country of origin of imports. The possibility that traded products incorporating patents, copyrights or industrial designs will be copied, or that brand names or services marks will be used, by competitors without creates a strong disincentive for innovation, investment and trade. This section discusses (1) the origins of the *TRIPS Agreement*, and (2) the objectives and principles of this Agreement.

2.1   Origins of the *TRIPS Agreement*

International agreements to strengthen and harmonise protection in the field of IP law exist since the late nineteenth century. However, they were plagued by deficiencies. In particular, they were fragmented in their coverage of IP rights; they lacked effective enforcement standards and systems for the settlement of disputes; and they often had very limited membership, with non-members being notorious violators of IP rights.[3] At the outset of the Uruguay Round negotiations in 1986, some participants noted that:

trade distortions and impediments were resulting from, among other things: the displacement of exports of legitimate goods by unauthorized copies, or of domestic sales by imports of unauthorized copies; the disincentive effect that inadequate protection of intellectual property rights had on inventors and creators to engage in research and development and in trade and investment; the deliberate use in some instances of intellectual property right protection to discourage imports and encourage local production, often of an inefficient and small-scale nature; and the inhibiting effect on international trade of disparities in the protection accorded under different legislations.[4]

Hence, the *TRIPS Agreement* was negotiated to address these problems. Developed countries in general, and the United States in particular, were the driving force behind these negotiations. Although developing countries initially

---

3 See e.g. the *Paris Convention for the Protection of Industrial Property (1967)*, the *Berne Convention for the Protection of Literary and Artistic Works (1971)*, the *International Convention for the Protection of Performers, Producers of Phonograms and Broadcasting Organizations (1961)* (the '*Rome Convention*') and the *Treaty on Intellectual Property in Respect of Integrated Circuits (1989)*.

4 Negotiating Group on Trade-Related Aspects of Intellectual Property Rights, Including Trade in Counterfeit Goods, Note by the Secretariat, MTN.GNG/NG11/1, dated 10 April 1987, para. 4. Reference was also made to trade problems arising from restrictive business practices linked to intellectual property rights. See *ibid.* On the pre-Uruguay Round 'history' of the *TRIPS Agreement*, Taubman, Wager and Watal noted: 'In the Tokyo Round, there was a proposal to negotiate rules on trade in counterfeit goods resulting in a draft agreement on Measures to Discourage the Importation of Counterfeit Goods. However, negotiators did not reach agreement. In 1982, pursuant to a work programme agreed by trade ministers, a revised version of a draft agreement on trade in counterfeit goods was submitted. This draft was referred to a group of experts in 1984, which submitted its report a year later ... It produced a report on Trade in Counterfeit Goods that recommended that joint action was probably needed, but could not decide on the appropriate forum. It left it to the GATT Council to make a decision.' See A. Taubman, H. Wager and J. Watal (eds.), *A Handbook on the WTO TRIPS Agreement* (Cambridge University Press, 2012), 5–6.

objected to the inclusion of negotiations on IP protection on the Uruguay Round agenda and would never truly embrace these negotiations, they came to realise that they were better off with multilateral disciplines than being subject to bilateral pressure to improve IP protection.[5]

2.2 Objectives and Principles of the *TRIPS Agreement*

The objectives of the *TRIPS Agreement* clearly reflect the concerns of negotiators, mentioned above. The Preamble identifies as the main objectives of the *TRIPS Agreement*:

> to reduce distortions and impediments to international trade ... taking into account the need to promote effective and adequate protection of intellectual property rights, and to ensure that measures and procedures to enforce intellectual property rights do not themselves become barriers to legitimate trade.

The various objectives of the *TRIPS Agreement* are sometimes in conflict with each other. As aptly noted by Thomas Cottier:

> Lack of, or insufficient protection [of intellectual property rights] amounts to *de facto* restrictions on market access, as exported products will be replaced by both generic and copied products that free ride on research and development, investment in creative activities and in quality control and product differentiation undertaken elsewhere. On the other hand, lack of appropriate limitations on rights may unduly hamper the flow of goods and services. *The real issue is one of balancing different policy goals.*[6]

The *TRIPS Agreement* reflects the effort to achieve this balance. According to Carlos Correa:

> The TRIPS Agreement must be viewed as a means for the realization of public policy objectives via the 'inducement to innovation' *and* the access to the results thereof by those who need them. In other words the objectives of the patent system would not be fulfilled if it only served to induce innovations to the benefit of those who control them.[7]

Article 7 of the *TRIPS Agreement*, entitled 'Objectives', reflects the rationale of the *TRIPS Agreement* to create a balance between these competing goals. It states:

> The protection and enforcement of intellectual property rights should contribute to the promotion of technological innovation and the transfer and dissemination of technology, to the *mutual advantage* of producers and users of technological knowledge and in a manner conducive to *social and economic welfare*, and to a *balance* of rights and obligations.[8]

---

5 See P. Drahos, 'Developing Countries and International Intellectual Property Standard-Setting', *Journal of World Intellectual Property*, 2002, 774.

6 T. Cottier, 'The Agreement on Trade-Related Aspects of Intellectual Property Rights', in P. F. J. Macrory, A. E. Appleton and M. G. Plummer (eds.), *The World Trade Organization: Legal, Economic and Political Analysis* (Springer, 2005), 1054. Emphasis added.

7 C. M. Correa, *Trade-Related Aspects of Intellectual Property Rights: A Commentary on the TRIPS Agreement* (Oxford University Press, 2007), 94.

8 Emphasis added. While couched in hortatory language ('should' instead of 'shall'), the fact that this provision is placed in the operative part of the agreement rather than in its Preamble highlights its importance in

The objective of creating an equilibrium between rewarding creators of IP and protecting the public interest in disseminating IP is also present in Article 8 of the *TRIPS Agreement*, entitled 'Principles'. Paragraph 1 of Article 8 recognises that Members may adopt measures 'necessary to protect public health and nutrition' and to 'promote the public interest in sectors of vital importance to their socio-economic and technological development'. Paragraph 2 of Article 8 suggests that Members take appropriate measures to counteract abuse of IP rights by right holders, or anti-competitive practices.[9] The types of measures that could fall within the scope of Article 8 are in some respects similar to those falling within the scope of Article XX of the GATT 1994, however, whereas Article XX provides for a general exception for measures that are otherwise GATT-inconsistent, the relevance of Article 8 is limited by the requirement that measures referred to therein be *consistent* with the provisions of the *TRIPS Agreement*.[10] Thus, rather than creating an exception from *TRIPS* disciplines for measures serving public policy objectives, Article 8 is best seen as enunciating a fundamental principle of the *TRIPS Agreement*, to be taken into account, along with Article 7, when interpreting and applying its remaining provisions.

In *Canada – Pharmaceutical Patents (2000)*, the European Communities challenged provisions of Canada's patent law that allowed producers of generic medicines, before the expiry of the patent term, to stockpile generic products and use patented products to prepare their submissions for marketing authorisation of a generic version. While Canada conceded that these provisions violated Article 28.1 of the *TRIPS Agreement*, which grants exclusive rights to patent holders, it relied on the exception in Article 30 to justify its measures, and argued that the objectives and principles of Articles 7 and 8 of the *TRIPS Agreement* should inform the interpretation of Article 30. The panel in *Canada – Pharmaceutical Patents (2000)* held that:

Article 30's very existence amounts to a recognition that the definition of patent rights contained in Article 28 would need certain adjustments. On the other hand, the three limiting conditions attached to Article 30 testify strongly that the negotiators of the Agreement did not intend Article 30 to bring about what would be equivalent to a renegotiation of the basic balance of the Agreement. Obviously, the exact scope of Article 30's authority will depend on the specific meaning given to its limiting conditions. The words of those conditions must be examined with particular care on this point. Both the goals and the limitations stated in Articles 7 and 8.1 must obviously be borne in mind when doing so as well as those of other provisions of the TRIPS Agreement which indicate its object and purposes.[11]

As an important further development since *Canada – Pharmaceutical Patents (2000)*, the *Doha Declaration on the TRIPS Agreement and Public Health*

---

informing the interpretation of the *TRIPS Agreement*. See D. Gervais, *The TRIPS Agreement: Drafting History and Analysis*, 2nd edn (Sweet & Maxwell, 2003), 116.

9 Specifically, Article 8.2 refers to appropriate measures needed to prevent 'the resort to practices which unreasonably restrain trade or adversely affect the international transfer of technology'.

10 See also Panel Report, *EC – Trademarks and Geographical Indications (Australia) (2005)*, paras. 7.245–7.246; and Panel Report, *EC – Trademarks and Geographical Indications (US) (2005)*, paras. 7.209–7.210.

11 Panel Report, *Canada – Pharmaceutical Patents (2000)*, para. 7.26.

reaffirms the right of WTO Members to use fully the provisions in the *TRIPS Agreement*, which provide flexibilities for Members in order to protect public health.[12] It states:

Accordingly ... while maintaining our commitments in the TRIPS Agreement, we recognize that these flexibilities include:

(a) In applying the customary rules of interpretation of public international law, *each provision* of the TRIPS Agreement shall be read in the light of the object and purpose of the Agreement *as expressed, in particular, in its objectives and principles.*[13]

Questions and Assignments 15.1

What is intellectual property (IP)? What is the link between international trade and the protection of IP rights? Is the *TRIPS Agreement* the first international agreement addressing the protection of IP rights? What are the objectives of the *TRIPS Agreement*? What is the role of Articles 7 and 8 of the *TRIPS Agreement*? Compare Article 8 of the *TRIPS Agreement* with Article XX of the GATT 1994. What is the importance of the *Doha Declaration on the TRIPS Agreement and Public Health* in this context?

3 SCOPE OF APPLICATION OF THE *TRIPS AGREEMENT*

This section discusses both the substantive and temporal scope of application of the *TRIPS Agreement*.

3.1 Substantive Scope of Application

Article 1.3 of the *TRIPS Agreement* requires Members to accord the treatment provided for in this Agreement to 'nationals' of other Members.[14] 'Nationals' of other Members are understood as:

those natural or legal persons that would meet the criteria for eligibility for protection provided for in the Paris Convention (1967), the Berne Convention (1971), the Rome Convention and the Treaty on Intellectual Property in Respect of Integrated Circuits, were all Members of the WTO members of those Conventions.

---

12 See Ministerial Conference, *Doha Declaration on the TRIPS Agreement and Public Health*, WT/MIN(01)/DEC/2, dated 20 November 2001, para. 4. On the legal status of this Declaration, see above, pp. 50–4.

13 Ministerial Conference, *Doha Declaration on the TRIPS Agreement and Public Health*, WT/MIN(01)/DEC/2, dated 20 November 2001, para. 5. Emphasis added.

14 Given that the *TRIPS Agreement* confers IP protection on the 'nationals' of WTO Members, but separate customs territories (that may be WTO Members) do not confer nationality, a supplementary definition was required for 'nationals' in the case of separate customs territories that are WTO Members. These nationals are defined in footnote 1 to the *TRIPS Agreement* as 'persons, natural or legal, who are domiciled or who have a real and effective industrial or commercial establishment in that customs territory'. Note that the panel in *EC – Trademarks and Geographical Indications (US) (2005)* stated that the European Communities is not a 'separate customs territory Member' of the WTO and its nationals are therefore not defined by the terms of this footnote. See Panel Report, *EC – Trademarks and Geographical Indications (US) (2005)*, paras. 7.141–7.171; see also Panel Report, *EC – Trademarks and Geographical Indications (Australia) (2005)*, paras. 7.191–7.205.

The *TRIPS Agreement* does not define the concept of intellectual property. In-stead it specifies which categories of IP rights are covered by its provisions. Article 1.2 provides:

For the purposes of this Agreement, the term 'intellectual property' refers to all categories of intellectual property that are the subject of Sections 1 through 7 of Part II.

Thus, clearly the *TRIPS Agreement* does *not* cover every form of IP right. Sec-tions 1 to 7 of Part II of the *TRIPS Agreement* cover: (1) copyright and related rights; (2) trademarks; (3) geographical indications; (4) industrial design; (5) patents; (6) layout-designs of integrated circuits; and (7) protection of undis-closed information. It should be borne in mind, however, that the categories of IP rights covered by the *TRIPS Agreement* are not always clearly delineated, and are not limited to those explicitly mentioned in the titles of sections 1 to 7. In *US – Section 211 Appropriations Act (2002)*, the panel had to interpret Article 2.1 of the *TRIPS Agreement* in relation to 'trade names', which, although not explicitly mentioned in the *TRIPS Agreement*, are referred to in Article 1.2 of the *Paris Convention (1967)*. The panel read the references in Article 1.2 of the *TRIPS Agreement* to 'all categories' as an indication that this Article contains an exhaustive list.[15] The Appellate Body disagreed with this analysis. It stated:

[T]he subject of Sections 1 through 7 of Part II deals not only with the categories of intel-lectual property indicated in each section *title*, but with other *subjects* as well. For example, in Section 5 of Part II, entitled 'Patents', Article 27(3)(b) provides that Members have the option of protecting inventions of plant varieties by *sui generis* rights (such as breeder's rights) instead of through patents. Under the Panel's theory, such *sui generis* rights would not be covered by the *TRIPS Agreement*. The option provided by Article 27(3)(b) would be read out of the *TRIPS Agreement*.[16]

With regard to 'trade names', the Appellate Body ruled that WTO Members have an obligation under the *TRIPS Agreement* to provide protection to trade names, since Article 2.1 of the *TRIPS Agreement* explicitly incorporates Article 8 of the *Paris Convention (1967)* into the TRIPS Agreement. The latter provision cov-ers only the protection of trade names and has no other subject.[17] In general, the categories of IP rights covered by the *TRIPS Agreement* are those expressly mentioned in Sections 1 to 7 of Part II *as well as* those in the incorporated con-ventions that are the '*subject*' of these Sections.

The *TRIPS Agreement* does not cover every *aspect of IP protection* for the covered categories of IP rights. For example, it expressly excludes the issue of exhaustion of IP rights from its coverage.[18] Other aspects of the protection of

---

15 See Panel Report, *US – Section 211 Appropriations Act (2002)*, para. 8.26.
16 Appellate Body Report, *US – Section 211 Appropriations Act (2002)*, para. 335.
17 *Ibid.*, paras. 336–8 and 341.
18 See below, pp. 970–1. Note that Members are nevertheless required to respect the non-discrimination princi-ples in respect of exhaustion of rights.

IP rights that are not mentioned in the *TRIPS Agreement* or in the incorporated provisions of the World Intellectual Property Organization (WIPO) conventions are also excluded from the disciplines of the agreement.[19]

3.2   Temporal Scope of Application

Article 70 of the *TRIPS Agreement* deals with the protection of existing subject-matter, i.e. the temporal scope of application of the *TRIPS Agreement*. Article 70.1 specifies certain acts which do *not* give rise to obligations under the *TRIPS Agreement*. It states:

> This Agreement does not give rise to obligations *in respect of acts which occurred* before the date of application of the Agreement for the Member in question.[20]

In other words, the *TRIPS Agreement* does not apply retroactively to acts that occurred before its 'date of application' for a Member.[21] In contrast, Article 70.2 of the *TRIPS Agreement* provides that the Agreement does create obligations in respect of subject-matter that existed at the date of application. It provides, in relevant part:

> Except as otherwise provided for in this Agreement, this Agreement gives rise to obligations *in respect of all subject-matter existing* at the date of application of this Agreement for the Member in question, and which is *protected* in that Member on the said date, or which meets or comes subsequently to meet the criteria for protection under the terms of this Agreement ...[22]

In *Canada – Patent Term (2000)*, Canada relied on Article 70.1 to justify that its (Old) Patent Act, which granted a patent protection term of seventeen years, did not confer the twenty-year term of protection required by Article 33 of the *TRIPS Agreement*. The Appellate Body interpreted the phrase 'acts which occurred before the date of application' as encompassing acts of public authorities as well as acts of private or third parties.[23] Where such acts 'occurred' (were done, carried out or completed) before the date of application of the *TRIPS Agreement* for a Member, Article 70.1 provides that the *TRIPS Agreement* does not give rise to obligations in respect of those '*acts*'.[24] However, the Appellate Body noted the fundamental importance of distinguishing in respect of IP rights between 'acts' and the 'rights' created by those acts.[25] For example, the grant of a patent is an 'act' conferring various substantive rights, such as national

---

19 See e.g. Panel Report, *Indonesia – Autos (1998)*, para. 14.275. With regard to these aspects of IP rights, Members do not have to ensure a minimum level of protection and to provide non-discriminatory treatment (under the *TRIPS Agreement*).

20 Emphasis added.

21 The 'date of application' refers to the dates at which different transitional periods for developed, developing and least-developed countries expire, as discussed below. See below, pp. 1011–2.

22 Emphasis added.

23 See Appellate Body Report, *Canada – Patent Term (2000)*, para. 54.

24 See *ibid*., para. 55.   25 *Ibid*., para. 56.

treatment, MFN treatment, and term of protection. The Appellate Body then identified the key question before it in *Canada – Patent Term (2000)* as follows:

if patents created by 'acts' of public authorities under the Old Act continue to be in force on the date of application of the *TRIPS Agreement* for Canada (that is, on 1 January 1996), can Article 70.1 operate to exclude those patents from the scope of the *TRIPS Agreement*, on the ground that they were created by 'acts which occurred' before that date?[26]

The Appellate Body answered this question in the negative. It acknowledged that an 'act' is something that is 'done', and that the use of the phrase 'acts which occurred' suggests that what was done is now complete or ended.[27] However, it pointed out that this 'excludes situations, including existing rights and obligations, that have *not* ended'.[28] It noted that, if 'acts which occurred' would be interpreted to cover all continuing situations involving patents granted before the date of application of the *TRIPS Agreement*, then:

Article 70.1 would preclude the application of virtually the whole of the *TRIPS* Agreement to rights conferred by the patents arising from such 'acts'.[29]

Questions and Assignments 15.2

Who is subject to the obligations of the *TRIPS Agreement*? To whom does the *TRIPS Agreement* give rights? What is the substantive scope of application of the *TRIPS Agreement*? Give two examples of aspects of the protection of IP rights that are not covered by the *TRIPS Agreement*. To what extent does the MFN treatment obligation apply to these aspects? Are the disciplines of the *TRIPS Agreement* applicable to a Member with regard to IP rights acquired before the date of application of the *TRIPS Agreement* for the Member concerned?

4   GENERAL PROVISIONS AND BASIC PRINCIPLES OF THE *TRIPS AGREEMENT*

Part I of the *TRIPS Agreement* contains the general provisions and basic principles that apply to all covered areas of IP. Article 1.1 of the *TRIPS Agreement* obliges Members to 'give effect' to its provisions. However, it expressly states that Members are 'free to determine the appropriate method' of implementing their obligations under the Agreement within their own legal systems and practice.[30] In addition, Article 1.1 provides that Members are free, but not

---

26 *Ibid.*, para. 57.   27 See *ibid.*, para. 58.   28 *Ibid.*   29 *Ibid.*, para. 59.

30 Note that, in *EC – Trademarks and Geographical Indications (US) (2005)*, the United States Article 1.1 based on the fact that the EC's inspection structure requirements for the protection of geographical indications conditioned the protection on the adoption by other Members of structures that the EC unilaterally determines to be equivalent to its own. The panel disagreed, holding that the evidence before it did not establish that these inspection structures concerned the systems of protection of *other* WTO Members; rather, they only ensured compliance with product specifications, which are a feature of the EC's system of protection. See Panel Report, *EC – Trademarks and Geographical Indications (US) (2005)*, paras. 7.762–7.766.

obliged, to implement more extensive protection than that required by the *TRIPS Agreement*. This firmly establishes the nature of the *TRIPS Agreement* as setting a *minimum level* of IP protection. The flexibility available to Members with regard to *how* they give effect to their *TRIPS* obligations is an important tool in balancing the competing policy goals mentioned above.[31] However, the flexibility available to Members is obviously not without limits. When, in *India - Patents (US) (1998)*, in interpreting India's obligation under Article 70.8(a) of the *TRIPS Agreement*,[32] the Appellate Body recalled the 'important general rule' of Article 1.1, and noted:

> Members, therefore, are free to determine how best to meet their obligations under the *TRIPS Agreement* within the context of their own legal systems. And, as a Member, India is 'free to determine the appropriate method of implementing' its obligations under the *TRIPS Agreement* within the context of its own legal system.[33]

However, in this case, the Appellate Body, like the panel, was not persuaded that the 'administrative instructions' given by India to its patent office to accept 'mailbox' applications as required under Article 70.8(a) would prevail over the conflicting and mandatory provisions of the Indian Patents Act.[34] Therefore, despite the flexibility provided in Article 1.1, India was found to have failed to properly implement its obligations under Article 70.8(a) of the *TRIPS Agreement*.[35]

This section discusses the basic principles laid down in Part I of the *TRIPS Agreement*. More specifically, it addresses: (1) the relationship between the *TRIPS Agreement* and WIPO conventions; (2) the national treatment obligation; (3) the most-favoured-nation treatment obligation; and (4) the issue of exhaustion of IP rights.

4.1 Relationship Between the *TRIPS Agreement* and WIPO Conventions

The *TRIPS Agreement* builds upon the standards of IP protection enshrined in the IP conventions administered by the World Intellectual Property Organization (WIPO). It does so by incorporating by reference specific provisions of the relevant conventions, namely, the *Paris Convention for the Protection of Industrial Property of 1883*, as revised in the Stockholm Act of 1967 (the *Paris Convention (1967)*), the *Berne Convention for the Protection of Literary and Artistic Works*

---

31 See, for example, the flexibility in determining domestic limitations and exceptions to copyright under the 'three-step test' and other relevant provisions, discussed below, pp. 977–9.
32 This provision allows Members availing themselves of transitional arrangements under Part VI of the *TRIPS Agreement* to delay patent protection for pharmaceutical and agricultural chemical products subject to the requirement that they provide a 'means' by which patent applications in those fields can be filed. These applications are often referred to as 'mailbox applications' and Article 70.8 is called the 'mailbox provision'.
33 Appellate Body Report, *India – Patents (US) (1998)*, para. 59.
34 See *ibid.*, paras. 69–70.
35 See *ibid.*, para. 71. See also Panel Report, *Canada – Patent Term (2000)*, para. 6.94, where the panel noted that: 'Article 1.1 gives Members the freedom to determine the appropriate method of implementing [the two requirements at issue], but not to ignore either requirement.'

of 1886, as revised in the Paris Act of 1971 (the *Berne Convention (1971)*), the *International Convention for the Protection of Performers, Producers of Phonograms and Broadcasting Organizations of 1961* (the *Rome Convention*) and the *Treaty on Intellectual Property in Respect of Integrated Circuits of 1989* (the *IPIC Treaty*). The obligations of the *TRIPS Agreement* must therefore be read together with the relevant WIPO conventions.

However, the *TRIPS Agreement* does more than simply incorporate the substantive provisions of these conventions. Developed-country negotiators of the *TRIPS Agreement* viewed the existing WIPO conventions as 'inadequate to address the needs of their business sectors in the "post-industrial era" or "information age"'.[36] Therefore, the *TRIPS Agreement* supplements and innovates the rules of the relevant WIPO conventions, as well as expressly provides additional protection in some areas. In addition, it creates an obligation under municipal law for Members to have a system in place to ensure the enforcement of the protected IP rights, and links them to the effective and binding dispute settlement system of the WTO.[37]

The relationship between the WIPO conventions and the *TRIPS Agreement* is set out in Article 2 of the *TRIPS Agreement*. Article 2.1 of the *TRIPS Agreement* explicitly obliges Members to comply with Articles 1 to 12 and 19 of the *Paris Convention (1967)* in respect of Parts II, III and IV of the *TRIPS Agreement*. Therefore, even WTO Members that are not Parties to the *Paris Convention (1967)* must comply with these provisions.[38] Article 2.2 of the *TRIPS Agreement* provides that nothing in Parts I to IV of the *TRIPS Agreement* shall derogate from Members' obligations under the *Paris Convention (1967)*, the *Berne Convention (1971)*, the *Rome Convention* or the *IPIC Treaty*. This non-derogation clause does not create new obligations but seeks to ensure that Members do not apply their *TRIPS* obligations in a manner that results in a violation of their obligations under the above-mentioned WIPO conventions. In addition, various provisions in Part II of the *TRIPS Agreement* dealing with different categories of IP rights incorporate certain provisions of the relevant WIPO conventions. With regard to the *Berne Convention (1971)*, the *Paris Convention (1967)* and the *IPIC Treaty*, these incorporation clauses oblige all WTO Members to comply with the incorporated articles of the WIPO conventions, and make them binding even on those WTO Members that are not Parties to WIPO conventions.[39]

---

36 *Course on Dispute Settlement in International Trade, Investment and Intellectual Property – Module 3.14. WTO: TRIPS*, UNCTAD Document EDM/Misc.232/Add.18 (2003), 11.

37 See D. Matthews, *Globalising Intellectual Property Rights: The TRIPs Agreement* (Routledge, 2002), 46. These enforcement obligations are discussed below, p. 1002.

38 See Appellate Body Report, *US – Section 211 Appropriations Act (2002)*, para. 125.

39 See, for example, Article 9.1 of the *TRIPS Agreement*, which obliges Members to comply with Articles 1 to 21, and the Appendix to the *Berne Convention (1971)* and Article 35 of the *TRIPS Agreement*, which obliges Members to provide protection to layout-designs of integrated circuits in accordance with Articles 2 to 7 (except Article 6.3), 12 and 16.3 of the *IPIC Treaty*. Note that no similar provision exists with regard to the *Rome Convention*, which continues to bind only its Contracting Parties.

Questions and Assignments 15.3

What kind of 'flexibility' does Article 1.1 of the *TRIPS Agreement* give to Members? Which provisions of WIPO conventions are incorporated by reference in the *TRIPS Agreement*? Does the *TRIPS Agreement* do more than incorporate these provisions? If so, what and why does the *TRIPS Agreement* do more? What is the relationship between the *TRIPS Agreement* and the WIPO conventions referred to therein?

4.2   The National Treatment Obligation

The principles of national treatment and MFN treatment, familiar from the discussion of the non-discrimination obligations under the GATT 1994 and the GATS in Chapters 4 and 5 of this book, apply also in the context of the *TRIPS Agreement*.[40] However, there are some differences in their formulation in the *TRIPS Agreement* in order to take into account the intangible nature of IP rights.

The national treatment obligation of the *TRIPS Agreement*, in Article 3.1, requires each Member to accord to nationals of other Members treatment 'no less favourable' than it accords to its own nationals in respect of IP protection.[41] As discussed above, Article 1.2 of the *TRIPS Agreement* defines the term 'intellectual property'.[42] Footnote 3 to Article 3.1 in turn defines the meaning of the term 'protection' of IP for purposes of Articles 3 and 4, and provides that it:

shall include matters affecting the availability, acquisition, scope, maintenance and enforcement of intellectual property rights as well as those matters affecting the use of intellectual property rights *specifically addressed in this Agreement*.[43]

The national treatment obligation of Article 3 thus applies only to the categories of IP rights covered by the *TRIPS Agreement*. While 'protection' of those rights includes 'matters affecting the availability, acquisition, scope, maintenance and enforcement', 'matters affecting the use' of those rights are included only to the extent covered by the Agreement.[44] Unlike Article III of the GATT 1994 and Article XVII of the GATS, the national treatment obligation in Article 3 of the *TRIPS Agreement* applies to 'nationals' as defined in Article 1.3, rather than to 'like products' or 'like services or service providers'. This is because IP rights are intangible, and attach to an IP right holder, rather than to the product or service in which these rights are embodied.

---

40 See above, p. 316 and 350.

41 Note that the *TRIPS Agreement* incorporates, in addition, three national treatment obligations of pre-existing IP conventions, namely: Article 2 of the *Paris Convention (1967)* (incorporated by Article 2.1 of the *TRIPS Agreement*); Article 5 of the *Berne Convention (1971)* (incorporated by Article 9.1 of the *TRIPS Agreement*); and Article 5 of the *IPIC Treaty* (incorporated by Article 35 of the *TRIPS Agreement*). See e.g. Panel Report, *EC – Trademarks and Geographical Indications (US) (2005)*, footnote 166 to para. 7.131.

42 See above, p. 957.

43 Emphasis added. On the 'limited' scope of application of the national treatment obligation of Article 3 of the *TRIPS Agreement*, see Panel Report, *Indonesia – Autos (1998)*, para. 14.275.

44 See C. M. Correa, *Trade-Related Aspects of Intellectual Property Rights: A Commentary on the TRIPS Agreement* (Oxford University Press, 2007), 62.

The Appellate Body addressed the national treatment obligation in the *TRIPS Agreement* for the first time in *US – Section 211 Appropriations Act (2002)*. In this case, the Appellate Body observed the 'fundamental significance of the obligation of national treatment ... in the *TRIPS Agreement*',[45] and noted that:

[i]ndeed, the significance of the national treatment obligation can hardly be overstated. Not only has the national treatment obligation long been a cornerstone of the Paris Convention and other international intellectual property conventions. So, too, has the national treatment obligation long been a cornerstone of the world trading system that is served by the WTO.[46]

The Appellate Body stated that the national treatment obligation is 'a fundamental principle underlying the *TRIPS Agreement*, just as it has been in what is now the GATT 1994'.[47] It agreed with the panel that, because the language of Article 3.1 of the *TRIPS Agreement* is similar to that of Article III:4 of the GATT 1994, the case law concerning Article III:4 of the GATT 1994 'may be useful in interpreting the national treatment obligation in the *TRIPS Agreement*'.[48]

In applying the national treatment obligation of Article 3.1 in *US – Section 211 Appropriations Act (2002)*, the Appellate Body pointed out that Section 211(a)(2) of the US Appropriations Act, on its face, imposed an 'extra hurdle' on successors-in-interest to the confiscated trademark who were not US nationals, and that hurdle did not apply successors-in-interest that were US nationals. More importantly, non-nationals faced the additional problem that under the terms of Section 211(a) of the Appropriations Act, their trademark would not be recognised, validated or enforced by US courts. Although it was not very likely that in practice foreign nationals would actually have to overcome both 'hurdles', according to the Appellate Body 'even the *possibility* that non-United States successors-in-interest face two hurdles is *inherently less favourable* than the undisputed fact that United States successors-in-interest face only one'.[49] Therefore, the Appellate Body found that the United States had violated the national treatment obligation in Article 3.1 of the *TRIPS Agreement*.[50]

The panel in *EC – Trademarks and Geographical Indications (2005)* also discussed the national treatment obligation of Article 3.1 of the *TRIPS Agreement*. The measure at issue in that case was an EC regulation with two sets of detailed procedures for the registration of geographical indications ('GIs') for agricultural products and foodstuffs. The first procedure (Articles 5–7) applied to the names of geographical areas located in the European Communities. The second procedure (Articles 12a and 12b) applied to the names of geographical areas located in third countries outside the European Communities. Furthermore additional conditions (Article 12.1) required that a third country must provide reciprocal

---

45 Appellate Body Report, *US – Section 211 Appropriations Act (2002)*, para. 240.
46 *Ibid.*, para. 241.   47 *Ibid.*, para. 242.   48 *Ibid.*   49 *Ibid.*, para. 265.
50 See *ibid.*, para. 268. The Appellate Body also found that the United States acted inconsistently with Article 2.1 of the *Paris Convention (1967)*. See *ibid.*

and equivalent protection for GIs to those available in the European Communities (known as the 'reciprocity and equivalence conditions').[51] The complainants (the United States and Australia) claimed that the EC regulation at issue was inconsistent with the national treatment obligation in Article 3.1 of the *TRIPS Agreement*, because it imposed conditions of reciprocity and equivalence on the availability of protection.[52] The panel identified two elements for establishing an inconsistency with the national treatment obligation of Article 3.1 of the *TRIPS Agreement*: (1) the measure at issue must relate to the protection of intellectual property; and (2) the nationals of other Members must be accorded 'less favourable' treatment than the nationals of the Member whose measure is challenged.[53] In examining the *first* element of this two-tier test, the panel pointed out that it was undisputed that 'designations of origin' and 'geographical indications', as defined in the EC regulation at issue, fell within the category of 'geographical indications', i.e. the subject-matter of Section 3 of Part II of the *TRIPS Agreement*, and were therefore part of a category of intellectual property within the meaning of the *TRIPS Agreement*.[54] The panel concluded that:

> this claim concerns the 'protection' of intellectual property, as clarified in footnote 3 to the TRIPS Agreement, within the scope of the national treatment obligation in Article 3 of that Agreement.[55]

Turning to the *second* element of the two-tier test under Article 3.1 of the *TRIPS Agreement*, that is, whether 'less favourable treatment' is accorded to nationals of other Members, the panel noted:

> It is useful to recall that Article 3.1 of the TRIPS Agreement combines elements of national treatment both from pre-existing intellectual property agreements and GATT 1994. Like the pre-existing intellectual property conventions, Article 3.1 applies to 'nationals', not products. Like GATT 1994, Article 3.1 refers to 'no less favourable' treatment, not the advantages or rights that laws now grant or may hereafter grant, but it does not refer to likeness.[56]

The panel pointed out that Article 3 prohibits not only measures, which *on their face* discriminate between the nationals of a Member and foreign nationals, but also *de facto* discriminatory measures. The panel referred to the case law regarding less favourable treatment under Article III:4 of the GATT 1994, which

---

51 See Panel Report, *EC – Trademarks and Geographical Indications (US) (2005)*, paras. 7.57–7.75 and 7.102; and Panel Report, *EC – Trademarks and Geographical Indications (Australia) (2005)*, para. 7.109–7.125 and 7.152.

52 See Panel Report, *EC – Trademarks and Geographical Indications (US) (2005)*, para. 7.104; Panel Report, *EC – Trademarks and Geographical Indications (Australia) (2005)*, para. 7.154. Note that the United States and Australia also claimed that the EC regulation was inconsistent with the national treatment obligation of Article 2.1 of the *Paris Convention (1967)*, as incorporated by Article 2.1 of the *TRIPS Agreement*.

53 See Panel Report, *EC – Trademarks and Geographical Indications (US) (2005)*, para. 7.125; Panel Report, *EC – Trademarks and Geographical Indications (Australia) (2005)*, para. 7.175.

54 See Panel Report, *EC – Trademarks and Geographical Indications (US) (2005)*, para. 7.128; and Panel Report, *EC – Trademarks and Geographical Indications (Australia) (2005)*, para. 7.178.

55 Panel Report, *EC – Trademarks and Geographical Indications (US) (2005)*, para. 7.129; and Panel Report, *EC – Trademarks and Geographical Indications (Australia) (2005)*, para. 7.179.

56 Panel Report, *EC – Trademarks and Geographical Indications (US) (2005)*, para. 7.131; and Panel Report, *EC – Trademarks and Geographical Indications (Australia) (2005)*, para. 7.181.

has been interpreted as including situations where the application of formally identical legal provisions would in practice accord less favourable treatment.[57] The panel held:

> We consider that this reasoning applies with equal force to the no less favourable treatment standard in Article 3.1 of the TRIPS Agreement. In our view, even if the provisions of the Regulation are formally identical in the treatment that they accord to the nationals of other Members and to the European Communities' own nationals, this is not sufficient to demonstrate that there is no violation of Article 3.1 of the TRIPS Agreement.[58]

The panel recalled that the panel and Appellate Body in *US – Section 211 Appropriations Act (2002)*[59] found that the appropriate standard for 'no less favourable treatment' under Article 3 of the *TRIPS Agreement* is that developed by the GATT panel in *US – Section 337 Tariff Act (1989)* under Article III of the GATT.[60] The panel in *EC – Trademarks and Geographical Indications (2005)* thus proceeded to examine whether the difference in treatment affected the 'effective equality of opportunities' between the nationals of other Members and the European Communities' nationals with regard to the protection of IP rights, to the detriment of nationals of other Members.[61] The equivalence and reciprocity conditions of the EC regulation at issue were held by the panel to modify the effective equality of opportunities to obtain protection of intellectual property.[62] Those conditions, according to the panel, constituted a significant 'extra hurdle'[63] to obtaining GI protection that did not apply to geographic areas located within the European Communities. The panel concluded:

> [T]he equivalence and reciprocity conditions modify the effective equality of opportunities with respect to the availability of protection to persons who wish to obtain GI protection under the Regulation, to the detriment of those who wish to obtain protection in respect of geographical areas located in third countries, including WTO Members. This is less favourable treatment.[64]

The EC regulation at issue referred to the location of geographical indications, whereas the national treatment obligation in Article 3.1 of the *TRIPS Agreement* refers to treatment accorded to 'nationals'. Therefore the panel had to determine how less favourable treatment accorded under the EC regulation with respect

---

57 See Panel Report, *EC – Trademarks and Geographical Indications (US) (2005)*, para. 7.173; and Panel Report, *EC – Trademarks and Geographical Indications (Australia) (2005)*, para. 7.207.
58 Panel Report, *EC – Trademarks and Geographical Indications (US) (2005)*, para. 7.176; and Panel Report, *EC – Trademarks and Geographical Indications (Australia) (2005)*, para. 7.210.
59 See Panel Report, *US – Section 211 Appropriations Act (2002)*, paras. 8.130–8.131; and Appellate Body Report, *US – Section 211 Appropriations Act (2002)*, para. 258.
60 See Panel Report, *US – Section 337 Tariff Act (1989)*, para. 5.11.
61 See Panel Report, *EC – Trademarks and Geographical Indications (US) (2005)*, para. 7.134; Panel Report, *EC – Trademarks and Geographical Indications (Australia) (2005)*, para. 7.184.
62 See Panel Report, *EC – Trademarks and Geographical Indications (US) (2005)*, para. 7.139; and Panel Report, *EC – Trademarks and Geographical Indications (Australia) (2005)*, para. 7.189.
63 Here the panel referred to the approach of the Appellate Body in *US – Section 211 Appropriations Act (2002)* to an 'extra hurdle' imposed only on foreign nationals. See Appellate Body Report, *US – Section 211 Appropriations Act (2002)*, para. 268.
64 Panel Report, *EC – Trademarks and Geographical Indications (US) (2005)*, para. 7.140; and Panel Report, *EC – Trademarks and Geographical Indications (Australia) (2005)*, para. 7.190.

to the *availability of protection* affects the treatment accorded to the *nationals* of other Members and that accorded to the European Communities' *nationals* for the purposes of Article 3.1 of the *TRIPS Agreement*.[65] The fact that the EC regulation, on its face, provided formally identical treatment to the nationals of other Members and to the European Communities' nationals was not considered to be sufficient to demonstrate that there was no violation of Article 3.1 of the *TRIPS Agreement*. The panel then proceeded to examine whether the 'fundamental thrust and effect' of the regulation at issue was such that it affected the 'effective equality of opportunities' with regard to the protection of IP rights. Regarding the question of which nationals to compare for purposes of establishing whether less favourable treatment was conferred, the panel held that:

> the nationals that are relevant to an examination under Article 3.1 of the TRIPS Agreement should be those who seek opportunities with respect to the same type of intellectual property in comparable situations. On the one hand, this excludes a comparison of opportunities for nationals with respect to different categories of intellectual property, such as GIs and copyright. On the other hand, no reason has been advanced as to why the equality of opportunities should be limited *a priori* to rights with a territorial link to a particular Member.[66]

Therefore, the panel did not need to make a factual assumption that 'every person who wishes to obtain protection for a GI in a particular Member is a national of that Member'.[67] Having examined the provisions of the EC regulation at issue, the panel found that:

> the distinction made by the Regulation on the basis of the location of a GI will operate in practice to discriminate between the group of nationals of other Members who wish to obtain GI protection, and the group of the European Communities' own nationals who wish to obtain GI protection, to the detriment of the nationals of other Members. This will not occur as a random outcome in a particular case but as a feature of the *design and structure of the system*. This design is evident in the Regulation's objective characteristics, in particular, the definitions of 'designation of origin' and 'geographical indication' and the requirements of the product specifications. The structure is evident in the different registration procedures.[68]

The panel noted that the *TRIPS Agreement* itself recognises that discrimination based on residence and establishment will be a 'close substitute for nationality'.[69] In its view, the object and purpose of the *TRIPS Agreement*:

---

65 See Panel Report, *EC – Trademarks and Geographical Indications (US) (2005)*, para. 7.141; and Panel Report, *EC – Trademarks and Geographical Indications (Australia) (2005)*, para. 7.191.

66 Panel Report, *EC – Trademarks and Geographical Indications (US) (2005)*, para. 7.181; and Panel Report, *EC – Trademarks and Geographical Indications (Australia) (2005)*, para. 7.217.

67 Panel Report, *EC – Trademarks and Geographical Indications (US) (2005)*, para. 7.182; and Panel Report, *EC – Trademarks and Geographical Indications (Australia) (2005)*, para. 7.218.

68 Panel Report, *EC – Trademarks and Geographical Indications (US) (2005)*, para. 7.194; and Panel Report, *EC – Trademarks and Geographical Indications (Australia) (2005)*, para. 7.230. Emphasis added.

69 Panel Report, *EC – Trademarks and Geographical Indications (US) (2005)*, para. 7.198; and Panel Report, *EC – Trademarks and Geographical Indications (Australia) (2005)*, para. 7.234. Here the panel highlighted the criteria set out in footnote 1 to the *TRIPS Agreement* which it stated 'are clearly intended to provide close substitute criteria to determine nationality where criteria to determine nationality as such are not available in a Member's domestic law. These criteria are "domicile" and "real and effective industrial or commercial establishment".'

would be severely undermined if a Member could avoid its obligations by simply according treatment to its own nationals on the basis of close substitute criteria, such as place of production, or establishment, and denying treatment to the nationals of other WTO Members who produce or are established in their own countries.[70]

Therefore, the panel found that the reciprocity and equivalence conditions in the EC regulation respect the availability of GI protection, and thus violate Article 3.1 because the treatment accorded to the group of nationals of other Members was different from, and less favourable than, that accorded to the European Communities' nationals.[71]

The national treatment obligation in Article 3.1 of the *TRIPS Agreement* has exceptions. As noted by the panel in *EC – Trademarks and Geographical Indications (2005)*:

[t]he scope of the national treatment obligation in Article 3.1 of the TRIPS Agreement also differs from that of the national treatment obligation in Article III:4 of GATT 1994, as it is subject to certain exceptions in Articles 3.1, 3.2 and 5, one of which is inspired by the language of Article XX of GATT 1994.[72]

Article 3.1 exempts from the national treatment obligation the exceptions already provided for in the *Paris Convention (1967)*, the *Berne Convention (1971)*, the *Rome Convention* or the *IPIC Treaty*.[73] This exemption reflects the fact that IP treaties sometimes require reciprocity. Furthermore, the national treatment obligation applies to performers, producers of phonograms and broadcasting organisations only with respect to the rights provided in the *TRIPS Agreement*.[74] Therefore, the obligation does not cover other rights that holders of related rights may have under domestic laws or other international agreements. This avoids, for example, that Members who are not parties to the *Rome Convention* obtain 'through the back door',[75] any such other rights protected under this convention without committing to provide such protection themselves. In addition, Article 5 provides that the national treatment obligation of Article 3 does not apply to procedures for the acquisition of IP rights provided in multilateral agreements negotiated under the auspices of the WIPO.[76]

---

70 Panel Report, *EC – Trademarks and Geographical Indications (US) (2005)*, para. 7.199; and Panel Report, *EC – Trademarks and Geographical Indications (Australia) (2005)*, para. 7.235.

71 See Panel Report, *EC – Trademarks and Geographical Indications (US) (2005)*, paras. 7.204 and 7.213; and Panel Report, *EC – Trademarks and Geographical Indications (Australia) (2005)*, paras. 7.240 and 7.249.

72 *Ibid.*, paras. 7.211 and 7.247.

73 Note that Article 3.1 of the *TRIPS Agreement* provides that, in the case of two of these exceptions, those under Article 6 of the *Berne Convention (1971)* and Article 16.1(b) of the *Rome Convention*, notification to the Council for TRIPS is required if a Member intends to avail itself of them.

74 Article 3.2 of the *TRIPS Agreement* provides that the exceptions of Article 3.1 that relate to judicial and administrative procedures apply only to the extent necessary to secure compliance with laws and regulations that are not inconsistent with the *TRIPS Agreement* and where they are not applied in a way that constitutes a disguised restriction on trade. Compare this to Article XX(d) of the GATT 1994, discussed above, pp. 560–5.

75 C. M. Correa, *Trade-Related Aspects of Intellectual Property Rights: A Commentary on the TRIPS Agreement* (Oxford University Press, 2007), 63.

76 Note that the Article 5 exception applies also to the MFN obligation of Article 4 of the *TRIPS Agreement*.

Questions and Assignments 15.4

How does the national treatment obligation of the *TRIPS Agreement* differ from the national treatment obligations of the GATT 1994 and the GATS? Is the case law on national treatment of the GATT 1994 and the GATS of relevance to the application and interpretation of Article 3.1 of the *TRIPS Agreement*? What are the elements of the national treatment test under Article 3.1 of the *TRIPS Agreement*? Does Article 3.1 of the *TRIPS Agreement* cover both *de jure* and *de facto* discrimination? Discuss the finding on 'less favourable treatment' of the panel in *EC – Trademarks and Geographical Indications (2005)*. Are there any exceptions to the national treatment obligation of Article 3.1 of the *TRIPS Agreement*?

4.3   The Most-Favoured-Nation Treatment Obligation

Article 4 contains the MFN obligation of the *TRIPS Agreement*. It requires that any advantage, favour, privilege or immunity with regard to IP protection granted by a Member to the nationals of any other country be accorded immediately and unconditionally to the nationals of all other Members. We recall that Article 1.2 of the *TRIPS Agreement* defines the term 'intellectual property', and footnote 3 to Article 3.1 in turn defines the meaning of the term 'protection' of IP for purposes of Articles 3 and 4.[77] Members are required to provide MFN treatment only with respect to categories of IP rights covered by the Agreement. While 'protection' of those rights includes 'matters affecting the availability, acquisition, scope, maintenance and enforcement', 'matters affecting the use' of those rights are included only to the extent covered by the Agreement.[78]

Unlike the MFN treatment obligations of Article I:1 of the GATT 1994 and Article II:1 of the GATS, Article 4 of the *TRIPS Agreement* applies to 'nationals' as defined in Article 1.3, rather than to 'like products' or 'like services or service providers'. As noted above, this is because IP rights are intangible, and attach to an IP right holder, rather than to the product or service in which they are embodied. Interestingly, none of the pre-existing IP conventions contains an MFN treatment obligation. Thus, the *TRIPS Agreement* introduces such an obligation for the first time in the area of IP protection. In *US – Section 211 Appropriations Act (2002)*, the Appellate Body emphasised the importance of MFN treatment, which is key to the multilateral trading system, and that the *TRIPS Agreement* extends to IP right holders. It noted:

---

77 This footnote is quoted above, p. 962.
78 Note that Cottier considers that the MFN treatment obligation extends to all categories of IP protection covered by the *TRIPS Agreement*, and as a consequence Members that extend TRIPS-plus protection to certain countries are obliged by Article 4 to extend such protection to all WTO Members. Note that the *TRIPS Agreement* does not contain an exception to the MFN treatment obligation for regional trade agreements, similar to Article XXIV of the GATT 1994 and Article V of the GATS. See T. Cottier, 'The Agreement on Trade-Related Aspects of Intellectual Property Rights', in P. F. J. Macrory, A. E. Appleton and M. G. Plummer (eds.), *The World Trade Organization: Legal, Economic and Political Analysis* (Springer, 2005), 1068 and 1069. See contra C. M. Correa, *Trade-Related Aspects of Intellectual Property Rights: A Commentary on the TRIPS Agreement* (Oxford University Press, 2007), 66–7. Correa believes that footnote 3 limits the MFN principle to the rights specifically addressed in the *TRIPS Agreement* and incorporated IP conventions. Therefore, according to Correa, Members providing higher levels of IP protection, beyond that required by the *TRIPS Agreement*, under bilateral agreements (so-called 'TRIPS-plus' protection) need not extend that same protection to all WTO Members.

[T]he obligation to provide most-favoured-nation treatment has long been one of the cornerstones of the world trading system. For more than fifty years, the obligation to provide most-favoured-nation treatment in Article I of the GATT 1994 has been both central and essential to assuring the success of a global rules-based system for trade in goods. Unlike the national treatment principle, there is no provision in the Paris Convention (1967) that establishes a most-favoured-nation obligation with respect to rights in trademarks or other industrial property. However, the framers of the *TRIPS Agreement* decided to extend the most-favoured-nation obligation to the protection of intellectual property rights covered by that Agreement. As a cornerstone of the world trading system, the most-favoured-nation obligation must be accorded the same significance with respect to intellectual property rights under the *TRIPS Agreement* that it has long been accorded with respect to trade in goods under the GATT. It is, in a word, fundamental.[79]

Article 4 of the *TRIPS Agreement* is subject to exceptions. Advantages granted by a Member that drives from international agreements on judicial assistance or law enforcement need not be granted to all Members.[80] Further, the advantages granted in the *Rome Convention* and the *Berne Convention (1971)* on condition of reciprocity are excluded from the coverage of the MFN obligation of the *TRIPS Agreement*.[81] Members are also not required to provide on an MFN basis rights that performers, phonogram producers and broadcasting organisations may have under domestic laws or other international agreements but which are not protected under the *TRIPS Agreement*.[82] The most important exception in Article 4(d) relates to advantages that derive from international agreements 'related to the protection of intellectual property', which predate the entry into force of the *WTO Agreement*.[83] Such advantages need not be granted to all WTO Members on an MFN basis, provided that the relevant agreements have been notified to the Council for TRIPS, and they 'do not constitute an arbitrary or unjustifiable discrimination against nationals of other Members'.[84] In addition, Article 5 of the *TRIPS Agreement* provides that Article 4 does not apply to

---

79 Appellate Body Report, *US – Section 211 Appropriations Act (2002)*, para. 297. As the arguments advanced by both parties in relation to the alleged violation of MFN treatment were basically the same as those they relied upon in respect of the alleged violation of national treatment, discussed above, the Appellate Body held, for the same reasons *mutatis mutandis*, that a violation of Article 4 had been established. See *ibid.*, paras. 305–19. See also above, p. 963.

80 See Article 4(a) of the *TRIPS Agreement*. Note that the agreements referred to are 'of a general nature and not particularly confined to the protection of intellectual property'.

81 See Article 4(b) of the *TRIPS Agreement*.

82 This is in line with the exception to the national treatment obligation in respect of rights of performers, phonogram producers and broadcasting organizations in the second sentence of Article 3.1 of the *TRIPS Agreement*. See above, p. 967.

83 Members have interpreted this exemption broadly. They have made clear in respective communications that future acts based on such agreements would also be exempted from the MFN treatment obligation. See the Notification under Article 4(d) of the Agreement: European Communities and its Member States, IP/N/4/EEC/1, dated 29 January 1996; ANDEAN Pact – The Notification under Article 4(d) of the Agreement: Bolivia, Colombia, Ecuador, Peru, Venezuela, IP/N/4/BOL/1, IP/N/4/COL/1, IP/N/4/ECU/1, IP/N/4/PER/1, IP/N/4/VEN/1, dated 19 August 1997; and MERCOSUR – Notification of Argentina, Brazil, Paraguay, Uruguay, IP/N/4/ARG/1, IP/N/4/BRA/1, IP/N/4/PRY/1, IP/N/4/URY/1, dated 14 July 1998.

84 Correa notes that this exception seems to imply that parties to agreements related to IP protection (such as free trade agreements with chapters on IP protection) that post-date the entry into force of the *WTO Agreement* are obliged to extend the advantages contained therein to all WTO Members. This would be the case despite the fact that WTO Members that are not parties to these agreements are not obliged to extend reciprocal advantages to such parties, which Correa regards as a 'troublesome implication' of this provision. See C. M. Correa, *Trade-Related Aspects of Intellectual Property Rights: A Commentary on the TRIPS Agreement* (Oxford University Press, 2007), 69.

procedures for the acquisition of IP rights that are protected under multilateral agreements negotiated under the auspices of WIPO.[85]

Questions and Assignments 15.5

How does the MFN treatment obligation of the *TRIPS Agreement* differ from the MFN treatment obligations of the GATT 1994 and the GATS? Is the case law on the MFN treatment obligations of the GATT 1994 and the GATS of relevance to the application and interpretation of Article 4 of the *TRIPS Agreement*? Is the MFN treatment obligation a 'novelty' among international rules on IP protection? What is the most important exception to the MFN treatment obligation of Article 4 of the *TRIPS Agreement*?

4.4   Exhaustion of Intellectual Property Rights

Intellectual property rights are often embodied in a product (for example, a book, compact disc or medicine). However, the rights exist independently of the products in which they may be embodied. Theoretically therefore, IP rights can 'follow' products indefinitely, even after they have been legitimately sold, allowing the IP right holder to control their resale. In order to balance the rights of the IP right holder with the interests of others, the doctrine of exhaustion of rights determines when the IP right holder's right to control the product in which the IP right is embodied ends. Note that exhaustion applies only to the right to control distribution (such as resale) of the product after it has been put on the market by or with the consent of the right holder.[86] It does not affect the essence of an IP right, namely, the right to exclude others from exploiting the IP right without the consent of the right holder (for example, by making pirated copies of a compact disc or copying a patented medicine).[87]

There are three possible approaches to the exhaustion of IP rights: (1) *national* exhaustion of rights, meaning that the first sale of a product exhausts IP rights to control the resale of the product only on the national market; the IP right holder retains these rights in other countries; (2) *regional* exhaustion of rights, meaning that the first sale of a product in a country that is a party to a regional agreement exhausts IP rights to control further distribution in other parties to the regional agreement; and (3) *international* exhaustion of rights, meaning that, once a product is sold by or with the consent of the right holder, whether on the domestic market or on a foreign market, the IP rights to control the

---

85 Note that, as stated above, the Article 5 exception applies also to the national treatment obligation of Article 3 of the *TRIPS Agreement*. See above, p. 967.

86 See T. Cottier, 'The Agreement on Trade-Related Aspects of Intellectual Property Rights', in P. F. J. Macrory, A. E. Appleton and M. G. Plummer (eds.), *The World Trade Organization: Legal, Economic and Political Analysis* (Springer, 2005), 1069. See, however, C. M. Correa, *Trade-Related Aspects of Intellectual Property Rights: A Commentary on the TRIPS Agreement* (Oxford University Press, 2007), 82, who argues that Article 6 of the *TRIPS Agreement* refers to 'IP rights' without qualification, and states that, therefore, the question arises whether exhaustion may be applied to all exclusive rights or only a sub-set thereof.

87 See T. Cottier, 'The Agreement on Trade-Related Aspects of Intellectual Property Rights', in P. F. J. Macrory, A. E. Appleton and M. G. Plummer (eds.), *The World Trade Organization: Legal, Economic and Political Analysis* (Springer, 2005), 1069.

further distribution of the product are exhausted both domestically and internationally.

International exhaustion makes it possible to allow the parallel importation of products that are subject to IP rights. This means that it is permitted to import and resell legally a product without the consent of the IP right holder, if that product was put on the market of the exporting country by or with the consent of the right holder. This is of great importance to developing countries, as it enables their importers to buy products that are subject to IP rights, such as patented medicines, wherever they are cheapest and to resell them on their domestic markets.

As negotiators were deeply divided on the issue of exhaustion, the *TRIPS Agreement* does not mandate a particular approach to the exhaustion of IP rights. Article 6 of the *TRIPS Agreement* expressly provides that nothing in this Agreement, leaving aside the obligations of national treatment and MFN treatment, shall be used to address the subject-matter of exhaustion of IP rights. Thus Members are free to choose their own approach to this matter. To alleviate concerns regarding the interpretation of Article 6 of the *TRIPS Agreement*, the *Doha Declaration on the TRIPS Agreement and Public Health* made clear that:

[t]he effect of the provisions in the TRIPS Agreement that are relevant to the exhaustion of intellectual property rights is to leave each Member free to establish its own regime for such exhaustion without challenge, subject to the MFN and national treatment provisions of Articles 3 and 4.[88]

While this statement does not add anything to the *TRIPS Agreement*, it does clarify that Members cannot be challenged in WTO dispute settlement under the *TRIPS Agreement* for allowing the international exhaustion of IP rights, and therefore permitting parallel importation.[89]

Questions and Assignments 15.6

Explain the concept of 'exhaustion' of IP rights. Why is the issue of exhaustion of IP rights important to international trade? Does the *TRIPS Agreement* regulate the issue of exhaustion? Do Members have any obligations under the *TRIPS Agreement* with regard to their national rules on the exhaustion of IP rights? What is the relevance of the *Doha Declaration on the TRIPS Agreement and Public Health* for the issue of exhaustion of IP rights?

---

88 Doha Ministerial Conference, *Declaration on the TRIPS Agreement and Public Health*, WT/MIN(01)/DEC/2, dated 20 November 2001, para. 5(d).
89 One of the main incentives for this clarification in the *Doha Declaration on the TRIPS Agreement and Public Health* was the fact that a large number of pharmaceutical firms challenged the South African Ministry of Health's authorisation of parallel importation of medicines under Section 15C of the South African Medicines and Related Substances Control Amendment Act, No. 90 of 1997. The challenge was withdrawn in 2001. As discussed in detail below, at pp. 999–1001, under the General Council Decision waiving the obligations of Article 31(f) of the *TRIPS Agreement*, Members are required to take reasonable measures to prevent re-exportation of essential medicines imported under the compulsory licence regime provided under the waiver. See Decision of the General Council of 30 August 2003, *Implementation of Paragraph 6 of the Doha Declaration on the TRIPS Agreement and Public Health*, WT/L/540 and Corr.1, dated 2 September 2003. See also the subsequent Decision of the General Council on the Amendment of the TRIPS Agreement of 29 July 2005, para. 4 of the Annex to the *TRIPS Agreement*.

5   SUBSTANTIVE PROTECTION OF INTELLECTUAL PROPERTY RIGHTS

Part II of the *TRIPS Agreement* contains the mandatory minimum standards of IP protection that Members are required to guarantee in their territories. These standards concern, more specifically, the availability, scope and use of those IP rights covered by the *TRIPS Agreement*. As noted above, the *TRIPS Agreement* does not cover every category of IP, but only deals with those seven categories specified in sections 1 to 7 of Part II of the Agreement.[90]

This section limits itself to an examination of four categories of the IP rights covered by the *TRIPS Agreement*, namely: (1) copyright and related rights; (2) trademarks; (3) geographical indications ('GIs'); and (4) patents. These four categories of IP rights have already been the subject of WTO dispute settlement.

5.1   Copyright and Related Rights

Section 1 of Part II of the *TRIPS Agreement* deals with copyright and related rights. It incorporates and supplements the relevant provisions of the *Berne Convention (1971)*.[91] Article 9.1 of the *TRIPS Agreement* expressly incorporates Articles 1 to 21 and the Appendix to the *Berne Convention (1971)*.[92] In Article 2, the *Berne Convention (1971)* contains a non-exhaustive list of protected works, which covers 'every production in the literary, scientific and artistic domain'.[93] Pursuant to Article 2.8 of the *Berne Convention (1971)*, news of the day or mere items of press information are clearly excluded from copyright protection. The protection of some other categories of works is optional; thus every Party may decide to what extent it wishes to protect works of applied art (Article 2.7), and political speeches (Article 2*bis*.1), and to what extent lectures, addresses and other oral works may be reproduced by the press, broadcast and communicated to the public.[94] Parties to the *Berne Convention (1971)* also have the possibility to limit the protection of works to their being fixed in some

---

90 See Panel Report, *EC – Trademarks and Geographical Indications (US) (2005)*, para. 7.598; and Panel Report, *EC – Trademarks and Geographical Indications (Australia) (2005)*, para. 7.598.

91 Note that the panel in *US – Section 110(5) Copyright Act (2000)* held: 'In the area of copyright, the Berne Convention and the TRIPS Agreement form the overall framework for multilateral protection. Most WTO Members are also parties to the Berne Convention. We recall that it is a general principle of interpretation to adopt the meaning that reconciles the texts of different treaties and avoids a conflict between them. Accordingly, one should avoid interpreting the TRIPS Agreement to mean something different than the Berne Convention except where this is explicitly provided for. This principle is in conformity with the public international law presumption against conflicts, which has been applied by WTO panels and the Appellate Body in a number of cases.' See Panel Report, *US – Section 110(5) Copyright Act (2000)*, para. 6.66.

92 Note, however, that the rights under Article 6*bis* of the *Berne Convention (1971)* have been expressly excluded. These relate to the 'moral rights' of authors, which refer to the inherent and inalienable rights of authors, aside from economic rights, such as the right to prevent distortion or modification of the author's work in a way that would negatively affect his or her reputation or honour. Under the *TRIPS Agreement*, Members are not obliged to extend protection to these 'moral rights'.

93 Article 2.1 of the *Berne Convention (1971)*.

94 See Article 2*bis*.2 of the *Berne Convention (1971)*.

material form.[95] For example, the protection of performances of a theatre play may be dependent on their being fixed in some form.

These provisions of the *Berne Convention (1971)* are supplemented by the provisions of the *TRIPS Agreement*. Article 10 of the *TRIPS Agreement* confirms that copyright protection covers two new types of works, namely, computer programs and compilations of data, and clarifies how protection is to be applied to them.

Under both the *Berne Convention (1971)* and the *TRIPS Agreement*, every Party is free to determine the *level* of originality or artistic creativity required for the work to be subject to copyright protection. The scope of copyright protection under the *TRIPS Agreement* is clarified in Article 9.2 as follows:

Copyright protection shall extend to expressions and not to ideas, procedures, methods of operation or mathematical concepts as such.

Thus, copyright protection is only granted to the 'expression' of an idea, not the idea itself, because ideas are seen as common goods that should be shared with all, whereas the expression thereof may be subject to property rights. Frederick Abbott illustrated the idea – expression dichotomy with the following example:

[T]he idea of writing a book about wizards and witches probably is as old as book writing itself ... [A]n author has earned a great deal of money by writing a popular series ... concerning a young man's coming of age in a school for wizards and witches. The author of this series cannot through copyright protection of her books prevent other authors from writing new books about wizards and witches. That would represent an attempt to control the use of an idea. What the author may be able to prevent is the use by others of a particular way of expressing an idea, such as describing specific individuals or the details in a storyline.[96]

Article 9.1 of the *TRIPS Agreement* expressly incorporates Articles 1 to 21 and the Appendix of the *Berne Convention (1971)*.[97] In Article 2, the *Berne Convention (1971)* contains a non-exhaustive list of 'copyrightable' works, which covers 'every production in the literary, scientific and artistic domain'.[98] The copyright provisions of the *Berne Convention (1971)* are supplemented by the recognition in the *TRIPS Agreement* of new rights regarding the protection of computer programs and compilations of data and related rights of performers and broadcasters. However, under both the *Berne Convention (1971)* and the *TRIPS Agreement*, every Party is free to determine the *level* of originality or artistic creativity required for the work to be subject to copyright protection.

In Article 5.1, the *Berne Convention (1971)* provides for two overlapping sets of rights, namely: (1) rights which the respective laws of the parties to the *Berne*

95 See Article 2.2 of the *Berne Convention (1971)*.
96 *Course on Dispute Settlement in International Trade, Investment and Intellectual Property – Module 3.14. WTO: TRIPS*, UNCTAD Document EDM/Misc.232/Add.18 (2003), 12–13.
97 Note, however, that the rights under Article 6*bis* of the *Berne Convention (1971)* have been expressly excluded. These relate to the 'moral rights' of authors, which refer to the inherent and inalienable rights of authors, aside from economic rights, such as the right to prevent distortion or modification of the author's work in a way that would negatively affect his or her reputation or honour. Under the *TRIPS Agreement*, Members are not obliged to extend protection to these 'moral rights'.
98 Article 2.1 of the *Berne Convention (1971)*.

Convention (1971) other than the country of origin grant (or may hereafter grant) to their nationals; and (2) rights specially granted by the *Berne Convention (1971)*. In *China – Intellectual Property Rights (2009)*, no party disputed that the 'works' which Chinese law denied copyright protection because they failed content review, included works falling within the definition of 'literary and artistic works' in Article 2.1 of the *Berne Convention (1971)*.[99] The panel in *China – Intellectual Property Rights (2009)* found:

> [a] government's right to permit, to control, or to prohibit the circulation, presentation, or exhibition of a work may interfere with the exercise of certain rights with respect to a protected work by the copyright owner or a third party authorized by the copyright owner. However, there is no reason to suppose that censorship will eliminate those rights entirely with respect to a particular work.[100]

The *Berne Convention (1971)* provides that authors of literary and artistic works shall have the exclusive rights to make and authorise the translation[101] and the reproduction of their works in any form, which includes any sound or visual recording.[102] Authors of dramatic, dramatico-musical and musical works enjoy the right to authorise the public performance of their works, as well as any communication to the public thereof, including translations.[103] The broadcasting or the communication to the public, by wire, rebroadcasting, loudspeaker or any other analogous instrument is also regarded as an exclusive right of authors of literary and artistic works.[104] In 1998, the United States requested consultations with Greece because a significant number of television stations in Greece regularly broadcasted motion pictures and television programmes without the authorisation of copyright owners and there appeared to be no effective provision or enforcement of remedies against copyright infringement in Greece.[105] The matter was resolved through consultations, as notified to the WTO in 2003.[106] Further, authors of literary works enjoy the exclusive right of authorising the public recitation of their works by any means or process and any communication thereof to the public.[107] In addition, the *Berne Convention (1971)* grants authors of literary or artistic works the right to authorise adaptations, arrangements and other alterations of their works,[108] as well as the cinematographic adaptation, the reproduction of these works, the public performance thereof and the communication to the public.[109] The author of a book, for example, would have to be asked before a producer of movies could adapt the story of the book into a screenplay.

---

99 See Panel Report, *China – Intellectual Property Rights (2009)*, para. 7.116.
100 *Ibid.*, para. 7.132.   101 See Article 8 of the *Berne Convention (1971)*.
102 See *ibid.*, Article 9.1 and 9.3.   103 See *ibid.*, Article 11.   104 See *ibid.*, Article 11*bis*.
105 See Request for Consultations by the United States, *Greece – Enforcement of Intellectual Property Rights for Motion Pictures and Television Programmes*, WT/DS125/1, dated 7 May 1998.
106 See Notification of Mutually Agreed Solution, *Greece – Enforcement of Intellectual Property Rights for Motion Pictures and Television Programmes*, WT/DS125/2, dated 26 March 2001.
107 See Article 11*ter* of the *Berne Convention (1971)*.
108 See *ibid.*, Article 12.   109 See *ibid.*, Article 14.

With regard to authors of original works of art and original manuscripts, Parties to the *Berne Convention (1971)* have the option, but no obligation, to grant them the right to an interest in any sale of the work subsequent to the first transfer by the author of the work, referred to as 'droit de suite'.[110] In contrast, Article 11 of the *TRIPS Agreement*, dealing with 'rental rights', contains a significant innovation – it requires the recognition of 'rental rights' in some cases. Specifically, Members to the *TRIPS Agreement* are required to provide authors (and their successors) of computer programs and cinematographic works to authorise or the right to prohibit the commercial rental to the public of originals or copies of their copyright works.[111] However, Article 11 exempts Members from this obligation in respect of cinematographic works unless such rental has led to widespread copying of the copyrighted works, which materially impairs the right of reproduction of the author. This implies that, in a Member that avails itself of this 'impairment test' in its domestic law, the right of authors of cinematographic works to authorise or prohibit the commercial rental of their works can be limited to situations where authors can prove that otherwise the copying of their works leads to the loss of considerable revenue. In respect of computer programs, this obligation does not apply to rentals where the program itself is not the essential object of the rental. Here, one can think of the example of global positioning software included in rental cars.

Copyright protection is not granted indefinitely, but is limited to a particular term of protection. According to Article 7.1 of the *Berne Convention (1971)*, incorporated by reference in the *TRIPS Agreement*, the minimum term of protection is the life of the author plus fifty years after his or her death. With regard to the duration of the protection of copyright when it is calculated on a basis other than the life of a natural person, Article 12 of the *TRIPS Agreement* provides:

Whenever the term of protection of a work, other than photographic work or a work of applied art, is calculated on a basis other than the life of a natural person, such term shall be *no less than* 50 years from the end of the calendar year of authorized publication, or, failing such authorized publication within 50 years from the making of the work, 50 years from the end of the calendar year of making.[112]

There are, however, exceptions to this basic rule in Article 7.1 of the *Berne Convention*. In the case of cinematographic works, the minimum term of protection, required by the *Berne Convention (1971)*, is fifty years after the work has been made available to the public with the author's consent, or, failing such an event, fifty years after the making.[113] Less than fifty years of protection are required for

110 See *ibid.*, Article 14*ter*.
111 Note that this is limited to 'commercial rental', and therefore not-for-profit rentals are not covered by this obligation.
112 Emphasis added. This provision solves the problem that arose under the *Berne Convention (1971)* with regard to the term of protection in countries which do not recognise legal persons as 'authors'. It provides for the term of protection where this is calculated 'on a basis other than the life of a natural person'.
113 See Article 7.2 of the *Berne Convention (1971)*.

three categories of works. Article 7.4 of the *Berne Convention (1971)* specifies that photographic works and works of applied art shall be protected for at least twenty-five years from the making of such a work.

Both the *Berne Convention (1971)* and the *TRIPS Agreement* provide limitations and exceptions to the strict application of the rules regarding exclusive rights. In other words, both agreements provide for the possibility of using protected works in particular cases without having to obtain the authorisation of the owner of the copyright. Some of the limitations require that the author be compensated, while others allow for the free use of copyrighted works in special cases. The way in which countries make use of these, in part, optional free uses of works is a matter of economic and social circumstances as well as cultural preferences and differs from country to country. These exceptions are then included in national law and therefore apply to individuals directly. The relevant provision in the *TRIPS Agreement* is Article 13, which is entitled 'Limitations and Exceptions' and states:

Members shall confine limitations or exceptions to exclusive rights to certain special cases which do not conflict with a normal exploitation of the work and do not unreasonably prejudice the legitimate interests of the right holder.

Article 13 of the *TRIPS Agreement* constitutes a binding guideline for WTO Members. It lays down the requirements that exceptions and limitations to exclusive rights provided for in national IP law have to meet. The limitations contained in the *Berne Convention (1971)* and in the *TRIPS Agreement* will be dealt with in turn.

The *Berne Convention (1971)* permits the free reproduction of protected works in certain special cases (Article 9.2); allows quotations and the use of works for teaching purposes (Article 10); permits the reproduction of newspaper or similar articles for the purpose of reporting current events (Article 10*bis*); and allows ephemeral (i.e. brief and temporary) recordings (Article 11*bis*.3). Consequently, if a Party to the *Berne Convention (1971)* has permitted the reproduction of articles already published in newspapers or periodicals on current topics, a broadcaster established in that country can use these articles in its broadcastings.

The rationale behind Article 13 of the *TRIPS Agreement*, quoted above, is the search for the 'appropriate balance between the rights of creators and the public interest in access to copyrighted works'.[114] Too many limitations could reduce the economic rewards to right holders; however, certain exceptions are desired in order to advance the public good. While Article 13 undisputedly applies to the newly created rights set out in the *TRIPS Agreement*, the question arises whether

---

114 UNCTAD–ICTSD, *Resource Book on TRIPS and Development: An Authoritative and Practical Guide to the TRIPS Agreement* (Cambridge University Press, 2005), 186.

it also creates a new exception to the existing rights in the *Berne Convention (1971)*. In *US – Section 110(5) Copyright Act (2000)*, the European Communities argued that Article 13 of the *TRIPS Agreement* applies only to those rights that were added to the *TRIPS Agreement*, and, therefore, not to those provisions of the *Berne Convention (1971)* that were incorporated into the *TRIPS Agreement* by reference.[115] The panel in this case addressed the scope of application of Article 13 of the TRIPS Agreement as follows:

> In our view, neither the express wording nor the context of Article 13 or any other provision of the TRIPS Agreement supports the interpretation that the scope of application of Article 13 is limited to the exclusive rights newly introduced under the TRIPS Agreement.[116]

According to the panel in *US – Section 110(5) Copyright Act (2000)*, Article 13 of the *TRIPS Agreement* sets out three cumulative requirements for limitations and exceptions to exclusive rights. They must: (1) be confined to certain special cases; (2) not conflict with a normal exploitation of the work; and (3) not unreasonably prejudice the legitimate interests of the right holder.[117] The panel emphasised from the outset that:

> Article 13 cannot have more than a narrow or limited operation. Its tenor, consistent as it is with the provisions of Article 9(2) of the Berne Convention (1971), discloses that it was not intended to provide for exceptions or limitations except for those of a limited nature.[118]

With regard to the *first requirement*, the panel in *US – Section 110(5) Copyright Act (2000)* found that the concept of 'certain special cases' prohibits broad exceptions of general application. Limitations under Article 13 'should be clearly defined and should be narrow in scope and reach'.[119] Note that the *Berne Convention (1971)* provides for special exceptions that allow the unauthorised use of copyrighted material, as explained above.[120] These exceptions can be invoked and relied upon regardless of Article 13 of the *TRIPS Agreement*.[121]

Whether a limitation or an exception conflicts with a normal exploitation of a work must be judged for each exclusive right individually.[122] In *US – Section 110(5) Copyright Act (2000)*, the panel referred in that regard to the empirical and normative component that has to be evaluated. According to the panel, the commercial use of a work is not necessarily in conflict with the normal exploitation. Such a conflict would exist, however, if the use of a work 'enter[ed] into economic competition with the ways the right holders normally extract economic value from that right'.[123] For example, there might be a conflict if copies of copyrighted works were sold on the market and thus reduced sales opportunities for the copyright holder. If copies of copyrighted work would be used for

---

115 See Panel Report, *US – Section 110(5) Copyright Act (2000)*, para. 6.75.
116 *Ibid.*, para. 6.80.   117 See *ibid.*, para. 6.97.   118 *Ibid.*
119 See *ibid.*, paras. 6.111–6.112.   120 See above, p. 976.
121 In *US – Section 110(5) Copyright Act (2000)*, para. 6.80.
122 See *ibid.*, para. 6.173.   123 *Ibid.*, para. 6.183.

research only, this would most likely not interfere with the normal exploitation of the copyright by the right holder.

Finally, the *third requirement* of Article 13 demands that an exception shall not 'unreasonably prejudice the legitimate interests of the right holder'. The panel in *US – Section 110(5) Copyright Act (2000)* ruled that 'legitimate interests' constitute both normative *and* legal positivist advantages of the right holder.[124] The normative concern for protecting interests could arguably refer to public policy interests such as free speech objectives, given that it is one of the objectives that underlie the protection of copyright. An 'unreasonable loss' to the copyright owner occurs if a limitation 'causes or has the potential to cause an unreasonable loss of income to the copyright owner'.[125] This is most likely not the case if the exception is limited to teaching or research purposes and applies to materials, such as fiction or news articles, that are not specifically produced for that purpose. A heavily commercial use, however, would probably not pass this test.

In *US – Section 110(5) Copyright Act (2000)*, the European Communities complained about the so-called 'business exemption' and 'homestyle exemption' of Section 110(5) of the US Copyright Act. These exemptions permitted the playing of radio and television music in public places such as bars, shops and restaurants, without paying a royalty fee. The United States argued that both exemptions met the conditions of Article 13 of the *TRIPS Agreement*. The panel found that the 'business exemption', which allowed the non-payment of royalties if the size of the establishment was limited to a certain square footage, did not comply with the requirements of Article 13. The panel stated that, in fact, the substantial majority of the eating and drinking establishments were covered by the 'business exemption' and therefore did not constitute a 'certain special case' to which Article 13 of the *TRIPS Agreement* refers.[126] With regard to the 'homestyle exemption', allowing small restaurants and retail outlets to amplify music broadcasts by the use of 'homestyle equipment' (i.e. equipment of a kind commonly used in private homes) only, the panel found that the conditions of Article 13 were fulfilled and that this exemption was therefore lawful.[127]

Under Article 14 of the *TRIPS Agreement*, special rights apply to performers, producers of phonograms and broadcasting organisations. According to Article 14.1, performers have the exclusive right to authorise the fixation, i.e. recording or taping, of their unfixed performances, the reproduction of such fixation and/or the broadcasting/communication to the public of their live performance. For example, a music band performing in a concert has the right to authorise or prohibit the recording of its performance. Furthermore, producers of phonograms enjoy the right to authorise or prohibit the reproduction of their sound recordings.[128] In this respect, note that, in 1997, the United States filed a complaint

124 See *ibid.*, para. 6.224.   125 *Ibid.*, para. 6.229.   126 See *ibid.*, para. 6.133.
127 See *ibid.*, para. 6.159.   128 See Article 14.2 of the *TRIPS Agreement*.

alleging that Ireland did not grant sufficient protection to producers and per-formers of sound recordings.[129] Ireland eventually amended its copyright law on various points to remedy this lack of protection.[130] According to Article 14.3 of the *TRIPS Agreement*, broadcasting organisations have the right to prohibit the re-fixation or rebroadcasting of broadcasts.

The term of protection for performers and producers of phonograms shall last at least fifty years from the end of the year in which the fixation was made or the performance took place.[131] Article 14.5, second sentence, of the *TRIPS Agreement* requires that broadcasting organisations be granted a minimum term of protection of twenty years from the year in which the broadcast took place.

With regard to the duration of protection for performers and producers of sound recordings, in 1996 the United States and the European Communities filed a complaint against Japan at the WTO. According to the complainants, Japanese law only granted protection to foreign sound recordings produced on or after 1 January 1971, the date on which Japan first provided specialised protection for sound recordings under its copyright law.[132] After consultations, this issue was resolved one year later by amendments to the Japanese copyright law pro-viding for protection to recordings produced between 1946 and 1971.[133]

Questions and Assignments 15.7

What is the coverage of copyright protection under the *TRIPS Agreement*? What is the rela-tionship between Article 9 of the *TRIPS Agreement* and Articles 1 to 21 of and the Appendix to the *Berne Convention (1971)*? Is a Member free to determine the *level* of originality or artistic creativity required for a work to be subject to copyright protection? What are the exclusive rights granted to the copyright owner under the *TRIPS Agreement* referring to? What is the *minimum* or *maximum* period of time for which Members shall give copyright protection under the *TRIPS Agreement*? Do the *TRIPS Agreement* and the *Berne Convention (1971)* provide for the possibility of using protected works in particular cases without hav-ing to obtain the authorisation of the copyright owner? Discuss the three-tier test for the application of Article 13 of the *TRIPS Agreement*.

5.2 Trademarks

Section 2 of Part II of the *TRIPS Agreement* deals with trademarks. Trade-marks are signs that aim to distinguish goods or services by communicating

---

129 See A. B. Zampetti, 'WTO Rules in the Audio-Visual Sector', *HWWA* Hamburg Report 229, 24.
130 See *Request for Consultations by the United States, Ireland – Measures Affecting the Grant of Copyright and Neighbouring Rights*, WT/DS82/1, dated 22 May 1997; *Request for Consultations by the United States, European Communities – Measures Affecting the Grant of Copyright and Neighbouring Rights*, WT/DS115/1, dated 12 January 1998; and *Notification of Mutually Agreed Solution*, WT/DS82/3, DS115/3, dated 13 September 2002.
131 Article 14.5, first sentence, of the *TRIPS Agreement*.
132 *Complaint by the United States and the European Communities, Japan – Measures Concerning Sound Re-cordings*, WT/DS28/1 and WT/DS42/1, dated 14 February 1996 and 4 June 1996.
133 See *Notification of a Mutually-Agreed Solution, Japan – Measures Concerning Sound Recordings*, WT/DS42/4, dated 17 November 1997; and *Notification of Mutually Agreed Solution, Japan – Measures Concerning Sound Recordings*, WT/DS28/4, dated 5 February 1997.

information about their source. These marks have economic value, as they can build up a reputation (for example, with regard to quality or reliability) and generate goodwill. Section 2 incorporates the rights of trademark owners set out in the *Paris Convention (1967)* into the *TRIPS Agreement* and strengthens them.[134]

Article 15.1 of the *TRIPS Agreement* defines the protectable subject-matter, i.e. what is capable of constituting a trademark and therefore eligible for registration as such, as follows:

> Any sign, or any combination of signs, capable of distinguishing the goods or services of one undertaking from those of other undertakings, *shall be capable of constituting a trademark*. Such signs, in particular words including personal names, letters, numerals, figurative elements and combinations of colours as well as any combination of such signs, *shall be eligible for registration as trademarks.* Where signs are not inherently capable of distinguishing the relevant goods or services, Members may make registrability depend on distinctiveness acquired through use. Members may require, as a condition of registration, that signs be visually perceptible.[135]

This provision covers both trademarks for goods and trademarks for services (otherwise known as 'service marks').[136] In principle, *distinctiveness* is required – whether inherent in the sign itself or acquired through use. As held by the Appellate Body in *US – Section 211 Appropriations Act (2002)*:

> If such signs are capable of distinguishing the goods or services of one undertaking from those of other undertakings, then they become *eligible for* registration as trademarks. To us, the title of Article 15.1 – 'Protectable Subject-Matter' – indicates that Article 15.1 embodies a *definition* of what can constitute a trademark. WTO Members are obliged under Article 15.1 to ensure that those signs or combinations of signs that meet the distinctiveness criteria set forth in Article 15.1 – and are, thus, *capable of constituting a trademark* – are *eligible for registration* as trademarks within their domestic legislation.[137]

In *US – Section 211 Appropriations Act (2002)*, the European Communities argued that, because Section 211(a)(1) of the US Appropriations Act prohibits registration of trademarks that are 'protectable', it is contrary to Article 15.1 of the *TRIPS Agreement*, as this provision obliges Members to register trademarks that meet the requirements of Article 15.1.[138] As emphasised by the Appellate Body in this case, the fact that a sign falls under the definition of Article 15.1 means only that it is *capable of registration*, not that Members are *obliged to register it*. The Appellate Body stated:

> [I]n our view, the European Communities sees an obligation in Article 15.1 that is not there. Identifying certain signs that are *capable of* registration and imposing on WTO Members an

134 For example, the protection of well-known trademarks in the *Paris Convention (1967)* is expanded.
135 Emphasis added.
136 While the *Paris Convention (1967)* obliges parties to protect service marks, it does not require them to provide for the registration of such marks. In this sense, the *TRIPS Agreement* increases the protection of the *Paris Convention (1967)*.
137 Appellate Body Report, *US – Section 211 Appropriations Act (2002)*, para. 154.
138 See *ibid.*, para. 149.

obligation to make those signs *eligible for* registration in their domestic legislation is not the same as imposing on those Members an obligation to register *automatically* each and every sign or combination of signs that are *capable of* and *eligible for* registration under Article 15.1. This Article describes which trademarks are 'capable of' registration. It does not say that all trademarks that are capable of registration 'shall be registered'. This Article states that such signs or combinations of signs 'shall be *eligible* for registration' as trademarks. It does not say that they 'shall be registered'.[139]

Therefore, according to the Appellate Body, Members are free under Article 15.1 to stipulate in their national legislation conditions for the registration of trademarks that do *not* address the definition of either 'protectable subject-matter' or what constitutes a trademark.[140] In particular, Article 15.2 provides that Members are permitted to deny trademark registration on 'other grounds' provided that they do not derogate from the *Paris Convention (1967)*. Such 'other grounds' are, as noted by the Appellate Body in *US – Section 211 Appropriations Act (2002)*, 'grounds *different from* those already mentioned in Article 15.1, such as lack of inherent distinctiveness of signs, lack of distinctiveness acquired through use, or lack of visual perceptibility'.[141] The Appellate Body stated in *US – Section 211 Appropriations Act (2002)*:

The right of Members under Article 15.2 to deny registration of trademarks on grounds other than the failure to meet the distinctiveness requirements set forth in Article 15.1 implies that Members are not obliged to register any and every sign or combination of signs that meet those distinctiveness requirements.[142]

As stated above, Article 15.2 requires that the other grounds for denial of trademark registration 'do not derogate from the provisions of the Paris Convention (1967)'. The question thus arises to what extent, if at all, 'Members are permitted to deny trademark registration on grounds *other than those expressly provided for* in the *TRIPS Agreement* and the Paris Convention (1967)'.[143] The Appellate Body in *US – Section 211 Appropriations Act (2002)* pointed out in this regard that Article 6.1 of the *Paris Convention (1967)* allows each party to determine conditions for the filing and registration of trademarks in its domestic legislation, provided that this is done consistently with the provisions of the *Paris Convention (1967)*.[144] These provisions set out internationally agreed

139 *Ibid.*, para. 155.
140 See *ibid.*, para. 156. The Appellate Body further pointed out that Article 6.1 of the *Paris Convention (1967)* allows parties to determine the conditions for filing and registration of trademarks in their national legislation. In the Appellate Body's view, Article 15.1 of the *TRIPS Agreement* limits the right of Members to determine the conditions for filing and registration of trademarks under their domestic legislation pursuant to Article 6.1 *only* as it relates to the distinctiveness requirements enunciated in Article 15.1. See *ibid.*, para. 165.
141 *Ibid.*, para. 158.
142 *Ibid.*, para. 159. One of such 'other grounds' mentioned in Article 15.2 is, as pointed out by the Appellate Body in *US – Section 211 Appropriations Act (2002)*, made explicit in Article 15.3, first sentence, which permits Members to condition registration of a trademark on use. See *ibid.*, para. 164. See further below, p. 982 and footnote 178 on p. 988.
143 *Ibid.*, para. 174.   144 See *ibid.*, para. 175.

grounds for denying registration,[145] as well as internationally agreed grounds for *not* denying registration.[146] Therefore, implicitly, Members have the right to refuse trademark registration under Article 6.1 of the *Paris Convention (1967)* on grounds other than those explicitly set out in the convention.[147] Thus, the Appellate Body found that:

'other grounds' for the denial of registration within the meaning of Article 15.2 of the *TRIPS Agreement* are not limited to grounds expressly provided for in the exceptions contained in the Paris Convention (1967) or the *TRIPS Agreement.*[148]

Therefore, Members are free to define in their own legislation the 'other grounds' for denying trademark registration, provided that they are not among those explicitly prohibited by the *Paris Convention (1967).*[149]

A controversial issue in the negotiation of the *TRIPS Agreement* was whether *use* could be required as a condition for the registration of a trademark.[150] Article 15.3 of the *TRIPS Agreement* reflects the compromise reached: Members may make registrability, but not the filing of an application for registration, dependent on use.[151] Pursuant to Article 15.4 of the *TRIPS Agreement*, the nature of the goods and services to which a trademark is applied may not be used as a ground to deny registration of the trademark.

In order to promote transparency, Article 15.5 of the *TRIPS Agreement* requires a Member to publish each trademark either before, or promptly after, it is registered. Members must provide an opportunity for petitions to cancel registration and *may* provide an opportunity for the registration of a trademark to be opposed.

Article 16 of the *TRIPS Agreement* sets out the exclusive rights conferred on trademark owners. It provides in paragraph 1 thereof:

The owner of a registered trademark shall have the exclusive right to prevent all third parties not having the owner's consent from using in the course of trade identical or similar

---

145 For example, Article 6*bis* of the *Paris Convention (1967)* requires the refusal of the registration of a well-known trademark by a third party, and Article 6*ter* covers prohibitions on the registration of State emblems, official hallmarks and emblems of international organisations. While Article 6*quinquies*(A) contains a general rule that every trademark duly registered in the country of origin shall be accepted for filing and protected as it is in other parties, Article 6*quinquies*(B) permits the denial of registration of such trademarks if they are devoid of distinctive character or have become customary, that are contrary to morality or public order, or infringe rights acquired by third parties.

146 See Appellate Body Report, *US – Section 211 Appropriations Act (2002)*, paras. 175–6. An example of a ground upon which registration may not be refused, mentioned by the Appellate Body, is that contained in Article 6.2 of the *Paris Convention (1967)*, which limits the legislative discretion of parties by providing that an application for registration by a national of a country of the Paris Union may not be refused on the ground that the national has not filed for registration or renewal in its country of origin. See *ibid.*, footnote 111 to para. 176.

147 See *ibid.*, para. 176.

148 *Ibid.*, para. 178. See also Panel Report, *US – Section 211 Appropriations Act (2002)*, paras. 8.53 and 8.70.

149 Appellate Body Report, *US – Section 211 Appropriations Act (2002)*, para. 177.

150 In Anglo-American legal systems, trademark rights can be created through use of the trademark without registration, and actual use is traditionally required as a condition for trademark registration. In civil law systems, trademarks are acquired through registration. See C. M. Correa, 'The TRIPS Agreement and Developing Countries', in P. F. J Macrory, A. E. Appleton and M. G. Plummer (eds.), The World Trade Organization: Legal, Economic and Political Analysis (Springer, 2005), 181.

151 In addition, a Member may not refuse to register a trademark *solely* on the ground that the intended use has not taken place within three years of the filing of the application.

signs for goods or services which are identical or similar to those in respect of which the trademark is registered where such use would result in a likelihood of confusion. In case of the use of an identical sign for identical goods or services, a likelihood of confusion shall be presumed. The rights described above shall not prejudice any existing prior rights, nor shall they affect the possibility of Members making rights available on the basis of use.

Therefore, a Member may decide for itself whether it will not only provide these exclusive rights to owners of registered trademarks, but also confer these rights on the basis of use. In *US – Section 211 Appropriations Act (2002)*, the European Communities challenged Section 211 of the US Omnibus Appropriations Act, which effectively prohibits registration and renewal – without the consent of the original owner or *bona fide* successor-in-interest – of trademarks and trade names used in connection with a business or assets that were confiscated without compensation by the Cuban government after the revolution. Under this provision, the trademark 'Havana Club' that had been confiscated by the Cuban government without compensation from its Cuban owners could not be registered or enforced in the United States. The trademark was later in the hands of a French–Cuban joint venture. The European Communities claimed that Section 211 of the Appropriations Act violated the rules of the *Paris Convention (1967)* on trademark registration and was inconsistent with the national treatment and MFN treatment obligations of the *TRIPS Agreement*. On appeal, the Appellate Body agreed with the panel that:

> neither Article 16.1 of the *TRIPS Agreement*, nor any other provision of either the *TRIPS Agreement* [or] the Paris Convention (1967), determines who owns or who does not own a trademark. Article 16.1 does not, in express terms, define how ownership of a registered trademark is to be determined. Article 16.1 confers exclusive rights on the 'owner', but Article 16.1 does not tell us who the 'owner' *is*. As used in this treaty provision, the ordinary meaning of 'owner' can be defined as the proprietor or person who holds the title or dominion of the property constituted by the trademark.[152]

The European Communities' argument that, under the *TRIPS Agreement*, the 'undertaking' that uses the trademark to distinguish its goods or services must be regarded as the owner of the trademark was rejected by the Appellate Body as having no basis in the text of the *TRIPS Agreement*.[153]

A few elements of the rights conferred under Article 16.1 of the *TRIPS Agreement* deserve attention. Note that the exclusive right is limited to the right to use the trademark 'in the course of trade'. Non-commercial use of trademarks is therefore not covered. Also, the owner is only granted the right to prevent the use of 'identical or similar signs' for goods or services that are 'identical or similar' to those in respect of which the trademark is registered. There is no definition of how similarity is to be determined, and this is left to Members to determine in their own legal systems. Note further that the exclusive right to

---

152 Appellate Body Report, *US – Section 211 Appropriations Act (2002)*, para. 195.
153 See *ibid.*, para. 194.

prevent use of a trademark is only granted 'where such use would result in a likelihood of confusion'.[154]

In *EC – Trademarks and Geographical Indications (2005)*, the complainants alleged a violation of Article 16.1 of the *TRIPS Agreement* by the EC regulation on the protection of geographical indications ('GIs') and designations of origin for agricultural products and foodstuffs. This regulation allowed for so-called 'coexistence', i.e. a legal regime under which a GI and a trademark can be used concurrently to some extent even though the use of one or both of them would otherwise infringe the rights conferred by the other. The complainants argued that the EC regulation did not ensure that an owner of a trademark was able to prevent uses of GIs, which would result in a 'likelihood of confusion' with a prior trademark.[155] The panel examined whether Article 16.1 of the *TRIPS Agreement* requires Members to make available to trademark owners the right to prevent confusing uses of signs, even where the signs are used as GIs. It noted:

Although each of the Sections in Part II provides for a different category of intellectual property, at times they refer to one another, as certain subject-matter may be eligible for protection by more than one category of intellectual property. This is particularly apparent in the case of trademarks and GIs, both of which are, in general terms, forms of distinctive signs. The potential for overlap is expressly confirmed by Articles 22.3 and 23.2, which provide for the refusal or invalidation of the registration of a trademark which contains or consists of a GI.[156]

Examining the text of Article 16.1, the panel noted that it contains no express or implied limitation with respect to GIs.[157] It held:

The text of Article 16.1 stipulates that the right for which it provides is an 'exclusive' right. This must signify more than the fact that it is a right to 'exclude' others, since that notion is already captured in the use of the word 'prevent'. Rather, it indicates that this right belongs to the owner of the registered trademark alone, who may exercise it to prevent certain uses by 'all third parties' not having the owner's consent. The last sentence provides for an exception to that right, which is that it shall not prejudice any existing prior rights. Otherwise, the text of Article 16.1 is unqualified.[158]

Therefore, the trademark owner has the exclusive right to prevent use of the trademark by all third parties, also GI holders, without the owner's consent.

Articles 16.2 and 16.3 of the *TRIPS Agreement* extend the protection of Article 6*bis* of the *Paris Convention (1967)* in respect of 'well-known' trademarks on

---

154 See C. M. Correa, 'The TRIPS Agreement and Developing Countries', in P. F. J Macrory, A. E. Appleton and M. G. Plummer (eds.), *The World Trade Organization: Legal, Economic and Political Analysis* (Springer, 2005), 186. Correa points out that Article 15.1 informs the meaning of 'confusion', i.e. confusion should be understood in relation to the capacity of the trademark to distinguish the similar/identical goods or services of one undertaking from those of another.

155 See Panel Report, *EC – Trademarks and Geographical Indications (US) (2005)*, para. 7.512; and Panel Report, *EC – Trademarks and Geographical Indications (Australia) (2005)*, para. 7.516.

156 Panel Report, *EC – Trademarks and Geographical Indications (US) (2005)*, para. 7.599; and Panel Report, *EC – Trademarks and Geographical Indications (Australia) (2005)*, para. 7.599.

157 See Panel Report, *EC – Trademarks and Geographical Indications (US) (2005)*, paras. 7.601 and 7.603; and Panel Report, *EC – Trademarks and Geographical Indications (Australia) (2005)*, paras. 7.601 and 7.603.

158 Panel Report, *EC – Trademarks and Geographical Indications (US) (2005)*, para. 7.602; and Panel Report, *EC – Trademarks and Geographical Indications (Australia) (2005)*, para. 7.602.

identical or similar goods to include, respectively: (1) 'well-known' trademarks on identical or similar *services*; and (2) 'well-known' trademarks on goods or services that are *not similar* to those in respect of which a trademark is registered. To determine whether a trademark is 'well known', Members must take account of the knowledge of the trademark in the relevant sector of the public, including that resulting from the promotion of the trademark.[159] Note that the knowledge need not be present in the public at large, but it is sufficient if it is present in the 'relevant sector' (for example, software users in the banking sector). However, the level of knowledge required for a mark to be 'well known' is left to Members to determine for themselves within their own legal systems. The extension of protection to 'well known' trademarks on goods or services that are not similar to those in respect of which the trademark is registered is limited to situations where the use of the trademark in relation to those goods or services would 'indicate a connection' between them and the trademark owner and thereby damage the latter's interests.[160] This aims to prevent 'dilution' of a trademark, i.e. where the value of the trademark is diminished by being associated with products that are, for example, of lesser quality.

The possibility to provide exceptions to trademark rights is contained in Article 17 of the *TRIPS Agreement*, which states:

Members may provide limited exceptions to the rights conferred by a trademark, such as fair use of descriptive terms, provided that such exceptions take account of the legitimate interests of the owner of the trademark and of third parties.

Note that this provision does not create an exception itself – it only allows Members to do so. The possibility to make such exceptions is, however, explicitly subject to two requirements, as identified by the panel in *EC – Trademarks and Geographical Indications (2005)*, namely: (1) the exception must be limited; and (2) the exception must satisfy the proviso that 'such exceptions take account of the legitimate interests of the owner of the trademark and of third parties'.[161]

With regard to the first requirement of Article 17 of the *TRIPS Agreement*, the panel agreed with the interpretation, made by the panel in *Canada – Pharmaceutical Patents (2000)*, of the identical term of 'limited exceptions' in Article 30 of the *TRIPS Agreement*, that '[t]he word "exception" by itself connotes a limited derogation, one that does not undercut the body of rules from which it is made'.[162] The panel in *EC – Trademarks and Geographical Indications (2005)* held:

The addition of the word 'limited' emphasizes that the exception must be narrow and permit only a small diminution of rights. The limited exceptions apply 'to the rights conferred by a trademark'. They do not apply to the set of all trademarks or all trademark owners.

---

159 See Article 16.2 of the *TRIPS Agreement*.
160 See Article 16.3 of the *TRIPS Agreement*.
161 See *EC – Trademarks and Geographical Indications (US) (2005)*, para. 7.648; and Panel Report, *EC – Trademarks and Geographical Indications (Australia) (2005)*, para. 7.648.
162 Panel Report, *Canada – Pharmaceutical Patents (2000)*, para. 7.30.

Accordingly, the fact that it may affect only few trademarks or few trademark owners is irrelevant to the question whether an exception is limited. The issue is whether the exception to the *rights conferred by a trademark* is narrow.[163]

Finding that only one right, namely, the exclusive right to prevent certain uses of a sign provided in Article 16.1, was conferred by the trademark at issue in this dispute, the panel in *EC – Trademarks and Geographical Indications (2005)* found it necessary to examine the exception of Article 17 'on an individual "per right" basis'.[164] According to the panel:

[t]his is a legal assessment of the extent to which the exception curtails that right. There is no indication in the text of Article 17 that this involves an economic assessment, although economic impact can be taken into account in the proviso. In this regard, we note the absence of any reference to a 'normal exploitation' of the trademark in Article 17, and the absence of any reference in Section 2, to which Article 17 permits exceptions, to rights to exclude legitimate competition. Rather, they confer, *inter alia*, the right to prevent uses that would result in a likelihood of confusion, which can lead to the removal of products from sale where they are marketed using particular signs, but without otherwise restraining the manufacture, sale or importation of competing goods or services.[165]

The panel held that the EC regulation at issue curtailed the trademark owner's right: (1) 'in respect of certain goods but not all goods identical or similar to those in respect of which the trademark is registered';[166] (2) 'against certain third parties, but not "all third parties"';[167] and (3) 'in respect of certain signs but not all signs identical or similar to the one protected as a trademark'.[168] Therefore, the panel found that the EC regulation at issue created a 'limited exception' within the meaning of Article 17 of the *TRIPS Agreement*.[169]

With regard to the second requirement of Article 17 of the *TRIPS Agreement*, namely, that the limited exceptions must satisfy the proviso that 'such exceptions take account of the legitimate interests of the owner of the trademark and of third parties', the panel in *EC – Trademarks and Geographical Indications (2005)* agreed with the interpretation of the panel in *Canada – Pharmaceutical Patents (2000)* of the term 'legitimate interests' of a patent owner and third parties in the context of Article 30 of the *TRIPS Agreement*.[170] The panel in *Canada – Pharmaceutical Patents (2000)* held that the term must be defined as:

163 Panel Report, *EC – Trademarks and Geographical Indications (US) (2005)*, para. 7.650; and Panel Report, *EC – Trademarks and Geographical Indications (Australia) (2005)*, para. 7.650.
164 Panel Report, *EC – Trademarks and Geographical Indications (US) (2005)*, para. 7.651; and Panel Report, *EC – Trademarks and Geographical Indications (Australia) (2005)*, para. 7.651.
165 Panel Report, *EC – Trademarks and Geographical Indications (US) (2005)*, para. 7.651; and Panel Report, *EC – Trademarks and Geographical Indications (Australia) (2005)*, para. 7.651.
166 Panel Report, *EC – Trademarks and Geographical Indications (US) (2005)*, para. 7.655; and Panel Report, *EC – Trademarks and Geographical Indications (Australia) (2005)*, para. 7.655.
167 Panel Report, *EC – Trademarks and Geographical Indications (US) (2005)*, para. 7.656; and Panel Report, *EC – Trademarks and Geographical Indications (Australia) (2005)*, para. 7.656.
168 Panel Report, *EC – Trademarks and Geographical Indications (US) (2005)*, para. 7.657; and Panel Report, *EC – Trademarks and Geographical Indications (Australia) (2005)*, para. 7.657.
169 See Panel Report, *EC – Trademarks and Geographical Indications (US) (2005)*, para. 7.661; and Panel Report, *EC – Trademarks and Geographical Indications (Australia) (2005)*, para. 7.661.
170 Panel Report, *EC – Trademarks and Geographical Indications (US) (2005)*, para. 7.663; and Panel Report, *EC – Trademarks and Geographical Indications (Australia) (2005)*, para. 7.663.

a normative claim calling for protection of interests that are 'justifiable' in the sense that they are supported by relevant public policies or other social norms.[171]

With respect to the 'legitimate interests' of the trademark owner and third parties in the context of Article 17 of the *TRIPS Agreement*, the panel in *EC – Trademarks and Geographical Indications (2005)* held:

The function of trademarks can be understood by reference to Article 15.1 as distinguishing goods and services of undertakings in the course of trade. Every trademark owner has a legitimate interest in preserving the distinctiveness, or capacity to distinguish, of its trademark so that it can perform that function. This includes its interest in using its own trademark in connection with the relevant goods and services of its own and authorized undertakings. Taking account of that legitimate interest will also take account of the trademark owner's interest in the economic value of its mark arising from the reputation that it enjoys and the quality that it denotes.[172]

The panel found that the EC regulation at issue took account of the trademark owner's rights in preserving the distinctiveness of its trademark in various ways. The panel emphasised that the proviso to Article 17 requires only that exceptions 'take account' of the legitimate interests of the owner of the trademark.[173] The panel subsequently examined whether the EC regulation took account of the legitimate interests of third parties. The panel identified as relevant third parties consumers and GI users,[174] and determined that the interests of these third parties were taken into account in the EC regulation at issue.[175] Therefore, the panel found the EC regulation at issue to be justified by Article 17 of the *TRIPS Agreement*.[176]

Unlike copyright, trademarks can be protected for an unlimited period. Article 18 of the *TRIPS Agreement* provides that trademarks 'shall be renewable indefinitely'. Although Members may require that trademark registrations be renewed, this may not be more often than once every seven years. However, a trademark registration may be cancelled if a Member requires use to maintain a registration, as permitted by Article 19 of the *TRIPS Agreement*. Such a requirement may lead to the cancellation of the trademark registration only after an uninterrupted period of at least three years, and not if the non-use was for

171 Panel Report, *Canada – Pharmaceutical Patents (2000)*, para. 7.69.
172 Panel Report, *EC – Trademarks and Geographical Indications (US) (2005)*, para. 7.664; and Panel Report, *EC – Trademarks and Geographical Indications (Australia) (2005)*, para. 7.664.
173 There is no reference to 'unreasonabl[e] prejudice' to those interests, unlike the provisos in Articles 13, 26.2 and 30 of the *TRIPS Agreement* and Article 9.2 of the *Berne Convention (1971)* as incorporated by Article 9.1 of the *TRIPS Agreement*, suggesting that a lesser standard of regard for the legitimate interests of the owner of the trademark is required. See Panel Report, *EC – Trademarks and Geographical Indications (US) (2005)*, para. 7.671; and Panel Report, *EC – Trademarks and Geographical Indications (Australia) (2005)*, para. 7.671.
174 See Panel Report, *EC – Trademarks and Geographical Indications (US) (2005)*, paras. 7.676, 7.680 and 7.681; and Panel Report, *EC – Trademarks and Geographical Indications (Australia) (2005)*, paras. 7.675 and 7.679.
175 See Panel Report, *EC – Trademarks and Geographical Indications (US) (2005)*, para. 7.686; and Panel Report, *EC – Trademarks and Geographical Indications (Australia) (2005)*, para. 7.684.
176 See Panel Report, *EC – Trademarks and Geographical Indications (US) (2005)*, para. 7.688; and Panel Report, *EC – Trademarks and Geographical Indications (Australia) (2005)*, para. 7.686.

valid reasons due to obstacles to such use.[177] Valid reasons include, for example, import restrictions or other government requirements for goods or services protected by the trademark.[178]

Article 20 prohibits unjustifiable encumbrances on trademarks by means of 'special requirements' such as use with another trademark or in a special form or manner that is detrimental to its capability to distinguish the goods or services of one undertaking from those of another. In *Indonesia – Autos (1998)*, the United States claimed that the Indonesian National Car Programme was inconsistent with Article 20. The panel disagreed, holding in this regard that:

> if a foreign company enters into an arrangement with [an Indonesian] Pioneer company it does so voluntarily and in the knowledge of any consequent implications for its ability to use any pre-existing trademark. In these circumstances, we do not consider the provisions of the National Car Programme as they relate to trademarks can be construed as 'requirements', in the sense of Article 20.[179]

Finally, note that, under Article 21 of the *TRIPS Agreement*, Members are free to determine conditions on the licensing and assignment of trademarks. The only limitations on this freedom, also contained in Article 21, are: (1) the prohibition on compulsory licensing of trademarks;[180] and (2) the requirement that Members allow the transfer of a trademark with or without the transfer of the business to which it belongs.

Questions and Assignments 15.8

What are 'trademarks'? Are Members free under Article 15.1 of the *TRIPS Agreement* to lay down in their national legislation conditions for the registration of trademarks and the grounds for denying such registration? Can a Member refuse to register a trademark that is not used? What, pursuant to the *TRIPS Agreement*, must fall within the exclusive rights conferred on trademark owners? Are there special rules on the protection of 'well-known' trademarks? Can Members limit the rights conferred on trademark owners? Is there a *minimum* or *maximum* period of time for which Members shall give protection to trademarks under the *TRIPS Agreement*? Can Members freely determine the conditions on the licensing and assignment of trademarks under the *TRIPS Agreement*?

5.3 Geographical Indications

The quality, characteristics or reputation of a product are sometimes determined by where it comes from, i.e. its geographical origin. Geographical indications

---

177 Article 5C (1) of the *Paris Convention (1967)* also allows the cancellation of a trademark for non-use after a reasonable period if the trademark holder does not justify his inaction. However, the reasonable period is not specified. In this regard the *TRIPS Agreement* supplements the *Paris Convention (1967)*.

178 Note that the use of a trademark by someone other than the owner will be recognised as 'use' of the trademark for purposes of maintaining the registration if such use is subject to the control of the trademark owner. See Article 19.2 of the *TRIPS Agreement*.

179 Panel Report, *Indonesia – Autos (1998)*, para. 14.277.

180 Correa notes that compulsory licences have rarely been granted in the field of trademarks, so Article 21 is merely preventative of an unlikely future event. See C. M. Correa, 'The TRIPS Agreement and Developing Countries', in P. F. J Macrory, A. E. Appleton and M. G. Plummer (eds.), *The World Trade Organization: Legal, Economic and Political Analysis* (Springer, 2005), 202.

(such as 'Champagne', 'Parma' ham, 'Bohemian' crystal, 'Orkney' beef, 'Tequila', 'Gorgonzola' cheese and 'Darjeeling' tea)[181] are place names that are used to identify the products that originate in these places and have the characteristics associated with that place. The provision of protection to geographical indications was a contentious issue in the Uruguay Round negotiations. Section 3 of Part II of the *TRIPS Agreement* reflects the compromise reached.

Geographical indications ('GIs') are defined in Article 22.1 of the *TRIPS Agreement* as:

indications which identify a good as originating in the territory of a Member, or a region or locality in that territory, where a given quality, reputation or other characteristic of the good is *essentially attributable to its geographical origin.*[182]

In terms of this definition, it is clear that, in order to qualify for GI protection, it is not necessary to show that the product from that geographical area is *in fact* better or different from a similar product that originates elsewhere. It may also be established that a particular reputation or goodwill has been built in a particular place with regard to that product.[183] The 'indication' used does not have to be the place name itself, but may also be a name or symbol that is understood by the public as identifying a specific geographical origin (for example, 'Basmati' rice).[184] Note that a geographical indication is *not* the same as an indication of origin, such as 'Made in India', which only specifies the place where the product was produced, without indicating any associated product attributes. A geographical indication is also different from a trademark. A trademark identifies the *undertaking* offering the product or service on the market, whereas a GI indicates only the *place* where the product is produced. Several undertakings may use the same GI.[185]

The protection of geographical indications required under the *TRIPS Agreement* is specified in two provisions: (1) Article 22.2 of the *TRIPS Agreement*, which sets out the standard level of protection to be accorded to *all* products; this protection focuses on preventing misuse of GIs so as to mislead the public or constitute unfair competition; and (2) Article 23 of the *TRIPS Agreement*, which provides a higher or enhanced level of protection for *wines and spirits*;

---

181 These are frequently given examples of geographical indications. However, inclusion in this illustrative list should not be read as an affirmation that these names are 'geographical indications' within the meaning of Article 22.1 of the *TRIPS Agreement*.

182 Emphasis added.

183 It may be harder to prove that a particular reputation is essentially attributable to a geographical location, than that a product characteristic or the product quality are so attributable. It will be up to the Member in which GI protection is sought to determine whether the conditions for acquiring a GI are met, within the limits set by Article 22.1. See C. M. Correa, *Trade-Related Aspects of Intellectual Property Rights: A Commentary on the TRIPS Agreement* (Oxford University Press, 2007), 220.

184 For example, 'Ouzo' is associated with Greece and 'Grappa' with Italy, and symbols such as the Eiffel Tower and the Matterhorn are widely associated with France and Switzerland respectively. See *ibid.*, 212, footnotes 12 and 13.

185 As several undertakings may be producing the relevant product in the identified geographical location, the GI may be combined with a trademark in order to identify a particular producer within the geographical area. See *ibid.*, 210.

this protection must be provided even if misuse would not mislead the public. These two levels of protection will now be discussed in more detail.

Pursuant to Article 22.2 of the *TRIPS Agreement*, Members must protect GIs for all products by providing interested parties with the 'legal means' to prevent: (1) use of any means in the designation or presentation of the good that misleads the public as to the geographical origin of the good; and (2) use that constitutes unfair competition under Article 10*bis* of the *Paris Convention (1967)*. The form that these 'legal means' take is left up to the Member involved.[186] Pursuant to Article 22.4 of the *TRIPS Agreement*, the protection against use of a GI that 'misleads the public' is extended to the use of 'homonymous' GIs. This prevents the use of a GI that is literally true as to the origin of the product, but falsely represents to the public that the product originates in another place with the same name. To avoid the use of a GI that 'misleads the public', producers may use additions such as 'imitation', 'like' or 'type' (for example, 'Roquefort-type' cheese or 'Delft-style' pottery). It is for the authorities in the Member where GI protection is provided to determine if public confusion is effectively avoided in this way.[187]

The enhanced GI protection for wines and spirits provided in Article 23 of the *TRIPS Agreement* requires Members to provide interested parties with legal means to prevent the use of a GI identifying a wine or a spirit for a wine or a spirit not originating in the place indicated by the GI in question. This is the case even if use of these GIs would *not* cause the public to be misled nor lead to unfair competition. According to Article 23.1 of the *TRIPS Agreement*, a Member must make it possible for the holder of a GI to prevent the use of the GI on the non-originating product even if confusion is prevented by an indication of the true origin of the product, the translation of the GI or the use of terms such as 'like' or 'type' (for example, 'Champagne-like' or 'Bordeaux-type') to distinguish products originating outside the place attributed to the GI.[188] Article 23.3 of the *TRIPS Agreement* deals with the use of homonymous GIs for wines (not for spirits) whose use is not misleading under Article 22.4.[189] It provides that both GIs shall be protected and the Member concerned must determine the practical conditions under which the homonymous GIs will be differentiated from each other. Such conditions must ensure that the producers concerned are treated equitably and that consumers are not misled.

Under Article 24.4 of the *TRIPS Agreement*, Members agree to negotiate with a view to increasing the protection of individual GIs under Article 23.

---

186 Note that Members are obliged, under Article 22.3 of the *TRIPS Agreement*, to refuse or to invalidate trademark registration where the trademark is a GI with respect to goods not originating in the indicated territory, if the use of the GI in the trademark is of such a nature as to mislead the public as to the true place of origin of the product.
187 See C. M. Correa, *Trade-Related Aspects of Intellectual Property Rights: A Commentary on the TRIPS Agreement* (Oxford University Press, 2007), 231.
188 With regard to footnote 4 dealing with the enforcement of the protection, see below, p. 1003.
189 For example, 'Rioja' wine is produced in both Spain and Argentina. See D. Gervais, *The TRIPS Agreement: Drafting History and Analysis*, 2nd edn (Sweet & Maxwell, 2003), 197, footnote 60.

The expansion of coverage of the higher level of protection of Article 23 of the *TRIPS Agreement* beyond GIs for wines and spirits to other products is being discussed under the Doha Work Programme as a so-called outstanding implementation issue.[190] Members are deeply divided on this issue. Some Members advocate the extension of the higher level of protection of Article 23 to other products as a way to differentiate their products more effectively from those of their competitors, and to prevent other Members from 'usurping' their GIs. Others see the protection reflected in Article 22 as sufficient and are concerned that added protection would restrict legitimate marketing practices. They also point out that since a number of Members have received many immigrants who have brought with them their cultural traditions, including names and terms, it would be culturally insensitive for Members, predominantly those from which these people had migrated, to try to claim back terms that had been used for decades without being contested.[191]

Article 23.4 of the *TRIPS Agreement* provides for negotiations in the Council for TRIPS to establish a multilateral system of notification and registration of geographical indications for wines in those Members participating in the system, in order to facilitate the protection of GIs for wines. Although this provision refers only to wines, paragraph 18 of the Doha Ministerial Declaration provides for negotiations on the establishment of a multilateral system of notification and registration of geographical indications for wines and spirits, with a view to completing the work started in the Council for TRIPS on the implementation of Article 23.4.[192] These negotiations were to be completed in 2003, but, due to the strongly diverging positions of Members, no agreement has been reached on such a system to date. Key issues on which disagreement exists are: what legal effect, if any, registration of a GI in such a 'multilateral register' should Members be required to accord; to what extent, if at all, should this effect apply to Members that choose not to participate in the system; and whether the administrative and financial costs of implementing such a system for individual governments would outweigh the possible benefits.[193]

190 See Ministerial Conference, Doha Ministerial Declaration, WT/MIN(01)/DEC/1, dated 20 November 2001, paras. 12 and 18.
191 On the positions taken by Members in these negotiations, see Trade Negotiations Committee, Note by the Secretariat, *Issues Related to the Extension of the Protection of Geographical Indications Provided for in Article 23 of the TRIPS Agreement to Products Other Than Wines and Spirits: Compilation of Issues Raised and Views Expressed*, TN/C/W/25, WT/GC/W/546, dated 18 May 2005, para. 14.
192 See Ministerial Conference, *Doha Ministerial Declaration*, WT/MIN(01)/DEC/1, dated 20 November 2001, para. 18.
193 The WTO Secretariat has made a useful compilation of the proposals and comments received on this issue. See Council for TRIPS, Special Session, Note by the Secretariat, *Side-by-Side Presentation of Proposals*, TN/IP/W/12, dated 14 September 2005. See also Report by the Director-General, *Issues Related to the Extension of the Protection of Geographical Indications Provided for in Article 3 of the TRIPS Agreement to Products other than Wines and Spirits and Those Related to the Relationship between the TRIPS Agreement and the Convention on Biological Diversity*, TN/C/W/61, WT/GC/W/633, dated 21 April 2011, highlighting the divergence of views among Members.

In order to prevent that the provisions on GI protection in the *TRIPS Agreement* lead to a reduction in the protection already provided for by some Members, Article 24.3 of the *TRIPS Agreement* contains an 'anti-rollback' provision, which states:

In implementing this Section, a Member shall not diminish the protection of geographical indications that existed in that Member immediately prior to the date of entry into force of the WTO Agreement.

The above obligation applies indefinitely and prohibits any reduction in the level of protection for GIs, even if the protection remains above the standards mandated by the *TRIPS Agreement*.[194]

The *TRIPS Agreement* sets out a number of permissible exceptions to GI protection in paragraphs 4 to 9 of Article 24 of the *TRIPS Agreement*. Note, for example, that Article 24.5 of the *TRIPS Agreement* provides that the protection of GIs shall not prejudice prior trademark rights that were acquired in good faith. Under this exception, the fact that a trademark is identical with or similar to a GI shall not prejudice the eligibility for or validity of the registration of the trademark if it has been applied for, registered or acquired through use, in good faith, either: (1) before the provisions of Section 3 of Part II became applicable in the Member concerned; or (2) before the GI was protected in its country of origin.[195] Article 24.4 of the *TRIPS Agreement* contains an exception of GI protection to wines and spirits, allowing under specific conditions continued and similar use of a geographical indication of another Member when that GI has been used continuously and with respect to the same goods or services. As a final example of an exception to GI protection, consider Article 24.6 of the *TRIPS Agreement*. Pursuant to Article 24.6, a Member is not obliged to provide protection to a GI of another Member that is identical with a term that is customary in common language as the common name for goods or services in its territory. This takes account of the fact that some GIs have become common terms for particular products.[196]

Questions and Assignments 15.9

What are 'geographical indications'? Are Members required to give protection to geographical indications under the *TRIPS Agreement*? Is Argentina required under Article 22.2 of the *TRIPS Agreement* to prohibit the marketing in Argentina of a domestically produced cheese identified on the label as a 'Roquefort-type' cheese? Is France allowed to prohibit the marketing of this product in France? Is your answer to the previous two questions the same if the product concerned is a 'Bordeaux-type' wine?

194 Note the difference with Article 65 of the *TRIPS Agreement*, discussed below. See below, p. 1011.
195 For an analysis of the scope and nature of Article 24.5 of the *TRIPS Agreement* as well as possible conflicts between the protection of GIs and trademarks, see Panel Report, *EC – Trademarks and Geographical Indications (US) (2005)*, paras. 7.604–7.625; Panel Report, *EC – Trademarks and Geographical Indications (Australia) (2005)*, paras. 7.604–7.625.
196 Note that Members availing themselves of the use of the exceptions provided for in Article 24 of the *TRIPS Agreement* must be willing to enter into negotiations under Article 24.1 about their continued application to individual geographical indications.

5.4 Patents

Minimum requirements for patent protection are set out in Section 5 of Part II of the *TRIPS Agreement*. Article 27.1 of the *TRIPS Agreement* defines the patentable subject-matter as follows:

Subject to the provisions of paragraphs 2 and 3, patents shall be available for any inventions, whether products or processes, in all fields of technology, provided that they are new, involve an inventive step and are capable of industrial application.

Thus, when requested, patent protection must be granted to any invention in any field, provided three requirements are met: (1) the invention is new; (2) it involves an inventive step; and (3) it is capable of industrial application. Furthermore, Article 27.1 of the *TRIPS Agreement* provides:

Subject to paragraph 4 of Article 65, paragraph 8 of Article 70 and paragraph 3 of this Article, patents shall be available and patent rights enjoyable without discrimination as to the place of invention, the field of technology and whether products are imported or locally produced.

In addition to the general non-discrimination obligations set out in Articles 3 and 4 of the *TRIPS Agreement* discussed above, with regard to patents, Article 27.1 thus prohibits discrimination regarding the availability and enjoyment of patent rights based on: (1) the place of invention; (2) the field of technology; and (3) whether products are imported or locally produced.[197]

Articles 27.2 and 27.3 of the *TRIPS Agreement* allow Members to exclude certain inventions from patentability. Article 27.2 provides that:

Members may exclude from patentability inventions, the prevention within their territory of the commercial exploitation of which is necessary to protect *ordre public* or morality, including to protect human, animal or plant life or health or to avoid serious prejudice to the environment, provided that such exclusion is not made merely because the exploitation is prohibited by their domestic law.

It is likely that, in line with case law on the concept of public order and public morality under the GATS, this exception will take into account national perceptions that differ across Members.[198] Note that health and the environment are illustrative examples only, as indicated by the word 'including'. The link between the use of the exception and the prevention of commercial exploitation of the invention in the territory of the Member aims to ensure that this exception is not used to deny patent protection to an invention on public order or morality grounds, while the invention itself is in fact exploited commercially in the Member. Article 27.3 of the *TRIPS Agreement* allows the exclusion from patentability of: (1) diagnostic, therapeutic and surgical methods for the treatment of humans or animals; and (2) plants and animals other than micro-organisms, and

---

197 For a dispute involving alleged discrimination based on the field of technology, see Panel Report, *Canada – Pharmaceutical Patents (2000)*, para. 7.105.
198 See above, pp. 585–90.

essentially biological processes for the production of plants or animals other than non-biological and microbiological processes.[199]

The exclusive rights conferred on patent owners are set out in Article 28 of the *TRIPS Agreement*. Article 28.1 of the *TRIPS Agreement* provides:

A patent shall confer on its owner the following exclusive rights:

(a) where the subject-matter of a patent is a product, to prevent third parties not having the owner's consent from the acts of: making, using, offering for sale, selling, or import-ing[200] for these purposes that product;

(b) where the subject-matter of a patent is a process, to prevent third parties not having the owner's consent from the act of using the process, and from the acts of: using, offering for sale, selling, or importing for these purposes at least the product obtained directly by that process.

Article 28.2 of the *TRIPS Agreement* gives patent owners the additional right to assign, or transfer by succession, the patent and to conclude licensing contracts.

The filing of patent applications is usually subject to conditions. In terms of Article 29.1 of the *TRIPS Agreement*, Members must require patent applicants to disclose the invention 'in a manner sufficiently clear and complete' for a person skilled in the art to be able to carry out the invention. Members may also require the applicant to disclose the best way of carrying out the invention known to the inventor. In addition, Members may require the applicant to provide information about his or her foreign applications for or grants of patents.[201]

There are two provisions in the *TRIPS Agreement* allowing for exceptions to the exclusive rights conferred by a patent: (1) the 'limited exceptions' provision of Article 30 of the *TRIPS Agreement*; and (2) the 'compulsory licences' provi-sion of Article 31 of the *TRIPS Agreement*. Article 30 of the *TRIPS Agreement* states:

Members may provide limited exceptions to the exclusive rights conferred by a patent, provided that such exceptions do not unreasonably conflict with a normal exploitation of the patent and do not unreasonably prejudice the legitimate interests of the patent owner, taking account of the legitimate interests of third parties.

In *Canada – Pharmaceutical Patents (2000)*, the European Communities chal-lenged the regulatory review and stockpiling exceptions in Canada's patent law. Canada conceded that these provisions were inconsistent with Article 28.1 of the *TRIPS Agreement*, which grants exclusive rights to patent holders.[202] However,

---

199 Note in respect of this exclusion that Members are, however, required to provide for the protection of plant *varieties* either by patents or by an 'effective *sui generis* system', or by any combination thereof. See Article 27.3(b), second sentence, of the *TRIPS Agreement*.

200 Footnote 6 to the *TRIPS Agreement* notes that '[t]his right, like all other rights conferred under this Agree-ment in respect of the use, sale, importation or other distribution of goods, is subject to the provisions of Article 6'. Article 6 provides that nothing in the *TRIPS Agreement* shall be used to address the issue of exhaustion of IP rights: see above, pp. 970–1.

201 See Article 29.2 of the *TRIPS Agreement*.

202 See Panel Report, *Canada – Pharmaceutical Patents (2000)*, para. 7.12.

it relied on the exception of Article 30 of the *TRIPS Agreement* to justify its measures, and argued that the objectives and principles of Articles 7 and 8 of the *TRIPS Agreement* should inform the interpretation of Article 30.[203] The panel in *Canada – Pharmaceutical Patents (2000)* identified *three* cumulative requirements that must be met to qualify for an exception under Article 30: (1) the exception must be 'limited'; (2) the exception must not 'unreasonably conflict with a normal exploitation of the patent'; and (3) the exception must not 'unreasonably prejudice the legitimate interests of the patent owner, taking account of the legitimate interests of third parties'.[204] Turning to the first requirement, the panel chose a narrow interpretation, holding that such interpretation is more appropriate:

when the word 'limited' is used as part of the phrase 'limited exception'. The word 'exception' by itself connotes a limited derogation, one that does not undercut the body of rules from which it is made. When a treaty uses the term 'limited exception', the word 'limited' must be given a meaning separate from the limitation implicit in the word 'exception' itself. The term 'limited exception' must therefore be read to connote a narrow exception – one which makes only a *small diminution of the rights in question.*[205]

On a literal reading of the text, the panel focused on the extent to which rights have been curtailed, rather than on the economic impact, to determine whether the exception was 'limited'. The panel supported this conclusion by referring to the fact that the other two requirements of Article 30 'ask more particularly about the economic impact of the exception, and provide two sets of standards by which such impact may be judged'.[206] In examining the extent to which the stockpiling exception curtailed the patent owner's rights to exclude 'making' and 'using' the patented product, the panel noted that this exception sets no limitation at all on the quantity of the product that could be produced and stockpiled pending expiry of the patent.[207] The panel thus found that the stockpiling exception constituted a *substantial* curtailment of the exclusive rights to be granted to patent owners under Article 28.1 and was thus not a 'limited' exception.[208] With regard to the regulatory review exception, however, the panel found that it was a 'limited' exception as required by Article 30. It held:

It is 'limited' because of the narrow scope of its curtailment of Article 28.1 rights. As long as the exception is confined to conduct needed to comply with the requirements of the regulatory approval process, the extent of the acts unauthorized by the right holder that are permitted by it will be small and narrowly bounded.[209]

With regard to the second requirement of Article 30 of the *TRIPS Agreement*, namely, that the exception must not 'unreasonably conflict with a normal exploitation of the patent', the panel in *Canada – Pharmaceutical Patents (2000)*

---

203 On Articles 7 and 8 of the *TRIPS Agreement*, see above, pp. 954–6 and 955.
204 See Panel Report, *Canada – Pharmaceutical Patents (2000)*, para. 7.20.
205 *Ibid.*, para. 7.30. Emphasis added.   206 *Ibid.*, paras. 7.31 and 7.49.
207 See *ibid.*, para. 7.34.   208 See *ibid.*, para. 7.36.   209 *Ibid.*, para. 7.45.

held that 'exploitation' refers to 'the commercial activity by which patent owners employ their exclusive patent rights to extract economic value from their patent'.[210] As to the meaning of 'normal', the panel noted that this word 'defines the kind of commercial activity Article 30 seeks to protect' and that it has both an empirical content (what is 'common' within a community) and a normative content (a standard of entitlement).[211] The panel agreed with Canada that the additional period of market exclusivity arising from using patent rights to prevent submissions for regulatory authorisation could not be seen as 'normal' exploitation.[212] Consequently, the panel held that the regulatory review exception did not conflict with the 'normal exploitation' of patents, under the second requirement of Article 30.

Finally, with regard to the third requirement of Article 30 of the *TRIPS Agreement*, namely, that the exception must not 'unreasonably prejudice the legitimate interests of the patent owner, taking account of the legitimate interests of third parties', the panel in *Canada – Pharmaceutical Patents (2000)* noted that similar considerations arose as under the second requirement.[213] In the case of the third requirement, the issue was:

whether patent owners could claim a 'legitimate interest' in the economic benefits that could be derived from such an additional period of *de facto* market exclusivity and, if so, whether the regulatory review exception 'unreasonably prejudiced' that interest.[214]

The European Communities claimed that 'legitimate' should be equated with 'lawful', implying that full respect for the legal interests reflected in Article 28.1 is necessary. The panel disagreed. It held:

To make sense of the term 'legitimate interests' in this context, that term must be defined in the way that it is often used in legal discourse – as a normative claim calling for protection of interests that are 'justifiable' in the sense that they are supported by relevant public policies or other social norms.[215]

Therefore, the panel held that the argument of the European Communities, which was based only on the legal rights of the patent owner under Article 28.1, 'without reference to any more particular normative claims of interest' did not show non-compliance with the third requirement of Article 30.[216] The European Communities raised a second argument with regard to the 'legitimate interests' requirement. It pointed out that, as patent owners are required to obtain marketing approval for their innovative products, they suffer delays that prevent them from marketing their products for a large part of the patent term, thereby reducing their period of market exclusivity. They should therefore be entitled

---

210 *Ibid.*, para. 7.54.   211 See *ibid.*   212 See *ibid.*, para. 7.57.
213 The key issue was again the fact that the exception would remove the additional period of *de facto* market exclusivity enjoyed by patent owners if they were permitted to employ their rights to exclude 'making', 'using' and 'selling' the patented product during the term of the patent to prevent potential competitors from preparing and/or applying for regulatory approval during the term of the patent.
214 Panel Report, *Canada – Pharmaceutical Patents (2000)*, para. 7.61.
215 *Ibid.*, para. 7.69.   216 *Ibid.*, para. 7.73.

to impose the same type of delay in connection with corresponding regulatory requirements for the market entry of competing products.[217] According to the panel, the 'primary issue was whether the normative basis of that claim rested on a widely recognized policy norm'.[218] Examining the approaches of various governments to this issue, the panel noted that governments are still divided in this regard. It then stated:

Article 30's 'legitimate interests' concept should not be used to decide, through adjudication, a normative policy issue that is still obviously a matter of unresolved political debate.[219]

Consequently, the panel held that Canada's regulatory review exception fell within the exception under Article 30 of the *TRIPS Agreement* and was thus not inconsistent with Article 28.1 thereof.[220]

Leaving aside Article 30 of the *TRIPS Agreement*, the other provision in the *TRIPS Agreement* allowing for exceptions to the exclusive rights conferred by a patent is Article 31. Article 31 relates to the exception for 'other use' of a patent without authorisation of the right holder. 'Other use' is defined as use other than that allowed under Article 30.[221] This 'other use' of a patent without the authorisation of the right holder is commonly known as *compulsory licensing*, although this term is not used in Article 31. Article 31 refers to the situation where:

the law of a Member allows for other use of the subject-matter of a patent without the authorization of the right holder, including use by the government or third parties authorized by the government.[222]

Article 31 of the *TRIPS Agreement* contains a detailed list of requirements for the grant of compulsory licences.[223] However, it does not limit the grounds on which compulsory licences may be granted.[224] It only mentions some possible grounds, such as: (1) public non-commercial use;[225] (2) national emergency;[226] (3) remedying of anti-competitive practices;[227] and (4) dependent patents (i.e. patents on improvements to an earlier patent-protected invention).[228] Due to concerns regarding the interpretation of this provision, the *Doha Declaration on the TRIPS Agreement and Public Health* confirms that:

[e]ach member has the *right* to grant compulsory licences and the *freedom to determine the grounds* upon which such licences are granted.[229]

---

217 See *ibid.*, para. 7.74. 218 *Ibid.*, para. 7.77. 219 *Ibid.*, para. 7.82. 220 See *ibid.*, para. 7.84.
221 See footnote 7 to Article 31 of the *TRIPS Agreement*.
222 Chapeau of Article 31 of the *TRIPS Agreement*.
223 See the conditions set out in paragraphs (a) to (l) of Article 31 of the *TRIPS Agreement*.
224 An exception to this is in the case of semiconductor technology, which may only be subject to compulsory licence for public non-commercial use and to remedy anti-competitive practices determined as such through a judicial or administrative process. See Article 31(c) of the *TRIPS Agreement*.
225 See Article 31(b) of the *TRIPS Agreement*. 226 See *ibid.*
227 See Article 31(k) of the *TRIPS Agreement*. 228 See Article 31(l) of the *TRIPS Agreement*.
229 Ministerial Conference, *Doha Declaration on the TRIPS Agreement and Public Health*, WT/MIN(01)/DEC/2, dated 20 November 2001, para. 5(b). Emphasis added.

However, Article 31 of the *TRIPS Agreement* lays down conditions for and limitations on an application for a compulsory licence for any particular use be considered on its individual merits. Therefore, compulsory licences cannot be granted with regard to broad categories of patents. Under Article 31(b) of the *TRIPS Agreement*, an attempt must have been made prior to applying for a compulsory licence to obtain authorisation from the patent holder to use the patent on reasonable commercial terms and conditions. Only if that attempt was unsuccessful within a reasonable period, can the compulsory licence be granted. However, there are three exceptions to this requirement: (1) cases of national emergency or other circumstances of extreme urgency; (2) cases of public non-commercial use; and (3) cases where the use is permitted to remedy an anti-competitive practice.[230]

The use of compulsory licences in cases of 'national emergency' could, for example, relate to the need to ensure affordable access to essential medicines to deal with public health crises. Compulsory licences may be used to authorise producers of generic medicines to copy a patented drug, without the consent of the right holder. The *Doha Declaration on the TRIPS Agreement and Public Health* recognises explicitly that, as part of the 'flexibilities' provided in the *TRIPS Agreement*:

[e]ach member has the right to determine what constitutes a national emergency or other circumstances of extreme urgency, it being understood that public health crises, including those relating to HIV/AIDS, tuberculosis, malaria and other epidemics, can represent a national emergency or other circumstances of extreme urgency.[231]

By including epidemics such as HIV/AIDS and malaria within the scope of the concept of 'national emergency or other situations of extreme urgency', the Doha Declaration clarified that situations of 'national emergency' or of 'extreme urgency' are not limited to short-term crises. In addition, by leaving Members the right to determine what is an emergency, it has been argued that the burden of proof shifts to the complaining party to show that an emergency does *not* in fact exist.[232]

Further requirements for the granting of compulsory licences, set out in subsequent paragraphs of Article 31 of the *TRIPS Agreement*, are: (1) that the scope and duration of the use of the patent shall be limited to the purpose for which it was authorised (paragraph (c)); (2) that such use shall be non-exclusive (paragraph (d)); (3) that such use shall be non-assignable except with that part of the

---

230 Note that, while the exceptions of national emergency and public non-commercial use are contained in Article 31(b), that of remedying an anti-competitive practice is reflected in Article 31(k) of the *TRIPS Agreement*. In the first case, the right holder must be notified as soon as is reasonably practicable, and in the second case as soon as there are demonstrable grounds to know that the patent will be used by or for the government.

231 Ministerial Conference, *Doha Declaration on the TRIPS Agreement and Public Health*, WT/MIN(01)/DEC/2, dated 20 November 2001, para. 5(c).

232 See C. M. Correa, 'The TRIPS Agreement and Developing Countries', in P. F. J. Macrory, A. E. Appleton and M. G. Plummer (eds.), *The World Trade Organization: Legal, Economic and Political Analysis* (Springer, 2005), 441.

enterprise or goodwill which enjoys such use (paragraph (e)); (4) that any such use shall be authorised predominantly for the supply of the domestic market of the authorising Member (paragraph (f));[233] (5) that authorisation of such use is liable to be terminated when the circumstances that led to it cease to exist (paragraph (g));[234] (6) that the right holder be paid adequate remuneration in the circumstances of each case (paragraph (h));[235] and (7) that the decision to authorise such use and the decision relating to the remuneration be subject to review by a court or other independent higher authority (paragraphs (i) and (j)).[236]

An important problem in complying with the requirement of Article 31(f) of the *TRIPS Agreement* arose with respect to the use of compulsory licences to ensure access to essential medicines in developing countries. Article 31(f), as set out above, requires that compulsory licences be provided 'predominantly for the supply of the domestic market'. However, some countries lack sufficient manufacturing capacity in pharmaceuticals to produce the necessary generic medicines themselves for their domestic market. Article 31(f) prevents other Members from granting compulsory licences to produce generic medicines predominantly for export. This constraint was expected to become more important in 2005 when some developing countries with significant generic industries and export capacities (such as India) became obliged to provide patent protection for pharmaceutical products pursuant to the special transition arrangement in Article 65.4 of the *TRIPS Agreement*.[237] The concern was raised that this would undermine the ability of developing countries, and in particular least-developed countries, with insufficient manufacturing capacity, to ensure access to affordable essential medicines. A first step towards resolving this serious problem was made in the *Doha Declaration on the TRIPS Agreement and Public Health*, which, in paragraph 6, instructed the Council for TRIPS to 'find an expeditious *solution* to this problem and to report to the General Council before the end of 2002'.[238] The General Council adopted, on 30 August 2003, a decision whereby

---

233 This requirement does not apply in cases of compulsory licences granted to remedy anti-competitive practices. See Article 31(k) of the *TRIPS Agreement*.

234 Under this paragraph, the competent authority is required to have the authority to review whether such circumstances continue to exist upon motivated request where compulsory licences were granted to remedy anti-competitive practices, competent authorities may refuse to terminate the authorisation if the anti-competitive practices are likely to recur. See Article 31(k) of the *TRIPS Agreement*.

235 The economic value of the authorisation must be taken into account in calculating the remuneration, under Article 31(h) of the *TRIPS Agreement*. In cases of compulsory licences to remedy anti-competitive practices, the need to correct such practices may be taken into account in determining the remuneration in terms of Article 31(k) of the *TRIPS Agreement*.

236 With respect to compulsory licences to permit the exploitation of a dependent patent (a patent that cannot be exploited without infringing another prior patent), three additional conditions apply: (1) the invention in the second patent must involve an important technical advance of considerable economic significance in relation to the first patent; (2) the owner of the first patent must be entitled to a cross-licence on reasonable terms to use the second patent; and (3) the use shall be non-assignable except with the assignment of the second patent. See Article 31(i) of the *TRIPS Agreement*.

237 See A. Taubman, H. Wager and J. Watal (eds.), *A Handbook on the WTO TRIPS Agreement* (Cambridge University Press, 2012), 184.

238 Ministerial Conference, *Doha Declaration on the TRIPS Agreement and Public Health*, WT/MIN(01)/DEC/2, dated 20 November 2001, para. 6. Emphasis added.

the obligations of Article 31(f) were waived in order to allow Members to export medicines produced under compulsory licence to Members with insufficient manufacturing capacity.[239] On 6 December 2005, the General Council took an important further step by adopting the decision to amend the *TRIPS Agreement* in order to resolve the conflict with Article 31(f) in a permanent manner.[240] When the amendment takes effect, a new Article 31*bis* as well as a new Annex will be added to the *TRIPS Agreement*, clarifying that the obligations of Article 31(f) do not apply with respect to the grant by a Member of a compulsory licence necessary for the production of a pharmaceutical product and its export to an 'eligible' importing Member in accordance with the terms set out in paragraph 2 of the new Annex to the *TRIPS Agreement*.[241] As discussed in Chapter 2 of this book, as of 5 November 2012, only seventy-two Members had notified their acceptance of the amendment.[242] Therefore, this amendment, agreed in December 2005, has yet to take effect.

To date, Rwanda and Canada are the only Members that have used the possibility provided under the waiver decision of 30 August 2003. Apotex, a Canadian pharmaceutical firm, exports to Rwanda TriAvir, a generic HIV medicine produced under a compulsory licence granted by Canada.[243] As the patent holders, GlaxoSmithKline and Boehringer Ingelheim, could indeed not come to an agreement with Apotex on a voluntary licence, Canada granted Apotex a compulsory licence to produce TriAvir for export to Rwanda.[244]

In May 2010, India and Brazil requested consultations with the European Union and the Netherlands regarding alleged repeated seizures on patent infringement grounds of generic drugs originating in India and other third countries when transiting through ports and airports in the Netherlands to Brazil and other third country destinations.[245] These seizures were made by applying the so-called 'manufacturing fiction' under which generic drugs actually manufactured in India and in transit to third countries were treated as if they had been manufactured

---

239 On waivers, see above, pp. 53–4. Recall that waivers adopted under Article IX of the *WTO Agreement*, as was the waiver at issue here, are *temporary* in nature. Note that the obligations under Article 31(h) of the *TRIPS Agreement* were also waived in the Decision of the General Council of 30 August 2003.

240 See General Council, *Amendment of the TRIPS Agreement: Decision of the General Council of 6 December 2005*, WT/L/641, dated 8 December 2005. Note that this is the first and thus far only decision to amend a WTO agreement. See above, p. 141.

241 Annex 2, paragraph 2, defines an 'eligible' importing Member as any least-developed-country Member; and any other Member that has notified the Council for TRIPS of its intention to use the Article 31*bis* system as an importer. Note that the notification does *not* need to be approved by any WTO body before the Article 31*bis* system may be used.

242 See above, pp. 116 and 141. See also www.wto.org/english/tratop_e/trips_e/amendment_e.htm. Note that the European Union notified its acceptance and did so also on behalf of the twenty-seven EU Member States.

243 On 4 October 2007, Canada notified the Council for TRIPS of its granting of a compulsory licence to Apotex. See *Notification under Paragraph 2(c) of the Decision of 30 August 2003 on the Implementation of Paragraph 6 of the Doha Declaration on the TRIPS Agreement and Public Health – Canada*, IP/N/10/CAN/1, dated 8 October 2007. There is a dedicated page on the WTO website for notifications of this kind, available at www.wto.org/english/tratop_e/trips_e/public_health_e.htm.

244 *Bridges Weekly Trade News Digest*, 25 July 2007.

245 See Request for Consultations by India, *European Union and a Member State – Seizure of Generic Drugs in Transit*, WT/DS408/1, dated 19 May 2010; and Request for Consultations by Brazil, *European Union and a Member State – Seizure of Generic Drugs in Transit*, WT/DS409/1, dated 19 May 2010.

in the Netherlands. India claimed violation of Article 31 of the *TRIPS Agreement*, read together with the provisions of the 2003 waiver decision, discussed above, because the measures at issue, *inter alia*, authorise interference with the freedom of transit of drugs that may be produced in, and exported from, India to WTO Members with insufficient or no capacity in the pharmaceutical sector that seek to obtain supplies of such products needed to address their public health problems. Reportedly, the consultations in this dispute resulted in a mutually agreed solution.[246] However, this solution has not been notified to the WTO.

The duration of patent protection is addressed in Article 33 of the *TRIPS Agreement*. It provides:

The term of protection available shall not end before the expiration of a period of twenty years counted from the filing date.[247]

Article 33 was at issue in *Canada – Patent Term (2000)* involving a challenge by the United States to Canada's patent legislation, which granted patent protection for only seventeen years for patents filed before 1 October 1989. Examining the terms of Article 33, the Appellate Body held:

In our view, the words used in Article 33 present very little interpretative difficulty. The 'filing date' is the date of filing of the patent application. The term of protection 'shall not end' before twenty years counted from the date of filing of the patent application.[248]

The Appellate Body rejected Canada's argument that a twenty-year period was in fact available under its regulatory practices and procedures, as every patent applicant has statutory and other means to delay the procedure so as to extend the period of patent protection to at least twenty years.[249] According to the Appellate Body, not only 'those who are somehow able to meander successfully through a maze of administrative procedures'[250] must have the opportunity to obtain the twenty-year patent term, but this opportunity:

must be a readily discernible and specific right, and it must be clearly seen as such by the patent applicant when a patent application is filed. The grant of the patent must be sufficient *in itself* to obtain the minimum term mandated by Article 33.[251]

Finally, note that Article 32 of the *TRIPS Agreement* requires that any decision to revoke or forfeit a patent be subject to an opportunity for judicial review.

Questions and Assignments 15.10

Must patents be available for 'any invention in any field' under the *TRIPS Agreement*? Are Members allowed to give patent protection exclusively to inventions made on their

---

246 See http://pib.nic.in/newsite/erelease.aspx?relid=73554.
247 Footnote 8 to this provision clarifies that Members that do not have a system of original grant may provide that the term of protection shall be calculated from the filing date in the system of original grant.
248 Appellate Body Report, *Canada – Patent Term (2000)*, para. 85.
249 See *ibid.*, para. 91.   250 *Ibid.*, para. 92.
251 *Ibid.* The Appellate Body pointed out that the text of Article 33 of the *TRIPS Agreement* does not support the notion of an 'effective' term of protection as distinguished from a 'nominal' term of protection. See *ibid.*, para. 95.

territory? What are the exclusive rights of patent holders under the *TRIPS Agreement*? What are the three requirements that must be met for an exception to be allowed under Article 30 of the *TRIPS Agreement*? On what grounds and under which conditions may a Member grant a compulsory licence? Discuss the rules applicable to compulsory licences for the production of essential medicines for export to developing-country Members with insufficient manufacturing capacity. What is the minimum duration of patent protection under the *TRIPS Agreement*?

6 ENFORCEMENT OF INTELLECTUAL PROPERTY RIGHTS

The protection of IP depends not only on substantive norms providing minimum standards of protection, but also on procedural rules that allow right holders to effectively enforce them. Therefore, the *TRIPS Agreement* includes rules on the enforcement of IP rights. The Preamble to the *TRIPS Agreement* reflects the recognition that new rules and disciplines were needed concerning 'the provision of effective and appropriate means for the enforcement of trade-related intellectual property rights, taking into account differences in national legal systems'. These rules on enforcement are contained in Part III of the *TRIPS Agreement*, entitled 'Enforcement of Intellectual Property Rights'. With regard to the coverage of Part III, the Appellate Body held in *US – Section 211 Appropriations Act (2002)* that this Part:

applies to all intellectual property rights covered by the *TRIPS Agreement*. According to Article 1.2 of the *TRIPS Agreement*, the term 'intellectual property' refers to 'all categories of intellectual property that are the subject of Sections 1 through 7 of Part II' of that Agreement.[252]

The panel report in *China – Intellectual Property Rights (2009)* noted that the concept of 'enforcement procedures', as used in Part III of the *TRIPS Agreement*, is an 'extensive' concept.[253] Part III deals with: civil and administrative procedures and remedies (Section 2); provisional measures (Section 3); special requirements related to border measures (Section 4); and criminal procedures (Section 5). Before dealing with these specific enforcement procedures, however, Part III first sets out a number of general obligations with regard to the enforcement of IP rights.

6.1 General Obligations

The general obligations with regard to enforcement of IP rights are contained in Article 41 of the *TRIPS Agreement*. Article 41.1 requires Members to ensure

---

252 Appellate Body Report, *US – Section 211 Appropriations Act (2002)*, para. 205.
253 See Panel Report, *China – Intellectual Property Rights (2009)*, para. 7.179. According to the panel, this is clear, among other things, from the text of Article 41.1 of the *TRIPS Agreement*, which specifies that these procedures include 'remedies'. See *ibid*. For example, Articles 44, 45, 46 and 50 of the *TRIPS Agreement* specify that the judicial authorities shall have the authority to make certain orders, such as injunctions, orders to pay damages, orders for the disposal or destruction of infringing goods, and provisional measures. See *ibid*.

that the enforcement procedures specified in Part III are available under their law 'so as to permit effective action' against infringement of IP rights protected in the *TRIPS Agreement*. This is specified as including expeditious remedies to *prevent* infringements and remedies to *deter* further infringements. As the panel in *China – Intellectual Property Rights (2009)* noted:

Where a Member chooses to make available other procedures – for enforcement of intellectual property rights or for enforcement of other policies with respect to certain subject-matter – that policy choice does not diminish the Member's obligation under Article 41.1 of the TRIPS Agreement to ensure that enforcement procedures as specified in Part III are available.[254]

Article 41.1 of the *TRIPS Agreement* further requires that enforcement procedures must be applied in a way that avoids creating barriers to legitimate trade and to provide safeguards against their abuse. A number of provisions supplement this general obligation. For example, Article 48 of the *TRIPS Agreement* provides for compensation of a party that has suffered injury due to abuse of enforcement procedures. Article 41.2 to 41.4 of the *TRIPS Agreement* sets out normal due process requirements. These paragraphs require that: (1) enforcement procedures be fair and equitable, and not unnecessarily costly, complicated or lengthy (Article 41.2); (2) decisions on the merits of a case be reasoned and preferably in writing, and be based on evidence on which the parties had an opportunity to be heard (Article 41.3); and (3) parties to a proceeding have the opportunity for judicial review of administrative decisions and of at least the legal aspects of judicial decisions (with the exclusion of acquittals in criminal cases) (Article 41.4). Article 41.5 of the *TRIPS Agreement* clarifies that Part III does not oblige Members to create a separate judicial system for the enforcement of IP rights, or create any obligation regarding the distribution of resources between enforcement of IP rights and other law enforcement. It clarifies that the enforcement of IP rights can take place through the existing law-enforcement system of a country, provided that the required level of enforcement specified in Part III is achieved.

6.2   Civil and Administrative Procedures and Remedies

The usual way of enforcing IP rights is through civil procedures initiated only at the request of or by the right holder but not *ex officio* by the Member State.[255] Article 42 of the *TRIPS Agreement* specifies that Members are required to make available to right holders civil *judicial* procedures for the enforcement of any IP right covered by the *TRIPS Agreement*. This means that the provision of only *administrative* enforcement procedures is insufficient.[256] Article 42 requires that

---

254 Panel Report, *China – Intellectual Property Rights (2009)*, para. 7.180.
255 See *ibid.*, para. 7.247.
256 An exception is made for the enforcement of the enhanced protection for GIs on wine and spirits, which may take place through administrative action rather than judicial proceedings. See footnote 4 to Article 23.1 of the *TRIPS Agreement*.

civil judicial procedures are 'fair and equitable'.[257] These requirements reflect normal due process rules applicable in civil proceedings.

Article 42 of the *TRIPS Agreement* was at issue in *US – Section 211 Appropriations Act (2002)*. The European Communities claimed that Sections 211(a)(2) and (b) of the US Appropriations Act violated Article 42 of the *TRIPS Agreement* as they expressly denied the availability of United States courts to enforce the rights targeted by Section 211.[258] The panel found that Section 211(a)(2) was inconsistent with Article 42.[259] It noted:

> While Section 211(a)(2) would not appear to prevent a right holder from initiating civil judicial procedures, its wording indicates that the right holder is not entitled to effective procedures as the court is *ab initio* not permitted to recognize its assertion of rights if the conditions of Section 211(a)(2) are met. In other words, the right holder is effectively prevented from having a chance to substantiate its claim, a chance to which a right holder is clearly entitled under Article 42, because effective civil judicial procedures mean procedures with the possibility of an outcome which is not pre-empted *a priori* by legislation.[260]

On appeal, the Appellate Body agreed with the panel that:

> the ordinary meaning of the term 'make available' suggests that 'right holders' are entitled under Article 42 to have *access* to civil judicial procedures that are effective in bringing about the enforcement of their rights covered by the Agreement ... The term 'right holders' ... also includes persons who claim to have legal standing to assert rights.[261]

The Appellate Body also noted that, as the term 'civil judicial procedures' is not defined in Article 42 of the *TRIPS Agreement*:

> [t]he *TRIPS Agreement* thus reserves, subject to the procedural minimum standards set out in that Agreement, a degree of discretion to Members on this, taking into account 'differences in national legal systems'.[262]

The Appellate Body then turned to the fourth sentence of Article 42 of the *TRIPS Agreement*, which requires that '[a]ll parties to such procedures shall be duly entitled to substantiate their claims and present all relevant evidence'. It noted that right holders are entitled thereby to choose how many and which claims to bring, to provide grounds for their claims and to bring all relevant evidence.[263] The Appellate Body stated:

> we understand that the rights which Article 42 obliges Members to make available to right holders are *procedural* in nature. These *procedural* rights guarantee an international minimum standard for nationals of other Members within the meaning of Article 1.3 of the *TRIPS Agreement*.[264]

257 See Appellate Body Report, *US – Section 211 Appropriations Act (2002)*, para. 207.
258 See *ibid.*, para. 208.
259 With regard to Section 211(b), the panel held that the European Communities had failed to explain the provisions referred to in the Section and had therefore not proved its case. See Panel Report, *US – Section 211 Appropriations Act (2002)*, para. 8.162.
260 *Ibid.*, para. 8.100.
261 Appellate Body Report, *US – Section 211 Appropriations Act (2002)*, paras. 215 and 217, referring to para. 8.95 of the Panel Report, *US – Section 211 Appropriations Act (2002)*.
262 Appellate Body Report, *US – Section 211 Appropriations Act (2002)*, para. 216.
263 See *ibid.*, paras. 219–20.   264 *Ibid.*, para. 221.

The Appellate Body then noted that Sections 211(a)(2) and (b) deal with the *substantive* requirements of ownership of trademarks in particular cases.[265] Further, it pointed out that the European Communities agreed with the United States that US Federal Rules of Civil Procedure apply to cases under Section 211 and guarantee 'fair and equitable ... civil judicial procedures'.[266] Referring to the argument of the European Communities that Sections 211(a)(2) and (b) limit the discretion of the courts by directing the courts to examine certain substantive requirements before, and to the exclusion of, other substantive requirements, the Appellate Body held:

> In our view, a conclusion by a court on the basis of Section 211, after applying the Federal Rules of Civil Procedure and the Federal Rules of Evidence, that an enforcement proceeding has failed to establish ownership – a requirement of substantive law – with the result that it is impossible for the court to rule in favour of that claimant's or that defendant's claim to a trademark right, does not constitute a violation of Article 42. There is nothing in the *procedural* obligations of Article 42 that prevents a Member, in such a situation, from legislating whether or not its courts must examine *each and every* requirement of substantive law at issue before making a ruling.[267]

Consequently, the Appellate Body found that Sections 211(a)(2) and (b) of the Appropriations Act were not, on their face, inconsistent with Article 42.[268]

The other provisions of the *TRIPS Agreement* relating to 'Civil and Administrative Procedures and Remedies' set out the powers that the judicial authorities involved are required to have in enforcement proceedings, such as: (1) the authority to require, in specific cases, the production of evidence by a party in whose control the evidence is (Article 43); (2) the authority to order a party to desist from an infringement, including to prevent the entry of infringing imports into channels of commerce in their jurisdiction after clearing customs (Article 44); and (3) the authority to order the infringer to pay damages and costs in certain cases (Article 45).[269]

6.3 Provisional Measures and Border Measures

Article 50 and Articles 51 to 60 of the *TRIPS Agreement* contain rules with regard to provisional measures and border measures, respectively, aiming at the prevention of IP infringements. Article 50 of the *TRIPS Agreement* requires judicial authorities to have the power to order 'prompt and effective provisional measures':

(a) to prevent an infringement of any intellectual property right from occurring, and in particular to prevent the entry into the channels of commerce in their jurisdiction of goods, including imported goods immediately after customs clearance;

(b) to preserve relevant evidence in regard to the alleged infringement.

---

265 See *ibid.*, para. 222.   266 See *ibid.*, para. 223.   267 *Ibid.*, para. 226.   268 See *ibid.*, para. 231.

269 Other remedies aimed at creating an effective *deterrent* to infringement of IP rights (e.g. by ordering the destruction of infringing goods without compensation) are provided for in Article 46 of the *TRIPS Agreement*.

Article 50 aims to deal with infringements that are taking place or are imminent.[270] It requires judicial authorities to have the authority to adopt provisional measures without hearing the other party (*inaudita altera parte*) where appropriate, in particular: (1) where any delay is likely to cause irreparable harm to the right holder, or (2) where there is a demonstrable risk of evidence being destroyed.

Article 51 of the *TRIPS Agreement* deals with measures applied *at the border* (i.e. applied to imports) in order to prevent IP infringements. Such measures can be applied when a right holder has valid grounds for suspecting that importation of counterfeit trademark or pirated copyright goods may take place.[271] While Article 50 of the *TRIPS Agreement* aims to prevent the introduction of the infringing product into commerce *after* it has cleared customs, Article 51 of the *TRIPS Agreement* addresses measures applied at the border *before* the release of the infringing product into free circulation by the customs authority. It provides for procedures to apply for the suspension by customs authorities of the release of the goods. While these border measures are required only for counterfeit trademark or pirated copyright goods, they *may* be extended to goods that involve infringements of other IP rights. Articles 52 to 60 of the *TRIPS Agreement* provide rules on the application of these border measures.

6.4 Criminal Procedures

Article 61 of the *TRIPS Agreement* deals with criminal procedures and penalties for infringement. It requires criminal procedures and penalties to be provided at least in cases of wilful trademark counterfeiting or copyright piracy on a commercial scale.[272] It requires the remedies of 'imprisonment and/or monetary fines sufficient to provide a deterrent, consistently with the level of penalties applied for crimes of a corresponding gravity'. In appropriate cases, the remedies must also include 'the seizure, forfeiture and destruction of the infringing goods and of any materials and implements the predominant use of which has been in the commission of the offence'.[273]

Questions and Assignments 15.11

Briefly summarise the enforcement efforts that the *TRIPS Agreement* requires Members to undertake. What do the due process requirements set out in Article 41 of the *TRIPS*

---

270 See Article 50.3 of the *TRIPS Agreement*. On this point, see C. M. Correa, *Trade-Related Aspects of Intellectual Property Rights: A Commentary on the TRIPS Agreement* (Oxford University Press, 2007), 433–8.

271 For a definition of 'counterfeit trademark goods' and 'pirated copyright goods', see footnote 14 to Article 51 of the *TRIPS Agreement*.

272 Members may, but are not obliged to, extend the application of criminal procedures and penalties to other cases of IP infringement, in particular where they are committed wilfully and on a commercial scale. The panel in *China – Intellectual Property Rights (2009)* did not endorse thresholds applied by China, but concluded that the factual evidence presented by the United States was inadequate to show whether or not the cases excluded from criminal liability met the TRIPS standard of 'commercial scale' when that standard is applied to China's marketplace. See Panel Report, *China – Intellectual Property Rights (2009)*, para. 7.614.

273 A. Taubman, H. Wager and J. Watal (eds.), *A Handbook on the WTO TRIPS Agreement* (Cambridge University Press, 2012), 152.

Agreement entail? Does the *TRIPS Agreement* require Members to establish IP courts to enforce IP rights within their territory? What are 'civil judicial procedures' within the meaning of Article 42 of the *TRIPS Agreement*? What is the difference between measures taken under Article 50 and measures taken under Article 51 of the *TRIPS Agreement*? When does the *TRIPS Agreement* require Members to provide criminal procedures and penalties for infringement of IP rights?

6.5 Acquisition and Maintenance of Intellectual Property Rights

Part IV of the *TRIPS Agreement* deals with the procedural aspects of the acquisition and maintenance of IP rights. For practical reasons, formalities and procedures apply to the acquisition of IP rights (for example, through the registration of a trademark or filing of a patent) and to their maintenance. Article 62.1 acknowledges that Members may require compliance with reasonable procedures and formalities as a condition for the acquisition or maintenance of the IP rights provided for in the *TRIPS Agreement*, except copyright and undisclosed information.[274] The *TRIPS Agreement* cautions that the effective protection of IP rights can be undermined if these procedural requirements are used to unfairly restrict the access to, and exercise of, these rights. Therefore, Article 62 of the *TRIPS Agreement* sets out the procedures and formalities for the acquisition and maintenance of IP rights. For example, Article 62.2 obliges Members to prevent unreasonable delays in procedures for the acquisition of IP rights, and Article 62.5 requires that decisions on the acquisition or maintenance of IP rights be subject to judicial or quasi-judicial review.

7 INSTITUTIONAL AND PROCEDURAL PROVISIONS OF THE *TRIPS AGREEMENT*

Parts V and VII of the *TRIPS Agreement* contain the provisions dealing with institutional and procedural arrangements. These provisions relate to: (1) the Council for TRIPS (Articles 68 and 71); (2) the transparency requirements (Article 63); (3) the rules on dispute settlement under the *TRIPS Agreement* (Article 64); (4) international cooperation between Members to prevent trade in goods that infringe IP rights (Article 69); and (5) the prohibition on reservations to the provisions of the *TRIPS Agreement* without the consent of other Members (Article 72). The most important of these provisions are briefly discussed in this section.

---

274 This is because, under Article 5.2 of the *Berne Convention (1971)*, copyrights cannot be subject to these types of formalities, and undisclosed information is by the very nature of the protected subject-matter not subject to registration. See C. M. Correa, Trade-Related Aspects of Intellectual Property Rights: A Commentary on the TRIPS Agreement (Oxford University Press, 2007), 467.

7.1   Council for TRIPS

Article 68 of the *TRIPS Agreement* provides for a 'Council for TRIPS' (also referred to as the 'TRIPS Council'), in which all WTO Members are represented.[275] Pursuant to Article 68, the tasks of the Council for TRIPS are: (1) to monitor the operation of the *TRIPS Agreement*, and, in particular, Members' compliance with their obligations thereunder; (2) to provide the possibility for Members to consult on matters relating to the trade-related aspects of IP rights; and (3) to carry out any other responsibilities assigned to it by the Members, and provide any assistance requested by them in the context of dispute settlement procedures.[276] In 2012, the TRIPS Council met three times. The TRIPS Council reports annually on its activities and developments regarding IP protection in the context of the WTO.[277] In carrying out its functions, the TRIPS Council may consult with or seek information from any source it deems appropriate. Within a year of its first meeting, the TRIPS Council was required to seek to establish appropriate arrangements for cooperation with WIPO. A cooperation agreement was concluded between the WTO and WIPO in 1995, and came into force on 1 January 1996.[278]

7.2   Transparency

Interestingly, the transparency provisions of the *TRIPS Agreement* are contained in Part V, entitled 'Dispute Settlement and Prevention'. This indicates that transparency with regard to IP protection is regarded as a way of preventing disputes between Members. Article 63 of the *TRIPS Agreement* lays down transparency obligations on Members. Under Article 63.1, Members are required, with regard not only to laws and regulations, but also to judicial decisions and administrative rulings of general application pertaining to the subject-matter of the *TRIPS Agreement*, to publish them or, if this is impracticable, to make them publicly available in a manner that enables governments and IP right holders to become acquainted with them.[279] Article 63.2 requires Members to notify the TRIPS Council of any laws and regulations referred to in Article 63.1, to facilitate the Council's review of the operation of the *TRIPS Agreement*. Article 63.3 requires Members to supply information of the sort referred to in Article 63.1 or with regard to specific judicial decisions or administrative rulings in response to a written request by another Member.[280]

---

275 See also above, p. 125.
276 Additional tasks of the TRIPS Council are, for example, set out in Articles 23.4 and 24.2 of the *TRIPS Agreement* (with regard to GIs) and Article 66.1 of the *TRIPS Agreement* (with regard to the extension of the transitional period for least-developed countries).
277 See e.g. Council for TRIPS, *Annual Report (2012)*, IP/C/62, dated 26 November 2012.
278 See www.wto.org/english/thewto_e/coher_e/wto_wipo_e.htm.
279 The subject-matter of the *TRIPS Agreement* is defined as 'the availability, scope, acquisition, enforcement and prevention of the abuse of IP rights'. Article 63.1 further requires that agreements between Members or their governmental agencies concerning the subject-matter of the *TRIPS Agreement* also be published.
280 See Article 63.4 of the *TRIPS Agreement*. Note that 'confidential information' is exempted from this obligation.

In *India – Patents (US) (1998)*, the panel found a violation by India of the transparency obligation in Article 63.1 due to the fact that an administrative ruling regarding the mechanism for the implementation of the 'mailbox' system for patent applications under Article 70.8(a) of the *TRIPS Agreement* had not been published or made publicly available.[281] India's argument that the existence of the mailbox system was recognised in a written answer by the government to a question in Parliament was rejected by the panel, which pointed out that such a way of conveying information could not be regarded as a sufficient means of publicity under Article 63.1 of the *TRIPS Agreement*.[282]

7.3 Dispute Settlement

One of the great achievements of the *TRIPS Agreement* is that it brings disputes regarding IP protection under the effective and enforceable mechanism for dispute settlement contained in the Dispute Settlement Understanding (DSU). Article 64.1 of the *TRIPS Agreement* provides that the rules of Articles XXII and XXIII of the GATT 1994, as elaborated and applied by the DSU, apply to the settlement of disputes under that agreement, except as otherwise specifically provided therein. As noted by the Appellate Body in *India – Patents (US) (1998)*:

> As one of the covered agreements under the DSU, the *TRIPS Agreement* is subject to the dispute settlement rules and procedures of that Understanding.[283]

To date, thirty-two disputes have been initiated involving complaints under the *TRIPS Agreement*.[284] Of these, ten have resulted in panel reports and three eventually in Appellate Body reports.[285] Members have been found to have acted inconsistently with their obligations under the *TRIPS Agreement* in ten disputes.[286]

The *TRIPS Agreement* contains a specific provision deviating from the normal WTO dispute settlement rules. As discussed in Chapter 3 of this book, under normal dispute settlement rules, Members can bring three types of complaints: violation complaints, non-violation complaints and situation complaints.[287] There was strong resistance from developing countries during the Uruguay Round

---

281 This finding was reversed by the Appellate Body on procedural grounds, as the terms of reference of the panel did not include Article 63 of the *TRIPS Agreement*. See Appellate Body Report, *India – Patents (US) (1998)*, paras. 85–6.

282 See Panel Report, *India – Patents (US) (1998)*, para. 7.48.

283 Appellate Body Report, *India – Patents (US) (1998)*, para. 29.

284 Seventeen of these disputes, or 53 per cent, were initiated by the United States. See www.worldtradelaw.net/dsc/database/searchcomplaints.asp.

285 See www.worldtradelaw.net/dsc/database/trips.asp.

286 See *India – Patents (US) (1997)*; *Indonesia – Autos (1998)*; *India – Patents (EC) (1998)*; *Canada – Pharmaceutical Patents (2000)*; *US – Section 110(5) Copyright Act (2000)*; *Canada – Patent Term (2000)*; *US – Section 211 Appropriation Act (2002)*; *EC – Trademarks and Geographical Indications (Australia) (2005)*; *EC – Trademarks and Geographical Indications (US) (2005)*; and *China – Intellectual Property Rights (2009)*.

287 See above, pp. 173–5.

negotiations against inclusion of non-violation and situation complaints as a cause of action under the *TRIPS Agreement*, as they were concerned that this would create the possibility to extend the protection of the *TRIPS Agreement* beyond that specified in its provisions.[288] For this reason, Article 64.2 of the *TRIPS Agreement* provided that, for a period of five years from the entry into force of the *WTO Agreement*, no non-violation or situation complaints could be brought under the *TRIPS Agreement*. The moratorium under Article 64.2 of the *TRIPS Agreement* expired on 1 January 2000.[289] Under Article 64.3, the Council for TRIPS was directed to examine the scope and modalities for non-violation and situation complaints and make recommendations to the Ministerial Conference for approval. Any decision of the Ministerial Conference to adopt such recommendations or to extend the moratorium must be made by consensus.[290] The moratorium has been extended a number of times, under which Members have agreed not to initiate non-violation or situation complaints under the *TRIPS Agreement* and to continue the examination of modalities for such complaints.[291] To date, no agreement has been reached on such modalities.

Questions and Assignments 15.12

What does the transparency obligation under the *TRIPS Agreement* entail? Are all disputes between Members on rights and obligations under the *TRIPS Agreement* subject to the rules and procedures of the DSU? Can Members initiate non-violation complaints under the *TRIPS Agreement*?

8   SPECIAL AND DIFFERENTIAL TREATMENT OF DEVELOPING-COUNTRY MEMBERS

The implementation of the obligations under the *TRIPS Agreement* requires regulatory capacity and an infrastructure for enforcement. This may create problems for developing-country Members in particular. The *TRIPS Agreement* thus provided, and to some extent still provides, for transitional periods for implementation of the obligations, and provides for technical cooperation.

---

288 Abbott notes two specific concerns of developing countries, namely, that developed countries would: (1) claim that the TRIPS provisions are intended to provide IP right holders with market access, not just protection of their IP rights; and (2) try to use the non-violation cause of action to 'expand the literal language of the TRIPS Agreement in light of whatever their "expectations" might have been about its effects'. F. M. Abbott, 'TRIPS in Seattle: The Not-So-Surprising Failure and the Future of the TRIPS Agenda', *Berkeley Journal of International Law*, 2000, 172.

289 With regard to Article 64.2 of the *TRIPS Agreement*, see Appellate Body Report, *India – Patents (US) (1998)*, paras. 36–42.

290 See Article 64.3 of the *TRIPS Agreement*.

291 This agreement was last renewed at the 2011 Geneva Ministerial Conference. See Ministerial Conference, Ministerial Declaration on *TRIPS Non-Violation and Situation Complaints*, WT/L/842, dated 19 December 2011.

8.1 Transitional periods

Article 65.1 of the *TRIPS Agreement* provided a *one-year* implementation period for *all* Members from the entry into force of the *WTO Agreement*. Pursuant to Article 65.2 of the *TRIPS Agreement*, developing-country Members, and certain Members with economies in transition,[292] could delay implementation of the provisions of the *TRIPS Agreement* (other than Articles 3, 4 and 5) for a further four years, until 1 January 2000.[293] An additional five-year implementation period was added to this initial period by Article 65.4 of the *TRIPS Agreement* in respect of product patent protection for those developing-country Members which did not provide such protection to particular areas of technology at the time when the *TRIPS Agreement* became applicable to them under Article 65.2 of the *TRIPS Agreement*.[294] These transitional periods have now all come to an end. Only least-developed-country Members still 'benefit' from a transitional period. In view of their 'special needs and requirements', their 'economic financial and administrative constraints', and their need for 'flexibility to create a viable technological base', least-developed-country Members were given, in Article 66 of the *TRIPS Agreement*, a transitional period of eleven years, starting from the date of the entry into force of the *WTO Agreement*. The transitional period was thus due to expire on 1 January 2006. However, in November 2005, the TRIPS Council decided to further extend the transitional period until 1 July 2013, or until the the date on which the Member involved graduates from least-developed-country status, whichever date is the earlier.[295]

Paragraph 7 of the *Doha Declaration on the TRIPS Agreement and Public Health* states that least-developed-country Members will not be obliged, with respect to pharmaceutical products, to implement the obligations of the *TRIPS Agreement* regarding patents and the protection of undisclosed information or to enforce these IP rights until 1 January 2016. The TRIPS Council was directed to take the necessary action to give effect to this, pursuant to Article 66.1 of

---

292 Note that only Members in transition from a centrally planned economy to a free-market economy that were undertaking structural reform of their IP systems and facing 'special problems' in preparing and implementing IP laws could make use of this additional transitional period. See Article 65.3 of the *TRIPS Agreement*.

293 Note that the transitional periods of Article 65 of the *TRIPS Agreement* do not apply to Article 70.8 (known as the 'mailbox' provision). See Panel Report, *India – Patents (US) (1998)*, para. 7.27. On Members' obligations under the 'mailbox' provision, see Appellate Body Report, *India – Patents (US) (1998)*, para. 58.

294 Note that Article 65.5 of the *TRIPS Agreement* contains an 'anti-rollback' obligation, i.e. an obligation that, during the implementation period, no changes could be made to national legislation that resulted in a lesser degree of consistency with the *TRIPS Agreement*. On Article 65.5 of the *TRIPS Agreement*, see also Panel Report, *Indonesia – Autos (1998)*, para. 14.282.

295 See Council for TRIPS, Decision of 29 November 2005, *Extension of the Transition Period under Article 66.1 for the Least-Developed Country Members*, IP/C/40, dated 30 November 2005. On a further extension of the transitional period, see Council for TRIPS, *Request for an Extension of the Transitional Period under Article 66.1 of the TRIPS Agreement*, Communication from Haiti on behalf of the LDC Group, IP/C/W/583, dated 5 November 2012. See also Geneva Ministerial Conference, Decision of 17 December 2011, *Transition Period For Least-Developed Countries under Article 66.1 of the TRIPS Agreement*, WT/L/845, dated 19 December 2011. The TRIPS Council was asked to submit a report to the next Ministerial Conference regarding the request of the LDC Members for the extension of the period of implementation under Article 66.1 of the *TRIPS Agreement*.

the *TRIPS Agreement*. In accordance with this direction, on 27 June 2002, the TRIPS Council approved a decision extending until 2016 the implementation period for least-developed-country Members with regard to *certain* obligations with respect to *pharmaceutical products*.[296] In addition, on 8 July 2002, the General Council approved a waiver exempting least-developed countries from the obligation under Article 70.9 of the *TRIPS Agreement* to provide exclusive marketing rights for any new drugs in the period when they do not provide patent protection.[297]

8.2   Technical Assistance and Transfer of Technology

Article 67 of the *TRIPS Agreement* obliges developed-country Members to provide technical and financial assistance to developing- and least-developed-country Members, upon request and on mutually agreed terms and conditions. Such assistance includes helping with the preparation of legislation for the protection and enforcement of IP rights and the prevention of their abuse, and support for the establishment and maintenance of the relevant national offices and agencies, including training their staff. To make information on available technical assistance accessible and to facilitate the monitoring of compliance with the obligation of Article 67, developed-country Members have agreed to submit descriptions of their technical and financial cooperation programmes annually. Intergovernmental organisations have also presented, on the invitation of the TRIPS Council, information on their activities in order to promote transparency.[298] The Decision of the TRIPS Council of 29 November 2005 provided for further commitments on technical assistance for least-developed-country Members to help them prepare to implement the Agreement.[299]

Developed-country Members are also obliged, under Article 66.2 of the *TRIPS Agreement*, to provide incentives to their enterprises and institutions to promote the transfer of technology to least-developed-country Members so that they can create a 'sound and viable technological base'. In order to establish a mechanism for ensuring the monitoring and full implementation of the obligations

---

296 Council for TRIPS, *Extension of the Transition Period under Article 66.1 of the TRIPS Agreement for Least-Developed Country Members for Certain Obligations with Respect to Pharmaceutical Products, Decision of the Council for TRIPS of 27 June 2002*, IP/C/25, dated 1 July 2002. The TRIPS Council noted that it considered paragraph 7 of the *Doha Declaration on the TRIPS Agreement and Public Health* to be a 'duly motivated request' by least-developed-country Members under Article 66.1 for the extension of their transitional period.

297 See General Council, *Least-Developed Country Members – Obligations under Article 70.9 of the TRIPS Agreement with Respect to Pharmaceutical Products. Decision of 8 July 2002*, WT/L/478, dated 12 July 2002.

298 See www.wto.org/english/tratop_e/trips_e/intel9_e.htm. The information from developed-country Members, intergovernmental organisations and the WTO Secretariat on their technical cooperation activities with regard to the *TRIPS Agreement* is circulated in documents in the IP/C/W/ series.

299 See Council for TRIPS, Decision of 29 November 2005, *Extension of the Transitional Period under Article 66.1 for Least-Developed-Country Members*, IP/C/40, dated 30 November 2005.

in Article 66.2, as instructed in the *Doha Decision on Implementation-Related Issues and Concerns*,[300] the TRIPS Council adopted a decision on 19 February 2003.[301] In terms of this decision, developed-country Members must submit annual reports on actions taken or planned in pursuance of their commitments under Article 66.2.[302] The TRIPS Council must review these submissions at its end-of-year meeting each year, and Members shall have an opportunity to pose questions, request additional information and 'discuss the effectiveness of the incentives provided in promoting and encouraging technology transfer to least-developed-country Members in order to enable them to create a sound and viable technological base'.[303]

9   SUMMARY

The *Agreement on Trade-Related Aspects of Intellectual Property Rights* (the '*TRIPS Agreement*') reflects the recognition that trade and intellectual property protection are closely connected. The achievements in liberalisation of trade through disciplines on trade barriers can be greatly undermined if the IP rights related to the traded goods or services are not respected. The *TRIPS Agreement* is arguably the most innovative of the WTO agreements. It was the first trade agreement to establish positive regulatory obligations for Members to ensure a minimum level of protection and enforcement of IP rights in their territories. The need to balance the competing interests of holders of IP rights on the one hand and the public interest on the other forms the basic rationale underlying the rights and obligations laid down in the *TRIPS Agreement*. The *Doha Declaration on the TRIPS Agreement and Public Health* reaffirms the right of WTO Members to use, to the full, the provisions in the *TRIPS Agreement*, providing flexibilities for Members in order to protect public health.

The *TRIPS Agreement* builds upon the standards of IP protection enshrined in pre-existing IP conventions administered by the World Intellectual Property Organization (WIPO). It does so by incorporating by reference specific provisions of the relevant conventions, namely, the *Paris Convention (1967)*, the *Berne Convention (1971)*, the *Rome Convention* and the *IPIC Treaty*. The obligations of

300 See Ministerial Conference, *Doha Decision on Implementation-Related Issues and Concerns*, WT/MIN(01)/17, dated 20 November 2001, para. 11.2.

301 See Council for TRIPS, Decision of 19 February 2003, *Implementation of Article 66.2 of the TRIPS Agreement*, IP/C/28, dated 20 February 2003.

302 Members must provide new detailed reports every third year and, in the intervening years, provide updates to their most recent reports. These reports must be submitted prior to the last Council meeting scheduled for the year in question. See *ibid.*, para. 1.

303 *Ibid.*, para. 2. Paragraph 3 of this decision sets out the information which must be provided in these annual submissions.

the *TRIPS Agreement* must, therefore, be read together with the relevant WIPO conventions. However, the *TRIPS Agreement* does more than simply incorporate the substantive provisions of these conventions. It supplements and updates the rules of the relevant WIPO conventions, as well as expressly provides new rules in some areas. In addition, it creates an obligation on Members to have a system in place for the enforcement of the protected IP rights, and links them to the effective and enforceable dispute settlement system of the WTO.

The *TRIPS Agreement* does *not* cover every form of IP right, but only those expressly mentioned in Sections 1 to 7 of Part II *as well as* those in the incorporated conventions that are the 'subject-matter' of these Sections. These Sections address: (1) copyright and related rights; (2) trademarks; (3) geographical indications; (4) industrial design; (5) patents; (6) layout-designs of integrated circuits; and (7) protection of undisclosed information. The *TRIPS Agreement* does not apply retroactively to *acts* that occurred before its 'date of application' for a Member. In contrast, the *TRIPS Agreement* does create obligations in respect of *subject-matter* that existed at the date of application of the *TRIPS Agreement.*

The *TRIPS Agreement* obliges Members to 'give effect' to its provisions, but leaves Members 'free to determine the appropriate method' of implementing their obligations under the *TRIPS Agreement* within their own legal systems and practice. In addition, Members may, but are not obliged to, implement more extensive protection than that laid down in the *TRIPS Agreement.* The *TRIPS Agreement* therefore lays down a *minimum level* of harmonised IP protection.

The non-discrimination obligations of national treatment and MFN treatment apply also in the context of the *TRIPS Agreement.* However, there are some differences in their formulation compared to the national treatment and MFN treatment obligations of the GATT 1994 and the GATS, in order to take into account the intangible nature of IP rights. These obligations apply only to the IP rights covered by the *TRIPS Agreement* (including in the incorporated conventions) and apply to 'nationals' as defined in Article 1.3 of the *TRIPS Agreement*, rather than to 'like products' or 'like services or service providers' as is the case in the GATT 1994 and GATS respectively. Both the national treatment and the MFN treatment obligations in the *TRIPS Agreement* are subject to specific exceptions.

The *TRIPS Agreement* does not mandate a particular approach to the exhaustion of IP rights. Members are free to choose their own approach to this matter, provided that they apply their chosen approach in a non-discriminatory manner.

Part II of the *TRIPS Agreement* contains the mandatory minimum standards of IP protection that Members are obliged to provide in their territories to nationals of other Members. Sections 1 to 7 of Part II contain standards relating to various categories of IP rights (including copyright, trademarks, geographical indications and patents) and set out, as a minimum, the *subject-matter* which is eligible for protection, the scope of the *rights conferred* by the relevant category of intellectual property and permitted *exceptions* to those rights.

The protection of IP depends not only on substantive norms providing minimum standards of protection, but also on procedural rules providing effective means to enforce them. Part III of the *TRIPS Agreement* therefore contains rules on enforcement of IP rights. This constitutes a significant innovation by which the *TRIPS Agreement* supplements the existing WIPO conventions and strengthens the protection of IP rights. Members are required to ensure that the enforcement procedures specified in Part III are available under their law 'so as to permit effective action' against infringement of IP rights protected in the *TRIPS Agreement*, including by providing expeditious remedies to *prevent* infringements and remedies to *deter* further infringements. In general, Members are required to have civil *judicial* procedures available for the enforcement of any IP right covered by the *TRIPS Agreement*. Criminal procedures and penalties must be provided at least in cases of wilful trademark counterfeiting or copyright piracy on a commercial scale.

Part IV of the *TRIPS Agreement* deals with the procedural aspects of the acquisition and maintenance of IP rights. It allows Members to require compliance with procedures and formalities as a condition for the acquisition or maintenance of IP rights (except copyright and undisclosed information), but limits these to what is 'reasonable'.

Part V of the *TRIPS Agreement* sets out rules with regard to transparency and dispute settlement. Members are required to publish not only laws and regulations, but also judicial decisions and administrative rulings of general application pertaining to the subject-matter of the *TRIPS Agreement*. If this is impracticable, Members must make them publicly available in a manner that enables governments and IP right holders to become acquainted with them. The WTO dispute settlement rules and procedures, discussed in Chapter 3, apply to disputes under the *TRIPS Agreement*. The *TRIPS Agreement* contains one special dispute settlement rule, with regard to the possible causes of action. For a period of five years from the entry into force of the *WTO Agreement*, no non-violation or situation complaints could be brought under the *TRIPS Agreement*. This moratorium has been extended a number of times, but no agreement has yet been reached on modalities for such complaints.

Members consult on all matters pertaining to the *TRIPS Agreement* in the TRIPS Council. The TRIPS Council is composed of all WTO Members.

Finally, the *TRIPS Agreement* acknowledges the difficulties developing-country Members may face in implementing their obligations under that

Agreement. It thus provided, and still continues to provide, for least-developed-country Members, for transition periods for implementation of the obligations, and contains commitments on technical cooperation and incentives for transfer of technology.

Exercise 15: Malaria

Southland is a small, tropical least-developed country which joined the WTO three years ago. In Southland, malaria is endemic, and more than 60,000 people die from this disease each year. Last year, after a decade of very costly research, MalNet Inc., a company based in Richland, brought a new kind of insecticide-treated mosquito net (ITN) on the market. MalNet applied for, and was granted, a patent on its 'revolutionary' ITN in most countries of the world, including Southland and Newland. This new kind of ITN has been shown to be highly effective and is in great demand. Unfortunately, the MalNet ITNs are expensive. They currently sell for €50 per square metre. Most people in Southland cannot afford these life-saving nets at that price. A few months ago, the Ministry of Health of Southland decided that it would import this new kind of ITN from Newland. In Newland, GlobalSolutions produces this kind of ITN under a compulsory licence granted by the Government of Newland. The ITNs produced by GlobalSolutions sell for €10 per square metre. According to MalNet, both Newland and Southland act inconsistently with their obligations under the *TRIPS Agreement*, and it wants the Government of Richland to take action on its behalf. While investigating this matter, MalNet's lawyers 'discovered' that, in both Southland and Newland, scientific publications concerning public health issues are copyright protected for a period of 5 years only.

You are a junior lawyer working for the Ministry of Trade of Richland, and you have been asked to write a brief on the legal aspects of the two issues referred to above, in order to allow your Minister to decide whether to take any action against Southland and/or Newland.

16 Future Challenges

The challenges facing the WTO and the multilateral trading system in the years to come are multiple and formidable. As discussed in Chapter 1 of this book, international trade can make a significant contribution to economic development and prosperity in both developed and developing countries. International trade has realised this potential – albeit to varying degrees – in many countries. Over the past two decades, this has particularly been the case in Asia. It is, however, undisputed that not all countries, and within countries not all sections of the population, have benefitted from international trade. For the potential of international trade to be realised, there must be: (1) good governance at the national level; (2) a further reduction of trade barriers; (3) more development aid; and (4) better international cooperation and global governance of economic globalisation and international trade. Without the national and/or international action required in these four areas, international trade will not bring prosperity to all, but, on the contrary, is likely to result in more income inequality, social injustice, environmental degradation and cultural homogenisation. This book on the law and the policy of the WTO touches upon each of the national and international actions required, but deals primarily with the requirement of global governance, i.e. global management and regulation, of international trade.

Under the GATT (1948–94), and clearly even more so since the establishment of the WTO in 1995, the international community has made significant progress towards ensuring global governance of international trade. This book discusses in detail the institutions created and the substantive and procedural rules agreed upon, applied and enforced, in order to promote 'rules-based', rather than 'power-based', international trade. 'Rules-based' international trade is to the benefit of all, especially when the rules take into account the differences in economic development between countries. While much has already been achieved, more needs to be done, and this is so for two main reasons. First, some of what was done and agreed upon in the past was not done well, and current shortcomings, inequities and failures must be addressed. Different WTO Members have different shortlists of shortcomings, inequities and failures that they wish to address,

1017

but all would agree that the WTO and its law is 'work in progress'. Secondly, since the establishment of the WTO, the world has changed significantly. Emerging economies have become major traders and will become even more so in the future. The geopolitical balance of global economic power is shifting away from the European Union and the United States to China, India, Brazil and other emerging economies. This shift cannot but lead to an adjustment in the contributions to be made by, and the responsibility of, the industrialised countries, on the one hand, and emerging economies, on the other, to the good functioning of the multilateral trading system. Also, the nature of trade in today's global economy is rapidly changing from trade in goods and services to trade in tasks and value-added, whereby few products sold to a final consumer are wholly produced in one country, but most products sold to a final consumer are, on the contrary, the result of a global value chain – a chain of inputs and tasks produced in many different countries that eventually lead to the product sold to the final consumer. Throughout history, global and regional value chains have always existed, but what is different in today's global economy is the extent, pervasiveness and depth of these chains. The changing nature of trade cannot but give rise to fundamental questions regarding the way in which international trade is currently managed and regulated.

It is not the ambition of this book to discuss at any length the challenges facing the WTO and the multilateral trading system in the years to come. After having completed a 1,000-page voyage through the land of WTO law and policy, even the most enthusiastic reader of this book may long for a well-deserved rest before taking up other books and reports to find out what may or should happen to the WTO and the multilateral trading system in the future. Also, other authors may be less constrained, and are undoubtedly better placed, to look ahead and offer public advice on what should be done. Please refer in particular to the forthcoming report of the WTO Panel on Defining the Future of Trade, and other publications by governments of WTO Members, international organisations, NGOs and academics.[1] This book limits itself to a short, non-exhaustive list of future challenges.

The challenges facing the WTO and the multilateral trading system include, but are not limited to the following: (1) the further liberalisation and international regulation of trade in goods and services (within and/or outside the current Doha Round negotiations); (2) the adaptation of the WTO's political institutions and processes to the shifting geopolitical balance of global economic power, in order to make those institutions and processes more effective; (3) the preservation, and further development, of the WTO's unique and well-functioning dispute settlement

---

1 See e.g. the collection of short essays edited by R. Meléndez-Ortiz, C. Bellmann and M. Rodriguez Mendoza (eds.), *The Future and the WTO: Confronting the Challenges* (International Centre for Trade and Sustainable Development (ICTSD), 2012); and the forthcoming WTO World Trade Report 2013 on *Shaping Factors of World Trade over the Next Decades* (WTO, forthcoming 2013).

system to ensure the security and predictability of the multilateral trading system; (4) the relationship between international trade and the protection of the global ecosystem (e.g. global warming) as well as the local environment (e.g. water, air and soil pollution); (5) the relationship between international trade and minimum labour standards; (6) the relationship between international trade and food security and access to fresh water; (7) the further integration of developing countries, and in particular least-developed countries, into the multilateral trading system; and (8) the expansion of the WTO's mandate in the areas of international investment, competition policy, energy policy, and monetary policy and currency valuation.

While these and other challenges are daunting, it would be a mistake to underestimate the robustness and resilience of the WTO and the multilateral trading system. It has been stated – and not without justification – that multilateralism in the trade as well as in other fields is currently in crisis.[2] Be that as it may, if humanity is to thrive, there is no alternative to international institutions and rules that manage and regulate international trade to the benefit of all. However, the journey ahead will require the international community to navigate with courage and vision in stormy and uncharted waters.

---

2 See the contributions made at the 2012 WTO Public Forum on 'Is Multilateralism in Crisis?', 24–26 September 2012, at www.wto.org/english/forums_e/public_forum12_e/public_forum12_e.htm.

INDEX